# Restored
# Hamilton County
# Ohio
# MARRIAGES

# 1808-1849

—Part One—

**Indexed by**

*Jeffrey G. Herbert*

HAMILTON COUNTY CHAPTER
THE OHIO GENALOGICAL SOCIETY
CINCINNATI, OHIO

HERITAGE BOOKS
2020

# HERITAGE BOOKS

*AN IMPRINT OF HERITAGE BOOKS, INC.*

## Books, CDs, and more—Worldwide

For our listing of thousands of titles see our website
at
www.HeritageBooks.com

Published 2020 by
HERITAGE BOOKS, INC.
Publishing Division
5810 Ruatan Street
Berwyn Heights, Md. 20740

International Standard Book Numbers
Paperbound: 978-0-7884-4605-4
Clothbound: 978-0-7884-9050-7

# TABLE OF CONTENTS

Important Note to Researchers ......................... v

Number of Marriages by Church and Year ................ vii

List of Codes and Sources ...........................viii

Alphabetical Listing of Grooms ........................ 1

Alphabetical Listing of Brides ....................... 323

## Important Note to Researchers

It is important that the user of this index take a few minutes to read this introduction in order to get the most from this index, and to understand why a name may not be found, or if it is found, where to find additional information if available.

On March 24, 1884 a great tragedy struck Cincinnati. A riot started that evening in the downtown area and resulted in the burning of the Hamilton County Courthouse. This fire destroyed many of the records that had been kept previously in the courthouse, one of which was marriage license applications and returns. Apparently many of the 'older' records (before 1860) were stored in another part of the courthouse and did not sustain as extensive damage as those from the period 1860 until March 1884, however, the license returns before 1860 have entire month gaps where there are no records surviving, and some records are missing first or last names. Since this index is concerned with the time period before 1850, it is important to note that there were several previous fires that completely or partially destroyed the courthouse. In 1812 the first brick courthouse on 5th Street between Walnut and Main was accidentally burnt by soldiers. In 1819 a new building was constructed on 10th Street, now known as Court Street. This building was completely destroyed in July 1849 when a neighboring slaughter house caught on fire and the flames spread to the roof of the courthouse. For several years county business was conducted on the upper floors of a nearby slaughter house nicknamed the 'Pork House Court House'. Construction on a new building was started in 1851, which served the county until the March 1884 fire completely destroyed that building.

The reconstructed licenses at the courthouse today for the period before 1850 comprise approximately 50% of the total licenses applied for during this time period. This index is an attempt to reconstruct and supplement as much of that data as possible for the time period before December 1849. This index contains almost 23,000 marriages which occurred in Hamilton County before 1850.

The primary base of information for this index is the restored marriage license applications and returns that are still available at the Hamilton County Courthouse. To try to compensate for some gaps in the restored marriage licenses available, and also to help the researcher locate additional sources of information, church records were checked, when available and permitted, and these are so indicated in the code column. In the cases where the code indicates a church, this is the actual date when the marriage occurred. During these early days, however, many churches did not keep records of marriages. These were recorded by the individual minister who performed the marriage, and kept as his private records, all of which have been subsequently lost. During the 1820's and 1830's time period, there are entire months and years where gaps exist in the surviving marriage records at the courthouse. Also, to date no publication of marriage licenses in newspapers have been found to supplement the gaps in the courthouse records as was the case in the 1870's and 1880's. Unfortunately this information about early inhabitants of Hamilton County may be lost to us forever.

There may be a great deal of spelling variations in the way a first or last name may be spelled. This might be due to the 'Americanization' of a name after the immigrant lived here for a few years. Also most of the names in church registers were not written in English during this time. All of the German Protestant churches kept their records in German and used the Old German script style of handwriting, which makes interpretation very difficult. Almost all of the Catholic churches kept their records in Latin, which can make translation to an equivalent English name difficult. For example, the name 'Jacob' in Latin can be translated into English as either 'James' or 'Jacob', also the name 'Joanna' in Latin can be translated into English as 'Johanna', 'Joanne', 'Joan' or 'Jane'. In addition, some common spelling variations to watch for, are the frequent interchangeability of the letters 'C' and 'K' (e.g. Carl/Karl).

The unique German letters and their usual English equivalents are listed below as an aid to the reader. Any unique German letter that was recorded, would be translated as found below.

ä translated into English as 'ae'
ö translated into English as 'oe'
ü translated into English as 'ue'
ß translated into English as 'ss'

Some examples are as follows: (Schäfer = Schaefer), (Schröder = Schroeder), (Müller = Mueller), (Bußmann = Bussmann).

# NUMBER OF MARRIAGES BY CHURCH AND YEAR
###### ★ ★ ★ ★ ★ ★  ★ ★  ★ ★ ★ ★ ★ ★ ★ ★  ★ ★  ★ ★ ★ ★ ★ ★  ★ ★ ★  ★ ★ ★ ★

## Protestant Churches
###### ★ ★ ★ ★ ★ ★ ★ ★ ★ ★  ★ ★ ★ ★ ★ ★ ★

| CODE | 1840 | 1841 | 1842 | 1843 | 1844 | 1845 | 1846 | 1847 | 1848 | 1849 |
|------|------|------|------|------|------|------|------|------|------|------|
| A |    |    | 5  | 10 | 20 | 27 | 30 | 49 | 78 | 83 |
| B |    |    |    |    |    | 4  | 29 | 27 | 39 | 43 |
| C |    |    |    | 35 | 41 | 54 | 63 | 79 | 103 | 145 |
| D | 4  | 10 | 3  | 4  | 2  | 5  | 12 | 9  | 16 | 17 |
| E |    |    |    |    |    |    | 1  | 8  | 5  | 7  |
| F | 49 | 51 | 70 | 62 | 61 | 75 | 85 | 88 | 98 | 112 |
| G | 53 | 31 | 36 | 48 | 52 | 72 | 84 | 77 | 133 | 129 |
| H |    |    |    |    |    |    |    |    |    | 3  |
| I | 9  | 18 | 13 | 11 | 8  | 8  | 12 | 12 | 24 | 10 |

## Catholic Churches
###### ★ ★ ★ ★ ★ ★ ★ ★  ★ ★ ★ ★ ★ ★ ★

| CODE | 1840 | 1841 | 1842 | 1843 | 1844 | 1845 | 1846 | 1847 | 1848 | 1849 |
|------|------|------|------|------|------|------|------|------|------|------|
| AA |    |    | 42 | 136 | 178 | 245 | 189 | 222 | 190 | 189 |
| BB | 56 | 65 | 61 | 77 | 70 | 82 | 76 | 77 | 128 | 161 |
| CC |    |    |    |    |    |    |    | 37 | 54 | 92 |
| DD |    |    |    |    |    |    |    |    |    | 14 |
| EE |    |    |    |    |    | 3  | 146 | 230 | 268 | 247 |
| FF | 217 | 207 | 176 | 94 | 79 | 103 | 88 | 110 | 111 | 100 |
| GG |    |    |    |    |    |    | 28 | 44 | 49 | 140 |
| HH |    |    |    |    |    | 1  | 3  | 3  | 5  | 8  |
| II |    |    |    |    |    |    |    |    | 82 | 163 |

## List of Codes and Sources

| Code | Protestant Churches | Dates | Source |
|------|---------------------|-------|--------|
| A. | St. Peter German Evangelical | 1842 - 1849 | LDS 1514064 |
| B. | St. Paul German Evangelical | 1845 - 1849 | LDS 1514059 |
| C. | St. Matthaeus German Evangelical | 1843 - 1849 | LDS 1548046 |
| D. | St. Paul Episcopal (4th St.) | 1834 - 1849 | Episcopal Archives |
| E. | Zion German Evangelical | 1846 - 1849 | LDS 1510057 |
| F. | North German Lutheran | 1840 - 1849 | PLCHC |
| G. | St. John's Unitarian (12th and Elm St.) | 1839 - 1849 | LDS 1510039 |
| H. | Concordia Evangelical Lutheran | 1849 - 1849 | LDS 1514042 |
| I. | Christ Episcopal Church | 1818 - 1849 | LDS 1955202 |

| Code | Roman Catholic Churches | Dates | Source |
|------|-------------------------|-------|--------|
| AA. | Old St. Mary | 1842 - 1849 | Archives of Cinti Archdiocese |
| BB. | St. Peter in Chains Cathedral | 1839 - 1849 | Archives of Cinti Archdiocese |
| CC. | St. Joseph | 1846 - 1849 | Archives of Cinti Archdiocese |
| DD. | St. Michael | 1847 - 1849 | Archives of Cinti Archdiocese |
| EE. | St. John the Baptist | 1845 - 1849 | Archives of Cinti Archdiocese |
| FF. | Holy Trinity | 1834 - 1849 | Archives of Cinti Archdiocese |
| GG. | St. Xavier | 1846 - 1849 | Archives of Cinti Archdiocese |
| HH. | St. James (White Oak) | 1845 - 1849 | Archives of Cinti Archdiocese |
| II. | St. Philomena | 1848 - 1849 | Archives of Cinti Archdiocese |

| Code | Source | Source |
|------|--------|--------|
| CH | Original Hamilton County Courthouse Marriage License Books | LDS or Courthouse |
| RCH | Restored Hamilton County Courthouse Marriage License Books | LDS or Courthouse |

PLCHC = Public Library of Cincinnati and Hamilton County (Main Branch)
LDS = Latter Day Saints (Morman) Church Library

| Grooms | Brides | Date of Marriage | Code |
|--------|--------|------------------|------|
| ****** | ****** | **** ** ******** | **** |
| ----, ---- | Stonemetz, Ann | 28, Aug. 1817 | RCH |
| ----, ---- | Ferry, Cynthia | 1, Oct. 1817 | RCH |
| ----, ---- | Bamn, Sarah | 2, Oct. 1817 | RCH |
| ----, ---- | Parsel, Mary | 30, Oct. 1817 | RCH |
| ----, ---- | Seran, Mary | 10, Nov. 1817 | RCH |
| ----, ---- | Kelly, Mary | 13, Nov. 1817 | RCH |
| ----, ---- | Orr, Jane | 20, Nov. 1817 | RCH |
| ----, ---- | Worrel, Lydia | 27, Nov. 1817 | RCH |
| ----, ---- | Carell, Mary | 15, 1817 | RCH |
| ----, ---- | Campbell, Elisabeth | 28, Feb. 1818 | RCH |
| ----, ---- | Murphy, Jane | 9, Apr. 1818 | RCH |
| ----, ---- | Davis, Margaret | 7, May 1818 | RCH |
| ----, ---- | Chandler, Sarah | 1, Oct. 1818 | RCH |
| ----, ---- | Ward, Polly | 11, Mar. 1819 | RCH |
| ----, ---- | Brown, Hannah | 6, Apr. 1819 | RCH |
| ----, ---- | Hartman, Sophia C. | 19, Aug. 1819 | RCH |
| ----, ---- | Foster, Belinda | 14, Sept 1819 | RCH |
| ----, ---- | Whitehead, Heltia | 9, Aug. 1821 | RCH |
| ----, ---- | Giffin, Ann | 20, Dec. 1821 | RCH |
| ----, ---- | McDonald, Emily | 18, Oct. 1823 | RCH |
| ----, ---- | Hutchison, May | 30, Apr. 1824 | RCH |
| ----, ---- | Mason, Sarah | 27, May 1824 | RCH |
| ----, ---- | Rose, Elizabeth | 9, Apr. 1825 | RCH |
| ----, ---- | Brown, Sarah | 10, May 1826 | RCH |
| ----, ---- | Cutter, Maria | 19, May 1826 | RCH |
| ----, ---- | Moon, Mary M. | 28, May 1826 | RCH |
| ----, ---- | Miller, Anna Agnes | 4, July 1826 | RCH |
| ----, ---- | Band, Elisabeth | 8, Aug. 1826 | RCH |
| ----, ---- | Smith, Elisabeth | 10, Aug. 1826 | RCH |
| ----, ---- | Gland, Soffie | 24, Aug. 1826 | RCH |
| ----, ---- | Folger, Lydia | 19, Oct. 1826 | RCH |
| ----, ---- | Jones, Elisabeth | 2, Nov. 1826 | RCH |
| ----, ---- | Greene, Maria A. | 14, July 1827 | RCH |
| ----, ---- | Palmer, Lucretia | 22, Feb. 1832 | RCH |
| ----, ---- | Roohh, Mary Ann | 21, Mar. 1832 | RCH |
| ----, ---- | Ramsdale, Julian | 6, May 1832 | RCH |
| ----, ---- | Denham, Elmira | 6, Jan. 1833 | RCH |
| ----, ---- | Perkins, Deborah | 4, Apr. 1833 | RCH |
| ----, ---- | Case, Mahala | Apr. 1833 | RCH |
| ----, ---- | Burke, Rachel | 26, Aug. 1833 | RCH |
| ----, ---- | Bascom, Elisabeth | 27, Aug. 1833 | RCH |
| ----, ---- | Abbott, Elisabeth | Aug. 1833 | RCH |
| ----, ---- | Wolf, Elisabeth | 7, Oct. 1833 | RCH |
| ----, ---- | Bellfield, Rebecca | 12, Nov. 1833 | RCH |
| ----, ---- | Gillens, Margaret | 28, Nov. 1833 | RCH |
| ----, ---- | Hudson, Edina | 30, Nov. 1833 | RCH |
| ----, ---- | Guvard, | 14, Dec. 1833 | RCH |
| ----, ---- | Sparr, Harriet | 26, Dec. 1833 | RCH |
| ----, ---- | Sperd, Mary | Dec. 1833 | RCH |
| ----, ---- | Lowry, Elisabeth | 8, 1833 | RCH |
| ----, ---- | Carnes, Sarah | 19, 1833 | RCH |
| ----, ---- | Law, Catharine | 23, 1833 | RCH |
| ----, ---- | Foster, Catharine | 1833 | RCH |
| ----, ---- | Mitchell, Rachel | 1833 | RCH |
| ----, ---- | Wilkens, Susan | 1833 | RCH |
| ----, ---- | Winings, | 8, Jan. 1834 | RCH |
| ----, ---- | Hampton, Sarah J. | 25, Mar. 1834 | RCH |
| ----, ---- | Williamson, Mary A. | Mar. 1834 | RCH |
| ----, ---- | Scothean, Weger | 15, May 1834 | RCH |
| ----, ---- | Scroggen, C. | 31, Aug. 1834 | RCH |
| ----, ---- | McDonough, Amanda | 20, Sept 1834 | RCH |
| ----, ---- | Turner, | 2, Oct. 1834 | RCH |
| ----, ---- | Gibbs, Nancy | 1834 | RCH |
| ----, ---- | VanMiddlesworth, E. | 14, Mar. 1835 | RCH |
| ----, ---- | Archibald, Mary | May 1835 | RCH |
| ----, ---- | Green, Margaret | 15, June 1835 | RCH |
| ----, ---- | Link, Julia | 9, July 1835 | RCH |
| ----, ---- | Colvin, Zelphia | 5, Aug. 1835 | RCH |
| ----, ---- | Robertson, Christina | 27, Aug. 1835 | RCH |

| Grooms | Brides | Date of Marriage | Code |
|--------|--------|------------------|------|
| ----, ---- | King, Jane | 2, Nov. 1835 | RCH |
| ----, ---- | Howell, | 12, Nov. 1835 | RCH |
| ----, ---- | Rudd, Ann | 13, Nov. 1835 | RCH |
| ----, ---- | McWright, B. | Nov. 1835 | RCH |
| ----, ---- | Levitt, Sarah B. | 13, Dec. 1835 | RCH |
| ----, ---- | Hedgeland, Catharine | 15, Dec. 1835 | RCH |
| ----, ---- | Kennedy, Elisabeth | 1835 | RCH |
| ----, ---- | Shands, Mary Ann | 16, June 1835 | RCH |
| ----, ---- | Coovert, Abigail | 5, Jan. 1836 | RCH |
| ----, ---- | Campbell, Mary | 18, Jan. 1836 | RCH |
| ----, ---- | Hartley, Sarah | 19, Jan. 1836 | RCH |
| ----, ---- | Ewings, Rebecca | 17, Mar. 1836 | RCH |
| ----, ---- | Bunion, Minerva | 20, Mar. 1836 | RCH |
| ----, ---- | Hervey, Tomson | 28, Apr. 1836 | RCH |
| ----, ---- | Spears, Hannah | 8, Aug. 1836 | RCH |
| ----, ---- | Braster, Charlotte | 19, Aug. 1836 | RCH |
| ----, ---- | Sifton, Sarah | 26, Aug. 1836 | RCH |
| ----, ---- | Pearson, Matilda | 11, Sept 1836 | RCH |
| ----, ---- | Whiteside, Caroline | 22, Sept 1836 | RCH |
| ----, ---- | Tolliver, Charlotte | 10, Oct. 1836 | RCH |
| ----, ---- | Morsell, Amelia | 11, Nov. 1836 | RCH |
| ----, ---- | Bishop, Hannah | 14, Nov. 1836 | RCH |
| ----, ---- | Hemphill, Martha | 22, Dec. 1836 | RCH |
| ----, ---- | Barrett, Lucy D. | 16, 1836 | RCH |
| ----, ---- | Thompson, Ann | 25, Jan. 1837 | RCH |
| ----, ---- | Groves, Mary M. | 24, Mar. 1837 | RCH |
| ----, ---- | Redrow, Mary Ann | 26, Mar. 1837 | RCH |
| ----, ---- | Fish, Sarah Ailis | 20, Aug. 1837 | RCH |
| ----, ---- | Hubbard, Mary | 2, Sept 1837 | RCH |
| ----, ---- | Woodward, Joanna | 4, Sept 1837 | RCH |
| ----, ---- | Graham, Catharine | 8, Oct. 1837 | RCH |
| ----, ---- | Striggens, Rebecca | 1837 | RCH |
| ----, ---- | Brigman, Margaret | 1, Nov. 1837 | RCH |
| ----, ---- | Newman, Christina | 21, Dec. 1837 | RCH |
| ----, ---- | Peck, Catharine | 1837 | RCH |
| ----, ---- | Humphries, Mary | 6, Feb. 1838 | RCH |
| ----, ---- | Hagle, Elisabeth | 15, Mar. 1838 | RCH |
| ----, ---- | Corbin, Mary | 21, Mar. 1838 | RCH |
| ----, ---- | Guard, Sarah | 7, June 1838 | RCH |
| ----, ---- | Danensink, Henrietta | 26, Sept 1838 | RCH |
| ----, ---- | Cheackley, Elisabeth | 26, Dec. 1837 | RCH |
| ----, ---- | Helking, Maria | 17, Sept 1844 | RCH |
| ----, ---- | Peterson, Jemimia | 30, Nov. 1844 | RCH |
| ----, ---- | Charters, Anna C. | 10, Dec. 1844 | RCH |
| ----, ---- | Finch, Adeline | 23, Dec. 1844 | RCH |
| ----, ---- | Deters, Mary | 19, Sept 1844 | RCH |
| ----, ---- | Karr, Angeline | 1, Jan. 1849 | RCH |
| ----, ---- | Morgan, Ann | 1, Mar. 1849 | RCH |
| ----, ---- | Ludwig, Mathilda | 15, Mar. 1849 | RCH |
| ----, ---- | VanHorn, Margaret | 28, Mar. 1849 | RCH |
| ----, ---- | Cottle, Rebecca | 29, Mar. 1849 | RCH |
| ----, ---- | Wiley, Jane | 4, Apr. 1849 | RCH |
| ----, ---- | Tyrill, Demaris | Apr. 1849 | RCH |
| ----, ---- | Morgan, Sarah | 24, July 1849 | RCH |
| ----, Aaron | Jackson, Ann | 16, Sept 1824 | RCH |
| ----, Aaron | Coder, Lydia N. | 9, June 1836 | RCH |
| ----, Abijah | Swigolar, Rebecca | 7, Mar. 1849 | RCH |
| ----, Abraham | Harvey, Lydia | 2, Jan. 1818 | RCH |
| ----, Abraham | Crossman, Catharine | 27, Apr. 1836 | RCH |
| ----, Alexander | Sturge, Martha | 1, June 1818 | RCH |
| ----, Alexis | Foster, Patience | 2, Oct. 1823 | RCH |
| ----, Alpheus | Fisk, Sarah | 5, Mar. 1824 | RCH |
| ----, Americus | Devit, Mary | 24, Dec. 1823 | RCH |
| ----, Andrew | Crane, Henrietta | 4, Nov. 1836 | RCH |
| ----, Andrew | Davis, Phoebe | 30, July 1838 | RCH |
| ----, Anton | Lienhard, Sarah | 7, Nov. 1843 | RCH |
| ----, Asap. | Simmons, Charity | 3, Oct. 1821 | RCH |
| ----, August | Lowe, Susan E. | 25, June 1836 | RCH |
| ----, Barnaby | Bolser, Sarah | 10, Aug. 1837 | RCH |
| ----, Barney | Connel, Elisabeth | 14, Jan. 1838 | RCH |
| ----, Basel E. | Griffith, | 25, Dec. 1836 | RCH |

| Grooms<br>****** | Brides<br>****** | Date of Marriage<br>**** ** ******** | Code<br>**** |
|---|---|---|---|
| ----, Benjamin | Carro, Mary | 14, Oct. 1817 | RCH |
| ----, Benjamin | Rose, Jane | 18, Jan. 1821 | RCH |
| ----, Benjamin | Viars, Rachel | 23, Nov. 1837 | RCH |
| ----, Caleb | Williams, Margaret | 5, Mar. 1824 | RCH |
| ----, Charles | Smith, Eleanor | 13, Apr. 1823 | RCH |
| ----, Charles | Comstock, Maria | 12, Dec. 1833 | RCH |
| ----, Charles | Barber, Parmelia | 9, Aug. 1838 | RCH |
| ----, Charles | Nevols, Lucretia | 5, Sept 1838 | RCH |
| ----, Charles | Baltimore, Susan | 21, Dec. 1844 | RCH |
| ----, Charles | Sherman, Elisabeth | 4, July 1848 | RCH |
| ----, Charles | Billings, Sarah | 11, Mar. 1849 | RCH |
| ----, Clinton | Wusby, Elis. Jane | 13, May 1840 | RCH |
| ----, Columbus | Doane, Malinda | 4, Sept 1825 | RCH |
| ----, Cornelius | Green, Charlotte | 21, Apr. 1818 | RCH |
| ----, Cornelius | Balser, Rebecca | 29, Dec. 1826 | RCH |
| ----, D. | Fullerton, Elisabeth | 30, Dec. 1817 | RCH |
| ----, Daniel | Hubble, Mary | 24, Dec. 1823 | RCH |
| ----, Daniel | West, Susan | 12, Apr. 1826 | RCH |
| ----, Daniel | Cobb, Abigail | 8, May 1826 | RCH |
| ----, Daniel | Stratton, Mary | 8, Aug. 1835 | RCH |
| ----, David | Gillespie, | 12, Oct. 1817 | RCH |
| ----, David | Misner, Sarah | 16, Nov. 1820 | RCH |
| ----, David | Case, Eunice | 8, Nov. 1832 | RCH |
| ----, Durham | Hole, Keziah | 16, Apr. 1818 | RCH |
| ----, Edward | Bradford, Margaret | 31, Mar. 1824 | RCH |
| ----, Eli | Patmore, Rachel | 28, June 1827 | RCH |
| ----, Elijah | Stewart, Esther | 23, Nov. 1817 | RCH |
| ----, Elijah | Hudson, Elisabeth | 3, May 1821 | RCH |
| ----, Elijah | Hartford, Naomi | 27, Dec. 1824 | RCH |
| ----, Elijah | Scudder, Mary | 22, Oct. 1826 | RCH |
| ----, Elisha | Whitney, Susan | 8, Feb. 1827 | RCH |
| ----, Elston | Stewart, Elisabeth | 7, Feb. 1839 | RCH |
| ----, Ephraim | Burnett, Elisabeth H | 15, June 1820 | RCH |
| ----, Foster | Morgan, Eleanor | 24, Feb. 1839 | RCH |
| ----, Francis | Green, Mary Ellen | 26, Sept 1843 | RCH |
| ----, George | Dawson, Elisabeth | 2, Jan. 1818 | RCH |
| ----, George | Hartman, Elisabeth | 20, Mar. 1823 | RCH |
| ----, George | Boswell, Nancy | 29, May 1823 | RCH |
| ----, George | Arbuckle, Margaret | July 1833 | RCH |
| ----, George | Johnston, Jane | 26, Sept 1833 | RCH |
| ----, George | Law, Amanda | Dec. 1835 | RCH |
| ----, George | Cameron, Mary | 23, Feb. 1836 | RCH |
| ----, George | Herron, Hannah | 21, Dec. 1842 | RCH |
| ----, Gibson | Norris, Polly | 28, Feb. 1826 | RCH |
| ----, Griffin | Bibbs, Dorcas | 2, June 1826 | RCH |
| ----, Henry | Thorp, Sarah | 2, Jan. 1818 | RCH |
| ----, Henry | Cox, Sarah | 6, Aug. 1821 | RCH |
| ----, Henry | Wakefield, Lydia | 27, Apr. 1824 | RCH |
| ----, Henry | Nasheny, Mary | 10, Nov. 1836 | RCH |
| ----, Henry | Frazier, Sarah Ann | 1, Jan. 1837 | RCH |
| ----, Henry | Dorsey, Elisabeth | Jan. 1839 | RCH |
| ----, Henry William | Brown, Ann | 29, Dec. 1836 | RCH |
| ----, Isaac | Rodgers, Anna Elis. | 7, May 1818 | RCH |
| ----, Isaac | VanDyke, Catharine | 11, June 1821 | RCH |
| ----, Isaac | Nitchy, Sarah | 27, Apr. 1824 | RCH |
| ----, Isaac | Moore, Mary | 30, June 1836 | RCH |
| ----, Israel | Cameron, Elisabeth | 18, May 1834 | RCH |
| ----, Israel | Dunn, Mary Elisabeth | 14, Apr. 1835 | RCH |
| ----, J. | Burley, Margaret | 21, Oct. 1817 | RCH |
| ----, J. | Brynah, Betsy | 8, Jan. 1820 | RCH |
| ----, J. | Smith, Agnes A. | 20, Sept 1838 | RCH |
| ----, Jackson | Gammel, | 7, July 1825 | RCH |
| ----, Jacob | Aldridge, Ruth | 2, Nov. 1817 | RCH |
| ----, Jacob | Tucker, Susanna | 14, May 1818 | RCH |
| ----, Jacob | Montgomery, Mary A. | 8, June 1834 | RCH |
| ----, Jacob | Markly, Elisabeth | 5, Sept 1838 | RCH |
| ----, James | Fall, Mary | 26, Sept 1817 | RCH |
| ----, James | Burrows, Nancy | 21, Mar. 1818 | RCH |
| ----, James | Cummins, Jane | 11, June 1818 | RCH |
| ----, James | Brady, Catharine | 27, June 1824 | RCH |
| ----, James | Minn, Sophronia | 26, Jan. 1826 | RCH |

| Grooms | Brides | Date of Marriage | Code |
|--------|--------|------------------|------|
| ****** | ****** | **** ** ******** | **** |
| ----, James | McMackin, Emma Ann | 14, Feb. 1832 | RCH |
| ----, James | Delmeson, | 27, Nov. 1835 | RCH |
| ----, James | Richard, Julia Anna | 29, Sept 1836 | RCH |
| ----, James | Betts, Mary Ann | 19, Aug. 1838 | RCH |
| ----, James | Wune, Mary H. | 22, June 1839 | RCH |
| ----, James | Williams, Jane | 3, Aug. 1843 | RCH |
| ----, James | Winterbaum, Mary A. | 28, Aug. 1844 | RCH |
| ----, James A. | Abbot, Hannah | 22, Jan. 1824 | RCH |
| ----, Jasper | Netlin, Elisabeth | 18, Jan. 1836 | RCH |
| ----, Jerry | Westcott, Hester A. | 11, Apr. 1836 | RCH |
| ----, Job | Miller, Mariah | 24, Apr. 1825 | RCH |
| ----, Johan | Hudson, Catharine A. | 29, Mar. 1849 | RCH |
| ----, John | Townley, Elisabeth | 19, Aug. 1817 | RCH |
| ----, John | Wood, Elisabeth | 4, Sept 1817 | RCH |
| ----, John | Shulenbeyer, | 21, Nov. 1817 | RCH |
| ----, John | Jackson, Harriet | 28, June 1818 | RCH |
| ----, John | Hayden, Charity | 19, Oct. 1820 | RCH |
| ----, John | Linscott, Nancy | 5, Apr. 1821 | RCH |
| ----, John | Inhook, Betsy | 23, Apr. 1821 | RCH |
| ----, John | Watson, Jane | 22, May 1821 | RCH |
| ----, John | Hay, Mary Ann | 5, July 1821 | RCH |
| ----, John | Marshall, Isabella | 2, Jan. 1823 | RCH |
| ----, John | Jones, Hannah | 20, May 1823 | RCH |
| ----, John | Humphie, Patience | 10, July 1823 | RCH |
| ----, John | Bales, Ruth | 14, Oct. 1823 | RCH |
| ----, John | Davis, Nancy | 14, Dec. 1823 | RCH |
| ----, John | Hutchinson, Eleanor | 6, Apr. 1825 | RCH |
| ----, John | Shears, Margaret | 12, Jan. 1836 | RCH |
| ----, John | Rowan, Mary | 21, Nov. 1837 | RCH |
| ----, John | Lee, Susanna | 31, May 1838 | RCH |
| ----, John | Ross, Rebecca | 19, July 1838 | RCH |
| ----, John | Gibbons, Ann | 24, July 1838 | RCH |
| ----, John | King, Elisabeth | 25, Dec. 1842 | RCH |
| ----, John | Bodan, Lucind | 5, Apr. 1843 | RCH |
| ----, John | Wolf, Lydia | 3, Jan. 1844 | RCH |
| ----, John | Duncan, Elis. Martha | 14, Nov. 1844 | RCH |
| ----, John | Lynch, Margaret | 28, Aug. 1845 | RCH |
| ----, John | Martin, Almira | 4, Mar. 1849 | RCH |
| ----, John Heinrich | Kammers, Elisabeth | 7, Aug. 1845 | RCH |
| ----, Jonathan | Hood, Rachel | 11, Nov. 1828 | RCH |
| ----, Joseph | Bryant, Milli | 10, Mar. 1825 | RCH |
| ----, Joseph | Hart, Mary Ann | 1, Apr. 1832 | RCH |
| ----, Joseph | Fulton, Martha | 31, May 1836 | RCH |
| ----, Joshua | Wake, Juliann | 27, Mar. 1825 | RCH |
| ----, Lendly | Scofield, Emeline | 16, Feb. 1839 | RCH |
| ----, Leonard | Asa, Clarissa | 20, Apr. 1826 | RCH |
| ----, Louis | Calments, Jane W. | Aug. 1839 | RCH |
| ----, Mathias | Peters, Sarah | 20, Nov. 1828 | RCH |
| ----, Michael | Moore, Louisa | 26, Dec. 1822 | RCH |
| ----, Michael | O'Donnell, Bridget | 7, Oct. 1849 | GG |
| ----, Morris | Karr, Rebecca Ann | 21, Dec. 1833 | RCH |
| ----, Nathan | Faris, Jerusha | 17, June 1824 | RCH |
| ----, Neeton | Burroughs, Rebecca | 2, June 1818 | RCH |
| ----, Oliver | Tuder, Elisabeth | 25, June 1826 | RCH |
| ----, P. | Grady, Nancy | 14, Feb. 1818 | RCH |
| ----, Patrick | Born, Cilona | 7, Apr. 1818 | RCH |
| ----, Patrick | Latin, Sarah | 1, Aug. 1825 | RCH |
| ----, Patrick | English, | 15, May 1836 | RCH |
| ----, Paul | Palmer, Almira | 12, Oct. 1817 | RCH |
| ----, Peter | Ready, Leah | 3, Apr. 1818 | RCH |
| ----, Peter | Rowland, Hannah | 24, Oct. 1833 | RCH |
| ----, Peter | Jones, Ann | 12, May 1836 | RCH |
| ----, Philipp | Shaysgreen, Ann | 5, Apr. 1836 | RCH |
| ----, Price | Johnson, Hannah | Aug. 1823 | RCH |
| ----, Randolph | Robinson, Millie | 24, Feb. 1825 | RCH |
| ----, Reason | Davis, Elisabeth Ann | 20, Nov. 1817 | RCH |
| ----, Reuben | Glason, Sally | 11, Sept 1817 | RCH |
| ----, Reuben | Bell, Cindeley C. | 15, Apr. 1824 | RCH |
| ----, Reuben | Miller, Elisabeth | 3, July 1848 | RCH |
| ----, Richard | Cummins, Louise | 5, Feb. 1818 | RCH |
| ----, Richard | Osborne, May | 30, Nov. 1825 | RCH |

| Grooms | Brides | Date of Marriage | Code |
|--------|--------|------------------|------|
| ****** | ****** | **** ** ******** | **** |
| ----, Richard | Jackson, Sarah | 8, Aug. 1826 | RCH |
| ----, Richard | Roberts, Mary | 17, Mar. 1849 | RCH |
| ----, Robert | McKnight, Ann | 13, June 1818 | RCH |
| ----, Robert | McGill, Elisabeth | 10, June 1824 | RCH |
| ----, Robert | Downs, Melinda | 14, Aug. 1825 | RCH |
| ----, Robert | Hurrell, Nancy | 23, Feb. 1826 | RCH |
| ----, Robert | Hannaford, Harriet | 12, Apr. 1838 | RCH |
| ----, Robert | Miller, Lucinda | 3, July 1843 | RCH |
| ----, Robert | Ross, Sarah Frances | 21, Aug. 1845 | RCH |
| ----, Samuel | Smith, Happy | 12, Apr. 1821 | RCH |
| ----, Samuel | Rennet, Rebecca | 29, June 1825 | RCH |
| ----, Samuel | Snider, Susan | 11, Aug. 1827 | RCH |
| ----, Samuel | Miller, Maria Anna | 19, Nov. 1828 | RCH |
| ----, Samuel | Buker, Damans | 30, Nov. 1836 | RCH |
| ----, Samuel | McPhearson, Sarah | 31, Oct. 1844 | RCH |
| ----, Samuel A. | Groff, Sarah | 19, Feb. 1826 | RCH |
| ----, Solomon | Clark, Phoebe Ann | Sept 1835 | RCH |
| ----, Stephen | Gorman, Susan | 18, Sept 1823 | RCH |
| ----, Sylvester | Smith, Mary | 17, May 1836 | RCH |
| ----, T. | Sparks, Nancy | 2, Dec. 1820 | RCH |
| ----, Theodore | Williams, Sarah Jane | 31, Mar. 1841 | RCH |
| ----, Theophilus | Edwards, Deborah | 10, Sept 1835 | RCH |
| ----, Thomas | Dodge, Ecry | 25, Aug. 1818 | RCH |
| ----, Thomas | Webb, Sally | 25, Mar. 1821 | RCH |
| ----, Thomas | Davis, Mary Ann | 25, Dec. 1831 | RCH |
| ----, Thomas | Farrell, Ellen | 14, July 1848 | RCH |
| ----, Thomas | Dowling, Mary Ann | 26, Aug. 1848 | RCH |
| ----, Timothy | Knapp, Martha | 20, Sept 1817 | RCH |
| ----, Timothy | Edwards, Betsy | 27, Mar. 1825 | RCH |
| ----, William | Wilson, Hannah | 3, Sept 1816 | RCH |
| ----, William | Thomas, Harriet | 18, Dec. 1817 | RCH |
| ----, William | Clark, Mary | 20, Apr. 1818 | RCH |
| ----, William | Nelson, Elisabeth | 1, June 1818 | RCH |
| ----, William | Walker, Elisabeth | 24, Mar. 1821 | RCH |
| ----, William | Pine, Rosanna | 6, Feb. 1823 | RCH |
| ----, William | Wilson, Mary | 12, Feb. 1824 | RCH |
| ----, William | Bellis, Hannah | 4, July 1824 | RCH |
| ----, William | Hildreth, Mary | 23, Dec. 1824 | RCH |
| ----, William | Ramsey, Elisabeth | 31, Aug. 1826 | RCH |
| ----, William | Ringwood, Catharine | 28, Nov. 1826 | RCH |
| ----, William | Davis, Maria | Nov. 1826 | RCH |
| ----, William | Bowers, Mary | 26, Apr. 1827 | RCH |
| ----, William | Hubbard, Mary | 26, Apr. 1832 | RCH |
| ----, William | Hughes, | 4, June 1835 | RCH |
| ----, William | Arnold, Malinda | Oct. 1835 | RCH |
| ----, William | Jones, Sidney | 30, Sept 1836 | RCH |
| ----, William | Tate, Jane | 2, Nov. 1836 | RCH |
| ----, William | Sondermann, Margaret | 15, Feb. 1837 | RCH |
| ----, William | Wolverton, Rebecca | 7, Apr. 1839 | RCH |
| ----, William | Morris, Jane | 29, Sept 1844 | RCH |
| ----, William | Curtis, Elisabeth | 11, Aug. 1845 | RCH |
| ----, William | Hefron, Bridget | 24, Jan. 1846 | RCH |
| ----, William | Ward, Phebe | 20, Sept 1847 | RCH |
| ----, William | Lang, Matilda A. | 28, Oct. 1847 | RCH |
| ----, William H. | Barrett, Jane | 24, Dec. 1836 | RCH |
| ----, William Isaac | Moore, Ann | 4, May 1834 | RCH |
| ---chell, Sylvester | Cole, Eleanor | 22, July 1821 | RCH |
| ---dan, Silas | Covaer, Susan | 6, May 1836 | RCH |
| ---eagland, James | Thompson, Susan | 11, Sept 1839 | RCH |
| ---goner, George | Mullen, Rebecca | 21, June 1827 | RCH |
| ---it, William | Neff, Mary Ann | 31, Oct. 1826 | RCH |
| ---ker, Joseph | Geyer, Anna | 29, Mar. 1849 | RCH |
| ---kins, | Street, Mary C. | 30, Dec. 1836 | RCH |
| ---ll, | Shane, Jane | 21, July 1837 | RCH |
| ---nistin, M. | Davis, Ann | 16, June 1837 | RCH |
| ---sper, Thomas | Lake, Elisabeth | 18, Jan. 1827 | RCH |
| ---ster, O. | Parker, Priscilla | 4, Sept 1838 | RCH |
| ---thins, Cornelius | Bean, Susannah | 1, Aug. 1825 | RCH |
| ---tington, Thomas | Redish, Mary | 26, Mar. 1818 | RCH |
| ---way, John | Carran, Susan | 30, June 1818 | RCH |
| --adley, Anson | Whitlock, Elisabeth | 3, Feb. 1833 | RCH |

| Grooms | Brides | Date of Marriage | Code |
| ****** | ****** | **** ** ******** | **** |
| --awan, | Graves, Julia | 7, Dec. 1837 | RCH |
| --nsworth, Paul | Fulton, Martha | 21, Oct. 1844 | RCH |
| --rius, Edward | Daudes, Sophia | 5, Mar. 1839 | G |
| --rott, | Askew, Mary Ann | 9, May 1833 | RCH |
| -ainard, Hanson | Read, Mary | 19, Oct. 1817 | RCH |
| -arnel, Christopher | Gross, Elisabeth | 11, Aug. 1817 | RCH |
| -orris, Benjamin | McQuinley, Martha A. | 8, Mar. 1849 | RCH |
| | | | |
| A---, John | Markeye, Sarah | 17, Oct. 1835 | RCH |
| A---, Omar | Muckelmann, Mary | 30, July 1844 | RCH |
| Abborger, Simon | Child, Sarah Ann | 27, June 1849 | RCH |
| Abbot, Christopher | Watkins, Elisabeth | 23, Mar. 1820 | RCH |
| Abbott, August | Parker, Abigail | 6, July 1847 | RCH |
| Abbott, David | Brown, Elisabeth | 10, Jan. 1833 | RCH |
| Abbott, Hiram | Blinn, Caroline | 22, Feb. 1846 | RCH |
| Abbott, John | Thomas, Jane | 19, Mar. 1844 | RCH |
| Abbott, Nathaniel | Clark, Susannah | 2, Dec. 1846 | RCH |
| Abbott, Robert | Thompson, Elcy | 4, Nov. 1842 | RCH |
| Abbott, Thomas | Thompson, Ruth Ann | 30, Dec. 1845 | RCH |
| Abbott, William | Gordon, Phebe A. | 1, June 1846 | RCH |
| Abbott, William H. | Thomas, Ruth | 28, July 1836 | RCH |
| Abel, Friedrich | Messmann, Anna Maria | 14, Nov. 1848 | FF |
| Abel, Johan Gerhard | Grobmeyer, Maria A. | 31, May 1842 | FF |
| Abel, Johan Joseph | Grobmeyer, A Gertrud | 29, Apr. 1845 | FF |
| Abele, Johan Heinric | Evers, Maria Anna | 21, June 1846 | FF |
| Abker, John Henry | Mollring, Anna Maria | 16, Nov. 1843 | RCH |
| Able, Elijah | ----, Mary Ann | 16, Feb. 1847 | RCH |
| Abrams, James | Gifford, Freelove | 23, Feb. 1820 | RCH |
| Abrams, James | Williamson, Ann | 18, Jan. 1833 | RCH |
| Abrams, John | Davis, Elisabeth | 2, July 1846 | RCH |
| Abrams, Joseph | Case, Hannah | 30, Mar. 1823 | RCH |
| Abrams, Swain | McClintic, Elisabeth | 20, Aug. 1846 | RCH |
| Achenkamp, Dietrich | Wahms, Catharine | 31, Jan. 1847 | AA |
| Acher, Abraham | O'Neal, Elisabeth | 21, Feb. 1819 | RCH |
| Achterfeld, Gerhard | Reneke, Anna Maria | 27, June 1847 | FF |
| Acker, Jacob | Grobs, Salome | 5, Dec. 1848 | G |
| Ackermann, Alexander | Daum, Catharina | 7, Oct. 1849 | G |
| Ackermann, Bernard | Determann, Catharina | 12, Apr. 1842 | FF |
| Ackermann, Conrad | Staut, Magdalena | 20, May 1849 | C |
| Ackermann, Daniel | Spaeth, Helen | 29, Nov. 1843 | C |
| Ackermann, J. Georg | Stevens, Maria | 28, Jan. 1847 | G |
| Ackermann, Joseph | Eicher, Catharina | 23, Nov. 1841 | FF |
| Ackermann, Mathias | Schuetz, Barbara | 17, Sept 1846 | EE |
| Ackett, Israel | Miller, Mary A. | 9, May 1836 | RCH |
| Ackley, David | Leighton, Elisabeth | 28, Mar. 1833 | RCH |
| Ackley, Hezekiah | Jones, Clarissa | 18, July 1837 | RCH |
| Ackley, John | Scott, Lydia | 21, Aug. 1846 | RCH |
| Ackmann, Heinrich | Heemann, Elisabeth | 7, Oct. 1845 | AA |
| Acley, Hezekiah | Bennett, Lorina | 17, Jan. 1834 | RCH |
| Adam, Franz | Remlinger, Theresa | 23, May 1844 | AA |
| Adam, Mathias | Kuhn, H. P. Susanna | 22, Aug. 1849 | G |
| Adam, Valentin | Schaller, Apollonia | 1, Feb. 1848 | EE |
| Adams, Alexander | Tiebort, Esther Y. | 6, Oct. 1846 | I |
| Adams, Alfred | Coolidge, Rebecca | 1, May 1836 | RCH |
| Adams, Amos B. | Merrell, Charlotte | 5, Dec. 1843 | RCH |
| Adams, Andrew | Brown, Elisabeth | 8, Mar. 1838 | RCH |
| Adams, Andrew | Nase, Susan | 23, June 1842 | RCH |
| Adams, Andrew | Hudson, Elisabeth | 18, July 1842 | RCH |
| Adams, Cordy | Featherman, Nancy | 2, July 1846 | RCH |
| Adams, David | Kitchell, Matilda | 5, Aug. 1824 | RCH |
| Adams, George W. | Heath, Ann M. | 25, Feb. 1838 | RCH |
| Adams, Heinrich | Peters, Julia | 18, July 1843 | AA |
| Adams, Henry J. | Gibson, Abby | 16, Sept 1841 | D |
| Adams, James | Coulman, Mary | 2, July 1842 | RCH |
| Adams, James | Striemetz, Mary Ann | 18, Apr. 1846 | RCH |
| Adams, James | Walker, Margaret | 23, Mar. 1847 | RCH |
| Adams, James | Strickels, Mary Ann | 18, Apr. 1847 | BB |
| Adams, John | Conroy, Mary | 26, Nov. 1849 | BB |
| Adams, John W. | Swift, Eliza | 11, Sept 1823 | RCH |
| Adams, Louis | Budenkopf, Catharine | 7, Dec. 1847 | G |
| Adams, Marvin | Dobins, Catharine M. | 12, July 1835 | RCH |

| Grooms | Brides | Date of Marriage | Code |
|--------|--------|------------------|------|
| ****** | ****** | **** ** ******* | **** |
| Adams, Robert | Gibson, Martha | 27, June 1841 | RCH |
| Adams, Samuel | Pa---, Elisabeth | 19, June 1822 | RCH |
| Adams, Solomon | Lancaster, Lucy | 21, Dec. 1848 | RCH |
| Adams, Thomas J. | Bogie, Isabella | 22, May 1821 | I |
| Adams, Urban H. | Pruden, Mary A. | 14, Feb. 1839 | RCH |
| Adams, William | Green, Elisabeth | 13, Aug. 1845 | RCH |
| Adams, William A. | Cassilly, Mary | 12, Oct. 1842 | I |
| Addis, Albert | Lyons, Catharine Ann | 28, Mar. 1847 | RCH |
| Addison, Cyrus | Lee, Louise | 2, Aug. 1834 | RCH |
| Addison, Patrick | Johnson, Hannah | 24, May 1847 | RCH |
| Adel, Gerhard H. | Bruns, Anna Maria | 24, Feb. 1846 | AA |
| Ader, Jacob | Meitzler, Apollonia | 24, June 1845 | AA |
| Ader, Wilhelm | Ande, Elisabeth | 14, May 1844 | AA |
| Adkins, Edward | Strewoner, Hannah | 13, Oct. 1844 | RCH |
| Adkins, Emery | Symms, Catharine | 24, Nov. 1843 | RCH |
| Adkins, Henry | Conklin, Isabella | 14, Oct. 1847 | RCH |
| Adkins, Silas | Harvey, Phebe | 3, Dec. 1832 | RCH |
| Adler, Leon | August, Dina | 9, Apr. 1848 | RCH |
| Adler, Levi | Maholt, Sarah | 9, May 1847 | RCH |
| Aelen, Johan Albert | Schrand, Angela | 9, Aug. 1846 | AA |
| Affezar, Peter | Zenileger, Catharine | 14, Dec. 1837 | RCH |
| Agar, William | Strohver, Jane | 13, Oct. 1845 | RCH |
| Agar, William | Daughaday, Lydia | 5, June 1849 | RCH |
| Agin, Buroughs | Smith, Sarah Jane | 3, Aug. 1848 | RCH |
| Agner, Allen | ----, ---- | 16, Mar. 1826 | RCH |
| Agnes, Daniel M. | Ray, Mary A. | 4, Oct. 1838 | RCH |
| Agnew, James | Freeman, Mary Ann | 2, Jan. 1848 | RCH |
| Agnew, William | Butler, Jane | 15, Aug. 1847 | RCH |
| Agus, Thomas | Rust, Sarah | 27, Sept 1832 | RCH |
| Ahlborn, Wilhelm | Deller, Catharina | 31, Aug. 1841 | FF |
| Ahlering, Friedrich | Arnsen, Elisabeth | 11, May 1843 | FF |
| Ahlering, Friedrich | Strategier, Elis. | 13, June 1847 | FF |
| Ahlering, Heinrich | Meyer, Maria | 3, Oct. 1844 | F |
| Ahlering, Johan B. | Gerdhabrig, Elisabet | 19, Nov. 1848 | II |
| Ahlers, Friedrich | Bierhorst, Caroline | 15, June 1843 | A |
| Ahlers, Herman H. | Tingers, Maria Anna | 24, Oct. 1847 | EE |
| Ahlers, Herman Hein. | Hofleins, Maria | 8, Apr. 1847 | A |
| Ahlers, Johan H. | Heilemann, Anna M. | 4, Feb. 1849 | EE |
| Ahlers, Johan Heinr. | Thile, Bernardina | 10, Oct. 1843 | FF |
| Ahlers, John Bernard | Zulagen, A.M. Cath. | 6, Feb. 1841 | F |
| Ahlert, Friedrich | Gebel, Gertrud | 6, Feb. 1849 | EE |
| Ahrens, Bernard H. | Kabes, Anna M. | 15, Jan. 1839 | FF |
| Ahrens, Conrad | Rodkamp, Margaretha | 19, Feb. 1847 | C |
| Ahrens, John Gerhard | Grammann, Margaretha | 29, Jan. 1839 | FF |
| Ahrens, Wilhelm | Brueggemann, Anna | 12, Nov. 1849 | F |
| Ahrens, Wilhelm | Gotting, Anna Maria | 14, Apr. 1846 | FF |
| Ahrham, Joseph W. | Hunt, Aaclaw | 12, Oct. 1835 | FF |
| Ahring, Friedrich | Meyer, Elisabeth | 12, Nov. 1844 | F |
| Ahring, Georg Heinr. | Wilke, A.M. Louise | 4, Sept 1845 | F |
| Aicher, | Wallis, Amanda | 6, Dec. 1825 | RCH |
| Aiken, Macauley | Mix, Clara B. | 1, May 1845 | D |
| Aitchenson, James | Anthony, Cordelia | 14, May 1824 | RCH |
| Aitken, George | Preston, Eleanor | 21, June 1846 | RCH |
| Akers, James | Fagan, Mary A. | 24, Apr. 1844 | RCH |
| Akins, Samuel | Farin, Catharine | 9, July 1820 | RCH |
| Akins, Thomas O. | Ward, Martha | 26, Feb. 1834 | RCH |
| Albels, Foster | Slunck, Catharine | 24, June 1832 | RCH |
| Albers, Bernard | Harbering, Elisabeth | 7, Nov. 1843 | FF |
| Albers, Bernard | Kester, Maria Anna | 26, Apr. 1846 | AA |
| Albers, Eilard | Raters, Angela | 21, Oct. 1845 | RCH |
| Albers, Eilard | Husmann, Maria Cath. | 11, Jan. 1849 | FF |
| Albers, Gerhard | Linnemann, Catharine | 8, Apr. 1845 | AA |
| Albers, Gerhard E. | Raders, Angela | 23, Oct. 1845 | AA |
| Albers, Gerhard H. | Knollenberg, Cath. M | 28, Feb. 1844 | F |
| Albers, Heinrich | Wilmer, Theresa | 27, Feb. 1838 | FF |
| Albers, Heinrich | Woltring, Maria | 13, Feb. 1838 | FF |
| Albers, Heinrich G. | VorderWuesten, Maria | 8, May 1841 | F |
| Albers, Herman H. | Weheidem, Anna | 30, Aug. 1846 | EE |
| Albers, J. Christoph | Vornholt, M. Louise | 8, Feb. 1844 | F |
| Albers, J. Friedrich | Droppelmann, Elis. | 12, June 1849 | II |
| Albers, Johan Theo. | Hoppe, Elisabeth | 1, Nov. 1846 | AA |

| Grooms<br>***** | Brides<br>***** | Date of Marriage<br>**** ** ******** | Code<br>**** |
|---|---|---|---|
| Albert, Adam | Wilson, Sybilla | 25, May 1843 | RCH |
| Albert, Eduard | Berger, Christina | 22, Oct. 1843 | G |
| Albig, Johan | Schmidt, Maria | 23, Jan. 1849 | G |
| Albrecht, Christian | Hoffer, Catharina | 11, Oct. 1836 | FF |
| Albrecht, G. Wilhelm | Finke, Doretta | 15, Nov. 1849 | G |
| Albrecht, Georg | Goss, Ballina | 26, Apr. 1836 | FF |
| Albricht, John | Yunbin, Barbara | 7, Aug. 1847 | RCH |
| Albright, James | Marshall, Rebecca | 3, Oct. 1847 | RCH |
| Albright, John | Webb, Bulah | 10, May 1843 | RCH |
| Alcoke, James B. | Creager, Emily | 9, Nov. 1842 | RCH |
| Alcoke, William | Bowen, Susan E. | 16, Feb. 1834 | RCH |
| Alcorn, John G. | Mann, Rachel | 13, Mar. 1834 | RCH |
| Alder, Samuel J. | Robbins, Lucy W. | 25, Aug. 1819 | RCH |
| Alder, Ulrich | Kugler, Josepha | 13, Apr. 1846 | A |
| Aldrich, Gustav | Grim, Permelia | 28, Aug. 1837 | RCH |
| Aldrich, Patrick | Allen, Elisabeth | 22, June 1834 | RCH |
| Aldrich, Taylor | Jackson, Anna | 2, May 1831 | RCH |
| Aldridge, Lewy | Tull, Mary Ann | 30, Mar. 1836 | RCH |
| Alert, Gerhard | Sturk, Catharine | 2, May 1843 | AA |
| Alexander, Heinrich | VonNieta, Eva | 4, Aug. 1840 | G |
| Alexander, Heinrich | Hallebach, Rosina | 25, Oct. 1846 | G |
| Alexander, Hugh | McConnell, James | 27, June 1842 | RCH |
| Alexander, James | Browne, Elisabeth | 16, Aug. 1841 | RCH |
| Alexander, Nathaniel | Brandroff, Rachel | Oct. 1844 | RCH |
| Alexander, P. | Doty, Margaret | 16, Mar. 1848 | RCH |
| Alexander, Robert | Shield, Ann M. | 21, Nov. 1833 | RCH |
| Alexander, Thomas | Martin, Margaret | 6, June 1835 | RCH |
| Alexander, Thomas | Hyndmann, Martha | 9, June 1847 | RCH |
| Alexander, Thomas | Newton, Jane | 28, Aug. 1847 | RCH |
| Alexander, Washing. | Clark, Ann | 1, Aug. 1848 | RCH |
| Alexander, William | Fry, Elisabeth | 20, July 1820 | RCH |
| Alexander, William | Vaughn, Caroline | 30, Sept 1836 | RCH |
| Alexander, William | Hall, Nancy | 26, May 1849 | RCH |
| Alf, Bernard Herman | Bernsen, Maria Cath. | 15, Jan. 1846 | AA |
| Alf, Franz | Schulte, Maria | 15, Apr. 1849 | II |
| Alf, Gerhard H. | Herzog, Elisabeth | 28, Jan. 1845 | AA |
| Alf, Herman | Gers, M. Elisabeth | 8, Feb. 1849 | II |
| Alf, Johan Wilhelm | Lin, Maria Adelheid | 25, Aug. 1846 | EE |
| Alf, Theodor | Schippers, Margaret | 13, Feb. 1849 | II |
| Alfers, Johan Gerh. | Gomann, Catharine | 18, Aug. 1846 | AA |
| Alfing, Bernard | Linnenkugel, Elis. | 3, Nov. 1847 | FF |
| Alfing, Friedrich | Amkemeyer, Margaret | 3, June 1847 | B |
| Alfink, Wilhelm | Wilwin, Christina | 17, Mar. 1842 | RCH |
| Alfred, | Shearer, Amy | 31, Dec. 1820 | RCH |
| Alfred, James | Bennett, Nelly | 14, July 1826 | RCH |
| Alfrid, John A. | Wil---, Nancy | 26, Dec. 1822 | RCH |
| Algair, Thomas | Coates, Elisabeth | 7, Aug. 1836 | RCH |
| Alhring, Heinrich | Graentt, Maria Anna | 15, Nov. 1842 | FF |
| Alick, Adam | Mueller, Margaretha | 20, Feb. 1849 | EE |
| Alig, Andreas | Gebensbauer, Cath. | 28, Nov. 1844 | AA |
| Alig, Nicolaus | Wessel, Elisabeth | 15, Jan. 1845 | AA |
| Alker, Barney | Hadebach, Maria | 2, Dec. 1838 | FF |
| Allabaugh, John | Callahan, Mary J. | 17, Feb. 1846 | BB |
| Allbecker, Johan | Paul, Barbara | 27, Jan. 1841 | FF |
| Allbritt, | Evatt, Rebecca | 28, Jan. 1822 | RCH |
| Allch, Bernard Herm. | Benson, M. Catharine | 14, Jan. 1846 | RCH |
| Allcorn, William | Row, Anna Maria | 11, Oct. 1846 | RCH |
| Allee, William | ----, ---- | 14, Oct. 1823 | RCH |
| Allen, Alexander | Ruppell, Sarah | 13, Mar. 1838 | RCH |
| Allen, Caleb | Hastings, Caroline | 3, Aug. 1835 | I |
| Allen, Caleb | Bassett, Polly | 31, Oct. 1841 | RCH |
| Allen, Charles | Avis, Mary L. | 22, Feb. 1844 | D |
| Allen, Ebenezer | Semler, Elisabeth | 28, Aug. 1845 | RCH |
| Allen, Edward P. | Vannie, Sarah | 28, Oct. 1835 | RCH |
| Allen, Enoch | Kruse, Phoebe | Aug. 1845 | RCH |
| Allen, George | VanZant, Mary E. | 24, Dec. 1841 | RCH |
| Allen, George | Thompson, Jane | 13, Feb. 1847 | RCH |
| Allen, George | Brown, Charlotte | 4, Aug. 1847 | RCH |
| Allen, George D. | Hamilton, Mary Ann | 26, July 1832 | RCH |
| Allen, Harrison | Perry, Maria | 25, Dec. 1845 | RCH |
| Allen, Hiram | Jackson, Almira | 9, Jan. 1823 | RCH |

| Grooms | Brides | Date of Marriage | Code |
|--------|--------|------------------|------|
| ****** | ****** | **** ** ******** | **** |
| Allen, Ira D. | Gibbs, Hannah | 5, Aug. 1840 | RCH |
| Allen, J.A. | Fisk, Jane | Feb. 1827 | RCH |
| Allen, Jacob | Burnett, Maria | 27, July 1840 | RCH |
| Allen, James | Stine, Lavina | 16, Sept 1837 | RCH |
| Allen, James Alfred | Bashiers, Alice | 15, Feb. 1847 | RCH |
| Allen, Jedediah | Mistlynn, Elisabeth | 17, Nov. 1840 | RCH |
| Allen, John | Tucker, Sarah Ann | 25, Feb. 1834 | RCH |
| Allen, John | Mead, Sarah | 8, Jan. 1842 | RCH |
| Allen, John | Reeder, Cornelia | 4, Nov. 1846 | RCH |
| Allen, John W. | Ball, Esther | 17, Mar. 1837 | RCH |
| Allen, Jonathan | Whitaker, Nancy | 21, May 1834 | RCH |
| Allen, Joseph | Thompson, Mary | 6, Dec. 1845 | RCH |
| Allen, Robert S. | Heylands, Elisabeth | 2, Aug. 1834 | RCH |
| Allen, Samuel | Riddle, Emeline | 3, Apr. 1849 | RCH |
| Allen, Seth | Moore, Sarah | 4, Apr. 1847 | RCH |
| Allen, Thomas | Walker, Mary | 10, Apr. 1843 | RCH |
| Allen, W.C. | Jeffries, Emily | 18, Sept 1841 | RCH |
| Allen, William | Orr, Mary | 27, Sept 1821 | RCH |
| Allen, William | McHenry, Catharine | 5, Oct. 1841 | RCH |
| Allen, William | Gold, Margaret | 18, Oct. 1843 | RCH |
| Allen, William | Williams, Sarah | 31, Jan. 1844 | RCH |
| Allers, John Fred. | Smearson, Anna P. | 12, July 1836 | RCH |
| Alley, Andreas | ---bauer, | Nov. 1844 | RCH |
| Alley, Benjamin | ----, ---- | Nov. 1844 | RCH |
| Allgeier, Heinrich | Ihrig, Maria Elis. | 4, May 1841 | FF |
| Allgeier, Michael S. | Anderson, Henrietta | 31, Dec. 1849 | BB |
| Allgeier, Paul | Reichert, Elisabeth | 13, June 1849 | CC |
| Allgeier, Sebastian | Snyder, Sarah A. | 4, Feb. 1845 | BB |
| Allhands, John | Winter, Margaret | 25, Aug. 1843 | RCH |
| Allison, Archibald | Morrison, Amy | 9, Feb. 1834 | RCH |
| Allison, John | Hamilton, Arabella | 2, Apr. 1848 | RCH |
| Allison, John T. | ----, Rebecca | 20, Feb. 1823 | RCH |
| Alloways, John | Elsrate, Sarah | 17, May 1847 | RCH |
| Alms, George | Berenz, Louise | 25, Apr. 1837 | F |
| Alms, Gerhard Heinr. | Hespe, Friedricka D. | 17, Oct. 1849 | F |
| Alms, Heinrich Aug. | Nohring, Cath. M. | 25, Nov. 1841 | F |
| Alms, Herman Friedr. | Duhme, Margaretha M. | 9, June 1842 | F |
| Alms, Wilhelm H. | Duhme, A.Maria Elis. | 16, Dec. 1845 | G |
| Almy, Giles M. | Sanborn, Elvira B. | 6, July 1841 | I |
| Almy, Philipp | Marshall, Synthia | 21, Dec. 1825 | RCH |
| Alpin, Andrew | Merie, Margaret | 17, Mar. 1817 | RCH |
| Alsberle, | Loffer, Maria | 3, Sept 1844 | AA |
| Alshire, Joel | Williams, Nancy Ann | 24, Mar. 1844 | RCH |
| Alt, Johan Gerhard | Welsch, Barbara | 24, Aug. 1847 | EE |
| Altehoff, Herman | Nuxol, M. Elisabeth | 10, Oct. 1847 | AA |
| Alten, John | Toy, Mary | 9, June 1838 | RCH |
| Altenau, James | McFolard, Jane | 21, Mar. 1835 | RCH |
| Altstadter, Michael | Kerbel, Veronica | 28, Jan. 1840 | FF |
| Alves, William | Taylor, Hannah | 13, Aug. 1845 | RCH |
| Always, Charles | E---, Christina | 18, Aug. 1822 | RCH |
| Aman, Conrad | Ankenbauer, Margaret | 1, Aug. 1847 | EE |
| Aman, Lawrence | Quick, Catharine | 4, Jan. 1827 | RCH |
| Amann, Arnold | Apgar, Anna | 21, Nov. 1843 | RCH |
| Amann, Heinrich | Heth, Anna Maria | 14, Oct. 1845 | AA |
| Amberg, David | Leeser, Rosetta | 3, Nov. 1845 | RCH |
| Amberg, Moses | Newman, Sophia | 19, Oct. 1843 | RCH |
| Amberg, Wilhelm | Eberle, Elisabeth | 13, Feb. 1838 | FF |
| Ambros, Alois | Schaffer, Wilhelmina | Apr. 1847 | RCH |
| Amburg, Hezekiah | Neiler, Hannah | 22, Dec. 1846 | RCH |
| Amburg, Samuel | Gruenbaum, Regina | 13, Dec. 1845 | RCH |
| Ammermann, Andrew | Kelley, Frances Mary | 12, Aug. 1837 | RCH |
| Ammermann, Elbert | Bolser, Olive | 16, Jan. 1836 | RCH |
| Ammermann, John | Hatt, Anna | 13, May 1837 | RCH |
| Amps, Joseph | Hagen, Maria | 23, Apr. 1849 | EE |
| Ams, Gregor | Dinger, Crescentia | 22, June 1848 | EE |
| Amyotte, Francis | Lammont, Elisabeth | 21, Feb. 1842 | BB |
| An---, Peter | Hatfield, Elisabeth | 27, Nov. 1817 | RCH |
| Anawalk, Elias | Fleming, Jane | 6, June 1833 | RCH |
| Anders, James | Karr, Mary | 16, Mar. 1834 | RCH |
| Anders, Joseph | Guild, Amanda | 25, July 1849 | RCH |
| Anderson, | King, Mariah | 10, June 1823 | RCH |

| Grooms | Brides | Date of Marriage | Code |
|--------|--------|------------------|------|
| ****** | ****** | **** ** ******** | **** |
| Anderson, Adam | Newkirk, Lydia Ann | 30, Apr. 1843 | RCH |
| Anderson, Alex M. | Bakewell, Sarah | 29, Mar. 1826 | I |
| Anderson, Alexander | Beach, Nancy Ann | 1834 | RCH |
| Anderson, Andrew | Tivers, Leah | 2, Oct. 1834 | RCH |
| Anderson, Chamberlin | Jones, Ann | 19, May 1842 | RCH |
| Anderson, Charles | Loring, Elisabeth | 24, May 1842 | RCH |
| Anderson, Edon | Lumley, Mary | 28, Sept 1841 | RCH |
| Anderson, George | Brown, Rhoda | 17, Mar. 1834 | RCH |
| Anderson, George L. | Humphreys, Emeline | 15, June 1842 | I |
| Anderson, Hayden | Tatman, Sarah Ann | 8, Nov. 1846 | RCH |
| Anderson, Hugh | Feeney, Ann | 26, Apr. 1841 | RCH |
| Anderson, Israes | Julet, Jane | 1, Aug. 1832 | RCH |
| Anderson, Jacob | Bishop, Lydia Ann | 30, Mar. 1826 | RCH |
| Anderson, Jacob | Sunman, Mary | 31, Dec. 1843 | RCH |
| Anderson, James | Till, Mary | 8, Aug. 1833 | RCH |
| Anderson, James | Alford, Mary Ann | 1, Mar. 1837 | RCH |
| Anderson, James | Burgen, Catharine | 21, Mar. 1844 | RCH |
| Anderson, James | Miller, Susan | 14, June 1846 | RCH |
| Anderson, James | Hudson, Elisabeth | 19, Dec. 1846 | RCH |
| Anderson, James | Long, Elisabeth | 4, Feb. 1847 | RCH |
| Anderson, John | Clark, Mary | 3, Jan. 1826 | RCH |
| Anderson, John | Torrence, Mariah | 14, June 1827 | RCH |
| Anderson, John | Riske, Mary Ann | 26, Mar. 1833 | RCH |
| Anderson, John | Newton, Elisabeth A. | 20, Dec. 1833 | RCH |
| Anderson, John | Tapley, Elisabeth | 5, May 1841 | RCH |
| Anderson, John | Amyotte, Sophia | 15, Jan. 1842 | RCH |
| Anderson, John | Row, Margaret E. | 15, Nov. 1846 | RCH |
| Anderson, John | Monrow, Abigail | 4, Feb. 1847 | RCH |
| Anderson, John | Scott, Jane | 18, Mar. 1847 | RCH |
| Anderson, John | Dennis, Mary Jane | 11, Oct. 1848 | RCH |
| Anderson, John | Manifold, Margaret | 24, Apr. 1849 | RCH |
| Anderson, John G. | Anderson, Mary | 9, Jan. 1826 | RCH |
| Anderson, John G. | Hoover, Tabitha | 18, Dec. 1836 | RCH |
| Anderson, Joseph | McLean, Maria | 7, June 1832 | RCH |
| Anderson, Kewett | Chamberlain, Cath. | 25, July 1822 | RCH |
| Anderson, Larz | Longworth, Catharine | 10, Sept 1834 | D |
| Anderson, Levi | Guinup, Ruth | 26, Feb. 1847 | RCH |
| Anderson, Morgan | Phillips, America | 21, Mar. 1833 | RCH |
| Anderson, Robert | Hutchins, Sarah | 8, May 1836 | RCH |
| Anderson, Robert J. | Writing, Mary Jane | 17, July 1839 | RCH |
| Anderson, Samuel | Wood, Cassy | 22, Apr. 1826 | RCH |
| Anderson, Samuel | Johnson, Catharine | 29, Sept 1836 | RCH |
| Anderson, Samuel | Berry, Rachel | Dec. 1842 | RCH |
| Anderson, Samuel | Cosgrove, Elisabeth | 1, July 1849 | BB |
| Anderson, Thomas | Yeatman, Isabella | 18, Sept 1817 | RCH |
| Anderson, Thomas | Rigdon, Naomi | 27, Sept 1846 | RCH |
| Anderson, William | Schaefer, Mary | 5, Oct. 1835 | RCH |
| Anderson, William | Clark, Jane D. | 5, Oct. 1837 | RCH |
| Anderson, William C. | Howell, Elisabeth M. | 23, Jan. 1836 | RCH |
| Anderson, William C. | Yeatman, Anna Maria | 16, May 1837 | I |
| Anderson, Younger | Burritt, Maria | 16, Jan. 1847 | RCH |
| Andreas, Christoph | Ferbig, Anna Maria | 3, Jan. 1849 | A |
| Andreas, John | Calvin, Margaret | 20, Sept 1846 | RCH |
| Andreas, John | Wesel, Barbara | 16, Sept 1847 | RCH |
| Andree, Jacob | Hutt, Susanna | 14, May 1834 | RCH |
| Andres, Jacob | Wirmel, Barbara | 7, Sept 1845 | AA |
| Andres, Johan | Rumel, Elisabeth | 7, Aug. 1849 | A |
| Andres, Matthias | Roeter, Catharina | 26, May 1841 | FF |
| Andress, Charles | Marshall, | 14, Oct. 1824 | RCH |
| Andress, Frederick | Worthington, Mary | 9, May 1833 | RCH |
| Andrew, | Boyer, Anna | 23, May 1838 | RCH |
| Andrew, Henry C. | Conclin, Jane | 31, July 1848 | RCH |
| Andrew, Jacob P. | Pottenger, Elis. J. | 3, Apr. 1834 | RCH |
| Andrew, William C. | Johnston, Adeline | 4, Aug. 1847 | RCH |
| Andrews, Abraham | Newberger, Margaret | 18, Jan. 1849 | RCH |
| Andrews, Andrew | Harris, Hulda | 18, Dec. 1846 | RCH |
| Andrews, Charles | Maranda, Priscilla | 3, Oct. 1841 | RCH |
| Andrews, Charles | Young, Mary Jane | 6, Sept 1849 | RCH |
| Andrews, James | Ross, Sarah | 22, Oct. 1845 | RCH |
| Andrews, John | Mann, Sarah | 24, Oct. 1832 | RCH |
| Andrews, John | Boyd, Elisabeth | 30, Apr. 1846 | RCH |

| Grooms | Brides | Date of Marriage | Code |
|--------|--------|------------------|------|
| ****** | ****** | **** ** ******** | **** |
| Andrews, Joseph | Smith, Mary | 13, Apr. 1837 | RCH |
| Andrews, Joseph | Corwin, Ann | 14, Nov. 1841 | RCH |
| Andrews, Joseph | Morris, Caroline | 9, Aug. 1847 | RCH |
| Andrews, Joseph M. | ----, Esther | 17, Nov. 1822 | RCH |
| Andrews, Mark | Gerrity, Mary | 27, Apr. 1849 | GG |
| Andrews, Nicolaus | Wood, Matilda | 18, Mar. 1840 | RCH |
| Andrews, Richard | Holmes, Elisabeth | 30, July 1846 | RCH |
| Andrews, Robert | Law, Ann | 16, Oct. 1838 | RCH |
| Andrews, Robert | Law, Jane | 24, Sept 1846 | RCH |
| Andrews, Rupert R. | Harris, Cordelia M. | 27, Dec. 1832 | RCH |
| Andrews, Samuel | Grose, Maria W. | 10, Sept 1842 | RCH |
| Andrews, Samuel | McCormick, Mary | 6, June 1848 | RCH |
| Andrews, Thomas | Baker, Mary Ann | 1, Nov. 1845 | RCH |
| Andrews, William | Dewell, Harriet | 21, Apr. 1836 | RCH |
| Ange, Solomon G. | Damiael, Maria B. | 23, Jan. 1834 | RCH |
| Angelo, Adison | Cline, Mary E. | 26, Nov. 1837 | RCH |
| Angern, Johan G. | Plogmann, Josephina | 22, July 1849 | EE |
| Angersbach, Joseph M | Laux, Theresa | 14, Sept 1847 | AA |
| Angevine, Charles | Skaats, Catharine E. | 5, Nov. 1845 | RCH |
| Angher, Jacob | Mitchell, Frances A. | 1, Mar. 1833 | RCH |
| Angle, Solomon | McCune, Julia | 9, Dec. 1845 | RCH |
| Ankenbauer, Georg | Runzer, Maria Magdal | 25, Oct. 1846 | EE |
| Ankenbauer, Johan | Kamper, Anna Maria | 23, Nov. 1843 | AA |
| Ankenbauer, Joseph | Bittner, Margaretha | 31, Jan. 1843 | FF |
| Ankenbauer, Martin | Boijour, Maria | 11, May 1845 | FF |
| Ankenbrock, Johan H. | Kramer, Gertrud | 8, June 1841 | FF |
| Anley, Richard | Harris, Rachel | 9, Feb. 1826 | RCH |
| Annear, John | Sooney, Nancy | 16, May 1843 | RCH |
| Anselm, Joseph | Thiemann, Sophia | 14, Dec. 1841 | RCH |
| Anselm, Joseph | Guddorf, Cath. (Mrs) | 2, Dec. 1849 | CC |
| Anstaedt, Adam | Baumgartner, Cath. | 1, Oct. 1848 | A |
| Anten, David | Clark, Mary Ann | 28, June 1846 | RCH |
| Anthes, Peter | Meyer, Dorothea | 12, Jan. 1845 | G |
| Anthony, Joseph | Bentley, Sarah | 3, Oct. 1824 | RCH |
| Anthony, William T. | Merry, Ann Elisabeth | 6, Nov. 1833 | RCH |
| Antram, Joseph | Armistead, Alcina | 23, July 1849 | RCH |
| Anxel, Stephan | Helem, Elisabeth | 12, Apr. 1842 | FF |
| Apenbrog, Francis | Webers, Anna Maria | 13, Oct. 1846 | EE |
| Apfelbeck, Michael | Welsch, Catharine | 13, Oct. 1845 | FF |
| Apgar, Benaya | Arbuckle, Ruth | 10, Oct. 1843 | RCH |
| Apgar, David | Cregar, Amelia | 29, Apr. 1844 | RCH |
| Apgar, Jacob | Riker, Emeline | 29, Aug. 1848 | RCH |
| Apgar, Matthias | Sears, Sophia | 21, Aug. 1844 | RCH |
| Apgar, Peter | Busatt, Sarah | 12, Nov. 1841 | RCH |
| Apke, Bernard H. | Ahaus, Maria Elis. | 12, Aug. 1849 | EE |
| Aple, John S. | Beayl, Phebe | 1, Dec. 1833 | RCH |
| Apple, John | Rickett, Sarah | 25, July 1821 | RCH |
| Apple, William | Gerard, Nancy | 4, Feb. 1847 | RCH |
| Applegate, Aaron | Black, Jane | 19, June 1819 | RCH |
| Applegate, Amos | Humble, Elisabeth | 3, Dec. 1841 | RCH |
| Applegate, Daniel | Brinkdal, Sophia | 8, June 1824 | RCH |
| Applegate, David | Hills, Martha | 19, Apr. 1821 | RCH |
| Applegate, Henry | Applegate, Margaret | 26, Nov. 1820 | RCH |
| Applegate, Israel | Colsher, Mary | 22, Dec. 1822 | RCH |
| Applegate, James | Leming, Martha | 19, June 1834 | RCH |
| Applegate, John | Funk, Elisabeth | 29, May 1844 | RCH |
| Applegate, Lewis | Stout, Mary | 1, Dec. 1841 | RCH |
| Applig, S. | Burrows, Sarah T. | 16, Jan. 1834 | RCH |
| Arbaugh, Albert | Geno, Margaret | 12, Apr. 1849 | RCH |
| Arbuckle, Joseph | Miller, Mary | 29, Aug. 1842 | RCH |
| Archer, John | McQuillin, Elisabeth | 18, Dec. 1846 | RCH |
| Archinger, Anton | Boeh, Rigarta | 6, Aug. 1848 | FF |
| Aregood, George | Dunn, Elisabeth | 3, Jan. 1839 | RCH |
| Arent, Daniel | Gartner, Theresa | 8, Jan. 1838 | FF |
| Arfkamp, Simon | Aedorn, Rek. | 18, Dec. 1849 | RCH |
| Arft, J Christian A. | Agness, Anna Maria | 25, Oct. 1849 | A |
| Argadine, William | Mannel, Rosanna | 16, July 1842 | RCH |
| Argedine, Robert | Stratton, Matilda | 17, Oct. 1837 | RCH |
| Argo, Ebenezer | Yapel, Amanda | 4, Oct. 1842 | RCH |
| Arison, Thomas S. | Collins, Elisabeth | 10, Oct. 1833 | RCH |
| Arling, Francis H. | Grothe, Maria Elis. | 24, Jan. 1847 | EE |

| Grooms<br>****** | Brides<br>****** | Date of Marriage<br>**** ** ******** | Code<br>**** |
|---|---|---|---|
| Arling, J. Heinrich | Behne, Elisabeth | 9, May 1837 | FF |
| Armatage, Henry | Morrison, Maria | 11, Oct. 1847 | RCH |
| Armbricht, Ludwig | Bode, Wilhelmina | 25, Dec. 1846 | RCH |
| Armbruster, Bernard | Abba, Maria Anna | 14, Jan. 1845 | AA |
| Armbruster, Dominick | Welsch, Maria Cath. | 4, Oct. 1849 | EE |
| Armbruster, Johan | Kramer, Maria | 10, Apr. 1849 | EE |
| Armbruster, Thomas | Heim, Elisabeth | 17, Aug. 1837 | FF |
| Armistead, George M. | Hubble, Elcy | 17, Feb. 1820 | RCH |
| Armistedt, Seymour | Ferris, Maria | 3, Nov. 1847 | RCH |
| Armstead, Henry | Cleland, Hester | 23, Mar. 1834 | RCH |
| Armstead, Richard | Weiff, Ann D. | 18, Dec. 1833 | RCH |
| Armsted, Reuben | Shilton, Emily | 14, Dec. 1848 | RCH |
| Armstrong, Andrew | Askew, Mary | 20, May 1819 | RCH |
| Armstrong, Andrew | Smith, Francis | 19, Sept 1849 | RCH |
| Armstrong, Arthur | Scilling, Pricilla | 24, Oct. 1837 | RCH |
| Armstrong, Benjamin | Walters, Margaret | 25, Sept 1849 | RCH |
| Armstrong, George W. | Jackson, Chesiphy | 15, Dec. 1833 | RCH |
| Armstrong, Grandson | Prith, Harriet | 13, Oct. 1841 | RCH |
| Armstrong, Hamilton | Smith, Hetty | 3, Oct. 1843 | RCH |
| Armstrong, James | Smith, Sarah | 13, Apr. 1820 | RCH |
| Armstrong, James | Donald, Sarah Ann | 20, Apr. 1839 | RCH |
| Armstrong, James | Roszel, Louise | 24, June 1847 | RCH |
| Armstrong, John | Brown, Ann | 2, Feb. 1832 | RCH |
| Armstrong, John | Fostick, Frances | 25, Dec. 1849 | RCH |
| Armstrong, John H. | Russell, Theodocia | 25, Mar. 1849 | RCH |
| Armstrong, John L. | Taber, Ann | 13, Dec. 1832 | RCH |
| Armstrong, Joseph B. | Harslet, | 22, Dec. 1824 | RCH |
| Armstrong, Lafayette | Dudley, Charlotte | 15, Oct. 1845 | I |
| Armstrong, Marshall | Lyons, Henrietta | 25, Feb. 1847 | RCH |
| Armstrong, Nathaniel | Millspaugh, Charlott | 9, Nov. 1843 | RCH |
| Armstrong, Robert | Vail, Eleanor | 13, Feb. 1834 | RCH |
| Armstrong, Robert | Burley, Jane | 1, Oct. 1835 | D |
| Armstrong, Robert | Wood, Catharine | 19, Apr. 1842 | RCH |
| Armstrong, Robert | Kellogg, Margaret | 30, Sept 1845 | RCH |
| Armstrong, Robert G. | Simmons, Mary Jane | 25, Nov. 1847 | BB |
| Armstrong, Thomas | McSorley, Rebecca | 16, Aug. 1821 | I |
| Armstrong, William | Halstead, Patience | 10, July 1825 | RCH |
| Arndt, George | Woeber, Magdalena | 6, July 1848 | RCH |
| Arnhold, Wilhelm F. | Harms, Maria | 13, Oct. 1844 | F |
| Arnkens, Herman | Schmiederbernd, M. | 21, May 1848 | AA |
| Arnold, Calvin | Phelps, Jane | 6, July 1841 | RCH |
| Arnold, Christian | Vogel, Margaret | 19, Mar. 1847 | RCH |
| Arnold, Jerry | Reed, Becky | 22, Dec. 1849 | RCH |
| Arnold, Paul | Keil, Maria | 28, July 1844 | RCH |
| Arnold, Thomas | Perkins, | 23, Feb. 1826 | RCH |
| Arnold, Thomas H. | Hanson, Harriet | 6, May 1840 | RCH |
| Arnold, William | Sloop, Catharine | 6, Oct. 1818 | RCH |
| Arnold, William | Hedge, Christine | May 1849 | RCH |
| Arnot, Christopher | Vorhees, Sarah | 11, Dec. 1836 | RCH |
| Arnstall, Adam | Schwein, M. | 21, Oct. 1841 | RCH |
| Arnt, George | Little, Caroline | 31, Dec. 1846 | RCH |
| Arnzen, J. Heinrich | Carl, Isabella | 28, Mar. 1849 | RCH |
| Arons, David | Craig, Mary Ann | 14, Mar. 1847 | RCH |
| Arons, Garrett | Dumont, Harriet L. | 6, Sept 1843 | RCH |
| Arris---, William H. | Kibby, Harriet | 9, Mar. 1840 | I |
| Arrison, | Fuller, Margaret | 6, Feb. 1824 | RCH |
| Arterburn, William | Goff, Letitia | 6, Nov. 1845 | RCH |
| Arthaus, Heinrich | Steinkamp, Elisabeth | 25, Apr. 1847 | CC |
| Arthins, William | VanWinkle, Ann | 1, Sept 1840 | RCH |
| Arthonstall, George | Swail, Marian | 7, June 1827 | I |
| Arthurs, John | Evans, Nancy | 30, Oct. 1835 | RCH |
| Arthurs, Nicolaus | Cobb, Charlotte | 5, Apr. 1836 | RCH |
| Arthurs, William | VanZant, Elisabeth | 7, Feb. 1822 | RCH |
| Arthurton, Joseph | Simonson, Elisabeth | 9, Oct. 1833 | RCH |
| Arthurton, Milton | Simonson, Sarah | 9, Oct. 1833 | RCH |
| Artmann, Bernard | Meyer, Maria Anna | 16, Nov. 1847 | EE |
| Artsch, Nicolaus | Hoffmann, Barbara | 31, May 1847 | C |
| Arvare, Francis | Smith, Catharine | 7, Oct. 1839 | RCH |
| Ary, Samuel | Davis, Prudo | 22, Sept 1834 | RCH |
| As---, John | Cooper, Elisabeth | 7, Jan. 1836 | RCH |
| Aschenauer, Francis | Ammann, Anna | 10, Oct. 1847 | AA |

| Grooms | Brides | Date of Marriage | Code |
|--------|--------|------------------|------|
| ****** | ****** | **** ** ******** | **** |
| Ash, James | Bliss, Mary Ann | 8, Feb. 1836 | RCH |
| Ashbrock, Thomas | Goodwin, Margaret | 17, Aug. 1835 | RCH |
| Ashburn, Richard | Williams, Mary | 27, Oct. 1818 | RCH |
| Ashby, | Cook, Mary | 18, Jan. 1837 | RCH |
| Ashby, James | Beam, Elvira | 16, Dec. 1847 | RCH |
| Ashcraft, Benjamin | Cox, Emeline | 1, Jan. 1822 | RCH |
| Ashcraft, Benjamin | Barkitt, Sarah | 27, Aug. 1834 | RCH |
| Ashcraft, Hiram | Murphy, Amanda | 20, July 1836 | RCH |
| Ashcraft, Jesse | Miller, Mary | 3, Nov. 1841 | RCH |
| Ashcraft, Robert S. | Ugle, Mary | 20, Feb. 1845 | RCH |
| Ashcraft, Samuel | White, Agnes | 23, Sept 1842 | RCH |
| Ashcraft, Thomas | Dean, Mary Ann | 22, May 1849 | RCH |
| Asher, Edmund | Law, Adaline | 28, Feb. 1836 | RCH |
| Asher, Francis | Fair, Catharine | 30, May 1835 | RCH |
| Asher, William | Woolman, Phebe | 16, Oct. 1841 | RCH |
| Ashford, Zebulon | Miller, Margaret | 19, Dec. 1847 | RCH |
| Ashlaw, Joseph | Ashton, Margaret | 11, Sept 1837 | RCH |
| Ashley, Stephen | B---, Emeline | 4, June 1835 | RCH |
| Ashman, James | Clarkson, Mary A. | 14, Jan. 1849 | RCH |
| Ashton, James | Jones, Lydia | 3, May 1846 | RCH |
| Ashton, James H. | Davidson, A. Elis. | 13, July 1848 | RCH |
| Ashton, John | Cordingley, Calista | 4, July 1847 | RCH |
| Askew, Lewis | Vandever, Ingebe | 3, Nov. 1836 | RCH |
| Askew, Lewis | Bernan, Jane | 31, Aug. 1842 | RCH |
| Asmus, Friedrich | Steinert, Barbara | 1, Apr. 1839 | G |
| Asmus, Ludwig | Hembler, Maria | 27, Apr. 1848 | G |
| Aspey, Harvey | Staughton, Catharine | 9, Apr. 1826 | RCH |
| Aspey, John | Hutchinson, Isabella | 6, May 1844 | I |
| Aspinal, | Catternale, Emma | 1, Jan. 1834 | I |
| Aspinwall, Benjamin | Thornhill, Elisabeth | 4, Dec. 1833 | RCH |
| Assling, Herman H. | Blanke, Margaretha | 19, Nov. 1846 | B |
| Assmann, J. Bernard | Gerke, Maria Elis. | 19, July 1846 | FF |
| Aszmann, Heinrich | Wellmann, M Caroline | 21, Sept 1848 | RCH |
| Atchinson, John | Holliday, Belinda | 5, Apr. 1849 | RCH |
| Athearn, Frederick | Patterson, Elisabeth | 19, Mar. 1833 | RCH |
| Atherton, Elijah | Arnold, Mary | 19, Aug. 1843 | RCH |
| Atherton, George | Bonnell, Adelia | 30, Aug. 1846 | RCH |
| Athison, William | Park, Elisabeth W. | 28, Mar. 1835 | RCH |
| Athmer, Bernard | Puthoff, Elisabeth | 26, Nov. 1844 | FF |
| Atkerson, Sirens | Maddox, Nancy | 31, Jan. 1846 | RCH |
| Atkins, Mark | Williams, Mary Ann | 9, Dec. 1846 | RCH |
| Atkinson, Ashly | Bailey, Mercy B. | June 1849 | RCH |
| Atkinson, Daniel | Thatcher, Summervile | 16, Jan. 1825 | RCH |
| Atkinson, Francis | Shepler, Harriet | 4, Oct. 1832 | RCH |
| Atkinson, Francis | Wright, Ann | 13, Mar. 1838 | RCH |
| Atkinson, George | Blaco, Elisabeth | 4, May 1847 | RCH |
| Atkinson, John | Downey, Angela | 22, June 1846 | BB |
| Atkinson, Joseph | Mueller, Jane | 25, Apr. 1844 | RCH |
| Atkinson, Richard | Cobb, Almira | 14, Apr. 1849 | RCH |
| Aton, Adnon | Long, | 18, Apr. 1826 | RCH |
| Atrip, William | Bennington, Keziah | 29, Dec. 1847 | RCH |
| Attee, Charles | Hampton, Sarah Jane | 26, May 1847 | RCH |
| Attermeyer, Heinrich | Fruehling, Maria | 25, Jan. 1842 | FF |
| Attwell, Roger | Fones, Amanda | 10, Oct. 1847 | RCH |
| Atvessen, Heinrich H | Kroeger, Maria Anna | 15, Aug. 1847 | FF |
| Atwell, John | Ray, Mary | 9, May 1838 | RCH |
| Atwood, Ephraim | Robinson, Peggy | 18, Aug. 1818 | RCH |
| Atwood, F. | McLaughlin, Nancy | 13, Jan. 1848 | RCH |
| Au---, Dudley | Copeland, Emily | 3, June 1821 | RCH |
| Auberman, William | Place, Lucy A. | 22, Feb. 1840 | I |
| Aubke, Francis | Kolkmeyer, Catharine | 16, Nov. 1842 | AA |
| Aubke, Johan Heinric | Meier, Clara Maria | 31, Aug. 1845 | F |
| Aubrey, Richard J. | Faulconer, Ann | 22, July 1839 | RCH |
| Aue, Friedrich | Thiesing, Sophia | 1, Aug. 1844 | F |
| Auel, Conrad | Ezel, Maria | 18, Dec. 1849 | G |
| Auer, Georg | Bass, Charlotte | 26, July 1846 | A |
| AufdenKamp, Carl | Greiwe, Caroline | 12, Dec. 1843 | RCH |
| AufderHaar, Adolph W | Brinkmeyer, Christin | 21, Oct. 1846 | RCH |
| AufderHaar, Jacob | Doetmeier, Anna M. | 4, Sept 1845 | C |
| AufderHaar, Jacob R. | Robaum, Anna Maria | 13, Sept 1849 | C |
| AufderHaar, Rudolph | Settle, Elisabeth | 28, Jan. 1842 | RCH |

| Grooms | Brides | Date of Marriage | Code |
|--------|--------|------------------|------|
| ***** | ***** | **** ** ******** | **** |
| AufderHeide, Bernard | Bohn, Elisabeth | 10, Mar. 1842 | F |
| AufderHeide, Bernard | Schulte, Louise | 25, Feb. 1848 | F |
| AufderHeide, Heinric | Ekelmann, Catharine | 25, Oct. 1845 | F |
| Aufheil, Michael | Hollinger, Rosanna | 30, Jan. 1837 | FF |
| Augar, George | Danby, Sarah | Nov. 1848 | I |
| Auger, Martin | Wickersham, Cath. | 8, Apr. 1819 | RCH |
| Augur, Daniel | Clayton, Mary | 22, Oct. 1818 | RCH |
| Augur, James | Wainwright, Jeruska | 18, Oct. 1848 | RCH |
| August, Lewis | Adler, Nancy | 29, Sept 1845 | RCH |
| Aul, Christoph | Schroewers, Sophia | 20, Dec. 1849 | B |
| Aulvers, Franz | Brase, Sophia | 15, July 1846 | C |
| Auman, John | Bickett, Ann | 30, Oct. 1843 | BB |
| Aumueller, Paul | Reizmer, Anna Marg. | 25, Nov. 1846 | RCH |
| Aupke, Friedrich | Fischer, Christina | 20, Feb. 1848 | AA |
| Aupke, Georg | Mittendorf, Louise | 21, Mar. 1848 | F |
| Aupke, Johan Fried. | Schaeper, Regina | 18, Sept 1849 | AA |
| Aurndall, Thomas | France, Elisabeth | 12, Aug. 1848 | RCH |
| Auspacher, Abraham | Rothschild, Babette | 18, Sept 1843 | RCH |
| Austen, David | Pecket, Cordelia H. | 5, Nov. 1844 | I |
| Austin, Henry | Hicks, Sarah | 25, July 1839 | RCH |
| Austin, James | Smith, Maria | 28, Mar. 1839 | RCH |
| Austing, Johan Bern. | Theilen, Catharine | 24, Apr. 1845 | AA |
| Auth, Nicolaus | Feldmann, Agnes | 18, July 1847 | EE |
| Authers, Thomas | Starmes, Lucinda | 2, July 1836 | RCH |
| Averdick, Matthias | Toschlag, Helena | 1, Nov. 1846 | AA |
| Averweser, Gerhard H | Alers, Elis. Christ. | 29, Nov. 1846 | A |
| Avery, Charles | Bakewell, Martha P. | 7, June 1847 | I |
| Avery, Cladius | Hopaugh, Lucy | 29, July 1845 | RCH |
| Avery, Guy C. | Towner, Betsy | 3, Jan. 1822 | RCH |
| Avery, Humphrey | ----, ---- | 7, Aug. 1834 | RCH |
| Avery, Jonas | Tumig, Juliana | 2, June 1825 | RCH |
| Avis, Charles | Hargraves, Mary Ann | 24, June 1837 | RCH |
| Avy, Joseph | Hoffmann, | 4, Dec. 1818 | RCH |
| Aydelotte, B.P. | Fosdick, Elizabeth | 21, June 1841 | I |
| Aydelotte, Isaac | Vorhees, Mary | 30, June 1836 | RCH |
| Aydelotte, James R. | List, Amelia | 7, Jan. 1834 | RCH |
| Ayer, John M. | VanEaton, Mary | 29, Oct. 1847 | RCH |
| Ayer, William | Stansbury, Mary Ann | 15, Oct. 1848 | RCH |
| Ayler, | Phillips, Rebecca | 5, Apr. 1838 | RCH |
| Aylward, Charles | Poland, Elisabeth | 10, July 1843 | RCH |
| Ayres, Abijah | Hunter, Eleanor | 6, Oct. 1820 | RCH |
| Ayres, August | Jones, Elizabeth | 1, Mar. 1846 | RCH |
| Ayres, Cyrus D. | Goldtrap, Jane | 5, Nov. 1833 | RCH |
| Ayres, Daniel | Wise, Mary | 23, Oct. 1845 | RCH |
| Ayres, Darias | Rosebrough, | 26, Aug. 1824 | RCH |
| Ayres, Elisha | Sorter, Mary | 22, Jan. 1833 | RCH |
| Ayres, Elisha | Hamilton, Catharine | 12, June 1841 | RCH |
| Ayres, Isaiah | Mastin, Sarah | 21, Dec. 1820 | RCH |
| Ayres, Joel | Stockham, Frances A. | 24, Apr. 1834 | RCH |
| Ayres, Joel | Fuller, Margaret | 7, May 1843 | RCH |
| Ayres, Mark | Mason, Maria A. | 23, Sept 1846 | RCH |
| Ayres, Richard | Stout, Ruth | 9, Dec. 1832 | RCH |
| Ayres, Samuel | Snider, Ethelinda | 3, Nov. 1841 | RCH |
| Ayres, Stephen | Stout, Priscilla | 9, May 1836 | RCH |
| Ayres, Stephen | Ayres, Elisabeth | 21, Apr. 1845 | RCH |
| | | | |
| B---, Bates | Grane, Charlotte | 8, Jan. 1836 | RCH |
| B---, Charles | Kinghead, Mary | 17, Mar. 1844 | RCH |
| B---, Isaac | Kerr, Jane | 14, Aug. 1838 | RCH |
| B---, James F. | Brandruff, Hannah | 1, Nov. 1826 | RCH |
| B---, Jefferson | Pickens, Caroline | 12, July 1825 | RCH |
| B---, Jerome | Green, | Nov. 1844 | RCH |
| B---, John | Dugan, Catharine | 18, July 1825 | RCH |
| B---, John | Anderson, Hannah | 29, Dec. 1831 | RCH |
| B---, Lewis | Rose, Sarah | 16, Mar. 1825 | RCH |
| Baandson, Joseph P. | D---, Maria | 20, Nov. 1839 | RCH |
| Babb, David B. | Totten, Elisabeth | 29, Apr. 1849 | RCH |
| Babbit, Calvin | Darrow, Mary | 17, Aug. 1833 | RCH |
| Babbitt, Andrew | Gaithers, Cordelia | 31, Dec. 1849 | RCH |
| Babbitt, Hathaway | Wilson, Margaretha | 1, June 1849 | RCH |
| Babbot, William W. | Siselow, Mary | 21, Jan. 1824 | RCH |

| Grooms<br>****** | Brides<br>****** | Date of Marriage<br>**** ** ******** | Code<br>**** |
|---|---|---|---|
| Babbs, Charles | Risk, Elisabeth | 14, June 1843 | RCH |
| Babbs, William | Minshall, Christina | 21, Jan. 1847 | RCH |
| Babcock, David | Johnson, Elisabeth | 3, May 1835 | RCH |
| Babcock, Edward | Wilson, Malary | 13, Oct. 1833 | RCH |
| Babcock, Jonathan | Morrisy, Betsy P. | 2, Apr. 1820 | RCH |
| Babeng, Abraham | Hart, Catharine | 21, Apr. 1833 | RCH |
| Bach, Carl | Katzenborn, Louisa | 28, Nov. 1849 | C |
| Bach, Georg | Hoffmann, Eva Marg. | 8, Jan. 1847 | RCH |
| Bach, Johan Adam | Schetter, Judith | 21, Nov. 1848 | AA |
| Bachelor, William | Skillman, Louise J. | 16, Nov. 1848 | RCH |
| Bacher, Heinrich | Mannweiler, Elisabet | 31, July 1842 | G |
| Bachhus, Carl | Goecher, Matilda | 2, Sept 1835 | RCH |
| Bachle, Anton | Fuchs, Ursula | 30, Jan. 1848 | EE |
| Bachmann, Franz | Knorr, M. Barbara | 6, Jan. 1848 | C |
| Bachmann, Fridolin | Rister, Theresa | 22, Aug. 1847 | EE |
| Bachmann, Gervas | Wiederle, Magdalena | 23, Nov. 1846 | FF |
| Bachmann, Johan | Evans, Elisabeth | 6, May 1839 | RCH |
| Bachmann, Johan | Flach, Maria Anna | 14, Jan. 1846 | CC |
| Bachmann, Meyndus | Guy, Elisabeth | 4, July 1847 | RCH |
| Bachmann, Peter | Graw, Anna Catharine | 29, Mar. 1848 | C |
| Bachmann, Peter | Schuler, Elisabeth | 30, Oct. 1849 | CC |
| Bachmann, Peter | Auberger, Catharine | 21, Sept 1848 | EE |
| Bachouse, Benjamin | Taylor, Catharine | 11, Mar. 1846 | RCH |
| Backel, John | Friedle, Barbara | 25, Sept 1849 | RCH |
| Backer, Adolph Hein. | Mueller, L. Maria | 29, May 1845 | C |
| Backhaus, Johan | Duden, Dorothea | 22, Mar. 1843 | A |
| Backinstos, Benjamin | Barcum, Elisabeth | 25, Oct. 1832 | RCH |
| Backmann, J. Gerhard | Woellers, Anna Maria | 23, Feb. 1841 | FF |
| Bacon, Horace | McClaurin, Margaret | 9, July 1844 | RCH |
| Bacon, Isaac | Wilmuth, Mary J. | 21, Feb. 1847 | RCH |
| Bacon, Isaac W. | Armstrong, Elisabeth | 1, Nov. 1843 | RCH |
| Bacon, Jacob | Kerr, Harriet | 28, Oct. 1819 | RCH |
| Bacon, James | Lewis, Maria | 22, Sept 1842 | RCH |
| Bacon, James H. | Eberle, Catharine M. | 12, Dec. 1833 | I |
| Bacon, John | Ludlow, Elisabeth | 1, Mar. 1820 | RCH |
| Bacon, John | Ponner, Ruth | 4, Apr. 1841 | RCH |
| Bacon, Joseph | Atkins, Sarah | 29, Sept 1841 | RCH |
| Bacon, Nathan | ----, ---- | 5, Jan. 1835 | RCH |
| Bacon, William | Holmes, Martha | 2, July 1844 | RCH |
| Bade, George Peter | Seadel, Elisabeth | 29, Aug. 1845 | RCH |
| Badel, Stephan | Wuest, Elisabeth | 25, Oct. 1847 | RCH |
| Badern, Johan Conrad | Mansars, Margaretha | 9, Oct. 1849 | C |
| Badger, Benjamin | Pauly, Jane | 3, Oct. 1837 | RCH |
| Badger, William | Rapalee, Mary Ann | 6, Oct. 1846 | RCH |
| Badgley, James | Ditmann, Rachel | 24, June 1846 | RCH |
| Badgley, John | Davis, Mary Ann | 24, Dec. 1846 | RCH |
| Badgley, Robert | Hancock, Nancy | 17, Apr. 1843 | RCH |
| Badin, James | Rogers, Ann | 6, May 1849 | GG |
| Badmann, Hiram | Jones, Mary Ann | 5, Jan. 1832 | RCH |
| Bado, Nicolaus | Gruen, Elisabeth | 26, July 1842 | FF |
| Baechtler, Georg L. | Benningsdorf, Elis. | 27, June 1848 | C |
| Baeke, Bernard | Knabke, Elisabeth | 26, Sept 1837 | FF |
| Baer, Francis | Olinger, Christina | 1, July 1837 | FF |
| Baer, Johan | Esler, Veronica | 2, May 1847 | CC |
| Baerhle, Ferdinand | Lipps, Rosa | 30, Sept 1849 | II |
| Baermann, Matthias | Keller, Maria Louisa | 27, Apr. 1841 | FF |
| Baesel, Heinrich | Becker, Elisabeth | 18, Jan. 1844 | G |
| Baeter, Bernard Hein | Reisinger, M Gertrud | 26, Sept 1837 | FF |
| Bagge, Heinrich Jos. | Macke, Anna M. | 2, Sept 1849 | AA |
| Baggot, William | Phelan, Catharine | 1, Jan. 1848 | BB |
| Bagley, | Bush, Hannah | 16, May 1849 | RCH |
| Bagley, Thomas | Murray, Elisabeth | 7, Feb. 1847 | BB |
| Bagly, Robert | Lane, Louise | 24, Jan. 1846 | RCH |
| Bahe, Herman | Meyer, Anna | 28, Dec. 1839 | G |
| Bahlmann, J. Caspar | Hausharpel, Cath. E. | 29, June 1847 | AA |
| Bahning, Carl | Horzmann, Cath. Elis | 13, Jan. 1841 | F |
| Bahr, Joseph | Ziegler, Doretta | 28, Dec. 1849 | RCH |
| Baich, William | Lowe, Elisabeth | 20, July 1846 | RCH |
| Baier, Martin | Krues, Anna Maria | 7, Nov. 1844 | AA |
| Baier, Peter | Scherrer, Maria | 9, Apr. 1843 | C |
| Bailey, Aaron E. | Schock, Amelia | 4, Aug. 1839 | RCH |

| Grooms | Brides | Date of Marriage | Code |
|--------|--------|------------------|------|
| ****** | ****** | **** ** ******** | **** |
| Bailey, Benjamin | Dodson, Agnes | 21, Apr. 1837 | RCH |
| Bailey, Conrad | Mills, Louise M. | 11, Jan. 1846 | RCH |
| Bailey, Daniel | Epley, Hannah | 30, Dec. 1843 | RCH |
| Bailey, Edward | Woolever, Sidney | 23, Nov. 1848 | RCH |
| Bailey, Herford | Wanson, Catharine | 21, Sept 1834 | RCH |
| Bailey, Jerry | Lamb, Jane | 29, Nov. 1847 | RCH |
| Bailey, John | Jones, Nancy | 11, Dec. 1836 | RCH |
| Bailey, John | May, Nancy | 2, June 1847 | RCH |
| Bailey, Leonard | Brown, Ann | 28, Mar. 1846 | RCH |
| Bailey, Palmon | Lumley, Ann | 25, May 1843 | RCH |
| Bailey, Reuben | Reynolds, Elisabeth | 8, Feb. 1849 | RCH |
| Bailey, Samuel | Anderson, Margaret | 21, July 1846 | RCH |
| Bailey, Stephen | Mourgon, Sarah | 25, Mar. 1838 | RCH |
| Bailey, Thomas | Gregg, Susan | 16, Oct. 1848 | RCH |
| Bailey, William | Wilson, Margaret Ann | 14, July 1844 | RCH |
| Bailey, William | Cast, Susan | 20, June 1845 | RCH |
| Bailiff, Phineas | Dean, Nancy | 21, Dec. 1837 | RCH |
| Bain, John W. | Pollack, Mary | 10, Sept 1844 | RCH |
| Bair, Samuel | McKinney, Ann | Dec. 1844 | RCH |
| Baird, James S. | Bevis, Charlotte | 21, Jan. 1836 | RCH |
| Baker, Andrew | Morris, Mary | 8, Nov. 1847 | BB |
| Baker, Arnold | McFana--, Elisabeth | 21, Feb. 1822 | RCH |
| Baker, Arnold | Orr, Mary | 4, Apr. 1849 | RCH |
| Baker, Charles | Alvord, Jemima | 29, Apr. 1846 | RCH |
| Baker, David | Vaughan, Jane | 20, Mar. 1834 | RCH |
| Baker, David | Isgrig, Rachel | 25, Mar. 1841 | RCH |
| Baker, George W. | Taylor, Isabella | 28, Aug. 1834 | RCH |
| Baker, Greenbury | McCracken, Charlotte | 7, Nov. 1848 | RCH |
| Baker, H. | Pindall, Mary Ann | 15, Sept 1825 | RCH |
| Baker, Henry | Scofield, Eliza | 6, Apr. 1825 | RCH |
| Baker, Henry James | Conklin, Elis. Jane | 8, Feb. 1838 | RCH |
| Baker, Jacob | Payne, Lucinda | 18, Sept 1845 | RCH |
| Baker, John | Longstable, | 1, Oct. 1817 | RCH |
| Baker, John | Ball, Hanett | 25, May 1832 | RCH |
| Baker, John | Porter, Sarah | 9, Nov. 1835 | RCH |
| Baker, John | ----, Rachel Ann | 12, May 1839 | RCH |
| Baker, Joseph B. | Boyce, Lucia Ann | 28, Sept 1837 | RCH |
| Baker, Martin | Morrow, Olive | 21, Jan. 1846 | RCH |
| Baker, Melyne | Lane, Mary | 26, May 1826 | RCH |
| Baker, Nathan | ----, Rebecca | 20, July 1835 | RCH |
| Baker, Samuel | Ellis, Elisabeth | 25, Oct. 1835 | RCH |
| Baker, Stephen | Hussey, Sophia | 20, Dec. 1849 | RCH |
| Baker, Thomas | McDonald, Sarah | 16, Apr. 1835 | RCH |
| Baker, Thomas | Fisher, Elisabeth | 27, Jan. 1836 | RCH |
| Baker, William | King, Mary | 19, May 1842 | RCH |
| Baker, William | Piercefield, Mary | 4, Mar. 1847 | RCH |
| Bakewell, German | Schaffer, Anna Elis. | 16, Nov. 1843 | RCH |
| Bal---, Jesse W. | Harris, Eleanor | 17, Aug. 1824 | RCH |
| Balangy, James | Davis, Elisabeth | 17, Jan. 1818 | RCH |
| Balauf, Peter | Babbitt, Amanda | 20, Aug. 1835 | RCH |
| Balcons, Constantin | Weston, Anna C. | 15, Aug. 1839 | RCH |
| Baldock, Milton | Ross, Virginia | 29, Jan. 1842 | RCH |
| Baldridge, N. | Griffey, Martha | 30, Apr. 1849 | RCH |
| Baldwin, | Miller, Sarah | 3, Dec. 1822 | RCH |
| Baldwin, Amos S. | Turner, Keziah | 9, Dec. 1819 | RCH |
| Baldwin, Charles | McAdams, Rebecca | 6, Aug. 1848 | RCH |
| Baldwin, Ebenezer | Casan, Ruth | 2, May 1819 | RCH |
| Baldwin, George | Jenks, Julia | 24, May 1836 | RCH |
| Baldwin, Henry | Augustia, Julia | 28, June 1835 | RCH |
| Baldwin, James | Spencer, Rhoda | 13, May 1847 | RCH |
| Baldwin, John | Roll, Abigail | 13, Sept 1836 | RCH |
| Baldwin, John | Secrist, Sarah Jane | 12, Apr. 1846 | RCH |
| Baldwin, John | Jones, Marietta | 22, Mar. 1847 | RCH |
| Baldwin, John | Sloop, Priscilla | 16, Sept 1849 | RCH |
| Baldwin, John W. | Raxter, Elizabeth | 15, Oct. 1846 | RCH |
| Baldwin, Joseph | Williams, Mary | 18, Oct. 1836 | RCH |
| Baldwin, Levi | Bohanan, Catharine | 8, Apr. 1836 | RCH |
| Baldwin, Philander | Green, Perlina | 21, Nov. 1819 | RCH |
| Baldwin, Robert | Tatman, Harriet | 25, Oct. 1843 | RCH |
| Baldwin, William | Corwin, Elisabeth M. | 23, Sept 1837 | RCH |
| Balke, Casper H. | Teglers, A. Margaret | 15, Feb. 1849 | RCH |

| Grooms | Brides | Date of Marriage | Code |
|--------|--------|------------------|------|
| ***** | ***** | **** ** ******** | **** |
| Ball, D. Blackhall W | Denny, Rebecca | 3, June 1827 | I |
| Ball, Danforth E. | Morten, Maria A. | 13, 1834 | RCH |
| Ball, E.H. | Bowlen, Elisabeth | 28, May 1834 | RCH |
| Ball, Ezekiel | Crane, Mary | 8, Aug. 1823 | RCH |
| Ball, Jacob T. | Scofield, Emeline | 15, Apr. 1833 | RCH |
| Ball, Ludwig | Diebold, Maria Magd. | 3, Oct. 1847 | EE |
| Ball, Rice | Goodin, Lydia | 18, June 1835 | RCH |
| Ball, Thomas | Smith, Rachel | 29, Aug. 1847 | RCH |
| Ballance, Charles | England, Elisabeth | 26, Jan. 1836 | D |
| Ballance, John H. | Whiteside, Mathilda | 23, Dec. 1834 | RCH |
| Ballauf, Louis | Friedeborn, Henriett | 10, Mar. 1842 | G |
| Ballauf, Wilhelm | Storch, Josephine | 10, June 1847 | G |
| Ballay, Francis | ----, Mary Magdalena | 20, Dec. 1834 | RCH |
| Balling, Johan Georg | Gebauer, Catharine | 26, July 1842 | A |
| Ballinger, Martin | Endres, Catharina | 12, Oct. 1840 | FF |
| Ballmeyer, Ernst H. | Hofmeister, M. Elis. | 25, Dec. 1847 | F |
| Ballness, Joseph | Dudley, Lucy | 14, Jan. 1821 | RCH |
| Balls, Moses | Newbrough, Margaret | 27, Sept 1835 | RCH |
| Ballweber, Simon | Kugler, Gertrud | 24, Nov. 1842 | FF |
| Balser, George | Layman, Lydia | 6, Dec. 1821 | RCH |
| Balser, George | Sanburn, Harriet | 21, Sept 1843 | RCH |
| Balser, Henry A. | Landon, Barbary | 19, Mar. 1834 | RCH |
| Balser, Jacob | Gough, Margaret | 11, Mar. 1825 | RCH |
| Balsley, Jacob A. | Runyon, Mary R. | 1, June 1848 | RCH |
| Balter, Samuel | Hodgson, Elisabeth | 1, Mar. 1819 | RCH |
| Balwin, John | Baptist, Frances | 22, Sept 1841 | RCH |
| Bambeck, Balthasar | Steigerwald, Cath. | 2, Jan. 1849 | EE |
| Bamberg, William | O'Donnell, Mary | 18, June 1849 | BB |
| Bamberger, Charles | Joseph, Lena | 15, Aug. 1843 | RCH |
| Bammer, Christian | Eckardt, Caroline | 9, Jan. 1846 | RCH |
| Bang---, William | McMains, Abigail | 22, Feb. 1839 | RCH |
| Banister, Alfred | Poe, Elisabeth | 15, Apr. 1838 | RCH |
| Banister, James | Oldenbaugh, Sarah | 19, July 1849 | RCH |
| Banister, William | Brewer, Susan | 25, Oct. 1838 | RCH |
| Banks, F. | Wiggins, Verinda | 22, May 1845 | A |
| Banks, Herman | Fesgan, Margaret | 15, Aug. 1849 | RCH |
| Banks, Hiram | Jones, Elis. Jane | 22, Sept 1833 | RCH |
| Banks, Jedediah | Hardin, Elisabeth | 1822 | RCH |
| Banks, John | Flinn, Susan | 11, May 1833 | RCH |
| Banks, William | Pye, Jane | 27, July 1846 | RCH |
| Bann, John | Kline, Helen | 22, Nov. 1846 | BB |
| Bannecke, John | Kamlin, Catharine | 6, June 1836 | RCH |
| Bannin, Roger | Costello, Mary | 30, Oct. 1843 | BB |
| Banning, Asa | ----, Elisabeth | 18, Mar. 1835 | RCH |
| Bannister, Isaac | C---, Sarah | 7, July 1835 | RCH |
| Bannister, William | Myers, Elisabeth | 29, July 1844 | RCH |
| Bans, Mathias | Scheirer, Barbara | 6, May 1846 | EE |
| Banser, Johan | Dixler, Kunigunda | 3, June 1845 | AA |
| Bantz, Jacob | Billman, Elisabeth | 6, Sept 1835 | RCH |
| Baptist, George J. | Lewis, Lucinda | 8, Feb. 1837 | RCH |
| Barbank, Lester | Simmons, Eliza | 14, Mar. 1822 | RCH |
| Barben, John | Biddinger, Emeline | 1, Aug. 1847 | RCH |
| Barber, Hiram | Sprawley, Elisabeth | 3, Feb. 1837 | RCH |
| Barbian, Peter | Zei, Walburga | 23, Sept 1849 | EE |
| Barbor, Johan Bern. | Tengers, Anna Maria | 14, Oct. 1849 | EE |
| Barbour, Charles V. | Smith, Nancy E. | 8, Apr. 1819 | RCH |
| Barbour, John | Snelson, Elisabeth | 26, June 1849 | RCH |
| Barcus, Richard | Hubbard, Hannah | 26, Jan. 1843 | RCH |
| Bard, John | ----, Mary | 22, 1818 | RCH |
| Bard, Sylvester | Mayhew, Louise | 5, Nov. 1845 | RCH |
| Bardes, Heinrich | Thomer, Elisabeth | 30, Jan. 1849 | G |
| Bardes, Henry | Knerr, Catharina | 2, Dec. 1849 | G |
| Barenfield, William | Geppert, Barbara | 29, Aug. 1841 | RCH |
| Barenhorst, Bernard | Storing, Margaretha | 21, May 1848 | II |
| Barfield, William | Bacon, Margaret | 23, Nov. 1845 | RCH |
| Bargdolt, John | Stout, Sarah | 16, Dec. 1841 | RCH |
| Bargert, Johan | Rulers, Agnes | 29, Apr. 1845 | AA |
| Barges, Johan | Westermann, Elis. | 7, Aug. 1838 | FF |
| Barhorst, Friedrich | Frampelmeyer, Maria | 30, May 1843 | F |
| Bari, Jacob | Schauer, Anna | 25, Nov. 1849 | II |
| Baril, George | Rafferty, Margaret | 6, Nov. 1849 | GG |

| Grooms ***** | Brides ***** | Date of Marriage **** ** ******** | Code **** |
|---|---|---|---|
| Baril, Isaac | LaCount, Ellen | 14, Oct. 1845 | RCH |
| Barkeling, Johan H. | Tenger, Euphemia | 20, Jan. 1846 | AA |
| Barker, Azias | Adams, Catharine | 23, Mar. 1848 | RCH |
| Barker, Emery | Robinson, Martha | 9, Dec. 1844 | RCH |
| Barker, Henry | Ayers, Ellen | 17, Aug. 1846 | RCH |
| Barker, Hiram | Brown, Rebecca | 21, Dec. 1819 | RCH |
| Barker, John | Braden, Mary Ann | 29, May 1847 | RCH |
| Barker, William | Maynard, Susan | 6, Sept 1841 | RCH |
| Barker, William | Wood, Martha Ann | 22, Aug. 1846 | RCH |
| Barker, Zachariah | Brown, Mary | 17, June 1824 | RCH |
| Barkley, Joseph | Johnson, Maria | 9, Mar. 1849 | RCH |
| Barkley, Samuel | Grodin, Adaline | Apr. 1839 | RCH |
| Barkmann, Francis | Eusterkemper, Elis. | 8, Sept 1840 | FF |
| Barkshire, Milton | Miller, Frances | 2, Sept 1846 | RCH |
| Barkshire, Samuel | Newman, Frances | 28, Mar. 1846 | RCH |
| Barleon, Basil | Adam, Anna Maria | 20, May 1849 | CC |
| Barnard, Foster | Burns, Indiana | 23, Jan. 1842 | RCH |
| Barnard, George | Kendall, Sarah W. | 9, Jan. 1844 | I |
| Barnard, Matthias | Wertz, Elisabeth | 21, Apr. 1835 | RCH |
| Barnard, Richard | Ingey, Indiana | 1, Jan. 1835 | RCH |
| Barnard, Zacheus | Lawrence, Eunice | 7, Feb. 1819 | RCH |
| Barnes, Alexander | Norris, Allasana | 21, Feb. 1833 | RCH |
| Barnes, Alfred | Todd, Florence | 21, Mar. 1844 | I |
| Barnes, Allen W. | O'Donnell, Ann | 6, Dec. 1847 | C |
| Barnes, Alva T. | Ingersoll, Elisabeth | 17, Aug. 1848 | RCH |
| Barnes, Andrew J. | Geward, Julianna | 13, Dec. 1834 | RCH |
| Barnes, Dennis | Danforth, Emily | 2, June 1836 | RCH |
| Barnes, John | Bloom, Rachel | 11, Oct. 1835 | RCH |
| Barnes, John | Wilson, Margaret | 26, Aug. 1843 | RCH |
| Barnes, Joshua | Cross, Sarah | 3, Feb. 1836 | RCH |
| Barnes, Nelson | Oden, Elisabeth | 1, June 1834 | RCH |
| Barnes, Thomas | Steelman, Martha A. | 4, Oct. 1842 | RCH |
| Barnes, William | McGee, Semiramis | 11, Dec. 1846 | RCH |
| Barnes, Zacheus | Stilwell, Rachel | 31, Jan. 1819 | RCH |
| Barnet, Robert W. | Groesbeck, Margaret | 19, Oct. 1836 | RCH |
| Barnett, James | Watson, Sarah Jane | 18, June 1844 | RCH |
| Barnett, John | Harrison, Mehaley | 11, July 1833 | RCH |
| Barnett, John | Ashby, Jane | 22, June 1848 | RCH |
| Barney, Chester | McCollough, Amanda | 6, June 1847 | RCH |
| Barney, David F. | Parker, Sarah | 23, Apr. 1836 | RCH |
| Barnhard, Philipp | Clark, Abigail | 5, June 1833 | RCH |
| Barnhart, Adam | Schollert, Margaret | 21, Dec. 1848 | RCH |
| Barnhart, Daniel | Williams, Anna | 5, Sept 1842 | RCH |
| Barnhart, Jacob | McClane, Mary | 2, June 1841 | RCH |
| Barns, Abraham | Seel, Martha Ann | 10, Oct. 1843 | RCH |
| Barns, Harrison | Poole, Acenth | 8, Apr. 1837 | RCH |
| Barnus, Joseph | Shipman, Sarah | 6, May 1836 | RCH |
| Barnwell, George | Crosman, Sarah | 7, Apr. 1836 | RCH |
| Baron, George F. | McKenny, Margaret | 20, Apr. 1845 | BB |
| Barost, Heinrich | Suder, Catharina | 23, Aug. 1838 | FF |
| Barr, Baldwin | Wilson, Catharine | 31, Dec. 1846 | RCH |
| Barr, Benjamin | Cooke, Nancy Ann | 23, July 1846 | RCH |
| Barr, Lemuel | Alston, Elmina | 13, Dec. 1845 | RCH |
| Barr, Samuel | Adams, Julia Ann | 30, Aug. 1835 | RCH |
| Barr, Samuel S. | Moller, Clara P. | 9, Sept 1847 | BB |
| Barr, Stephen | Ferrell, Charlotte | 27, Oct. 1841 | RCH |
| Barr, William | Burch, Jenetta | 10, Nov. 1846 | RCH |
| Barr, William T. | Lifler, Mary | 31, Dec. 1832 | RCH |
| Barrett, Amos | Martin, Elisabeth | 18, Feb. 1844 | RCH |
| Barrett, Austin | Kingsley, Jane | 7, Feb. 1849 | RCH |
| Barrett, D. | Conner, Elisabeth | 7, Aug. 1834 | RCH |
| Barrett, Edward | Cushin, Bridget | 6, Aug. 1841 | BB |
| Barrett, George | Bedford, Elisabeht | 17, Mar. 1849 | RCH |
| Barrett, John | Palmer, Rachel | 7, Nov. 1846 | RCH |
| Barrett, Jonathan | Davis, Ellen | 19, Dec. 1843 | RCH |
| Barrett, Joseph | Dailey, Caroline | 24, Sept 1846 | RCH |
| Barrett, William | Martin, Sarah | 11, Aug. 1844 | RCH |
| Barrett, William S. | Crain, Anna (Mrs) | 11, Oct. 1843 | RCH |
| Barrett, Wilson | Firget, Mary Ann | 29, Jan. 1839 | RCH |
| Barri, Jacob | Sebauer, Anna Maria | 25, Nov. 1849 | RCH |
| Barrigan, James | Dwyer, Bridget | 6, June 1849 | RCH |

| Grooms<br>****** | Brides<br>****** | Date of Marriage<br>**** ** ******** | Code<br>**** |
|---|---|---|---|
| Barron, Patrick | Carr, Mary | 7, Jan. 1845 | BB |
| Barrow, Archibald | Bunton, Celia | 12, Feb. 1837 | RCH |
| Barrow, Bennett | D---, Hannah | 25, Jan. 1835 | RCH |
| Barry, John | Lafferty, Margaret | 11, Sept 1838 | RCH |
| Barry, Martin | Flynn, Ann | 12, Aug. 1841 | BB |
| Barry, Patrick | Mahoney, Mary Ann | 3, Sept 1848 | BB |
| Barry, Thomas | Limerick, Mary | 1, Jan. 1844 | RCH |
| Barry, Thomas | Gibby, Sarah | 30, July 1846 | RCH |
| Barry, William | Flinn, Margaret H. | 30, Aug. 1835 | RCH |
| Barson, John | Laird, Rebecca | 16, Nov. 1841 | RCH |
| Bartel, Heinrich | Greiwe, Maria Elis. | 3, Oct. 1849 | F |
| Bartell, John L. | Law, Lucinda | 25, Sept 1848 | RCH |
| Bartels, Barthold | Bahn, Anna | 27, Feb. 1844 | C |
| Bartels, Carl | Weingaertner, Cath. | 20, Aug. 1849 | C |
| Bartels, Francis | Miller, Anna Clara | 8, Dec. 1846 | RCH |
| Bartels, George | Nessenius, Augusta | 27, May 1842 | RCH |
| Bartels, Johan Georg | Meier, Anna Maria | 20, May 1848 | CC |
| Barth, Ehrhardt | Selzer, Barbara | 15, Feb. 1848 | G |
| Barth, Jacob | Baumann, Magdalena | 12, Sept 1848 | EE |
| Barth, Johan | Diebold, Christina | 10, Apr. 1845 | G |
| Barth, John | Knauer, Margaretha | 14, Dec. 1846 | RCH |
| Barthling, Ernst | Buring, Johanna | 4, Sept 1841 | RCH |
| Bartholomai, Valent. | Dickhaut, A. Martha | 7, Nov. 1848 | G |
| Bartholomew, Jacob | Empson, Catharine | 16, July 1844 | RCH |
| Bartlett, Charles | VanSickle, Nancy | 2, Nov. 1843 | RCH |
| Bartlett, David | Elsworth, Felic. | 2, May 1833 | RCH |
| Bartlett, H.H. | Wallace, Caroline W. | 9, Oct. 1832 | RCH |
| Bartlett, Nathan | Comstock, Nancy | 24, June 1821 | RCH |
| Bartlett, William | Mason, Mary | 18, Feb. 1837 | RCH |
| Bartlett, William | Winter, Mathilda | 25, July 1846 | RCH |
| Bartlett, William H. | Andrews, Elisabeth C | 23, Mar. 1836 | RCH |
| Bartlow, Oliver M. | Shuecrop, Martha | 2, Feb. 1833 | RCH |
| Barton, Joseph | Johnevin, Mary Polly | 19, July 1833 | RCH |
| Barton, Julius | Hand, Mary | 4, Apr. 1844 | RCH |
| Barton, Miers | Woods, Lucinda | 12, Jan. 1833 | RCH |
| Barton, R.S. | Woods, Margaret | 2, Aug. 1849 | RCH |
| Barwise, Edward | Wilson, Matilda | 1, Apr. 1847 | RCH |
| Barwise, Thomas | Collins, Julia | 7, Feb. 1822 | RCH |
| Barwise, William | Layman, Ellen | 28, Nov. 1822 | RCH |
| Bascoe, Thomas | Rollers, Mildred | 16, May 1844 | RCH |
| Bascom, Caleb | Hidden, C. | 16, Nov. 1835 | RCH |
| Bascom, Thomas | Fisher, Angeline | 12, Feb. 1838 | RCH |
| Basinga, Joseph | Klock, Catharina | 26, Mar. 1839 | RCH |
| Bass, John | Smith, Susan | 1, July 1847 | RCH |
| Bassett, Joel R. | ----, Elisabeth | 20, Mar. 1838 | RCH |
| Bassett, John | Taylor, Catharine | 29, Apr. 1849 | RCH |
| Bassett, John | Philipps, Mary | 4, Feb. 1849 | BB |
| Bassett, John L. | Price, Sarah J. | 19, Feb. 1835 | RCH |
| Bassett, Samuel | Davis, Marian | 4, Oct. 1848 | RCH |
| Bassit, Charles | Edwards, Mary | 12, Aug. 1820 | RCH |
| Bassit, Isaac | Stiles, Sarah | 25, July 1820 | RCH |
| Bast, John | Hoffmann, Barbara | 9, Jan. 1838 | FF |
| Bastel, John C. | Frazer, | May 1839 | RCH |
| Batchelder, | Knox, Sarah | 18, July 1822 | RCH |
| Batchelder, George | Avis, Susannah | 5, May 1847 | I |
| Batchelor, Francis | Frazier, Margaret | 3, May 1847 | RCH |
| Batchelor, Francis | King, Georgianna | 30, Apr. 1849 | RCH |
| Batcher, John | Zoleis, Catharina | 9, May 1849 | RCH |
| Bate, Samuel | Grosvenor, Martha | 29, Mar. 1849 | RCH |
| Bateman, Aaron | Hictemul, Sophia | 17, Mar. 1825 | RCH |
| Bateman, Edgar | Ince, Elisabeth | 9, Aug. 1842 | RCH |
| Bateman, Henry | Markland, Hannah | 23, Jan. 1849 | RCH |
| Bateman, John | Phillips, Mary Ann | 2, Feb. 1847 | BB |
| Bateman, Noah | Goff, Sarah | 12, Oct. 1820 | RCH |
| Bateman, William | Langdon, Mary Jane | 14, Aug. 1842 | RCH |
| Batemann, Heinrich | Bone, Maria | 22, Feb. 1849 | C |
| Bates, Asa | Dunn, Mary | 12, Oct. 1820 | RCH |
| Bates, Asahel C. | Bobo, Meeky | 16, Apr. 1818 | RCH |
| Bates, Cass | Shepherd, Nelly | 21, Sept 1842 | RCH |
| Bates, Ethan | Beresford, Elisabeth | 8, Apr. 1840 | RCH |
| Bates, Harrison | Cole, Pauline | 10, May 1848 | RCH |

| Grooms<br>****** | Brides<br>****** | Date of Marriage<br>**** ** ******** | Code<br>**** |
|---|---|---|---|
| Bates, Henry M. | Fawcett, Mary A. | 10, Jan. 1838 | RCH |
| Bates, Isaac | McDougal, Adelheid | 30, Nov. 1840 | RCH |
| Bates, James | Post, Henrietta | 16, Feb. 1842 | RCH |
| Bates, Joshua | Olmstead, Elisabeth | 28, Dec. 1836 | RCH |
| Bates, Richard | Pretter, Nancy | 9, Feb. 1835 | RCH |
| Bates, Samuel | Grandin, Hannah | 22, Mar. 1842 | RCH |
| Bates, William | Ackley, Elisabeth | 15, Mar. 1841 | RCH |
| Bates, William | Winn, Sophia | 22, Feb. 1842 | RCH |
| Batey, James | Gano, Maria | 11, July 1840 | RCH |
| Bath, David | Lapp, Victoria | 4, Oct. 1849 | AA |
| Bath, Nicolaus | Guetz, Maria | 11, Feb. 1847 | AA |
| Batman, Josiah | ----, Mary | 8, Feb. 1835 | RCH |
| Battenberg, Daniel | Elsten, Elisabeth | 17, Feb. 1833 | RCH |
| Battenburg, Jacob | VanHorn, Nancy | 13, Feb. 1834 | RCH |
| Bauce, John G. | Ross, Ann | 4, Sept 1834 | RCH |
| Bauch, Georg | Reichert, Maria | 13, Oct. 1844 | G |
| Bauer, Adam | Zimmermann, Margaret | 15, Nov. 1846 | EE |
| Bauer, Andreas | Beck, Eva | 19, Aug. 1845 | AA |
| Bauer, Bernard | Bock, Apollonia | 25, Oct. 1848 | EE |
| Bauer, Conrad | Ludwig, Elisabeth | 4, Apr. 1847 | RCH |
| Bauer, George F. | Christel, Maria | 27, Oct. 1848 | RCH |
| Bauer, Gottlieb | Trauerbach, M. Elis. | 29, Oct. 1849 | C |
| Bauer, Ignatz | Brantweisen, Christ. | 3, July 1847 | C |
| Bauer, Johan | Loge, Catharine | 1, Oct. 1843 | C |
| Bauer, Johan Casper | Spaeth, Wilhelmina | 24, Oct. 1847 | G |
| Bauer, John | Hinas, Elisabeth | Feb. 1843 | RCH |
| Bauer, John | Schoenlaub, Elisabet | 16, Feb. 1843 | G |
| Bauer, Jonathan | Thomas, Rebecca | 14, Sept 1837 | RCH |
| Bauer, Joseph | Schwatzer, | Aug. 1849 | RCH |
| Bauer, Michael | Hiddler, Kunigunda | 5, Mar. 1848 | EE |
| Bauer, Peter | Held, Anna | 26, Oct. 1847 | AA |
| Bauer, Sebastian | Bernhard, Margaretha | 23, Jan. 1848 | FF |
| Bauer, Valentin | Fuster, Sibylla | 1, Oct. 1839 | G |
| Bauer, Wilhelm | Delp, Katharina | 15, Oct. 1848 | A |
| Bauerle, Frederick | Linck, Christina | 12, Sept 1848 | RCH |
| Bauerle, Leonard J. | Leidenberger, Cath. | 2, Dec. 1849 | A |
| Bauerle, Max Joseph | Bonert, Barbara | 17, Nov. 1849 | EE |
| Baughman, John | Carr, Lucinda | 16, Sept 1846 | RCH |
| Baughman, Robert | Armstrong, Margaret | 7, June 1842 | RCH |
| Baughman, William | Armstrong, Sarah | 12, July 1837 | RCH |
| Bauker, Joseph | Schwartz, Maria L. | 23, Nov. 1835 | FF |
| Baum, Adam | Wuest, Margaretha | 9, Jan. 1844 | G |
| Baum, Valentin | Bangert, Babette | 18, Oct. 1849 | G |
| Baum, William | Kain, Matilda C. | 15, Nov. 1846 | RCH |
| Baumann, Christian | Bauer, Amalia | 5, Aug. 1844 | C |
| Baumann, Ignatz | Helmer, Magdalena | 20, Feb. 1848 | EE |
| Baumann, Isidor | Stephen, Anna Maria | 1, Oct. 1844 | AA |
| Baumann, John | Aldinger, Maria | 28, Sept 1841 | RCH |
| Baumann, Joseph | Scheiner, Barbara | 23, Nov. 1841 | FF |
| Baumann, Michael | Frey, Barbara | 23, Feb. 1841 | G |
| Baumann, Michael | Volk, Anna Maria | 5, June 1843 | AA |
| Baumbusch, Francis | Schoener, Catharina | 9, Apr. 1837 | FF |
| Baumeister, Bernard | Huelsmann, Maria E. | 7, Jan. 1849 | CC |
| Baumeister, William | Gashmann, Johanna C. | 15, Aug. 1847 | F |
| Baumer, Bernard Jos. | Deye, Catharine Elis | 1, July 1849 | EE |
| Baumer, Heinrich | Wissling, Elisabeth | 14, Jan. 1845 | AA |
| Baumer, Johan Heinr. | Freihage, Anna Maria | 6, Jan. 1846 | RCH |
| Baumer, Joseph | Berlage, Maria Anna | 16, May 1843 | AA |
| Baumgartner, Georg | Riegert, Barbara | 25, Mar. 1844 | C |
| Baumgartner, James | Hyme, Catharine | 2, Feb. 1845 | BB |
| Baumgartner, Joseph | Rapp, Francisca | 10, Jan. 1837 | FF |
| Baumgartner, Joseph | Judey, Louise | 30, Dec. 1849 | BB |
| Baumgratz, John | McLaughlin, Jane | 14, Dec. 1844 | RCH |
| Bave, Israel | Smith, Phebe Jane | 20, Sept 1845 | RCH |
| Bavvet, Thomas | Conley, Mary W. | 26, Jan. 1834 | RCH |
| Bawin, William | Westo--, Hannah | 8, Dec. 1819 | RCH |
| Baxley, James | Parker, Maria | 16, Aug. 1845 | RCH |
| Baxter, John M. | Vorhees, Hetty | 8, Dec. 1845 | RCH |
| Baxter, Paul | Parmar, Polly | 15, Sept 1836 | RCH |
| Baxter, Samuel | Scull, Eliza Ann | 1, July 1824 | RCH |
| Baxter, William | Patterson, Sarah W. | 19, Jan. 1835 | RCH |

| Grooms<br>***** | Brides<br>***** | Date of Marriage<br>**** ** ******** | Code<br>**** |
|---|---|---|---|
| Baxter, William W. | Clark, Elisabeth A. | 4, Oct. 1838 | RCH |
| Bayer, Friedrich | Michael, Agnes | 3, Sept 1844 | AA |
| Bayer, Gustav | Palmer, Mindwell | 20, Apr. 1848 | RCH |
| Bayer, Martin | Kraus, Anna Maria | 7, Nov. 1844 | RCH |
| Bayerle, Peter | Schmidt, Dorothea C. | 10, Sept 1835 | RCH |
| Baymiller, Jacob | Pearson, Ann L. | 7, Sept 1819 | RCH |
| Be---, John | Williamson, Sarah | 16, May 1824 | RCH |
| Beadle, Benjamin G. | Brown, Lydia | 15, June 1833 | RCH |
| Beagle, Andrew | Goodin, Fanny | 25, Feb. 1837 | RCH |
| Beal, William | Day, Abigail | 1, Feb. 1820 | RCH |
| Beale, John | Bradford, Sarah | 7, Sept 1847 | RCH |
| Beale, William B. | Long, Mary | 17, Oct. 1822 | RCH |
| Beales, James | Shaw, Cynthia | 6, Feb. 1847 | RCH |
| Beall, Bazil | Creach, Susan | 19, Mar. 1844 | RCH |
| Beall, Benoni | Low, Sarah | 26, July 1846 | RCH |
| Beall, Charles | Roberts, Mary L. | 21, Nov. 1848 | RCH |
| Beall, Henry | Estell, Mary | 23, Oct. 1823 | RCH |
| Beall, William | S---, Margaret | 5, Nov. 1823 | RCH |
| Beals, Jesse | Smith, Mary Ann | 11, Feb. 1847 | RCH |
| Beamon, Justus | Jones, Sally | 30, July 1818 | RCH |
| Bean, Alexander | Bean, Eleanor | 9, Sept 1820 | RCH |
| Bean, Thomas | King, Alice | 6, June 1821 | RCH |
| Bean, William | Clark, Francis | 29, May 1849 | RCH |
| Beardsley, Joseph H. | Macy, Charlotte P. | 4, Dec. 1845 | D |
| Bears, John | Stevens, Margaret | 4, July 1847 | RCH |
| Beattie, John | Wade, Melissa | 9, Apr. 1846 | RCH |
| Beattie, Thomas T. | Burnes, Jane A. | 10, Aug. 1830 | I |
| Beatty, David | Bell, Sarah Jane | 24, Dec. 1849 | RCH |
| Beatty, Ebenezer | Hughes, Mary | 28, Apr. 1844 | BB |
| Beatty, James | Rees, Amarilla | 19, May 1842 | RCH |
| Bechbehammer, Chas. | Goslin, Sarah | 4, June 1836 | RCH |
| Bechel, Anton | Schaefer, Eva | 27, June 1848 | AA |
| Bechler, Johan | Halftermeyer, Anna M | 7, Aug. 1838 | FF |
| Bechmann, Justinian | Friedensdorf, Cath. | 1, Oct. 1843 | G |
| Becht, Friedrich J. | Bobinger, Catharine | 30, Jan. 1848 | C |
| Bechtel, Ludwig | Amolsch, Christina | 2, May 1847 | C |
| Bechtel, Wendel | Volls, Anna Maria | 1, May 1849 | AA |
| Bechtold, Andreas | Bauer, Eva | 27, Oct. 1840 | FF |
| Bechtold, Andrew | Bein, Barbara | 7, Dec. 1848 | RCH |
| Bechtold, B. Joachim | Katz, Christina R. | 7, July 1842 | FF |
| Bechtold, Georg | Gollat, Rosina | 20, Feb. 1849 | EE |
| Bechtold, Peter | Wolf, Maria | 4, July 1844 | RCH |
| Beck, Andreas | Schulz, Christina | 17, Sept 1848 | EE |
| Beck, Freeman | Chalmers, Mary | 22, Oct. 1840 | RCH |
| Beck, Heinrich | Baulsa, Maria | 5, Mar. 1839 | RCH |
| Beck, Jacob | Biegelmeier, Sarah | 8, Feb. 1849 | RCH |
| Beck, Jacob | Ruf, Theresa (Mrs) | 26, Nov. 1849 | EE |
| Beck, Johan | Mueller, Walburga | 6, July 1835 | FF |
| Beck, Johan | Conrad, Margaretha | 15, Jan. 1847 | C |
| Beck, Johan Theodor | Streit, Maria Ther. | 22, Nov. 1847 | EE |
| Beck, John A. | Laflin, Margaret C. | 3, Aug. 1848 | RCH |
| Beck, Joseph | Stolzenberg, Maria | 2, Jan. 1843 | AA |
| Beck, Lorenz | Eigner, Maria Anna | 19, Aug. 1849 | CC |
| Beck, Michael | Brill, Caroline | 5, Oct. 1848 | G |
| Beck, Peter | Gesmann, Barbara | 12, Dec. 1848 | A |
| Beckel, Thomas | McAdams, Elisabeth | 22, May 1838 | RCH |
| Beckenhaupt, John | Peter, Caroline | 22, Apr. 1847 | RCH |
| Becker, Albert | Bischof, Dorothea | 28, May 1840 | G |
| Becker, Andreas | Blum, Eva | 21, Oct. 1848 | G |
| Becker, Caspar | Therwort, Anna Maria | 26, Dec. 1848 | CC |
| Becker, Christian | Thesing, Maria Elis. | 25, Dec. 1847 | RCH |
| Becker, David | Wolf, Margaret | 25, Dec. 1849 | G |
| Becker, Henry | Meiers, Florentine | 3, Feb. 1846 | RCH |
| Becker, Hieronymus | Lange, Elisabeth | 28, June 1846 | AA |
| Becker, Johan | Waltas, Catharine | 8, Feb. 1846 | C |
| Becker, Johan Clemen | Carnol, Catharina | 26, Apr. 1836 | FF |
| Becker, Johan Heinr. | Ohms, Anna Maria | 16, June 1848 | RCH |
| Becker, Johan Heinr. | Vocht, Anna Maria | 4, Sept 1849 | B |
| Becker, John Carl | Mollenkamp, Elisabet | 6, Jan. 1848 | G |
| Becker, Peter | Stoll, Sarah | 30, June 1842 | RCH |
| Becker, Theodor | Caspers, Gesina | 21, Nov. 1848 | II |

| Grooms<br>***** | Brides<br>***** | Date of Marriage<br>**** ** ******** | Code<br>**** |
|---|---|---|---|
| Becker, Wilhelm | Bayer, Catharine | 24, Sept 1846 | C |
| Becket, Thomas | Jones, Sarah E. | 14, Oct. 1841 | RCH |
| Becking, Francis C. | Warden, Rebecca J. | 9, May 1848 | BB |
| Beckkroeger, Klaus H | Meckworth, Maria E. | 25, Nov. 1849 | RCH |
| Becklehammer, Joseph | Gould, Sarah | 15, Aug. 1841 | RCH |
| Beckley, Jesse | Jones, Margaret | 7, May 1846 | RCH |
| Beckmann, Andreas | Schaller, Barbara | 20, Sept 1849 | EE |
| Beckmann, Bernard | Greimann, Catharine | 7, Sept 1845 | AA |
| Beckmann, Dietrich | Schulte, Anna Maria | 10, Feb. 1846 | AA |
| Beckmann, Friedrich | Rehmann, Anna Maria | 21, Dec. 1848 | B |
| Beckmann, H. Gerhard | Strieker, A. Maria | 29, Feb. 1848 | II |
| Beckmann, Heinrich | Boedecker, A. Maria | 26, Jan. 1836 | FF |
| Beckmann, Heinrich | Benkos, Maria Anna | 22, May 1838 | FF |
| Beckmann, Heinrich | Bardendink, Elisabet | 13, Feb. 1844 | AA |
| Beckmann, Heinrich | Keiser, Lucia | 13, Dec. 1849 | RCH |
| Beckmann, Heinrich | Ricker, Catharine | 22, Sept 1846 | AA |
| Beckmann, Heinrich | Sicker, Gesina | 27, May 1849 | FF |
| Beckmann, Henry | Bergerdick, Elisabet | 13, Feb. 1844 | RCH |
| Beckmann, Johan H. | Schulten, Sophia | 31, Mar. 1848 | C |
| Beckmann, Johan Hein | Finck, Theresa | 7, Jan. 1840 | FF |
| Beckmann, Johan Herm | Sandel, Euphemia | 14, Feb. 1843 | AA |
| Beckmann, Johan Herm | Lammers, Theresa | 7, May 1848 | AA |
| Beckmann, Johan Theo | Sprakel, Theresa | 24, Oct. 1847 | EE |
| Beckmann, Theodor | Bramlage, Gertrud | 10, May 1842 | FF |
| Beckwith, Travice | Vanbar, Rebecca | 26, Mar. 1818 | RCH |
| Beckwith, William | Harris, Sarah Ann | 24, July 1846 | RCH |
| Becuder, Samuel | Billiod, Margaret | 9, July 1843 | RCH |
| Bedel, Andreas | Riester, Regina | 24, Oct. 1847 | HH |
| Bedel, Jacob Aloys. | Enneser, Rosina | 10, Jan. 1842 | FF |
| Bedel, Johan | Link, Carolina | 30, May 1848 | A |
| Bedel, Johan | Alig, Maria | 7, Jan. 1849 | EE |
| Bedel, Joseph | Fischer, Elisabeth | 6, Jan. 1848 | EE |
| Bedel, Stephan | Wist, Maria Elis. | 26, Oct. 1847 | EE |
| Bederkellen, Heinric | Schumaker, M. Engel | 6, Oct. 1849 | F |
| Bedgood, F.C. | Griffin, Emeline | 21, May 1849 | RCH |
| Bedgood, George | Knight, Martha | 20, May 1844 | RCH |
| Bedgood, James E. | Dudley, Clarissa | 19, Jan. 1836 | RCH |
| Bedient, Zalm-- | Wright, Mary Ann | 22, Aug. 1838 | RCH |
| Bee, James | Wooley, Mary | 19, Aug. 1824 | RCH |
| Beebe, Lewis | Grow, Adeline | 30, Dec. 1848 | RCH |
| Beebe, Samuel | Wheeler, Susannah | 14, May 1839 | RCH |
| Beeching, John | Gill, Ann | 25, Mar. 1847 | RCH |
| Beekley, James | Jones, Catharine | 14, Aug. 1842 | RCH |
| Beekley, John | Highlands, Mary Ann | 27, June 1847 | RCH |
| Beel, Johan | Wuebbel, Christina | 12, Jan. 1845 | AA |
| Beeler, David | Gaston, Elis. Jane | 29, Dec. 1836 | RCH |
| Beeler, Peter | Scully, Mary Francis | 6, July 1845 | BB |
| Beelsy, David | Burns, Elisabeth | 5, July 1849 | RCH |
| Beermann, Bernard H. | Niemeyer, Maria F. | 21, Nov. 1847 | EE |
| Beermann, Friedrich | Holthaus, Maria | 27, Feb. 1849 | RCH |
| Beers, Charles | Leonard, Maria | 10, Nov. 1845 | RCH |
| Beesey, Matthew | Link, Rosanna | 5, May 1836 | RCH |
| Beesley, John W. | Wanis, Sarah | 23, Oct. 1839 | RCH |
| Beessear, James | Fost, Ruth | 21, Apr. 1839 | RCH |
| Beesten, Herman | Buehning, Carolina | 28, Sept 1847 | AA |
| Behl, Johan | Seifert, Anna Maria | 19, Jan. 1841 | FF |
| Behl, Peter | Arnold, Sarah | 9, Aug. 1844 | RCH |
| Behler, Jacob | Kahn, Elisabeth | 12, May 1842 | RCH |
| Behne, Johan Herman | Albers, Marg. Adel. | 10, Nov. 1842 | FF |
| Behner, Adam | Mueller, Gertrud | 29, May 1838 | FF |
| Behning, August | Schmising, Agnes | 12, June 1849 | AA |
| Behr, Georg | Distler, Maria | 11, June 1845 | FF |
| Behre, Heinrich | Thoellen, Elisabeth | 11, Nov. 1846 | F |
| Behrens, Friedrich A | Wernax, Elisabeth | 26, Oct. 1848 | AA |
| Behrens, Herman | Date, Elisabeth | 27, Feb. 1838 | RCH |
| Behrens, Johan | Pardieck, Catharina | 17, July 1838 | FF |
| Behringer, Xavier | Klack, Catharina | 16, Mar. 1839 | FF |
| Behrmann, Heinrich | Schmeding, Anna M. | 30, Oct. 1838 | FF |
| Behrmann, Michael | Krin, Catharina | 23, Oct. 1849 | AA |
| Beide, Wilhelm Hein. | Kobelmann, Regina | 21, Dec. 1848 | C |
| Beiderhake, Johan B. | Brueggemann, Angela | 7, Sept 1845 | AA |

| Grooms | Brides | Date of Marriage | Code |
|--------|--------|------------------|------|
| ***** | ***** | **** ** ******** | **** |
| Beile, Carl | Tappe, Theresa | 26, Apr. 1846 | FF |
| Beile, Johan Gerhard | Bockhorst, Christina | 10, Nov. 1846 | AA |
| Beiler, Martin | Stelzer, Dominica | 8, Oct. 1848 | EE |
| Beilmann, Herman Bd. | Niemeyer, Bernardina | 23, Jan. 1848 | EE |
| Beimkampen, Georg H. | Niemann, Charlotte | 19, Oct. 1844 | F |
| Beinhart, Michael | Mayer, Barbara | 12, Apr. 1849 | RCH |
| Beiring, F.W Theodor | Dippel, Maria Cath. | 27, June 1844 | F |
| Beiser, Andreas | Graf, Helena | 31, Aug. 1848 | EE |
| Beiser, Andrew | Theinig, Eliza | 29, Dec. 1849 | RCH |
| Beitmann, Carl | Giese, Francisca | 23, Aug. 1842 | FF |
| Beitmann, Gerhard | Borgeding, Catharine | 24, May 1849 | II |
| Beitz, Valentin | Hoffmann, Kunigunda | 4, Oct. 1849 | A |
| Bekemeyer, Ernst | Ebler, Anna M. | 16, May 1843 | RCH |
| Bekemeyer, Johan H.G | Wibblemann, Anna M.C | 16, May 1843 | RCH |
| Bel---, Benjamin | Clark, Rebecca | 12, Nov. 1817 | RCH |
| Belange, John | Jones, Mami | 12, Nov. 1840 | RCH |
| Belangee, Charles | Carr, Margaret | 14, Aug. 1842 | RCH |
| Belangee, Samuel | Bedunnah, Phoebe | 15, Aug. 1847 | RCH |
| Belangie, Joseph | Kirby, Maria | 27, Nov. 1842 | RCH |
| Belans, John | Greene, Susanna | 23, Apr. 1826 | RCH |
| Belany, Daniel | Turner, Sarah | 9, Oct. 1819 | RCH |
| Belcher, Samuel | Delaney, Rachel | 3, Nov. 1837 | RCH |
| Beler, James | Jackson, Mary | 10, Feb. 1834 | RCH |
| Belfore, Nathaniel | Dundy, Jane | May 1843 | RCH |
| Belknap, Henry P. | Williams, Mary | 11, Mar. 1836 | RCH |
| Bell, Andrew | Gilbert, Sarah M. | 9, Dec. 1832 | RCH |
| Bell, David R. | Somburson, | 6, Apr. 1826 | RCH |
| Bell, James | Campbell, Hetty | 25, Apr. 1835 | RCH |
| Bell, James | McCain, Nancy | 2, Oct. 1835 | RCH |
| Bell, James | Ward, Mary Ann | 8, Oct. 1836 | RCH |
| Bell, James | Dickson, Jane | 28, Nov. 1849 | RCH |
| Bell, James M. | Sandlin, Louisiana | 9, Nov. 1847 | RCH |
| Bell, Joseph | Foley, Mary | 1, Sept 1847 | RCH |
| Bell, Michael | Adamson, Sarah | 31, May 1836 | RCH |
| Bell, Peter | Martin, Fanny A. | 1, Jan. 1849 | RCH |
| Bell, Shaber | Gilkey, Mary | 8, May 1842 | RCH |
| Bell, Thomas | Sanderlin, Indiana | 7, Apr. 1847 | RCH |
| Bell, William | Cross, Elisabeth | 20, Dec. 1821 | RCH |
| Bell, William | Rigdell, Sarah | 4, Aug. 1842 | RCH |
| Belleding, Joseph | Reser, Nympha | 9, May 1842 | FF |
| Bellis, James | Strong, Amy | 7, Jan. 1844 | RCH |
| Bellows, Isaac | Mary, Abigail | 29, Sept 1838 | RCH |
| Bellows, William A. | Dawson, Eleanor | 11, Sept 1838 | RCH |
| Belter, Bernard H. | Fraulmann, Charlotte | 19, Aug. 1843 | F |
| Belter, Friedrich W. | Rodefeld, Charlotte | 24, Jan. 1846 | G |
| Belter, Heinrich | Allendick, Elisabeth | 15, Oct. 1839 | FF |
| Belton, William | Moore, Elisabeth | 17, May 1841 | BB |
| Belville, J.R. | Folger, Harriet | 11, Oct. 1838 | RCH |
| Belzner, Michael | Dietz, Barbara | 28, Nov. 1847 | RCH |
| Bemann, Johan | Watschen, Julia | 20, Nov. 1845 | F |
| Bencher, Louis | Klemens, Catharine | 4, Dec. 1849 | RCH |
| Bencler, Peter | Damiael, Catharine | 8, Feb. 1834 | RCH |
| Bendecker, Conrad | Roessmann, Carolina | 27, Oct. 1847 | C |
| Bendell, John | Gay, Frances | Jan. 1848 | RCH |
| Bender, Abraham | Coppen, Elisabeth | 10, Oct. 1841 | RCH |
| Bender, Jacob | Hogans, Elisabeth | 20, July 1847 | RCH |
| Bendlage, Johan Bd. | Deiters, Euphemia | 6, Feb. 1848 | AA |
| Bene, Adam | Lampert, Sophia | 13, Nov. 1845 | RCH |
| Benedict, Alexander | Cleveland, Sarah | 31, July 1842 | RCH |
| Benedict, Spencer | Ward, Frances | 25, July 1849 | RCH |
| Benge, Joel | Boon, Matilda | 19, Aug. 1838 | RCH |
| Bengemann, Theodore | Langemeyer, Gertrud | 25, June 1846 | AA |
| Bengler, Gerhard H. | Stevens, Anna Maria | 9, Aug. 1842 | FF |
| Benham, Levi | Morris, Charlotte | 14, Mar. 1837 | RCH |
| Bening, John F. | Meyers, Mary | 25, July 1849 | RCH |
| Benjamin, Clayborn | Lemmon, Elisabeth | 21, Dec. 1845 | RCH |
| Benke, J. Dietrich | Ruprecht, Cath. D. | 20, Jan. 1846 | B |
| Benken, B.D. | Cahle, Theresa | 7, Jan. 1849 | AA |
| Benker, Johan | Oesten, Maria | 7, Mar. 1848 | A |
| Benkert, Johan | Eimer, Eva | 2, May 1843 | FF |
| Benkhof, Johan Bd. | Mairing, Anna Elis. | 14, Oct. 1849 | EE |

| Grooms<br>****** | Brides<br>****** | Date of Marriage<br>**** ** ******* | Code<br>**** |
|---|---|---|---|
| Benkofer, Gerhard | Roller, Gertrud | 20, Aug. 1848 | EE |
| Benlage, Gerhard H. | Heidemann, Theresa | 27, Jan. 1846 | AA |
| Benn, Benjamin | Hamilton, Priscilla | 15, Feb. 1842 | RCH |
| Bennart, Nicolaus | Evers, Sophia | 7, Feb. 1849 | RCH |
| Benne, Bernard Hein. | Lampe, Elisabeth | 13, Apr. 1847 | AA |
| Benne, Heinrich | Bredick, Elisabeth | 4, Mar. 1845 | AA |
| Benne, Johan Ernst | Dickhaus, Katharina | 24, Sept 1848 | AA |
| Bennefield, William | Kain, Jane | 8, Apr. 1819 | RCH |
| Bennefield, William | Hunt, Mary | 25, Apr. 1822 | RCH |
| Bennet, George | Penick, Betsey | 20, Jan. 1825 | RCH |
| Bennet, Monroe | Purdy, Florinda | 25, June 1848 | G |
| Bennet, Morris | Sherer, Barbara | 19, Feb. 1824 | RCH |
| Bennet, Reuben | Durham, Sarah | 10, Nov. 1842 | RCH |
| Bennet, Valentine | Phelps, Prudence | 28, July 1825 | RCH |
| Bennett, | Hawkins, Nancy | 27, Dec. 1821 | RCH |
| Bennett, | Cole, Catharine | 13, Sept 1849 | RCH |
| Bennett, Alfred | Pork---, Mary | 24, May 1837 | RCH |
| Bennett, Andrew | Ewan, Mary M. | 5, Mar. 1844 | RCH |
| Bennett, Burress | Allen, Margaret | 29, Apr. 1846 | RCH |
| Bennett, Charles | Garriott, Harriet | 19, Aug. 1845 | RCH |
| Bennett, David | Coleman, Rachel | 26, Aug. 1844 | RCH |
| Bennett, George | Kore, Charlotte | 10, Nov. 1845 | RCH |
| Bennett, James | Powell, Mary | 22, Mar. 1846 | RCH |
| Bennett, James | Graham, Mary Ann | 10, May 1846 | RCH |
| Bennett, Joseph | Roge, Norvey | 14, Mar. 1839 | RCH |
| Bennett, Joseph B. | McCormick, Lydia | 17, Apr. 1848 | RCH |
| Bennett, Littleton | Dudley, Ellen C. | 2, May 1849 | I |
| Bennett, Robert | Burton, Elisabeth | 18, May 1827 | RCH |
| Bennett, Vinton | Silsbee, Mary | 22, May 1843 | RCH |
| Bennett, William | Montgomery, Mary | 5, Apr. 1821 | RCH |
| Benning, Heinrich | Recker, Francisca | 11, Feb. 1849 | II |
| Benninghaus, Gerhard | Niemeyer, Maria(Mrs) | 5, Nov. 1844 | AA |
| Bennington, James | Johnston, Jane | 10, July 1848 | RCH |
| Bennington, Samuel | Cox, Nancy | 15, Sept 1847 | RCH |
| Benry, Bernard | Brink, Gesina | 28, Nov. 1843 | AA |
| Bensen, Peter | Sharp, Elisabeth | 3, Jan. 1833 | RCH |
| Bensmann, Herman | Michael, Mary Ann | 27, Nov. 1849 | RCH |
| Benson, | Stesinger, Nancy | 22, Nov. 1837 | RCH |
| Benson, Benjamin | Fosdick, Anna | 6, Nov. 1845 | RCH |
| Benson, Blakely | Scofield, Elisabeth | 3, Sept 1835 | RCH |
| Benson, Francis | Little, Caroline | Oct. 1844 | RCH |
| Benson, Jackson | Schofield, Margaret | 30, May 1846 | RCH |
| Benson, James | Nelson, Mary Ann | 6, Sept 1849 | RCH |
| Benson, James | McGinn, Elisabeth | 2, May 1847 | BB |
| Benson, Mathers | Kyser, Mary Ann | 14, Dec. 1820 | RCH |
| Benson, Peter | Brookaw, Ann V. | 27, Oct. 1838 | RCH |
| Benson, Zacheus | Flowers, Rosanna | 1, Aug. 1839 | RCH |
| Benter, Dietrich | Knollenberg, Friedr. | 26, May 1842 | F |
| Bentley, John | Thompson, Virginia | 23, July 1849 | RCH |
| Bently, A.W. | Davie, Angeline C. | 26, Mar. 1834 | RCH |
| Bently, Samuel | Ludlum, Sarah | 4, July 1821 | RCH |
| Benton, Durett | Cox, Salomea | 7, May 1849 | RCH |
| Benton, Frederick | Snider, Susan | 10, Sept 1848 | RCH |
| Benton, John | Wolf, Sarah | June 1823 | RCH |
| Bentz, John | Coil, Catharine | 1, Mar. 1842 | RCH |
| Benz, Francis | Scholl, Regina | 6, Sept 1844 | AA |
| Benzer, Friedrich A. | Hulfemann, Charlotte | 29, June 1848 | C |
| Benzmann, Herman | Michael, A. Maria | 27, Nov. 1849 | II |
| Bepman, Henry | Mullen, Mary | 27, Nov. 1839 | RCH |
| Beppler, Eduard | Wilde, Margaretha | 1, Oct. 1848 | G |
| Berbering, Ferdinand | Ehrmantraut, Sophia | 7, Aug. 1848 | EE |
| Berdes, Ludwig | Faust, Sophia | 3, Feb. 1845 | AA |
| Berdin, Roman | Liber, Juliana | 2, Aug. 1847 | FF |
| Berding, Johan H. | Pinemeier, Maria E. | 30, May 1848 | EE |
| Bereman, David | Wilson, Margaret | 25, Dec. 1834 | RCH |
| Beresford, Richard | Sutton, Elisabeth | Aug. 1832 | I |
| Beresford, Richard | Wunder, Catharine | 18, Sept 1845 | RCH |
| Beresford, William | Packer, Helen | 22, May 1844 | RCH |
| Berg, Carl | Veille, Louisa | 9, July 1835 | FF |
| Berg, Jacob | Huch, Sarah | 14, Dec. 1843 | RCH |
| Berg, Jacob | Golle, Elisabeth | 13, Sept 1849 | RCH |

| Grooms ****** | Brides ****** | Date of Marriage **** ** ******** | Code **** |
|---|---|---|---|
| Berger, Christopher | Meyer, Gertrud | 6, Aug. 1839 | FF |
| Berger, Georg | Fetter, Barbara | 12, Oct. 1843 | G |
| Berger, Heinrich | Spicker, Margaretha | 19, Sept 1847 | FF |
| Berger, Herman | Wolterings, Anna M. | 28, July 1840 | FF |
| Berger, Peter | Cook, Elizabeth | 8, Nov. 1846 | BB |
| Bergerot, Johan Bap. | Roidague, Judith | 7, Jan. 1836 | FF |
| Bergheger, Friedrich | Mueller, Catharine | 10, Mar. 1846 | AA |
| Berghegger, Johan F. | Spellbring, Anna M. | 7, Sept 1842 | FF |
| Bergjohann, Wilhelm | Lehmeier, Caroline | 30, May 1849 | C |
| Bergmann, Bonaface | Meiers, Fanny | 12, May 1842 | RCH |
| Bergmann, Conrad | Schott, Catharine | 1, Aug. 1848 | EE |
| Bergmann, Friedrich | Stricker, Agnes | 21, Jan. 1840 | FF |
| Bergmann, Georg | Mueller, Mary | 28, May 1844 | AA |
| Bergmann, Heinrich | Hoene, Margaretha | 10, Apr. 1845 | AA |
| Bergmann, Johan Fr. | Luhring, Maria D. | 14, Oct. 1841 | F |
| Bergmann, Johan H. | Sickmann, M. Elis. | 28, Oct. 1849 | FF |
| Bergmann, Karl | Meinze, Louise | 9, Aug. 1846 | G |
| Bergmann, Theodor | Burkhof, Anna Maria | 5, Oct. 1841 | FF |
| Bergmann, Wilhelm | Meyers, Sophia | 29, June 1848 | F |
| Berheide, Anton Wm. | Busse, Bernardina | 10, Oct. 1847 | AA |
| Berheide, Johan H. | Feldmann, Gesina | 24, June 1845 | AA |
| Berington, William | Gastiage, Delila | 5, Nov. 1836 | RCH |
| Berlage, Francis | Roberg, A. Maria | 29, Apr. 1849 | II |
| Berling, Anton | Hausmann, Maria | 24, Apr. 1838 | FF |
| Berlitz, Jacob | Wagemann, Margaretha | 7, Jan. 1845 | A |
| Bermann, David | Heidelbach, Theresa | 12, Oct. 1847 | RCH |
| Berna, John | Verner, Magdalena | Aug. 1847 | RCH |
| Bernard, G.M. | Kernnard, Caroline | 24, May 1849 | RCH |
| Bernard, Johan | Barnickel, Maria | 24, May 1841 | FF |
| Bernard, John | Bassmann, Mary E. | Nov. 1849 | RCH |
| Bernard, Nicolaus | Beck, Mary A. | 27, June 1847 | RCH |
| Berndt, Louis F. | Deeg, Margaret | 24, Dec. 1847 | G |
| Bernemann, Johan H. | Spillbrink, Elis(Mrs | 7, Oct. 1849 | AA |
| Bernert, Ludwig | Graf, Magdalena | 18, Aug. 1845 | AA |
| Bernhard, Andreas | Pfaff, Catharine | 14, Oct. 1841 | RCH |
| Bernhard, Bernard | Huber, Genofeva | 16, Jan. 1849 | EE |
| Bernhard, Jakob | Luchoder, Magdalena | 10, Apr. 1849 | C |
| Bernhard, Louis | Steimer, Mary | 17, Feb. 1848 | RCH |
| Bernhardt, Georg | Meyers, Maria | 27, Sept 1849 | RCH |
| Bernhardt, Johan | Fischer, Caroline | 27, Aug. 1849 | G |
| Berning, Anton | Koors, Maria Anna | 6, Feb. 1848 | FF |
| Berning, Bernard | Bullermann, Elis. | 30, Sept 1849 | FF |
| Berning, Johan Herm. | Heidger, Euphemia A. | 2, July 1848 | AA |
| Berninger, Sebastian | Hartmann, Maria Anna | 27, Nov. 1847 | EE |
| Berns, Joseph | Niehaus, Anna Maria | 3, June 1845 | FF |
| Bernzott, Johan | Stueckel, Anna Maria | 30, Oct. 1845 | AA |
| Berren, Jonathan | Beall, Hester | 8, Mar. 1846 | RCH |
| Berry, Alexander | Wilson, Clarissa | 27, Sept 1849 | RCH |
| Berry, Archibald | Looker, Amelia | 5, Mar. 1846 | RCH |
| Berry, August | Scheu, Mary | 31, Mar. 1846 | RCH |
| Berry, David | Wainwright, Maria | 19, Nov. 1844 | RCH |
| Berry, George W. | Parker, Lucretia | 13, Feb. 1848 | RCH |
| Berry, James | Ryan, Elisabeth | 4, Nov. 1834 | RCH |
| Berry, John H. | Adams, Rachel | 11, Dec. 1845 | RCH |
| Berry, Luke | O'Neil, Ann | 14, Mar. 1846 | GG |
| Berry, Washington | Jonas, Susan C. | 11, June 1839 | RCH |
| Berry, William | Cox, Mary Elisabeth | 10, July 1834 | RCH |
| Berryman, Eli | Chambers, Phoebe | 28, Oct. 1838 | RCH |
| Berryman, James | Lord, Alice | 5, July 1821 | RCH |
| Berst, Heinrich | Rathgens, Elis. M. | 13, June 1847 | A |
| Berte, Heinrich | VonderHeide, Maria | 30, Apr. 1846 | AA |
| Berte, Joseph | VonLehmen, Margaret | 14, May 1839 | FF |
| Berte, Joseph | Timpermann, Margaret | 18, Apr. 1847 | AA |
| Berting, Heinrich | Schroeder, Angela | 9, Apr. 1844 | AA |
| Bertke, Theodor | Heidmann, Maria F. | 7, June 1849 | FF |
| Bertlein, Adam | Schmick, Ursula | 13, July 1840 | FF |
| Bertling, Adolph | Renk, Eva Catharina | 28, Oct. 1841 | FF |
| Bertram, James | Ritter, Maria | 29, Aug. 1846 | HH |
| Bertram, Leonard | Bach, Apollonia | 19, Aug. 1849 | EE |
| Bertram, Peter | Matthewson, Jennetta | 6, Feb. 1847 | RCH |
| Bertsch, Jacob | Hermann, Regina | 6, Apr. 1842 | FF |

| Grooms | Brides | Date of Marriage | Code |
|--------|--------|------------------|------|
| ****** | ****** | **** ** ******** | **** |
| Berwiller, Nicolaus | Reis, Gertrud | 13, May 1839 | FF |
| Bess, William | Isgrig, Rebecca | 18, May 1842 | RCH |
| Bessey, Lyman | Farmer, Mahala | 22, Sept 1822 | RCH |
| Bessler, Wolfgang | Seibert, Magdalena | 19, Aug. 1845 | AA |
| Bessler, Wolfgang | Schuh, Rosina | 29, Apr. 1849 | EE |
| Best, Jacob | Rosenberg, Barbara | 28, Jan. 1839 | FF |
| Best, Joseph B. | Tucker, Theodosia | 22, June 1838 | RCH |
| Best, Karl | Weber, Rosina | 26, Dec. 1848 | RCH |
| Best, Martin | Hayden, Jane E. | 23, Sept 1849 | RCH |
| Best, Robert | Davis, Martha | 5, Dec. 1832 | RCH |
| Bestbrock, Theodor | Lobmeyer, Catharine | 16, July 1848 | EE |
| Besten, Joseph | Kunk, Elisabeth | 14, Jan. 1849 | AA |
| Bestermann, Bernard | Brueggemann, Louisa | 12, July 1842 | FF |
| Besuden, Heinrich | Wuerdemann, Margaret | 18, May 1848 | B |
| Betherford, Philipp | Summerfield, Elis. | 13, May 1833 | RCH |
| Bethurst, John | Hillman, Maria | 7, June 1836 | RCH |
| Betscher, Casper | Meier, Adelheid | 4, Oct. 1849 | FF |
| Bettenbrock, Friedr. | Fricken, Catharina M | 22, Oct. 1840 | F |
| Betterston, William | Halsted, Amelia | 13, Feb. 1848 | RCH |
| Bettinger, Eberhard | Koerber, Elisabeth | 7, Mar. 1848 | CC |
| Bettinger, Peter | Roth, Elisabeth | 28, Feb. 1848 | FF |
| Bettinghaus, Clamer | Bramsche, Emilia M. | 6, Oct. 1845 | F |
| Bettle, John | Wright, Mary | 30, Oct. 1842 | BB |
| Bettmann, Moritz | Morhring, Flora | 9, Oct. 1845 | RCH |
| Betts, Andrew | Bengle, Rachel | 4, Nov. 1832 | RCH |
| Betts, John | Kelly, | 13, Nov. 1823 | RCH |
| Betts, John | Martin, Sarah Ann | 16, May 1844 | RCH |
| Betts, Oliver | Brant, Elisabeth | 15, Feb. 1844 | RCH |
| Betts, Samuel | Saxton, Louisa | 3, Sept 1844 | RCH |
| Betts, William | Andrews, Susan | 1, Feb. 1820 | RCH |
| Betz, Michael | Kuhn, Elisabeth | 23, Apr. 1844 | FF |
| Betz, Pancratz | Mohnlein, Christina | 15, Aug. 1847 | EE |
| Betzer, George F. | Heitmann, mary | 18, Sept 1843 | RCH |
| Betzhold, Francis | Veit, Walburga | 25, Oct. 1846 | AA |
| Beuchel, Jacob | Trettel, Margaretha | 11, July 1846 | EE |
| Beuck, J. Dietrich | Linnemann, M. Elis. | 20, Jan. 1846 | B |
| Beuscheider, Gilbert | Stewart, Margaret | 22, Apr. 1838 | RCH |
| Beuse, Theodor | Wiggermann, Anna | 7, Jan. 1849 | FF |
| Bevan, John | Lawdon, Hannah | 28, Mar. 1822 | RCH |
| Bevan, Philipp | Davis, Anna J. | 14, June 1849 | RCH |
| Bevan, Thomas | Dean, Hulda | 10, Nov. 1845 | RCH |
| Bevans, William | Alfirld, Nancy | 17, Feb. 1833 | RCH |
| Bevington, James | Irwin, Nancy | 20, July 1843 | RCH |
| Bevis, Benjamin A. | Howard, Lydia | 8, Aug. 1833 | RCH |
| Bevis, David | Stout, A. | 14, Jan. 1836 | RCH |
| Bevis, James | Reed, Abigail | 5, Nov. 1835 | RCH |
| Bevis, James | Shipman, Rebecca | 24, Aug. 1843 | RCH |
| Bevis, Jesse | Williamson, Nancy | 28, Oct. 1842 | RCH |
| Bevis, Martin | Stout, Eleanor | 5, Jan. 1833 | RCH |
| Bew, John | Hubener, Dorothea | 12, Oct. 1841 | RCH |
| Beyer, Georg | Bauer, Elisabeth | 20, Apr. 1840 | G |
| Bezolt, Valentin | Braun, Maria Anna | 14, Nov. 1847 | EE |
| Bias, Garrett | Linscott, Polly | 1, Mar. 1821 | RCH |
| Bick, Bernard | Schippers, Anna M. | 26, Jan. 1847 | AA |
| Bickerdyke, Robert | Ball, Mary Ann | 27, Apr. 1847 | I |
| Bickham, Thomas | Davis, Missouri | 20, Jan. 1840 | RCH |
| Bicknell, William | Ellis, Mariah | 31, Jan. 1844 | RCH |
| Bickwermet, Bernard | Tille, Maria | 20, June 1837 | FF |
| Biddinger, William | Owens, Rhoda | 29, Aug. 1847 | RCH |
| Biddle, | Anderson, Mary | 1, July 1836 | RCH |
| Biddle, Lewis | English, Mary Ann | 11, June 1837 | RCH |
| Biddle, William | Weston, Electa | 12, Oct. 1843 | RCH |
| Biddle, William B. | ----, Mary | 30, July 1835 | RCH |
| Bidwell, Gilbert | Collins, Emeline | 13, Sept 1847 | RCH |
| Bieber, Andreas | Ahlbrinck, M. Angela | 19, Sept 1841 | FF |
| Biedinger, Johan | Lieberich, Elisabeth | 28, Sept 1847 | C |
| Biedinger, Nicolaus | Weber, Catharine | 2, Dec. 1844 | G |
| Biedinger, Peter | Bankhardt, Maria | 2, June 1847 | C |
| Biegelberger, Jacob | Krenser, Caroline | 3, May 1846 | RCH |
| Biehl, Jacob | Schneider, Elisabeth | 3, Aug. 1844 | A |
| Bielefeld, Heinrich | Schumacher, Maria A. | 26, May 1846 | FF |

| Grooms<br>***** | Brides<br>***** | Date of Marriage<br>**** ** ******* | Code<br>**** |
|---|---|---|---|
| Bierbaum, Ernst | Mayers, Johanna M.C. | 19, Sept 1849 | C |
| Bierbaum, Georg P. | Guendling, Louisa | 14, June 1846 | FF |
| Biermann, Friedrich | Nulkamper, Christina | 5, Apr. 1849 | B |
| Biesenbach, Adolph | Meyer, Agnes | 27, June 1843 | AA |
| Biesenbach, Christ. | Fischer, Catharine | 11, Feb. 1847 | RCH |
| Bieste, Johan H. | Lester, Catharina | 15, Apr. 1834 | RCH |
| Biethenharn, Heinric | Feldmann, Anna | 10, Jan. 1847 | AA |
| Bigdon, John | Barr, Mariah | 19, Oct. 1824 | RCH |
| Biger, Peter | Seifert, Barbara | 18, Sept 1849 | G |
| Bigford, Adonisum | Hopkins, Sarah H. | 25, Mar. 1819 | RCH |
| Bigger, George D. | Parvin, Delia M. | 25, Apr. 1842 | I |
| Biggler, Jacob | Jones, Ruth | Mar. 1836 | RCH |
| Biggs, David | Valentine, Magdalena | 31, Oct. 1832 | RCH |
| Biggs, James M. | Andrew, Nancy Ann | 22, Sept 1833 | RCH |
| Biggs, John S. | Randall, Elisabeth | 8, Oct. 1832 | RCH |
| Biggs, Peter | Stout, M. | 18, Aug. 1838 | RCH |
| Bigham, William | Clark, Jane | 12, Oct. 1824 | RCH |
| Bigler, George | Hilburn, Toloma | 30, Nov. 1833 | RCH |
| Bigler, John | Kepler, Rosina | 20, Sept 1846 | RCH |
| Biker, Johan Friedr. | Engelschroeder, Anna | 14, Jan. 1841 | FF |
| Biles, Charles | Edgar, Mary | 8, Jan. 1843 | RCH |
| Biles, George | Bogen, Margaret(Mrs) | 5, Oct. 1841 | I |
| Biles, Thompson | Armstrong, Martha A. | 26, Feb. 1844 | RCH |
| Bille, Heinrich | Renkus, Elisabeth | 5, Feb. 1839 | FF |
| Billenstein, John | Rieget, Catharine | 14, Mar. 1842 | RCH |
| Billerbeck, Clemens | Pille, M. Catharina | 27, Apr. 1835 | FF |
| Billert, Johan | Doerer, Margaretha | 12, Oct. 1845 | A |
| Billiam, Michael | Tangemann, Augusta C | 18, Feb. 1849 | C |
| Billinger, Casper | Taylor, Elisabeth | 13, June 1841 | RCH |
| Billings, E.S. | Dustin, Levina | 31, Mar. 1834 | RCH |
| Billings, James | S---, Abba | 2, July 1835 | RCH |
| Billingsley, Adam | Tucker, Mary | 15, Feb. 1846 | RCH |
| Billingsley, Charles | Willis, Elisabeth | 26, May 1824 | RCH |
| Binder, Constantine | Kubber, Eva | 16, Feb. 1847 | CC |
| Binder, Nicolaus | Steder, Magdalena | 22, May 1845 | AA |
| Bindhammer, H. Ernst | Bettmann, Anna Maria | 5, July 1845 | A |
| Bindhammer, Paul | Carle, Maria Anna | 26, Nov. 1846 | FF |
| Binger, Johan H. | Amenscamp, Maria | 19, Nov. 1848 | EE |
| Binges, Edward | Bogart, Eliza | 3, Mar. 1825 | RCH |
| Binges, James | ----, Mary | 2, Feb. 1825 | RCH |
| Bingham, William | Sloop, Sarah | 12, Aug. 1841 | RCH |
| Binghaus, Tracy | Garrison, Rebecca | 9, Oct. 1840 | RCH |
| Bingle, James S. | Kendrick, Sarah | 16, Feb. 1841 | RCH |
| Bingle, William | Johnston, Phoebe | 6, Aug. 1826 | RCH |
| Bingle, William | Jinks, Nancy | 21, Feb. 1842 | RCH |
| Binker, Johan H. | Fehr, Anna | 2, Sept 1849 | AA |
| Binkey, John | Brown, Julia Ann | 7, June 1839 | RCH |
| Binney, Mathias | Linck, Rosanna | 27, Apr. 1836 | RCH |
| Binsach, Johan | Siefert, Barbara | 25, Feb. 1837 | FF |
| Binty, Jesse | Finch, Mary | 8, Sept 1839 | RCH |
| Binzack, Peter | Noll, Regina | 20, July 1841 | FF |
| Birch, Elias | Cameron, Jane | 14, Nov. 1842 | RCH |
| Birch, William | Gibson, Agnes | 10, Jan. 1847 | RCH |
| Birckenhau, Heinrich | Geisler, Margaretha | 25, Apr. 1836 | FF |
| Bird, | Jadis, Ruth | 23, May 1827 | RCH |
| Bird, Henry | Holmes, Catharine | 23, Aug. 1833 | RCH |
| Bird, Ira H. | Symmonds, Julia A. | 8, July 1840 | RCH |
| Bird, John | Murphy, Margaret | 13, July 1849 | BB |
| Bird, William | Hughes, Jane | 12, June 1842 | RCH |
| Birdsell, Moses | Winsor, Emily | 20, Nov. 1840 | RCH |
| Birer, Melchior | McQuillan, Margaret | 16, Aug. 1842 | BB |
| Bires, James | Barnes, Sophronia | 11, Feb. 1847 | RCH |
| Birhelt, Thomas | Bagshaw, Ann | 1, Jan. 1848 | RCH |
| Birkle, Mathias | Feinthel, Magdalena | 11, Dec. 1843 | G |
| Birney, Dion | Crawford, Sarah | 13, Aug. 1845 | RCH |
| Birney, William | Hoffmann, Catharine | 12, Nov. 1846 | D |
| Bische, Dietrich | Meyers, Maria | 10, Oct. 1843 | FF |
| Bishop, Alfred | Smiley, Nancy | 17, June 1847 | RCH |
| Bishop, Joel | Parson, Mary | 21, Mar. 1822 | RCH |
| Bishop, John | Merchant, Thirza | 23, Mar. 1833 | RCH |
| Bishop, John | Hildreth, Any Ann | 28, Jan. 1847 | RCH |

| Grooms<br>****** | Brides<br>****** | Date of Marriage<br>**** ** ******** | Code<br>**** |
|---|---|---|---|
| Bishop, John | Crisser, Mary Ann | 10, Dec. 1849 | RCH |
| Bishop, Jonathan | McCrary, Marinda | 15, Aug. 1842 | RCH |
| Bishop, Samuel | Hoge, Elisabeth H. | 7, Oct. 1841 | I |
| Bishop, Samuel | Smith, Mary Ann | 21, Nov. 1848 | RCH |
| Bisop, Lornezo Dow. | Hardin, Ellen | 3, June 1834 | RCH |
| Bissell, Israel M. | Mead, Augusta T. | 22, Mar. 1831 | I |
| Bissmann, Israel M. | Clay, Margaret | 18, Jan. 1826 | RCH |
| Bitt, Joseph | Stewart, Nancy | 10, Apr. 1834 | RCH |
| Bitter, Bernard | Braun, Maria | 6, Aug. 1839 | FF |
| Bitters, David | Shott, Catharine | 21, Dec. 1834 | RCH |
| Bittihoeffer, Fred. | Veith, Friedricka | 12, Nov. 1833 | RCH |
| Bittinger, Philipp | Bertny, Catharina | 26, Feb. 1839 | G |
| Bittle, Hezekiah | Everson, Ann | 16, Nov. 1820 | RCH |
| Bittner, Adam | Bachmann, Catharine | 26, July 1848 | EE |
| Bjorkland, Peter | Bauer, Catharine | 27, Mar. 1843 | RCH |
| Blaas, Friedrich Wm. | Bimson, Maria | 23, Mar. 1848 | A |
| Black, Adam | Martin, Isabella | 27, June 1842 | RCH |
| Black, David | Thompson, Celia | 20, Feb. 1818 | RCH |
| Black, David | Beard, Lucinda | 21, Aug. 1842 | RCH |
| Black, David A. | Guess, Cynthia Ann | 7, Jan. 1836 | RCH |
| Black, David P. | Williams, Theresa | 6, Aug. 1848 | RCH |
| Black, George | Meyers, Rachel | 9, Nov. 1843 | RCH |
| Black, Jacob | Flanigan, Nancy | 21, Aug. 1836 | RCH |
| Black, James | McMeen, Nancy | 17, Oct. 1837 | RCH |
| Black, Jeffrey | Fay, Catharine | 19, May 1844 | RCH |
| Black, Johan | Linnemann, Catharine | 16, Jan. 1844 | FF |
| Black, Josiah | McLain, Glowina | 5, Apr. 1847 | RCH |
| Black, Mahlon | Burrows, Adaline | 11, July 1847 | RCH |
| Black, Milo | Clausen, Priscilla | 5, Dec. 1843 | RCH |
| Black, Morris W. | Martin, Elisabeth | 27, Dec. 1835 | RCH |
| Black, Reuben | Rands, Catharine | 16, June 1846 | RCH |
| Black, Samuel | Lewis, Hannah | 31, Mar. 1842 | RCH |
| Black, William | English, Letitia | 5, Sept 1844 | RCH |
| Blackall, Truman | Levi, Rachel | 17, Dec. 1843 | RCH |
| Blackback, Daniel | Calhoun, Nancy J. | 21, July 1841 | RCH |
| Blackburn, David | Spurier, Carsa | 9, Feb. 1819 | RCH |
| Blackburn, Edward C. | Norris, Virginia | 16, Jan. 1844 | I |
| Blackburn, John | Everet, Elisabeth | 27, Mar. 1820 | RCH |
| Blackburn, Samuel | Holmes, Mary A. | 24, Nov. 1836 | RCH |
| Blackburn, Thomas R. | Stillman, Lucilia M. | 3, Oct. 1832 | I |
| Blackenmore, Thomas | Hopson, Emily | 24, Oct. 1839 | RCH |
| Blackman, Alonzo | Ward, Alvira Jane | 7, Oct. 1847 | RCH |
| Blackman, John B. | Goldswell, Catharine | 10, May 1835 | RCH |
| Blackman, John L. | McFeely, Hannah | 28, July 1839 | RCH |
| Blackman, Lamor | Huffman, Elisabeth | 31, May 1838 | RCH |
| Blackmann, Herman | Weri, Maria Elis. | 28, Jan. 1845 | AA |
| Blackstone, Benjamin | Morris, Mary J. | 20, Apr. 1848 | RCH |
| Blaco, John | Remlinger, Ann | 21, July 1849 | RCH |
| Bladel, Heinrich | Gschwind, Hannah | 18, Nov. 1845 | A |
| Blades, Parnell | Sedam, Nancy | 30, Sept 1832 | RCH |
| Blaesy, Carl | Koch, Catharine | 18, Nov. 1845 | EE |
| Blair, Greenville | Rickets, Lucinda | 7, July 1847 | RCH |
| Blair, M. | Taylor, Elisabeth | 28, May 1834 | RCH |
| Blair, McClean L. | Walker, Caroline S. | 10, Apr. 1845 | I |
| Blair, McLean | Gerrard, Sarah Belle | 11, May 1843 | RCH |
| Blair, Samuel | Lafferty, Mary Ann | 28, Apr. 1843 | RCH |
| Blair, William | Addison, Clarissa | 14, May 1843 | RCH |
| Blake, Henry | Robinson, Sarah | 25, Sept 1845 | RCH |
| Blake, James | Leonard, Ann | 26, Sept 1847 | GG |
| Blake, Michael | Wall, Mary | 22, May 1839 | BB |
| Blake, Robert | Helms, Elisabeth | 13, Mar. 1847 | RCH |
| Blake, Thomas C. | Bishop, Lavina | 12, Oct. 1819 | RCH |
| Blake, William B. | Andrews, Rebecca | 17, May 1834 | RCH |
| Blakeley, John | Harvey, Anna Eveline | 10, Aug. 1842 | RCH |
| Blakemore, John | Denman, Abigail | 30, Oct. 1845 | RCH |
| Blancey, William | Cobb, Phebe o. | 6, Dec. 1846 | RCH |
| Blaney, Lawrence | Melley, Nancy | 13, July 1844 | RCH |
| Blank, Carl | Lange, Emma | 10, June 1845 | FF |
| Blank, Johan | Brosamer, Maria Anna | 29, Oct. 1843 | FF |
| Blankemeyer, Heinric | Schlademann, Anna | 26, Oct. 1848 | B |
| Blanken---, Abraham | McGlaughlin, Jane | 10, Oct. 1825 | RCH |

| Grooms<br>****** | Brides<br>****** | Date of Marriage<br>**** ** ******** | Code<br>**** |
|---|---|---|---|
| Blankenbuhler, Johan | Reidel, Kunigunda | 22, Apr. 1849 | A |
| Blankmann, Bernard H | Lueken, Maria Angela | 26, Jan. 1847 | CC |
| Blannon, George | Halstead, | 18, Sept 1825 | RCH |
| Blanst, Elisha | Shepherd, Mary Jane | 9, Nov. 1848 | RCH |
| Blase, Adam H. | Wilken, Catharine | 18, June 1846 | F |
| Blasford, Francis | Matthews, Rebecca | 14, Apr. 1840 | RCH |
| Blasie, Christian | Angert, Maria | 30, Dec. 1849 | CC |
| Blatchford, Henry | Crossman, Martha | 17, June 1844 | I |
| Bleaks, David | Church, Susan | 3, Dec. 1846 | RCH |
| Bleck, Peter P. | Kerb, Maria Anna | 17, Aug. 1841 | FF |
| Bleckmann, Carl H. | Nienaber, Elisabeth | 19, Nov. 1844 | AA |
| Bleckmann, Carl Hein | Trentmann, Louisa A. | 20, Apr. 1841 | FF |
| Bledsod, Abraham | Egliston, Diana | 28, Aug. 1834 | RCH |
| Blehs, Heinrich | Rechtin, Maria Anna | 21, Nov. 1847 | AA |
| Bleimann, Bernard H. | Godkinn, Catharine | 11, Aug. 1840 | FF |
| Bleimeier, Joseph | Stork, Maria E. | Nov. 1844 | RCH |
| Bleistner, John | Heinemann, Catharine | 17, June 1844 | RCH |
| Blen, Douglas | Jones, Chary | 25, Dec. 1817 | RCH |
| Blene, Elisha | Jones, Ann | 28, July 1848 | RCH |
| Blenke, Michael | Ensfelder, Catharina | 17, Oct. 1848 | FF |
| Blesch, Michael | Hipp, Barbara | 27, June 1847 | G |
| Blesch, Philipp | Kleinmann, Salome | 12, Nov. 1848 | A |
| Blesch, Sebastian | Weismann, Johanna B. | 16, Dec. 1849 | G |
| Blesi, Samuel | Jung, Margaret | 14, May 1849 | RCH |
| Bley, Theodor | Sander, Maria Helena | 9, May 1843 | AA |
| Blick, Robert | Caldwell, Ellen J. | 6, June 1849 | RCH |
| Blim, Enos | Fruhman, Evaline | 16, Mar. 1837 | RCH |
| Blinn, Asa | Weston, Lucy | 3, July 1843 | RCH |
| Blinn, Enos | Abbott, Clarissa | 1, Jan. 1845 | RCH |
| Blinn, James | Nye, Emily | 27, Apr. 1842 | RCH |
| Blinn, Lorenzo | Hubbard, Elisabeth | 15, Jan. 1836 | RCH |
| Blinn, Orra | Layman, Laura | 26, Sept 1843 | RCH |
| Blircker, Daniel | Merwe, Martha | 20, Nov. 1821 | RCH |
| Bliss, George | Dodge, Margaret | 28, Dec. 1836 | RCH |
| Bliss, Oliver H. | Douglass, Caroline | 27, Nov. 1842 | RCH |
| Bloch, Simon | Daniel, Fanny | 25, May 1847 | RCH |
| Block, Ernst | Niemann, Margaret | 15, Mar. 1849 | RCH |
| Block, Ernst | Brueggemann, Sophia | 11, Apr. 1848 | C |
| Block, Larus | Levi, Barbara | 8, Sept 1841 | RCH |
| Blodget, Dennis | Ferguson, Elisabeth | 7, Oct. 1838 | RCH |
| Blodget, William D. | Hapion, Pauline | 15, Aug. 1848 | BB |
| Bloe--, Joseph | Aughter, Fanny | 15, Aug. 1817 | RCH |
| Bloebaum, Henry Wm. | Scholen, Maria | 17, Sept 1846 | B |
| Bloemer, J. Heinrich | Hehemann, A.M. Clara | 29, Oct. 1839 | FF |
| Bloemer, Johan B. | Nedler, Bernardina | 17, June 1849 | AA |
| Blome, Bernard Hein. | Schroeder, Maria A. | 11, June 1845 | FF |
| Blome, Heinrich Otto | Wempe, Maria Anna | 12, Sept 1847 | FF |
| Blome, Johan Heinric | Hueninghake, M Engel | 22, Aug. 1847 | AA |
| Blomer, Andreas | Blomer, Margaretha | 7, Oct. 1849 | II |
| Bloom, George | Hart, Rachel | 11, Apr. 1842 | RCH |
| Bloomburgh, William | Sponsler, Amanda | 30, Sept 1832 | RCH |
| Bloomer, George A. | Kencher, Mary | 5, Aug. 1838 | RCH |
| Bloomingdale, Chas. | Ezekiel, Eve | 2, July 1844 | RCH |
| Blossom, Matthew | Smith, Mercy | 3, July 1844 | RCH |
| Blount, Ambrose | Hansel, Rebecca | 14, Apr. 1846 | RCH |
| Blue, Henry | Beckwith, Becky | 24, Mar. 1837 | RCH |
| Blum, Abraham | Haas, Caroline | 23, Sept 1849 | RCH |
| Blum, Amand | Aman, Elisabeth | 20, Dec. 1848 | RCH |
| Blum, Anton | Wirth, Elisabeth | 11, Nov. 1844 | G |
| Blum, Carl | Rottenkirch, Cath. | 1, Oct. 1848 | EE |
| Blum, Friedrich | Petersohn, Elisabeth | 16, May 1847 | A |
| Blurze, Alexander | Hill, Hannah | 19, Apr. 1834 | RCH |
| Bluse, Adam Henry | Heckers, Maria Engel | 13, Dec. 1848 | F |
| Blythe, Benjamin | Ruse, Mary | 9, Sept 1844 | RCH |
| Blythe, John | Murphy, Mary Ann | 23, Nov. 1836 | RCH |
| Boack, Heinrich | Englebusch, Maria | 14, May 1834 | RCH |
| Boady, George W. | Bentrum, Charlotte | 26, May 1842 | RCH |
| Boal, Edward | Williams, Susan | 5, May 1838 | RCH |
| Boaman, Henry | Botts, Elisabeth | 17, May 1840 | RCH |
| Bob, August | Steidel, Maria | 26, Nov. 1848 | C |
| Boberg, Heinrich | Kubermann, Clara | 30, Jan. 1849 | AA |

| Grooms | Brides | Date of Marriage | Code |
|--------|--------|------------------|------|
| ****** | ****** | **** ** ******** | **** |
| Boberg, Wilhelm | Franks, M. Elisabeth | 12, Apr. 1842 | FF |
| Boberg, William | Stille, Sophia | 15, July 1842 | RCH |
| Bobinger, Jacob | Boh, Louise | 13, July 1849 | C |
| Bobinger, Johan | Schroeder, Catharine | 21, June 1842 | FF |
| Bochard, Carl | Hitzelmann, Charlott | 26, Sept 1848 | C |
| Bockel, Johan | Friedel, Barbara | 25, Sept 1849 | EE |
| Bocklage, Gerhard H. | Wobeler, Elisabeth | 20, Jan. 1849 | CC |
| Bockmann, Bernard H. | Puthoff, Anna | 2, July 1844 | AA |
| Bockmann, Friedrich | Ruske, Maria Elis. | 28, Apr. 1846 | EE |
| Bockting, Bernard | Meyer, Maria Anna | 17, Apr. 1849 | EE |
| Bodde, Wilhelm | Honnigfort, Maria | 10, Feb. 1848 | AA |
| Bode, Gerhard Wm. | Fiedeldei, Catharine | 28, July 1840 | FF |
| Bode, Heinrich | Buehner, Margaretha | 23, Dec. 1841 | F |
| Bode, Johan Heinrich | Krusemeyer, Sophia | 9, Sept 1847 | F |
| Bodeker, Johan Hein. | Pille, Maria Elis. | 12, Apr. 1842 | FF |
| Bodine, Elisha | Stites, Mary | 28, June 1821 | RCH |
| Bodine, Zelah | Scogin, Sarah | 18, May 1836 | RCH |
| Bodley, Thomas J. | Miller, Rebecca | 20, Oct. 1838 | RCH |
| Boebinger, Johan | Rapp, Maria | 28, Mar. 1839 | G |
| Boebinger, Michael | Rehmund, Elisabetha | 4, Jan. 1844 | G |
| Boeck, Bartholomew | Wirst, Magdalena | 21, Oct. 1847 | EE |
| Boeck, Johan | Voelker, Catharine | 6, Mar. 1843 | C |
| Boecking, Anton | Borgess, Elisabeth | 27, Feb. 1848 | FF |
| Boeckmann, Friedrich | Neupol, Maria | 25, Sept 1849 | EE |
| Boeckmann, Joseph | Huelsmann, M Gertrud | 23, Jan. 1844 | FF |
| Boedecker, Johan H. | Fairmann, Elisabeth | 19, Jan. 1836 | FF |
| Boedeker, J. Herman | Luetmerding, Agnes | 4, May 1845 | FF |
| Boedker, Gerhard | Gerwe, Maria Anna | 26, Nov. 1848 | EE |
| Boegel, Adam | Derfer, Catharine | 22, July 1844 | A |
| Boeggemann, Johan H. | Naber, Maria Elis. | 27, Apr. 1847 | AA |
| Boeh, Mathias | Jaeger, Francisca | 8, Feb. 1846 | FF |
| Boehm, Lorenz | Rabding, Margaretha | 17, May 1849 | B |
| Boehm, Simon | Ehrmann, Magdalena | 26, July 1846 | G |
| Boehmann, Heinrich | Berns, Elisabeth | 8, Oct. 1839 | FF |
| Boehmer, B. Heinrich | Brune, A. Elisabeth | 18, Nov. 1849 | II |
| Boehmer, Casper H. | Springmeier, Maria L | 24, Dec. 1847 | C |
| Boehmer, Henry Adolf | Amelung, C Henrietta | 2, Nov. 1843 | F |
| Boehmer, Joseph | Kleintrimpe, Anna M. | 18, July 1837 | FF |
| Boehn, Nicolaus | Kraemer, Francisca | 22, Nov. 1842 | AA |
| Boehne, Gerhard H. | Jansen, Maria Anna | 29, Sept 1846 | AA |
| Boehne, Johan D. | Widde, Maria Elis | 23, Sept 1849 | EE |
| Boehne, Johan Heinr. | Koenig, Anna Elis. | 13, Feb. 1844 | FF |
| Boehne, Johan Theo. | Gangelsbrink, Elis. | 7, Oct. 1846 | EE |
| Boehne, John Henry | Moellers, Anna Maria | 3, Oct. 1843 | RCH |
| Boehning, Heinrich | Steinmann, Dorothea | 16, July 1840 | F |
| Boekinkamp, Franz H. | Wilkens, Catharine | 25, Feb. 1847 | B |
| Boekmann, Gerhard | Buenger, Theresa | 21, Nov. 1847 | FF |
| Boellinger, Georg | Schneider, Sarah | 20, Dec. 1843 | RCH |
| Boene, Bernard | Elbers, Maria | 26, Feb. 1835 | FF |
| Boerstler, Adam | Keizer, Susannah | 19, Dec. 1849 | RCH |
| Boerum, Joseph | Crummins, Mary | 3, July 1844 | RCH |
| Boescher, Joseph | Schaefer, Catharine | 26, Mar. 1845 | AA |
| Boesherz, Johan | Raufhacke, Elisabeth | 18, May 1845 | FF |
| Boetz, Johan | Brand, Barbara | 18, Jan. 1847 | EE |
| Bofing, Johan Fried. | Kohs, Bernardina | 8, Jan. 1847 | RCH |
| Bogart, Abraham | Bridges, Patsy | 22, Sept 1836 | RCH |
| Bogart, Alvin | Wheeler, Mary | 3, Apr. 1834 | RCH |
| Bogart, Edward | Boyer, Frances | 14, Aug. 1845 | RCH |
| Bogart, Helmus | Noble, Mary | 5, Jan. 1842 | RCH |
| Bogart, Isaac | Williams, Phebe T. | 8, July 1834 | RCH |
| Bogart, John | Stokes, Emma | 23, Sept 1841 | RCH |
| Bogart, Peter | Fox, Mary | 15, Nov. 1838 | RCH |
| Bogener, Bernard | Dickmann, Maria Elis | 29, Jan. 1839 | FF |
| Bogener, Bernard | Reismann, Theresa | 27, Sept 1846 | AA |
| Bogenschuetz, Carl | Meyer, Ursula | 8, Oct. 1846 | EE |
| Bogenschuetz, Carl | Schelter, Anna Maria | 28, June 1848 | EE |
| Bogenschultz, Dennis | Schelter, Wilhelmina | 19, Oct. 1843 | AA |
| Bogert, Thomas | Ayres, Emeline | 8, Nov. 1843 | RCH |
| Boggs, Andrew | Frazer, Diema | 22, Aug. 1844 | RCH |
| Boggs, Joseph R. | Ford, Rachel | 6, June 1848 | RCH |
| Boggs, Robert | Niles, Elisabeth | 6, Apr. 1826 | RCH |

| Grooms<br>***** | Brides<br>***** | Date of Marriage<br>**** ** ******** | Code<br>**** |
|---|---|---|---|
| Boggs, Samuel | Brooks, Emily | 7, Apr. 1836 | RCH |
| Boggs, Samuel | Brooks, Emily | 8, Apr. 1841 | RCH |
| Boggs, William | ----, Catharine | 15, May 1835 | RCH |
| Bogott, William | Crane, Sarah | 2, July 1846 | RCH |
| Bohl, Mathias | Walter, Margaretha | 10, Apr. 1845 | A |
| Bohlander, Dietrich | Zoller, Charlotte | 1, Dec. 1846 | RCH |
| Bohlander, Georg | Numants, Elisabeth | 22, Aug. 1844 | C |
| Bohlander, Johan | Detchenhaus, Louise | 18, May 1847 | G |
| Bohlander, Johan | Mueller, Clarissa | 27, Sept 1849 | G |
| Bohlinger, Jacob | Kelsch, Maria Anna | 4, June 1839 | FF |
| Bohm, Charles | Friedmann, Louise | 26, Dec. 1845 | RCH |
| Bohm, Friedrich | Knauring, Babette | 6, Apr. 1849 | RCH |
| Bohm, Marcus | Rothschild, Janeda | 24, May 1842 | RCH |
| Bohmann, Johan Gott. | Hund, Caroline Fr. | 29, May 1849 | E |
| Bohmann, Joseph | Dreyer, Maria Elis. | 16, May 1849 | FF |
| Bohn, Stephen | Carter, Nancy Jane | 4, Nov. 1833 | RCH |
| Bohner, Joseph | Munzemeyer, Catharin | 10, Jan. 1849 | AA |
| Bohnert, Anton | Schantz, Magdalena | 29, May 1849 | G |
| Bohr, Nicolaus | Kramer, Francisca | 22, Nov. 1842 | RCH |
| Bohrer, Anthony | Fleury, Mary | 4, July 1849 | RCH |
| Bohrer, Georg A. | Neumann, Caroline | 11, Feb. 1849 | G |
| Bois, Henry | Pepples, Elisabeth | 17, Sept 1846 | RCH |
| Boker, Nelson | Collins, Anna | 27, Sept 1836 | RCH |
| Boland, Michael | Wise, Elisabeth | 10, Dec. 1825 | RCH |
| Bolander, M. Amos | Wolf, Malinda | 1837 | RCH |
| Bolander, William | Thorp, Harriet | 24, Apr. 1839 | RCH |
| Bole, Robert | Dennis, Anna | 23, Dec. 1846 | RCH |
| Boley, Ludwig | Traeger, Juliana | 11, June 1848 | G |
| Boling, S. | Gregg, Nancy | 17, May 1835 | RCH |
| Bollenberg, Johan | Kamphaus, Catharine | 10, Jan. 1847 | AA |
| Bolling, Andrew | Doolittle, Margaret | 25, Apr. 1843 | RCH |
| Bollinger, Johan | Gasser, Agatha | 19, July 1841 | FF |
| Bollinger, Martin | Reis, Eva | 13, Nov. 1849 | AA |
| Bollinger, Melchior | Evans, Ann | 27, Mar. 1849 | RCH |
| Bolsel, Reason | Scanck, Mary | 14, Apr. 1836 | RCH |
| Bolser, John H. | Parvin, Rebecca | 12, Nov. 1834 | RCH |
| Bolser, Joseph | Caughlin, Ellen | 27, July 1834 | RCH |
| Bolser, Mahlon | Jones, Mary Elisabet | 20, Aug. 1846 | RCH |
| Bolser, Reason | McGill, Fanny | 11, Sept 1834 | RCH |
| Bolser, Samuel | Coughlin, Hannah | 19, Oct. 1833 | RCH |
| Bolte, Johan Heinric | Speckmann, Christina | 2, Oct. 1845 | F |
| Bolton, Samuel | White, Esther | 8, Aug. 1841 | RCH |
| Bolze, Heinrich | Gasser, Liberata | 9, Feb. 1847 | EE |
| Bon, Joseph H. | Koetting, Maria | 7, Dec. 1848 | EE |
| Bonaparte, Solomon | Oldfield, Louise | 4, May 1844 | RCH |
| Bond, Benjamin | Moore, Martha | 21, July 1846 | RCH |
| Bond, David | Dorsee, Hoger | 23, Nov. 1838 | RCH |
| Bond, John | Livermore, Martha | 8, Nov. 1846 | RCH |
| Bond, John | McWilliams, Cath. | 8, Sept 1846 | BB |
| Bond, Samuel | Tindall, Anna | 3, Jan. 1821 | RCH |
| Bond, Silas | Meals, Martha Ann | 2, Sept 1841 | RCH |
| Bond, Thomas J. | Howell, Rebecca | 30, Apr. 1838 | RCH |
| Bone, William | Shellhouse, Julia A. | 10, June 1840 | RCH |
| Bonelken, Joseph | Boehmers, Gertrud | 17, Aug. 1847 | EE |
| Boner, Harvey | Stewart, Louise | 17, Mar. 1844 | RCH |
| Bonert, August | Ott, Maria Anna | 31, Oct. 1847 | AA |
| Bonett, Reuben | Kelly, Betsy | 14, May 1820 | RCH |
| Bonham, David | Tebow, Martha | 20, Oct. 1847 | RCH |
| Bonham, Elijah | VanDolah, Mary Ann | 13, Oct. 1843 | RCH |
| Bonham, Ezra | Ewing, Elisabeth N. | 4, Feb. 1845 | RCH |
| Bonham, George W. | Blackburn, Harriet | 24, May 1846 | RCH |
| Bonham, Hezekiah | Buxton, Jane | 23, Feb. 1841 | RCH |
| Bonham, Nehemiah | Harris, Deborah | 2, Mar. 1846 | RCH |
| Boning, Friedrich | Kohorst, Bernardina | 10, Jan. 1847 | AA |
| Bonne, Wilhelm | Thimhorst, Maria | 26, Oct. 1843 | RCH |
| Bonnel, John | Benedict, Sarah E. | 13, May 1847 | RCH |
| Bonnel, Stephen H. | Castner, Mary | 14, Feb. 1833 | RCH |
| Bonnell, Aaron | Dackey, Margaret | 29, Jan. 1837 | RCH |
| Bonnell, Allison C. | Looker, Catharine C. | 1, Nov. 1835 | RCH |
| Bonnell, Jonathan | Oliver, Martha | 9, Oct. 1843 | RCH |
| Bonnell, Joseph | Dunham, Hannah | 17, Dec. 1822 | RCH |

| Grooms<br>****** | Brides<br>****** | Date of Marriage<br>**** ** ******** | Code<br>**** |
|---|---|---|---|
| Bonnell, Marcus | Rifner, Martha | 8, Dec. 1842 | RCH |
| Bonnell, Samuel | Gilliland, Nancy | 7, Oct. 1824 | RCH |
| Bonnell, Samuel | Centre, Maria | 6, Feb. 1834 | RCH |
| Bonnell, Samuel | Wells, Alice Jane | 5, Oct. 1837 | RCH |
| Bonnell, William B. | Polser, Harriet | 18, Dec. 1834 | RCH |
| Bonner, Samuel | Hammel, Roxanna | 25, Oct. 1838 | RCH |
| Bonnham, John | Hammit, Eliza | 28, Apr. 1825 | RCH |
| Bonninger, Nicolaus | Niemann, Sophia | 21, July 1842 | G |
| Bonsheim, Ephram | Friedmann, Theresa | 24, July 1847 | RCH |
| Bonte, Francis | Lany, Olivia | 3, Jan. 1842 | BB |
| Bonte, John | Cross, Rohanna | 7, Jan. 1837 | RCH |
| Bonte, Peter | Blanchard, Frances | 2, May 1843 | RCH |
| Bontell, Georg | Brooks, Marietta | 14, Apr. 1846 | RCH |
| Booker, James | Wiley, Emeline | 17, Apr. 1842 | RCH |
| Bookman, Casper | Nitten, Elisabeth | 19, Jan. 1837 | RCH |
| Booley, John H. | Ailn---, A. Mary | 4, July 1837 | RCH |
| Boones, Isaac F. | Ferguson, Mary | 5, Sept 1824 | RCH |
| Boorgalter, John | Friend, Elisabeth | 26, Mar. 1849 | RCH |
| Boorom, Adam | Addis, Eva | 1, Oct. 1843 | RCH |
| Boorom, Jonathan | Remley, Mary | 28, Mar. 1833 | RCH |
| Boose, Thomas | Craig, Mary | 2, Dec. 1824 | RCH |
| Boosfeld, Christian | Borgmann, Lucia | 23, Nov. 1847 | FF |
| Booso, Meinrad | Meyers, Hester | 22, June 1849 | RCH |
| Booth, Addison | Woods, Maria | 25, Apr. 1833 | RCH |
| Boothby, Charles | Serls, Jane | 21, Aug. 1849 | RCH |
| Boothby, William | Davis, Louise | 5, May 1842 | RCH |
| Boots, E. | Ravenscraft, Mary | 29, Apr. 1849 | RCH |
| Boots, Erastus | Vallandingham, Elis. | 20, July 1844 | RCH |
| Boots, Erastus | Ayres, Ellen | 4, Aug. 1844 | RCH |
| Boplin, David | Sharman, Amely | 1, Apr. 1824 | RCH |
| Borche, Friedrich | Heisemann, Friedrika | 2, May 1848 | G |
| Borcheding, Friedr. | Gunther, Maria | 24, Nov. 1849 | G |
| Borchelt, Friedrich | Nollmann, Maria | 22, Feb. 1844 | RCH |
| Borchelt, Johan Hein | Frankampf, Christina | 22, Apr. 1847 | B |
| Borcherding, Henry | Korshner, Caroline | 6, Dec. 1842 | RCH |
| Borcherding, William | Ringer, Ann | 17, Sept 1846 | RCH |
| Borchers, Carl Georg | Schwenker, Sophia | 12, Aug. 1843 | F |
| Borchers, Friedrich | Stahl, Louise | 9, Feb. 1843 | F |
| Borden, | Upjohn, | 1827 | I |
| Borden, Joseph | West, Caroline | 29, Mar. 1842 | RCH |
| Borden, Samuel | Y---, Sarah | 14, July 1819 | RCH |
| Bordin, Joseph | Richardson, Henriett | 15, Feb. 1833 | RCH |
| Borgeding, Joseph | Beckmann, Elisabeth | 11, Oct. 1846 | AA |
| Borger, Johan Anton | Schuhmacher, Carolin | 24, Apr. 1849 | II |
| Borger, Peter | Ruh, Maria | 20, May 1849 | EE |
| Borgerding, Francis | Kramer, Maria | 14, Aug. 1849 | EE |
| Borgerding, Heinrich | Dusselhorst, Cath. | 7, Jan. 1847 | AA |
| Borgert, Bernard | Rolfzen, Elisabeth | 7, Jan. 1847 | AA |
| Borgert, Johan Fr. | Laumann, Elisabeth | 17, Jan. 1847 | AA |
| Borgmann, Johan | Klinghammer, Anna M. | 9, May 1848 | AA |
| Borgmann, Johan | Frilling, Anna Maria | 15, Apr. 1849 | FF |
| Borgmann, Joseph | Deters, Catharine | 20, May 1845 | FF |
| Borgsted, Johan | Wiebold, Anna Adel. | 5, Mar. 1846 | F |
| Borgstede, Johan H. | Meyer, Wilhelmina | 3, Nov. 1842 | F |
| Borgstedt, J Gerhard | Kramer, Catharina M. | 12, Dec. 1840 | F |
| Boring, Ezra | Barnes, Rebecca | 4, Oct. 1842 | RCH |
| Borkas, Heinrich | Austin, Agnes | 5, Jan. 1836 | FF |
| Borman, Joseph | Veiler, Rhoda | 25, May 1834 | RCH |
| Borner, Carl Friedr. | Strueve, Friedricka | 9, Oct. 1846 | G |
| Bornet, Jacob | Bruederli, Maria | 17, July 1849 | DD |
| Borntraeger, Francis | Sonneburg, Sophia | 22, Jan. 1846 | FF |
| Borntraeger, Ludwig | Dickmann, M. Anna | 4, June 1847 | AA |
| Bornwasser, Carl | Meininger, Maria | 18, Nov. 1849 | A |
| Boroff, Samuel | Brooks, Sarah | 3, Sept 1818 | RCH |
| Borrowman, Thomas | Wilson, Isabella | 31, Dec. 1846 | RCH |
| Borsch, Anton | Doslittle, Anna | 1, July 1844 | AA |
| Bortsch, Johan | Malgolt, Agnes | 25, May 1846 | EE |
| Borwarth, Francis | Dopler, Barbara | 24, Sept 1839 | FF |
| Bory, Edward Adolph | Luppe, Adele | 9, Dec. 1847 | BB |
| Bosch, Johan | Bonewits, Rebecca | 25, Apr. 1843 | C |
| Bosche, Heinrich | Foos, Barbara | 15, May 1849 | HH |

| Grooms<br>****** | Brides<br>****** | Date of Marriage<br>**** ** ******** | Code<br>**** |
|---|---|---|---|
| Bose, Johan Heinrich | Meyer, Elisabeth S. | 21, Sept 1843 | F |
| Bosendick, Johan H. | Mese, Anna | 2, June 1840 | FF |
| Bosse, Heinrich | Kemper, Maria | 6, Feb. 1844 | AA |
| Bosse, Johan Heinric | Wichmann, Margaretha | 30, Apr. 1840 | F |
| Bosse, Johan Heinric | Bruns, Dorothea | 7, Apr. 1846 | F |
| Bosse, Wilhelm | Topie, Maria E. | 22, Feb. 1842 | F |
| Bossekamp, John H. | Moellers, M. Elis. | 14, Apr. 1846 | RCH |
| Bossell, Asbury | Farnel, Emma | 7, July 1839 | RCH |
| Bossen, Alexnder | Babcock, Mary | 8, Sept 1846 | RCH |
| Bossert, John Edward | Lynch, Ann Mary | 25, Aug. 1847 | BB |
| Bossfoo, Thomas | Singer, Mary Jane | 10, Jan. 1841 | RCH |
| Bostnagel, Joseph | Knoses, Catharina | 8, Jan. 1838 | FF |
| Bostwick, David | Gould, Julia | 25, Sept 1848 | RCH |
| Boswell, C. | Hatch, Cynthia | 20, Oct. 1836 | RCH |
| Boswell, George W. | McGinnis, Anna Elis. | 5, Dec. 1847 | RCH |
| Boswell, William | Boots, Parmelia | 1, July 1844 | RCH |
| Botkin, Alexander | St.Clair, Jane | 20, Sept 1835 | RCH |
| Bott, Sebastian | Sauerbier, Elisabeth | 8, Apr. 1847 | RCH |
| Bott, Sebastian | Kleinpeter, Catharin | 11, Sept 1847 | EE |
| Botta, Vincent | Botta, Carol | 20, July 1848 | GG |
| Bottes, William | Avey, Elisabeth | 6, June 1847 | RCH |
| Botz, Friedrich | Hoffmann, Maria | 3, Aug. 1841 | FF |
| Botz, Henry | Chera, Elisabeth | 19, June 1848 | RCH |
| Botz, John | Phlum, Christina | 24, Mar. 1842 | RCH |
| Bougart, George | Voight, Apollonia | 29, Sept 1842 | RCH |
| Bountow, William | Myers, Elisabeth | 16, Apr. 1834 | RCH |
| Bourgoin, Alexis J. | Mosier, Elisabeth | 14, June 1849 | D |
| Bousners, Herman | Torrent, Emeline | 28, Nov. 1832 | RCH |
| Bouthly, James | Nalker, Experience | 28, Oct. 1843 | RCH |
| Bouttet, Francis | Lannx, Olive | 28, Dec. 1841 | RCH |
| Boutwell, B.F. | ----, Jane | 22, May 1843 | RCH |
| Bovieri, Valentine | Rittinger, Ursula | 12, Sept 1848 | HH |
| Bowar, Philipp | Pierson, Sarah | 18, Dec. 1842 | RCH |
| Bowdle, Daniel | Dickey, Catharine | 18, Oct. 1832 | RCH |
| Bowen, Benjamin | Goldstrap, Harriet | 7, May 1849 | RCH |
| Bowen, Clovis | Snider, Mary Jane | 25, Dec. 1842 | RCH |
| Bowen, Clovis | Hunt, Lucinda | 29, Aug. 1847 | RCH |
| Bowen, David | Brooks, Abigail | 20, Nov. 1819 | RCH |
| Bowen, Handy D. | Bamety, Mary Jane | 27, Sept 1836 | RCH |
| Bowen, Pardour | Farris, Narcissa | 10, May 1849 | RCH |
| Bowen, William | Carpenter, Salina | 8, Oct. 1846 | RCH |
| Bower, William | ----, Elisabeth | 23, May 1821 | RCH |
| Bowers, Adam | Stone, Sarah | 7, May 1844 | RCH |
| Bowers, August | Cole, C. | 27, Sept 1838 | RCH |
| Bowers, Henry | Cox, Hannah | 10, June 1847 | RCH |
| Bowers, Joseph | Phillips, Rachel | 21, Jan. 1845 | BB |
| Bowers, Mathias | Yancy, Fanny | 25, Dec. 1845 | RCH |
| Bowers, Samuel | ----, Mary | 31, Aug. 1826 | RCH |
| Bowers, William | Kitchel, Irene | 9, Oct. 1822 | RCH |
| Bowers, William | Kinley, Mary Ann | 6, June 1847 | RCH |
| Bowes, John | Ryan, Jane A. | 14, June 1847 | BB |
| Bowes, Samuel | Shuls, Sarry | 6, Nov. 1825 | RCH |
| Bowing, Johan H. | Meyer, Maria Elis. | 27, Nov. 1838 | FF |
| Bowler, Robert | Pendelton, Susan L. | 20, Oct. 1842 | I |
| Bowles, Jefferson | Ferguson, Elisabeth | 15, Apr. 1847 | RCH |
| Bowlin, Jesse | Martin, Catharine | 22, Mar. 1846 | RCH |
| Bowlsby, John | Sloan, Desdemona | 24, June 1849 | RCH |
| Bowman, Alexander D. | Thornton, Mildred | 25, Oct. 1837 | I |
| Bowman, Christopher | Buffington, Elisabet | 4, Feb. 1849 | RCH |
| Bowman, Daniel | Martin, Charlotte | 19, May 1842 | RCH |
| Bowman, Daniel | Read, Sarah Jane | 19, Dec. 1846 | RCH |
| Bowman, David | Katz, Hannah | 19, Mar. 1847 | RCH |
| Bowman, Henry | Townsend, Easton | 2, Nov. 1834 | RCH |
| Bowman, Henry A. | Eastland, Anna Elis. | 23, Mar. 1848 | RCH |
| Bowman, Isidore | Steffen, Anna Maria | 1, Oct. 1844 | RCH |
| Bowman, Jacob | Wise, Elisabeth | 25, Oct. 1842 | RCH |
| Bowman, Jesse | Anderson, Elvira | 6, Jan. 1847 | RCH |
| Bowman, John | Segewick, Elisabeth | 20, Sept 1845 | RCH |
| Bowman, Robert | Cochran, Nancy Ann | 13, Sept 1847 | RCH |
| Bowman, William | Grayson, Maria E. | 4, Nov. 1847 | RCH |
| Bowser, John Henry | Johns, Anna Elis. | 19, Apr. 1849 | RCH |

| Grooms | Brides | Date of Marriage | Code |
|--------|--------|------------------|------|
| ****** | ****** | **** ** ******** | **** |
| Bowtell, George W. | Oliver, Phoebe | 15, Sept 1835 | RCH |
| Bowyer, Adiah | Dyer, Mary Ann | 24, Feb. 1833 | RCH |
| Boxstetter, Casper | Macke, Elisabeth | 3, Oct. 1838 | FF |
| Boyce, James | McGallop, Emily | June 1835 | RCH |
| Boyce, William | Baker, Mary | 11, Oct. 1846 | RCH |
| Boyd, John W. | Morton, Eveline | 22, Mar. 1842 | RCH |
| Boyde, David | Smith, Sarah | 13, June 1848 | A |
| Boye, Johan Heinrich | Hennecke, Beke | 21, Oct. 1848 | B |
| Boyer, Gilbert | Lemmon, Mary J. | 12, Feb. 1845 | RCH |
| Boyer, John | Morris, Esther | 30, Dec. 1819 | RCH |
| Boyer, John | Ayres, Eleanor | 22, May 1822 | RCH |
| Boyer, Louis | Bailey, Deborah Ann | 16, Dec. 1845 | RCH |
| Boyer, Zachariah | Flinn, Anna S. | 21, Sept 1842 | RCH |
| Boyle, Edward | Dawson, Rachel | 29, May 1844 | RCH |
| Boyle, James | Freel, Ellen | 15, Nov. 1848 | RCH |
| Boyle, Michael | Moghan, Joanna | 24, Apr. 1846 | RCH |
| Boyle, Walter | Good, Sarah Ann | Dec. 1844 | RCH |
| Boyle, William | Patterson, Hartensia | 22, May 1842 | RCH |
| Boyles, Cyrus | Crail, Mary W. | 7, Aug. 1834 | RCH |
| Boyles, Johnson | Gardner, Elisabeth J | 26, Sept 1841 | RCH |
| Boyles, Johnson | Gardner, Harriet | 10, Nov. 1845 | RCH |
| Boylin, Michael | Crajjin, Ann | 5, Nov. 1849 | GG |
| Boynton, Alonzo | Martin, Eliza | 25, Mar. 1849 | RCH |
| Bozorth, William | Newbery, Mary Ann | 7, Oct. 1843 | RCH |
| Br---, Thomas | Polke, Julia Anna | 24, Feb. 1825 | RCH |
| Br---, William | Walker, Ann | 28, Mar. 1838 | RCH |
| Bracken, Daniel J. | Snyder, Susan | 20, Aug. 1848 | BB |
| Bracken, John | Boyd, Elisabeth | 1, Apr. 1847 | RCH |
| Bracken, William | Ingalls, Lucy | 2, Nov. 1842 | RCH |
| Brackenridge, Wm. | Simpson, Mary | 16, Nov. 1843 | RCH |
| Brackman, Johan Theo | Dargeloh, Agnes | 11, July 1837 | FF |
| Brackmann, Herman H. | Niehaus, A Charlotte | 11, Feb. 1846 | G |
| Braclin, James | Hiles, Phebe | 26, Mar. 1837 | RCH |
| Bradbury, George W. | Wright, Anna R. | 20, Oct. 1843 | D |
| Bradfisch, Johan | Rupert, Agnes | 5, Sept 1844 | G |
| Bradford, Chancey D. | Palmer, Louise L. | 9, Nov. 1831 | I |
| Bradford, David | Charters, Mary Ann | 2, July 1822 | RCH |
| Bradford, David V. | Hawkins, Harriet | 2, June 1839 | RCH |
| Bradford, James | Rhodes, Elisabeth | 30, Dec. 1843 | RCH |
| Bradford, M.C. | Jones, Catharine A. | 9, July 1839 | RCH |
| Bradford, Thomas | Hannah, Susan M. | 3, Sept 1845 | RCH |
| Brading, John | Inskip, Lydia | 19, Dec. 1848 | RCH |
| Bradish, John | Moran, Jane | 11, Oct. 1840 | BB |
| Bradley, Benjamin | Veasey, Amanda | 12, Dec. 1846 | RCH |
| Bradley, Bonaparte | Girard, Hannah | 21, July 1847 | RCH |
| Bradley, Henry | Stearns, Artimeria | 1, Oct. 1842 | RCH |
| Bradley, Henry | McVicker, Sarah | 29, Aug. 1843 | RCH |
| Bradley, Henry | Riley, Jane | 29, Aug. 1846 | RCH |
| Bradley, Isaac | Pemiston, Jane | 28, Jan. 1847 | RCH |
| Bradley, James | Tunny, Deborah | 9, Nov. 1842 | RCH |
| Bradley, John | Dean, Lavina | 20, Aug. 1844 | RCH |
| Bradley, Josiah L. | Angus, Mary Ann | 31, Dec. 1835 | RCH |
| Bradley, William | Thompson, Sophia | 25, Jan. 1833 | RCH |
| Bradley, William | Iddings, Margaret | 3, Sept 1846 | RCH |
| Bradman, John | Wardall, Maria | 12, Jan. 1837 | RCH |
| Bradstreet, John M. | Price, Mary Ann | 14, Mar. 1834 | RCH |
| Bradstreet, Samuel | Magrewe, Amanda | 1, July 1841 | RCH |
| Brady, A.M. | Bird, Mary Ann | 10, Feb. 1841 | RCH |
| Brady, Charles | Lawrence, Ann | 14, Jan. 1838 | RCH |
| Brady, James | Darcy, Catharine | 25, Apr. 1842 | BB |
| Brady, James | Barnet, Mary | 3, Mar. 1847 | RCH |
| Brady, James | Heffernan, Jane | 6, Sept 1847 | BB |
| Brady, Joseph C. | VanDuzen, Mary | 16, Sept 1832 | RCH |
| Brady, Solomon | Hahn, Betty | 20, Sept 1849 | RCH |
| Braemer, Theodor | Meyer, Lucinda | 12, Sept 1847 | AA |
| Brahm, David | Bauer, Catharine | 16, Feb. 1845 | C |
| Brake, Abraham | Littlepage, Elisabet | 5, Apr. 1841 | RCH |
| Braker, John | Lewis, Louise Ann | 30, June 1842 | RCH |
| Brambb, William | Beard, Angeline | 13, June 1849 | RCH |
| Bramble, Major | Stites, Margaret | 19, Mar. 1818 | RCH |
| Bramkamp, Dietrich | Dunmeyer, Catharine | 11, Nov. 1841 | RCH |

| Grooms | Brides | Date of Marriage | Code |
|--------|--------|------------------|------|
| ****** | ****** | **** ** ******** | **** |
| Bramkamp, Heinrich W | Hollen, Dorothea | 4, Sept 1849 | F |
| Bramlage, Herman H. | Urlage, Elisabeth | 23, May 1849 | AA |
| Bramlage, Ludwig | Fankmann, Catharine | 5, May 1847 | FF |
| Bramlage, Wilhelm | Frankmann, Elisabeth | 7, Feb. 1847 | FF |
| Bramland, James | Cannon, Harriet | 16, May 1834 | RCH |
| Bramsche, J. Gerhard | Lanfersick, Cath. E. | 3, Oct. 1848 | F |
| Bramsche, Johan G. | Tielen, Anna Maria | 17, Nov. 1846 | F |
| Brand, Herman | Buschmann, Anna M. | 7, June 1849 | AA |
| Brand, Herman Hein. | Eckelmann, Maria A. | 4, June 1849 | F |
| Brand, Jonathan | Mewhinney, Sarah | 23, June 1844 | RCH |
| Brand, Joseph | Schatmann, Maria | 20, Sept 1846 | RCH |
| Brandehoff, Johan | Bens, Susanna Adel. | 8, Oct. 1848 | II |
| Brandeis, | Dembitz, Friedricka | 9, Sept 1849 | RCH |
| Brandeis, Samuel | Wehle, Caroline | 9, Sept 1849 | RCH |
| Brandes, James | Lykins, Nancy Jane | 7, July 1846 | RCH |
| Brandibury, Jacob | Thrilkill, Margaret | 17, 1822 | RCH |
| Brandley, Michael | Miederin, Theresa | 27, Jan. 1844 | RCH |
| Brandon, Paul | Tibbs, Sylvia Ann | 13, Sept 1843 | RCH |
| Brandriff, Andrew | Cornelius, Emeline | 22, Dec. 1849 | RCH |
| Brandstetter, Isidor | Spinner, Julia | 28, Nov. 1848 | EE |
| Brandt, Carl | Doepke, Dorothea | 29, Jan. 1846 | G |
| Brandt, Dietrich | April, Sarah | 20, Sept 1846 | G |
| Brandt, Friedrich L. | Rohlfing, Sophia | 21, Oct. 1847 | F |
| Branick, Edward | Cassidy, Rose | 7, May 1840 | BB |
| Brannan, John | Moulter, Margaret | 19, Apr. 1847 | RCH |
| Brannon, James | Jackson, Rebecca | 13, May 1846 | RCH |
| Brant, Johan Heinric | Herzog, Anna Maria | 24, Nov. 1842 | AA |
| Brase, William | Wermeyer, Louise | 2, Nov. 1843 | RCH |
| Brashears, Benjamin | Lepperson, Mary | 20, May 1834 | RCH |
| Brashears, Gassaway | Laws, Amelia C. | 28, Dec. 1836 | RCH |
| Brasher, Lawrence | Larison, Enry | 2, Sept 1841 | RCH |
| Brasier, William | McKee, Rachel | 7, Sept 1820 | RCH |
| Brasier, William | Johnson, Caroline | 24, July 1842 | RCH |
| Brates, Jacob | Salzmann, Mary Ann | 13, Dec. 1849 | RCH |
| Bratton, John W. | Hamilton, Rachel | 24, May 1849 | RCH |
| Bratzler, Charles | Yost, Elisabeth | 16, Jan. 1848 | RCH |
| Brauer, Friedrich | Tappenhoff, Anna | 3, Sept 1841 | RCH |
| Braun, | Stifel, Anna Barbara | 4, Sept 1849 | RCH |
| Braun, Friedrich | Mueller, Margaretha | 29, Aug. 1847 | EE |
| Braun, Georg | Russ, Anna | 11, June 1848 | EE |
| Braun, Joel | Ritzer, Eveline | 11, July 1844 | RCH |
| Braun, Johan | Lutz, Anna Maria | 2, Feb. 1847 | EE |
| Braun, Joseph | Veit, Crescentia L. | 18, June 1848 | EE |
| Braun, Michael | Buetner, Maria | 15, Apr. 1847 | EE |
| Braun, Peter | Foutz, Mary | 18, Sept 1849 | RCH |
| Braun, Simon | Riedinger, Brigitta | 27, July 1847 | AA |
| Braun, Ulrich | Fischer, Margaretha | 9, Nov. 1845 | AA |
| Braun, Valentin | Rondler, Cecilia | 11, Apr. 1847 | EE |
| Braun, William | Graham, Margaret | 24, May 1849 | RCH |
| Brause, Friedrich | Stricker, Maria | 20, Sept 1842 | F |
| Braxner, Christian | Negley, Dorothea | 24, May 1849 | RCH |
| Braxon, David | Tobias, Emily | 17, Apr. 1849 | RCH |
| Bray, Robert | Jones, Mary | 14, Nov. 1848 | RCH |
| Bray, William N. | Robbins, Mary Ann | 15, Nov. 1847 | RCH |
| Brayard, | Sine, Theresa | 25, Nov. 1838 | RCH |
| Brecht, Carl | Jackel, Hermina | 23, Oct. 1849 | FF |
| Brecker, Gottfried | Langkamp, Bernardina | 4, Jan. 1848 | AA |
| Breckweg, Theodor | Wolken, Anna | 14, May 1848 | AA |
| Brecount, Clark | Sampson, Elisabeth M | 21, Apr. 1839 | RCH |
| Brecount, David | Hugle, Sarah | 22, June 1843 | RCH |
| Brecount, Gideon | Humes, Jane | 31, Dec. 1818 | RCH |
| Bredehoft, Paul | Duden, Anna | 16, Apr. 1849 | F |
| Bree, Johan | Noetker, Gertrud | 16, Aug. 1846 | AA |
| Bree, Johan | Meyer, Anna Maria | 6, Aug. 1848 | FF |
| Breed, Jacob | Heyner, Friedricka | 23, Sept 1841 | RCH |
| Breeding, John | Harper, Elisabeth | 21, Dec. 1848 | RCH |
| Breedland, Thomas | Foley, Elender | 19, Dec. 1819 | RCH |
| Brees, Evan | Cormick, Catharine | 24, Sept 1835 | RCH |
| Brees, Henry | Bangs, Susan | 21, June 1847 | RCH |
| Brees, Samuel | Jones, Letitia | 27, Dec. 1843 | RCH |
| Breeze, William G. | Wiggins, Adeline | 31, June 1840 | D |

| Grooms | Brides | Date of Marriage | Code |
|--------|--------|------------------|------|
| ****** | ****** | **** ** ******** | **** |
| Brefort, Wilhelm F. | Eilers, Anna Elis. | 21, Oct. 1846 | F |
| Breggs, Gree--- | Swift, Jane | 10, Oct. 1823 | RCH |
| Brehm, Andreas | Meyers, Rosannah | 25, Nov. 1846 | RCH |
| Breitenbach, Aloys | Nordmann, Carolina | 12, Nov. 1848 | EE |
| Brelage, Francis | Richter, Catharina | 26, Apr. 1836 | FF |
| Brem, Andreas | Putscher, Maria Anna | 4, Feb. 1849 | EE |
| Brem, Georg | Schmidt, Maria | 30, Oct. 1849 | EE |
| Bremenkamp, Herman H | Heidemann, Adelheid | 31, Jan. 1843 | FF |
| Bremer, Friedrich | Walters, Margaretha | 18, Apr. 1844 | F |
| Brendel, Andreas | Zanna, Theresa | 24, June 1846 | EE |
| Brendel, Johan | Franz, Margaretha | 21, Feb. 1839 | G |
| Brendel, Johan | Miller, Margaretha | 29, Oct. 1839 | G |
| Brender, Simon | Werter, Josephina | 4, Sept 1849 | EE |
| Brengelmann, Bernard | Rohlfing, Christina | 2, May 1849 | F |
| Brennan, John | Solomon, Maria | 5, Mar. 1832 | RCH |
| Brennan, Martin | White, Jane | 7, Nov. 1848 | BB |
| Brennan, Patrick | Flannagan, Ellen | 21, Aug. 1842 | BB |
| Brennan, Thomas | Openheimer, A. Elis. | 21, June 1842 | BB |
| Brennan, William | Cottam, Anna | 30, Apr. 1848 | BB |
| Brenton, William H. | Bills, Elisabeth | 12, Sept 1849 | RCH |
| Brentzinghafer, Geo. | Curnes, Margaret | 30, Apr. 1832 | RCH |
| Breslan, Hugh | Boyle, Elisabeth | 31, Jan. 1842 | BB |
| Bretelkamp, Bernard | Schuhmacher, Marg. | 29, Feb. 1849 | C |
| Brett, William | White, Adeline | 21, Aug. 1845 | RCH |
| Brettel, Joseph | Deilkes, Jerusha | 13, Feb. 1844 | RCH |
| Bretten, Mathias | VanBerndt, Elisabeth | 8, Aug. 1848 | EE |
| Brew---, Bernard Wm. | Chos, Anna C. | 26, June 1844 | RCH |
| Brewer, Christopher | Sherman, Lavina | 11, June 1847 | RCH |
| Brewster, John R. | Hilton, Julia | 26, Apr. 1849 | BB |
| Brichler, Georg | Wirtz, Gertrud | 8, Aug. 1847 | EE |
| Brick, Thomas | Freshower, Rachel | 18, Aug. 1844 | RCH |
| Brickell, Daniel | Weeks, Philena | 21, Mar. 1846 | RCH |
| Brickler, Nicolaus | Hovermuhle, Eva Marg | 7, July 1835 | FF |
| Brickwede, Nicolaus | Glassing, Catharine | 16, Oct. 1849 | EE |
| Bridge, B.H. | Gainer, Nancy | 25, Sept 1823 | RCH |
| Bridge, Fronick D. | Witney, Mary Elis. | 29, Apr. 1841 | RCH |
| Bridge, William | Hummel, Matilda J. | 15, Apr. 1837 | RCH |
| Bridges, David | Lines, Fanny | 27, Oct. 1822 | RCH |
| Bridges, Harrison | Gordon, Ellen | 10, Aug. 1848 | RCH |
| Bridges, James | Hahn, Hester | 16, Sept 1841 | RCH |
| Bridges, Joel | Grayson, Maria | Nov. 1841 | RCH |
| Bridges, Joel | Carl, Levina | 8, Jan. 1846 | RCH |
| Bridges, Joseph | Pavey, Mary | 3, Oct. 1845 | RCH |
| Bridwell, Martin | Hamilton, Martha | 6, May 1848 | RCH |
| Brierly, William | Gross, Rebecca | 4, Jan. 1835 | RCH |
| Brigel, Conrad | Mimmel, Kunigunda | 9, Jan. 1838 | FF |
| Briggs, Abraham | Bailey, Jane S. | 13, Oct. 1842 | RCH |
| Briggs, James | Wolf, Elizabeth | 16, Dec. 1849 | RCH |
| Briggs, William | Suiter, Ellen | 20, Feb. 1842 | RCH |
| Bright, Ethelbert | Rud, Elisabeth M. | 12, Mar. 1839 | RCH |
| Bright, J. | Stewart, Almira | 6, Mar. 1823 | RCH |
| Brightmore, Mark | Mortimore, Ann | 25, July 1838 | RCH |
| Brigmann, John A. | Braker, Angelina | 4, May 1848 | RCH |
| Briler, Anton | Stoll, Jacobina | 11, Nov. 1849 | C |
| Briley, John | Newland, Martha Ann | 25, Nov. 1842 | RCH |
| Brill, Adam | Dewein, Christina | 15, Aug. 1849 | A |
| Brill, Johan | Diener, Theresa | 10, June 1845 | AA |
| Brimstone, William | Clendening, Mary | 21, Nov. 1833 | RCH |
| Brimstone, William | Caldwell, Elizabeth | 8, May 1849 | I |
| Brinckner, Heinrich | Holters, Elisabeth | 26, May 1837 | RCH |
| Brindle, James | Brown, Maria | 28, Nov. 1844 | RCH |
| Briner, John | Nect, Hannah M. | 9, Jan. 1834 | RCH |
| Bringelmann, Bernard | Dreyer, M. Catharine | 17, Nov. 1844 | FF |
| Bringermann, Friedr. | Schottner, Christina | 20, Nov. 1849 | FF |
| Brinker, Dietrich H. | Wendeln, M. Gertrud | 5, May 1846 | AA |
| Brinkers, J. Bernard | Tebben, Margaretha | 25, Nov. 1849 | II |
| Brinkers, Johan H. | Heitmeyer, Catherine | 12, Nov. 1848 | EE |
| Brinkers, Johan Herm | Thole, Margaretha | 10, May 1842 | FF |
| Brinkly, John | Harrison, Ellen | 30, Apr. 1833 | RCH |
| Brinkmann, Bernard | Wiegelmann, Agnes | 23, June 1849 | FF |
| Brinkmann, Francis | Macke, Maria Agnes | 22, Jan. 1839 | FF |

| Grooms<br>****** | Brides<br>****** | Date of Marriage<br>**** ** ******** | Code<br>**** |
|---|---|---|---|
| Brinkmann, Francis | Widekamp, Clara(Mrs) | 31, Jan. 1843 | AA |
| Brinkmann, Friedrich | Winner, Mary | 8, Oct. 1842 | RCH |
| Brinkmann, Friedrich | Ohlmann, Margaret | 26, Sept 1846 | RCH |
| Brinkmann, Friedrich | Kruzen, Catharine E. | 20, Dec. 1849 | C |
| Brinkmann, Friedrich | Tunemakers, Anna M. | 21, Nov. 1849 | F |
| Brinkmann, Heinrich | Hatke, Bernardina | 29, Jan. 1835 | FF |
| Brinkmann, J Gerhard | Rammler, Margaretha | 25, May 1848 | FF |
| Brinkmann, Joseph | Otten, Agnes | 2, Mar. 1848 | CC |
| Brinkmann, Mathias | Schildmeyer, Elis. | 19, Nov. 1848 | EE |
| Brinkmann, Rudolph | Meyers, Martha Maria | 30, Apr. 1846 | C |
| Brinkmann, Wilhelm | Steinaker, Maria | 24, Nov. 1842 | RCH |
| Brinkmeier, Bernard | VanHolle, Anna | 6, Nov. 1849 | EE |
| Brinkmeier, Friedric | Heger, Margaretha | 5, Dec. 1849 | RCH |
| Brinkmeyer, Friedric | AufderHar, Christina | 30, Oct. 1840 | G |
| Brinkmeyer, Friedric | Relpis, Sophia | 26, Jan. 1846 | A |
| Brinkmeyer, Friedric | Balser, Sophia | 2, Nov. 1848 | A |
| Brinkmeyer, Gerhard | Exler, Margaret(Mrs) | 7, Oct. 1849 | AA |
| Brinkmeyer, Henry | Ottemeyer, Theresa | 26, Nov. 1849 | RCH |
| Brinkmeyer, Herman H | Beinicke, Cath.(Mrs) | 25, Apr. 1849 | E |
| Brinkmeyer, Johan | Domhoff, Anna Maria | 7, Oct. 1847 | F |
| Brinkmeyer, Johan H. | Attermeyer, Theresa | 27, Nov. 1849 | AA |
| Brinkmeyer, Wilhelm | Thimhorst, Elisabeth | 26, Oct. 1843 | RCH |
| Brisbane, John | Risk, Elisabeth | 14, July 1843 | RCH |
| Brisbon, Arthur | Goshorn, Sarah | 8, Mar. 1835 | RCH |
| Brisby, Autker | Burtsfield, Elis. A. | 14, Oct. 1838 | RCH |
| Briscoe, William | Corbin, Susannah | 1, Aug. 1849 | D |
| Britsch, Christopher | Kellermann, Barbara | 10, Nov. 1846 | RCH |
| Britsch, Christopher | Niemeyer, Catharine | 5, July 1848 | RCH |
| Britt, Thomas | Henry, Mary | 22, Feb. 1846 | BB |
| Britting, Conrad | Borgerding, Margaret | 4, Aug. 1849 | RCH |
| Britton, John | Starks, Susan | 12, Aug. 1832 | RCH |
| Brivery, Augustin | Anderson, Phoebe | 24, Dec. 1849 | RCH |
| Bro---, Jacob | Leffeth, Margaretha | 30, Mar. 1837 | RCH |
| Broadbury, Samuel | Baion, Catharine | 4, Apr. 1831 | RCH |
| Broadwell, Harland | Leaf, Elisabeth | 15, July 1847 | RCH |
| Broadwell, Henry | Wainwright, Ann Elis | 16, Jan. 1834 | RCH |
| Broadwell, Joseph P. | Sheckel, Prudence A. | 16, Apr. 1844 | BB |
| Broadwell, Linnaus | Goldson, Mary Jane | 19, Dec. 1842 | RCH |
| Broadwell, Samuel | Perry, Caroline | 2, May 1842 | RCH |
| Broady, Alexander | Miller, Elisabeth | 1, July 1847 | RCH |
| Brocaw, Michael | Braden, Margaret | 18, Feb. 1836 | RCH |
| Brock, Jeremiah | Peters, Elisabeth | 13, Oct. 1845 | RCH |
| Brock, John | Felinger, Barbara | 7, July 1847 | RCH |
| Brockamp, Herman | Nuxol, M. Catharine | 8, Jan. 1846 | AA |
| Brockamp, Johan Bd. | Lange, Maria Elis. | 21, Nov. 1843 | AA |
| Brockamp, Johan H. | Meyer, Anna M. Agnes | 13, Aug. 1839 | FF |
| Brockamp, Johan H. | Lange, Elisabeth | 21, Nov. 1847 | FF |
| Brockamp, Joseph | Kreutzjans, Anna | 9, Nov. 1848 | II |
| Brockamp, Joseph | Feldmann, Elisabeth | 27, May 1849 | II |
| Brockell, John | Brown, Martha | 27, Dec. 1846 | RCH |
| Brockell, Joseph | Higby, Harriet | 12, Nov. 1820 | RCH |
| Brockell, Joseph | Hastings, Eleanor | 3, June 1842 | RCH |
| Brockensick, Heinr. | Bohm, Maria | 22, Aug. 1844 | F |
| Brocker, Theodor Bd. | Dicks, Catharine G. | 18, Feb. 1849 | RCH |
| Brockhaus, Bd. Theo. | Wolf, Anna Maria | 27, June 1848 | FF |
| Brockhaus, Bernard | Thalken, Gesina | 22, Apr. 1845 | AA |
| Brockhaus, Bernard W | Schwindler, Adelheid | 10, May 1842 | FF |
| Brockhoff, J. Hein. | Strubbe, M. Elis. | 4, Mar. 1847 | F |
| Brockmann, Bernard | Henke, Anna Maria | 9, Nov. 1845 | AA |
| Brockmann, Bernard H | Handorf, M. Adelheid | 22, July 1841 | FF |
| Brockmann, Christian | Naunt, Margaretha | 21, Oct. 1841 | RCH |
| Brockmann, Friedrich | Luhan, Christina | 17, Sept 1844 | RCH |
| Brockmann, Friedrich | Lihn, Christina | 17, Sept 1844 | AA |
| Brockmann, Friedrich | Kunne, Catharina A. | 9, May 1847 | AA |
| Brockmann, Heinrich | Stuckhoff, Christina | 22, Nov. 1842 | FF |
| Brockmann, Heinrich | Ahlers, Catharina | 29, Oct. 1848 | II |
| Brockmann, Herman B. | Meier, Charlotte | 1, Mar. 1848 | F |
| Brockmann, Herman H. | Ahrmanns, A. Cath. D | 13, Apr. 1848 | B |
| Brockmann, J Gerhard | Dierkers, Elisabeth | 9, Aug. 1842 | F |
| Brockmann, Johan H. | Braidhold, Anna M.C. | 29, Nov. 1849 | B |
| Brockmann, Joseph | Lackmann, Gertrud | 16, Feb. 1847 | AA |

| Grooms | Brides | Date of Marriage | Code |
|--------|--------|------------------|------|
| ***** | ***** | **** ** ******** | **** |
| Brockmann, Joseph | Riesenbeck, Wilhel. | 1, Feb. 1849 | II |
| Brockmann, Theodor | Deting, Elisabeth | 12, Jan. 1841 | FF |
| Brockmeier, Heinrich | Bohne, Anna Maria | 26, Oct. 1848 | C |
| Brockmeyer, Bernard | Niemanns, M. Engel M | 18, Oct. 1849 | C |
| Brockschmidt, Chris. | Luening, Gertrud | 8, Aug. 1848 | AA |
| Brockschmidt, Fried. | Donselmann, Margaret | 23, Aug. 1849 | RCH |
| Brockschmidt, Gerh. | Voss, Maria Louise | 4, Sept 1845 | F |
| Brockschmidt, Joseph | Busch, M. Elisabeth | 22, Nov. 1837 | FF |
| Brodbeck, Stephen | Elrenz, Margaretha | 22, May 1838 | FF |
| Brodwolf, John | Meyer, Friedricka | 11, July 1844 | RCH |
| Broecker, Theodor | Diecks, Cathariine | 16, Apr. 1849 | CC |
| Brogan, Dennis | Higgins, Ann | 26, Nov. 1848 | GG |
| Brogan, William | Kidd, Margaret | 22, Oct. 1842 | RCH |
| Broggen, Heinrich | Akamp, Maria | 6, Apr. 1842 | FF |
| Brohard, George | Miller, Hannah | 21, Aug. 1834 | RCH |
| Brokamp, Bernard | Wehmhof, Anna Maria | 3, May 1849 | FF |
| Brokamp, Heinrich | Kramer, Catharine | 17, Sept 1844 | AA |
| Brokamp, Johan | Strieker, Anna Maria | 5, Feb. 1849 | AA |
| Brokamp, Johan Heinr | Kenkel, Anna M.(Mrs) | 4, June 1844 | FF |
| Brokaw, Isaac | Cook, Electa | 31, May 1849 | RCH |
| Brokaw, John | Brisbin, Nancy | 16, Sept 1843 | RCH |
| Brokaw, John | Williams, Susan | 28, Nov. 1849 | RCH |
| Brokenshire, James | Wallace, Margaret | 25, July 1844 | RCH |
| Brollmann, Herman | Kroeger, Josephina | 21, May 1848 | II |
| Brollmann, Michael | Fisher, Jane | 28, July 1847 | RCH |
| Bromer, Heinrich | Freyhage, Anna Maria | 7, Jan. 1846 | AA |
| Bromm, Johan Gerhard | Renzmann, M. Angela | 19, May 1841 | FF |
| Bromwell, Henry | Averal, Sarah | 21, Nov. 1844 | RCH |
| Bromwell, Robert | Coke, Harriet | 25, Sept 1845 | RCH |
| Bron, Bernard Heinr. | Fels, Adelheid | 30, Apr. 1844 | FF |
| Bronson, George H. | Almy, Catharine B. | 30, Dec. 1846 | D |
| Brooke, E. Smith | Keller, Jane | 15, July 1844 | RCH |
| Brooks, Amanah H. | Leiper, Elisabeth | 20, Feb. 1834 | RCH |
| Brooks, Cyrus | Dunport, Mary E. | 19, Sept 1838 | RCH |
| Brooks, Daniel | Barwise, Mary Ann | Apr. 1823 | RCH |
| Brooks, Daniel | Hoke, Susanna | 24, Oct. 1833 | RCH |
| Brooks, Edward | Herbst, Letitia | 30, Nov. 1848 | BB |
| Brooks, George | Rankin, Ann | 18, Jan. 1834 | RCH |
| Brooks, Isaac | Seymour, Sarah | 31, May 1842 | RCH |
| Brooks, Jackson | King, Nancy | 8, Oct. 1845 | RCH |
| Brooks, James | Bennett, Druce. | 21, July 1818 | RCH |
| Brooks, John | Foster, Rachel | 14, Jan. 1819 | RCH |
| Brooks, John | Turvin, Elizbeth | 1, July 1846 | RCH |
| Brooks, John H. | St.John, Elisabeth | 17, June 1841 | RCH |
| Brooks, Joseph | Dennis, Elisabeth | 30, Sept 1841 | RCH |
| Brooks, Joseph | Hutchinson, M. Jane | 4, Feb. 1849 | RCH |
| Brooks, Peter W. | Moeller, Jane | 31, Mar. 1834 | RCH |
| Brooks, Randal | Clay, Adaline | 7, Feb. 1846 | RCH |
| Brooks, Theodore | Hoff, Catharine | 29, Mar. 1839 | RCH |
| Brooks, Valentine | Hoack, Margaret A. | 10, Jan. 1838 | RCH |
| Brooks, William | Harding, Rachel | 25, Feb. 1846 | RCH |
| Broom, Cyrus | Rogers, Nancy | 1, Feb. 1821 | RCH |
| Broondle, Daniel | Wheeler, Edith | 19, Apr. 1834 | RCH |
| Brophy, Joseph | Brophy, Mary Ann | 15, Aug. 1848 | BB |
| Broquest, Joseph | Seger, Mary | 13, July 1847 | GG |
| Bros, Carl | Schott, Kunigunda | 27, Jan. 1846 | EE |
| Brosamle, Friedrich | Brosamle, Barbara | 25, June 1847 | RCH |
| Brosemann, Ernst | Neider, Maria | 13, June 1849 | F |
| Brosemer, S. Joseph | Ohnemus, Catharina | 7, Jan. 1836 | FF |
| Brosmer, Lawrence | Lans, Maria | 7, Jan. 1847 | EE |
| Brosmer, Xavier | Groh, Clara | 8, Jan. 1844 | FF |
| Brossart, Francis M. | Hermann, Margaretha | 22, May 1842 | FF |
| Brossart, John | Fischer, Margaret | 28, July 1845 | RCH |
| Brosser, Carl | Steinmann, Johanna M | 28, June 1836 | FF |
| Brotherton, Elber | Bownell, Levisa | 12, Oct. 1834 | RCH |
| Brotherton, James H. | Snyder, Ann L. | 7, Mar. 1849 | D |
| Broudbent, Robert | Preston, Lucy | 4, May 1844 | RCH |
| Browell, Gilbert | Scott, Jemima | 18, Apr. 1834 | RCH |
| Brower, John | Craig, Catharine A. | 22, May 1842 | RCH |
| Brown, | Beekle, Catharine | 27, Nov. 1844 | RCH |
| Brown, A. | Robinson, Ann | 20, Sept 1825 | RCH |

| Grooms<br>****** | Brides<br>****** | Date of Marriage<br>**** ** ******** | Code<br>**** |
|---|---|---|---|
| Brown, Aaron | Spencer, Rachel | 9, Nov. 1820 | RCH |
| Brown, Aaron | VanZant, Rebecca | 31, Mar. 1844 | RCH |
| Brown, Alexander | Peck, Phoebe | 21, Apr. 1819 | RCH |
| Brown, Alexander | Meyers, Sarah | 21, Feb. 1847 | RCH |
| Brown, Andrew | McKinney, Martha | 3, Sept 1835 | RCH |
| Brown, Anton | Sundy, Elisabeth | 22, Feb. 1849 | RCH |
| Brown, Archibald | McKay, Flora | 31, July 1845 | RCH |
| Brown, Beckley T. | Hardenbrook, Erychem | 18, Apr. 1833 | RCH |
| Brown, Benjamin | Miller, Melissa | 4, Mar. 1843 | RCH |
| Brown, Charles | Maloney, A. Isabella | 18, July 1843 | RCH |
| Brown, Charles S. | Smith, Maria | 6, May 1849 | RCH |
| Brown, Chasteen | Dobb, Rebecca M | 29, Apr. 1846 | RCH |
| Brown, David | Winslow, Anna Elis. | 3, Nov. 1836 | RCH |
| Brown, David | Buner, Sarah Jane | 4, Dec. 1848 | RCH |
| Brown, David O. | Alter, Harriet | 10, Sept 1834 | RCH |
| Brown, Eathan | Huffman, Mary Jane | 19, Aug. 1841 | RCH |
| Brown, Edward | Cook, Emeline | 28, Feb. 1833 | RCH |
| Brown, Edward | Smith, Agnes | 16, Oct. 1845 | RCH |
| Brown, Elisha | Brown, Ann | 19, June 1836 | RCH |
| Brown, Elnathon | Sturgis, Martha | 22, Nov. 1843 | RCH |
| Brown, Ephraim | Johnson, Gillean | 2, Feb. 1836 | RCH |
| Brown, Ethan | Thorpe, Nancy | 12, Dec. 1833 | RCH |
| Brown, Ferdinand | Klapper, Sophia | 27, May 1846 | RCH |
| Brown, George | Saile, Mary | 3, Dec. 1833 | I |
| Brown, George | Carter, Lucinda | 30, Mar. 1848 | RCH |
| Brown, George | Wallace, Elizabeth | 31, Dec. 1849 | RCH |
| Brown, George W. | Lacy, Hester Ann | 20, Jan. 1847 | RCH |
| Brown, Hamilton | Switzer, Elisabeth | 13, Apr. 1843 | RCH |
| Brown, Harvey | Hood, Mary Jane | 20, Apr. 1844 | RCH |
| Brown, Henry | Hays, Martha | 26, Sept 1834 | RCH |
| Brown, Henry | Lee, Mary | 24, Feb. 1846 | RCH |
| Brown, Henry | Greenwood, Jane | 25, May 1846 | RCH |
| Brown, Henry B. | Dobson, Elisabeth | 29, July 1837 | RCH |
| Brown, Herick | Marvin, Amanda | 29, Nov. 1832 | RCH |
| Brown, Hiram | Swallow, Mary S. | 15, Dec. 1842 | RCH |
| Brown, Hope M. | Anderson, Sarah E. | 15, Jan. 1833 | RCH |
| Brown, Isaac | Dawson, Lucinda | 29, Nov. 1834 | RCH |
| Brown, Isaac B. | Sloan, Emily | 4, July 1833 | RCH |
| Brown, Israel | R---, Jane | 11, Nov. 1826 | RCH |
| Brown, Israel | Goe, Catharine B. | 15, Nov. 1835 | RCH |
| Brown, Jacob | Griffin, Charlotte | 29, Sept 1845 | RCH |
| Brown, James | Hilt, Matilda | 9, July 1843 | RCH |
| Brown, James H. | Walls, Winifred | 19, Aug. 1841 | RCH |
| Brown, Jenks | Williams, Rachel | 14, Aug. 1823 | RCH |
| Brown, Jeremiah | ----, Hannah | 14, Aug. 1821 | RCH |
| Brown, John | Storm, Hannah | 11, Nov. 1817 | RCH |
| Brown, John | Kains, | 9, Sept 1824 | RCH |
| Brown, John | Sargent, Martha | 5, Nov. 1833 | RCH |
| Brown, John | Williams, Louisa | 13, June 1834 | RCH |
| Brown, John | Ackly, Elisabeth | 16, June 1834 | RCH |
| Brown, John | Griffin, Elisabeth | 11, Oct. 1837 | RCH |
| Brown, John | Parker, Esther | 30, Apr. 1839 | RCH |
| Brown, John | Rapp, Magdalena | 18, Apr. 1837 | FF |
| Brown, John | Huddlester, Elis. | 18, May 1843 | RCH |
| Brown, John | Spencer, Ruth Ann | 25, Nov. 1843 | RCH |
| Brown, John | McLean, Mary | 25, Dec. 1843 | RCH |
| Brown, John | Cox, Nancy Ann | 26, Mar. 1846 | RCH |
| Brown, John | Fitzgibbon, Mary | 29, Aug. 1847 | BB |
| Brown, John Henry | Foster, Mary Ann | 1, July 1840 | RCH |
| Brown, John L. | Phelman, Sarah | 16, Dec. 1841 | RCH |
| Brown, John M. | Sage, Sarah | 12, Dec. 1832 | RCH |
| Brown, John P. | Longsteth, Barbara | 25, Aug. 1825 | RCH |
| Brown, John W. | ----, Mary | 16, July 1835 | RCH |
| Brown, Joseph | Feldmann, Maria | 31, Aug. 1839 | FF |
| Brown, Joseph | Sweeney, Mary Ellen | 21, Feb. 1844 | RCH |
| Brown, Joseph A. | Barcus, Hannah | 23, June 1833 | RCH |
| Brown, Joseph M. | Shnashu, Lucy Ann | 11, Apr. 1839 | RCH |
| Brown, Mathias | Moffit, Sarah | 25, Dec. 1823 | RCH |
| Brown, Matthew | Brown, Martha | 13, May 1847 | RCH |
| Brown, Michael | Bennett, Martha | 9, June 1844 | RCH |
| Brown, Nicolaus | Walker, Margaret | 3, Aug. 1837 | RCH |

| Grooms<br>****** | Brides<br>****** | Date of Marriage<br>**** ** ******** | Code<br>**** |
|---|---|---|---|
| Brown, Origin | McKoy, Mary Ann | 21, Mar. 1833 | RCH |
| Brown, Oscar | Lewis, Milley | 4, Aug. 1825 | RCH |
| Brown, Peter L. | Wright, Anna Maria | 9, Nov. 1848 | D |
| Brown, Philipp | Cilley, Martha | 22, Feb. 1835 | RCH |
| Brown, Richard | Wallace, Ann | 29, Dec. 1841 | RCH |
| Brown, Robert | Murphy, Elisabeth | 25, Mar. 1818 | RCH |
| Brown, Robert | Brittain, Sally | 21, Aug. 1822 | RCH |
| Brown, Robert | Cayley, Elisabeth | 15, Mar. 1842 | RCH |
| Brown, Samuel | Faweits, Susan | 18, May 1837 | RCH |
| Brown, Samuel J. | ---mken, Caster | 30, Apr. 1839 | RCH |
| Brown, Thomas | Darby, Susan | 28, Nov. 1843 | RCH |
| Brown, Thomas | Compton, Maria | 21, Dec. 1849 | RCH |
| Brown, Thomas M. | Ward, Anna Elisabeth | 22, Dec. 1836 | RCH |
| Brown, Valorus | Willey, Olive | 15, Dec. 1845 | RCH |
| Brown, Vincent | Goshorn, Rachel | 21, Mar. 1821 | RCH |
| Brown, William | Fowler, Eleanor | 27, July 1826 | RCH |
| Brown, William | Street, Jane | 3, Dec. 1832 | RCH |
| Brown, William | Fargo, Jane | 7, Apr. 1838 | RCH |
| Brown, William | Reeves, Ellen | 5, Nov. 1842 | RCH |
| Brown, William B. | Hoogland, Minerva | 2, Dec. 1847 | RCH |
| Brownand, John | Cordner, Rosetta | 14, Sept 1834 | RCH |
| Browne, Alfred | James, Martha | 29, Dec. 1846 | RCH |
| Browne, James | Burke, Helen | 29, May 1846 | BB |
| Brownfield, John | Oliver, Elisabeth | 30, Apr. 1847 | RCH |
| Browning, George | Holmes, Martha A. | 2, Apr. 1846 | I |
| Brownrigg, Samuel | Williamson, Sarah | 1, Jan. 1846 | D |
| Browns, Homan | Johnson, Allaid | 15, June 1842 | RCH |
| Broxtermann, Heinr. | Riker, Christina | 29, July 1845 | FF |
| Bru---, B. | Tume, Carolina Maria | 21, Jan. 1846 | RCH |
| Brua, Jacob | Hegner, Friedricka | 25, Sept 1841 | G |
| Brubacher, Jacob | Wiggers, Margaret L. | 27, Aug. 1846 | G |
| Bruce, Benjamin | Tume, Caroline M. | 22, Jan. 1846 | BB |
| Bruce, Isaac | Ray, Catharine M. | Oct. 1844 | RCH |
| Bruce, Joseph | Riston, Margaret | 17, Aug. 1819 | RCH |
| Bruch, Jacob | Langfeld, Margaretha | 20, Aug. 1848 | G |
| Bruck, Ignatz | Walter, Ottilia | 3, Nov. 1846 | EE |
| Bruckenschmidt, Fr. | Grosse, Maria Angela | 21, May 1840 | FF |
| Brucker, John | Lewis, Donara Ann | 30, June 1842 | G |
| Bruckmann, Philipp | Seibert, Elisabeth | 5, Nov. 1847 | C |
| Bruckmeier, Georg H. | Tebers, Anna Maria | 27, Mar. 1849 | F |
| Bruederle, Georg F. | Hotzenbohler, Chris. | 20, Nov. 1845 | C |
| Bruegge, Johan Hein. | Lammers, Catharine | 11, June 1845 | FF |
| Brueggemann, Bernard | Luettel, Adelheid | 14, May 1848 | AA |
| Brueggemann, Christ. | Stillen, Maria Elis. | 1, June 1841 | FF |
| Brueggemann, Francis | Schmidt, M Catharine | 9, June 1842 | RCH |
| Brueggemann, Francis | Kunck, Elisabeth | 16, Aug. 1842 | AA |
| Brueggemann, Friedr. | Veschmeyer, Frances | 8, May 1838 | FF |
| Brueggemann, Gerhard | Grewe, M. Margaretha | 14, Oct. 1849 | AA |
| Brueggemann, Heinric | Willer, Elisabeth | 22, Nov. 1846 | AA |
| Brueggemann, Johan | Hagemann, Theresa | 26, Aug. 1845 | AA |
| Brueggemann, Johan H | Wessendorf, Anna M. | 23, Nov. 1845 | AA |
| Bruegging, Lambert | Lutkenhoff, Johanna | 12, May 1846 | AA |
| Bruem, Michael | Strubel, Barbara | 21, Apr. 1842 | G |
| Bruemmer, Friedrich | Hungerkamp, Sophia | 4, Dec. 1845 | G |
| Bruemmer, Johan Herm | Schottelkote, Elis. | 12, Jan. 1843 | AA |
| Bruen, Edward | Hewit, Emily | 2, Apr. 1836 | RCH |
| Bruening, August | Bermann, Elisabeth | 9, Nov. 1845 | AA |
| Bruening, Herman F. | Krause, Elisabeth A. | 27, Feb. 1845 | G |
| Bruening, Herman Wm. | Burghardt, Nancy | 22, Apr. 1847 | G |
| Bruening, J Friedric | ZuLagen, Catharine A | 21, Apr. 1843 | F |
| Bruening, Johan D. | Thole, Margaretha | 29, May 1849 | F |
| Bruening, Johan H. | Schwenker, Louise | 28, Nov. 1847 | F |
| Bruening, Johan H. | ----, Maria Angela | 19, Aug. 1845 | AA |
| Bruenington, | Lamar, Sarah S. | 6, Apr. 1837 | RCH |
| Brullmann, Georg J. | VonderHeide, Elis. | 8, Aug. 1837 | FF |
| Brumleve, Clemens | Grove, Francisca | 15, Feb. 1846 | FF |
| Brummer, Johan Bd. | Ahlering, Elisabeth | 12, Apr. 1842 | FF |
| Brummerhaus, Heinric | Bremerkamp, Adelheid | 23, Jan. 1848 | FF |
| Brund, Johan | Keizer, M. Magdalena | 28, June 1849 | C |
| Brune, Bernard | Niehaus, Elisabeth | 30, Jan. 1848 | AA |
| Brunes, Gerhard | Morwessel, Maria A. | 7, Jan. 1847 | CC |

| Grooms | Brides | Date of Marriage | Code |
|--------|--------|------------------|------|
| ***** | ***** | **** ** ******** | **** |
| Bruning, Heinrich W. | Shepmans, Anna M. | 13, Sept 1849 | A |
| Bruning, Joseph | Schmidt, Catharine | 3, June 1849 | II |
| Brunland, Heinrich | Altrup, Margaretha | 16, Sept 1846 | F |
| Brunner, Johan | Schaefer, Rosina | 11, Feb. 1841 | FF |
| Brunner, Johan Georg | Bader, Margaretha | 30, July 1844 | FF |
| Brunner, Philipp | Belinger, Magdalena | 20, May 1839 | FF |
| Brunner, Philipp | Schneider, Magdalena | 2, Sept 1849 | FF |
| Brunner, Samuel | Levy, Caroline | 29, Aug. 1849 | RCH |
| Brunning, Herman | Schweers, Mary | 7, May 1849 | RCH |
| Bruns, Bernard | Nieberding, Elisabet | 14, Oct. 1849 | II |
| Bruns, Heinrich | Schmidt, Sophia | 27, Mar. 1845 | F |
| Bruns, Heinrich | Hinkers, Henrietta | 21, June 1848 | F |
| Bruns, Heinrich J. | Grawe, Maria Elis. | 24, Oct. 1844 | AA |
| Bruns, Henry | Carson, Wilhelmina | 18, Jan. 1844 | RCH |
| Bruns, J. Herman | Jansen, Adelheid | 12, July 1842 | FF |
| Bruns, Johan | Freling, Maria Elis. | 5, May 1836 | FF |
| Bruns, Johan | Meyer, Margaretha | 18, Feb. 1841 | F |
| Bruns, Johan | Schumacher, Susanna | 7, Jan. 1846 | EE |
| Bruns, Johan Bernard | Hoersmann, Maria A. | 25, Apr. 1847 | FF |
| Bruns, Johan Heinric | Baumann, Elisabeth | 5, May 1846 | AA |
| Bruns, John | Bourne, Cynthia | 1, Oct. 1822 | RCH |
| Bruns, John Bernard | Wilms, Maria Gesina | 18, June 1839 | FF |
| Bruns, Theodor | Puthoff, Anna M. | 8, Oct. 1839 | FF |
| Bruns, Theodor | Brinkmeyer, Catharin | 14, Feb. 1844 | AA |
| Brunsmann, Heinrich | Hackmann, Regina | 30, Aug. 1849 | C |
| Brunson, Daniel | Clark, Mary Ann | 13, Nov. 1832 | RCH |
| Brunson, Daniel | Lloyd, Mary | 20, May 1841 | D |
| Brusche, Fridolin | Ziegler, Margaretha | 18, Oct. 1849 | II |
| Bruscker, Ernst | Oswald, Catharine | 31, July 1846 | C |
| Brush, Alfred C. | Douglass, Nancy | 29, Apr. 1848 | D |
| Brush, Israel | Frazier, Mary | 7, Oct. 1824 | RCH |
| Brutting, J. Charles | Gow, Nancy | 25, Apr. 1844 | RCH |
| Bryan, George | Diely, E. | Oct. 1834 | RCH |
| Bryan, William | Murray, Ann | 30, May 1842 | RCH |
| Bryant, James | Middleton, Mary | 24, Dec. 1823 | RCH |
| Bryant, James | Kincade, Margaret | 8, Sept 1836 | RCH |
| Bryant, John | Daily, Elisabeth | 30, June 1846 | RCH |
| Bryant, William | Lyon, Harriet | 3, July 1838 | RCH |
| Bryce, Peter | Meier, Elisabeth | 24, July 1849 | RCH |
| Bryce, William | Craig, Isabella | 4, Dec. 1849 | RCH |
| Bryer, Joseph | ----, Elisabeth | 7, July 1835 | RCH |
| Bryson, Ambrose | Walker, Mary | 6, Jan. 1841 | I |
| Bu---, John | Tribant, Mary S. | 23, July 1836 | RCH |
| Buchanan, Jonah | Thompson, Charlotte | 6, July 1847 | RCH |
| Buchanan, Joseph | Teater, Susan | 25, Nov. 1819 | RCH |
| Buchanan, Robert | Riggle, Sarah Jane | 29, Apr. 1847 | RCH |
| Buchanan, Sampson | Luckey, Minerva | 21, Mar. 1833 | RCH |
| Buchanan, William | Myrick, Mary | 27, Oct. 1817 | RCH |
| Buchanon, Joseph | McDougal, | 28, Dec. 1844 | RCH |
| Buchholz, Friedrich | Kahle, Sophia | 1, Feb. 1840 | F |
| Buchholz, Leopold | Jaeger, Magdalena | 29, Oct. 1848 | II |
| Buck, Friedrich W. | Heggefort, Louise M. | 5, June 1849 | A |
| Buck, Harmon C. | Craig, Nancy | 16, Mar. 1820 | RCH |
| Buck, James | Graham, | 16, Nov. 1820 | RCH |
| Buckel, Michael | Grohel, Margaretha | 12, June 1840 | FF |
| Buckels, Aaron | Dwinney, Catharine | 12, Nov. 1848 | RCH |
| Bucker, George | Ready, Matilda | 4, Sept 1843 | RCH |
| Buckhart, David | Short, Elisabeth | 4, Sept 1836 | RCH |
| Buckingham, | Jackson, Melinda | 23, Sept 1849 | RCH |
| Buckingham, Andrew | Ramsey, Louise | 1, June 1847 | RCH |
| Buckingham, Frederic | Harris, Elisabeth | 15, May 1834 | RCH |
| Buckingham, George W | Cramore, Elisabeth | 13, Apr. 1834 | RCH |
| Buckingham, James | Elliott, Mary | 3, Mar. 1849 | RCH |
| Buckingham, John | Guest, Margaret | 31, Mar. 1844 | RCH |
| Buckingham, Levi | Bell, Elisabeth | 3, Dec. 1818 | RCH |
| Buckingham, Levi | Black, Margaret | 31, Dec. 1846 | RCH |
| Buckingham, Matthew | Crossman, Caroline | 30, Sept 1821 | RCH |
| Buckingham, Nimrod | Snider, Sarah Ann | 24, Aug. 1834 | RCH |
| Buckingham, William | Plumridge, Jane | 4, Oct. 1836 | RCH |
| Buckle, David | Bearing, Francisca | 27, Apr. 1835 | FF |
| Bucklein, Henry | Fredlaleir, C. | 5, Dec. 1835 | RCH |

| Grooms | Brides | Date of Marriage | Code |
|--------|--------|------------------|------|
| ***** | ***** | **** ** ******** | **** |
| Buckley, | Sultan, Sarah | 22, June 1834 | RCH |
| Buckley, Thomas | Day, Joanne | 16, Feb. 1843 | BB |
| Buckner, Commodore | Scott, Nancy | 29, May 1844 | RCH |
| Buckner, William | Green, Adeline | 4, Feb. 1847 | RCH |
| Buckner, William | Read, Charlotte E. | 10, May 1848 | D |
| Buckney, Francis | Martin, Julia | 31, Jan. 1844 | RCH |
| Budd, William | Robinson, Nancy | 16, Nov. 1842 | RCH |
| Budd, William | Stoddart, Mary | 17, Apr. 1844 | RCH |
| Budde, Heinrich | Lapp, Catharina | 21, Nov. 1837 | FF |
| Budde, Johan Herman | Hoelscher, Catharine | 27, Oct. 1849 | CC |
| Buddeke, Heinrich | Ratermann, Maria | 15, May 1838 | FF |
| Budeck, Herman Hein. | Enneking, Maria Elis | 11, Nov. 1841 | FF |
| Budeke, B.H. | Schrant, Anna Gesina | 17, June 1849 | AA |
| Budke, Conrad | Moorhaus, Maria Cath | 29, Dec. 1842 | F |
| Budke, John Dietrich | Henning, Elisabeth | 17, May 1842 | FF |
| Budke, Wilhelm R. | Wibbeler, Elisabeth | 8, Feb. 1849 | C |
| Buechler, Johan | Bauer, Julia | 26, Nov. 1846 | B |
| Bueck, Jacob | Ritter, Sarah | 5, Aug. 1819 | RCH |
| Buecke, Fidel | Bininger, Caroline | 6, Dec. 1849 | RCH |
| Buecker, Franz Jos. | Dillmann, Lucia | 4, Nov. 1845 | AA |
| Buecker, Johan Ernst | Meier, M. Margaretha | 8, Sept 1849 | F |
| Bueckmann, Johan | Stuckenberg, Marg. | 8, May 1847 | F |
| Buehle, Martin | Lang, Barbara | 13, Oct. 1846 | FF |
| Buehnen, J. Martin | Schaefer, Christina | 5, May 1839 | G |
| Buehter, Heinrich | Imhoff, Longina | 29, Oct. 1848 | AA |
| Buek, Heinrich | Bauten, Maria | 5, Nov. 1839 | FF |
| Buekel, David | Felix, Catharina | 23, Jan. 1837 | FF |
| Bueker, Sebastian | Wirin, Maria Anna | 1, June 1840 | FF |
| Buel, Eli | Hoal, | 8, Apr. 1838 | RCH |
| Buel, Leonard | Jones, Abigail | 3, July 1833 | I |
| Buell, Israel | Adams, Rosannah | 31, Oct. 1846 | RCH |
| Bueltel, J. Bernard | Schmitz, M. Theresa | 12, Oct. 1847 | FF |
| Bueltner, Martin | Amerein, Anna Maria | 23, Feb. 1841 | FF |
| Buening, Anton | Boking, Agnes | 4, Feb. 1847 | AA |
| Buening, Georg | Steffen, Catharine | 16, May 1844 | F |
| Buening, Johan Hein. | Rahe, Maria Elis. | 27, Oct. 1846 | RCH |
| Buente, Friedrich | Dohmann, Sophia B. | 6, June 1844 | C |
| Buercker, Johan | Luebbert, Catharina | 9, Mar. 1848 | E |
| Buerckle, Barthol. | Kruch, Margaretha | 15, June 1835 | FF |
| Buerker, Johan Hein. | Wolke, Maria | 8, Nov. 1842 | FF |
| Buerker, Joseph | Heil, Elisabeth | 13, Feb. 1848 | AA |
| Buerkle, Anton | Metz, Elisabeth | 23, May 1847 | G |
| Buerkle, F. Xavier | Wagner, Agatha | 27, Jan. 1842 | FF |
| Buerkle, Martin | Burkhart, Anna Maria | 20, Sept 1846 | EE |
| Buerkle, Pius | Pott, Barbara | 27, Feb. 1848 | II |
| Buersner, J. Mathias | Seemann, Maria Anna | 10, Aug. 1847 | EE |
| Buesching, Friedrich | Schnitker, Maria | 8, June 1848 | C |
| Bueter, J. Bernard | Ficker, M. Adelheid | 25, Apr. 1847 | FF |
| Bueter, Wilhelm | Meyer, Gertrud | 9, Jan. 1848 | AA |
| Buetke, Heinrich Wm. | Oberklein, Julia | 10, Nov. 1843 | RCH |
| Buety, Andreas | Lemminger, Maria A. | 4, Sept 1849 | AA |
| Buffington, Richard | Sumpter, Elisabeth | 21, Oct. 1845 | RCH |
| Bugg, Franz Anton | Bruns, Caroline | 29, June 1847 | G |
| Bugg, Henry | Skinner, Elisabeth | 20, Mar. 1841 | RCH |
| Bugh, William | Forrest, Margaret | 13, Oct. 1848 | RCH |
| Bugle, Fidel | Benninger, Carolina | 6, Dec. 1849 | II |
| Buhlmann, Dietrich | Sturig, Elisabeth | 9, May 1843 | AA |
| Buhmann, Heinrich | Niemeyer, Caroline | 11, Nov. 1842 | F |
| Buhne, Johan H. | Strieker, Theresa | 5, Feb. 1849 | AA |
| Buhners, Bernard | Bahlmann, M. Helena | 25, Sept 1849 | FF |
| Buhnut, Bernard | Kamluck, Elisabeth | 18, Jan. 1848 | AA |
| Buhr, Herman Friedr. | Spanhorst, Catharina | 16, May 1847 | AA |
| Buhr, Joseph | Herd, Regina | 1, June 1836 | FF |
| Buhrer, Georg | Freund, Maria | 9, July 1848 | AA |
| Buhrmann, Heinrich | Bentz, Maria | 16, Apr. 1834 | RCH |
| Bulbsheid, Nathaniel | Taubrust, Rebecca | 5, Nov. 1835 | RCH |
| Bulfinch, John | Turner, Mary | 9, Sept 1846 | RCH |
| Bullington, Lemuel | Rany, Hannah | 25, Mar. 1835 | RCH |
| Bullington, Moses | Johnson, Susan | 9, Sept 1843 | RCH |
| Bullock, Orin | Collins, Deborah | 20, Aug. 1836 | RCH |
| Bulser, John | Coest, Catharine | 23, Apr. 1835 | RCH |

| Grooms<br>****** | Brides<br>****** | Date of Marriage<br>**** ** ******** | Code<br>**** |
|---|---|---|---|
| Bulte, Johan H. | Hetlich, Anna | 29, Oct. 1848 | AA |
| Bulter, Joseph | Rollmann, Maria Anna | 6, Jan. 1846 | AA |
| Bulthaup, Heinrich R | Westmeier, M. Elis. | 23, Feb. 1843 | C |
| Bultmann, Dietrich L | Bode, Dorothea | 12, Aug. 1847 | B |
| Bun, Edwin | Pickering, Susannah | 31, Aug. 1842 | RCH |
| Bund, Anton | Redecker, Maria Elis | 9, Nov. 1841 | FF |
| Bund, Friedrich | Wilking, M. Carolina | 19, Oct. 1841 | FF |
| Bund, Heinrich | Kroene, Maria A. | 6, Oct. 1846 | AA |
| Bundley, Moses | Reese, Hannah | 4, Sept 1823 | RCH |
| Bundy, James | Phillips, Elisabeth | 24, Dec. 1833 | RCH |
| Bundy, John | Pallor, Sarah | 13, Feb. 1834 | RCH |
| Bune, Johan Heinrich | Stricker, Anna Maria | 30, July 1844 | AA |
| Bunkard, Charles | Starbuck, Elisabeth | 8, July 1841 | RCH |
| Bunken, William | O'Neal, Catharine | 7, Feb. 1849 | GG |
| Bunker, Carl | Toerner, M Elisabeth | 9, Jan. 1838 | FF |
| Bunker, Herman D. | Heitmeyer, Elisabeth | 1, June 1845 | AA |
| Bunnel, Benjamin | Davis, Margaret | 15, Mar. 1832 | RCH |
| Bunnell, Josiah | Tucker, Rachel | 3, May 1846 | RCH |
| Bunnemeier, J.B. | Bode, Maria Engel | 23, Apr. 1849 | II |
| Bunnemeyer, Johan H. | Sudbeck, Maria Anna | 7, Jan. 1849 | FF |
| Bunsemeyer, Herman H | Meyer, Dorothea | 30, Sept 1849 | C |
| Bunte, Francis H. | Rosenmeyer, Maria J. | 4, Oct. 1846 | EE |
| Bunte, Henry | S---, Henrietta | 23, Feb. 1837 | RCH |
| Buntee, Henry | Piatt, Elisabeth | 16, Sept 1834 | RCH |
| Bunten, William | Davis, Susannah | 1, June 1844 | RCH |
| Bunts, Richard | Brown, Sally | 18, July 1825 | RCH |
| Bunyan, Thomas | Muller, Mary | 17, Mar. 1820 | RCH |
| Burback, Benedict | Eichenlaub, Cath. | 13, May 1834 | RCH |
| Burbrink, Johan H. | Moehring, Maria | 17, Dec. 1846 | A |
| Burch, Heinrich | Lohmann, Elisabeth H | 3, June 1847 | FF |
| Burch, Porter | Allen, Catharine | 17, June 1826 | RCH |
| Burchfield, Perry | Tryon, Deborah | 1, June 1846 | RCH |
| Burd, Joseph | Clark, Susan | 6, Sept 1843 | RCH |
| Burd, Thomas | McCollouch, Eleanora | 21, Sept 1837 | RCH |
| Burd, Thomas | Griffin, Mary Ann | 15, July 1838 | RCH |
| Burdge, Jonathan | Winans, Margaretha | 9, Mar. 1849 | RCH |
| Burdge, Thomas | Winans, Elisabeth | 10, Sept 1845 | RCH |
| Burdsal, Caleb | Beach, Mary | 13, Sept 1846 | RCH |
| Burdsal, Samuel | Turner, Mary | 30, July 1833 | RCH |
| Burdsall, Abner | Nonnamaker, Anna | 8, Oct. 1846 | RCH |
| Burdsall, Solomon | Denny, Elisabeth(Mrs | 28, Apr. 1847 | BB |
| Burg, David | Pendleton, Erie | 3, June 1847 | RCH |
| Burged, David | Andrew, Mary A. | 28, Oct. 1839 | RCH |
| Burger, August | Moormann, Anna M. | 24, Oct. 1847 | AA |
| Burger, Cletus | Geyer, Gertrud | 21, Jan. 1845 | FF |
| Burger, Herman H. | Bodinghaus, Cath. | 9, Oct. 1838 | FF |
| Burger, Johan | Froelich, Louisa | 5, Feb. 1841 | FF |
| Burger, Johan | Mahler, Barbara | 25, May 1841 | FF |
| Burger, John V. | Blenting, | Sept 1844 | RCH |
| Burger, Joseph | Ronnebaum, Elisabeth | 24, Aug. 1843 | AA |
| Burger, Peter | Beck, Rosina | 19, Sept 1844 | AA |
| Burger, Philipp H. | Muehl, Barbara | 9, Feb. 1841 | FF |
| Burget, Henry | Punch, Sarah Jane | 15, May 1844 | RCH |
| Burget, Peter | Huber, Nothburga | 2, Sept 1844 | RCH |
| Burgett, William | Bloome, Edith | 19, Nov. 1835 | RCH |
| Burggrefe, Johan | Goldhoff, Anna | 24, Sept 1844 | AA |
| Burghard, F. Joseph | Weber, Maria Anna | 12, Apr. 1842 | FF |
| Burghard, Johan | Streitmann, Catharin | 5, June 1843 | C |
| Burghard, Johan | Eisenmann, Eva | 23, June 1840 | FF |
| Burghard, Joseph | Pauhl, Anna Maria | 15, Apr. 1847 | FF |
| Burghardt, Georg F. | Hohe, Nancy Barbara | 27, Feb. 1845 | G |
| Burgmann, Herman L. | Scheper, Elisabeth | 18, Jan. 1846 | AA |
| Burgoyne, Erastus | Lowe, Susanna | 2, Mar. 1834 | RCH |
| Burgoyne, John | Montgomery, Frances | 27, Sept 1826 | RCH |
| Burgtorf, George H. | Wechter, Julia | 27, July 1847 | RCH |
| Burk, George | Thorp, Elisabeth | 20, Apr. 1833 | RCH |
| Burk, Thomas | Dolan, Ann | 18, Jan. 1847 | RCH |
| Burkard, John George | Richer--, Ann Marg. | 25, Nov. 1840 | RCH |
| Burkart, Charles | Ryan, Margaret | 16, Nov. 1848 | RCH |
| Burkart, Georg | Bauer, Maria | 17, Oct. 1847 | AA |
| Burke, Alexis | Woolever, Mary | 27, Feb. 1834 | RCH |

| Grooms<br>****** | Brides<br>****** | Date of Marriage<br>**** ** ******** | Code<br>**** |
|---|---|---|---|
| Burke, Edmond | Ryan, Jane | 21, May 1849 | BB |
| Burke, George M. | Patterson, Margaret | 27, Apr. 1833 | RCH |
| Burke, Glendy | Carneal, Sallie | 11, June 1844 | I |
| Burke, Heinrich | Gosmit, Henrietta | 15, Nov. 1848 | F |
| Burke, Henry | Minean, Agnes | 29, July 1843 | RCH |
| Burke, Joseph | Jones, Mary | 23, Mar. 1833 | RCH |
| Burke, Luke | Patterson, Mary | 30, June 1848 | BB |
| Burke, Patrick | Clancy, Catharine | 30, Mar. 1845 | BB |
| Burke, William | Lane, Mary (Mrs) | 17, Aug. 1842 | RCH |
| Burke, William | Powers, Catharine | 12, Nov. 1848 | BB |
| Burke, William W. | Rees, Mary N. | 16, Sept 1818 | RCH |
| Burkhalter, Solomon | Cortelyou, Elisabeth | 1, Sept 1835 | RCH |
| Burkhandtsmeier, G. | Seibert, Catharine | 25, June 1848 | C |
| Burkhard, Johan | Riester, Monica | 31, Aug. 1843 | FF |
| Burkhard, Leonard | Zollies, Margaretha | 17, Apr. 1846 | RCH |
| Burkhard, Xavier | Kiefer, Louise | 29, Apr. 1847 | A |
| Burkhardt, Ferdinand | Bechtel, Rosa | 27, Nov. 1849 | FF |
| Burkhardt, J. Georg | Riedel, A. Margaret | 25, Oct. 1840 | G |
| Burkhart, Philipp | Seifert, Catharine | 25, Nov. 1847 | EE |
| Burkitt, James | Culbertson, Elis. | 13, Nov. 1836 | RCH |
| Burkley, John | Washington, F. (Mrs) | 1, Nov. 1832 | RCH |
| Burks, Aaron | Basket, Ann | 14, Nov. 1842 | RCH |
| Burmann, Friedrich | Holthaus, Lena Adel. | 25, June 1846 | C |
| Burmann, Wilhelm H. | Schulz, Maria | 27, June 1849 | F |
| Burn, William | Coogan, Julia | 7, Nov. 1848 | BB |
| Burnard, Charles | Cutter, Abigail | 4, June 1822 | RCH |
| Burnes, James | Stewart, Margaret | 23, July 1818 | RCH |
| Burnet, Isaac | Bryant, Rebecca | 26, Apr. 1844 | RCH |
| Burnett, John | Bowman, Mary A. | 12, May 1836 | RCH |
| Burnett, Patrick | Coughlin, Mary | 29, Apr. 1849 | GG |
| Burnham, N.C. | Pancoast, Maria A. | 22, Oct. 1842 | RCH |
| Burnhart, John | Roll, Elisabeth Ann | 13, Mar. 1844 | RCH |
| Burnholdt, Jurgen | Diers, Hannah | 24, Sept 1849 | RCH |
| Burnitz, George W. | Moore, Charlotte | 15, Apr. 1819 | RCH |
| Burnker, J. Bernard | Tubbis, Helena Maria | 18, Feb. 1840 | FF |
| Burns, Isaac | Codton, Hannah | 23, Sept 1841 | RCH |
| Burns, James | Ferguson, Ruth | 11, Feb. 1836 | RCH |
| Burns, James A. | Varney, Charlotte | 12, May 1840 | RCH |
| Burns, Johan | Siegmann, Margaretha | 4, Nov. 1847 | F |
| Burns, John | Todd, Jane | 6, May 1847 | RCH |
| Burns, Jonathan R. | Mills, Susan A. | 30, Dec. 1835 | RCH |
| Burns, Joseph | McKnight, Jane | 23, Feb. 1826 | RCH |
| Burns, Lawrence | Ogg, Hannah | 20, May 1847 | RCH |
| Burns, Patrick | Monahan, Sarah | 5, Oct. 1848 | BB |
| Burns, Peter | ----, Nancy | 1837 | RCH |
| Burns, Philipp | Clayton, Malinda | 11, July 1844 | RCH |
| Burns, Theodore S. | Ridlin, Patience | 8, Mar. 1838 | RCH |
| Burns, Thomas | Huston, Jeanet | 19, Sept 1822 | RCH |
| Burnside, David | Estell, Hannah | 28, Sept 1834 | RCH |
| Burnside, Solomon | ----, Letty | 23, Sept 1837 | RCH |
| Burridge, Charles | Bangs, Elisabeth | 29, Jan. 1824 | RCH |
| Burrmann, August | Buehler, Catharine | 10, Nov. 1842 | F |
| Burroughs, James | Cook, Mary Ann | 13, Mar. 1838 | RCH |
| Burroughs, John | Hemphill, Margaret | 16, Nov. 1845 | RCH |
| Burroughs, Thomas | Perry, Ann D. | 18, Aug. 1846 | RCH |
| Burrows, Abraham | Danburg, Lydia | 4, July 1842 | RCH |
| Burrows, Benjamin | Dent, Eleanor | 4, Aug. 1833 | RCH |
| Burrows, James | Lynchard, Nancy | 16, Feb. 1843 | RCH |
| Burrows, John M. | Gennage, Sarah | 1, Dec. 1836 | RCH |
| Burry, Edmund | Monks, Lucinda | 29, July 1837 | RCH |
| Burscht, Francis X. | Volz, Maria Anna | 16, Aug. 1841 | FF |
| Burst, Johan | Oliger, Catharina | 20, Aug. 1835 | FF |
| Burt, Clement N. | Holins, Frances | 18, Dec. 1823 | RCH |
| Burt, H. | Kneling, Anna Maria | 1, Sept 1834 | RCH |
| Burt, Moses | Jones, Mary Frances | 19, May 1835 | RCH |
| Burt, Samuel | Allen, Mary E. | 22, Mar. 1843 | RCH |
| Burten, Henry | Conant, Margaret | 5, Mar. 1834 | RCH |
| Burton, Edmond | Cortlegan, Elisabeth | 16, Feb. 1836 | RCH |
| Burton, F. | Salyer, Mary A. | 22, June 1836 | RCH |
| Burton, James | Ramsey, Kesiah | 12, May 1836 | RCH |
| Burton, Ottoway | Harweson, Ann | 23, June 1847 | RCH |

| Grooms<br>****** | Brides<br>****** | Date of Marriage<br>**** ** ******** | Code<br>**** |
|---|---|---|---|
| Burton, Robert | Burton, Catharine | 4, Oct. 1837 | RCH |
| Bury, James | Byington, Elisabeth | 31, May 1838 | RCH |
| Busam, Gregor | Sander, Maria Anna | 14, July 1839 | FF |
| Busbalder, Johan H. | Fortcamp, Gertrud | 21, Jan. 1849 | EE |
| Buscell, Joseph | ----, Catharine | 8, July 1834 | RCH |
| Busch, Anton | Baumeister, Elisabet | 25, June 1848 | FF |
| Busch, Bernard | Post, Elisabeth | 17, Feb. 1835 | FF |
| Busch, Bernard | Koch, Maria Anna | 23, Sept 1849 | CC |
| Busch, Johan B. | Olverman, Catharina | 10, June 1834 | RCH |
| Busch, Johan Heinric | Post, Maria Anna | 5, Jan. 1836 | FF |
| Busch, Matthias | Gingal, Catharina | 7, Nov. 1848 | FF |
| Busch, William | Schaller, Phebe | 6, Apr. 1847 | G |
| Buschen, Johan Herm. | Warmes, Margaretha | 16, May 1847 | EE |
| Buscher, Anton | Schlebbe, Catharine | 20, Feb. 1848 | FF |
| Buscher, Friedrich | Wilking, Catharine | 15, Aug. 1848 | F |
| Buschheim, Friedrich | Wehling, Philippina | 5, Oct. 1847 | C |
| Buschmann, Cord H. | Visselmann, Sophia | 18, Oct. 1849 | G |
| Buschmann, Joseph | Brockhorst, Elis. | 30, Oct. 1838 | FF |
| Buschmann, Louis Wm. | Nebeler, Caroline W. | 20, May 1847 | B |
| Buschnell, A.L. | Hastings, Sarah | 11, Apr. 1837 | RCH |
| Buse, Johan Matthias | Zetlage, Elisabeth | 13, Feb. 1844 | FF |
| Buse, Ludwig | Hartmann, Sophia | 27, Oct. 1842 | FF |
| Bush, Asa M. | Beach, Mary Ann | 16, Aug. 1837 | RCH |
| Bush, Conrad | Turner, Jane | 1, Feb. 1838 | RCH |
| Bush, George W. | Sterling, Elisabeth | 13, Aug. 1846 | RCH |
| Bush, James | Granger, Elisabeth | 2, Dec. 1848 | RCH |
| Bush, John | Moxley, Ersly | 14, Aug. 1846 | RCH |
| Bush, William | Marrow, Clarissa | 29, Dec. 1841 | RCH |
| Bushmann, Heinrich | VonDrele, A. Gertrud | 30, Jan. 1838 | FF |
| Bushnell, Jason | Holt, Nancy Ann | 9, Aug. 1847 | RCH |
| Busjan, Herman H. | Wimelder, Anna Maria | 3, Nov. 1847 | EE |
| Buske, | Hunefield, Catharine | Sept 1836 | RCH |
| Busse, Conrad | Rogelmueller, Henr. | 9, Nov. 1848 | F |
| Busse, Friedrich | Asbrock, Elisabeth | 2, Dec. 1847 | F |
| Busse, Friedrich | Eichert, Catharine | 19, Jan. 1847 | G |
| Busse, Gerhard | Uphaus, Margaretha | 20, Oct. 1840 | FF |
| Busse, Heinrich | Schuemeyer, Wilhel. | 10, Apr. 1849 | F |
| Busse, Heinrich | Rupke, Anna Maria | 31, Aug. 1847 | AA |
| Busse, Herman | Sitterdink, Maria | 7, Nov. 1840 | F |
| Busse, Johan Heinric | Post, Anna Catharine | 18, Oct. 1846 | FF |
| Busse, Theodor Bd. | Huerstmann, Bernar. | 9, Jan. 1845 | AA |
| Busset, Francis | Langerbecker, Maria | 12, Sept 1836 | FF |
| Butcher, George | Gibson, Rebecca | 12, June 1824 | RCH |
| Butcher, James | Becke, Georgiana | 15, Aug. 1836 | RCH |
| Buten, Bernard | Engelbert, Catharine | 26, Nov. 1844 | FF |
| Buthof, Bernard | God, Anna Maria | 14, July 1840 | FF |
| Butke, Herman Rudolf | Lobaum, A.M. Elis. | 5, June 1845 | F |
| Butler, Charles | Hertom, Lydia | 2, Nov. 1840 | RCH |
| Butler, Cyrus | Easton, Margaret J. | 13, June 1840 | RCH |
| Butler, Edward | Smith, Margaret | 18, Feb. 1847 | RCH |
| Butler, Enoch | Willey, Hannah | 3, Aug. 1834 | RCH |
| Butler, Francis | Hill, Margaret | 14, Dec. 1843 | RCH |
| Butler, Frederick | Comen, Mary | 19, Oct. 1841 | RCH |
| Butler, George | Jones, Dicy | 5, Sept 1833 | RCH |
| Butler, Isaac H. | Looker, Pamela B. | 7, Jan. 1835 | RCH |
| Butler, Isaac N. | Gibson, Nancy | 22, June 1836 | RCH |
| Butler, John | Tynack, Elisabeth | 11, Apr. 1836 | RCH |
| Butler, Joseph C. | Laverty, Alice B. | 1, Sept 1847 | BB |
| Butler, Matthew | Brown, Margaret | 28, Nov. 1847 | GG |
| Butler, Mills | Thom, Caroline | 28, Sept 1848 | RCH |
| Butler, Peterson | Naylor, Ann | 25, Feb. 1841 | RCH |
| Butler, Robert | Carter, Dicy | 20, June 1833 | RCH |
| Butler, Simon | Kinsley, Mary | 1, Aug. 1844 | BB |
| Butler, Stephen | Marshall, Hannah J. | 11, Dec. 1839 | RCH |
| Butler, Thomas | Patterson, Jane | 25, Oct. 1841 | RCH |
| Butler, Thomas | Quinlan, Ann | 10, July 1845 | BB |
| Butler, W.J. | McDonald, Mary | 14, Sept 1834 | RCH |
| Butler, William | Robb, Mary Ann | 9, Nov. 1845 | RCH |
| Butscha, Johan | Weiler, Barbara | 7, Oct. 1839 | FF |
| Buttemueller, Joseph | Monsch, Magdalena | 22, May 1838 | FF |
| Butter, Dietrich | Kettler, Catharina | 27, Nov. 1849 | AA |

| Grooms | Brides | Date of Marriage | Code |
|--------|--------|------------------|------|
| ****** | ****** | **** ** ******** | **** |
| Butterfield, Alegern | Veach, Anna Maria | 24, Dec. 1843 | RCH |
| Butterfield, James | Rasher, Hannah | 19, Aug. 1819 | RCH |
| Butterfield, Jeremy | Willey, Sarah Jane | 20, Mar. 1844 | RCH |
| Butterfield, Nathan | McRoberts, Cynthia | 17, May 1847 | RCH |
| Butterfield, Nathan. | VanTruss, Hannah | 26, Sept 1841 | RCH |
| Butterworth, George | Colebow, Mary | 8, July 1844 | RCH |
| Buttles, Lucian | Disney, Mary E. | 13, June 1844 | RCH |
| Buttner, Henry | Goetz, Margaretha | 13, Feb. 1848 | RCH |
| Buttrick, Erastus | Kincaid, Margaret | 17, Aug. 1844 | RCH |
| Butts, Henry | Dean, Charlotte | 7, Dec. 1841 | RCH |
| Butts, Perry | Taylor, Martha | 25, Aug. 1834 | RCH |
| Butts, William | Loper, Amy | 21, Dec. 1845 | RCH |
| Butz, | Volsiefer, Theresa | 4, July 1838 | FF |
| Butz, Andreas | Demming, Maria Anna | 3, Sept 1849 | RCH |
| Butz, Georg Valentin | Fritz, Eva Margaret | 24, Sept 1843 | G |
| Buxton, Aaron | Pierson, Rebecca | 23, Oct. 1846 | RCH |
| Buxton, Moses | Peat, Elisabeth | 29, Nov. 1843 | RCH |
| Buxton, Nathan | Mann, Sarah Jane | 7, Sept 1847 | RCH |
| Buxton, William | Lawrence, Elisabeth | 1, Feb. 1838 | RCH |
| Buxton, William M. | ----, Catharine | Aug. 1826 | RCH |
| Bw---, John L. | Pearce, Temperance | 2, July 1820 | RCH |
| Bw---, Robert | Whalen, Olivia | 9, Nov. 1820 | RCH |
| Byam, Theodor | Byam, Mary | 18, Nov. 1835 | RCH |
| Byers, Philip | Gromup, Mary | 5, July 1821 | RCH |
| Byers, Samuel F. | Taylor, Mary | 15, Sept 1832 | RCH |
| Byfield, George | Simonson, Magdalena | 21, May 1820 | RCH |
| Byington, Charles | Heath, Selma Ann | 25, Aug. 1836 | RCH |
| Byington, Edward | Warham, Mary | 30, Apr. 1838 | RCH |
| Byington, Zebulon | Upton, Sarah | 23, Oct. 1822 | RCH |
| Byram, Samuel | Seeds, Maria | 24, Mar. 1836 | RCH |
| Byrn, John | Keys, Mary Jane | 24, Jan. 1847 | RCH |
| Byrne, James | Cox, Catharine (Mrs) | 3, July 1843 | BB |
| Byrne, John | McHugh, Ellen | 28, June 1849 | RCH |
| Byrne, Michael | King, Bridget | 29, May 1849 | RCH |
| Byrne, Michael | Crains, Sarah | 30, Apr. 1849 | BB |
| Byrne, Peter | Rowan, Bridget | 19, Aug. 1843 | BB |
| Byrne, Peter A. | Linnahan, Winan | 26, Apr. 1843 | BB |
| Byrne, Thomas | Reynolds, Mary A. | 18, Jan. 1838 | RCH |
| Byrnes, Patrick | Dooley, Ann (Mrs) | 17, Sept 1842 | BB |
| Byrns, James | Doyle, Winifred(Mrs) | 30, Sept 1842 | BB |
| Byron, Charles | Caringer, Margaret | 26, Sept 1842 | RCH |
| Byron, Michael | Farley, Margaret | 9, July 1840 | BB |
| Bywaters, Edward | Smith, Margaret | 30, Dec. 1849 | BB |
| Bywaters, Thomas | Rittenhouse, Sarah J | 6, Dec. 1845 | RCH |
| | | | |
| C---, Jacob | Brand, Delilah | 6, May 1839 | RCH |
| C---, John | Howe, Sarah M. | 10, June 1826 | RCH |
| C---, John | Gardner, Janet Mary | 27, July 1826 | RCH |
| C---, Joseph | Fox, Jemima | 9, July 1816 | RCH |
| C---, Joseph | Woodward, Elis. Jane | 5, Sept 1839 | RCH |
| C---, Josiah | Corwine, Margaret L. | 30, Aug. 1833 | RCH |
| C---, William | Day, Nancy | 11, Oct. 1823 | RCH |
| C---, William J. | McKinsey, Elisabeth | 19, Aug. 1817 | RCH |
| C---sh, Spencer | Corbin, Anna | 13, Aug. 1839 | RCH |
| Ca---, Henry | Rice, Romela Andrus | 18, June 1818 | RCH |
| Caasmann, Heinrich | Mertens, Gertrud | 1, May 1849 | AA |
| Cabel, Elijah | Fowler, Pamela | 5, Sept 1822 | RCH |
| Cable, David | ----, Isabella | 9, May 1839 | RCH |
| Cable, Luther | Armstead, Amanda | 6, Aug. 1843 | RCH |
| Cady, Benjamin | Lining, Catharine | 7, Nov. 1820 | RCH |
| Cady, Charles | Kiersted, Abigail | 1, Nov. 1842 | I |
| Cady, Henry H. | Harsha, Mary Ann | 2, Sept 1832 | RCH |
| Cady, John N. | Craner, Louise | 28, Aug. 1849 | RCH |
| Cady, Nathan | Banister, Frances | 28, Mar. 1839 | RCH |
| Cady, Nathan | Bonnell, Sarah | 14, Jan. 1848 | RCH |
| Caes---, Sylvester | Frame, Elisabeth | 31, July 1839 | RCH |
| Cafferty, Jonathan | Parsons, Grace | 17, Oct. 1841 | RCH |
| Cage, Richard | Dawson, Patsey Ann | 25, Aug. 1846 | RCH |
| Cahill, Hugh | Marshall, Margaret | 23, Feb. 1846 | GG |
| Cahill, James | Wallis, Elisabeth | 16, Sept 1843 | BB |
| Cahill, John F. | Frakes, Anna Elis. | 22, Dec. 1849 | GG |

| Grooms<br>****** | Brides<br>****** | Date of Marriage<br>**** ** ******** | Code<br>**** |
|---|---|---|---|
| Cahins, Valentin | Weiss, Eva | 1, Jan. 1843 | C |
| Cain, Francis | Anderson, Mary | 19, Sept 1845 | RCH |
| Cain, John W. | Young, Mary Ann | 15, Apr. 1834 | RCH |
| Cain, Joseph | Nelson, J. | 13, Mar. 1838 | RCH |
| Cainwood, John | Gray, Phoebe | 23, Nov. 1826 | RCH |
| Calder, William | Alden, Mary Elis. | 27, July 1847 | RCH |
| Caldwell, Albert E. | Weller, Mary | 23, May 1841 | RCH |
| Caldwell, David | Hicks, Mary Ann | 6, Apr. 1847 | RCH |
| Caldwell, James | Gibson, Jane | 12, Apr. 1842 | RCH |
| Caldwell, Jerry | Caldwell, Catharine | 21, Dec. 1826 | RCH |
| Caldwell, John | James, Mary Ann | 26, Sept 1844 | RCH |
| Caldwell, John D. | Downes, Mary J. | 11, Dec. 1838 | RCH |
| Caldwell, Ross | Glendenning, Mary | 1, Oct. 1846 | RCH |
| Caldwell, William | Corry, Harriet | 3, Jan. 1844 | RCH |
| Calhorn, Alexander | Bramble, Elisabeth | 20, Sept 1836 | RCH |
| Calhoun, Alexander | Huntress, Amelia | 24, Feb. 1839 | RCH |
| Call, George | Beadle, Elisabeth | 9, Feb. 1843 | RCH |
| Callaghan, Bernard | McNulty, Mary | 28, May 1848 | BB |
| Callaghan, Joseph | Flannagan, Margaret | 13, July 1845 | BB |
| Callaghan, Michael | McLevy, Ann | 20, Nov. 1843 | BB |
| Callahan, Henry | Metcalf, Sarah | 4, Jan. 1844 | RCH |
| Callahan, James | Jackson, Emeline | 24, Nov. 1843 | RCH |
| Callahan, John | Cosgrove, Mary | 2, Dec. 1843 | BB |
| Callahan, Patrick | Busch, Julia | 22, Dec. 1847 | RCH |
| Callern, Christian | Ehrhardt, Maria | 29, Nov. 1847 | C |
| Calloway, Thomas | Cannon, Mary | 13, Nov. 1843 | RCH |
| Calloway, William | Bonham, Mary C. | 27, Oct. 1847 | RCH |
| Callum, William | McLain, Nancy | 8, Aug. 1839 | RCH |
| Calmitz, Jareat | Lytle, Hannah J. | 29, Sept 1841 | RCH |
| Calwell, Daniel W. | Berlew, Emily | 28, Mar. 1833 | RCH |
| Camal, Patrick T. | Parker, Julia A. | 3, Nov. 1842 | BB |
| Cambeis, Georg Adam | Rapp, Elisabeth | 28, Feb. 1843 | AA |
| Cambron, Stephen | Stephens, Francis A. | 3, Feb. 1846 | BB |
| Camel, Joseph | ----, Elizabeth | 10, Mar. 1825 | RCH |
| Camell, Arthur | Howell, Nancy Ann | 5, July 1837 | RCH |
| Camell, Thornton | Burrows, Sarah | 19, Jan. 1826 | RCH |
| Cameron, Allen | Broadwell, Maria | 14, Sept 1844 | RCH |
| Cameron, Bernard J. | McQuelland, Martha | 25, Jan. 1838 | RCH |
| Cameron, Daniel | Norris, Margaret | 25, July 1839 | RCH |
| Cameron, Ebenezer | Plummer, Sarah | 19, Aug. 1841 | RCH |
| Cameron, John | Tilloson, Elisabeth | 10, May 1832 | RCH |
| Cameron, John | Smith, Mary | 12, Apr. 1846 | RCH |
| Cameron, John M. | Price, Sally | 23, Aug. 1821 | RCH |
| Cameron, Robert | Bowes, Sarah A. | 26, Dec. 1843 | RCH |
| Cameron, Wesley M. | Starbolt, | 12, July 1836 | RCH |
| Cameron, William | Ryder, Martha Jane | 13, Dec. 1842 | RCH |
| Camoist, William | Roberson, Jane | 17, Nov. 1825 | RCH |
| Camp, Rodney | Smith, Harriet | 14, July 1840 | RCH |
| Campbell, | Hillhouse, Martha J. | 3, June 1849 | RCH |
| Campbell, | Golden, Sarah | 17, June 1849 | RCH |
| Campbell, Alexander | Foster, Maria | 17, Oct. 1841 | RCH |
| Campbell, Alexander | Pasmore, Margaret | 1, Aug. 1843 | RCH |
| Campbell, Allen H. | Love, Sarah A. | 3, Dec. 1837 | RCH |
| Campbell, Andrew | Martin, Margaret C. | 19, Nov. 1846 | BB |
| Campbell, Bartley | Baker, Christina | 14, Sept 1848 | RCH |
| Campbell, Daniel | Doyle, Mary | 11, Aug. 1849 | GG |
| Campbell, David | Pasmore, Ann | 16, Nov. 1843 | RCH |
| Campbell, Edwin R. | Wright, Sarah Jane | 17, May 1849 | D |
| Campbell, Eleazar | Snider, Eliza Jane | 10, Jan. 1849 | RCH |
| Campbell, Elisha | Hayden, Nancy | 17, Nov. 1842 | RCH |
| Campbell, Francis | Barrow, Sarah | 24, Dec. 1843 | RCH |
| Campbell, George W. | Suitor, Mary | 19, May 1842 | RCH |
| Campbell, Hugh | Allen, Jane | 12, Nov. 1831 | RCH |
| Campbell, Isaac | Cox, Sarah | 19, July 1820 | RCH |
| Campbell, Jacob | Reland, Eleanor | 31, Dec. 1833 | RCH |
| Campbell, James | Bryant, Martha Ann | 27, June 1825 | RCH |
| Campbell, James | Timberlake, Nancy | 3, Aug. 1834 | RCH |
| Campbell, James | Hammell, Phoebe | 24, May 1837 | RCH |
| Campbell, James | Thompson, Deborah | 13, Aug. 1837 | RCH |
| Campbell, James | Pickin, Elisabeth | 29, Nov. 1843 | RCH |
| Campbell, James | Patton, Christina | 14, Sept 1848 | RCH |

| Grooms<br>****** | Brides<br>****** | Date of Marriage<br>**** ** ******** | Code<br>**** |
|---|---|---|---|
| Campbell, James | Mountford, Mary | 15, Aug. 1849 | RCH |
| Campbell, James P. | Drake, Harriet E. | 4, June 1839 | D |
| Campbell, John | Walker, Joanna | 19, Aug. 1824 | RCH |
| Campbell, John | Griffin, Rebecca | 7, Mar. 1833 | RCH |
| Campbell, John | Walthenrath, Cath. | 30, Mar. 1843 | RCH |
| Campbell, John | Strong, Mary | 27, Sept 1846 | RCH |
| Campbell, Joseph | Arnold, Elisabeth | 3, Dec. 1832 | RCH |
| Campbell, Joseph | Jones, Jane | 20, Sept 1838 | RCH |
| Campbell, Joseph | McDermott, Margaret | 26, Sept 1846 | BB |
| Campbell, Levi | Campbell, Sarah | 25, Sept 1849 | RCH |
| Campbell, Michael | Lose, Elisabeth | 30, Sept 1839 | RCH |
| Campbell, Morgan | Robinson, Nancy | 26, Aug. 1847 | RCH |
| Campbell, Obediah | ----, ---- | 2, Mar. 1823 | RCH |
| Campbell, Peter | Maher, Martha | 22, Feb. 1846 | BB |
| Campbell, Peter | Morris, Elisabeth | 20, Aug. 1848 | BB |
| Campbell, Philipp | Corday, Mary | 16, Dec. 1838 | RCH |
| Campbell, Samuel | Pevey, Ann | 2, Oct. 1834 | RCH |
| Campbell, Samuel | Cannon, Alice | 16, July 1846 | RCH |
| Campbell, Tristram | Lilley, Ellen | 9, Oct. 1845 | RCH |
| Campbell, William | Campbell, Ellen | 11, Sept 1834 | RCH |
| Campbell, William | Hazelton, Mary | 4, Sept 1843 | RCH |
| Campbell, William | Pugh, Ann | 29, Sept 1846 | RCH |
| Campbell, William G. | Ripley, Mary D. | 4, Apr. 1839 | RCH |
| Camron, Daniel | Haines, Sarah | 29, Jan. 1818 | RCH |
| Camson, C. | Thompson, Cynthia | 20, Oct. 1833 | RCH |
| Canaan, John | Brooks, Maria | 20, Oct. 1819 | RCH |
| Canfield, B. | Kise, Margaret P. | 4, May 1823 | RCH |
| Canfield, David | Bland, Jane | 21, Sept 1846 | RCH |
| Cangeman, Bernard | Meyer, Elisabeth | 22, Apr. 1834 | RCH |
| Cann, John | Storms, Catharine | 30, Oct. 1834 | RCH |
| Cannon, Adam | Orr, Maria Anna | 4, Feb. 1847 | RCH |
| Cannon, Hewit P. | Hinkley, Eleanor | 2, June 1832 | RCH |
| Cannon, Patrick | McHugh, Mary | 24, Sept 1848 | BB |
| Cannon, Peter | Travis, Catharine | 15, Aug. 1840 | BB |
| Cannon, Robert | Bennett, Elisabeth | 15, Apr. 1843 | RCH |
| Cannon, Theophilus | Humber, Charlotte | 21, May 1840 | RCH |
| Canole, William | Code, Bridget | 22, Oct. 1838 | RCH |
| Caorier, Horatio | Woodruff, Hannah | 25, Oct. 1834 | RCH |
| Capp, Henry B. | Butler, Lucy | 16, Feb. 1823 | RCH |
| Capron, James | Norris, Sarah | 22, Apr. 1821 | RCH |
| Carbert, Thomas | Scott, Catharine | 24, Sept 1845 | RCH |
| Cardivelt, John | Dair, Mary | 4, Nov. 1832 | RCH |
| Cardwell, John H. | Montgomery, Caroline | 21, Jan. 1841 | RCH |
| Carey, George | Faris, Jane | 14, June 1849 | D |
| Carey, James | McNally, Bridget | 31, July 1848 | GG |
| Carey, John | Foreman, Margaret | 17, Feb. 1846 | RCH |
| Carey, Joseph | Williams, Catharine | 11, June 1848 | RCH |
| Carey, Michael | Kohane, Bridget | 18, Feb. 1844 | BB |
| Carey, Milo | Gountre, Nancy | 25, May 1837 | RCH |
| Carey, Patrick | Stanton, Margaret | 17, Apr. 1843 | BB |
| Carey, Samuel F. | Allen, Maria Louise | 18, Oct. 1836 | RCH |
| Carey, Thomas | Jones, Sarah | 15, Sept 1833 | RCH |
| Cargill, Austin | Grymour, Amelia | 11, Aug. 1822 | RCH |
| Carhart, John | ----, May | 27, Jan. 1825 | RCH |
| Carl, Cornelius | Tullis, Elisabeth | 25, Dec. 1845 | RCH |
| Carl, Gilbert T. | Douglass, Elisabeth | 13, Aug. 1826 | RCH |
| Carland, Patrick | Voorhes, Jemima | 25, Jan. 1849 | RCH |
| Carle, William | Ward, Louise | 25, May 1837 | RCH |
| Carley, James S. | H---, Mary | 21, Mar. 1820 | RCH |
| Carlin, William | Cook, Catharine | 25, Dec. 1843 | RCH |
| Carlisle, James | Owens, Hester | 12, Mar. 1848 | RCH |
| Carlisle, James M. | Boriff, Sarah | 6, Dec. 1826 | RCH |
| Carlisle, Samuel | Graves, Margaret | 7, Dec. 1837 | RCH |
| Carll, Ephraim | Loring, Jane | 20, Aug. 1842 | RCH |
| Carlton, Charles W. | Webb, Phebe Ann | 6, Apr. 1841 | RCH |
| Carlton, Isaac | Jackson, Jane | 20, Nov. 1834 | RCH |
| Carmical, John | Gerard, Amy | 20, June 1847 | RCH |
| Carmican, Samuel | Glass, Nancy | 22, Nov. 1836 | RCH |
| Carmichael, Neil | Linfoot, Rosetta | 21, Dec. 1842 | RCH |
| Carnahan, George | Risk, Elisabeth Jane | Nov. 1841 | RCH |
| Carnahan, Isaac | Casey, Rowena | 9, Jan. 1836 | RCH |

| Grooms<br>***** | Brides<br>***** | Date of Marriage<br>**** ** ******** | Code<br>**** |
|---|---|---|---|
| Carnahan, J. | Edmondson, Abigail | 4, July 1834 | RCH |
| Carnahan, James | Cummings, Sarah | 18, Sept 1846 | RCH |
| Carnahan, Thomas | Hubbard, Amelia | 2, Dec. 1841 | RCH |
| Carnathan, Robert | Conner, Mary | 9, Nov. 1820 | RCH |
| Carneal, Louis | Lawrence, Maria | 27, Nov. 1845 | RCH |
| Carnes, Peter | Hand, Elisabeth | 14, Oct. 1832 | RCH |
| Carnes, Peter | Whitney, Harriet | 21, Mar. 1842 | RCH |
| Carnes, Samuel | Forden, Jane | 4, July 1847 | RCH |
| Carnes, William | Hoalt, Eleanor | 5, Aug. 1846 | RCH |
| Carney, Andrew | Doherty, Catharine | 21, Feb. 1841 | BB |
| Carney, Edward | Wilson, Jane | 21, June 1844 | RCH |
| Carney, Francis | Sheridan, Catharine | 25, Apr. 1838 | RCH |
| Carney, Hugh | Bingham, Susanna | 25, June 1841 | BB |
| Carney, John | McDonald, Bridget | 15, Feb. 1849 | BB |
| Carney, Patrick | Langdon, Ellen | 11, Jan. 1843 | BB |
| Carns, Jesse | Bassett, Cynthia | 22, Apr. 1824 | RCH |
| Caron, Ferdinand | Koese, Barbara | 29, Oct. 1835 | FF |
| Caron, Peter | Rapp, Catharina | 10, Nov. 1835 | FF |
| Carpenter, Calvin | Horare, Anna Maria | 19, Nov. 1833 | RCH |
| Carpenter, Ezra | Andrews, Sarah P. | 14, May 1833 | RCH |
| Carpenter, John | Bun---, Maria | 23, Sept 1819 | RCH |
| Carpenter, Michael | Habblemann, Mary Ann | 22, Jan. 1847 | RCH |
| Carpenter, Samuel | Carman, Louise | 1, Oct. 1846 | RCH |
| Carpenter, William | Fowler, Malinda | 11, July 1847 | RCH |
| Carpenter, William A | Williams, Rachel | 20, Feb. 1849 | RCH |
| Carr, Alfred | Wells, Amanda | 19, Nov. 1845 | RCH |
| Carr, Dan. | Titus, Hannah | 20, Sept 1835 | RCH |
| Carr, David | Hunter, Maria | 3, Dec. 1845 | RCH |
| Carr, Francis | Upjohn, Mary Ann | 1, Aug. 1822 | I |
| Carr, George | Stout, Sarah Ann | 15, Sept 1849 | RCH |
| Carr, James | Cook, Sarah | 10, Oct. 1834 | RCH |
| Carr, James | Segar, Catharine | 21, Apr. 1841 | RCH |
| Carr, James | Hou---, Elisabeth | 15, Dec. 1845 | RCH |
| Carr, James O. | Picket, Elisabeth A. | 14, Mar. 1833 | RCH |
| Carr, John | Scowden, Emma J. | 11, Oct. 1838 | RCH |
| Carr, John | Holland, Martha | 8, July 1847 | RCH |
| Carr, Joseph V. | Arnold, Susan E. | 31, Aug. 1833 | RCH |
| Carr, Thomas | Lane, Anna | 25, Aug. 1833 | RCH |
| Carrel, Hercules | Jones, Mary | 23, July 1839 | RCH |
| Carrell, Joseph | Boon, Phoebe | 2, July 1825 | RCH |
| Carrier, Charles | Peoples, Elisabeth H | 3, July 1838 | RCH |
| Carrigan, Stephan | Keeshan, Mary A. | 2, Feb. 1845 | BB |
| Carrmann, William | Winter, Elisabeth | 5, Nov. 1845 | RCH |
| Carrol, Hugh | Morrisy, Cattura F. | 31, Jan. 1820 | RCH |
| Carroll, James | Kilburn, Elisabeth | 5, Apr. 1846 | RCH |
| Carroll, James | Kingsley, Margaret | 1, May 1848 | BB |
| Carroll, John | Donnegan, Elisabeth | 30, Aug. 1842 | BB |
| Carroll, Michael | Carroll, Joanne | 24, May 1848 | BB |
| Carroll, Michael | Fuchs, Anna Maria | 22, Nov. 1848 | EE |
| Carroll, Philipp | Hogan, Anna | 26, Nov. 1849 | GG |
| Carroll, William | Carroll, Catharine | 25, Nov. 1841 | RCH |
| Carroll, William | Dorsey, Mary A. | 14, Aug. 1848 | BB |
| Carrow, Peter | Raff, Catharine | 18, Oct. 1835 | RCH |
| Carrydel, Barnabus | Orr, Catharine Ann | 31, Mar. 1836 | RCH |
| Carson, David | Goe, Margaret W. | 2, Sept 1837 | RCH |
| Carson, Enoch | Williams, Julia A. | Apr. 1847 | RCH |
| Carson, J. | Terry, Margaret | 2, Aug. 1821 | RCH |
| Carson, Lumis | Carr, Amelia | 1, Jan. 1849 | RCH |
| Carson, Robert | Nichols, Hannah | 12, Mar. 1843 | RCH |
| Carson, William | Butler, Margaret J. | 16, May 1842 | RCH |
| Cart, Casper | Hehmann, Julia | 29, Aug. 1839 | FF |
| Carter, Allison | Smith, Charlotte | 7, Dec. 1835 | RCH |
| Carter, Henry | Stokes, Emma | 10, Dec. 1844 | RCH |
| Carter, Henry | Hull, Abigail | 22, Feb. 1849 | RCH |
| Carter, Horace | Holbrock, Perris | 1, Mar. 1838 | RCH |
| Carter, James H. | Roberts, Margaret | 31, Dec. 1847 | D |
| Carter, John J. | Henoch, Louise | 3, May 1834 | RCH |
| Carter, Jonathan | Byrunes, Elisabeth | 8, Jan. 1838 | RCH |
| Carter, Louis | Banks, Rosannah | 25, Sept 1839 | RCH |
| Carter, Nathan | Beck, Mary | 22, Feb. 1846 | RCH |
| Carter, Roger | Carden, Mary | 1, Jan. 1846 | RCH |

| Grooms<br>****** | Brides<br>****** | Date of Marriage<br>**** ** ******** | Code<br>**** |
|---|---|---|---|
| Carter, Valentine C. | Perin, Rebecca | 11, Mar. 1832 | RCH |
| Carter, Vincent S. | Foreman, Elisabeth | 18, Nov. 1832 | RCH |
| Carter, William | Hamilton, Anna E. | 18, Nov. 1841 | RCH |
| Cartlyou, John | Hole, Elizabeth | 30, Mar. 1825 | RCH |
| Cartmann, Thomas | Langmeyer, Anna | 22, Feb. 1848 | RCH |
| Cartmill, Elias | Ward, Susan | 4, May 1843 | RCH |
| Cartwright, John | Duvall, Matilda | 24, Dec. 1844 | RCH |
| Cartwright, John H. | Cartwright, Elisabet | 28, Nov. 1847 | RCH |
| Carty, Uriah | Sprague, Lorena | 12, July 1835 | RCH |
| Carver, Albert | Huble, Sarah | 26, Nov. 1826 | RCH |
| Carver, William H. | Ferris, Mary Ann | 2, May 1848 | RCH |
| Carwood, John | Burnham, Winifred | 1, Apr. 1833 | RCH |
| Carwood, Joseph | Booney, | 17, Apr. 1834 | RCH |
| Cary, Christopher | Robinson, Sarah Ann | 10, Aug. 1835 | RCH |
| Cary, Freeman G. | Mean, Melvina | 4, Apr. 1833 | RCH |
| Cary, Irvin | Jones, Martha | 27, Sept 1849 | RCH |
| Cary, Warren | Harrison, Elisabeth | 24, Dec. 1846 | RCH |
| Cary, William | McCary, Elisabeth | 6, Dec. 1843 | RCH |
| Cary, William W. | Smith, Hannah | 30, Apr. 1835 | RCH |
| Case, Dominick | Scheaman, Theresa | 8, Sept 1844 | BB |
| Case, Henry | Caldwell, Emily Jane | 8, June 1841 | RCH |
| Case, Henry | Adams, Mary Ann | 8, Feb. 1844 | RCH |
| Case, Nicolaus | Bender, Caroline | 16, May 1844 | BB |
| Case, Thomas | Arnold, Augustina | 10, Nov. 1836 | RCH |
| Casey, Charles | Charles, Candes | 6, Sept 1832 | RCH |
| Casey, Charles E. | Minner, Sarah | 2, Dec. 1847 | RCH |
| Casey, David D. | Holland, Emsey | 30, Mar. 1823 | RCH |
| Casey, George H. | Tapley, Caroline M. | 20, July 1848 | RCH |
| Casey, James | Langford, Sarah | 23, Apr. 1849 | GG |
| Casey, John | Saybrooks, Prisilla | 27, Feb. 1820 | RCH |
| Casey, Joshua | Jobe, Sarah A. | 31, Mar. 1839 | RCH |
| Casey, Maurice | McCarthy, Catharine | 20, Sept 1839 | BB |
| Casey, Thomas | Han---, Elisabeth | 21, Dec. 1837 | RCH |
| Casey, William | Johnson, Maria | 17, Mar. 1833 | RCH |
| Casey, Wilson | Comte, Mary Atte | 2, May 1833 | RCH |
| Cash, Jesse | York, Milly | 9, Sept 1842 | RCH |
| Cashman, Thomas | O'Kain, Ann | 25, Oct. 1849 | BB |
| Casled, Nathaniel | Knabb, Mary | 2, Dec. 1819 | RCH |
| Casley, Archibald | Miller, Matilda | 28, Nov. 1837 | RCH |
| Casner, John | McGrew, Margaret | 30, Apr. 1843 | RCH |
| Casper, Jacob | Hegner, Eleanor | 3, June 1844 | RCH |
| Cass, David | Rupel, Nancy | 29, Jan. 1838 | RCH |
| Cassady, Andrew | Maguire, Susan | 1, Oct. 1849 | BB |
| Cassel, John | Moon, Elisabeth F. | 27, June 1847 | RCH |
| Cassel, Joseph | Herron, Mary | 1, Mar. 1843 | RCH |
| Cassidy, Edward | Young, Frances (Mrs) | 3, June 1843 | BB |
| Cassidy, Henry | Crowley, Ellen | 9, Dec. 1849 | GG |
| Castard, David C. | Susans, Elisabeth A. | 27, June 1840 | RCH |
| Casteel, Jacob | Logan, Mary Ann | 13, Sept 1849 | RCH |
| Castel, Peter | Dowling, Mary | 22, Mar. 1842 | RCH |
| Castens, Heinrich L. | Aul, M. Friedricka | 24, Feb. 1848 | B |
| Castigan, John | Caraher, Elizabeth | 5, Apr. 1847 | GG |
| Castle, Barket | Walker, Mary | 13, Oct. 1834 | RCH |
| Castler, Joseph | Crater, Clarissa | 27, Jan. 1820 | RCH |
| Castner, Jacob | Riggs, Amanda | 13, Apr. 1844 | RCH |
| Caston, Levi | Rudisell, Catharine | 20, Aug. 1846 | RCH |
| Casue, Alexander | Felter, Sarah | 16, Feb. 1836 | RCH |
| Caswell, Daniel J. | Wilson, Mary | 2, May 1822 | I |
| Cathell, J. | Wells, Trypena | 22, Apr. 1822 | RCH |
| Cathol, John | Phelpps, Mary | 29, Sept 1840 | RCH |
| Catterlin, Solomon | Withau, Hannah | 13, Nov. 1838 | RCH |
| Catternale, Henry | Catternale, Eliz. | 3, Oct. 1832 | I |
| Cattley, Peter | VanPelt, Catharine | 22, May 1823 | RCH |
| Caulfield, Robert | Burnside, Jane | 15, Feb. 1837 | RCH |
| Caunant, Hardy C. | Cargill, Ellen | 27, Feb. 1837 | RCH |
| Cautnoe, Charles | Shepard, Elisabeth | 17, Oct. 1837 | RCH |
| Cavalli, Hugo L. | Burckhart, Henrietta | 2, Oct. 1845 | G |
| Cavanaugh, Peter | Chamberlain, Julia A | 9, Jan. 1838 | RCH |
| Cavanaugh, Thomas | Reilly, Jane | 3, June 1839 | BB |
| Cavemann, Bernard | Bringmeier, Elisabet | 24, Jan. 1846 | RCH |
| Caves, William | Spencer, Alice | 4, Aug. 1835 | RCH |

| Grooms<br>***** | Brides<br>***** | Date of Marriage<br>**** ** ******** | Code<br>**** |
|---|---|---|---|
| Caward, Philipp | Graninger, Mariah | 1, Jan. 1826 | RCH |
| Cawin, George | Vist, Margaret | 15, Nov. 1843 | RCH |
| Cawk, Henry | Athop, Maria | 23, Apr. 1834 | RCH |
| Caywood, John | Robinson, Elisabeth | 22, Dec. 1847 | RCH |
| Cazell, Friedrich | Saltson, Rosanna | 19, Jan. 1821 | RCH |
| Cecil, James | Morrison, Emily | 23, May 1843 | RCH |
| Center, Hartzell | Slaughter, Sarah | 7, Feb. 1849 | RCH |
| Centner, Christoph | Robert, Henrietta | 8, Feb. 1842 | FF |
| Chadwick, Cyrus | Walker, Elisabeth | 6, May 1834 | RCH |
| Chadwick, Darwin | Graham, Emily | 6, Nov. 1844 | RCH |
| Chadwick, Samuel | Roberts, Ann | 7, Nov. 1835 | RCH |
| Chain---, James L. | Moore, Caroline | 2, Oct. 1823 | RCH |
| Chalfant, Jonathan | Thompson, Louise | 15, Nov. 1843 | RCH |
| Chalfont, Johnson | Hamblin, Minerva | 31, Dec. 1848 | RCH |
| Chamberlain, Daniel | Reed, Nancy | 25, Nov. 1835 | RCH |
| Chamberlain, J.L. | Pain, Lea--- F. | 18, Jan. 1825 | RCH |
| Chamberlain, James | Vance, Jane | 16, Dec. 1841 | RCH |
| Chamberlain, John | Williams, Mary | 4, Sept 1842 | RCH |
| Chamberlain, Nathan. | Dunbar, Mary Ann | 6, Aug. 1847 | RCH |
| Chamberlain, Nathan. | McDaniel, Ruth Ann | 8, Aug. 1849 | RCH |
| Chamberlain, Robert | Mullen, Elisabeth | 8, June 1836 | RCH |
| Chamberlain, Seymore | Salsbury, Mary | 28, Feb. 1847 | RCH |
| Chamberlain, Tyler | Snider, Euphemia | 25, Dec. 1836 | RCH |
| Chamberlin, John | Hand, Margaret | 2, May 1847 | RCH |
| Chamberlin, William | Whitaker, Frances | 10, Nov. 1836 | RCH |
| Chambers, Benjamin | Carls, Ceney | 25, June 1847 | RCH |
| Chambers, David | Hoffman, Rebecca | 30, Jan. 1837 | RCH |
| Chambers, Enoc | Marshall, Hannah | 29, Mar. 1833 | RCH |
| Chambers, Francis T. | Felinger, Elizabeth | 18, Apr. 1848 | I |
| Chambers, George W. | DeGraw, Mary Ann | 12, Mar. 1843 | RCH |
| Chambers, George W. | Gibbs, Elisabeth | 10, Dec. 1848 | RCH |
| Chambers, Jacob | Houts, Mary Ann | 2, June 1833 | RCH |
| Chambers, Jacob | Hauls, Morgan (Mrs) | 3, June 1833 | RCH |
| Chambers, James | Collins, Mary | 21, Oct. 1819 | RCH |
| Chambers, James | Linton, Ann | 15, Aug. 1844 | RCH |
| Chambers, John | Bonte, Jane Elis. | 4, Oct. 1841 | RCH |
| Chambers, Joseph | Freshower, Sarah | 23, Oct. 1838 | RCH |
| Chambers, Pius | Chamberlain, Ann | 13, Nov. 1844 | BB |
| Chambers, Theodore | Finley, Susan | 11, Jan. 1846 | BB |
| Chambers, William | Bowers, Catharine | 21, Jan. 1836 | RCH |
| Champion, Thomas | Moore, Martha | 23, Nov. 1826 | RCH |
| Chancy, Andrew | Mott, Sophia | 29, Mar. 1819 | RCH |
| Chandler, Charles | Tracy, Mary Ann | 31, Jan. 1842 | RCH |
| Chandler, James W. | --evis, Mary | 20, June 1841 | RCH |
| Chandler, John | Hopkins, Charlotte | 10, Sept 1846 | RCH |
| Chandler, John W. | Cunningham, Margaret | 4, July 1819 | RCH |
| Chandler, Joseph | Kent, Anna | 13, July 1847 | RCH |
| Channing, William E. | Fuller, Ellen | 24, Sept 1841 | D |
| Chaphan, John | Bryant, Mary | 24, Aug. 1837 | RCH |
| Chapman, Charles | Munday, Jane | 4, Jan. 1836 | RCH |
| Chapman, Henry | Drake, Julia | 6, July 1841 | RCH |
| Chapman, Robert T. | Curtis, May | 2, Sept 1825 | RCH |
| Chapman, William B. | Caosman, Margaret | 9, Apr. 1839 | RCH |
| Chapman, William Hy. | Allison, Elisabeth | 1, May 1843 | RCH |
| Charlton, James | Brown, Jane | 13, Nov. 1847 | RCH |
| Charp, Bernard | Ward, Mary | 23, Apr. 1839 | RCH |
| Charter, George | Carneally, Bridget | 17, June 1843 | RCH |
| Chartlerworth, Wm. | Cranshaw, Elisabeth | 30, Dec. 1836 | RCH |
| Chase, Nathan | Willey, Catharine | 15, Nov. 1832 | RCH |
| Chase, Rabon | Tollover, Linda | 4, Oct. 1832 | RCH |
| Chase, Salmon P. | Smith, Eliza Ann | 26, Sept 1839 | D |
| Chase, Salmon P. | Ludlow, Sarah Belle | 6, Nov. 1846 | RCH |
| Chase, William H. | Boyer, Elisabeth A. | 21, Aug. 1842 | RCH |
| Chasebrough, Robert | Davis, Mary Ann | 1, Jan. 1848 | RCH |
| Chattaway, Job | Haywood, Sarah | 1, Oct. 1847 | RCH |
| Chatterlin, Solomon | Witham, Elisabeth | 11, May 1837 | RCH |
| Chatton, Jonathan | Martin, Julia | 24, Dec. 1840 | RCH |
| Chaves, Harrison | Clark, Winney | 14, Dec. 1846 | RCH |
| Chavios, William | Scott, Elisabeth | 20, June 1842 | RCH |
| Chavlier, L. | Stokes, Mary | 8, Feb. 1821 | RCH |
| Check, George | Deford, Avis | 11, Nov. 1840 | RCH |

| Grooms | Brides | Date of Marriage | Code |
|--------|--------|------------------|------|
| ****** | ****** | **** ** ******** | **** |
| Cheek, Lazarus | Curtis, Mary Ann | 10, July 1844 | RCH |
| Cheesman, Edward | Stone, Amelia | 17, Oct. 1846 | RCH |
| Cheetham, John | Briggs, Mary Ann | 13, Oct. 1842 | RCH |
| Cheever, George | Gould, Helen Elis. | 19, Sept 1847 | RCH |
| Cheever, William | Jackson, Margaret | 6, July 1844 | RCH |
| Cheevers, John M. | Harp, Helen | 13, Feb. 1818 | RCH |
| Cheneworth, Richard | Hough, Jane H. | Nov. 1844 | RCH |
| Chenoweth, William | Korsen, Henrietta | 11, Apr. 1849 | RCH |
| Cheny, Robert | Stevens, Mary | 27, Nov. 1835 | RCH |
| Chermink, Heinrich | Meyer, Margaretha | 8, Jan. 1844 | AA |
| Chesebrough, William | Taylor, Margaret J. | 4, Mar. 1847 | RCH |
| Chidlaw, Benjamin | Hughes, Rebecca | 28, July 1842 | RCH |
| Childers, Dudley | Benham, Julia A. | 3, July 1836 | RCH |
| Childers, James D. | Kelpan, Sarah Ann | 24, Aug. 1836 | RCH |
| Childs, Charles | Baldridge, Elisabeth | 15, Mar. 1847 | RCH |
| Childs, Elijah | Porter, Margaret | 9, Dec. 1846 | RCH |
| Childs, Michael | Gutmann, Jede | 27, Dec. 1845 | RCH |
| Childs, William | Tait, Elisabeth | 1, June 1837 | RCH |
| Chiles, John | Morgan, Elisabeth | 7, July 1847 | RCH |
| Chinch, Jeremiah | Ludlum, Harriet | 16, Apr. 1826 | RCH |
| Chinn, Chichester | Hatfield, Catharine | 22, Oct. 1842 | RCH |
| Chisholm, George | King, Mahala | 18, Nov. 1839 | RCH |
| Chisman, David | ----, Lucinda | 23, Jan. 1823 | RCH |
| Chister, Joseph | McMaster, Hannah | 14, May 1838 | RCH |
| Chollar, London | Keech, Caroline | 7, Sept 1848 | RCH |
| Chote, Albin | Haddock, Elisabeth | 9, Jan. 1821 | RCH |
| Chrismann, Daniel | McKinney, Martha | 3, Sept 1835 | RCH |
| Chrismann, Joseph | Rapp, Maria | 14, Dec. 1837 | FF |
| Christ, Henry | Ragle, Elisabeth | 3, Dec. 1835 | RCH |
| Christ, Johan | Walter, Elisabeth | 18, July 1848 | EE |
| Christian, David | Sand, Priscilla | 30, Sept 1839 | RCH |
| Christian, George | Sansey, Charlotte | 27, Aug. 1844 | RCH |
| Christie, John | Reilly, Cecilia | 2, Jan. 1847 | GG |
| Christina, John | Kana, Anna Maria | 17, Nov. 1843 | RCH |
| Christmann, Daniel | Bester, Maria | 20, Feb. 1845 | C |
| Christmann, Daniel | Faut, Regina | 4, Feb. 1849 | C |
| Christmann, Jacob | Werling, Catharine | 10, June 1849 | RCH |
| Christmann, Jacob | Krummel, Catharine | 26, Oct. 1845 | G |
| Christmann, Johan F. | Seelig, Theresa | 8, June 1847 | AA |
| Christmann, Nicolaus | Eyl, Anna Christina | 2, Aug. 1843 | FF |
| Christmann, Peter | Noll, Elisabeth | 2, Dec. 1849 | C |
| Christopher, William | Lynes, Rebecca | 26, July 1821 | RCH |
| Christopher, William | Beall, Mary | 24, Apr. 1843 | RCH |
| Christy, Andrew | Corritt, Julia | Jan. 1822 | RCH |
| Chue, Heinrich | Goetz, Maria Barbara | 22, June 1835 | FF |
| Chumney, David A. | Beach, Catharine | 13, Dec. 1848 | RCH |
| Chumney, Franklin | Benson, Rebecca | 14, Apr. 1841 | RCH |
| Chunbill, Gilbert | Black, Jane | 25, July 1839 | RCH |
| Church, Milo | Frost, Ann | 28, Sept 1847 | RCH |
| Churchill, David | Clifton, Frances Ann | 22, Feb. 1825 | RCH |
| Churchill, Noble | Ryland, Margaret | 26, Nov. 1835 | RCH |
| Cifalo, Alexander | Trap, Maria | 23, Nov. 1841 | RCH |
| Cilley, Bradbury | Hedges, Harriet | 13, Mar. 1834 | RCH |
| Cilly, Benjamin | McCormick, Martha | 28, Feb. 1822 | RCH |
| Ciolia, Francis | Lempert, Josephine | 15, May 1843 | AA |
| Cissna, Charles | Higgins, Mary Jane | 12, Jan. 1847 | RCH |
| Ciste, John | Foster, Harriet | 31, Dec. 1846 | RCH |
| Claassen, Claus | Mohlenkamp, Catharin | 23, Dec. 1847 | F |
| Clam---, Samuel | Whiteside, Maria | 5, Feb. 1818 | RCH |
| Clancey, John | Lynch, Honora | 4, Feb. 1849 | GG |
| Clancy, James | Abbott, Mathilda Ann | 8, Oct. 1840 | BB |
| Clancy, John | Dempsey, Ann | 19, Aug. 1838 | RCH |
| Clancy, William | Cate, Margaret | 7, Jan. 1840 | BB |
| Clapem, George | Pease, Lucretia | 26, Sept 1841 | RCH |
| Clark, | Askin, Elisabeth | 16, Jan. 1823 | RCH |
| Clark, Abraham | Kitchel, Irene | 30, Jan. 1823 | RCH |
| Clark, Abram | Wear, Emily | 25, May 1849 | RCH |
| Clark, Alexander | Snyder, Hannah | 16, Sept 1844 | RCH |
| Clark, Alfred | Davis, Margaret | 29, Sept 1845 | RCH |
| Clark, Andrew | ----, ---- | 10, Feb. 1847 | RCH |
| Clark, August | Sargent, Helena B. | 5, Mar. 1839 | RCH |

| Grooms<br>****** | Brides<br>****** | Date of Marriage<br>**** ** ******** | Code<br>**** |
|---|---|---|---|
| Clark, Benjamin | Berwin, Julia Ann | 5, Feb. 1837 | RCH |
| Clark, Caleb | Williamson, Maria | 30, Nov. 1844 | RCH |
| Clark, Carril | Miller, Mary Ann | 24, July 1835 | RCH |
| Clark, Charles | Clippen, Prudence | 6, Feb. 1842 | RCH |
| Clark, Charles | Frasee, Emeline | 16, Nov. 1843 | RCH |
| Clark, Charles | Mathews, Rachel | 29, Nov. 1844 | RCH |
| Clark, Charles T. | Hall, Louise J. | 10, Mar. 1839 | RCH |
| Clark, Cyrus | Richards, Sarah | 9, Feb. 1847 | RCH |
| Clark, Edward | Jackson, Mary | 9, May 1842 | RCH |
| Clark, Edward | Conners, Mary | 3, Aug. 1844 | BB |
| Clark, Enos | Dickson, Mary | 13, Sept 1845 | RCH |
| Clark, George | McLaughlin, Mary Ann | 14, Feb. 1836 | RCH |
| Clark, George | Bagott, Nancy | 14, Aug. 1845 | RCH |
| Clark, George | Clark, Lydia | 20, May 1847 | RCH |
| Clark, Henry | Skyum, Mary | 28, June 1832 | RCH |
| Clark, Hugh | Hurley, Ann | 22, Oct. 1846 | GG |
| Clark, Ira | Burnet, Ruth | 3, Oct. 1833 | RCH |
| Clark, Isaac | Patterson, Elisabeth | 25, Dec. 1832 | RCH |
| Clark, J.D. | Fithian, Ruth | 1, Oct. 1837 | RCH |
| Clark, James | Millspaugh, Polly | 23, July 1822 | RCH |
| Clark, James | Kinney, Elisabeth | 25, Nov. 1824 | RCH |
| Clark, James | ----, ---- | 20, July 1835 | RCH |
| Clark, James | Kelso, Frances | 20, Nov. 1837 | RCH |
| Clark, James | Black, Sarah | 28, Nov. 1841 | RCH |
| Clark, James | Aldred, Margaret | 14, Nov. 1842 | RCH |
| Clark, James | Boyce, Sarah | 13, June 1847 | RCH |
| Clark, James | Harrison, Mary | 17, Feb. 1848 | RCH |
| Clark, James N. | Warner, Rachel | 16, Sept 1832 | RCH |
| Clark, Jeremiah M. | Tessel, Samantha | 25, Oct. 1821 | RCH |
| Clark, John | Reed, Christina | 23, Apr. 1818 | RCH |
| Clark, John | Scoby, Almira | 10, Aug. 1819 | RCH |
| Clark, John | Mackey, Mary | 25, May 1823 | RCH |
| Clark, John | Goudy, Sarah | 3, Apr. 1825 | RCH |
| Clark, John | Benham, Mary | 2, Sept 1833 | RCH |
| Clark, John | Thistwell, Ann | 16, Mar. 1834 | RCH |
| Clark, John | Holt, Mary | 6, Aug. 1834 | RCH |
| Clark, John | Walsh, Martha | 25, Aug. 1845 | RCH |
| Clark, John | Cary, Lilah | 22, June 1846 | RCH |
| Clark, John | Tomlin, Lydia | 26, Jan. 1847 | RCH |
| Clark, John | Rittenhouse, Mary | 30, June 1849 | RCH |
| Clark, John B. | Dean, Abigail | 26, Oct. 1826 | RCH |
| Clark, Jonathan | Burmidge, Ann | 12, Aug. 1838 | RCH |
| Clark, Jonathan | Taylor, Jane | 29, Nov. 1849 | RCH |
| Clark, Joseph | Whitlock, Julia Ann | 14, Jan. 1837 | RCH |
| Clark, Josiah | McCalla, Amanda | 21, Feb. 1847 | RCH |
| Clark, Matthew | Hopes, Martha Ann | 8, Apr. 1833 | RCH |
| Clark, Michael | Thompson, Riney | 1, Mar. 1825 | RCH |
| Clark, Nathan | Taylor, Margaret | 12, Sept 1818 | RCH |
| Clark, Nelson | Merrill, Mary | 7, Apr. 1846 | RCH |
| Clark, Ozro | Menge, Harriet | 5, Sept 1847 | RCH |
| Clark, Patrick | Kendall, Mary Ann | 18, Sept 1843 | BB |
| Clark, Powell | Johnson, Jane | 20, Nov. 1845 | RCH |
| Clark, Robert | Lawrie, Marion | 25, Apr. 1846 | RCH |
| Clark, Shelby | Millspaugh, Sarah J. | 24, Oct. 1833 | RCH |
| Clark, Squire | Tucker, Nancy | 25, July 1846 | RCH |
| Clark, Stephan | Lightfoot, Wealthy | 4, Jan. 1849 | RCH |
| Clark, Theophilius | Beeler, Margaret | 23, June 1844 | RCH |
| Clark, Thomas | Barton, Eliza H. | 18, Oct. 1825 | RCH |
| Clark, Thomas | Reilly, Mary | 18, Sept 1843 | BB |
| Clark, William | Hicks, Lucia Ann | 5, Jan. 1832 | RCH |
| Clark, William | Luke, Mary | 14, July 1834 | I |
| Clark, William | Taylor, Grace | 4, Feb. 1847 | RCH |
| Clark, William | Tyre, Elisabeth | 19, Mar. 1847 | RCH |
| Clark, William | Paddock, Elisabeth | 10, Oct. 1848 | RCH |
| Clark, William H. | Bartels, Catharine | 28, June 1847 | C |
| Clark, Zerah | Stout, Sarah A. | 20, Apr. 1839 | RCH |
| Clarke, | McCleland, Elisabeth | 3, Oct. 1822 | RCH |
| Clarke, Francis | Wilson, Louise | 9, Sept 1841 | RCH |
| Clarke, Jacob | Madden, Catharine | 11, Jan. 1849 | GG |
| Clarke, Joseph | Mills, Mary | 13, Sept 1837 | RCH |
| Clary, Oliver | O'Donnell, Catharine | 15, May 1838 | RCH |

| Grooms | Brides | Date of Marriage | Code |
|--------|--------|------------------|------|
| Clasby, Charles | Barnard, Lydia | 25, Oct. 1818 | RCH |
| Clason, Lewis | Morris, Silvina | 13, Jan. 1834 | RCH |
| Clason, Lewis | Rutledge, Lucy A. | 24, Oct. 1847 | RCH |
| Claudius, August | Charles, Susanna | 5, July 1848 | G |
| Clausheide, Johan F. | Johannes, Gesina | 3, Dec. 1849 | F |
| Clausheide, Johan H. | Krieger, Louise | 26, July 1843 | F |
| Clauson, George | Bloomfield, Elis. | 28, Feb. 1841 | RCH |
| Claxmeyer, Friedrich | Dalinghaus, M. Elis. | 3, Jan. 1843 | AA |
| Claxton, Thomas | Mann, Emily | 19, Dec. 1847 | RCH |
| Clay, Henry | Gentry, Sarah | 29, Sept 1845 | RCH |
| Clay, Ralph A. | Gassaway, Lucy Ann | 13, Oct. 1841 | I |
| Clay, William | Hall, Sarah | 19, Aug. 1834 | RCH |
| Claypoole, James T. | Allibone, Eliza | 14, Aug. 1823 | I |
| Clayton, Anderson J. | Sattsman, Sarah | 16, June 1818 | RCH |
| Clayton, Andrew P. | Morgin, Nancy | 5, Nov. 1823 | RCH |
| Clayton, Isaac | Carman, Eleanor | 26, Mar. 1844 | RCH |
| Clayton, James | Coon, Sarah | 2, Nov. 1845 | RCH |
| Clayton, John B. | Wescott, Sarah | 14, Mar. 1822 | RCH |
| Clayton, Richard | Jenkins, Jane | 24, Jan. 1843 | RCH |
| Clayton, Richard | Jenkins, Mary Ann | 31, Mar. 1844 | RCH |
| Clayton, Thomas | Rose, Mary | 12, June 1838 | RCH |
| Clear, Daniel | Alexander, Elisabeth | 15, July 1832 | RCH |
| Cleary, Edmund | Burke, Mary | 30, Sept 1843 | BB |
| Cleaver, Levi | Thompson, Mary Ann | 8, Mar. 1849 | RCH |
| Cleaver, Richard | Bright, Lydia | 3, Jan. 1823 | RCH |
| Clegg, David | Williams, Hannah | 25, Dec. 1848 | RCH |
| Clegg, Thomas | Coleman, Rebecca | 23, July 1844 | RCH |
| Cleland, James | Hammer, Elisabeth | 12, May 1834 | RCH |
| Clemand, Cornelius | Hoolahan, Margaret | 14, Feb. 1848 | BB |
| Clement, Martin | Hoffmann, Sophia | 9, Jan. 1838 | FF |
| Clement, Robert | Lawrence, Charlotte | 27, Feb. 1848 | RCH |
| Clements, | Strobridge, Maria M. | 27, Sept 1849 | RCH |
| Clementz, Friedrich | Kaummel, Louise | 13, Nov. 1849 | A |
| Clemeyer, Johan F. | Dammans, Friedricka | 8, Feb. 1848 | A |
| Clemmer, Jacob | Clement, Jane | 14, Oct. 1845 | RCH |
| Clemmons, John C. | Mayall, Susan | 7, Oct. 1832 | RCH |
| Clendening, Evert | Gilmore, Margaret | 15, Dec. 1836 | RCH |
| Clendening, Evert | Grisley, Ann | 8, Feb. 1846 | RCH |
| Clendening, Robert | Wilkins, Hannah | 1, Mar. 1843 | RCH |
| Clenenger, Shobal | Wright, Elisabeth | 5, Aug. 1833 | RCH |
| Clephane, Julius | Bush, Eleanor | 4, May 1847 | RCH |
| Cleveland, George | Vessels, Betsey | 6, Jan. 1838 | RCH |
| Cleveland, Milton | Edmans, Sarah | 11, Jan. 1835 | RCH |
| Cleveland, Thomas J. | Stansifer, Sarah E. | 21, Mar. 1844 | RCH |
| Clew, Duffiel | Thompson, Rachel | 4, Dec. 1842 | RCH |
| Clifford, William | Wheeler, Ellen | 28, Aug. 1844 | RCH |
| Climer, Henry | Miller, M. Matilda | 29, June 1847 | RCH |
| Cline, Alexander | Keefe, Mary | 6, Jan. 1848 | GG |
| Cline, John | Gregg Nancy A. | 23, Nov. 1837 | RCH |
| Cline, William | Anten, Elisabeth | 1, Mar. 1843 | RCH |
| Clingman, John | Harrison, Elisabeth | 18, May 1840 | RCH |
| Clingman, John A. | Nash, Nancy | 10, Aug. 1837 | RCH |
| Clinort, Samuel | Gest, Ellen B. | 27, Apr. 1841 | RCH |
| Clobes, John | Hamilton, Irene | 7, Dec. 1847 | RCH |
| Cloe, Wencel. | Stocker, Louise | 3, June 1849 | EE |
| Cloft, Clinton | Turs, Sarah | 5, July 1849 | RCH |
| Cloon, Samuel | Clemens, Martha M. | 9, Aug. 1847 | RCH |
| Cloonin, Alfred | Stoops, Eddy | 23, May 1833 | RCH |
| Clossin, David | Kain, Almira | 30, Nov. 1845 | RCH |
| Cloud, Daniel | Mayall, Mary | 20, June 1842 | RCH |
| Cloud, Francis | Grove, Wilhelmina | 25, Aug. 1846 | FF |
| Cloud, Jared | Gardner, Ann | 24, Dec. 1840 | RCH |
| Cloud, Mason J. | Farrar, Elisabeth | 30, Nov. 1826 | RCH |
| Clough, Ezekiel | Huddart, Mary A. | 23, Apr. 1838 | RCH |
| Clough, John | Marshall, Harriet | 22, Sept 1849 | RCH |
| Clough, Moses | Richardson, Emeline | 29, Mar. 1835 | RCH |
| Clouser, Francis | McCallough, Mary J. | 1, Oct. 1845 | RCH |
| Clouser, John | Bartlett, Fanny | 21, July 1842 | RCH |
| Cloyer, Andrew | Grove, Esther | 17, Apr. 1823 | RCH |
| Cloyer, Joab | Ashmore, Eva Ann | 30, Jan. 1848 | RCH |
| Clyde, Andrew | Lovelace, Louise | 25, Dec. 1843 | RCH |

| Grooms | Brides | Date of Marriage | Code |
| ***** | ***** | **** ** ******** | **** |
| Clyde, John Edward | Fotrell, Sarah | 6, Mar. 1845 | RCH |
| Coates, James | Williams, Elisabeth | 26, Nov. 1848 | RCH |
| Coates, William | Endicott, Eunice | 6, Oct. 1846 | RCH |
| Coats, John T. | Parks, Jane | 31, Aug. 1834 | RCH |
| Coats, Matthew H. | Allen, Beulah W. | 10, Apr. 1836 | RCH |
| Cobb, Samuel | Jackson, Minerva | 11, Jan. 1849 | RCH |
| Cobbs, Henry H. | Stansbury, Elisabeth | 12, Oct. 1836 | RCH |
| Coblenz, Charles | Dinkelpahl, Henriett | 31, Mar. 1842 | RCH |
| Cobourn, Joseph R. | Easton, Martha | 30, Oct. 1834 | RCH |
| Coburg, Harmon | Enneking, Elisabeth | 8, Jan. 1842 | FF |
| Coburn, Adam | Cambra, Nancy | 27, Feb. 1843 | RCH |
| Coburn, Henry | Fosdick, Elisabeth | 26, May 1836 | RCH |
| Cochlin, Timothy | Hearney, Mary | 21, Nov. 1847 | GG |
| Cochran, Hiram | Snider, Rosina | 8, June 1841 | RCH |
| Cochran, J. | Stark, Elisabeth | 24, Dec. 1840 | RCH |
| Cochran, Roswell | Crowell, Mary Jane | 24, Sept 1846 | RCH |
| Cochran, Simon | Lind, Catharine | 20, Apr. 1842 | RCH |
| Cock, Alfred | Hoover, Susan | 2, July 1835 | RCH |
| Cock, William W. | Gardner, Jane | 5, Aug. 1820 | RCH |
| Cocklin, Thomas | Coffee, Mary Ann | 7, Feb. 1841 | BB |
| Cockrell, Francis | Goddard, Elisabeth | 19, Oct. 1841 | RCH |
| Coddington, Benjamin | Whitroh, Isabella | 24, Dec. 1818 | RCH |
| Coddington, Benjamin | Paley, Catharine | 12, Aug. 1832 | RCH |
| Coddington, Georg W. | Hulbert, Mary E. | 13, June 1849 | RCH |
| Coddington, John | Cox, Mary Ann | 20, Sept 1843 | RCH |
| Cody, James | McAuliffe, Mary | 18, Feb. 1849 | BB |
| Cody, John | English, Mary | 6, Oct. 1839 | BB |
| Cody, Patrick | Hughes, Louise | 19, Apr. 1839 | BB |
| Coen, John D. | Wedderstrand, Mary C | 9, July 1846 | D |
| Coen, Thomas | Gideon, Louise J. | 25, Oct. 1846 | RCH |
| Coff---, Frederick | Taylor, Lydia | 9, Oct. 1826 | RCH |
| Coffey, Malachy | Glaven, Elisabeth | 1, May 1847 | GG |
| Coffey, William | Barker, Prudence | 25, Apr. 1838 | RCH |
| Coffin, Benjamin | Bennett, Charity | 23, Nov. 1837 | RCH |
| Coffin, Charles | Davis, Susan J. | 17, Mar. 1833 | RCH |
| Coffin, Dennis | McKee, Naomi | 30, Dec. 1845 | RCH |
| Coffin, George W. | Meisner, Amelia | 28, Apr. 1838 | RCH |
| Coffin, Samuel | Waring, Rachel | 15, Feb. 1820 | RCH |
| Coffin, William G. | Israel, Hannah | 20, Apr. 1840 | RCH |
| Coghlan, James | Wood, Jane | 21, Sept 1843 | RCH |
| Cohen, Philipp | Kaufmann, Caroline | 21, June 1847 | RCH |
| Cohen, Solomon | Workum, Rachel | 21, Mar. 1844 | RCH |
| Coil, Jamel | Herrnez, Lorina | 8, Mar. 1841 | RCH |
| Coil, Joseph | Hastings, Electa | 27, Oct. 1842 | RCH |
| Coischler, Nicolaus | Heumann, Magdalena | 20, May 1834 | RCH |
| Cok---, George M. | Roberts, Rachel | 21, July 1825 | RCH |
| Colb, Abraham | Johnson, Catharine A | 15, Jan. 1841 | RCH |
| Colb, Johan | Bathmann, Johanna | 24, Sept 1844 | AA |
| Colburn, Charles | Symmes, Mary | 29, July 1847 | RCH |
| Colburn, William | Thomas, Sophronia | 12, Feb. 1845 | RCH |
| Colby, Isaac | Crosly, Nancy | 18, Jan. 1820 | RCH |
| Colchasire, Alfred | Young, Emily | 9, Aug. 1848 | RCH |
| Colclaser, Frederick | Jerome, Verilda | 29, Oct. 1848 | D |
| Cole, Adam | Shull, Elisabeth | 13, Feb. 1818 | RCH |
| Cole, Alexander | Hill, Elisabeth | 20, Sept 1848 | RCH |
| Cole, Edwin | Lucas, Jane | 7, Apr. 1846 | RCH |
| Cole, Glasgoe | Stogers, Rhoda | 31, Aug. 1849 | RCH |
| Cole, Henry | Grimes, Maria | 24, Apr. 1835 | RCH |
| Cole, Horace | Harbin, Elisabeth | 8, June 1842 | RCH |
| Cole, Israel | Cram, Mirilda | 26, Oct. 1842 | RCH |
| Cole, James | Pipeo, Catharine | 28, Dec. 1834 | RCH |
| Cole, Jeremiah | Shull, Mary Ann | 9, Nov. 1837 | RCH |
| Cole, John | Cooper, Mary Ann | 7, Nov. 1837 | RCH |
| Cole, John | Finan, Ellen (Mrs) | 27, June 1848 | BB |
| Cole, John A. | Casey, Elisabeth | 14, Feb. 1849 | RCH |
| Cole, Milo | Lacy, Mary | 21, June 1824 | RCH |
| Cole, Richard | Frost, Hannah | 5, Nov. 1835 | RCH |
| Cole, Samuel | McDaniel, Emily | 16, May 1839 | RCH |
| Cole, Thomas | Purdy, Elisabeth | 19, Aug. 1849 | RCH |
| Cole, William J. | Shide, Catharine | 13, Jan. 1837 | RCH |
| Cole---, Nathaniel | Willyard, Elisabeth | 10, Aug. 1841 | RCH |

| Grooms ****** | Brides ****** | Date of Marriage **** ** ******** | Code **** |
|---|---|---|---|
| Coleby, Abner | Knuckles, Mary | 26, July 1838 | RCH |
| Coleman, Adbel | Butler, Rachel | 18, Mar. 1821 | RCH |
| Coleman, Andreas | Linneberg, M.E. | 22, Apr. 1834 | RCH |
| Coleman, Benjamin | Barnes, Melinda | 29, Oct. 1825 | RCH |
| Coleman, Benjamin | Gilmore, Elisabeth | 13, Oct. 1836 | RCH |
| Coleman, C.W. | Forden, Angeline | 10, June 1849 | RCH |
| Coleman, Charles | Wagner, Louise | 21, Feb. 1837 | F |
| Coleman, David | Smith, Patsey | 6, Jan. 1848 | RCH |
| Coleman, Jacob | Taylor, Nancy | 19, Dec. 1822 | RCH |
| Coleman, Jacob | Martin, Anna | 13, Nov. 1825 | RCH |
| Coleman, Jacob | Wilson, Susan | 13, Mar. 1834 | RCH |
| Coleman, James | Morris, Elisabeth | 26, Feb. 1835 | RCH |
| Coleman, John | Wood, Catharine | 5, Sept 1843 | RCH |
| Coleman, John | Cunningham, Mary | 23, Sept 1849 | GG |
| Coleman, John W. | Simrins, Eva | 4, July 1821 | RCH |
| Coleman, John W. | Woodward, Lucia Anna | 23, Oct. 1834 | I |
| Coleman, Robert | Carlisle, Anna M. | 30, Mar. 1844 | RCH |
| Coleman, Samuel | Sharp, Lucy Ann | 19, Aug. 1843 | RCH |
| Coleman, W. | Miner, Cynthia | 24, Sept 1845 | RCH |
| Coles, A.B. | Morse, Rebecca | 31, Mar. 1849 | RCH |
| Colgan, Michael | Luck, Lucy | 12, Aug. 1848 | RCH |
| Collard, Enoch | Thornton, Elisabeth | 18, Dec. 1845 | RCH |
| Collard, James | Thom---, Mary | 16, Sept 1819 | RCH |
| Collard, William | Swerns, Rebecca | 10, Oct. 1846 | RCH |
| Colles, Jones V. | Long, Catharine | 2, Oct. 1834 | RCH |
| Collet, Peter | Minher, Magdalena | 7, July 1846 | EE |
| Colley, John | Hampton, Caroline A. | 12, Oct. 1843 | RCH |
| Collier, Albert | Morgan, Elisabeth | 19, Feb. 1846 | RCH |
| Colling, T.J. | Bumiss, Maria | 31, Oct. 1847 | RCH |
| Collings, John | Cox, Catharine | 3, Nov. 1823 | RCH |
| Collingwood, Daniel | Newman, Mary | 26, Apr. 1843 | RCH |
| Collins, Andrew | Hill, Susan | 30, Jan. 1834 | RCH |
| Collins, Charles | Driskill, Caroline | 16, Jan. 1843 | RCH |
| Collins, Christopher | Matthews, Catharine | 16, May 1840 | BB |
| Collins, Edmund | Taylor, Elisabeth | 3, Aug. 1842 | RCH |
| Collins, Edward | Sheilly, Lydia | 8, Aug. 1834 | RCH |
| Collins, Edward | Smith, Mary | 9, Aug. 1846 | RCH |
| Collins, Ensley | Keys, Emily | 23, Sept 1845 | RCH |
| Collins, Francis | Lehman, Mary Ann | 14, July 1842 | RCH |
| Collins, George | Sargent, Sarah | 13, Apr. 1820 | RCH |
| Collins, George | Lewis, Harriet | 1, July 1847 | RCH |
| Collins, Gustavus | Utley, Caroline | 17, Dec. 1822 | RCH |
| Collins, Henry | Wallace, Barbara | 21, Aug. 1842 | RCH |
| Collins, Henry | Brown, Sarah | 27, Jan. 1843 | RCH |
| Collins, James | Sargent, Martha A. | 21, Jan. 1836 | RCH |
| Collins, Jesse | Jones, Mary Ann | 21, Aug. 1843 | RCH |
| Collins, John | Smith, Martha | 22, Aug. 1845 | RCH |
| Collins, Joseph H. | Judkins, Martha A. | 16, Jan. 1849 | RCH |
| Collins, Levi | Grazen, Elisabeth | 27, Feb. 1848 | RCH |
| Collins, Major R. | McMahon, Jane | 20, May 1847 | RCH |
| Collins, Marcus | Hoffmann, Sarah | 10, Sept 1844 | RCH |
| Collins, Martin C. | Folger, Lydia S. | 21, Apr. 1835 | RCH |
| Collins, Moses | Irwing, Molly | 23, Nov. 1837 | RCH |
| Collins, William | Everett, Sarah (Mrs) | 2, Jan. 1844 | RCH |
| Collins, William | Hickey, Mary | 31, May 1849 | GG |
| Collins, William H. | Brinkerhoff, Rebecca | 18, Apr. 1825 | RCH |
| Collopy, Michael | Kearney, Mary Ann | 31, Oct. 1849 | BB |
| Collopy, Patrick | Clancy, Bridget | 24, Sept 1848 | BB |
| Colmes, Reuben | Disbrowe, Polly | 4, Dec. 1821 | RCH |
| Colpe, Ellis | Burt, Clarinda | 16, Oct. 1834 | RCH |
| Colsher, Joseph | Lamford, Lucinda | 13, Oct. 1836 | RCH |
| Colter, Andrew | Stewart, Martha | 11, July 1839 | RCH |
| Colter, John | Lemmon, Harriet | 10, Oct. 1847 | RCH |
| Colter, John | Johnson, Elisabeth | 10, Jan. 1849 | RCH |
| Colton, John W. | Miller, | 7, Apr. 1835 | RCH |
| Colts, Abraham | Thomas, Emily | 12, June 1839 | RCH |
| Columbia, John | Chambers, Sarah | 3, Jan. 1820 | RCH |
| Colven, John | ----, Margaret | 4, Dec. 1822 | RCH |
| Colville, Andrew | Hammond, Mary Ann T. | 26, Dec. 1848 | BB |
| Colvin, Thomas | Conn, Hannah | 9, July 1826 | RCH |
| Colwell, James | Jones, Caroline | 28, May 1848 | RCH |

| Grooms | Brides | Date of Marriage | Code |
|--------|--------|------------------|------|
| Combs, Alfred | Frankenstein, Maria | 15, May 1849 | RCH |
| Combs, John | Stratton, Dorcus | 15, July 1823 | RCH |
| Comley, James D. | Pennington, Francis | 18, Sept 1849 | RCH |
| Comley, Richard N. | Saunders, Julia E. | 8, May 1833 | RCH |
| Comly, William F. | Judkins, Sarah | 19, Oct. 1836 | RCH |
| Common, Robert A. | Boles, Jane | 28, July 1835 | RCH |
| Comnitz, Daniel | Richardson, Maria | 15, Aug. 1841 | RCH |
| Comps, N.W. | Bowen, E.M. | 7, Nov. 1838 | RCH |
| Compton, Azaiah | Flemings, Alice | 29, Dec. 1846 | RCH |
| Compton, Ira S. | Campbell, Martha | 21, Jan. 1835 | RCH |
| Compton, John | Bunyon, | 27, Aug. 1835 | RCH |
| Compton, Nathan | Walls, Nancy S. | 23, Feb. 1836 | RCH |
| Compton, Reuben S. | LaBoyteaux, Basheba | 25, Nov. 1824 | RCH |
| Compton, William A. | VanAndof, Caroline | 24, Dec. 1837 | RCH |
| Comstock, James | Nicholas, Mary | 25, Sept 1834 | RCH |
| Comstock, Stephen | Butler, Caroline | 13, June 1847 | RCH |
| Comstock, William | Foote, Catharine A. | 25, May 1847 | I |
| Conahan, Charles | Montford, Sarah C. | 9, Oct. 1838 | RCH |
| Conahan, John | Gross, Mary Ann | 17, Nov. 1846 | BB |
| Conclin, William | Borden, Louise | 17, July 1821 | RCH |
| Conde, Abner | Henshaw, Elvira | 29, Jan. 1844 | RCH |
| Condon, William | Morehead, Elisabeth | 28, Mar. 1843 | RCH |
| Cone, Charles | Jones, Elmira | 12, Feb. 1846 | RCH |
| Cones, William | Thompson, Margaret | 1, Dec. 1845 | RCH |
| Coney, Edward | Pearson, Ann | 8, Nov. 1843 | I |
| Conger, | Fuller, Margaret | 21, Jan. 1841 | RCH |
| Congo, Samuel | Gilbert, Melissa | 8, July 1843 | RCH |
| Congo, William | Johnson, Nancy | 30, Apr. 1842 | RCH |
| Conk, William | Stevenson, Martha | 22, Jan. 1833 | RCH |
| Conklin, | Bush, Morrice | 27, Dec. 1837 | RCH |
| Conklin, Benjamin C. | Evan, Sarah | 1, Nov. 1820 | RCH |
| Conklin, Elias D. | ----, ---- | 31, May 1835 | RCH |
| Conklin, Henry | Donelan, Christine | 29, Apr. 1841 | I |
| Conklin, Richard | ----, Margaret | 17, Sept 1818 | RCH |
| Conklin, Stephan | Mills, Sarah | 31, May 1821 | RCH |
| Conkling, Isaac | Carman, Mary | 3, Mar. 1847 | RCH |
| Conkling, John | Connett, Amanda | 23, Feb. 1834 | RCH |
| Conkling, Joseph | Fitten, Josephine | 22, May 1840 | RCH |
| Conkling, Richard | Renten, Lucy | 12, Nov. 1845 | RCH |
| Conkling, Stephen | Forgey, Mary | 22, Mar. 1848 | RCH |
| Conkling, William | Windling, Elisabeth | 25, Jan. 1846 | RCH |
| Conlan, Eugene | Rousch, Mary Ann | 22, Apr. 1847 | BB |
| Conlan, Jeremiah | Ames, Ellen | 11, Feb. 1849 | BB |
| Conlan, Jeremiah | Ames, Ellen | 11, Feb. 1849 | BB |
| Conlan, Michael | Duffy, Martha | 22, May 1842 | BB |
| Conley, John | McHenry, Mary Ann | 13, June 1820 | RCH |
| Conn, Aaron | Wentworth, Jane | 8, Aug. 1848 | RCH |
| Conn, Edward | Stewart, Elizabeth | 13, Feb. 1825 | RCH |
| Conn, James | Hurdus, Hannah | 16, Nov. 1817 | RCH |
| Connel, Henry | Butt, Anna | 16, Mar. 1819 | RCH |
| Connel, Joseph | Winston, Rebecca | 25, Aug. 1837 | RCH |
| Connell, James | Green, Catharine | 17, Apr. 1845 | BB |
| Connell, Joseph B. | Morrey, Sarah Jane | 5, Apr. 1849 | RCH |
| Connell, Michael | Lawler, Catharine | 29, Apr. 1849 | BB |
| Connell, Patrick | McCarthy, Catharine | 14, Oct. 1847 | BB |
| Connell, Paul | Folger, Mary | 23, Sept 1832 | RCH |
| Connelly, Charles | Dunn, Catharine | 19, Sept 1842 | BB |
| Connelly, John | Cunningham, Elis. A. | 17, July 1834 | RCH |
| Connelly, Michael | Cox, Lavinia | 4, Feb. 1840 | BB |
| Connelly, Peter | Murphy, Mary | 21, Oct. 1849 | GG |
| Connelly, Thomas | Lawlor, Catharine | 19, Feb. 1849 | GG |
| Conner, Benjamin | Dillard, Nancy | 14, Feb. 1839 | RCH |
| Conner, Charles | McC---, Sarah A. | 15, Oct. 1837 | RCH |
| Conner, Francis | Shields, Bridget | 8, May 1849 | RCH |
| Conner, Thomas | Disbrow, Jane | 3, June 1844 | RCH |
| Connery, Edmund | Poole, Susan | 19, June 1838 | I |
| Connet, Ira | Wiggins, Mary | 12, Sept 1833 | RCH |
| Connet, Lot D. | Mann, Elisabeth | 30, Dec. 1819 | RCH |
| Connolly, John | Murphy, Ann | 4, May 1842 | BB |
| Connolly, Patrick | Walter, Elisabeth A. | 28, June 1839 | BB |
| Connolly, Patrick | Loughan, Margaret | 27, Nov. 1847 | BB |

| Grooms<br>***** | Brides<br>***** | Date of Marriage<br>**** ** ******** | Code<br>**** |
|---|---|---|---|
| Connolly, Thomas | Gillen, Mary | 5, Aug. 1849 | BB |
| Connolly, Walter | Lawler, Mary | 17, June 1849 | BB |
| Connoly, George | Smith, Harriet | 3, Feb. 1841 | RCH |
| Connor, | Sheppard, Margaret | 23, July 1825 | RCH |
| Connor, George | Black, Elisabeth | 2, Sept 1819 | RCH |
| Connor, Thomas | Sullivan, Mary | 9, Oct. 1849 | GG |
| Connor, Wesley | Wheaton, Abigail | 12, Dec. 1844 | RCH |
| Connwell, Robert B. | Blake, Delia | 17, June 1835 | RCH |
| Conover, | ----, Priscilla | 12, May 1836 | RCH |
| Conover, James | Morten, Tabitha J. | 31, Oct. 1848 | RCH |
| Conover, Peter | Jones, Mary | 21, July 1836 | RCH |
| Conover, Peter | Bodine, Anna Elis. | 11, Nov. 1847 | RCH |
| Conover, William H. | Diar, Ann | 10, Nov. 1840 | RCH |
| Conrad, Conrad | Burgotten, Margaret | 25, Oct. 1840 | G |
| Conrad, Daniel | Symms, Melissa | 9, Jan. 1847 | RCH |
| Conrad, Jacob | Lacy, Anna H. | 24, Nov. 1846 | RCH |
| Conrad, Jacob | Kramer, Margaretha | 25, Apr. 1847 | EE |
| Conrad, Peter | Meral, Magdalena | 14, May 1848 | II |
| Conrad, Phineas B. | Scull, Rosanna | 21, Oct. 1824 | RCH |
| Conrad, Valentin | Walton, Elisabeth | 3, Feb. 1845 | A |
| Conretins, Maxwell | Peokey, Catharine | 15, May 1834 | RCH |
| Conrey, Jonathan | Elliott, Mary J. | 26, Mar. 1846 | RCH |
| Conroy, Peter | McDermott, Catharine | 23, July 1849 | BB |
| Constable, Christoph | Clark, Jane | 22, Dec. 1826 | RCH |
| Constable, Hiram | Bodine, Emily | 4, Nov. 1835 | RCH |
| Constable, Jacob | Tucker, Sarah | 21, Feb. 1838 | RCH |
| Constable, Napthaly | Bornan, Nancy J. | 3, Mar. 1842 | RCH |
| Constans, Peter | Spidel, Caroline | 15, Aug. 1849 | RCH |
| Converse, Edward | McClurey, Harriet | 30, July 1845 | RCH |
| Conway, Bernard | Morgan, Catharine | 13, June 1839 | BB |
| Conway, Mason | Bavis, Elisabeth | 9, Sept 1849 | RCH |
| Conway, Thomas | Light, Sarah | 29, Mar. 1835 | RCH |
| Conway, Thomas | Lynch, Catharine | 23, July 1848 | BB |
| Conway, William C. | Rittenhouse, Marg. | 28, Mar. 1848 | RCH |
| Conway, Wilton | Burns, Laura | 15, Oct. 1846 | RCH |
| Cony, Francis | Clarke, Bridget | 4, Feb. 1849 | GG |
| Coodier, Francis | Vatton, Catharine | 20, May 1834 | RCH |
| Cook, | Muttock, Elis. Jane | 30, Nov. 1842 | RCH |
| Cook, Alfred | ----, Nancy | 2, Mar. 1837 | RCH |
| Cook, Anthony | Cornish, Martha | 25, Oct. 1845 | RCH |
| Cook, Benjamin | Fitzwater, Sarah | 21, Nov. 1842 | RCH |
| Cook, Benjamin | Graham, Mary | 15, Aug. 1847 | RCH |
| Cook, Bernard | Moran, Ellen | 24, Sept 1848 | BB |
| Cook, Elihu | Thorp, Joan | 17, Dec. 1826 | RCH |
| Cook, George | German, Harriet | 6, Nov. 1817 | RCH |
| Cook, George | McKeag, Ann | 18, May 1843 | RCH |
| Cook, Henry | Cook, Mary | 10, Nov. 1844 | BB |
| Cook, Henry | Gentry, Susannah | 21, Mar. 1846 | RCH |
| Cook, J.R. | Gentry, Catharine | 26, Dec. 1843 | RCH |
| Cook, Jacob | Walker, Charity | 8, May 1849 | RCH |
| Cook, James | King, Rhoda | 28, Dec. 1842 | RCH |
| Cook, James Sandford | Lemmon, Rachel | 22, Feb. 1846 | RCH |
| Cook, Jesse S. | Theis, Elisabeth Ann | 12, Sept 1819 | RCH |
| Cook, John | Conover, Amanda | 29, Aug. 1844 | RCH |
| Cook, Joseph | Cook, Catharine | 25, Apr. 1841 | RCH |
| Cook, Lee | Rankin, Mary | 24, Sept 1846 | RCH |
| Cook, Lewis | Sylvester, Louise | 14, Oct. 1843 | RCH |
| Cook, Milton | Pettis, Rebecca Ann | 15, Nov. 1847 | RCH |
| Cook, Reece G. | Ready, Fanny | 16, Nov. 1826 | RCH |
| Cook, Robert | Wright, Julia | 29, Dec. 1842 | RCH |
| Cook, Samuel | Cockplias, Narcissa | 13, Apr. 1837 | RCH |
| Cook, Samuel | Dollin, Frances | 8, Nov. 1820 | I |
| Cook, Sylvester | McPherson, Sally | 9, Dec. 1844 | RCH |
| Cook, William | Cobb, Sarah Ann | Oct. 1844 | RCH |
| Cook, William B. | Martin, Elisabeth | 31, May 1846 | RCH |
| Cook, William E. | Burns, Martha Jane | 24, Dec. 1849 | RCH |
| Cooke, Edward | Hughes, Mary Ann | 11, Feb. 1842 | RCH |
| Cooke, William | Musick, Charity | 30, Sept 1848 | RCH |
| Cool, Heinrich | Durbin, E. Adelheid | 14, May 1839 | FF |
| Cooley, Jabez | James, Mary | 31, Mar. 1833 | RCH |
| Cooley, William | Stewart, Sarah | 16, June 1844 | RCH |

| Grooms<br>****** | Brides<br>****** | Date of Marriage<br>**** ** ******** | Code<br>**** |
|---|---|---|---|
| Coolidge, William | Merrie, Sophia Ann | 11, Sept 1825 | RCH |
| Coolidge, William | Philpot, Elisabeth | 27, Apr. 1843 | RCH |
| Coombs, Elijah | Hilts, Margaret | 8, June 1848 | RCH |
| Coombs, Samuel | Davis, Hester | 21, Dec. 1838 | RCH |
| Coon, William August | Langrel, Mary A. | 23, Nov. 1837 | RCH |
| Cooney, John | Ellis, Ann | 3, Feb. 1841 | BB |
| Coons, Charles | Cox, Catharine | 21, Jan. 1841 | RCH |
| Coons, Frederick | Holland, Elisabeth | 15, Nov. 1832 | RCH |
| Coons, George | McDonald, Grace | 29, July 1832 | RCH |
| Coons, John | Gardner, Elisabeth | 4, Aug. 1826 | RCH |
| Coons, John | Wilson, Ann | 8, Apr. 1832 | RCH |
| Coons, John M. | Floyd, Mary | 13, May 1826 | RCH |
| Coons, Joseph | McColony, Sophia | 16, May 1833 | RCH |
| Coons, Valentine | Burdick, Mary Jane | 27, Aug. 1846 | RCH |
| Cooper, Christopher | Clark, Elisabeth Ann | 28, June 1842 | RCH |
| Cooper, Daniel | Monsy, Martha | 1, Apr. 1846 | RCH |
| Cooper, Edmond | Sewards, Mary | 21, Mar. 1818 | RCH |
| Cooper, H. | Nunn, Sarah | 27, 1836 | RCH |
| Cooper, Isaac | Wathin, Nancy K. | 5, Sept 1821 | RCH |
| Cooper, James | Buckingham, Jane | 28, Apr. 1844 | RCH |
| Cooper, James M. | Ross, Elisabeth A. | 10, Oct. 1833 | RCH |
| Cooper, Jochonias | Center, Mary | 28, June 1846 | RCH |
| Cooper, John | Weber, Eva | 18, Apr. 1836 | FF |
| Cooper, John | Oliver, Helen | 8, May 1848 | RCH |
| Cooper, Jonas | Price, Elizabeth | 27, Dec. 1821 | I |
| Cooper, Joseph | ----, ---- | Jan. 1832 | RCH |
| Cooper, Joseph | Leslie, Mary Ann | 7, Mar. 1849 | RCH |
| Cooper, Lot | McMurray, Mary | 25, Jan. 1821 | RCH |
| Cooper, Milton | Oliver, Margaret | 16, Nov. 1834 | RCH |
| Cooper, Robert | Smith, Mary Ann | 12, Oct. 1837 | RCH |
| Cooper, Samuel | Gile, Anna | 7, Nov. 1846 | RCH |
| Cooper, Spencer | Porter, Laura | 21, July 1838 | RCH |
| Cooper, William | Haris, Lucinda | 2, July 1844 | RCH |
| Cooper, William | Hollowell, Caroline | 11, July 1847 | RCH |
| Cooper, William W. | Tucker, Mary E. | 29, June 1835 | RCH |
| Coopers, John | Winters, Sally | 1837 | RCH |
| Cooplen, Isaac | B---, Ruth | 23, Sept 1819 | RCH |
| Coors, Heinrich | Stuewe, Maria | 7, Dec. 1848 | B |
| Copeland, Willis | Meader, Amanda | 8, Oct. 1846 | RCH |
| Coppin, Edward | Norton, Malissa | 26, May 1842 | RCH |
| Coppin, Joseph | King, Sarah | 12, Apr. 1842 | RCH |
| Coppin, Joseph | Cusick, Mary Ellen | 18, Mar. 1848 | RCH |
| Coppin, William | Roberts, Mary | 18, Sept 1846 | RCH |
| Coprey, Lewis | Divine, Margaret | 28, May 1849 | D |
| Corban, William | Hey, Ann | 23, Mar. 1819 | RCH |
| Corben, Edwin | Taylor, Anna M. | 22, Feb. 1849 | D |
| Corbin, Henry | Drake, Lydia | 30, Apr. 1844 | RCH |
| Corbin, John | Peterson, Mary | 26, May 1833 | RCH |
| Corbin, John | Gardner, Sophia | 30, May 1844 | RCH |
| Corbley, | Mills, Mary | 11, June 1818 | RCH |
| Corbly, Newton | Crosby, Matilda | 27, Feb. 1834 | RCH |
| Corboy, Patrick | Farmer, Mary Lucinda | 3, Oct. 1841 | BB |
| Corcoran, Andrew | Molloy, Elisabeth | 30, Oct. 1843 | BB |
| Corcoran, Paul | Killoran, Julia | 29, Jan. 1849 | BB |
| Cord, Charles R. | Sutton, Deborah | 25, Mar. 1849 | RCH |
| Cordell, Calvin | Burr, Orvelia | 6, Aug. 1843 | RCH |
| Cordery, Michael | Jones, Philena | 11, July 1844 | RCH |
| Cordes, Dietrich | Kleinschmidt, Doroth | 14, Dec. 1847 | F |
| Cordes, Friedrich | Gaberding, Sophia | 31, Aug. 1848 | G |
| Cordes, Gerhard | Sonderhaus, Anna M. | 25, Nov. 1840 | FF |
| Cordesmann, H. Jos. | Elsmann, Francisca | 4, Feb. 1840 | FF |
| Cordmann, Benjamin | Wright, Mary Jane | 25, Oct. 1848 | RCH |
| Cordry, John | Curtis, Nancy | 2, July 1842 | RCH |
| Corell, Johan | Peiser, Dorothea | 18, Mar. 1849 | G |
| Corey, John | Gorth, Rufina | 27, Dec. 1844 | RCH |
| Corlein, William H. | Yearing, Harriet | 20, Nov. 1848 | RCH |
| Cormick, John H. | Foster, Caroline | 27, Apr. 1848 | RCH |
| Cormyny, John | Grove, Mary | 29, Jan. 1837 | RCH |
| Cornelius, Charles | Broaday, Martha | 5, Feb. 1844 | RCH |
| Cornelius, James | McMannus, Rebecca | 19, Apr. 1846 | RCH |
| Cornelius, James | Goudy, Ruthamy | 25, Dec. 1849 | RCH |

| Grooms | Brides | Date of Marriage | Code |
|--------|--------|------------------|------|
| ****** | ****** | **** ** ******** | **** |
| Cornelius, Lorenz | Leinsemann, Magdal. | 25, Dec. 1849 | A |
| Cornell, William | Gaston, Martha | 13, Mar. 1847 | RCH |
| Cornelle, Louis | Stanger, Caroline | 19, June 1849 | G |
| Cornelly, Granville | Connor, Harriet | 11, Oct. 1832 | RCH |
| Cornish, Joseph | Jones, Sarah | 30, May 1833 | RCH |
| Correl, Johan | Wagner, Catharine | 6, Sept 1846 | G |
| Corrigan, William | Bailey, Eliza | 3, June 1824 | RCH |
| Corwain, Henry | Maddox, Margaret | 15, Apr. 1819 | RCH |
| Corwein, George | Rust, Margaretha | 13, Apr. 1847 | C |
| Corwin, Benjamin | Stockman, Maria | 18, Nov. 1832 | RCH |
| Corwin, Daniel W. | Lowring, Harriet | 17, Jan. 1838 | RCH |
| Corwin, Erastus | Reynolds, Susan | 19, Mar. 1846 | RCH |
| Corwin, Henry | Cooper, Louise | 18, Jan. 1837 | RCH |
| Corwin, Samuel | Fnell, Amelia | 21, Nov. 1841 | RCH |
| Cory, James M. | Stagg, Elisabeth Ann | 14, Aug. 1818 | RCH |
| Cory, Jonathan L. | Ross, Hetty | 8, June 1820 | RCH |
| Cosberline, | Miller, Mary | 1, Jan. 1827 | RCH |
| Cosby, David | Lyons, Hannah J. | 8, Feb. 1849 | RCH |
| Cosby, Samuel Mills | Cosby, Elisabeth | 21, Jan. 1841 | RCH |
| Cosby, William | Bray, Martha | 20, Sept 1840 | RCH |
| Cosden, William | Holland, Sarah Jane | 16, Jan. 1842 | RCH |
| Cosgrove, John N. | Gardner, Susan | 31, Dec. 1844 | RCH |
| Cosgrove, Otaway J. | Fitzgerald, Cath. | 7, Feb. 1842 | BB |
| Cosgrove, Thomas | Quinn, Margaret | 11, June 1843 | BB |
| Coss, James | Lee, Susan | 26, Feb. 1846 | RCH |
| Coss, James | Smith, Margaret | 8, Aug. 1847 | RCH |
| Costelli, Constantin | Moriano, M Magdalena | 10, June 1841 | FF |
| Costello, Anthony | Schniveley, Mary A. | 25, June 1848 | BB |
| Costello, Thomas | Reynolds, Mary Ann | 5, Sept 1846 | RCH |
| Costieman, John | Bird, Doshia Ann | 2, Feb. 1836 | RCH |
| Coston, Thomas | Burns, Mary Ann | 22, Dec. 1841 | RCH |
| Cotes, Benjamin F. | Godfrey, Ann | 4, Apr. 1836 | RCH |
| Cottam, Richard | Rolef, Mary Elisabet | 30, Apr. 1844 | RCH |
| Cotter, Bernard | Snier, Theresa | 24, June 1849 | RCH |
| Cotteral, George | Brown, | Sept 1844 | RCH |
| Cottle, John | Ames, Catharine | 15, Dec. 1849 | RCH |
| Cottle, Peter | Goudy, Catharine | 7, Oct. 1824 | RCH |
| Cottle, Rodman | Benson, Mary Jane | 3, Apr. 1846 | RCH |
| Cottman, Thomas | Dunlap, Lanza | 10, Apr. 1836 | RCH |
| Cotton, Israel | Kertenon, Nancy | 26, Feb. 1818 | RCH |
| Cotton, Richard | Ladley, Lydia Ann | 23, Sept 1841 | RCH |
| Cotton, William | Budd, Mary Ann | 28, Nov. 1844 | RCH |
| Cottrell, George W. | McLelland, Elisabeth | 29, Oct. 1848 | RCH |
| Cotts, John | Gibson, Arietta | 6, Dec. 1848 | RCH |
| Cotty, William | Leeds, Elisabeth | 1, Mar. 1849 | RCH |
| Couch, Chancey | McDaniel, Nancy Jane | 26, Jan. 1835 | RCH |
| Coughlin, Daniel | Laughlin, Prisilla | 26, Jan. 1820 | RCH |
| Coughlin, Jeremiah | Cronin, Ellen | 6, Apr. 1845 | BB |
| Coughlin, John | Calkin, Mary F. | 29, Oct. 1843 | BB |
| Coughlin, William | Ingle, Sarah Jane | 11, Jan. 1848 | RCH |
| Coughlin, William | Andreae, Elis. (Mrs) | 13, July 1849 | BB |
| Coulson, Edward | Smith, Maria | 24, Dec. 1846 | RCH |
| Coulson, Thomas | Bascoe, Margaret | 27, July 1836 | RCH |
| Coulson, William | Nightengale, Ann | 25, May 1842 | RCH |
| Coulter, Henry | Thompson, Elisabeth | 17, June 1847 | RCH |
| Coulter, William | Loveday, Susan | 5, Apr. 1838 | RCH |
| Cousins, James | Ralls, Sarah A. | 24, Aug. 1847 | RCH |
| Cousins, Samuel | Hailstock, Julia | 27, Oct. 1840 | RCH |
| Couts, John | Whitaker, Jane Lee | 26, July 1832 | RCH |
| Coutz, George | Taylor, Elisabeth | 12, May 1841 | RCH |
| Couvin, Erastus | Gray, Jane | 20, June 1839 | RCH |
| Couzins, Jacob | Williamson, Elis. | 6, May 1832 | RCH |
| Coval, Willis | Mueller, Elisabeth | 10, Aug. 1842 | RCH |
| Covall, T. | Goldtrap, Nancy | 12, Dec. 1835 | RCH |
| Coverdale, Matthew | Jinkins, Deborah | 20, Apr. 1822 | RCH |
| Covert, George | Bogart, Mary Ann | 25, Sept 1847 | RCH |
| Covert, John | McManama, Malinda | 31, Aug. 1842 | RCH |
| Cowan, Humphrey | Fulcher, Martha | 10, Sept 1847 | RCH |
| Cowan, Terry | Rare, Margaret | 27, Nov. 1836 | RCH |
| Cowan, William | Ward, Sophia | 15, Mar. 1822 | RCH |
| Cowel, Samuel | Harney, Harriet | 16, June 1836 | RCH |

| Grooms ****** | Brides ****** | Date of Marriage **** ** ******** | Code **** |
|---|---|---|---|
| Cowender, Alexander | McGurr, Maria | 7, Jan. 1824 | RCH |
| Cowgwill, Madison | Campbell, Elis. Jane | 15, June 1847 | RCH |
| Cowing, Ewing | Alston, Mary Jane | 18, Aug. 1847 | RCH |
| Cox, | Connucan, Susannah | 8, Jan. 1824 | RCH |
| Cox, | Wilkens, Elisabeth | 11, Feb. 1836 | RCH |
| Cox, Aaron | Crane, Rebecca | 11, Mar. 1841 | RCH |
| Cox, Abial | McDonald, Elisabeth | 26, July 1821 | RCH |
| Cox, Alexander | Hawkins, Sarah Ann | 27, May 1841 | RCH |
| Cox, Alexander | Turner, Martha J. | 30, June 1844 | RCH |
| Cox, Andrew | Maphet, Margaret | 25, Mar. 1824 | RCH |
| Cox, Charles B. | Tuttle, Abigail | 9, Apr. 1839 | RCH |
| Cox, David | Crawford, Sarah | 13, Oct. 1843 | RCH |
| Cox, Griffin | Gates, Susan | 19, July 1838 | RCH |
| Cox, Hiram | Chamberlin, Sarah | 7, May 1846 | BB |
| Cox, James | Tanner, Caroline | 28, Apr. 1825 | RCH |
| Cox, James | Megrew, | Sept 1844 | RCH |
| Cox, John | Smith, Lucy Ann | 14, Aug. 1838 | RCH |
| Cox, John | Bartlett, Hannah | 19, Sept 1841 | RCH |
| Cox, John F. | Sutton, Ellen | 25, Sept 1848 | RCH |
| Cox, John M. | Walker, Bulah | 2, Feb. 1834 | RCH |
| Cox, Jonathan | Patterson, Mary | 23, Mar. 1849 | RCH |
| Cox, Meridith | Scogin, Ruth | 27, Dec. 1832 | RCH |
| Cox, Oliver | Higbee, Elisabeth | 12, June 1849 | RCH |
| Cox, Robertson | Camieon, Nancy | 18, Aug. 1825 | RCH |
| Cox, Thomas | Connueton, Jane | 28, Nov. 1835 | RCH |
| Cox, Thomas J. | Davis, Maria | 1, June 1840 | RCH |
| Cox, Thompson | Patterson, Susan | 18, Aug. 1844 | RCH |
| Cox, Tunis | Satler, Sarah | 5, Apr. 1842 | RCH |
| Coy, John | Coy, Sarah | 23, Sept 1838 | RCH |
| Coy, Robert | Smith, Laura | 24, Feb. 1848 | RCH |
| Coyle, Edward | Holcomb, Amanda M. | 8, Nov. 1846 | BB |
| Coyne, Thomas | McGervy, Joanne | 6, Sept 1849 | GG |
| Cozort, David | Addis, Rebecca | 25, May 1834 | RCH |
| Crabb, Henry | Allen, Alley | 1, Apr. 1846 | RCH |
| Crabrelle, Christian | Kendrix, A. | 29, Mar. 1838 | RCH |
| Craft, James | Applegate, Rebecca | 27, May 1847 | RCH |
| Cragan, John | VanDyke, Mary Ann | 5, July 1835 | RCH |
| Craig, George | Blackwell, Mary | 22, May 1849 | RCH |
| Craig, James C. | Douglas, Sarah Jane | 22, Oct. 1840 | RCH |
| Craig, James H. | Burnside, Eliza Jane | 7, May 1848 | RCH |
| Craig, Johnson | Pringle, Isabella | 27, Sept 1841 | RCH |
| Craig, Peter | Ewing, Charity | 20, Oct. 1838 | RCH |
| Craig, Robert | Howard, Margaret | 16, Dec. 1848 | RCH |
| Craig, Samuel | Carr, Sarah | 5, June 1849 | RCH |
| Crail, Thomas J. | Magdala, Mary | 4, Aug. 1836 | RCH |
| Crain, Alfred | Ludlow, Henrietta | 22, Nov. 1848 | RCH |
| Crain, David | Stewart, M Catharine | 8, July 1847 | RCH |
| Crain, Ebenezer | Curry, Mary Ann | 21, Nov. 1837 | RCH |
| Crain, George C. | Boughman, Reuben | 3, Nov. 1833 | RCH |
| Crain, John M. | Mahan, Sarah | 30, Sept 1843 | RCH |
| Crain, Jonathan | Ricker, Catharine | 6, Apr. 1843 | RCH |
| Crain, William | Springer, Polly Ann | 10, May 1835 | RCH |
| Crambert, Georg | Hoeckmann, Anna M. | 28, Sept 1835 | FF |
| Cramer, Anton | Heidaker, Catharina | 8, Jan. 1835 | FF |
| Cramer, Friedrich | Meyer, Maria | 9, May 1843 | AA |
| Cramer, George | Hollenshade, Cathar. | 11, Sept 1849 | RCH |
| Cramer, Heinrich | Handmann, Catharine | 27, Dec. 1847 | G |
| Crampton, Henry | Andrews, Mary | 12, July 1826 | RCH |
| Cranc, Jeremiah | Millard, Elisabeth A | 14, Nov. 1837 | RCH |
| Crandel, Solomon | Smith, Malinda | 26, Dec. 1822 | RCH |
| Crane, Benjamin | Armstrong, Casander | 8, May 1842 | RCH |
| Crane, Ebenezer | Lavowe, Mary | 13, Dec. 1832 | RCH |
| Crane, John | Jones, Mary E. | 6, June 1844 | RCH |
| Crane, John M. | Harper, Sarah | 28, Dec. 1837 | RCH |
| Crane, Patrick | Gouldrick, Ellen | 18, July 1844 | RCH |
| Crane, Thomas | Coleman, Mary | 6, July 1848 | BB |
| Crane, Thristen | Owens, Ann | 25, May 1820 | RCH |
| Crane, Uriah | Hamna, Caroline | 8, Sept 1836 | RCH |
| Crane, William | Anderson, Catharine | 6, July 1826 | RCH |
| Cranmer, Thomas | Muck, Barbara | 15, June 1849 | RCH |
| Cranston, Adoniram | Fulmer, Catharine | 8, Nov. 1846 | RCH |

| Grooms ***** | Brides ***** | Date of Marriage **** ** ******** | Code **** |
|---|---|---|---|
| Craow, Asahel | Sob, Sarah | 12, Apr. 1833 | RCH |
| Crary, Alonzo | Palmer, Mary | 12, Apr. 1842 | RCH |
| Crary, John M. | Sargent, Mary | 12, Apr. 1833 | RCH |
| Crary, Samuel | Cox, Elisabeth | 27, Nov. 1844 | RCH |
| Crary, Silas | Ripley, Susan | 7, Dec. 1848 | RCH |
| Craven, | Markland, Cinthia | 21, Jan. 1819 | RCH |
| Craven, Cushun | Mulford, Harriet P. | 14, Sept 1820 | RCH |
| Craven, George | ----, Jane | 26, June 1834 | RCH |
| Craven, Harmon | Martin, Nancy | 24, Dec. 1841 | RCH |
| Craven, John | Bean, Ellen | 14, Apr. 1834 | RCH |
| Crawford, Charles | Campbell, Ann | 30, Jan. 1847 | RCH |
| Crawford, E. | McCleese, Henrietta | 28, Nov. 1849 | RCH |
| Crawford, Job. | Denny, Sarah | 16, Mar. 1823 | RCH |
| Crawford, John | Bradford, Mary Jane | 26, Aug. 1845 | RCH |
| Crawford, John A. | Arthur, Mary | 28, Mar. 1826 | RCH |
| Crawford, Levi | Hamilton, Anna M. | 1, Dec. 1845 | RCH |
| Crawford, Robert | Davis, Elisabeth | 1, Aug. 1842 | RCH |
| Crawford, Thomas | Williamson, Elisabet | 24, Sept 1848 | RCH |
| Crawford, William | Kennedy, Elisabeth | 18, Aug. 1842 | RCH |
| Crawford, William | Willets, Alice | 4, Oct. 1846 | RCH |
| Crawford, William | McPherson, Mary Jane | 19, Sept 1848 | RCH |
| Crawford, William | Smith, Rosanna | 20, Feb. 1849 | GG |
| Crawl, Peter W. | Smotherman, Jane | 1, Apr. 1841 | RCH |
| Cray, Nicolaus | Barker, Nancy | 15, Aug. 1833 | RCH |
| Creasser, | Thornton, Mary A. | 28, Mar. 1849 | RCH |
| Creasser, Thomas | Rider, Mary Ann | 9, Nov. 1844 | RCH |
| Credo, Bernard | Prey, Mary | 29, Dec. 1836 | RCH |
| Creger, Peter | Nemyer, Rebecca | 29, Sept 1847 | RCH |
| Creighton, Thomas | Francisco, Jane | 11, Aug. 1846 | RCH |
| Creighton, William | Goshorn, Lorena | 30, Sept 1843 | RCH |
| Crelow, Samuel | Hinton, Elisabeth | 7, Dec. 1835 | RCH |
| Crench, John | Flinchpaugh, Hannah | 20, Oct. 1843 | RCH |
| Creogh, John | Williamson, Emily | Nov. 1849 | RCH |
| Creppel, Frederick | Bird, Margaret | 4, Mar. 1846 | RCH |
| Crew, | Bowen, Mary Jane | 31, Aug. 1849 | RCH |
| Crew, Thomas | Hand, Elisabeth | 15, Dec. 1844 | RCH |
| Criager, John | Apgar, Amelia | 22, Dec. 1836 | RCH |
| Crichton, Andrew | McCoy, Virginia Ann | 27, May 1844 | RCH |
| Crigni, Michael | Berenfery, Mary | 5, Nov. 1848 | II |
| Criman, W.A. | Branson, | 24, Nov. 1831 | RCH |
| Crippen, Abraham | Jones, Julia Ann | 22, Oct. 1844 | RCH |
| Crippen, William G. | Crosby, Eleanor | 8, Apr. 1841 | RCH |
| Crist, Cyrenus | Bennet, Celinda | 25, Mar. 1834 | RCH |
| Crist, Ebenezer | Terwillegar, Sarah | 2, Oct. 1842 | RCH |
| Crist, Edward | Robertson, Mary A. | 21, Apr. 1849 | RCH |
| Crist, Elias | Black, Sarah | 27, May 1841 | RCH |
| Crist, Jacob F. | Betts, Sarah | 3, Oct. 1832 | RCH |
| Crist, Moses | Yoast, Margaret | 3, Jan. 1833 | RCH |
| Critchfield, Joshua | Hitchens, Ruth | 7, Sept 1820 | RCH |
| Crittenden, George W | Stewart, Susan | 16, Nov. 1835 | RCH |
| Croh, Heinrich | Klein, Wilhelmina | 4, Aug. 1835 | FF |
| Croker, William | McGillion, Anna | 27, Feb. 1848 | BB |
| Cronan, Cornelius | Walsh, Joann | 30, Dec. 1849 | GG |
| Cronan, Dennis | Butler, Ellen | 15, Sept 1844 | BB |
| Cronan, Timothy | O'Donnell, Mary | 8, Dec. 1840 | BB |
| Crone, Asa | Smith, Mary | 25, Jan. 1842 | RCH |
| Cronin, Patrick | Mahoney, Margaret | 5, Sept 1846 | RCH |
| Cronin, Timothy | White, Margaret | 26, Aug. 1849 | BB |
| Crook, Christopher | Bowser, Louise | 16, Oct. 1833 | RCH |
| Crookshank, E.D. | Lincoln, Mary | 4, Apr. 1833 | RCH |
| Crookshank, George | Fauver, Elisabeth | 21, May 1843 | RCH |
| Cropper, Cyrus | Busheart, Nancy | 4, Mar. 1819 | RCH |
| Cropsey, Andrew | Harrington, Mary J. | 21, Apr. 1847 | RCH |
| Crosby, Joshua E. | Stibbs, Sarah Ann | 2, June 1836 | RCH |
| Crosby, Rufus | Rains, Elizabeth | 30, July 1848 | RCH |
| Crosley, | Corbly, Elisabeth | 7, May 1818 | RCH |
| Crosley, John | King, Elisabeth | 8, Oct. 1845 | RCH |
| Crosley, Josiah | Jones, Julia Ann | 9, May 1844 | RCH |
| Crosley, Richmond | Beheimer, Glarwina | 12, Apr. 1846 | RCH |
| Cross, Charles | Whiteside, Louise | 17, June 1834 | RCH |
| Cross, Jacob | Thacker, Elisabeth | 15, Dec. 1833 | RCH |

| Grooms<br>***** | Brides<br>***** | Date of Marriage<br>**** ** ******** | Code<br>**** |
|---|---|---|---|
| Cross, Joshua | Hole, Martha | 12, Sept 1819 | RCH |
| Cross, Noah | Rau---, Catharine | 12, Apr. 1833 | RCH |
| Cross, Oliver | Botkin, Nancy | 14, Jan. 1834 | RCH |
| Cross, William | Green, Sarah | 9, Jan. 1821 | RCH |
| Cross, William | Miller, Mary A. | 17, Dec. 1837 | RCH |
| Crossin, Henry | Bland, Bridget | 3, Sept 1848 | BB |
| Crossman, Peter | Howard, Catharine | 28, Aug. 1844 | RCH |
| Crossmann, Lewis | Patton, Elizabeth | 8, Oct. 1846 | RCH |
| Crouse, Charles | Hampe, Louise | 24, Aug. 1836 | RCH |
| Crowder, John | Searcy, Pocahontis | 30, Mar. 1846 | RCH |
| Crowell, Archable | Wess, Susan | 23, Oct. 1823 | RCH |
| Crowell, Benjamin | Creech, Margaret | 25, Jan. 1827 | RCH |
| Crowell, John | Morris, Jane | 13, Dec. 1835 | RCH |
| Crowell, John | Spahr, Emily | 28, Oct. 1846 | RCH |
| Crowell, Nelson | McHenry, Susannah | 9, Dec. 1847 | RCH |
| Crowell, William | Thacker, Catharine | 18, May 1831 | RCH |
| Crowen, Anthony | McClean, Bridget | 30, Apr. 1843 | BB |
| Crowin, Richard M. | Quinton, M. Elis. | 15, Feb. 1842 | RCH |
| Crowley, Daniel | Malone, Catharine | 16, Sept 1849 | BB |
| Crowley, Daniel | O'Mahoney, Mary | 18, Nov. 1849 | BB |
| Crowley, Henry | Kaufmann, Jeannette | 29, Dec. 1845 | G |
| Crozier, | Enyart, Abjah | 14, June 1818 | RCH |
| Cruel, Joseph Rand. | Spruel, J. | 8, Dec. 1841 | BB |
| Crues, James H. | Crane, Catharine | 17, July 1834 | RCH |
| Cruise, John | Moores, Margaret | 8, Nov. 1848 | RCH |
| Cruise, Robert | Kealey, Jane | 11, July 1847 | BB |
| Crummet, Thomas | Whitford, Hester Ann | Oct. 1844 | RCH |
| Crummins, J. | Newton, Joanne H. | 6, Jan. 1845 | BB |
| Crump, Francis Hein. | Moormann, Elisabeth | 5, Jan. 1836 | FF |
| Cruser, Aaron | Varness, Mary Ann | 2, May 1833 | RCH |
| Cryer, Edwin | Alexander, Mary Jane | 6, July 1843 | RCH |
| Cryer, Thomas | Morten, Charlotte | 15, Apr. 1849 | RCH |
| Cryer, William | Harrison, Nelly | 2, Feb. 1843 | RCH |
| Cryne, Thomas | Gilday, Ellen | 15, Apr. 1849 | GG |
| Cuder, Samuel | Avenger, Catharine | 8, Feb. 1826 | RCH |
| Cuique, Michael | Bergenseng, Mary | 11, Oct. 1848 | RCH |
| Culker, Heinrich | Scrive, Clara | 23, Jan. 1838 | FF |
| Cullam, James | Silvers, Betsey | 6, Jan. 1825 | RCH |
| Cullen, Thomas | Cass, Bridget | 14, Sept 1849 | RCH |
| Cullen, Thomas | Connelly, Mary | 8, July 1849 | BB |
| Cullin, Edward | Wing, Catharine | 10, Aug. 1842 | RCH |
| Cullom, George | Applegate, Malvina | 15, Sept 1833 | RCH |
| Cullom, Reuben | Goudy, Emily | 25, Nov. 1832 | RCH |
| Cullum, Allen G. | Smith, Elisabeth | 23, Apr. 1835 | RCH |
| Cullum, George | Stevens, Jaen | 28, Jan. 1847 | RCH |
| Cullum, George | Winship, Eliza Jane | 26, Dec. 1847 | RCH |
| Cullum, Thomas | Akers, | 15, Aug. 1839 | RCH |
| Culpeper, Hardy | Bills, Mary | 29, July 1818 | RCH |
| Culshaw, Josephus | Belanger, Phebe | 28, Feb. 1833 | RCH |
| Culvert, Orrin | Sharrer, Elisabeth | 20, Dec. 1841 | RCH |
| Cumberland, Martin | French, Anna | 27, Dec. 1817 | RCH |
| Cumming, James | Delap, Lucinda | 8, Mar. 1836 | RCH |
| Cumming, John | Graham, Mary Ann | 12, July 1821 | RCH |
| Cummings, Caleb P. | Campton, Cynthia | 1, Feb. 1842 | RCH |
| Cummings, George | Campbell, Rebecca | 6, May 1847 | RCH |
| Cummings, James | Cain, Mary | 31, May 1849 | RCH |
| Cummins, Adam | ----, Margaret | Sept 1836 | RCH |
| Cummins, Alexander | Freeman, Lavina | 28, Sept 1848 | RCH |
| Cummins, James | Morrey, Mary Alice | 31, Mar. 1846 | RCH |
| Cummins, John S. | Carpenter, Olive | 16, Oct. 1836 | RCH |
| Cummins, Patrick | Dugan, Mary Ann | 9, Jan. 1849 | BB |
| Cummins, William | Ellison, Martha | 2, Nov. 1842 | RCH |
| Cummon, John | Gibson, | 9, Nov. 1824 | RCH |
| Cunenberg, Heinrich | Trempe, Elisabeth | 11, Feb. 1840 | FF |
| Cuney, Richard Rowl. | Miller, Clarissa | 7, Apr. 1829 | I |
| Cunningham, Arthur | Goldtrap, Mary | 4, Mar. 1819 | RCH |
| Cunningham, Frederic | Taylor, Mary Jane | 10, Aug. 1845 | RCH |
| Cunningham, Frederic | McDonald, Sarah | 30, July 1846 | RCH |
| Cunningham, James | Rosbrough, Elisabeth | 28, Dec. 1820 | RCH |
| Cunningham, James | Fosdick, Harriet | 5, Sept 1846 | RCH |
| Cunningham, Jesse | Baxter, Jane | 16, June 1825 | RCH |

| Grooms | Brides | Date of Marriage | Code |
|--------|--------|------------------|------|
| ****** | ****** | **** ** ******** | **** |
| Cunningham, John | Fry, Lucinda J. | 14, Aug. 1842 | RCH |
| Cunningham, John | Letter, Eleanor | Jan. 1843 | RCH |
| Cunningham, Joseph | Long, Mary Ann | 2, Jan. 1846 | RCH |
| Cunningham, Michael | Rourke, Catharine | 22, July 1844 | BB |
| Cunningham, Richard | Miovett, Sarah | 8, Jan. 1832 | RCH |
| Cunningham, Samuel | ----, M. | 30, Dec. 1819 | RCH |
| Cunningham, William | Price, Sarah | 14, Dec. 1823 | RCH |
| Cunningham, William | Flanagan, Margaret | 4, May 1849 | GG |
| Cuny, Henry A. | Gilmore, Margaret | 8, Aug. 1838 | RCH |
| Cure, Herman Heinr. | Gausepohl, Maria A. | 7, Jan. 1836 | FF |
| Curle, Herman | Borgeding, Agnes | 23, Nov. 1845 | AA |
| Curley, George | Robinson, Sarah | 25, Dec. 1844 | RCH |
| Curley, Luke | Conlan, Sarah | 10, Feb. 1846 | BB |
| Currey, Thomas H. | Secrist, Lydia Ann | 4, May 1848 | RCH |
| Curry, Isaac | Robinson, Mary A. | 31, Dec. 1848 | RCH |
| Curry, James | Breen, Sarah | 12, Sept 1844 | RCH |
| Curry, Ross | West, Sarah | 9, July 1842 | RCH |
| Curry, Ross | Brown, Mary | 13, May 1847 | RCH |
| Curtis George | Kemper, Ellen | 8, Nov. 1843 | RCH |
| Curtis, | Potter, Eunice | 28, Aug. 1823 | RCH |
| Curtis, Benjamin | Howlings, Amanda | 4, May 1844 | RCH |
| Curtis, Herschel | Schatzmann, Julia | 22, Jan. 1846 | RCH |
| Curtis, Isham | Mosy, Rachel | 14, Sept 1820 | RCH |
| Curtis, John | Tibbets, Mary | 2, Sept 1819 | RCH |
| Curtis, John | Clark, Hester Ann | 25, Jan. 1846 | RCH |
| Curtis, John G. | Longworth, Elizabeth | 15, Oct. 1848 | I |
| Curtis, Joseph | Jackson, Maria | 13, Oct. 1846 | RCH |
| Curtis, Lucius | Brown, Frances | 5, Sept 1847 | RCH |
| Curtis, Nathan | Clark, Ellen | 20, Sept 1842 | RCH |
| Curtis, Richard | Gibbs, Mary | 16, June 1836 | RCH |
| Curtis, Stephen B. | Ferrel, Ophelia | 23, June 1833 | RCH |
| Curtis, William | Addis, Elisabeth | 11, Nov. 1819 | RCH |
| Curtis, William G. | Miller, Elisabeth | 1, Aug. 1849 | RCH |
| Curton, Anthony | Rude, Catharine | 10, Dec. 1844 | RCH |
| Curtwing, Joseph | Taylor, Ann S. | 21, Apr. 1835 | RCH |
| Curwood, John | Turner, Phebe | 5, Oct. 1845 | RCH |
| Cushing, David | Lamb, Sarah | 28, Sept 1846 | RCH |
| Cushing, John | Brady, Catharine | 5, July 1846 | BB |
| Cusick, Thomas J. | Byron, Jane | 14, Sept 1839 | BB |
| Custard, John | Chambers, Margaret | 21, May 1818 | RCH |
| Cutaiar, Joseph | Stephens, Helena | 12, June 1839 | BB |
| Cutler, Willard | Fitch, Mary Jane | 1, Dec. 1845 | RCH |
| Cutter, Alpheus | Riddle, Martha Jane | 18, Aug. 1847 | RCH |
| Cutter, Robert | Conn, Maria | 8, Nov. 1826 | RCH |
| Cyler, George | Hammond, Sophia | 11, Sept 1841 | RCH |
| D---, Charles D. | Lyman, Sarah P. | 12, June 1832 | I |
| D---, George | Robinson, Elisabeth | 31, Jan. 1826 | RCH |
| D---, John | Whitaker, Elisabeth | 25, Jan. 1827 | RCH |
| D---, Robert T. | Haines, Elizabeth S. | 30, Nov. 1825 | RCH |
| D---, William | Sweet, Louise Ann | 12, Nov. 1826 | RCH |
| D---, William | Brooks, Lucinda | 24, June 1838 | RCH |
| Dackey, Henry | Walker, Rebecca | 24, Dec. 1844 | RCH |
| Dackey, John | Armstrong, Sarah | 1, Aug. 1843 | RCH |
| Dacy, Timothy | Buckley, Julia | 27, Apr. 1849 | RCH |
| Daeger, Peter | Wilkin, Elisabeth | 26, Nov. 1843 | G |
| Daenzer, Johan | Schrass, Margaretha | 10, Aug. 1841 | FF |
| Daeters, Heinrich | Ebers, Anna Rosalia | 26, Nov. 1839 | FF |
| Dagner, Louis | VordemHolz, Anna M.L | 27, Oct. 1849 | F |
| Dahlmann, Herman F. | Buckshorn, Johanna | 14, June 1849 | G |
| Dahmann, J. Heinrich | Moormann, Catharine | 30, Apr. 1844 | FF |
| Dahmann, Joseph | Rockes, M. Elisabeth | 17, May 1842 | FF |
| Dahmann, Wilhelm | Huelsmann, Elisabeth | 28, Jan. 1846 | FF |
| Daiker, Severin | Weishar, Clara | 2, Aug. 1849 | RCH |
| Dail, Robert | Daily, Mary | 21, May 1842 | RCH |
| Dailey, Benjamin | Rue, Louise | 10, Feb. 1836 | RCH |
| Dailey, Christopher | Coval, Maria | 27, Dec. 1849 | RCH |
| Daily, John | Ryan, Ann | 15, Aug. 1847 | GG |
| Daily, Thomas | Caughlan, Honora | 19, Dec. 1849 | GG |
| Dair, John F. | Martin, Julia Ann | 8, Aug. 1832 | RCH |
| Daisey, Thomas | Martin, Rachel | 31, Jan. 1822 | RCH |

| Grooms<br>****** | Brides<br>****** | Date of Marriage<br>**** ** ******** | Code<br>**** |
|---|---|---|---|
| Dakes, Jacob P. | John, Syble Jane | 6, Nov. 1836 | RCH |
| Dale, Daniel | Kemball, Elisabeth | 5, June 1834 | RCH |
| Dale, Jeremiah | Ross, Hannah | 22, Oct. 1829 | I |
| Dale, Richard C. | Mason, Sophia | 2, Mar. 1819 | RCH |
| Dale, Sidney | Lockmann, Emeline | 3, Oct. 1843 | RCH |
| Dales, George W. | Butler, Prudence | 15, Jan. 1841 | RCH |
| Daley, William | Williams, Margaret | 10, Oct. 1847 | GG |
| Dallar, Friedrich | Kiel, Theresa | 8, June 1840 | FF |
| Dallas, Michael | Garman, Elisabeth | 1, May 1849 | RCH |
| Dallheim, Jacob | Bonegel, Barbara | 21, Apr. 1846 | EE |
| Dallinghaus, Ferd. | Rolfes, Carolina | 4, July 1847 | AA |
| Dallmann, Rudolph | Grothaus, Charlotte | 5, July 1848 | F |
| Dallyhide, William | Byrne, Sarah | 23, Oct. 1842 | RCH |
| Dalrymple, Andrew | Stewart, Mary | 8, Dec. 1846 | RCH |
| Dalton, Ellis | Shields, Mary | 7, June 1847 | RCH |
| Dalton, James | Clancy, Julia | 3, July 1842 | BB |
| Dalton, James | Halley, Loretha | 16, Mar. 1848 | RCH |
| Dalton, John | Smith, Lavina | 15, Aug. 1843 | RCH |
| Dalton, Lawrence | Ryan, Frances | 23, Oct. 1837 | RCH |
| Daly, David | Faudree, Hannah | 13, Aug. 1818 | RCH |
| Daly, Erastus H. | Knowlton, R. | 10, Aug. 1834 | RCH |
| Daly, Ira W. | Rood, Polly | 9, Mar. 1820 | RCH |
| Daly, Patrick | Armstrong, Catharine | 20, Feb. 1848 | BB |
| Damm, John | Zoller, Dorothea | 25, June 1846 | RCH |
| Dana, Joseph | Johnson, Martha | 31, May 1836 | RCH |
| Danbury, D. | Foster, Catharine | 2, Jan. 1824 | RCH |
| Dandridge, Alexander | Pendleton, Martha E. | 4, May 1843 | I |
| Danford, Joseph | Joyce, Rachel | 9, May 1838 | RCH |
| Danforth, Nathan | Fowler, Margaret | 28, June 1821 | RCH |
| Danglade, J.L.A. | Siebenthal, Anna | 18, Feb. 1824 | RCH |
| Daniel, Heinrich | Vetter, Catharine | 17, Apr. 1843 | G |
| Daniel, John | Huniston, Mary E. | 24, Aug. 1844 | RCH |
| Daniel, Richard | Comerford, Bridget | 13, Mar. 1848 | BB |
| Daniels, Hector | O'Neill, Julia | 18, Nov. 1846 | RCH |
| Daniels, Michael O. | Holsted, Ann | 5, Feb. 1833 | RCH |
| Daniels, Stacey | Rush, Margaret | 27, Dec. 1849 | RCH |
| Danks, Joseph | Rees, Harriet | 20, June 1835 | RCH |
| Dannettel, H. Conrad | Kattau, Lucia D. | 18, Mar. 1840 | F |
| Dannettel, Heinrich | Ortmann, Caroline | 26, Jan. 1843 | F |
| Dannettel, Heinrich | Dolbeling, Carolina | 9, Oct. 1849 | B |
| Dannettel, Johan | Langhorst, Sophia | 21, Apr. 1846 | F |
| Dannettel, R. | Kattan, Louise | 16, Apr. 1849 | RCH |
| Dans, Herman | Lowenstein, Jenette | 9, Aug. 1849 | RCH |
| Dansbach, Jacob | Bauenschwender, Phil | 20, Sept 1849 | EE |
| Danser, Smith | Wile, Lucretia | 10, July 1842 | RCH |
| Danson, James | Kitchel, Huldy | 4, Nov. 1834 | RCH |
| Dappeth, Henry S. | Rau---, Frances | 8, Jan. 1839 | RCH |
| Darby, Levi | Crossly, Sarah | June 1825 | RCH |
| Darby, Thomas | Wood, Mary Jane | 22, Mar. 1848 | RCH |
| Darby, William | Smith, Nancy | 18, Feb. 1834 | RCH |
| Dardio, Christian | Muller, Catharine | 25, Mar. 1849 | RCH |
| Darhaw, Samuel | ----, Susannah | 10, Nov. 1821 | RCH |
| Dark, John | Brooks, Nancy Ann | 21, Mar. 1847 | RCH |
| Darlage, Herman G. | Niermeier, Caroline | 17, Sept 1846 | B |
| Darlage, Johan H. | Helmkamp, Catharine | 12, Dec. 1844 | F |
| Darling, George | McCollough, Maria | 9, Apr. 1849 | RCH |
| Darling, John | Gillet, Cynthia | 27, Sept 1842 | RCH |
| Darling, Lucius | Ward, Malina Ann | 27, Feb. 1833 | RCH |
| Darling, Thomas | Anderson, Margaret | 3, May 1836 | RCH |
| Darr, Michael | Hill, Elisabeth | 1, June 1847 | RCH |
| Darrell, Daniel | Westcott, Phebe | 16, Mar. 1842 | RCH |
| Darrell, Thomas | French, Caroline | 25, Nov. 1841 | RCH |
| Darrington, William | Dean, Sarah | 29, May 1842 | RCH |
| Darrow, Milton | Bennett, Josephine | 5, Oct. 1848 | RCH |
| Dart, Diedat | Malfort, Anna | 27, Apr. 1823 | RCH |
| Dart, George | Gross, Julia | 29, Sept 1841 | RCH |
| Darton, Richard | Irwin, Sarah | 7, Sept 1841 | RCH |
| Darum, Daniel | Ries, Henrietta | 29, Apr. 1846 | G |
| Dasenbrock, Bernard | Doerger, Anna Maria | 17, May 1846 | AA |
| Dasey, John | Lighten, Catharine | 18, Feb. 1849 | GG |
| Dater, Adam | Mattel, Charlotte | 2, Apr. 1846 | A |

| Grooms<br>***** | Brides<br>***** | Date of Marriage<br>**** ** ******** | Code<br>**** |
|---|---|---|---|
| Dater, Gebhard | Fein, Louise | 16, Mar. 1843 | A |
| Dater, Johan | Harsch, Cath. Elis. | 31, Oct. 1844 | A |
| Daters, Heinrich | Elerns, Sinners Rose | 26, Mar. 1839 | RCH |
| Daugherty, Bernard | McBride, Cecilia | 26, July 1849 | RCH |
| Daugherty, John | Ross, Margaret | 23, Oct. 1845 | RCH |
| Daum, Michael | Heinrich, Margaretha | 29, Aug. 1848 | EE |
| Dauth, Friedrich | Linginger, Eleanora | 30, July 1848 | C |
| Davee, Isaac | Fishvater, Eleanor | 18, Dec. 1834 | RCH |
| Davenport, Cyrus | Doan, Ruth | 25, Nov. 1832 | RCH |
| Davenport, Cyrus | Stevens, Mary Ann | 8, July 1847 | RCH |
| Davenport, D.G. | McDannel, Lettice | 19, Oct. 1846 | RCH |
| Davenport, Darius | Barr, Emma C. | 18, Apr. 1820 | RCH |
| Davenport, Darius | Wooley, Sarah | 25, Dec. 1834 | RCH |
| Daveson, Daniel | Blackleach, Jane | 24, Dec. 1845 | RCH |
| Davey, Isaac | Hicks, Elisabeth | 11, Dec. 1833 | RCH |
| David, Daniel T. | Pierson, Martha W. | 11, Jan. 1837 | RCH |
| David, Joseph | Kahn, Sarah | 22, Sept 1847 | RCH |
| David, Theobald | Lambers, M. Gesina | 1, Mar. 1849 | II |
| Davidmeyer, Conrad | Korte, Catharine M. | 18, Jan. 1842 | FF |
| Davidson, Alfred | Charters, Anna L. | 19, Nov. 1837 | RCH |
| Davidson, Edward | Pierce, Cordelia | 2, Aug. 1848 | RCH |
| Davidson, John | Madison, Mary | 2, Jan. 1843 | RCH |
| Davidson, John | Sidle, Henrietta | 29, Mar. 1843 | I |
| Davidson, Michael | Hosbrook, Maria | 12, Dec. 1833 | RCH |
| Davidson, Thomas | Ward, Maria | 20, Nov. 1834 | RCH |
| Davidson, William | Hill, Nancy | 11, May 1837 | RCH |
| Davie, M.C. | Wood, Frances M. | 13, Apr. 1836 | RCH |
| Davies, John | Collins, Ann | 7, July 1849 | RCH |
| Davies, John D. | Jones, Mary | 2, June 1849 | RCH |
| Davis, | Waller, Tharissa | 29, Nov. 1822 | RCH |
| Davis, | Sutton, Rebecca P. | 11, May 1823 | RCH |
| Davis, Abraham | Morris, Elisabeth | 12, Aug. 1819 | RCH |
| Davis, Adam | Hossert, Margaretha | 26, Oct. 1835 | FF |
| Davis, Alexander | Low, Susan | 26, Sept 1837 | RCH |
| Davis, Benjamin | Carson, Mary | 13, Dec. 1834 | RCH |
| Davis, Benjamin | Cahoun, Rhoda | 6, Aug. 1837 | RCH |
| Davis, Benjamin | McLean, Amanda J. | 11, Oct. 1846 | RCH |
| Davis, Charles | Boyer, Fanny | 30, Aug. 1841 | RCH |
| Davis, Charles J. | Mornson, Mariah | Apr. 1835 | RCH |
| Davis, Corbly | Link, Elisabeth Jane | 14, July 1843 | RCH |
| Davis, Daniel D. | Belch, Julzan | 14, Aug. 1832 | RCH |
| Davis, Daniel M. | Edwards, Mary | 19, Apr. 1842 | RCH |
| Davis, David | Harris, Nancy | 1, June 1839 | RCH |
| Davis, David | Clark, Priscilla | 27, Mar. 1844 | RCH |
| Davis, Edward | Lapp, Mary Ann | 23, Aug. 1847 | RCH |
| Davis, Eli | Howard, Peggy | 17, Aug. 1826 | RCH |
| Davis, Enoch | Freckling, Elisabeth | 15, Apr. 1835 | RCH |
| Davis, Eparimondas | Griffing, Louise | 15, May 1842 | RCH |
| Davis, George | Baldwin, Perlina | 26, Nov. 1843 | RCH |
| Davis, George | Child, Elisabeth | 14, May 1846 | RCH |
| Davis, George | Barman, Elisabeth | 27, July 1847 | RCH |
| Davis, Heinrich | Mangold, Cath. Elis. | 23, Jan. 1840 | F |
| Davis, Henry | Brooks, Harriet A. | 26, Dec. 1833 | RCH |
| Davis, Henry F. | West, Ellen Maria | 3, Oct. 1832 | I |
| Davis, Hiram | Evans, Phebe | 11, Apr. 1844 | RCH |
| Davis, Hiram | Kettlewell, Rachel | 27, Dec. 1846 | RCH |
| Davis, Horace | Williams, Elisabeth | 12, Aug. 1848 | RCH |
| Davis, Isaac | Small, Jessie | 7, Jan. 1846 | RCH |
| Davis, Jacob | Kilwell, Emily | 10, Apr. 1842 | RCH |
| Davis, James | McHaly, Sarah | 28, Jan. 1822 | RCH |
| Davis, James | Webb, Ann | 9, Apr. 1825 | RCH |
| Davis, James | Lockhard, Jennette | June 1835 | RCH |
| Davis, James | Dean, Mary | 28, Oct. 1837 | RCH |
| Davis, James | Wright, Christina | Mar. 1843 | RCH |
| Davis, James | Tarmon, Martha | 9, May 1844 | RCH |
| Davis, James | Allen, Barbara E. | 14, May 1846 | RCH |
| Davis, Jesse E. | Allen, Mary F. | 14, Nov. 1847 | RCH |
| Davis, Job | Lippencott, Mary | 23, Jan. 1847 | RCH |
| Davis, John | Chambers, H. | 30, Oct. 1824 | RCH |
| Davis, John | Plunket, Margaret | 9, Sept 1837 | RCH |
| Davis, John B. | Batchelder, Elisabet | 19, July 1846 | RCH |

| Grooms ****** | Brides ****** | Date of Marriage **** ** ******** | Code **** |
|---|---|---|---|
| Davis, John H. | Ashman, Ann H. | 22, Jan. 1849 | RCH |
| Davis, John J. | Shiner, Barbara | 22, June 1837 | RCH |
| Davis, John S. | Hasselmann, Elisabet | 24, Feb. 1848 | RCH |
| Davis, Jonathan | McMahon, Phoebe | 3, Nov. 1834 | RCH |
| Davis, Joseph | Parrott, Jane | 9, May 1849 | RCH |
| Davis, Levi | Swanger, Sarah | 6, May 1846 | RCH |
| Davis, Louis | McGuire, Catharine | 22, Feb. 1844 | RCH |
| Davis, Oliver | Potter, Elizabeth | 11, Oct. 1846 | RCH |
| Davis, Philipp | Burke, Isabella | 12, Aug. 1847 | GG |
| Davis, Richard | Ball, Rebecca | 3, Nov. 1836 | RCH |
| Davis, Richard | Skillman, Catharine | 15, Apr. 1847 | RCH |
| Davis, Robert | Rosebery, Harriet | 26, June 1833 | RCH |
| Davis, Robert | Marriott, Elisabeth | 13, Sept 1846 | RCH |
| Davis, Robert | VandeVere, Mary | 29, Aug. 1848 | RCH |
| Davis, Samuel | Williams, Jane | 16, Jan. 1823 | RCH |
| Davis, Samuel | ----, Levina | 16, Dec. 1824 | RCH |
| Davis, Samuel | Boyd, Lydia | 9, Oct. 1834 | RCH |
| Davis, Samuel | Coleman, Hannah | 19, Nov. 1835 | RCH |
| Davis, Samuel | Clark, Rohanna | 28, Feb. 1842 | RCH |
| Davis, Samuel | Duvall, Elisabeth | 1, Jan. 1843 | RCH |
| Davis, Thomas | Hays, Elisabeth | 25, Dec. 1844 | RCH |
| Davis, William | Davis, Ann | 28, Mar. 1822 | RCH |
| Davis, William | Lupton, Mary | 2, Apr. 1822 | RCH |
| Davis, William | Moore, Sarah | 29, Apr. 1834 | RCH |
| Davis, William | Birch, Catharine | 3, Dec. 1844 | RCH |
| Davis, William | O'Donnell, Mary | 30, Mar. 1842 | BB |
| Davis, William | Flumigan, Mary Jane | 3, Mar. 1848 | RCH |
| Davis, William | Shields, Catharine J | 20, Sept 1848 | RCH |
| Davis, William | Hahn, Elisabeth | 16, June 1849 | RCH |
| Davishead, Alexander | Mayhead, Mary C. | 5, Mar. 1822 | RCH |
| Davison, Andrew | Kitchell, Rebecca | 26, May 1842 | RCH |
| Davison, Benjamin | Keys, Anna M. | 6, Oct. 1842 | RCH |
| Davison, James | Crary, Mary | 13, Feb. 1844 | RCH |
| Davison, John | Smith, Margaret | 12, July 1847 | RCH |
| Davison, William | Cooper, Phebe | 18, Oct. 1841 | RCH |
| Davitt, John | Oppenlander, Wilhel. | 25, Dec. 1849 | RCH |
| Davy, Isaac | Greenham, Mary | 28, Nov. 1824 | RCH |
| Dawson, | Robbins, Mary Ann | 23, Sept 1823 | RCH |
| Dawson, James | Thompson, Elisabeth | 30, Oct. 1823 | RCH |
| Dawson, Jeremiah | Loring, Catharine | 6, May 1838 | RCH |
| Dawson, Leroy | Spunauger, Elisabeth | 19, Aug. 1849 | RCH |
| Dawson, Moses | Evans, Sarah | 6, Oct. 1836 | RCH |
| Dawson, Nicolaus | Coulter, Margaret | 16, Oct. 1833 | RCH |
| Dawson, Stephen | Wright, Martha | 27, July 1844 | RCH |
| Dawson, Thomas | Oliver, Eliza | 22, Dec. 1830 | I |
| Dawson, Thomas | Nash, Julia | 17, May 1844 | RCH |
| Dawson, William | Hastings, Alice | 24, Oct. 1843 | RCH |
| Day, Aaron C. | Debolt, Rachel | 9, Mar. 1820 | RCH |
| Day, Allen | Frakes, Ruth | 25, July 1844 | RCH |
| Day, Amacy | Seining, Lucy | 23, Nov. 1832 | RCH |
| Day, James | Brooks, Elisabeth | 14, Oct. 1835 | RCH |
| Day, John | Whetzel, Lavina | 27, Dec. 1821 | RCH |
| Day, John | Goss, Enevoet | 11, Sept 1834 | RCH |
| Day, John | Hays, Margaret | 22, July 1849 | BB |
| Day, Lambert | Hoffmann, Louise | 11, June 1843 | F |
| Day, Lewis | Tait, Georgiana | 31, Oct. 1833 | RCH |
| Day, Nicolaus | Kennedy, Ellen | 29, Oct. 1848 | RCH |
| Day, Robert | Symmes, Ann | 18, Jan. 1849 | RCH |
| Day, Robert | Donnelly, Rosanna | 10, June 1849 | RCH |
| Day, Samuel | Stephens, Elisabeth | 19, June 1819 | RCH |
| Day, Samuel | Sharp, Ann | 1, Mar. 1827 | RCH |
| Day, Samuel | Pearce, Harriet | 9, Aug. 1846 | RCH |
| Day, Stephen | Lefebre, Catharine | 11, Feb. 1827 | RCH |
| Day, William | Ault, Elizabeth | 3, Oct. 1847 | RCH |
| Dayton, Luther | Strong, Phebe | 14, Apr. 1842 | RCH |
| Dayton, Sherman | Duvall, Susan | 13, Apr. 1848 | RCH |
| Dayton, Walter | Page, Martha | 5, Apr. 1844 | RCH |
| DeCamp, | Ward, Elisabeth | 19, Jan. 1826 | RCH |
| DeCamp, Daniel | Lee, Eleanor | 20, July 1835 | RCH |
| DeCamp, Henry | Sargent, Mary Jane | 10, Mar. 1836 | RCH |
| DeCamp, James | Evans, Joanna | 17, May 1838 | RCH |

| Grooms | Brides | Date of Marriage | Code |
|--------|--------|------------------|------|
| ****** | ****** | **** ** ******** | **** |
| DeCamp, Job | Jacobs, Margaret | 2, May 1844 | RCH |
| DeCamp, John | Hildreth, Serena | 2, June 1844 | RCH |
| DeCamp, Lambert | Folger, Elisabeth | 5, June 1844 | RCH |
| DeCamp, Mahlen | Mills, Malinda | 24, Feb. 1839 | RCH |
| DeCamp, Mahlon | Gibson, Elisabeth | 9, Oct. 1845 | RCH |
| DeColproter, Zaevi T | Wilham, Mary | 14, June 1832 | RCH |
| DeFerris, Ephraim | Moore, Elisa | 12, Nov. 1833 | RCH |
| DeGraw, Abraham | Cornelius, Mary | 29, Dec. 1841 | RCH |
| DeGraw, Wesley | Auter, Caroline | 18, July 1849 | RCH |
| DeHaven, Alpheus | Tilison, Didamus | 23, Aug. 1832 | RCH |
| DeHogel, Wilhelm | Ruschan, Elisabeth | 26, Nov. 1839 | FF |
| DeLargy, James | Brennan, Margaret | 7, Jan. 1845 | RCH |
| DePugh, William | Keelon, Matilda G. | 12, June 1843 | RCH |
| DeRodes, Joseph H. | Rolison, Elisabeth | 3, July 1849 | RCH |
| DeSerisy, Edward | Cox, Margaret | 10, July 1818 | RCH |
| DeSerisy, Louis | Reid, Margaret | 27, Aug. 1845 | RCH |
| DeSeusy, Melancthon | Hays, Frances Ann | 14, Jan. 1848 | RCH |
| DeSilver, John | Geiger, Lavina | 26, Nov. 1844 | RCH |
| DeVrooe, Francis | Thery, Susan | 5, Dec. 1849 | RCH |
| DeVroun, Johan | Klatte, Maria Angela | 3, Nov. 1840 | FF |
| DeWitt, Zachariah | Pitman, Rebecca | 14, Jan. 1832 | RCH |
| DeYoung, Moses | Jacobs, Isabella | 7, Apr. 1848 | RCH |
| Dean, Charles | Isgrigg, Elisabeth | 15, Mar. 1849 | RCH |
| Dean, Edward | Dean, Comforth | 30, Dec. 1824 | RCH |
| Dean, Henry A. | Senior, Emma | 9, Aug. 1848 | RCH |
| Dean, Jackson | Sloten, Harriet | 7, Jan. 1847 | RCH |
| Dean, James | Lang, Louise | 26, Jan. 1846 | RCH |
| Dean, Joseph | Howarth, Orpha | 31, Jan. 1846 | RCH |
| Dean, Levi | Paine, Alvina | 3, Mar. 1849 | RCH |
| Dean, Noble | Wilkinson, Mary | 4, July 1833 | RCH |
| Dean, Noble | VanSicklen, Mary Ann | 11, June 1841 | RCH |
| Dean, Thomas | Page, Margaret L. | 21, July 1839 | RCH |
| Dean, Thomas | Rynear, Elisabeth | 21, July 1844 | RCH |
| Deans, John W. | Wescott, Nancy A. | 7, Dec. 1837 | RCH |
| Deary, William | Bodwell, Jane | 3, June 1825 | RCH |
| Debeno, Anton | Koler, Magdalena | 3, Sept 1846 | EE |
| Debolt, Andrew | Segmann, Susan | 8, Aug. 1822 | RCH |
| Debolt, Archibald | ----, Elisabeth | 25, Dec. 1835 | RCH |
| Debolt, Henry | Gerard, Rachel | 22, Oct. 1818 | RCH |
| Debolt, Henry | Muchmore, Rebecca | 28, May 1835 | RCH |
| Debzell, Alexander | Todhunter, Harriet A | 27, Oct. 1835 | RCH |
| Decaitrit, John H. | Hening, Elisabeth | 22, Apr. 1822 | RCH |
| Decatur, Thomas | Swaik, Mary Ann | 13, June 1846 | RCH |
| Dechinger, Wilibald | Brandt, Theresa | 26, Oct. 1847 | EE |
| Deck, Christian | Lang, Elisabeth | 21, Oct. 1847 | F |
| Deck, Heinrich | Ei, Barbara | 5, Jan. 1847 | C |
| Deck, James | Brown, Ann | 21, Apr. 1824 | RCH |
| Decker, Adolph | Pierson, Hester A. | 23, Dec. 1841 | RCH |
| Decker, Bernard | Enneking, Catharine | 11, Jan. 1842 | FF |
| Decker, Christoph | Beniks, Maria | 11, May 1839 | FF |
| Decker, Francis | Snyder, Catharine | 9, Nov. 1837 | RCH |
| Decker, Francis | Brink, Maria | 12, July 1842 | FF |
| Decker, George | Chenenet, Ann | 24, Apr. 1848 | GG |
| Decker, H. Heinrich | Schildmeyer, Maria A | 7, May 1842 | FF |
| Decker, James | Jackson, Elizabeth | 2, Dec. 1849 | RCH |
| Decker, Johan Heinr. | Grubens, Maria Engel | 28, Oct. 1846 | C |
| Decker, Joseph | Muensler, Susanna | 14, May 1848 | A |
| Decker, Josiah | Whittberger, Susan | 9, May 1822 | RCH |
| Decker, Lorenz | Whittaker, Wilhelmin | 25, Oct. 1846 | B |
| Decker, Stewart | Reed, Elisabeth E. | 21, Mar. 1833 | RCH |
| Decynin, Jacob | Meyer, Catharina | 17, Oct. 1839 | G |
| Deders, J. Dietrich | Reckers, Louisa | 25, Nov. 1848 | II |
| Deegin, Alonzo | Steele, Malinda | 16, Sept 1847 | RCH |
| Deeters, Abraham | Pellewessel, Agnes | 20, Apr. 1836 | FF |
| Deeters, Reuben | Faulkner, Hagar | 28, June 1846 | RCH |
| Deevit, G.V.H. | Pearson, Mary | 19, May 1819 | RCH |
| Defrus, T. | Gebles, Josephina | 2, Nov. 1847 | EE |
| Dehne, Carl | Brokamp, Lisette | 10, Oct. 1843 | AA |
| Dehner, Daniel | Koenig, Rosina | 25, Nov. 1845 | FF |
| Dehoyd, Wilhelm | Bushan, Elisabeth | 26, Mar. 1839 | RCH |
| Deibkes, Stephen | Read, Catharine | 15, May 1834 | RCH |

| Grooms<br>***** | Brides<br>***** | Date of Marriage<br>**** ** ******** | Code<br>**** |
|---|---|---|---|
| Deie, Johan W. | Nagel, Carolina | 15, Oct. 1848 | EE |
| Deierlein, Friedrich | Maur, Friedricka | 19, Nov. 1849 | C |
| Deising, Friedrich | Meyers, Cath. Sophia | 10, Dec. 1847 | F |
| Deiss, Gottlieb | Kline, Christina | 15, Feb. 1844 | RCH |
| Deitsch, Julius | Lyens, Johanna | 21, Aug. 1849 | RCH |
| Deitz, Henry | Dick, Mary | 6, Dec. 1841 | RCH |
| Deitzer, Heinrich | Keizer, Catharine | 24, Nov. 1848 | RCH |
| Deken, Herman Heinr. | Otten, M. Elisabeth | 2, Nov. 1841 | FF |
| Dekot, Gerhard J. | Moeller, M. Euphemia | 26, May 1846 | AA |
| Deland, Henry | Annis, Margaret | 26, Aug. 1848 | RCH |
| Delaney, Bernard | Gallagher, Mary | 18, June 1846 | BB |
| Delaney, Daniel | Burns, Mary | 25, Oct. 1849 | GG |
| Delaney, Isaac | Clary, Julia Ann | 13, Sept 1837 | RCH |
| Delaney, Jacob | Montgomery, Elis. | 17, Sept 1839 | RCH |
| Delaney, John | Herron, Ellen | 18, June 1849 | GG |
| Delaney, Joseph | Wharm, Elisabeth | 11, Apr. 1837 | RCH |
| Delaney, Patrick | Ennis, Mary | 30, Nov. 1848 | GG |
| Delaney, Thomas | ----, Catharine | 30, Sept 1849 | GG |
| Delargy, Hugh | McGraw, Bridget | 30, Jan. 1838 | RCH |
| Delaware, John | Griffin, Hester | 8, Nov. 1842 | RCH |
| Delfendahl, Johan H. | Gaetje, Adelheid | 29, Nov. 1848 | F |
| Delkhisen, Joseph | Sinebery, M. Cath. | 16, Feb. 1836 | FF |
| Dell, Jacob | Knapp, Wilhelmina | 20, Dec. 1836 | RCH |
| Deller, Peter | Scherer, Elisabeth | 21, Jan. 1849 | EE |
| Dellerman, Andreas | Pitroff, Anna | 26, Aug. 1849 | EE |
| Dellinghunt, William | Jolly, Emeline | 7, Sept 1841 | RCH |
| Delorac, Michael | Whitlock, Rebecca | 7, Dec. 1843 | RCH |
| Delthoster, Heinrich | Eggers, Angela | 17, Aug. 1848 | B |
| Delworth, John | Parry, Mary | 15, Dec. 1841 | D |
| Delzell, Alexander | Deaty, Amanda | 29, Dec. 1844 | RCH |
| Demand, Mathias | Langesher, Francisca | 2, Feb. 1847 | EE |
| Demarce, William | King, Orilda Ann | 16, Feb. 1846 | RCH |
| Demarest, Charles | Wilson, Susan | 1, May 1847 | RCH |
| Demass, Peter | Stewart, Elisabeth | 28, July 1822 | RCH |
| Demeoris, Jacob | Parks, Rebecca | 23, Feb. 1819 | RCH |
| Demire, Richard | Jenkins, Jane | 22, Jan. 1822 | RCH |
| Demler, Johan | Unschuld, Catharine | 4, July 1848 | A |
| Dempsey, Thomas | Bailey, Eleanor | 28, Sept 1847 | RCH |
| Demsey, Dennis | McDaniel, Mary | 15, Aug. 1847 | GG |
| Demuth, Jacob | Haf, Friedricka | 12, June 1848 | EE |
| Denham, | Tibbetts, | 11, Sept 1834 | RCH |
| Denham, Robert | Holliday, Ida | 7, July 1844 | RCH |
| Deninger, Clemens | Meyer, Adelheid | 2, Aug. 1838 | FF |
| Denis, Martin | Burcker, Veronica | 7, July 1835 | FF |
| Deniston, James | Gaddis, Isabella | 1, July 1847 | RCH |
| Deniston, Thompson | Miller, Mary | 2, Sept 1824 | RCH |
| Denk, Valentin | Ries, Elisabeth | 24, Apr. 1849 | CC |
| Denman, Edmund | Lyon, Elvira | 4, June 1846 | RCH |
| Denman, John | Meeker, Isabella | 29, Oct. 1843 | RCH |
| Denman, Nathaniel | Snyder, Catharine | 20, Nov. 1842 | RCH |
| Denn, James | McCormick, Elisabeth | 29, Oct. 1848 | RCH |
| Dennerlien, Wolf. | Gebhardt, Catharine | 4, Feb. 1847 | G |
| Dennhart, Valentine | Kuhn, Sophia Barbara | 1, Nov. 1842 | A |
| Dennich, Johan | Hutmacher, Magdalena | 24, Sept 1846 | C |
| Dennies, Johan H. | Macke, Anna Maria | 27, Jan. 1846 | EE |
| Dennig, Johan | Ressler, Louisa | 9, June 1844 | FF |
| Dennis, Alonzo | Snell, Sarah C. | 16, Aug. 1849 | RCH |
| Dennis, Andrew | Williams, Patience | 15, Apr. 1835 | RCH |
| Dennis, Benjamin | Beeson, Charlotte | 31, Jan. 1838 | I |
| Dennis, James | Sharer, Sarah | 14, Feb. 1844 | RCH |
| Dennis, John | Mallally, Elisabeth | 7, Nov. 1845 | RCH |
| Dennis, Joseph | Vogelbach, Barbara | 28, Jan. 1845 | FF |
| Dennison, Joshua | Gress, Margaret | 1, May 1848 | RCH |
| Denniston, James | Barnes, Frances J. | 4, Oct. 1842 | RCH |
| Denny, Henry Hall | Conroy, Elisabeth | 21, June 1843 | BB |
| Denny, Joseph J. | Card, Elisabeth | 19, Sept 1837 | RCH |
| Denochweiler, Anton | Harth, Jacobina | 25, Nov. 1849 | C |
| Densing, James | Arnoll, Sarah | 21, Mar. 1839 | RCH |
| Dent, John T. | Smith, A. (Mrs) | 4, Oct. 1832 | RCH |
| Dentinger, Francis | Huber, Magdalena | 6, May 1847 | AA |
| Denver, James | Molloy, Ethel | 18, June 1848 | GG |

| Grooms<br>****** | Brides<br>****** | Date of Marriage<br>**** ** ******** | Code<br>**** |
|---|---|---|---|
| Denz, Adolph | Biegelmeyer, Julia | 12, Apr. 1849 | FF |
| Depeker, Friedrich | Landwehr, Maria | 11, Jan. 1838 | FF |
| Depenbrock, Rudolph | Klus, Anna Maria | 21, Oct. 1849 | AA |
| Depew, John | Robinson, Sarah | 25, Oct. 1846 | RCH |
| Depke, John Henry | Berenz, Catharine | 25, Apr. 1837 | F |
| Deple, Andrew | Erkenbrecher, Maria | 22, May 1843 | RCH |
| Deppe, Friedrich | Verlhus, Maria | 3, Feb. 1835 | FF |
| Deppe, Heinrich | Hockagen, Maria | 9, May 1837 | F |
| Deppe, Herman | Huenefeld, Elisabeth | 3, June 1845 | F |
| Depper, Christian | Hellmann, Anna M. | 29, Jan. 1839 | FF |
| Depre, Eberhard | Schmidt, M Elisabeth | 6, June 1843 | C |
| Derden, Duden E. | Kamlin, Catharine | 24, May 1836 | RCH |
| Dereol, George | Hatten, Louise | 11, May 1833 | RCH |
| Derig, Joseph | Musser, Caroline | 20, Mar. 1843 | RCH |
| Derkes, Joseph | Oligers, Margaretha | 7, Jan. 1840 | FF |
| Dernnen, Nathaniel | Taulman, Mary | 20, Nov. 1833 | RCH |
| Derrick, Frederick | Galvin, Mary Ann | 7, Apr. 1849 | BB |
| Derrick, Frederick | Galvin, Mary A. | 7, Apr. 1849 | BB |
| Desbury, George | Baeyorten, Mary Ann | 7, Sept 1834 | RCH |
| Deserens, Henry | Murdock, Mary Ann | 15, May 1836 | RCH |
| Dessen, Henry | Ninkas, Louise | 31, Oct. 1844 | A |
| Dessert, Joseph | Reinoth, Sophia | 4, July 1844 | AA |
| Dessert, Paul | Aibe, Rosanna | 27, Dec. 1849 | RCH |
| Detatron, Leonhard | Hepp, Barbara | 14, Mar. 1848 | RCH |
| Deters, Francis H. | Kortmann, M. Cath. | 7, Jan. 1846 | FF |
| Deters, Franz Wm. | Redecker, Engel | 14, May 1844 | AA |
| Deters, Johan Heinr. | Luecken, Josephine | 17, Nov. 1844 | FF |
| Dethlehen, Henry | ----, Sophia | 18, Aug. 1835 | RCH |
| Detith, Townsend | Brooks, A. | 4, Nov. 1838 | RCH |
| Detman, George | Mooney, Sarah | 18, Apr. 1839 | RCH |
| Detmer, Casper Hein. | Voske, M. Elisabeth | 19, Sept 1843 | FF |
| Detmering, Friedrich | Bahnkamp, Elisabeth | 19, Oct. 1848 | F |
| Detmering, Heinrich | Portschen, Apollonia | 28, Aug. 1849 | F |
| Detter, Gerhard H. | Schlichte, Margaret | 16, Apr. 1839 | FF |
| Dettermann, Friedric | Poper, Anna Christin | 9, Feb. 1847 | EE |
| Dettmer, Bernard | Liening, Catharina M | 22, Apr. 1841 | FF |
| Dettmer, Joseph | Rusche, Caroline | 19, Oct. 1845 | FF |
| Deuker, Wilhelm | Meyer, Anna | 27, June 1845 | F |
| Deutsch, Bernard | Eckert, Louise | 10, July 1849 | RCH |
| Deutsch, Jacob | Kirchner, Maria E. | 27, Dec. 1845 | RCH |
| Deutsch, Johan Jacob | Kachmer, Maria Eva | 11, Jan. 1846 | AA |
| Deutschmann, John | Dickhaut, A. Elis. | 12, July 1848 | G |
| Devine, James | Geshing, Mary | 27, June 1839 | BB |
| Devine, Jesse | Riser, Mira | 1, Sept 1842 | RCH |
| Devlin, James C. | Treat, Nancy Jane | 10, Jan. 1847 | BB |
| Devoss, David | Watson, Mary Ann | 21, Mar. 1843 | RCH |
| Dewein, Conrad | Kranzer, Catharine | 18, Feb. 1845 | C |
| Dewein, Isaac | Leathers, Mary | 2, July 1835 | RCH |
| Dewsin, George | Ewan, Helena | 20, Sept 1843 | RCH |
| Dick, Abraham | Meyer, Maria | 24, Mar. 1846 | C |
| Dick, Bernard H. | Schloemer, M. Gesina | 14, Oct. 1849 | AA |
| Dick, Christian | Kepken, Catharine | 28, June 1842 | RCH |
| Dick, Georg | Hauck, Anna Catharin | 31, May 1841 | G |
| Dick, George | Ogden, Deddy A. | 27, Feb. 1849 | RCH |
| Dick, James | Ramsay, Mary | 1, Feb. 1843 | RCH |
| Dick, Johan | Hey, Susanna | 1, July 1845 | C |
| Dick, John R. | Grue, Lucinda M. | 5, May 1825 | RCH |
| Dick, Theodor Nick. | Wallhaus, Anna | 19, Feb. 1849 | II |
| Dick, William | Argat, Sarah | 6, Dec. 1841 | RCH |
| Dickbruder, J. Hein. | Hackmann, Lucy Helen | 29, Apr. 1847 | F |
| Dickens, Gustav | Glass, Julia | 18, Sept 1846 | RCH |
| Dickerson, John | Hahn, Mary | 1, Nov. 1834 | RCH |
| Dickerson, John | Gould, Catharine | 26, May 1842 | RCH |
| Dickhaus, Bernard | Husmann, Gertrud | 9, Nov. 1845 | AA |
| Dickhaus, Friedrich | Gosemeyer, Friedrika | 11, May 1847 | AA |
| Dickhaus, Friedrich | Middendorf, Dina | 21, Jan. 1849 | AA |
| Dickhof, Heinrich | Webers, Elisabeth | 25, Nov. 1849 | CC |
| Dickhoff, Gerhard H. | Timmer, Elisabeth | 10, Oct. 1847 | AA |
| Dickhoff, Johan H. | Kipp, Catharine | 8, Jan. 1845 | AA |
| Dickhoff, John | Kipp, Elisabeth | 3, June 1849 | RCH |
| Dickinson, Darius | Cowings, Lydia | 29, July 1848 | RCH |

| Grooms<br>****** | Brides<br>****** | Date of Marriage<br>**** ** ******** | Code<br>**** |
|---|---|---|---|
| Dickinson, Isaiah | Ferguson, Elisabeth | 23, Feb. 1847 | RCH |
| Dickinson, James | Kendall, Sybel | 13, Sept 1837 | RCH |
| Dickmann, Carl Aug. | Kennewig, Johanna J. | 26, Feb. 1849 | F |
| Dickmann, Christian | Schafsdick, Maria E. | 6, Sept 1842 | FF |
| Dickmann, Frank H. | Himmelmeyer, Maria | 9, Jan. 1848 | AA |
| Dickmann, Friedr. H. | Mueller, Margaret E. | 7, Sept 1843 | F |
| Dickmann, Friedrich | Fischer, Elisabeth | 9, Sept 1837 | FF |
| Dickmann, Herman G. | Mohrhaus, Cath. Marg | 4, Sept 1845 | F |
| Dickmann, Johan Bd. | Luers, Anna Maria | 12, Oct. 1847 | AA |
| Dickmann, Johan H. | Kellermann, Anna M. | 10, June 1849 | AA |
| Dickmann, Matthias | Fortmann, Dina | 21, Nov. 1848 | FF |
| Dickmann, Wilhelm | Bolton, Maria | 22, Oct. 1846 | B |
| Dickmeyer, Bernard | Lebbermann, Louise | 8, Jan. 1845 | AA |
| Dickrede, Dietrich | Gossmann, Maria Elis | 16, June 1846 | FF |
| Dicks, David | Ferguson, Mary | 1, Mar. 1843 | RCH |
| Dicks, Isaac | Moore, Sophia | 22, Mar. 1847 | RCH |
| Dickscheid, Wendelin | Schubert, Louise | 1, May 1849 | C |
| Dickson, Edward | Broens, Ellen | 6, Aug. 1839 | RCH |
| Dickson, James | Smith, Mary J. | 26, Nov. 1843 | RCH |
| Dickson, James | Taylor, Caroline T. | 5, Nov. 1846 | I |
| Dickson, Samuel | Blackburn, Martha | 26, Feb. 1834 | RCH |
| Dickson, Thomas | Graham, Hannah | 28, June 1843 | RCH |
| Dickson, Thomas | Weinders, Ann | 25, May 1848 | RCH |
| Diebel, Peter | Meiners, Gertrud | 7, Jan. 1849 | EE |
| Diebold, Carl | Stoll, Louise | 9, Sept 1849 | A |
| Diebold, Michael | Wurtz, Regina | 4, Feb. 1845 | AA |
| Diebolt, Conrad | Bader, Margaretha | 3, Nov. 1842 | FF |
| Diebolt, Lawrence | Zenk, Barbara | 27, Sept 1847 | EE |
| Diechaus, Herman | Otte, Louise | 21, Dec. 1848 | F |
| Dieck, Johan Georg | Wissmann, Margaretha | 31, Oct. 1847 | C |
| Dieck, Louis | Windeler, Maria Anna | 26, Sept 1848 | G |
| Dieckmann, Franz H. | Barlage, Anna Maria | 23, Apr. 1844 | AA |
| Dieckmeyer, Hein. P. | Manns, Louise | 7, Sept 1843 | F |
| Diederichs, Ferdinan | Schnicke, Louise E. | 22, Mar. 1846 | G |
| Diefenbach, Philipp | Eberle, Christina | 15, Aug. 1847 | RCH |
| Diefenbacher, Alex. | Weis, Barbara | 30, Nov. 1844 | RCH |
| Diefendorf, Oliver | Cutter, Caroline | 26, Oct. 1848 | RCH |
| Diehl, Adam | Braun, Agnes | 7, Dec. 1848 | C |
| Diehl, Jacob | Becker, Anna Maria | 23, May 1839 | G |
| Diehl, Jacob | Bechler, Elisabeth | 1, Feb. 1844 | C |
| Diehl, Jacob | Laberheim, Christina | 27, Oct. 1842 | AA |
| Diehm, Francis | Pinngers, Margaret | 24, Apr. 1849 | RCH |
| Diek, Georg | Weiss, Maria | 5, Nov. 1839 | FF |
| Diekely, Joseph | Metzler, Agatha | 3, Aug. 1840 | FF |
| Diekmann, Henry | Geise, Elisabeth | 16, Oct. 1834 | FF |
| Diel, Casper | Gesser, Maria | 29, July 1844 | RCH |
| Diener, Anton | Gindling, Barbara | 3, May 1842 | FF |
| Dierauf, Francis | Fess, Kunigunda | 1, Aug. 1847 | EE |
| Dierfuss, Wendel | Krissinger, Eva | 24, Nov. 1842 | AA |
| Dierker, Dietrich | Dierker, Catharine | 7, May 1848 | FF |
| Dierker, Heinrich | Kluesener, Gertrud | 17, May 1842 | FF |
| Dierkes, Johan Diet. | Nagels, Maria Elis. | 22, Sept 1841 | F |
| Dierking, Georg H. | Kuntz, Maria Marg. | 23, Mar. 1843 | F |
| Diers, Herman H. | Posse, Margaretha | 25, Nov. 1849 | EE |
| Diers, John Henry | Schwepmann, Johanna | 19, June 1849 | RCH |
| Diersmann, Wilhelm H | Amaling, Catharine W | 12, Sept 1844 | F |
| Diester, George | Stuckenberg, Carolin | 16, Jan. 1847 | RCH |
| Dietemeier, Adam | Geiger, Emilia | 30, Apr. 1849 | F |
| Dieting, Friedrich | Drogen, Sophia | 17, Sept 1840 | F |
| Dietmann, Benedict | Bleh, Maria Anna | 19, Aug. 1847 | EE |
| Dietrich, Conrad | Feeher, Susannah | 12, Aug. 1845 | RCH |
| Dietrich, Jacob | Engel, Clara | 25, Nov. 1842 | FF |
| Dietrich, Johan | Heinmann, Anna Maria | 3, Jan. 1846 | RCH |
| Dietrich, Johan H. | Hake, Dorothea W. | 25, June 1846 | F |
| Dietrich, Joseph | Heer, Maria | 5, May 1840 | FF |
| Dietrich, Mathias | First, Catharine | 28, Feb. 1843 | AA |
| Dietsch, William | Bach, Maria | 30, Oct. 1848 | RCH |
| Dietz, Friedrich W. | Wuest, Catharine | 27, Sept 1849 | C |
| Diezer, Mathias | Eveline, Kunigunda | 17, Oct. 1848 | RCH |
| Digby, Theodore | Stone, Frances | 18, Mar. 1847 | RCH |
| Diggin, Louis | Huger, Christina | 17, Dec. 1835 | RCH |

| Grooms<br>****** | Brides<br>****** | Date of Marriage<br>**** ** ******** | Code<br>**** |
|---|---|---|---|
| Dignan, Jeremiah | Crofton, Mary | 9, Sept 1846 | BB |
| Dignan, Timothy | Keough, Mary | 16, Oct. 1841 | BB |
| Dilg, Christian | Runk, Eva Elisabeth | 4, May 1847 | G |
| Dilg, Jacob | Angert, Catharine | 9, Feb. 1847 | EE |
| Dilg, Peter | Story, Catharina | 2, Jan. 1843 | G |
| Dill, John G. | Crisman, Ann | 15, May 1833 | RCH |
| Dill, Richard | Adams, Ann | 31, Dec. 1845 | RCH |
| Dill, Samuel | Knowles, Sarah Ann | 22, Dec. 1842 | RCH |
| Dill, William J. | Smith, Anna F. | 31, Dec. 1849 | RCH |
| Dille, Philipp | Diller, Theresa | 14, Jan. 1845 | AA |
| Dille, Squire | Feast, Mary | 21, Apr. 1818 | RCH |
| Dilley, Henry | Hawkins, Mary | 23, Sept 1833 | RCH |
| Dillhof, Francis | Bohmann, Gertrud | 8, May 1838 | FF |
| Dilling, John | Wurzbacher, Margaret | 28, May 1848 | G |
| Dillinoann, Richard | Dill, Jane | 19, Apr. 1820 | RCH |
| Dilliplim, Joseph | Cullom, Juliana | 3, Nov. 1825 | RCH |
| Dillmann, Adam | Dreyer, Cath. Marg. | 21, Aug. 1844 | A |
| Dillmann, Adam | Dreyer, Catharine | 24, Feb. 1845 | AA |
| Dillmann, Heinrich | Warth, Friedricka | 15, June 1848 | G |
| Dilson, W. Sidney | Chapman, Ellen B. | 11, Nov. 1839 | D |
| Dilts, John M. | Brigman, Catharine | 16, June 1839 | RCH |
| Dimmick, Edward | Richardson, Sarah | 2, July 1834 | RCH |
| Dimock, Edward | Stone, Mary Ann | 20, Sept 1833 | RCH |
| Dimond, Cornelius | Carter, Adelia | 28, Apr. 1846 | RCH |
| Dinge, Matthias | Redelstaffer, Marg. | 13, Aug. 1848 | II |
| Dinger, Joseph | Kraus, Margaretha | 19, Apr. 1849 | EE |
| Dinghausen, Friedric | VordemHolz, Magdalen | 26, Nov. 1846 | G |
| Dingler, Daniel | Koch, Catharine | 18, July 1847 | G |
| Diniar, James | Hoepf, Ursula | 1, May 1849 | HH |
| Dinkelbeihler, John | Schindler, Margaret | 8, Oct. 1846 | RCH |
| Dinkelspeel, Joseph | Lippshig, Caroline | 7, Jan. 1842 | RCH |
| Dinser, Fidel | Schmitt, Catharine | 28, Oct. 1845 | FF |
| Dinser, Martin | Miller, Maria Eva | 24, July 1843 | FF |
| Dinsinon, Samuel | Hall, Sarah | 10, Jan. 1837 | RCH |
| Dinsmore, Jonathan | Powerfield, Rachel | 11, July 1838 | RCH |
| Dipkemper, Francis | Hohncamp, Bernardina | 20, Feb. 1848 | EE |
| Dirauft, Georg | Gast, Margaretha | 16, Jan. 1848 | EE |
| Dirckmann, Bernard | Godemeyer, Maria Ann | 4, Nov. 1841 | FF |
| Dirick, Anton | Andres, Magdalena | 28, Oct. 1845 | AA |
| Dirig, Joseph | Hicks, Mary A. | 19, Dec. 1848 | RCH |
| Dirken, Johan F. | Funke, Elisabeth | 17, Sept 1848 | AA |
| Dirksmeyer, Georg | Wellmann, Maria | 8, Feb. 1842 | FF |
| Dischinger, Jacob | Find, Elisabeth | 7, May 1848 | RCH |
| Dischinger, Raimond | Disterer, Agatha | 25, June 1844 | AA |
| Dismann, Heinrich | Stoerr, Friedricka | 21, May 1844 | AA |
| Disney, David T. | Carter, Sarah | 1, Sept 1825 | RCH |
| Disney, William | Woods, Mary | 8, Apr. 1833 | RCH |
| Disney, William | Wood, Ellen | 12, Mar. 1842 | RCH |
| Diss, Franz Joseph | Wagner, Josephine | 4, Feb. 1845 | AA |
| Dister, George | Amann, Rose | 18, July 1844 | RCH |
| Diston, William L. | Lahmanousky, Anna | 12, Sept 1837 | RCH |
| Ditmars, John | Tigner, Mary Ann | 25, Aug. 1847 | RCH |
| Dittey, Thomas | McCullough, Elisabet | 15, Apr. 1847 | RCH |
| Divelly, James | Ullery, Mary J. | 29, July 1849 | RCH |
| Dively, Isaac | Allbright, Margaret | 23, Feb. 1826 | RCH |
| Diviney, Nelson | Ferris, Cynthia A. | 22, Nov. 1843 | RCH |
| Dix, Heinrich | Erfmann, Regina | 22, May 1849 | RCH |
| Dixon, Charles | Bailey, Sally | 4, Dec. 1849 | RCH |
| Dixon, Charles E. | Armstrong, Elisabeth | 29, Aug. 1843 | BB |
| Dixon, Ethan | Kail, Frances | 2, July 1846 | RCH |
| Dixon, George | Dury, Sarah | 11, Sept 1843 | RCH |
| Dixon, James | Wright, Jane | 9, Feb. 1846 | RCH |
| Dixon, Mordecai | Couch, Esther | 29, Mar. 1846 | RCH |
| Dixon, Richard | Collins, Maria | 1, Feb. 1827 | RCH |
| Do---, Simon | Jacobs, Electa | 5, Sept 1826 | RCH |
| Doach, Lewis | Keller, Maria | 24, Apr. 1834 | RCH |
| Doan, Isaac | Dumphey, Tootella | 29, Nov. 1839 | RCH |
| Doan, Josiah S. | Loomis, Lucretia | 17, Mar. 1836 | RCH |
| Doans, William | Smith, Elisabeth | 20, Jan. 1819 | RCH |
| Dobbel, Heinrich | Ribben, Rosetta | 22, Jan. 1841 | F |
| Dobell, William T. | Hall, Catharine | 25, Dec. 1846 | RCH |

| Grooms | Brides | Date of Marriage | Code |
|--------|--------|------------------|------|
| ****** | ****** | **** ** ******** | **** |
| Dober, William | Reis, Cider | 17, May 1836 | RCH |
| Dobson, Benjamin | Luck, Sarah | 7, Apr. 1847 | RCH |
| Dochter, Thomas J. | Bledsoe, Cynthia A. | 23, Mar. 1848 | RCH |
| Doclsetzch, Franz | Bants, Johanna | 12, Sept 1836 | RCH |
| Dodas, James | Gibbs, Charlotte | 23, Dec. 1840 | RCH |
| Dodd, Aaron G. | Bigelow, Mary | 24, Dec. 1823 | RCH |
| Dodd, Daniel | Newkirk, Elisabeth | 16, Jan. 1842 | RCH |
| Dodd, Jedderthorn | Barge, Elisabeth | 23, Feb. 1836 | RCH |
| Dodd, John | Jennings, Susan | 30, June 1842 | RCH |
| Dodd, Joseph | Smith, Julia Ann | 23, Dec. 1841 | RCH |
| Dodd, Samuel | Cullum, Harriet | 10, June 1844 | RCH |
| Dodd, Thomas | Bennett, Mary | 27, Oct. 1844 | RCH |
| Dodd, Thomas M. | Susan, Adaline | 7, Jan. 1836 | RCH |
| Dodds, | Fulton, Elisabeth | 31, May 1849 | RCH |
| Dodge, Venning | Watson, Caroline | 20, Sept 1842 | RCH |
| Dodson, Charles W. | Bales, Sarah | 13, May 1838 | RCH |
| Dodsworth, Thomas | Outsoby, Sarah Maria | 5, May 1842 | RCH |
| Dodsworth, Thomas | Bean, Susanna | 31, Dec. 1846 | RCH |
| Dodt, Bernard H. | Schulze, Maria Anna | 14, Feb. 1843 | AA |
| Dodt, Johan | Schildmeier, Agnes | 29, Oct. 1848 | CC |
| Dodthage, Wilhelm | Staggenborg, Elis. | 15, Nov. 1846 | FF |
| Dodtmann, Heinrich | Timmelmann, Margaret | 3, May 1836 | FF |
| Doehling, Joseph | Scheiner, Kunigunda | 13, Oct. 1845 | FF |
| Doeker, Francis | Bingmann, Helena | 1, May 1838 | FF |
| Doel, Andreas | Haemmel, Margaretha | 28, Dec. 1840 | FF |
| Doell, Georg | Pfaff, Catharine | 29, Feb. 1848 | EE |
| Doeller, Fried. Aug. | Klein, Maria | 3, July 1848 | B |
| Doeller, Peter | Dreizigacher, Barb. | 31, Jan. 1846 | AA |
| Doelli, Heinrich | Hegen, Theresa | 2, Apr. 1848 | G |
| Doen, Alexander | Iliff, Priscilla | 4, June 1843 | RCH |
| Doepke, Dietrich | Heidner, Dorothea | 8, Feb. 1848 | C |
| Doepke, Friedrich | Kruse, Anna | 8, Mar. 1846 | G |
| Doepke, Johan Heinr. | Haskamp, Anna Marg. | 27, Jan. 1842 | F |
| Doepker, John F. | Klines, Caroline | 1, June 1848 | RCH |
| Doepp, George | Loekers, Kunigunda | 15, Jan. 1846 | RCH |
| Doeppe, Franz | Young, Lena | 12, Oct. 1847 | RCH |
| Doerfer, Georg | Opelt, Elisabeth | 28, Sept 1845 | AA |
| Doerfler, Johan | Endelein, Barbara | 30, Jan. 1849 | EE |
| Doerfler, Joseph | Rentler, Anna M. | 24, Mar. 1842 | RCH |
| Doerger, Johan | Siemer, Maria | 24, Sept 1848 | FF |
| Doering, Charles | McLaughlin, Nancy | 11, Oct. 1843 | RCH |
| Doering, Johan Hein. | Heim, Barbara | 11, Jan. 1842 | FF |
| Doerler, Cornelius | Meyer, Sabina | 25, June 1844 | AA |
| Doermann, Daniel | Huss, Helena | 27, Sept 1845 | RCH |
| Doerner, Johan Hein. | Holtmeier, Maria E. | 16, May 1848 | EE |
| Doerr, Carl | Appel, Kunigunda | 15, Nov. 1846 | G |
| Doerr, Jacob | Keller, Margaretha | 13, June 1848 | A |
| Doerr, Nicolaus | Martin, Christina | 4, May 1843 | AA |
| Doerring, Lawrence | Bosold, Anna Maria | 18, Nov. 1848 | EE |
| Doggett, James | B----, Laura | Sept 1845 | RCH |
| Dohan, James | Boulger, Jane M. | 4, Oct. 1847 | BB |
| Doherty, Anthony | Gibbons, Bridget | 28, Apr. 1847 | GG |
| Doherty, Charles | Glasgow, Ann | 15, Jan. 1849 | GG |
| Doherty, John | Sweeney, Rose | 11, Feb. 1843 | BB |
| Doherty, John | Manning, Sarah | 17, Aug. 1845 | RCH |
| Doherty, Joseph | Smith, Elisabeth | 27, Mar. 1833 | RCH |
| Doherty, William | Dennis, Mary | 17, Oct. 1848 | BB |
| Dohm, Ferdinand | Blumhanf, Louise | 17, July 1848 | C |
| Dohrmann, Friedrich | Wind, Sophia | 27, July 1847 | RCH |
| Dolan, John | Whelan, Margaret | 7, Sept 1845 | BB |
| Dolan, John | Bradley, Sarah Ann | 9, May 1847 | BB |
| Dolan, Michael | Boyce, Mary | 25, Aug. 1847 | RCH |
| Dole, Bernard | Klostermann, Maria | 15, Apr. 1847 | EE |
| Dole, Jonathan | Morris, Maria | 3, Mar. 1835 | RCH |
| Doll, Francis | Baumgartner, Rosina | 3, Oct. 1847 | EE |
| Doll, Jacob | Spies, Rosa | 13, Aug. 1848 | EE |
| Doll, Lazarus | Goetz, Catharine | 27, Feb. 1848 | EE |
| Doll, Matthias | Hund, Victoria | 26, May 1836 | FF |
| Doll, Matthias | Spinner, Catharina | 4, Oct. 1849 | AA |
| Doll, Nicholas | Dups, Magdalena | 1, Feb. 1847 | RCH |
| Dollmann, Herman | Miller, Catharine | 13, Jan. 1845 | AA |

| Grooms ****** | Brides ****** | Date of Marriage **** ** ******** | Code **** |
|---|---|---|---|
| Dollmann, Johan G. | Otten, Gertrud | 21, Feb. 1843 | AA |
| Dollweber, Anton | Baumer, Theresa | 24, Nov. 1846 | AA |
| Doly, James | Reine, Ann | 19, Aug. 1849 | GG |
| Domhoff, Johan Wm. | Bockshorn, M Lisette | 16, Aug. 1849 | G |
| Donahower, Louis | Ashton, Maria | 10, Nov. 1844 | RCH |
| Donalds, Samuel | Parks, Sarah | 4, Apr. 1848 | RCH |
| Donaldson, Francis | Guilford, Anna | 7, Oct. 1846 | RCH |
| Donaldson, George | Guilford, Apollonia | 24, May 1847 | RCH |
| Donaldson, James F. | Harrison, Elisabeth | 1, May 1823 | RCH |
| Donally, Bernard | Stuart, Josephine | 15, Nov. 1845 | RCH |
| Donato, Joseph | Liuirys, Mary | 14, Oct. 1847 | GG |
| Donen, George W. | Wescot, | 15, Feb. 1824 | RCH |
| Doneriael, John | Bailey, Frances | 9, Feb. 1834 | RCH |
| Dones, John | Davis, Mercy | 8, Sept 1843 | RCH |
| Dongas, William | Magnes, Ellen | 29, Nov. 1840 | BB |
| Donicus, Joseph | Sponsel, Magdalena | 14, Oct. 1846 | C |
| Donies, Herman | Darpel, Rosina | 21, Nov. 1847 | AA |
| Donley, John | McGill, Mary | 7, July 1841 | BB |
| Donley, Thomas | Harran, Mary | 4, Feb. 1845 | BB |
| Donne, William H.D. | Noble, Amelia R. | 21, May 1834 | I |
| Donnelly, Anthony | Major, Mary Ellen | 10, June 1849 | GG |
| Donnelly, Cornelius | Murphy, Mary | 18, Mar. 1838 | RCH |
| Donnelly, Edward | Thorp, Catharine | 25, Feb. 1847 | RCH |
| Donnolly, John | Butler, Catharine | 30, Sept 1849 | BB |
| Donnolly, Nicolaus | Walsh, Ellen | 18, Jan. 1843 | BB |
| Donoghue, Daniel | Cavanaugh, Sarah J. | 13, May 1849 | BB |
| Donohue, Charles | Elliott, Sarah | 3, Apr. 1844 | BB |
| Donohue, Charles | Sullivan, Mary | 27, Sept 1846 | GG |
| Donohue, Edward | Brown, Elisabeth | 17, Sept 1836 | RCH |
| Donohue, George | McNelly, Ann | 6, May 1839 | BB |
| Donough, John | Southerland, Susan | 20, Jan. 1849 | RCH |
| Donough, John P. | Mahard, Ester | 3, Nov. 1835 | RCH |
| Donough, Michael | Cassidy, Ellen | 27, Oct. 1843 | BB |
| Donough, Robert | Coleman, Elisabeth | 25, Feb. 1843 | RCH |
| Donovan, Michael | Murphy, Catharine | 28, Aug. 1841 | BB |
| Donsbeck, | Ranenschwender, P. | 20, Sept 1849 | RCH |
| Donvia--, Corydon | Daughty, Rachel | 25, July 1839 | RCH |
| Dooley, James | Flynn, Ann | 20, May 1849 | GG |
| Doolittle, Charles | Fitzpatrick, Mary A. | 21, Dec. 1848 | RCH |
| Doolittle, Samuel | Miles, Sarah | 23, Nov. 1834 | RCH |
| Door, Artemas | Ward, Susan | 21, Feb. 1847 | RCH |
| Dopke, Johan Fried. | Schanker, Margaret | 11, Sept 1849 | RCH |
| Dopkey, Aaron | Murray, | 5, Apr. 1832 | RCH |
| Dopper, Johan Theo. | Hagen, Anna Margaret | 25, Apr. 1848 | EE |
| Doppler, Andreas | Gisler, Maria | 22, May 1837 | FF |
| Doppler, Christian | Woll, Barbara | 31, May 1849 | EE |
| Doppler, Heinrich | Geier, Elisabeth | 17, Aug. 1835 | FF |
| Dor, Christoph | Kopp, Elisabeth | 15, Aug. 1848 | II |
| Doran, James | Carrigan, Elisabeth | 26, Jan. 1834 | RCH |
| Doran, Michael | Weir, Mary Jane | 17, Jan. 1847 | RCH |
| Doranbus, John | Meyer, Mary | Sept 1847 | RCH |
| Dorbecke, Herman H. | Kuhlmann, Anna Maria | 18, Oct. 1846 | FF |
| Dorcherr, Johan | Moormann, Maria Anna | 28, Oct. 1849 | EE |
| Doren, Peter | Hill, Polly | 25, Nov. 1819 | RCH |
| Dorflinger, David | Bonnet, Barbara | 23, Feb. 1841 | FF |
| Doris, James | Manin, Sarah | 30, May 1839 | RCH |
| Dorman, James | Betst, Lydia | 10, Jan. 1822 | RCH |
| Dorman, John C. | Binnett, S. Ann | 4, May 1837 | RCH |
| Dorman, Samuel | Dawson, Susan | 8, May 1846 | RCH |
| Dormann, Heinrich | Schuhmacher, Anna M. | 6, Nov. 1838 | FF |
| Dorn, Baltzar | Clark, Harriet | 20, Nov. 1845 | RCH |
| Dornbrick, Heinrich | Brueggenschmidt, E. | 17, Sept 1848 | EE |
| Dornbusch, Johan Bd. | Mair, Maria Anna | 3, Oct. 1847 | EE |
| Dornseifer, Heinrich | White, Charlotte | 9, Oct. 1847 | RCH |
| Dorr, Philipp | Chertz, Elisabeth | 23, May 1843 | RCH |
| Dorr---, Thomas | Denmann, Rebecca | 11, Jan. 1827 | RCH |
| Dorrell, Michens | King, Rebecca | 8, Aug. 1839 | RCH |
| Dorsch, Johan | Betz, Kunigunda | 16, Sept 1847 | EE |
| Dorset, Peter | Grimmer, M Elisabeth | 25, Oct. 1836 | FF |
| Dorsey, Edward | Sweeney, Mary | 7, Feb. 1848 | RCH |
| Dorst, Isaac | Weiss, Elisabeth | 14, Aug. 1845 | C |

| Grooms | Brides | Date of Marriage | Code |
|--------|--------|------------------|------|
| ****** | ****** | **** ** ******** | **** |
| Dosch, Johan | Boelinger, Sophia | 16, Nov. 1845 | FF |
| Doscher, Heinrich | Ludken, Margaretha | 4, Jan. 1844 | G |
| Dosmann, Friedrich | Schmidt, Anna M. | 27, Nov. 1849 | EE |
| Doss, Martin | Thompson, Sarah | 25, Mar. 1835 | RCH |
| Dothwait, Timothy | Oliver, Hannah | 16, July 1826 | RCH |
| Doty, | Hayt, Charlotte | 21, July 1823 | RCH |
| Doty, Curtis | Thompson, Elisabeth | 3, Dec. 1845 | RCH |
| Doty, John | Lawson, Hannah | 20, Jan. 1847 | RCH |
| Doty, Shelton | Addis, Anna Maria | 1, Nov. 1848 | RCH |
| Doty, William | Bryant, Harriet | 22, Apr. 1844 | RCH |
| Doudle, Isaac | Hull, Rebecca | Aug. 1841 | RCH |
| Dougherty, Edward | Murphy, Bridget | 26, Apr. 1846 | BB |
| Dougherty, Jacob | Barkalow, Catharine | 11, Mar. 1821 | RCH |
| Dougherty, James | Cassilly, Elisabeth | 31, Oct. 1848 | BB |
| Dougherty, John | Hoper, Mary | 26, July 1832 | RCH |
| Dougherty, John | McDonough, Bridget | 25, Jan. 1846 | BB |
| Dougherty, Neal | Rafferty, Ellen | 11, Sept 1844 | RCH |
| Dougherty, Richard | ----, Mary | 12, Oct. 1819 | RCH |
| Dougherty, William | Brennan, Mary | 14, Jan. 1840 | BB |
| Dougherty, William | McCoy, Ann | 30, Aug. 1842 | BB |
| Doughty, A. | Daily, Jane Ann | 25, Dec. 1841 | RCH |
| Doughty, Moses C. | Chusman, Ann P. | 31, May 1832 | RCH |
| Doughty, William | Guthrie, Martha | 16, Nov. 1843 | RCH |
| Douglas, Ralph N. | Brout, Elisabeth | 2, Feb. 1834 | RCH |
| Douglas, Samuel | Doty, Elisabeth Ann | 2, Sept 1843 | RCH |
| Douglas, William W. | Shewrer, Catharine | 24, Sept 1818 | RCH |
| Douglass, David | Naylor, Tirza S. | 10, Apr. 1833 | RCH |
| Douglass, William | Barnes, Rebecca | 14, Mar. 1824 | RCH |
| Douglass, William | Carson, Elisabeth A. | 12, Feb. 1835 | RCH |
| Douglass, William | Hillings, Maria Anna | 22, Feb. 1848 | RCH |
| Dove, John Alexander | Pasley, Susan Ann | 8, Nov. 1848 | RCH |
| Dow, Carlisle | Park, Mary Ann | 28, Sept 1843 | RCH |
| Dowler, Samuel L. | McCoy, Elenor | 7, Aug. 1834 | RCH |
| Dowler, Thomas | Snyder, Mary | 14, May 1842 | RCH |
| Dowling, Patrick | Hayden, Helen | 20, Aug. 1848 | BB |
| Downard, Thomas | Harmon, Mary Ann | 28, Mar. 1848 | RCH |
| Downey, Christopher | Galloway, Amanda | 19, May 1846 | RCH |
| Downey, Wesley | Roberts, Amelia | 22, Nov. 1838 | RCH |
| Downs, Andrew J. | Munday, Margaret | 7, May 1839 | BB |
| Downs, Charles A. | Jones, Clarissa | 16, May 1848 | RCH |
| Downs, Simpkins | Goosbury, Mary Jane | 28, Mar. 1849 | RCH |
| Downs, Thomas | Weiler, Mary | 26, Dec. 1846 | RCH |
| Doyle, Christopher | Hanlon, Catharine | 5, Nov. 1844 | BB |
| Doyle, James | Flannagan, Abby | 8, Dec. 1840 | BB |
| Doyle, James | Flemming, Mary | 21, Oct. 1849 | BB |
| Doyle, John | Clark, Ann C. | 18, Feb. 1834 | RCH |
| Doyle, Martin | Mulally, Mary | 24, Oct. 1847 | GG |
| Doyle, Michael | Lightfoot, Susan | 13, June 1844 | RCH |
| Doyle, Michael | Donovan, Mary | 23, Sept 1841 | BB |
| Doyle, Thomas | Seale, Aurelia | 16, Aug. 1847 | RCH |
| Doyle, Thomas H. | ----, Cordelia | 3, Oct. 1835 | RCH |
| Dra---, Hanson | Ross, Abigail | 27, Apr. 1826 | RCH |
| Drach, Conrad | Mack, Maria | 23, Nov. 1848 | C |
| Drake, | Harrison, Ann | 29, Mar. 1821 | RCH |
| Drake, Aaron | Spooner, Amanda | 15, Mar. 1847 | RCH |
| Drake, Francis | Ferris, Catharine | 19, Feb. 1835 | RCH |
| Drake, John M. | Thomas, Harriet | 10, Dec. 1835 | RCH |
| Drake, Josiah | Kugler, Catharine | 24, Apr. 1833 | RCH |
| Drake, Lewis | Gaston, Mary A. | 10, May 1849 | RCH |
| Drake, Louis | Goodapple, Ann | 13, Feb. 1844 | RCH |
| Drake, Oliver F. | Waring, Elisabeth | 30, Oct. 1832 | RCH |
| Drake, Thomas | Mills, Lydia Ann | 18, Mar. 1841 | RCH |
| Draper, William | Hilmar, Rachel | 17, Sept 1837 | RCH |
| Draper, William | Jennings, Sarah | 9, Aug. 1842 | RCH |
| Drausfeld, Henry F. | Ruffner, Eliza Ann | 7, May 1848 | RCH |
| Draxmeyer, Bernard | Hunt, Josephine | 7, June 1847 | EE |
| Dreby, John | Cawein, Maria | 20, Oct. 1836 | RCH |
| Drees, Herman A. | Wessling, Maria Adel | 20, May 1849 | EE |
| Dreher, Bernard L. | Strang, Johanna | 25, Nov. 1849 | AA |
| Dreier, Heinrich | Benzmann, M. Anna | 28, Oct. 1849 | II |
| Dreier, J. Wilhelm | Sanders, A. Gertrud | 7, Nov. 1847 | FF |

| Grooms | Brides | Date of Marriage | Code |
|--------|--------|------------------|------|
| ****** | ****** | **** ** ******** | **** |
| Dreier, Johan Heinr. | Witte, Anna Maria | 4, June 1839 | FF |
| Dreier, Johan Heinr. | Hilker, Margaretha | 10, Jan. 1849 | F |
| Drenley, Friedrich | Baumgartner, Maria | 24, May 1836 | FF |
| Drescher, | Werling, Maria A. | 19, Aug. 1849 | RCH |
| Drescher, Andrew | Grosshinser, Christ. | 17, Aug. 1847 | RCH |
| Drescher, Casper | Schmidt, Louise | 4, Feb. 1849 | C |
| Dresing, Friedrich | Everhardt, Catharine | 30, Nov. 1843 | A |
| Dressel, Jacob | Kirskadon, Jane | 25, Mar. 1847 | RCH |
| Dressel, Peter | Steinberg, Johanna R | 9, Mar. 1841 | F |
| Dressel, William | Taylor, Elisabeth | 8, Oct. 1848 | RCH |
| Dresser, Thomas | Jackson, Sarah Ann | 7, Apr. 1836 | RCH |
| Dressmann, Bernard | Wanstrad, Catharina | 11, Nov. 1841 | FF |
| Dressmann, J. Herman | Toepke, Anna Maria | 4, Nov. 1841 | FF |
| Dretlein, Heinrich | Schmall, Margaretha | 29, Sept 1840 | FF |
| Drew, Benjamin | Taylor, Lydia | 2, Aug. 1849 | RCH |
| Drew, Harrison | Lacy, Elisabeth | 1, Mar. 1846 | RCH |
| Drewer, Ebenezer | Chambers, Nancy | 10, Mar. 1836 | RCH |
| Dreyer, Gerhard H. | Korte, Dina | 16, Jan. 1849 | RCH |
| Dreyer, Herman Bd. | Focke, Maria Elis. | 5, Aug. 1849 | FF |
| Dreyer, Wilhelm | Koenig, Gerhard | 4, Feb. 1845 | AA |
| Dreymann, Friedrich | Hellmann, M. Helena | 9, Feb. 1846 | FF |
| Driehaus, Herman | Arnhold, Caroline | 15, Aug. 1842 | F |
| Drier, Robert | Kerwin, Margaret | 4, July 1825 | RCH |
| Drinkwater, Henry | ----, Catharine | 20, Aug. 1821 | RCH |
| Drisbrow, William | VanGorder, Betsey | 22, Dec. 1842 | RCH |
| Driscoll, Timothy | Driscoll, Mary | 4, Sept 1842 | BB |
| Driskell, John | Gouldman, Ann | 18, Oct. 1848 | RCH |
| Driver, George | Parker, Elisabeth | 1, Apr. 1849 | RCH |
| Driver, Lucian | Shingledecker, Mary | 2, Apr. 1844 | RCH |
| Drocher, Heinrich | Wenling, M. Anna | 19, Aug. 1849 | II |
| Drochter, Johan Bd. | Wedding, Cath. (Mrs) | 30, Sept 1845 | AA |
| Droege, Friedrich | Basthaus, Elisabeth | 6, July 1843 | A |
| Droege, Heinrich | Bosse, M. Elisabeth | 20, Feb. 1845 | F |
| Droege, J Friedrich | Fidelar, Louise | 1, July 1847 | F |
| Droege, Johan Carl | Bosse, Johanna A. | 26, May 1842 | F |
| Droste, Herman Hein. | Igelmann, Catharine | 21, Oct. 1847 | B |
| Droste, J. Dietrich | Heitlagen, A. Regina | 25, Jan. 1844 | F |
| Droste, J. Dietrich | Ellerkamp, Elisabeth | 21, Jan. 1848 | B |
| Droste, Johan F. | Nuehring, Sophia | 5, Oct. 1843 | F |
| Droste, Johan Herman | Hehe, Clara Elenora | 16, Sept 1847 | B |
| Druckelmann, Friedr. | Hunefeld, Elisabeth | 24, Mar. 1842 | RCH |
| Drude, Heinrich | Lendler, Louise | 23, Dec. 1845 | F |
| Drum, Carl | Hainz, Elisabeth | 5, July 1849 | C |
| Drum, Thomas | McCarthy, Ann | 11, Sept 1835 | RCH |
| Drumm, Edward | McGarahan, Catharine | 4, Apr. 1842 | BB |
| Drumm, Jacob | Bader, Philippina | 28, June 1844 | C |
| Drummond, | Stagg, Mary A. | 18, Jan. 1838 | RCH |
| Drumon, John | Andrews, Phebe | 15, July 1835 | RCH |
| Dryden, James | Winton, Caroline | 27, Sept 1846 | RCH |
| Dryer, A. | Louis, Sally | 22, May 1823 | RCH |
| Dryfuss, Wolf | Childs, Eva | 20, May 1848 | RCH |
| Dubber, Heinrich L. | Kolkmeier, Clara L. | 19, Oct. 1847 | RCH |
| Dubenkrap, Joseph | Freitag, Anna Sophia | 27, Jan. 1846 | FF |
| Duberty, John | Garrison, Sarah L. | 22, May 1842 | RCH |
| Dubois, George W. | McIlvaine, Mary | 16, Aug. 1848 | I |
| Dubois, Herman | Nicoll, Mary Ann | 10, Feb. 1847 | RCH |
| Dubois, John | Butler, Unis. | 11, Dec. 1834 | RCH |
| Dubois, John M. | Ward, Nancy | 6, July 1844 | RCH |
| Dubois, Joseph | Orr, Mary | 6, Jan. 1847 | RCH |
| Dubois, William S. | Williams, Sarah | 17, Feb. 1841 | RCH |
| Duchemin, George | Roll, Susan Ann | 26, Nov. 1845 | RCH |
| Duchemin, James | Bacon, Mary | 29, Oct. 1846 | RCH |
| Duchemin, Peter | Davis, Lucy | 10, Apr. 1834 | RCH |
| Duchemin, Peter | Guistan, Maria L. | 14, June 1834 | RCH |
| Duchemin, Peter | Bacon, Elisabeth | 14, Apr. 1844 | RCH |
| Duck, Louis Theodor | Rapp, Philippina | 4, Apr. 1844 | G |
| Duckey, John H. | McCauley, Mary A. | 20, Jan. 1835 | RCH |
| Dudel, Herman | Siefker, Catharine | 29, Jan. 1845 | AA |
| Duden, Johan | Dregen, Maria | 18, Sept 1845 | G |
| Dudenhoffer, Johan | Meyer, Magdalena | 29, July 1837 | FF |
| Dudley, Ambrose | Cuny, Clara | 6, July 1837 | I |

| Grooms<br>****** | Brides<br>****** | Date of Marriage<br>**** ** ******** | Code<br>**** |
|---|---|---|---|
| Dudley, James M. | Lewis, Mary Ann | 29, Jan. 1843 | RCH |
| Dudley, Moses | Carl, Ellen | 22, Aug. 1847 | RCH |
| Duedel, Herman | Koch, Katharina | 15, Feb. 1848 | AA |
| Duell, Francis | Hubing, Friedricka | 11, Aug. 1846 | EE |
| Duemers, Bernard | Luepke, Philomena | 21, Oct. 1849 | FF |
| Duer, Joseph | Schute, Veronica | 1, Oct. 1839 | FF |
| Duerenkemper, Fried. | Placke, Gertrud | 17, Aug. 1845 | AA |
| Duerk, Andreas | Koch, Maria | 4, May 1848 | EE |
| Duerk, Anton | Klein, Christina | 6, Feb. 1837 | FF |
| Duerr, Francis | Ritt, Barbara | 24, Jan. 1843 | FF |
| Duerstock, Bernard | Meimann, Margaretha | 9, Jan. 1844 | AA |
| Duerstock, Bernard | Wendel, Anna Maria | 1, Sept 1844 | FF |
| Duerstock, Heinrich | Kroeger, Theresa | 17, June 1849 | II |
| Duerstock, J Bernard | Radweg, Elisabeth | 13, June 1848 | FF |
| Duerstock, Johan H. | Terwin, Anna Maria | 21, May 1848 | AA |
| Dues, Heinrich | Wehry, Catharine | 15, Apr. 1849 | FF |
| Dues, Johan Bernard | Robers, Gertrud | 23, Aug. 1846 | AA |
| Dueshaus, Bernard | Lueker, Anna | 15, Aug. 1848 | EE |
| Duesing, Friedrich W | Meyer, Cath. Sophia | 10, Dec. 1846 | F |
| Duesing, Johan Hein. | Jasper, M. Anna | 2, May 1847 | AA |
| Duetemeyer, Johan | Niedehesper, Cath. | 3, June 1847 | F |
| Duetmann, J. Casper | Schumpe, Elisabeth | 17, Sept 1848 | AA |
| Duettmann, Wilhelm | Hondorf, Gertrud | 4, July 1847 | AA |
| Duff, Richard | Warsaw, Julia Ann | 19, Oct. 1843 | BB |
| Duffe, Christopher | Robinson, Susan | 10, Sept 1848 | RCH |
| Duffield, Charles | Cloon, Sarah | 24, Mar. 1842 | RCH |
| Duffy, Francis | Rogers, Rosanna | 4, Jan. 1846 | BB |
| Duffy, Lawrence | Quinley, Mary | 4, May 1845 | BB |
| Duffy, Michael | Bradley, Letitia | 10, Aug. 1848 | BB |
| Duffy, Nicolaus | Considine, Mary | 19, Aug. 1841 | BB |
| Duffy, Nicolaus | Patridge, Bridget | 24, Oct. 1845 | BB |
| Duffy, Peter | Kennedy, Ann | 29, Oct. 1848 | GG |
| Duffy, Thomas | Moore, Catharine | 14, July 1846 | GG |
| Duffy, Thomas W. | Stone, Ann Ellen | 1, Oct. 1843 | BB |
| Dugan, Hugh | Florer, Indian | 15, Apr. 1843 | RCH |
| Dugan, James | Lopers, Mary Jane | 19, May 1848 | RCH |
| Dugan, James | O'Brien, Honora | 2, Feb. 1845 | BB |
| Dugan, John H. | McConnell, Sarah | 20, July 1848 | RCH |
| Duhan, August | Berleton, Felicty | 7, Feb. 1842 | BB |
| Duhan, Joseph | McKeown, Margaret | 8, Nov. 1849 | BB |
| Duhme, Herman | McNicoll, Mary Ann | 1, Feb. 1847 | RCH |
| Duhme, Herman Heinr. | Kassauer, Louisa C. | 10, Oct. 1840 | F |
| Duhmeyer, Michael | Sauer, Richardina | 4, July 1847 | AA |
| Dujardin, V. | Cardinal, Josephine | 22, Sept 1844 | RCH |
| Duksen, Johan Jacob | Schaeper, Maria Anna | 23, Oct. 1849 | II |
| Duley, Zeacloe | Bennet, Lydia | 29, Apr. 1832 | RCH |
| Dull, Charles | Fithian, Sarah | 21, Mar. 1842 | RCH |
| Dullivan, Harrison W | ----, Ann | May 1832 | RCH |
| Dulweber, Theodor | Frankmann, M. Engel | 3, Aug. 1845 | AA |
| Dumann, Heinrich | Moellers, Susanna M. | 23, May 1847 | FF |
| Dumass, Benjamin | B---, Maria | 14, Oct. 1819 | RCH |
| Dumick, Wilhelm | Mayhew, Josephina | 23, Aug. 1841 | FF |
| Dumm, Heinrich | Heinrich, Elisabeth | 28, July 1849 | II |
| Dumont, Charles | Erickson, Susannah | 6, Aug. 1846 | RCH |
| Dumont, Dominick | Bricler, Gertrud | 14, Aug. 1845 | RCH |
| Dumont, Richard | Sharp, Margaret S. | 20, July 1842 | RCH |
| Dunaway, Elias | Chrisman, Margaret | 26, Feb. 1837 | RCH |
| Dunbar, Annanias | Meeker, Phoebe | 8, Jan. 1819 | RCH |
| Dunbar, Malzar | Vincent, Sarah | 26, Nov. 1841 | RCH |
| Dunbar, Robert W. | Sampson, Harriet | 8, Nov. 1835 | RCH |
| Duncan, Alexander | St.Clair, Frances | 22, June 1837 | RCH |
| Duncan, David | Crosset, Jane | 20, Oct. 1842 | RCH |
| Duncan, James | Hawkins, Rebecca | 13, Aug. 1843 | RCH |
| Duncan, John | Ridlin, | 3, Sept 1837 | RCH |
| Duncan, Richard | Kelly, Mary | 7, May 1841 | BB |
| Duncan, Thomas | Calder, Mary Ann | 16, Nov. 1848 | RCH |
| Duncan, Thomas H. | Burnes, Margaret | 13, Nov. 1834 | RCH |
| Duncan, William | Simmons, Hannah | 18, Dec. 1845 | RCH |
| Dunce, William | Kitchel, Mary | 27, Jan. 1835 | RCH |
| Dungoen, Thomas | Rybolt, Sarah | 5, May 1839 | RCH |
| Dunham, David | Wil---, Catharine | 14, Feb. 1822 | RCH |

| Grooms | Brides | Date of Marriage | Code |
|--------|--------|------------------|------|
| ****** | ****** | ****  **  ******** | **** |
| Dunham, Eliphalet | Enos, Matilda | 7, Dec. 1845 | RCH |
| Dunham, Huseford | Judkins, Sally D. | 17, Apr. 1820 | RCH |
| Dunham, Joseph B. | Porter, Catharine T. | 7, Feb. 1833 | RCH |
| Dunham, Joseph C. | Stevens, Elisabeth A | 29, Mar. 1848 | RCH |
| Dunham, Josiah | Horbly, Margaret | 16, Jan. 1834 | RCH |
| Dunham, Levi | Thompson, Mary A. | 22, Mar. 1838 | RCH |
| Dunham, Levi | Wile, Caroline | 20, Dec. 1849 | RCH |
| Dunham, Seth | Mahew, Hannah | 1, June 1820 | RCH |
| Dunham, Thomas E. | Elder, Mary | 1, Aug. 1839 | RCH |
| Dunham, William | McLean, Elisabeth L. | 16, Feb. 1841 | RCH |
| Dunker, Anton | Reidelmann, Elis. | 3, Nov. 1846 | AA |
| Dunker, Johan | Dunheimer, Rosina | 18, May 1846 | EE |
| Dunkerson, Robert | Graham, Rebecca | 3, Dec. 1841 | RCH |
| Dunlap, James | Limerick, Jane | 23, Oct. 1835 | RCH |
| Dunlap, John P. | Carmichael, Elis. | 28, May 1834 | RCH |
| Dunlap, Joseph | Wright, Sarah | 19, May 1846 | RCH |
| Dunlap, Robert | Scudder, Sybel | 17, Mar. 1839 | RCH |
| Dunlop, James S. | Bowman, Catharine J. | 15, Jan. 1846 | RCH |
| Dunlop, John | Hays, Isabella | 29, May 1844 | RCH |
| Dunlop, Robert | Howe, Rebecca | 26, May 1842 | RCH |
| Dunlop, Robert | Hazlewood, Nancy | 30, June 1844 | RCH |
| Dunn, Beracha | Boyle, Artemesia | 28, Feb. 1846 | RCH |
| Dunn, Brasillia | Gaston, Margaret | 25, Feb. 1841 | RCH |
| Dunn, Caleb | McFeely, Sarah | 3, July 1843 | RCH |
| Dunn, Cornelius | Boyle, Mary | 1, May 1849 | RCH |
| Dunn, Jeremiah | Robinson, Elisabeth | 25, Sept 1817 | RCH |
| Dunn, Jeremiah | Wickhoff, Jane | 29, Oct. 1835 | RCH |
| Dunn, John | Ryan, Mary | 10, Sept 1849 | BB |
| Dunn, John W. | Dunbar, Roxanna | 22, Mar. 1843 | RCH |
| Dunn, Michael | Ryan, Mary | 21, Oct. 1849 | GG |
| Dunn, Owen | Byrns, Margaret | 31, July 1848 | BB |
| Dunn, Thomas | Ryan, Mary Ann | 8, July 1846 | BB |
| Dunnahew, Thomas | Stroat, Julia | 5, Dec. 1833 | RCH |
| Dunning, | Haroil, Rebecca | 12, Aug. 1849 | RCH |
| Dunning, Ezra | Sheron, Phebe | 11, Apr. 1849 | RCH |
| Dunning, Robert | Perkins, Hannah | 20, Oct. 1841 | RCH |
| Dunning, Samuel | Boyce, Margaret | 14, Aug. 1843 | RCH |
| Dunseth, John | Hart, Mary H. | 28, Nov. 1844 | RCH |
| Dunsman, Robert | Rouch, Ellen | 18, May 1843 | RCH |
| Dunston, Joseph | Mills, Sarah | 11, Oct. 1846 | RCH |
| Dunton, Isaac | Belville, Sarah | 21, Jan. 1847 | RCH |
| Dunz, Georg | Vennemann, Maria | 18, Oct. 1846 | AA |
| Dupas, Thomas | Plage, Anna Maria | 13, Nov. 1849 | EE |
| Dupler, Carl | Ropf, Mary Eva | 29, Feb. 1848 | G |
| Duppernell, John | Baehr, Regina | 31, Aug. 1848 | G |
| Dupps, Christian | Huber, Anna (Mrs) | 29, Apr. 1845 | AA |
| Dupps, Raymond | Lambert, Victoria | 17, Jan. 1843 | AA |
| Dupruit, Langsdon | Danforth, Judith | 9, Sept 1824 | RCH |
| Dups, Wendel | Huetche, Louisa | 22, Sept 1840 | FF |
| Durall, Otto | Prather, Mary Ann | 16, June 1835 | RCH |
| Duran, James | Shiner, Margaret | 17, June 1847 | RCH |
| Duran, John | Riggs, | Oct. 1826 | RCH |
| Dureis, Charles H. | Balcain, Barbara | 6, June 1839 | RCH |
| Durghusing, J Rudolf | Hartemueller, Elis. | 22, Nov. 1836 | FF |
| Durham, Aquilla | Thompson, Sarah | 23, Dec. 1841 | RCH |
| Durham, Daniel | Clark, Catharine | 23, Sept 1834 | RCH |
| Durham, John | Martin, Maria | 29, Oct. 1846 | RCH |
| Durham, John W. | Lowrey, Margaret E. | 24, Dec. 1834 | RCH |
| Durham, Joshua | Poor, Nancy | 28, Feb. 1842 | RCH |
| Durham, Stephen | Clark, Elisabeth Ann | 7, Mar. 1837 | RCH |
| Durham, Winfield | Wilmington, Narcissa | 4, July 1844 | RCH |
| Durigan, Patrick | Dooling, Ellen | 22, Apr. 1845 | BB |
| Durkee, Henry | Tumy, Elisabeth | 28, Feb. 1833 | RCH |
| Durkes, Heinrich | Beddels, Maria Anna | 14, Oct. 1849 | EE |
| Durkey, John | Woodret, Eunice | 28, Apr. 1833 | RCH |
| Durrell, John | McQuillan, Sarah | 16, June 1836 | RCH |
| Durrell, Joseph E. | Stewart, Maria | 3, Oct. 1848 | RCH |
| Durst, Carl | Brunner, Theresa | 31, Dec. 1837 | FF |
| Dury, Francis | Gibson, Louise | 18, Dec. 1846 | RCH |
| Dusinberg, Cornelius | Lamson, Maria | 21, Nov. 1845 | RCH |
| Dusmann, Henry | Sturick, Friedricka | 21, May 1844 | RCH |

| Grooms<br>****** | Brides<br>****** | Date of Marriage<br>**** ** ******** | Code<br>**** |
|---|---|---|---|
| Dutmann, Wilhelm | Schmeider, Anna M. | 3, Oct. 1839 | FF |
| Duval, George W. | Fry, Maria | 17, Jan. 1833 | RCH |
| Duval, James | Williams, Jane | 12, Apr. 1849 | RCH |
| Duvall, John | Ireland, Laura Ann | 13, Aug. 1844 | RCH |
| Duvel, Casper | Meiers, Catharine | 17, Apr. 1849 | II |
| Duveneck, Dietrich H | Wehrmann, M. Elis. | 9, Jan. 1840 | F |
| Duvy, George | Dixon, Elisabeth | 28, Dec. 1834 | RCH |
| Dwinell, Benjamin | Richardson, Angela | 19, Oct. 1843 | RCH |
| Dwyer, Francis | Reynolds, Bridget | 20, Nov. 1848 | BB |
| Dwyer, John | Walch, Elisabeth | 3, Jan. 1847 | BB |
| Dyer, Charles | Cordry, Emeline | 4, Aug. 1844 | RCH |
| Dyer, Charles B. | Langtry, Elisabeth | 4, Dec. 1832 | RCH |
| Dyer, Elisha | Gregory, Frances | 2, Mar. 1841 | RCH |
| Dyer, John G. | Allen, Harriet | 23, Nov. 1842 | RCH |
| Dyett, Joshua | Williams, Sarah | 10, Sept 1845 | RCH |
| Dynan, John | Early, Catharine | 19, Nov. 1848 | GG |
| Dyran, John | Farmer, Mary D. | 1, Dec. 1836 | RCH |
| Dyrssen, Theodor | Kottmeyer, Christina | 25, Apr. 1847 | C |
| | | | |
| E---, Johnson | Teming, Deborah | Dec. 1833 | RCH |
| Eadons, Joseph | McIntyre, Ann | 19, Mar. 1818 | RCH |
| Eagan, Peter | Foley, Catharine | 25, Jan. 1846 | BB |
| Eagelmann, Johan F. | Hebeler, Carolina | 24, Oct. 1849 | F |
| Eagleson, John | Stinson, Hannah | 12, Mar. 1849 | D |
| Earhart, John | Boosa, Margaret | 18, Dec. 1845 | RCH |
| Earhart, William | Ward, Marietta | 23, Jan. 1844 | RCH |
| Earle, J.F. | Carpenter, Abby | 4, Oct. 1832 | RCH |
| Earle, Thomas | Waters, Mary Ann | 14, Mar. 1844 | RCH |
| Earls, Robert | McCarty, Elisabeth | 10, Nov. 1841 | RCH |
| Early, Dangerfield | Jones, Georgiana | 22, Nov. 1845 | RCH |
| Early, Daniel | Williams, Mary Ann | 1, Oct. 1846 | RCH |
| Early, John | Martin, America | 26, Nov. 1845 | RCH |
| Earnshaw, Henry | Lawrence, Catharine | 22, Mar. 1849 | RCH |
| Easley, John W. | Robertson, Sarah | 4, Sept 1848 | RCH |
| Easterly, Ezra | Sallee, Mary Jane | 12, Oct. 1843 | RCH |
| Eastland, William W. | West, Anna Maria | 21, Feb. 1833 | RCH |
| Eastman, Henry | Stephenson, Margaret | 15, May 1845 | RCH |
| Easton, George | Calnon, Florinda | 30, May 1839 | RCH |
| Easton, John | Coates, Ann | 19, Sept 1846 | RCH |
| Easton, Rufus | Warner, Sarah | 12, May 1843 | RCH |
| Easton, Shadford | Reed, Elisabeth | 18, Nov. 1841 | RCH |
| Eaton, George | Harrison, Betsey | 1, June 1847 | RCH |
| Eaton, John | Allen, Elisabeth | 29, Mar. 1847 | RCH |
| Ebbeler, Johan | Trehaus, Christina | 23, Nov. 1847 | EE |
| Ebbensteiner, Conrad | Heimbur, Barbara | 18, Jan. 1849 | EE |
| Ebener, Johan | Gerard, Catharina | 11, June 1848 | AA |
| Ebenschweiger, David | Hollinger, Crescent. | 12, July 1841 | FF |
| Eberhard, Christoph | Thoelmann, Catharine | 27, May 1847 | B |
| Eberhardt, Ferdinand | Mingesen, Margaret | 5, May 1835 | RCH |
| Eberhardt, Franz C. | Kunkler, Mathilda | 6, July 1847 | C |
| Eberhardt, Heinrich | Koch, Johanna | 1, Jan. 1846 | G |
| Eberhardt, Wilhelm | Beck, Jacobina | 19, Oct. 1848 | G |
| Eberle, Francis H. | Phillips, Mary C. | 5, July 1840 | BB |
| Eberlin, George | Yost, Margaret | 11, Oct. 1843 | RCH |
| Eberlin, William | Leitz, Albertine | 1, Nov. 1847 | RCH |
| Ebers, Friedrich | Strangemann, Sophia | 9, Sept 1835 | RCH |
| Ebers, Gerhard H. | Bruns, Adelheid | 29, Sept 1846 | EE |
| Ebersole, Clayton | Drake, Elisabeth | 17, Feb. 1849 | RCH |
| Ebersole, Henry | Humphrey, Elisabeth | 31, July 1838 | RCH |
| Ebersole, Jacob E. | Ferris, Catharine | 27, Dec. 1836 | RCH |
| Eberz, Nicolaus | Stolz, Elisabeth | 4, Feb. 1849 | FF |
| Ebrenz, Ferdinand | Eppich, Elisabeth | 10, Jan. 1843 | FF |
| Eccles, Henry | Johnston, Jane | 30, June 1847 | RCH |
| Echtermann, Bernard | Nabbe, Catharina | 7, Nov. 1848 | AA |
| Eck, Georg | Weiss, Catharine | 21, Sept 1845 | C |
| Eck, Levi | Gingricha, Elisabeth | 17, Mar. 1847 | RCH |
| Eckel, Georg | Wermuth, Catharina | 11, Nov. 1838 | FF |
| Eckel, Johan | Rosenberger, Maria | 11, May 1841 | FF |
| Eckelmann, Bernard P | Schnelker, Maria | 3, Mar. 1842 | RCH |
| Eckelmann, Philipp | Pruss, Maria Engel | 24, Oct. 1843 | G |
| Eckert, Christian | Eckert, Sophia | 13, Sept 1849 | C |

| Grooms<br>****** | Brides<br>****** | Date of Marriage<br>**** ** ******** | Code<br>**** |
|---|---|---|---|
| Eckert, John | Berry, Charlotte | 9, Nov. 1848 | RCH |
| Eckert, Mathias | Hoefer, Magdalena | 3, Sept 1848 | C |
| Eckert, Michael | Reis, Elisabeth | 13, June 1843 | AA |
| Eckert, Valentin | Meyer, Carolina | 19, May 1846 | AA |
| Eckman, Addison S. | McGowan, Margaret | 14, Oct. 1847 | BB |
| Eckmann, Addison | Allison, Mary Ann | 15, Sept 1844 | RCH |
| Eckmann, Jacob | Raney, Mary | 22, Apr. 1844 | RCH |
| Eckstein, Paul | Gieringer, Julia | 27, Jan. 1840 | FF |
| Ecler, Gerhard H. | Schroeder, Maria M. | 14, Jan. 1849 | CC |
| Eddy, Gideon | ----, Susan | 22, July 1839 | RCH |
| Eddy, Thomas | White, Ann | 6, Aug. 1845 | RCH |
| Edeberger, Moses | Curtis, Rachel | 22, July 1841 | RCH |
| Eden, William | Stonesiffer, Polly | 25, Feb. 1819 | RCH |
| Edge, John | Molloy, Margaret | 16, Oct. 1848 | BB |
| Edinger, William F. | Barnes, Susan | 29, July 1844 | RCH |
| Edmiston, William | Roll, Phebe A. | 12, Jan. 1849 | RCH |
| Edmonds, Horace S. | Smith, Sarah A. | 1, May 1833 | RCH |
| Edmonson, John | Sherby, Mary Ann | 3, Apr. 1833 | RCH |
| Edmonson, Robert | ----, Casandra | 17, Sept 1834 | RCH |
| Edmundson, Edward | Richardson, Ruth | 29, July 1819 | RCH |
| Edrehi, Isaac | Meyers, Hannah | 12, Nov. 1847 | RCH |
| Edrington, William | King, Josephine | 21, June 1843 | RCH |
| Edvington, Edmond | Hewlett, Levina | 22, Mar. 1834 | RCH |
| Edward, Evan | Isaac, Ann | 4, June 1839 | RCH |
| Edward, John S. | Rokenfield, Susan | 24, Oct. 1839 | RCH |
| Edwards, Alexander | Ware, Letitia | 27, Dec. 1833 | RCH |
| Edwards, Amos | Natheizon, Jane | 23, Oct. 1834 | RCH |
| Edwards, Asa | Parker, Elisabeth | 28, June 1835 | RCH |
| Edwards, David | Clement, Juliana | 28, July 1834 | RCH |
| Edwards, Edwin | Risinger, Sarah | 16, May 1847 | RCH |
| Edwards, George W. | Jones, Catharine | 17, Mar. 1844 | RCH |
| Edwards, Isaac | Lawyer, Alice | 1, Apr. 1819 | RCH |
| Edwards, Isaac | McCoy, Nancy | 14, Jan. 1823 | RCH |
| Edwards, James | Scull, Elisabeth J. | 1, Sept 1841 | RCH |
| Edwards, Job | Stanbath, Harriet | 7, Mar. 1825 | RCH |
| Edwards, John | Philpot, Anna | 30, June 1844 | RCH |
| Edwards, John | Williams, Ann | 25, Feb. 1847 | RCH |
| Edwards, John C. | Marshall, Phoebe | 28, Sept 1826 | RCH |
| Edwards, Ludwig | Jones, Catharine | 1, June 1849 | RCH |
| Edwards, Peyton | Nutt, Hannah | 8, Dec. 1833 | RCH |
| Edwards, Robert | Wood, Mary | 18, Mar. 1832 | RCH |
| Edwards, Samuel | Sutton, Mary | 29, Jan. 1835 | RCH |
| Edwards, Samuel | Parmeter, Amelia M. | 19, May 1842 | RCH |
| Edwards, Thomas | Pugh, Mary | 18, Feb. 1843 | RCH |
| Edwards, Thomas | Study, Louise J. | 7, Oct. 1845 | RCH |
| Edwards, W. | Simes, Alpha | 31, Dec. 1845 | RCH |
| Edwards, William | Hoogland, Catharine | Oct. 1844 | RCH |
| Efers, John Andreas | Schmidt, Helena | 23, Oct. 1844 | C |
| Effray, Alexander | Burns, Susan Ann | 21, Nov. 1848 | RCH |
| Efgemann, Bernard H. | Buermann, Gertrud | 11, June 1848 | II |
| Efkemann, Johan | Brining, Margaretha | 23, Jan. 1848 | EE |
| Eg---, Isaac W. | Huston, Mary | 14, July 1835 | RCH |
| Egan, Cornelius | Wallace, Ann | 6, Sept 1849 | BB |
| Egan, John | Lynch, Joann | 15, Oct. 1848 | BB |
| Egbers, Johan G. | Keutz, Euphemia A. | 30, Jan. 1848 | EE |
| Egbers, Theodor | Stern, Anna Maria | 11, Jan. 1842 | FF |
| Egbert, Gerhard | Thomas, Margaretha M | 7, Sept 1843 | FF |
| Eger, Peter | Schweinlein, Elis. | 3, Oct. 1845 | RCH |
| Eggelmeyer, Johan W. | Nieporte, Barbara | 7, Feb. 1847 | EE |
| Eggermann, Heinrich | Schlickermann, Cath. | 5, Sept 1849 | II |
| Eggermeier, Georg H. | Brommer, M Elisabeth | 4, Nov. 1849 | II |
| Eggermeier, Heinrich | Notbranks, Dina | 9, May 1847 | FF |
| Eggert, Johan H. | Hausmann, Henrietta | 9, Nov. 1846 | B |
| Egglishan, Richard | Grinstone, Jane | 12, May 1831 | RCH |
| Eglessen, Heinrich | Bauer, Anna Maria | 15, Aug. 1847 | FF |
| Egleston, William | Level, Catharine | 27, Nov. 1846 | RCH |
| Egli, Joseph E. | Gut, Carolina | 9, Sept 1847 | EE |
| Egloff, Johan | Doll, Agnes | 12, Jan. 1841 | FF |
| Egner, James | Burnes, Emily | 30, Apr. 1835 | RCH |
| Egner, Michael | Erdmann, Elisabeth | 6, Nov. 1842 | RCH |
| Ehebauer, Jacob | Hein, Anna Eva | 17, Oct. 1848 | RCH |

| Grooms<br>***** | Brides<br>***** | Date of Marriage<br>**** ** ******** | Code<br>**** |
|---|---|---|---|
| Ehler, Elias | Dunn, Mary Jane | 17, Oct. 1842 | RCH |
| Ehlers, Albert | Castens, Margaretha | 2, Oct. 1848 | F |
| Ehlers, Heinrich | Blank, Louise | 20, Feb. 1845 | F |
| Ehlers, Johan Fried. | Burmeister, Carolina | 3, Dec. 1849 | A |
| Ehlmann, Bernard | Beck, Catharine | 10, Dec. 1849 | F |
| Ehme, Johan Andreas | Mueller, Maria | 30, Oct. 1849 | G |
| Ehrenfried, Heinrich | Meyer, Dorothea | 13, Mar. 1845 | G |
| Ehresmann, Friedrich | Berger, Catharine | 2, Dec. 1844 | RCH |
| Ehresmann, Michael | Hoffmann, Catharine | 13, Mar. 1846 | G |
| Ehrhardt, Christian | Schindeldecker, Char | 2, Feb. 1845 | C |
| Ehrhardt, Christoph | Schroeder, Dorothea | 13, July 1843 | G |
| Ehrhardt, Georg | Weber, Catharine | 6, Apr. 1845 | C |
| Ehrhardt, Philipp | Arnold, Elisabeth | 4, Nov. 1845 | C |
| Ehrmantraut, Johan | Bauber, Theresa | 11, Nov. 1849 | EE |
| Ehrmantraut, Michael | Gehlers, Margaretha | 4, July 1848 | EE |
| Ehtermeier, Francis | Basse, Maria Adel. | 22, Oct. 1848 | CC |
| Eibert, Casper | Schaefer, Elisabeth | 9, Feb. 1841 | FF |
| Eichelberger, Jacob | Weissmann, Philipina | 12, July 1842 | G |
| Eichelberger, Wendel | Lemdermer, Eva | 23, Mar. 1844 | RCH |
| Eichelberger, Wendel | Schwartz, Gertrud | 14, May 1844 | FF |
| Eichelmann, Balthas. | Fehr, Josephina | 18, Aug. 1840 | FF |
| Eichenlaub, Georg | Dauth, Wilhelmina | 8, Oct. 1848 | C |
| Eichenlaub, Johan A. | Duirck, Margaretha | 6, Nov. 1845 | EE |
| Eichenlaub, Valentin | Wolsieper, Catharina | 13, Aug. 1839 | FF |
| Eicher, Francis | Ackermann, Rosa | 30, July 1839 | FF |
| Eicher, Franz | Bohlander, Margaret | 22, Aug. 1844 | C |
| Eicher, Jacob | Widmer, Barbara | 25, Oct. 1842 | FF |
| Eicher, Johan | Lampert, Walburga | 29, Mar. 1842 | FF |
| Eicher, Michael | Habig, Genofeva | 20, Feb. 1848 | CC |
| Eichert, Wilhelm | Metzger, Margaretha | 22, Aug. 1848 | G |
| Eichler, Heinrich | Meyer, Carolina | 16, Jan. 1841 | F |
| Eichner, Michael | Derrer, Anna Barbara | 16, Nov. 1846 | RCH |
| Eichtstadt, Johan | Poeppie, Elisabeth | 14, Oct. 1849 | B |
| Eigelyard, Andrew | Sheeman, Susan | 5, Aug. 1841 | RCH |
| Eigmann, Herman H. | Grothaus, Helena | 3, May 1849 | G |
| Eilers, Heinrich | Ruttland, Angela | 1, Aug. 1843 | AA |
| Eilers, Herman | Steffens, Euphemia | 27, Aug. 1844 | AA |
| Eilers, Johan Herm. | Wekenborg, Adelheid | 16, Aug. 1846 | AA |
| Einboom, Heinrich | Albrecht, Elisabeth | 1, Nov. 1845 | FF |
| Einstein, Joseph | Levi, Rachel | 24, Mar. 1847 | RCH |
| Eisberg, Friedrich W | Kleine, M. Elisabeth | 11, Feb. 1841 | F |
| Eisemann, Joseph | Ries, Barbara | 16, June 1846 | RCH |
| Eisen, Anton | Rapp, C. | 3, Sept 1848 | AA |
| Eisenhardt, Adolph | Freund, Dorothea | 27, Sept 1849 | C |
| Elber, Wilhelm | Strotmann, Sophia | 30, Oct. 1838 | FF |
| Elbrige, William | Buckner, Susan | 1, May 1844 | RCH |
| Elder, Edward | Beamar, Louise | 8, Aug. 1844 | RCH |
| Elder, James | Powlan, Rosanna | 12, Apr. 1844 | RCH |
| Eldridge, Ebenezer | Devie, Ellen | 21, June 1842 | RCH |
| Eldridge, Nimrod | Smith, Frances | 3, Oct. 1842 | RCH |
| Elfering, Ernst | Wendemuth, Margaret | 16, Mar. 1848 | RCH |
| Elfers, Bernard H. | Holtlein, Caroline | 8, June 1848 | F |
| Elfers, Heinrich | Bierbaum, Margaretha | 17, Aug. 1848 | F |
| Elias, | Rose, Matilda | 27, Sept 1849 | RCH |
| Elison, Isaac S. | ----, Anna | 14, July 1825 | RCH |
| Elkins, John | Howard, Delsey | 28, Dec. 1835 | RCH |
| Elkins, William | Wile, Susanna | 6, Mar. 1820 | RCH |
| Ell, Peter | Feger, Adelheid | 30, Apr. 1839 | FF |
| Ellemann, Heinrich | Schwabe, Lisette | 23, Nov. 1843 | G |
| Ellenberger, John | Ponder, Harriet | 22, Feb. 1846 | RCH |
| Ellenbrock, Johan H. | Jacobs, Agatha | 7, June 1846 | EE |
| Ellerhorst, Louis | Dahms, Sophia | 8, Aug. 1846 | F |
| Ellermann, Friedrich | Baier, Anna | 25, July 1848 | EE |
| Ellermann, Heinrich | Platen, Catharine | 9, Dec. 1845 | RCH |
| Ellermann, Johan | Sicken, Wilhelmina | 30, Nov. 1849 | RCH |
| Ellick, Joseph | Snyder, Mary | 31, Dec. 1845 | RCH |
| Ellinger, Jacob | Davis, Jane | 30, Dec. 1843 | RCH |
| Ellinghaus, Christ. | Dammeyer, Sophia W. | 31, May 1849 | B |
| Elliott, John | Cameron, Martha | 24, Oct. 1847 | RCH |
| Elliott, Joseph | Johnson, Lavina | 9, Feb. 1843 | RCH |
| Elliott, Michael | Plow---, Elisabeth | 25, Oct. 1838 | RCH |

| Grooms | Brides | Date of Marriage | Code |
|--------|--------|------------------|------|
| ****** | ****** | **** ** ******** | **** |
| Elliott, Michael | Pilcher, Evelyn | 14, Sept 1847 | RCH |
| Elliott, Noah | Fisher, Elis. Ann | 30, July 1844 | RCH |
| Elliott, Noah | Johnson, Susan | 21, Dec. 1847 | RCH |
| Elliott, Samuel | Wood, Elisabeth | 22, Feb. 1844 | RCH |
| Elliott, Simon | Robinson, Maria | 12, Feb. 1818 | RCH |
| Elliott, Thomas R. | Jones, Hannah | 29, Oct. 1847 | RCH |
| Elliott, William | Long, Sarah | 1, Feb. 1826 | RCH |
| Elliott, William | Campbell, Elis. Jane | 14, Sept 1843 | RCH |
| Elliott, William | Pecky, Harriet | 15, Oct. 1843 | RCH |
| Elliott, William | Sawyer, Sallie F. | 5, June 1849 | I |
| Ellis, Absalom | Walton, Nancy | 30, Jan. 1844 | RCH |
| Ellis, Absolom | Ellis, Mary | Oct. 1844 | RCH |
| Ellis, Charles | ----, Catharine | 17, Aug. 1846 | BB |
| Ellis, James | Lomux, Frances | 25, Jan. 1849 | RCH |
| Ellis, John | Menifee, Frances A. | 30, Aug. 1843 | RCH |
| Ellis, John | Carlsen, Maria | 8, Jan. 1848 | G |
| Ellis, Joseph | Jacobus, Margaret | 30, Jan. 1842 | RCH |
| Ellis, Reason | Sterling, | 11, May 1835 | RCH |
| Ellis, William | McConnell, Jane L. | 31, Dec. 1833 | RCH |
| Ellis, William | Henderson, Elizabeth | 24, Mar. 1846 | RCH |
| Ellison, Andrew B. | Ennis, Rachel A.H. | 23, Oct. 1833 | RCH |
| Ellring, Heinrich | Witthof, Maria Anna | 19, Nov. 1844 | AA |
| Ells, John | Patterson, Eleanor | 13, July 1842 | RCH |
| Ellsing, Henry | Schneider, Anna M. | Nov. 1844 | RCH |
| Elsas, Jacob | Fechheimer, Jeanette | 20, Aug. 1844 | RCH |
| Elsbernd, Gerhard | Hohenberg, Gertrud | 9, Jan. 1848 | EE |
| Elsche, Gerhard | Bagge, Maria Angela | 19, July 1846 | AA |
| Elsche, Gerhard H. | Husmann, Katharina | 30, Apr. 1848 | AA |
| Elses, Joseph | Lutz, Anastasia | 30, Sept 1849 | EE |
| Elsesser, Francis | Schick, Anna Maria | 17, Jan. 1847 | EE |
| Elsing, Heinrich | Dahlmann, Elisabeth | 30, July 1846 | AA |
| Elsing, Johan H. | Tehring, Anna Gesina | 23, Sept 1849 | EE |
| Elstner, John | Rains, Mary | 13, Mar. 1823 | RCH |
| Elston, William | McKee, Emma | 19, May 1842 | RCH |
| Elstro, Francis | Brockmann, Louise | 6, Sept 1849 | II |
| Elstro, Heinrich | Huermann, Catharine | 27, Nov. 1847 | RCH |
| Elstro, Johan H. | Middendorf, Anna M. | 24, Feb. 1846 | AA |
| Elus, Wilhelm | Clarmann, Maria | 16, Sept 1838 | FF |
| Elwell, Samuel | Ogden, Mary | 15, Sept 1845 | RCH |
| Elwell, Thomas | Sheldon, Bula | 14, June 1822 | RCH |
| Ely, George W. | Noble, Lydia | 27, July 1845 | RCH |
| Ely, Jacob W. | Ganoe, Mary Jane | 4, Nov. 1836 | RCH |
| Ely, Nathan | Firgers, Jane | 3, Sept 1821 | RCH |
| Elyea, John | Stump, Jane | 17, Feb. 1838 | RCH |
| Embich, Michael D. | Pyne, Matilda M. | 23, Jan. 1842 | BB |
| Emeck, David | Lahr, Catharine | 28, Jan. 1840 | FF |
| Emers--, Andrew M. | How, Amy | 25, Dec. 1817 | RCH |
| Emery, Andrew | Weller, Julia | 14, Oct. 1846 | RCH |
| Emery, Arthur | Price, Eleanor | 30, July 1845 | RCH |
| Emery, John P. | Noble, Emeline J. | 30, July 1834 | RCH |
| Emge, Wilhelm | Noll, Barbara | 9, May 1844 | AA |
| Emlich, Christoph | Roessner, Bernardina | 12, Sept 1849 | RCH |
| Emmeleth, Justus | Wagner, Philippina | 6, Apr. 1843 | G |
| Emmenecker, Peter | Jung, Margaret(Mrs) | 3, Feb. 1846 | FF |
| Emmens, John | Williams, Susan | 9, Nov. 1842 | RCH |
| Emmert, Jacob | Scheid, Friedricka | 18, Jan. 1848 | C |
| Emmerth, Friedrich | Martin, Elisabeth | 23, Feb. 1842 | RCH |
| Emmett, Alexander | Davis, Margaret | 3, Aug. 1843 | RCH |
| Emmitt, James | Audrey, Isabella | 8, July 1819 | RCH |
| Emmons, William | Pierson, Rebecca | 4, Apr. 1833 | RCH |
| Emory, Charles | Crane, Mary | 11, Mar. 1833 | RCH |
| Emosy, James | Coon, Sally | 10, July 1823 | RCH |
| Empson, John H. | Riley, Nancy | 14, Nov. 1833 | RCH |
| Empson, Thomas | Stokes, Sophia | 1, Jan. 1845 | RCH |
| Empson, Thomas | Wright, Susan | 20, Dec. 1846 | RCH |
| Emrich, Johan | Baum, Apollonia | 23, Sept 1847 | A |
| Emrie, J.R. | Longwell, Emma | 30, Nov. 1847 | RCH |
| Endebrock, Johan H. | Ohe, Sophia M. Magd. | 29, Aug. 1844 | F |
| Enderlin, Theobald | Hub, Barbara | 29, Jan. 1846 | A |
| Enders, Demarcus | Benefield, Rhoda | 14, Nov. 1834 | RCH |
| Endres, Philipp | Doehling, Catharine | 29, Aug. 1847 | EE |

| Grooms | Brides | Date of Marriage | Code |
|--------|--------|------------------|------|
| ****** | ****** | **** ** ******** | **** |
| Enfmeyer, J. Conrad | Wullter, Maria M.E. | 4, Oct. 1849 | C |
| Engbers, Johan H. | Moellers, A Margaret | 7, Nov. 1837 | FF |
| Engehausen, Heinrich | Fieselmann, Cath. M. | 3, Feb. 1844 | F |
| Engehausen, Heinrich | Fricke, Louise | 7, July 1840 | G |
| Engel, Adam | Story, Maria | 20, June 1839 | G |
| Engel, Conrad | Reichenbacher, Elis. | 10, Aug. 1845 | RCH |
| Engel, Heinrich | Liegel, Catharine | 13, Jan. 1846 | EE |
| Engel, Heinrich | Brunstein, Margaret | 27, Aug. 1849 | EE |
| Engel, John | Goss, Apollonia | 18, Oct. 1846 | RCH |
| Engel, Joseph | Baberger, Margaretha | 11, Nov. 1845 | AA |
| Engel, Ludwig | Hatzenbuhler, Cathar | 11, Mar. 1848 | G |
| Engel, Wilhelm | Sundermann, Louise | 4, Mar. 1841 | F |
| Engelhardt, Conrad | Lorenz, Catharine | 10, Mar. 1842 | RCH |
| Engelhardt, Johan | Wuestefeld, Louise | 15, Oct. 1844 | AA |
| Engelhardt, Michael | Buss, Elisabeth | 24, Jan. 1842 | G |
| Engelhart, Adam | Krake, Elisabeth | 14, Oct. 1849 | EE |
| Engelhart, J Philipp | Kaehny, Elisabeth | 23, June 1842 | FF |
| Engelhart, Johan | Moeller, Margaret | 3, Nov. 1845 | RCH |
| Engelhart, Michael | Buse, Elisabeth | 24, Jan. 1842 | RCH |
| Engelke, Carl | Idepohl, Caroline | 26, July 1848 | RCH |
| Engelke, Friedrich | Helmsing, Catharine | 1, June 1840 | FF |
| Engelker, Heinrich R | Loehrkamp, Cath Elis | 9, Oct. 1845 | F |
| Engelking, Conrad | Went, Louise | 9, Mar. 1847 | RCH |
| Engelking, Heinrich | Meyer, Christina | 8, June 1835 | RCH |
| Engert, Adam | Baumann, Margaretha | 23, Sept 1835 | FF |
| Engesser, Mathias | Riesterer, Agnes | 20, Feb. 1848 | EE |
| Engle, James | Naylor, Margaret | 5, Apr. 1846 | RCH |
| Engler, Anton | Geisler, Regina | 24, Aug. 1835 | FF |
| Engler, Heinrich | Griming, Anna Maria | 7, Jan. 1847 | FF |
| Engler, Joseph | Gertisen, Agatha | 6, Oct. 1840 | FF |
| Englert, Johan | Brickner, Barbara | 20, May 1844 | AA |
| Englert, Joseph | Knivel, Barbara | 3, Sept 1844 | AA |
| Englert, Joseph | Riepperger, Louisa | 4, May 1847 | EE |
| Englisch, Carl | Lonx, Sarah | 24, Aug. 1847 | C |
| English, Isaac | Henes, Catharine | 16, May 1847 | RCH |
| English, Jeremiah | Ross, Nancy | 29, May 1819 | RCH |
| English, Job S. | Stathard, Laome | 23, Feb. 1819 | RCH |
| English, Leon | Guilchrist, Alice | 7, Oct. 1849 | GG |
| English, William | McElive, Amanda | 5, July 1847 | RCH |
| Enkick, Friedrich | Brokamp, Anna Maria | 23, Jan. 1840 | FF |
| Enle, John | Sayre, Sarah | 17, Aug. 1826 | RCH |
| Ennekamp, Johan H. | Teppenhof, Anna C. | 14, Sept 1841 | RCH |
| Enneking, Bernard | Schmidt, Anna Maria | 9, Jan. 1844 | AA |
| Enneking, Franz | Huesmann, Margaretha | 10, Oct. 1847 | AA |
| Enneking, Friedrich | Tiemann, Hanna | 13, Apr. 1845 | AA |
| Enneking, Heinrich | Nienaber, Agnes | 29, Aug. 1843 | FF |
| Enneking, Johan Bd. | Helmkamp, M. Elis. | 5, Oct. 1843 | FF |
| Enneking, Johan H. | Schildmeyer, Gertrud | 14, May 1844 | AA |
| Enneking, Joseph | Fangmann, Elisabeth | 29, Sept 1846 | AA |
| Enneking, Joseph | Fortmann, Elisabeth | 29, Sept 1849 | CC |
| Enness, John B. | Clingman, Susan | 11, Oct. 1826 | RCH |
| Enos, Benjamin | Evans, Jane | 30, June 1838 | RCH |
| Enos, John | Ellis, Mary | 19, May 1838 | RCH |
| Enos, Joshua | Layton, Louise | 3, June 1843 | RCH |
| Enos, William | Waldeck, Rebecca | 2, Nov. 1848 | RCH |
| Ensign, Horton | Jones, Martha G. | 28, Dec. 1847 | RCH |
| Ensign, Sampson | Johnson, Mary Jane | 28, June 1843 | RCH |
| Ensley, Peter | VanZant, Phoebe | 26, Sept 1835 | RCH |
| Enteman, Friedrich | Baumgartner, Anna | 25, Aug. 1848 | RCH |
| Enters, Johan | Eckers, Regina | 24, July 1849 | C |
| Entwistle, William | Denton, Elisabeth A. | 3, May 1842 | RCH |
| Entwistle, William | Bell, Susan | 14, Mar. 1844 | RCH |
| Enyart, | Harrison, Mary | 13, Feb. 1838 | RCH |
| Enyart, Joel | Rowen, Susannah | 7, Mar. 1822 | RCH |
| Enyart, Thomas | ----, Mary | 14, Oct. 1819 | RCH |
| Enzenberger, Jacob | Hauck, Magdalena | 11, July 1844 | RCH |
| Eovet, Joseph B. | Hoor, Rebecca | 16, Jan. 1834 | RCH |
| Eple, Valentin | Burkhart, Apollonia | 30, June 1840 | FF |
| Epley, James | Conger, Sarah | 4, Jan. 1846 | RCH |
| Epley, Mark | Underwood, Jule Ann | 7, July 1833 | RCH |
| Eply, James C. | Montgomery, Tawson | 25, Dec. 1844 | RCH |

| Grooms ***** | Brides ***** | Date of Marriage **** ** ******** | Code **** |
|---|---|---|---|
| Eply, William | Montgomery, Ann | 12, Apr. 1838 | RCH |
| Eppe, Matthew | Redant, Emily | 16, Nov. 1842 | RCH |
| Epperson, James | Hill, Caroline | 11, July 1834 | RCH |
| Epperson, William | McCormick, Sarah | 30, Oct. 1817 | RCH |
| Eppertson, Anthony | Mullen, Mary | 19, Nov. 1837 | RCH |
| Eppinger, Herman | May, Esther | 31, Mar. 1843 | RCH |
| Eppinghoff, Bernard | Rufers, Adelheid | 7, Oct. 1845 | AA |
| Eppinghoff, Herman H | Losekamp, Helena A. | 27, Feb. 1848 | EE |
| Epple, Francis C. | Gordon, Catharine | 4, Apr. 1837 | RCH |
| Epply, John | Manser, Harriet | 3, Sept 1844 | RCH |
| Epps, Edward | Bibb, Anna Maria | 28, Mar. 1843 | RCH |
| Epps, Matthew | Johnson, Ann | 8, July 1849 | RCH |
| Epscomb, George | Adams, Ann | 9, Sept 1836 | RCH |
| Epstein, S. | Steinhart, Mary | 11, Apr. 1847 | RCH |
| Erb, Lorenz | Butschin, Catharine | 20, June 1841 | G |
| Erd, Francis Ignatz | Lambert, M Benedicta | 25, Nov. 1845 | FF |
| Erdmann, Friedrich | Herrmann, Catharine | 15, Oct. 1848 | C |
| Ergs, Franklin | Hopper, Jemima | 19, May 1840 | RCH |
| Erhardt, Adam | Vogel, Margaretha | 29, Oct. 1843 | A |
| Erhardt, Georg | Triner, Louise | 30, July 1848 | A |
| Erhardt, Michael | Meyer, Anna Maria | 4, Feb. 1841 | G |
| Erickson, Martin | Wescott, Mary Emily | 25, Sept 1845 | RCH |
| Ernst, Georg | Kihl, Elisabeth | 19, July 1846 | EE |
| Ernst, Gerhard | Greler, Maria Anna | 18, Jan. 1842 | FF |
| Ernst, Henry M. | McDonald, Sarah Ann | 21, Oct. 1826 | RCH |
| Ernst, Jacob | Swager, Elisabeth | 6, June 1849 | RCH |
| Ernst, Johan | Klein, Apollonia | 19, June 1835 | FF |
| Ernst, Louis | Gertner, Eva | 2, May 1847 | EE |
| Ernst, Samuel | Skinner, Elisabeth | 13, Jan. 1821 | RCH |
| Ernst, Wilhelm | Wessling, Adelheid | 28, Oct. 1849 | EE |
| Ernstes, Caspar H. | Bedenbecker, Elis. | 28, Nov. 1844 | AA |
| Ernstesmann, Casper | Dunhoft, Elisabeth | 24, May 1842 | FF |
| Ertel, Daniel | Suter, Elisabeth | 2, Oct. 1823 | RCH |
| Ertel, Friedrich | Walter, Barbara | 29, June 1846 | G |
| Ertel, Jacob | Stueve, Wilhelmina | 23, May 1839 | FF |
| Ertel, Leonhard | Horn, Maria | 10, May 1847 | EE |
| Ertell, Daniel | Booram, Lydia | 30, Sept 1819 | RCH |
| Ertell, Valentine | Sutten, Catharine | 10, Mar. 1818 | RCH |
| Erths, Jacob | Boram, Malinda | 2, Dec. 1834 | RCH |
| Erven, Isaac | Gossage, Elisabeth | 15, Jan. 1833 | RCH |
| Erven, Robert | Hammel, Harriet | 8, Apr. 1849 | RCH |
| Erwin, Andrew | Michaels, Rosanna | 4, Mar. 1844 | RCH |
| Erwin, Columbus | Guynn, Elisabeth A. | 3, Mar. 1844 | RCH |
| Erwin, Enoch | Creager, Mary | 30, Jan. 1844 | RCH |
| Esberg, George W. | Stubbs, Elisabeth | 27, June 1844 | RCH |
| Eschhacke, Friedrich | Wubler, Catharine | 5, Aug. 1845 | AA |
| Eshelmann, Isaac | Marriott, Sarah Ann | 30, Jan. 1849 | RCH |
| Espel, Johan Heinric | Aumann, Bernardina | 21, Feb. 1843 | FF |
| Espenscheid, Heinr. | Rice, Elisabeth | 29, Mar. 1842 | RCH |
| Espenscheid, John | Legner, Barbara | 13, Dec. 1841 | RCH |
| Espenschot, Henry | Lents, Amelia | 5, Feb. 1846 | RCH |
| Espy, Thomas | Morten, | 7, Sept 1826 | RCH |
| Essel, Johan Georg | Arnold, Barbetta | 6, June 1847 | RCH |
| Essert, Martin | Hahn, Elisabeth | 2, Sept 1847 | C |
| Esslinger, Peter | Baus, Anna | 19, Oct. 1841 | FF |
| Este, David | Miller, Louise | 13, May 1829 | I |
| Este, David K. | H---, Lucy S. | 30, Sept 1819 | RCH |
| Estell, William | Graham, Harriet | 7, Oct. 1832 | RCH |
| Estep, Richard | Noble, Frances | 4, July 1842 | RCH |
| Estep, Thomas | Smith, Sarah | 29, Jan. 1842 | RCH |
| Eton, Heinrich | Marriott, Elisabeth | 25, Nov. 1847 | RCH |
| Eubank, Martin | Hunt, Mary B. | 12, Oct. 1841 | RCH |
| Euler, Conrad | Gross, M. Elisabeth | 7, Nov. 1847 | G |
| Eumy, Jesse | Conkling, Rosalinda | 28, Dec. 1848 | RCH |
| Eusterkemper, Johan | Kuhlenberg, Maria | 14, Jan. 1849 | AA |
| Evan, William | McCorkhill, Henrieta | 12, Apr. 1834 | RCH |
| Evans, | Sellman, Elisabeth | 20, May 1836 | RCH |
| Evans, Abraham | Jones, Ann | 5, Jan. 1824 | RCH |
| Evans, Charles | Kincaid, Mary H. | 4, Oct. 1843 | RCH |
| Evans, Charles N. | ----, ---- | May 1839 | RCH |
| Evans, Daniel | Lewis, Elisabeth Ann | 9, July 1844 | RCH |

| Grooms<br>****** | Brides<br>****** | Date of Marriage<br>**** ** ******** | Code<br>**** |
|---|---|---|---|
| Evans, Daniel | Phipps, Mary | 21, May 1848 | RCH |
| Evans, David | Brown, Sarah | 19, Oct. 1820 | RCH |
| Evans, David | Morgan, Margaret | 16, Apr. 1846 | RCH |
| Evans, David | Thomas, Mary | 16, Mar. 1847 | RCH |
| Evans, Elijah | VanSant, Mary | 7, Mar. 1841 | RCH |
| Evans, Evan | Jones, Jane | 8, June 1844 | RCH |
| Evans, Evan | Field, Lucy | 20, May 1847 | RCH |
| Evans, Francis | Cox, Elisabeth | 10, Mar. 1833 | RCH |
| Evans, Israel | Schooley, Ann Elis. | 2, Apr. 1835 | RCH |
| Evans, James G. | Lyon, Mary J. | 15, Feb. 1849 | RCH |
| Evans, James J. | McMahan, Maria T. | 28, Apr. 1834 | RCH |
| Evans, James R. | Sweet, Martha | 26, Jan. 1836 | RCH |
| Evans, John | ----, Anna Elisabeth | 6, Mar. 1838 | RCH |
| Evans, John | Dillon, Elisabeth | 1, Oct. 1839 | RCH |
| Evans, John P. | Cobb, Emily | 2, Sept 1841 | RCH |
| Evans, John W. | Samuel, Mary | 19, Oct. 1839 | RCH |
| Evans, Joseph | Sampson, Anna B. | 14, Dec. 1842 | RCH |
| Evans, Lewis | Carey, Sarah Ann | 7, Oct. 1834 | RCH |
| Evans, Louis | Jones, Mary | 8, Nov. 1845 | RCH |
| Evans, Oliver | Evans, Harriet | 1, Jan. 1837 | RCH |
| Evans, Patrick | Landregan, Margaret | 20, June 1849 | GG |
| Evans, Seth | Brown, Winnifred | 26, Oct. 1848 | RCH |
| Evans, William | Stilwell, Mary | 1, July 1819 | RCH |
| Evans, William | Deisgal, Bridget | 27, July 1843 | RCH |
| Evans, William | Thomas, Elisabeth | 9, May 1846 | RCH |
| Evans, William | Thomas, Jane | 6, Oct. 1848 | RCH |
| Evarts, Sylvanus | Haywood, Elisabeth | 29, Apr. 1820 | RCH |
| Evelen, F.A. | ----, ---- | 22, Aug. 1838 | RCH |
| Evens, Bartley B. | Perkinson, | 13, Mar. 1827 | RCH |
| Evens, Daniel T. | Atherton, Caroline | 16, Sept 1824 | RCH |
| Evens, Oliver | Linfoot, Hannah | 29, Mar. 1842 | RCH |
| Everest, Charles M. | Silver, Lydia | 2, Mar. 1834 | RCH |
| Everett, Thomas | Cook, Amanda M. | 14, Mar. 1833 | RCH |
| Everett, William H. | Broadwell, Amanda | 14, Mar. 1837 | D |
| Everhardy, Michael | Becker, Margaretha | 28, Feb. 1843 | AA |
| Everhart, Daniel G. | Johnson, Mary Ann | 14, Feb. 1836 | RCH |
| Everling, Charles | Robbins, Susan | 20, June 1847 | RCH |
| Evers, Herman | Mittendorf, Katharin | 17, Nov. 1849 | EE |
| Evers, Herman | Wilke, Anna Maria | 3, Sept 1848 | FF |
| Evers, Johan Heinric | Hartmann, Elisabeth | 16, May 1847 | AA |
| Eversall, Jacob | Brown, Mary Jane | 28, June 1847 | RCH |
| Eversfield, John | Sheely, Mary | 7, Feb. 1849 | RCH |
| Everslage, Dietrich | VanderAnder, Carol. | 23, May 1847 | FF |
| Everslage, Joseph | Bockerstette, Cath. | 24, Oct. 1847 | FF |
| Eversmann, Franz J. | Stuerenberg, Anna C. | 25, July 1847 | AA |
| Eversmann, Herman H. | Grossrechtin, Ther. | 1, Nov. 1845 | FF |
| Eversmann, Herman P. | Schwermann, Maria T. | 30, May 1847 | FF |
| Eversmann, J Gerhard | Tepe, Maria Anna | 2, Nov. 1845 | FF |
| Eversmann, Johan H. | Muthers, Maria | 8, Dec. 1841 | F |
| Eversol, Bartholomew | Nolt, Martha Ann | 15, June 1833 | RCH |
| Everson, Albert | Roll, Sarah Jane | 4, Aug. 1844 | RCH |
| Everson, Benjamin | Newell, Maria | 20, Jan. 1842 | RCH |
| Everson, George | Addis, Adaline | 27, Apr. 1826 | RCH |
| Everson, John | Morgan, Fidela | 5, Dec. 1843 | RCH |
| Eversull, Henry | Fowler, Henrietta | 28, Aug. 1842 | RCH |
| Eversull, John | Morrison, R. | 16, June 1835 | RCH |
| Eversull, John | Black, Caroline | 4, Dec. 1845 | RCH |
| Eveslage, Heinrich | Cordes, Maria Cath. | 9, June 1836 | FF |
| Evinger, David | Joiner, M. Caroline | 21, Dec. 1841 | RCH |
| Evinger, Thomas | Miller, Elisabeth | 25, Apr. 1822 | RCH |
| Evins, Benjamin | Gilmore, Elisabeth | 29, July 1819 | RCH |
| Ewald, Heinrich | Gerholtz, Catharine | 22, Jan. 1843 | C |
| Ewald, Wilhelm Fr. | Kruse, Friedricka | 3, July 1842 | F |
| Ewald, Wilhelm H. | Kettermann, Catharin | 20, June 1848 | CC |
| Ewan, John | Fox, Marinda | 29, Dec. 1846 | RCH |
| Ewen, Charles | Vaughn, Sarah | 27, Feb. 1842 | RCH |
| Ewin, Levi | Burner, Eleanor | 11, May 1836 | RCH |
| Ewing, Henry | VanDike, Phebe J. | Dec. 1840 | RCH |
| Ewing, Israel | Coombs, Elisabeth | 30, Dec. 1833 | RCH |
| Ewing, James A. | Allen, Sarah | 14, Feb. 1844 | RCH |
| Ewing, Johan Albert | Heidemann, Maria Ann | 3, Sept 1849 | FF |

| Grooms<br>****** | Brides<br>****** | Date of Marriage<br>**** ** ******** | Code<br>**** |
|---|---|---|---|
| Ewing, Johan Heinric | Blommel, Margaretha | 7, Jan. 1849 | FF |
| Ewing, John | Boyd, Mary Ann | 23, May 1825 | RCH |
| Ewing, John | McLain, Elisabeth | 26, Jan. 1842 | RCH |
| Ewing, John | Kimball, Augusta | 5, June 1846 | RCH |
| Ewing, Jonathan | Vanonsan, Deborah | 25, June 1836 | RCH |
| Ewing, Joseph M. | Fry, Rachel | 19, Oct. 1848 | RCH |
| Ewing, Robert | Nash, Catharine | 10, Dec. 1840 | RCH |
| Ewing, William | Moore, Martha | 4, July 1849 | BB |
| Ewing, Wilson | Allen, Nancy | 6, May 1839 | RCH |
| Ewings, Enos | Waller, Jane | 10, Aug. 1826 | RCH |
| Exler, Heinrich | Lankemper, Elisabeth | 27, May 1849 | AA |
| Exler, Herman Anton | Feldmann, Agnes | 27, Oct. 1849 | CC |
| Eyer, Henry | Vochlein, Catharine | 22, May 1849 | RCH |
| Ezekiel, Eleazer | Johnson, Selina | 7, Dec. 1841 | RCH |
| Ezekiel, Mosely | Oppenheimer, Julia | 16, July 1842 | RCH |
| | | | |
| F---, Daniel | Ettell, Marianna | 29, July 1824 | RCH |
| F---, Thomas | Jackson, Abigail | 13, Nov. 1817 | RCH |
| Fa---, Solomon | Guenin, Sarah | 28, Sept 1826 | RCH |
| Facker, Abraham | Barrett, Sarah Ann | 26, Aug. 1841 | RCH |
| Faeger, Johan | Bugenmeier, Christin | 24, June 1836 | FF |
| Faeger, Nicolaus | Collinberg, Elis. | 8, Sept 1835 | RCH |
| Faesig, Philipp | Leitner, M. Cecilia | 22, Nov. 1840 | FF |
| Fagan, Joseph | Martin, Mary (Mrs) | 15, Dec. 1836 | RCH |
| Fagin, Aaron | Elless, Anna W. | 10, Jan. 1843 | RCH |
| Fagin, Aaron | Black, Jemimah | 17, Dec. 1846 | RCH |
| Fagin, Jackson | Stump, Sarah | 10, Feb. 1842 | RCH |
| Fagin, John | Woodruff, Elisabeth | 9, Aug. 1849 | RCH |
| Fagin, Louis | Morgan, Ruth T. | 10, Apr. 1838 | RCH |
| Fagley, Caleb | Park, Rebecca | 31, Oct. 1821 | RCH |
| Fah---, Johan | Meister, Anna | 28, Oct. 1847 | C |
| Fahey, John | Cooper, Sarah Ann | 18, July 1843 | RCH |
| Fahjen, Heinrich | Steinkamp, Catharine | 31, Aug. 1843 | F |
| Fahjin, Jacob | Steinkamp, Anna M. | 27, Nov. 1845 | F |
| Fahlbusch, Carl | Ismael, Friedricka | 26, Nov. 1842 | RCH |
| Fahling, Clemens | Uptmore, Maria | 26, Sept 1839 | FF |
| Fahnhoen, Joseph | Thole, M. Helena | 30, Sept 1849 | II |
| Fahrbach, Michael | Fulwalder, Maria | 22, June 1848 | G |
| Faije, Johan | Buhrmann, Maria | 14, Nov. 1843 | F |
| Failer, John H. | Wham, Nancy | 25, Oct. 1836 | RCH |
| Fair, Robert | Brooks, Mary | 31, Aug. 1832 | RCH |
| Fairchild, Charles | Tucker, Maria | 7, Jan. 1849 | RCH |
| Fairchild, Walter | Wallace, Susan | 22, Oct. 1836 | RCH |
| Fairclough, Thomas | Leach, Harriet | 17, Sept 1849 | RCH |
| Fais, Georg | Schrimmel, Theckla | 23, Oct. 1849 | EE |
| Falemsby, Theodore | Hunter, Patience | 18, Feb. 1841 | RCH |
| Falk, Joseph | Schmieder, Barbara | 29, Apr. 1849 | EE |
| Falke, Bernard H. | Fiddeldin, Mary | 3, Sept 1844 | AA |
| Falke, Heinrich | Heiser, Julia | 7, Mar. 1848 | EE |
| Falkenberg, Charles | Scarborough, Rachel | 2, June 1849 | RCH |
| Fall, Georg | Urlage, Catharine | 5, Mar. 1848 | EE |
| Falley, Alfred | Camon, Mary | 14, Apr. 1836 | RCH |
| Fallon, John | Fallon, Bridget | 19, Feb. 1849 | BB |
| Fangemann, Heinrich | Wickenberg, M Angela | 24, Aug. 1836 | FF |
| Faning, Henry | Parker, Isabella | 21, Aug. 1823 | RCH |
| Fannally, Richard | Conway, Alice | 23, Nov. 1846 | RCH |
| Fanning, John | Burke, Bridget | 19, Oct. 1848 | BB |
| Fanning, John | Burnst, Ann | 1, Nov. 1846 | GG |
| Fanning, Michael | Kennedy, Cath. (Mrs) | 6, June 1842 | BB |
| Fanning, William | Westcott, Roxanna | 28, Mar. 1839 | RCH |
| Fanshaw, William D. | Higgins, Mary Louise | 15, July 1847 | BB |
| Fanssett, Robert | Wallace, Elisabeth | 19, Jan. 1842 | RCH |
| Farbeck, Johan | Flory, Catharine | 30, Nov. 1843 | FF |
| Faren, Charles O. | ----, Sarah | 6, May 1819 | RCH |
| Farish, John | McGregor, Mary | 8, July 1846 | RCH |
| Fark, Henry | Witten, Mary | 16, Dec. 1843 | RCH |
| Farlen, Daniel | Appelbeck, Catharine | 28, Jan. 1849 | GG |
| Farley, James | Weller, Laura | 3, Nov. 1841 | RCH |
| Farley, John | Duffey, Margaret | 18, Oct. 1845 | RCH |
| Farley, Thomas | Webb, Sarah O. | 25, June 1838 | RCH |
| Farm--, Peter | Mack, Rosina | 23, Sept 1845 | RCH |

| Grooms | Brides | Date of Marriage | Code |
|--------|--------|------------------|------|
| ****** | ****** | **** ** ******** | **** |
| Farmohr, Heinrich | Latt, Agnes | 15, Jan. 1839 | FF |
| Farnum, Reuben | Birdsell, Caroline | 6, July 1842 | RCH |
| Farquar, Lewis | Francher, Elisabeth | 26, July 1847 | RCH |
| Farrar, Matthew | Wells, Sarah | 29, Nov. 1821 | RCH |
| Farrar, Thomas | S---, Jane | 24, Mar. 1825 | RCH |
| Farrell, Barney | Shandley, Catharine | 16, Aug. 1842 | BB |
| Farrell, James | Hartley, Mary Ann | 20, Apr. 1840 | BB |
| Farrell, James | McFall, Mary | 15, May 1846 | RCH |
| Farrell, John | Duffy, Bridget | 10, July 1848 | BB |
| Farrelly, Patrick | Murray, Ann | 13, Aug. 1848 | BB |
| Farren, | Thornell, Anna | Nov. 1844 | RCH |
| Farris, Thomas | Doerrer, Rachel | 29, July 1845 | RCH |
| Farris, William | Grace, Emeline | 1, Nov. 1846 | RCH |
| Fars, Peter | Winger, Sibella | 12, Aug. 1847 | EE |
| Farsarber, Harris | Link, Jane | 27, July 1847 | RCH |
| Farwert, Francis | Cheerbrook, Maria | 1, Nov. 1836 | FF |
| Farwick, Bernard | Steyermann, Dina | 20, Apr. 1841 | FF |
| Fasanach, Gottfreid | Birkle, Catharine | 2, Sept 1847 | EE |
| Fasche, Otto Heinric | Vaner, Elisabeth | 14, May 1844 | FF |
| Fasset, J.B. | Williams, Abigail | 25, Aug. 1832 | RCH |
| Faster, William | Vaness, Sarah | 2, Sept 1826 | RCH |
| Fath, Johan Adam | Helms, Bernardina | 1, Sept 1846 | EE |
| Fatherton, Thomas | Flynn, Hannah | 26, Mar. 1845 | BB |
| Fauber, | Steig, Anna | 10, Sept 1849 | RCH |
| Faul, Gottfried | Faber, Friedricka S. | 18, June 1843 | G |
| Faulkner, David | Minkley, Mary Ann | 20, Feb. 1844 | RCH |
| Faulkner, William | Casine, Margaret | 14, Aug. 1844 | RCH |
| Faulstick, Thaddeus | Culo, Susanne Cath. | 20, June 1847 | G |
| Faunry, Joseph | Cullom, Margaret | 26, Sept 1822 | RCH |
| Faussett, George | Robinson, Alvina | 17, July 1843 | RCH |
| Faust, George | Gray, Hannah | 20, Mar. 1836 | RCH |
| Faust, Jesse | Norris, Margaret | 15, July 1834 | RCH |
| Faust, Peter | Cunningham, Rebecca | 11, Feb. 1835 | RCH |
| Faw, Jonathan | Marshall, Elisabeth | 7, Aug. 1842 | RCH |
| Fawcett, William | Morgan, Elisabeth | 3, Feb. 1848 | BB |
| Fay, Cutting | Miller, Elisabeth | 1, June 1820 | RCH |
| Fay, Peter | Lynnan, Bridget | 16, Sept 1849 | BB |
| Faye, Johan | Buermann, Maria | 14, Nov. 1843 | F |
| Featherling, George | Dean, Sarah | 5, Apr. 1821 | RCH |
| Featherly, Truman | Evans, Charlotte | 1, Jan. 1846 | RCH |
| Febiger, George | Smith, Caroline | 5, Apr. 1849 | D |
| Fechheimer, M. | Thurnauer, Nanni | 10, May 1849 | RCH |
| Fechheimer, Samuel | Bernard, Caroline | 13, Oct. 1845 | RCH |
| Fechter, Bernard | Haendle, Sabina | 16, Oct. 1848 | EE |
| Fedders, Heinrich | Wellinghof, Elis. | 23, July 1838 | FF |
| Fedders, Heinrich | Werning, Maria | 7, Nov. 1848 | CC |
| Fedders, Johan | Orth, Anna Maria | 2, Apr. 1839 | FF |
| Fee, Hugh A. | Eldridge, Elisabeth | 28, Oct. 1836 | RCH |
| Feeley, Patrick | O'Brien, Ann | 29, Dec. 1848 | BB |
| Feely, Martin | McLaughlin, Ann M. | 30, Oct. 1843 | BB |
| Feeney, Eugene | Gainor, Elisabeth J. | 7, Apr. 1838 | RCH |
| Feeny, Patrick | Cantwell, Ellen | 19, Feb. 1849 | BB |
| Feeser, Jacob | Sampson, Margaret | 29, Mar. 1838 | RCH |
| Feger, Joseph | Emhart, Sophia Fr. | 28, May 1840 | FF |
| Feger, Lorenz | Graf, Maria Anna | 2, Apr. 1840 | FF |
| Fegley, Samuel | Craver, Dina | 21, Aug. 1844 | RCH |
| Fehrenbruck, Herman | Schott, Lisette | 15, Oct. 1848 | C |
| Fehring, Wilhelm | Schneider, Maria A. | 21, Jan. 1847 | AA |
| Feich, Valentin | Baum, Catharine | 15, Jan. 1846 | G |
| Feid, Johan | Roese, Catharine | 2, Apr. 1846 | G |
| Feiltes, Johan | Bauer, Maria | 10, Dec. 1842 | AA |
| Fein, Gerhard Bd. | Wulfkotter, Anna M. | 10, Sept 1844 | AA |
| Fein, Louis | Daudel, Regina | 21, Sept 1843 | A |
| Feingar, Solomon | McFarline, Nancy | 10, Mar. 1831 | RCH |
| Feldhake, Friedrich | Glinkamp, Elisabeth | 1, Nov. 1848 | AA |
| Feldhaus, Heinrich | Behmer, Catharine | 22, June 1848 | G |
| Feldkamp, J Heinrich | Bredeweg, Elisabeth | 11, Sept 1845 | F |
| Feldmann, Bernard | Helmers, Maria | 3, Nov. 1840 | FF |
| Feldmann, Gerhard J. | Medel, M. Adelheid | 25, Apr. 1847 | AA |
| Feldmann, Heinrich | Beckmann, Anna Maria | 20, Nov. 1838 | FF |
| Feldmann, Heinrich | Ossenbeck, Elisabeth | 27, Sept 1842 | FF |

| Grooms | Brides | Date of Marriage | Code |
|--------|--------|------------------|------|
| Feldmann, Herman | Nutbusch, Maria Elis | 9, Jan. 1844 | AA |
| Feldmann, Herman | Schroeder, Maria E. | 14, Oct. 1849 | CC |
| Feldmann, J. Herman | Dickhaus, Maria Elis | 9, May 1847 | AA |
| Feldmann, Johan Bd. | Frieling, Elisabeth | 6, Feb. 1844 | AA |
| Feldmann, Johan D. | Schuette, M. Angela | 18, Apr. 1847 | AA |
| Feldmann, Johan E. | Hanfeld, Anna Maria | 25, Apr. 1847 | EE |
| Feldmann, Johan H. | Reling, A. Adelheid | 7, Nov. 1837 | FF |
| Feldmann, Johan H. | Pape, M. Gertrud | 27, Feb. 1838 | FF |
| Feldmann, Johan Wm. | Hobbe, Maria Elis. | 31, Jan. 1847 | EE |
| Feldmann, Wilhelm H. | Schulte, Anna Maria | 8, June 1843 | C |
| Feldmann, Wilhelm H. | Heidt, Catharina | 30, Oct. 1849 | G |
| Feldschneider, Bd. | Boeh, Maria Anna | 9, Sept 1845 | AA |
| Feldschneider, Johan | Niemann, Charlotte | 18, Jan. 1842 | FF |
| Feldwisch, Heinrich | Steinkamp, M. Angela | 21, Dec. 1847 | E |
| Feliehmann, Philipp | Steigleiter, Cath. | 18, Apr. 1848 | A |
| Feliger, John | Ryan, Ann C. | 3, May 1849 | BB |
| Felix, Francis | Marion, Magdalena | 8, Aug. 1837 | FF |
| Felix, Friedrich | Weber, Maria | 14, Aug. 1849 | EE |
| Felix, Georg Peter | Sussidor, Barbara | 9, Oct. 1849 | EE |
| Felix, Johan | Runzer, Catharina | 5, Jan. 1835 | FF |
| Felix, Michael | Robein, Barbara | 20, Apr. 1841 | FF |
| Felix, Michael | Hofreider, Magdalena | 9, Sept 1849 | EE |
| Felker, Heinrich | Ahrens, A. Maria | 20, Apr. 1847 | FF |
| Fellner, Francis | Fleddermann, Cath. | 20, Aug. 1846 | AA |
| Felter, Dietrich | Gotke, Adelheid | 25, Sept 1849 | FF |
| Felter, Granville | Dukes, Edith | 13, Oct. 1846 | RCH |
| Felter, William | Vo---, Mary | 14, 1822 | RCH |
| Felters, Andrew | Snider, Mary | 8, Oct. 1846 | RCH |
| Feltmann, William H. | Klenne, Caroline | 17, June 1847 | RCH |
| Felty, August | Sparks, Mary | 2, Mar. 1843 | RCH |
| Fendt, Casimer | Stamm, Maria | 31, Oct. 1848 | G |
| Fenelon, Thomas | Crosson, Margaret | 7, May 1846 | RCH |
| Fenger, Friedrich | Gers, Elisabeth | 29, June 1847 | AA |
| Fenger, Heinrich | Schmutten, Agnes | 12, Sept 1847 | AA |
| Fenker, Johan B. | Voss, Catharine | 21, Nov. 1843 | AA |
| Fennell, James | Scott, Thamar | 2, Sept 1843 | RCH |
| Fennell, John | Kyle, Margaret | 1, Feb. 1839 | RCH |
| Fennemann, Herman H. | Gausepohl, Cath. A . | 5, Dec. 1848 | F |
| Fennemann, J. Herman | Wanneck, Marg. Adel. | 20, Apr. 1843 | F |
| Fennemann, Philipp | Restock, Catharine | 15, May 1849 | RCH |
| Fennmeyer, Johan | Schulte, Katharina E | 9, July 1848 | AA |
| Fenton, George | Bray, Elisabeth Ann | 17, Jan. 1847 | RCH |
| Fenton, Jacob | Wright, Sarah | 22, Apr. 1819 | RCH |
| Fenton, James | Mann, Sarah T. | 3, Nov. 1847 | RCH |
| Fenton, Marsh | Rolff, Elisabeth | 13, Apr. 1826 | RCH |
| Fenton, Roswell | Bray, Sarah | 23, Feb. 1842 | RCH |
| Fenton, William | Riffy, Lavicy | 13, Jan. 1843 | RCH |
| Fenzer, Anton | Muhring, Lisetta | 19, Nov. 1848 | AA |
| Feppe, Heinrich | Feldhaus, Marg. Elis | 4, Aug. 1840 | FF |
| Ferbon, George C. | Jones, Sarah H. | 14, Sept 1848 | RCH |
| Fereday, Charles | Gilbert, Mary Ann | 3, Dec. 1833 | RCH |
| Fereo, Christian A. | Hesing, Lisette | 6, Mar. 1848 | AA |
| Ferguson, | Bartlett, | 27, Dec. 1833 | RCH |
| Ferguson, | Leads, Sarah | 20, Aug. 1835 | RCH |
| Ferguson, Anthony H. | Mewhim, Matilda | 6, Nov. 1834 | RCH |
| Ferguson, Charles | Tyre, Mary | 7, Nov. 1834 | RCH |
| Ferguson, Daniel | ----, Henrietta | 11, Apr. 1819 | RCH |
| Ferguson, Daniel | Moore, Dorothea | 4, Apr. 1844 | RCH |
| Ferguson, Edward | Terreyck, Mary | 24, Dec. 1843 | RCH |
| Ferguson, Isaac | Carr, Nancy | 1, Dec. 1841 | RCH |
| Ferguson, Jacob H. | Irwin, Mary | 14, July 1834 | RCH |
| Ferguson, James | Corbley, Nancy | 31, May 1837 | RCH |
| Ferguson, James | Miller, Emma | 4, Sept 1842 | RCH |
| Ferguson, James | Whalon, Elisabeth | 14, Mar. 1848 | RCH |
| Ferguson, John | Byard, Mary Ann | 17, Oct. 1822 | RCH |
| Ferguson, Robert M. | Dumand, Phoebe | 30, July 1835 | RCH |
| Ferguson, Thomas | Thompson, Clara | 3, May 1848 | RCH |
| Ferguson, William | Hammit, Beulah | 13, July 1825 | RCH |
| Fering, B. Theodor | Bruemmerhaus, Chris. | 25, May 1847 | FF |
| Fermer, Thomas | Ross, Ann | 30, Apr. 1836 | RCH |
| Ferning, Casper | Kohorst, Catharina | 2, Apr. 1839 | FF |

| Grooms ***** | Brides ***** | Date of Marriage **** ** ******** | Code **** |
|---|---|---|---|
| Ferral, Harrison | Martin, Margaret | 1, Jan. 1846 | RCH |
| Ferrar, John | Winton, Martha B. | 23, Nov. 1835 | RCH |
| Ferrel, Emanuel J. | Price, Lydia | 25, May 1847 | RCH |
| Ferrel, John Wesley | Martin, Mary | 1, Feb. 1846 | RCH |
| Ferrell, Andrew | Stevens, Elisabeth | 14, Aug. 1848 | RCH |
| Ferrell, James W. | Martin, Alegam | 22, May 1841 | RCH |
| Ferrell, William | Barr, Nancy J. | 28, Dec. 1841 | RCH |
| Ferrill, Peter | Engard, J. | 13, Mar. 1821 | RCH |
| Ferrily, Luke | Jones, Patty | 26, June 1847 | RCH |
| Ferrin, James | Regan, Sophia | 14, Mar. 1821 | RCH |
| Ferris, Isaac | Buxton, Sarah A. | 28, Sept 1848 | RCH |
| Ferris, John | E---, Margaret | 1, Feb. 1825 | RCH |
| Ferris, John | Foreman, Harriet | 26, Apr. 1838 | RCH |
| Ferris, John | Minshall, Mary | 9, Apr. 1847 | RCH |
| Ferris, Samuel | Williams, Selina | 1, Sept 1842 | RCH |
| Ferris, Samuel M. | Ferris, Mary Z. | 6, Nov. 1838 | RCH |
| Ferris, Solomon | Stites, | 9, July 1818 | RCH |
| Ferris, William L. | Brown, Ann Elizabeth | 14, Dec. 1839 | I |
| Ferry, Aaron | Burke, Louise | 20, Apr. 1838 | RCH |
| Fesbeck, Adolph | Harmeier, Sophia | 30, Dec. 1845 | RCH |
| Fess, Henry | Herren, Barbara | 5, Aug. 1849 | RCH |
| Fessender, Benjamin | Leveret, Charlotte A | 24, Nov. 1829 | I |
| Fessender, Stephen | McBay, Henrietta | 23, Oct. 1838 | RCH |
| Fessler, Fidel | Gehrlich, Kunigunda | 18, Jan. 1842 | FF |
| Fessler, Georg | Kayser, Salome | 12, May 1844 | C |
| Fessler, Joseph | Diering, Catharina | 13, Sept 1841 | FF |
| Fester, Georg | Vogel, Catharine | 11, Apr. 1847 | A |
| Feth, Mathias | Bussen, Anna Maria | 17, Nov. 1849 | EE |
| Fette, Anton | Klophage, Elisabeth | 20, Sept 1849 | FF |
| Fetter, David E. | Ryan, Lucinda | 27, Nov. 1832 | RCH |
| Fetter, Heinrich | Burger, Catharine | 18, Oct. 1842 | G |
| Fetter, Jacob | Sampson, Mary | 31, Aug. 1841 | RCH |
| Fetter, Samuel | Huffmann, Mary | 29, Feb. 1848 | RCH |
| Fetzer, Johan | Wilke, Friedricka | 10, Dec. 1849 | RCH |
| Fetzer, Melchior | Stauss, Wil. | 6, Aug. 1844 | AA |
| Fetzer, Michael | Staus, Wilgefort | 6, Aug. 1844 | RCH |
| Feucht, Christopher | Bauman, Margaret | 24, Dec. 1846 | RCH |
| Feustel, Michael | Lehnbeuter, Barbara | 18, Feb. 1847 | EE |
| Fey, Georg Peter | Dewein, Margaretha | 27, May 1847 | C |
| Fey, Johan Nicolaus | Pitlinger, Catharine | 12, Jan. 1849 | EE |
| Fey, Nicholas | Genser, Elisabeth | 26, Sept 1846 | C |
| Fey, Wilhelm | Bank, Hedwig | 4, July 1849 | A |
| Feyman, Peter | Sound, Mary | 3, May 1849 | GG |
| Fibbe, Herman Hein. | Thoele, Maria Anna | 30, July 1848 | AA |
| Fibisch, Stanislaus | Bender, Mary | 29, July 1849 | BB |
| Fichter, Francis A. | Schmidt, Anna Maria | 8, Jan. 1849 | CC |
| Fick, Warren G. | Mayhew, Adeline | 12, Aug. 1834 | RCH |
| Fickbusch, Heinrich | Walstenmann, Sophia | 11, Nov. 1847 | C |
| Ficke, Herman Fried. | Schaefer, Ottilia P. | 3, Jan. 1840 | F |
| Ficken, Jacob | Heine, A. Margaretha | 24, Oct. 1844 | F |
| Ficken, Johan | Helmig, Caroline | 16, Aug. 1846 | F |
| Ficker, Johan | Poelling, E Adelheid | 7, July 1846 | FF |
| Fickers, Bernard H. | Bruegge, Clara | 16, Feb. 1847 | AA |
| Fidg---, Martin | Edmundson, Eunice | 8, Aug. 1836 | RCH |
| Fieber, Nicolaus | Wise, Catharine | 10, Mar. 1837 | RCH |
| Fieber, Simon | Hauck, Elisabeth | 19, Aug. 1836 | RCH |
| Fieber, Simon | Kaltern, Magdalena | 20, Dec. 1836 | RCH |
| Fieber, Simon | Will, Catharine | 1, Oct. 1845 | RCH |
| Fiebiger, Theophilus | Wey, Magdalena | 4, Mar. 1841 | G |
| Fiedeldey, Johan H. | Himm, Maria Anna | 12, Nov. 1846 | EE |
| Fiedler, Johan | Hoefer, Amalia | 17, Nov. 1848 | FF |
| Field, Albert | Smith, Ann | 16, Oct. 1842 | RCH |
| Field, Richard | Blaeque, Dessina | 20, Oct. 1842 | RCH |
| Field, Robert | Anderson, Lurena | 4, Oct. 1841 | RCH |
| Fields, Daniel | Quick, Mary J. | 28, Nov. 1845 | RCH |
| Fieler, Valentin | Kebberland, Margaret | 5, Jan. 1835 | FF |
| Fiernan, James | Story, Missouri | 24, Jan. 1843 | RCH |
| Fife, Alfred | Buckner, Harriet | 31, Aug. 1836 | RCH |
| Fihe, Theodor | Goediger, A. Cath. | 25, Nov. 1840 | FF |
| Fihner, Bernard | Floeder, Maria | 28, Sept 1841 | FF |
| Fike, Johan | Beckmann, Catharine | 7, Feb. 1843 | AA |

| Grooms ***** | Brides ***** | Date of Marriage **** ** ******** | Code **** |
|---|---|---|---|
| Filer, Nelson | White, Sarah | 10, Sept 1835 | RCH |
| Filla, William | Howard, Arminta | 27, Aug. 1845 | RCH |
| Fille, Leonard | Holthaus, Maria | 3, June 1849 | II |
| Filley, Lucius | Jones, Christina | 20, Mar. 1849 | RCH |
| Fillmore, August | Lockwood, Hannah | 29, June 1848 | RCH |
| Fillmore, Levins | Trowbridge, Mary | 3, Apr. 1838 | RCH |
| Fils, Medard | Rhine, Catharine | 17, Mar. 1843 | RCH |
| Filten, Thomas | Hawkins, Mary | 31, Aug. 1834 | RCH |
| Fin---, Patrick | Grogan, Mary Ann | 19, Mar. 1849 | RCH |
| Finan, Bernard | Butler, Margaret | 11, Sept 1841 | BB |
| Finch, Benson | Littlefield, Lydia | 11, July 1838 | RCH |
| Finch, Charles C. | Farmer, Miranda | 14, Feb. 1847 | BB |
| Finch, Conrad | Harrington, Louise | 27, June 1842 | RCH |
| Finch, Hardin | Allen, Rebecca | 5, Nov. 1845 | RCH |
| Finch, Henry | VanHorne, Jane | 4, 1825 | RCH |
| Finch, Henry | Grigg, Elisabeth | 14, Sept 1842 | RCH |
| Finch, Henry H. | Barfield, Mary | 17, Jan. 1834 | RCH |
| Finch, Joel | Saxton, Harriet | 29, June 1844 | RCH |
| Finch, John | Copeland, Eliza | 13, Jan. 1819 | RCH |
| Finch, Marcus A. | Howell, Amelia F. | 20, Sept 1849 | D |
| Finch, Samuel | Permit, Harriet | 30, Aug. 1841 | RCH |
| Finch, Thomas | Carr, Elisabeth H. | 16, Oct. 1844 | RCH |
| Finch, William | Young, Frances M. | 21, June 1838 | RCH |
| Finck, Friedrich | Schmidt, Margaretha | 5, July 1849 | G |
| Finck, Heinrich | Brand, Maria | 20, Sept 1849 | B |
| Findlay, Andrew | Cole, Caroline | 3, Aug. 1848 | RCH |
| Findlay, Samuel B. | Duncan, Elisabeth | 7, Dec. 1837 | RCH |
| Findlay, William B. | Vaun, Lydia | 12, Sept 1822 | RCH |
| Findley, Simon | Wood, Anna Elisabeth | 8, Aug. 1842 | RCH |
| Finegan, James | Nelson, Nancy | 12, Aug. 1821 | RCH |
| Finegan, James | Burroughs, Temperan. | 20, Apr. 1826 | RCH |
| Fink, Christian H. | Meyer, Sophia | 25, Aug. 1842 | F |
| Fink, Franz H. | Harlbrink, Anna M. | 11, June 1849 | F |
| Fink, Friedrich | Mueller, Elisabeth | 2, July 1846 | G |
| Fink, Heinrich Bern. | Hiehmann, Charlotte | 28, Feb. 1844 | G |
| Fink, Jacob | Meyer, Barbara | 9, Aug. 1837 | FF |
| Fink, Johan Heinrich | Wessling, Catharine | 27, Nov. 1845 | AA |
| Fink, Wilhelm | Kelsch, Salome | 29, Mar. 1849 | G |
| Finkba---, William | Swift, Maria | 5, June 1824 | RCH |
| Finke, Francis H. | Fraulker, Maria | 1, Aug. 1847 | CC |
| Finke, Franz Heinric | Harbedank, Anna M. | 15, Oct. 1846 | B |
| Finke, Friedrich | Delerein, Wilhelmina | 26, June 1837 | FF |
| Finke, Gerhard F. | Schump, Maria E. | 9, Sept 1849 | RCH |
| Finke, Heinrich | Kadenbruck, Louise | 7, Dec. 1848 | F |
| Finke, Heinrich Wm. | Siefke, Catharina M. | 1, July 1840 | G |
| Finke, J. Friedrich | Kammen, Louise | 21, Oct. 1847 | F |
| Finke, Johan Heinric | Wusthoff, Louise | 13, Mar. 1849 | A |
| Finley, Alexander | Barr, Ann Ellen | 19, Oct. 1837 | I |
| Finley, Preston | Byrd, Susan | 17, Jan. 1843 | RCH |
| Finley, William | Charters, Ellen | 9, Nov. 1845 | RCH |
| Finn, Johan | Ott, Elisabeth | 26, Sept 1847 | AA |
| Finney, Ira | Messich, Elisabeth | 17, Aug. 1837 | RCH |
| Finney, James | Minor, Rebecca | 13, Mar. 1839 | RCH |
| Finney, John | Spencer, Ruth | 22, Nov. 1837 | RCH |
| Finney, John | Clark, Mary A. | 23, Nov. 1841 | BB |
| Finney, John | Young, Sarah | 12, Apr. 1846 | RCH |
| Finney, Thomas | Green, Mary | 7, Mar. 1833 | RCH |
| Finney, Thomas | Runyan, Martha A. | 16, Sept 1849 | RCH |
| Finnigan, Francis | Reenan, Mary | 10, Apr. 1849 | GG |
| Finnigan, John | Kelly, Ellen | 25, Oct. 1841 | BB |
| Finnigan, Michael | Kelly, Margaret | 8, June 1844 | BB |
| Finnigan, Richard | McAndrew, Mary | 27, May 1849 | BB |
| Finny, John | Gormly, Mary A. | 14, May 1848 | GG |
| Finsh, Henry B. | Seldon, Eliza | 4, Nov. 1824 | RCH |
| Firke, Heinrich | Kallmeyer, Elisabeth | 19, May 1842 | F |
| Firleck, Louis | ----, Sarah Ann | 17, Apr. 1839 | RCH |
| Firth, Friedrich | Hankins, Elisabeth | 17, Mar. 1842 | RCH |
| Fischbach, Jacob | Roark, Sarah | 1, Aug. 1847 | RCH |
| Fischer, Anton | Miller, Elisabeth | 9, Jan. 1843 | AA |
| Fischer, August | Haugh, Elisabeth | 5, Sept 1847 | RCH |
| Fischer, Balthasar | Pistner, Elisabeth | 17, Jan. 1837 | FF |

| Grooms | Brides | Date of Marriage | Code |
|--------|--------|------------------|------|
| ****** | ****** | **** ** ******* | **** |
| Fischer, Bernard F. | Schroeder, Carolina | 5, Nov. 1848 | II |
| Fischer, Carl | Reisch, Victoria | 21, Nov. 1848 | C |
| Fischer, Friedrich | Mueller, Catharina | 30, Dec. 1849 | H |
| Fischer, Friedrich | Reis, Margaretha | 16, Aug. 1846 | EE |
| Fischer, Friedrich | Neurohr, Anna Maria | 28, June 1848 | EE |
| Fischer, Georg | Dahmann, Maria Anna | 26, Nov. 1844 | FF |
| Fischer, Gerhard L. | Kamp, Agnes A. | 22, July 1849 | EE |
| Fischer, Heinrich | Busch, Maria | 16, Aug. 1842 | FF |
| Fischer, Jacob | Klinger, Anna | 27, May 1849 | II |
| Fischer, Johan | Senbert, Anna Maria | 20, Sept 1846 | EE |
| Fischer, Johan Adam | Leckers, Dorothea L. | 5, Feb. 1846 | F |
| Fischer, Johan Fried | Fortmann, Elisabeth | 13, July 1837 | FF |
| Fischer, Joseph | Hagedorn, Elisabeth | 25, Jan. 1848 | AA |
| Fischer, Joseph | Bauer, Elisabeth | 20, Feb. 1849 | EE |
| Fischer, Joseph A. | Vollenweiter, Emilia | 23, Oct. 1849 | A |
| Fischer, Martin | Oehler, Maria | 30, Nov. 1848 | EE |
| Fischer, Michael | Kline, Magdalena | 18, Mar. 1844 | RCH |
| Fischer, Peter | Schoening, Anna M. | 16, Sept 1845 | AA |
| Fischer, Peter | Mueller, Katharina | 25, June 1848 | AA |
| Fischer, Wilhelm | Bender, Sophia | 11, Sept 1845 | C |
| Fischvogt, J. Fried. | Korf, Sophia Marg. | 8, Feb. 1849 | B |
| Fish, Daniel W. | Claypole, Harriet | 26, Nov. 1837 | RCH |
| Fish, Davis A. | Williams, Elisabeth | July 1824 | RCH |
| Fish, Eli | Williams, Sarah | 2, Dec. 1841 | RCH |
| Fish, Isaac L. | Phillips, Mary A. | 16, Oct. 1845 | BB |
| Fish, Thomas | Turner, Eliza | 20, May 1824 | RCH |
| Fishburn, Samuel | Sornts, Jane R. | 8, Oct. 1833 | RCH |
| Fisher, Adam | Moore, Catharine | 14, May 1846 | RCH |
| Fisher, Daniel | Cook, Harriet | 4, Apr. 1843 | RCH |
| Fisher, Daniel | Johnson, Sally | 25, Apr. 1846 | RCH |
| Fisher, Edmund L. | Manyar, Rebecca | 25, Mar. 1832 | RCH |
| Fisher, Frederick C. | Hopkins, Rachel A. | 3, Mar. 1841 | RCH |
| Fisher, George | McDonald, Mary | 28, May 1844 | RCH |
| Fisher, Henry C. | Haven, Caroline S. | 1, July 1848 | D |
| Fisher, Isaac | Hamilton, Maria | 23, Aug. 1846 | RCH |
| Fisher, James | Parker, Margaret | 17, Sept 1818 | RCH |
| Fisher, James | Dawson, Rebecca | 19, Feb. 1843 | RCH |
| Fisher, James | Priest, Mary E. | 5, Aug. 1843 | RCH |
| Fisher, James | Bowers, Edy | 24, May 1849 | RCH |
| Fisher, John | Gasner, Rebecca | 17, July 1834 | RCH |
| Fisher, Jonathan | Titus, Elisabeth | 12, Nov. 1835 | RCH |
| Fisher, Joseph | Tice, Esther | 31, Mar. 1844 | RCH |
| Fisher, Myers | Johnson, Susan | 22, Nov. 1831 | RCH |
| Fisher, Robert J. | Jameson, Catharine | 21, Jan. 1836 | I |
| Fisher, Samuel C. | Norris, Sarah Ann | 26, Nov. 1837 | RCH |
| Fisher, Stephen | Foderce, Sarah F. | 24, Oct. 1844 | RCH |
| Fisher, William | Sayer, Joanna | 9, Dec. 1844 | RCH |
| Fisher, William | Gordon, Hannah | 30, Oct. 1845 | RCH |
| Fisher, William | Williams, Lydia | 27, Mar. 1847 | RCH |
| Fishwater, Thomas | Stiles, Augusta | 9, Sept 1832 | RCH |
| Fisk, Benjamin | Moore, Ellen | 11, May 1842 | RCH |
| Fisk, Ebenezer | Stephens, Elisabeth | 11, June 1843 | RCH |
| Fisk, John | Johnson, Elisabeth | 15, Oct. 1842 | RCH |
| Fisk, Nathan | Willis, Hannah | 6, Sept 1818 | RCH |
| Fisk, Valorus | Shirly, Sarah | 27, Sept 1842 | RCH |
| Fisk, William | Fagley, Rebecca | 15, Mar. 1846 | RCH |
| Fisse, Johan Heinric | Wessels, Maria Elis. | 30, July 1839 | FF |
| Fist, Ellis | Maloney, Ann | 24, Sept 1835 | RCH |
| Fister, Jacob | Gephardt, Louise | 18, Apr. 1843 | RCH |
| Fisting, Anton | Snippe, Maria Elis. | 26, Nov. 1838 | FF |
| Fisting, Francis | Mueller, Maria Anna | 23, Aug. 1842 | FF |
| Fitch, A. | Grady, M.A. | 4, Apr. 1833 | RCH |
| Fitch, James M. | Bushnell, Jane E. | 9, Aug. 1838 | RCH |
| Fitch, Joseph | Cordington, Varinda | 12, Nov. 1841 | RCH |
| Fithian, Daniel | Ellsworth, Mary E. | 26, Apr. 1848 | RCH |
| Fitzgerald, John | Burns, Ellen | 11, Oct. 1847 | RCH |
| Fitzgerald, John | Hill, Joanne | 15, Aug. 1847 | GG |
| Fitzgerald, Patrick | Mackey, | 16, May 1835 | RCH |
| Fitzgerald, Peter | Walsh, Anna | 11, June 1835 | RCH |
| Fitzgerald, Peter | Coulter, Martha | 10, Oct. 1848 | D |
| Fitzhugh, George W. | Weatherby, Amelia | 24, Aug. 1835 | RCH |

| Grooms | Brides | Date of Marriage | Code |
|--------|--------|------------------|------|
| ****** | ****** | **** ** ******** | **** |
| Fitzhugh, George W. | Dalton, Martha | 19, June 1849 | RCH |
| Fitzmorris, John | Quinn, Bridget | 19, Nov. 1848 | GG |
| Fitzpatrick, Andrew | Manning, Ann | 23, Nov. 1847 | GG |
| Fitzpatrick, John | Harrington, Mary | 25, July 1847 | BB |
| Fitzpatrick, Matthew | Burke, Margaret | 16, Aug. 1842 | BB |
| Fitzpatrick, Patrick | Boyle, Ann | 29, Jan. 1834 | RCH |
| Fitzpatrick, Thomas | Carroll, Elisabeth | 21, Oct. 1848 | BB |
| Fitzsimmons, Benj. | Krouse, Alvina | 3, Oct. 1841 | RCH |
| Fitzsimmons, Bernard | McCoy, Ann | 15, Nov. 1846 | BB |
| Fitzsimmons, William | McAleer, Ellen | 14, May 1840 | BB |
| Fitzsimmons, William | Adams, Maria | 22, Aug. 1847 | RCH |
| Fitzwater, Henry | Brown, Anna | 2, Oct. 1843 | RCH |
| Fl---, Moses | Risp, Margaret | 4, July 1827 | RCH |
| Flach, Carl | Jung, Maria Anna | 25, June 1848 | EE |
| Flagg, Jacob J. | Tropton, Hannah | 14, Sept 1834 | RCH |
| Flagg, Martin H. | Cory, Hetty | 22, Dec. 1825 | RCH |
| Flagge, Franz H. | Kreiming, Catharine | 12, Nov. 1846 | RCH |
| Flake, Georg Heinric | Brocker, Maria Anna | 15, July 1849 | FF |
| Flanagan, George | Allen, Mary J. | 14, Apr. 1847 | RCH |
| Flanagan, James | Farley, Bridget | 25, Apr. 1840 | BB |
| Flanagan, James | Dowd, Catharine | 2, Aug. 1841 | BB |
| Flanagan, John | Robinson, Mary Jane | 9, May 1849 | RCH |
| Flangher, David | Beeler, Matilda | 30, Apr. 1844 | RCH |
| Flannagan, Edward | Connoughton, Bridget | 28, Aug. 1842 | BB |
| Flannery, Michael | Philipps, Mary | 25, July 1849 | BB |
| Flaspohler, Heinrich | Holdmeyer, M. Elis. | 1, July 1849 | II |
| Flatcher, William | Buckingham, Gydier | 13, Oct. 1839 | RCH |
| Flatery, Henry | Hafferon, Margaret | 13, May 1849 | GG |
| Flattery, Martin | McGlain, Margaret | 6, June 1848 | BB |
| Flaxmeyer, Anton | Hauser, Catharine | 2, July 1848 | RCH |
| Fleak, Alfred | Derman, Elisabeth | 4, July 1834 | RCH |
| Fleck, Heinrich | Breindt, Caroline | 20, Dec. 1849 | RCH |
| Fleckenstein, Conrad | Oberbeck, Elisabeth | 12, Oct. 1843 | AA |
| Fleckenstein, Johan | Gass, Elisabeth | 23, May 1848 | EE |
| Flecksteiner, Alex. | Worst, Margaretha | 14, Feb. 1847 | EE |
| Fleddermann, Bernard | Kenwinkel, Dorothea | 15, Jan. 1846 | AA |
| Fleig, Anton | Hurst, Balbina | 3, Feb. 1848 | EE |
| Fleisch, Stephan | Bauer, Regina | 8, Feb. 1842 | FF |
| Fleischmann, Charles | Ayniel, Lucille | 23, Dec. 1834 | RCH |
| Fleisen, Theodore | Kaiser, Margaret | 9, Jan. 1847 | RCH |
| Fleming, | Coddington, Martha | 17, Aug. 1826 | RCH |
| Fleming, Alexander | Bratton, Joanna | 15, Nov. 1842 | RCH |
| Fleming, David | Seller, Sarah | 7, Apr. 1844 | RCH |
| Fleming, Francis | Bell, Mary | 28, Nov. 1835 | RCH |
| Fleming, Jesse | Flinchpaugh, Polly | 4, Mar. 1847 | RCH |
| Fleming, John H. | W---, Asenath | 2, Dec. 1824 | RCH |
| Fleming, John R. | Bundy, Martha | 6, Oct. 1842 | RCH |
| Fleming, Thomas | Pelton, Sarah | 19, June 1849 | RCH |
| Fleming, Thomas | O'Hare, Margaret | 10, Aug. 1845 | BB |
| Fleming, William | Gibson, Sarah | 28, July 1833 | RCH |
| Flemming, Henry | Wells, Caroline | 8, Feb. 1837 | RCH |
| Flemming, J. | Hamilton, Hannah | 2, July 1849 | RCH |
| Flerlage, John G. | Brundiers, Christine | 4, Nov. 1846 | BB |
| Fletcher, Robert | Haines, Mary Ann | 25, Dec. 1834 | RCH |
| Fletcher, Solon | Richards, Adeline | 12, Nov. 1846 | RCH |
| Fletcher, William W. | Buckingham, Lydia | 1837 | RCH |
| Flick, Francis | Herzog, M. Josephina | 15, Nov. 1836 | FF |
| Flick, Franz | Zimmermann, Helena | 29, Sept 1849 | A |
| Flick, Joseph | Graff, Francisca | 6, Apr. 1847 | EE |
| Flick, Michael | Mueller, Maria Anna | 19, Aug. 1836 | FF |
| Flimnis, John E. | Bradbin, Dorcas | 15, Feb. 1839 | RCH |
| Flin, Stephan | Smedley, Joanna | 25, Dec. 1822 | RCH |
| Flinchpaugh, David | Flemin, Maria | 17, Mar. 1842 | RCH |
| Flinchpaugh, Henry | Creech, Cynthia Ann | 9, Mar. 1843 | RCH |
| Flinn, Ambrose | Earhart, Priscilla | Jan. 1845 | RCH |
| Flinn, Jacob | Muchmore, Sarah | 3, Sept 1820 | RCH |
| Flinn, James | Kennedy, Sophronia | 27, Oct. 1823 | RCH |
| Flinn, Jesse | Wilson, Sarah Ann | 15, Apr. 1847 | RCH |
| Flinn, Patrick | McDonald, Catherine | 27, Feb. 1849 | GG |
| Flinn, Patrick | Seihane, Mary | 29, July 1849 | GG |
| Flinn, Peter | Linehart, Bridget | 25, June 1848 | BB |

| Grooms ***** | Brides ***** | Date of Marriage **** ** ******** | Code **** |
|---|---|---|---|
| Flinn, Vincent J. | Robinson, Alasana | 29, Apr. 1833 | RCH |
| Flinn, William | Jones, Margaret Ann | 25, Sept 1842 | RCH |
| Flinn, William | Bland, Rebecca | 28, July 1846 | RCH |
| Flint, Daniel | Arthur, Mary | 1, Apr. 1819 | RCH |
| Floders, Johan Herm. | Trentmann, Elisabeth | 15, Oct. 1848 | AA |
| Flodmann, Gerhard H. | Otting, Anna Maria | 21, Apr. 1846 | AA |
| Flohr, Carl | Wolf, Barbara | 30, Sept 1845 | AA |
| Flomerfelt, George | McKiney, Susannah | 20, June 1823 | RCH |
| Flood, Daniel | O'Neill, Ellen | 16, Aug. 1846 | BB |
| Flood, Joel | Honor, Rhoda | 19, Aug. 1846 | RCH |
| Floork, John | Derrough, Sally | 24, Mar. 1836 | RCH |
| Flori, Jacob | Schweitzer, C.(Mrs) | 22, Feb. 1841 | FF |
| Flow--, Zachariah | Ingersoll, Sally Ann | 8, May 1825 | RCH |
| Flowers, James | Mean, Ann | 12, Sept 1834 | RCH |
| Flowers, Michael B. | Colter, Catharine | 5, Oct. 1820 | RCH |
| Flowry, Alfred | Pool, Mary | 6, Feb. 1847 | RCH |
| Floyd, Samuel | Ch---, Maria | 17, Apr. 1838 | RCH |
| Floyd, Thomas | Ayres, Maria | 11, Jan. 1835 | RCH |
| Fluckhuff, Francis | Brockmann, Elisabeth | 22, Oct. 1848 | AA |
| Flugel, Adam | Werner, Barbara | 27, Feb. 1838 | RCH |
| Flynn, Edward | Creely, Ann | 11, Oct. 1849 | BB |
| Flynn, James | Quinlan, Margaret | 6, May 1849 | BB |
| Flynn, John | Kelly, Mary | 13, Apr. 1841 | BB |
| Flynn, Patrick | Maguire, Mary | 2, Nov. 1849 | BB |
| Flynn, Patrick | Irwin, Mary | 9, Dec. 1849 | GG |
| Flynn, Thomas | Nolan, Mary | 13, Jan. 1840 | BB |
| Fobbe, Clemens | Kotte, Catharina | 9, Oct. 1849 | II |
| Fobe, Johan Caspar | Kellinghaus, Elis. | 21, Nov. 1847 | EE |
| Fochs, | Eisenmann, Francisca | 6, May 1849 | RCH |
| Foecke, Heinrich | Winter, Theresa | 27, Aug. 1848 | II |
| Foegle, Balthasar | Kleine, M. Magdalena | 1, Apr. 1845 | FF |
| Foegle, Joseph | Voigt, Johanna | 8, Aug. 1843 | FF |
| Foerht, Jacob | Wirthlein, Christina | 21, Jan. 1845 | FF |
| Foerster, J. Tobias | Reager, Margaret | 15, Aug. 1843 | RCH |
| Foest, Johan Aloys | Ganters, M Christina | 24, Nov. 1847 | EE |
| Fogarty, James | Yager, Sarah Ann | 18, Nov. 1843 | RCH |
| Fogarty, John | Hughes, Mary | 3, July 1844 | BB |
| Fogarty, Patrick | Ging, Margaret | 6, July 1846 | BB |
| Fogarty, Patrick | Ryan, Bridget | 18, Feb. 1849 | BB |
| Fogg, John | Burch, Anna | 1, Jan. 1829 | I |
| Fohr, Leonard | Gerbet, Agatha | 23, Jan. 1842 | RCH |
| Foley, Daniel | Brenney, Julia | 28, Oct. 1849 | GG |
| Foley, Henry | Titus, Rose Ann | 16, July 1835 | RCH |
| Foley, Michael | Wuerst, Catharine | 1, Sept 1846 | EE |
| Foley, Thomas | Gallagher, Mary | 19, Apr. 1840 | BB |
| Folger, Alexander | Heffley, Eleanor | 29, Jan. 1835 | RCH |
| Folger, Charles | Clayton, Elisabeth | 26, Apr. 1835 | RCH |
| Folger, George | Laird, Anna | 19, May 1847 | RCH |
| Folger, Jethro | Macy, Margaret | 16, July 1818 | RCH |
| Folger, John | Swain, Emma | 13, Nov. 1817 | RCH |
| Folger, Richard | Ross, Eleanor | 14, Nov. 1835 | RCH |
| Folger, Seth W. | Washburn, Mary | 4, June 1837 | RCH |
| Folger, Thomas B. | Risk, Catharine | 23, June 1836 | RCH |
| Folke, Casper | Weber, Catharina | 6, Jan. 1835 | FF |
| Folleck, James | Teeple, Margaret | 7, July 1835 | RCH |
| Follen, John | Adkins, Clarissa | 11, May 1836 | RCH |
| Foller, Johan | Schart, Elisabeth | 24, Jan. 1847 | A |
| Follin, August | Reeder, Caroline | 6, Sept 1847 | RCH |
| Folsom, Samuel | Davis, Sophia | 28, Nov. 1847 | RCH |
| Fonekous, Jacob | Larabee, Abigail | 7, Mar. 1821 | RCH |
| Fones, Jacob | Stillwell, Louise | 24, Mar. 1836 | RCH |
| Foor, David | Burdsall, Jedijah | 22, Oct. 1846 | RCH |
| Foos, John | Linville, Elisabeth | 7, Oct. 1845 | RCH |
| Foos, Thomas | Linville, Jane | 30, Aug. 1847 | RCH |
| Foote, Andrew | Wane, Abigail | 12, Sept 1837 | RCH |
| Forber, John | Sisson, Emily | 6, Aug. 1818 | RCH |
| Forbes, | Dayton, Elisabeth | 2, Aug. 1849 | RCH |
| Forbes, Samuel | Rittenhouse, Elis. | 4, Sept 1841 | RCH |
| Forbes, Thomas | Marshall, Hannah | 3, June 1832 | RCH |
| Forbes, Thomas | Redinbo, Sarah | 4, Feb. 1843 | RCH |
| Force, Munson | McKee, Martha | 25, Aug. 1843 | RCH |

| Grooms | Brides | Date of Marriage | Code |
|--------|--------|------------------|------|
| ****** | ****** | **** ** ******** | **** |
| Ford, Alexander | Reeves, Mary E. | 7, Oct. 1846 | RCH |
| Ford, Charles | Richardson, Mary Ann | 11, Apr. 1844 | RCH |
| Ford, Elias | Snider, Martha | 28, May 1843 | RCH |
| Ford, Hiram | Ingram, Elisabeth | 13, May 1835 | RCH |
| Ford, Isaiah | Kemper, Frances | 11, June 1842 | RCH |
| Ford, James | Hall, Susan | 11, Aug. 1847 | RCH |
| Ford, John W. | Byer, Mary | 27, Aug. 1839 | RCH |
| Ford, Joseph | Wardage, Phoebe K. | 9, Apr. 1820 | RCH |
| Ford, Michael | Reany, Margaret | 3, Sept 1848 | BB |
| Ford, Nicholas W. | Page, Martha H. | Mar. 1834 | I |
| Ford, Samuel | Curry, Abigail | 2, May 1836 | RCH |
| Ford, Smith | Fox, Frances | 16, June 1847 | RCH |
| Ford, William | Lundlum, Mary | 8, Jan. 1847 | RCH |
| Fordney, Beats | Semar, Mary A. | 11, Oct. 1845 | RCH |
| Forg---, Isaac | Chrisinore, Charlott | 21, Jan. 1838 | RCH |
| Forhach, Jacob | Vogel, Anna Barbara | 3, June 1849 | C |
| Forman, James | Hammel, Mary Jane | 24, Mar. 1847 | RCH |
| Forman, John M. | Millhoff, | Feb. 1845 | RCH |
| Former, Rufus | Shipman, Susan Ann | 2, May 1833 | RCH |
| Forquer, Charles | Morris, Euphemia | 24, Apr. 1839 | RCH |
| Forrells, Edward | Owens, Mary Ann | 1, Feb. 1836 | RCH |
| Forrest, Ernst | Frank, Maria | 17, Sept 1849 | F |
| Forrest, Regen | Pierce, Sarah | 21, Sept 1835 | RCH |
| Forrester, Augustine | Miller, Elisabeth | 14, Apr. 1849 | RCH |
| Forsha, Samuel W. | Kently, Hannah | 28, July 1825 | RCH |
| Forsha, William | Collins, Elisabeth L | July 1824 | RCH |
| Forshey, C.G. | Williams, Martha | 31, Aug. 1843 | RCH |
| Forster, Georg | Schmidt, Margaretha | 29, Jan. 1849 | HH |
| Fortmann, Anton | Sanders, Gertrud | 24, Feb. 1846 | AA |
| Fortmann, Heinrich | Wiegelmann, Anna M. | 16, Feb. 1836 | FF |
| Fortmann, Herman | Duncan, Margaret | 5, May 1844 | RCH |
| Fortmann, Herman H. | Finke, Catharine | 4, Oct. 1849 | F |
| Fortmann, J Heinrich | Biederbeck, Gertrud | 3, Oct. 1848 | II |
| Fortmer, Meridith | Edwards, Melly | 6, May 1837 | RCH |
| Fortune, Patrick | Slaughter, Elisabeth | 28, June 1848 | BB |
| Forvers, Charles | Duvall, Rebecca | 11, Aug. 1833 | RCH |
| Forwett, Heinrich | ----, Catharina | 20, Oct. 1840 | F |
| Fosdick, Henry N. | Harkness, | 28, Jan. 1836 | RCH |
| Fosdick, Samuel | Wood, Sarah Ann | 13, Jan. 1836 | RCH |
| Fosdick, William | Tylie, Amelia A. | 9, Sept 1841 | RCH |
| Foss, Joseph | Fowble, Harriet | 12, Dec. 1818 | RCH |
| Fossenkemper, Henry | VonBergen, Maria | 10, Aug. 1843 | F |
| Fosser, Samuel | Babb, Martha | 26, Mar. 1845 | RCH |
| Fossin, Morris | Moore, Caroline | 13, May 1849 | RCH |
| Foster, Charles | Turner, Elisabeth | 1, Feb. 1835 | RCH |
| Foster, David | Johnson, Ruth Ann | 25, Dec. 1843 | RCH |
| Foster, Elijah | Delaney, Catharine | 18, Mar. 1847 | RCH |
| Foster, Francis | Thomas, Sarah | 8, Sept 1844 | RCH |
| Foster, George | McCullock, Jane | 24, June 1835 | RCH |
| Foster, Hamilton | Bradley, Emily | 28, Dec. 1841 | RCH |
| Foster, Henry | Baxter, Triplen(Mrs) | 10, June 1841 | RCH |
| Foster, James | Bargett, Susannah | 20, May 1846 | RCH |
| Foster, James | Pruden, Hannah | 20, Jan. 1848 | RCH |
| Foster, Jesse | Shelton, Susan M. | 5, Feb. 1846 | RCH |
| Foster, John | Kilburn, Hannah | 15, Feb. 1821 | RCH |
| Foster, John | Foster, Eleanor | 6, May 1824 | RCH |
| Foster, Ralph | Craddock, Elisabeth | 9, Feb. 1846 | RCH |
| Foster, Robert | Waldsmith, Catharine | 25, Nov. 1833 | RCH |
| Foster, Seneca | Ferrel, Paulina | 29, Apr. 1819 | RCH |
| Foster, Seth | Huntington, Anna M. | 3, Dec. 1846 | RCH |
| Foster, Thomas J. | Williamson, Anna L. | 1, Nov. 1832 | RCH |
| Foster, William | Townsend, Mandana | 4, Feb. 1836 | RCH |
| Foster, William C. | Smith, Martha Ann | 28, June 1830 | RCH |
| Foster, William S. | Kilgour, Elisabeth | 12, Sept 1822 | RCH |
| Foster, William T. | Cosperce, Mary Clara | 22, Feb. 1848 | BB |
| Fottrell, Andrew | Fottrell, Sarah | 26, June 1836 | RCH |
| Foulger, Seth | Clasby, Lydia | 13, Apr. 1820 | RCH |
| Foulks, George | Manning, Jemima | 24, Oct. 1847 | RCH |
| Fowble, Jacob | Bowen, Mary | 21, July 1819 | RCH |
| Fowler, Abraham | Erwin, Cynthia Ann | 26, May 1846 | RCH |
| Fowler, Alanson | McRoberts, Lucy B. | 3, June 1827 | RCH |

| Grooms | Brides | Date of Marriage | Code |
| ****** | ****** | **** ** ******** | **** |
| Fowler, David | Reese, Nancy | 30, July 1835 | RCH |
| Fowler, Jacob | Ferguson, Sarah | 4, May 1825 | RCH |
| Fowler, John | Sharp, Sarah | 23, Aug. 1847 | RCH |
| Fowler, John | McDonald, Elisabeth | 27, Mar. 1848 | RCH |
| Fowler, Samuel | Cromwell, Morgiana | 31, Oct. 1843 | RCH |
| Fowler, William | Bayard, Elisabeth | 13, June 1844 | RCH |
| Fowler, William P. | Woods, Altha | 9, June 1841 | RCH |
| Fox, Benjamin | Jones, Eliza Jane | 23, Dec. 1849 | RCH |
| Fox, Charles | Miller, Mary | 25, Nov. 1824 | RCH |
| Fox, George | Fry, Elisabeth | 1, Oct. 1837 | RCH |
| Fox, Jack | Dempsey, Julia | 1, Nov. 1847 | BB |
| Fox, Jacob L. | Heinthover, Mary Ann | 4, June 1833 | RCH |
| Fox, John | Haughton, Martha | 18, Oct. 1821 | RCH |
| Fox, Samuel | Bostick, Elisabeth | 22, Mar. 1838 | RCH |
| Fox, Silas | Enos, Hannah | 3, Sept 1837 | RCH |
| Fox, Silas | McDale, America | 23, Feb. 1846 | RCH |
| Fox, Thomas | Benson, Margaret | 23, Jan. 1842 | RCH |
| Fox, Thomas | Stop, Christina | 23, Sept 1848 | RCH |
| Fox, Thomas | Mooney, Mary | 26, Nov. 1849 | BB |
| Fox, Thomas | Hyland, Catharine | 11, Nov. 1849 | BB |
| Foy, Francis | Flannigan, Mary | 11, Jan. 1843 | BB |
| Foy, Francis | Coleman, Jane | 25, Nov. 1846 | GG |
| Foy, George D. | McAll, Rachel M. | 29, Mar. 1835 | RCH |
| Fragge, Joseph | Feldhaus, Gertrud | 11, Nov. 1849 | AA |
| Frake, Heinrich | Buddelemier, Carolin | 8, Nov. 1849 | II |
| Fraley, Frederick | Williamson, Louise | 16, Aug. 1842 | RCH |
| Fralisch, Samuel | Laly, Hester | 28, July 1839 | RCH |
| Frame, Wilhelm | Schuhmacher, Cath. | 15, Nov. 1849 | II |
| Framm, Sebastian | Brunner, Maria | 16, May 1838 | FF |
| Frances, James | May, Emily | 3, Feb. 1833 | RCH |
| Francis, Abraham | Smith, Caroline | 29, Oct. 1842 | RCH |
| Francis, Abraham | Daily, Minerva | 21, July 1847 | RCH |
| Francis, August | Hoeveler, M. Cath. | 27, June 1840 | FF |
| Francis, Henry | Ingrim, Catharine | 14, Oct. 1843 | RCH |
| Francis, Lewis | Singleton, Ellen | 5, Aug. 1843 | RCH |
| Francis, Thomas | Preston, Mary Ann | 27, Aug. 1843 | RCH |
| Francisca, John | Mitchell, Jane | 28, May 1841 | RCH |
| Francisco, Albert | Covert, Minerva | 16, Dec. 1844 | RCH |
| Francisco, Samuel | Wise, Deborah | 24, Oct. 1833 | RCH |
| Francois, Anton | Lods, Susan | 3, June 1832 | RCH |
| Frank, August W. | Rupp, A.M. Margaret | 9, Oct. 1845 | G |
| Frank, Charles B. | Wehler, Anna Maria | 28, Mar. 1841 | F |
| Frank, Henry | Block, Caroline | 7, Mar. 1842 | RCH |
| Frank, Henry | Silverman, Fanny | 14, June 1848 | RCH |
| Frank, Johan B. | Frap, Catharine(Mrs) | 8, Apr. 1844 | AA |
| Frank, Michael | Keeberline, Margaret | 3, Aug. 1835 | FF |
| Frank, Michael | Siemer, Charlotte | 1, May 1849 | G |
| Frank, William | Niedermeier, Ernes. | 24, Oct. 1848 | RCH |
| Franke, Bernard | Schulting, Gesina | 10, Sept 1844 | AA |
| Franke, Casper | Brinkmann, Clara | 23, Aug. 1843 | AA |
| Frankemelle, Bernard | Huenemann, Elisabeth | 20, Feb. 1849 | EE |
| Frankenberg, Herman | Aulkenmeyer, Louisa | 29, Oct. 1848 | AA |
| Franklin, Friedrich | Eaton, Adelheid A. | 27, Aug. 1849 | RCH |
| Franklin, Henry | Rothschild, Fanny | 6, Oct. 1843 | RCH |
| Franklin, John | Simpson, Melinda | Nov. 1842 | RCH |
| Franklin, Stephen | Bruse, Charlotte | 31, Aug. 1845 | RCH |
| Franklin, William | Smith, Mary Elis. | 12, Sept 1841 | RCH |
| Franks, Frederick | Stockman, Margaret | 25, July 1824 | RCH |
| Franlte, Johan | Pabst, Elisabeth | 1, Aug. 1843 | AA |
| Franz, Friedrich | Ahring, Henrietta | 2, Nov. 1843 | F |
| Franzer, Conrad | Bauer, Elisabeth | 20, May 1841 | G |
| Frasee, William | Randall, Mariah | 12, Apr. 1838 | RCH |
| Frauenknacht, Rudolf | Huber, Jacobina | 9, Sept 1849 | A |
| Frazee, | Kincaid, Elisabeth | 23, Jan. 1823 | RCH |
| Frazee, John | Pray, Hannah | 9, Aug. 1845 | RCH |
| Frazer, | McCormick, Elisabeth | 6, June 1848 | RCH |
| Frazer, George | Woodruff, Harriet | 16, Apr. 1821 | RCH |
| Frazer, Jonas | Ackley, Sarah | 6, Aug. 1824 | RCH |
| Frazer, Joseph | Hardesty, Azura | 11, Aug. 1831 | RCH |
| Frazer, Rudolph | Wise, Caroline | 3, Sept 1841 | RCH |
| Frazer, Samuel | Moore, Frances | 24, Dec. 1842 | RCH |

| Grooms<br>****** | Brides<br>****** | Date of Marriage<br>**** ** ******** | Code<br>**** |
|---|---|---|---|
| Frazer, William | Kitchell, Jemima | 6, May 1819 | RCH |
| Frazer, William | Baxter, Mary Ann | 3, Dec. 1846 | RCH |
| Frazey, John | Leach, Mary | 16, Apr. 1844 | RCH |
| Frazier, | Looker, Elisabeth | May 1839 | RCH |
| Frazier, Alexander | Ludlow, Elisabeth | 27, Aug. 1845 | RCH |
| Frazier, Anthony | Stewart, Hannah | 15, Dec. 1844 | RCH |
| Frazier, B. | Plummer, Ellen | 30, Aug. 1826 | RCH |
| Frazier, Benjamin | Fox, Darby | 3, Oct. 1836 | RCH |
| Frazier, George | Foley, Sidney A. | 23, Dec. 1849 | RCH |
| Frazier, James | Patterson, Amanda | 12, Dec. 1849 | RCH |
| Frazier, Jeremiah | Hughes, Mary | 1, June 1848 | RCH |
| Frazier, Recompense | Bonnel, Abigail | 19, Oct. 1820 | RCH |
| Freat, Isaac | Nortle, Jane M. | 17, Aug. 1841 | RCH |
| Frech, Johan C. | Mergenthaler, Fried. | 6, July 1845 | G |
| Frechtling, Johan H. | Bucks, Wilhelmina S. | 21, June 1849 | C |
| Freck, Simon | Zurwick, Elisabeth | 19, May 1849 | RCH |
| Frecking, Friedrich | Hellebusch, M. Elis. | 30, Oct. 1847 | FF |
| Frecking, H. Arnold | Wilbring, Elisabeth | 31, May 1838 | FF |
| Frecking, J. Bernard | Recking, Maria Engel | 1, May 1849 | FF |
| Frecks, Franz | Schmutte, Mary | 16, July 1844 | AA |
| Frederick, Nicolaus | Banker, Barbara | 27, Nov. 1838 | FF |
| Fredrich, Johan | Hermann, Maria | 7, Oct. 1834 | FF |
| Fredrich, Pierre | Hackenger, Agnes | 24, Oct. 1845 | RCH |
| Free, Atkin | Orr, Catharine L. | 13, June 1839 | RCH |
| Freear, Jeremiah | Lapp, Mary | 25, Oct. 1846 | RCH |
| Freely, James | Rany, Ann | 8, Feb. 1849 | GG |
| Freeman, Benjamin P. | Hamilton, Elisabeth | 22, Dec. 1825 | RCH |
| Freeman, Matherson | Bowers, Sarah | 3, Jan. 1821 | RCH |
| Freeman, Nathan | Goddard, Jane | 28, Aug. 1847 | RCH |
| Freeman, Sam. | Mouser, Barbara | 25, Oct. 1849 | RCH |
| Freeman, William | Burns, Margaret | 16, May 1847 | BB |
| Freer, Joseph | Korte, Maria Helena | 8, Feb. 1842 | FF |
| Fregan, Noah | Cooley, Mary | 11, Feb. 1836 | RCH |
| Frei, Ludwig | Knerr, Catharine | 6, June 1848 | G |
| Freid, Elias | Hupp, Barbara | 30, May 1844 | AA |
| Freis, Georg | Beck, Rosa | 5, Feb. 1839 | FF |
| Freis, Simon | Steyart, Maria | 5, Feb. 1839 | FF |
| Freise, Joseph | Huelskotter, Louise | 7, Feb. 1843 | AA |
| Freiss, Jacob | Doholly, Ann (Mrs) | 25, Apr. 1847 | BB |
| Freiss, Jacob | Ehrenweill, Helena | 9, Jan. 1849 | DD |
| Freitman, Levi | Freitman, Barbara | 4, Oct. 1841 | RCH |
| Frekers, Johan | Brueggemann, Elis. | 13, Feb. 1848 | AA |
| Frels, Johan Gerhard | Franke, M.L.Dorothea | 31, Jan. 1840 | F |
| French, George | Porter, Elisabeth | 16, May 1838 | RCH |
| French, Henry | Voller, Mary | 19, Sept 1833 | RCH |
| French, James | McGilliard, Abigail | 26, Nov. 1822 | RCH |
| French, Joseph | Freeland, Elisabeth | 22, Sept 1818 | RCH |
| French, Joseph L. | Quillin, Emily | 2, June 1841 | RCH |
| French, Lewis | Sargent, Mary M. | 10, Sept 1841 | RCH |
| French, Samuel | Poland, Nancy A. | 9, Oct. 1832 | RCH |
| Frentzer, Friedrich | S---, Barbara | 4, Oct. 1849 | C |
| Frercking, Friedrich | Henricks, Mary | 14, Oct. 1847 | A |
| Freund, Georg | Lehmann, Maria | 19, Nov. 1844 | FF |
| Freund, Joseph | Rausch, Anna Maria | 30, July 1848 | EE |
| Freundt, Ernst | Arndt, Bertha | 26, Apr. 1849 | C |
| Frey, Johan | Martz, Anna Maria | 11, Mar. 1841 | G |
| Frey, John C. | Atherton, Elisabeth | 30, Oct. 1824 | RCH |
| Frey, Joseph | Oehler, Maria | 13, Jan. 1835 | FF |
| Frey, Nicolaus | Katter, Catharine | 22, Aug. 1843 | RCH |
| Freye, Johan Heinric | Stuckwisch, Engel | 15, Oct. 1846 | F |
| Freyer, Philipp | Ulrich, Louise | 23, Dec. 1849 | C |
| Freyhacke, Henrich | Reiners, Bernardina | 12, Jan. 1836 | FF |
| Freyss, Lorenz Bd. | Albrecht, Anna Maria | 28, May 1844 | RCH |
| Freytag, Anton | Young, Susanna | 10, Sept 1844 | AA |
| Freytag, Valentin | Schermann, Elisabeth | 25, Sept 1839 | FF |
| Frezee, Anthony | Chapin, Margaret | 23, Nov. 1843 | RCH |
| Fricht, Ignatz | Bauer, Anna Maria | 5, Oct. 1835 | FF |
| Frichtmann, Dietrich | Glover, Drusilla | 23, May 1849 | RCH |
| Frick, Joseph | Verle, Francisca | 24, May 1836 | FF |
| Frick, Lorenz | Hang, Eva | 1849 | RCH |
| Frick, Sebastian | Havert, Caecilia | 28, Nov. 1837 | FF |

| Grooms | Brides | Date of Marriage | Code |
|--------|--------|------------------|------|
| ****** | ****** | **** ** ******** | **** |
| Fricke, Clement | Grove, Theresa | 14, June 1846 | FF |
| Fricke, Friedrich C. | Brown, Harriet | 1, Sept 1842 | F |
| Fricker, Joseph | Baumgartner, Sarah | 9, Sept 1839 | FF |
| Fridell, Michael | Gering, Maria | 14, Aug. 1838 | FF |
| Friedeborn, August | Tron, Mathilda | 25, June 1846 | G |
| Friedlein, Johan | Oester, Margaretha | 7, Jan. 1847 | A |
| Friedmann, Michael | Schaffer, Dorothea | 12, Oct. 1846 | RCH |
| Friedmann, Solomon | Miller, Fanny | 19, Feb. 1846 | RCH |
| Friedmann, Wilhelm | Stutzinger, Elisa | 9, Dec. 1849 | G |
| Friedrich, Bernard | Wilgelmann, Cath. M. | 14, Aug. 1835 | FF |
| Friedrich, Heinrich | Casper, Elisabeth | 24, July 1849 | G |
| Friedrich, Johan A. | Kolb, Barbara | 15, Aug. 1848 | EE |
| Friedrich, Pius | Heckinger, Agnes | 4, Nov. 1845 | FF |
| Friend, George H. | Bradford, Elisabeth | 15, June 1843 | RCH |
| Friend, John | Foster, Phebe F. | 6, Nov. 1842 | RCH |
| Friend, Wellington | Wycoff, Catharine E. | 9, Mar. 1838 | RCH |
| Friendling, George | Henke, Anna M. | 8, Feb. 1844 | RCH |
| Fries, Georg | Scheinhof, Barbara | 2, Feb. 1847 | EE |
| Fries, Ludwig | Sauer, Margaretha | 7, Oct. 1839 | FF |
| Fries, Michael | Kipperger, Barbara | 25, Feb. 1843 | AA |
| Fries, Michael | Scheinhof, Maria A. | 2, Feb. 1847 | EE |
| Fries, Sylvester | Lerbee, Selome | 2, Nov. 1845 | RCH |
| Friks, Heinrich | Buhr, Anna Gesina | 31, Jan. 1843 | AA |
| Frilling, Johan | Pund, Catharina M.B. | 9, Feb. 1836 | FF |
| Frilling, Johan | Trennekamp, Elis. | 20, May 1847 | FF |
| Frintz, Michael | Monroe, Cornelia | 9, Aug. 1847 | RCH |
| Frisbie, J.W. | DeCamp, Sarah | 14, July 1819 | RCH |
| Frische, Everhard | Linnemann, Catharine | 24, Apr. 1838 | FF |
| Frische, Everhard | Steins, Maria | 10, Jan. 1846 | RCH |
| Frische, Johan H. | Wuebbel, Elisabeth | 29, Feb. 1848 | EE |
| Frishe, C. | Thalen, Henrietta | 8, Apr. 1837 | F |
| Friske, Edward | Stueve, Maria Adel. | 11, Jan. 1846 | AA |
| Fritsch, Anton | Zeis, Agnes | 4, Feb. 1849 | II |
| Fritsch, Georg | Wendel, Helena | 21, Jan. 1847 | C |
| Fritsch, Georg | Streibick, Cordula | 10, Jan. 1848 | CC |
| Fritsch, Heinrich | Hohnhorst, Regina | 18, Aug. 1835 | FF |
| Fritsch, Johan Carl | Panck, Louise | 10, Mar. 1849 | C |
| Fritsch, Simon | Schmeyer, Regina | 26, July 1841 | FF |
| Fritsche, Francis | Mojes, Anna Maria | 28, Mar. 1837 | FF |
| Fritz, Anton | Broquet, Maria Anna | 10, Jan. 1837 | FF |
| Fritz, Joseph | Huck, Martha | 12, Oct. 1843 | AA |
| Froehlig, Georg | Grille, Dorothea | 27, Jan. 1848 | B |
| Froemmer, Peter | Dimung, Barbara | 29, July 1843 | FF |
| Froendhoff, Johan H. | Hackmann, Theresa | 9, Sept 1849 | AA |
| Frohliger, Stephen | Plaetner, Maria | 26, Oct. 1835 | FF |
| Frohmann, Johan | Cook, Louise | 23, Feb. 1843 | RCH |
| Frohndorf, Philipp J | Muehl, Eva | 8, Oct. 1839 | FF |
| Frolling, Johan | Brill, Catharine | 17, Oct. 1847 | FF |
| Fromhold, J. Georg | Linnemann, Catharine | 29, Oct. 1848 | II |
| Fromme, Bernard | Koellner, Elisabeth | 19, Apr. 1849 | AA |
| Frommel, Johan | Schuler, Margaretha | 11, Nov. 1849 | CC |
| Frommeyer, Edward | Fiedeldei, Anna M. | 24, Oct. 1848 | AA |
| Frommeyer, Gerhard | Melcher, Maria Elis. | 1, Oct. 1848 | EE |
| Fron, Benjamin | Washington, Elis. | 7, June 1840 | RCH |
| Froning, Bernard | Wehrkamp, Elisabeth | 21, Oct. 1849 | CC |
| Frost, Abraham | Phares, Anny | 18, Oct. 1834 | RCH |
| Frost, Isaac | Hutchinson, Nancy | 22, Feb. 1838 | RCH |
| Frost, Isaac | Morck, Rebecca | 7, Apr. 1842 | RCH |
| Frost, Jacob L. | Hegerman, Charlotte | 3, Dec. 1843 | RCH |
| Frost, Nicolaus | Freidly, Catharine | 23, Nov. 1820 | RCH |
| Frost, William | Toney, Melvina | 11, Nov. 1842 | RCH |
| Frost, Wolf | Kohn, Hannah | 8, Apr. 1842 | RCH |
| Fruct, Jacob | Schraffenberger, M. | 14, May 1848 | C |
| Fruddenburg, Isaac | Bassett, Dorcas | 11, Aug. 1818 | RCH |
| Fruechte, Heinrich | Ricke, Wilhelmina | 13, Dec. 1849 | C |
| Fruelling, Friedrich | Meyer, Maria Elis. | 11, Feb. 1847 | EE |
| Fruhwald, Friedrich | Koehler, Barbara | 28, July 1844 | RCH |
| Frumme, Meinrad | Wichmann, Maria | 30, Jan. 1849 | FF |
| Frushour, David | Boothby, Martha | 11, Dec. 1842 | RCH |
| Fry, Elias | Huppman, Barbara | 15, May 1844 | RCH |
| Fry, Samuel | Harris, Jane | 14, Oct. 1845 | RCH |

| Grooms | Brides | Date of Marriage | Code |
|--------|--------|------------------|------|
| ****** | ****** | **** ** ******** | **** |
| Fryberger, Joseph | Bassett, Julia | 18, Dec. 1833 | RCH |
| Frye, Johan Gerhard | Hahnroth, Christina | 28, Mar. 1849 | C |
| Frylor, Henry | Smith, Mary | 18, May 1818 | RCH |
| Fryrote, Heinrich | Jarson, Maria Engel | 20, Feb. 1838 | FF |
| Fryvogel, Solomon | Colter, Catharine | 25, Sept 1836 | RCH |
| Fuchs, Conrad Theo. | Faehr, Susanna | 26, Aug. 1845 | FF |
| Fuchs, Friedrich | Hust, Eva | 30, June 1840 | G |
| Fuchs, Jacob | Kredel, Anna | 30, Jan. 1845 | G |
| Fuchs, Johan | Heinrich, Maria | 27, Aug. 1846 | C |
| Fuchs, Martin | Pfeifer, Josephina | 16, June 1846 | FF |
| Fuchs, Nicolaus | Zech, Philippina | 23, July 1842 | G |
| Fuchs, Peter | Koehler, Catharine | 22, May 1845 | G |
| Fuchs, Valentin | Schmidt, Theresa | 13, Mar. 1849 | II |
| Fuchs, Wilhelm | Goetz, Christina C. | 2, Jan. 1849 | A |
| Fuelle, Jacob | Grove, Anna | 3, Feb. 1841 | FF |
| Fuerst, Georg | Distler, Margaretha | 25, Nov. 1845 | AA |
| Fuerst, Nicolaus | Schalh, Anna Maria | 14, Dec. 1844 | RCH |
| Fuerst, Nicolaus | Fuerst, Maria Anna | 7, Jan. 1845 | FF |
| Fuescher, Johan H. | Egbers, Christina | 5, Sept 1848 | EE |
| Full, Lewis | Chris---, Elisabeth | 21, Mar. 1837 | RCH |
| Fuller, Daniel | Johnson, Elisabeth | 31, Dec. 1818 | RCH |
| Fuller, Edgar | Gerard, Cecilia | 1, June 1849 | RCH |
| Fuller, Robert C. | Martin, Laura A. | 17, Apr. 1847 | I |
| Fuller, Shubal | Scott, Catharine | 26, Nov. 1848 | RCH |
| Fuller, Sydney | Thurston, Mary Alice | 15, June 1848 | RCH |
| Fuller, Sylvanus | Cole, Olive | 26, Dec. 1849 | RCH |
| Fullerton, James | Little, Jane | 6, Jan. 1837 | RCH |
| Fulton, Asahel | Stewart, Anna Elis. | 9, Sept 1846 | RCH |
| Fulweiler, John | Moore, Frances Ann | 4, Dec. 1838 | D |
| Funk, Isaac | Moore, Elisabeth | 1, Nov. 1840 | RCH |
| Funke, Heinrich | Grothaus, Catharina | 5, May 1847 | FF |
| Funke, Herman Heinr. | ----, ---- | 29, Oct. 1844 | F |
| Furiermuth, Joseph | Moeller, Matilda | 22, Apr. 1845 | AA |
| Furness, Robert | McComas, M Elisabeth | 26, Nov. 1845 | RCH |
| Furnish, Garrett | Bales, Mary Jane | 9, Aug. 1847 | RCH |
| Furnish, Henry | Crowder, Malinda J. | 3, June 1847 | RCH |
| Furst, David | Reiss, Caroline | 10, Oct. 1845 | RCH |
| Fuss, Joseph | Stark, Elisabeth | 17, Aug. 1848 | EE |
| Fussner, Mathias | Schmidt, Anna Maria | 30, May 1843 | AA |
| Fye, John | Turner, Mary | 24, Feb. 1846 | RCH |
| | | | |
| G---, George S. | Lyon, Elisabeth | 16, July 1826 | RCH |
| G---, James | McIntire, Martha | 5, Oct. 1820 | RCH |
| G---, James | Gregory, Rebecca | 25, Dec. 1831 | RCH |
| G---, Richard | Graham, Hannah | 2, Oct. 1828 | RCH |
| G---, William | Heazlitt, Sarah | 1, Dec. 1845 | RCH |
| G---zell, Daniel | Guffin, Charlotte | 24, Nov. 1825 | RCH |
| Ga---, Stephen | Yans, Henrietta | 26, Sept 1844 | RCH |
| Gabel, Conrad | Greve, Margaretha | 20, Apr. 1845 | C |
| Gabriel, Johan | Fischer, Walburga | 7, Sept 1841 | FF |
| Gabriel, John | Marther, Rebecca | 15, Sept 1842 | RCH |
| Gabriel, Mathias | Krautwasser, Friedr. | 26, Jan. 1847 | G |
| Gabriel, Peter | Geissler, Margaretha | 13, May 1847 | EE |
| Gaeking, Gerhard J. | Stuehring, Anna M. | 24, Nov. 1846 | AA |
| Gaertner, Adam | Hoff, Catharine | 28, Apr. 1840 | FF |
| Gafeny, Owen O. | Yost, Emily S. (Mrs) | 7, June 1848 | D |
| Gaffert, Horrast | Coleman, Elisabeth | 20, June 1841 | RCH |
| Gafga, Jacob | Strohle, Elisabeth | 24, June 1849 | FF |
| Gage, Gideon | Garrison, Mary Ann | 16, Jan. 1835 | RCH |
| Gagin, Enoch | Eisell, Mary Ann | 9, June 1835 | RCH |
| Gahnenn, J. Gerhard | Wepker, M. Elisabeth | 27, Sept 1849 | II |
| Gahrer, Anton | Leitner, Theresa | 21, July 1845 | AA |
| Gahrer, Benedict | Kloke, Christina | 22, Apr. 1845 | AA |
| Gail, Amos | Jackson, Lucinda | 30, Aug. 1843 | RCH |
| Gain, William | Getzendanner, Mary | 8, Nov. 1837 | RCH |
| Gaines, Henry | Carson, Acksah J. | 16, Apr. 1847 | RCH |
| Gaines, Richard | Cheney, Clarinda | 29, Apr. 1844 | RCH |
| Gains, Isam. | Clark, Elisabeth | 16, Dec. 1819 | RCH |
| Gaiser, Jacob | Weber, Magdalena | 9, July 1848 | G |
| Gaity, Bryan | Snyder, Ann | 25, Apr. 1847 | RCH |
| Gakken, Clemens | Schroeter, Wilhelmin | 8, May 1844 | AA |

| Grooms | Brides | Date of Marriage | Code |
|--------|--------|------------------|------|
| Gal---, Thomas | McCormick, Lucinda | 30, June 1825 | RCH |
| Galbreath, James | Cole, Nancy | 27, Nov. 1836 | RCH |
| Galbreath, John D. | Smith, Mary C. | 18, Dec. 1849 | RCH |
| Gale, John H. | Lawrence, Hannah | 29, May 1837 | RCH |
| Gall, Heinrich | Balke, A. Friedricka | 31, Dec. 1846 | RCH |
| Gall, William | Stewart, Mary A. | 19, Dec. 1842 | RCH |
| Gallagher, Charles | Nash, Mary | 6, Jan. 1846 | BB |
| Gallagher, Francis | McGrorey, Ann | 23, Jan. 1848 | BB |
| Gallagher, George | Hull, Julia | 3, Nov. 1845 | RCH |
| Gallagher, John | Fury, Catharine | 5, Aug. 1849 | GG |
| Gallagher, Philipp | Burnham, Mary Jane | 18, Jan. 1847 | BB |
| Gallagher, Thomas | Lindley, Caroline | 11, Nov. 1845 | RCH |
| Gallagher, Thomas | Manion, Jane | 17, July 1848 | BB |
| Gallagher, William | Devine, Mary | 17, May 1844 | BB |
| Gallagher, William G | Kanty, Sarah | 13, Mar. 1833 | RCH |
| Gallart, Caspar | Hutzler, Margaretha | 18, Apr. 1847 | EE |
| Gallass, Henry | Viar, Rebecca | 12, Dec. 1836 | RCH |
| Gallbaugh, John S. | Robinson, Elisabeth | 14, May 1848 | RCH |
| Gallenhaus, Friedric | Grower, Maria Adel. | 8, May 1849 | EE |
| Gallis, Michael | Mulligan, Ann | 29, Nov. 1849 | BB |
| Galloway, A.M. | Keller, | 1, Mar. 1848 | RCH |
| Galloway, Joseph W. | Galloway, Elisabeth | 24, Feb. 1835 | RCH |
| Galloway, Samuel | Wallen, Joan | 2, Nov. 1843 | RCH |
| Galloway, William | Bond, Jane | 6, Sept 1837 | RCH |
| Galloway, William | Laurence, Ann | 18, Oct. 1848 | RCH |
| Gallup, Francis | Talbott, Elisabeth | 25, July 1847 | RCH |
| Galura, Sebastian | Guerth, Ruffina | 2, June 1846 | EE |
| Galvin, James | Burke, Hannah | 15, Sept 1844 | BB |
| Gama, Joseph | Littig, Catharine | 20, June 1839 | FF |
| Gamble, Alexander | McCallon, Mary | 3, July 1838 | RCH |
| Gamble, David | Skeen, Margaret | 24, July 1849 | RCH |
| Gamble, James | Norris, Elisabeth | 21, Mar. 1833 | RCH |
| Gambrel, Hugh | ----, Sarah | 9, May 1826 | RCH |
| Gambrell, Alexander | Crain, Amanda | 10, Feb. 1825 | RCH |
| Gamel, Johan | Brakensick, Maria | 2, Sept 1849 | AA |
| Gammersill, Thomas | Head, Mary | 3, Nov. 1823 | RCH |
| Gan, Peter | Abrams, Nancy | 24, Mar. 1824 | RCH |
| Gangloff, Michael | Zoller, Elisabeth | 2, Dec. 1849 | C |
| Ganning, Joshua | Turner, Charlotte | 3, Nov. 1836 | RCH |
| Gano, Aaron G. | Burley, Frances | 12, May 1818 | RCH |
| Gano, Charles | Thompson, Margaret | 13, Mar. 1841 | RCH |
| Gano, Charles | Harkness, Jane | 21, Nov. 1843 | RCH |
| Gano, Howell | Wilshire, Elisabeth | 13, Apr. 1848 | RCH |
| Gano, Samuel | Stevens, Elisabeth | 12, May 1839 | RCH |
| Gano, Stephen | Rufner, Pamelia | 27, Mar. 1819 | RCH |
| Gano, William | Bennet, Emily | 28, May 1839 | BB |
| Gans, Johan | Bonns, Carolina | 28, Nov. 1839 | FF |
| Gansheimer, Christ. | Heck, Barbara | 31, Oct. 1849 | G |
| Ganson, James | Moor, Mary | 25, Mar. 1825 | RCH |
| Ganter, Cassian | Hebel, Catharine | 29, Dec. 1842 | RCH |
| Gantzshier, Philipp | Beutel, Barbara | 25, July 1847 | RCH |
| Garath, John | Zick, Anna | 11, Aug. 1842 | RCH |
| Garbrock, J. Caspar | Wernke, Elisabeth | 9, Sept 1849 | AA |
| Garbrock, J. Casper | Gerbes, M. Theresa | 16, May 1847 | AA |
| Gard, Hiram | Gard, Hannah Ann | 23, Oct. 1835 | RCH |
| Gardewein, Heinrich | Schoenhof, Catharina | 25, Aug. 1842 | FF |
| Gardiner, Carl | Ebberts, Maria | 14, July 1844 | G |
| Gardner, Andrew | Homer, Mary | 26, Jan. 1841 | RCH |
| Gardner, Bernard | Weber, Sophia | 5, Jan. 1835 | FF |
| Gardner, Burrows | Fountain, Susan | 25, Apr. 1842 | RCH |
| Gardner, David | Porter, Mary | 14, Oct. 1838 | RCH |
| Gardner, David | Newell, Jane | 21, June 1846 | RCH |
| Gardner, Erastus | Engle, Ellen | 13, Nov. 1836 | RCH |
| Gardner, George | Morehouse, Maria | 11, Feb. 1823 | RCH |
| Gardner, Julius | Jack, Sarah Ann | 20, Apr. 1833 | RCH |
| Gardner, Lewis B. | Piles, Susan Jane | 28, Jan. 1836 | RCH |
| Gardner, Lewis W. | Richmond, Electa | 17, Mar. 1836 | RCH |
| Gardner, Martin | Wighaus, Maria | 5, Sept 1844 | AA |
| Gardner, Robert | Nichols, Julia | 20, Jan. 1842 | RCH |
| Gardner, Robert | Woodruff, Mary Ann | 28, Aug. 1845 | RCH |
| Gardner, Samuel | Ludlow, Elmira | 29, Sept 1845 | RCH |

| Grooms<br>***** | Brides<br>***** | Date of Marriage<br>**** ** ******** | Code<br>**** |
|---|---|---|---|
| Gardner, Thomas | Keown, Rebecca | 5, July 1849 | D |
| Gardner, W. | Craig, Elisabeth | 31, May 1849 | RCH |
| Gardner, William | Rice, Maria | 20, July 1841 | RCH |
| Gares, Jonathan | Nonnamacher, Cath. | 26, May 1842 | RCH |
| Garesche, Alexander | Carnes, Laura | 8, May 1849 | GG |
| Garlich, Matthias | Maimann, Elisabeth | 16, Sept 1849 | II |
| Garmhausen, Bernard | Engelhausen, Louise | 3, Jan. 1849 | F |
| Garmore, William | Chew, Aseneth | 8, June 1843 | RCH |
| Garnett, William | Truitt, Doshia | 22, Dec. 1846 | RCH |
| Garrard, David | Garrard, Sarah | 20, Jan. 1821 | RCH |
| Garrard, David | Stites, Ann | 24, Mar. 1835 | RCH |
| Garrard, John H. | Knight, Rachel | 14, Feb. 1822 | RCH |
| Garrard, Matheson | Campbell, Ann | 18, Feb. 1826 | RCH |
| Garrard, William | Reno, Lavina | 2, Apr. 1822 | RCH |
| Garratt, Charles | Thorp, Christina | 18, June 1846 | RCH |
| Garre, Bernard | Rinert, Catharine | 4, Feb. 1836 | FF |
| Garretson, | Corry, Sarah | 18, Mar. 1838 | RCH |
| Garretson, Andrew | McDu---, Sarah L. | 29, July 1837 | RCH |
| Garretson, George | Wells, Amelia | 11, Nov. 1832 | RCH |
| Garretson, Owen | Roberts, Jane | 30, May 1842 | RCH |
| Garrett, Cyrus | Reed, Sarah | 1, Apr. 1837 | RCH |
| Garrett, Elmus | Smith, Mary | 19, May 1842 | RCH |
| Garrett, James | Larner, Jane | 18, Oct. 1839 | RCH |
| Garrett, John | Harvey, Dorothea | 8, Sept 1841 | RCH |
| Garrett, Lewis | Morris, Elisabeth M. | 4, Mar. 1847 | RCH |
| Garrett, William | Weston, Laura | 29, Mar. 1846 | RCH |
| Garrey, William | Tillitson, Mary | 13, Apr. 1820 | RCH |
| Garriot, James | Scudder, Matilda | 19, Nov. 1842 | RCH |
| Garrish, Francis | Bacon, Ann | 14, Dec. 1846 | RCH |
| Garrison, B. | West, Mary Jane | 1, June 1837 | RCH |
| Garrison, David | Boots, Belinda | 7, Jan. 1844 | RCH |
| Garrison, Edward R. | Miller, Margaret | 21, Oct. 1832 | RCH |
| Garrison, Isaac | Moore, Mary | 3, Mar. 1844 | RCH |
| Garrison, Israel | Garrison, Lida | 15, Oct. 1835 | RCH |
| Garrison, John | ----, Caroline | 25, Jan. 1827 | RCH |
| Garrison, John | Knox, Elisabeth | 15, Jan. 1835 | RCH |
| Garrison, John | Handy, Margaret | 29, Oct. 1845 | RCH |
| Garrison, John A. | Taylor, Ann | 22, Mar. 1835 | RCH |
| Garrison, Jonathan | Emery, Margaret | 19, May 1836 | RCH |
| Garrison, Stephen W. | Gross, Julia | 14, Sept 1835 | RCH |
| Garrison, William | Williamson, Elis. | 20, May 1841 | RCH |
| Garrotts, Gregory | Borgett, Francisca | 9, Apr. 1836 | RCH |
| Garroutte, Theodore | Allen, Mary | 22, Aug. 1847 | RCH |
| Gartner, Michael | Morgnereth, Bernar. | 6, Feb. 1849 | EE |
| Gartsides, Gabriel | Gibson, Elisabeth | 2, Oct. 1833 | RCH |
| Garvey, Daniel | Kelley, Elisabeth | 13, Sept 1847 | GG |
| Garwood, Nicolaus | Rollan, Mary A. | 8, June 1847 | RCH |
| Garwood, Samuel | Dudley, Elis. Ann | 18, Aug. 1847 | RCH |
| Gary, James | Gallagher, Mary | 20, Apr. 1845 | BB |
| Gary, John | Server, Mary Ann | 11, June 1842 | RCH |
| Gary, John | Watkins, Ellen | 19, Oct. 1844 | RCH |
| Gary, Richard | Carpenter, Elisabeth | 14, Jan. 1847 | RCH |
| Gaskill, John C. | Singer, Catharine | Dec. 1844 | RCH |
| Gaskill, William | Love, Amanda | 16, Feb. 1846 | RCH |
| Gass, Henry W. | Lewis, Jane | 17, Mar. 1848 | RCH |
| Gass, Richard | Chew, Ann | 1, Aug. 1833 | RCH |
| Gasser, Anton | Herzog, Maria | 29, May 1838 | FF |
| Gasser, Anton | Bauer, Theresa | 24, Jan. 1843 | FF |
| Gasser, Martin | Heisler, Catharine | 1, May 1849 | C |
| Gasser, Mathias | Lang, Albina | 27, Nov. 1843 | FF |
| Gassoway, Henry C. | Allen, Elisabeth | 7, Sept 1844 | RCH |
| Gassoway, John | Barkason, Mary | 18, May 1848 | RCH |
| Gastader, Jacob | Schneider, Cecilia | 6, Dec. 1846 | A |
| Gaston, Hugh | Gordon, Margaret | 19, Mar. 1818 | RCH |
| Gaston, John H. | ----, Mary | 3, Apr. 1823 | RCH |
| Gatchell, Horatio | Crane, Anna Maria | 27, Nov. 1842 | RCH |
| Gate, Joseph | Herd, Ann Elisabeth | 6, Oct. 1846 | I |
| Gates, John | Collins, Margaret | 20, Sept 1837 | RCH |
| Gates, John | Collingwood, Elis. | 7, Apr. 1841 | RCH |
| Gates, Uriah | Gaunt, Susanna | 29, Jan. 1818 | RCH |
| Gathard, Nathan | Sparks, Martha | 23, Mar. 1844 | RCH |

| Grooms<br>****** | Brides<br>****** | Date of Marriage<br>**** ** ******** | Code<br>**** |
|---|---|---|---|
| Gatting, Joseph | Heilmann, Anna | 21, Sept 1848 | EE |
| Gatzen, Herman | Schierholt, Anna | 19, July 1844 | A |
| Gaukermann, Matthias | Lange, Dina | 30, Sept 1849 | II |
| Gault, Samuel E. | Rawes, | 9, May 1826 | RCH |
| Gaurd, Joseph | Decker, Hannah | 25, Nov. 1838 | RCH |
| Gausepohl, J Bernard | Kraft, Anna Elis. | 28, Nov. 1846 | FF |
| Gausepohl, Johan G. | Meyer, Elisabeth | 22, Oct. 1846 | C |
| Gausepohl, Johan H. | Stuke, M. Catharina | 7, Feb. 1849 | AA |
| Gausmann, Gerhard | Dickmeyer, Louise M. | 5, Apr. 1848 | F |
| Gauspohl, Carl | Kreienbrink, Anna C. | 14, Nov. 1844 | AA |
| Gauter, John | Strueve, Carolina | 5, Jan. 1836 | RCH |
| Gay, John | Buckley, Sarah | 10, Feb. 1842 | RCH |
| Gayer, Gottlieb | Dick, Catharina | 7, Sept 1839 | G |
| Gaylord, H.H. | Tunis, Joann | 27, Nov. 1832 | RCH |
| Gazart, Hiram | Dumford, Amanda | 24, Mar. 1849 | RCH |
| Gazlay, Albert | Buck, Elisabeth | 15, Apr. 1827 | RCH |
| Gazlay, James N. | Williams, Rebecca | 13, Apr. 1820 | RCH |
| Gazlay, Thomas J. | Boyce, Elisabeth | 21, Mar. 1819 | RCH |
| Gazley, Allen W. | Kizer, Susan | 14, Sept 1848 | RCH |
| Gebbe, Heinrich | Brockmann, Catharine | 10, Jan. 1843 | AA |
| Gebberly, Enoch | Fowler, Nancy | 6, Nov. 1842 | RCH |
| Gebbert, Lorenz | Heitz, Magdalena | 9, June 1835 | FF |
| Gebel, Heinrich | Habicht, Maria | 15, Aug. 1848 | II |
| Gebel, Peter | Schuhmacher, Elis. | 20, Aug. 1844 | FF |
| Gebhard, Jacob | Plettner, Maria Anna | 27, Apr. 1847 | AA |
| Gebhard, Lorenz | Bender, Catharine | 13, Dec. 1840 | G |
| Gebhart, Anton | Wolf, Maria | 19, Aug. 1849 | EE |
| Gebhart, Johan | Reinhart, Theresa | 27, Apr. 1843 | AA |
| Geddes, John | Harris, Sarah A. | 4, Aug. 1835 | RCH |
| Gee, George | Gregg, Mary Ann | 10, July 1846 | RCH |
| Geeding, Aaron | Case, Elmira | 22, Feb. 1844 | RCH |
| Gees, Heinrich | Depweg, Maria | 28, Apr. 1840 | FF |
| Geeting, Isaac | Watson, Caroline | 9, Apr. 1842 | RCH |
| Geggus, Philipp | Shipman, Louise | 29, Sept 1847 | RCH |
| Gegner, Conrad | Esel, Anna M. | 1841 | RCH |
| Gegner, George | Bader, Johanna | 7, Nov. 1845 | RCH |
| Gehbauer, John | Packen, Marai | 13, Mar. 1847 | RCH |
| Geheber, Heinrich | Wahl, Elisabeth | 16, July 1848 | G |
| Gehers, Christoph F. | Hartmann, Sophia | 22, Nov. 1849 | A |
| Gehle, H.C. Herman | Arassener, Charlotte | 24, June 1841 | G |
| Gehles, Martin | Ott, Margaretha | 3, Nov. 1840 | FF |
| Gehring, Christian | Koch, Anna Maria | 26, May 1849 | RCH |
| Gehring, Johan Hein. | Bosmann, Elisabeth | 23, Feb. 1841 | FF |
| Gehringer, Martin | --recker, Louise | 3, Apr. 1840 | F |
| Gehrlich, Isidor | Kraft, Margaretha | 13, May 1845 | AA |
| Gehrlich, Johan H. | Kempf, Maria Anna | 18, Feb. 1849 | EE |
| Gehrling, Jacob | Pfirsing, Eva | 5, Mar. 1848 | EE |
| Gehuzes, Edward | Allen, Julia | 18, Sept 1848 | GG |
| Geibolt, John | Brown, Magdalena | 27, Apr. 1844 | RCH |
| Geider, Heinrich | Sehlamp, M. Barbara | 25, Dec. 1845 | G |
| Geier, Joseph | Bremer, Anna Maria | 7, Mar. 1849 | RCH |
| Geiger, Arbogast | Hunt, Agatha | 7, Oct. 1845 | FF |
| Geiger, Columban | Priu, Francisca | 18, Apr. 1837 | FF |
| Geiger, Gerhard | Drechsel, Catharina | 9, Mar. 1839 | G |
| Geiger, Henry | Hauck, Maria | 4, Aug. 1835 | RCH |
| Geiger, Johan H. | Fischer, Petronella | 6, Nov. 1848 | CC |
| Geiger, Landelin | Brosemer, Ursula | 19, Apr. 1836 | FF |
| Geiler, Friedrich | Jung, Elisabeth | 27, June 1848 | B |
| Geiler, Jacob | Schnell, Henrietta | 30, May 1844 | G |
| Geiler, Johan | Hemler, Elisabeth | 24, Dec. 1844 | G |
| Geilfus, Louis | Brua, Alphonia | 22, May 1844 | RCH |
| Geimann, Conrad | Wolf, Margaretha | 6, Feb. 1837 | FF |
| Geirhart, Casper | Hoffner, Mary Ann | 16, Oct. 1834 | RCH |
| Geis, Bernard | Bund, Maria Anna | 12, May 1840 | FF |
| Geise, Heinr. Arnold | Kallage, Theresa | 12, July 1842 | FF |
| Geise, Heinrich | Flick, Regina | 16, Feb. 1847 | EE |
| Geise, Johan Heinr. | Messmann, M. Agnes | 23, May 1843 | FF |
| Geise, Johan Heinric | Boeckmann, Anna | 9, Apr. 1839 | FF |
| Geiser, Michael | Gabriel, Barbara | 4, Sept 1836 | FF |
| Geisler, Otto | Breson, Christina | 20, Aug. 1845 | RCH |
| Geismann, Johan H. | Brengelmann, Anna | 13, July 1843 | F |

| Grooms | Brides | Date of Marriage | Code |
|--------|--------|------------------|------|
| ****** | ****** | **** ** ******** | **** |
| Geisse, Heinrich | Glick, Regina | 1, Feb. 1847 | RCH |
| Geissmann, Johan H. | Wiemann, Sophia E. | 29, Mar. 1849 | C |
| Geist, Heinrich Wm. | Pottebaum, Caroline | 19, June 1845 | F |
| Geist, Wilhelm Fried | Wissmann, Henrietta | 31, Oct. 1844 | F |
| Geix, Johan Philipp | Heilmann, Barbara | 4, Oct. 1846 | EE |
| Gelace, | Mellor, Maria | 28, Oct. 1838 | RCH |
| Gell, Anton | Brendel, Magdalena | 2, May 1848 | EE |
| Gellenbeck, Bernard | Schrage, Elisabeth | 9, Jan. 1839 | FF |
| Gellenbeck, Gerhard | Kraemer, Mary | 13, July 1847 | AA |
| Gellenbeck, Heinrich | Ronnebaum, Maria | 14, Nov. 1843 | AA |
| Gellhaus, Johan | Trimpe, Maria E. | 30, Jan. 1848 | AA |
| Gels, Johan Gerhard | Schulte, Maria Engel | 9, May 1843 | FF |
| Gelson, James | Smith, Ann | 15, Feb. 1847 | BB |
| Geltzon, Charles | Rye, Elisabeth B. | 31, July 1849 | BB |
| Gemeiner, Andreas | Scharold, Barbara | 20, Sept 1849 | EE |
| Gentle, Thomas | Turner, Mary Jane | 22, Aug. 1845 | RCH |
| Gentle, William | Ray, Jarasia | 18, Jan. 1837 | RCH |
| Gentrup, Friedrich | Borgeding, Maria | 3, May 1849 | C |
| Gentrup, H Andreas W | Meyers, Carolina Wm. | 16, Dec. 1847 | C |
| Gentry, John | Gillen, Nancy | 29, Nov. 1843 | RCH |
| Gentry, Nicholas | Terry, Susan | 24, Mar. 1847 | RCH |
| Gentry, Nicholas | Lathean, Margaret | 31, Dec. 1849 | RCH |
| Geny, James | Chusmann, Sarah | 12, Jan. 1842 | RCH |
| George, George | Bryant, Mary Ann | 13, Mar. 1833 | RCH |
| George, John | Hall, Phebe | 2, Nov. 1843 | RCH |
| Gephardt, Anton | Markstein, Magdalena | 12, Dec. 1848 | EE |
| Gerald, Georg | Musching, Sophia | 11, May 1844 | AA |
| Gerard, Abner | Muchmore, Mary | 21, Sept 1848 | RCH |
| Gerardy, Nicolaus | Piepers, Elisabeth | 12, Aug. 1847 | A |
| Gerber, Andreas | Adams, Mary Ann | 15, July 1846 | RCH |
| Gerbes, Herman Jos. | Wenke, M. Anna | 16, Sept 1849 | AA |
| Gerding, Dietrich | Erpenbeck, Maria A. | 7, Nov. 1843 | AA |
| Gerding, John | Witten, Mary J. | 4, Mar. 1844 | RCH |
| Gerdsen, Herman H. | Mesloh, Marg. Magdel | 16, Nov. 1848 | F |
| Gerdser, Henry | Toele, Anna | 3, June 1841 | RCH |
| Gerhard, J. Nicolaus | Hassforter, Eva Marg | 8, Feb. 1841 | FF |
| Gerhard, Johan Hein. | Luer, Cath. Elis. | 25, Mar. 1847 | C |
| Gerhard, Leonard | Herbert, Maria | 17, Jan. 1845 | AA |
| Gerhardt, Herman T. | Andrews, Margaret | 27, Jan. 1847 | RCH |
| Gerig, Michael | McIntire, Catharine | 30, Apr. 1835 | RCH |
| Gerin, William H. | Lindsey, Jane | 11, Apr. 1839 | RCH |
| Gering, Anton | Theibel, Maria | 11, Sept 1838 | FF |
| Gering, Johan Georg | Scharold, Maria | 23, Apr. 1849 | EE |
| Geringer, Nicolaus | Allbecker, Walburga | 13, June 1837 | FF |
| Gerke, Johan Bernard | Gritter, Anna Marg. | 20, May 1849 | CC |
| Gerken, Wilhelm | Meyer, Elisabeth | 27, Sept 1842 | AA |
| Gerlach, Francis | Besler, Anna | 9, June 1849 | II |
| Gerlach, Philipp | Karg, Margaretha | 24, Dec. 1849 | F |
| Gerlag, Stephen | Grab, Margaretha | 22, June 1847 | FF |
| Gerlemann, Johan H. | Maschus, Adelheid M. | 17, Apr. 1849 | AA |
| Gerling, Johan | Tembru, Anna | 10, Feb. 1846 | EE |
| German, Wilhelm | Nunn, Anna Maria | 8, Oct. 1846 | FF |
| Germann, Anton | Ernst, Julia | 12, Sept 1839 | FF |
| Germann, Bernard | Fortmann, Anna Maria | 29, June 1848 | FF |
| Germann, Johan | Stephan, Magdalena | 12, Jan. 1835 | FF |
| Gerner, Eugene | Bessler, Margaretha | 19, Sept 1842 | AA |
| Gerner, Wilhelm | Jergens, Catharine | 29, Oct. 1848 | F |
| Gerrard, John | Hays, Sarah | 7, May 1834 | RCH |
| Gerrard, John | Merrett, Rachel | 5, Oct. 1842 | RCH |
| Gerreson, Moses | Jackman, Susan | 29, Dec. 1822 | RCH |
| Gerson, Wolf | Devinson, Caroline | 24, June 1847 | RCH |
| Gerve, J. Heinrich | Funke, Catharine | 19, Oct. 1847 | FF |
| Gerve, Joseph | Meuermann, Catharina | 30, Oct. 1849 | FF |
| Gervers, Francis | Stenspohl, Anna C. | 11, June 1844 | FF |
| Gervers, Johan F. | Kerkhof, A Christina | 24, Oct. 1846 | EE |
| Gerwe, Johan Mathias | Grove, Christina | 24, May 1842 | FF |
| Gerwin, Anton | Schroer, Anna Maria | 18, Nov. 1845 | AA |
| Gessert, Henry | Dunheimer, Theresa | 29, Aug. 1844 | BB |
| Gessner, Michael | Wild, Regina | 31, Dec. 1849 | EE |
| Gessner, Paul | Denk, Maria | 7, Jan. 1845 | AA |
| Gest, Joshua | ----, Sarah | 9, 1818 | RCH |

| Grooms<br>****** | Brides<br>****** | Date of Marriage<br>**** ** ******** | Code<br>**** |
|---|---|---|---|
| Gest, Nathaniel H. | Castren, Ellen | 24, Mar. 1835 | RCH |
| Gest, Reuben | Phillips, Rachel | 11, Mar. 1819 | RCH |
| Gethard, John | Johnston, Julia | 17, Feb. 1842 | RCH |
| Gethers, Richard | Carson, Phebe | 12, Aug. 1841 | RCH |
| Gettrich, Johan Hein | Thung, | 1, Nov. 1847 | C |
| Getzendanner, James | Ross, Elisabeth | 26, Feb. 1833 | RCH |
| Gewe, E. | Hemmelgarn, Elisa. | 20, Apr. 1847 | AA |
| Geyer, Anton | Hoffmann, Margaret | 20, Mar. 1846 | RCH |
| Geyer, Christian G. | Dautel, Rosina | 23, Nov. 1843 | G |
| Geyer, Johan | Touger, Elisabeth D. | 27, Dec. 1840 | G |
| Geyer, Ludwig | Hisling, Barbara | 11, Mar. 1847 | G |
| Ghoell, Joseph | Weber, Juliana | 25, Nov. 1847 | EE |
| Gibb, | Fisher, Mary | 30, Aug. 1837 | RCH |
| Gibbens, Francis | Huddard, Ann | 13, Dec. 1835 | RCH |
| Gibbin, Leonard | Aubrey, Sarah | 25, Dec. 1834 | RCH |
| Gibble, Edward | Kelpan, Mary Jane | 10, Oct. 1841 | RCH |
| Gibbon, John | Evans, Sarah | 11, Nov. 1841 | RCH |
| Gibbon, John | O'Brien, Ann | 6, Aug. 1849 | BB |
| Gibbons, | Holgarth, Mary | 19, Nov. 1837 | RCH |
| Gibbons, John | Miller, Isabella | 13, Mar. 1843 | RCH |
| Gibbons, John | Aikens, Mary Ann | 27, Aug. 1849 | RCH |
| Gibbons, Thomas H. | Worth, Elisabeth | 1, July 1834 | RCH |
| Gibbs, Aaron | Oakman, Elisabeth | 19, Apr. 1837 | RCH |
| Gibbs, Anson | Hopper, Mary A. | 20, June 1833 | RCH |
| Gibbs, Benjamin | Short, Mary A. | 26, Feb. 1846 | RCH |
| Gibbs, Byron | Quigley, Sarah | 10, Oct. 1841 | RCH |
| Gibbs, Edwin | Lafler, Elisabeth | 16, Jan. 1823 | RCH |
| Gibbs, George | Chambers, Mary M. | 5, Feb. 1848 | I |
| Gibbs, George W. | McFall, Keziah | 21, May 1821 | RCH |
| Gibbs, James | Sipe, Elisabeth | 2, June 1833 | RCH |
| Gibbs, John | Gibbs, Hannah | 30, Apr. 1819 | RCH |
| Gibbs, Richard | Russell, Hepzibah | 13, Apr. 1840 | RCH |
| Gibbs, William | Looker, Helen M. | 18, Sept 1836 | RCH |
| Gibbs, William F. | Eaton, Elisabeth Ann | 10, Mar. 1836 | RCH |
| Gibner, Joseph | Davis, Anna J. | 10, June 1843 | RCH |
| Gibson, | Carnahan, Catharine | 20, Sept 1849 | RCH |
| Gibson, Alfred | Cole, Margaret | 8, Dec. 1822 | RCH |
| Gibson, Hiram | Miller, Mary Ann | 5, Dec. 1843 | RCH |
| Gibson, Isaac | Bruce, Nancy | 4, May 1837 | RCH |
| Gibson, John | McShane, Elisabeth | 21, Sept 1842 | RCH |
| Gibson, Joshua | Reddish, Sarah | 15, Feb. 1843 | RCH |
| Gibson, Thomas | Harrison, Elisabeth | 20, Mar. 1844 | RCH |
| Gibson, Thomas | Henry, Caroline | 10, July 1847 | RCH |
| Gibson, William | McNicol, Louise | 2, Jan. 1837 | RCH |
| Gibson, William | Miller, Leah | 23, Sept 1842 | RCH |
| Giese, Johan | Dinghauser, Anna M. | 4, July 1843 | F |
| Giese, Joseph | Kleemann, A. Gertrud | 13, Feb. 1849 | FF |
| Gieske, Herman | Meyers, Johanna C. | 15, May 1846 | RCH |
| Giesker, Gerhard | Hitzemann, Louise | 4, Jan. 1849 | C |
| Giesker, Wilhelm | Meyers, Lucia | 12, Nov. 1849 | F |
| Giesting, Georg | Welage, Anna Maria | 31, Jan. 1847 | AA |
| Giffin, James | Fowler, Rachel | 10, Aug. 1820 | RCH |
| Giffin, John | Carter, Mary | 8, Aug. 1844 | RCH |
| Giffin, Robert | Taylor, Sarah | 26, July 1822 | RCH |
| Giffin, William | Casey, Elisabeth | 28, July 1844 | RCH |
| Gifford, Robert | Docking, Clarissa | 24, Nov. 1825 | RCH |
| Gilas, Othor | Rohe, Catharine | 30, May 1847 | EE |
| Gilberd, John E. | Gogen, Mary Elis. | 28, May 1849 | RCH |
| Gilbert, Joseph | Morrison, Minerva | 12, Dec. 1843 | RCH |
| Gilbert, Samuel | Munson, Cordelia | 5, Aug. 1847 | RCH |
| Gilchrist, James | ----, ---- | 27, Apr. 1826 | RCH |
| Gilcrist, Michael | Curneen, Alitia | 20, Apr. 1845 | BB |
| Gildea, Patrick | Snee, Catharine | 21, Jan. 1849 | GG |
| Gilead, Johan | Roberts, Doras | 1, Nov. 1849 | A |
| Gilerack, James | Lacky, Rebecca | 20, Jan. 1820 | RCH |
| Giles, Benjamin | Longshore, Rachel | 28, Oct. 1847 | RCH |
| Giles, George B. | Gardner, Deborah | 16, July 1827 | RCH |
| Gilker, Wilhelm | Altenthal, Anna M. | 16, Feb. 1841 | FF |
| Gilkey, James | Gilkey, Lucinda | 26, Mar. 1842 | RCH |
| Gilkey, Luman | Post, Mary | 14, Feb. 1846 | RCH |
| Gill, | Runyan, Keziah | 12, Apr. 1818 | RCH |

| Grooms | Brides | Date of Marriage | Code |
|--------|--------|------------------|------|
| Gill, James | Barrington, Ann | 14, Aug. 1845 | RCH |
| Gill, John | Gill, Mary Jane | 3, Jan. 1837 | RCH |
| Gill, John | Lawson, Mary | 16, June 1848 | BB |
| Gillan, Isaac | Stewart, Nancy | 21, Oct. 1841 | RCH |
| Gillespie, Brown | Jay, Hannah | 16, Aug. 1835 | RCH |
| Gillespie, John | Smith, Lucy Ann | 2, Mar. 1833 | RCH |
| Gillian, J.S.M. | Preston, Alizale | 6, Aug. 1835 | RCH |
| Gilligeman, Hugh | Coleman, Margaret | 5, Nov. 1832 | RCH |
| Gilliland, William | Carson, Emeline | 30, Dec. 1848 | RCH |
| Gillman, John | Denman, Ann | 2, Aug. 1821 | RCH |
| Gilman, | Utt, Elisabeth | 16, July 1837 | RCH |
| Gilman, Ichabod | Weddocks, Lydia | 7, May 1818 | RCH |
| Gilman, James G. | Decker, Eveline | 30, Dec. 1820 | RCH |
| Gilman, Nikolaus | Lyon, Rhoda | 1, Jan. 1824 | RCH |
| Gilmore, Alfred | Messer, Frances | 16, Aug. 1849 | RCH |
| Gilmore, Gordon | Bennefield, Elisabet | 8, June 1844 | RCH |
| Gilmore, James | Stibbs, Mary Jane | 18, July 1842 | RCH |
| Gilmore, Robert | Miller, Elisabeth | 22, Aug. 1848 | RCH |
| Gilp, Simon | Gilp, Catharine | 22, Nov. 1846 | AA |
| Gilpin, Thomas | Cane, Emmeline | 31, Mar. 1844 | RCH |
| Gilpin, William | Savage, Elis. Jane | 7, Apr. 1849 | RCH |
| Gilroy, James | Green, Rosanna | 19, Aug. 1849 | GG |
| Gilwer, John W. | Wardell, Frances | 16, Apr. 1839 | RCH |
| Gimbel, Peter | Keller, Charlotte | 8, Sept 1842 | G |
| Ginandt, Wilhelm | Alz, Eva | 18, Feb. 1849 | G |
| Ginn, Alver | Scollin, Rhoda | 4, Aug. 1836 | RCH |
| Ginnis, William | Jarcet, Mary | 9, Aug. 1836 | RCH |
| Girot, Jean Etiene | Corrigeux, Theresa F | 13, June 1847 | GG |
| Girten, Peter | Dilg, Catharine | 6, Sept 1848 | RCH |
| Giselan, Aaron | Peake, Ruth | 17, Mar. 1821 | RCH |
| Gissler, Philipp | Schlosser, Carolina | 3, Apr. 1845 | AA |
| Gist, Rob C. | Dorsey, Mary F. | 10, Jan. 1832 | I |
| Gistermann, Joachim | Kline, Magdalena | 16, Sept 1843 | RCH |
| Gitchell, Joseph | Collins, Caroline | 1, Feb. 1849 | RCH |
| Gittel, Heinrich | Eberhard, Elisabeth | 12, Oct. 1840 | G |
| Givner, Peter | Sterlz, Elisabeth | 23, July 1833 | RCH |
| Gladman, Archibald | Ha---, Mary | 14, Jan. 1819 | RCH |
| Gladstone, Thomas | Johnston, Rachel | 3, May 1847 | I |
| Glanemann, Wilhelm | Luebbe, M. Anna | 1, July 1849 | AA |
| Glardon, Christopher | Banks, Martha | 24, Nov. 1846 | RCH |
| Glardon, Joseph | Francis, Mary F. | 13, Jan. 1835 | RCH |
| Glascoe, James S. | Hill, Frances A. | Dec. 1832 | RCH |
| Glaser, Christian | Sieger, Louise | 24, Jan. 1842 | RCH |
| Glaser, Jacob | Stahl, Margaretha | 31, Oct. 1843 | G |
| Glaser, Mathias | Fillian, Catharine | 4, Sept 1849 | EE |
| Glasgow, Lafayette | Shaw, Lydia | 29, Apr. 1846 | RCH |
| Glasmeyer, Gerhard H | Brockamp, Elisabeth | 9, Jan. 1848 | AA |
| Glass, David | Champion, Phoebe | 10, Feb. 1820 | RCH |
| Glass, Emery R. | Bryarly, Sarah R. | 1, Aug. 1848 | RCH |
| Glass, Heinrich | Thinnes, Susanna | 23, Feb. 1846 | AA |
| Glass, Jacob | Dusky, Nancy M. | 27, Sept 1834 | RCH |
| Glass, John | Schalaub, Margaret | 14, Sept 1847 | RCH |
| Glass, Michael | Kessinger, Lavina | 15, Oct. 1847 | RCH |
| Glasser, Friedrich | Wurst, Magdalena | 29, Oct. 1839 | FF |
| Glassferd, Alexander | Roberts, Margaret | 10, Mar. 1825 | RCH |
| Gleie, Joseph | Dabeck, Clara | 1, Oct. 1848 | AA |
| Gleim, George | Bayer, Margaret | 25, Feb. 1846 | RCH |
| Glenn, James | Miller, Jane | 6, Oct. 1830 | RCH |
| Glenn, John | Williams, Harriet | 28, Nov. 1848 | RCH |
| Glenn, Leonard | Gates, Rhiner | 12, Aug. 1834 | RCH |
| Glenn, Lewis | Lewis, Lucy Mary | 22, Mar. 1843 | RCH |
| Glennon, John | Holleran, Rosanna | 23, June 1844 | BB |
| Glennon, Michael | Campbell, Mary | 26, Oct. 1849 | BB |
| Gles, Peter | Hoffmann, Barbara | 22, Jan. 1849 | II |
| Glindmeier, Bernard | Rekers, Catharine | 15, June 1849 | CC |
| Glins, Heinrich | Wellinghof, Catharin | 14, Feb. 1847 | AA |
| Glinz, Joseph | Moormann, Theresa | 29, Aug. 1847 | EE |
| Glismann, Heinrich D | Moeller, Christina | 24, Dec. 1845 | C |
| Glisson, Caleb | Summers, Frances | 3, Apr. 1834 | RCH |
| Glockner, Leo | Kessner, Elisabeth | 9, Jan. 1848 | CC |
| Gloeckner, Georg | Faul, Magdalena | 16, Sept 1843 | G |

| Grooms<br>\*\*\*\*\*\* | Brides<br>\*\*\*\*\*\* | Date of Marriage<br>\*\*\*\* \*\* \*\*\*\*\*\*\*\* | Code<br>\*\*\*\* |
|---|---|---|---|
| Gloem, Roman | Weber, Magdalena | 14, Feb. 1847 | EE |
| Glovdin, Peter C. | Grinthm, Cassandra | 29, Mar. 1832 | RCH |
| Glover, William | Pasely, Mary | 14, Nov. 1841 | RCH |
| Gmeiner, Hieronymus | Spinner, Theresa | 5, Sept 1847 | AA |
| Gnahn, Johan | Faehr, Elisabeth | 1, Feb. 1844 | G |
| Gnau, Georg Adam | Sieber, Maria | 27, Nov. 1848 | CC |
| Gnau, Johan | Seim, Walburga | 15, Jan. 1839 | FF |
| Gnau, Joseph | Hock, Barbara | 23, Apr. 1844 | AA |
| Goady, Robert | Cochran, Anna | 25, July 1822 | RCH |
| Goble, Samuel B. | Doty, Elisabeth | 6, Aug. 1836 | RCH |
| Goble, William B. | Gage, Elisabeth | 13, May 1833 | RCH |
| Gochstatter, Friedr. | Rapp, Margaretha | 5, Sept 1839 | G |
| Gockrell, William | Slaughter, Elisabeth | 3, July 1842 | RCH |
| Godden, Edward | Smart, Mary W. | 14, May 1844 | RCH |
| Godemann, Joseph | Kemper, M. Gertrud | 1, Nov. 1846 | FF |
| Godert, John | Vonderact, Louisa | 7, June 1835 | RCH |
| Godke, Bernard H. | Likers, Adelheid | 28, Nov. 1837 | FF |
| Godson, George | Degman, America | 4, Jan. 1842 | RCH |
| Godt, Johan Heinrich | Makentepe, Elisabeth | 24, Jan. 1837 | FF |
| Goebel, Carl F. | Gebhardt, Magdalena | 4, Nov. 1847 | G |
| Goecker, Bernard H. | Niemeier, Catharine | 12, Sept 1849 | F |
| Goeddel, Peter | Stamm, Fiebeehn | 5, Aug. 1845 | RCH |
| Goedecke, Friedrich | Wolken, Margaret | 9, Oct. 1848 | RCH |
| Goediker, Johan H. | Richter, Catharine | 14, Nov. 1843 | AA |
| Goehbel, Johan | Dop, Anna Maria | 20, Oct. 1842 | AA |
| Goehring, Andreas | Korn, Catharine | 24, Apr. 1848 | B |
| Goeke, Bernard L. | Tenbusch, Carolina | 21, Sept 1845 | AA |
| Goeke, Joseph | Gerdemann, Anna M. | 7, Jan. 1847 | AA |
| Goeke, Mathias | Stricker, Elisabeth | 16, Aug. 1842 | AA |
| Goekens, Clemens | Schroeder, Adelheid | 8, May 1844 | RCH |
| Goekens, Clement | Strieker, Catharina | 27, Nov. 1849 | AA |
| Goeker, J Gottfried | Schlomer, Rosina | 2, Oct. 1849 | C |
| Goeller, Johan | Raif, Maria Anna | 6, May 1845 | FF |
| Goepper, Michael | Bicker, Catharine | 2, Feb. 1845 | G |
| Goer, Henry | Kelly, Mary | 9, Sept 1819 | RCH |
| Goeswein, Johan | Meyer, Kunigunda | 26, July 1846 | EE |
| Goetemoeller, Wm. | Mullmann, Anna Maria | 4, Dec. 1849 | RCH |
| Goetke, Caspar H. | Taphorn, Margaretha | 3, Aug. 1848 | AA |
| Goetke, Johan Heinr. | DeHaide, Maria Cath. | 21, Nov. 1847 | FF |
| Goetken, Georg Herm. | Wilmes, A. Christina | 30, Jan. 1844 | FF |
| Goettel, Jacob | Latterner, Catharine | 24, May 1846 | RCH |
| Goetter, Bernard H. | Henke, Maria | 20, Feb. 1848 | EE |
| Goetter, Johan Hein. | Buschian, Anna M. | 23, May 1848 | EE |
| Goettke, Rudolf | Kruesmann, M. Anna | 18, Nov. 1847 | AA |
| Goetz, Adam | Wuest, Maria Anna | 4, Feb. 1839 | FF |
| Goetz, Johan | Bickner, Elisabeth | 26, Dec. 1844 | RCH |
| Goetz, Johan | Benker, Christina | 12, July 1840 | G |
| Goetz, Joseph | Brausch, Margaretha | 3, Aug. 1841 | FF |
| Goetz, Philipp | Lam, Barbara | 12, Aug. 1849 | EE |
| Goetz, Valentin | Weising, Barbara | 20, Mar. 1848 | HH |
| Goforth, Thomas J. | Matthews, Elisabeth | 15, Mar. 1826 | RCH |
| Gogin, Aaron | McGarvey, Nancy | 14, Apr. 1825 | RCH |
| Gognan, Edward | Kenney, Elisabeth | 19, Nov. 1849 | BB |
| Goin, George | Danby, Charlotte | 11, Oct. 1832 | RCH |
| Going, Johan Friedr. | Buscher, M Catharine | 15, May 1845 | AA |
| Goins, John H. | Sanders, Martha | 12, Apr. 1849 | RCH |
| Gold, James | Biddinger, Catharine | 3, Mar. 1842 | RCH |
| Gold---, Thomas | Scott, Sally | 1, Feb. 1827 | RCH |
| Golden, Charles | Gold, Emeline | 1, Nov. 1833 | RCH |
| Golden, Isaac | Shearrer, Jane | 12, Mar. 1837 | RCH |
| Goldenburg, John | Fosdick, Eveline | 30, Apr. 1841 | RCH |
| Golder, John | Neff, Catharine J. | 12, Nov. 1846 | RCH |
| Golding, Aaron | Garish, Sophia | 5, Mar. 1822 | RCH |
| Golding, Robert | Steele, Lydia Ann | 1, Nov. 1846 | RCH |
| Goldkamp, Ferdinand | Brockschmidt, Gertr. | 14, Apr. 1836 | FF |
| Goldschmidt, Carl | Meyers, Sophia | 9, Aug. 1848 | G |
| Goldschmidt, Clemens | Wolking, Catharina | 13, June 1837 | FF |
| Goldsmith, David | Crosley, Syltha | 7, June 1835 | RCH |
| Goldsmith, David | Straus, Fanny | 8, May 1849 | RCH |
| Goldsmith, Hersch | Scheinhaus, Hannah | 17, Apr. 1846 | RCH |
| Goldson, George | Markland, Matilda | 30, Oct. 1845 | RCH |

| Grooms | Brides | Date of Marriage | Code |
|--------|--------|------------------|------|
| ****** | ****** | **** ** ******** | **** |
| Goldstein, Isaac | Katz, Regina | 9, Apr. 1848 | RCH |
| Goldsworth, Vinson | McIntire, Elisabeth | 29, Feb. 1824 | RCH |
| Goldtrap, Isaac | Rollins, Rebecca | 11, Apr. 1849 | RCH |
| Goldtrap, William | Cunningham, Jeanet | 25, May 1820 | RCH |
| Goldtrap, William | Hunt, Naomi | 15, Dec. 1825 | RCH |
| Golladay, John | Tracy, Lucretia | 25, Apr. 1834 | RCH |
| Gombey, James | Newcumliker, Barbara | 3, Dec. 1818 | RCH |
| Gondy, Hugh | Benn, Rebecca | 8, Feb. 1821 | RCH |
| Gonly, William | West, Hannah | 9, Sept 1819 | RCH |
| Gonsly, Amos | Grant, Hulda | 17, Aug. 1823 | RCH |
| Gooch, Frederick | Beeler, Margaret | 27, Nov. 1843 | RCH |
| Gooch, Henry | Stoddart, Clarissa | 27, May 1841 | D |
| Good, John | Cooke, Helen M. | 9, May 1849 | RCH |
| Good, Robert | Kelly, Susan A. | 30, Oct. 1839 | I |
| Good, William | Pierce, Anna M. | 31, Dec. 1846 | RCH |
| Goodall, William | Roberts, Winnifred | 21, Feb. 1844 | RCH |
| Goodhue, Daniel F. | Rogers, Elisabeth | 25, Aug. 1835 | RCH |
| Goodhue, George | Graves, Elisabeth | 29, Apr. 1847 | RCH |
| Goodhue, William | Knoblaugh, Margaret | 11, Sept 1849 | RCH |
| Goodin, Samuel H. | Green, Ellen | 9, Sept 1840 | D |
| Goodloe, James | Neaver, Marian | 11, Nov. 1819 | RCH |
| Goodman, August | Grandin, Lucy | 7, July 1847 | RCH |
| Goodman, Conrad | Bigler, Jane | 28, May 1846 | RCH |
| Goodman, George | Hill, Mary Jane | 25, Dec. 1849 | RCH |
| Goodwin, Christopher | Malone, Maria | 29, Sept 1836 | RCH |
| Goodwin, Edward | Williams, Elmira | 29, Sept 1843 | RCH |
| Goodwin, James | Allen, Amanda | 21, May 1846 | RCH |
| Goodwin, Moses | Goshorn, Jane | 9, Aug. 1844 | RCH |
| Goodwin, Nicodemus | McRoberts, Martha | 18, Nov. 1846 | RCH |
| Goodwin, Robert | Fleming, Syntha | 17, Oct. 1825 | RCH |
| Goos, August Wilhelm | Schmidt, Maria Cath. | 24, Apr. 1849 | II |
| Goos, Gottfried Sieg | Nentrup, A.M. Cath. | 18, Aug. 1847 | FF |
| Gooseman, Charles | Ugle, Althea | 29, Oct. 1843 | RCH |
| Gopin, Henry | Morrison, Maria | 11, Jan. 1849 | RCH |
| Gordon, | Cressup, Eliza Jane | 18, Sept 1849 | RCH |
| Gordon, George H. | White, Ellen | 8, June 1836 | RCH |
| Gordon, Gilbert | Montart, Charlotte | Nov. 1841 | RCH |
| Gordon, Harvey | Davis, Mary | 17, Sept 1847 | RCH |
| Gordon, James | Campbell, Catharine | 2, Oct. 1845 | RCH |
| Gordon, Jesse J. | Sost, Sarah | 7, Dec. 1835 | RCH |
| Gordon, John | Cartlavins, Elis. | 25, Aug. 1833 | RCH |
| Gordon, John | Wood, Rebecca | 22, Dec. 1836 | RCH |
| Gordon, John | Harris, Mary | 27, Sept 1837 | RCH |
| Gordon, John | Muchmore, Eunice | 7, Sept 1843 | BB |
| Gordon, John B. | Higbee, Margaret | 31, Dec. 1835 | RCH |
| Gordon, John B. | N---, Laura | 29, Oct. 1837 | RCH |
| Gordon, John T. | Vorhees, Sarah | 9, May 1836 | RCH |
| Gordon, Jonas | Huffmann, Isabella | 26, Oct. 1848 | RCH |
| Gordon, Jonathan | Haisher, Jane | 29, July 1824 | RCH |
| Gordon, Nathaniel | Smith, Ann | 13, Nov. 1845 | RCH |
| Gordon, Richard | Davenport, Mary Ann | 23, Mar. 1837 | RCH |
| Gordon, Tapsley | Spinet, Mary | 21, July 1835 | RCH |
| Gordon, William | Hanson, Jane | 16, Apr. 1825 | RCH |
| Gordon, William L. | Weeks, Sarah J. | 24, Sept 1848 | RCH |
| Gorgan, Christopher | Murphy, Margaret | 1, Nov. 1846 | GG |
| Gorline, John | Albright, Susan | 7, Jan. 1844 | RCH |
| Gorman, Ephraim | Billingsly, Amanda | 23, June 1844 | RCH |
| Gorman, Frederick | Holening, Margaret | 11, Jan. 1834 | RCH |
| Gorman, Henry | Crossan, Lucretia | 29, Dec. 1842 | RCH |
| Gorman, James | Hutchinson, Rachel | 13, May 1826 | RCH |
| Gormley, James | O'Neil, Ann Mary | 15, Aug. 1848 | BB |
| Gorwine, Matthias | Corbley, Elisabeth | 29, Jan. 1820 | RCH |
| Gosemeyer, Johan H. | Fischer, Maria Anna | 9, Jan. 1844 | AA |
| Goshorn, Andrew | Ross, Sarah | 14, May 1835 | RCH |
| Goshorn, James | Carnahan, Margaret | 6, Aug. 1846 | RCH |
| Goshorn, John C. | Williams, Sarah | 3, Feb. 1844 | RCH |
| Goshorn, Nicolaus | Cox, Mary Ann | 10, Mar. 1842 | RCH |
| Goshorn, William | Daggett, Eliza Jane | 20, Apr. 1847 | RCH |
| Gosling, George | Leper, Jane | 10, June 1840 | RCH |
| Gosling, John | Bird, Sarah | 6, Aug. 1844 | RCH |
| Gosling, Samuel | Cook, Content | 24, Dec. 1833 | RCH |

| Grooms<br>****** | Brides<br>****** | Date of Marriage<br>**** ** ******** | Code<br>**** |
|---|---|---|---|
| Gosling, Samuel | Smith, Susan H. | 3, Nov. 1848 | RCH |
| Gosmann, Bernard H. | Seifers, Catharine W | 13, June 1848 | RCH |
| Gosmeier, Johan | Bohmkamp, Margaretha | 3, Feb. 1846 | FF |
| Gosney, George | Knight, America | 15, Sept 1843 | RCH |
| Goss, Johan Mathias | Remping, Maria | 16, Aug. 1836 | FF |
| Gossel, Friedrich W. | Strothmann, Margaret | 19, Mar. 1842 | RCH |
| Gossett, David | Price, Amanda | 11, Aug. 1845 | RCH |
| Gossin, Henry | Bowman, Catharine | 1, Nov. 1821 | I |
| Gossin, William | Mortimer, Eliza Ann | 21, June 1846 | RCH |
| Gossinger, Friedrich | Oevermann, Anna M. | 2, May 1843 | FF |
| Gossler, J Friedrich | Lisler, Barbara | 19, Dec. 1844 | RCH |
| Gotge, Wilhelm | Stakenborg, Sophia | 26, Oct. 1847 | C |
| Gotmann, Bernard H. | Meyer, Elisabeth | 27, Nov. 1838 | FF |
| Gott, Francis C. | Boerger, Agnes | 9, Jan. 1848 | CC |
| Gott, Heinrich And. | Buhre, Anna Maria | 23, Sept 1845 | FF |
| Gottbehode, Johan H. | Hugenberg, Gertrud | 26, Apr. 1846 | EE |
| Gottbehote, Johan H. | Pille, Maria Agnes | 15, May 1849 | FF |
| Gouck, Frederick | Fawver, Charlotte | 12, Dec. 1833 | RCH |
| Goudy, Abram | Gaskell, Lydia Ann | 6, July 1843 | RCH |
| Gough, John C. | Sampson, Elisabeth | 4, Oct. 1838 | RCH |
| Goulcher, John | Park, Margaretha | 11, May 1833 | RCH |
| Gould, Alfred | Boyd, Eleanor | 25, Dec. 1848 | RCH |
| Gould, George | Schmidt, Maria | 16, Jan. 1844 | RCH |
| Gould, George W. | Fish, Elisabeth B. | 16, Mar. 1835 | RCH |
| Gould, Jackson | Markley, Phebe | 17, Mar. 1842 | RCH |
| Gould, Matthew | Carter, Elisabeth | 9, Aug. 1820 | RCH |
| Gould, William | Kischler, Abaline | May 1843 | RCH |
| Gould, William | Hey, Catharine | 25, July 1847 | RCH |
| Govermann, Francis | Glaspohl, Maria | 2, Jan. 1838 | FF |
| Gowan, Benjamin | Ball, Agnes | 3, Dec. 1848 | RCH |
| Gowdy, Samuel | Williamson, Rachel | 12, Mar. 1818 | RCH |
| Gowdy, Thomas | Hurnan, Ruth | 7, Sept 1836 | RCH |
| Gra---, John | Tomlinson, Sarah | 10, Jan. 1839 | RCH |
| Grace, Benjamin | Rhoads, Elisabeth | 26, July 1827 | RCH |
| Graeber, Francis | Waechter, Maria | 20, Nov. 1834 | FF |
| Graef, Ludwig | Kalp, Philippina | 23, Nov. 1846 | RCH |
| Graessel, John Georg | Horn, Cath. Marg. | 4, June 1846 | A |
| Graewe, H. Heinrich | Butz, M. Elisabeth | 1, Feb. 1844 | G |
| Graf, Johan | Reibly, Maria | 30, June 1839 | G |
| Graf, John | Fey, Amelia | 4, July 1849 | A |
| Graf, Joseph | Froehlich, Elisabeth | 4, Aug. 1840 | G |
| Graff, August | Schmidt, Elisabeth | 12, Jan. 1842 | RCH |
| Graff, Friedrich | Wieland, Margaretha | 4, Jan. 1841 | F |
| Graff, Ludwig | Hessel, Wilhel.(Mrs) | 25, Nov. 1846 | AA |
| Graffell, Antonio | Miller, Dorothea | Oct. 1847 | RCH |
| Gragoff, William | Goforth, Mary Jemima | 3, Sept 1833 | RCH |
| Graham, George | Johnson, Joanna | 18, Feb. 1819 | RCH |
| Graham, Henry | Bowman, Mary | 11, Jan. 1842 | RCH |
| Graham, Holmes | Munroe, Lucinda | 12, Aug. 1847 | RCH |
| Graham, James | Johns, | 6, Oct. 1825 | RCH |
| Graham, James | Logan, Jane | 12, Mar. 1842 | RCH |
| Graham, James | Hunt, Grizelda | 24, Jan. 1844 | BB |
| Graham, James | Neville, Cornelia B. | 9, Oct. 1844 | BB |
| Graham, John | Hiner, Ellen | 28, Sept 1834 | RCH |
| Graham, John | Merct, Martha | 17, Jan. 1836 | RCH |
| Graham, John | Patterson, Susan | 12, Oct. 1848 | RCH |
| Graham, Joseph S. | Tanner, Elisabeth | 3, Oct. 1832 | RCH |
| Graham, Robert | Dawson, Susan | 20, Feb. 1844 | RCH |
| Graham, Robert C. | Lemmon, Polly | 1, Oct. 1826 | RCH |
| Graham, Robert R. | Crawford, Triditha | 19, Jan. 1835 | RCH |
| Graham, Thomas | Symmes, Elisabeth | 29, Sept 1819 | RCH |
| Graham, Thomas | Rosebrook, Rebecca | 4, Sept 1842 | RCH |
| Graham, William | Price, Harriet | 17, Mar. 1847 | RCH |
| Graher, Johan F. | Buck, Maria Elis. | 13, Sept 1849 | C |
| Gramann, Heinrich | Egbert, M. Anna | 16, Jan. 1838 | FF |
| Gramann, J. Bernard | Brinkmann, Carolina | 11, May 1841 | FF |
| Grampp, Michael | Jacobi, Susanna | 23, May 1848 | G |
| Grandbeck, Daniel | Schenck, Charlotte | 23, June 1842 | RCH |
| Grandemann, Gerhard | VordemBerge, Marg. | 5, Mar. 1847 | F |
| Granger, John | Iddings, Elisabeth | 2, July 1842 | RCH |
| Grant, Abner | Nash, Elisabeth | 9, Sept 1832 | RCH |

| Grooms<br>***** | Brides<br>***** | Date of Marriage<br>**** ** ******** | Code<br>**** |
|---|---|---|---|
| Grant, Amasa C. | Spicer, Sarah | 4, Oct. 1820 | RCH |
| Grant, John | Hugle, Mary Ann | 7, Apr. 1825 | RCH |
| Grant, John W. | Bateman, Anna | 17, Dec. 1818 | RCH |
| Grant, Nathan | Nash, Keturah G. | 20, Dec. 1835 | RCH |
| Grant, Wilhelm | Hammerle, Emilia | 15, Aug. 1848 | AA |
| Grant, William | Owens, Elisabeth | 16, June 1836 | RCH |
| Grant, William | Wilson, Elisabeth | May 1843 | RCH |
| Grant, William | Adams, Mary | 12, Sept 1847 | RCH |
| Grant, William | Smith, Mary Ann | 1, July 1847 | D |
| Grapvine, Nehemiah | Stewart, Elisabeth | 13, Jan. 1846 | RCH |
| Grass, Michael | Peter, Eva | 27, Sept 1849 | EE |
| Grasser, Jacob | Hilmann, Elisabeth | 14, Sept 1847 | A |
| Grau, John | Brice, Barbara | 29, Mar. 1847 | RCH |
| Grautmann, Christian | Reineke, Cath. Elis. | 9, May 1847 | F |
| Grautmann, Heinrich | Monning, Catharine | 15, Nov. 1849 | F |
| Grave, William | Pieper, Clara | 10, Jan. 1849 | RCH |
| Graver, Johan Hein. | Luepken, Anna M. | 29, July 1848 | AA |
| Graves, Anthony | Grismer, Mary Ann | 7, Nov. 1846 | RCH |
| Graves, George | Hazzard, Laura A. | 30, May 1842 | RCH |
| Gray, | Porter, Martha | 7, Dec. 1844 | RCH |
| Gray, Anthony | Carroll, Susan | 5, July 1849 | GG |
| Gray, Bettniel | Anderson, Mary | 23, Sept 1841 | RCH |
| Gray, Daniel | Carter, Polly | 5, Oct. 1823 | RCH |
| Gray, David | Evans, Mary Eleanor | 3, Jan. 1843 | RCH |
| Gray, Edmund | Shafer, Mary | 12, Mar. 1846 | RCH |
| Gray, George | Robertson, Anna | 25, Mar. 1838 | RCH |
| Gray, James | Colston, Nelly | 26, Sept 1833 | RCH |
| Gray, Jeremiah | Newmanly, Susan | 25, Sept 1836 | RCH |
| Gray, John | Hopper, Mary Ann | 23, Nov. 1842 | RCH |
| Gray, Moses | Crary, Abigail | 2, July 1848 | RCH |
| Gray, Thomas | Hancock, Betsy A. | 14, May 1836 | RCH |
| Gray, Thompson | Hidley, Martha | 2, Mar. 1843 | RCH |
| Gray, William | Faist, Amanda | 8, June 1837 | RCH |
| Grays, William | Donn, Lucy | 8, Feb. 1838 | RCH |
| Grayson, Edward | Applegate, Jane | 29, Nov. 1849 | RCH |
| Greasley, William | Wilkins, Susan | 19, Nov. 1844 | RCH |
| Greatrake, Henry | Crocket, Elizabeth | 7, June 1846 | RCH |
| Greeley, Michael | Mehran, Bridget | 8, June 1846 | BB |
| Greely, Daniel | Brown, Nancy H. | 8, Oct. 1818 | RCH |
| Green, Albert | McFarland, Rachel | 9, Aug. 1846 | RCH |
| Green, Amos | Webber, Amanda | 26, Aug. 1838 | RCH |
| Green, Bendego | Wooleaver, Rebecca | 11, Jan. 1847 | RCH |
| Green, Benjamin | Powers, Elisabeth | 20, May 1833 | RCH |
| Green, Benjamin | Bargar, Winney | 27, Dec. 1846 | RCH |
| Green, Caleb B. | Jones, Sarah E. | 8, Sept 1834 | RCH |
| Green, Charles | Ogden, Martha | 20, Feb. 1824 | RCH |
| Green, Daniel | Haney, Catharine | 12, June 1841 | BB |
| Green, Edward | Moseley, Maria | 9, Dec. 1844 | RCH |
| Green, Fenton | Dustin, Sarah B. | 16, Sept 1832 | RCH |
| Green, Franklin | Mays, Nicey | 30, June 1842 | RCH |
| Green, George | Stephens, Frances | 19, Mar. 1833 | RCH |
| Green, George | Sprong, Catharine | 16, July 1846 | RCH |
| Green, Horace | Shanks, Sarah | 4, Sept 1834 | RCH |
| Green, Jacob | Adler, Caturie | 10, June 1819 | RCH |
| Green, James | Henry, Catharine | 20, Oct. 1845 | BB |
| Green, John | Comstock, Thankful | 31, Dec. 1818 | RCH |
| Green, John M. | Peters, Dolly R. | 4, July 1834 | RCH |
| Green, Josiah H. | Hand, Jane | 26, Apr. 1838 | RCH |
| Green, Lazarus | Cord, Hannah M. | 24, Sept 1842 | RCH |
| Green, Matthew | Fanning, Ellen | 25, May 1846 | GG |
| Green, Matthew | Melany, Bridget | 11, Feb. 1849 | GG |
| Green, Orry | Spraig, Ellis | 21, Oct. 1821 | RCH |
| Green, P.R.M. | Merriet, Martha Ann | 13, Oct. 1833 | RCH |
| Green, Robert | Jordan, Frances | 17, Dec. 1845 | RCH |
| Green, Russell | Bassett, Olive | 8, July 1819 | RCH |
| Green, Silas | Bird, Mary Jane | 4, July 1848 | RCH |
| Green, Stephen | Lovejoy, Mary | 3, June 1847 | RCH |
| Green, Thomas | Tobin, Eliza | 27, Dec. 1849 | RCH |
| Green, Thomas G. | Bonsell, Margaret | 11, Mar. 1837 | RCH |
| Green, Timothy | Richards, Mary | 11, Nov. 1839 | RCH |
| Green, William | Jones, Caroline | 28, Jan. 1849 | RCH |

| Grooms<br>****** | Brides<br>****** | Date of Marriage<br>**** ** ******** | Code<br>**** |
|---|---|---|---|
| Green, William N. | Stockwell, Elis. B. | 11, Nov. 1840 | D |
| Greenas, Thomas | Mixer, Mary Ann | 27, Nov. 1834 | RCH |
| Greene, John R. | Stuart, Jane | 4, Nov. 1841 | RCH |
| Greene, O. | Kilgour, Sarah | 23, Oct. 1841 | RCH |
| Greene, Sam. | Coleman, Hannah | 15, Oct. 1836 | RCH |
| Greene, Willard | Stone, Annis | 21, Aug. 1845 | RCH |
| Greenham, Joseph | Millthrop, Hannah | 20, Mar. 1846 | RCH |
| Greenhaus, Samuel | VanKirk, Elisabeth | 13, Dec. 1845 | RCH |
| Greenlead, William | Milligan, Agnes R. | 12, Aug. 1834 | RCH |
| Greenleaf, Samuel | Heuston, M. | 4, Oct. 1822 | RCH |
| Greentree, Simon | Storey, Margaret | 26, Oct. 1848 | RCH |
| Greenville, John | Stewart, Sarah | 23, June 1844 | RCH |
| Greenwell, Robert | Mills, Martha | 10, Mar. 1836 | RCH |
| Greenwell, William | Cathy, Rachel | 22, Jan. 1835 | RCH |
| Greenwood, | Hopson, Phebe Jane | 14, 1836 | RCH |
| Greenwood, George | Houc---, Elisabeth | 18, Nov. 1844 | RCH |
| Greenwood, James | Hubbard, Delilah | 20, June 1846 | RCH |
| Greg, Arnold | Dressmann, M Gertrud | 17, July 1838 | FF |
| Gregel, Jacob | Dressing, Elisabeth | 24, June 1841 | RCH |
| Greger, George | Leeds, Rudy | 27, Mar. 1818 | RCH |
| Gregory, Francis H. | Hollabard, Caroline | 2, July 1849 | RCH |
| Gregory, John | Haff, Cynthia Ann | 25, Apr. 1839 | RCH |
| Gregory, John | Irwin, Abigail | 23, July 1848 | RCH |
| Gregory, Lorenzo | Smith, Jane | 21, Jan. 1844 | RCH |
| Gregory, Richard | Neville, America | 10, July 1836 | RCH |
| Greib, Johan Otto | Barberger, Carolina | 1, Nov. 1845 | FF |
| Greif, Franz | Glass, Catharine | 19, Apr. 1846 | G |
| Greife, Johan Georg | Kolkmeyer, Anna M. | 26, Oct. 1845 | FF |
| Greine, Johan Heinr. | Geise, Caroline | 8, May 1849 | F |
| Greskamp, Herman | Schratz, Christina | 22, Dec. 1848 | II |
| Gressard, Frederick | Keller, Theresa | 4, July 1845 | BB |
| Greting, Simon | Miller, Charlotte | 13, Aug. 1839 | RCH |
| Greve, Bernard | Herbeding, Sophia | 22, July 1849 | II |
| Greve, Gerhard | Fisse, Theresa | 30, Nov. 1845 | AA |
| Greve, J. Gerhard | Wehof, Catharine | 20, Aug. 1848 | II |
| Grevenkamp, J.B. | Greve, Anna M.G. | 23, Jan. 1849 | II |
| Grevers, Bernard H. | Eithoff, Hermina | 16, Sept 1849 | AA |
| Grewe, Joseph | Grevenkamp, Anna M. | 26, Nov. 1848 | FF |
| Grey, Harvey | West, Harriet | 9, Sept 1833 | RCH |
| Greybehl, Johan | Derrebecken, Louise | 15, Jan. 1843 | RCH |
| Grideon, James | Moran, Rebecca | 6, July 1848 | RCH |
| Gridley, Chester P. | Ferris, Elisabeth | 12, Nov. 1833 | RCH |
| Gridley, Francis | Duvall, Caroline | 20, Sept 1846 | RCH |
| Grief, Johan | Stab, Anna | 27, Jan. 1846 | FF |
| Grieme, Dietrich | Lange, Anna Maria | 3, May 1846 | AA |
| Gries, Michael | Rauch, Katharine | 25, Oct. 1849 | EE |
| Gries, Nicolaus | Busets, Francisca | 17, May 1836 | FF |
| Griese, Gerhard H. | Wickmann, Katharine | 9, Sept 1849 | EE |
| Griese, Johan H. | Schneider, Maria | 30, Nov. 1843 | AA |
| Griese, Johan Herman | Huelsmann, Elisabeth | 13, Jan. 1846 | AA |
| Griese, Joseph | Tienhers, Margaretha | 16, June 1845 | AA |
| Grieves, John | Longley, Amanda | 2, Mar. 1847 | RCH |
| Griffen, Edmund | Tills, Phebe | 16, Feb. 1837 | RCH |
| Griffin, | Ferguson, Margaret T | 4, Mar. 1836 | RCH |
| Griffin, Abraham | Darden, Sarah | 24, Sept 1846 | RCH |
| Griffin, George P. | Neville, Mary A. | 17, Dec. 1837 | RCH |
| Griffin, James | Campbell, Nancy | 13, Dec. 1821 | RCH |
| Griffin, John | Morrison, | Dec. 1842 | RCH |
| Griffin, John | Autenheimer, Louise | 27, Aug. 1846 | G |
| Griffin, John B. | Forbes, Anna Elis. | 15, June 1849 | RCH |
| Griffin, Patrick | McGovern, Mary | 12, Sept 1847 | BB |
| Griffin, Peter | Moak, Caroline | 22, Jan. 1842 | RCH |
| Griffin, Peter | Lawler, Mary | 27, June 1841 | BB |
| Griffin, Philipp | Casey, Honora | 20, Dec. 1849 | BB |
| Griffin, Stephen | Crane, Rachel | 14, May 1846 | RCH |
| Griffing, George B. | Allen, Hannah | 7, Dec. 1833 | RCH |
| Griffith, Bohtha | Mosbom, Aceneth | 25, Nov. 1845 | RCH |
| Griffith, David | Lawrence, Elisabeth | 18, Dec. 1834 | RCH |
| Griffith, Humphrey | Davis, Margaret | 26, July 1849 | RCH |
| Griffith, Jack | Scot, Huberta | 19, May 1842 | RCH |
| Griffith, Lewis | Childers, Julia Ann | 27, Jan. 1844 | RCH |

| Grooms | Brides | Date of Marriage | Code |
|--------|--------|------------------|------|
| ****** | ****** | **** ** ******** | **** |
| Griffith, Samuel | Lockwood, Ellen | 25, Oct. 1846 | RCH |
| Griffith, T. | Edwards, Elisabeth | 26, May 1849 | RCH |
| Griffith, Thomas H. | Henry, Caroline | 17, Aug. 1848 | RCH |
| Griffith, William | Haven, Hester A. | 10, Aug. 1842 | RCH |
| Griffiths, James | McNicol, Elisabeth | 14, May 1843 | RCH |
| Griffiths, James | Rees, Jane | 21, Oct. 1845 | RCH |
| Grifis, John | Garrison, Theresa | 28, June 1849 | RCH |
| Grigg, James | Leright, Elisabeth | 30, Sept 1841 | RCH |
| Grillet, John | Brown, | 20, July 1826 | RCH |
| Grimes, James | McMahon, Nancy | 9, Dec. 1823 | RCH |
| Grimes, Martin | Martin, Theresa | 12, Sept 1842 | BB |
| Grimes, Robert F. | Moore, Effie | 17, Mar. 1833 | RCH |
| Grimm, Aloys | Brodbeck, Theresa | 4, Jan. 1849 | EE |
| Grimm, Daniel | Helmboldt, Magdalena | 10, May 1842 | G |
| Grimm, Jacob | Riepperger, Carolina | 28, June 1848 | EE |
| Grimme, Heinrich | Rekers, Anna Adel. | 26, Aug. 1845 | AA |
| Grimme, Herman H. | Buning, A. Theresa | 11, May 1843 | AA |
| Grimmeisen, Nikolaus | Theiss, Elisabeth | 15, Mar. 1849 | G |
| Grimmelsmann, Hein. | Meyer, Johanna | 26, June 1849 | AA |
| Grinkemeyer, Herman | Fedders, Anna Maria | 23, Aug. 1842 | FF |
| Grinkemeyer, Johan | Ruechelmann, Cath. | 15, Apr. 1849 | EE |
| Grinnell, Thomas | Woolsey, Sarah M. | 2, Sept 1836 | RCH |
| Grinsteiner, Georg | Reit, Maria | 23, Jan. 1844 | AA |
| Griser, Louis | Evers, Catharine | 6, Feb. 1848 | B |
| Grisewell, Adam H. | Sieks, Catharine | 16, Jan. 1845 | F |
| Grismore, George | Hinkler, Anna | 11, May 1826 | RCH |
| Gro, Georg | Perring, Catharina | 28, Jan. 1836 | FF |
| Groat, Francis | Page, Armenia | 11, Jan. 1847 | RCH |
| Groben, Ambrose | Diehl, Catharine | 30, July 1842 | FF |
| Grobmeier, Heinrich | Kessens, M Elisabeth | 24, Aug. 1841 | FF |
| Grobmeyer, J Rudolph | Losemeyer, Anna B. | 21, Aug. 1838 | FF |
| Groene, Frank | Willenkamp, Maria | 26, Apr. 1849 | B |
| Groene, Heinrich | Tiehaus, Theresa | 14, May 1844 | AA |
| Groene, Heinrich | Junker, Catharina | 9, Nov. 1848 | AA |
| Groene, Herman | Moellenkamp, Thekla | 12, Aug. 1845 | FF |
| Groene, J. Gerhard | Langenkamp, Maria | 6, Feb. 1848 | AA |
| Groene, Johan Herman | Kustermeyer, Elis. | 26, Oct. 1847 | AA |
| Groenefeld, Johan G. | Reselage, Agnes | 3, Nov. 1848 | CC |
| Groeniger, Ludwig | Dallwigs, Elisabeth | 23, Mar. 1847 | C |
| Groenland, Herman M. | Dressel, Johanna R. | 1, Feb. 1849 | G |
| Groesbeck, Abraham | Burnham, Ann E. | 6, Sept 1846 | BB |
| Groffer, Heinrich | Ohler, Maria | 10, Feb. 1848 | F |
| Grogan, Edward | Thompson, Rachel | 26, Jan. 1844 | BB |
| Grogan, Patrick | Brown, Elisabeth | 15, Apr. 1847 | BB |
| Groghan, John | Wales, Mary | 1, May 1841 | BB |
| Groh, John | Friedrich, Louise | 24, Feb. 1848 | G |
| Groh, Michael | Lang, Regina | 31, Oct. 1843 | AA |
| Groh, Michael | Reis, Maria Anna | 16, Aug. 1842 | FF |
| Grohman, Samuel | Blyford, Martha J. | 8, Aug. 1842 | RCH |
| Grolmann, Georg | Cordes, Clara | 14, Oct. 1849 | II |
| Grone, Herman | Mollenkamp, Thecla | 26, July 1845 | RCH |
| Groneweg, Henry Phil | Strick, Dorothea E. | 6, Nov. 1847 | A |
| Grooms, George | Bennefield, Elis. | 3, Apr. 1834 | RCH |
| Groppe, Phillip Wm. | Werle, Margaretha | 4, Nov. 1845 | AA |
| Grosch, Philipp | Bachelor, Jane | 8, May 1841 | RCH |
| Grosche, Johan Georg | Spath, Margaret | 26, Dec. 1847 | RCH |
| Groschwitz, Carl Th. | Eckardt, Maria Elis. | 27, May 1844 | G |
| Groshardt, Herman | Amann, Rosalia | 25, Aug. 1846 | FF |
| Gross, Anton | Hinkel, Magdalena | 31, May 1849 | II |
| Gross, Frederick | Shinn, Maria Anna | 10, Nov. 1846 | RCH |
| Gross, Gideon O. | Dunlap, Elisabeth | 17, Aug. 1836 | RCH |
| Gross, John | Woodward, Ann H. | 10, June 1834 | RCH |
| Gross, Joseph | Graham, Sarah | 30, Apr. 1819 | RCH |
| Gross, Peter | Barger, Elisabeth | 17, Oct. 1848 | AA |
| Gross, Simon | Jefferson, Sarah | 8, May 1836 | RCH |
| Grossemeyer, Conrad | Brocamp, Elisabeth | 31, Dec. 1848 | EE |
| Grossenbrink, Fried. | Ortmann, Elisabeth | 29, Apr. 1849 | FF |
| Grosser, Baptist | Habner, Margaretha | 6, Aug. 1848 | HH |
| Grosskopf, Andreas | Knupper, Barbara | 23, July 1848 | FF |
| Grossmann, Andreas | Gruen, Catharine | 13, Mar. 1849 | G |
| Grossmann, J. Anton | Huep, Catharine E. | 9, Aug. 1839 | FF |

| Grooms | Brides | Date of Marriage | Code |
| ****** | ****** | **** ** ******** | **** |
| Grossmann, Joseph | Bedel, Eva Maria | 24, June 1845 | AA |
| Grossmann, Michael | Fischer, Lucia | 24, Sept 1842 | RCH |
| Grossmuecke, Francis | Bauer, Barbara | 5, May 1836 | FF |
| Grote, Johan Gerhard | Burwinkel, Catharine | 11, Sept 1849 | CC |
| Grotenkamp, Heinrich | Sendhof, Catharina | 4, Nov. 1849 | FF |
| Grotenkemper, Henry | ----, Catharine | 15, Dec. 1849 | RCH |
| Grothaus, David | Kentner, Helena | 24, Oct. 1848 | EE |
| Grothaus, Herman | Meyer, Anna M. | 1, Dec. 1842 | F |
| Grothaus, Johan H. | Klate, Margaretha C. | 27, Nov. 1845 | F |
| Grothaus, Rudolph | Stickforth, Maria | 21, Dec. 1848 | G |
| Grothaus, Wilhelm F. | Bruening, Caroline | 23, Dec. 1849 | G |
| Grotjann, Dietrich | Stimmermann, Marg. | 13, Aug. 1843 | C |
| Grottendick, Friedr. | Buchholz, M. Sophia | 28, June 1848 | F |
| Grove, Benjamin B. | Redrow, Mary Ann | 25, July 1835 | RCH |
| Grover, George | Andrews, Hepza D. | 28, May 1844 | RCH |
| Groves, John | Ashby, Maria | 19, June 1838 | RCH |
| Groves, William | Beall, Margaret | 13, Sept 1846 | RCH |
| Groves, William | Richardson, Elis. A. | 24, June 1847 | RCH |
| Grow, Anson | Henderson, Mary | 10, Feb. 1833 | RCH |
| Grow, William D.E. | Dorthwatt, Elenor | 6, Jan. 1825 | RCH |
| Groyer, John J. | Nordicke, Rachel | 26, May 1837 | RCH |
| Grubbs, | Smith, Margaret | 21, Nov. 1844 | RCH |
| Grube, Johan Wilhelm | Hoppenjans, Anna M. | 6, Aug. 1848 | EE |
| Gruber, Johan D. | Fries, Margaretha | 12, Nov. 1848 | II |
| Grudley, Chester | Thomas, Lydia | 5, Dec. 1848 | RCH |
| Gruener, John | Holfelder, Regina | 28, Jan. 1844 | RCH |
| Gruenloh, Bernard | Alberding, Maria | 20, June 1843 | FF |
| Gruenwald, Thaddeus | Petz, Kunigunda | 7, Aug. 1848 | EE |
| Grueter, Herman | Steffens, Caroline | 13, May 1849 | FF |
| Gruetter, Gerhard | Zurline, Margaretha | 11, Nov. 1840 | FF |
| Grulinger, Carl | Hoffmann, Maria | 26, May 1838 | FF |
| Grumbine, Jeremiah | Shaw, Mary A. | 25, Jan. 1845 | RCH |
| Grunder, Jacob | Jung, Josephina | 23, Jan. 1849 | EE |
| Gruner, Anton | Meisel, Margaretha | 11, Jan. 1844 | G |
| Grunkemeier, Johan H | Romann, Elisabeth | 26, May 1838 | FF |
| Gruse, Johan Heinr. | Determann, Catharine | 21, May 1848 | EE |
| Gruter, Gerhard | Kuhlmann, Maria Anna | 23, Sept 1849 | FF |
| Gschwind, Johan | Brodbeck, Anna M. | 7, Mar. 1848 | CC |
| Gu---, Benjamin | Wright, Elisabeth | May 1843 | RCH |
| Gu---, Valentin | Jegly, Catharina | 13, May 1834 | RCH |
| Guard, Alexander | Miller, Elisabeth | 19, Sept 1837 | RCH |
| Guard, Bailey | Hays, Catharine | 10, June 1841 | RCH |
| Guard, James | Hays, Lucy | 25, Feb. 1841 | RCH |
| Guard, Timothy | ----, Rebecca | 2, Sept 1837 | RCH |
| Guard, William | Wanrial, Susan | 12, Oct. 1820 | RCH |
| Gude, Herman | Seiger, Gertrud | 18, Feb. 1840 | FF |
| Gude, Joseph | Heitgers, Margaretha | 16, Nov. 1847 | AA |
| Guedecker, Herman | Macke, M. Catharine | 13, Feb. 1840 | FF |
| Guehe, Johan Anton | Zumbroegel, Elis. | 7, Oct. 1849 | AA |
| Guelker, | Dopker, Catharine | 25, Sept 1849 | RCH |
| Guelker, Joseph | Kespers, Margaret | 20, Jan. 1847 | RCH |
| Guelker, Wilhelm | Volkering, Catharina | 3, Nov. 1836 | FF |
| Guenthner, Michael | ----, ---- | Sept 1847 | RCH |
| Guess, Harvey | Jones, Mary | 8, Feb. 1838 | RCH |
| Guester, Leonard | String, Anna Maria | 3, May 1836 | FF |
| Guffing, William | Baldwin, Angelina | 24, May 1846 | RCH |
| Gugel, Jacob | Bauer, Elisabeth | 30, Sept 1847 | G |
| Gugselle, Sebastian | Burgart, Francisca | 9, Sept 1837 | FF |
| Guild, Benjamin | Ford, Marrandy | 1, Jan. 1832 | RCH |
| Guild, Harvey | Byron, Amanda | 21, Oct. 1843 | RCH |
| Guilfoil, Thomas | Bird, Nancy | 28, Nov. 1843 | RCH |
| Guilford, George | B---, Jane Elisabeth | 18, Apr. 1824 | RCH |
| Guilford, Nathan | ----, Elisabeth | 28, Oct. 1819 | RCH |
| Guilford, William | Kirby, Charlotte | 5, Oct. 1847 | RCH |
| Guin, John R. | Pray, Ann | 3, July 1838 | RCH |
| Guinan, William | Dougherty, Joann | 15, Apr. 1849 | GG |
| Guion, David | Ganns, Catharine | 7, Aug. 1836 | RCH |
| Guion, John P. | Sprague, Wealthy | 16, July 1835 | RCH |
| Guire, | Mount, Melvina | 12, July 1849 | RCH |
| Guiterman, Alexander | Rauh, Amelia | 18, Dec. 1846 | RCH |
| Guitman, Joseph | Eishburg, Bertha | 26, Mar. 1848 | RCH |

| Grooms | Brides | Date of Marriage | Code |
|--------|--------|------------------|------|
| ****** | ****** | **** ** ******** | **** |
| Gulick, Henry | Pool, Angela | 6, Oct. 1842 | RCH |
| Gulick, Jacob | Shaf---, Catharine F | 14, Mar. 1820 | RCH |
| Gulick, John | Aiken, Elisabeth | 15, Apr. 1849 | BB |
| Gulick, John | Aiken, Elisabeth | 15, Apr. 1849 | BB |
| Gulker, Wilhelm | Wischmeier, A.M. | 17, Sept 1848 | II |
| Gullett, Jesse | Mayall, Mary | 15, May 1836 | RCH |
| Gumminger, Balthasar | Guetlien, Kunigunda | 2, Jan. 1849 | EE |
| Gunbo, John | Taylor, Mary A. | 20, July 1839 | RCH |
| Gundel, John George | Dorfer, Anna M. | 10, Aug. 1845 | RCH |
| Gundersheimer, Henry | Bossinger, Getta | 29, Mar. 1844 | RCH |
| Gunkel, Henry Ferd. | Stoszmeister, Henr. | 22, May 1849 | G |
| Gunkel, Johan | Steffens, Helen | 6, Feb. 1849 | FF |
| Gunkle, John | Fox, Araminta | 13, Dec. 1849 | RCH |
| Gunn, John | Keegan, Mary | 4, June 1842 | RCH |
| Gunning, Thomas | Cassidy, Ann | 15, Mar. 1838 | RCH |
| Gunter, Johan | Horst, Elisabeth | 11, Apr. 1847 | A |
| Gunther, Andreas | Mueller, Louise | 13, May 1849 | G |
| Gunther, Johan | Pepermann, Maria | 25, Feb. 1845 | G |
| Gunthner, J. Michael | Bomkamp, Maria | 8, Oct. 1844 | AA |
| Guntmann, Johan Wm. | Kunk, Theresa | 27, Feb. 1848 | AA |
| Gusinon, Samuel | Dowell, Mary | 3, July 1823 | RCH |
| Gusmore, George | Scott, Charlotte | 23, Mar. 1836 | RCH |
| Gustav, Carl | Meyer, Margaretha | 2, Apr. 1848 | G |
| Gut, Herman | Engel, Adelheid | 10, Oct. 1844 | AA |
| Gute, Johan Gerhard | Meyer, Elisabeth | 9, Feb. 1841 | FF |
| Guth, Mathias | Beck, Catharine | 26, Apr. 1846 | EE |
| Guthrie, Alexander | Ross, Francis | 8, Sept 1842 | RCH |
| Guthrie, David | Black, Sarah Jane | 13, July 1847 | RCH |
| Guthrie, John L. | Guthrie, Elisabeth | 12, Nov. 1820 | RCH |
| Gutmann, Dietrich | Boerger, Elisabeth | 23, Nov. 1845 | AA |
| Gutmann, J. Heinrich | Clumper, Christina | 31, Dec. 1839 | FF |
| Gutzwiller, Aloysius | Bleile, Maria | 30, Nov. 1848 | FF |
| Guy, Samuel | VanWormer, Clarnia | 27, Aug. 1835 | RCH |
| Guysi, John | McKim, Emma | 2, Mar. 1846 | RCH |
| Gwaltney, Abr. S. | Durham, Sarah | 24, Feb. 1833 | RCH |
| Gwaltney, James | Sater, Sarah | 7, Feb. 1843 | RCH |
| Gwaltney, Josiah | Atherton, Mary Ann | 12, Sept 1847 | RCH |
| Gwaltney, Samuel | Wheaton, Sarah | 5, Dec. 1819 | RCH |
| Gwin, Alexander | Smith, Abby | 31, Oct. 1846 | RCH |
| Gwin, William | West, Sabina | 18, Nov. 1847 | RCH |
| Gwinn, John W. | Dailey, Patience | 3, Sept 1826 | RCH |
| Gwinner, Ernst | Rockey, Caroline | 22, Aug. 1847 | G |
| Gwinup, George | Marshall, Margaret | 16, Sept 1818 | RCH |
| Gwyrine, David | McClain, Sarah | 20, May 1834 | RCH |
| Gynod, William | Carl, Neinery | 26, Apr. 1834 | RCH |
| | | | |
| H---, Henry | Stuckler, Catharine | 21, June 1825 | RCH |
| H---, James W. | Cottle, Sarah | Apr. 1833 | RCH |
| H---, Jesse | Ray, Ann W. | 7, Oct. 1844 | RCH |
| H---, John | Landon, Elisabeth | 13, Nov. 1828 | RCH |
| H---, John | Ruse, Penelope | 11, Aug. 1836 | RCH |
| H---, Joseph | Thompson, Susanna | 16, Feb. 1818 | RCH |
| H---, Louis | Dunham, Catharine | 25, Nov. 1835 | RCH |
| H---, William | Patterson, Martha | 1, Jan. 1818 | RCH |
| H---, William | Burnet, Ann | 13, Nov. 1828 | RCH |
| H---, William | Tribby, Elisabeth N. | 24, Aug. 1833 | RCH |
| H---, William | Dunwodie, Rebecca | 9, July 1835 | RCH |
| Ha---, Amos | McQuord, Polly | 3, May 1826 | RCH |
| Ha---, Daniel H. | Ames, Olivia | 24, May 1832 | RCH |
| Ha---, Josiah | Marsh, Lydia | 7, Feb. 1821 | RCH |
| Haag, Simon | Darirn, Mary | 17, Oct. 1845 | RCH |
| Haager, Johan | Specht, Magdalena | 3, Feb. 1848 | EE |
| Haalammert, William | Sundermann, Catharin | 21, Dec. 1843 | RCH |
| Haas, Johan | Dorsch, Maria | 26, Aug. 1849 | A |
| Haas, Johan Casper | Huber, Louise | 21, Feb. 1849 | RCH |
| Haas, John | Edle, Margaret | 26, Oct. 1845 | RCH |
| Haas, John | Ochs, Anna | 6, Aug. 1849 | RCH |
| Haase, Wilhelm | Auer, Barbara | 31, Jan. 1849 | A |
| Habedank, Henry | Sneger, Friedricka | 3, Apr. 1837 | RCH |
| Habel, Heinrich | Hussmann, Maria | 15, June 1841 | FF |
| Haber, Jacob | Hann, Anna M. | 5, May 1834 | RCH |

| Grooms<br>****** | Brides<br>****** | Date of Marriage<br>**** ** ******** | Code<br>**** |
|---|---|---|---|
| Haberkorn, Charles | Bofinger, Mathilda | 14, Oct. 1849 | G |
| Haberle, Aloisius | Schuler, Elisabeth | 23, Feb. 1835 | FF |
| Habick, Anton | Arne, Maria | 4, Aug. 1840 | FF |
| Habig, Ambrose | Doll, Francisca | 18, Aug. 1840 | FF |
| Habig, Michael | Auer, Kunigunda | 7, Aug. 1849 | CC |
| Hablicie, Christian | Schafer, Mary | 28, June 1836 | RCH |
| Habn, | Barrow, Lucinda | 23, Dec. 1838 | RCH |
| Hack, Peter | Dick, Victoria | 22, June 1847 | CC |
| Hack, Urban | Larin, Theresa | 25, Apr. 1839 | FF |
| Hacke, Wilhelm | Pluemer, M. Engel | 19, June 1845 | F |
| Hackett, Joseph | Avery, Henrietta | 27, Oct. 1846 | RCH |
| Hackman, Gerhard E. | Bruemmer, A Margaret | 16, Oct. 1849 | AA |
| Hackmann, Ernst H. | Tappin, Maria Marg. | 8, May 1849 | C |
| Hackmann, Friedrich | Severing, M. Engel | 8, July 1845 | G |
| Hackmann, Heinrich | Baumer, Anna Maria | 29, June 1837 | FF |
| Hackmann, Heinrich | Klatte, Dorothea | 5, Dec. 1844 | F |
| Hackmann, Heinrich | Helms, Maria Anna | 17, May 1842 | FF |
| Hackmann, Heinrich F | Rosing, Sophia A. | 2, May 1849 | F |
| Hackney, Joseph | Gibbs, Elisabeth | 9, Apr. 1837 | RCH |
| Hackstadt, Georg H. | Schroeder, Margaret | 5, Sept 1844 | F |
| Hackstadt, Henry R. | Rinkhorst, Lucinda | 5, Aug. 1841 | RCH |
| Haddix, Nimrod | Meeker, Sarah | 3, May 1844 | RCH |
| Haddleston, | Hathorn, Mary | 9, Feb. 1822 | RCH |
| Haden, Sylvannus | Murcell, Susannah | 14, Oct. 1846 | RCH |
| Hadley, Samuel P. | Taylor, Martha | 15, Aug. 1833 | RCH |
| Hadnall, James | Stewart, Nancy | 15, Feb. 1843 | RCH |
| Haefner, Georg | Seitzer, Sophia | 14, May 1844 | AA |
| Haettrich, Christoph | Wegmann, Maria | 16, Aug. 1840 | FF |
| Haffner, Xavier | Fritsch, Maria | 25, Aug. 1840 | FF |
| Hafner, Anton | Clemens, Margaretha | 9, Apr. 1839 | FF |
| Haft, Friedrich | Henning, Gertrud | 16, July 1848 | C |
| Hag, Anthony | Baries, | 29, Dec. 1846 | RCH |
| Hag, Johan | Wolfsefer, Barbara | 22, Oct. 1839 | FF |
| Hagan, James | McFalls, Cynthia | 6, Apr. 1842 | RCH |
| Hagedorn, | Paust, Maria | 22, Sept 1849 | RCH |
| Hagedorn, Johan H. | Vrocklage, Dina | 18, Oct. 1846 | AA |
| Hagedorn, Joseph | Hallermann, Elisabet | 12, Nov. 1848 | II |
| Hageman, Benjamin | Graham, Mary Ann | 5, Sept 1832 | RCH |
| Hageman, Benjamin | Graham, Lucinda | 14, Oct. 1834 | RCH |
| Hageman, James | Swing, Clarinda | 28, Oct. 1835 | RCH |
| Hageman, William | Middleton, Catharine | 7, Oct. 1835 | RCH |
| Hagemann, Albert | Heinbuch, A. Sabina | 1, June 1849 | G |
| Hagemann, Heinrich | Fischer, M. Theresa | 18, Jan. 1842 | FF |
| Hagemann, Johan | Hutchinson, Mary A. | 4, Sept 1849 | RCH |
| Hagemann, Johan Bd. | Weiering, Angela | 13, Jan. 1846 | EE |
| Hagemann, Johan Ferd | Engelbert, Catharine | 12, May 1846 | EE |
| Hagemeyer, Heinrich | Scholmeier, Catharin | 7, Jan. 1847 | F |
| Hagen, Friedrich | Schroeder, Catharine | 7, Jan. 1847 | AA |
| Hagen, Louis | Schroeder, Elisabeth | 18, Oct. 1849 | F |
| Hagenberg, Gerhard | VondemFange, Maria | 11, Nov. 1841 | RCH |
| Hagenberg, Heinrich | Bushklaus, Maria | 21, Dec. 1848 | C |
| Hagenhorst, Wilhelm | Sollman, Elisabeth | 21, Sept 1843 | F |
| Hagerman, Christian | McCullough, Elis. | 14, Nov. 1837 | RCH |
| Hagerman, Peter | Dorsey, Clarissa | 4, May 1820 | RCH |
| Hagerty, Alexander | Kelly, Ann | 15, Aug. 1849 | BB |
| Hagerty, James | Horley, Catharine | 26, Nov. 1849 | RCH |
| Hagerty, Peter Wm. | McGowan, Anna | 1, Nov. 1847 | GG |
| Haggarty, Robert | Troy, Mary | 27, Feb. 1848 | BB |
| Haggarty, William | McElroy, Mary | 18, May 1843 | BB |
| Haggarty, William | Sullivan, Mary | 4, Sept 1848 | RCH |
| Haggerty, Maurice | Rider, Catharine | 4, July 1838 | RCH |
| Haglage, Joseph | Fick, Maria Anna | 22, Nov. 1846 | AA |
| Hahl, Jacob | Pohlender, Barbara | Feb. 1836 | RCH |
| Hahn, Adam | Klingler, Maria Anna | 27, Nov. 1848 | EE |
| Hahn, Heinrich | Barnhart, Catharine | 31, Aug. 1843 | RCH |
| Hahn, Johan | Weber, Elisabeth | 9, Jan. 1844 | FF |
| Hahn, Johan | Wagner, Rosina | 28, Oct. 1849 | EE |
| Hahn, John | Hatfield, Ann | 12, Feb. 1832 | RCH |
| Hahn, Justics | Clark, Nancy | 20, Oct. 1847 | RCH |
| Hahn, Louis | Sucher, Rebecca | 27, Dec. 1847 | G |
| Hahn, Maximillian | Heide, Theresa | 8, Nov. 1842 | FF |

| Grooms<br>***** | Brides<br>***** | Date of Marriage<br>**** ** ******** | Code<br>**** |
|---|---|---|---|
| Hahn, William | Crosley, Ruth | 15, Feb. 1842 | RCH |
| Hahnbacher, Johan | Thomas, Dorothea | 23, Jan. 1849 | C |
| Hahnhauser, Jacob | Mueller, Francisca | 29, Nov. 1838 | FF |
| Hahnhorst, J Theodor | Hehemann, Charlotte | 11, July 1839 | FF |
| Hahood, Thomas | Guerkle, Margaret | 8, June 1841 | RCH |
| Haht, Martin | Kraus, Margaretha | 28, Jan. 1845 | AA |
| Haider, Jakob | Clement, Maria | 28, Jan. 1845 | AA |
| Haigh, Simon | Connelly, Mary | 26, Jan. 1846 | RCH |
| Haight, Benjamin J. | Coolidge, Hetty B. | 26, June 1835 | I |
| Haight, John | ----, Rebecca | 24, Sept 1835 | RCH |
| Hailman, Jonathan | McChesney, Nancy H. | 25, July 1826 | RCH |
| Haim, John | Gray, Levina | 19, Oct. 1842 | RCH |
| Hain, Friedrich | Marx, Susan | 10, May 1844 | RCH |
| Haines, John | Gill, Margaret Jane | 18, June 1846 | RCH |
| Haing, Georg | Litel, Maria | 21, Sept 1848 | EE |
| Hair, Jacob | Hunt, Susan | 21, Apr. 1819 | RCH |
| Haka, Andrew | Jackwert, Anne | 30, Apr. 1849 | RCH |
| Haldasmon, Thomas J. | Gilman, Sarah Ann | 2, July 1834 | RCH |
| Haldemann, Walter | Metcalfe, Elisabeth | 31, Oct. 1844 | RCH |
| Hale, Alexander | Christian, Frances | 1, Aug. 1837 | RCH |
| Hale---, John | Edington, Mary | 23, Aug. 1818 | RCH |
| Hales, Allen | Walker, Caroline | 25, Dec. 1843 | RCH |
| Hales, Charles | Lewis, Margaret | 27, May 1849 | RCH |
| Haley, Patrick | Ryan, Anna | 31, Dec. 1849 | RCH |
| Haliass, Hanion | Long, Sarah | 28, Apr. 1839 | RCH |
| Halis, Charles | Kell, Mary Ann | 17, Nov. 1833 | RCH |
| Hall, Benjamin | Newell, Sarah | 18, Aug. 1847 | RCH |
| Hall, Daniel | Stoughton, Nancy | 28, Dec. 1836 | RCH |
| Hall, David | Bust, Elisabeth | 23, Feb. 1843 | BB |
| Hall, David | Riley, Sarah | 19, May 1847 | RCH |
| Hall, Elnathan | Rayher, Catherine A. | 14, Mar. 1844 | RCH |
| Hall, Ephraim | Calshan, Dareus | 1, Apr. 1821 | RCH |
| Hall, Frederick | Loomis, Elisabeth | 20, Nov. 1847 | RCH |
| Hall, George | Haymon, Mary | 9, July 1842 | RCH |
| Hall, Henry | Haurting, Ann Mary | 11, Oct. 1844 | A |
| Hall, Jacob | ----, Nancy | 27, June 1824 | RCH |
| Hall, James | Peason, Elisabeth | 19, May 1833 | RCH |
| Hall, James C. | Oliver, Harriet | 13, Aug. 1835 | I |
| Hall, James H. | Leerels, Matilda | 25, Aug. 1834 | RCH |
| Hall, Jeremiah | Dixon, Lucinda | 18, June 1833 | RCH |
| Hall, Jeremiah | Briscoe, Maria | 7, July 1836 | RCH |
| Hall, John | Longstreat, Margaret | 26, Aug. 1838 | RCH |
| Hall, John | Dicks, Cornelia | 3, Dec. 1843 | RCH |
| Hall, John | Christman, Christina | 7, Mar. 1844 | RCH |
| Hall, John | Doan, Martha A. | 4, Apr. 1848 | RCH |
| Hall, John | Dunseth, Ann | 19, Mar. 1846 | D |
| Hall, John C. | Falkner, Anna | 26, Sept 1841 | RCH |
| Hall, John C. | Roach, Julia | 14, Sept 1846 | RCH |
| Hall, Joseph W. | Norton, Elisabeth W. | 31, Sept 1839 | RCH |
| Hall, Mathew | Carson, Elizabeth J. | 3, Oct. 1848 | RCH |
| Hall, Patrick | Atchinson, Elisabeth | 19, Oct. 1840 | BB |
| Hall, Robert | Douglas, Emma | 23, Apr. 1842 | I |
| Hall, Robert | Watts, Margaret | 24, July 1849 | RCH |
| Hall, Robert S. | Davinna, Hester Ann | 3, June 1836 | RCH |
| Hall, Stephen | Ferry, Cynthia Ann | 13, May 1819 | RCH |
| Hall, Sylvester | Watson, Harriet | 11, Mar. 1846 | RCH |
| Hall, Thomas | King, Mary | 8, Aug. 1839 | RCH |
| Hall, William | Niles, Ann | 6, Apr. 1823 | RCH |
| Hall, William | Redeford, Martha | 9, Feb. 1840 | RCH |
| Hall, William | Johnson, Mary Ann | 5, Jan. 1844 | RCH |
| Hall, William | Miner, Elisabeth | 28, Apr. 1847 | RCH |
| Hallam, Jonathan | Gilpin, Sidney A. | 23, May 1836 | RCH |
| Hallem, Daniel S. | Sterling, Hannah | 1, May 1833 | RCH |
| Haller, Anton | Brodbeck, Catharine | 9, Aug. 1847 | EE |
| Haller, Conrad | Koerner, Christina | 15, May 1842 | RCH |
| Hallermann, Bernard | Peisker, Gertrud | 8, May 1849 | RCH |
| Hallinan, William | Byrne, Elisabeth | 16, Sept 1849 | GG |
| Halmer, Philipp | Stagburger, Harriet | 9, Apr. 1849 | RCH |
| Halstead, James | Folger, Elisabeth | 31, Oct. 1838 | RCH |
| Halstead, Nicholas | Dennins, Jerusha | 12, June 1825 | RCH |
| Haltemes, Johan B. | Muehlering, Maria E. | 24, Dec. 1849 | F |

| Grooms<br>****** | Brides<br>****** | Date of Marriage<br>**** ** ******** | Code<br>**** |
|---|---|---|---|
| Haltenhof, Carl | Martin, Eva | 17, Feb. 1848 | G |
| Halter, Christian | Schott, Maria Anna | 24, Oct. 1847 | EE |
| Ham, Gustav | Webster, Martha A. | 14, May 1848 | RCH |
| Hamann, Conrad | Rehm, Anna | 28, Sept 1841 | FF |
| Hamant, Lambert | Bardo, Maria | 21, Nov. 1847 | FF |
| Hamar, James | ----, Margaret | 31, Oct. 1822 | RCH |
| Hambleton, Eli | Moss, Margaret | 20, Jan. 1845 | RCH |
| Hambleton, James | Howard, Elisabeth | 15, Dec. 1844 | RCH |
| Hambleton, John | Samson, Susan | 19, Nov. 1842 | RCH |
| Hamblin, Robert | Goggan, Elisabeth | 14, June 1835 | RCH |
| Hambo, Stephan | Scheibli, Anna | 22, May 1849 | AA |
| Hamel, Andrew | Schull, Anna | 21, Mar. 1842 | RCH |
| Hamel, Samuel | Cummins, Lavina | 17, May 1846 | RCH |
| Hamel, Stephen | Johns, Eleanor | 18, June 1846 | RCH |
| Hames, | Humphrey, Margaret | 25, Nov. 1844 | RCH |
| Hamill, William | Boyd, Mary Ann | 20, May 1846 | RCH |
| Hamilton, Alexander | Mortimer, Sarah | 25, May 1839 | RCH |
| Hamilton, Amos | McCord, Margaret | 25, Dec. 1836 | RCH |
| Hamilton, Anthony | Sladick, Maria | 9, June 1827 | RCH |
| Hamilton, C.M. | O'Connor, Margaret | 7, Apr. 1849 | RCH |
| Hamilton, Edward | Keefe, Mary | 10, Oct. 1847 | GG |
| Hamilton, George | Clark, Huldah | 9, Feb. 1844 | RCH |
| Hamilton, Hannabel | Arnold, Mary Ann | 29, Jan. 1842 | RCH |
| Hamilton, Henry | Applegate, Lucinda | 24, Dec. 1833 | RCH |
| Hamilton, Henry | Williams, Caroline | 31, Dec. 1833 | RCH |
| Hamilton, Hugh S. | Dabney, Caroline | 28, June 1836 | RCH |
| Hamilton, James | McBride, Sarah | 31, Aug. 1843 | RCH |
| Hamilton, John J. | Leak, Mary | 17, Nov. 1833 | RCH |
| Hamilton, Joseph | Rhoades, Sarah | 9, Jan. 1843 | RCH |
| Hamilton, Lorenzo | Edwards, Sophia | 1, Oct. 1843 | RCH |
| Hamilton, Samuel | Boon, Ann | 2, Aug. 1826 | RCH |
| Hamilton, Samuel | Adams, Amanda M. | 28, Apr. 1842 | RCH |
| Hamilton, Samuel R. | Bigger, Abigail M. | 24, Oct. 1833 | RCH |
| Hamilton, Theodore | Gossett, Eleanor A. | 26, June 1844 | RCH |
| Hamlin, Leonard | Truesdale, Melinda | 15, Feb. 1836 | RCH |
| Hammann, Christoph | Pund, Josephine | 4, July 1847 | EE |
| Hammann, Xavier | Dopler, Brigitta | 25, Sept 1838 | FF |
| Hammel, Andrew | Riggs, Lucretia Ann | 9, June 1835 | RCH |
| Hammel, Andrew | McKimm, Mary | 7, May 1840 | RCH |
| Hammel, Conrad | Winkler, Magdalena | 5, Apr. 1849 | C |
| Hammel, Jacob | Kalbfleisch, Barbara | 4, Jan. 1849 | A |
| Hammel, John | Menelly, Ellen | 17, Aug. 1837 | RCH |
| Hammel, John | Morton, Mary Ann | 30, Mar. 1847 | RCH |
| Hammel, Joseph | Mullen, Mary | 13, Sept 1849 | RCH |
| Hammel, Samuel | Clark, Agelah J. | 21, Apr. 1849 | RCH |
| Hammer, Lorenz | Geist, Maria Anna | 13, Oct. 1840 | FF |
| Hammer, Peter Jos. | Wuertz, Anna Maria | 17, Jan. 1843 | AA |
| Hammerle, Francis | Moster, Rosina | 20, Feb. 1848 | AA |
| Hammerschmidt, Leon. | Minzenbach, Gertrud | 22, Dec. 1848 | B |
| Hammes, Peter | Busch, Wilhel.(Mrs) | 25, Nov. 1847 | AA |
| Hammett, Andrew | Black, Elisabeth | 1, Sept 1840 | BB |
| Hammit, John | Sprague, Sally | 3, Oct. 1820 | RCH |
| Hammitt, Samuel | Seal, Elisabeth | 17, May 1846 | RCH |
| Hammon, James | Lynn, Nancy | 10, Aug. 1845 | RCH |
| Hammon, John | Princeton, Nancy | 25, June 1842 | RCH |
| Hammon, Oliver | Beaty, Elisabeth | 29, Nov. 1848 | RCH |
| Hammond, Aaron | Wilson, Harriet | 5, Oct. 1837 | RCH |
| Hammond, Andrew | Henderson, Elisabeth | 13, Aug. 1837 | RCH |
| Hammond, Charles | Bloomfield, Anna | 30, Apr. 1849 | RCH |
| Hammond, James | Dowle, Sarah | 7, May 1842 | RCH |
| Hammond, Joseph | Hilton, Minerva | 12, Jan. 1848 | RCH |
| Hammond, Joseph W. | Johnson, Mary Jane | 6, Apr. 1848 | RCH |
| Hammond, Timothy | Adams, Elisabeth | 4, Dec. 1833 | RCH |
| Hammont, Matthew | Collon, Mary Ann | 8, Aug. 1839 | RCH |
| Hampf, Johan | Schulte, Elisabeth | 22, Oct. 1839 | FF |
| Hampton, William | Cain, Mary J. | 7, Apr. 1847 | RCH |
| Han---, John | VordemBerger, Anna | 11, Apr. 1849 | RCH |
| Hanaley, Jabez | Vantrece, Charlotte | 18, Nov. 1840 | RCH |
| Hanauer, Johan | Schneider, Margaret | 12, Sept 1840 | FF |
| Hanauer, Joseph | Roos, Mathilda | 27, July 1844 | RCH |
| Hanbold, Nicolaus | Schmidt, Margaretha | 2, Nov. 1841 | RCH |

| Grooms<br>****** | Brides<br>****** | Date of Marriage<br>**** ** ******** | Code<br>**** |
|---|---|---|---|
| Hanbredel, Andreas | Wietheuper, Anna | 28, May 1844 | AA |
| Hancock, Daniel | Patterson, Rachel | 25, Jan. 1821 | RCH |
| Hancock, James | Pinney, Elisabeth | 31, Aug. 1847 | RCH |
| Hancock, Stanford | Ingersoll, Elisabeth | 24, Aug. 1833 | RCH |
| Hand, Ellis | Evans, Ellen | 23, May 1847 | RCH |
| Hand, Elmore | Creach, Elisabeth | 15, Mar. 1835 | RCH |
| Hand, Joseph | Shepard, Elisabeth | 10, Nov. 1839 | RCH |
| Hand, L. | Coleman, Catharine | 1, Jan. 1836 | RCH |
| Hand, Samuel | Whitesides, Jane | 27, July 1841 | RCH |
| Hand, Sylvester | Innes, Margaret | 22, Aug. 1844 | RCH |
| Hand, Valentin | Mueller, Elisabeth | 29, May 1840 | FF |
| Hand, William | Raymond, Ann | 11, Aug. 1826 | RCH |
| Hand, William | Hammond, Elisabeth | 27, Apr. 1836 | RCH |
| Handfeld, Wilhelm H. | Wilhelm, Margaretha | 7, Nov. 1843 | AA |
| Handford, Thadeus | Morten, Catharine | 8, Dec. 1845 | RCH |
| Handlen, Alexander | Kineon, Catharine | 28, Aug. 1839 | BB |
| Handlin, Francis | Rutledge, Seraphina | 15, Oct. 1846 | RCH |
| Handmann, Anton | Hohne, Margaretha | 1, June 1848 | II |
| Handtmann, Friedrich | Sucher, Veronica | 16, Feb. 1847 | G |
| Handy, John | Applegate, Elisabeth | 23, July 1844 | RCH |
| Handy, Robert | Cummings, Elisabeth | 6, Feb. 1844 | RCH |
| Hanegreef, John | For---, Jemima | 10, Oct. 1822 | RCH |
| Hanes, William | McBride, Elisabeth | 21, Dec. 1845 | RCH |
| Haney, Matthew | Porter, Martha | 17, May 1848 | BB |
| Hanfbauer, Johan | Schorr, Anna | 9, Sept 1849 | G |
| Hanfeld, Johan Herm. | Hoppens, Euphemia | 12, Jan. 1847 | AA |
| Hangs, Lorenz | Burghard, Ruth | 16, Apr. 1839 | FF |
| Hankens, John S. | LaBoyteaux, Caroline | 14, Feb. 1838 | RCH |
| Hankins, John | Hancock, Orpha | 29, Aug. 1847 | RCH |
| Hankinson, Josiah | Fisk, Elisabeth | 4, Oct. 1820 | RCH |
| Hanks, Albert | Jungman, Anna | 3, May 1847 | RCH |
| Hanks, Arthur | Billings, Elisabeth | 21, Feb. 1843 | RCH |
| Hanlan, Timothy | English, Marge | 30, Aug. 1847 | GG |
| Hanley, Anton | Fager, Maria Anna | 26, Apr. 1839 | FF |
| Hanlon, James | St.John, Hannah | 19, June 1842 | BB |
| Hanly, Harvey | Stotsenburg, Elis. | 16, Feb. 1826 | RCH |
| Hann, George | Morrison, Margaret | 7, Sept 1847 | RCH |
| Hanna, James | Cooke, Edmonia | 28, Oct. 1842 | RCH |
| Hanna, Jonathan | McLean, Mary | 30, Oct. 1823 | RCH |
| Hannaford, Richard | Tanner, Rebecca | 8, Apr. 1838 | RCH |
| Hannaford, Richard | Fuller, Rosanna | 1, June 1846 | RCH |
| Hannegan, Patrick | Brophy, Catharine | 30, July 1848 | BB |
| Hanneklau, Carl | Kettler, Elisabeth | 21, Oct. 1847 | FF |
| Hanners, James B. | Arbuckle, Nancy | 31, Mar. 1844 | RCH |
| Hanning, Friedrich | Kemp, Friedricka | 23, Feb. 1842 | F |
| Hannon, Bartholomew | Dwyer, Ann | 27, Sept 1846 | BB |
| Hannon, Patrick | Campbell, Mary | 7, Sept 1847 | BB |
| Hannon, Patrick | Reid, Catharine | 19, Oct. 1847 | BB |
| Hanon, James | Coleman, Ellen | 18, June 1848 | GG |
| Hans, Jacob | Wild, Kunigunda | 3, Jan. 1846 | G |
| Hans, Jakob | Will, Philippina | 13, Mar. 1848 | A |
| Hanschen, Wilhelm | Dieckmann, Cath. W. | 15, Nov. 1849 | C |
| Hanselman, Christoph | Hanselman, Christina | 23, Mar. 1823 | I |
| Hanselman, Jacob | Borger, Betsy | 5, Apr. 1825 | RCH |
| Hanselmann, Adam | Kenkel, Anna Cath. E | 13, July 1847 | AA |
| Hansen, Andreas P. | Johnsen, Elvina | 18, Sept 1847 | A |
| Hansen, Joseph | Hopping, Margaretha | 3, Sept 1848 | AA |
| Hansford, Garret | Clark, Elisabeth | 15, Dec. 1819 | RCH |
| Hansmann, Aloysius | Lindener, Eva | 26, Nov. 1844 | AA |
| Hanson, Calvin | Cochran, Mary Ann | 19, Dec. 1843 | RCH |
| Hansz, Johan | Schreiber, Elisabeth | 2, Nov. 1843 | C |
| Happ, Bartholomew | Beinmann, Elisabeth | 9, Apr. 1839 | FF |
| Happock, John | Farnes, Nancy | 28, Mar. 1822 | RCH |
| Harbaugh, David | Thomas, Mary | 6, Apr. 1820 | RCH |
| Harbaugh, Hamilton | Haites, Mary Helen | 1, May 1839 | RCH |
| Harbes, Johan Heinr. | Speckmann, Louise W. | 15, Oct. 1846 | G |
| Harbeson, Robert | Staply, Elisabeth | 25, Apr. 1844 | RCH |
| Harbold, George | Herberger, Elisabeth | 2, July 1846 | RCH |
| Harbough, Daniel | Colvin, Catharine | 20, June 1834 | RCH |
| Harcourt, William | Freeman, Mahala | 15, Sept 1834 | RCH |
| Hardebeck, Bernard | Lot, Elisabeth | 24, Nov. 1840 | FF |

| Grooms | Brides | Date of Marriage | Code |
|--------|--------|------------------|------|
| ****** | ****** | **** ** ******** | **** |
| Hardebeck, Gerhard | Focken, M. Elisabeth | 20, Feb. 1838 | FF |
| Hardebeck, Heinrich | Farenbarens, Cath. | 20, Feb. 1838 | FF |
| Hardebeck, Herman | Mehrings, Anna Maria | 30, Oct. 1843 | FF |
| Hardeiz, Joshua | Carrick, Elisabeth | 10, Feb. 1833 | RCH |
| Hardemann, F. Heinr. | Nedermann, Wilhelmin | 2, Dec. 1847 | F |
| Hardenbrock, Henry | Copton, Catharine | 19, Dec. 1835 | RCH |
| Hardenstein, Otto | Haven, Harriet | 3, Aug. 1843 | RCH |
| Hardesty, Samuel | Emiley, Nancy | 15, Dec. 1842 | RCH |
| Hardgrove, Rowland | Burberry, Sarah | 25, Nov. 1845 | RCH |
| Hardie, Francis | Todd, Elisabeth | 19, Oct. 1836 | RCH |
| Hardin, James | Dawson, Mary | 24, June 1834 | RCH |
| Hardin, Josiah | Cottle, Susan | 30, Dec. 1819 | RCH |
| Hardin, William | Chamberland, Marg. | 26, May 1844 | RCH |
| Harding, Carpenter | Voorhees, Ann | 11, Jan. 1836 | RCH |
| Harding, David | Ferguson, Oney | 24, May 1825 | RCH |
| Harding, Jesse | Walden, Nancy | 5, June 1846 | RCH |
| Harding, John | Boal, Frances S. | 24, Nov. 1835 | RCH |
| Harding, Lyman | Shephard, Mary P. | 4, Jan. 1837 | I |
| Harding, William | Tunnel, Harriet | 1, Dec. 1845 | RCH |
| Hardinghaus, Heinric | Messmann, Elisabeth | 17, May 1836 | FF |
| Hardlage Heinrich G. | Wanstrat, M. Gertrud | 29, Sept 1840 | FF |
| Hardway, Friedrich | McGrew, Margaret | 20, Aug. 1849 | RCH |
| Hardy, Charles | Wallace, Isabella | 18, Nov. 1846 | RCH |
| Hardy, John | Bozart, Sarah | 3, May 1847 | RCH |
| Hardy, Joseph | Shannon, Catharine | 20, May 1841 | RCH |
| Hardy, Patrick | ----, A. | 28, May 1835 | RCH |
| Hare, Anton | Ougley, Catharine | 10, June 1847 | RCH |
| Harger, Peter | Woodin, Rebecca | 6, Aug. 1834 | RCH |
| Hargrave, Hannibal | Whalon, Elisabeth | 12, Dec. 1832 | RCH |
| Hargrave, Peter | Nickons, Rebecca | 3, June 1846 | RCH |
| Hargraves, Hercules | Mills, Ann | 24, Mar. 1836 | RCH |
| Harker, Anthony E. | Birdsall, Maria L. | 7, May 1834 | RCH |
| Harker, Jacob | Johnson, Sarah | 13, July 1826 | RCH |
| Harker, Joseph | Maline, Susannah | 19, Feb. 1822 | RCH |
| Harker, Samuel | Daniel, Elis. Ann | 1, Jan. 1834 | RCH |
| Harkin, Peter | Reilly, Bridget | 18, May 1848 | BB |
| Harkness, Charles | Harkness, Elisabeth | 29, July 1843 | RCH |
| Harley, David S. | Symmonds, Elisabeth | 28, May 1839 | RCH |
| Harley, Theodore S. | Little, Martha | 13, Oct. 1842 | RCH |
| Harlin, Michael | Heeny, Mary | 30, Aug. 1847 | RCH |
| Harlin, Samuel | Lee, Mary M. | 30, Oct. 1848 | RCH |
| Harlough, Henry | Myers, Elisabeth | 23, Apr. 1835 | RCH |
| Harlow, Hiram | Eveleth, Harriet | 25, Dec. 1832 | RCH |
| Harlow, Orlando | Coleman, Mary | 8, Jan. 1844 | RCH |
| Harman, William | Jackson, Margaret | 29, July 1848 | RCH |
| Harmann, Gerhard H. | Becker, Catharina | 30, Sept 1849 | II |
| Harmann, Herman Ant. | Burk, Elisabeth | 13, Aug. 1848 | II |
| Harmeier, Heinrich H | Dollmann, A. Elis. | 12, Nov. 1848 | II |
| Harmeier, J. Rudolph | Kallmeyer, Louise B. | 11, Nov. 1841 | F |
| Harmer, Stacy | Rogers, Hannah | 23, Oct. 1820 | RCH |
| Harmeyer, Georg F. | Schwenghaus, Anna M. | 25, May 1843 | F |
| Harmon, Benjamin | Bronson, Julia | 25, July 1843 | RCH |
| Harms, Friedrich | Gasekins, Catharine | 24, Mar. 1842 | RCH |
| Harness, Solomon | McNeal, Anna Maria | 15, Jan. 1835 | RCH |
| Harney, Matthew | Ryan, Winnifred | 4, June 1848 | BB |
| Harnish, Johan | Mattis, Barbara | 2, Aug. 1841 | F |
| Harnold, Jacob | Gruh, Barbara | 1, Nov. 1838 | FF |
| Harold, Andrew | Barwich, Susannah | 5, Oct. 1846 | RCH |
| Harold, Ezekiel P. | ----, Frances | 23, Sept 1832 | RCH |
| Harp, David | Smith, Harriet | 21, Oct. 1847 | RCH |
| Harper, Abel | Sp---, Catharine | 21, Mar. 1820 | RCH |
| Harper, Goodlow | Highgate, Sarah | 1, Oct. 1846 | RCH |
| Harper, Hamilton | Loder, Catharine | 22, Feb. 1847 | RCH |
| Harper, James | Grissup, Mary A. | 11, Oct. 1838 | RCH |
| Harper, Josiah | Rose, Elisabeth | 8, June 1843 | RCH |
| Harper, Samuel | Moris, Catharine | 20, June 1833 | RCH |
| Harper, Thomas | Russell, Sarah | 5, Apr. 1835 | RCH |
| Harper, William | Hughfly, Mary Louise | 20, Sept 1821 | RCH |
| Harr, Georg | Hammer, Francisca | 18, Feb. 1849 | C |
| Harradeth, Andrew | Easley, Mary | 14, May 1818 | RCH |
| Harrah, William | Foster, Hannah | 25, Nov. 1848 | RCH |

RESTORED HAMILTON COUNTY MARRIAGE RECORDS --- 1808 - 1849

| Grooms | Brides | Date of Marriage | Code |
|------|------|------|------|
| Harrell, Josiah | Hodge, Mary | 2, May 1844 | RCH |
| Harrer, Johan | Raken, Leonora | 14, Feb. 1847 | B |
| Harrie, Arthur | Coppin, Susannah | 26, Sept 1833 | RCH |
| Harrington, Daniel | Ray, Mary | 31, Jan. 1842 | RCH |
| Harrington, David | Williams, Mary A. | 26, July 1849 | RCH |
| Harrington, Dennis | Reed, Catharine | 21, July 1844 | BB |
| Harrington, James | McDowal, Ann | 10, June 1826 | RCH |
| Harrington, James J. | Spalding, Caroline | 10, Feb. 1847 | BB |
| Harrington, Whitford | Gould, Catharine | 1, Mar. 1842 | I |
| Harris, | Wheeler, Elisabeth | 5, Aug. 1849 | RCH |
| Harris, Abner | Hardin, Sarah | 17, Jan. 1849 | RCH |
| Harris, Abraham | Ezekiel, Bethsheba | 22, Sept 1847 | RCH |
| Harris, Andrew | Decoster, Lydia Ann | 13, Oct. 1842 | RCH |
| Harris, Benjamin | ----, ---- | 30, Sept 1819 | RCH |
| Harris, Caleb | Davis, Mary Ann | 12, Nov. 1846 | RCH |
| Harris, Calvin | Dunn, Edith | 21, May 1835 | RCH |
| Harris, David | Roderick, Mary | 2, Aug. 1847 | RCH |
| Harris, Edward | James, Sarah | 18, Oct. 1842 | RCH |
| Harris, Edward | Williams, Ann | 19, Apr. 1847 | RCH |
| Harris, Frederick | Grasson, Sophia | 1, June 1848 | RCH |
| Harris, Hardin | Caldwell, Mary | 5, Feb. 1846 | RCH |
| Harris, James | Taylor, Julia | 31, May 1847 | RCH |
| Harris, James B. | Baldwin, Sarah W. | 23, Oct. 1822 | RCH |
| Harris, Jeremiah | Rust, Elisabeth | 10, Dec. 1834 | RCH |
| Harris, John | Hall, Mary Ann | 17, Jan. 1833 | RCH |
| Harris, John | Casner, Mary | Nov. 1833 | RCH |
| Harris, John | LaCount, Frances | 4, Dec. 1845 | RCH |
| Harris, John | Linman, Tamar | 8, Sept 1846 | RCH |
| Harris, John | King, Emily A. | 19, Nov. 1846 | RCH |
| Harris, John C. | Ford, Martha | 20, July 1849 | RCH |
| Harris, Jonathan | Davis, Elisabeth | 21, Mar. 1848 | RCH |
| Harris, Jonathan | Reager, Susan | 12, Apr. 1849 | RCH |
| Harris, Joseph | Thompson, Elisabeth | 28, Aug. 1843 | RCH |
| Harris, Nathaniel | Nelson, Margaret | 13, Jan. 1846 | RCH |
| Harris, Robert | Reeder, Phebe H. | 27, Feb. 1836 | RCH |
| Harris, Shaddrach | Cord, Luezer J. | 1, Nov. 1846 | RCH |
| Harris, Thomas | Floyd, Lucy | 6, Feb. 1846 | RCH |
| Harris, Wiley | Harris, Susan | 26, Dec. 1846 | RCH |
| Harris, William | Stuart, Mary | 22, Feb. 1842 | RCH |
| Harris, William | Addis, Sarah | 1, Oct. 1843 | RCH |
| Harris, William | Perry, Sarah Jane | 19, Aug. 1849 | RCH |
| Harris, William | Ray, Martha | 8, May 1848 | BB |
| Harris, William Hy. | Rose, Mary Ann | 2, Sept 1848 | RCH |
| Harris, William L. | Rouse, Parmelia | 6, June 1839 | RCH |
| Harrison, Charles | Enyart, Mary Ann | 20, Jan. 1836 | RCH |
| Harrison, Clark | Smith, Elizabeth | 19, Mar. 1846 | RCH |
| Harrison, David T. | Boughman, Mary | 3, Mar. 1819 | RCH |
| Harrison, Edwin | Wyeth, Amanda | 8, Jan. 1837 | RCH |
| Harrison, George | Randall, Rebecca | 6, Jan. 1820 | RCH |
| Harrison, George | Davis, Maria L. | 11, Dec. 1845 | RCH |
| Harrison, Henry | Sinclair, Margaret | 25, Sept 1841 | RCH |
| Harrison, Henry | Thurmann, Tinsey | 22, Dec. 1844 | RCH |
| Harrison, Henry | Gibson, Josephine E. | 2, Feb. 1847 | RCH |
| Harrison, Hiram | Baker, Margaret Ann | 13, Sept 1846 | RCH |
| Harrison, James | Parker, Sarah | 27, Aug. 1841 | RCH |
| Harrison, James F. | Alston, Caroline W. | 20, Sept 1848 | I |
| Harrison, John | Ellett, Elisabeth | 13, Nov. 1823 | RCH |
| Harrison, John | Wescott, Abigail | 28, Feb. 1837 | RCH |
| Harrison, Joseph | Harrison, Sarah | 16, May 1819 | RCH |
| Harrison, Lewis | Stake, Margaret | 21, Aug. 1832 | RCH |
| Harrison, Livingston | Pierson, Mary | 23, Oct. 1822 | RCH |
| Harrison, Noah | Witham, Nancy Ann | 25, May 1820 | RCH |
| Harrison, Richard | Lamier, | 27, Apr. 1818 | RCH |
| Harrison, Samuel | Berryman, Alice | 19, Oct. 1822 | RCH |
| Harrison, Samuel | Roark, Catharine | 22, Feb. 1834 | RCH |
| Harrison, Samuel | McCoffee, M. Juliett | 1, Feb. 1843 | RCH |
| Harrison, Thomas | Gaston, Phoebe | 17, Dec. 1818 | RCH |
| Harrison, Thomas | C---, Jehila | 7, Mar. 1820 | RCH |
| Harrison, Thomas | Cooke, Sally | 4, Oct. 1842 | RCH |
| Harrison, Thomas P. | Merrie, Mary Ann | 17, May 1838 | D |
| Harrison, William | Armstrong, Powne | 25, Oct. 1836 | RCH |

| Grooms<br>****** | Brides<br>****** | Date of Marriage<br>**** ** ******** | Code<br>**** |
|---|---|---|---|
| Harrison, William | Lesche, Sarah Jane | 8, Dec. 1845 | RCH |
| Harrod, Elijah | Staughton, Elisabeth | 8, Jan. 1832 | RCH |
| Harroll, William | Tomkins, Harriet | 28, Feb. 1846 | RCH |
| Harrow, Thomas | Lowe, Mary Ann | 26, June 1837 | RCH |
| Harroway, Samuel | Mankin, Rosa | 12, June 1834 | RCH |
| Harsch, Gottlieb | Schafer, Elisabeth | 8, Jan. 1849 | A |
| Harsch, Johan | Etzel, Margaretha | 2, Jan. 1848 | A |
| Harsha, Thomas | Lumley, Sarah | 14, July 1844 | RCH |
| Harshay, James | Crommett, Rachel | 14, Feb. 1845 | RCH |
| Hart, A. | Trountstein, Carolin | 22, Apr. 1849 | RCH |
| Hart, Abraham | R---, Elisabeth | 12, Feb. 1821 | RCH |
| Hart, Alfred | Boarder, Caroline | 21, Feb. 1843 | RCH |
| Hart, Asher | Wilson, Jane | 11, Jan. 1844 | RCH |
| Hart, Henry N. | Church, Jane Elis. | 25, Sept 1838 | D |
| Hart, Henry R. | Dodd, Mary W. | 8, June 1848 | RCH |
| Hart, Isaac | Johnston, Elisabeth | 20, Aug. 1849 | RCH |
| Hart, James | Edmondson, Cassandra | 2, Apr. 1843 | RCH |
| Hart, John | Mahar, Mary | 27, July 1845 | BB |
| Hart, Matthew | Moreland, Mary Ann | 5, Feb. 1846 | BB |
| Hart, Nathan | Reitzenberger, Jetta | 9, Mar. 1847 | RCH |
| Hart, Samuel M. | Pugh, Mary A. | 3, June 1841 | I |
| Hart, Silas | Holt, Elizabeth | 27, Oct. 1846 | RCH |
| Hart, Thomas | Higginson, Elisabeth | 26, Nov. 1844 | BB |
| Hart, Thomas | Dunn, Olivia | 25, Nov. 1849 | BB |
| Hart, William | Hoglen, Hannah | 14, Feb. 1833 | RCH |
| Harter, Benedict | Mueller, Victoria | 19, Nov. 1846 | HH |
| Harter, Lafayette | Williams, Catharine | 5, July 1849 | RCH |
| Hartgrove, Nelson | McMillan, Catharine | 22, May 1842 | RCH |
| Harthorn, Francis | Brown, Martha Jane | 20, Feb. 1846 | RCH |
| Harthorn, Gilman | Cary, Maria L. | 2, May 1833 | RCH |
| Hartig, Adam | Albach, Elisabeth | 13, Feb. 1844 | RCH |
| Harting, Friedrich | Dittmann, Caroline | 6, Apr. 1848 | G |
| Hartje, Johan Herman | Poppe, Margaret R. | 15, Apr. 1847 | B |
| Hartke, J. Gerhard | Winkeljohan, Anna | 26, Nov. 1844 | AA |
| Hartke, Joseph | Feldmann, Maria Anna | 16, Apr. 1844 | AA |
| Hartke, William | Scott, Ann | 23, Apr. 1834 | RCH |
| Hartlaub, Philipp | Backofer, Johanna | 9, Nov. 1848 | FF |
| Hartley, Abner | Frazer, Sarah | 10, Mar. 1836 | RCH |
| Hartley, George | Smorzka, Elisabeth | 17, Jan. 1847 | RCH |
| Hartley, James | McDowell, Elisabeth | 7, Jan. 1839 | D |
| Hartley, Josiah | Hackweller, Elis. | 10, Sept 1835 | RCH |
| Hartley, Richard | Doty, Hannah | 19, Nov. 1842 | RCH |
| Hartman, John Henry | Blackmeyer, Catharin | 14, July 1838 | RCH |
| Hartman, Moses | Athaus, Elizabeth | 12, Sept 1825 | RCH |
| Hartmann, | Schlueter, Elisabeth | 3, Aug. 1849 | RCH |
| Hartmann, Carl | Horn, Barbara | 12, July 1849 | B |
| Hartmann, Conrad | Linat, Elisabeth | 25, Oct. 1840 | G |
| Hartmann, Dietrich | AufderMarsh, Cath. | 13, May 1847 | F |
| Hartmann, Gerhard | Mollinghoff, Theresa | 19, Sept 1847 | FF |
| Hartmann, H.H. | Brinkmann, Bernardin | 27, Mar. 1849 | RCH |
| Hartmann, Johan Jos. | Alig, Elisabeth | 9, Jan. 1848 | EE |
| Hartmann, Joseph | Mickel, Anna Maria | 12, Oct. 1847 | EE |
| Hartmann, Michael | Ziegler, Barbara | 23, July 1848 | EE |
| Hartnagel, Joseph | Butz, Juliana | 18, Feb. 1849 | AA |
| Harton, John | VanAusdol, Catharine | Dec. 1844 | RCH |
| Hartpence, Daniel E. | Ross, Elvira | 26, June 1836 | RCH |
| Hartpence, Isaac | Meginnis, Margaret | 11, Feb. 1837 | RCH |
| Hartpence, James B. | Riggs, Lucinda | 28, Feb. 1822 | RCH |
| Hartshorn, Charles | Baum, Eleanor | 30, Nov. 1841 | I |
| Hartshorn, Johan | Schooley, Elisabeth | 4, Nov. 1847 | RCH |
| Hartsough, Ephraim | ----, Julia Ann | 23, Feb. 1839 | RCH |
| Hartweg, Jacob | Hutt, Caroline | 13, May 1848 | G |
| Hartwell, August | Challoner, Anna E. | 6, Dec. 1844 | RCH |
| Hartwell, Jonathan | Shaw, Mary J. | 18, Nov. 1845 | I |
| Hartwell, Shattuck | Mussey, Catharine | 26, July 1849 | RCH |
| Hartwell, Winthrop | Ault, Naomi | 25, Dec. 1845 | RCH |
| Harves, John Henry | Schwirmann, Catharin | 18, June 1846 | G |
| Harvey, Albert | Bledsoe, Julia | 19, June 1838 | RCH |
| Harvey, George | Morten, Tabitha | 14, Mar. 1843 | RCH |
| Harvey, Joel B. | ----, Elisabeth | 28, Mar. 1822 | RCH |
| Harvey, Owen | McDonald, Catharine | 4, June 1842 | RCH |

| Grooms<br>****** | Brides<br>****** | Date of Marriage<br>**** ** ******** | Code<br>**** |
|---|---|---|---|
| Harvey, Samuel C. | Dunn, Louisa | 7, Oct. 1834 | RCH |
| Harvey, Solomon | Morten, Viola | 5, Nov. 1845 | RCH |
| Harvie, Charles | Kramer, Clarion | 4, June 1843 | RCH |
| Harwood, Charles | Wilson, | 19, June 1838 | RCH |
| Harzel, William | Ely, Elisabeth | 5, Aug. 1834 | RCH |
| Harzmeyer, Georg | Gardelmann, Johanna | 19, Nov. 1849 | G |
| Has, Anton | Eicher, Margaretha | 15, Apr. 1839 | FF |
| Hasch, Andreas | Leiss, Carolina | 12, Oct. 1841 | FF |
| Haschan, Philipp | Schevene, Elisabeth | 30, Apr. 1839 | FF |
| Haskell, John | Bolds, Mary | 13, Oct. 1833 | RCH |
| Haskins, Isaac | Bogass, Milley | 1, Nov. 1823 | RCH |
| Haskinson, John H. | Lord, Rebecca Ann | 5, Dec. 1825 | RCH |
| Haslan, John | Yates, Mary | 12, Sept 1846 | RCH |
| Hasler, Eli | Devine, Maria | 3, Aug. 1849 | RCH |
| Haslet, John | Cummings, Ann | 14, Mar. 1833 | RCH |
| Hasley, William | Enos, Henrietta | 16, Apr. 1849 | RCH |
| Hasluck, Daniel S. | VanDyke, Fidelia R. | 31, May 1842 | D |
| Hass, Conrad | Bruns, Engel | 3, June 1847 | RCH |
| Hass, Georg | Detsch, Louisa | 30, Oct. 1848 | EE |
| Hasse, Lorenz Wm. | Krieg, Francisca | 11, May 1841 | FF |
| Hasselbeck, Stephen | Jaeger, Margaretha | 2, June 1840 | FF |
| Hasselberger, Valen. | Schneider, Francisca | 28, Oct. 1847 | CC |
| Hassen, Thomas | Tharburn, Sophia | 8, Feb. 1849 | BB |
| Hassenpflug, Daniel | Groeninger, Catharin | 11, Sept 1848 | C |
| Hassler, Friedrich | Lansh, Dorothea | 1, Jan. 1849 | A |
| Hasson, William | Sherman, Ann | 23, Mar. 1837 | RCH |
| Hastar, James | Aygan, Phebe | 15, Sept 1846 | RCH |
| Hasting, Francis | Douglass, Caroline | 28, Sept 1832 | RCH |
| Hatcher, John | Witham, F. Nancy | 23, Nov. 1841 | RCH |
| Hatfield, | Webb, Elisabeth | 27, Mar. 1842 | RCH |
| Hatfield, Andrew | Pyle, Margaret | 5, July 1846 | RCH |
| Hatfield, George | Ayres, Jane | 18, June 1839 | I |
| Hatfield, George | Trousdale, Hannah | 11, Sept 1849 | RCH |
| Hatfield, Joseph | Crosby, Elisabeth | 15, Mar. 1836 | RCH |
| Hatfield, William | Debolt, Jane | 6, Aug. 1836 | RCH |
| Hathaway, Eleazar | Abbott, Rachel | 23, July 1822 | RCH |
| Hathaway, Henry | Corn, Lydia | 15, Mar. 1821 | RCH |
| Hathaway, Henry | Hall, Jane | 17, Mar. 1846 | RCH |
| Hathaway, William | Simons, Seleigh | 6, Feb. 1833 | RCH |
| Hathorn, John G. | Stephens, Mary | 5, Sept 1839 | RCH |
| Hathorn, Samuel | Johnson, Lucinda | 12, Feb. 1835 | RCH |
| Hatsledd, | Maish, Anna | 7, Jan. 1823 | RCH |
| Hatt, James | Griffith, Clarissa | 24, Mar. 1847 | RCH |
| Hatt, John | Runyan, Martha | 27, Nov. 1841 | RCH |
| Hatt, Lewis | Pine, Mary Jane | 23, May 1847 | RCH |
| Hatt, William | Hubbard, Sarah | 25, Jan. 1838 | RCH |
| Hattick, Adam | Aulbeck, Elisabeth | 13, Feb. 1844 | AA |
| Hattmann, Heinrich | Schneider, Magdalena | 16, May 1842 | F |
| Haubner, Michael | Stubenvoll, Barbara | 14, Nov. 1844 | AA |
| Haubold, Frederick | Kalter, Mary | 10, Apr. 1844 | RCH |
| Haubold, George | Aldrich, Laura | 26, Mar. 1848 | RCH |
| Haubold, Jacob | Schmidt, Margaretha | 26, Mar. 1843 | RCH |
| Hauck, Columbus | Norton, Julia | 4, Feb. 1844 | RCH |
| Hauck, Georg J. | Arnold, Margaretha | 17, Mar. 1842 | G |
| Hauck, Jacob | Hornberger, Maria | 5, June 1837 | RCH |
| Hauck, Jacob | Meusch, Maria | 30, Apr. 1840 | G |
| Hauck, Jacob | Pinger, Christina | 23, June 1846 | RCH |
| Hauck, John | Rodacker, Catharine | 14, Mar. 1819 | RCH |
| Hauck, Joseph | Wengert, Anna Maria | 8, June 1840 | RCH |
| Hauck, Louis | Weber, Maria | 19, May 1842 | RCH |
| Hauck, Michael | Steiner, Catharine | 12, July 1842 | G |
| Hauck, Michael | Siemer, Johanna | 1, May 1849 | RCH |
| Hauck, Nicolaus | Fils, Francisca | 21, Feb. 1843 | AA |
| Haud, Friedrich | Zapf, Anna Maria | 8, May 1849 | HH |
| Hauenschild, Friedr. | VonBeren, Catharine | 16, Mar. 1847 | C |
| Hauer, Michael | Fais, Clarissa | 3, June 1841 | G |
| Hauey, Daniel | McCain, Catharine | 19, Nov. 1818 | RCH |
| Hauft, Johan Georg | Unrein, Dorothea | 7, June 1846 | C |
| Haug, Jacob | Waltrig, Christine | 3, Nov. 1844 | G |
| Haughenford, David | Sefton, Eleanor | 12, May 1836 | RCH |
| Hauling, Perry | Cook, Elisabeth | 13, May 1848 | RCH |

| Grooms<br>****** | Brides<br>****** | Date of Marriage<br>**** ** ******** | Code<br>**** |
|---|---|---|---|
| Hauschild, J Michael | Kohlschank, Maria | 5, Jan. 1845 | C |
| Hausenkamp, Henry | Hodeis, Maria | 9, Feb. 1849 | RCH |
| Hauser, David | Wuest, Catharine | 1, May 1847 | C |
| Hauser, Leonhard | Hauser, Magdalena | 8, May 1848 | RCH |
| Hauser, Mathias | Bettinger, Adelheid | 13, Aug. 1848 | FF |
| Hausfeld, Joseph | Fiscus, Angela | 7, Jan. 1840 | FF |
| Hausfelt, Joseph | Moormann, Agnes | 2, Feb. 1836 | FF |
| Hausmann, Alois | Hoffmann, Ursula | 1, Aug. 1848 | EE |
| Hausmann, Ferdinand | Higert, Caecilia | 20, Feb. 1849 | DD |
| Hausmann, Georg | Feldmann, Agnes | 22, Aug. 1839 | FF |
| Hausmann, Wilhelm | Lueckens, Sophia | 16, Dec. 1847 | C |
| Hausner, Johan | Zerin, Theresa | 27, Aug. 1848 | FF |
| Hausstadter, Rudolph | Katterjohan, Elis. | 2, Nov. 1848 | C |
| Hautz, Michael | Phillips, Elisabeth | 12, Aug. 1838 | RCH |
| Havekotte, Friedrich | Wulfeck, Gertrud(Mrs | 19, Feb. 1845 | F |
| Havekotte, Heinrich | Burs, Maria Engel | 21, June 1842 | F |
| Havely, | Mahone, Mary | 12, Apr. 1849 | RCH |
| Havens, Joel | Crummy, Nancy Ann M. | 2, Apr. 1849 | G |
| Haverbeck, A. | Bushman, Gertrud | 15, Apr. 1834 | RCH |
| Haverkamp, Johan H. | Meyers, Catharine M. | 18, June 1846 | B |
| Haverkamp, Johan H. | Marischen, Carolina | 28, Nov. 1848 | AA |
| Havickhorst, Heinric | Weber, Elisabeth | 8, Oct. 1848 | II |
| Haviland, Isaac | Benson, Mary | 10, Aug. 1845 | RCH |
| Hawen, Langdon | Symmes, Elisabeth | 25, Nov. 1845 | RCH |
| Hawes, Dan | Pyle, Josephine | 14, Oct. 1846 | RCH |
| Hawey, Isaac | Blackburn, Sarah A. | 2, Apr. 1838 | RCH |
| Hawk, Mashen | Matschler, Tutineo | 5, May 1834 | RCH |
| Hawk, Samuel | Day, Artemesia | 3, May 1837 | RCH |
| Hawk, William | Willey, Margaret | 11, Dec. 1833 | RCH |
| Hawkins, Carvil | Skinmore, Ascherz | 28, Mar. 1833 | RCH |
| Hawkins, Daniel | Edmunds, Sarah | 18, Nov. 1845 | RCH |
| Hawkins, Joseph | Gray, Jane | 2, Aug. 1843 | RCH |
| Hawkins, Philipp | Hatfield, Elisabeth | 14, July 1843 | RCH |
| Hawkins, Regin | Roy, Hester Ann | 1, Jan. 1846 | RCH |
| Hawkins, Reuben | St.Clair, Sarah | 30, Nov. 1820 | RCH |
| Hawkins, Richard | Hale, Mary Ann | 14, Oct. 1833 | I |
| Hawkins, Samuel | VanEaton, Lucinda | 15, Jan. 1835 | RCH |
| Hawkins, Thomas | Burdsal, Hester J. | 11, Feb. 1847 | RCH |
| Hawley, Franklin | McMaster, Jane | 16, May 1839 | RCH |
| Hawley, Robert | Wainwright, Mary E. | 28, Oct. 1847 | RCH |
| Hawlings, Joel W. | Ridwell, Leandis | 24, Aug. 1836 | RCH |
| Hawn, Emmanuel | Colvin, Hannah | 21, Sept 1842 | RCH |
| Hawpe, George | Wilson, Rebecca | 14, Nov. 1844 | RCH |
| Hay, John | Walker, Harriet | 1, Jan. 1835 | RCH |
| Hay, Michael | Hay, Ann | 1, Nov. 1820 | RCH |
| Hay, Robert | Caseman, Lydia | 8, Dec. 1842 | RCH |
| Hay, William | Weatherby, Anna | 6, Sept 1847 | RCH |
| Haycock, George | Knowlden, Ann | 1, Oct. 1846 | RCH |
| Haycock, Hamilton | Patton, Isabella | 9, July 1835 | I |
| Hayden, Alfred | Burley, Esther B. | 4, June 1827 | I |
| Hayden, Blemons | Cook, | 13, Nov. 1828 | RCH |
| Hayden, Hosea | Hayden, Rebecca | 27, July 1823 | RCH |
| Hayden, John | McCotter, Sarah | 24, Apr. 1834 | RCH |
| Hayden, Joseph | Lawson, Elisabeth | 25, Apr. 1842 | RCH |
| Hayden, Lot | Simpson, Margaret | 12, Oct. 1820 | RCH |
| Hayes, Charles | Lewis, Jane | 16, Nov. 1847 | RCH |
| Hayes, Dennis C. | Barry, Margaret | 10, May 1839 | BB |
| Hayes, James C. | Stevens, Mary | 27, May 1843 | RCH |
| Hayes, Job C. | McCause, Mary | 23, Mar. 1836 | RCH |
| Hayes, William L. | Dunn, Eliza | 14, Mar. 1840 | I |
| Hayman, Henry | Casner, Jane | 5, Sept 1846 | RCH |
| Hayner, William | Ritter, Catharine | 16, Feb. 1843 | RCH |
| Hays, Georg P. | Kraft, Catharine | 4, Feb. 1849 | C |
| Hays, James | Iliff, Catharine | 12, Oct. 1834 | RCH |
| Hays, Nelson | Blackstone, Rachel | 12, May 1847 | RCH |
| Hays, Oliver C. | Jones, Cynthia Ann | 15, Jan. 1836 | RCH |
| Hays, Oliver C. | Hatt, Leah Ann | 18, June 1839 | RCH |
| Hays, Patrick | Mullins, Catharine | 5, Sept 1842 | BB |
| Hays, Thomas H. | Street, Mandiana | 21, May 1832 | RCH |
| Hays, Thomas R. | Crowell, Catharine | 12, June 1836 | RCH |
| Hays, William | McCarthy, Ellen | 15, Aug. 1847 | GG |

| Grooms<br>****** | Brides<br>****** | Date of Marriage<br>**** ** ******** | Code<br>**** |
|---|---|---|---|
| Haythorn, Edward | Niblett, Ann | 17, Nov. 1842 | RCH |
| Haythorne, Edward | Wisely, Phebe | 11, Sept 1836 | RCH |
| Haywood, Christopher | Park, Susan | 12, July 1834 | RCH |
| Haywood, John | Wilson, Angeline | 29, Dec. 1832 | RCH |
| Haywood, Samuel | Bennett, Elisabeth | 16, Mar. 1847 | RCH |
| Hazard, Robert | Mixer, Elisabeth | 30, Sept 1842 | RCH |
| Hazelwood, Andrew | ----, Anna Maria | 22, Jan. 1823 | RCH |
| Hazelwood, Robert | Madison, Fanny Mary | 14, Dec. 1847 | RCH |
| Hazen, Burton | Ready, Sarah | 5, Nov. 1835 | RCH |
| Hazen, Lev. | Earnot, Elisabeth | 15, July 1827 | RCH |
| Hazenbuhler, Peter | Bohenn, Catharine | 26, Mar. 1846 | C |
| Hazlett, John | Noble, Sarah Jane | 31, Oct. 1848 | RCH |
| Head, James | Nessmith, Mary Jane | 22, July 1847 | RCH |
| Head, Patrick | Reilly, Rosanna | 31, Aug. 1840 | BB |
| Head, William | Battis, Martha | 14, June 1849 | RCH |
| Healy, John | Purcell, Hannah | 4, Feb. 1849 | RCH |
| Healy, Michael | Kernon, Margaret | 1, Sept 1849 | RCH |
| Healy, Patrick | Reilly, Catharine | 7, Oct. 1849 | BB |
| Hearn, Edward | Palmer, Sarah | 25, Aug. 1838 | RCH |
| Hearn, Stephen | Miller, Achsah | 8, June 1849 | RCH |
| Hearne, James | Rogers, Hester | 4, Aug. 1844 | RCH |
| Hearne, Purnel | Nobel, Anna Maria | 22, Apr. 1849 | RCH |
| Heash, Moses | Larowe, Lydia | 4, June 1825 | RCH |
| Heath, Isaac | Williams, Charlotte | 14, Jan. 1847 | I |
| Heath, John | Passage, Elisabeth | 26, Aug. 1848 | RCH |
| Heath, John W. | Sander, Jane | 2, Nov. 1837 | RCH |
| Heath, Samuel | Tallertest, Jane | 13, Oct. 1833 | RCH |
| Heath, Thomas | Scofield, Deborah | 4, Nov. 1843 | RCH |
| Heath, Thomas | Delvin, Elisabeth | 22, Nov. 1843 | RCH |
| Heath, Thomas | Shaw, Lucinda | 11, Feb. 1849 | RCH |
| Heather, Uziah | Laird, Mary E. | 10, June 1844 | RCH |
| Heatherington, John | Selman, Effie | 19, Mar. 1848 | RCH |
| Heaton, Isaac | Kell---, Jane | 18, May 1819 | RCH |
| Heaton, John H. | Salmon, Eleanor | 6, Jan. 1848 | RCH |
| Heaver, William | Ross, Margaret | 18, Feb. 1847 | RCH |
| Heayes, Anthony L. | Johnson, Hannah | 15, Jan. 1824 | RCH |
| Hebauf, John | Weist, Catharine | 27, Jan. 1847 | RCH |
| Hebbeler, Adam | Ruese, Maria | 5, Mar. 1846 | F |
| Hebbig, Michael | Herfel, Margaret | 18, July 1849 | RCH |
| Heberlein, Georg | Waldmann, Magdalena | 13, Oct. 1845 | C |
| Heberlein, Georg | Knott, Catharine | 2, Sept 1849 | C |
| Hebler, Johan Hein. | Franzmann, M. Anna | 27, Apr. 1847 | AA |
| Hechinger, Anton | Eichert, Anna Maria | 14, Apr. 1845 | FF |
| Hechler, Andreas | Karet, M. Barbara | 12, Oct. 1844 | C |
| Hechler, Peter | Baumann, Barbara | 18, Nov. 1849 | CC |
| Hecht, Jacob | Fischer, Jane | 27, Mar. 1847 | RCH |
| Hecht, Johan | Eder, Veronica | 19, Apr. 1846 | FF |
| Heckel, Herman | Berning, Maria Anna | 12, Nov. 1844 | AA |
| Heckel, Melchior A. | Nistler, Regina | 14, Sept 1836 | RCH |
| Heckendorfer, Fried. | Araus, Eva Maria | 19, June 1840 | G |
| Hecker, Benjamin | Leu---, Hannah | 28, May 1820 | RCH |
| Hecking, Anton | Hemann, Louisa | 5, Feb. 1848 | EE |
| Heckinger, Thomas | Arunes, Gertrud | 10, Jan. 1843 | FF |
| Heckle, Joseph | Germann, Helena | 12, Jan. 1835 | FF |
| Heckmann, Bernard | Merten, Elisabeth | 6, Nov. 1849 | II |
| Heckmann, James | Parson, Jennette | 18, Aug. 1846 | RCH |
| Heckmann, Peter | Schwein, Maria | 18, Mar. 1847 | A |
| Hecksterkamp, Hein. | Elfers, Gesina Elis. | 3, Oct. 1847 | AA |
| Heckwelder, George | Stewart, Maria Jane | 6, May 1848 | RCH |
| Hectel, Johan | Burkhardt, Elisabeth | 17, Dec. 1839 | G |
| Hede, Joseph | Good, Matilda | 10, Oct. 1836 | RCH |
| Hedenberg, William | Bryant, Mary J. | 16, Apr. 1846 | RCH |
| Hederick, Georg | Hartmann, Elisabeth | 24, Apr. 1838 | FF |
| Hederig, Johan | Eichenlaub, Elis. | 19, Feb. 1838 | FF |
| Heders, Johan H. | Gockmann, Gertrud | 7, Oct. 1849 | EE |
| Hedge, Samuel | Campbell, Elisabeth | 16, Sept 1838 | RCH |
| Hedger, Robert | Coddington, Emeline | 19, Aug. 1844 | RCH |
| Hedges, Benjamin | Van---, Rachel | 17, Mar. 1822 | RCH |
| Hedges, Clayborn | Drennan, Sarah J. | 4, Feb. 1847 | RCH |
| Hedges, John | Shull, Catharine | 6, July 1843 | RCH |
| Hedgland, James | Evans, Elisabeth | 16, Jan. 1834 | RCH |

| Grooms | Brides | Date of Marriage | Code |
|--------|--------|------------------|------|
| ****** | ****** | **** ** ******** | **** |
| Hee, Peter | Helfrich, Catharine | 24, Jan. 1847 | EE |
| Heed, Anton | Litter, Maria | 22, Sept 1846 | AA |
| Heeg, Benjamin | Bradley, Eveline | 26, July 1838 | RCH |
| Heeg, Heinrich | Flick, Charlotte | 27, Apr. 1842 | RCH |
| Heeke, Heinrich | Theil, Maria Anna | 12, Apr. 1842 | FF |
| Heelis, James | Frazier, Mary | 26, Sept 1820 | RCH |
| Heemann, Johan Georg | Rohrmann, A. Theresa | 13, Oct. 1846 | EE |
| Heeney, William | Scully, Margaret | 18, Aug. 1845 | BB |
| Heer, Anton | Schmidt, Maria | 5, May 1835 | FF |
| Heerdt, Adam | Eberhardt, Catharine | 31, Oct. 1844 | G |
| Hees, Joseph | Goldschmidt, Lena | 29, Oct. 1845 | RCH |
| Heffermann, William | Berry, Hannah | 9, Sept 1849 | RCH |
| Heffernan, Michael | Larkin, Catharine | 28, May 1848 | BB |
| Heffernan, Patrick | White, Mary Ann | 9, Jan. 1844 | BB |
| Heffner, Anton | Henting, Eva | 4, Feb. 1835 | FF |
| Hefter, Nicolaus | Burckly, Anna M. | 29, June 1834 | RCH |
| Hegemann, Leonard | Bruering, Catharine | 29, Nov. 1849 | RCH |
| Hegenbuch, Heinrich | Bermann, Elise | 29, Aug. 1844 | G |
| Hegener, Anton Theo. | Koelmann, Theresa C. | 17, Sept 1848 | AA |
| Heger, Adam | Genzheimer, Elisabet | 4, July 1847 | AA |
| Heger, Heinrich | Rah, Philomena | 29, Apr. 1849 | EE |
| Hegner, Gottfried | Heifelmann, Barbara | 5, July 1848 | C |
| Hehemann, Francis J. | Spaunhorst, M. Elis. | 9, Apr. 1837 | FF |
| Hehemann, Heinrich | Ossendarp, Cath Elis | 23, Oct. 1838 | FF |
| Hehet, Henry | Stanfers, Mary | 20, Aug. 1844 | RCH |
| Hehmann, Francis Wm. | Wendt, Clara Maria | 6, Sept 1846 | FF |
| Heibeck, Friedrich | Mauntz, Ann | 28, July 1849 | RCH |
| Heick, Philipp | Kramp, Margaretha | 13, Mar. 1845 | G |
| Heid, Philipp | Litzenberger, Elis. | 8, June 1846 | RCH |
| Heidacker, Heinrich | Espes, Agnes | 6, Nov. 1839 | FF |
| Heidacker, Heinrich | Brauer, Elisabeth | 1, Sept 1840 | FF |
| Heidelbach, Simon | Amborg, Nancy | 22, Aug. 1847 | RCH |
| Heidenreich, Christ. | Holtmeyer, Louise | 7, Dec. 1843 | F |
| Heidenreich, Christ. | Meschwerth, Catharin | 22, May 1849 | F |
| Heiderkamp, Gerhard | Wendt, Anna Marg. | 22, June 1845 | AA |
| Heidkamp, Bernard J. | Baumer, Maria Agnes | 11, Jan. 1848 | AA |
| Heidmann, Ferdinand | Dickhaus, Anna Maria | 10, May 1836 | FF |
| Heidmann, Heinrich | Jaste, Maria | 11, Nov. 1845 | F |
| Heidmeyer, Casper | Putthof, Carolina | 18, Nov. 1849 | FF |
| Heidrich, J. Philipp | Kartbucher, Louise | 26, Nov. 1841 | F |
| Heidt, Friedrich D. | Kefer, Anna | 12, Aug. 1847 | B |
| Heien, Theodor | Kaiser, Margaretha | 9, Jan. 1848 | FF |
| Heiermann, Johan | Kron, Maria | 22, Nov. 1848 | EE |
| Heigel, | Sering, Sally | 3, Apr. 1823 | RCH |
| Heighway, Samuel | Hawkins, Caroline | 22, Dec. 1842 | RCH |
| Heiing, Bernard | Jebbing, Margaretha | 7, Oct. 1849 | II |
| Heil, Friedrich | Lerch, Maria | 13, June 1847 | RCH |
| Heil, Jacob | Becker, Mary | 20, Jan. 1848 | RCH |
| Heil, Leonhard | Bonet, Maria | 27, Feb. 1848 | EE |
| Heil, Philipp | Pistor, Louise | 21, Mar. 1849 | RCH |
| Heil, Wilhelm | Ring, Francisca | 1, Feb. 1838 | FF |
| Heilemann, Johan Bd. | Dudai, Elisabeth | 29, Apr. 1849 | EE |
| Heillert, Wilhelm | Mueller, Sophia | 7, Sept 1843 | G |
| Heilmann, Johan | Sponsel, Margaretha | 20, May 1849 | C |
| Heilmann, Peter | Grossmann, Anna M. | 6, Mar. 1848 | EE |
| Heim, Andreas | Reiner, Magdalena | 13, Feb. 1845 | G |
| Heim, Francis | Wirthlein, Christina | 24, Apr. 1837 | FF |
| Heim, Philipp | Zeller, Anna Maria | 25, Apr. 1843 | AA |
| Heim, Wilhelm | Busalt, Barbara | 3, Jan. 1847 | EE |
| Heimburger, Johan | Stenger, Barbara | 23, Jan. 1844 | AA |
| Heimsch, Louis | Heinsmann, Maria | 1, Dec. 1849 | EE |
| Heimseth, Heinrich | Droege, Anna Maria | 27, Dec. 1849 | RCH |
| Heindrich, Martin | Kraus, Margaretha | 23, Nov. 1847 | RCH |
| Heine, Conrad | Mueller, Dorothea | 8, Feb. 1841 | F |
| Heine, Thomas | Smith, Mary Jane | 10, Dec. 1846 | RCH |
| Heineke, Francis | Reis, Maria Anna | 10, May 1846 | AA |
| Heinemann, Anton | Imholte, Agnes | 19, June 1849 | AA |
| Heininger, Johan | Ritter, M. Josephine | 18, May 1847 | FF |
| Heinlein, Georg | Stroebel, Elisabeth | 19, Nov. 1848 | G |
| Heinlein, Heinrich | Duetschli, Barbara | 9, Apr. 1849 | CC |
| Heinlein, Johan | Banger, Maria | 30, June 1841 | G |

| Grooms | Brides | Date of Marriage | Code |
|--------|--------|------------------|------|
| Heinrich, Andreas | Metz, Maria | 28, Nov. 1837 | FF |
| Heinrich, Andreas | Herbrand, Anna (Mrs) | 26, Aug. 1849 | AA |
| Heinrich, John | Speiser, Cevalli | 6, Mar. 1848 | G |
| Heinrich, Martin | Deutsch, Anna Maria | 9, May 1842 | FF |
| Heinrich, Michael | Helfrich, Barbara | 5, Aug. 1845 | FF |
| Heinrichs, Carl | Posse, Amalia | 16, Nov. 1848 | C |
| Heins, Carl | Blinns, Maria | 2, Dec. 1844 | C |
| Heintz, Carl | Weismann, Catharina | 2, Dec. 1847 | G |
| Heinzelmann, Georg | Kappauf, Friedricka | 30, June 1840 | G |
| Heippert, Isaac | Bauman, Fanny | 31, Jan. 1843 | RCH |
| Heisinger, Philipp | Bolley, Mary Ann | 13, Oct. 1847 | RCH |
| Heisler, Johan | Rosenberger, Magdal. | 29, Dec. 1840 | FF |
| Heitcamp, B Herman | Egbers, A. Maria | 7, May 1848 | II |
| Heitkemper, Johan G. | Streubing, Elisabeth | 6, Aug. 1848 | EE |
| Heitmann, Francis | Hemann, M. Elisabeth | 26, July 1838 | FF |
| Heitmann, J. Bernard | Uphoff, Catharine | 2, May 1847 | FF |
| Heitmeyer, Carl | Niepenget, Elisabeth | 21, Nov. 1843 | AA |
| Heitmeyer, Johan F. | Stroebel, M. Barbara | 4, June 1846 | G |
| Heitz, Carl | Pfau, Louise | 30, June 1848 | B |
| Helber, Johan Jacob | Stuehr, Barbara | 24, Dec. 1848 | G |
| Helborn, Henry | Sater, Dorcas | 22, Sept 1836 | RCH |
| Held, Andreas | Mueller, Catharine | 10, Nov. 1846 | EE |
| Held, Paul | Merklin, Barbara | 31, Oct. 1847 | HH |
| Helde, Bernard | Steiert, Sophia | 29, Apr. 1844 | FF |
| Helenberger, George | Hanbold, Eva | 3, Jan. 1837 | RCH |
| Helker, Joseph | Hapelkemper, Anna M. | 16, July 1848 | EE |
| Helleberg, Carl G. | Frank, Anna Elis. | 26, Apr. 1846 | G |
| Heller, August | Nurings, Caroline | 23, Mar. 1843 | C |
| Heller, Herman | Weis, Dina | 23, Sept 1847 | RCH |
| Hellmann, Herman | Fruehling, Anna | 11, May 1841 | FF |
| Hellmann, Jacob | Wehe, Catharine | 16, Aug. 1849 | G |
| Hellmig, Johan H. | Gressen, Maria Anna | 30, Nov. 1848 | EE |
| Hellstein, Johan | Hollwek, Katharine | 27, Nov. 1849 | EE |
| Hellstern, Joseph | Meyer, Barbara | 10, Jan. 1842 | FF |
| Helm, Adam | Runge, Charlotte | 30, Mar. 1845 | F |
| Helm, Adam Heinrich | Surer, Anna Maria | 19, July 1848 | F |
| Helm, Henry | Miller, Ann B. | 19, July 1846 | RCH |
| Helm, John L. | Mesusan, Elisabeth | 17, Feb. 1832 | RCH |
| Helmbach, Adam | Schneider, Caroline | 22, Jan. 1847 | RCH |
| Helmbacher, Peter | Wagner, Margaretha | 13, Sept 1846 | EE |
| Helmeking, Herman H. | Reimers, Maria | 21, Aug. 1848 | F |
| Helmering, Friedrich | Grube, Charlotte W. | 31, Dec. 1848 | RCH |
| Helmering, Friedrich | Kaiser, Wilhelmina | 3, Sept 1846 | F |
| Helmich, Johan G. | Meyers, Maria Elis | 18, Apr. 1847 | EE |
| Helmich, John C. | Pearson, Nancy | 30, Sept 1837 | RCH |
| Helmich, Joseph | Welle, Angela | 2, July 1838 | FF |
| Helmich, Joseph | Gels, Maria Angela | 16, Apr. 1844 | FF |
| Helmig, Henry | Attig, Catharine | 15, Nov. 1842 | RCH |
| Helmig, J. Rudolph | Meyer, Maria | 15, Nov. 1848 | F |
| Helming, Johan Henr. | Hagedorn, Maria | 31, May 1847 | E |
| Helmkamp, Christoph | Eberle, Elisabeth | 10, Sept 1844 | AA |
| Helmkamp, Friedrich | Rathgens, Johanna A. | 7, Mar. 1847 | A |
| Helmreich, Conrad | Lotze, Dorothea | 19, Oct. 1843 | G |
| Helmreich, Conrad | Selzer, Mary | 4, Jan. 1849 | RCH |
| Helms, Bernard | Niehoff, Anna Angela | 7, Nov. 1847 | AA |
| Helms, Friedrich | Niemann, Elisabeth | 16, Feb. 1847 | AA |
| Helms, Johan H. | Wessendorf, Theresa | 14, Nov. 1843 | AA |
| Helmsing, J.Heinrich | Hafeld, Anna Maria | 29, Aug. 1844 | F |
| Helmstetter, Johan S | Wilzbacher, Margaret | 7, Jan. 1846 | EE |
| Helwig, Adam | Ott, Catharine | 4, Feb. 1840 | FF |
| Helwig, Charles | Simmiling, Anna J. | 21, June 1849 | B |
| Helwig, Herman | Lange, Maria | 13, July 1845 | AA |
| Hemann, Andreas | Brocamp, Catharine | 9, Jan. 1849 | EE |
| Hemann, Friedrich | Wilke, Anna Maria | 26, May 1838 | FF |
| Hemann, Gerhard | Koestermeier, Bern. | 12, Oct. 1847 | EE |
| Hemat, Peter | Stehling, Catharine | 3, Sept 1848 | EE |
| Hemesath, Friedrich | Rueter, Bernardina | 5, Mar. 1848 | AA |
| Hemler, Wilhelm | Reisinger, M. Anna | 26, Sept 1837 | FF |
| Hemmer, Jacob | Stephen, Margaretha | 27, Sept 1841 | FF |
| Hemmer, John H. | Hemmer, Sophia | 3, July 1849 | RCH |
| Hemmer, William | Sundermann, Christin | 9, Nov. 1843 | RCH |

| Grooms<br>***** | Brides<br>***** | Date of Marriage<br>**** ** ******** | Code<br>**** |
|---|---|---|---|
| Hempfling, Johan | Dallwings, Elisabeth | 27, Nov. 1849 | A |
| Hempfner, Michael | Hoffmann, Maria Anna | 20, July 1841 | FF |
| Hemphill, Edward | Jones, Elisabeth | 28, Dec. 1844 | RCH |
| Hemphill, Griffin | Culver, Elisabeth | 22, Feb. 1846 | RCH |
| Hemsath, Heinrich | Richter, Julia | 14, May 1846 | F |
| Hemsche, Herman | Corwin, Anna | 2, Jan. 1845 | A |
| Hen---, Daniel | Leopold, Louise | 9, Sept 1839 | RCH |
| Henckman, Allen | Hardy, Mary | 4, Feb. 1846 | RCH |
| Henderson, Benjamin | ----, Sarah | 6, Dec. 1821 | RCH |
| Henderson, Elias | Taylor, Mary | 24, Mar. 1825 | RCH |
| Henderson, James | Reding, Eleatora | 11, Dec. 1841 | RCH |
| Henderson, Joseph | Jackson, Alice | 14, July 1836 | RCH |
| Henderson, Joseph | Florer, Sarah Jane | 15, Apr. 1848 | RCH |
| Henderson, Josiah | Mullen, Mary | 29, Sept 1835 | RCH |
| Henderson, Robert | Goff, Jane | 5, July 1835 | RCH |
| Henderson, William | Laughlin, Elisabeth | 17, Jan. 1833 | RCH |
| Henderson, William H | Sullivan, Eleanor | 13, Feb. 1840 | RCH |
| Henderson, William J | Chalfant, Rebecca | 27, June 1849 | A |
| Hendler, Carl | Schatzmann, Elis. | 3, Sept 1849 | C |
| Hendricks, David | M---, Mary | 2, July 1819 | RCH |
| Hendricks, Leonard | Riddle, Catharine | 26, Sept 1818 | RCH |
| Hendricks, Thomas | Morgan, Elisabeth | 25, Sept 1845 | RCH |
| Hendrickson, Charles | Rose, Elisabeth | 5, June 1843 | RCH |
| Hendrixon, Elijah | Gibson, Nancy Jane | 5, July 1849 | RCH |
| Hendy, James | Langtry, Mary Ann | 29, May 1834 | I |
| Hengehausen, Ferd. | Fletschinger, Cath. | 17, Apr. 1849 | G |
| Hengehold, Philipp | Specking, Elisabeth | 23, Jan. 1848 | FF |
| Hengehold, Wilhelm | Roberg, Juliana | 3, Nov. 1844 | FF |
| Hengelbrock, Heinric | Austrup, M.G. | 30, Jan. 1849 | AA |
| Hengler, George | Freeman, Nancy | 20, Mar. 1823 | RCH |
| Henk, John | Frazer, Mary | 1, Dec. 1847 | RCH |
| Henke, Bernard | Hulemann, Catharina | 7, Oct. 1838 | FF |
| Henke, Bernard | Boller, Elisabeth | 5, Oct. 1842 | AA |
| Henke, Christian | Treben, Catharine | 3, Feb. 1846 | RCH |
| Henke, Johan Chris. | Aubke, M. Angela | 2, Sept 1849 | AA |
| Henkly, John | Davidson, Catharine | 25, Dec. 1831 | RCH |
| Henkmann, Heinrich | Goebel, Anna Maria | 22, Jan. 1849 | EE |
| Henlich, Christoph | Resener, Dina | 11, Sept 1849 | CC |
| Henman, Abraham | Stickle, Margaret | 30, Dec. 1824 | RCH |
| Henn, Carl | Leibold, Margaretha | 12, Aug. 1841 | G |
| Henn, Friedrich | Dyrson, Johanna | 27, Jan. 1846 | G |
| Henn, John | Hoech, Catharine | 30, Mar. 1848 | G |
| Henne, Georg | Weghorst, Louisa | 15, Nov. 1849 | G |
| Henne, Jacob | Schlichte, Magdalena | 20, May 1847 | AA |
| Hennel, Jacob | Braun, Barbara | 30, Apr. 1839 | FF |
| Hennessy, John | Collins, Ann | 3, Nov. 1844 | BB |
| Hennesy, Michael | Davis, Alma Ann | 29, Dec. 1840 | RCH |
| Henni, Georg Heinric | Ohe, Christina Elis. | 10, Oct. 1844 | F |
| Henni, William | Mayalls, Myra | 17, Nov. 1824 | RCH |
| Henning, Carl F. | Knaus, Babette | 8, May 1849 | RCH |
| Henning, Heinrich | Ridder, Lena | 16, Sept 1847 | F |
| Henning, J. Bernard | Wehrmann, Catharine | 17, Oct. 1848 | FF |
| Hennings, George | Derr, Elisabeth | 22, Sept 1845 | RCH |
| Hennisee, Jacob | Schaffer, Margaret | 2, Nov. 1845 | RCH |
| Henri, Henry | McGinn, Bridget | 15, Oct. 1848 | GG |
| Henrichsmann, Bern. | Kemper, Elisabeth | 15, Aug. 1847 | EE |
| Henrici, Johan | Bindmann, Josephine | 30, May 1847 | G |
| Henrie, Arthur | Heren, Patience | 21, Dec. 1843 | RCH |
| Henrie, Daniel | Bayer, Nancy | 2, Mar. 1837 | RCH |
| Henrie, George | ----, Rhoda | 8, Jan. 1822 | RCH |
| Henrie, Harvey | Wilsey, Amey | 2, Oct. 1837 | RCH |
| Henrie, William N. | Baker, Anna Maria | 22, Feb. 1848 | RCH |
| Henry, Andrew A. | Morrison, Frances | 28, May 1841 | RCH |
| Henry, David | Andrews, Martha J. | 29, July 1849 | RCH |
| Henry, Edward | Whalen, Ann | 7, May 1840 | BB |
| Henry, Hugh | Baxter, Eleanor | 12, Feb. 1844 | RCH |
| Henry, Jacob E. | Saffa, Hanna E. | 29, Mar. 1839 | RCH |
| Henry, James | Bell, Ann | 14, Sept 1819 | RCH |
| Henry, James | Wakefield, Mary | 25, Jan. 1820 | RCH |
| Henry, John | Cahill, Sarah | 10, Oct. 1843 | BB |
| Henry, John | McClenan, Jane | 8, Feb. 1847 | BB |

| Grooms | Brides | Date of Marriage | Code |
|--------|--------|------------------|------|
| Henry, John B. | Codington, Louise | 28, Mar. 1841 | RCH |
| Henry, R.B. | Kennedy, Charlotte | 13, July 1838 | RCH |
| Henry, Robert | Guffis, Caroline | Nov. 1848 | RCH |
| Henry, William | Mansfield, Sally | 15, July 1818 | RCH |
| Henry, William | Relpin, Jane | 15, July 1840 | RCH |
| Henscher, Heinrich | Lebbe, Maria Anna | 18, Aug. 1842 | FF |
| Henscher, Johan Bd. | Strategir, Catharine | 18, Nov. 1845 | AA |
| Hensen, Bernard | Banke, Anna Maria | 17, Nov. 1844 | FF |
| Hensen, Bernard | Trimpe, Maria Anna | 6, May 1849 | EE |
| Hensen, Herman | Meyermann, Theresa | 18, May 1847 | EE |
| Henshy, Elkana | Friend, Sarah | 25, May 1834 | RCH |
| Hentze, Frederick | Goshorn, Sarah | 20, Aug. 1838 | RCH |
| Henzel, Johan Georg | Winand, Anna Maria | 11, Aug. 1849 | C |
| Henzler, Johan | Pieper, Bernardina | 2, Dec. 1847 | AA |
| Hepp, Daniel | Eiswart, Adaline | 29, June 1846 | RCH |
| Heppner, Johan | Gerlach, Margaretha | 26, Nov. 1840 | FF |
| Herancourt, Georg M. | Jungling, Barbara | 6, Apr. 1847 | A |
| Herbe, Lawrence | Freund, Maria | 7, Jan. 1849 | EE |
| Herberding, Francis | Brinkmann, Bernardin | 10, Oct. 1847 | FF |
| Herberg, Adolph | Schwartz, Friedricka | 5, Nov. 1848 | C |
| Herberger, Francis | Linder, Elisabeth | 24, Aug. 1845 | AA |
| Herbermann, Heinrich | Birkemeyer, Catharin | 4, July 1843 | AA |
| Herbermann, Heinrich | Bloemer, Bernardina | 28, Apr. 1846 | AA |
| Herbermann, Heinrich | Grotmann, M. Anna | 21, Oct. 1849 | II |
| Herbert, Adam | Bergmann, Anna M. | 23, Nov. 1842 | AA |
| Herbi, Johan B. | Hoffmann, Magdalena | 7, Mar. 1848 | CC |
| Herblin, Francis | Quige, Elisabeth F. | 13, Aug. 1845 | A |
| Herboltzheimer, John | Mueller, Elisabeth | 19, Aug. 1844 | RCH |
| Herbst, George | Wirtz, Magdalena | 31, Jan. 1844 | RCH |
| Herbst, J. Leonard | Oerdel, A. Margaret | 1, July 1847 | RCH |
| Herbstreit, Joseph | Siefert, Catharine | 30, Aug. 1844 | RCH |
| Herbstreit, Matthias | Strecker, Ursula | 4, Aug. 1842 | FF |
| Hercules, David | Logan, Elisabeth | 4, Aug. 1842 | RCH |
| Hercules, William | Hamilton, Mary | 16, Nov. 1843 | RCH |
| Herculess, James | Murdock, Sarah Jane | 13, May 1843 | RCH |
| Herder, Gustav | Gebhardt, Elisabeth | 1, Sept 1844 | G |
| Herenberger, Johan W | Stadelbauer, Cath. | 5, Dec. 1847 | A |
| Herider, Jacob | Vantreese, Nancy | 28, Aug. 1818 | RCH |
| Herker, Heinrich | Farber, Angela | 14, Jan. 1849 | II |
| Herman, John | Cooper, Mary | 10, Feb. 1839 | RCH |
| Hermann, August | Backoffen, Johanna | 10, Jan. 1847 | FF |
| Hermann, Gabriel | Abraham, Mary | 6, Oct. 1843 | RCH |
| Hermann, Jacob | Gruenstein, Magdal. | 27, Jan. 1842 | FF |
| Hermann, Jacob | Pfar, Catharine | 8, Aug. 1847 | EE |
| Hermann, Johan | Lamott, Barbara | 9, May 1848 | EE |
| Hermann, John | Wilson, Mary | 5, Oct. 1843 | RCH |
| Hermann, Ludwig | Kempf, Maria | 24, Aug. 1845 | AA |
| Hermann, Solomon | Schwartz, Barbara | 24, Apr. 1846 | RCH |
| Hermes, Bernard | Goeke, Elisabeth | 6, Feb. 1844 | AA |
| Hermes, Bernard | Borders, Catharina | 15, Sept 1840 | FF |
| Hermes, Bernard | Hude, Josephine | 20, June 1848 | CC |
| Hermesch, Johan H. | Meyer, Gertrud | 13, May 1849 | AA |
| Hermoeller, Bernard | Schlatbaum, Elisabet | 15, Nov. 1846 | AA |
| Herndon, James | Taylor, Maria | 5, Apr. 1849 | RCH |
| Hernneshied, | Wehe, Gertrud | 18, Nov. 1844 | RCH |
| Heroh, Andreas | Fiernkoes, Margaret | 9, Aug. 1846 | EE |
| Herold, Andreas | Barbig, Susanna | 11, Oct. 1846 | AA |
| Herold, Johan | Barwick, Christina | 3, Nov. 1846 | EE |
| Heron, John | Robertson, Jane | 6, June 1849 | RCH |
| Herr, George | Middlewood, Frances | 22, June 1833 | RCH |
| Herrald, Zimri | Broadwell, | 19, Mar. 1820 | RCH |
| Herren, William | Akers, Rachel | 20, Jan. 1822 | RCH |
| Herrin, William | Charlton, Rebecca | 19, July 1817 | RCH |
| Herrmann, Friedrich | Hanft, Johanna | 7, Mar. 1848 | C |
| Herrmann, Laurenz | Weimer, Margaret | 12, Apr. 1849 | RCH |
| Herron, Andrew C. | Gray, Mary | 11, Oct. 1835 | RCH |
| Herron, Cornelius | Rollins, Martha | 13, Feb. 1848 | RCH |
| Herron, John | Ingersoll, Patience | 24, Mar. 1839 | RCH |
| Herschede, Heinrich | Limberg, Maria Anna | 10, Sept 1846 | AA |
| Hershler, Solomon | Weiler, Caroline | 12, Apr. 1847 | RCH |
| Hersinger, Philipp V | Pauck, Henriette E. | 9, Mar. 1841 | G |

| Grooms | Brides | Date of Marriage | Code |
|--------|--------|------------------|------|
| Herth, Jacob | Johrs, Elisabeth | 19, Nov. 1848 | A |
| Hertie, Johan Heinr. | Huntemann, Elisabeth | 12, June 1846 | B |
| Hertner, J. Stephan | Hanfbauer, Christina | 26, Aug. 1847 | RCH |
| Herves, Joseph V. | Armstrong, Sarah | 12, Feb. 1832 | RCH |
| Hervey, Thomas J. | Prouty, Anna Janette | 27, Dec. 1843 | RCH |
| Herwig, Johan H. | Steinle, Catharine | 17, Oct. 1848 | EE |
| Herzog, Carl | Marks, Elisabeth | 18, Dec. 1844 | RCH |
| Herzog, Carl | Theiss, Carolina | 30, Apr. 1849 | G |
| Herzog, Carl | Braun, Cecilia | 16, Sept 1847 | EE |
| Herzog, Carl | Weiss, Barbara | 28, Aug. 1849 | EE |
| Herzog, Friedrich | Brinkmann, Margaret | 6, May 1849 | II |
| Herzog, Georg | Hunt, Elisabeth | 14, Apr. 1834 | RCH |
| Herzog, Gottfried | Pefer, Rosina | 9, Sept 1841 | RCH |
| Herzog, Johan | Ross, Maria Anna | 6, May 1849 | EE |
| Herzog, Lorenz | Eyert, Cathariner | 14, Sept 1845 | RCH |
| Herzog, Wilhelm | Schaffer, Catharine | 1, Nov. 1846 | RCH |
| Hesbacher, Cornelius | Walter, Anna Maria | 11, Sept 1847 | EE |
| Heskamp, Bernard | Meyer, Catharine | 20, Aug. 1844 | AA |
| Heskamp, Bernard | Nordmann, Elisabeth | 1, Apr. 1845 | AA |
| Hesler, Joseph | Surenbrock, Anna M. | 7, Feb. 1847 | AA |
| Hespe, Heinrich | Stratmann, Caroline | 29, Sept 1842 | F |
| Hess, Anthony | Fey, Margaret | 4, Mar. 1846 | RCH |
| Hess, Jacob | Woodruff, Nancy | 22, Apr. 1823 | RCH |
| Hess, Johan | Arnz, Catharine | 19, Sept 1841 | EE |
| Hess, Johan | Kepp, Elisabeth | 9, Oct. 1849 | EE |
| Hess, John | Runyen, Eleanor | 12, Aug. 1832 | RCH |
| Hess, Martin | Flint, Elisabeth | 11, May 1833 | RCH |
| Hess, Michael | Littel, Maria | 16, Nov. 1841 | FF |
| Hess, Philipp | Schmidt, Elisabeth | 18, Oct. 1842 | RCH |
| Hess, Samuel | Lodley, Catharine | 19, Oct. 1835 | RCH |
| Hess, Thomas P. | Hoffner, Elisabeth | 27, Mar. 1841 | RCH |
| Hessang, Georg | Dieste, Dorothea | 11, Feb. 1849 | C |
| Hesse, Francis | Lohmann, Bernardina | 20, June 1848 | CC |
| Hesse, Georg | Heimkreuter, Elis. | 8, Feb. 1848 | EE |
| Hesselbeck, Peter | Rehbold, Catharine | 30, Oct. 1845 | FF |
| Hesselbrock, Fried. | Klein, Elisabeth | 30, Sept 1845 | AA |
| Hesselbrock, Herman | Hopster, A. Maria | 12, Sept 1849 | AA |
| Hesseling, J. Herman | Elsen, Anna Maria | 18, Feb. 1849 | CC |
| Hesselmann, Henry | Kramer, Anna Maria | 18, Sept 1846 | RCH |
| Hessing, Joseph | Simon, Helena | 27, Jan. 1835 | FF |
| Hesskamp, Gerhard H. | Deyer, Anna Maria | 2, June 1846 | AA |
| Hessler, Conrad | Piestner, Anna Maria | 30, Apr. 1840 | FF |
| Hessler, Ludwig | Leder, Dorothea | 9, Oct. 1838 | FF |
| Hessler, Michael | Sauer, Catharina | 25, Mar. 1839 | G |
| Hester, Michael | Hagen, Biddy | 17, Feb. 1840 | RCH |
| Hestop, Benjamin | Ferguson, Emily | 15, May 1833 | RCH |
| Hetlage, Heinrich | Petermann, Margaret | 7, Aug. 1849 | B |
| Hett, Matthias | Kramer, Magdalena | 19, Nov. 1839 | FF |
| Hette---, William | Hunter, Phebe | 3, June 1836 | RCH |
| Hetterich, Heinrich | Kling, Catharine | 13, June 1843 | C |
| Hetterick, Lawrence | Hamilton, Mary Ann | 2, Oct. 1842 | RCH |
| Hettesheimer, Daniel | Stevens, Catharine | 11, Apr. 1847 | RCH |
| Hettweis, Carl Leo. | Schmidt, Christina | 23, Jan. 1848 | C |
| Hetzel, George | Renkel, Mary | 5, Dec. 1842 | RCH |
| Hetzler, David | Thornell, Mary Ann | 3, Aug. 1843 | RCH |
| Hetzler, Joseph | Geasin, | 25, Nov. 1828 | RCH |
| Hetzler, Volser | Briant, Margaret | 22, Nov. 1821 | RCH |
| Heuber, Sebastian | Keker, Theresa (Mrs) | 21, July 1835 | FF |
| Heuer, Benjamin | Hamer, Catharine | 29, Apr. 1849 | BB |
| Heuer, Friedrich | Bruns, Louise | 25, Feb. 1848 | F |
| Heuer, Johan Heinric | Waelder, Elisabeth H | 6, Sept 1849 | RCH |
| Heuerkamp, Clemens | Zurline, Theresa | 17, Aug. 1843 | AA |
| Heuermann, J Gerhard | Hehemann, Henrietta | 11, Feb. 1844 | FF |
| Heuermann, Johan Bd. | Schroermeyer, Lucia | 17, May 1849 | AA |
| Heuetle, Johan | Hermueller, Veronica | 16, Sept 1849 | AA |
| Heulsmann, Johan H. | Cordes, Anna Magdal. | 30, Jan. 1849 | F |
| Heumann, August | Logemann, Adelheid | 28, Jan. 1849 | RCH |
| Heumann, Heinrich | Froning, Helena | 13, June 1847 | CC |
| Heune, Georg Heinric | Bonning, Sophia Wil. | 28, May 1848 | G |
| Heuser, Heinrich M. | Pohlmann, Johanna | 1, July 1848 | A |
| Heveringlam, James | Wheeler, Edith | 20, Jan. 1833 | RCH |

| Grooms<br>****** | Brides<br>****** | Date of Marriage<br>**** ** ******** | Code<br>**** |
|---|---|---|---|
| Hewing, Bernard H. | Gerken, Maria Helena | 22, Apr. 1849 | CC |
| Hewit, Samuel | Chase, Martha | 30, Dec. 1819 | RCH |
| Hewitt, Charles | Chase, Lucinda | 4, Mar. 1844 | RCH |
| Hewitt, Daniel | Moak, Caroline | 22, Feb. 1842 | RCH |
| Hewitt, Nathan | Church, Rhoda | 15, May 1825 | RCH |
| Hewitt, William L. | Plappert, Catharine | 2, Apr. 1848 | RCH |
| Hewkirk, John | McKoy, Rebecca | 27, Sept 1821 | RCH |
| Hewlett, Jeremiah | Huntington, Amelia | 17, Oct. 1842 | RCH |
| Hews, | Fenton, Amanda | 9, May 1839 | RCH |
| Hey, Bartley | Paull, Elizabeth | 17, Sept 1825 | RCH |
| Hey, Joseph | Matchett, Sophia | 8, Dec. 1842 | RCH |
| Hey---, Aaron | Jones, Elisabeth | 14, Apr. 1844 | RCH |
| Heyden, Juvel | Mevan, Ann | 8, Nov. 1832 | RCH |
| Heye, Ernst Wilhelm | Beinkampen, Friedr. | 13, Dec. 1849 | A |
| Heyer, Dietrich F. | Lrig, Bernardina S. | 11, Jan. 1849 | C |
| Heyer, Dietrich F. | Oberhelmann, Sophia | 24, Oct. 1849 | C |
| Heyl, Nicolaus | Fritz, Apollonia | 15, Oct. 1835 | RCH |
| Heyler, Christoph | Bader, Barbara | 20, Apr. 1847 | G |
| Heylman, John P. | Taylor, Mary Ann | 10, Nov. 1841 | RCH |
| Heylton, Thomas | Morton, Anna H. | 9, Dec. 1844 | RCH |
| Hi---, Matthew | McLocklin, Polly | 4, Oct. 1820 | RCH |
| Hibbard, King | Twigg, Phoebe | 2, Nov. 1826 | RCH |
| Hick, Henry | Smith, Elisabeth | 4, Sept 1839 | RCH |
| Hickcox, Elisha C. | Berry, Elce R. | 15, June 1821 | I |
| Hickenman, Ithamar | Tarter, Angeline | 11, Aug. 1833 | RCH |
| Hickerman, Joseph | Preston, Sary | 16, Jan. 1834 | RCH |
| Hickey, John | Fehelly, Mary | 16, Sept 1845 | BB |
| Hickman, Henry | Swem, Dulcinda | 21, May 1846 | RCH |
| Hickman, Jesse | Green, Elisabeth A. | 31, May 1842 | RCH |
| Hickmann, John S. | Ball, Maria | 28, Feb. 1833 | RCH |
| Hickox, Nathan | Myers, Eliza Jane | 6, June 1846 | RCH |
| Hicks, Andrew | Shank, Anna | 6, Dec. 1842 | RCH |
| Hicks, David | Chambers, Sarah | 16, Apr. 1843 | RCH |
| Hicks, James | Whetstone, Caroline | 31, May 1838 | RCH |
| Hicks, James | Harrison, Martha A. | 14, June 1842 | RCH |
| Hicks, John | ----, Jane | 18, Aug. 1839 | RCH |
| Hicks, Joseph | Glarden, Martha E. | 8, Oct. 1848 | RCH |
| Hicks, Mortimor | Baylor, Frances | 2, Jan. 1848 | RCH |
| Hicks, Thomas | Rash, Betsy | 1, Nov. 1845 | RCH |
| Hicks, Wiley | Mills, Angeline | 20, Feb. 1843 | RCH |
| Hicks, Wiley | Taylor, Clara Ann | 10, Dec. 1848 | RCH |
| Hicks, William | Schafer, Caroline | 20, Mar. 1844 | RCH |
| Hide, Joseph | McGowen, Catharine | 16, Nov. 1843 | RCH |
| Hieber, Carl | Klotzen, Maria | 6, Aug. 1848 | G |
| Hier, Jacob | Bollinger, Julianna | 16, June 1840 | FF |
| Hiffler, John | Mitchell, Elisabeth | 2, Apr. 1835 | RCH |
| Hiffron, Daniel | Brochel, Martha A. | 2, Apr. 1848 | RCH |
| Higbee, John | Wright, Louise | 19, Mar. 1846 | RCH |
| Higby, Henry | Hayslitt, | 22, Apr. 1825 | RCH |
| Higdon, Benjamin | Truss, Mary | 11, Feb. 1836 | RCH |
| Higdon, Henry | Lee, Jane Ann | 19, Mar. 1844 | RCH |
| Higdon, Peter | Burke, Harriet | 2, Sept 1849 | RCH |
| Higgins, Cyrus | Fin, Mary | 6, Aug. 1819 | RCH |
| Higgins, George | Fanning, Isabella | 5, Sept 1849 | BB |
| Higgins, John | Slattery, Margaret | 18, July 1843 | BB |
| Higgins, John M. | Berbeck, Elisabeth | 22, Mar. 1838 | RCH |
| Higgins, Patrick | Shield, Bridget | 23, Apr. 1846 | AA |
| Higgins, Peter | Moffitt, Mary | 12, Sept 1848 | RCH |
| Higgins, Vandorn | Tucker, Mary | 25, May 1826 | RCH |
| Higgins, William | Booth, Sarah | 1, Dec. 1825 | RCH |
| Higgins, William T. | Gilbreath, Elisabeth | 15, Oct. 1846 | D |
| Highland, G. | Farmer, Electa | 8, Feb. 1821 | RCH |
| Highlands, Andrew | Adams, Mary M. | 25, Aug. 1825 | RCH |
| Highlands, John | Smith, Margaret | 3, Sept 1833 | RCH |
| Hight, Nicolaus | Aunis, Sarah | 16, Jan. 1842 | RCH |
| Hightower, London | Taylor, Carey | 24, May 1844 | RCH |
| Hilands, William | Smith, Sarah | 20, June 1822 | RCH |
| Hilbert, Edward | Sturz, Maria Antonia | 21, Oct. 1847 | EE |
| Hildebrand, Christ. | Kirchhof, Johanna | 25, July 1848 | B |
| Hildebrandt, Daniel | Cochran, Elisabeth | 1, Jan. 1835 | RCH |
| Hildreth, David | VanZant, Sarah | 23, Sept 1849 | RCH |

| Grooms<br>****** | Brides<br>****** | Date of Marriage<br>**** ** ******** | Code<br>**** |
|---|---|---|---|
| Hildreth, Jonathan | Connet, Mary | 19, Sept 1822 | RCH |
| Hildreth, Joseph | Craig, Lilas | 21, Apr. 1836 | RCH |
| Hildreth, William | Sweet, Philinda | 11, Sept 1836 | RCH |
| Hilge, Ernst | Vornhardt, Cath. E. | 18, June 1847 | C |
| Hilge, Friedrich | Vahrenhorst, Wilhel. | 8, Jan. 1847 | C |
| Hilge, Heinrich | VorderMark, Friedr. | 11, Mar. 1847 | C |
| Hilge, Wilhelm | Lammers, Wilhelmina | 10, June 1847 | C |
| Hilgedick, Wilhelm | Kokner, Elisabeth | 10, Feb. 1848 | C |
| Hilgemann, Ernst J. | Herrmann, Friedricka | 28, Dec. 1849 | RCH |
| Hilgemann, Friedrich | Duewelius, Dorothea | 26, Nov. 1842 | F |
| Hilger, Friedrich | Arodtmann, Charlotte | 17, July 1840 | G |
| Hilker, Dietrich | Stickfort, Catharine | 17, Oct. 1844 | F |
| Hilker, Herman H. | Stewen, Maria Elis. | 22, June 1848 | G |
| Hill, Adam | Hopwood, Ann | 10, Oct. 1819 | RCH |
| Hill, Alfred | Webb, Harriet | 24, Sept 1845 | RCH |
| Hill, Alinson | Simmonds, Emily | 5, June 1842 | RCH |
| Hill, Benjamin | Bowen, Elisabeth | 1, Sept 1838 | RCH |
| Hill, Benjamin | Sheemer, Barbara | 21, Dec. 1841 | RCH |
| Hill, Benjamin | Brooks, Jane | 11, Apr. 1849 | RCH |
| Hill, Benjamin A. | Munjoir, Mary M. | 9, Apr. 1839 | RCH |
| Hill, Caleb | Bowin, Barbara Ann | 20, Apr. 1836 | RCH |
| Hill, Charles | Robison, Susanna | 30, Dec. 1841 | RCH |
| Hill, D. | Shull, Margaret | 1, Apr. 1826 | RCH |
| Hill, David | Johns, Letitia | 20, Feb. 1834 | RCH |
| Hill, David | Gilmore, Elisabeth | 22, Feb. 1846 | RCH |
| Hill, Dennis | Fisher, Isabella | 12, Sept 1835 | RCH |
| Hill, Edmond | Wilmurth, Amanda | 29, Aug. 1847 | RCH |
| Hill, Edward | VanDuzen, Elisabeth | 9, Mar. 1841 | RCH |
| Hill, Edward | Lehmanowsky, Pauline | 7, Nov. 1843 | RCH |
| Hill, Elsey | Sharer, Hannah | 26, Sept 1841 | RCH |
| Hill, Francis | Beetle, Louise | 26, Mar. 1846 | RCH |
| Hill, Francis | Babcock, Electa | 27, Jan. 1847 | RCH |
| Hill, George | Wayt, Elisabeth | 6, Oct. 1835 | RCH |
| Hill, George | Dunham, Elizabeth | 1, Apr. 1848 | I |
| Hill, George M. | Rhodes, Frances | 10, Apr. 1839 | RCH |
| Hill, Heinrich | Broom, Catharina | 22, Sept 1838 | FF |
| Hill, Henry | Boram, Rebecca | 24, Dec. 1840 | RCH |
| Hill, Henry B. | Auten, Mary Jane | 2, May 1849 | RCH |
| Hill, Horris | Shellenberger, Elis. | 4, May 1819 | RCH |
| Hill, James | Shay, Ellen Ann | 10, May 1842 | RCH |
| Hill, Jediah | Cash, Elisabeth | 1, June 1843 | RCH |
| Hill, Jesse | Hand, Sarah Ann | 5, Dec. 1837 | RCH |
| Hill, Joseph | Jenkins, Jennie | 11, Nov. 1847 | I |
| Hill, Joseph S. | McKinnell, Anna | 3, July 1845 | D |
| Hill, Lemuel | Rue, Elisabeth | 30, May 1843 | RCH |
| Hill, Martin | Hill, Mary A. | 15, Jan. 1838 | RCH |
| Hill, Nathan | Miller, Elisabeth | 18, Oct. 1818 | RCH |
| Hill, Philipp | Conover, Amelia | 25, May 1848 | RCH |
| Hill, Richard | Count, Lucinda | 19, Apr. 1837 | RCH |
| Hill, Robert | Risk, Grace M. | 21, Sept 1848 | RCH |
| Hill, Sylvester | Dyer, Martha | 15, Oct. 1843 | RCH |
| Hill, Walter | Lytle, Rebecca | 25, Aug. 1846 | RCH |
| Hill, William | Smith, Julia | 1, July 1839 | RCH |
| Hill, William | Sater, Elisabeth | 20, July 1843 | RCH |
| Hill, William | Smither, Nancy | 6, Aug. 1845 | RCH |
| Hille, Bernard H. | Revermann, Elisabeth | 2, Aug. 1842 | FF |
| Hille, Johan Heinric | Rembeck, M Elisabeth | 28, Sept 1841 | FF |
| Hillebrand, Bernard | Dirches, Bernardina | 30, May 1848 | EE |
| Hillebrand, Joseph | Heitmeyer, Anna M. | 14, Jan. 1849 | FF |
| Hiller, Gustav A. | Glocke, Julia | 18, Jan. 1849 | G |
| Hiller, Heinrich | Walker, Catharine | 9, Aug. 1842 | RCH |
| Hiller, Herman H. | Borcherding, Marg. | 23, Apr. 1846 | F |
| Hillermann, W.J. | Robinson, Elisabeth | 10, Feb. 1849 | RCH |
| Hillers, Heinrich | Ropking, A Catharine | 1, Jan. 1849 | II |
| Hillhouse, Henry | Wescott, Sarah | 20, Jan. 1820 | RCH |
| Hills, Alfred | McCash, Eleanor | 29, Oct. 1835 | RCH |
| Hills, George H. | Wiley, Elisabeth | 31, May 1845 | RCH |
| Hills, Townsend | Cochrane, Elisabeth | 21, July 1844 | RCH |
| Hillyer, Charles | Costello, Catharine | 25, Apr. 1847 | BB |
| Hilman, James | Hoffmann, Malinda | 26, Feb. 1835 | RCH |
| Hilmers, Clemens | Michael, M. Anna | 1, May 1849 | II |

| Grooms | Brides | Date of Marriage | Code |
|--------|--------|------------------|------|
| ****** | ****** | **** ** ******** | **** |
| Hilterbrand, Joshua | Mundary, Martha Ann | 2, Jan. 1845 | RCH |
| Hilton, George | Leaverty, Honora | 20, June 1842 | RCH |
| Hilton, John | Lamburn, Margaret | 31, Oct. 1819 | RCH |
| Hilton, Joseph | Kennedy, Elisabeth | 25, Nov. 1846 | RCH |
| Hilton, Robert | Atchinson, Isabella | 4, July 1846 | RCH |
| Hilton, Theophilus | Porter, Lydia | 20, Nov. 1819 | RCH |
| Hilton, Thomas J. | Patterson, Irene | 22, Feb. 1849 | BB |
| Himler, Johan | Back, Felicitas | 28, June 1848 | EE |
| Himmelgarten, Johan | Roemer, Maria Agnes | 17, Nov. 1840 | FF |
| Himmelmeyer, Johan | Gellhaus, Antoinette | 29, Apr. 1849 | AA |
| Hinck, William | Hill, Catharine | 3, Sept 1826 | RCH |
| Hindenon, Lewis | Netles, Rachel Ann | 21, Sept 1831 | RCH |
| Hinderness, Friedric | Woltring, Elisabeth | 13, Apr. 1847 | AA |
| Hinders, Dietrich | Ritscher, Catharine | 8, Nov. 1843 | AA |
| Hindmann, John F. | Morgan, Martha J. | 11, June 1843 | RCH |
| Hine, Andrew | Copes, Elisabeth | 3, Jan. 1836 | RCH |
| Hiner, David | Baker, Christina | 4, Sept 1843 | RCH |
| Hiner, David | Lippencott, H. | 31, May 1849 | RCH |
| Hiner, Ezekiel | Wiggins, Mary Jane | 26, July 1847 | RCH |
| Hiner, George | Shiner, Amanda | 18, Nov. 1845 | RCH |
| Hines, John | Shane, Catharine | 10, Oct. 1819 | RCH |
| Hingson, Richard | Wright, Catharine | 30, Nov. 1845 | RCH |
| Hink, P. | Wallace, Jane W. | 12, Mar. 1835 | RCH |
| Hinke, Heinrich | Elsemann, Gertrud | 7, Nov. 1837 | FF |
| Hinkebein, Meinrad | Behrens, Maria | 10, July 1849 | II |
| Hinkinson, Ezekiel | Crane, Mary | 19, Jan. 1826 | RCH |
| Hinkle, Anthony | Shillinger, Francis | 4, Apr. 1842 | RCH |
| Hinman, Conrad | Jeltz, Elisabeth | 19, Aug. 1819 | RCH |
| Hinnenkamp, Anton | Fiedeldei, Elisabeth | 31, July 1845 | FF |
| Hinsdale, T. | Loring, Susan M. | 30, Nov. 1836 | RCH |
| Hinterlang, Martin | Hornberger, Maria | 6, Nov. 1849 | EE |
| Hinton, Elijah | Farrer, Hannah | 2, Feb. 1834 | RCH |
| Hinton, William | Stone, Eunice | 30, Oct. 1845 | RCH |
| Hinton, William | Seiderberg, Elisabet | 15, Aug. 1848 | RCH |
| Hinzemann, Heinrich | Mueller, Dorothea | 30, Sept 1849 | G |
| Hippel, Bernard E. | Schuler, Barbara | 22, Aug. 1847 | CC |
| Hipple, Benjamin | King, Amanda | 17, Sept 1843 | RCH |
| Hirel, Martin | Rudicil, Patsey | 5, July 1842 | RCH |
| Hireman, John H. | Torphy, Catharine | 10, May 1849 | BB |
| Hirsch, Anton | Kleinmann, Carolina | 2, Feb. 1847 | FF |
| Hirsch, Friedrich | Gruen, Catharina | 25, Oct. 1849 | G |
| Hirsch, Heinrich | Weil, Jennette | 29, Oct. 1848 | RCH |
| Hirsch, Jonas | Hiller, Caroline | 28, Apr. 1848 | RCH |
| Hirsh, Georg Jacob | Kempf, Catharine | 4, Feb. 1845 | AA |
| Hirst, Samuel | Lowry, Vileniet A. | 24, Aug. 1847 | RCH |
| Hirt, Heinrich | Hipp, Maria | 13, Aug. 1848 | A |
| Hirt, Heinrich | Kress, Elisabeth | 30, June 1848 | G |
| Hirtheis, Joseph | Hipoltsteiner, Barb. | 29, May 1849 | HH |
| Hiryton, Abraham | Mahoney, Deborah | 1, Dec. 1832 | RCH |
| Hiser, Solomon | Masters, Julia Ann | 31, May 1849 | RCH |
| Hitchings, Joseph | Holland, Ellen | 5, Jan. 1832 | RCH |
| Hitchler, John | McCann, Rosetta | 16, Aug. 1847 | BB |
| Hixson, James | Randall, Mary | 5, Mar. 1844 | RCH |
| Ho---, | Walker, Sarah | 26, Mar. 1836 | RCH |
| Hoack, Friedrich | Maier, Magdalena | 20, Oct. 1836 | F |
| Hoagland, Ralph | Hunt, Rebecca Ann | 28, Mar. 1825 | RCH |
| Hoard, Elijah | Hall, Susan | 19, Sept 1848 | RCH |
| Hoban, Patrick | Purcell, Catharine | 4, Feb. 1849 | RCH |
| Hoban, Patrick | Miles, Bridget (Mrs) | 8, Oct. 1848 | BB |
| Hobele, Johan | Hobele, Maria | 20, Apr. 1847 | EE |
| Hoberg, Johan Heinr. | Fraser, Maria | 15, Nov. 1848 | F |
| Hobin, Francis | Gent, Justina | 12, June 1849 | RCH |
| Hobing, Wendel | Krug, Kunigunda | 10, Sept 1844 | AA |
| Hobkemeyer, Rudolph | Fruechte, Christina | 11, May 1848 | G |
| Hobley, Joseph | Brown, Mary L. | 4, May 1841 | RCH |
| Hobs, John | Walker, Mary | 5, May 1836 | RCH |
| Hobson, James | Wright, Mary A. | 31, Dec. 1845 | RCH |
| Hock, Joseph | Voll, Elisabeth | 9, Sept 1847 | RCH |
| Hocker, Matthias | Bruns, Elisabeth | 23, Jan. 1849 | II |
| Hockmann, J Heinrich | Ellermann, Louise | 10, Apr. 1845 | F |
| Hodapp, Martin | Deutschle, Perpetua | 2, Aug. 1842 | FF |

| Grooms<br>****** | Brides<br>****** | Date of Marriage<br>**** ** ******** | Code<br>**** |
|---|---|---|---|
| Hodge, Adam | Carson, Mary M. | 13, Dec. 1846 | RCH |
| Hodge, Ariel | Bennet, Louise M. | 7, Oct. 1842 | RCH |
| Hodge, Robert | Spence, | 20, Apr. 1835 | RCH |
| Hodge, Thomas | Thompson, Hannah | 10, Mar. 1818 | RCH |
| Hodgson, William | Shepherd, Lena | 17, June 1844 | RCH |
| Hoebene, Benedict | Steifel, Louise | 14, Apr. 1843 | RCH |
| Hoeckel, Heinrich | Hielpert, Barbara | 25, May 1846 | A |
| Hoeffling, Michael | Albrecht, Catharine | 28, Nov. 1847 | CC |
| Hoefler, Georg F. | Blaese, Maria Anna | 27, Aug. 1848 | CC |
| Hoefling, Adam | Menninger, Anna M. | 16, July 1848 | CC |
| Hoegemann, Johan H. | Ballmann, Bernardina | 11, Oct. 1846 | AA |
| Hoeger, Michael | Scheidler, Josephina | 29, Oct. 1848 | EE |
| Hoeger, Theodor | Schuerbachs, Cath. | 10, July 1839 | FF |
| Hoehing, Johan Georg | Kreiser, Magdalena C | 27, June 1846 | G |
| Hoehn, Francis L. | Marschall, Margaret | 30, Apr. 1849 | CC |
| Hoel, | Riley, Mary E. | 1, Aug. 1849 | RCH |
| Hoel, George W. | Hoper, Catharine | 6, Dec. 1834 | RCH |
| Hoel, William | Case, | 27, June 1826 | RCH |
| Hoelber, Christoph G | Bernhardt, Christina | 10, Aug. 1848 | C |
| Hoelker, Dietrich | Kleine, Elisabeth | 18, June 1844 | AA |
| Hoelker, Herman | Hess, Elisabeth | 17, Sept 1848 | CC |
| Hoelker, Johan | Pelke, Catharina | 29, Sept 1840 | FF |
| Hoelscher, Bernard H | Hillen, Maria Angela | 26, Sept 1847 | AA |
| Hoelscher, Carl | Reiser, Rosina | 23, Sept 1849 | CC |
| Hoelscher, Herman F. | Kempmeyer, Catharine | 8, Nov. 1846 | EE |
| Hoelscher, Wilhelm | Lohmann, Margaretha | 15, Nov. 1837 | FF |
| Hoenig, Johan H. | Wensing, Clara | 31, Jan. 1847 | EE |
| Hoening, Anton | Meyer, Anna Margaret | 31, May 1847 | EE |
| Hoening, Carl | Pabst, Aloysia | 16, Feb. 1847 | EE |
| Hoening, Theodor | Huelsgen, Maria Elis | 30, May 1846 | EE |
| Hoensing, Gottfried | Sturwell, Maria A. | 26, Mar. 1839 | RCH |
| Hoer, Philipp | Mickle, Maria | 6, Feb. 1849 | A |
| Hoersmann, Anton | Brockmann, Dorothea | 18, June 1848 | AA |
| Hoesbing, Herman | Luhn, Margaretha | 14, Feb. 1843 | FF |
| Hoesch, Georg | Seeger, Margaretha | 3, Dec. 1846 | C |
| Hoesdebink, Wilhelm | Holtmeyer, Anna M. | 13, Feb. 1848 | EE |
| Hoevelmeyer, Herman | Dierkers, Anna Cath. | 7, Feb. 1847 | EE |
| Hoey, Bernard | Mullen, Fannie | 3, Sept 1849 | RCH |
| Hoey, William | Snider, Sarah | 12, June 1849 | RCH |
| Hof, Constantin | Goffine, Elisabeth | 12, May 1840 | FF |
| Hof, Nicolaus | Kraft, Anna Maria | 13, Jan. 1846 | EE |
| Hofer, Randolph | Lehman, Regina | 26, June 1834 | RCH |
| Hoff, Anton | Geise, Louise | 4, Feb. 1839 | FF |
| Hoff, Georg | Jedele, Elisabeth | 24, Apr. 1848 | FF |
| Hoff, Jacob | Lang, Magdalena | 9, May 1848 | FF |
| Hoff---, Andrew | Stonesifter, Elis. | 6, Jan. 1825 | RCH |
| Hoffer, Francis | Eller, Martha | 18, July 1836 | FF |
| Hoffer, Georg | Elbert, Margaretha | 24, Nov. 1848 | EE |
| Hoffer, John | Woodruff, Martha | 10, Dec. 1840 | RCH |
| Hoffermann, J. Hein. | Ahaus, M. Louisa | 30, Jan. 1849 | FF |
| Hoffhaus, Heinrich | Thie, Maria Theresa | 11, Feb. 1849 | CC |
| Hoffman, John | Smith, Elenna | 21, Sept 1826 | RCH |
| Hoffmann, Adam | Reis, Margaretha | 14, Mar. 1837 | FF |
| Hoffmann, Balthasar | Windrich, Margaretha | 12, June 1849 | EE |
| Hoffmann, Carl | Baus, Maria | 12, Feb. 1836 | FF |
| Hoffmann, Edelbert | Pfeffer, Catharine | 5, July 1847 | EE |
| Hoffmann, Elias | ----, ---- | 30, Oct. 1823 | RCH |
| Hoffmann, Francis A. | Helms, Maria Anna | 9, Jan. 1844 | FF |
| Hoffmann, Friedrich | Gitermann, Barbara | 1, May 1849 | EE |
| Hoffmann, G Heinrich | Abel, Maria Anna | 9, Sept 1849 | FF |
| Hoffmann, Georg | Wagner, Maria | 1, Jan. 1845 | HH |
| Hoffmann, Georg H. | Voss, A. Margaretha | 19, Aug. 1845 | FF |
| Hoffmann, Georg L. | Kalb, Catharine | 7, Aug. 1849 | RCH |
| Hoffmann, Georg Phil | Feyer, Maria (Mrs) | 15, Nov. 1849 | FF |
| Hoffmann, Gerhard | Pund, Carolina | 13, July 1841 | FF |
| Hoffmann, Gottfried | Sohnlein, Kunigunda | 17, Aug. 1845 | C |
| Hoffmann, Heinrich | Huber, Charlotte | 31, Dec. 1848 | II |
| Hoffmann, Henry | Rinehart, Jane | 29, July 1842 | RCH |
| Hoffmann, Jacob | Whitney, Abby | 16, Sept 1841 | RCH |
| Hoffmann, Jacob | Hornampke, Doris | 28, Dec. 1849 | F |
| Hoffmann, Johan | Hammerschmidt, Elis. | 5, Aug. 1839 | FF |

| Grooms<br>****** | Brides<br>****** | Date of Marriage<br>**** ** ******** | Code<br>**** |
|---|---|---|---|
| Hoffmann, Johan | Bedelberger, Marg. | 11, Dec. 1848 | RCH |
| Hoffmann, Johan | Hofmeister, Catharin | 23, Nov. 1845 | C |
| Hoffmann, Johan | Rutz, Magdalena(Mrs) | 21, Sept 1847 | AA |
| Hoffmann, Johan | Rettelberger, Marg. | 11, Dec. 1848 | EE |
| Hoffmann, Johan H. | Kampmeyer, Catharine | 6, Jan. 1848 | EE |
| Hoffmann, John | Maypole, Sarah | 13, May 1838 | RCH |
| Hoffmann, John | Schmidt, Margaretha | 21, Dec. 1845 | RCH |
| Hoffmann, Michael | Trefser, Rosina | 28, June 1843 | G |
| Hoffmann, Nicolaus | Block, Helena | 12, Nov. 1848 | AA |
| Hoffmann, Peter | Merz, Eva | 24, Nov. 1840 | FF |
| Hoffmann, Peter | Dant, Barbara | 13, Feb. 1847 | RCH |
| Hoffmann, Peter | Reis, Veronica | 7, May 1848 | EE |
| Hoffmann, Philipp | Hackinger, M. Alice | 13, Sept 1849 | BB |
| Hoffmann, Valentin | Mentel, Martha Elis. | 9, Dec. 1845 | G |
| Hoffmann, Wilhelm | Freygang, Anna Maria | 2, Aug. 1842 | FF |
| Hoffmann, William | Daniels, Martha | 9, Oct. 1836 | RCH |
| Hoffmann, Wolfgang | Schwarz, Margaretha | 23, Jan. 1845 | G |
| Hoffmeyer, Heinrich | Linneweber, Louise | 21, Nov. 1844 | F |
| Hoffner, Adonijah | Doen, Mary | 8, Jan. 1837 | RCH |
| Hoffner, Jacob | Marsden, Elisabeth | 1, June 1820 | RCH |
| Hoffner, James | Balsell, Catharine | 6, Oct. 1823 | RCH |
| Hoffner, James | Moonie, Amanda | 26, Sept 1841 | RCH |
| Hoffner, James | Ege, Eliza Ann | 16, Apr. 1846 | RCH |
| Hoffner, John | McGill, Lenah | 31, May 1846 | RCH |
| Hoffner, Peter | Hester, Anna C. | 7, Dec. 1848 | RCH |
| Hoffner, Samuel | Balsell, Catharine | 6, Nov. 1823 | RCH |
| Hoffner, Samuel | Bolser, | 24, May 1827 | RCH |
| Hoffner, Thomas | Smith, Abigail | 10, Nov. 1836 | RCH |
| Hoffner, Thomas | Ege, Sarah Jane | 2, Nov. 1843 | RCH |
| Hofgesang, Caspar | Hoffmann, Margaretha | 1, Nov. 1849 | EE |
| Hofknecht, Johan | Regus, Margaretha | 14, Dec. 1845 | C |
| Hofmann, Peter | Gasser, Maria Anna | 4, Feb. 1845 | AA |
| Hofreiter, John | Efger, Maria Cath. | 26, Dec. 1849 | RCH |
| Hofreiter, Sebastian | Roedinger, Crescent. | 6, Oct. 1846 | AA |
| Hofrogge, Anton | Post, Gertrud | 8, Nov. 1842 | AA |
| Hofschulte, Wilhelm | Balgenort, Margaret | 27, Oct. 1840 | FF |
| Hofsetz, Peter | Bauer, Barbara | 31, Oct. 1848 | A |
| Hofstetter, Reinhard | Adam, Maria | 31, Jan. 1843 | AA |
| Hofue, Jacob | Camfield, Sarah | 29, Sept 1833 | RCH |
| Hog, Robert | Cregan, Jane | 18, Jan. 1838 | RCH |
| Hogan, John | Hubbard, Margaret | 10, Aug. 1826 | RCH |
| Hogan, Joseph | Mathews, Catharine | 25, July 1847 | RCH |
| Hogan, Philipp | Alterman, Ally | 12, June 1834 | RCH |
| Hoge, Heinrich | Arodtmann, Maria | 17, July 1840 | G |
| Hogeback, Johan H. | Kotte, Maria Anna | 11, July 1847 | EE |
| Hogeback, Johan H. | Finker, Adelhaid | 30, Sept 1849 | EE |
| Hoget, Thomas | Devine, Elisabeth | 18, Jan. 1846 | RCH |
| Hoggeford, John | Bowers, Charlotte | 4, July 1832 | I |
| Hogland, John | Bassett, Catharine | 12, Nov. 1846 | RCH |
| Hoglen, James | Caendem, Maria | 4, Nov. 1838 | RCH |
| Hogue, John | Hornden, Hannah | 6, Nov. 1846 | RCH |
| Hohl, Heinrich | Gehefer, Catharine | 6, Nov. 1847 | F |
| Hohlenkamp, Herman | Wilbes, Maria Adel. | 28, May 1848 | EE |
| Hohmann, Heinrich | Starbe, Anna Maria | 14, May 1839 | FF |
| Hohn, Peter | Alexander, Mary | 22, Feb. 1849 | RCH |
| Hohnhorst, Gerhard H | Stuerwald, Catharina | 12, July 1842 | FF |
| Hohnstedt, Henry | Bohning, Sophia | 9, Mar. 1847 | RCH |
| Hohrn, John Leonard | Fiber, Johanna | 26, Sept 1841 | RCH |
| Hoing, Gottfried A. | Sturwald, M Adelheid | 26, Nov. 1839 | FF |
| Hoit, William | Sheldon, Julia | 11, Oct. 1837 | RCH |
| Hoke, Abraham | Amot, Mary B. | 13, Apr. 1848 | RCH |
| Hoke, David | Brill, Lucetta | 18, Oct. 1845 | RCH |
| Holber, Andrew | Stepps, Isabella | 26, Aug. 1839 | RCH |
| Holcomb, Sylvander | Dean, Mary | 1, Jan. 1838 | RCH |
| Holden, Henry | Frost, Georgianna | 23, May 1849 | RCH |
| Holden, William | Johnson, Sarah | 23, Sept 1845 | RCH |
| Holdenfula, James | Raw, Charlotte | 24, Sept 1836 | RCH |
| Holderfield, William | Mann, Amanda | 7, Aug. 1843 | RCH |
| Holdkamp, Eberhard | Lichtenberg, Elis. | 17, Nov. 1849 | EE |
| Holdkamp, Heinrich | Diege, Elisabeth | 11, Nov. 1849 | EE |
| Holdzkorn, William | Laird, Amanda | 18, Feb. 1846 | RCH |

| Grooms<br>***** | Brides<br>***** | Date of Marriage<br>**** ** ******** | Code<br>**** |
|---|---|---|---|
| Hole, David | May, Sarah B. | 12, Apr. 1832 | RCH |
| Hole, Edmund | Ryan, Sarah | 12, Apr. 1821 | RCH |
| Holeand, William | Shill, Ann | 25, Sept 1834 | RCH |
| Holenkamp, Wilhelm | Bischof, Elisabeth | 11, Jan. 1848 | FF |
| Holenshade, James C. | McIntire, Hannah | 25, June 1849 | RCH |
| Holford, Frederick | Weissmann, Louise | 11, Apr. 1843 | RCH |
| Holla---, Palmer | VanAusdol, Esther | 4, Sept 1839 | RCH |
| Holland, Calvin M. | Grey, Elisabeth | 14, Apr. 1837 | RCH |
| Holland, Claburn | Bates, Rose Ann | 28, Oct. 1847 | RCH |
| Holland, James | Bolles, Lydia | 27, July 1845 | RCH |
| Holland, James M. | Brown, Jane | 26, Feb. 1834 | RCH |
| Holland, James P. | Woodington, Matilda | 30, Apr. 1841 | RCH |
| Holland, Jesse | McGlenn, Margaret | 14, Mar. 1842 | RCH |
| Holland, John | Barnet, Polly | 14, Nov. 1822 | RCH |
| Holland, John | West, Mary | 12, Jan. 1834 | RCH |
| Holland, Jonathan | Allenton, Sarah | 14, Dec. 1834 | RCH |
| Holland, Perry | Harcourt, Cynthia | 6, Aug. 1843 | RCH |
| Holland, Perry | Allen, Nancy A. | 5, Nov. 1848 | RCH |
| Holland, Zacherias | Morrison, Susanna | 27, Mar. 1835 | RCH |
| Hollard, Thomas | Patterson, Margaret | 15, Jan. 1834 | RCH |
| Holle, Ernst Wilhelm | Kleine, Maria Sophia | 9, May 1849 | F |
| Holle, Theodor | Piehl, Caroline | 22, May 1845 | F |
| Hollen, Stephen Wm. | Frecking, Elisabeth | 18, Jan. 1842 | FF |
| Hollenbach, Herman | Ertel, Maria Anna | 21, Jan. 1844 | FF |
| Hollenbeck, Christ. | Landwehr, Charlotte | 11, June 1841 | F |
| Hollenbeck, Martin | Solmon, Anna Sophia | 20, June 1844 | RCH |
| Hollenbeck, Wilhelm | Droste, Cath. Elis. | 25, Feb. 1847 | B |
| Hollende, B.Heinrich | Flechtenkotter, Ther | 27, Aug. 1849 | II |
| Hollenkamp, Bernard | Grueter, M Elisabeth | 9, May 1847 | FF |
| Hollenkamp, Gerhard | Reinken, M. Gertrud | 12, May 1839 | FF |
| Hollenkamp, Heinrich | Goerting, Margaretha | 11, Feb. 1849 | II |
| Hollenkamp, Heinrich | Wellmeier, Theresa | 23, Oct. 1849 | II |
| Hollenkamp, Johan | Kruse, Maria | 17, Jan. 1841 | FF |
| Hollenkamp, Johan G. | Depweg, Elisabeth | 3, Aug. 1841 | FF |
| Holler, Peter | Groeser, Margaretha | 8, Aug. 1847 | EE |
| Hollerah, Wilhelm | Dickhaus, Mary | 6, Apr. 1845 | AA |
| Hollet, Heinrich | Herbert, Elisabeth | 15, Nov. 1849 | AA |
| Holley, Samuel | Bonnell, Lackey Ann | 21, July 1822 | RCH |
| Holley, Samuel | Dosh, Susan | 15, June 1845 | BB |
| Holliday, Horace | Armstrong, Susannah | 27, June 1848 | I |
| Holliday, James | Holliday, Rebecca | 22, July 1844 | RCH |
| Holliday, Joseph | Smith, Susan | 20, May 1847 | RCH |
| Hollin, Henry P. | Colshear, Elisabeth | 24, Dec. 1836 | RCH |
| Hollinan, John | Montgomery, Elis. | 19, Aug. 1849 | BB |
| Holling, Heinrich | Alber, Sophia | 23, Feb. 1848 | EE |
| Hollinger, Alexander | Eckstein, Lutgardis | 12, Jan. 1841 | FF |
| Hollister, Bradley | McDade, Bridget | 14, July 1845 | BB |
| Hollmann, Johan H. | Stockhoff, Clara E. | 4, Feb. 1849 | AA |
| Hollmeyer, Karl | Kerselsberger, Gen. | 12, Jan. 1843 | AA |
| Holloway, Thomas | Fear, Elisabeth | 26, Nov. 1845 | RCH |
| Hollowell, Amos | Dickerson, Anna Elis | 1, Jan. 1846 | RCH |
| Hollowell, James B. | VanDusen, Sophia | 28, Oct. 1847 | RCH |
| Holmes, Cornelius | ----, ---- | 25, Sept 1834 | RCH |
| Holmes, Ezekiel | Goulden, Bridget | 15, Dec. 1848 | RCH |
| Holmes, William | Mills, Ann | 22, Mar. 1827 | RCH |
| Holmes, William | Buffington, Elisabet | 2, Nov. 1847 | RCH |
| Holmes, William | Roberg, Sophia | 14, Feb. 1847 | GG |
| Holmet, William | ----, Nancy | 9, Jan. 1823 | RCH |
| Holmick, Valentin | Reilly, Eliza | 30, Dec. 1849 | RCH |
| Holowell, Benjamin | Bidinger, Sarah | 24, Mar. 1842 | RCH |
| Holroh, Heinrich | Els, Maria Catharina | 11, Nov. 1840 | FF |
| Holroyd, Edward | Tucker, Hannah | 8, Nov. 1841 | I |
| Holstead, David | Sheridan, Ann | 30, Sept 1848 | GG |
| Holstead, Ira | Harper, Lydia | 23, Feb. 1826 | RCH |
| Holstermann, Clement | Harmann, Regina | 18, July 1847 | EE |
| Holt, Aaron | Sayres, Jane | 11, Aug. 1819 | RCH |
| Holt, Bernard Herman | Viertag, A. Adelheid | 7, Jan. 1840 | FF |
| Holt, William | VanWinkle, Mary | 1, Oct. 1837 | RCH |
| Holtel, Gerhard Bd. | Deiker, Maria Elis. | 16, Feb. 1847 | AA |
| Holters, Bernard | Stuerwald, Helena | 16, Jan. 1848 | FF |
| Holters, Johan Hein. | Wilke, Maria Cath. | 21, Oct. 1845 | FF |

| Grooms ****** | Brides ****** | Date of Marriage **** ** ******** | Code **** |
|---|---|---|---|
| Holtgrewe, Carl H. | Michael, Maria Elis. | 27, Feb. 1848 | AA |
| Holthaus, Bartholom. | Tillmann, Maria Elis | 7, Sept 1847 | EE |
| Holthaus, Bernard H. | Brune, Anna Maria | 9, Sept 1849 | AA |
| Holthaus, Herman | Baumers, Elisabeth | 30, Oct. 1849 | II |
| Holtheide, Herman H. | Kellermann, Catharin | 2, Mar. 1848 | AA |
| Holtkamp, B. Joseph | Tillmann, Catharine | 30, Jan. 1849 | II |
| Holtkamp, Johan B. | Ninker, Charlotte | 11, Dec. 1845 | F |
| Holtkamp, Joseph | Husmann, Theresa | 9, Sept 1845 | AA |
| Holtmann, Francis H. | Bauten, M. Elisabeth | 21, Nov. 1847 | AA |
| Holtmeyer, Francis | Overbeck, M. Elis. | 14, July 1840 | FF |
| Holtmeyer, Francis | Bauten, Dina | 28, Oct. 1849 | AA |
| Holtzinger, George | Thompson, Frances | 2, May 1847 | RCH |
| Holtzinger, Jacob | Myers, Elisabeth | 5, Oct. 1848 | RCH |
| Holweg, Jacob | Schildering, Adel. | 23, Sept 1849 | AA |
| Holz, Ignatz | Bechtel, Maria Anna | 12, July 1842 | FF |
| Holzberger, George | Gugel, Margaret | 22, Dec. 1846 | RCH |
| Holzhausen, Johan J. | Winkelmann, F Louise | 2, Sept 1849 | E |
| Holzner, Johan | Ganz, Elisabeth | 4, Oct. 1849 | EE |
| Holzwart, Georg | Harsch, Barbara | 23, July 1848 | A |
| Homan, David | Strickland, Elis. | 13, Mar. 1833 | RCH |
| Homan, Francis | Pierce, Sarah | 6, May 1846 | RCH |
| Homan, John | Alexander, Elisabeth | 24, Dec. 1846 | RCH |
| Homan, Mark | Harbaugh, Catharine | 16, May 1833 | RCH |
| Homann, Albert | Benoelken, Catharine | 3, Oct. 1848 | II |
| Homann, Herman H. | Acker, Margaretha | 17, Nov. 1846 | AA |
| Hombach, Ludwig J. | Sipp, Rachel Louise | 3, June 1848 | G |
| Hombach, Peter | Gehbauer, Maria Anna | 5, Dec. 1848 | G |
| Homer, James H. | Mitchell, Margaret | 1, July 1846 | GG |
| Homer, John | Lincoln, Ann | 5, Jan. 1832 | RCH |
| Homer, Thomas | Whitelaw, Mary | 13, Sept 1846 | RCH |
| Homm, Samuel L. | Swift, Elisabeth C. | 22, June 1826 | RCH |
| Hommelmeyer, Johan | Helwig, Theresa | 26, Aug. 1845 | AA |
| Hompky, Johan | Thiesholz, Anna | 26, Aug. 1840 | G |
| Honefinger, Herman | Hackmann, Anna Maria | 22, Feb. 1842 | F |
| Honeyman, William H. | Rage, Rebecca | 1, May 1833 | RCH |
| Honeywell, Charles | Ross, Mary Ann | 20, Oct. 1834 | RCH |
| Honigfeld, Heinrich | Hesselmann, Maria A. | 26, Aug. 1849 | EE |
| Honking, Herman | Schneider, Margaret | 18, Oct. 1842 | F |
| Honkomp, Friedrich | Rabe, Bernardina | 3, Feb. 1842 | FF |
| Honkomp, Heinrich | Hausfeld, Anna M. | 2, Sept 1841 | FF |
| Honnek, Anton | Biele, Francisca | 28, Dec. 1835 | FF |
| Honroth, F. Adolph | Telljohann, Christin | 31, May 1849 | C |
| Honroth, William | Katterheinrich, Chr. | 21, Feb. 1846 | RCH |
| Hood, John | Stewart, Rosanna | 26, Aug. 1846 | RCH |
| Hood, John C. | Abercrombe, Mary | 8, Aug. 1843 | RCH |
| Hood, Jonathan | Dodd, Louise | 1, May 1842 | RCH |
| Hood, Rowly | Wright, Elisabeth | 25, Dec. 1819 | RCH |
| Hood, Thomas | Kite, Elisabeth | 22, Dec. 1821 | RCH |
| Hoog, Victor | Finn, Louise | 16, Aug. 1848 | RCH |
| Hoogland, John | Brown, Catharine | 15, Oct. 1835 | RCH |
| Hoogland, William C. | Howard, Miranda | 21, Sept 1843 | RCH |
| Hook, Arthur | Allen, Margaret | 27, June 1839 | RCH |
| Hook, Firman | Bogenschuetz, Regina | 7, Jan. 1847 | EE |
| Hook, Ira G. | Williamson, Charlott | 30, June 1835 | RCH |
| Hook, Israel | Gosney, Nancy | 12, Jan. 1843 | RCH |
| Hooks, John | Charter, Susan C. | 10, Dec. 1844 | RCH |
| Hool, Joseph | Graham, Lucy A. | 23, Feb. 1838 | RCH |
| Hoole, Samuel | Phillips, Rebecca | 20, Jan. 1833 | RCH |
| Hooper, Jacob | Johnson, Lucinda | 30, Jan. 1838 | RCH |
| Hooper, John | Doyle, Elisabeth | 15, Sept 1841 | RCH |
| Hooper, Joseph J. | McGinnis, Amanda | 1, Feb. 1838 | RCH |
| Hooper, Stephen | Hatch, Mary Ann | 22, Oct. 1846 | RCH |
| Hoops, George | Fain, Adelheid | 31, Aug. 1843 | RCH |
| Hoops, John | Columbia, Rebekah | 3, Apr. 1820 | RCH |
| Hoops, Wilhelm N. | Meyer, Anna Adel. | 21, May 1847 | F |
| Hoover, Isaac | Dur---, Rose Ann | 28, Jan. 1841 | RCH |
| Hoover, Samuel J. | Cross, Mary | 7, Dec. 1836 | RCH |
| Hopeck, Johan | Moser, Catharine | 15, Aug. 1843 | AA |
| Hopf, Michael | Wogenhauser, Maria | 14, Feb. 1843 | AA |
| Hopf, Valentin | Rau, Maria | 23, Oct. 1849 | AA |
| Hopings, Francis | Rose, Parmelia | 24, Feb. 1839 | RCH |

| Grooms<br>****** | Brides<br>****** | Date of Marriage<br>**** ** ******** | Code<br>**** |
|---|---|---|---|
| Hopkins, Alonzo | Isgrigg, Hannah | 19, Apr. 1849 | RCH |
| Hopkins, George | Clark, Mary | 3, Feb. 1833 | RCH |
| Hopkins, George W. | McHenry, Margaret | 31, Dec. 1831 | RCH |
| Hopkins, Isaac | Messuk, Elisabeth | 13, Feb. 1834 | RCH |
| Hopkins, Isaac W. | Green, Sarah J. | 23, Aug. 1820 | RCH |
| Hopkins, Jacob | Jones, Elisabeth | 9, Jan. 1847 | RCH |
| Hopkins, John C. | Watts, Sidney | 13, Feb. 1837 | RCH |
| Hopkins, John N. | Perry, Mary C. | 3, Nov. 1840 | RCH |
| Hopkins, Richard | Baldridge, Mary | 15, Mar. 1847 | RCH |
| Hopkins, Robert | Rybolt, Margaret | 27, Mar. 1847 | RCH |
| Hopkins, Samuel | Graves, Elisabeth | 10, Dec. 1843 | RCH |
| Hopkins, Samuel M. | Christy, Elisabeth | 11, Sept 1833 | RCH |
| Hopkins, William | Winters, Lucy | 3, May 1818 | RCH |
| Hopkins, William | Hobbs, Laura | 16, July 1842 | RCH |
| Hopkins, William | Waggoner, Mary | 6, Oct. 1848 | RCH |
| Hopkins, William H. | Rogers, Elisabeth | 21, Mar. 1837 | RCH |
| Hopkinson, Joseph | Lavil, Mary | 4, July 1848 | RCH |
| Hople, Peter | Doll, Maria Anna | 8, Sept 1842 | FF |
| Hoppe, Herman | Schmidt, Francisca | 28, Aug. 1848 | A |
| Hopper, Abraham | Johsnon, Miriam | 22, Feb. 1849 | RCH |
| Hopper, Garrett | Wood, Ann | 5, Dec. 1839 | RCH |
| Hopper, Garrett | Johnson, Rebecca A. | 1, Mar. 1848 | RCH |
| Hopper, Jonathan | Perry, Elisabeth Ann | 19, Oct. 1834 | RCH |
| Hopper, Joseph L. | Dirk, Mary J. | 4, Jan. 1838 | RCH |
| Hopper, Morris | Webb, Hannah | 12, May 1834 | RCH |
| Hopper, Morris | West, Susan | 20, Mar. 1838 | RCH |
| Hopper, William | Cary, Martha | 15, Feb. 1844 | RCH |
| Hoppin, Jonathan | Maish, Ann Elis. | 7, Dec. 1824 | RCH |
| Hoppin, Samuel | Sullivan, Ann | 22, Oct. 1833 | RCH |
| Hopping, Caleb L. | Graff, Mary | 10, Sept 1837 | RCH |
| Hopping, Edward | Karr, Eleanor | 27, Sept 1832 | RCH |
| Hopping, Robert | Fauver, Catharine | 5, Sept 1837 | RCH |
| Hopple, Jacob | Tudor, Ann C. | 26, Dec. 1843 | RCH |
| Hopple, Madison | DeSezure, Nancy C. | 21, Apr. 1846 | RCH |
| Hoppmann, Friedrich | Kohlmann, Martha | 13, Feb. 1849 | RCH |
| Hopps, Henry | Mayhew, Catharine | 21, Apr. 1842 | RCH |
| Hopps, James | Brislie, Elisabeth | 15, Mar. 1846 | RCH |
| Hopster, Heinrich | Rohe, Anna Maria | 7, Feb. 1847 | FF |
| Horan, Finton | Sweeney, Eliza Jane | 25, June 1846 | RCH |
| Hordorf, Andreas | Meier, Anna Barbara | 19, Oct. 1843 | RCH |
| Horgan, Dennis | Donahue, Sarah | 3, Sept 1849 | RCH |
| Hork, Edward | Campbell, Sarah | 5, Jan. 1837 | RCH |
| Horm, Philipp | Straub, Anna | 6, Apr. 1845 | FF |
| Horm, Wendel | Oehler, Caroline | 22, June 1843 | FF |
| Horman, Eli | Jackson, Betsy | 23, Oct. 1836 | RCH |
| Hormann, Friedrich | Wellmann, Christina | 10, Nov. 1840 | F |
| Horn, Jacob | Bobinger, Elisabeth | 7, Aug. 1849 | C |
| Horn, Johan | Schwab, Philippina | 17, Mar. 1849 | CC |
| Horn, Werner | Wippelmann, Elisabet | 16, Sept 1848 | RCH |
| Hornberger, John | Loge, Catharine | 15, May 1837 | RCH |
| Hornemann, Friedrich | Holl, Charlotte | 6, July 1848 | F |
| Hornemann, Henry | Fletcher, Margaret | 13, Sept 1849 | RCH |
| Horner, Isaac | Finn, Rhoda | 13, Mar. 1836 | RCH |
| Horner, John | Clark, Phoebe | 22, Jan. 1838 | RCH |
| Horner, John | Tansansda, Mary Jane | 15, Aug. 1839 | RCH |
| Horney, Thornton | Goodall, Martha | 2, Jan. 1844 | RCH |
| Hornflewr, Jud | Rogers, Susan T. | 27, May 1838 | RCH |
| Horning, August | Aele, Wilhelmina | 14, May 1848 | C |
| Hornish, Bazaleel | Cook, Clara | 24, July 1844 | RCH |
| Hornschemeier, Johan | Meyer, M. Elisabeth | 7, Jan. 1849 | AA |
| Hornung, Heinrich | Schinkel, Catharine | 3, Dec. 1849 | RCH |
| Horr, Elnathan | Campbell, Elisabeth | 17, May 1841 | RCH |
| Horr, Philipp | Jacklelst, Mary | 19, Feb. 1844 | RCH |
| Horra---, James | Freeland, Elisabeth | 24, May 1821 | RCH |
| Horrake, Jonathan | Harris, Malinda | 23, Oct. 1833 | RCH |
| Horrocks, John | Gardner, Harriet | 12, May 1836 | RCH |
| Horrocks, John F. | Fagley, Harriet | 17, Aug. 1843 | RCH |
| Horsely, William | Ehler, Mary | 24, Dec. 1833 | RCH |
| Horst, Heinrich | Wolfard, Kunigunda | 8, Oct. 1839 | FF |
| Horstmann, Herman | Detmar, A.M. | 5, July 1846 | AA |
| Horstmann, J. Heinr. | Detmer, A Margaretha | 29, June 1848 | FF |

| Grooms<br>***** | Brides<br>***** | Date of Marriage<br>**** ** ******** | Code<br>**** |
|---|---|---|---|
| Horstmann, John B. | Froelinger, Sophia | 23, Oct. 1844 | BB |
| Horstmann, Nicolaus | Bruns, Charlotte | 22, Nov. 1849 | AA |
| Horther, Jacob | Herzog, Margaret | 27, Dec. 1846 | RCH |
| Horton, George | Roll, Mary Ellen | 24, Mar. 1846 | RCH |
| Horton, Gilbert | Shattuck, Sarah | 4, Jan. 1848 | RCH |
| Horton, Henry H. | McRoberts, Lucetta | 20, Nov. 1845 | RCH |
| Horton, John | Hill, Jane | 6, Jan. 1836 | RCH |
| Horton, Louis | Barker, Almira | 12, Oct. 1837 | RCH |
| Horton, Nicolaus | Smith, Elisabeth A. | 10, June 1846 | RCH |
| Horton, Samuel | Amos, Emeline | 31, Aug. 1845 | RCH |
| Hosbrock, Daniel | Hinkel, Mary Ellen | 28, Feb. 1848 | RCH |
| Hosbrook, Harvey | Robinson, Miriam | 8, June 1841 | RCH |
| Hosbrook, Percy | Duval, Phebe | 4, June 1836 | RCH |
| Hosdings, James | Higgins, Margaret A. | 19, June 1834 | RCH |
| Hoseier, Isaac | Winton, Jane M. | 10, Oct. 1843 | RCH |
| Hoskin, Henry | Mitchell, Mary Ann | 26, Nov. 1849 | RCH |
| Hoskins, William | Cooley, Nancy | 10, Mar. 1844 | RCH |
| Hosper, Gerhard | Post, Maria Anna | 20, Oct. 1835 | FF |
| Hosquiter, Gonst | Fost, H. Ann | 20, Oct. 1835 | RCH |
| Hoss---, Henry | Swartz, Charlotte | 23, Jan. 1824 | RCH |
| Hostmeier, Rudolph | Starker, Louise | 5, Mar. 1846 | C |
| Hotchkiss, August | ----, ---- | 28, Feb. 1824 | RCH |
| Hotchkiss, William J | Loomis, Sarah A. | 24, Dec. 1832 | RCH |
| Hough, Henry | Waltemeier, Elisabet | 7, Jan. 1843 | RCH |
| Hough, Thomas | Ranney, Mary | 14, Oct. 1843 | RCH |
| Houghton, Thomas | Jackson, Prudence | 4, May 1820 | RCH |
| Houilbon, Dominick | Hauck, Barbara | 21, Sept 1844 | RCH |
| House, Edwin | Fottrell, Mary | 19, May 1844 | RCH |
| House, Erwin | Davis, Margaret | 30, Aug. 1848 | RCH |
| House, William | Horitan, Susan | 15, Apr. 1819 | RCH |
| Houshold, George | Williams, Sarah | 2, May 1833 | RCH |
| Houss, John | Brue, Mary | 30, Oct. 1839 | RCH |
| Houston, James S. | Long, Nancy | 5, Jan. 1837 | RCH |
| Houston, William | Smith, Sarah | 14, Dec. 1837 | RCH |
| Houston, William | Brown, Ellen | 31, July 1838 | RCH |
| Houts, Benjamin | Miller, Catharine | 9, Jan. 1823 | RCH |
| Houts, Jacob | Case, Elisabeth | 12, Mar. 1849 | RCH |
| Hovekamp, Joseph | Bennike, Maria Anna | 7, Feb. 1843 | AA |
| Hovey, James | Morrow, Ursula | 30, June 1844 | RCH |
| How, John | Morris, Louise | 25, Sept 1835 | RCH |
| How, Johnson | Bowram, Elizabeth | 26, Oct. 1847 | RCH |
| How, Nathan A. | Abell, Elisabeth | 31, Jan. 1827 | RCH |
| How---, George | McCleary, Mary | 25, Sept 1834 | RCH |
| Howard, Abner | Green, Hannah | 24, Mar. 1836 | RCH |
| Howard, Charles P. | Noble, Nancy A. | 15, Sept 1835 | RCH |
| Howard, Ezekiel | Jones, Jane | 16, June 1844 | RCH |
| Howard, Fielding | Peoss, Levisa | 26, Feb. 1841 | RCH |
| Howard, George | Whitten, M. Augusta | 27, May 1848 | RCH |
| Howard, Hiram | Harrison, Isabella | 27, Apr. 1843 | RCH |
| Howard, James | Irwin, Mary M. | 6, May 1842 | RCH |
| Howard, James | Padget, Elisabeth | 9, Apr. 1844 | RCH |
| Howard, John | ----, ---- | 16, Apr. 1835 | RCH |
| Howard, John | Lowry, Ann E. | 5, Apr. 1841 | I |
| Howard, Nicolaus | Hart, Newretta | 19, Oct. 1841 | RCH |
| Howard, Philipp | Wikoff, Sarah | 1, June 1843 | RCH |
| Howard, Richard | Pepin, Josephine D. | 26, May 1843 | RCH |
| Howard, Samuel | Balton, Sarah | 30, Nov. 1824 | RCH |
| Howard, Washington | Isgrigg, Elisabeth | 12, Sept 1833 | RCH |
| Howard, William | Morris, Mary | 22, Oct. 1837 | RCH |
| Howarth, James | Leadbeater, Sarah | 22, Sept 1834 | RCH |
| Howarth, James | Jackson, Ruth | 24, June 1847 | RCH |
| Howarth, John | Smith, Catharine | 13, Oct. 1822 | RCH |
| Howe, Ernst | Berkmann, Elisabeth | 4, Dec. 1844 | RCH |
| Howe, H. Tracy | Coolidge, Sarah T. | 21, Sept 1835 | D |
| Howe, Jacob | Alley, Susan | 10, Oct. 1841 | RCH |
| Howe, Joseph | Marsh, Fanny Elis. | 9, Apr. 1843 | RCH |
| Howe, Silas | Webb, Nancy | 29, Aug. 1838 | RCH |
| Howell, Alfred | Kidwell, Verlinda | 10, Apr. 1844 | RCH |
| Howell, David | Phillips, Sarah | 11, Nov. 1848 | RCH |
| Howell, David | Bear, Mary | 2, Apr. 1849 | RCH |
| Howell, George | Fenton, Josephine | 13, Aug. 1842 | RCH |

| Grooms<br>****** | Brides<br>****** | Date of Marriage<br>**** ** ******** | Code<br>**** |
|---|---|---|---|
| Howell, Hazel | Hall, Huldah | 2, Nov. 1847 | RCH |
| Howell, Herman | Bottom, Elisabeth | 11, Feb. 1847 | RCH |
| Howell, Hezekiah | Virgin, Sarah | 20, Oct. 1823 | RCH |
| Howell, John B. | Crist, Mary C. | 19, June 1833 | RCH |
| Howell, Lewis | Salathiel, Mary Jane | 21, Oct. 1846 | RCH |
| Howell, Seely P. | Dunn, Margaret | 13, Apr. 1841 | RCH |
| Howes, James M. | Betts, Mary | 31, Oct. 1841 | RCH |
| Howley, Thomas | Barrett, Margaret | 17, Jan. 1844 | BB |
| Hoy, David | Cook, Maria | 4, Apr. 1846 | RCH |
| Hoy, John | Clarke, Ladonia | 28, Mar. 1847 | RCH |
| Hoys, Robert | Budd, Huldah | 18, June 1818 | RCH |
| Hreile, Anton | Mueller, Maria Eva | 15, Aug. 1839 | FF |
| Hubart, Phineas | Johnson, Lydia | 13, Oct. 1836 | RCH |
| Hubbard, Dawson | Tartershell, Lucy | 3, May 1832 | RCH |
| Hubbard, Enoch V. | Miller, Elisabeth | 12, Sept 1833 | RCH |
| Hubbard, Milton S. | Siebentholb, Elis. | 31, Dec. 1831 | RCH |
| Hubbell, Ephraim | Carnahan, Mary S. | 12, Nov. 1848 | RCH |
| Hubbell, Nathaniel S | McChesney, Elisabeth | 6, Aug. 1818 | RCH |
| Hubbell, Thomas B. | Benson, Elisabeth A. | 26, Dec. 1844 | RCH |
| Hubbell, William M. | Campbell, Rebecca | 11, Jan. 1843 | RCH |
| Hube, Herman | Precht, Margaretha | 3, Aug. 1848 | F |
| Huber, Carl | Bittenbring, Wilhel. | 18, Dec. 1849 | G |
| Huber, Friedrich | Oswald, Elisabeth | 18, Oct. 1842 | RCH |
| Huber, Jacob | Littinney, Adeline | 9, Jan. 1848 | I |
| Huber, Johan | Meyer, Catharine | 27, Feb. 1838 | FF |
| Huber, Johan Nep. | Jerger, Aloysia | 26, July 1842 | FF |
| Huber, Joseph | McCabe, Mary | 25, Mar. 1849 | BB |
| Huber, Joseph | McCabe, Mary | 25, Mar. 1849 | BB |
| Huber, Joseph | Geisler, Josephina | 15, Feb. 1848 | FF |
| Huber, Joseph W. | Stertenkamp, Elis. | 7, Jan. 1845 | RCH |
| Huber, Peter | ----, Anna | 28, May 1849 | RCH |
| Huber, Philipp | Grans, Maria Anna | 3, Nov. 1847 | RCH |
| Huber, Thomas | Meister, Catharina | 2, May 1836 | FF |
| Huber, Xavier | Danheimer, Louisa | 10, Apr. 1837 | FF |
| Hubert, Heinrich | Leopold, Friedricka | 22, Nov. 1848 | F |
| Hubert, Johan Georg | Thompson, Catharine | 14, Feb. 1847 | G |
| Hubert, William | Ponder, Ann | 7, June 1827 | RCH |
| Hubing, Anton | Schapker, Catharine | 14, Oct. 1845 | FF |
| Huck, Charles | Doelo, Hannah | 11, Dec. 1834 | RCH |
| Huck, Georg M. | Sebach, Elisabeth | 29, Nov. 1849 | B |
| Huckemeyer, Heinrich | Busch, Ernestine | 28, Nov. 1848 | B |
| Hudard, William | Higby, Caroline | 30, Mar. 1841 | RCH |
| Huddleston, William | Robinson, Margaret | 14, Oct. 1817 | RCH |
| Hudepohl, J Heinrich | Flaspohler, Gertrud | 2, Aug. 1848 | FF |
| Hudepohl, Ludwig | Macke, Agnes | 11, Nov. 1841 | FF |
| Hudepohl, Ludwig | Knieremmer, Maria | 27, Nov. 1849 | AA |
| Hudnut, More | Wonnan, Sarah | 10, Aug. 1844 | RCH |
| Hudon, Samuel | Mann, Sarah | 4, Mar. 1837 | RCH |
| Hudson, Elijah D. | Miller, Keziah | 28, Nov. 1841 | RCH |
| Hudson, Guy | Goodwin, Mary M. | 1, Aug. 1824 | RCH |
| Hudson, James | ----, Mary Jane | 2, May 1836 | RCH |
| Hudson, James | Eberle, Mary | 16, Oct. 1848 | RCH |
| Hudson, John W. | Dales, Mary Ann | 23, Aug. 1832 | RCH |
| Hudson, Matthew T. | Bute, Rebecca | 23, Oct. 1835 | RCH |
| Hudson, Nathaniel | Hockins, Maria | 9, Sept 1847 | RCH |
| Hudson, Stanton | Burks, Irena | 28, July 1846 | RCH |
| Huebner, August | Buchheid, Margaretha | 28, May 1843 | G |
| Hueg, Nicolaus | Schmidt, Louise | 27, Nov. 1849 | EE |
| Huege, Ernst Wilhelm | Finkler, Catharina | 7, Dec. 1848 | A |
| Huelke, Joseph | Kaspar, Margaretha | 31, Jan. 1847 | AA |
| Huelker, Dietrich | Herbermann, Catharin | 2, May 1843 | AA |
| Huellmann, Heinrich | VonderHeide, Elis. | 18, Apr. 1847 | AA |
| Huels, Heinrich | Kemper, Theresa | 14, Feb. 1843 | FF |
| Huelshof, Johan Geo. | Brenemann, Catharine | 14, Jan. 1840 | FF |
| Huelsing, Johan G. | Muellering, Anna M. | 19, Aug. 1849 | CC |
| Huelsmann, Bernard | Hungkem, Catharine | 4, Feb. 1849 | II |
| Huelsmann, Conrad | Werner, M. Elisabeth | 7, Nov. 1847 | AA |
| Huelsmann, Heinrich | Tobe, Maria | 5, June 1845 | FF |
| Huelsmann, Johan H. | Nordloh, Helena | 2, May 1848 | AA |
| Huelsmann, Joseph | Grafen, Anna Elis. | 24, Jan. 1847 | EE |
| Huenemann, Johan | Manns, Maria | 19, Oct. 1843 | F |

| Grooms<br>****** | Brides<br>****** | Date of Marriage<br>**** ** ******** | Code<br>**** |
|---|---|---|---|
| Huenemeier, J. Hein. | Moffert, J. Amalia W | 19, Oct. 1849 | F |
| Huening, Heinrich | Dwent, Elisabeth | 11, Nov. 1849 | EE |
| Hues, Joseph | Pickens, Sarah | 19, Nov. 1833 | RCH |
| Hueser, Bernard | Vrocklage, Theresa | 31, Oct. 1847 | AA |
| Huesing, Bernard | Weitzel, M. Gertrud | 25, Jan. 1846 | FF |
| Huesmann, Francis | Meyer, Agnes | 22, Apr. 1845 | AA |
| Huesmann, Heinrich | Lamping, Catharina | 25, Sept 1849 | AA |
| Huesmann, Joseph | Hoedebeke, Elisabeth | 15, Nov. 1846 | FF |
| Huesmann, Ludwig | Schmidt, Maria | 11, June 1844 | FF |
| Huess, Johan | Groh, Anna Maria | 22, Oct. 1839 | FF |
| Hueston, Samuel | Long, Jane | 16, Feb. 1836 | RCH |
| Hueston, Samuel | Kruson, Margaretha | 26, Feb. 1847 | RCH |
| Huewe, Friedrich | Laumann, Carolina | 17, May 1849 | AA |
| Hufe, Johan Heinrich | Jimken, Metta Ann | 7, Dec. 1845 | F |
| Huff, Asa J. | Tague, Mary | 6, Feb. 1822 | RCH |
| Huff, Enos | Caster, Sarah | 21, Oct. 1832 | RCH |
| Huff, John | Peoples, Catharine | 29, Oct. 1837 | RCH |
| Huff, William | Burlew, Sarah | 16, Sept 1832 | RCH |
| Huffmann, Allen | Huffmann, Elisabeth | 1837 | RCH |
| Huffmann, Allen | Gillmann, Barbara | 7, Oct. 1847 | RCH |
| Huffmann, Herman H. | Peters, Christina | 15, Aug. 1845 | F |
| Huffmann, Jacob | Gardner, Mary | 4, Apr. 1846 | RCH |
| Hufnagel, George | Hanfbauer, Magdalena | 9, Aug. 1846 | RCH |
| Hufnagel, Lorenz | Vogel, Catharine | 23, Feb. 1848 | C |
| Hufts, John | Ehlers, Margaret | 9, Oct. 1845 | RCH |
| Hugh, David | Hurnes, Matilda | 9, Mar. 1834 | RCH |
| Hughes, David | Chambers, Mary | 31, Aug. 1844 | RCH |
| Hughes, Edward Jos. | Lewis, Elisabeth | 13, Sept 1845 | BB |
| Hughes, Frederick | Davis, Rebecca A. | 7, Nov. 1837 | RCH |
| Hughes, Henry | Burt, Sarah | 11, Sept 1817 | RCH |
| Hughes, Henry C. | Dairs, Elisabeth | 29, Mar. 1849 | RCH |
| Hughes, Israel | Stemitz, Ruth | 5, Aug. 1841 | RCH |
| Hughes, James | Stonemetz, Martha A. | 24, Aug. 1837 | RCH |
| Hughes, James | Morrow, Elizbeth | 25, June 1846 | RCH |
| Hughes, John | Glasgow, Lucinda | 24, Sept 1835 | RCH |
| Hughes, John | Patmore, Elisabeth | 5, Sept 1838 | RCH |
| Hughes, John | Clark, Mary B. | 22, Feb. 1843 | RCH |
| Hughes, Leopold | Lewis, Mary | 10, Sept 1845 | BB |
| Hughes, Mathew | McGovern, Rose | 7, June 1849 | RCH |
| Hughes, Richard | Thomas, Ann | 4, Aug. 1848 | RCH |
| Hughes, Robert | Hammond, Sarah | 12, Mar. 1836 | RCH |
| Hughes, Rowland | Ridlin, Martha Ann | 13, Dec. 1849 | RCH |
| Hughes, Thomas | Maloney, Mary | 14, Nov. 1841 | RCH |
| Hughes, Thomas | Jones, Ann J. | 15, Nov. 1845 | RCH |
| Hughes, William | Davidson, Emily | 23, Sept 1839 | BB |
| Hughes, William A. | Bartley, Delilah | 13, Aug. 1848 | RCH |
| Hughs, Jonathan | Joyce, Margaret | 1, June 1846 | RCH |
| Hughs, Paul H. | Pirkins, Mathilda | 9, Nov. 1833 | RCH |
| Hugle, John | Terry, Mary | 13, Feb. 1842 | RCH |
| Hugo, Carl | Benten, Charlotte | 16, Dec. 1847 | C |
| Hugo, Henry | Schmidt, Margaret | 25, Aug. 1849 | G |
| Hugo, Herman Ludwig | Moeller, Charlotte W | 20, Feb. 1845 | F |
| Hukill, Richard | Pyle, Emily | 8, July 1844 | RCH |
| Hulbert, Thomas | Hadley, Paulina | 17, May 1839 | RCH |
| Hulbert, William | Wood, Amelia | 6, July 1837 | RCH |
| Hulick, Isaac | Niles, Ruth | 10, June 1827 | RCH |
| Hulings, Isaac | Lawrence, Mary | 29, Feb. 1824 | RCH |
| Hulings, Thomas | Eckwell, Christina | 27, Oct. 1848 | RCH |
| Hull, James | Cake, Martha E. | 10, Feb. 1842 | RCH |
| Hull, James | Turner, Ann | 10, Mar. 1846 | RCH |
| Hull, Thomas | Thompson, Flora | 21, Oct. 1847 | RCH |
| Hulle, Conrad | Stueve, Anna Maria E | 20, Oct. 1835 | FF |
| Huller, Adam | Reis, Anna Maria | 4, Feb. 1849 | EE |
| Hullermann, Bernard | Pasker, Gertrud | 30, Apr. 1849 | CC |
| Hullgath, Joseph | Goodall, Ann | 21, Mar. 1842 | RCH |
| Hulsmeyer, Bernard H | Becker, Gertrud | 28, June 1845 | AA |
| Hulzforster, George | Scheland, Caroline W | 28, Oct. 1847 | RCH |
| Hulzler, Albert | Geisler, Catharina | 3, May 1836 | FF |
| Humbert, Heinrich | Upsholter, Adelheid | 21, May 1844 | FF |
| Humbert, Herman H. | Brinker, Maria Anna | 21, Oct. 1849 | FF |
| Humbert, Johan Wm. | Niemann, Anna Maria | 31, Oct. 1847 | EE |

| Grooms<br>****** | Brides<br>****** | Date of Marriage<br>**** ** ******** | Code<br>**** |
|---|---|---|---|
| Humble, James | Barker, Jane | 17, June 1847 | RCH |
| Humble, John | Brodie, Ellen | 31, Jan. 1834 | RCH |
| Humble, John | Coats, Elisabeth | 13, June 1846 | RCH |
| Hume, Charles | McDonough, Adelia | 4, July 1844 | BB |
| Hume, Charles | Tilton, Mary | 3, Jan. 1846 | RCH |
| Hume, James H. | Dowd, Ann | 22, July 1838 | RCH |
| Hume, Thomas | Dowd, Ann | 22, July 1838 | RCH |
| Humel, Johan | Fehr, Elisabeth | 13, Feb. 1838 | FF |
| Humes, Thomas | Brown, Elisabeth | 27, Nov. 1832 | RCH |
| Humhagen, Andreas | Elsen, Louise | 1, Oct. 1848 | C |
| Hummel, David | Deystein, Dorothea | 6, Nov. 1848 | C |
| Hummel, Ferdinand | Ganter, Elisabeth | 12, Nov. 1848 | C |
| Hummel, Jacob | Niemert, Elisabeth | 29, Aug. 1836 | FF |
| Hummer, Jacob | Liedel, Maria Anna | 11, June 1848 | FF |
| Humphrey, Edwin | Humphrey, Phebe | 11, Apr. 1846 | RCH |
| Humphrey, Henry W. | Menegh, Sidney | 3, Dec. 1847 | RCH |
| Humphrey, Hugh | Lovell, Elisabeth | 30, May 1843 | RCH |
| Humphrey, Samuel | Reed, Elisabeth | 3, May 1837 | RCH |
| Humphrey, Samuel | Banks, Susan | 31, May 1849 | RCH |
| Humphrey, Thomas | Galvin, Esther | 15, Apr. 1844 | BB |
| Humphreys, Guy | Brown, Rachel | 12, Oct. 1847 | RCH |
| Humphreys, Joseph | Pendery, Martha | 13, Mar. 1833 | RCH |
| Humphries, Guy W. | Holmes, Susan | 16, Mar. 1843 | RCH |
| Humphries, William | Golden, Susan | 14, July 1833 | RCH |
| Hunber, George | Woo--, Martha | 4, Oct. 1832 | RCH |
| Hund, Silver | Orth, Elisabeth | 4, July 1848 | EE |
| Hund, Xavier | Kramer, Maria | 4, June 1844 | AA |
| Hune, Johan Joseph | Westemeyer, Anna M. | 13, Apr. 1847 | AA |
| Hunefelt, Johan | Teulker, Catharine | 3, Feb. 1849 | F |
| Hunemann, Bernard | Kolbert, Maria | 7, Feb. 1849 | F |
| Hungeling, Johan | Kuhne, Anna Margaret | 24, Sept 1844 | AA |
| Hungerford, Richard | Joyce, Adelheid | 28, Jan. 1847 | RCH |
| Hungler, Andrew | Harcourt, Julia | 3, Dec. 1848 | RCH |
| Hunkamp, Francis Jos | Busch, Catharina E. | 7, Jan. 1836 | FF |
| Hunley, Harrison | Thomas, Sarah | 15, Aug. 1844 | RCH |
| Hunn, Michael | Stehr, Flangina | 29, Apr. 1844 | FF |
| Hunsaker, George | Coddington, Emeline | 8, Sept 1844 | RCH |
| Hunster, Thomas | Smith, Laura | 20, Dec. 1843 | RCH |
| Hunt, Aaron | Tullis, Mary Jane | 21, Jan. 1849 | RCH |
| Hunt, Albert | Stewart, Martha | 19, Dec. 1846 | RCH |
| Hunt, Alfred | Delap, Rebecca | 18, Nov. 1834 | RCH |
| Hunt, Alonzo | Manifold, Elisabeth | 9, Aug. 1842 | RCH |
| Hunt, Edward | Stump, Catharine L. | 12, Nov. 1848 | RCH |
| Hunt, George | Littel, Caroline | 31, Dec. 1846 | RCH |
| Hunt, Isaac | Pittman, Jane | 1835 | RCH |
| Hunt, James | VanZant, Drucilla | 10, Nov. 1844 | RCH |
| Hunt, James C. | Ellsworth, Anna | Nov. 1844 | RCH |
| Hunt, James G. | Palmer, Sarah E. | 2, Sept 1849 | RCH |
| Hunt, John H. | Green, Elisabeth | 6, Sept 1832 | RCH |
| Hunt, John T. | Miller, Rebecca | 12, Mar. 1839 | RCH |
| Hunt, Joshua | Mahbai--, Mary | 14, Aug. 1819 | RCH |
| Hunt, Lewis | Gardner, Mary B. | 8, Aug. 1830 | RCH |
| Hunt, M. | Runyan, Rebecca | 10, June 1821 | RCH |
| Hunt, Matthew | Schevene, Anna | 20, Apr. 1848 | RCH |
| Hunt, Peter | Guthrey, Mary | 25, Nov. 1837 | RCH |
| Hunt, Thomas | Murphy, Mary Ann | 13, Apr. 1826 | RCH |
| Hunt, Thomas | Eperson, Elisabeth | 28, Dec. 1833 | RCH |
| Hunt, Thomas | Brown, Jane | 8, Aug. 1848 | RCH |
| Hunt, William | Harvey, Jerusha | 28, Jan. 1839 | RCH |
| Hunt, William | Logan, Rebecca | 12, Aug. 1847 | RCH |
| Hunt, William | Burdorf, Catharine | 13, Apr. 1849 | E |
| Huntemann, Heinrich | Friedelage, Anna | 9, June 1842 | F |
| Hunter, | Vanueter, Polly | 28, Oct. 1819 | RCH |
| Hunter, | Bailey, (Mrs) | 17, May 1824 | I |
| Hunter, Abraham | Brown, Nancy | 16, Apr. 1843 | RCH |
| Hunter, Alexander | Campbell, Catharine | 20, Apr. 1846 | RCH |
| Hunter, Cortice | White, Almina | 17, Oct. 1837 | RCH |
| Hunter, David P. | Steward, Sarah | 7, June 1824 | RCH |
| Hunter, Edmund | Bell, Margaret | 27, June 1838 | RCH |
| Hunter, Edward | Hargraves, Sarah | 9, June 1842 | RCH |
| Hunter, Enos C. | Halstead, Abiah | 17, Dec. 1818 | RCH |

| Grooms<br>***** | Brides<br>***** | Date of Marriage<br>**** ** ******** | Code<br>**** |
|---|---|---|---|
| Hunter, James G. | Osborn, Elisabeth J. | 16, Oct. 1832 | RCH |
| Hunter, John | Riggles, Mary | 7, Sept 1826 | RCH |
| Hunter, John | Day, Polly Ward | 12, Apr. 1843 | RCH |
| Hunter, Joseph | Wiley, Ann | 20, June 1844 | RCH |
| Hunter, Louis | Wilkins, Rebecca | 16, Mar. 1843 | RCH |
| Hunter, Moses H. | Hammon, Catharine | 16, Feb. 1843 | I |
| Hunter, Ralph | Musser, Mary Jane | 22, Nov. 1846 | RCH |
| Hunter, Robert | Mathers, Mary Jane | 28, Nov. 1849 | RCH |
| Hunter, William | Bailey, Martha | 17, Feb. 1824 | RCH |
| Hunter, William | Lilly, Mary A. | 1, Feb. 1838 | RCH |
| Hunter, William | Harvey, Elisabeth | 17, Feb. 1842 | RCH |
| Hunter, William | Wright, Sophia | 16, Apr. 1846 | RCH |
| Hunting, Richard | Odell, Susan | 24, Oct. 1837 | RCH |
| Huntington, Henry D. | Johnston, Sarah H. | 12, May 1846 | D |
| Huntington, John | Canfield, Jeanette H | 30, Sept 1845 | D |
| Huntington, Thomas | Williamson, Frances | 5, Dec. 1848 | RCH |
| Huntley, Charles W. | Huncherly, Elisabeth | 20, Mar. 1835 | RCH |
| Hurd, Leander | Nicolaus, Mary Elis. | 24, Aug. 1845 | RCH |
| Hurd, Theodore | Maheu, Juliana | 16, Feb. 1837 | RCH |
| Hurlaender, Eberhard | Henkemer, Catharina | 23, Oct. 1849 | C |
| Hurlaender, Friedric | Henkaus, Bernardina | 6, Nov. 1849 | C |
| Hurlbut, Thomas | Tweedy, Jane | 27, Mar. 1848 | RCH |
| Hurley, Dennis | Berry, Ann | 30, Dec. 1849 | BB |
| Hurley, Thomas | Prout, Margaret | 26, Aug. 1849 | GG |
| Hurley, Thomas | McNally, Ann | 19, Dec. 1849 | GG |
| Hurly, Dennis | Kain, Catharine | Aug. 1849 | RCH |
| Hurming, Heinrich W. | Kabbel, Louise Marg. | 12, Apr. 1849 | B |
| Hursch, August F. | Denman, Louisa | 28, Apr. 1836 | RCH |
| Hurst, Friedrich | Kissel, Margaret | 19, Dec. 1846 | RCH |
| Hurst, Rochus | Hartmann, Maria Anna | 27, July 1847 | AA |
| Hurst, Thomas | Gildersleve, Phebe | 28, Feb. 1836 | RCH |
| Hurst, Thomas | Meyer, Maria | 30, May 1847 | G |
| Hurstmann, Herman | Tepe, Bernardina | 27, June 1848 | AA |
| Hurston, Parul | Philips, Esther | 15, Jan. 1822 | RCH |
| Hurt, Francis | Smith, Lucina | 26, Nov. 1848 | RCH |
| Huschard, Georg | Lang, Margaretha | 23, Nov. 1841 | FF |
| Huseker, Heinrich | Hornemann, Jaen | 27, Jan. 1848 | B |
| Huser, Herman | Schroeder, M. Louise | 20, Feb. 1848 | FF |
| Huser, Philipp | Knopf, Felicitas | 29, Sept 1840 | FF |
| Husmann, Andreas | Wiemueller, Anna M. | 11, Apr. 1847 | EE |
| Husmann, Heinrich | Japper, Bernardina | 25, July 1847 | AA |
| Hussey, Patrick | Quinn, Jane | 27, Mar. 1848 | BB |
| Hussey, Thomas | Padlock, Phoebe | 8, June 1820 | RCH |
| Hussing, Clemens | Holbrook, Catharine | 26, Sept 1847 | FF |
| Hussmann, Heinrich | Recker, Maria Lucia | 29, Aug. 1847 | EE |
| Hust, Anton | Wuerz, Maria | 6, May 1849 | EE |
| Hust, Heinrich | Reinhart, Barbara | 4, Sept 1845 | C |
| Hust, Jacob | Haar, Margaret | 14, Nov. 1844 | C |
| Hust, Valentin | Schneider, Caroline | 25, Apr. 1844 | C |
| Husted, Josiah | Haney, Elisabeth | 12, Jan. 1834 | RCH |
| Husted, Samuel | Husted, Fanny | 16, Apr. 1842 | RCH |
| Huston, Harp | Bevis, Sarah | 3, Nov. 1842 | RCH |
| Huston, James | Logan, Elisa | 24, Jan. 1822 | RCH |
| Huston, James | Voorhees, Rebecca | 6, Aug. 1844 | RCH |
| Huston, John | McCombs, Letitia | 29, Jan. 1846 | RCH |
| Huston, Joseph M. | Covolt, Mary S. | 24, Dec. 1833 | RCH |
| Huston, Robert | Chambers, Margaret | 17, June 1824 | RCH |
| Huston, William | Gorman, Anna M. | 4, Feb. 1836 | RCH |
| Hutcheson, James | Humphreys, Elisabeth | 24, Nov. 1843 | RCH |
| Hutchins, Charles | Golden, Elvira | 14, June 1821 | RCH |
| Hutchinson, Amos | Shannon, Julia A. | 4, Jan. 1838 | RCH |
| Hutchinson, Asa | Rude, Susanna | 20, July 1816 | RCH |
| Hutchinson, Charles | Sampson, Frances | 12, Sept 1841 | RCH |
| Hutchinson, Francis | Honna, Ann | 14, Jan. 1837 | RCH |
| Hutchinson, Howell | Ferris, Mary | 23, May 1833 | RCH |
| Hutchinson, Joel | Dugan, Mary Ann | 21, June 1841 | RCH |
| Hutchinson, John | Humphreys, Charlotte | 26, July 1825 | RCH |
| Hutchinson, John | Dunham, Adeline | 14, Feb. 1847 | RCH |
| Hutchinson, Jonathan | Hopkins, Martha | 29, June 1836 | RCH |
| Hutchinson, Levi | Ruddish, Yownna | 25, Apr. 1833 | RCH |
| Hutchinson, Lewis | ----, Sophia | 14, June 1838 | RCH |

| Grooms | Brides | Date of Marriage | Code |
|--------|--------|------------------|------|
| Hutchinson, Lindsay | Nichols, Elisabeth | 4, Mar. 1846 | RCH |
| Hutchinson, Samuel | Hawkins, Sarah | 14, Apr. 1819 | RCH |
| Hutchinson, W.C. | Smith, Sarah M. | 8, Mar. 1825 | RCH |
| Hutchinson, William | Guard, Dorcas | 1, Apr. 1841 | RCH |
| Hutchison, Azariah | Chambers, Maria Anna | 28, Jan. 1846 | RCH |
| Hutchison, Samuel | Brown, Nancy | 21, Mar. 1822 | RCH |
| Huth, Jacob | Klein, Barbara | 3, Oct. 1847 | EE |
| Huth, John | Saal, Theresa | 14, Mar. 1849 | RCH |
| Hutle, Jacob | Brown, Catharine | 6, Jan. 1833 | RCH |
| Hutler, Herman | Kramers, Catharine | 27, Feb. 1838 | FF |
| Hutmacher, Friedrich | Lattimore, Margaret | 15, Feb. 1844 | C |
| Hutsenpiller, Hippus | Flowers, Elisabeth | 17, Oct. 1842 | RCH |
| Hutte, Henry | Wietholter, Catharin | 6, Oct. 1845 | RCH |
| Hutte, John | Karkemlein, Verona | 10, Sept 1849 | RCH |
| Huttenbauer, John | Morgan, Mary Ann | 30, July 1849 | RCH |
| Huttoce--, Abel | Duface, Letty | 5, Mar. 1818 | RCH |
| Hutton, John | Stapley, Ann | 2, July 1843 | RCH |
| Hutts, Francis | Gifford, Nancy | 28, Feb. 1822 | RCH |
| Hutzelmann, August | Henning, Kunigunda | 20, Sept 1845 | RCH |
| Hutzelmann, Michael | Diehl, Catharine | 25, Jan. 1848 | G |
| Hutzler, Carl | Geisler, Kunigunda | 11, Apr. 1837 | FF |
| Hutzler, Carl | Forster, Magdalena | 28, Oct. 1845 | FF |
| Huvert, Herman | Kramer, Catharine | 8, Feb. 1849 | II |
| Hyams, Isaac | Lazarus, Elisabeth | 11, Aug. 1849 | RCH |
| Hyams, Nathan | Fetchwinger, Frances | 19, Dec. 1846 | RCH |
| Hyath, John | Moore, Hannah | 13, Dec. 1832 | RCH |
| Hyatt, Cornelius | Taylor, Elisabeth | 24, Feb. 1846 | RCH |
| Hyatt, Elisha | Grounds, Catharine | 25, Jan. 1849 | RCH |
| Hyatt, Fredding B. | Glascoe, Elisabeth | 25, Mar. 1834 | RCH |
| Hyatt, James | Thurston, Elisabeth | 9, Aug. 1848 | RCH |
| Hyatt, John H. | Bottes, Leodocia | 3, Dec. 1840 | RCH |
| Hyatt, Joshua | Howell, Phebe | 29, July 1844 | RCH |
| Hyatt, Mesbuck | Crane, Marvilla | 12, Sept 1833 | RCH |
| Hyatt, Milton | Woodward, Abigail | 6, Dec. 1845 | RCH |
| Hyatt, Thomas | Decker, Sarah | 12, Oct. 1843 | RCH |
| Hyatt, William | Wilder, Harriet | 4, Dec. 1836 | RCH |
| Hyland, John | Kearney, Catharine | 29, Nov. 1849 | BB |
| Hyman, Charles | Simon, Hannah | 17, Oct. 1846 | RCH |
| Hyne, David | Andrews, Emma | 8, Dec. 1849 | RCH |
| Hynes, Thomas | Rafferty, Bridget | 20, Dec. 1849 | RCH |
| Hyter, John | Looker, Louise | 7, Feb. 1844 | RCH |
| | | | |
| Icent, John | Gibson, Lucretia | 15, Dec. 1841 | RCH |
| Ickelsauer, Georg F. | Turkin, Anna Maria | 16, Aug. 1846 | RCH |
| Idoux, Francis Jos. | Marischen, Carolina | 6, July 1846 | AA |
| Idoux, Francis Jos. | Frischolz, Maria | 7, Jan. 1847 | FF |
| Igel, George | Ochs, Anna | 18, Sept 1846 | RCH |
| Igrigg, Daniel | Underwood, Mary | 6, Dec. 1841 | RCH |
| Ihlbrock, Dietrich | Eilermann, Margaret | 7, Nov. 1844 | F |
| Ihlbrock, Dietrich H | Kemper, Maria | 28, Dec. 1847 | F |
| Ihle, Michael | Bakehaus, Anna | 24, Mar. 1846 | RCH |
| Iliff, Samuel | Robeson, Catharine | 20, Oct. 1819 | RCH |
| Iliff, Thomas | Tosana, Josephine | 16, Apr. 1844 | RCH |
| Illig, Martin | Lentz, Eva Maria | 6, Jan. 1845 | FF |
| Ilsby, Washington | Call, Mary Ann | 4, Mar. 1842 | RCH |
| Ilwett, John B. | Ferris, Mary | 21, June 1834 | RCH |
| Imbusch, Bernard H. | Scheiper, Anna Cath. | 2, May 1847 | AA |
| Ime---, John | Lawrence, Ann B. | 27, June 1821 | RCH |
| Imegart, Johan | Eisberg, Louise | 22, Oct. 1846 | F |
| Imel, Leonard | Wert, Elisabeth | 10, Aug. 1847 | C |
| Imhof, Martin | Scherer, Magdalena | 14, Jan. 1849 | AA |
| Imhoff, John | Wygatt, Sarah | 31, Mar. 1833 | RCH |
| Imhoff, Joseph | Uhlenbrock, Maria | 17, July 1847 | CC |
| Imholte, Johan | Schroten, Maria Elis | 2, May 1848 | FF |
| Imholtz, Heinrich | Russe, Anna E. | 17, Sept 1842 | F |
| Immegart, Friedrich | Hutchinson, Sarah | 12, Oct. 1848 | RCH |
| Immel, Jacob | Johnson, Elisabeth | 24, Dec. 1844 | RCH |
| Immenhart, Heinrich | Funk, Friedricka | 20, Jan. 1848 | F |
| Immig, B. Herman | Theising, A. Cath. | 12, Nov. 1848 | II |
| Immil, Joseph | Lowe, Mary | 14, Oct. 1841 | RCH |
| Imorde, Heinrich | Nieters, M. Adelheid | 13, Feb. 1848 | FF |

| Grooms | Brides | Date of Marriage | Code |
|--------|--------|------------------|------|
| ****** | ****** | **** ** ******** | **** |
| Imsicke, Bernard | Raitler, Josephina | 7, Mar. 1848 | AA |
| Imsicke, Joseph | Enneking, Anna Maria | 7, Jan. 1845 | AA |
| Imwalde, Herman | Markes, Maria | 4, Oct. 1848 | II |
| Imwolle, Johan Hein. | Koesters, M. Elis. | 30, July 1839 | FF |
| Inderrieden, Anton | Decker, Maria Agnes | 10, Jan. 1843 | AA |
| Inderrieden, Francis | Rabe, Anna M. | 28, Aug. 1838 | FF |
| Inderrieden, Johan H | Wehmhof, Elisabeth | 1, Aug. 1847 | FF |
| Inderstrodt, Ernst H | Albers, Charlotte W. | 13, July 1843 | F |
| Inderstrodt, Heinric | Schmidt, Louise | 10, Feb. 1848 | F |
| Inderstroth, Friedr. | Hasberger, Anna M. | 16, Sept 1847 | F |
| Ingalls, Abraham | Mitchell, Elisabeth | 5, Dec. 1844 | RCH |
| Ingels, Chester | Bishop, Ada | 8, Feb. 1819 | RCH |
| Inger---, Owen | James, Lucinda | 8, Sept 1836 | RCH |
| Ingersall, Arthur | Skinner, Julia Ann | 26, Aug. 1834 | RCH |
| Ingersoll, Henry | Wile, Lucretia | 13, Mar. 1821 | RCH |
| Ingersoll, James | Hughes, Martha Ann | 18, June 1842 | RCH |
| Ingersoll, James | Tucket, Elisabeth | 9, Sept 1844 | RCH |
| Ingersoll, Nathan | Dene, Margaret | 2, Aug. 1824 | RCH |
| Ingersoll, Van | Hancock, Elmira | 23, Feb. 1833 | RCH |
| Ingle, Henry B. | E---, Mary | 25, June 1841 | RCH |
| Inglehard, Nicolaus | Gano, Frances Mary | 18, July 1837 | RCH |
| Ingram, Edward | Ingram, Ivy | 11, Oct. 1845 | RCH |
| Ingram, Peter | Boswel, Elsy | 13, Oct. 1833 | RCH |
| Inkamp, Philipp | Petters, Cath. (Mrs) | 13, Feb. 1838 | FF |
| Inkrot, Bernard | Valding, Maria | 4, Nov. 1845 | AA |
| Inloes, Edward J. | Duvall, Elizabeth J. | 5, Nov. 1846 | RCH |
| Innes, Robert | Williams, Laura J. | 30, Dec. 1849 | RCH |
| Innes, William | Locke, Mary | 13, May 1846 | RCH |
| Inness, James | Lewis, Sarah | 29, Jan. 1846 | RCH |
| Innis, David | Hand, Harriet | 3, May 1847 | RCH |
| Intertwart, Ernst | Consood, Margaret | May 1839 | RCH |
| Ireland, | Sampson, Mary H. | 19, Jan. 1825 | RCH |
| Ireland, Alexander | Isgrigg, Martha | 22, Nov. 1846 | RCH |
| Ireland, George | VanBlonk, Sarah | 30, Nov. 1833 | RCH |
| Ireland, Isaac | Fisk, Mary | 28, Dec. 1821 | RCH |
| Ireland, Isaac | Petty, Louise | 7, May 1836 | RCH |
| Ireland, Jonathan | Coulter, Elisabeth | 2, June 1836 | RCH |
| Ireland, Joseph | Blackway, Elisabeth | 10, Feb. 1848 | RCH |
| Ireland, Robert | Morgan, Sophia E. | 20, May 1837 | RCH |
| Ireland, William | Peckinpaugh, Elis. | 17, Apr. 1849 | RCH |
| Irey, Otto | Gardner, Harriet | 14, Nov. 1845 | RCH |
| Irion, Thomas | Jacobi, Barbara | 15, May 1849 | G |
| Irons, James | Whetstone, Catharine | 6, June 1844 | RCH |
| Irvin, | Tucker, Emeline | 7, Nov. 1837 | RCH |
| Irvin, James | McCormick, Margaret | 5, Nov. 1837 | RCH |
| Irvin, Joseph | Bouser, Sarah | 14, July 1833 | RCH |
| Irvin, Thomas | Pomroy, Mary R. | 19, Dec. 1835 | RCH |
| Irving, George | Krewson, Mary | 25, Dec. 1841 | D |
| Irwin, Alexander | Irwin, Sarah | 10, Mar. 1818 | RCH |
| Irwin, Alexander | Reilly, Catharine | 12, Dec. 1846 | GG |
| Irwin, Benjamin J. | Harleton, Charity | 1, Nov. 1835 | RCH |
| Irwin, James | Meehan, Nanely | 7, Sept 1837 | RCH |
| Irwin, James | McAffee, Elisabeth | 3, Apr. 1838 | RCH |
| Irwin, James F. | Sassing, Lydia | 20, Mar. 1833 | I |
| Irwin, John | Shipman, Hannah | 17, Aug. 1839 | RCH |
| Irwin, Thomas | Pryall, Ann | 9, Jan. 1848 | BB |
| Irwin, William F. | Whiteman, Harriet | 12, Oct. 1848 | RCH |
| Isaacs, Abraham | Levi, Frances | 28, Oct. 1845 | RCH |
| Isbell, Thomas | Howlett, Lucy | 24, Oct. 1845 | RCH |
| Isdell, Robert | Ramsay, Sarah | 31, Oct. 1837 | RCH |
| Iseler, David | Baker, Margaret | 14, May 1838 | RCH |
| Isensee, John | Albert, Babette | 7, Apr. 1847 | RCH |
| Isgrig, Henry | Stoughton, Harriet | 7, Jan. 1838 | RCH |
| Isgrigg, Eli | Winings, Christina | 13, Nov. 1836 | RCH |
| Isgrigg, Henry | Acceinstead, Hester | 12, Aug. 1841 | RCH |
| Isgrigg, James | Noble, Julia | 19, Apr. 1849 | RCH |
| Isgrigg, Michael | Waggoner, Catharine | 29, Mar. 1836 | RCH |
| Ismeurt, Louis | Miller, Justina | 10, Sept 1848 | GG |
| Israels, Isaac | McClellan, Hester | 7, Mar. 1833 | RCH |
| Ivory, Bartlet | Stur, Sarah | 21, Jan. 1847 | RCH |
| Izzard, William S. | Moore, Mary | 17, Nov. 1834 | RCH |

| Grooms<br>****** | Brides<br>****** | Date of Marriage<br>**** ** ******** | Code<br>**** |
|---|---|---|---|
| Jack, James | Mahoney, Mary | 30, June 1835 | RCH |
| Jackson, | Tebbs, Nancy | 2, Aug. 1838 | RCH |
| Jackson, | Parrish, Martha | 7, Aug. 1849 | RCH |
| Jackson, Ander. | Sword, Elisabeth | 30, June 1836 | RCH |
| Jackson, Andrew | Bavis, Margaret | 15, Feb. 1842 | RCH |
| Jackson, Ansen W. | Clark, Elisabeth | 20, Nov. 1821 | RCH |
| Jackson, Benjamin | Black, Fanny | 8, Apr. 1824 | RCH |
| Jackson, Charles | ----, ---- | 8, June 1819 | RCH |
| Jackson, Charles | Joycelin, Mary H. | 16, May 1822 | RCH |
| Jackson, David | Jones, Sarah | 23, Mar. 1837 | RCH |
| Jackson, Edmund | Frainly, Rosanna | 1, Feb. 1834 | RCH |
| Jackson, George A. | Morris, Juliana | 27, Mar. 1821 | RCH |
| Jackson, George A. | Hiersted, Mary A. | 9, Oct. 1832 | I |
| Jackson, Hamilton | Anderson, Sarah A. | 16, Aug. 1838 | RCH |
| Jackson, Henry J. | Lovejoy, Ann | 23, Nov. 1825 | RCH |
| Jackson, Hugh | Collins, Mary | 22, Oct. 1849 | GG |
| Jackson, James | Tucker, Amy | 3, Apr. 1833 | RCH |
| Jackson, James | Pinehart, Sarah | 18, Apr. 1833 | RCH |
| Jackson, James | Miller, Sarah | 12, Dec. 1847 | RCH |
| Jackson, James | Mallanlee, Maria A. | 1, Mar. 1848 | RCH |
| Jackson, James | Lewis, Lucy | 20, Mar. 1848 | RCH |
| Jackson, James | Grant, Mary Jane | 26, Feb. 1849 | RCH |
| Jackson, James P. | Clarke, Helen | 3, June 1840 | BB |
| Jackson, John | Jouelin, Hannah M. | 28, Sept 1820 | RCH |
| Jackson, John | Lucas, Jane | 27, Feb. 1838 | RCH |
| Jackson, John | McFarlan, Sarah | 12, June 1844 | RCH |
| Jackson, John | McFarlan, Mary | 25, Mar. 1846 | RCH |
| Jackson, John | Bogart, Ellen | 9, Sept 1849 | RCH |
| Jackson, John | McGurin, Julia | 18, Sept 1849 | GG |
| Jackson, John R. | Makepeace, Elisabeth | 20, Apr. 1837 | RCH |
| Jackson, Joseph | Riddle, Nancy | 19, Aug. 1834 | RCH |
| Jackson, Richard | Carney, Elisabeth | 16, Jan. 1842 | RCH |
| Jackson, Richard | Brown, Isabella | 10, Oct. 1844 | RCH |
| Jackson, Robert | Crowder, Elisabeth | 14, May 1849 | RCH |
| Jackson, Thomas | Andrews, Catharine | 8, Aug. 1848 | RCH |
| Jackson, Thomas M. | Collins, Maria S. | 24, May 1821 | I |
| Jackson, William | Mead, Mary Ann | 6, June 1847 | RCH |
| Jacob, Christian | Haller, Mary Barbara | 22, Dec. 1845 | RCH |
| Jacob, Conrad | Oetzel, Elisabeth | 13, July 1846 | G |
| Jacob, Daniel | Scheiber, Barbara | 28, Aug. 1847 | C |
| Jacob, Johan | Brand, Maria Anna | 17, Oct. 1847 | AA |
| Jacob, John | Hart, Filena | 1, May 1842 | RCH |
| Jacob, John Peter | Weindel, Margaretha | 10, Dec. 1845 | RCH |
| Jacob, Martin | Seibel, Eva | 4, Feb. 1841 | FF |
| Jacob, Simon | Stein, Elisabeth | 7, Jan. 1840 | FF |
| Jacobi, Heinrich | Kabauf, Elisabeth | 28, Sept 1843 | RCH |
| Jacobs, Asa | Cooper, Lucy Ann | 3, Mar. 1844 | RCH |
| Jacobs, Jacob | Adams, Lucretia | 19, Mar. 1835 | RCH |
| Jacobs, James | Matthews, Leah | 14, Apr. 1846 | RCH |
| Jacobs, James | Gibbs, Mary F. | 19, Dec. 1847 | RCH |
| Jacobs, James M. | Borders, Elis. Ann | 23, May 1849 | RCH |
| Jacobs, Johan | Kessling, Elisabeth | 29, May 1838 | FF |
| Jacobs, Johan | Neil, Margaretha | 30, June 1848 | B |
| Jacobs, Ludwig | Stillwell, Emilia | 15, Feb. 1844 | C |
| Jacobs, Peter | Trier, Barbara | 7, Jan. 1845 | AA |
| Jacobs, Richard | McCain, Charlotte | 3, Oct. 1822 | RCH |
| Jacobs, Samuel H. | Hopkins, Lida K. | 3, July 1834 | RCH |
| Jacobs, William | Kilbourn, Electra | 8, Mar. 1820 | RCH |
| Jacobs, William | Parker, Elisabeth | 8, Sept 1842 | RCH |
| Jacobus, Th. Dwight | Mosier, Hannah F. | 18, June 1848 | D |
| Jaeger, Christian | Schatzmann, Margaret | 3, July 1849 | C |
| Jaeger, Conrad | Schmidt, Catharine | 23, May 1844 | C |
| Jaeger, Francis | Ripperger, Genofeva | 6, May 1845 | AA |
| Jaeger, Geo. Michael | Gephardt, Maria | 26, Nov. 1848 | C |
| Jaeger, Georg H. | Kiehl, Francisca | 22, Aug. 1847 | EE |
| Jaeger, George | Carr, Mary Ann | 16, Feb. 1842 | RCH |
| Jaeger, Heinrich | Stephan, Juliana | 30, Mar. 1835 | FF |
| Jaeger, Heinrich | Morbach, Barbara | 7, Jan. 1847 | AA |
| Jaeger, J. Christoph | Schnell, Maria Anna | 15, Jan. 1846 | G |
| Jaeger, Joseph | Scherer, Magdalena | 23, June 1840 | FF |

| Grooms<br>****** | Brides<br>****** | Date of Marriage<br>**** ** ******** | Code<br>**** |
|---|---|---|---|
| Jaeger, Joseph | Uhl, Sophia | 17, Oct. 1847 | FF |
| Jaeger, Michael | Uhl, Christina | 4, Jan. 1846 | AA |
| Jaeger, Stephan | Schweer, Josephina | 11, Apr. 1844 | FF |
| Jaehlin, Jacob | Geldmacher, Ernestin | 23, July 1848 | C |
| Jaess, Joseph | Mermel, Barbara | 9, Oct. 1843 | RCH |
| Jagness, John Henry | Lemand, Elisabeth | 7, Oct. 1849 | BB |
| Jahraus, J. Valentin | Sinn, Anna Maria | 11, July 1848 | A |
| Jakaway, Orison | Allen, Mary | 20, June 1835 | RCH |
| Jakes, Joshua | McGillard, Elisabeth | 15, Feb. 1838 | RCH |
| Jakob, Simon | Eisemann, Christina | 6, Apr. 1842 | RCH |
| James, B.W. | Forsythe, Martha | 30, Apr. 1849 | RCH |
| James, David A. | Bakewell, Elisabeth | 27, May 1841 | I |
| James, George | String, Sarah | 11, Aug. 1844 | RCH |
| James, Henry | Disney, Amelia Maria | 12, Apr. 1836 | RCH |
| James, Joseph | Neamiah, Sarah | 6, Mar. 1837 | RCH |
| James, Joseph | Picket, Sarah Jane | 30, Aug. 1845 | RCH |
| James, Joseph Junius | Keating, Margaret | 30, June 1826 | I |
| James, Seth | Price, Mary | 4, Oct. 1846 | RCH |
| James, Thomas S. | Knowle, Louise | 23, Feb. 1837 | RCH |
| James, Uriah | Wood, Oliver | 6, May 1847 | RCH |
| James, William | Weekly, Elisabeth | 5, Jan. 1837 | RCH |
| Jameson, Jordan | Joyce, Elisabeth A. | 9, July 1838 | RCH |
| Janally, Anthony | Colvin, Nancy | 2, Oct. 1819 | RCH |
| Jandy, William | Weary, Catharine | 28, Aug. 1837 | RCH |
| Janni, Johan Friedr. | Demolder, Wilhelmina | 20, Apr. 1847 | FF |
| Janning, Herman | Wuerdmann, Gertrud | 1, Apr. 1845 | AA |
| Jansen, Arnold | Rattermann, Catharin | 31, Jan. 1848 | CC |
| Jansen, Arnold | Rechtine, Theresa | 25, Sept 1849 | FF |
| Jansen, Heinrich | Bauer, Margaretha | 28, Aug. 1846 | CC |
| Jansen, Herman | Forstiege, Magdalena | 13, Jan. 1846 | FF |
| Jansen, Jacob | Richter, Elisabeth | 13, May 1849 | FF |
| Jansen, Johan | Wintering, Anna M. | 7, Jan. 1846 | EE |
| Jansen, Johan Herm. | Tepe, Hanna Cath. | 1, Sept 1846 | AA |
| Jansen, Joseph | Mueller, Elisabeth | 16, May 1842 | FF |
| Jansen, Luke | Schmidt, Maria | 10, Sept 1844 | AA |
| Jansen, Weert | Meyer, H.S. Caroline | 13, Apr. 1845 | G |
| Janson, Heinrich | Mette, Bernardina | 18, Feb. 1840 | FF |
| Janson, Rudolph | Linnemann, Margaret | 28, June 1846 | AA |
| Janssen, Wert. | Frey, Christina | 20, Dec. 1849 | RCH |
| January, Theodore | Brewster, Martha | 13, July 1836 | RCH |
| Jaquish, William | Vice, Mary Ellen | 14, May 1847 | RCH |
| Jarrell, Jonathan | Low, Mary | 13, Nov. 1843 | RCH |
| Jarret, Abner | Hoell, Amy | 19, Sept 1822 | RCH |
| Jaske, Bernard H. | Buerte, Anna Maria | 5, Nov. 1848 | EE |
| Jasper, Francis | Klaus, Elisabeth | 15, Aug. 1846 | AA |
| Jass, Carl | Eller, Rosina | 24, June 1845 | C |
| Jaubert, Pierce | Ridley, Nancy | 2, Oct. 1822 | RCH |
| Jeatman, Walker | Burrows, Charlotte | 9, Dec. 1818 | RCH |
| Jefferies, Benjamin | Pavie, Sarah | 17, Aug. 1834 | RCH |
| Jeffers, Alexander | Gordon, Anna | 12, Oct. 1820 | RCH |
| Jeffers, Caleb | Boggs, | 15, Sept 1825 | RCH |
| Jeffers, Constantine | Mints, Ruth | 3, Sept 1833 | RCH |
| Jefferson, | Epeneton, | 24, July 1834 | RCH |
| Jefferson, Peter | Clarkson, Mary | 13, Jan. 1825 | RCH |
| Jefferson, Richard | Dunn, Helen | 27, May 1849 | GG |
| Jeffries, James | Stoot, Elisabeth | 26, Jan. 1846 | RCH |
| Jeffries, John | VanAusdol, Mary | 12, Apr. 1842 | RCH |
| Jeffries, Thomas | M---, Sarah | 30, Sept 1824 | RCH |
| Jehlich, Johan | Hoffmann, Anna Maria | 16, May 1848 | EE |
| Jelges, Bernard H. | Fisbeck, M Catharina | 22, Aug. 1848 | FF |
| Jelleff, Charles | Bird, Martha | 20, May 1847 | RCH |
| Jelliff, Benjamin | Bird, Sarah | 15, Oct. 1843 | RCH |
| Jencks, L.B. | Beauchamp, Sarah | 10, Sept 1834 | RCH |
| Jenkins, Albert | Flemmins, Else | 2, Nov. 1842 | RCH |
| Jenkins, Benjamin | Mahoney, Elisabeth | 24, Feb. 1844 | RCH |
| Jenkins, Daniel | Fotrell, Harriet | 19, July 1847 | RCH |
| Jenkins, David T. | Magnus, Sarah | 7, Nov. 1837 | RCH |
| Jenkins, Henry | Burdsal, Sarah | 18, Jan. 1845 | RCH |
| Jenkins, Henry W. | French, Harriet | 2, Dec. 1847 | RCH |
| Jenkins, John | Ritter, Ann | 12, Sept 1837 | RCH |
| Jenkins, Justice | Pearce, Miranda | 6, Mar. 1843 | RCH |

| Grooms<br>\*\*\*\*\*\* | Brides<br>\*\*\*\*\*\* | Date of Marriage<br>\*\*\*\* \*\* \*\*\*\*\*\*\*\* | Code<br>\*\*\*\* |
|---|---|---|---|
| Jenkins, Riley | Fisk, Eveline | 25, Dec. 1846 | RCH |
| Jenkins, Thomas | Phillips, Ellen | 15, Jan. 1846 | RCH |
| Jenks, Edward T. | Farmer, Martha | 31, Dec. 1836 | RCH |
| Jenks, Jediah | Atkinson, Betsey | 25, Oct. 1843 | RCH |
| Jenks, Joseph S. | Green, Isabella M. | 24, May 1833 | RCH |
| Jenner, James | Shaw, Ann | 10, June 1846 | RCH |
| Jenner, Peter | Hesselbach, Magdal. | 28, Jan. 1845 | AA |
| Jennings, | Angerwere, Susan E. | 30, Nov. 1837 | RCH |
| Jennings, Charles | Burnet, Gertrud | 6, Sept 1842 | RCH |
| Jennings, Dennis | Johns, Elisabeth | 8, July 1847 | RCH |
| Jennings, Redmond | Murran, Bridget | 18, Feb. 1849 | BB |
| Jennings, Thomas | Thompson, Ellen | 19, Oct. 1836 | RCH |
| Jennings, Thomas | Donlon, Helen | 7, Aug. 1848 | BB |
| Jennings, William | Martin, Louise | 16, Mar. 1846 | RCH |
| Jennison, James | Parker, Francis A. | 19, Mar. 1849 | RCH |
| Jerger, Joseph | Habich, Apollonia | 13, Jan. 1846 | FF |
| Jergins, Philipp | Steffen, Maria | 21, Jan. 1845 | FF |
| Jerkins, William H. | Platt, Amelia E. | 9, Sept 1839 | RCH |
| Jerome, Isaac | Craig, Catharine | 15, Apr. 1846 | RCH |
| Jessoy, John | Trub, Ann | 22, July 1849 | RCH |
| Jessup, Elisha | Randle, Charlotte | 12, Sept 1837 | RCH |
| Jessup, George | Ashton, Julia | 28, Dec. 1841 | RCH |
| Jessup, Isaac | Snodgrass, Abigail | 3, Nov. 1820 | RCH |
| Jessup, Isaac | Banning, Charity | 29, Dec. 1845 | RCH |
| Jessup, Israel | Brecount, Matilda | 23, Mar. 1837 | RCH |
| Jessup, Oliver | Barnes, Deliverance | 30, Nov. 1843 | RCH |
| Jessup, William | Regs, Christina | 4, Mar. 1838 | RCH |
| Jessup, William | McConnell, Charity | 27, Apr. 1843 | RCH |
| Jester, Eli | Caldwell, Catharine | 27, Aug. 1845 | RCH |
| Jeude, Herman | Stein, Agnes | 3, Feb. 1842 | FF |
| Jewel, William | Stearns, Nancy | 2, Apr. 1844 | RCH |
| Jewett, Evi L. | Lenis, Sarah K. | 24, Oct. 1831 | RCH |
| Jewett, Isaac | Chandler, Matilda | 15, Apr. 1840 | RCH |
| Jinson, William | Wuest, Ann | Mar. 1834 | RCH |
| Joannigmann, Mathias | Hartker, Catharine | 23, Jan. 1849 | II |
| Joes, George | Koch, Margaretha | 30, Oct. 1842 | RCH |
| Johan, Friedrich | Hemgreiner, Ottilia | 24, Aug. 1847 | EE |
| Johanigmann, Johan | Hofschneider, Elis. | 31, Aug. 1847 | EE |
| Johannemann, Joseph | Buening, Maria Anna | 24, Nov. 1840 | FF |
| Johannemann, Joseph | Hermueller, Elis. | 24, Mar. 1849 | AA |
| Johanning, Bernard | Willenbrink, Cath. | 25, Sept 1839 | FF |
| Johanning, Heinrich | Behrens, Christina | 29, Nov. 1846 | B |
| Johanning, J. Herman | Trimpe, Elisabeth | 28, Feb. 1843 | AA |
| Johantgen, Peter | Lemox, Maria | 11, Mar. 1845 | G |
| John, James | Cook, Abigail | 3, Dec. 1832 | RCH |
| John, John S. | Jenkins, Harriet | 22, Apr. 1838 | RCH |
| John, Oliver | Johnson, Rebecca | 22, Feb. 1838 | RCH |
| Johns, James | Williamson, D.A. | 5, Apr. 1834 | RCH |
| Johns, James | Thompson, Ann | 5, Apr. 1842 | RCH |
| Johns, James W. | Huston, Harriet | 1, Feb. 1842 | RCH |
| Johns, Robert | Minus, Jenett | 10, Oct. 1842 | RCH |
| Johnson, | Byw---, Olivia | 9, Dec. 1844 | RCH |
| Johnson, | Sarrar, Mary A. | 16, Aug. 1849 | RCH |
| Johnson, Abel | Ashley, Martha | 1, July 1847 | RCH |
| Johnson, Alexander | Ferguson, Margaret | 10, Sept 1833 | RCH |
| Johnson, Alexander | Wallace, L. | 26, Sept 1833 | RCH |
| Johnson, Alexander | Hagerty, Clarissa | 16, Mar. 1842 | RCH |
| Johnson, Alexander | Randall, Jane | 13, July 1843 | RCH |
| Johnson, August | Gilbert, Caroline | 5, Jan. 1847 | RCH |
| Johnson, Benjamin | Hay, Mary A. | 3, Aug. 1839 | RCH |
| Johnson, Calvin | Lewis, Sarah E. | 7, June 1846 | RCH |
| Johnson, Campbell | Sanford, Jerusha | Dec. 1824 | RCH |
| Johnson, Charles | Allen, Mary | 18, Sept 1823 | RCH |
| Johnson, Charles | Cashnill, Mary | 20, Nov. 1840 | RCH |
| Johnson, Charles | Stuttard, Elisabeth | 13, Sept 1841 | RCH |
| Johnson, Charles | Corbley, Rebecca | 17, Oct. 1841 | RCH |
| Johnson, Charles | Grant, Julia Ann | 1, Nov. 1842 | RCH |
| Johnson, Charles | Markley, Elisabeth | 30, Apr. 1843 | RCH |
| Johnson, Charles | Cockson, Lucinda | 29, May 1844 | RCH |
| Johnson, Charles | Henry, Rebecca | 13, Oct. 1846 | RCH |
| Johnson, Charles D. | Curtis, Chaoville | 19, Oct. 1834 | RCH |

| Grooms | Brides | Date of Marriage | Code |
|--------|--------|------------------|------|
| ****** | ****** | **** ** ******** | **** |
| Johnson, Charles J. | Brecount, Minerva | 1, May 1834 | RCH |
| Johnson, Daniel | Campbell, Caroline | 28, Feb. 1836 | RCH |
| Johnson, David | Palmer, Jane | 24, Dec. 1842 | RCH |
| Johnson, Ebenezer | Rawl, Elisabeth | 23, Feb. 1836 | RCH |
| Johnson, Elisha | Bates, Sarah | 27, Dec. 1824 | RCH |
| Johnson, Elisha B. | Huff, Eunice | 14, July 1836 | RCH |
| Johnson, Elmore | Bennett, Elisabeth | 6, Jan. 1844 | RCH |
| Johnson, George | Hardin, Sarah Ann | 21, Apr. 1846 | RCH |
| Johnson, Gideon | Jessup, Edith | 29, Oct. 1837 | RCH |
| Johnson, H. | Allen, Abigail W. | 15, Jan. 1836 | RCH |
| Johnson, Harrison | Harmmel, Catharine | 25, Aug. 1839 | RCH |
| Johnson, Henry | McFeely, Mary | 29, Oct. 1833 | RCH |
| Johnson, Henry | Conor, Ary. | 15, Dec. 1833 | RCH |
| Johnson, Henry | Taylor, Phebe | 29, May 1843 | RCH |
| Johnson, Hiram | White, Elisabeth | 29, May 1836 | RCH |
| Johnson, Hiram | Newell, Phoebe | 30, Aug. 1846 | RCH |
| Johnson, Hiram | Owens, Martha Jane | 24, Sept 1846 | RCH |
| Johnson, Jackson | Brown, Georgiana | 24, Sept 1842 | RCH |
| Johnson, James | Cormick, Sarah | 19, May 1822 | RCH |
| Johnson, James | McCombs, Jane | 17, Jan. 1839 | RCH |
| Johnson, James | Baker, Olive | 4, Apr. 1839 | RCH |
| Johnson, James | Hutchison, Eleanor | 23, May 1839 | RCH |
| Johnson, James | Pierson, Jane E. | 22, July 1842 | RCH |
| Johnson, James A. | White, Catharine | 8, Feb. 1848 | RCH |
| Johnson, James C. | Smith, Theodorca | 13, Feb. 1834 | RCH |
| Johnson, James R. | Simmermann, Deborah | 11, Jan. 1838 | RCH |
| Johnson, James R. | Wintercass, Ann | 7, June 1848 | RCH |
| Johnson, James T. | Hamet, Mary | 8, Jan. 1823 | RCH |
| Johnson, Jepthah | Estill, Betsy | 22, Mar. 1819 | RCH |
| Johnson, John | ----, Martha | 18, July 1835 | RCH |
| Johnson, John | Dickerson, Elisabeth | 1, Jan. 1839 | RCH |
| Johnson, John | Robinson, Charlotte | 24, Apr. 1839 | RCH |
| Johnson, John | Getzendanner, Emily | 16, Mar. 1842 | RCH |
| Johnson, John | Barcus, Rebecca | 18, Aug. 1842 | RCH |
| Johnson, John | Britton, Marcella | 25, Dec. 1847 | RCH |
| Johnson, John | Heath, Sarah Jane | 22, June 1849 | RCH |
| Johnson, John J. | Summerfield, Susan | 4, Apr. 1833 | RCH |
| Johnson, John R. | Cook, Isabella | 19, June 1838 | RCH |
| Johnson, John R. | Freeman, Rebecca | 9, Feb. 1848 | RCH |
| Johnson, John W. | Hopping, Phebe | 20, Sept 1843 | RCH |
| Johnson, Joseph | McQueen, Elisabeth | 20, Sept 1846 | RCH |
| Johnson, Joseph | Joyce, Isabella | 11, Apr. 1847 | RCH |
| Johnson, Lewis | Hoffner, Margaret | 22, Feb. 1837 | RCH |
| Johnson, Mariot | Graham, Martha | 18, Oct. 1843 | RCH |
| Johnson, Moses | Hughes, Louise | 20, Jan. 1847 | RCH |
| Johnson, Noble | Todd, Mary A. | 25, Oct. 1837 | RCH |
| Johnson, Peter | Mason, Catharine | 6, Apr. 1836 | RCH |
| Johnson, Peter | Ward, Margaret | 7, Dec. 1845 | RCH |
| Johnson, Robert | Ash, Lucinda | 4, Oct. 1842 | RCH |
| Johnson, Robert | Spahr, Sarah | 18, Feb. 1844 | RCH |
| Johnson, Robert | Carson, Adeline | 14, May 1844 | RCH |
| Johnson, Robert | Brown, Julia | 4, Sept 1847 | RCH |
| Johnson, S. | Baker, Margaret | 24, July 1834 | RCH |
| Johnson, Samuel | Moulton, M Elisabeth | 3, Jan. 1844 | RCH |
| Johnson, Samuel | Whann, Charlotte | 2, Aug. 1844 | RCH |
| Johnson, Samuel | Farrell, Bridget | 18, Nov. 1847 | BB |
| Johnson, Seth S. | Hornel, Sarah S. | 13, June 1839 | RCH |
| Johnson, Thomas | Blauvel, Johanna | 24, June 1839 | RCH |
| Johnson, Thomas | Hinds, Margaret | 22, June 1840 | BB |
| Johnson, Thomas | Atkinson, Jane | 9, July 1848 | RCH |
| Johnson, Thomas J. | Johnson, Mary B. | 1, May 1838 | RCH |
| Johnson, Willard | Esterby, Jane | 5, Mar. 1834 | RCH |
| Johnson, William | Dawson, Elisabeth | 2, June 1836 | RCH |
| Johnson, William | Mitchell, Elisabeth | 28, Oct. 1843 | RCH |
| Johnson, William | Cox, Deborah | 12, Nov. 1845 | RCH |
| Johnson, William | Littell, Elisabeth | 27, Mar. 1846 | RCH |
| Johnson, William | Workmann, Mary Jane | 31, Aug. 1846 | RCH |
| Johnson, William | Bois, Elisabeth | 20, Sept 1846 | RCH |
| Johnson, William | Irvin, Mary Ann | 22, Oct. 1846 | RCH |
| Johnson, William | Gano, Lucretia | 1, Feb. 1847 | RCH |
| Johnson, William | Schofield, Theodotia | 11, Jan. 1849 | RCH |

| Grooms | Brides | Date of Marriage | Code |
|--------|--------|------------------|------|
| Johnson, William H. | Scofield, Mary | 24, Sept 1837 | RCH |
| Johnson, William Hy. | Hafley, Elisabeth | 31, May 1849 | GG |
| Johnson, William M. | Jarned, Clara | 23, June 1841 | RCH |
| Johnson, William P. | Wilsbacher, Henrica | 23, Apr. 1839 | FF |
| Johnston, | Lucas, Mary | 21, July 1822 | RCH |
| Johnston, | Keeling, Mary Helen | 18, June 1849 | RCH |
| Johnston, Alexander | Purcell, Harriet | 17, Dec. 1845 | RCH |
| Johnston, Anthony | Frost, Martha | 19, Aug. 1842 | RCH |
| Johnston, Benjamin | Barmore, Ester | 5, Aug. 1824 | RCH |
| Johnston, Charles | Gaines, Sarah | 6, Nov. 1845 | RCH |
| Johnston, Franklin | Stump, Elisabeth | 10, Jan. 1838 | RCH |
| Johnston, Isaac | Forbes, Mary | 8, Mar. 1821 | RCH |
| Johnston, J. | Loer, Hannah | 29, Oct. 1836 | RCH |
| Johnston, John | Soda, Elisabeth | 25, Oct. 1836 | RCH |
| Johnston, John | Patterson, Mary | 28, Oct. 1841 | RCH |
| Johnston, John | Henderson, Agnes | 19, Feb. 1846 | RCH |
| Johnston, John G. | Salor, Anna Maria | 6, Apr. 1834 | RCH |
| Johnston, John R. | Hardin, Louise | 2, Apr. 1844 | RCH |
| Johnston, Jonathan | Miller, Rebecca | 21, Feb. 1837 | RCH |
| Johnston, Joseph | Pettit, Mary A. | 30, Dec. 1845 | RCH |
| Johnston, Louis | Tharp, Susan | 10, Jan. 1842 | RCH |
| Johnston, Milton | John, Mary | 9, Nov. 1820 | RCH |
| Johnston, Samuel | Wilson, Margaret E. | 4, Dec. 1820 | I |
| Johnston, Samuell | Bailey, Mary Jane | 28, Feb. 1844 | RCH |
| Johnston, Shadrock | Jones, Patience | 8, Mar. 1822 | RCH |
| Johnston, Thomas | Terwilleger, Mary | 19, July 1846 | RCH |
| Johnston, Thomas B. | Johnston, Louise C. | 14, July 1833 | RCH |
| Johnston, William | Reyland, Anna Elis. | 12, Aug. 1847 | RCH |
| Johnston, William | Boyd, Martha | 22, Mar. 1849 | RCH |
| Johnston, William S. | Bartow, Clarissa | 22, Feb. 1821 | I |
| Joiner, Jordan | Penker, Rachel | 11, June 1824 | RCH |
| Joines, | Lockwood, Mariah | 19, Feb. 1838 | RCH |
| Joker, John | Bulten, Elisabeth | 16, Aug. 1844 | RCH |
| Jolliffe, Amos | Williamson, Cretia A | 3, Sept 1848 | RCH |
| Jolly, William | Prather, Elisabeth | 10, May 1838 | RCH |
| Jones, | Welmington, Ann | 2, Oct. 1817 | RCH |
| Jones, | Jones, Winnefred | 9, Mar. 1824 | RCH |
| Jones, | Stevens, Sarah | 4, Apr. 1849 | RCH |
| Jones, Aaron | Belville, Elisabeth | 8, Jan. 1844 | RCH |
| Jones, Alfred | Mathews, Caroline | 2, Aug. 1841 | RCH |
| Jones, Alner | Bennett, Emily | 27, Mar. 1849 | RCH |
| Jones, Cadwalader | Reese, Ann | 11, Oct. 1846 | RCH |
| Jones, Caleb | Tibbetts, Anna | 31, July 1837 | RCH |
| Jones, Castilla | ----, Patsy Wilson | 17, Sept 1818 | RCH |
| Jones, Charles | Stewart, Laura | 20, Sept 1842 | RCH |
| Jones, Charles | Wiggins, Ann | 21, Oct. 1842 | RCH |
| Jones, Charles | Ludlow, Charlotte | 11, July 1843 | RCH |
| Jones, Charles | Smith, Elisabeth | 27, Nov. 1845 | RCH |
| Jones, Charles C. | Chambers, Margaret | 20, Oct. 1842 | BB |
| Jones, Christopher | Taulman, Eunice | 18, Jan. 1820 | RCH |
| Jones, Daniel | Jones, Martha | 26, Apr. 1843 | RCH |
| Jones, Daniel | Leinbach, Ann | 26, Feb. 1846 | RCH |
| Jones, Daniel | Turner, Martha Jane | 26, Apr. 1846 | RCH |
| Jones, Daniel | Wiley, Juliet | 13, Dec. 1848 | RCH |
| Jones, David | Waurn, Elisabeth | 20, Nov. 1821 | RCH |
| Jones, David | Evans, Susan | 7, June 1844 | RCH |
| Jones, David | Treasure, Fanny | 3, Aug. 1849 | RCH |
| Jones, Dudley C. | Lark, Onea | 19, Dec. 1842 | RCH |
| Jones, E. Glover | Young, Frances | 15, Apr. 1844 | RCH |
| Jones, Enoch | Keller, Sarah | 26, Sept 1843 | RCH |
| Jones, Ephraim | Wilson, Amelia | 24, Mar. 1846 | RCH |
| Jones, Ephraim B. | Leonard, Elisabeth | 4, Sept 1833 | RCH |
| Jones, Evan | Jones, Mary | 26, Dec. 1832 | RCH |
| Jones, Evan | Jones, Mary Ann | 12, Nov. 1841 | RCH |
| Jones, Evan | Davis, Mary | 24, Feb. 1846 | RCH |
| Jones, Evan W. | Davis, Mary | 28, Dec. 1844 | RCH |
| Jones, George | Hill, Anna | 5, Apr. 1844 | RCH |
| Jones, George G. | Aydelotte, Hannah M. | 22, Oct. 1845 | I |
| Jones, George M. | Stewart, Isabella | 24, Mar. 1825 | RCH |
| Jones, George W. | Febbeger, Harriet | 23, Aug. 1832 | I |
| Jones, George W. | Murphy, Eleanor | 18, Sept 1848 | RCH |

| Grooms | Brides | Date of Marriage | Code |
|--------|--------|------------------|------|
| ****** | ****** | **** ** ******** | **** |
| Jones, George W. | Tibbatts, Jane T. | 3, Jan. 1849 | I |
| Jones, Gilbert | Niles, Catharine | 24, Aug. 1843 | RCH |
| Jones, Gilbert | Decker, Caroline | 29, Nov. 1845 | RCH |
| Jones, Henry | Gray, Nancy | 25, Feb. 1819 | RCH |
| Jones, Henry W. | Cooper, Dolly | 22, Jan. 1834 | RCH |
| Jones, Hugh | Davis, Mary D. | 24, July 1847 | RCH |
| Jones, Hugh H. | Hughey, Mary | 2, Apr. 1849 | RCH |
| Jones, Isaiah | Slaughter, Leah | 1, Sept 1819 | RCH |
| Jones, Jacob | Connor, Sarah Ann | 17, Apr. 1836 | RCH |
| Jones, James | Newom, Elisabeth | 7, June 1821 | RCH |
| Jones, James | Johnson, Susan | 20, Dec. 1834 | RCH |
| Jones, James | Harris, Amelia | 27, Mar. 1847 | RCH |
| Jones, James | Phillips, Ellen | 31, July 1847 | RCH |
| Jones, James | Garner, Catharine J. | 16, Sept 1847 | RCH |
| Jones, James J. | Lefever, Anna | 17, Dec. 1834 | RCH |
| Jones, Jenkins | Evans, Mary W. | 12, July 1841 | RCH |
| Jones, Jesse | Ward, Mary Jane | 16, Apr. 1844 | RCH |
| Jones, Jesse | Hall, Margaret | Oct. 1849 | RCH |
| Jones, Jesse | Conners, Bridget | 7, Feb. 1847 | BB |
| Jones, Jesse D. | Hughes, Mary | 26, Sept 1832 | RCH |
| Jones, John | Terwilliger, Fanny | 29, Nov. 1821 | RCH |
| Jones, John | Bailey, | 10, Aug. 1825 | RCH |
| Jones, John | Semms, Rebecca | 12, Feb. 1835 | RCH |
| Jones, John | Karr, Alice | 1, Mar. 1842 | RCH |
| Jones, John | Bellville, Amelia | 30, Nov. 1846 | RCH |
| Jones, John | Pyle, Elisabeth | 8, Apr. 1847 | RCH |
| Jones, John | Higbee, Sarah | 4, Apr. 1849 | RCH |
| Jones, John | Tilbury, Sidney | 26, Aug. 1849 | RCH |
| Jones, John D. | Johnston, Elizabeth | 22, Sept 1823 | I |
| Jones, John F. | Edwards, Mary | 6, May 1848 | RCH |
| Jones, John G. | Brewster, Elisabeth | 14, Apr. 1846 | D |
| Jones, John H. | Bailey, P.C. | 3, Oct. 1838 | RCH |
| Jones, John R. | Tudor, Elisabeth | 30, Sept 1848 | RCH |
| Jones, John S. | Hatfield, Margaret | 25, Jan. 1824 | RCH |
| Jones, Jona | Hughes, Mary | 5, Nov. 1841 | RCH |
| Jones, Jonathan | Wallace, Rebecca | 12, Feb. 1835 | RCH |
| Jones, Jonathan | Fields, Sarah Jane | Sept 1845 | RCH |
| Jones, Joseph | Cox, Catharine | 24, Mar. 1842 | RCH |
| Jones, Joshua | Coons, Rachel | 6, Oct. 1833 | RCH |
| Jones, Josiah | Hamilton, Sarah Ann | 13, Feb. 1837 | RCH |
| Jones, Leroy | Price, Mary M. | 16, Aug. 1846 | RCH |
| Jones, Lewis | Sterlin, Catharine | 16, Feb. 1843 | RCH |
| Jones, Lorenzo | Rose, Sarah | 13, Nov. 1845 | RCH |
| Jones, Ludwell | Keller, Elisabeth | 31, May 1843 | RCH |
| Jones, Martin | Hogeman, Susan | 23, Sept 1846 | RCH |
| Jones, Morgan | Griffith, Elisabeth | 26, May 1847 | RCH |
| Jones, Moses | --iest, | 30, Nov. 1826 | RCH |
| Jones, Nathan | Defreese, Christiana | 5, Oct. 1824 | RCH |
| Jones, Newman O. | Creager, Caroline | 23, Feb. 1844 | RCH |
| Jones, Owen | Hughes, Mary | 19, Nov. 1835 | RCH |
| Jones, Paul | Davis, Elisabeth | 8, Dec. 1840 | RCH |
| Jones, Paul | Renner, Mary | 27, Nov. 1844 | RCH |
| Jones, Philemon | Goudy, Margaret | 3, Feb. 1842 | RCH |
| Jones, Philipp | Hammel, Harriet A. | 11, Oct. 1832 | RCH |
| Jones, Reuben | Smiley, Malinda | 28, Dec. 1843 | RCH |
| Jones, Richard | Price, Margaret | 30, May 1849 | RCH |
| Jones, Robert | Logan, | 14, Nov. 1824 | RCH |
| Jones, Robert | Roberts, Jane | 10, Sept 1847 | RCH |
| Jones, Salmon | Williams, Elisabeth | 2, Oct. 1838 | RCH |
| Jones, Samuel | Bloom, Nancy | 2, Sept 1819 | RCH |
| Jones, Samuel | Larrison, Catharine | 19, Apr. 1821 | RCH |
| Jones, Samuel | Harris, Sarah | 22, Aug. 1822 | RCH |
| Jones, Samuel | Jones, Sarah | 15, Mar. 1824 | RCH |
| Jones, Samuel | Colley, Margaret | 7, Apr. 1836 | RCH |
| Jones, Samuel | Shannon, Elisabeth | 24, Apr. 1836 | RCH |
| Jones, Samuel | Wallace, Nancy | 12, May 1836 | RCH |
| Jones, Samuel | Pool, Elisabeth | Nov. 1841 | RCH |
| Jones, Samuel | Cameron, Hester T. | 15, Dec. 1847 | RCH |
| Jones, Seneca | Leishof, Elisabeth | 17, Nov. 1840 | RCH |
| Jones, Thomas | Hill, Elisabeth | 22, Sept 1835 | RCH |
| Jones, Thomas | Sears, Martha | 11, Mar. 1844 | RCH |

| Grooms<br>***** | Brides<br>***** | Date of Marriage<br>**** ** ******** | Code<br>**** |
|---|---|---|---|
| Jones, Thomas | Johnson, Susan | 30, Mar. 1844 | RCH |
| Jones, Thomas | Gray, Lydia Ann | 5, Dec. 1848 | RCH |
| Jones, Thomas C. | Alley, Lydia | 16, July 1848 | RCH |
| Jones, Thomas P. | Cain, Levina | 2, July 1835 | RCH |
| Jones, William | Goodwin, Caroline | 8, Mar. 1822 | RCH |
| Jones, William | Oldham, Sarah | 9, Jan. 1832 | RCH |
| Jones, William | Carr, Margaret | 2, June 1836 | RCH |
| Jones, William | Reilly, Catharine | 3, July 1839 | BB |
| Jones, William | Heath, Ann | 4, Oct. 1841 | RCH |
| Jones, William | Griffin, Charlotte | 5, Feb. 1843 | RCH |
| Jones, William | Gray, Rachel | 9, Feb. 1843 | RCH |
| Jones, William | Dawson, Elisabeth | 12, Sept 1843 | RCH |
| Jones, William | Dever, Mary Ann | 9, Sept 1846 | RCH |
| Jones, William D. | Longworth, Charlotte | 12, Mar. 1821 | I |
| Jones, Zachariah | Farmer, Mary | 9, Feb. 1837 | RCH |
| Jonlyn, August | Jackson, Parmela | 22, Mar. 1820 | RCH |
| Jonte, John G. | Genin, Mary J. | 26, Sept 1833 | RCH |
| Jonte, Peter F. | ----, ---- | 1835 | RCH |
| Jop, Jacob | Weise, Margaretha | 23, May 1840 | G |
| Jordan, James | Stout, Eleanor | 7, Sept 1842 | RCH |
| Jorden, David | Ashley, Martha Ann | 30, Mar. 1842 | RCH |
| Jorden, John | Hill, Poney | 28, Mar. 1833 | RCH |
| Joseph, Elewize | Williams, Jane | 7, Nov. 1836 | RCH |
| Joseph, Francis | Sitter, Catharina | 21, Nov. 1839 | FF |
| Joseph, J.G. | Symonds, Rebecca | 25, Dec. 1833 | RCH |
| Josephs, Joseph | Maas, Jette | 10, Jan. 1848 | RCH |
| Josinger, Bernard H. | Schoene, Catharine | 15, Aug. 1849 | CC |
| Jouck, Joseph | Morrison, Louise | 22, Sept 1839 | RCH |
| Jourdan, Isaac | Williams, Elisabeth | 29, Jan. 1848 | C |
| Jourdan, James | Leighton, Mary | 7, Mar. 1821 | RCH |
| Joutsey, John | Davis, Elisabeth | 10, May 1818 | RCH |
| Joyce, David | Sedam, Sarah | 4, Jan. 1838 | RCH |
| Joyce, Hiram | Joyce, Elisabeth | 22, Mar. 1843 | RCH |
| Joyce, James | Bowers, Mary Ann | 1, Nov. 1835 | RCH |
| Joyce, John | Gibbons, Mary | 20, Aug. 1848 | BB |
| Joyce, Valentine | Gambel, Elisabeth | 20, Mar. 1841 | RCH |
| Joyner, Josiah | Stevens, Letta | 3, Jan. 1844 | RCH |
| Judah, Judah | Moeritz, Caroline | 28, Aug. 1843 | RCH |
| Judd, | Hill, Barbara | 30, Apr. 1826 | RCH |
| Judd, Daniel | Rosebery, Frances | Oct. 1844 | RCH |
| Judd, David | Merritt, Elisabeth | 1, Sept 1836 | RCH |
| Judd, Ezias | French, Cynthia | 19, Aug. 1847 | RCH |
| Judge, Patrick | Moran, Ann | 9, Oct. 1849 | GG |
| Judkins, William | Palmer, Mary | 7, Sept 1841 | RCH |
| Juell, Georg | Hagemann, Helena | 30, Sept 1849 | A |
| Juen, Lawrence | Popp, Catharine | 17, Aug. 1847 | EE |
| Juengling, Gottlob | Harsch, Barbara | 18, Apr. 1843 | G |
| Juergens, Gerhard | Hoeckermann, Maria | 18, Mar. 1847 | B |
| Jugling, Gottlieb | Harshe, Barbara | 17, Apr. 1843 | RCH |
| Julian, William F. | Richardson, Margaret | 7, Dec. 1832 | RCH |
| Julich, Conrad | Voltshart, Catharine | 16, July 1848 | C |
| Jung, Andreas | Kutzler, Margaretha | 12, Dec. 1836 | FF |
| Jung, Daniel | Jung, Philippina | 12, Oct. 1848 | C |
| Jung, Georg | Buttner, Margaretha | 2, May 1839 | FF |
| Jung, Gerhard | Sommer, M. Angela | 27, May 1837 | FF |
| Jung, Johan | Schrempt, Kunigunda | 10, Jan. 1848 | EE |
| Jung, Johan | Rauh, Barbara | 16, Jan. 1845 | FF |
| Jung, Theobald | Blum, Thecla | 19, Oct. 1848 | CC |
| Jung, Wilhelm | Conrad, Maria | 28, Dec. 1847 | C |
| Jungbluth, J. Jacob | Jacob, Barbara C. | 25, June 1839 | FF |
| Junior, | See, Cecilia | 3, May 1849 | RCH |
| Junker, Heinrich | Barting, Maria | 21, May 1846 | F |
| Junkin, John | Peat, Adelheid | 12, Apr. 1849 | RCH |
| Junnemann, Heinrich | Lindley, Martha | 6, May 1849 | RCH |
| Juppenlatz, Georg M. | Pflueger, Catharine | 30, Oct. 1849 | A |
| Juppenlatz, Jacob | Loermann, Christina | 13, Dec. 1845 | RCH |
| Jurgens, J Friedrich | Beckmann, Johanna C. | 14, Sept 1848 | F |
| Justice, James | Howard, Harriet | 8, Apr. 1834 | RCH |
| Justice, Jesse | Briant, Mary | 26, Sept 1833 | RCH |
| K---, James | Goff, Elisabeth | 27, Nov. 1835 | RCH |

| Grooms<br>***** | Brides<br>***** | Date of Marriage<br>**** ** ******* | Code<br>**** |
|---|---|---|---|
| K---, James | Dremmond, Maria | 19, July 1839 | RCH |
| Kabes, Gerhard | Zurline, Maria Anna | 9, Nov. 1841 | FF |
| Kaeferlein, Andreas | Kalblein, Elisabeth | 20, Oct. 1840 | FF |
| Kaegin, Polycarp | Guetler, Magdalena | 2, May 1848 | AA |
| Kaeszer, J. Gerhard | Migrunt, Catharine | 1, Dec. 1847 | RCH |
| Kaetter, Heinrich | Hammilin, Dorothea | 25, Feb. 1846 | RCH |
| Kafemann, Bernard | Brinkmeyer, Elis. | 29, Jan. 1846 | EE |
| Kafenbrink, Anton | Embertink, Maria A. | 8, Jan. 1839 | FF |
| Kafkemeyer, Heinrich | Mueller, Anna Maria | 16, Oct. 1838 | FF |
| Kah, Ludwig | Ludwig, Sarah | 16, Nov. 1846 | G |
| Kahl, Johan Bernard | Korte, Catharina E. | 10, May 1842 | FF |
| Kahle, Friedrich | Wierville, Christina | 2, July 1841 | G |
| Kahn, Johan | Jergen, Margaretha | 19, Apr. 1846 | EE |
| Kahn, Samuel | Ray, Caroline | 6, Jan. 1848 | RCH |
| Kain, Franklin | Humphreys, Malinda | 4, Nov. 1843 | RCH |
| Kain, Franklin | Moore, Nancy | 4, Apr. 1847 | RCH |
| Kain, James | ----, ---- | 6, June 1826 | RCH |
| Kain, Michael | Kelly, Catharine | 27, Feb. 1840 | BB |
| Kaiser, Carl | Walker, Christina | 16, Dec. 1849 | C |
| Kaiser, Heinrich | Hormann, Christine | 29, Aug. 1844 | G |
| Kaiser, Heinrich | Batsch, Friedricka | 2, Apr. 1849 | A |
| Kaiser, Jacob | Heilmann, Catharine | 25, Oct. 1846 | FF |
| Kaiser, Joseph | Straus, Caroline | 3, Aug. 1846 | RCH |
| Kalb, Friedrich | Schoettle, Eleanor | 21, May 1848 | EE |
| Kalb, Wolfgang | Scheiderin, Margaret | 2, Jan. 1840 | FF |
| Kallenbach, Ludwig | Henderson, Sarah | 1, May 1848 | I |
| Kallendorf, Friedric | Anfort, Wilhelmina | 6, Apr. 1849 | F |
| Kallmeier, Friedrich | Schwane, Maria | 28, July 1849 | II |
| Kalter, Paul | Everlein, Caroline | 22, Sept 1840 | G |
| Kamann, Heinrich P. | Kamann, Anna Maria | 23, Apr. 1842 | F |
| Kamden, Heinrich | Ellermann, Maria | 3, Aug. 1843 | F |
| Kamle, Friedrich | Brinkschmidt, Louise | 8, Feb. 1849 | C |
| Kammann, Heinrich | Hacke, Rike | 2, May 1844 | F |
| Kammer, Jacob | Hilgert, Catharine | 22, Sept 1846 | EE |
| Kammerer, Gottlieb | Conrad, Elisabeth | 7, Dec. 1843 | G |
| Kammeyer, Friedrich | Willen, M.G. | 17, June 1849 | AA |
| Kamp, Gerhard Heinr. | Classmeier, Catharin | 29, Sept 1848 | E |
| Kamp, Joseph | Mescher, Gertrud | 16, June 1846 | AA |
| Kamp, Peter | Schoepner, Adelheid | 16, July 1849 | CC |
| Kampelmann, Bernard | Berte, Catharine | 24, Apr. 1838 | FF |
| Kamper, Herman D. | Teben, Maria | 19, Nov. 1846 | F |
| Kamphaus, Johan | Poehling, Gesina | 26, Aug. 1849 | CC |
| Kamphaus, Joseph | Miller, Maria (Mrs) | 24, Sept 1844 | AA |
| Kampmann, Georg | Unluecke, Maria Anna | 10, June 1845 | FF |
| Kane, Michael | Armstrong, H. | 15, Feb. 1836 | RCH |
| Kane, Michael | Mullen, Sarah | 3, Sept 1849 | BB |
| Kane, Thompkins | Gray, Jane | 16, Aug. 1849 | RCH |
| Kanzer, Conrad | Wuest, Susanna | 15, Oct. 1848 | G |
| Kaplard, Stephen | Smith, Sarah | 30, Sept 1841 | RCH |
| Kappauff, Carl | Fender, Sabina | 3, Jan. 1844 | C |
| Kappel, Adam | Gebhardt, Katharina | 23, Apr. 1848 | G |
| Kapps, Johan Heinric | Lenger, Maria Anna | 15, Oct. 1839 | FF |
| Karbel, Joseph | Clement, Theresa | 25, Sept 1838 | FF |
| Karbrink, H. Andreas | Schulte, Anna Maria | 13, Aug. 1840 | F |
| Karl, Joseph | Hoefling, Francisca | 7, Apr. 1845 | AA |
| Karli, Johan Joseph | Fleitz, Jacobina | 16, May 1848 | EE |
| Karn, Michael | Sander, Francisca | 14, July 1839 | FF |
| Karney, Lewis | Johnson, Marie E. | 13, Sept 1849 | RCH |
| Karr, Henry | Jones, Charlotte | 12, Oct. 1837 | RCH |
| Karr, James | Martin, Margaret | 10, Mar. 1836 | RCH |
| Karr, John | Morgan, Mary | 29, Dec. 1833 | RCH |
| Karr, Stephan | Garriss, Catharine | 23, Feb. 1848 | RCH |
| Karr, Walter | Scogin, Catharine | 14, Oct. 1838 | RCH |
| Karr, William | Jamison, Mary Jane | 15, Apr. 1847 | RCH |
| Karrenbrock, Bernard | Bockmeier, Elisabeth | 12, Jan. 1841 | FF |
| Karrmann, Ferdinand | Tilly, Julia | 24, Apr. 1848 | G |
| Karsch, John | Espenscheid, Marg. | 29, Apr. 1849 | G |
| Karsnert, Theobald | Allbecker, Walburga | 20, July 1835 | FF |
| Karthaus, Bernard | Fischer, Maria Anna | 10, May 1842 | FF |
| Kartmann, Theodor | Wolmering, Elisabeth | 17, Jan. 1843 | FF |
| Kasten, Johan Fried. | Brueggemann, Anna M. | 23, May 1848 | F |

| Grooms | Brides | Date of Marriage | Code |
|--------|--------|------------------|------|
| ****** | ****** | **** ** ******** | **** |
| Kastens, Herman H. | Brueggemann, Doroth. | 8, Jan. 1849 | F |
| Kasting, Franz Henry | Dickruger, Sophia D. | 8, Oct. 1846 | F |
| Kasting, Ludwig | Moenks, Engel | 1, Jan. 1843 | RCH |
| Kastler, Nicolaus | Volz, Tecla | 10, June 1845 | AA |
| Kastner, Anthony | Harsensale, Mary Ann | 7, May 1842 | RCH |
| Kastner, Anthony | Stewart, Anna Elis. | 16, Apr. 1844 | RCH |
| Katenbrock, Johan | Pont, Catharina | 3, Mar. 1835 | FF |
| Kathmann, Clemens | Schirberg, A. Maria | 18, Nov. 1849 | II |
| Kathmann, Herman | Helling, M. Gesina | 13, Sept 1846 | AA |
| Kattein, Conrad | Kissling, Gottlieba | 13, Nov. 1848 | A |
| Kattenbrink, Heinric | Pohlmann, Catharine | 24, Sept 1846 | F |
| Kattenhorn, Martin F | Dreyer, Hedwig | 9, June 1840 | F |
| Katterheinrich, A. | Eggers, M. Carolina | 25, Oct. 1849 | C |
| Katterheinrich, A. | Hausmann, Wilhelmina | 4, Jan. 1848 | E |
| Katterheinrich, H.L. | Nienker, M Christine | 14, Apr. 1840 | G |
| Katterjohan, Henry | Elshof, Sophia | 5, Apr. 1849 | RCH |
| Kattmann, Herman H. | Scherrer, Maria Elis | 25, Oct. 1849 | C |
| Katzenbuhler, August | Raumann, Catharina | 25, July 1848 | AA |
| Katzenstein, Theo. | Fricke, M. Anna | 25, Apr. 1847 | AA |
| Katzenstein, Theodor | Schaps, Maria | 19, Aug. 1849 | II |
| Katzung, Louis | Scherfenberg, Elis. | 9, Feb. 1847 | RCH |
| Kaufermann, Johan H. | Drees, Elisabeth | 9, Jan. 1848 | CC |
| Kauffmann, Jacob | Strauss, Elisabeth | 1, Aug. 1848 | RCH |
| Kauffmann, Johan | Ball, Maria | 1, Feb. 1836 | FF |
| Kauffmann, Johan L. | Barrett, Hannah E. | 3, Aug. 1848 | RCH |
| Kaufmann, Andreas | Rude, Theresa | 27, May 1844 | AA |
| Kaufmann, Heinrich E | Crippen, Elisabeth C | 13, Dec. 1848 | RCH |
| Kaufmann, Michael | Altschul, Mina | 2, Jan. 1847 | RCH |
| Kaufmann, Simon | August, Friedricka | 30, Dec. 1848 | RCH |
| Kaufmann, Solomon | Moss, Fanny | 26, Sept 1846 | RCH |
| Kaup, Herman | Schumacher, Helen | 7, Jan. 1847 | FF |
| Kaupel, Johan H. | Ruling, Maria Adel. | 18, Apr. 1843 | AA |
| Kausch---, Jacob | Luekert, Mary | 6, Sept 1848 | RCH |
| Kaussmann, Michael | Fey, Barbara | 30, Oct. 1848 | C |
| Kauther, Philipp J. | Egelhof, Christine | 23, Aug. 1844 | G |
| Kautz, David | Griffith, Harriet | 25, Dec. 1836 | RCH |
| Kautz, John | Tanley, Hannah | 17, Sept 1843 | RCH |
| Kay, James | Newton, Rebend | 15, Dec. 1818 | RCH |
| Kayser, Johan Hein. | Schneider, Clara M. | 9, Jan. 1848 | AA |
| Kazdenfer, Johan | Steinmann, Friedrika | 5, Nov. 1848 | C |
| Ke---, John | Schireher, Caroline | 28, Mar. 1837 | RCH |
| Kealy, Edward | Richardson, Susan | 8, Feb. 1843 | RCH |
| Kean, Lewis | Price, Emeline | 12, Mar. 1837 | RCH |
| Kearb, Orlando | Munday, Ophilia | 26, July 1841 | RCH |
| Kearnes, Michael | Beltz, Mary | 6, Dec. 1832 | RCH |
| Kearney, Edward | Keenan, Nancy Ann | 27, May 1849 | BB |
| Kearney, Francis | O'Neill, Eleanor | 12, Jan. 1840 | BB |
| Kearney, Michael | Flynn, Mary Ann | 4, Nov. 1849 | BB |
| Kearns, Valentine | Williams, Hannah | 27, Aug. 1846 | RCH |
| Keating, George | Lockhart, America | 14, Apr. 1842 | RCH |
| Keating, John | Wheelright, Mary R. | 24, Apr. 1826 | I |
| Keating, Loftus | Long, Rachel | 27, Sept 1845 | RCH |
| Keating, Thomas | Warren, Honora | 23, Oct. 1848 | GG |
| Keck, William | Parker, Ann | 8, Apr. 1846 | RCH |
| Keefe, John | Cohen, Mary | 5, Feb. 1846 | BB |
| Keefe, Joseph | Turner, Sarah | 24, Apr. 1843 | BB |
| Keegan, John | Moran, Ann | 20, May 1849 | BB |
| Keegan, John | Wiley, Susan | 22, Nov. 1848 | BB |
| Keegan, Thomas | Reilly, Ellen | 28, Dec. 1843 | BB |
| Keeler, Benjamin | Carlin, Margery | 27, Dec. 1821 | RCH |
| Keeler, Edwin | Allington, Sarah | 15, Nov. 1846 | RCH |
| Keeler, Jesse | Shull, Anna | 23, Apr. 1826 | RCH |
| Keeler, John | Vallandingham, Sarah | 4, June 1846 | RCH |
| Keeler, John | Durham, Rachel | 13, Sept 1849 | RCH |
| Keeler, Philander | Keely, Susan S. | 11, Dec. 1831 | RCH |
| Keely, Pierce | McCoy, Margaret | 20, Nov. 1820 | RCH |
| Keen, Daniel | Jones, Frances | 29, Mar. 1846 | RCH |
| Keen, Oliver | Clay, Sally | Mar. 1843 | RCH |
| Keenan, Patrick | Tone, Catharine | 20, Jan. 1849 | RCH |
| Keer, John | Pager, Agnes | 23, Mar. 1838 | RCH |
| Kees, Daniel | Sears, Harriet | 21, June 1844 | RCH |

| Grooms | Brides | Date of Marriage | Code |
|--------|--------|------------------|------|
| ****** | ****** | **** ** ******** | **** |
| Keesham, John | McCarthy, Catharine | 12, Apr. 1841 | BB |
| Keger, Basil | Gahrer, Sophia | 21, July 1845 | AA |
| Kehler, Christian | Kechler, Maria | 23, Feb. 1841 | FF |
| Kehnke, Johan | Feldschneider, Maria | 11, Oct. 1840 | F |
| Keidel, Andreas | Hefferin, Anna D. | 23, Jan. 1849 | C |
| Keidel, Geo. Michael | Mars, Margaretha | 15, Oct. 1848 | C |
| Keidel, Heinrich | Schmidt, Johanna | 19, June 1842 | G |
| Keifer, Gerhard | Ungrund, Maria Cath. | 4, Dec. 1847 | EE |
| Keifert, Xavier | Falk, Magdalena | 8, Jan. 1849 | RCH |
| Keim, Johan | Eyer, Louise | 20, Apr. 1847 | A |
| Keiser, J. Heinrich | Etter, Maria | 20, May 1838 | FF |
| Keiser, John | Mitchell, Rebecca | 5, Aug. 1846 | GG |
| Keith, Robert | Hulse, Catharine | 7, June 1846 | GG |
| Keith, Thomas | White, Elisabeth F. | 22, Oct. 1845 | RCH |
| Keithorn, Bernard H. | Gerdsen, A.M. Elis. | 2, Feb. 1845 | F |
| Kel---, Charles F. | Gazlay, Elisabeth | 21, June 1821 | RCH |
| Kell, William | ----, Mary | Sept 1826 | RCH |
| Kellaher, Matthew | O'Connell, Margaret | 4, Nov. 1849 | BB |
| Kelle, Gerhard H. | Stagemann, Cath. G. | 5, Feb. 1839 | FF |
| Keller, Burget | Spun, Margaretha | 22, July 1839 | FF |
| Keller, Franz | Jauch, Maria | 24, Dec. 1848 | A |
| Keller, Friedrich | Hentz, Rosalia | 12, Oct. 1848 | EE |
| Keller, George | Meyers, Bertha | 27, June 1844 | RCH |
| Keller, Jacob | Brooks, Louise | 1, Aug. 1844 | RCH |
| Keller, Johan | Zwick, Ottilia | 7, Aug. 1843 | AA |
| Keller, Johan H. | Wissmann, Anna Ther. | 18, Aug. 1846 | EE |
| Keller, Johan H. | Lange, Maria Agnes | 24, Nov. 1848 | EE |
| Keller, John | Runyan, Rebecca | 11, May 1841 | BB |
| Keller, Martin | Phillips, Elisabeth | 23, Feb. 1849 | RCH |
| Keller, Philipp | Mateter, Elisabeth | 8, Jan. 1838 | FF |
| Keller, Philipp | Shuck, Philippina | 10, Feb. 1848 | A |
| Keller, Stephen | Krapp, Margaretha | 17, June 1847 | RCH |
| Keller, Valentin | Brown, Catharine | 27, Aug. 1839 | FF |
| Keller, Wilhelm M. | Hess, Margaretha | 14, Aug. 1849 | C |
| Keller, William | Kennedy, Mary Jane | 4, May 1843 | RCH |
| Kellermann, Francis | Buitsch, Maria | 10, Oct. 1847 | EE |
| Kellermann, Joseph | Overbeck, Catharine | 1, Nov. 1846 | FF |
| Kelley, Daniel | Crosby, Ann | 7, Dec. 1836 | RCH |
| Kelley, Dennis | Stone, Mary | 28, July 1837 | RCH |
| Kelley, John H. | Laughlin, Elisabeth | 6, Jan. 1848 | RCH |
| Kelley, Milton | Brily, Ann | 25, Nov. 1841 | RCH |
| Kelley, Moses | Ford, Catharine Ann | 15, Oct. 1845 | RCH |
| Kellinger, Anton | Woertlin, Johanna | 30, Jan. 1848 | II |
| Kellogg, Charles | Brown, Margaret | 30, Oct. 1836 | RCH |
| Kellogg, Charles Hy. | Bockey, Mary E. | Oct. 1844 | RCH |
| Kellogg, James | Reeder, Adeline | 11, Nov. 1843 | RCH |
| Kelly, Andrew | Johnson, Bridget | 21, Dec. 1839 | BB |
| Kelly, Archibald | Martin, Jane | 14, Feb. 1841 | RCH |
| Kelly, Charles | Bloomfield, Lydia | 12, Dec. 1843 | RCH |
| Kelly, Daniel | Martin, Catharine | 4, Apr. 1847 | RCH |
| Kelly, Everhan | Crosbing, Margaret | 11, Apr. 1838 | RCH |
| Kelly, James | Quinn, Bridget | 7, Sept 1845 | BB |
| Kelly, James | Connolly, Ann | 4, Feb. 1849 | BB |
| Kelly, John | Hubbard, Matilda | 1, June 1834 | RCH |
| Kelly, John | Martin, Mary A. | 3, May 1836 | RCH |
| Kelly, John | Metzel, Mary | 5, May 1836 | RCH |
| Kelly, John | West, Susan | 6, Aug. 1839 | RCH |
| Kelly, John | Knowlton, Elisabeth | 7, Nov. 1841 | RCH |
| Kelly, John | White, Ann | 10, June 1841 | BB |
| Kelly, John | McGuiness, Mary Ann | 18, Aug. 1845 | BB |
| Kelly, John | Ward, Bridget | 21, July 1846 | GG |
| Kelly, John H. | Myres, Barbara | 4, May 1820 | RCH |
| Kelly, John R. | Merrill, Mathilda | 7, Mar. 1844 | RCH |
| Kelly, Joseph | Collins, Ann | 27, Oct. 1839 | BB |
| Kelly, Matthew | Fagin, Nancy | 20, May 1843 | RCH |
| Kelly, Michael | Erwin, Mary | 31, May 1846 | GG |
| Kelly, Morris | Summers, Nancy | 2, Nov. 1842 | RCH |
| Kelly, Patrick | Rawle, Ann | 20, Sept 1843 | BB |
| Kelly, Patrick | Bradley, Sarah | 16, Apr. 1844 | BB |
| Kelly, Patrick | Crager, Margaret | 20, May 1849 | GG |
| Kelly, Peter | Cavany, Winnie | 20, May 1849 | GG |

| Grooms | Brides | Date of Marriage | Code |
|--------|--------|------------------|------|
| ****** | ****** | **** ** ******** | **** |
| Kelly, Samuel | Gardner, Margaret A. | 6, Dec. 1849 | RCH |
| Kelly, Thomas | Lackey, Rosanna | 26, July 1849 | BB |
| Kelly, William | Heffernan, Esther | 7, June 1843 | BB |
| Kelly, William | Roe, Elisabeth Ann | 16, Aug. 1846 | RCH |
| Kelm, William | Conklin, Anna Maria | 26, May 1844 | RCH |
| Kelsall, Thomas | Gooch, Emma | 6, Nov. 1845 | D |
| Kelsay, Joseph | Allen, Elisabeth | 21, Sept 1843 | RCH |
| Kelsey, Benjamin | Hall, Elvira | 12, Oct. 1846 | RCH |
| Kelsey, Naaman | Barbour, Sarah Jane | 12, May 1842 | D |
| Kelsh, Michael | Hellmann, Catharina | 16, May 1837 | FF |
| Kelso, William | Martin, Susanna | 26, Apr. 1838 | RCH |
| Kelting, Joseph | Martin, Elisabeth | 20, Sept 1832 | RCH |
| Kembel, Johan | Schwab, Anna Maria | 23, Nov. 1845 | FF |
| Kemerly, Daniel | Steward, Mary | 24, July 1832 | RCH |
| Kemp, Jacob | Burnham, Phebe | 30, Dec. 1843 | RCH |
| Kempel, Peter | Lipps, Francisca | 24, Oct. 1848 | EE |
| Kemper, Anton | Faber, Christina | 29, Oct. 1848 | FF |
| Kemper, Bernard | Meyer, Wilhelmina | 20, Feb. 1838 | FF |
| Kemper, Charles | Terry, Margaret | 24, Aug. 1847 | RCH |
| Kemper, Jacob | Metcalfe, Mary Jane | 4, Aug. 1847 | RCH |
| Kemper, James | Jones, Mathilda | 14, Sept 1843 | RCH |
| Kemper, Samuel | Hall, Elizabeth | 29, Mar. 1846 | RCH |
| Kemper, Stephen | Minshall, Mary | 9, Apr. 1844 | RCH |
| Kempf, Laurenz | Deters, Gertrud | 29, Sept 1846 | EE |
| Kempf, Mathias | Mohr, Regina | 10, Sept 1848 | EE |
| Kempf, Peter | Aschenbrenner, Cath. | 22, June 1847 | FF |
| Kempker, Johan Hein. | Hoeveler, M. Adel. | 12, Nov. 1848 | AA |
| Kempton, William | Singer, Nancy | 11, May 1847 | RCH |
| Kems, Thomas | Scowden, Sarah Ann | 24, Dec. 1835 | RCH |
| Kena, Daniel | McDonald, Mary | 9, Nov. 1837 | RCH |
| Kendall, Addison | Buckingham, Margaret | 20, Sept 1842 | RCH |
| Kendall, Alonzo | Lee, Mary | 5, Feb. 1849 | RCH |
| Kendall, Charles | Dunham, Sarah | 15, Dec. 1846 | RCH |
| Kendall, Joseph A. | Blackburn, M. | 26, July 1837 | RCH |
| Kendall, Omar | Parker, Margaret | 6, Oct. 1845 | RCH |
| Kendall, Raymond | Weaver, Abby | 6, Nov. 1847 | RCH |
| Kendall, Wilson S. | Taylor, Clarissa | 18, Feb. 1836 | RCH |
| Kendrick, Charles | Ludlow, Amanda | 9, Dec. 1844 | RCH |
| Kendrick, James | Skidmore, Eunice | 12, Sept 1847 | RCH |
| Kennard, Joseph L. | Palmer, Amelia B. | 28, Nov. 1837 | I |
| Kennedy, Benjamin | Baxter, Ann | 12, Feb. 1835 | RCH |
| Kennedy, David | Anton, Elisabeth | 6, June 1839 | RCH |
| Kennedy, James | Man, Joann | 27, Nov. 1841 | BB |
| Kennedy, James | McDermott, Catharine | 4, Feb. 1849 | GG |
| Kennedy, John | Schwab, Maria | 7, Sept 1844 | RCH |
| Kennedy, Patrick | Fitzgibbon, Ellen | 10, July 1843 | BB |
| Kennet, John | Gassaway, Elisabeth | 17, Nov. 1834 | I |
| Kennet, William C. | Thomsit, Nancy | 24, Sept 1835 | RCH |
| Kennett, John | Wade, Mary E. | 3, Mar. 1846 | I |
| Kenny, Dennis | Greeley, Ann (Mrs) | 8, Oct. 1848 | BB |
| Kenny, Patrick | Hamilton, Catharine | 11, Nov. 1842 | BB |
| Kenricks, J. Gerhard | Bagge, Elisabeth | 19, Jan. 1845 | FF |
| Kent, Horatio | Fox, Adelia | 31, Jan. 1842 | RCH |
| Kent, James | Vallandingham, Elis. | 24, Aug. 1846 | RCH |
| Kent, Thomas | Armitage, Matilda | 24, July 1836 | RCH |
| Kenton, Henry | Crawford, Sarah | 30, Apr. 1846 | RCH |
| Keogh, Patrick | Kelly, Margaret | 22, Apr. 1849 | BB |
| Keppen, Gerhard H. | Treckler, Theresa E. | 24, Oct. 1848 | AA |
| Keppler, Gottlob | Gessler, Caroline | 20, Aug. 1848 | G |
| Ker, Clarkson | Conklin, Mary | 19, Feb. 1818 | RCH |
| Kerber, Charles | Shirth, Mary Ann | 4, Jan. 1827 | RCH |
| Kerkhoff, Dominick | Berte, Elisabeth | 20, Feb. 1848 | FF |
| Kern, Rudolph | Emmert, Catharine | 20, Oct. 1842 | RCH |
| Kernan, Michael | McGovern, Margaret | 7, Jan. 1845 | BB |
| Kerndorfer, Johan | Klausen, Rosina | 8, Nov. 1848 | C |
| Kerner, Christoph | Steigerwald, Barbara | 19, Nov. 1849 | AA |
| Kerns, Bartholomew | McHugh, Ann | 26, July 1847 | BB |
| Kerr, John D. | Miller, Elisabeth | 19, Apr. 1821 | RCH |
| Kersch, Peter | Ohlick, Regina | 8, Dec. 1849 | EE |
| Kersen, Johan | Kallmann, M. Theresa | 30, Sept 1849 | II |
| Kersen, Theodor | Tindermann, Catharin | 9, Jan. 1848 | FF |

| Grooms<br>****** | Brides<br>****** | Date of Marriage<br>**** ** ******** | Code<br>**** |
|---|---|---|---|
| Kersker, Johan G. | Robben, Anna Maria | 10, Oct. 1847 | EE |
| Kerth, Johan | Koeler, Catharine | 1, Jan. 1846 | A |
| Kerth, Karl | Goetz, Barbara | 7, June 1847 | C |
| Kerwin, Jeremy | Donohue, Catharine | 4, Nov. 1849 | GG |
| Kerwin, Michael | Ryan, Catharine | 18, Feb. 1849 | GG |
| Kerwin, Thomas | Murphy, Margaret | 14, Aug. 1849 | GG |
| Kesselring, Martin | Bentz, Maria | 11, Oct. 1849 | C |
| Kessen, J. Heinrich | Baumer, Maria Anna | 8, June 1841 | FF |
| Kessen, Johan | Huelskamp, Bernardin | 17, Oct. 1847 | AA |
| Kessing, Heinrich | Brueggemann, Anna M. | 8, Apr. 1847 | C |
| Kessing, Herman H. | Schroeder, M. Elis. | 23, Apr. 1844 | FF |
| Kessinger, Samuel | Ireland, Elisabeth | 19, Nov. 1835 | RCH |
| Kessler, Balthasar | Ankenbauer, Dorothea | 9, May 1843 | AA |
| Kessler, Herman | Meyers, Charlotte | 31, May 1847 | RCH |
| Kessler, Johan Bapt. | Brand, Maria Anna | 3, Feb. 1835 | FF |
| Kessler, Peter | Brown, Rachel | 20, Mar. 1848 | RCH |
| Kessler, Valentin | Havert, Catharina | 24, Sept 1839 | FF |
| Kestner, Friedrich | Kestner, Henrietta | 7, Mar. 1849 | F |
| Ketcham, Ira | Steele, Elisabeth | 29, Oct. 1821 | RCH |
| Ketchum, Benjamin | Benn, Rhoda | 17, Aug. 1826 | RCH |
| Ketchum, James | Tud---, Mary Ann | 15, Sept 1836 | RCH |
| Ketchum, William | King, Elisabeth Jane | 10, Apr. 1848 | RCH |
| Ketteler, Carl | Schroeder, Elisabeth | 8, Feb. 1848 | AA |
| Kettelmann, Heinrich | Ronnebaum, M. Agnes | 9, Nov. 1849 | II |
| Kettle, James | Tullis, Sarah Ann | 18, Aug. 1843 | RCH |
| Kettler, Gerhard | Knabmeier, Gesina | 21, Jan. 1849 | II |
| Kettler, Johan Bd. | Wuennemann, Euphemia | 22, June 1847 | AA |
| Kettlewell, Joseph | Paul, Elisabeth | 15, Apr. 1847 | RCH |
| Kettmann, Bernard H. | Baters, Maria Adel. | 21, Sept 1848 | EE |
| Kettmann, Heinrich | Geers, Anna Maria | 16, July 1848 | EE |
| Keuper, Joseph | Reismann, Gertrud | 19, Oct. 1845 | FF |
| Keuter, Heinrich | Griffenkamp, Maria A | 4, June 1839 | FF |
| Keuvers, Joseph | Schevienhar, Gertrud | 12, May 1839 | FF |
| Key, Samuel | Kisinger, Mary | 20, Jan. 1825 | RCH |
| Key, William | Reid, Agnes | 18, Dec. 1843 | RCH |
| Keygon, John | Meeker, Jane Ann | 10, Nov. 1845 | RCH |
| Keys, John F. | Bagley, Elisabeth H. | 13, July 1836 | RCH |
| Keys, Richard | Sterrett, Mary E. | 13, May 1846 | RCH |
| Keys, Samuel | May, Amanda M. | 25, Nov. 1846 | RCH |
| Keyt, Alonzo | Hamlin, Susanna | 10, Oct. 1848 | RCH |
| Kibby, Jarvis | Clark, Elisabeth | 20, Jan. 1820 | RCH |
| Kidd, Friedrich | Hawkins, Anna | 24, Feb. 1842 | RCH |
| Kiderlin, William L. | Longworth, Lucia A. | 20, June 1848 | I |
| Kidman, Richard | Cox, Matilda | 15, May 1837 | RCH |
| Kiefer, Daniel | White, Maria | 30, Oct. 1845 | A |
| Kiefer, George | Cushman, Eliza | 27, Oct. 1833 | I |
| Kiefer, Ignatz | Schewni, Catharine | 4, Oct. 1842 | AA |
| Kiefer, Jacob | Busse, Amelia | 4, June 1846 | G |
| Kiefer, Johan | Schultheiss, Dora | 8, Apr. 1849 | G |
| Kiefer, John | Albrecht, Magdalena | 18, July 1848 | G |
| Kiefer, Joseph | Hettesheimer, Carol. | 1, July 1848 | AA |
| Kiefer, Philipp | Wacker, Maria | 8, July 1845 | G |
| Kiefer, Philipp | Weber, Barbara | 29, June 1847 | G |
| Kiefer, Xavier | Jerger, Genofeva | 22, Nov. 1846 | FF |
| Kieffe, Daniel | McCarthy, Margaret | 2, May 1847 | GG |
| Kiegler, Johan | Proes, Maria | 7, Nov. 1842 | AA |
| Kiendit, Johan Hein. | Turner, Catharine | 17, July 1845 | AA |
| Kienker, Johan H. | Ronnebaum, M.A. | 26, Aug. 1849 | AA |
| Kiepe, Friedrich | Kammann, Maria | 11, Apr. 1844 | F |
| Kiernan, James | McBride, Martha | 4, Feb. 1849 | BB |
| Kiersted, John H. | Daudal, Godiva | 3, Nov. 1835 | RCH |
| Kifmeyer, Bernard H. | Ruwe, Anna Maria | 7, May 1848 | AA |
| Kiggan, Nicholas | Shane, Josephine | 19, Dec. 1848 | RCH |
| Kihr, Michael | Herbach, Anna M(Mrs) | 7, Oct. 1841 | FF |
| Kilgour, Abraham | Shotz, Elisabeth | 25, June 1849 | RCH |
| Kilgour, John | Cunnen, Mary Ann | 22, Aug. 1840 | RCH |
| Kilian, Jacob | Story, Barbara | 17, Aug. 1841 | FF |
| Kilkelly, Edward | Martin, Margaret | 13, Nov. 1848 | BB |
| Kilkenny, Anthony | Robinson, Bridget | 27, Aug. 1849 | GG |
| Kilker, J. Gerhard | Nichting, Anna Maria | 18, Aug. 1841 | FF |
| Killing, Patrick | Palmer, Elisabeth M. | 18, July 1837 | RCH |

| Grooms<br>***** | Brides<br>***** | Date of Marriage<br>**** ** ******** | Code<br>**** |
|---|---|---|---|
| Killison, John | Scott, Catharine | 4, Nov. 1820 | RCH |
| Killough, James | Brownrigg, Catharine | 10, Aug. 1837 | RCH |
| Killough, James | Davis, Mary | 8, Sept 1841 | RCH |
| Kilzer, Georg | Burkhart, Katharina | 15, July 1847 | AA |
| Kimball, Abel | Francisco, Mary A. | 19, Nov. 1845 | RCH |
| Kimball, Benjamin | Chapin, Lydia | 5, Feb. 1846 | RCH |
| Kimball, Isaac | Dailey, Mary | 17, May 1837 | RCH |
| Kimball, Isaac | Wollen, Elisabeth | 10, Mar. 1843 | RCH |
| Kimball, John | Hawkins, Maria M. | 19, Apr. 1844 | RCH |
| Kimble, William | Jeffers, Esther | 21, Apr. 1846 | RCH |
| Kina, Daniel | Byrne, Elisabeth | 7, Jan. 1819 | RCH |
| Kincade, Alexander | Livingston, Mary | 24, Oct. 1844 | RCH |
| Kincaid, George L. | Bauchmed, Elisabeth | 31, July 1834 | RCH |
| Kincaid, Thomas | Argo, Phoebe | 30, Dec. 1833 | RCH |
| Kindrub, J. Bernard | Bramlage, M. Cath. | 7, July 1840 | FF |
| Kine, Luke | Ernst, Emilia Mary | 28, Aug. 1836 | RCH |
| King, | Boman, Tracy Ann | 24, 1836 | RCH |
| King, Benjamin | McCurdy, Margaret | 27, Feb. 1823 | RCH |
| King, Conrad | Bonn, Apollonia(Mrs) | 7, Jan. 1841 | FF |
| King, Daniel | Smith, Cynthia | June 1849 | RCH |
| King, David | Caldwell, Almona | 9, Nov. 1826 | RCH |
| King, Edward | McNaughton, Sarah A. | 24, May 1841 | I |
| King, Frederick | Heigelman, Christina | 10, May 1836 | RCH |
| King, George | Robeson, Mary | 16, Apr. 1839 | RCH |
| King, Henry | Martin, Mary Ann | 14, Apr. 1844 | RCH |
| King, James | Byrne, Mary | 9, Apr. 1844 | BB |
| King, John | Jones, Rachel | 6, May 1839 | RCH |
| King, John | Luke, Mary | 17, Nov. 1834 | I |
| King, Jonathan | W---, Susan | May 1839 | RCH |
| King, Justin | Lampson, Mary | 28, June 1826 | RCH |
| King, Justin | Hunt, Elisabeth D. | 1, Aug. 1835 | RCH |
| King, Leander | Gwinnis, Temperence | 24, July 1825 | RCH |
| King, Michael | Hagemann, Catharine | 14, Jan. 1840 | FF |
| King, Peter | Wooster, Jane | 10, Mar. 1842 | RCH |
| King, Rufus | Rivers, Margaret | 18, May 1843 | I |
| King, Samuel | Gans, Susan | 2, June 1833 | RCH |
| King, W.J. | Pangburn, Parmelia | 6, May 1849 | RCH |
| King, William | Drake, Mary | 31, Jan. 1822 | RCH |
| King, William | Gammott, Nancy | 27, Dec. 1831 | RCH |
| Kingston, William | Allen, Mary Ann | 19, Aug. 1847 | RCH |
| Kinnan, John | Porter, Sarah | 17, Sept 1843 | RCH |
| Kinner, Butler | Rish, Ruhanna Ann | 11, Sept 1832 | RCH |
| Kinney, John | Evans, Jane | 21, Mar. 1822 | RCH |
| Kinney, John | Johnson, Julia A. | 10, Oct. 1839 | RCH |
| Kinney, John | Goins, Mary | 11, June 1849 | RCH |
| Kinney, Joseph | Collins, Jane | 20, June 1839 | RCH |
| Kinney, Patrick | Hamilton, Catharine | 11, Nov. 1842 | RCH |
| Kinnison, James | Gry---, Peggy | 6, June 1822 | RCH |
| Kinsella, James P. | Dunn, Eleanora | 9, Sept 1848 | BB |
| Kinsey, David | Beck, Julia A. | 31, Jan. 1843 | BB |
| Kinsey, Edmund | McFarland, Sarah Ann | 3, Aug. 1834 | RCH |
| Kinsey, Parson | Pancoast, Mary | 28, July 1845 | RCH |
| Kinsey, Samuel | Kinsey, Rachel | 13, Aug. 1846 | RCH |
| Kinzinger, Joseph | Kinzinger, Katharine | 20, June 1848 | G |
| Kipfenberger, Philip | Cottier, Maria | 11, May 1847 | FF |
| Kipp, Friedrich | Evers, Anna F. | 7, June 1849 | RCH |
| Kipp, Friedrich Wm. | Sommermeyer, Wilhel. | 22, Feb. 1848 | C |
| Kipp, Herman | Meyers, Catharine | 13, Nov. 1845 | C |
| Kipper, Johan | Semer, Barbara | 15, June 1843 | AA |
| Kippes, Anton | Duehl, Catharine | 30, Jan. 1848 | EE |
| Kirby, James | Ball, Hannah | 14, Oct. 1819 | RCH |
| Kirby, James | Taylor, Cordelia | 24, Feb. 1846 | RCH |
| Kirby, John | Celstrip, Hannah | 3, Oct. 1832 | RCH |
| Kirby, Josiah | Hargy, Catharine | 4, June 1837 | RCH |
| Kirby, Thomas | Price, Mary | 13, Nov. 1842 | RCH |
| Kircher, Francis | Siefert, Maria | 16, Oct. 1834 | FF |
| Kircher, Johan Adam | Imm, Catharina | 28, May 1849 | AA |
| Kirchhoff, Ludwig | Rentz, Maria | 30, Apr. 1840 | FF |
| Kirchmer, Francis | Beck, Catharine | 5, Feb. 1845 | A |
| Kirchner, Franz M. | Bechler, Magdalena | 6, Feb. 1848 | C |
| Kirchner, John | Meyer, Philippina | 23, Nov. 1841 | RCH |

| Grooms<br>****** | Brides<br>****** | Date of Marriage<br>**** ** ******** | Code<br>**** |
|---|---|---|---|
| Kirchner, Louis | Heckmann, Elisabeth | 7, Feb. 1843 | RCH |
| Kirk, James | Winters, Elizabeth | 26, Dec. 1849 | GG |
| Kirk, Thomas | Thompson, Mary | 5, Sept 1848 | RCH |
| Kirkpatrick, Stephen | Sears, Mary | 24, Sept 1846 | RCH |
| Kirley, Daniel | Gerhard, Mary | 23, July 1848 | GG |
| Kirn, Samuel | House, Susannah | 28, Mar. 1824 | RCH |
| Kirsch, Balthasar | Veith, Regina | 31, Dec. 1849 | EE |
| Kirsch, John | Lehmann, Magdalena | 24, Jan. 1844 | RCH |
| Kirsten, Anton | Foerster, Caecilia | 12, May 1846 | AA |
| Kirwan, Thomas | Markey, Catharine | 10, Nov. 1847 | GG |
| Kisker, Herman Phil. | Hanke, Theresa | 16, July 1848 | AA |
| Kisker, J. Heinrich | Rohlfing, Maria | 7, Nov. 1849 | F |
| Kissel, Georg | Fuldelar, Maria | 19, Nov. 1849 | A |
| Kissinger, George W. | Mills, Susan | 3, Dec. 1849 | RCH |
| Kissinger, William | Stuart, Elisabeth | 3, Feb. 1842 | RCH |
| Kistner, Eduard | Burghardt, Charlotte | 2, Jan. 1845 | G |
| Kistner, Ernst F. | Burghart, Charlotte | 1, Jan. 1844 | RCH |
| Kistner, John | Meerbus, Maria | 25, Nov. 1848 | RCH |
| Kistner, Theodor | Schelle, Maria Anna | 4, June 1848 | FF |
| Kitcham, Israel | Richardson, Elmira | 28, Mar. 1822 | RCH |
| Kitchel, Aaron | Munson, Lydia H. | 4, Oct. 1835 | RCH |
| Kitchel, Samuel | Leaming, Judah | 13, Mar. 1825 | RCH |
| Kitchell, Cyrus | Richardson, Delia | 21, Sept 1848 | RCH |
| Kitchell, Daniel | Crist, Elisabeth | 19, Sept 1833 | RCH |
| Kitchen, John | Mooney, Catharine | 21, Apr. 1822 | RCH |
| Kite, George | Beach, Patty | 4, Sept 1819 | RCH |
| Kite, Hiram | Warren, Rosannah S. | 21, July 1847 | RCH |
| Kitte, Bernard | Becker, Wilhelmina | 10, Feb. 1847 | AA |
| Kittel, Jacob | Weissmann, Elisabeth | 15, Nov. 1845 | G |
| Kittelring, Martin | Cosmann, Anna Maria | 22, Sept 1840 | G |
| Kitts, David H. | Meyers, Elisabeth | 28, Sept 1843 | RCH |
| Kitts, Joseph | Ray, Maria Elisabeth | 20, Apr. 1847 | RCH |
| Kitzner, Michael | Krum, Barbara | 9, Nov. 1843 | FF |
| Kizer, Emanuel | Frazier, Rebecca | 25, Jan. 1834 | RCH |
| Kizer, Philipp | Gamble, | 21, Apr. 1832 | RCH |
| Kizer, William | Williams, Nancy | 25, Feb. 1819 | RCH |
| Klanke, Johan Heinr. | Brengelmann, Maria | 23, May 1849 | F |
| Klar, Ignatz | Frueh, Christina | 29, May 1847 | FF |
| Klari, Friedrich | Ensinger, Rosina | 1, Jan. 1849 | A |
| Klarmann, Georg | Ott, Barbara | 13, Apr. 1847 | FF |
| Klarmann, Georg | Meier, Theresa | 19, Aug. 1849 | FF |
| Klasen, Herman | Ramp, Helena | 21, Apr. 1846 | AA |
| Klatte, Caspar | Gerwe, Margaretha | 24, Apr. 1849 | CC |
| Klatte, Johan | Kleine, Maria Agnes | 24, Apr. 1849 | CC |
| Klatte, Johan Heinr. | Hillen, Maria Engel | 2, Nov. 1848 | F |
| Klaus, Dominick | Trimpe, Maria Anna | 21, May 1844 | AA |
| Klaus, Dominick | Fischer, Maria Elis. | 25, Aug. 1842 | FF |
| Klaus, Dominick | Hoppenjans, Catharin | 19, Aug. 1849 | FF |
| Klaus, Johan Bernard | Gessen, M. Elisabeth | 29, June 1841 | FF |
| Klaus, Johan Bernard | Trentmann, Cath. E. | 3, Oct. 1843 | FF |
| Klaus, Johan Heinric | Meyer, Anna Maria | 4, Mar. 1846 | AA |
| Klausing, Bernard | Rudde, Maria Anna | 16, Jan. 1849 | II |
| Klaw, Michael | Wertheimer, Rose | 24, Feb. 1847 | RCH |
| Kleb, Joseph | Seifert, Amalia | 16, Sept 1849 | II |
| Klee, Nicolaus | Hartig, Margaretha | 1, Apr. 1845 | AA |
| Kleekamp, Johan | Meyer, Sophia | 24, Feb. 1842 | F |
| Kleekamp, Johan Fr. | Surenkamp, Maria | 28, Oct. 1841 | F |
| Klefot, Friedrich | Settlage, Julianna | 20, Apr. 1847 | AA |
| Kleibacher, Friedric | Stickfers, Elisabeth | 25, Feb. 1847 | F |
| Kleier, Gerhard | Rickamp, Catharine | 31, Oct. 1847 | CC |
| Kleier, John Bernard | Springmeier, Louise | 3, Feb. 1848 | F |
| Kleimeyer, Heinrich | Dunker, Maria | 28, Nov. 1849 | F |
| Klein, Andreas | Hulzelberger, Marg. | 11, July 1836 | FF |
| Klein, Casper | Duffner, Maria Anna | 29, Nov. 1849 | FF |
| Klein, Georg | Schulz, Elisabeth | 17, Aug. 1848 | B |
| Klein, Georg P. | Knochl, Margaretha | 9, July 1848 | EE |
| Klein, Heinrich | Begelberger, Maria | 24, Nov. 1834 | FF |
| Klein, Heinrich | Macke, Maria | 26, Jan. 1836 | FF |
| Klein, Herman | Biscus, Maria | 27, Nov. 1838 | FF |
| Klein, Jacob | Deter, Francisca | 25, July 1844 | A |
| Klein, Johan B. | Ritzert, Theresa | 28, June 1849 | EE |

| Grooms<br>****** | Brides<br>****** | Date of Marriage<br>**** ** ******** | Code<br>**** |
|---|---|---|---|
| Klein, Joseph | Dickhaus, M. Agnes | 8, Aug. 1837 | FF |
| Klein, Lawrence | Schuler, Barbara | 15, June 1847 | EE |
| Klein, Michael | Nies, Margaretha | 15, Apr. 1849 | A |
| Klein, Nicolaus | Schwartz, Anna Maria | 24, Aug. 1847 | RCH |
| Kleinberg, Joseph | Kenken, Anna Maria | 6, July 1845 | AA |
| Kleinberg, Theodor | Hinsla, Bernardina | 26, Oct. 1849 | CC |
| Kleine, David | Roth, Anna Maria | 23, Nov. 1840 | FF |
| Kleine, Friedrich | Linnenkugel, Elis. | 3, Aug. 1845 | AA |
| Kleine, Heinrich | Wipler, Anna Maria | 22, Sept 1840 | F |
| Kleine, Herman | Kestner, Dorothea | 18, June 1843 | AA |
| Kleine, Joseph | Steinke, Maria Anna | 29, Jan. 1839 | FF |
| Kleine, Joseph | Bruns, Gesina | 27, Nov. 1849 | EE |
| Kleinekruthof, Jos. | Wermann, Catharina | 11, Sept 1838 | FF |
| Kleinekruthop, Jos. | Sieve, M. Catharina | 17, Nov. 1840 | FF |
| Kleinfelder, Jacob | Stuck, Elisabeth | 4, Jan. 1847 | G |
| Kleinfelter, Jacob | Weaer, Mary | 26, May 1849 | RCH |
| Kleinhaus, Johan | Hetzel, Margaretha | 27, Nov. 1843 | FF |
| Kleinmann, Abraham | Wolff, Magdalena | 11, July 1844 | RCH |
| Kleinmann, Gottfried | Kleinmann, Maria | 30, Dec. 1840 | G |
| Kleinmann, Johan | Lehmkuhle, Catharina | 4, June 1848 | AA |
| Kleinschmidt, Ernst | Glindkamp, Anna M. | 2, Feb. 1843 | F |
| Kleintrimpe, Bernard | Wille, Elisabeth | 29, Sept 1846 | AA |
| Klekamp, Heinrich | Meyers, Catharine | 16, Dec. 1847 | C |
| Klem, George M. | Schaaf, Barbara | 14, Sept 1849 | RCH |
| Klemann, Johan Theo. | Fai, Crescentia | 10, Oct. 1848 | EE |
| Klemeier, Johan | Henniger, Charlotte | 19, Apr. 1849 | C |
| Klen, Johan | Hausmann, Catharine | 22, Feb. 1842 | F |
| Klene, Bernard | Reke, Carolina | 6, Feb. 1848 | AA |
| Klene, Bernard | Zurbecke, Gertrud | 7, Jan. 1845 | FF |
| Klene, Francis | Rauth, Christina | 9, Feb. 1841 | FF |
| Klene, Herman | Wigmann, Maria Elis. | 17, Apr. 1849 | II |
| Klenke, Herman Hein. | Janzen, Dorothea | 12, Feb. 1839 | FF |
| Klenke, Johan H. | Trentmann, Elisabeth | 26, Nov. 1844 | AA |
| Klenke, Joseph | Luening, Maria | 3, Oct. 1847 | AA |
| Kleyer, Friedrich W. | Piepers, Maria Elis. | 19, Jan. 1846 | F |
| Kleyer, Heinrich | Greiven, Anna Maria | 2, Feb. 1843 | RCH |
| Kliber, Francis | Schumm, Margaretha | 20, Apr. 1841 | FF |
| Klimper, Anton | Arens, Anna Maria | 4, Feb. 1849 | EE |
| Kling, Franz | Staeble, Caroline | 29, Jan. 1846 | G |
| Kling, J.H. | Hauck, Catharina | 9, May 1848 | II |
| Kling, Johan | Hoffmann, Catharine | 9, Jan. 1844 | FF |
| Klinge, Justin | Rebekkam, Gesina | 27, Feb. 1848 | AA |
| Klingenberg, Heinric | Kuhlmann, Theresa | 30, May 1847 | AA |
| Klingwart, John | Knobe, Sophia | 16, Mar. 1846 | RCH |
| Klink, Charles | Black, Julia | 3, Sept 1843 | RCH |
| Klinker, Christopher | Mergevot, Margaret | 27, Aug. 1835 | FF |
| Klinker, J. Heinrich | Repking, Sophia | 13, Sept 1848 | F |
| Klinler, Georg | Alendorf, Christina | 14, Oct. 1849 | II |
| Klintemeier, Bernard | Rayers, Catharine | 15, June 1849 | RCH |
| Klintworth, Christ. | Zix, Wilhelmina | 11, Nov. 1849 | G |
| Klippel, Joseph | Magly, Margaret | 29, Aug. 1844 | RCH |
| Klipser, Charles N. | Thornell, Sarah | 13, Sept 1836 | RCH |
| Klister, Herman | Schaten, Elisabeth | 31, Dec. 1848 | AA |
| Klock, William | Brua, Friedricka | 17, June 1844 | RCH |
| Klocke, Heinrich | Heyer, Margaretha | 1, Aug. 1844 | G |
| Klocke, Ludwig | Stembring, Elisabeth | 7, May 1846 | G |
| Klockenkemper, Henry | Moenning, Elisabeth | 9, Jan. 1844 | FF |
| Kloeb, Joseph | Geisert, | 6, Sept 1849 | RCH |
| Kloelb, Lorenz | Nadler, Mathilda | 10, Jan. 1847 | FF |
| Klopf, Johan | Durst, Catharine | 6, June 1847 | CC |
| Klopf, Johan | Seifert, Barbara | 6, July 1847 | CC |
| Klopf, Martin | Hoffmann, Maria Anna | 16, Sept 1839 | FF |
| Klopfer, Friedrich | Bauer, Anna | 22, Aug. 1848 | A |
| Kloppenberg, Friedr. | Doepke, Catharine | 3, Sept 1848 | G |
| Klopper, Heinrich | Wehmeier, Johanna | 7, Aug. 1849 | RCH |
| Klos, Jacob | Krummel, Louise | 19, Aug. 1849 | C |
| Klostermann, Carl | Korte, Maria | 26, Nov. 1844 | AA |
| Klostermann, Heinric | Consen, Gertrud | 26, Apr. 1840 | FF |
| Klostermann, Johan H | Kohl, Elisabeth | 10, Apr. 1847 | FF |
| Klostermann, Johan J | Busse, Anna Elis. | 11, May 1845 | AA |
| Klostermann, Joseph | Steinemann, Maria | 14, Oct. 1849 | AA |

| Grooms<br>****** | Brides<br>****** | Date of Marriage<br>**** ** ******** | Code<br>**** |
|---|---|---|---|
| Klostermann, Rudolph | Rump, Maria Anna | 11, Sept 1848 | CC |
| Kluck, Heinrich | Branchendee, Anna | 10, Oct. 1848 | AA |
| Klueber, Anton | Schaefer, Margaretha | 4, Jan. 1848 | CC |
| Klueber, Heinrich | Brand, Elisabeth | 28, May 1844 | FF |
| Klueber, Johan | Kessler, Ursula | 23, Jan. 1844 | FF |
| Klueber, Johan | Baus, Barbara | 3, Aug. 1847 | CC |
| Klueber, Johan Jos. | Zwirlein, Anna Marg. | 26, Dec. 1847 | EE |
| Klueber, Philipp | Scheerer, Elisabeth | 10, Dec. 1848 | G |
| Klueckert, Adam | Memmel, Kunigunda | 24, July 1849 | EE |
| Kluemper, Joseph | Brueggemann, Angela | 3, May 1846 | FF |
| Kluenberg, Heinrich | Piening, Agnes | 1, Nov. 1849 | AA |
| Kluesener, Casper | Imwald, Juliana | 11, Jan. 1842 | FF |
| Kluesener, Heinrich | Stoewer, Maria Anna | 7, Oct. 1849 | AA |
| Kluesener, Johan | Evermann, Johanna | 27, Oct. 1842 | AA |
| Kluesener, Theodor | Vaske, Maria | 6, Feb. 1848 | II |
| Kluesner, Bernard T. | Wintering, Anna M. | 15, Nov. 1846 | EE |
| Klug, Valentin | Braindl, Catharine | 14, May 1848 | EE |
| Kluker, Wilhelm | Muellering, Maria A. | 29, Aug. 1849 | F |
| Klump, Joseph | Purst, Agatha | 14, Aug. 1849 | EE |
| Klumpp, Peter | Steckenreider, Susan | 19, Apr. 1849 | RCH |
| Klusmann, Friedrich | Tabke, Johanna | 21, Oct. 1847 | G |
| Klusmann, Georg H. | Gaus, Sophia Louise | 1, Dec. 1846 | RCH |
| Klusmann, Heinrich | Bunnemeier, Dina | 14, Oct. 1849 | II |
| Klusmann, Heinrich L | Mueller, Sophia L. | 6, Sept 1849 | B |
| Klusmann, Ludwig | Tapking, Caroline | 10, May 1849 | B |
| Klute, Johan Heinric | Hutte, Sophia Doroth | 14, Oct. 1847 | F |
| Knab, Adam | Boerin, Eva | 11, Sept 1848 | A |
| Knab, Peter | Reising, Elisabeth | 28, Apr. 1849 | II |
| Knabe, Anton | Meyer, Catharine | 16, May 1843 | AA |
| Knabel, Hieronymus | Doll, Genofeva | 2, Jan. 1840 | FF |
| Knabel, Jacob | Jung, Christina | 11, Nov. 1840 | FF |
| Knabel, Simon | Mein, Magdalena | 8, May 1837 | FF |
| Knabke, Albert | Lammers, Gertrud | 14, Nov. 1837 | FF |
| Knaebel, Georg | Erhard, Friedricka | 26, Apr. 1846 | EE |
| Knagge, Johan Heinr. | Holleid, M. Sophia | 29, May 1845 | AA |
| Knagge, Theodor | Haumann, Catharina | 18, May 1841 | FF |
| Knapke, Bernard | Brundeis, Maria | 29, Jan. 1839 | FF |
| Knapke, Francis | Meier, Bernardina | 18, Apr. 1839 | FF |
| Knapp, Casper | Greven, Maria | 19, Nov. 1846 | FF |
| Knapp, Gottlieb | Koch, Catharina | 30, Nov. 1849 | G |
| Knapp, Heinrich | Hautmann, Josephina | 12, May 1839 | FF |
| Knapp, Johan | Ladenberger, Elis. | 31, Mar. 1847 | G |
| Knapp, Johan Friedr. | Scheid, Kunigunda | 1, Sept 1845 | C |
| Knapp, John | Baughman, Margaret | 29, Dec. 1819 | RCH |
| Knapper, William | Vail, Jane | 19, May 1825 | RCH |
| Knauer, Christian | Knauring, Carolina | 4, Nov. 1849 | C |
| Knebel, Andreas | Knebel, Carolina | 20, July 1835 | FF |
| Knebel, Georg L. | Knerr, Elisabeth | 4, July 1848 | A |
| Knecke, Gottfried | Miller, Catharina | 13, May 1834 | RCH |
| Kneeland, Phil. | Barringer, Caroline | 17, Apr. 1846 | RCH |
| Kneelor, Valentin | Markle, Magdalena | 15, Apr. 1834 | RCH |
| Knicely, Jesse C. | Greene, Mary S. | 26, Mar. 1837 | RCH |
| Knicely, John | Bodin, Fanny | 1, Feb. 1838 | RCH |
| Knickmann, Heinrich | Trimble, Carolina | 18, Aug. 1835 | FF |
| Knickmann, Heinrich | Klookens, Margaretha | 11, Sept 1845 | F |
| Knickmann, Heinrich | Brandt, Maria (Mrs) | 3, June 1847 | F |
| Knickmann, Heinrich | Fudler, Anna | 6, Sept 1848 | F |
| Knickmeier, Henry | Hartmann, Lucy | 27, Aug. 1845 | RCH |
| Knider, Samuel | Crane, Clarissa | 6, Sept 1849 | RCH |
| Knight, | Turner, Nancy | 25, Apr. 1836 | RCH |
| Knight, Albert G. | Gazley, Delia | 12, Nov. 1832 | RCH |
| Knight, Benjamin | Adamson, Frances | 19, July 1838 | RCH |
| Knight, Charles | Tucker, Phebe | 30, Mar. 1835 | RCH |
| Knight, Henry | Buel, Abigail | 23, Oct. 1836 | RCH |
| Knight, Henry W. | Martin, Mary Elis. | 29, Aug. 1835 | RCH |
| Knight, James | Smith, Mary A. | 24, Nov. 1833 | RCH |
| Knight, John | Bradshaw, Anna Elis. | 6, Nov. 1845 | RCH |
| Knight, John W. | Stevens, Elisabeth | 6, Dec. 1846 | RCH |
| Knight, Thomas | McHugh, Bridget | 25, June 1848 | GG |
| Knippenberg, Friedr. | Foskel, Catharine | 14, Mar. 1847 | RCH |
| Knobbe, Bernard | Borger, Lucia | 31, Oct. 1849 | II |

| Grooms | Brides | Date of Marriage | Code |
|--------|--------|------------------|------|
| ****** | ****** | **** ** ******** | **** |
| Knoebel, Theobald H. | Nageleisen, Maria V. | 14, Aug. 1848 | AA |
| Knoepfler, Michael | Oberli, Elisabeth | 8, Oct. 1848 | EE |
| Knoke, Frederick | Schultz, Mary | 25, Aug. 1846 | RCH |
| Knoop, Peter | Stammler, Caroline | 9, Mar. 1848 | RCH |
| Knoph, Thompson | Brownson, Lucinda | 30, June 1834 | RCH |
| Knost, Friedrich | Rehme, M. Elisabeth | 5, Oct. 1843 | G |
| Knost, Friedrich | Vollmer, Henrietta | 20, Dec. 1849 | G |
| Knost, Heinrich | Ahlering, Doris | 16, Sept 1847 | F |
| Knost, Henry | Havekotte, M. Elis. | 6, Apr. 1837 | RCH |
| Knostmann, Carl | Niehaus, Cath. Elis. | 21, June 1846 | FF |
| Knostmann, Gerhard F | Hobers, Anna Maria | 4, Jan. 1849 | B |
| Knostmann, Wilhelm | Darlinghaus, A. Elis | 16, Dec. 1844 | RCH |
| Knoth, Andreas | Schrindharin, Chris. | 7, Aug. 1847 | RCH |
| Knoth, Andreas | Bauer, Catharine | 20, Sept 1846 | G |
| Knott, Arthur | Dumford, Elisabeth | 11, June 1848 | RCH |
| Knowle, Levi | Davis, Jane | 27, Dec. 1835 | RCH |
| Knowles, William | Chavore, Mary | 15, June 1837 | RCH |
| Knowlton, Francis | Foster, Fanny | 3, Dec. 1837 | RCH |
| Knowlton, Hiram | Stevenson, Mary | 10, Sept 1835 | RCH |
| Knowlton, Sherman | Monahan, Dorcas | 13, May 1847 | RCH |
| Knox, Charles | Rogers, Mary | 29, Aug. 1848 | RCH |
| Knox, Evan | Jones, Ann | 25, May 1847 | RCH |
| Knox, James M. | Stevenson, Amelia | 7, Dec. 1848 | RCH |
| Knox, John | Nalor, Nancy | 11, Nov. 1819 | RCH |
| Knox, John | Detchler, Sarah | 3, Jan. 1848 | RCH |
| Knox, Joseph H. | Cable, Elmira | 3, Feb. 1844 | RCH |
| Knox, William H. | Davies, Eleanor | 23, May 1849 | RCH |
| Knuefer, Bernard | Huewe, Anna Maria | 30, Oct. 1845 | AA |
| Knueven, J. Herman | Reling, Maria Anna | 13, Feb. 1838 | FF |
| Knueven, J. Herman | Rufers, Johanna | 23, Feb. 1841 | FF |
| Knuf, Johan Herman | Hoedlers, Maria Anna | 24, Jan. 1843 | AA |
| Knufener, Philipp | Meyer, Maria | 14, Feb. 1838 | FF |
| Knust, Friedrich | Bregemann, Maria | 10, June 1847 | G |
| Knust, Heinrich | Meyers, Maria | 17, Apr. 1845 | G |
| Kober, Leonard | Krebs, Julia | 2, Dec. 1849 | RCH |
| Koch, Adam | Heerdt, Elisabeth | 9, July 1844 | G |
| Koch, Bernard Heinr. | Schmidt, Louise | 9, May 1848 | RCH |
| Koch, Felix | Folz, Magdalena | 21, Sept 1846 | EE |
| Koch, Georg Michael | Stroebel, Sybilla | 27, Nov. 1845 | C |
| Koch, Heinrich | Bierbaum, Sophia | 19, Oct. 1843 | F |
| Koch, Heinrich Johan | Lucas, Cath. Sophia | 7, Mar. 1848 | C |
| Koch, Herman Heinric | Steinke, Anna Maria | 16, July 1848 | FF |
| Koch, Johan | Reis, Maria | 25, July 1837 | FF |
| Koch, Johan | Meyer, Rosina | 10, May 1842 | FF |
| Koch, Johan Baptist | Meyer, Magdalena | 24, May 1846 | A |
| Koch, Johan Dietrich | Ascherr, Dorothea | 16, May 1844 | G |
| Koch, Johan F. | Rechtin, Elisabeth | 8, Oct. 1848 | AA |
| Koch, Johan Georg | Lind, Elisabeth | 22, Aug. 1847 | G |
| Koch, Johan Heinrich | Schroten, M Adelheid | 15, July 1849 | RCH |
| Koch, Johan Heinrich | Friedeborn, Elisabet | 4, May 1848 | G |
| Koch, John | Nayeln, Elisabeth | 14, Oct. 1841 | RCH |
| Koch, Lorenz | Sparge, Catharine | 14, May 1843 | G |
| Koch, Ludwig | Eichert, Barbara | 13, June 1847 | RCH |
| Koch, Nicolaus | Gart, Maria Antonia | 6, Jan. 1847 | EE |
| Koch, Wilhelm | Aillen, Charlotte | 14, Aug. 1840 | G |
| Koch, Wilhelm | Niemann, Margaretha | 5, Dec. 1844 | G |
| Koch, Wilhelm Hein. | Moennig, Maria Elis. | 14, Nov. 1847 | AA |
| Koch, William J. | Hobbs, Jane | 15, Apr. 1844 | RCH |
| Kocher, Louis | Stohl, Anna | 28, Oct. 1849 | EE |
| Kochler, George | Reichenbecher, Maria | 25, Nov. 1845 | RCH |
| Kock, Bernard H. | Wigger, Elisabeth | 7, Jan. 1845 | AA |
| Kock, Georg | Sutter, Anna Maria | 30, Sept 1849 | EE |
| Kockmeyer, Bernard | Podt, Theresa | 10, Oct. 1847 | AA |
| Kockmeyer, Johan G. | Beidermuehl, Theresa | 4, June 1848 | EE |
| Kocks, Herman Heinr. | Bugge, M. Anna | 8, May 1849 | II |
| Koeber, Casper | Karret, Anna Maria | 20, July 1846 | AA |
| Koehl, Peter | Heiser, Maria | 18, Dec. 1844 | G |
| Koehler, Johan | Brunner, Catharina | 18, Feb. 1841 | FF |
| Koehler, Johan | Bittinger, Elisabeth | 18, Feb. 1846 | A |
| Koehler, Johan | Zoller, Elisabeth | 4, Sept 1849 | C |
| Koehler, Johan H. | Fischer, Margaret | 3, Oct. 1847 | RCH |

| Grooms | Brides | Date of Marriage | Code |
|--------|--------|------------------|------|
| ***** | ***** | **** ** ******** | **** |
| Koehler, Nicolaus | Steil, Mary | 13, July 1847 | RCH |
| Koehler, Philipp | Hellmann, Magdalena | 25, May 1848 | RCH |
| Koehne, Adolph Wm. | Strick, Charlotte | 8, Dec. 1842 | G |
| Koehne, H. | Slam---, Anna Marg. | 7, Jan. 1843 | RCH |
| Koehnken, Johan H. | Brandt, A. Catharine | 30, Nov. 1843 | C |
| Koelker, Herman Bd. | Kraemer, Maria Cath. | 25, June 1848 | CC |
| Koelker, Johan Hein. | Trick, Elisabeth | 27, Jan. 1846 | FF |
| Koelker, Stephen | Schwermann, Anna | 17, Nov. 1849 | EE |
| Koellein, Ludwig | Wocher, Josephine | 19, Mar. 1840 | G |
| Koellein, Otto | Koellein, Josephina | 23, Dec. 1849 | RCH |
| Koeller, Gerhard H. | Kamping, M. Adelheid | 27, June 1848 | AA |
| Koelsch, Francis | Silber, Catharine | 5, Nov. 1844 | FF |
| Koenemann, Wm. Henry | Lampen, Sophia | 13, Sept 1845 | G |
| Koenig, Ernst Heinr. | Meyer, Elisabeth | 5, Nov. 1846 | B |
| Koenig, Georg | Scheid, Philippina | 4, Apr. 1843 | C |
| Koenig, Gerhard H. | Boberg, Anna Gertrud | 6, Aug. 1845 | AA |
| Koenig, Johan | Simon, Susanna | 27, Dec. 1849 | G |
| Koenig, Johan | Mauerer, Rosa | 29, May 1845 | FF |
| Koenig, Johan Heinr. | Kiskers, Cath. Engel | 11, Oct. 1847 | B |
| Koenig, Peter | DeVose, Maria | 27, Feb. 1848 | EE |
| Koenig, Raymond | Lambert, Beatrice | 5, May 1842 | FF |
| Koenig, Valentin | Schweizer, Maria A. | 11, May 1837 | FF |
| Koeniger, Philipp | Jelliff, Lydia Ann | 25, Apr. 1842 | RCH |
| Koenning, Bernard | Heidemann, Maria | 4, Oct. 1846 | EE |
| Koers, J. Joseph | Arkenberg, Agnes | 18, Feb. 1849 | II |
| Koester, Christoph H | Sanders, Marg. Elis. | 7, Oct. 1849 | F |
| Koeter, Bernard | Vocke, M. Catharina | 17, Sept 1839 | FF |
| Koetter, Bernard H. | Meyer, Catharine | 19, Aug. 1849 | EE |
| Koetter, Bernard P. | Schnier, Theresa | 24, June 1849 | CC |
| Koetters, Bernard H. | Mays, Catharine | 19, Apr. 1849 | RCH |
| Kof, Georg | Kertz, Margaretha | 6, July 1840 | FF |
| Kofermann, Everhard | Niemeyer, Clara | 18, May 1846 | EE |
| Koge, Bernard H. | Mellerhaus, Maria E. | 30, Jan. 1849 | EE |
| Kohane, Patrick | Cushing, Bridget | 25, May 1839 | BB |
| Koherieser, Conrad | Hack, Theresa | 23, Nov. 1841 | FF |
| Kohl, Anton | Pfeifer, Maria | 21, Jan. 1847 | G |
| Kohl, Johan | Siemer, Carolina | 24, Feb. 1846 | AA |
| Kohlbrand, Christian | Strothmeyer, Elis. | 17, Sept 1843 | F |
| Kohle, Friedrich | Beckmann, Catharine | 28, Nov. 1844 | F |
| Kohlenberg, Friedric | Niemeyer, Adleheid | 3, Aug. 1841 | FF |
| Kohlenbrink, Herman | Steinecke, Julia(Mrs | 6, Dec. 1849 | H |
| Kohler, Bernard | Hueger, Barbara | 6, July 1846 | EE |
| Kohler, Henry | Kenner, Rosina | 9, Mar. 1848 | RCH |
| Kohlmann, Friedrich | Enkelmann, Anna M. | 12, Aug. 1847 | B |
| Kohne, Carl | Streutker, Charlotte | 30, Dec. 1847 | F |
| Kohr, Herman H. | Stiers, M. Adelheid | 1, Oct. 1839 | FF |
| Kohrhuf, Heinrich | Engelbert, Catharine | 22, Oct. 1844 | AA |
| Kohrs, Johan Heinric | Kelchmann, Anna M. | 19, Nov. 1844 | AA |
| Kohsmescher, Theodor | Himmelgarten, Anna M | 7, July 1840 | FF |
| Koke, Joseph | Brockmann, Agnes | 28, Jan. 1849 | II |
| Kolb, Adam | Becker, Margaretha | 7, Aug. 1845 | AA |
| Kolb, Friedrich | Taas, Maria | 22, Apr. 1848 | G |
| Kolb, Louis | Redding, Eleanor | 13, Oct. 1844 | BB |
| Kolb, Michael | Bensinger, Anna | 6, Nov. 1849 | G |
| Kolckmeier, Johan H. | Ewers, Anna Maria | 5, Nov. 1846 | A |
| Kolk, Johan | Fiege, Maria Anna | 8, Oct. 1848 | EE |
| Kolkmeyer, Gerhard F | Kettler, Angela | 27, Nov. 1849 | AA |
| Koll, Georg | Menyline, Barbara | 28, July 1835 | FF |
| Kollertz, John | Cooper, Elisabeth | 6, Feb. 1844 | RCH |
| Kollifarth, Franz | Appa, Anna Maria | 5, Oct. 1845 | AA |
| Kollmann, Gerhard H. | Moormann, Margaretha | 24, May 1849 | B |
| Kollmann, J. Bernard | Igermann, Elisabeth | 7, Feb. 1837 | FF |
| Kollmann, Johan | Hartmann, Elisabeth | 5, Nov. 1839 | FF |
| Kollmeier, Franz H. | Brinkers, Catharine | 29, Apr. 1847 | F |
| Kollstead, Johan | Listermann, Maria A. | 13, Apr. 1842 | FF |
| Kolmeyer, Friedrich | Plostert, Maria | 18, Dec. 1845 | F |
| Kolp, Jacob | Lemmon, Mary | 1, July 1834 | RCH |
| Kolthoff, C. Friedr. | Emsieck, M Elisabeth | 11, Aug. 1842 | F |
| Konen, Theodor | Wiechmann, Anna M. | 19, Aug. 1849 | CC |
| Konig, Johan | Hoefer, Maria Magdal | 6, Jan. 1847 | EE |
| Koo, Wilhelm Herman | Brink, Gesina A. | 28, Oct. 1849 | AA |

| Grooms<br>****** | Brides<br>****** | Date of Marriage<br>**** ** ******** | Code<br>**** |
|---|---|---|---|
| Koop, Herman | Forckenbeck, Maria A | 11, July 1848 | FF |
| Koors, Bernard | Bueter, Anna Marg. | 19, Feb. 1848 | FF |
| Koors, Friedrich | Tobbe, Wilhelmina | 24, Sept 1848 | II |
| Koors, J. Dietrich | Refermann, Margaret | 12, Nov. 1848 | FF |
| Koors, Johan Herman | Rewemann, Anna M. | 7, Nov. 1847 | AA |
| Koote, Herman | Winck, Margaretha | 28, Apr. 1836 | FF |
| Kopf, Carl | Meyer, Margaretha | 26, Nov. 1848 | G |
| Kople, Jacob | Schmock, Charlotte | 7, May 1835 | RCH |
| Kopp, Ludwig | Boepple, M. Theresa | 2, Jan. 1848 | G |
| Kopp, William | Boehle, Maria | 11, Nov. 1844 | RCH |
| Koppel, Daniel | Stern, Gustava | 26, Apr. 1848 | RCH |
| Koppel, Moses | Joseph, Babette | 16, Apr. 1844 | RCH |
| Korb, Adam | Hoetigger, Catharine | 29, July 1845 | FF |
| Korenz, Christoph | Bolster, Louise | 16, July 1840 | F |
| Korfhage, Johan G. | Dinkrefe, Francisca | 11, Mar. 1841 | FF |
| Koring, Heinrich Bd. | Kloker, Anna | 19, Nov. 1846 | F |
| Kornblet, Jacob | Fridenberg, Bena | 30, May 1843 | RCH |
| Kornmeyer, Carl | Fritmann, Elisabeth | 11, May 1841 | FF |
| Korte, Bernard Hein. | VonderHeide, Cath. E | 4, Nov. 1845 | FF |
| Korte, Franz Heinr. | Darlage, Maria Adel. | 28, Nov. 1844 | F |
| Korte, Franz Heinr. | Dartage, Catharine M | 3, Apr. 1849 | F |
| Korte, Gerhard | Hagenhof, Catharine | 10, Jan. 1843 | AA |
| Korte, Heinrich | Sanne, Doris | 6, Nov. 1849 | G |
| Korte, Herman H. | Brunes, Dina | 26, July 1846 | AA |
| Korte, Johan Gerhard | Thesing, Bernardina | 23, Apr. 1844 | AA |
| Korte, Johan Heinric | Huesken, Gesina | 7, Jan. 1847 | AA |
| Korte, Johan Heinric | Brinkmann, Anna M. | 2, July 1848 | AA |
| Kortgartner, Carl H. | Muhlenbruch, Cath. M | 23, Jan. 1845 | F |
| Kortmann, Gerhard | Kemper, Gertrud | 25, Aug. 1846 | AA |
| Korzenborn, Carl | Herrmann, Ernestine | 14, Mar. 1846 | C |
| Korzenborn, Wilhelm | Haas, Christina | 24, May 1849 | C |
| Kostermann, Henry | Plump, Maria Elis. | 4, Sept 1846 | B |
| Kotger, Rudolph | Lehmkol, Catharine | 5, May 1840 | G |
| Kotter, Anton | Koch, Gertrud | 29, Apr. 1849 | II |
| Kotting, J.G. | Rumps, Maria | 31, Oct. 1847 | FF |
| Kottmann, Bernard | Zumbrink, Angela | 22, Nov. 1846 | EE |
| Kountz, John | Marchant, Mary | 2, Oct. 1834 | RCH |
| Kowin, James | Gray, Adelia A. | 14, Sept 1848 | RCH |
| Kraas, William | Landwehr, Louise | 1, Dec. 1842 | RCH |
| Kracht, Theodor | Abrutz, Christina | 10, Apr. 1849 | B |
| Krack, Herman | Helmich, Catharine | 18, Feb. 1849 | EE |
| Krackt, Wilhelm | Trese, Agnes | 18, June 1848 | II |
| Kraemer, Bernard | Moormann, Agnes | 29, Sept 1836 | FF |
| Kraemer, Ferdinand | Wehming, Gertrud | 26, May 1846 | AA |
| Kraemer, J. Theodor | Brinker, Catharine | 21, May 1844 | FF |
| Kraemer, Johan Diet. | Zurline, A.M. | 9, Jan. 1848 | AA |
| Kraemer, Mathias | Brausch, Angela | 22, Nov. 1842 | AA |
| Kraeper, Heinrich | Baden, Charlotte | 7, Dec. 1848 | B |
| Krafeld, Herman | Ruhe, Elisabeth | 26, Apr. 1842 | FF |
| Kraft, Andreas | Graesser, Magdalena | 24, Apr. 1842 | RCH |
| Kraft, Georg Peter | Martin, Francisca | 23, Feb. 1841 | G |
| Kraft, Heinrich | Krop, Wilhelmina | 27, June 1844 | G |
| Kraft, Ignatz | Briggler, Christina | 8, Oct. 1848 | EE |
| Kraft, Johan | Reis, Carolina | 20, Aug. 1846 | EE |
| Kraft, Johan Adam | Faulhauber, Cath. | 17, Oct. 1847 | EE |
| Kraft, Nicolaus | Glaap, Maria | 16, Jan. 1843 | AA |
| Kraft, Nicolaus | Martiam, Regina | 4, Nov. 1847 | C |
| Kramel, Johan | Philipp, Maria | 30, July 1848 | EE |
| Kramer, Adolph | Hellenkamp, Margaret | 4, Feb. 1849 | II |
| Kramer, Bernard | Moormann, Bernardina | 11, July 1847 | AA |
| Kramer, Clemens | Bolk, Elisabeth | 26, July 1836 | FF |
| Kramer, Francis C. | Vocker, Maria Elis. | 21, May 1848 | EE |
| Kramer, Gerhard | Hackmann, Maria Anna | 4, Feb. 1836 | FF |
| Kramer, Heinrich | Loxterkamp, Maria | 23, Jan. 1838 | FF |
| Kramer, Heinrich | Brokamp, Elisabeth | 29, Nov. 1845 | AA |
| Kramer, Herman H. | Kalvelage, Catharine | 25, Oct. 1842 | AA |
| Kramer, Herman H. | Boman, Anna Maria E. | 28, Aug. 1849 | EE |
| Kramer, Herman Hein. | Barlage, Maria Cath. | 22, Apr. 1847 | AA |
| Kramer, Jacob | Gruhler, Anna | 23, Mar. 1849 | G |
| Kramer, Johan | Sullivan, Magdalena | 21, May 1839 | FF |
| Kramer, Johan F. | Precht, Dorothea | 7, Apr. 1846 | F |

| Grooms<br>****** | Brides<br>****** | Date of Marriage<br>**** ** ******** | Code<br>**** |
|---|---|---|---|
| Kramer, John | Wilke, Elisabeth | 27, Jan. 1848 | RCH |
| Kramer, John Henry | Frei, Barbara | 13, Nov. 1845 | G |
| Kramer, Xavier | Riegelsperger, Maria | 1, Dec. 1840 | FF |
| Kranz, Thomas | Black, Mary | 10, Oct. 1844 | RCH |
| Krasins, Johan | ----, Anna | 14, Oct. 1849 | C |
| Kratz, Conrad | Koehler, Louise | 5, May 1840 | G |
| Kratzemeyer, Friedr. | Kruse, Carolina | 28, Jan. 1841 | F |
| Kratzer, Andreas | Walter, Margaretha | 10, May 1847 | C |
| Kratzer, Georg | Juppenlatz, Dorothea | 24, Jan. 1848 | A |
| Kratzer, John Adam | Schneider, Anna M. | 17, Nov. 1842 | RCH |
| Kraus, Christoph | Zeus, Maria Anna | 7, Jan. 1841 | FF |
| Kraus, Conrad | Fleischmann, Theresa | 20, July 1847 | FF |
| Kraus, Jacob | Faher, Margaretha | 11, June 1846 | C |
| Kraus, Johan | Doerner, Marg. (Mrs) | 25, Nov. 1849 | EE |
| Kraus, Michael | Noehring, Maria Elis | 3, Sept 1849 | CC |
| Krause, Georg Carl | Schneider, Ursula | 7, Oct. 1849 | C |
| Krause, Johan Fr. | Wilbern, Maria Anna | 22, Nov. 1848 | F |
| Krauss, Jacob | Liehl, Elisabeth | 9, Oct. 1849 | C |
| Krauth, Georg Adam | Weisenborn, Maria | 18, Aug. 1846 | G |
| Krautler, Carl | Schallkopf, Friedr. | 7, Oct. 1849 | A |
| Krebs, Joseph | Balles, Maria Rosina | 26, Sept 1847 | EE |
| Kreckmer, Jacob | Karr, Caroline | 31, Aug. 1837 | FF |
| Kreeman, Michael | Butler, Helen | 14, May 1840 | BB |
| Krehenbrink, Heinric | Grotjohan, Elisabeth | 2, Nov. 1841 | FF |
| Kreider, Johan | Schondiger, Maria | 21, Sept 1848 | EE |
| Kreimer, Gerhard | Hoemer, Catharine G. | 28, Aug. 1849 | EE |
| Krein, Friedrich | Logel, Gertrud | 23, Apr. 1839 | FF |
| Kreinhagen, William | Gottschmidt, Charl. | 27, Dec. 1841 | RCH |
| Kreis, Johan Adam | Naumann, Wilhelmina | 10, Sept 1839 | G |
| Kreis, Wilhelm | Kraus, Bertha | 23, Dec. 1849 | A |
| Kreisel, Magnus | Eckart, Catharine | 15, Nov. 1849 | A |
| Kreke, Gerhard | Huesmann, Catharine | 5, Mar. 1848 | FF |
| Kreke, Henry Arnold | Fennemann, Maria E. | 12, Nov. 1846 | F |
| Kreke, Johan Bernard | Wolking, Wilhelmina | 3, Feb. 1841 | FF |
| Krekeler, Bernard | Siemer, Maria Elis. | 28, Jan. 1849 | AA |
| Krekeler, Ludwig | Wehking, Maria | 18, June 1846 | F |
| Krell, Valentin | Strale, Barbara | 27, Aug. 1839 | FF |
| Krempelmann, Christ. | Jahnson, Christina E | 4, Sept 1841 | FF |
| Krenning, Friedrich | Amelings, Henrietta | 25, May 1841 | F |
| Krenning, Heinrich | Spricks, Anna Cath. | 21, May 1846 | RCH |
| Krenning, J Heinrich | Schwarz, Anna Maria | 3, May 1845 | F |
| Krenning, Mathias | Hartmann, Maria | 22, Dec. 1849 | RCH |
| Kreple, Friedrich | Baumgartner, Marg. | 9, June 1846 | A |
| Kresberng, Bernard | Menge, Elisabeth | 9, Oct. 1849 | EE |
| Kresch, Gregor | Maurer, Rosa | 9, Sept 1849 | DD |
| Kress, Johan | Ehri, Susanna | 14, Sept 1849 | EE |
| Kretz, Johan | Hafer, Maria | 1, Sept 1837 | FF |
| Kreuson, Alexander | Storms, Julia Ann | 6, Nov. 1836 | RCH |
| Kreuter, Karl | Pflug, Eva | 4, Apr. 1847 | C |
| Kreutz, Jacob | Liar, Caroline | 18, July 1848 | EE |
| Kreutzjans, Christ. | Linnemann, Walburga | 29, July 1847 | FF |
| Kreutzmann, Casper | Wippertmann, Elis. | 9, Jan. 1849 | FF |
| Kreuzburg, Peter | Nurre, Maria Gertrud | 22, Feb. 1846 | EE |
| Kreyenhagen, Adolph | Brethold, A M Clara | 17, Dec. 1846 | B |
| Krieg, Carl | Ferris, Sabina | 30, Oct. 1846 | G |
| Krieg, Casper | Bohn, Margaretha | 29, Apr. 1847 | C |
| Krieg, Friedrich | Messerschmidt, Maria | 30, Aug. 1843 | G |
| Krieg, George | Kran, Christina | 26, Dec. 1843 | A |
| Krieg, Jacob | Zimpelmann, Catharin | 10, Feb. 1846 | C |
| Krieg, Johan | Hey, Elisabeth | 18, Nov. 1845 | C |
| Krieg, Johan | Wagner, Anna Maria | 14, July 1846 | C |
| Kriege, Eberhard R. | Ekelmann, Catharine | 24, Mar. 1840 | G |
| Krieger, Conrad | Frank, Elisabeth | 30, July 1846 | C |
| Krieger, Matthias | Hupke, Catharina M. | 21, Nov. 1837 | FF |
| Kriel, Michael | Dobmeier, Barbara | 11, Feb. 1849 | II |
| Krievenkamp, Johan B | Boeckmann, Anna M. | 21, Apr. 1836 | FF |
| Krigen, Thomas | VanBlaricum, Elis. | 19, June 1849 | RCH |
| Krimberg, Theodor | Mellmann, Maria Elis | 31, Aug. 1841 | FF |
| Krimm, Jacob F. | Staebler, Catharine | 9, Nov. 1845 | G |
| Kring, Jacob | Graus, Maria | 11, Jan. 1848 | C |
| Kripp, John | Belser, Louise | 2, Sept 1841 | RCH |

| Grooms | Brides | Date of Marriage | Code |
|--------|--------|------------------|------|
| ****** | ****** | **** ** ******** | **** |
| Krips, Peter | Esling, Elisabeth | 2, June 1842 | RCH |
| Krise, Johan | Kuese, Maria | 11, June 1839 | FF |
| Krite, Christian | Rohlfing, Wilhelmina | 12, Mar. 1846 | F |
| Krite, Friedrich | Finke, Friedricka | 2, Apr. 1846 | F |
| Kroeger, Bernard | Hinken, Cath. (Mrs) | 29, Sept 1846 | FF |
| Kroeger, Bernard | Huels, Dina | 12, Nov. 1848 | II |
| Kroeger, J. Clemens | Angelbeck, Margaret | 26, Aug. 1845 | AA |
| Kroeger, Johan H. | Masmann, Maria Anna | 23, Jan. 1844 | AA |
| Krogmann, Heinrich | Roske, Angela | 26, Apr. 1836 | FF |
| Krohme, Johan Fr. | Strubbe, Elisabeth | 29, Aug. 1848 | F |
| Krome, Friedrich | Klute, Elisabeth | 30, May 1840 | F |
| Kronathi, Wilhelm | Schaeper, Maria | 30, Aug. 1836 | FF |
| Krone, Ferdinand | Wormann, Anna Maria | 27, Apr. 1837 | FF |
| Kronimus, Georg | Nehlig, Margaretha | 13, Aug. 1848 | A |
| Kronlage, Heinrich | Settlage, Dorothea | 18, Sept 1838 | FF |
| Kronmiller, Henry | Sommer, Catharine | 18, Aug. 1846 | RCH |
| Kros, Conrad | Klersmann, Christina | 12, Sept 1836 | FF |
| Krude, Bernard | Cievens, Catharina | 19, Apr. 1836 | FF |
| Krug, Georg | Fuss, Barbara | 19, Feb. 1844 | AA |
| Krug, Johan | Tebald, Maria | 15, Sept 1846 | EE |
| Krug, Martin | Bauer, Elisabeth | 5, Aug. 1849 | RCH |
| Kruger, Joseph | Smith, Catharine | 1, Nov. 1846 | RCH |
| Krugmann, Johan | Stieve, Maria | 8, Nov. 1836 | FF |
| Krum, | Liggett, Jane | 15, Apr. 1849 | RCH |
| Krumm, Heinrich | Hutter, Elisabeth | 20, Nov. 1842 | G |
| Krumme, Wilhelm | Schulte, Caroline | 27, Dec. 1842 | F |
| Krummel, Godfried | Sieg, Margaretha | 18, Sept 1849 | A |
| Krumpelbeck, Francis | Quatmann, Carolina | 9, Nov. 1841 | FF |
| Krup, Johan Gerhard | Thiel, Anna Maria | 7, Jan. 1846 | AA |
| Krupp, Heinrich | Wehler, Sophia | 7, Oct. 1847 | F |
| Kruse, Arend | Quebbermann, Bernar. | 21, Oct. 1849 | AA |
| Kruse, Bernard | Leuges, Anna Maria | 10, Jan. 1843 | FF |
| Kruse, Conrad | Sauer, Charlotte | 5, Mar. 1846 | B |
| Kruse, Friedrich | Kriele, Louisa | 11, Nov. 1840 | F |
| Kruse, Heinrich | Bettenbrock, Engel | 1, Nov. 1848 | F |
| Kruse, Heinrich F. | Hobelmann, Catharine | 12, July 1848 | F |
| Kruse, Herman Rudolf | Piepers, Engel R. | 21, Jan. 1846 | F |
| Kruse, Johan Friedr. | Brodemeyer, Sophia | 5, Nov. 1840 | F |
| Kruse, Johan Heinr. | Schurmeyer, Wilhel. | 19, May 1847 | RCH |
| Kruse, Joseph | Balks, Agnes | 4, July 1843 | AA |
| Kruse, Wilhelm | Spronck, A. Margaret | 31, Aug. 1845 | F |
| Krusekamp, Friedrich | Rex, Maria | 9, Apr. 1846 | A |
| Krusting, Johan Bd. | Ruesemann, Anna M. | 26, Oct. 1847 | CC |
| Krutzins, Georg | Snider, Cath. Elis. | 3, Aug. 1844 | A |
| Kuber, Leonard | Schutter, Carolina | 30, Sept 1845 | AA |
| Kuchner, Balzer | Fogel, Catharine | 4, June 1844 | RCH |
| Kuck, Friedrich W. | Hilgemann, Christina | 28, Sept 1848 | C |
| Kuck, Heinrich | Hilgemann, Friedrika | 4, Mar. 1847 | C |
| Kuckherm, Friedrich | Schepperklaus, Anna | 21, May 1846 | C |
| Kuegeling, Francis J | Fering, Magdalena | 8, Aug. 1837 | FF |
| Kuehlefeld, Gerhard | Fangmann, Maria(Mrs) | 19, Nov. 1848 | EE |
| Kuehn, John | Kuntz, Catharine | 6, July 1842 | G |
| Kuehne, Heinrich | Schloemer, Margaret | 24, Jan. 1843 | AA |
| Kuehnle, Joseph | Bachmann, Elisabeth | 5, May 1845 | AA |
| Kuemich, Thomas | Jung, Elisabeth | 6, Apr. 1842 | F |
| Kuemmler, Adam | Hettesheimer, Cath. | 12, Dec. 1844 | C |
| Kuenel, Johan | Moritz, Catharina | 24, Dec. 1848 | G |
| Kuenke, Johan H. | Kruse, Maria Agnes | 29, Oct. 1848 | CC |
| Kuennen, Andreas | Wiemeyer, Maria | 13, Apr. 1845 | AA |
| Kuennen, J. Albert | Zurline, Catharine | 12, Jan. 1841 | FF |
| Kuester, Charles | Reiter, Christina | 21, Oct. 1848 | RCH |
| Kuestner, J. Georg | Hasselbacher, Sarah | 10, Apr. 1847 | RCH |
| Kuewen, Rudolph | Mohlenkamp, Margaret | 3, May 1846 | AA |
| Kufner, Adam | Adams, Catharine | 21, Feb. 1848 | A |
| Kugenmeister, Mich. | Kraus, Dorothea | 21, Nov. 1847 | EE |
| Kugler, John | West, Rebecca | 9, Mar. 1842 | RCH |
| Kugler, Peter P. | Rosenbaum, Angela A. | 3, Nov. 1838 | FF |
| Kuhl, Bernard | Helmer, Anna Angela | 18, Feb. 1849 | AA |
| Kuhl, Friedrich | Fritz, Catharine | 5, Jan. 1847 | G |
| Kuhlenberg, Johan H. | Guthke, Elisabeth | 16, Nov. 1847 | AA |
| Kuhlmann, Bernard | Fischer, Elisabeth | 17, Apr. 1838 | FF |

| Grooms<br>***** | Brides<br>***** | Date of Marriage<br>**** ** ******** | Code<br>**** |
|---|---|---|---|
| Kuhlmann, Bernard H. | Kurre, M. Elisabeth | 8, Aug. 1847 | FF |
| Kuhlmann, Clemens H. | Horstmann, M. Adel. | 23, May 1843 | FF |
| Kuhlmann, Eberhard | Richter, Catharine | 12, Nov. 1844 | AA |
| Kuhlmann, Friedrich | Danettel, Caroline | 10, Feb. 1846 | F |
| Kuhlmann, Heinrich | Wornhorn, Maria Cath | 12, July 1836 | FF |
| Kuhlmann, Heinrich | Kneser, Anna Maria | 12, Sept 1843 | FF |
| Kuhlmann, Herman Bd. | Kurey, Mary Elis. | 2, Aug. 1847 | RCH |
| Kuhlmann, J. | Schirbentz, Theresa | 9, Nov. 1848 | II |
| Kuhlmann, Johan H. | Neubauer, Elisabeth | 21, Oct. 1845 | AA |
| Kuhlmann, Joseph | Wesling, Maria Anna | 26, Oct. 1845 | AA |
| Kuhlmann, Joseph | Kohl, Catharine | 21, Jan. 1845 | FF |
| Kuhlmann, Wilhelm | Speckmann, Anna M. | 15, Aug. 1848 | AA |
| Kuhlo, Friedrich | Hemmer, Christina | 16, Feb. 1847 | G |
| Kuhlriefer, Ernst | Hummel, Maria | 19, Aug. 1847 | AA |
| Kuhn, Andrew | Shyrer, Louise D. | 18, May 1848 | RCH |
| Kuhn, Gabriel | Mill, Francisca | 27, Aug. 1844 | FF |
| Kuhn, Georg | Stein, Magdalena | 19, Apr. 1842 | FF |
| Kuhn, Georg Michael | Mueller, Adelheid | 19, Sept 1847 | AA |
| Kuhn, George | Robel, Margaret | 21, Oct. 1848 | RCH |
| Kuhn, John | Hartmann, Barbara | 26, Oct. 1845 | RCH |
| Kuhn, Ludwig | Haas, Catharine | 2, May 1847 | FF |
| Kuhn, Ludwig | Conrad, A. Maria | 14, May 1848 | II |
| Kuhn, Wilhelm | Pressler, Elisabeth | 3, Sept 1844 | AA |
| Kuhner, Theodor | Blersch, Maria | 22, Feb. 1849 | G |
| Kuling, Herman | Rufers, Anna Marg. | 7, Aug. 1844 | AA |
| Kulker, Alexander | Berte, Katharina | 27, Dec. 1847 | AA |
| Kummann, J Friedrich | Heckmann, A. Louise | 26, Aug. 1847 | B |
| Kunahan, Richard | Maroney, Julia | 22, Feb. 1841 | BB |
| Kunee, Baily S. | Wood, Abigail | 15, Jan. 1834 | RCH |
| Kunk, Francis | Hoffmann, Maria | 15, July 1849 | II |
| Kunk, Gerhard H. | Meinders, Gesina | 18, Jan. 1848 | EE |
| Kunkel, Heinrich | Sunderhausen, Maria | 26, Mar. 1846 | F |
| Kunker, J. Gerhard | Kraftfeld, Mary | 3, Oct. 1843 | AA |
| Kunkle, Johan | Elsasser, Margaretha | 20, Feb. 1838 | FF |
| Kunkler, Joseph | Schweitzer, Magdal. | 25, Apr. 1847 | FF |
| Kuntz, Anthony | Mangold, Mary | Feb. 1843 | RCH |
| Kuntz, Philipp | Knorr, Barbara | 9, Sept 1849 | C |
| Kunz, Andreas | Zittel, Anna Maria | 23, Sept 1847 | A |
| Kunz, George | Ordemann, Helena | 26, May 1842 | RCH |
| Kunz, Henry | Schleinemann, Elis. | 2, Nov. 1848 | RCH |
| Kunze, Friedrich Wm. | Walker, Wilhelmina | 28, May 1846 | F |
| Kunzler, John | Klein, Elizabeth | 15, Oct. 1846 | RCH |
| Kuper, Bernard Anton | Stuntebeck, Elis. | 27, Apr. 1837 | FF |
| Kuper, Johan Bernard | Shiper, Euphemia M. | 10, Oct. 1843 | AA |
| Kurlfinger, | Strubbe, Wilhelmina | 14, Sept 1848 | G |
| Kurre, Clemens | Doecker, Helena A. | 30, Sept 1849 | CC |
| Kurrenbrock, Joseph | Renneker, Anna Maria | 7, Sept 1845 | AA |
| Kurtz, Jacob | Weismann, Elisabeth | 6, May 1845 | G |
| Kurtz, Johan Heinric | Rotering, Johanna C. | 1, Feb. 1848 | FF |
| Kurz, Heinrich | Mueller, Catharina | 1, May 1849 | A |
| Kusch, Bernard | Buning, Maria Elis. | 13, Feb. 1844 | AA |
| Kustend, Christian | Wolfe, Mary | 19, Feb. 1849 | GG |
| Kuster, Heinrich | Rickes, Rebecca | 6, Apr. 1848 | B |
| Kuster, John Gerhard | Binninghaus, Angela | 28, July 1840 | FF |
| Kuster, Joseph | Buschmeier, Theresa | 9, July 1838 | FF |
| Kutting, Dietrich | Ehlen, Adelheid | 7, Jan. 1840 | FF |
| Kyle, Zacheus | Debolt, Elisabeth | 31, Dec. 1846 | RCH |
| Kyles, Thomas | Mapes, Rysiah | 19, Jan. 1837 | RCH |
| | | | |
| L'Hommidieu, Stephen | Hammond, Almy | 25, Apr. 1830 | I |
| LaBoyteaux, | Carso, Louise Jane | Jan. 1836 | RCH |
| LaBoyteaux, Daniel | Wolverton, Mahala | 21, July 1837 | RCH |
| LaBoyteaux, Ferman | Jessup, Lydia | 5, Feb. 1846 | RCH |
| LaBoyteaux, Gilbert | Stevens, Anna | 15, July 1847 | RCH |
| LaBoyteaux, LaFayett | Lowe, Almira A. | 8, Apr. 1847 | BB |
| LaBoyteaux, Paul | Tetherland, Betsy A. | 18, July 1818 | RCH |
| LaBoyteaux, William | Woodruff, Abigail | 2, June 1825 | RCH |
| LaDuc, Louis F. | Davis, Emily D. | 26, Nov. 1835 | RCH |
| LaDuke, Frederick | Ryland, Elisabeth | 7, Feb. 1835 | RCH |
| LaPierre, Joseph M. | Fannase, M. Datisa | 14, Mar. 1840 | BB |
| LaVanture, Drayton | Wescot, Zelphia | 24, Feb. 1839 | RCH |

| Grooms<br>****** | Brides<br>****** | Date of Marriage<br>**** ** ******** | Code<br>**** |
|---|---|---|---|
| Laacke, Gerhard | Niehaus, Elisabeth | 26, Nov. 1844 | AA |
| Laake, Bernard Henr. | VonHandorf, Maria E. | 11, Jan. 1846 | EE |
| Labave, James | Jones, Matilda | 28, Oct. 1841 | RCH |
| Labrot, August | Cromwell, Elisabeth | 21, Nov. 1844 | BB |
| Lacey, John | Stewart, Ann Jane | 3, Nov. 1843 | RCH |
| Lach, Peter Friedric | Troesch, Anna | 13, Nov. 1848 | AA |
| Lackens, Jacob | Russell, Eveline | 15, Feb. 1842 | RCH |
| Lackey, Ira | Merrit, Catharine | 20, Jan. 1822 | RCH |
| Lackner, Bernard | Kordes, Agnes | 4, Feb. 1849 | II |
| Lacroix, Jean Bapt. | Lanoux, Angela | 13, May 1833 | RCH |
| Lacy, Job | Hickman, Margaret | 4, Oct. 1836 | RCH |
| Lacy, Stephen | Shotts, Louise | 16, Apr. 1847 | RCH |
| Lacy, William | Saunderson, Salome | 16, Nov. 1823 | RCH |
| Ladd, Asa D. | McTinly, | 22, Dec. 1823 | RCH |
| Ladd, George | Sloan, Harriet | 11, Sept 1849 | RCH |
| Ladd, Robert | Wallace, Mary Ann | 7, Feb. 1842 | RCH |
| Ladd, William | White, Jean | 28, July 1847 | RCH |
| Ladder, John | Dobmeyer, Catharine | 23, July 1848 | GG |
| Ladenkotter, Joseph | Dirkers, Anna Maria | 4, May 1845 | AA |
| Lader, William | Wallace, Emily | 8, Feb. 1838 | RCH |
| Ladin, Johan | Ritter, Barbara | 5, Dec. 1846 | EE |
| Ladley, John J. | Hopkins, Ellen | 17, Apr. 1849 | RCH |
| Ladnsaw, John | Shannon, Rohanna | 23, Mar. 1837 | RCH |
| Laekamp, Johan Adam | Meyer, Anna Maria | 4, Mar. 1847 | RCH |
| Laestermann, Johan | Lis, Anna Maria | 24, Oct. 1843 | AA |
| Lafferty, James | Gardner, Mary | 19, Dec. 1844 | RCH |
| Lafferty, James | Zimmermann, Jane | 31, Dec. 1846 | RCH |
| Lafferty, John | Townshend, Sarah | 8, Mar. 1825 | RCH |
| Laforge, Jacob | Hartman, Catharine | 18, Feb. 1820 | RCH |
| Laforret, Johan B. | Lang, Barbara | 13, May 1847 | AA |
| Lafun, Michael | McKewn, Mary | 3, Nov. 1845 | RCH |
| Lage, Joseph | Stehmann, Catharine | 5, Nov. 1844 | AA |
| Lahady, Richard | Ryan, Ann | 8, Aug. 1847 | BB |
| Laheny, Thomas | O'Neil, Ellen | 18, June 1848 | GG |
| Lahmann, Abraham | Goldmann, Fanny | 23, Sept 1846 | RCH |
| Lahmann, Carl | Klanke, Henrietta | 20, Nov. 1849 | F |
| Lahmann, Gerhard | Westermann, Catharin | 5, Oct. 1845 | AA |
| Lahmann, Gerhard H. | Dickbreder, Maria | 7, May 1846 | F |
| Lahmering, J. Hein. | Pranton, Clara Elis. | 26, Apr. 1849 | B |
| Lahrmann, Heinrich | Schreiber, Henrietta | 1, Nov. 1849 | C |
| Lahuren, Christian T | Nuszbecklin, Maria E | 25, May 1848 | RCH |
| Laibe, Francis | Stricke, Francisca | 29, July 1848 | AA |
| Laing, Firman | LaBoyteaux, Almira | 6, May 1849 | RCH |
| Laitinger, Jacob | Tamer, Catharine | 19, Dec. 1848 | EE |
| Lake, Joseph | Griggs, Matty | 11, Aug. 1819 | RCH |
| Lakeman, James | Goodnow, Mary | 15, Oct. 1846 | RCH |
| Laman, John | Conover, Betsy Ann | 19, Apr. 1825 | RCH |
| Lamar, | Morten, Nancy | 30, Apr. 1849 | RCH |
| Lamb, George W. | Ogden, Sarah Jane | 30, Apr. 1849 | RCH |
| Lamb, Gilbert | Parker, Mary Jane | Oct. 1847 | RCH |
| Lamb, Joseph G. | Landon, Susan Lea | 15, Oct. 1834 | RCH |
| Lamb, Thomas S. | Kelly, Euphemia | 12, Sept 1848 | RCH |
| Lambdin, Thomas S. | McCormick, Jane | 12, Dec. 1833 | RCH |
| Lamber, Anton | Painter, Margaretha | 28, Apr. 1840 | FF |
| Lamber, Hubert | Wagner, Catharine | 30, Apr. 1840 | FF |
| Lambers, Bernard | Bene, Elisabeth(Mrs) | 8, Nov. 1846 | AA |
| Lambers, Bernard | Moeller, Elis. (Mrs) | 28, Oct. 1849 | AA |
| Lambers, J. Bernard | Hempen, Maria Helena | 25, Nov. 1849 | FF |
| Lambers, Johan Hein. | Bredeck, Anna Maria | 15, Apr. 1845 | AA |
| Lambers, Johan Herm. | Lang, Elisabeth | 25, Nov. 1849 | AA |
| Lambert, Benjamin | Smith, Eva | 29, Mar. 1848 | RCH |
| Lambert, Heinrich | Hoffmeister, Elis. | 19, Oct. 1848 | F |
| Lambert, Jacob | George, Maria Anna | 21, Jan. 1849 | II |
| Lambert, Simon | Joseph, Sarah | 20, Feb. 1849 | RCH |
| Lambert, Vincent | Pohl, Louisa | 12, May 1846 | EE |
| Lambur, Ludwig | Kampeis, Barbara | 15, Nov. 1842 | AA |
| Lamburn, Meacham | Gilbert, Hannah | 11, Nov. 1819 | RCH |
| Lame, Joseph | Philips, Nancy | 25, Jan. 1834 | RCH |
| Lamere, Nicolaus | ----, Fanny | 14, May 1818 | RCH |
| Lammer, Bernard H. | Deyer, Adelheid | 30, June 1846 | AA |
| Lammering, Johan Bd. | Terwelp, Maria Elis. | 16, June 1846 | EE |

| Grooms | Brides | Date of Marriage | Code |
|--------|--------|------------------|------|
| ****** | ****** | **** ** ******** | **** |
| Lammers, Franz Ferd. | Marke, Agnes | 7, May 1848 | II |
| Lammers, Johan | Brand, Catharina | 26, Aug. 1849 | AA |
| Lammers, Joseph | Stratmann, Gertrud | 7, Sept 1841 | FF |
| Lammes, Herman | Bruning, Maria | 3, Oct. 1848 | AA |
| Lamming, Samuel | Wallace, Sarah Ann | 16, Oct. 1822 | RCH |
| Lamont, Hugh | Giffin, Martha | 2, Oct. 1843 | RCH |
| Lamot, Roger | Wall, Elisabeth | 23, Mar. 1843 | RCH |
| Lamoth, Cyril | Maegdle, Magdalena | 29, Nov. 1849 | DD |
| Lamott, Nicolaus | Unger, Maria | 9, May 1848 | EE |
| Lamotte, Bernard J. | Stockdale, Elisabeth | 5, Apr. 1847 | RCH |
| Lampe, Christian | Dippel, Catharine | 11, July 1844 | G |
| Lampe, Francis | Wulfhorst, Angela | 25, Nov. 1845 | AA |
| Lampe, Heinrich | Flotemesch, M. Elis. | 6, Aug. 1848 | II |
| Lampe, Herman | Gellkamp, Anna | 15, Feb. 1846 | AA |
| Lampe, Johan | Mohlenkamp, Thecla | 11, Nov. 1849 | AA |
| Lampe, Johan Heinric | Schwenger, Louise | 24, Oct. 1843 | FF |
| Lampert, Cyprian | Spies, Maria Anna | 21, Nov. 1837 | FF |
| Lamphier, John | Shed, Sarah | 16, Apr. 1835 | RCH |
| Lamping, Anton | Bunte, Carolina | 1, Feb. 1846 | AA |
| Lamping, Joseph | Detters, M. Anna | 23, Oct. 1838 | FF |
| Lamsden, Nicolaus | Carter, Anna | 17, Dec. 1842 | RCH |
| Lamyn, Lewis | Cloud, Ann | 14, June 1839 | BB |
| Lan, Brian | Butler, Joann | 31, May 1846 | BB |
| Lancaster, Richard | Looker, Parmelia | 23, Aug. 1832 | RCH |
| Lancaster, Robert | Lumsden, Mary A. | Oct. 1844 | RCH |
| Lancaster, Washing. | Looker, Harriet C. | 26, June 1836 | RCH |
| Lancaster, Washing. | Bailey, Sarah | 7, Nov. 1847 | RCH |
| Lancaster, William | Lancaster, Malinda | 30, Apr. 1819 | RCH |
| Lancaster, William J | Ewing, | May 1834 | RCH |
| Lanchy, Thomas | Meir, Mary | 28, Apr. 1825 | RCH |
| Landeman, David | Sheddinger, Sarah | 19, Dec. 1836 | RCH |
| Landemann, Jacob | Scherer, Margaretha | 2, July 1848 | A |
| Landenberger, | Heinrich, Jane | 21, Aug. 1849 | RCH |
| Landerer, Max. | Winder, Johanna F. | 28, Oct. 1844 | RCH |
| Landes, John | Baley, Sarah | 4, July 1822 | RCH |
| Landey, Daniel | Martin, Hannah | 29, Aug. 1824 | RCH |
| Landon, William | Hardin, Prudence | 5, Aug. 1821 | RCH |
| Landon, William | Smith, Rachel | 22, Aug. 1824 | RCH |
| Landres, Heinrich G. | Lehmeier, Dorothea | 7, Jan. 1849 | C |
| Landreville, Cyprian | Hunter, Sophronia A. | 11, Nov. 1844 | BB |
| Landrigan, Patrick | Burrus, Bridget | 4, May 1845 | BB |
| Landser, Carl | Hank, Lucia | 21, May 1849 | EE |
| Landwehr, Anton | Lanfers, Bernardina | 5, Mar. 1848 | AA |
| Landwehr, Friedrich | Beckmann, Maria | 19, Feb. 1846 | C |
| Landwehr, Heinrich | Bruns, Maria Anna | 18, June 1848 | AA |
| Landwehr, Herman H. | Lacke, Maria Elis. | 28, Feb. 1843 | FF |
| Lane, Absolom | John, Mary Ann | 4, May 1834 | RCH |
| Lane, George | Hoffner, Urmanda | 27, Apr. 1843 | RCH |
| Lane, George | King, Amanda | 25, July 1844 | RCH |
| Lane, George | Seward, Elmira | 30, Aug. 1846 | RCH |
| Lane, Herman | Long, Isabella | 11, June 1818 | RCH |
| Lane, James | Test, Ann | 20, May 1837 | RCH |
| Lane, John | Sullivan, Bridget | 22, July 1849 | BB |
| Lane, Patrick | O'Connell, Margaret | 29, Oct. 1848 | BB |
| Lane, Robert | Jackson, Harriet | 29, Apr. 1846 | RCH |
| Lane, Wilson | Simpson, Jane | 18, Nov. 1833 | RCH |
| Lanfersick, J Conrad | Vedeler, Louise | 1, Sept 1842 | F |
| Lanfersick, J. Adam | Klacke, Louise | 4, June 1840 | F |
| Lanfersink, Johan | Lampe, Louise | 22, Oct. 1840 | F |
| Lang, Francis | Heide, Carolina | 10, Feb. 1848 | AA |
| Lang, Georg | Klein, Wilhelmina | 30, June 1846 | FF |
| Lang, Johan | Stephan, Sally | 21, Feb. 1839 | G |
| Lang, Johan | Aumann, Catharine | 11, June 1844 | AA |
| Lang, Johan | Haft, Margaretha | 24, Oct. 1847 | C |
| Lang, Johan | Meier, Maria | 18, July 1848 | F |
| Lang, Johan Jacob | Klotter, Louise | 7, May 1846 | C |
| Lang, John | Amann, Catharine | 11, June 1844 | RCH |
| Lang, John | Langerberger, Anna | 18, Sept 1846 | RCH |
| Lang, Martin | Faber, Theresa | 17, Apr. 1837 | FF |
| Lang, Michael | Hettinger, Maria | 9, Aug. 1842 | FF |
| Lang, Michael | Gehrlich, Maria J. | 7, Jan. 1845 | AA |

| Grooms<br>***** | Brides<br>***** | Date of Marriage<br>**** ** ******* | Code<br>**** |
|---|---|---|---|
| Lang, Nicolaus | Schweikard, Dorothea | 3, June 1847 | EE |
| Lang, Peter | Bruner, Barbara | 4, Aug. 1836 | FF |
| Lang, Robert | Thom, Barbara | 17, Apr. 1848 | RCH |
| Langdon, Charles | Green, Sarah | 2, Apr. 1826 | RCH |
| Langdon, Elam P. | Cromwell, Ann | 14, Oct. 1821 | RCH |
| Langdon, James D. | Ph---, Sally | 23, Dec. 1818 | RCH |
| Langdon, John | Manning, Mary Ann | 26, Mar. 1845 | BB |
| Langdon, Oliver | Bassett, Catharine | 31, Aug. 1824 | RCH |
| Langdon, Samuel | Lyons, Martha Jane | 20, Mar. 1849 | RCH |
| Langdon, Sylvester | Quackenbush, Elis. | 10, May 1848 | RCH |
| Lange, Anton | Rolfzen, Agnes | 29, Oct. 1848 | II |
| Lange, August | Thies, Maria | 24, June 1847 | F |
| Lange, Christoph | Brinkhoff, Carolina | 30, May 1848 | FF |
| Lange, Francis | Wellmann, Henriette | 22, Apr. 1843 | AA |
| Lange, Francis H. | Hessenfeld, Maria A. | 30, May 1847 | FF |
| Lange, Franz | Niehaus, Elisabeth | 9, Feb. 1847 | AA |
| Lange, Friedrich | Sonderbruck, | 19, Mar. 1840 | F |
| Lange, Friedrich | Schulten, Rosina | 22, Apr. 1849 | AA |
| Lange, Gerhard Jos. | Kessing, Maria Elis. | 5, Mar. 1844 | FF |
| Lange, Heinrich | Kleine, Caroline | 17, July 1846 | F |
| Lange, Herman H. | Lamping, Francisca | 26, Sept 1843 | AA |
| Lange, Herman Heinr. | Paske, Maria | 29, July 1845 | F |
| Lange, Herman Joseph | Kunst, Maria Cath. | 7, Sept 1847 | AA |
| Lange, Johan G. | Hille, M. Anna | 1, Oct. 1839 | FF |
| Lange, Johan Heinric | Evermann, Margaretha | 12, Nov. 1844 | AA |
| Lange, Johan Martin | Nichtern, Maria Anna | 2, July 1848 | FF |
| Lange, Nicolaus | Ripperger, Sibella | 21, Sept 1843 | AA |
| Langel, Anton | Jachtenfuss, Maria | 7, Nov. 1848 | EE |
| Langen, Bernard J. | Callage, Anna Chris. | 28, Oct. 1847 | FF |
| Langenberger, Fried. | Deierlein, Margaret | 20, Aug. 1848 | C |
| Langfermann, Joseph | Luebbehusen, Joseph. | 14, May 1848 | II |
| Langfritz, Johan | Hoinkein, Anna Maria | 9, July 1848 | C |
| Langhorst, Bernard F | Backmeier, Sophia | 7, Nov. 1849 | F |
| Langhorst, Christoph | Pottbaum, Wilhelmina | 21, Oct. 1847 | B |
| Langhorst, Wilhelm | Schmidt, Christina | 25, Jan. 1849 | G |
| Langley, Lewis | Taylor, Hannah F. | 9, Feb. 1834 | RCH |
| Langlin, John | Brennan, Rebecca | 16, May 1849 | GG |
| Langstredth, John | Hoffman, Catharine | 20, Feb. 1834 | RCH |
| Langstrom, Gideon | Clark, Anna Maria | 10, Oct. 1844 | RCH |
| Langtry, William | Beresford, Ann | 16, Oct. 1822 | I |
| Lanheady, Michael | Gill, Bridget | 23, Jan. 1848 | BB |
| Laning, John | ----, Elisabeth | 16, Nov. 1844 | RCH |
| Lanison, Robert | Crown, Nancy | 11, Apr. 1822 | RCH |
| Lanpacher, John | Kenroth, Maria Anna | 28, Apr. 1849 | RCH |
| Lanroth, George Jac. | Frurin, Catharine | 28, Sept 1843 | RCH |
| Lanston, John W. | Shaw, Helen M. | 6, Mar. 1837 | RCH |
| Lanz, Peter | Hauck, Maria | 22, June 1847 | G |
| Lanzing, Bernard H. | Kessler, Ursula | 16, Sept 1845 | FF |
| Lape, William | Taylor, Martha A. | 17, June 1847 | RCH |
| Lapold, Bernard | Drekeler, Catharina | 25, Sept 1838 | FF |
| Larabee, Thomas | Brower, Martha | 27, Mar. 1847 | RCH |
| Larber, Jacob | Danforth, Rachel A. | 14, Feb. 1842 | RCH |
| Larch, Charles | Beck, Theresa | 7, June 1849 | RCH |
| Laren---, Joseph | Doane, Mary | 10, Apr. 1821 | RCH |
| Larew, Malon | Hunus, Bridget | 24, Jan. 1834 | RCH |
| Larison, Amos | Hill, Rachel Ann | 3, Sept 1824 | RCH |
| Larison, George | Case, Julia Ann | 27, Mar. 1842 | RCH |
| Larkin, Joseph | Wood, Emeline | 5, June 1844 | RCH |
| Larkin, William | Leach, Jane | 22, May 1848 | RCH |
| Larmore, Matthew | Drake, Sarah Ann | 5, Sept 1847 | RCH |
| Larr, John | Scheve, Friedricka | 26, Dec. 1848 | C |
| Larue, Alison | Pursell, Priscilla | 6, Sept 1842 | RCH |
| Larue, Michael | Nichols, Polly | 27, May 1819 | RCH |
| Larydale, Robert H. | Corbin, Mary Ann | 28, Apr. 1833 | RCH |
| Lasaint, Franz | Renk, Catharine | 24, Dec. 1844 | RCH |
| Lash, James | Kennedy, Matilda | 26, Aug. 1841 | RCH |
| Latham, Leonard | Grimes, Amanda | 4, Apr. 1843 | RCH |
| Latham, Lowrey | Latham, Mary A. | 27, July 1826 | RCH |
| Latham, William | Johnson, Almira | 26, Jan. 1846 | RCH |
| Lathrop, Isaac | Gilber, Elenor | 20, Mar. 1834 | RCH |
| Latsch, Peter | Sweitzer, Felicitas | 11, Nov. 1846 | F |

| Grooms ***** | Brides ***** | Date of Marriage **** ** ******** | Code **** |
|---|---|---|---|
| Latta, Finley | Smith, Elisabeth Ann | 10, Mar. 1841 | RCH |
| Latten, Joseph | Schooly, Catharine | 24, Sept 1848 | RCH |
| Latterner, Peter | Fullhardt, Margaret | 6, Apr. 1845 | G |
| Laubel, Johan | Roegenberg, Wilhel. | 7, Dec. 1843 | C |
| Lauber, Jacob | Flading, Christina | 9, Dec. 1845 | G |
| Lauber, Johan | Eberhardt, Catharine | 15, Mar. 1849 | G |
| Lauberer, Max | Winter, Francisca | 28, Oct. 1844 | AA |
| Laudemann, Friedrich | Egalhoff, Elisabeth | 22, Feb. 1848 | A |
| Lauer, Peter | Herzog, Catharine | 23, Apr. 1839 | FF |
| Lauermann, Simon | Barth, Maria | 3, Aug. 1844 | G |
| Lauf, Ernst | Schwengel, Louisa | 25, Nov. 1849 | FF |
| Laufer, Michael | Arnold, Catharine | 14, Oct. 1841 | RCH |
| Laughlin, James | Roark, Phebe | 28, Jan. 1847 | RCH |
| Laughlin, Robert | Storms, Catharine | 29, May 1846 | RCH |
| Laughlin, Thomas | Pulse, Elisabeth | 24, Feb. 1844 | RCH |
| Laughlin, Thomas | Decoursey, Catharine | 7, June 1849 | GG |
| Laupacher, Johan | Neuroth, Margaretha | 28, Aug. 1849 | EE |
| Laurenz, Basil | Lippert, Catharine | 7, May 1848 | EE |
| Laut, Christian | Wiggers, Cath. Marg. | 15, June 1848 | B |
| Lauter, Adam | Warth, Caroline | 18, Dec. 1848 | G |
| Lauxtermann, Johan D | Yelkes, Anna Maria | 19, Nov. 1844 | AA |
| Lavall, Henry | Motherall, Elisabeth | 17, Sept 1826 | RCH |
| Laven, John | Cogans, Mary | 15, Oct. 1848 | GG |
| Lavey, Daniel | Sweeney, Ann | 21, June 1842 | BB |
| Lavinson, Isidor | Alcan, Caroline | 10, May 1849 | RCH |
| Law, William | Connelly, Ann | 27, Aug. 1846 | RCH |
| Law---, Daniel | Burrel, Rachel | 5, Jan. 1826 | RCH |
| Lawder, John | Sheldon, Rebecca | 17, May 1842 | RCH |
| Lawler, Charles | Ryan, Julia | 22, May 1838 | RCH |
| Lawler, Charles | Ryan, Mary | 4, Nov. 1844 | RCH |
| Lawler, Charles | Conway, Helen | 27, Nov. 1846 | BB |
| Lawler, Michael | Haggerty, Ann | 15, Apr. 1845 | BB |
| Lawless, Michael | Geraghty, Cecilia | 4, Mar. 1849 | BB |
| Lawless, Michael | Geraghty, Cecilia | 4, Mar. 1849 | BB |
| Lawrence, Allen | Schumacher, Ruth A. | 31, July 1842 | RCH |
| Lawrence, Emanuel | Whitemore, Ann | 8, Mar. 1834 | RCH |
| Lawrence, G.F. | Floyd, Louise | 14, Oct. 1835 | RCH |
| Lawrence, George W. | Miles, Louise | 12, Oct. 1836 | RCH |
| Lawrence, Holeten | Cook, Hulela | 31, Jan. 1822 | RCH |
| Lawrence, Isaac | Shiner, Elisabeth A. | 15, Nov. 1846 | RCH |
| Lawrence, Jacob | Memmen, Martha | 18, Oct. 1832 | RCH |
| Lawrence, James | Silvers, Margery | 10, Aug. 1820 | RCH |
| Lawrence, James | Green, Mary Ann | 6, May 1844 | RCH |
| Lawrence, John | S---, Matilda | 12, Mar. 1835 | RCH |
| Lawrence, Thomas | Davies, Hannah | 1, Aug. 1843 | RCH |
| Lawrence, William | Desbrow, Sarah Ann | 4, Apr. 1839 | RCH |
| Lawson, Benjamin S. | Robinson, Sarah | 15, Oct. 1831 | RCH |
| Lawson, Isaac | Allen, Elis. Jane | 27, June 1841 | RCH |
| Lawson, Isaac | Gould, Mary Ann | 22, Dec. 1846 | RCH |
| Lawson, Jesse | Brown, Elisabeth | 31, Oct. 1822 | RCH |
| Lawson, Joseph | Birdsall, Sarah Ann | 21, Dec. 1843 | RCH |
| Lawson, L.M. | Robinson, Anna Elis. | 14, Aug. 1848 | RCH |
| Lawson, Perry | Johnson, Elisabeth | 11, Aug. 1843 | RCH |
| Lawson, William | Griffin, Esther | 16, Feb. 1838 | RCH |
| Lawton, Alfred | Stewart, Jane Ann | 22, Nov. 1846 | RCH |
| Lawton, Charles | McCollough, Phoebe | 26, Sept 1849 | RCH |
| Lawton, Jeremiah | Kerns, Elisabeth | 26, Oct. 1826 | RCH |
| Lawton, John | Platt, Eunice | 5, Dec. 1846 | I |
| Lawyer, George H. | Pettit, Jane | 20, June 1839 | RCH |
| Lawzay, Peter | Pepin, Virginia | 24, Jan. 1844 | BB |
| Lay, Heinrich | Muhlberger, Eva Marg | 29, Jan. 1843 | C |
| Lay, John Jefferson | Freeman, Elis. Jane | 24, Jan. 1846 | RCH |
| Laycock, William | Timmons, Elisabeth | 23, Aug. 1838 | RCH |
| Layman, Alexander | Brewer, Sally | 1, Sept 1820 | RCH |
| Layman, Jeremiah | Cumming, Mary | 13, Jan. 1822 | RCH |
| Layman, John H. | Richards, Margaret | 4, Sept 1833 | RCH |
| Layman, Sirah B. | Letter, Charlotte | 7, Apr. 1841 | RCH |
| Layman, Wesley | Carter, Mary | 1, Apr. 1837 | RCH |
| Laymon, David | Mills, Hannah M. | 8, Feb. 1843 | RCH |
| Layton, Charles W. | Wheatley, Amelia | 16, Mar. 1848 | RCH |
| Layton, Joseph | VanBlarigan, Mary | 5, Sept 1822 | RCH |

| Grooms<br>****** | Brides<br>****** | Date of Marriage<br>**** ** ******** | Code<br>**** |
|---|---|---|---|
| Lazarus, Job | Goodman, Regina | 27, July 1849 | RCH |
| Lea, Edmund F. | Addison, Melissa E. | 15, May 1836 | I |
| Lea, James Henry | Campbell, Ellen | 3, May 1836 | I |
| Lea, Jarvis | Burrows, Sally | 30, Jan. 1822 | RCH |
| Leach, John | Bates, Elisabeth | 7, Dec. 1844 | RCH |
| Leach, Lewis | Stewart, Lucinda | 15, Sept 1843 | RCH |
| Leach, Thomas | Ramsey, Margaret | 22, Sept 1836 | RCH |
| Leadbetter, William | Black, Mary | 24, June 1835 | RCH |
| Leady, Herman L. | R---, Amanda M. | 17, May 1835 | RCH |
| Leaf, Aquilin | Vance, Sophia | 18, Jan. 1838 | RCH |
| Leahy, James | Croake, Joann | 19, Nov. 1846 | BB |
| Leary, Robert | Hartshorn, Maria | 16, Dec. 1849 | RCH |
| Leavenart, Mecandsi | Hayden, Drusilla | 28, Sept 1819 | RCH |
| Lebalt, John | Attem, Mary | 19, Jan. 1842 | RCH |
| Lebeaw, Charles | Patin, Wilhelmina | 30, May 1833 | RCH |
| Lebensberger, Joseph | Leopold, Rosina | 15, Sept 1846 | RCH |
| Leber, Wilhelm | Zeller, Margaretha | 8, Oct. 1840 | FF |
| Lebertmann, Johan H. | Bruening, Angela | 30, Sept 1849 | EE |
| Lechner, Friedrich | Vorter, Susannah | 20, July 1849 | RCH |
| Lechner, Simon | Hauck, Eva | 12, Feb. 1846 | A |
| Lecke, Friedrich | Ebening, Margaret | 26, Apr. 1847 | RCH |
| Leckner, Joseph | Settelmeyer, Louisa | 13, Oct. 1840 | FF |
| Lecky, Hugh | Crowley, Mary E. | 4, July 1846 | RCH |
| Leclair, Michael | Wolf, Anna | 7, Jan. 1847 | AA |
| Lecompt, Henry | Carr, Lucinda | 20, July 1842 | RCH |
| Lecount, William | Rynearson, Rosanna | 12, Sept 1837 | RCH |
| Ledeker, George | Lethen, Sophia | 7, Nov. 1847 | RCH |
| Ledel, Joseph | Mont, Elisabeth | 2, Mar. 1842 | RCH |
| Lederle, Jacob | Schulmeier, Louise | 11, Apr. 1848 | RCH |
| Ledler, John | Leening, Elisabeth | 23, Apr. 1834 | RCH |
| Lee, Bradley | Cole, Ann | 8, Apr. 1832 | RCH |
| Lee, C. | Morris, Rebecca | 6, Feb. 1823 | RCH |
| Lee, C. | Murphy, Sarah | 8, Aug. 1824 | RCH |
| Lee, David | Clark, Nancy | 31, Dec. 1818 | RCH |
| Lee, David | Carter, Nancy | 14, May 1834 | RCH |
| Lee, David | Gaston, Isabel | 10, Feb. 1848 | RCH |
| Lee, George | Wilson, Margaret Ann | 9, Aug. 1849 | RCH |
| Lee, Hugh A. | Eldridge, Elisabeth | May 1839 | RCH |
| Lee, James | Byington, Elisabeth | 1, Apr. 1842 | RCH |
| Lee, James H. | Lamley, Mary Jane | 3, Aug. 1843 | RCH |
| Lee, John | Inkes, Charlotte | 2, Aug. 1846 | RCH |
| Lee, Martin | McGearty, Ann | 3, Sept 1847 | GG |
| Lee, Prior | McDougall, Maria | 7, Mar. 1849 | RCH |
| Lee, Robert | Johnson, Cornelia | 8, Feb. 1849 | RCH |
| Lee, Thomas | Loughery, Margaret | 27, May 1843 | RCH |
| Lee, Thomas | Robbins, Mary Jane | 31, Oct. 1844 | RCH |
| Lee, Wesley | Schenck, Elisabeth | 24, Jan. 1844 | RCH |
| Lee, William | Lyons, Mary | 15, Dec. 1834 | RCH |
| Lee, William | Belanger, Hannah | 27, Sept 1846 | RCH |
| Lee, William H. | Abom, Sarah Jane | 22, Dec. 1835 | RCH |
| Lee, William L. | Hawkins, Eveline | 15, Aug. 1840 | I |
| Leer, David | Fox, Amanda | 7, Nov. 1843 | RCH |
| Leetch, William | Gailard, Hannah | 29, Mar. 1836 | RCH |
| Leever, Valentine | Hall, Mary L. | 22, May 1847 | RCH |
| Lefavour, Daniel | Morrison, Clementina | 3, Dec. 1848 | RCH |
| Lefeber, Philipp | Price, Sarah | 30, Aug. 1844 | RCH |
| Lefever, James | Boone, Sarah | 29, Dec. 1835 | RCH |
| Lefken, Johan Heinr. | Hudepohl, Theresa | 10, Jan. 1843 | AA |
| Lefken, Wilhelm | Meyerhoff, Mary A. | 20, Mar. 1848 | F |
| Lefler, John C. | Murdy, Margaret | 24, Feb. 1842 | RCH |
| Lefler, William | Kyson, Margaret | 27, Apr. 1820 | RCH |
| Leforce, Samuel | Beard, Elisabeth | 22, Mar. 1849 | RCH |
| Leftwick, Adison | Wait, Maria | 22, Dec. 1837 | RCH |
| Leger, Jean | Zablod, Victoria | 2, Oct. 1847 | RCH |
| Legg, Charles | Patterson, Hannah | 31, May 1846 | RCH |
| Legg, William C. | Meyers, Lydia | 1, Jan. 1818 | RCH |
| Lehan, John | Hardin, Sarah | 5, Oct. 1836 | RCH |
| Lehan, Mathew | Cronan, Elisabeth | 2, Dec. 1849 | GG |
| Lehfeld, Herman | Beckmann, Elisabeth | 7, Jan. 1847 | AA |
| Lehmann, Gerson | Block, Lena | 13, June 1848 | RCH |
| Lehmann, Herman | Widestetter, Maria A | 13, Feb. 1840 | FF |

| Grooms<br>****** | Brides<br>****** | Date of Marriage<br>**** ** ******** | Code<br>**** |
|---|---|---|---|
| Lehmas, Johan | Rudy, Maria | 6, Feb. 1843 | FF |
| Lehmkuhle, Anton | Westbrock, Mary | 24, Oct. 1843 | AA |
| Lehmkuhle, Diedrich | Hofhaus, Anna Maria | 7, Jan. 1846 | AA |
| Lehmkuhler, Ernst | Stillen, Friedricka | 29, July 1841 | G |
| Lehmkuhler, Ernst H. | Darlage, Anna M.C. | 23, Feb. 1844 | C |
| Lehnbeuter, Georg | String, Cunigunda | 14, June 1840 | FF |
| Lehneis, Conrad | Paunings, Cunigunda | 1, Jan. 1849 | A |
| Lehner, | Isham, Jane B. | 7, Aug. 1849 | RCH |
| Lehr, Georg | Schwarm, Magdalena | 8, Oct. 1848 | G |
| Lehrer, Pantaleon | Zimmermann, Elis. | 3, Apr. 1845 | AA |
| Lehrmann, Bernard | Bowing, Anna M. | 15, May 1838 | FF |
| Leib, Johan | Klein, Margaretha | 16, Feb. 1841 | FF |
| Leib, Michael | Schnetze, Francisca | 9, Jan. 1837 | FF |
| Leibeck, Sebastian | Staubach, Rosina | 19, Aug. 1845 | AA |
| Leibrock, Georg | Doerr, Anna Eva | 17, Dec. 1848 | C |
| Leiby, John A. | ----, Edna Jane | 16, Apr. 1837 | RCH |
| Leicht, Johan | Leicht, M. Barbara | 17, Jan. 1847 | G |
| Leicht, John Wendel | Kessner, Elisabeth | 20, Nov. 1842 | RCH |
| Leicht, Michael | Seifert, M Elisabeth | 5, Apr. 1847 | A |
| Leighton, Abel | Moore, Hannah | 28, Sept 1841 | RCH |
| Leighton, David | Ring, Eliza Ann | 8, Apr. 1847 | RCH |
| Leighton, John | Miller, Alcesta | 8, Apr. 1844 | RCH |
| Leimath, G. Jacob | Tharin, Catharine | 16, Oct. 1843 | FF |
| Leinfelder, Johan | Heeg, Elisabeth | 3, Sept 1847 | EE |
| Leining, Heinrich | Witharn, Agnes | 21, Aug. 1838 | FF |
| Leininger, Georg M. | Hanpert, Maria | 21, Nov. 1848 | EE |
| Leininger, J. Georg | Wendt, Louise | 3, June 1847 | RCH |
| Leininger, John Geo. | Hauck, Maria | 6, Oct. 1835 | RCH |
| Leininger, Nicolaus | Bedel, Rosina | 15, Apr. 1844 | FF |
| Leinman, Charles | Lutman, Catharine | 17, Apr. 1837 | RCH |
| Leiper, Sebastian | Sieyler, Julianna | 2, Nov. 1843 | AA |
| Leipold, Johan | Perks, Adelheid | 16, Sept 1841 | FF |
| Leiser, Sebastian | Dirk, Catharine | 17, July 1849 | EE |
| Leising, Heinrich | Wessels, Theresa | 14, May 1848 | EE |
| Leister, James | Craig, Drucilla | 15, Dec. 1845 | RCH |
| Leistner, Friedrich | Waldfahrer, Christ. | 3, May 1846 | C |
| Leitch, Richard | Pierson, Mary A. | 16, June 1843 | RCH |
| Leitenheimer, Jacob | Hoffmann, Elisabeth | 11, Dec. 1849 | EE |
| Leitsch, Robert | Bird, Elizabeth | 14, July 1848 | RCH |
| Leitt, Georg | Burghard, Augusta | 6, Nov. 1838 | FF |
| Leland, Elbridge | ----, ---- | 26, Dec. 1824 | RCH |
| Lelhoon, J.L.H. | Junger, Anna M. | 23, Apr. 1834 | RCH |
| Lelley, Charles | Rieber, Enis | 24, July 1832 | RCH |
| Leming, William | Huff, Charlotte | 14, Sept 1823 | RCH |
| Lemmann, Bernard | Spellmeyer, M. | 19, Nov. 1848 | AA |
| Lemmermichel, Henry | Averman, Maria E. | 6, Apr. 1834 | RCH |
| Lemmiger, Conrad | Zimmermann, Maria A. | 25, May 1846 | EE |
| Lemmon, David | Reeder, Rebecca Ann | 22, Dec. 1831 | RCH |
| Lemmon, David | Hill, Margaret | 16, Aug. 1834 | RCH |
| Lemmon, Elisha | Smith, Mary | 19, Jan. 1837 | RCH |
| Lemmon, William | Hudson, Lavina | 21, Oct. 1838 | RCH |
| Lemon, Jacob | Jones, Julia | 29, Dec. 1841 | RCH |
| Lemon, John | Andrews, Mary Ann | 28, May 1846 | RCH |
| Lemon, John | Ledley, Melinda | 31, Dec. 1846 | RCH |
| Lempler, William | Waldsmith, Elisabeth | 27, Nov. 1817 | RCH |
| Lemster, Jacob | Kleinmann, Maria | 21, Apr. 1846 | AA |
| Len, Johan | Wunderling, Pauline | 13, May 1849 | A |
| Lenahan, Jacob | McCombs, Elisabeth | 25, May 1849 | RCH |
| Lender, Heinrich | Baurichter, Maria A. | 1, Feb. 1842 | FF |
| Lenebauh, Samuel | Bump, Diadumia | 11, Aug. 1837 | RCH |
| Leng, Thomas | Sheldon, Catharine | 4, May 1833 | RCH |
| Lening, Thomas C. | Karnes, Catharine | 15, June 1832 | RCH |
| Lennis, Samuel | Hutchison, Catharine | 23, Apr. 1839 | RCH |
| Lennon, James | Casey, Ann | 26, Nov. 1848 | BB |
| Lentz, Samuel | Kurtz, Elisabeth | 15, Aug. 1849 | A |
| Lenz, Simon | Heinsheimer, Carolin | 18, June 1846 | RCH |
| Leonard, George L. | Amos, Mary Ann | 24, Apr. 1836 | RCH |
| Leonard, George W. | Farnham, Charlotte | 9, June 1835 | D |
| Leonard, John | Nall, Susan | 30, Jan. 1845 | RCH |
| Leonard, Richard | Davey, Margaret | 23, Oct. 1843 | BB |
| Leonard, Thomas | Butterworth, Ann | 15, Feb. 1838 | RCH |

| Grooms | Brides | Date of Marriage | Code |
|--------|--------|------------------|------|
| Leonard, William | Philley, Sarah Jane | 28, May 1843 | RCH |
| Leonhard, George | Obermeier, Eva M. | 3, Dec. 1846 | RCH |
| Leonhardt, Georg | Hummel, Dorothea(Mrs | 5, Sept 1846 | AA |
| Leonhardt, Johan H. | Molter, Elisabeth | 1, June 1846 | G |
| Leonhart, George | Salmon, M. Dorothea | 4, Sept 1846 | RCH |
| Leopold, Bernard | Ties, M. Catharina | 7, Nov. 1839 | FF |
| Leopold, Carl | Kessler, Louise | 19, July 1847 | A |
| Leopold, Herman | Elsas, Hannah | 4, Feb. 1842 | RCH |
| Leopold, J. Gottlieb | Sauer, Friedricka | 10, May 1848 | C |
| Leopold, John E. | Klein, Anna Catharin | 31, Dec. 1849 | RCH |
| Leopold, Morris | Goodhart, Rose | 15, Sept 1845 | RCH |
| Leopold, Wilhelm | Retzer, M. Elisabeth | 9, May 1843 | C |
| Leppert, Carl | Pfeiffer, Francisca | 14, Feb. 1843 | FF |
| Leppert, Jacob | Luck, Magdalena(Mrs) | 14, June 1842 | FF |
| Lepple, Mathias | Rothweiler, Rosina | 26, Oct. 1848 | A |
| Lerany, John | Clemens, Catharine | 14, Oct. 1841 | RCH |
| Lerrin, Caleb | Strong, Kesiah | 7, June 1818 | RCH |
| Lesaint, Franz | Rink, Catharine | 19, Aug. 1845 | G |
| Lesch, Johan | Doerr, Catharine | 24, July 1849 | EE |
| Leseberg, Christian | Decker, Catharine L. | 21, Mar. 1848 | F |
| Lesher, John | Crowell, Elisabeth | 9, Dec. 1832 | RCH |
| Leslie, Alfred | Eppleat, Margaret | 19, Jan. 1849 | RCH |
| Lessel, Peter | Wolsiefer, Elisabeth | 7, Feb. 1843 | FF |
| Lesterland, George | Leffler, Mary Ann | 31, July 1839 | RCH |
| Letford, John | Jones, Jane | 14, July 1846 | RCH |
| Letta, George W. | Wesley, Sarah | 28, Jan. 1845 | RCH |
| Lettig, Francis | Knopf, Anna Maria | 2, Mar. 1835 | FF |
| Leuer, Simon | Barnhart, Mary A. | 26, Oct. 1836 | RCH |
| Leuges, Georg | Herkenhoff, Catharin | 2, May 1837 | FF |
| Leunig, Heinrich | Abrutz, Emma | 30, Oct. 1849 | B |
| Leupold, Christian | Halbleib, Catharina | 5, Feb. 1841 | FF |
| Leutes, John | Boyles, Nancy | 30, June 1836 | RCH |
| Leuthstrom, William | Carey, Letitia | 12, Sept 1844 | RCH |
| Levan, Daniel | Webb, Catharine | 13, Sept 1849 | RCH |
| Leveque, Israel | Cox, Mary | 14, Sept 1849 | RCH |
| Leverid, J. Heinrich | Duning, Anna Marg. | 9, Jan. 1848 | FF |
| Levi, Alexander | Jacobs, Isabella | 27, July 1836 | RCH |
| Levi, Leopold | Heilbrenner, Jette | 20, Nov. 1848 | RCH |
| Levi, Louis | Starr, Ann | 9, Oct. 1848 | RCH |
| Levi, Michael | Silverman, Mary Ann | 20, Mar. 1844 | RCH |
| Levien, Sigmund | Moehring, Louise | 4, Jan. 1849 | RCH |
| Levinson, Jacob | Hirsch, Fanny | 25, Mar. 1844 | RCH |
| Levoy, Michael | Monfort, Mary Jane | 24, Nov. 1846 | BB |
| Levy, Matthew | McCloskey, Mary | 28, Oct. 1840 | BB |
| Levy, N. | O'Brien, Ann | 6, Aug. 1836 | RCH |
| Lewe, Christian | Schulte, Anna | 28, July 1849 | CC |
| Lewe, Heinrich | Schroeder, Anna | 7, Oct. 1849 | CC |
| Lewe, John Henry | Gudorff, Maria Anna | 8, Nov. 1845 | RCH |
| Lewis, | Frazier, L. | 3, Mar. 1848 | RCH |
| Lewis, Alexander | Corbin, Sarah | 28, July 1844 | RCH |
| Lewis, Anderson | Berring, Elisabeth | 28, Feb. 1833 | RCH |
| Lewis, Benjamin | Dougherty, Mary Ann | 10, Mar. 1840 | RCH |
| Lewis, Charles | Anderson, Margaret G | 19, June 1838 | RCH |
| Lewis, Charles | Wilson, Mary E. | 13, Oct. 1841 | BB |
| Lewis, Charles | C---, Caroline | 23, Mar. 1847 | RCH |
| Lewis, Charles | Hall, Sarah | 18, Apr. 1849 | RCH |
| Lewis, David | Regnes, Catharine | 1, Feb. 1836 | RCH |
| Lewis, Dyer | Bale, Delilah | 11, Oct. 1835 | RCH |
| Lewis, Ebenezer | Selers, Hannah | 23, Apr. 1818 | RCH |
| Lewis, Edward | Hull, Nancy | 16, Aug. 1844 | RCH |
| Lewis, Evan | Davis, Mary | 13, Feb. 1844 | RCH |
| Lewis, George | Wilson, Elisabeth J. | 8, Sept 1847 | RCH |
| Lewis, Henry | Stone, Mary | 12, June 1836 | RCH |
| Lewis, Ira R. | Hunt, Eliza | 22, Oct. 1822 | RCH |
| Lewis, Isaac | Preston, Elisabeth | 2, July 1846 | RCH |
| Lewis, James | Halt, Maria | 22, Dec. 1833 | RCH |
| Lewis, John | Lord, Ruth | 12, Sept 1818 | RCH |
| Lewis, John | Craig, Jane | 31, Jan. 1820 | RCH |
| Lewis, John | Sulton, Sarah | 26, Jan. 1842 | RCH |
| Lewis, John | McKinney, Bedelia | 1, Oct. 1847 | RCH |
| Lewis, John | Moles, Frances | 25, May 1849 | RCH |

| Grooms | Brides | Date of Marriage | Code |
|--------|--------|------------------|------|
| ****** | ****** | **** ** ******** | **** |
| Lewis, John H. | Wheeler, Cordelia | 5, Jan. 1844 | D |
| Lewis, John P. | Ramsey, Mary J. | 13, Feb. 1833 | RCH |
| Lewis, John S. | Makin, Ruth | 11, June 1848 | RCH |
| Lewis, John T. | ----, Lucinda | 13, Jan. 1825 | RCH |
| Lewis, Joseph | Parson, Mary Ann | 3, Nov. 1832 | RCH |
| Lewis, Joseph | Thornton, Ethalarila | 21, Nov. 1833 | RCH |
| Lewis, Joseph | Wakefield, Mary | 21, May 1835 | RCH |
| Lewis, Julian | Fort, Elisabeth | 10, May 1826 | RCH |
| Lewis, Luster | Chapman, Mary Jane | 25, Aug. 1842 | RCH |
| Lewis, Marion | Dodge, Polly | 26, Dec. 1824 | RCH |
| Lewis, Peter | Patterson, Margaret | 25, Feb. 1841 | RCH |
| Lewis, Reuben | Stevens, Matilda | 26, June 1842 | RCH |
| Lewis, Robert | Thompson, Sarah Jane | 29, Aug. 1841 | RCH |
| Lewis, Robert | Hubbard, Anna Sarah | 1, July 1846 | RCH |
| Lewis, Robert P. | Sponser, Nancy Ann | 11, Feb. 1835 | RCH |
| Lewis, Samuel | Goforth, Charlotte | 6, Aug. 1823 | RCH |
| Lewis, Simon | Babcock, | 9, Feb. 1818 | RCH |
| Lewis, Thatcher | Bennett, Elizabeth A | 29, Oct. 1846 | RCH |
| Lewis, Thomas | Rudel, Priscilla | 23, Jan. 1834 | RCH |
| Lewis, Thomas | Chambers, Jane | 17, July 1834 | RCH |
| Lewis, Thornton | Anderson, Dehla | 13, May 1847 | RCH |
| Lewis, W. | Wright, Hester A. | 18, June 1849 | RCH |
| Lewis, Watson | Jonlin, Nancy Elis. | 1, Sept 1819 | RCH |
| Lewis, William | Eddington, Nancy | 11, Sept 1833 | RCH |
| Lewis, William | Goudy, Amy | 4, Nov. 1845 | RCH |
| Lewis, William | Berkley, Elisabeth | 9, June 1849 | RCH |
| Lewis, William | Hughes, Elisabeth | 22, Sept 1849 | RCH |
| Lewton, Abraham | Lee, Melinda | 7, July 1825 | RCH |
| Lewton, Samuel | Campbell, Nancy | 11, June 1843 | RCH |
| Ley---, Samuel | Miller, Catharine | 14, Apr. 1825 | RCH |
| Leyrisse, Peter | Klare, Louise | 23, Feb. 1847 | GG |
| Leyton, Baird | Rose, Margaret | 27, Sept 1838 | RCH |
| Libbermann, Johan H. | Tenambergen, M. Elis | 27, June 1847 | AA |
| Libeau, Charles | Pile, Mary | 6, Dec. 1838 | D |
| Libert, Joseph | Tomlin, Lucy | 6, Nov. 1834 | RCH |
| Libke, Johan Joseph | Kihl, Margaretha M. | 2, Feb. 1847 | FF |
| Libler, Thomas | Lir, Anna Maria | 28, July 1840 | FF |
| Licher, Adam | Wichmann, Barbara | 17, Aug. 1845 | AA |
| Licher, J. Caspar | Schmits, M Elisabeth | 25, May 1847 | AA |
| Licher, Johan Caspar | Brinkmeyer, Catharin | 24, June 1849 | AA |
| Licht, Amos | Graffing, Helen | 2, Dec. 1841 | F |
| Licht, Jacob H. | Beyerle, M. Louise | 4, Nov. 1848 | F |
| Lichten, Adolph | Oberdorfer, Celia | 13, Apr. 1847 | RCH |
| Lichtenberg, August | Gerder, Anna | 11, Jan. 1848 | AA |
| Lichtenberg, Clement | Gehrs, Theresa | 21, Oct. 1849 | AA |
| Lichtenberg, Herman | Bolster, Anna Maria | 9, May 1848 | FF |
| Lichtendahl, Bernard | Benkenbusch, Alyda | 3, May 1849 | RCH |
| Lichtenfels, Jacob | Keicker, Franziska | 17, July 1849 | RCH |
| Lichtsin, Henry | Colmeier, Louise | 28, Jan. 1843 | RCH |
| Lickmeyer, Friedrich | Vleine, M.E. | 1, Apr. 1845 | RCH |
| Lidel, John Nicolaus | Reis, Josephina | 9, June 1840 | FF |
| Lieber, Joseph | Friedmann, Barbara | 10, Oct. 1843 | RCH |
| Lieber, Peter | Hauck, Francisca | 27, Jan. 1842 | G |
| Liebert, J. August | Gross, Elisabeth | 3, Dec. 1849 | A |
| Liebich, Johan | Hauser, Maria | 16, May 1848 | EE |
| Liedel, Peter | Engler, Regina | 8, Sept 1846 | FF |
| Liedere, Franz L. | Hesseling, Catharine | 6, Feb. 1844 | AA |
| Liening, J. Benrard | Muenker, M Elisabeth | 15, June 1841 | FF |
| Lieninger, Johan | Brugger, Maria | 25, Mar. 1849 | C |
| Lieston, Robert | Brown, Elisabeth | 27, Jan. 1844 | RCH |
| Liever, Bernard | Moehlenkamp, Gesina | 3, Feb. 1842 | FF |
| Light, Daniel | ----, H. | 5, Apr. 1835 | RCH |
| Light, James W. | Burdsill, Mary | 8, Mar. 1835 | RCH |
| Light, Simeon | Thompson, Rachel | 13, Sept 1835 | RCH |
| Lightfoot, William | Grason, Welthy | 4, Aug. 1840 | RCH |
| Lighthiger, Samuel | Budd, Elisabeth | 22, Dec. 1836 | RCH |
| Lightner, John J. | Grink, Catharine | 7, Jan. 1845 | BB |
| Lightser, John | Knox, Sarah | 11, Aug. 1832 | RCH |
| Liland, Bernard | Volker, Anna Helena | 13, Feb. 1844 | AA |
| Lilie, Heinrich | Wachendorf, Rachel | 21, Oct. 1841 | F |
| Liller, Michael | Dudenhoffer, Cath. | 22, June 1848 | C |

| Grooms | Brides | Date of Marriage | Code |
|--------|--------|------------------|------|
| ****** | ****** | **** ** ******** | **** |
| Lilley, Anderson | Bligs, Lucinda J. | 24, Dec. 1848 | RCH |
| Lilley, M.C. | Bickle, Sarah | 2, Apr. 1818 | RCH |
| Lillis, Patrick | Tracy, Ann | 12, Aug. 1849 | GG |
| Lilly, John | Dudenhoffer, Barbara | 22, Jan. 1842 | RCH |
| Limke, Clement | Engelkrode, Anna M. | 29, May 1849 | EE |
| Linck, Anthony | Heighty, Rosanna | 21, Dec. 1819 | RCH |
| Linck, Leonard | Boegetin, Cath. Marg | 28, July 1845 | RCH |
| Lind, Charles | Shober, Amanda | 5, Feb. 1846 | RCH |
| Lind, Richard | Miller, Elizabeth | 29, Sept 1847 | RCH |
| Lindemann, J. Herman | Kahrmann, M. Cath. | 4, June 1846 | F |
| Lindemann, Julius | Vordemann, Friedrika | 20, Aug. 1848 | G |
| Linder, Georg | Stanger, Catharine | 4, Jan. 1848 | G |
| Lindinger, Andreas | Meyer, Helena | 4, Sept 1848 | G |
| Lindlay, Jacob | Gillingham, Elisabet | 17, May 1842 | RCH |
| Lindle, Robert | ----, ---- | 23, Sept 1824 | RCH |
| Lindley, Abraham | L'Hommidieu, Sarah | 28, Feb. 1822 | RCH |
| Lindley, Francis | Segar, Elisabeth | 29, May 1841 | RCH |
| Lindley, John | Lodwick, Angeline | 27, Sept 1848 | RCH |
| Lindley, Tyler | Mullen, Sarah Belle | 4, Nov. 1847 | RCH |
| Lindmann, Lewis | Donaldson, Mary | 20, Apr. 1847 | RCH |
| Lindsay, John | Parker, Elisabeth | 14, Apr. 1844 | RCH |
| Lindsay, William | Hiatt, Elisabeth | 24, Aug. 1848 | RCH |
| Lindsey, David | Hawkins, Mary | 17, Jan. 1833 | RCH |
| Lindsey, Samuel | Turner, Edith | 25, July 1847 | RCH |
| Line, Abraham | Line, Sarah | 3, Aug. 1820 | RCH |
| Lingemann, Joseph | Gelhaus, Carolina | 7, Jan. 1840 | FF |
| Lingert, Johan | Pabst, Johanna | 26, Aug. 1847 | EE |
| Linghorst, Heinrich | Brockmann, Catharine | 23, Dec. 1845 | B |
| Lingo, Caleb | Finkbine, Margaret | 12, Sept 1833 | RCH |
| Lingo, Henry | McKain, Frances | 18, Dec. 1834 | RCH |
| Lingo, William | Johnson, Mary Ann | 13, Dec. 1835 | RCH |
| Linhart, John | Frazer, Margaret | 27, Oct. 1845 | RCH |
| Lining, Joseph Fran. | Krone, M. Catharina | 5, June 1838 | FF |
| Lining, Nicolaus | Hauck, Maria | 29, Sept 1845 | C |
| Link, Harper | Lowderbach, Patty | 21, Jan. 1836 | RCH |
| Link, Joseph | Murphy, Lydia | 31, Dec. 1835 | RCH |
| Linke, William | Thornell, Rachel | 5, Jan. 1834 | RCH |
| Linkenbach, Johan C. | Minor, Anna Margaret | 17, May 1849 | G |
| Linkert, Friedrich | Wiedholter, Friedr. | 21, Mar. 1849 | F |
| Linnehan, Patrick | Maloney, Catharine | 24, Nov. 1844 | BB |
| Linnemann, Francis H | Grever, Dorothea | 6, Nov. 1838 | FF |
| Linnemann, Heinrich | Moormann, Katharine | 24, Nov. 1842 | AA |
| Linnenkohl, Wilhelm | Ezel, Wilhelmina | 2, July 1843 | G |
| Linnenkugel, Friedr. | Strotmann, Maria C. | 5, Sept 1843 | FF |
| Linnert, John | Kohl, Babette | 29, June 1840 | A |
| Linsemann, Engelbert | Meyer, Magdalena | 28, Apr. 1840 | FF |
| Linsenmeyer, Louis | Harsch, Christina | 12, Aug. 1845 | G |
| Linsey, Thomas | ----, Elisabeth | 2, July 1835 | RCH |
| Linstriet, Wilhelm | AufderHaar, Cath. W. | 1, Dec. 1846 | C |
| Linsy, Samuel | Wingfield, Amanda | 15, Nov. 1832 | RCH |
| Linton, John W. | Hensley, Elisabeth | 13, Mar. 1836 | RCH |
| Lion, Moses | Ross, Elisabeth | 13, Nov. 1818 | RCH |
| Liper, John | Pfalzgraf, Maria | 28, May 1837 | RCH |
| Lipmann, Solomon | Hutchinson, Sarah A. | 30, May 1847 | RCH |
| Lippincott, Charles | Davis, Elisabeth | 30, June 1838 | RCH |
| Lippold, Johan H.C. | Ringemann, Clara | 20, Mar. 1849 | A |
| Lipps, Ferdinand | Thines, Catharine | 18, Aug. 1840 | FF |
| Lippus, Sebastian | Koch, Antonia | 20, Nov. 1849 | AA |
| Lipscomb, --llen | Mills, Mary | 8, June 1837 | RCH |
| Lipscomb, William | Knicely, Mary Ann | 31, July 1843 | RCH |
| Lisdenfeltzer, Nic. | Kister, Magdalena | 26, May 1843 | RCH |
| List, Bernard | Altenschulten, Engel | 1, Nov. 1846 | AA |
| List, John | P---, Carol | 9, Mar. 1836 | RCH |
| List, Joseph | Rittenhouse, Matilda | 7, Dec. 1846 | RCH |
| Listen, Michael | Brazil, Catharine | 3, Sept 1848 | BB |
| Lister, John | Brown, Rhoda | 9, Jan. 1844 | RCH |
| Listermann, Christ. | Felix, Catharine | 26, Apr. 1847 | EE |
| Listermann, Franz | Semler, Elisabeth | 20, Jan. 1846 | AA |
| Listermann, Johan | Eichenlaub, Theresa | 9, Feb. 1847 | EE |
| Listermann, Wilhelm | Mock, Maria | 12, Oct. 1847 | EE |
| Litchford, Abraham | Easley, Matilda | 12, July 1849 | RCH |

| Grooms | Brides | Date of Marriage | Code |
|--------|--------|------------------|------|
| ****** | ****** | **** ** ******** | **** |
| Litherbury, John | Weeks, Caroline | 24, Aug. 1824 | RCH |
| Litick, Joseph | Hechinger, Ver.(Mrs) | 26, May 1835 | FF |
| Litmer, Johan Casper | Hausmann, Bernardina | 5, Apr. 1842 | FF |
| Litoga, Joseph | Weber, Elisabeth | 11, Dec. 1845 | G |
| Littell, William M. | Garrison, Elisabeth | 6, Feb. 1835 | RCH |
| Littelmann, Herman F | Wachendorp, A Sophia | 2, Sept 1847 | F |
| Little, | Henry, Catharine | 23, Feb. 1837 | RCH |
| Little, Charles | Wilson, Catharine | 17, Feb. 1846 | RCH |
| Little, John | McKinney, Sarah Ann | 5, July 1845 | RCH |
| Little, John | Donahue, Catharine | 22, Feb. 1846 | GG |
| Little, Levi | Benson, Jane | 27, Dec. 1846 | RCH |
| Little, William | Rock, Mary | 30, July 1849 | BB |
| Littlefield, | Jones, Mary | 11, Dec. 1817 | RCH |
| Littlejohn, William | Myers, Ruth | 9, Sept 1847 | RCH |
| Litton, R.E. | Irwin, Ann E. | 9, July 1838 | RCH |
| Litzelberger, Jacob | Ritzer, Catharine | 26, Dec. 1843 | G |
| Litzenberg, M.N. | Morgan, Catharine W. | 26, Nov. 1839 | I |
| Liverpool, William | Shephard, Mary | 24, Sept 1849 | RCH |
| Livezey, Isaac | Sholcross, Elisabeth | 30, May 1838 | RCH |
| Livingston, Michael | Kaufmann, Rosina | 3, Feb. 1846 | RCH |
| Llewellyn, Robert | Knott, Abigail | 5, Sept 1842 | D |
| Lloyd, Alexander | Owens, Elisabeth | Apr. 1843 | RCH |
| Lloyd, Reuben | Case, Ludia | 31, July 1841 | RCH |
| Lloyd, Richard | Mansel, Amelia | 7, Apr. 1840 | RCH |
| Loar, John | Traver, Elisabeth | 23, Oct. 1842 | RCH |
| Lockard, John | Hickman, Marba | 2, Nov. 1833 | RCH |
| Locke, John | Morris, Mary | 17, Oct. 1825 | I |
| Lockhart, Jacob | Webb, Maria | 21, Nov. 1841 | RCH |
| Lockran, Robert | Garrison, Mary | 2, May 1839 | RCH |
| Lockwood, Charles | Rench, Nancy | 26, Dec. 1847 | RCH |
| Lockwood, Daniel | Shays, Frances Carol | 31, May 1837 | RCH |
| Lockwood, Daniel | Mulford, Gabriella | 26, Dec. 1848 | RCH |
| Lockwood, Ezekiel | Trobridge, Minerva | 1, Nov. 1821 | RCH |
| Lockwood, George | Milton, Rachel A. | 16, Feb. 1839 | RCH |
| Lockwood, George | Smith, Rosanna | 19, Feb. 1848 | RCH |
| Lockwood, Henry | Rish, Martha | 13, Mar. 1834 | RCH |
| Lockwood, Hiram | Raymond, Thirza | 10, Dec. 1842 | RCH |
| Lockwood, Isaac | Wunch, Elisabeth | 15, Nov. 1842 | RCH |
| Lockwood, James | Roberts, Ellen | 15, Aug. 1842 | RCH |
| Loder, Alford | Heald, Elisabeth | 21, Nov. 1837 | RCH |
| Loder, James | Hatchin, Jane S. | 24, Aug. 1839 | RCH |
| Lodge, Caleb T. | Irwin, L. | 12, Aug. 1827 | I |
| Lodwick, Lysle | Johnson, Mary Ann | 23, Sept 1833 | RCH |
| Loebker, Bernard H. | Borgess, Elisabeth | 21, Oct. 1849 | AA |
| Loebker, Heinrich | Schneider, Adelheid | 17, Oct. 1847 | AA |
| Loefer, Andreas | Derheger, Elisabeth | 16, July 1848 | II |
| Loeffler, Matthias | Geisler, Maria | 21, Jan. 1841 | FF |
| Loehmeyer, Johan Jos | Schroemeyer, Theresa | 15, Nov. 1846 | AA |
| Loercher, Friedrich | Lauer, Jeanette | 17, Nov. 1844 | G |
| Loes, Johan | Maichaim, Agnes | 27, Aug. 1839 | FF |
| Loesch, Johan | Weiss, Barbara | 7, Jan. 1849 | G |
| Loesche, Wilhelm | Eilers, Maria | 18, July 1848 | F |
| Loewenthal, Joseph | Wuest, Magdalena | 7, Jan. 1846 | EE |
| Loffink, George | Kim, Mary | 6, Apr. 1842 | RCH |
| Lofink, Georg | Gliem, Maria | 6, Apr. 1842 | G |
| Lofthouse, Patrick | Williams, Mary | 1, June 1846 | GG |
| Lofthouse, William | Wheatley, Anna | 16, July 1839 | RCH |
| Loga, | Haitenaker, Margaret | 5, Dec. 1836 | F |
| Logan, | Grimm, Elisabeth | 9, Aug. 1849 | RCH |
| Logan, John | Sommerville, Marg. | 16, Sept 1847 | RCH |
| Logan, John W. | Wilkins, Jane | 17, Apr. 1833 | I |
| Logan, William | Henrie, Caroline | 24, Dec. 1818 | RCH |
| Logar, James | Darling, Margaret | 16, Sept 1841 | RCH |
| Loge, John | Houck, Elisabeth | 28, May 1844 | RCH |
| Logen, Johan Philipp | Keissel, Margaretha | 26, Jan. 1845 | C |
| Lohmann, Anton | Kreiling, Elisabeth | 29, Aug. 1848 | AA |
| Lohmann, Bonaventure | Fels, Elisabeth | 15, Feb. 1849 | EE |
| Lohmann, Cord | Kestner, Sophia | 8, May 1847 | F |
| Lohmann, Dietrich | Westermann, Theresa | 25, Apr. 1847 | FF |
| Lohmann, Franz | Nolte, Mina | 16, Jan. 1849 | II |
| Lohmann, J. Gerhard | Renner, Maria Anna | 9, Jan. 1844 | AA |

| Grooms<br>****** | Brides<br>****** | Date of Marriage<br>**** ** ******** | Code<br>**** |
|---|---|---|---|
| Lohmann, J. Theodor | Bocklage, Bernardina | 22, Nov. 1846 | FF |
| Lohmeier, Herman | Kruse, Anna Maria | 17, July 1848 | F |
| Lohmueller, Bernard | Piter, Katharine | 27, Nov. 1849 | EE |
| Lohmueller, Gerhard | Stagen, Anna Elis. | 23, Dec. 1846 | F |
| Lohmueller, Johan A. | Mund, Catharine M. | 3, July 1846 | B |
| Lohmueller, Johan Bd | Lammen, Catharine A. | 7, May 1848 | EE |
| Lohmueller, Johan H. | Vallo, Maria Elis. | 23, Jan. 1848 | EE |
| Lohnsbach, Gustav | Laufhummern, Babette | 4, Aug. 1846 | RCH |
| Loipman, Richard | Walsh, Joann | 10, June 1835 | RCH |
| Lomere, Peter | Roll, Ann | 1, July 1821 | RCH |
| Lonecker, Abraham | Cook, Jane | 4, Jan. 1838 | RCH |
| Long, Alexander | Sammons, Cynthia | 27, Oct. 1842 | RCH |
| Long, George | Beal, Jane | 14, Apr. 1839 | RCH |
| Long, Henry | Kerr, Polly | 29, May 1823 | RCH |
| Long, Isaac | Smith, Sarah V. | 23, Nov. 1843 | RCH |
| Long, Jacob | Booram, Harriet | 7, Jan. 1847 | RCH |
| Long, James | Stephenson, Elis. | 5, Oct. 1824 | RCH |
| Long, John | Canby, Sarah | 22, Jan. 1820 | RCH |
| Long, John | Shaver, Catharine | 1, Mar. 1837 | RCH |
| Long, John | Cooper, Florinda | 6, May 1838 | RCH |
| Long, John | Brown, Rachel | 18, June 1842 | RCH |
| Long, Mathew | Felson, Elisabeth | 15, May 1838 | RCH |
| Long, Peter | White, Barbara | Sept 1845 | RCH |
| Long, Thomas | McMillan, Margaret | 18, Nov. 1824 | RCH |
| Long, William | Baker, Elisabeth | 4, July 1843 | RCH |
| Long, William | Adams, Harriet | 3, Feb. 1847 | RCH |
| Longe, Francis | Wellmann, Gertrud | Apr. 1843 | RCH |
| Longley, Abner | Bassett, Sophronia | 14, Aug. 1839 | RCH |
| Longley, Elias | Vater, Elisabeth | 13, May 1847 | RCH |
| Longnecker, Joseph | Cole, Jane | 5, Jan. 1837 | RCH |
| Longshore, Abner | O'Neill, Mary Ann | 1, May 1848 | BB |
| Longworth, Joseph | Rives, Anna | 13, May 1841 | D |
| Looker, Jeremiah | Kincade, Sarah | 27, Nov. 1847 | I |
| Looker, John M. | Jaquish, Martha | 5, Mar. 1846 | RCH |
| Looker, Lewis | True, Betsey | 28, Nov. 1848 | RCH |
| Looker, Lewis C. | Burroughs, Serepha | 16, June 1839 | RCH |
| Looker, Robert | Hooper, Sarah | 26, July 1838 | RCH |
| Looker, Robert A. | Gerard, Fidelia | 2, Sept 1849 | RCH |
| Looker, Samuel | Young, Francis Jane | 7, Aug. 1843 | RCH |
| Looker, William | Smith, Caroline | 25, May 1846 | RCH |
| Looten, Richard | Christian, Catharine | 17, Apr. 1833 | RCH |
| Lop---, John | Elam, Mary | 25, May 1843 | RCH |
| Loper, Enoch | Willey, Elisabeth | 24, Dec. 1841 | RCH |
| Loper, Isaac | McKorkill, Mary | 21, Aug. 1844 | RCH |
| Lorch, Isidor | Lyons, Babette | 23, Oct. 1848 | RCH |
| Lorch, Peter | Hartmann, Catharine | 17, Jan. 1843 | AA |
| Lord, Charles W. | West, Susan | 1, Oct. 1818 | RCH |
| Lord, Hosea | Murphy, Elisabeth C. | 3, Feb. 1844 | RCH |
| Lord, John | Bogert, Mary | 9, Dec. 1819 | RCH |
| Lord, Jonathan | Stewart, Sarah | 22, Jan. 1824 | RCH |
| Lord, Russell | Scott, Elisabeth | 29, Jan. 1849 | RCH |
| Loren, Matthew | Conlen, Mary | 9, Sept 1849 | GG |
| Lorenz, Jacob | Bradelin, Rhoda | 10, Mar. 1837 | RCH |
| Loring, Allen S. | Oliver, Elisabeth A. | 23, May 1841 | RCH |
| Loring, William | Austen, Harriet | 27, June 1844 | RCH |
| Lorkarn, Johan | Kreimer, Maria | 21, May 1848 | II |
| Lory, Joseph | Bowman, Susanna | 17, Feb. 1842 | RCH |
| Lorz, Blasius | Mair, Anna M. | 8, Oct. 1849 | EE |
| Losekamp, Heinrich | Mueller, Elisabeth | 16, Apr. 1846 | AA |
| Losekamp, J. Gerhard | Tecker, Elisabeth | 11, Jan. 1848 | AA |
| Losekamp, Johan Hein | Bush, Elisabeth | 3, Mar. 1840 | FF |
| Losey, Brazil | Shepherd, Mary | 20, Jan. 1820 | RCH |
| Losh, Joseph | Moss, Jane | 12, Oct. 1843 | RCH |
| Losh, Lot | Earhart, A. | 14, Aug. 1834 | RCH |
| Losson, William | Bean, Mary | 17, Mar. 1821 | RCH |
| Loth, Michael | Michelot, Eleanor | 16, Oct. 1849 | EE |
| Lots, Ernst | Espel, Catharine | 21, Dec. 1843 | RCH |
| Lott, John | Terry, Henriette | 18, May 1843 | G |
| Lottem, Bernard | Oetzel, Catharine | 12, Aug. 1845 | G |
| Lotterbach, Friedric | Bischhof, Margaret | 28, Sept 1843 | RCH |
| Lotz, Adam | Bernhardt, Susanna | 28, Sept 1848 | G |

| Grooms | Brides | Date of Marriage | Code |
|--------|--------|------------------|------|
| Lotz, Adolph | Behring, Magdalena | 18, Feb. 1840 | FF |
| Lotz, Bernard | Kohl, Dorothea | 30, Dec. 1847 | RCH |
| Lotz, Johan | Vogel, Barbara | 7, June 1849 | AA |
| Lotz, Peter | Hoff, Maria Elisabet | 8, Aug. 1843 | FF |
| Lotz, Peter | Henning, Maria | 25, Nov. 1849 | EE |
| Louder, John | Bruner, Elisabeth | 22, Aug. 1841 | RCH |
| Louderbach, Milton | Carter, Sarah | 30, June 1835 | RCH |
| Louderbeck, Jacob P. | Pittick, Marianne C. | 15, Feb. 1843 | D |
| Loughan, Christopher | Daley, Catharine | 22, Aug. 1847 | BB |
| Lougher, David | Price, Margaret | 13, June 1843 | RCH |
| Loughlan, Michael | Hocter, Ann | 24, Nov. 1849 | BB |
| Loughlin, Michael | Larkin, Sarah | 11, Oct. 1840 | BB |
| Louis, Adolph | Mayer, Juliet | 11, Oct. 1842 | RCH |
| Louis, Simon | Schild, Fanny | 2, Dec. 1846 | RCH |
| Loup, George | Simpson, Mary | 24, Apr. 1849 | RCH |
| Lovaldill, John B. | Pettit, Catharine | 20, Sept 1834 | RCH |
| Love, Henry | Wilson, Elisabeth | 4, Oct. 1820 | RCH |
| Love, John | Risinger, Letitia | 24, Nov. 1842 | RCH |
| Love, John | Rude, Sarah | 28, Dec. 1843 | RCH |
| Love, Richard | McDonough, Charlotte | 31, Dec. 1835 | RCH |
| Love, William | Keller, Christina | 5, Mar. 1833 | RCH |
| Love, William | Smith, Rebecca | 4, June 1849 | RCH |
| Lovejoy, Henry | Platt, Sarah | 9, July 1841 | RCH |
| Lovejoy, John | Frisby, Elisabeth | 1, July 1844 | RCH |
| Lovejoy, Samuel | Crusoe, Melissa | 7, June 1848 | RCH |
| Lovel, Washington M. | Bennett, Julia F. | 12, Nov. 1846 | RCH |
| Lovel, William | Sarver, Elizabeth | 7, Apr. 1825 | RCH |
| Lovelace, Seneca | Kindle, Susan Ann | 21, Dec. 1841 | RCH |
| Lovelave, Thomas | Thomas, Elisabeth | 24, Oct. 1833 | RCH |
| Lovell, Oliver | Russell, Sarah Jane | 9, Jan. 1843 | RCH |
| Loveridge, Friedrich | Boudy, Maria J. | 22, Sept 1843 | RCH |
| Lovet, William | Larrison, Elisabeth | 23, Jan. 1836 | RCH |
| Lovine, Elias | Kahn, Caroline | 14, Aug. 1846 | RCH |
| Loving, William | Kennedy, Lucy Jane | 15, Aug. 1849 | RCH |
| Low, Ebenezer W. | Sparks, Elisabeth | 16, Nov. 1833 | RCH |
| Lowe, George W. | Wright, Mary W. | 28, Oct. 1845 | RCH |
| Lowe, Heinrich | Brockhof, Maria | 27, Nov. 1845 | FF |
| Lowe, John m. | Dural, Mary | 2, Dec. 1837 | RCH |
| Lowe, Peter | Butler, Julia | 20, Apr. 1843 | RCH |
| Lowe, Richard | Hill, Mary | 15, Mar. 1832 | RCH |
| Lowenstein, Jacob | Cohen, Regina | 17, Feb. 1846 | RCH |
| Lower, George | Decker, Elisabeth | 6, May 1847 | RCH |
| Lowkamp, Johan Bd. | Niehaus, Elisabeth | 5, May 1846 | FF |
| Lowman, Jacob | Alexander, Malchen | 13, Apr. 1846 | RCH |
| Lowrey, Asbury | Guthrie, Isabella | 3, Dec. 1846 | RCH |
| Lowrey, Casper | Gray, Malinda | 9, Sept 1842 | RCH |
| Lowrie, John | Kinsbury, Esther | 29, June 1848 | RCH |
| Lowry, Monroe | Lape, Harriet | 19, May 1846 | RCH |
| Lowry, S.W. | Runyan, Lydia | 27, July 1845 | RCH |
| Lowry, Washington | McCall, Rebecca | 29, Apr. 1844 | RCH |
| Loxterkamp, Johan H. | Moellmann, Elisabeth | 26, May 1836 | FF |
| Lubbermann, Gerhard | Weibel, Maria Anna | 27, May 1849 | II |
| Lubke, Johan Heinric | AufdemBerge, Engel | 12, Apr. 1849 | F |
| Lubker, Johan Heinr. | Weber, Catharina | 30, Dec. 1834 | FF |
| Lucas, Edward | Meline, Catharine | 17, Feb. 1838 | RCH |
| Lucas, John | Warner, Sarah | 8, Jan. 1844 | RCH |
| Lucas, John M. | Morgan, Mary Ann | 28, May 1849 | RCH |
| Lucas, Mason | Lucas, Ann | 18, Sept 1848 | RCH |
| Lucas, Thomas | Misner, Mary | 5, Apr. 1821 | RCH |
| Luchtefeld, Casper H | Kintied, Bernardina | 19, Sept 1847 | FF |
| Luchtel, Albert | Toh, Adelheid | 22, Nov. 1846 | AA |
| Luchtenberg, Friedr. | Ahring, Anna Louise | 11, Dec. 1849 | F |
| Luck, William | Wratten, Jemima | 11, May 1833 | RCH |
| Lucken, B. Heinrich | Hartlaub, Christina | 8, Feb. 1849 | II |
| Lucker, Georg | Minard, Nancy | 19, Oct. 1841 | RCH |
| Luckett, William | Goode, Martha J. | 16, Feb. 1844 | RCH |
| Luckey, John S. | Walter, Amelia A. | 30, Apr. 1839 | RCH |
| Lucking, Joseph | Fangmann, Anna M. | 13, Nov. 1838 | FF |
| Ludder, Jacob | Jaeger, Maria Cath. | 4, Jan. 1836 | FF |
| Ludlow, Daniel W. | Collins, Catharine | 8, June 1834 | RCH |
| Ludlow, E.P. | Sayres, Eliza Jane | 5, Dec. 1849 | RCH |

| Grooms<br>****** | Brides<br>****** | Date of Marriage<br>**** ** ******** | Code<br>**** |
|---|---|---|---|
| Ludlow, George C. | Ludlum, Abzina | 15, July 1844 | RCH |
| Ludlow, Israel | Slocum, Helen A. | 24, June 1830 | I |
| Ludlow, James | Dunlap, Josephina | 30, Mar. 1819 | RCH |
| Ludlow, John | Niles, Hetty | 18, June 1818 | RCH |
| Ludlow, Philo | Kineham, Nancy | 10, Mar. 1825 | RCH |
| Ludlow, William | Bonnel, Abigail | 13, Sept 1846 | RCH |
| Ludwig, Carl Friedr. | Kauppel, Margaretha | 3, Sept 1839 | G |
| Ludwig, Erhard | Mohr, Catharina | 25, June 1840 | G |
| Ludwig, Friedrich | Schaffel, A. Elis. | 8, Oct. 1848 | C |
| Ludwig, Johan H. | Kolon, Elisabeth | 26, Aug. 1839 | G |
| Luebbe, Johan Heinr. | Mayers, Margaretha | 30, Sept 1847 | B |
| Luebbehusen, Johan H | Starkamp, Maria Elis | 15, May 1849 | EE |
| Luebber, J. Wilhelm | Lub---, Anna Cath. | 2, Dec. 1848 | C |
| Luebbermann, Johan B | Bockweg, Anna Maria | 21, Nov. 1843 | FF |
| Luebker, Heinrich | Burkelmann, Catharin | 30, Mar. 1848 | B |
| Luecken, Bernard | Gauspohl, M. Agnes | 8, Oct. 1840 | FF |
| Luecken, Bernard | Gossling, Dina | 27, Nov. 1849 | FF |
| Luecken, Herman H. | Ortmann, Maria Elis. | 17, Apr. 1845 | FF |
| Lueckmann, Gerhard H | Klaene, Maria Angela | 28, June 1846 | FF |
| Lueckmann, Johan G. | Bund, Maria Elisa | 28, May 1848 | EE |
| Luegers, Joseph | Peters, Anna | 30, June 1842 | FF |
| Luehn, Johan Bernard | Duetz, Maria Adel. | 20, Apr. 1847 | CC |
| Luehn, Johan Heinr. | Gersen, Anna Maria | 19, Jan. 1847 | CC |
| Luehn, Johan Wilhelm | Hamer, Theresa | 3, Oct. 1848 | EE |
| Lueker, Heinrich | Kunnemann, Charlotte | 27, Mar. 1845 | F |
| Luening, Johan | Imwalde, Elisabeth | 6, Nov. 1849 | II |
| Luers, J.B. | Roberg, Theresa | 19, Nov. 1848 | II |
| Lueske, Bernard H. | Schmiesing, Agnes | 17, Feb. 1846 | AA |
| Luetike, Hubert | Schroeder, Gertrud | 5, May 1846 | FF |
| Luetkenhaus, Johan G | Bockholt, Anna M. | 21, Jan. 1849 | EE |
| Luetkenhof, Johan C. | Frilling, Maria F. | 15, Nov. 1846 | EE |
| Luetteken, Ludwig | Barhorst, Elisabeth | 27, Feb. 1848 | AA |
| Luetterhen, Michael | Vogel, Rachel Barb. | 18, Feb. 1845 | G |
| Luft, Christoph | Blesch, Maria | 17, Feb. 1849 | G |
| Luft, John | Rasp, Magdalena | 26, Dec. 1848 | G |
| Lugos, Heinrich | Klein, Eleanor Helen | 7, Jan. 1840 | FF |
| Luhle, Johan | Wessel, Rebecca | 25, Oct. 1848 | AA |
| Luhmann, Bernard | Hulsmann, Catharine | 8, Jan. 1845 | AA |
| Luhring, Heinrich Wm | VonSeggern, M Sophia | 23, Mar. 1843 | F |
| Luhte, Herman | Wesendorf, M. Agnes | 4, Apr. 1837 | FF |
| Luhtel, Albert Herm. | Doenberg, Anna | 20, Feb. 1848 | AA |
| Luice, David | Geirrs, Adeline | Aug. 1833 | RCH |
| Luick, Joseph | Brown, Barbara Ann | 7, Oct. 1849 | BB |
| Luis, Joseph | Goetz, Magdalena | 2, May 1844 | AA |
| Luke, Samuel | Elvill, Elisabeth | 29, Apr. 1819 | RCH |
| Lukemeier, John Hy. | Krohme, Catharine | 25, Aug. 1847 | RCH |
| Lukens, Dietrich | Schmidt, Elisabeth | 3, Apr. 1849 | F |
| Lulai, Peter | Becker, Maria Anna | 20, July 1843 | AA |
| Lulcoth, Francis B. | Ramsey, Mary | 27, Feb. 1833 | RCH |
| Lull, Georg | Friedrich, Margaret | 6, Nov. 1837 | FF |
| Lullemann, Arnold H. | Stiens, Rebecca M. | 22, Nov. 1836 | FF |
| Lumby, Robert | Shipley, Mary Ann | 26, Apr. 1841 | RCH |
| Lunaveck, George | Cross, Lydia | 10, Dec. 1835 | RCH |
| Lunch, Thomas | Willmuth, Mary A. | 25, Dec. 1833 | RCH |
| Lund, Samuel | Lourey, Caroline | 28, Mar. 1837 | RCH |
| Lundy, Eli | Hyatt, Nancy | 13, June 1846 | RCH |
| Lunemann, Johan Theo | Voltering, Maria H. | 31, Oct. 1847 | EE |
| Lunenberger, Peter | Luebke, Catharina | 25, Nov. 1847 | FF |
| Lunlum, Wilhelm | Haddocks, Elisabeth | 27, Oct. 1841 | RCH |
| Lunnemann, Gerhard | Redermann, M.A. | 9, Feb. 1847 | AA |
| Lunweber, John | Evans, Mary Ann | 4, Sept 1844 | RCH |
| Lunz, Peter | Ultsch, Eva | 16, May 1847 | G |
| Lupton, Thomas | Ruly, Elisabeth | 11, Nov. 1839 | RCH |
| Lupton, William C. | Lyon, Isabella | 29, Jan. 1849 | RCH |
| Luser, George | Good, Elisabeth J. | 19, July 1848 | RCH |
| Lusk, James | Wainwright, Rachel | 28, Mar. 1843 | RCH |
| Lusk, James | Cook, Nancy Ann | 13, Oct. 1844 | RCH |
| Lusk, Uzal | Meady, Elizabeth | 25, Mar. 1847 | RCH |
| Luske, John Bernard | Windhorst, Maria | 20, Mar. 1849 | F |
| Luslow, John | Rilley, Sarah | 3, Apr. 1832 | RCH |
| Luther, John | Auppley, Mary | 1, Oct. 1835 | RCH |

| Grooms | Brides | Date of Marriage | Code |
|--------|--------|------------------|------|
| ****** | ****** | **** ** ******** | **** |
| Luther, John F. | Henderich, Magdalena | 22, Dec. 1842 | G |
| Lutherbeck, Bernard | Niehaus, Elisabeth | 4, July 1843 | AA |
| Lutkenhof, Engelbert | Bush, Gertrud | 3, Feb. 1846 | AA |
| Lutterbeck, Friedric | Weimann, Wilhelmina | 16, Mar. 1848 | G |
| Lutz, David | Howard, Elisabeth | 10, Feb. 1842 | RCH |
| Lutz, Heinrich | Monks, Elisabeth | 21, Jan. 1846 | F |
| Lutz, Johan | Hecker, Margaretha | 28, Aug. 1845 | AA |
| Lutz, John | Renner, Helena | 4, Sept 1848 | G |
| Lutzenberger, Conrad | Echternach, Helena | 15, June 1840 | G |
| Lwellan, John | Corotta, Mary (Mrs) | 1, Nov. 1849 | BB |
| Lyle, Charles | Mueller, Martha | 4, Oct. 1833 | RCH |
| Lyman, Azel | Noble, Amelia | 24, June 1846 | RCH |
| Lynch, Bernard | Hughes, Mary Ann | 7, Nov. 1843 | BB |
| Lynch, Dennis | Dacy, Mary | 28, Oct. 1849 | GG |
| Lynch, Edward | Howard, Eunice | 17, Apr. 1843 | RCH |
| Lynch, John | McDonald, Susan | 9, July 1849 | GG |
| Lynch, Michael | McCaigney, Ellen | 15, Apr. 1838 | RCH |
| Lynch, Michael | Kegan, Mary | 19, Oct. 1845 | BB |
| Lynch, Peter | Keegan, Catharine | 23, Jan. 1849 | BB |
| Lynchard, Henry | Hill, Elisabeth | 6, June 1837 | RCH |
| Lynde, | Carly, Sarah | 14, Sept 1832 | RCH |
| Lyndsey, Reuben | Lipscomb, Hannah | 22, June 1836 | RCH |
| Lynes, James | Conuty, Nelly | 12, Sept 1818 | RCH |
| Lynn, | Davis, Catharine | 17, Mar. 1824 | RCH |
| Lynn, Andrew M. | Ross, Jane C. | 9, Nov. 1848 | RCH |
| Lynn, Nathan | Pyle, Charlotte | 28, Sept 1826 | RCH |
| Lynnens, Friedrich | Buckner, Elizabeth J | 27, Oct. 1846 | RCH |
| Lyon, | Olney, Mary Matilda | 1, June 1834 | RCH |
| Lyon, Hamilton | Dwyer, Ann | 8, July 1843 | RCH |
| Lyon, James J. | Hull, Harriet | 26, Oct. 1843 | RCH |
| Lyon, John | Wilsey, Phebe | 22, Oct. 1837 | RCH |
| Lyon, Joseph | ----, Sarah Jane | 22, Oct. 1837 | RCH |
| Lyon, Leonard | Claypool, Elisabeth | 13, Apr. 1846 | RCH |
| Lyon, Peter | Miller, Ann | 5, Sept 1838 | RCH |
| Lyon, Samuel | Pearce, Ellen | 22, Feb. 1847 | RCH |
| Lyons, Dennis | Croney, Mary | 4, Nov. 1849 | GG |
| Lyons, Isaac | Weiler, Janette | 4, Oct. 1842 | RCH |
| Lyons, Matthew | Peers, Charlotte | 9, Aug. 1846 | RCH |
| Lyons, Michael | King, Catharine | 29, May 1846 | BB |
| Lyons, Thomas J. | Justis, Elisabeth | 1, Oct. 1843 | RCH |
| Lyson, James M. | Kent, Elisabeth D. | 1, Jan. 1833 | RCH |
| Lytle, William | Haines, Margaret | 27, Aug. 1822 | RCH |
| Lytle, William | Biddle, Hester | 9, Aug. 1842 | RCH |
| | | | |
| M---, David | Stites, Elisabeth | 26, June 1824 | RCH |
| M---, Friedrich L. | Campon, J.P. | 12, Nov. 1835 | RCH |
| M---, James | Bowman, Parmelia | 1835 | RCH |
| M---, John | Ferguson, Isabella | 25, Sept 1823 | RCH |
| M---, William | Powers, Mary | 10, June 1821 | RCH |
| M--annon, Matthew | Thompson, Jane | 30, June 1838 | RCH |
| Ma---, Clamor | Lovejoy, Harriet | 1, Dec. 1842 | RCH |
| Ma---, Orman | VanBlarigan, Cath. | 11, Aug. 1825 | RCH |
| Maag, Theodor | Bues, Catharina | 20, June 1837 | FF |
| Maas, Heinrich | Ollmann, Elisabeth | 1, Oct. 1846 | RCH |
| Maccatester, | Vallandingham, Rebec | 2, Dec. 1837 | RCH |
| Mace, John Wilson | Dailey, Bridget | 19, Apr. 1849 | RCH |
| Mack, Abraham | Satzmann, Rose | 1, Dec. 1845 | RCH |
| Mack, Francis H. | Nusbaum, Elisabeth | 19, June 1849 | FF |
| Mack, Henry | Mack, Rosalia | 15, Sept 1846 | RCH |
| Mack, Isaac | Payne, Ellenora | 21, May 1846 | RCH |
| Mack, Martin | Wertzmann, Sarah | 8, Dec. 1849 | RCH |
| Mack, Simon | Mack, Leonora | 12, Mar. 1849 | RCH |
| Macke, Bernard | Schoenhoff, Elis. | 18, July 1837 | FF |
| Macke, Bernard | Buthof, Maria Agnes | 14, July 1840 | FF |
| Macke, Clemens | Kostermeyer, Maria A | 20, Aug. 1840 | FF |
| Macke, Francis | Siefke, Anna Maria | 15, May 1838 | FF |
| Macke, Friedrich Wm. | Revermann, Helena | 12, Aug. 1849 | II |
| Macke, Herman Heinr. | Egbers, Anna Maria | 27, Feb. 1848 | FF |
| Macke, Johan Bernard | Hoelscher, Anna M. | 17, Nov. 1842 | FF |
| Macke, Johan Heinric | Wempe, Margaretha | 1, Nov. 1846 | AA |
| Macke, Johan Heinric | Niehaus, Maria Anna | 19, Sept 1847 | AA |

| Grooms<br>****** | Brides<br>****** | Date of Marriage<br>**** ** ******** | Code<br>**** |
|---|---|---|---|
| Macke, Wilhelm | Seuk, Elisabeth | 23, Nov. 1845 | AA |
| Mackel, Johan Philip | Everlein, Maria | 31, Mar. 1840 | G |
| Mackey, John | Renolds, Lucinda | 2, May 1841 | RCH |
| Mackridge, James | Shipley, Keturah | 8, Mar. 1835 | RCH |
| Maclay, Samuel | Stoddard, Rebecca | 16, Sept 1847 | RCH |
| Maclin, George | Harney, Elisabeth | 28, Mar. 1833 | RCH |
| Macracken, John | Brooks, Eliza | 22, Apr. 1847 | RCH |
| Macy, Charles | Duncan, Rachel | 16, Nov. 1846 | RCH |
| Macy, Frederick | Progas, Margaret | 8, Sept 1836 | RCH |
| Macy, Harrison | Andrews, Harriet | 18, May 1843 | RCH |
| Macy, Thomas | Cook, Eveline | 28, July 1846 | RCH |
| Madarg, William | Walker, Mary | 24, Nov. 1819 | RCH |
| Madden, John | Roe, Margaret | 2, Feb. 1833 | RCH |
| Madden, Michael | Hogan, Joann | 17, Aug. 1848 | GG |
| Madden, William | Hoovert, Mary Ann | 7, Aug. 1836 | RCH |
| Maddux, Edward | Ward, Fanny | 16, Feb. 1826 | RCH |
| Maddux, Tapley | Nold, Mary | 28, Sept 1848 | RCH |
| Madison, Reuben | Williams, Sophia | 8, Jan. 1844 | RCH |
| Maehl, Michael | Ireland, Maria L. | 19, Nov. 1848 | G |
| Maer, Heinrich | Waeler, Mary | 22, Dec. 1842 | RCH |
| Maertens, Georg | Bosse, Catharine | 31, May 1842 | G |
| Maesz, Heinrich | Kramer, Elisabeth | 2, Jan. 1847 | G |
| Maetzler, Peter | Sehi, Margaretha | 2, July 1840 | FF |
| Maffey, Anton | Birkle, Maria Anna | 22, May 1843 | AA |
| Mafford, Thomson | Ferris, Catharine | 28, Mar. 1833 | RCH |
| Maggini, John C. | McCloskey, Mary Ann | 28, Nov. 1844 | BB |
| Magie, Oliver | Clark, Nancy | 20, Aug. 1834 | RCH |
| Magill, John | Plonnet, Catharine | May 1839 | RCH |
| Magill, Wesley | Cook, Mary | 17, Mar. 1847 | RCH |
| Magly, Jacob | Klipple, Margaret | 4, Apr. 1844 | RCH |
| Magnass, Benjamin B. | Anderson, Mary | 27, Feb. 1820 | RCH |
| Magness, Alfred | Watts, Mary | 15, Feb. 1837 | RCH |
| Magness, William | Spellman, Catharine | 18, Feb. 1834 | RCH |
| Magnus, Friedrich | Mickel, Caroline | 25, Dec. 1849 | G |
| Maguire, Cornelius | Murray, Mary Ann | 24, Apr. 1845 | BB |
| Maguire, Nathan | Holland, Elisabeth | 7, Oct. 1824 | RCH |
| Maguire, Patrick | Brady, Susan | 3, Apr. 1845 | BB |
| Mahan, Michael | Cunningham, Ellen | 2, Feb. 1849 | RCH |
| Mahan, William | Boles, Deborah | 31, July 1836 | RCH |
| Mahee, Fountain | Price, Elisabeth | 18, Oct. 1838 | RCH |
| Maheerin, Edwin | Fearistine, Margaret | 14, July 1846 | RCH |
| Maher, Cornelius | Lyon, Jane | 24, June 1849 | BB |
| Maher, John | Foley, Joanne | 24, June 1849 | BB |
| Maher, John | Gleason, Ann | 3, Sept 1848 | GG |
| Maher, Nicolaus | Muldoon, Bridget | 22, Apr. 1849 | BB |
| Maher, Patrick | Farrell, Catharine | 22, Oct. 1848 | BB |
| Maher, Seth | Johnston, Lucy Ann | 13, July 1824 | RCH |
| Maher, Thomas | Burdins, Ann | 11, June 1848 | BB |
| Mahew, Alexander | Hawthorn, Rhoda M. | 2, Dec. 1824 | RCH |
| Mahew, Ebii | Miller, Agnes | 3, Feb. 1841 | RCH |
| Mahew, Joseph | Allen, Susan | 25, Dec. 1836 | RCH |
| Mahew, William | Davis, Mary | 21, Oct. 1833 | RCH |
| Mahlen, Thomas | Wilkerson, Sarah | 9, Jan. 1834 | RCH |
| Mahler, Frederick | Reiker, Louise | 18, May 1848 | RCH |
| Mahler, Michael | Spack, Margaretha | 2, Feb. 1847 | G |
| Mahlerwein, Georg P. | Koegel, Barbara | 20, Nov. 1842 | RCH |
| Mahnke, William | Ahring, Maria | 5, Feb. 1846 | F |
| Mahon, Edward | McCormack, Ellen | 7, Sept 1846 | BB |
| Mahon, Harry | Howe, Catharine | 29, Aug. 1838 | RCH |
| Mahon, Stephan | Cobb, Catharine | 30, May 1848 | GG |
| Mahon, Thomas | Ross, Sylvia Ann | 5, Apr. 1841 | RCH |
| Mahon, William | Bredin, Caroline | 30, Oct. 1834 | RCH |
| Mahoney, James | Lane, Elisabeth | 12, Oct. 1845 | BB |
| Mahoney, Timothy | Daly, Mary | 19, June 1849 | GG |
| Mahood, John | Campbell, Emeline | 17, Feb. 1844 | RCH |
| Mahorne, Joseph | Chind, Rachel | 20, July 1844 | RCH |
| Maier, Jacob | Hart, Betty | 12, Mar. 1849 | RCH |
| Maifeld, J. Gerhard | Noetker, Josephine | 18, May 1847 | FF |
| Maillet, John | Roidaget, Adelheid | 13, Jan. 1842 | BB |
| Main, Charles | Thatcher, Jane | 23, Oct. 1845 | RCH |
| Main, John A. | Sweet, Anna Maria | 31, Aug. 1841 | RCH |

| Grooms | Brides | Date of Marriage | Code |
|--------|--------|------------------|------|
| ****** | ****** | **** ** ******** | **** |
| Main, Mecom | Powers, Jane | 5, May 1822 | RCH |
| Mainken, Heinrich | Sanders, Maria Anna | 9, Nov. 1843 | AA |
| Mair, Anton | Deggers, Elisabeth | 25, Nov. 1849 | EE |
| Maisner, Jacob | Robinson, Agnes | 15, Jan. 1832 | RCH |
| Maitland, James | Clark, Jane | 10, Mar. 1836 | RCH |
| Makon, William | Breever, Hannah M. | 1, Sept 1839 | RCH |
| Malatt, Marshall | Burrows, Mary A. | 3, Aug. 1845 | RCH |
| Malcolm, James | McIntire, Ann | 19, Jan. 1842 | RCH |
| Malcom, William | Hull, Sarah | 25, Nov. 1832 | RCH |
| Malcomson, John | Waterfall, Ellen | 20, Sept 1847 | RCH |
| Maldoner, Joseph | Steger, Louise | 21, May 1849 | EE |
| Maleham, Daniel | Fenton, Elisabeth | 15, Mar. 1842 | RCH |
| Maley, Michael | Raiey, Nancy | 8, June 1840 | RCH |
| Mallon, Patrick | Neumann, Anna | 6, Oct. 1844 | BB |
| Malone, John | Hardesty, Drusy | 4, Feb. 1818 | RCH |
| Malory, Alfred | Ross, Catharine | 8, Apr. 1847 | RCH |
| Malory, David | Burk, Nancy | 30, Aug. 1819 | RCH |
| Malott, Andrew | Baldwin, Elisabeth | 27, June 1836 | RCH |
| Malotte, Joseph | Baitelbury, Lucinda | 18, Mar. 1824 | RCH |
| Malrick, Benjamin | Royal, Elisabeth | 15, May 1836 | RCH |
| Malso---, Charles | Alexander, Susan | 8, Aug. 1848 | RCH |
| Malson, James | Speeker, Minerva | 3, Apr. 1847 | RCH |
| Malta, Solomon | Whitelock, Elisabeth | 12, July 1838 | RCH |
| Malzer, Nathan | Ulfelter, Leah | 9, June 1843 | RCH |
| Man, Joseph | Hetzler, Catharine | 17, Nov. 1825 | RCH |
| Man---, Samuel | Williamson, Lucretia | 19, Mar. 1818 | RCH |
| Mandery, Jacob | Dick, Catharina | 17, Sept 1839 | FF |
| Mandler, Paul | Weber, Elisabeth | 3, Apr. 1845 | G |
| Mangold, Aloysius | Spinheide, Maria | 14, Apr. 1845 | AA |
| Mangold, Francis | Frank, Maria | 17, May 1849 | EE |
| Mangold, Sebastian | Waden, Catharina | 19, Nov. 1848 | II |
| Manhardt, Johan | Knoth, Christina | 25, Sept 1849 | C |
| Manifold, Henry | Davis, Martha Ann | 26, Oct. 1843 | RCH |
| Maniott, Isaac | Smith, Frances | Oct. 1844 | RCH |
| Manke, J. Dietrich | Benenn, Catharina | 20, Sept 1836 | FF |
| Manley, Benjamin | Webber, Catharine | 26, Jan. 1843 | RCH |
| Manley, Edward | Whipple, Louise | 29, Feb. 1848 | RCH |
| Manley, John | Strain, Sarah A. | 20, Apr. 1840 | RCH |
| Manley, Norman | Tibbs, H. | 11, Oct. 1832 | RCH |
| Mann, Alexander | Agnew, Phebe | 30, Sept 1845 | RCH |
| Mann, Benjamin | Burbeck, Harriet | 7, Jan. 1844 | RCH |
| Mann, Gerhard | Stickfort, Elisabeth | 6, Aug. 1844 | A |
| Mann, Gottlieb | Sperl, Anna | 28, Nov. 1849 | G |
| Mann, Horace | LaBoyteaux, Evaline | 22, Nov. 1837 | RCH |
| Mann, James | Bryon, Mary | 30, Dec. 1819 | RCH |
| Mann, John | Mahoney, Sarah | 8, Dec. 1832 | RCH |
| Mann, John R. | Butt, Catharine | 5, Oct. 1848 | RCH |
| Mann, John Wesley | Dew, Keziah | 19, Dec. 1847 | RCH |
| Mann, Nathan | Dunn, Mary | 15, Nov. 1842 | RCH |
| Mann, Thomas | Adams, Elisabeth | 16, Dec. 1844 | RCH |
| Mann, Thomas | Porter, Ann | 13, Apr. 1846 | RCH |
| Mannery, Enoch | Bacon, Alether | 28, Mar. 1833 | RCH |
| Manngott, Michael | Schwartz, Barbara | 19, Aug. 1844 | C |
| Manning, Francis | Meaker, Elisabeth | 5, Nov. 1845 | RCH |
| Manning, Stephen | --wescot, | 22, June 1839 | RCH |
| Manns, Hartley | Cobb, Mary E. | 1, July 1838 | RCH |
| Mansfield, Roswell | Morse, Waity | 5, Feb. 1836 | RCH |
| Manton, Louis | Whitecomb, Anna Elis | 23, Nov. 1843 | RCH |
| Mantor, Amzi C. | Wardall, Rebecca | 24, Apr. 1835 | RCH |
| Manuel, George W. | Manuel, Susan | 3, Dec. 1837 | RCH |
| Manwarning, Milton | Stone, Mary | 9, Apr. 1848 | RCH |
| Manzer, Engelbert | Blesse, Luitgardis | 4, Feb. 1839 | FF |
| Maphey, James | Evans, | 6, May 1834 | RCH |
| Maple, Joseph | Humphrey, Harriet | 25, Aug. 1845 | RCH |
| Mar---, William | Samison, Mary | 10, Oct. 1820 | RCH |
| Mara, Michael | Nugent, Margaret | 2, Sept 1849 | GG |
| Marbach, Nicolaus | Wolferburger, Theres | 1, May 1845 | AA |
| Marberger, Solomon | Smith, Elisabeth | 16, Sept 1841 | RCH |
| Marcel, Anton | Goins, Patsey | May 1849 | RCH |
| Marcello, Nicolaus | Maggini, Elisabeth L | 26, July 1843 | BB |
| March, Alanson | Woodruff, M. Louise | 14, May 1839 | RCH |

| Grooms<br>****** | Brides<br>****** | Date of Marriage<br>**** ** ******** | Code<br>**** |
|---|---|---|---|
| March, Enos | Harr, Mary | 11, Apr. 1839 | RCH |
| March, Oliver | Blackburn, Hannah | 11, May 1843 | RCH |
| Marchand, Louis | Kite, Laura | 31, July 1845 | RCH |
| Marchert, Nathan | Holmes, Maria | 31, Mar. 1839 | RCH |
| Marckley, Henry | Parvin, Tillithia | 16, Aug. 1821 | RCH |
| Mardis, Squire | Jenner, Elis. Jane | Oct. 1844 | RCH |
| Mare, Isaiah | Tebring, Charity M. | 10, Apr. 1834 | RCH |
| Marenthal, Israel | Straus, Fanny | 7, May 1844 | RCH |
| Marger---, John | Stephenson, Ann | 21, June 1821 | RCH |
| Marhoffer, Joseph | Rickert, Elisabeth | 27, Oct. 1840 | G |
| Mari, Martin | Beck, Maria Anna | 24, Oct. 1847 | EE |
| Marian, James | Molloy, Ellen | 19, Sept 1847 | BB |
| Marion, Luke | Martin, Bridget | 24, Aug. 1845 | BB |
| Marischen, Francis | Tenti, Maria Cath. | 20, Feb. 1848 | EE |
| Marke, Bernard | Nieheur, Gesina | 25, June 1848 | II |
| Markes, Herman Bd. | Wuebbelings, M. Cath | 20, Aug. 1848 | AA |
| Markgraf, Ludwig | Mentel, Elisabeth | 9, Mar. 1848 | G |
| Markland, Jefferson | Dale, Phebe Ann | 19, Apr. 1848 | RCH |
| Markland, Simeon | Stevens, Eliza Jane | 11, Mar. 1847 | RCH |
| Markland, Thomas | Richardson, Bathseba | 27, May 1819 | RCH |
| Markland, Thomas J. | Westcott, Mary Ann | 10, Apr. 1844 | RCH |
| Markland, William | Taylor, Mary Ann | 1, Aug. 1847 | RCH |
| Markley, John | Banks, Caroline | 3, Nov. 1845 | RCH |
| Markley, Moses | Sly, Malinda | 31, Mar. 1842 | RCH |
| Markley, William | Silver, Catharine L. | 1, Mar. 1848 | RCH |
| Markquerth, John | Shields, Sarah | 14, Oct. 1847 | RCH |
| Marks, David | Wertheimer, Sophia | 9, Apr. 1846 | RCH |
| Markstein, Carl | Zangermeister, Barb. | 7, Aug. 1848 | C |
| Markward, James | Churchill, Abigail | 13, Oct. 1846 | RCH |
| Marlach, Amadeus | Mermann, Margaretha | 21, Apr. 1846 | EE |
| Marlett, James | Boyle, Susannah | 4, Mar. 1846 | RCH |
| Marmardt, Peter | Rahm, Philippina | 9, Jan. 1844 | A |
| Marper, Michael | Brandt, Anna Maria | 9, May 1840 | FF |
| Marqua, Philipp Jac. | Moegly, Maria | 26, Dec. 1839 | G |
| Marr, George | Munch, Wilhelmina | 12, Apr. 1849 | RCH |
| Marr, J. Wolfgang | Keken, Elisabeth | 14, Sept 1846 | RCH |
| Marre, Joseph | Horff, Maria Anna | 2, Aug. 1839 | FF |
| Marringer, Nicolaus | Lucash, Margaretha | 9, June 1834 | RCH |
| Marriott, | Mains, Barbara | 29, Sept 1836 | RCH |
| Marriott, Andrew | Parker, Nancy | 12, Feb. 1824 | RCH |
| Marriott, Elijah | Owens, Louise | 5, Nov. 1843 | RCH |
| Marriott, John | Highlands, Rachel | 21, Sept 1845 | RCH |
| Marriott, Lewis | Adams, Jane | 12, Nov. 1848 | RCH |
| Marriott, William | Anderson, Sarah A. | 8, July 1836 | RCH |
| Mars, Francis Chris. | Koch, Veronica | 23, Feb. 1841 | FF |
| Marsch, George | Jones, Caroline | 20, Sept 1847 | RCH |
| Marsden, James | Barton, Mary | 15, Oct. 1832 | RCH |
| Marset, Dolly | Harrison, Louise | 16, Oct. 1835 | RCH |
| Marsh, Anderson | Wair, Harriet | 25, Nov. 1835 | RCH |
| Marsh, Andrew | Clemmer, A. Matilda | 22, Dec. 1840 | RCH |
| Marsh, August | Alvord, Hannah | 26, Aug. 1844 | RCH |
| Marsh, Ebenezer | Cox, Ann | 20, Sept 1832 | RCH |
| Marsh, Edward | Hale, Lucetta | 13, July 1846 | RCH |
| Marsh, Isaac | Folger, Margaret | 31, Dec. 1843 | RCH |
| Marsh, James | Stewart, Elisabeth | 12, Oct. 1837 | RCH |
| Marsh, John | Williams, Elisabeth | 9, Oct. 1834 | RCH |
| Marsh, John | Gillingham, Mary Ann | 20, July 1844 | RCH |
| Marsh, Jonathan | Taylor, Mary | 11, Mar. 1841 | RCH |
| Marsh, Nathan | Crossman, Elisabeth | 2, Nov. 1842 | RCH |
| Marsh, Samuel | Biddinger, Elisabeth | 4, Feb. 1847 | RCH |
| Marsh, Sylvester | Harmer, Sarah | 17, Mar. 1822 | RCH |
| Marsh, Theodore | Cunningham, Rachel | 17, Nov. 1845 | RCH |
| Marsh, Thomas H. | Hathaway, Elisabeth | 12, Sept 1836 | RCH |
| Marsh, Timothy | Pursel, Elisabeth | 1, Apr. 1819 | RCH |
| Marsh, Wales | Roll, Martha | 4, Sept 1841 | RCH |
| Marsh, William | Williams, Sarah O. | 8, Oct. 1833 | RCH |
| Marsh, William | Harker, Mary A. | 26, Feb. 1846 | RCH |
| Marsh, William | Hays, Sarah Ann | 4, June 1846 | RCH |
| Marshall, Anton | Dill, Margaret | 1, Nov. 1844 | RCH |
| Marshall, Anton | Ellison, Jane | 5, Nov. 1845 | RCH |
| Marshall, George | Wells, Esther | 29, Aug. 1844 | RCH |

| Grooms<br>****** | Brides<br>****** | Date of Marriage<br>**** ** ******** | Code<br>**** |
|---|---|---|---|
| Marshall, J.P. | Horner, Elisabeth | 2, Mar. 1834 | RCH |
| Marshall, James | Rodimbo, Elisabeth | 6, Dec. 1832 | RCH |
| Marshall, James | Hawkins, Elisabeth | 24, May 1842 | RCH |
| Marshall, John | De---, Rachel | 14, Oct. 1819 | RCH |
| Marshall, John | Herbert, Rachel | 19, Nov. 1824 | RCH |
| Marshall, Lebens | Voorhis, Belinda | 8, May 1838 | RCH |
| Marshall, Levi | Robinson, Elisabeth | 30, Oct. 1832 | RCH |
| Marshall, Peter | Boyd, Ellen | 7, May 1842 | RCH |
| Marshall, Richard | Wilmington, Mary | 28, Feb. 1822 | RCH |
| Marshall, Vincent C. | Pugh, Leah | 19, July 1820 | RCH |
| Marshall, William | Fogle, Julia | 30, Dec. 1840 | I |
| Marshall, William | Fandree, Cynthia | 21, Dec. 1846 | RCH |
| Martell, Carl L. | Keller, Kolistine | 2, Nov. 1846 | F |
| Marten, William | Noble, Sarah | 31, Mar. 1832 | RCH |
| Martin, Aaron | Lemmon, Rachel | 14, Mar. 1847 | RCH |
| Martin, Alfred | Kile, Elisabeth | 23, Mar. 1844 | RCH |
| Martin, Archibald | Crane, Sarah | 23, Jan. 1823 | RCH |
| Martin, Blasius | Schwarz, Maria | 21, Aug. 1843 | FF |
| Martin, Charles | Hezer, Louisa | 12, May 1833 | RCH |
| Martin, Ebenezer | Ley, Mary | 4, Nov. 1824 | RCH |
| Martin, Edward | Leary, Ann | 22, July 1847 | RCH |
| Martin, Enos | Sulgrove, Louisa A. | 10, Dec. 1844 | RCH |
| Martin, Ephraim | Smith, Ann | 3, Oct. 1832 | RCH |
| Martin, Fernando | Dunn, Zion M. | 10, Oct. 1844 | RCH |
| Martin, Francis D. | Jones, Rebecca E. | 5, Feb. 1841 | RCH |
| Martin, Georg | Kifer, El. Victoria | 16, June 1840 | FF |
| Martin, George | Snyder, Lydia | 3, Aug. 1842 | RCH |
| Martin, George | Ayer, Susannah | 18, Oct. 1847 | RCH |
| Martin, George | Bonsall, Mary P. | 1, Oct. 1849 | I |
| Martin, George W. | Sented, Sarah | 16, Feb. 1836 | RCH |
| Martin, Harrison H. | Callant, Elisabeth | 21, May 1834 | RCH |
| Martin, Henry | Cole, Maria | 16, Sept 1843 | RCH |
| Martin, Isaac | Johns, Margaret | 10, Jan. 1833 | RCH |
| Martin, Jacob | Hopper, Catharine | 19, Mar. 1843 | RCH |
| Martin, Jacob | Lammorth, Mary | 23, Mar. 1844 | RCH |
| Martin, Jacob | Hullinger, Elisabeth | 23, Sept 1848 | RCH |
| Martin, James | Cornnel, Sarah | 4, Sept 1833 | RCH |
| Martin, James | Allen, Ellen | 1, May 1846 | RCH |
| Martin, James | Brooks, Isabella | 6, Nov. 1846 | RCH |
| Martin, James D. | Master, Cloe | 8, Feb. 1824 | RCH |
| Martin, James H. | Miller, Jane E. | 4, Nov. 1835 | RCH |
| Martin, Johan | Eschenbrenner, Elis. | 19, June 1845 | C |
| Martin, Johan | Eschenbrenner, Elis. | 1, June 1846 | EE |
| Martin, John | Watkins, Catharine | 5, Sept 1824 | RCH |
| Martin, John | Glascow, Sophia | 2, Mar. 1834 | RCH |
| Martin, John | White, Catharine | 19, Mar. 1835 | RCH |
| Martin, John | Newman, Adaline | 21, Feb. 1846 | RCH |
| Martin, John | Little, Santha | 24, July 1847 | RCH |
| Martin, John | Rigdon, Sarah | 8, Aug. 1847 | RCH |
| Martin, John | Wilson, Elisabeth | 17, July 1846 | GG |
| Martin, Joseph | Northway, Clarinda | 4, Aug. 1835 | RCH |
| Martin, Joseph | Danes, Elisabeth | 8, Jan. 1837 | RCH |
| Martin, Joshua | Armstrong, Elisabeth | 6, Mar. 1844 | RCH |
| Martin, L. | Mitchell, Elisabeth | 10, May 1834 | RCH |
| Martin, Madison | Meyers, Elisabeth | 10, Apr. 1838 | RCH |
| Martin, Michael | Gibson, Ellen | 14, May 1849 | GG |
| Martin, Richard | Wallace, Nancy | 28, Mar. 1818 | RCH |
| Martin, Robert | Sorton, Martha Ann | 8, Nov. 1834 | RCH |
| Martin, Robert | Weeks, Margaret | 2, Mar. 1842 | RCH |
| Martin, Samuel | Taylor, Elis. Jane | 3, May 1837 | RCH |
| Martin, Thomas | Hazelett, Harriet | 25, Oct. 1846 | RCH |
| Martin, William | Vincent, Zerelda | 20, July 1843 | RCH |
| Martin, William | Harris, Christina | 20, Sept 1845 | RCH |
| Martin, William | Haines, Catharine | 13, Jan. 1848 | RCH |
| Martin, William | Ingersoll, Sophia | 20, Sept 1849 | RCH |
| Marty, Joseph | Horschinger, Margar. | 9, Sept 1846 | EE |
| Martz, Charles | Burkhardin, Catharin | 18, Oct. 1843 | RCH |
| Marvin, John | Grinstone, Nancy | 29, May 1831 | RCH |
| Marvin, Luke | Collins, Mary Ann | 22, Oct. 1846 | RCH |
| Marvin, Samuel R. | Hyde, Martha | 8, Mar. 1835 | RCH |
| Marx, Gottfried | Stall, Sarah | 23, Nov. 1846 | RCH |

| Grooms | Brides | Date of Marriage | Code |
|--------|--------|------------------|------|
| ****** | ****** | **** ** ******** | **** |
| Marzlaff, Stephan | Metzger, Apollonia | 16, Oct. 1849 | G |
| Marzlof, Paul | Reinlein, Mary Ann | 24, Oct. 1848 | BB |
| Masch, Joseph | Bramlage, Elisabeth | 26, Nov. 1839 | FF |
| Masche, Joseph | Linnemann, Elisabeth | 15, June 1841 | FF |
| Maschmeyer, Friedric | Luhrmann, Catharine | 1, Nov. 1844 | F |
| Mason, Abraham | Moore, Elisabeth | 9, Jan. 1838 | RCH |
| Mason, Adam | Barrows, Martha | 27, Sept 1841 | RCH |
| Mason, Alexander | Biles, Hester | 7, Apr. 1847 | RCH |
| Mason, Anders | Bruce, Keziah | 8, Aug. 1839 | RCH |
| Mason, David | Lendle, Emma | 25, June 1847 | F |
| Mason, Francis | Heying, Maria | 24, Aug. 1836 | FF |
| Mason, Freeman | Wright, Elisabeth | 8, May 1844 | RCH |
| Mason, Jacob | Carkle, Priscilla | 15, Dec. 1825 | RCH |
| Mason, Jacob | Smith, Nancy | 18, Dec. 1834 | RCH |
| Mason, James | Fosdick, Anna | 30, June 1823 | I |
| Mason, John | Gareis, Margaretha | 4, July 1848 | RCH |
| Mason, Jonathan R. | Price, Charlotte | 21, Aug. 1849 | I |
| Mason, Levi | ----, Louise | 20, Dec. 1818 | RCH |
| Mason, Lewis | Dustin, Melinda | Dec. 1824 | RCH |
| Mason, Reason | Waterhouse, Mary J. | 26, June 1837 | RCH |
| Mason, Wilkinson | McKinney, Martha | 22, June 1847 | RCH |
| Mason, William | Neave, Isabella | 25, Aug. 1846 | RCH |
| Massey, James | Kittle, Mary | 1, July 1848 | RCH |
| Massey, James | Dalby, Mary Jane | 7, Dec. 1848 | BB |
| Massey, Joseph | Curry, Elisabeth | 16, June 1842 | RCH |
| Massey, Lewis | Fetter, Amelia | 9, Oct. 1832 | RCH |
| Massmann, Ludwig | Baumer, Maria Anna | 11, Jan. 1842 | FF |
| Masters, Hiram | Gordon, Christina | 11, Apr. 1847 | RCH |
| Masters, John | Brevard, Josephine | 12, Aug. 1847 | RCH |
| Masters, Perry | Peters, Mary Ann | 3, Jan. 1825 | RCH |
| Masters, Thomas | Burton, Sally Ann | 13, Dec. 1836 | RCH |
| Masters, W.B. | Huffmann, Frances | 30, Mar. 1837 | RCH |
| Mastiller, Peter | Feniner, Elisabeth | 23, Aug. 1838 | RCH |
| Mastors, Dennis | Thompson, Julia Ann | 30, Apr. 1835 | RCH |
| Mastrub, Joseph | Wesselmann, Gertrud | 16, July 1848 | EE |
| Masun, Mattheus | Froehling, Margaret | 25, June 1848 | AA |
| Matheny, John | Morris, Margaret | 23, Mar. 1837 | RCH |
| Mather, Benjamin | Singer, Sarah | 6, June 1849 | RCH |
| Mathes, Wolfgang | Hoeffer, Henriette | 11, June 1848 | CC |
| Mathews, Christopher | Dawson, Nancy | 5, Aug. 1844 | RCH |
| Mathews, Christopher | Jones, Jane | 18, Aug. 1846 | RCH |
| Mathews, Christopher | Gentry, Nancy | 26, May 1847 | RCH |
| Mathews, Hannibal | Gilpin, Priscilla | 30, July 1843 | RCH |
| Mathews, Hannibal | Perry, Fanny | 22, Nov. 1846 | RCH |
| Mathews, James | West, Hannah | 17, Oct. 1833 | RCH |
| Mathews, James | Ayres, Julia Ann | 29, Oct. 1843 | RCH |
| Mathews, John H. | Wickersham, | July 1835 | RCH |
| Mathews, Joshua | Reed, Elisabeth | 14, Sept 1842 | RCH |
| Mathews, Peter | Dawson, Patsy | 17, Aug. 1835 | RCH |
| Mathews, Samuel | Farren, Isabella | 27, Jan. 1825 | RCH |
| Mathews, William | Emerson, Clarissa | 19, Apr. 1841 | RCH |
| Mathews, William | Phillips, Matilda | 1, July 1841 | RCH |
| Mathewson, Ariel | Reeves, Ellen | 23, Oct. 1842 | RCH |
| Mathias, Hamilton | Crew, Rosanna | 16, Feb. 1846 | RCH |
| Mathry, David | Williams, Margaret | 22, Nov. 1822 | RCH |
| Mathu, Thomas M. | Baker, Mary Ann | 8, Nov. 1840 | RCH |
| Matoon, Edwin | Langdon, Nancy B. | 10, Oct. 1833 | RCH |
| Matre, Joseph | Finn, Walburga | 23, Aug. 1846 | EE |
| Matre, Joseph | Seibert, Magdalena | 6, Nov. 1849 | EE |
| Matsenbaugh, Samuel | Gilmann, Sarah | 9, Dec. 1847 | RCH |
| Matson, Francis | Holland, Mary Ann | 1, Mar. 1848 | RCH |
| Matson, James | Collins, Ann | 10, Apr. 1846 | RCH |
| Matson, John | VonGorder, Milka | 6, Sept 1841 | RCH |
| Matson, Oliver | Taylor, Sarah | 9, June 1844 | RCH |
| Matson, Oliver | Stevenson, Louise | 5, Oct. 1848 | RCH |
| Matson, William | Hedges, Jane | 1, Mar. 1848 | RCH |
| Matt, Matthias | Folz, Maria Anna | 27, Sept 1847 | AA |
| Mattars, Edmund | Hays, Elisabeth | 9, Mar. 1837 | RCH |
| Mattel, Francis | Thiens, Margaretha | 19, Feb. 1849 | DD |
| Mattenheimer, Adam | Reis, Catharine | 24, Oct. 1847 | EE |
| Matter, Michael | Burgard, Margaret | 2, Jan. 1843 | C |

| Grooms<br>****** | Brides<br>****** | Date of Marriage<br>**** ** ******** | Code<br>**** |
|---|---|---|---|
| Mattheis, Christian | Hartmann, Maria | 17, Dec. 1849 | G |
| Matthes, Georg Mich. | Glass, Margaretha | 4, July 1849 | B |
| Matthes, Johan Paul | Baron, Rosina | 13, June 1847 | AA |
| Matthews, Albert | Hoyt, Elis. Jane | 4, Mar. 1841 | RCH |
| Matthews, Frederick | Ro---, Esther | 14, Nov. 1822 | RCH |
| Matthews, James | Chance, Jane | 22, Jan. 1843 | RCH |
| Matthews, James | Ellis, Jane | 21, Oct. 1847 | RCH |
| Matthews, James W. | Summers, Elisabeth | 3, Mar. 1844 | RCH |
| Matthews, John C. | Persons, Mary | 17, Mar. 1819 | RCH |
| Matthews, Robert | Choats, Mary | 3, Feb. 1842 | RCH |
| Matthews, Thomas | Bloom, Isabella | 30, Sept 1823 | RCH |
| Matthews, William | Caston, Margaret | 13, Dec. 1821 | RCH |
| Matthews, William | Bloodsoe, Elisabeth | 27, Apr. 1843 | RCH |
| Matthews, William | Nash, Mary | 20, Jan. 1847 | RCH |
| Matthews, William A. | Brown, Caroline | 23, May 1838 | RCH |
| Matthias, Francis | Maloy, Mary Jane | 29, Apr. 1848 | RCH |
| Matthias, Theobald | Knell, Nette | 28, Oct. 1849 | G |
| Matthus, Zachaeus | Gruhler, Anna | 5, Sept 1848 | G |
| Mattias, Francis | Molloy, Mary | 23, May 1848 | GG |
| Mattin, Joseph | Withorn, Wilhelmina | 15, Jan. 1839 | FF |
| Mattinger, George | Kirchner, Margaret | 30, June 1846 | RCH |
| Mattinger, Nicolaus | Klein, Philippina | 21, May 1844 | C |
| Mattmann, John | Dunlap, Elisabeth | 12, Aug. 1846 | RCH |
| Mattox, Lazarus | Johnson, Mary | 10, Nov. 1835 | RCH |
| Mattox, Solomon | Prayle, Ann | 26, Nov. 1835 | RCH |
| Mauderer, Joseph | Hermann, Theresa | 2, Nov. 1846 | EE |
| Maue, Friedrich H. | Hungerkamp, Friedr. | 11, June 1846 | G |
| Mauerer, Gustav | Thoerner, M. Angela | 8, June 1845 | FF |
| Mauntel, Friedrich | Brueggenschmid, Cath | 21, Nov. 1837 | FF |
| Mauntel, Friedrich | Boehning, Wilhelmina | 8, Dec. 1842 | F |
| Mauntel, Johan | Holthaus, Agnes | 13, Oct. 1846 | FF |
| Mauntel, Johan Hein. | Grewe, Elisabeth | 7, May 1848 | FF |
| Maupin, Alexander | Smyley, Mary | 4, Aug. 1836 | RCH |
| Maurath, Felix | Jacob, Josephine | 17, Oct. 1844 | AA |
| Maurer, Carl Friedr. | Maurer, Elisabeth C. | 29, July 1849 | A |
| Maurer, Friedrich | Lauber, Louise | 28, June 1840 | G |
| Maurer, Georg J. | Gerhardt, Christina | 16, Jan. 1845 | G |
| Maus, Casper | Dietrich, Magdalena | 17, May 1842 | FF |
| Maus, Nicolaus | Stefan, Barbara | 16, July 1844 | FF |
| Maus, Wendel | Scheitamann, Maria | 8, Feb. 1842 | FF |
| Maushorn, Franz | Schweigert, Victoria | 6, Aug. 1848 | II |
| Mawney, Lawrence | Cox, Rachel | 15, June 1834 | RCH |
| Mawson, William | Western, Sarah (Mrs) | 1, Nov. 1843 | D |
| Maxfield, Davas | Edmiston, Barbara | 1, Jan. 1836 | RCH |
| Maxfield, George | ----, Susan | Apr. 1826 | RCH |
| Maxon, Stephan | Roberts, Anna | 20, June 1843 | RCH |
| Maxwell, George | Adams, Submit | 14, Sept 1837 | RCH |
| Maxwell, Hugh B. | Henderson, Sophia | 2, Oct. 1832 | RCH |
| Maxwell, James | Johnston, Jane | 19, Sept 1848 | RCH |
| Maxwell, John | Gra---, Catharine | 2, Apr. 1838 | RCH |
| Maxwell, Joseph | Connover, Rebecca | 26, Oct. 1834 | RCH |
| Maxwell, Patrick | O'Neil, Mary | 18, Sept 1841 | BB |
| May, Franklin | Ban---, Matilda | 22, Oct. 1837 | RCH |
| May, George | Weis, Gertrud | 20, July 1849 | RCH |
| May, Job | Batton, | 31, Aug. 1826 | RCH |
| May, Johan | Bange, Elisabeth | 8, Sept 1849 | CC |
| May, Jonathan | Smith, Harriet | 20, Mar. 1841 | RCH |
| May, Michael | Flinn, Mary | 23, June 1840 | BB |
| May, Peter | Kunz, Margaretha | 26, Dec. 1847 | G |
| May, Robert | Parks, Elisabeth | 9, Mar. 1846 | RCH |
| May, Seator | Rinehart, Elisabeth | 11, Aug. 1833 | RCH |
| Mayer, Adolph | Phillipson, Rosa | 31, Oct. 1848 | RCH |
| Mayer, Clemens | Helms, Anna Maria | 5, Nov. 1839 | FF |
| Mayer, Friedrich Wm. | Hoekers, Maria | 11, Nov. 1847 | B |
| Mayer, Joseph | Weis, Clara | 3, Aug. 1849 | RCH |
| Mayers, Henry | Mulford, Mary | 13, Apr. 1839 | RCH |
| Mayers, Joseph | Mayers, Mary M. | 2, Aug. 1838 | RCH |
| Maygor, Michael | Smith, Laura | 25, July 1827 | RCH |
| Mayhew, Irwin | Sharp, Catharine | 21, Nov. 1832 | RCH |
| Mayhew, Mark | Allen, Jane A. | 7, Jan. 1836 | RCH |
| Mayhew, Rufus D. | Cammeron, Demmla | 19, Aug. 1838 | RCH |

| Grooms | Brides | Date of Marriage | Code |
|--------|--------|------------------|------|
| ***** | ***** | **** ** ******** | **** |
| Mayhew, Seth | Morris, Elisabeth | 30, Apr. 1839 | RCH |
| Mayhew, Thomas | Bassett, Margaret | 26, Nov. 1846 | RCH |
| Mayhood, Joseph | Openlader, Caroline | 27, Nov. 1845 | RCH |
| Mayhurst, John | Brisban, Mary Ann | 14, Feb. 1841 | RCH |
| Mayle, Ebenezer | Powell, Ann | 1, Feb. 1844 | RCH |
| Mayle, George F. | Dennis, Sarah | 10, Sept 1843 | RCH |
| Maylor, Archibald | Boyd, Melinda | 10, Nov. 1836 | RCH |
| Mayrose, Bernard | Redecker, Angela | 23, June 1846 | AA |
| Mc---, Brulen | Ringsily, Priscilla | 18, Oct. 1836 | RCH |
| McAfee, Edward | Minchel, Martha | 28, May 1844 | RCH |
| McAfee, William | Armstrong, Margaret | 28, Oct. 1832 | RCH |
| McAffee, Daniel | Small, Rachel | 18, Feb. 1837 | RCH |
| McAffee, John | Buzett, Jane | 9, July 1825 | RCH |
| McAffee, Patrick | Boyle, Elisabeth | 29, May 1841 | BB |
| McAllister, John | Lancaster, Malinda | 12, Apr. 1843 | RCH |
| McAndless, Thomas | Nolan, Ann | 20, Feb. 1849 | RCH |
| McAndrew, John | McGuire, Mary | 22, Nov. 1847 | BB |
| McArthur, Amos | Punch, Aller | 4, Mar. 1833 | RCH |
| McArthur, Edward | Leonard, Mary Ann | 7, Dec. 1834 | RCH |
| McArty, William | Setright, Ellen | 23, June 1841 | BB |
| McAvoy, Cornelius | Bonford, Julia | 12, June 1849 | GG |
| McAvoy, Luke | Medler, Catharine | 5, May 1839 | BB |
| McBride, James | Smith, Elisabeth | 8, Oct. 1841 | RCH |
| McBride, Lyman | Hare, Mary Ann | 13, Sept 1842 | RCH |
| McBride, William | Mixer, Elisabeth | 23, Feb. 1833 | RCH |
| McCabe, Eugene | Gaffney, Helen (Mrs) | 8, Nov. 1849 | BB |
| McCabe, Jacob | Lodwick, Jane E. | 21, May 1836 | RCH |
| McCabe, John | Cunningham, Mary | 18, June 1840 | BB |
| McCabe, Patrick | Brady, Ann | 10, Apr. 1842 | BB |
| McCabe, Patrick | Plunkett, Mary Ann | 7, Aug. 1848 | BB |
| McCabe, Peter | Gormly, Mary | 7, Apr. 1848 | GG |
| McCabe, Ross | Murphy, Catharine | 2, Nov. 1843 | BB |
| McCabe, Starkey | Nixin, Jane | 1, Apr. 1838 | RCH |
| McCaffey, William | P---, Mary Ann | 18, Dec. 1834 | RCH |
| McCaffrey, Bernard | McDermott, Mary Ann | 8, Apr. 1849 | BB |
| McCaffrey, James | Conlin, Anna | 14, Feb. 1836 | RCH |
| McCain, Robert | Barlow, Malvina | 19, Oct. 1845 | RCH |
| McCall, Archibald | Brady, Margaret | 29, June 1825 | RCH |
| McCall, David | Angus, Charlotte | 31, Oct. 1841 | RCH |
| McCall, Patrick | Sheridan, Mary | 13, Sept 1846 | GG |
| McCall, William | Guyger, Eunice | 26, Dec. 1848 | RCH |
| McCallister, James | Alexander, Lucy | 21, May 1840 | RCH |
| McCallister, Thomas | Simpson, Sophia | 7, June 1843 | RCH |
| McCameron, Samuel | Grau, Celir | 21, Mar. 1839 | RCH |
| McCammon, Joseph | Burns, Elis. Jane | 14, June 1833 | RCH |
| McCan, John | McDonough, Sally | 18, Oct. 1849 | GG |
| McCandless, Robert | White, Rachel | 11, Sept 1832 | RCH |
| McCann, John | McGarr, Mary | 4, May 1845 | BB |
| McCann, John N. | Tulley, Elisabeth | 28, Nov. 1839 | RCH |
| McCann, Michael | Cowan, Mary | 22, Feb. 1849 | RCH |
| McCannon, James | Johnson, Marshall | Nov. 1836 | RCH |
| McCardle, Patrick | Usher, Alice | 11, Apr. 1841 | BB |
| McCarren, James | Seideser, Henrietta | 22, Nov. 1842 | BB |
| McCarter, | McHugh, | 13, Feb. 1848 | BB |
| McCarter, John | Bishop, Henrietta | 6, Nov. 1843 | RCH |
| McCarthy, Cornelius | Dailey, Fanny | 3, Sept 1847 | GG |
| McCarthy, Edward | McGraw, Ellen | 18, July 1849 | BB |
| McCarthy, Jeremiah | Pennington, Ellen | 4, Oct. 1840 | BB |
| McCarthy, John | Mahoney, Helen | 3, Oct. 1847 | BB |
| McCarthy, Martin | Martin, Mary | 16, Sept 1835 | RCH |
| McCarthy, Michael | McCarthy, Helen | 28, Sept 1839 | BB |
| McCarthy, Owen | McKenna, Bridget | 23, Aug. 1848 | RCH |
| McCarthy, Timothy | Fleming, Mary | 14, May 1836 | RCH |
| McCartin, Patrick | Byron, Bridget | 23, Nov. 1843 | BB |
| McCarty, Josiah | Pitts, Lucy Ann | 28, Feb. 1847 | RCH |
| McCash, David | Bruin, Mary | 19, May 1836 | RCH |
| McCash, Israel | Loper, Sarah Ann | 11, June 1844 | RCH |
| McCauley, Henry | Hainan, Catharine | 20, July 1838 | I |
| McCay, James | Mathes, Phebe | 5, June 1834 | RCH |
| McChaney, John | Patterson, Flora | 8, Jan. 1824 | RCH |
| McChessney, Samuel | Cross, Martha | 13, Apr. 1826 | RCH |

| Grooms | Brides | Date of Marriage | Code |
|--------|--------|------------------|------|
| ****** | ****** | **** ** ******** | **** |
| McChroney, Robert | Conelin, Margaret | 6, Dec. 1831 | RCH |
| McClaid, Joseph | Elder, Margaret | 15, Dec. 1833 | RCH |
| McClain, Barnabas | Moore, Susannah | 8, Oct. 1845 | RCH |
| McClain, Edward | Robinson, Elisabeth | 24, Dec. 1845 | RCH |
| McClain, Harrison | BuKard, Caroline | 31, Aug. 1837 | RCH |
| McClain, Madison | Simpson, Mary Ann | 27, June 1847 | RCH |
| McClanahan, John | Bloomer, Elisabeth | 10, May 1836 | RCH |
| McClane, James | Wood, Malinda Emelin | 25, Sept 1823 | RCH |
| McCleary, John W. | Irwine, Anna Maria | 21, Dec. 1848 | RCH |
| McClellan, William | Whatson, Mary | 5, Mar. 1819 | RCH |
| McClelland, Alex. | Smith, Elisabeth A. | 18, Dec. 1835 | RCH |
| McClelland, John | Spencer, Lydia | 23, Mar. 1820 | RCH |
| McClelland, John | Moore, Frances M. | 9, Mar. 1837 | RCH |
| McClenend, James | Hageman, Levina | 21, Nov. 1832 | RCH |
| McClery, Andrew | Swint, Augusta | 1, Apr. 1846 | RCH |
| McClintock, John | Gerard, Hetty | 13, Dec. 1835 | RCH |
| McCloskey, Edward | Hyland, Mary Ann | 15, June 1843 | BB |
| McClosky, Bernard | Dolby, Mary Ann | 18, Apr. 1833 | RCH |
| McClure, David | Constable, Elisabeth | 1, Nov. 1848 | RCH |
| McClure, Edward | Sweet, Martha | 22, July 1838 | RCH |
| McClure, James | Morehead, Elisabeth | 13, Jan. 1824 | RCH |
| McClure, James | Wheeler, Sarah | 10, June 1844 | RCH |
| McClure, John | Allen, Catharine | 14, June 1821 | RCH |
| McClure, Joseph W. | Bateman, Ruth | 24, Feb. 1821 | RCH |
| McClury, James | Scott, Affy | 24, Apr. 1821 | RCH |
| McCluskey, Joseph | McCoy, Elisabeth | 18, June 1818 | RCH |
| McClutchey, John | Bassett, Emeline | 16, Nov. 1847 | RCH |
| McCollough, David | Murrell, Jane | 7, Dec. 1845 | RCH |
| McCollough, James | Cummins, Matilda J. | 20, Oct. 1847 | RCH |
| McCollough, Robert | Taylor, Sarah | 12, July 1849 | RCH |
| McColluck, James | Conklin, Charlotte | 17, Apr. 1842 | RCH |
| McComb, Robert | Kemper, Ann S. | 4, May 1841 | RCH |
| McConkey, Benjamin | Morsell, Hester | 30, June 1843 | RCH |
| McConnell, James | Hyndmann, Olivia | 7, Dec. 1848 | RCH |
| McConnell, John W. | Hill, Charlotte | 2, Apr. 1848 | RCH |
| McConnell, William | Clark, Elisabeth | 3, Jan. 1837 | RCH |
| McConville, John | Strickland, Jane | 23, Mar. 1848 | I |
| McCorckle, Thomas | Stone, Mary | 1, Sept 1833 | RCH |
| McCord, J.S. | Brown, Asenath | 12, Oct. 1842 | RCH |
| McCord, James | G---, Elisabeth | 18, Nov. 1824 | RCH |
| McCorkhill, Bricen | O'Neil, Lydia A. | 10, Nov. 1842 | RCH |
| McCormack, John | Glenn, Mary | 19, Apr. 1834 | RCH |
| McCormack, John C. | Hagen, Cordelia | 28, Apr. 1825 | RCH |
| McCormick, Charles | Littleton, Martha | 1, Apr. 1838 | RCH |
| McCormick, Charles | McVay, Rebecca | 13, June 1844 | RCH |
| McCormick, Dennis | O'Conner, Elisabeth | 8, May 1847 | GG |
| McCormick, Francis | Cinan, Martha | 2, Nov. 1844 | RCH |
| McCormick, George | Fleak, Nancy | 8, Dec. 1847 | RCH |
| McCormick, John | Halley, Elisabeth | 18, Aug. 1842 | RCH |
| McCormick, John | Nicholson, Ann | 19, Apr. 1846 | BB |
| McCormick, Mathew | Donovan, Margaret | 22, Nov. 1846 | BB |
| McCormick, Matthew | Elroy, Margaret | 3, July 1848 | GG |
| McCormick, Patrick | McCormick, Catharine | 12, Mar. 1844 | BB |
| McCormick, Robert | Levengood, Elisabeth | 14, Nov. 1842 | RCH |
| McCormick, Thomas | Byrum, Vanette | 28, Sept 1817 | RCH |
| McCormick, Thomas | Hunter, Eunice | 5, Jan. 1842 | RCH |
| McCormick, William | Edward, Julia | 28, Mar. 1844 | RCH |
| McCormick, William | Bywater, Ann Louise | 24, Nov. 1842 | BB |
| McCormick, William | Ham, Anna Maria | 26, Aug. 1845 | RCH |
| McCourt, Hugh | Denney, Ann | 3, May 1846 | BB |
| McCowen, George | Ervin, Mary | 27, May 1819 | RCH |
| McCoy, John | Young, Nancy | 20, June 1832 | RCH |
| McCoy, Oliver | Phipps, Jane | 4, Dec. 1845 | RCH |
| McCracken, George | Woolever, Louise | 23, Feb. 1843 | RCH |
| McCracken, Mark | Matson, Sarah | 5, Oct. 1820 | RCH |
| McCraken, William | Winters, Louisianna | 13, Apr. 1834 | RCH |
| McCreary, John | Stewart, Martha | 16, Nov. 1847 | BB |
| McCristal, William | Hosley, Cornelia | 25, Dec. 1842 | RCH |
| McCrumb, William | Ryan, Ann | 2, Dec. 1849 | RCH |
| McCue, Patrick | Higgins, Bridget | 2, Aug. 1846 | BB |
| McCullem, Daniel | McLean, Isabella | 2, Apr. 1835 | RCH |

| Grooms<br>***** | Brides<br>***** | Date of Marriage<br>**** ** ******** | Code<br>**** |
|---|---|---|---|
| McCullen, Owen | Murphy, Catharine | 23, Sept 1849 | GG |
| McCullock, | Merrie, Jane | 29, July 1819 | RCH |
| McCullon, William B. | Piatt, Arabella | 15, May 1826 | RCH |
| McCullough, Harry | ----, ---- | 4, Aug. 1836 | RCH |
| McCullough, Hugh | McMaster, Mary Ann | 12, Jan. 1826 | RCH |
| McCullough, Isaac | Mervin, Nancy | 28, Dec. 1835 | RCH |
| McCullough, James M. | Parvin, Melissa B. | 10, Feb. 1835 | RCH |
| McCullough, Joseph | Perry, Elisabeth | 1, Aug. 1844 | RCH |
| McCullough, Robert | Taylor, Sarah | 24, Dec. 1832 | RCH |
| McCullough, William | Moore, Matilda | 4, Sept 1833 | RCH |
| McCullough, William | Cummins, Anna Elis. | 14, Mar. 1849 | RCH |
| McCully, James | Coombs, Rachel | 24, Aug. 1843 | RCH |
| McCune, Joseph | Arbagust, Emeline | 2, Nov. 1837 | I |
| McCurdy, Jacob | Wentling, Mary Jane | 4, Mar. 1847 | RCH |
| McCurry, Henry | Bartlett, Mary | 31, May 1843 | RCH |
| McCurry, Henry | Coleman, Mary | 17, Jan. 1844 | RCH |
| McCusker, John | Hassen, Jane | 25, Apr. 1843 | BB |
| McDaniel, Mansfield | Young, Mary Ann | 8, Nov. 1835 | RCH |
| McDaniel, William | Anderson, Elisabeth | 27, Oct. 1835 | RCH |
| McDannold, William | Critse, Catharine | 1, Aug. 1833 | RCH |
| McDermit, Lachlin | Mills, Isabella | 24, Nov. 1842 | RCH |
| McDermott, Michael | Loughlin, Anna | 28, Apr. 1847 | AA |
| McDermott, Michael | Mulvihill, Ann | 11, Sept 1848 | BB |
| McDermott, William | Gill, Sarah D. | 12, July 1847 | RCH |
| McDevitt, Neal | McGinley, Mary Ann | 22, Nov. 1848 | RCH |
| McDole, Thomas | Eads, Mary Ann | 5, Dec. 1842 | RCH |
| McDonald, A. | Sayre, Cornelia | 24, May 1849 | RCH |
| McDonald, Andrew | Manley, Margaret A. | 24, Dec. 1837 | RCH |
| McDonald, Clifton | Empson, Cynthia | 20, Jan. 1842 | RCH |
| McDonald, Dennis | Welsh, Sarah | 25, Nov. 1849 | GG |
| McDonald, George | Selkirk, Jane Ann | 17, Apr. 1836 | RCH |
| McDonald, Harrison | Davis, Julia | 21, Apr. 1844 | RCH |
| McDonald, James | Windling, Sarah | 16, June 1844 | RCH |
| McDonald, James | Barmore, Maria | 9, Feb. 1847 | RCH |
| McDonald, John | Clark, Mariah C. | 25, Dec. 1823 | RCH |
| McDonald, John | Stewart, Maria | 6, Sept 1840 | RCH |
| McDonald, Matthew | Hill, Minerva | 10, Oct. 1844 | BB |
| McDonald, Patrick | McAllister, Ann | 25, Feb. 1840 | BB |
| McDonald, Peter | Johnson, Sarah Ann | 29, Nov. 1842 | BB |
| McDonald, Richard | Meyers, Charlotte | 20, Mar. 1843 | RCH |
| McDonald, Timothy | Waggoner, Elisabeth | 1, Apr. 1846 | RCH |
| McDonald, William | Smith, Harriet | 5, Apr. 1846 | RCH |
| McDonnell, John | Purcell, Margaret | 3, Aug. 1843 | BB |
| McDonnell, Patrick | Carroll, Mary | 15, Aug. 1843 | BB |
| McDonough, Jefferson | Sackett, E.C. | 25, Nov. 1834 | RCH |
| McDonough, John | McFarrell, Ann | 28, Nov. 1848 | BB |
| McDonough, Patrick | Kane, Mary Ann | 26, Nov. 1848 | BB |
| McDonough, Thomas | Green, Sophia | 1, Dec. 1846 | GG |
| McDougal, Addison | Turner, Emily | 17, Jan. 1844 | RCH |
| McDougal, Joseph | Barrett, Nancy | 9, July 1818 | RCH |
| McDowell, John | Bradley, Catharine | 4, Sept 1849 | RCH |
| McElfresh, John | Slinter, Clarissa | 13, June 1837 | RCH |
| McElroy, William | Byron, Helen | 23, Oct. 1849 | BB |
| McEwen, James | Vaughan, Phebe | 24, July 1842 | RCH |
| McEwen, James | Butler, Jane D. | 6, June 1847 | RCH |
| McFall, Benjamin | Patton, Ann | 9, Oct. 1834 | RCH |
| McFall, John J. | Daly, Mary | 19, Feb. 1849 | BB |
| McFann, Jonathan | Myrick, Hulda | 28, June 1848 | RCH |
| McFarlan, John | Jackson, Lydia | 16, Oct. 1845 | RCH |
| McFarlan, Joseph | Shiner, Elisabeth | 30, Oct. 1842 | RCH |
| McFarland, Amasa | Edstrom, Friedricka | 13, Feb. 1845 | RCH |
| McFarland, David | McCammon, Elisabeth | 21, Apr. 1839 | RCH |
| McFarland, James | Dickson, Alice | 7, Dec. 1848 | RCH |
| McFarlon, Robert | Budley, Sarah E. | 15, Jan. 1836 | RCH |
| McFeeler, Moses | Moreland, Ann | 21, Oct. 1822 | RCH |
| McFeeley, John | Wilson, Mary Ann | 13, May 1824 | RCH |
| McFeely, James | Hill, Rebecca | 26, Oct. 1833 | RCH |
| McFeely, James | Miniearo, Mary | 6, Aug. 1849 | RCH |
| McFreely, Elijah | Follock, Rachel | 7, May 1837 | RCH |
| McGarahan, Thomas | Dolan, Marcella | 8, Nov. 1847 | BB |
| McGatti, James | Butler, Ann | 26, Jan. 1836 | RCH |

| Grooms<br>****** | Brides<br>****** | Date of Marriage<br>**** ** ******** | Code<br>**** |
|---|---|---|---|
| McGaughey, George | Byfield, Hetty | 14, May 1818 | RCH |
| McGaw, Charles | White, Isabella | 4, Apr. 1833 | RCH |
| McGawly, James | Hernan, Joann | 17, Aug. 1846 | BB |
| McGechin, Thomas | Bishop, Thalia | 21, Dec. 1843 | RCH |
| McGee, Robert | Smith, Eliza Jane | 30, Nov. 1848 | RCH |
| McGee, Thomas | Miller, Nancy | 13, June 1835 | RCH |
| McGee, Thomas J. | Brown, Harriet | 22, Nov. 1842 | RCH |
| McGee, William | Stewart, Emily | 4, Apr. 1833 | RCH |
| McGhee, Harrison | Cheek, Catharine | 30, May 1839 | BB |
| McGibben, David | Sharp, Mary Ann | 14, Oct. 1847 | RCH |
| McGill, Fenton | McDonald, Margaret | 23, Aug. 1835 | RCH |
| McGill, Jacob | LaBoyteaux, Cath. | 10, Apr. 1818 | RCH |
| McGill, Jeremiah | Smith, Hattie Ann | 6, Aug. 1837 | RCH |
| McGillard, Reves | Gardner, Sarah | 1, Aug. 1833 | RCH |
| McGinily, Daniel | Hart, Catharine | 4, Dec. 1825 | RCH |
| McGinley, Andrew | Feiley, Bridget | 22, May 1842 | RCH |
| McGinley, Andrew | Feeley, Bridget | 22, July 1841 | BB |
| McGinty, Patrick | McLaughlin, Bridget | 7, Apr. 1849 | RCH |
| McGiven, David | Henry, Rosannah | 24, Nov. 1844 | BB |
| McGiveny, James | Mehan, Bridget | 24, June 1849 | GG |
| McGlade, Michael | Fury, Mary (Mrs) | 15, Apr. 1849 | BB |
| McGlade, Michael | Fury, Mary | 15, Apr. 1849 | BB |
| McGlin, Edward | Hughes, Mary | 29, Sept 1842 | RCH |
| McGlincey, Hugh | Reilly, Julia Agnes | 7, Jan. 1844 | BB |
| McGlone, Michael | Tiernan, Bridget | 8, May 1843 | BB |
| McGlothlin, Ezekiel | Holden, Henrietta | 24, June 1843 | RCH |
| McGlynn, William | Gleason, Sarah | 10, Aug. 1843 | BB |
| McGovern, Ferrel | McDermott, Ann | 19, Oct. 1846 | GG |
| McGovern, Thomas | Cannon, Sarah | 12, Feb. 1849 | BB |
| McGowan, Michael | Gilmartin, Mary | 25, Nov. 1849 | GG |
| McGowan, William | Waters, Catharine | 12, Feb. 1844 | RCH |
| McGrath, John | Shannon, Elisabeth | 11, May 1846 | RCH |
| McGrath, John | Mullally, Mary | 4, Feb. 1849 | BB |
| McGrath, William | Pierce, Matilda | 26, Oct. 1845 | BB |
| McGraw, John | Jukes, Mary Ann | 25, Oct. 1848 | RCH |
| McGreavy, Thomas | Goodrich, Winifred | 26, Sept 1847 | BB |
| McGreen, L. | Schulte, Elisabeth | 20, May 1849 | GG |
| McGregg, Francis | Gardner, Elisabeth | 2, Oct. 1842 | RCH |
| McGregor, Farquhar | McKibbon, Margaret | 1, Dec. 1848 | RCH |
| McGrew, Alend. | Fisher, Alvina | 10, Jan. 1822 | RCH |
| McGrew, Henry | Dick, Jane | 4, June 1846 | RCH |
| McGrew, James | Constable, Mary | 6, Aug. 1845 | RCH |
| McGroarty, Dennis | Maguire, Catharine | 20, Dec. 1849 | RCH |
| McGroy, John | Robinson, Caroline | 18, Sept 1849 | RCH |
| McGuffy, Alexander H | Drake, Elizabeth | 9, May 1839 | I |
| McGuier, William | Smith, Jane E. | 31, Aug. 1834 | RCH |
| McGuiffin, James | Laidd, Anna Maria | 20, Mar. 1833 | RCH |
| McGuillicuddy, John | Prindeville, Helen | 22, June 1845 | BB |
| McGuiness, Richard | Miller, Catharine | 19, Mar. 1837 | RCH |
| McGuinn, Patrick | McLaughlin, Hetty | 5, Dec. 1848 | BB |
| McGuinnis, Dennis | Boyle, Catharine | 11, Nov. 1849 | BB |
| McGuire, James | Cooper, Eleanora | 27, July 1837 | RCH |
| McGuire, John | Buckley, Honora | 29, Nov. 1849 | GG |
| McGuire, Martin | Moran, Catharine | 18, July 1847 | GG |
| McGuire, Thomas J. | Walden, Louisa | 18, Feb. 1834 | RCH |
| McGuire, William | Lacey, Sarah | 22, Dec. 1824 | RCH |
| McGurk, Michael J. | McAuliff, Mary C. | 29, Apr. 1841 | BB |
| McHale, Martin | Gallagher, Rosanna | 5, Mar. 1848 | BB |
| McHanch, George | Findle, Margaret | 20, May 1834 | RCH |
| McHann, Hugh A. | Lytle, Margaret | 8, Oct. 1837 | RCH |
| McHenry, Archibald | Donahue, Elisabeth | 13, Jan. 1841 | RCH |
| McHenry, John | Freathern, Martha | 30, July 1844 | RCH |
| McHenry, Peter | McGovern, Mary | 21, May 1848 | GG |
| McHenry, Samuel | Fagely, Rosella E. | 27, Dec. 1849 | RCH |
| McHenry, Van | Clemons, Nancy | 26, Nov. 1833 | RCH |
| McHugh, Bernard | McGraw, Joanne | 18, May 1846 | BB |
| McIntosh, William | Wood, Mary Jane | 22, June 1849 | RCH |
| McIntyre, Duncan | Kilgour, | 24, Sept 1839 | RCH |
| McKane, Jesse | Stites, Christiana | 3, Aug. 1825 | RCH |
| McKee, Daniel | Senior, Henrietta | 14, Nov. 1847 | BB |
| McKee, James | McNulty, Malinda | 11, Mar. 1846 | RCH |

| Grooms | Brides | Date of Marriage | Code |
|--------|--------|------------------|------|
| ****** | ****** | **** ** ******** | **** |
| McKee, John | Stewart, Mary | 26, Mar. 1818 | RCH |
| McKee, Joseph | Tom---, Drucilla | 4, Feb. 1819 | RCH |
| McKee, Thomas | Woodward, Caroline | 5, July 1842 | RCH |
| McKee, William | Flemming, Elisabeth | 30, Jan. 1836 | RCH |
| McKelvey, Patrick | Loney, Nancy Ann | 14, July 1835 | RCH |
| McKenna, George | Cassilly, Ann | 5, Sept 1839 | BB |
| McKenna, Leslie | Lowrey, Catharine | 17, Sept 1849 | RCH |
| McKenna, Thomas | Long, Laura | 28, June 1847 | RCH |
| McKenny, Reuben | Shires, Catharine | 26, Nov. 1848 | GG |
| McKenny, Seth | Gresham, Susan | 30, Jan. 1833 | RCH |
| McKeown, Bernard | McDonough, Catharine | 20, May 1849 | BB |
| McKeown, James | Cradall, Mary Jane | 2, Sept 1845 | RCH |
| McKeown, Patrick | Fanning, Bridget | 4, Dec. 1848 | BB |
| McKiernan, Michael | Ward, Bridget | 21, May 1846 | BB |
| McKim, William | Wilkins, Marietta | 16, Mar. 1842 | RCH |
| McKin, | Steward, Jane | 26, Oct. 1826 | RCH |
| McKiney, David | Flomerfelt, Mariah | 13, Dec. 1825 | RCH |
| McKinley, James | Lang, Margaret | 27, Nov. 1836 | RCH |
| McKinley, John | Dennis, Amy | 28, Dec. 1820 | RCH |
| McKinley, John | Lamphear, Frances W. | 29, Apr. 1839 | RCH |
| McKinnell, Charles | Tiebout, Mary Brooke | 28, Oct. 1847 | D |
| McKinney, Harmon | Davis, Charlotte | 30, Sept 1845 | RCH |
| McKinney, Isaac | McKown, Sarah | 24, July 1842 | RCH |
| McKinney, James | Mix, Jane | 30, Oct. 1845 | RCH |
| McKinney, John | Murrie, Malinda | 17, July 1834 | RCH |
| McKinney, John T. | Hall, Elisabeth A. | 26, June 1834 | RCH |
| McKittrick, Joseph | Traverse, Mary | 12, May 1839 | BB |
| McKnight, John | Washburn, Frances | 19, Dec. 1833 | RCH |
| McKnight, John | Kidney, Jane | 7, Aug. 1843 | RCH |
| McKnight, Josiah | Mc---, Martha Ann | 11, Feb. 1819 | RCH |
| McKnight, Robert | Clark, Sarah Jane | 2, Mar. 1842 | RCH |
| McKnown, Hiram | Cain, Elisabeth | 14, Dec. 1837 | RCH |
| McKoy, Theodore | Collins, Amelia | 9, Jan. 1846 | RCH |
| McLain, John | Underwood, Lavina | 21, June 1847 | RCH |
| McLain, Josiah | Whitiron, Priscilla | 21, Feb. 1848 | RCH |
| McLain, Thomas | Reeves, Caroline C. | 22, Dec. 1836 | RCH |
| McLanahan, Archibald | Woodburn, Elisabeth | 16, Aug. 1849 | RCH |
| McLane, John | Winn, Mary | 5, Apr. 1834 | RCH |
| McLane, John | Stewart, Elisabeth | 28, May 1848 | RCH |
| McLane, Joseph | Hunt, Delaw | 12, Oct. 1835 | RCH |
| McLaughlin, Bernard | Cassidy, Mary | 9, July 1849 | BB |
| McLaughlin, Charles | O'Donnell, Ellen | 27, Sept 1846 | GG |
| McLaughlin, Ezekiel | Tull, Margaret | 17, Apr. 1834 | RCH |
| McLaughlin, John | Dyer, Mary | 27, Sept 1842 | RCH |
| McLaughlin, Patrick | Miller, Mary | 1, Nov. 1848 | RCH |
| McLaughlin, Samuel | Wheeler, Mathilda | 6, May 1841 | RCH |
| McLaughlin, Stephan | Welsh, Eleanor | 13, Nov. 1849 | BB |
| McLaughlin, Thomas | Ryan, Mary Ann | 25, Oct. 1842 | BB |
| McLaughlin, Thomas | Dowd, Ellen | 17, June 1849 | BB |
| McLaughlin, William | Robinson, Mary | 4, Jan. 1825 | RCH |
| McLaughlin, William | Walton, Alasanna | 1, Nov. 1826 | RCH |
| McLaughlin, William | Brown, Mary | 5, Nov. 1845 | RCH |
| McLean, Allen | McNeal, Jane | 19, Sept 1837 | RCH |
| McLean, Benjamin | Wickham, Anna Elis. | 24, Jan. 1843 | RCH |
| McLean, Samuel | Hutchens, Anna E. | 17, Mar. 1846 | RCH |
| McLean, Thomas | Rowland, Mary Jane | 26, Apr. 1836 | RCH |
| McLean, William | Dunbar, Matilda | 20, Mar. 1835 | RCH |
| McLean, William | McLean, Eliz. (Mrs) | 6, Oct. 1847 | D |
| McLenand, Bernard | Sanders, Jean | 21, Sept 1841 | BB |
| McLeod, John | Condrick, Sarah Ann | 22, Mar. 1847 | RCH |
| McLowe, John | Mack, Mary | 5, June 1836 | RCH |
| McLuiths, James | Latham, Mary L. | 12, Sept 1834 | RCH |
| McMahan, Andrew | Orr, Hannah | 4, Nov. 1847 | RCH |
| McMahon, Benjamin | Bennett, Elisabeth F | 27, Jan. 1835 | RCH |
| McMahon, John | Hugunin, Rachel | 25, June 1819 | RCH |
| McMahon, John | Mathews, Martha | 4, Aug. 1842 | RCH |
| McMaken, James W. | Smith, Mary | 11, May 1848 | RCH |
| McMaken, John | Bacon, Sarah | 24, May 1836 | RCH |
| McManama, Andrew | Wood, Catharine | 2, Mar. 1847 | RCH |
| McManimore, Josiah | Barns, Mary | 16, Jan. 1834 | RCH |
| McMany, John | Jones, Mary | 14, Dec. 1826 | RCH |

| Grooms | Brides | Date of Marriage | Code |
|--------|--------|------------------|------|
| ****** | ****** | **** ** ******** | **** |
| McMeen, John R. | Long, Rebecca | 13, Dec. 1838 | RCH |
| McMeen, Joshua | Dailey, Elisabeth | 23, Nov. 1837 | RCH |
| McMichael, Isaac | Hager, Amelia | 26, Mar. 1848 | RCH |
| McMillen, Jesse | Johnson, Alvira | 4, Feb. 1835 | RCH |
| McMiller, R.G. | Ronalds, Rosannah | 4, Feb. 1824 | RCH |
| McMinn, George | Hatch, Elisabeth | 7, Mar. 1848 | RCH |
| McMullen, Hugh | Russell, Maria | 5, Oct. 1840 | RCH |
| McMullen, James | McCormick, Ellen E. | 14, June 1840 | BB |
| McMullin, Dennis | Monaghan, Ellen | 22, Oct. 1844 | BB |
| McMundell, Andrew | Moore, Rebecca | 19, Mar. 1846 | RCH |
| McMung, David | Miller, Susan | 17, May 1841 | RCH |
| McMurphy, Albert | Bennett, Eleanor | 16, Apr. 1844 | I |
| McMurphy, Samuel | Bates, M. Matilda | 1, May 1843 | RCH |
| McMurphy, Theodore | Bennett, Mary | 13, May 1845 | I |
| McMurray, Thomas | Risk, Elisabeth | 12, Aug. 1842 | RCH |
| McNair, Robert | McGregor, Elisabeth | 29, Dec. 1841 | RCH |
| McNally, John | Blodes, Elisabeth | 9, July 1846 | RCH |
| McNamara, Martin | Costello, Ann | 1, July 1844 | BB |
| McNamara, Preston | Chism, Mary Ann | 7, Sept 1843 | RCH |
| McNeal, Jacob | Dunbar, Lydia | 24, June 1819 | RCH |
| McNeeley, John | Hanney, Mary | 3, Mar. 1840 | BB |
| McNeely, Cyrus | Donaldson, Jane | 19, May 1837 | RCH |
| McNeely, James | Christmann, Magdalen | 14, Apr. 1849 | RCH |
| McNeil, Daniel T. | Quigley, Jane Ann | 9, May 1841 | BB |
| McNeil, Robert | Welsh, Elisabeth | 24, Oct. 1835 | RCH |
| McNeil, Robert | White, Elisabeth | 16, Feb. 1836 | RCH |
| McNelly, Martin | Byrne, Mary | 17, Sept 1849 | RCH |
| McNichols, James | Phillips, Bridget | 5, Feb. 1848 | BB |
| McNichols, Joseph | Westcott, Jane | 25, May 1840 | RCH |
| McNichols, Samuel | Couch, Emeline | 21, Jan. 1842 | RCH |
| McNicoll, John | Mellor, Elisabeth M. | 3, July 1842 | RCH |
| McNiff, James | Lenan, Margaret | 10, Jan. 1849 | BB |
| McNulty, David | Trimble, Sarah | 28, June 1849 | RCH |
| McNulty, John | Kegan, Margaret | 26, Apr. 1847 | BB |
| McNutt, Alexander | Ware, Robinson | 11, Sept 1837 | RCH |
| McPherson, A. | Dunham, Sarah | 23, Nov. 1824 | RCH |
| McPherson, John | Cook, Elisabeth E. | 21, May 1846 | RCH |
| McPike, John | Gr---, Lydia Jane | 9, Feb. 1820 | RCH |
| McQuaid, Charles | Elvins, Mariah | 2, July 1842 | RCH |
| McQualiaty, Peter | Murphy, Elisabeth | 18, Apr. 1840 | RCH |
| McQueen, Amon | Quigley, Sarah | 20, Aug. 1849 | RCH |
| McQuillan, Andrew | Mallard, Elisabeth | 8, Oct. 1839 | BB |
| McRibben, Jame s | Miller, Athelia | 18, Apr. 1834 | RCH |
| McRie, George | Marple, Maria | 5, Apr. 1832 | RCH |
| McRobert, R. | Bond, Susannah | 25, Oct. 1835 | RCH |
| McRoberts, Robert | Noble, Harriet | 27, June 1827 | RCH |
| McRoberts, William | McWilliams, Theresa | 10, July 1848 | BB |
| McVay, Abraham | Fairchild, Angeline | 18, July 1833 | RCH |
| McVay, John | Moore, Susan B. | 24, Sept 1848 | RCH |
| McVestal, J. | Dent, Violetta | 23, Sept 1833 | RCH |
| McWakefield, Joseph | Long, Nancy | 12, Aug. 1837 | RCH |
| McWilliams, Freeman | Slate, Mary Ann | 27, July 1845 | RCH |
| McWilliams, James | Duffin, Nancy | 3, June 1844 | RCH |
| McWilliams, John | Owen, Eliza | 29, Sept 1824 | RCH |
| McWithey, Ansil | Johns, Catharine | 22, Feb. 1845 | RCH |
| Meachan, James | Lee, Mary | 9, Apr. 1846 | RCH |
| Mead, John | Smith, Mary R. | 28, Sept 1843 | RCH |
| Mead, Patrick | Delaney, Margaret | 14, Apr. 1836 | RCH |
| Meader, Nathaniel | Athern, Lucretia | 11, June 1820 | RCH |
| Mealy, Martin | Mitchell, Sarah | 27, Sept 1847 | BB |
| Meara, Thomas | Wheeler, Angela | 2, Jan. 1849 | BB |
| Mears, Daniel | Huston, Deborah | 11, Oct. 1841 | RCH |
| Mears, William E. | Sutton, Hannah Ann | 20, Oct. 1835 | RCH |
| Meason, Isaac | Shephard, Narcissa L | 22, Mar. 1837 | I |
| Mechtersheimer, John | Grans, Elisabeth | 8, Apr. 1849 | RCH |
| Mecklenburg, Joseph | Schulte, Maria | 27, Feb. 1838 | FF |
| Meckli, | Meckli, Maria | 9, Oct. 1849 | A |
| Mecum, John | Goshorn, Esther | 14, Dec. 1842 | RCH |
| Medaris, John | Perry, Martha | 2, Mar. 1849 | RCH |
| Medary, John | Dubois, Lorinda | 19, May 1846 | RCH |
| Meddeke, Philipp | Stuntebeck, Elis. | 31, Aug. 1841 | FF |

| Grooms<br>****** | Brides<br>****** | Date of Marriage<br>**** ** ******** | Code<br>**** |
|---|---|---|---|
| Medeck, Peter | Unkerig, Philippina | 25, June 1848 | G |
| Meder, Daniel F. | Ferrell, Clarissa | 9, Oct. 1833 | RCH |
| Meder, Johan | Varkers, Catharina | 23, May 1841 | FF |
| Meek, A.H. | Hornet, Maria Anna | 26, Oct. 1832 | RCH |
| Meek, Alexander | Rhynearson, Susan | 20, Aug. 1836 | RCH |
| Meek, John P. | Lauter, Georgianna | 29, June 1843 | RCH |
| Meek, Simon | Moody, Elisabeth | 16, Aug. 1838 | RCH |
| Meeker, Moses | Shankleton, Elis. | 29, Jan. 1837 | RCH |
| Meeker, Ogden | Harper, Nancy | 17, Feb. 1841 | RCH |
| Meeks, Jacob | Hewley, Phebe | 29, Apr. 1834 | RCH |
| Meess, Nicolaus | Doerr, Pauline | 4, June 1848 | EE |
| Megener, John | Taulman, Amanda | 7, Oct. 1824 | RCH |
| Megie, John | Crane, Mary | Nov. 1841 | RCH |
| Megrue, Enoch | Levy, Ann | 24, Dec. 1842 | RCH |
| Megrue, Joseph | Megrue, Ruth C. | 26, Dec. 1844 | RCH |
| Mehan, Patrick | Harrigan, Rosanna | 24, May 1846 | GG |
| Mehin, Patrick | Cassady, Sarah | 22, July 1849 | BB |
| Mehl, Georg | Herencourt, Elisabet | 15, Apr. 1841 | G |
| Mehl, John | Stevens, Mary | 12, Mar. 1846 | RCH |
| Mehler, Georg | Luky, Carolina | 22, July 1849 | CC |
| Mehler, John | Bergen, Margaret | 13, Jan. 1842 | RCH |
| Mehling, Martin | McCanne, Catharine | 16, Sept 1841 | RCH |
| Mehne, Jacob | Jockers, Brigitta | 21, Aug. 1847 | A |
| Mehner, Lewis | Schillinger, Christ. | 24, Dec. 1848 | G |
| Meier, A.H. | Ronneke, Elisabeth | 17, Sept 1848 | II |
| Meier, Balthasar | Fuerst, Kunigunda | 16, Jan. 1845 | FF |
| Meier, Christian | Fai, Catharina | 18, Jan. 1841 | FF |
| Meier, Francis Jos. | Enneking, Agnes | 29, Apr. 1849 | FF |
| Meier, Franz Heinric | Rowekamp, Elisabeth | 26, Apr. 1849 | RCH |
| Meier, Friedrich | Oskamp, Elisabeth | 24, Jan. 1843 | FF |
| Meier, Friedrich | Gaines, Maria | 6, Aug. 1849 | RCH |
| Meier, Friedrich C. | Durens, Maria | 10, June 1848 | F |
| Meier, George | Scheib, Louise | 29, Apr. 1846 | RCH |
| Meier, Gerhard | Sicker, Maria | 13, Nov. 1849 | FF |
| Meier, H. Wilhelm | Eggers, Gertrud | 14, Nov. 1842 | F |
| Meier, Heinrich | Ves, Helena | 19, Jan. 1841 | FF |
| Meier, Heinrich | Froning, Elisabeth | 22, Aug. 1847 | CC |
| Meier, Heinrich | Fuesting, Margaretha | 24, Sept 1848 | CC |
| Meier, Henry | Fischer, Mary | 27, Dec. 1843 | RCH |
| Meier, Herman Heinr. | Bloemer, M Elisabeth | 20, May 1847 | FF |
| Meier, Johan | Weishaupt, Elisabeth | 16, Nov. 1849 | A |
| Meier, Johan | Schmidt, Margaretha | 4, Oct. 1846 | B |
| Meier, Johan Heinric | Schuhmacher, Antonet | 11, Nov. 1849 | CC |
| Meier, John | Postlerin, Cunigunda | 5, Jan. 1847 | RCH |
| Meier, John A. | Bergheit, Barbara | 12, June 1843 | RCH |
| Meier, Louis | Schaffer, Gertrud | 24, Oct. 1845 | RCH |
| Meier, Rudolph | Honstat, Margaret | 24, Sept 1846 | RCH |
| Meier, Stanislaus | Laninger, Theresa | 9, Jan. 1849 | II |
| Meier, Theodor | Hannebaum, Louisa | 6, Aug. 1848 | II |
| Meier, Wilhelm | Moritz, Anna | 20, Sept 1848 | F |
| Meierfeld, Henz | Maas, Caroline | 26, Mar. 1849 | RCH |
| Meiers, Johan | Schweers, Elisabeth | 23, May 1849 | II |
| Meiers, Johan Fr. Wm | Dinkelmann, Maria | 8, Aug. 1848 | F |
| Meiers, Joseph | Meiers, Elisabeth | 2, July 1839 | FF |
| Meighan, Andrew | Keweon, Ellen | 17, Sept 1843 | BB |
| Meighan, Lawrence | Dolan, Mary Ann | 10, Nov. 1839 | BB |
| Meikenhaus, Carl | Kramer, Margaretha | 22, July 1841 | F |
| Meiler, Francis | Sutmer, Catharine | 28, Jan. 1845 | AA |
| Meiners, Herman | Bergmann, Carolina | 7, July 1846 | AA |
| Meiners, Theodor | Drees, Maria | 6, May 1849 | II |
| Meinert, Heinrich | Wernke, Anna M. | 23, Sept 1849 | AA |
| Meines, Herman | Kramer, Agnes | 26, Nov. 1848 | II |
| Meingel, Joseph | Johnson, Sarah Ann | 27, Oct. 1841 | RCH |
| Meinhardt, Conrad | Nagel, Margaretha | 5, Aug. 1846 | G |
| Meinhardt, Peter | Gunther, Elisabeth | 13, Feb. 1848 | G |
| Meinken, Johan Bd. | Holtmeyer, Anna L. | 14, Oct. 1849 | EE |
| Meintz, Joseph | Davis, Lavina | 13, Aug. 1845 | BB |
| Meisel, Francis | Oehler, M. Magdalena | 4, Feb. 1845 | FF |
| Meisel, Wolfgang | Schoerger, Barbara | 9, Aug. 1847 | RCH |
| Meissel, Francis | Meier, Rosalia | 19, Oct. 1848 | CC |
| Mekeal, James | Mull, Susan | 19, Nov. 1845 | RCH |

| Grooms ****** | Brides ****** | Date of Marriage **** ** ******** | Code **** |
|---|---|---|---|
| Melcher, Friedrich | Kuper, Angela | 7, Jan. 1849 | II |
| Melcher, Heinrich | Neissard, Eva | 16, Oct. 1839 | G |
| Melcher, Joseph C. | Burnes, Elisabeth | 24, Nov. 1834 | RCH |
| Meldrum, Thomas G. | Healy, Mary | 15, May 1845 | BB |
| Melendy, Peter | Coddington, Martha | 20, Oct. 1846 | RCH |
| Meley, John T. | Moore, Sarah | 27, Nov. 1833 | RCH |
| Meley, Jonathan | Carson, Jane | 8, Mar. 1841 | RCH |
| Melg, Anton | Trendel, Katharine | 2, Oct. 1849 | EE |
| Meline, James P. | Rogers, M. Elisabeth | 27, Aug. 1846 | BB |
| Melish, Thomas | Bromwell, Maria | 15, May 1849 | RCH |
| Mell, George | Topler, Barbara | 1, Mar. 1836 | RCH |
| Mellage, Johan Hein. | Rammer, Elisabeth | 24, Aug. 1845 | AA |
| Melle, Herman | Unluecke, Margaretha | 21, Jan. 1845 | AA |
| Mellein, Johan Georg | Mueller, Aloysia | 26, July 1846 | EE |
| Mellen, William P. | Clarke, Martha Ann I | 15, Sept 1846 | D |
| Mellis, Francis | Gould, Julia | 31, Aug. 1842 | RCH |
| Melson, William | Ullerize, Sophia | 7, May 1849 | F |
| Menany, George | Holt, Rosetta | 23, Sept 1841 | RCH |
| Mench, Michael | Mock, Anna Maria | 25, July 1844 | AA |
| Mendelson, Solomon | Steinfields, Rose | 24, Dec. 1845 | RCH |
| Mendenhall, William | Morris, Julia C. | 24, Dec. 1839 | D |
| Mender, Nicolaus | Lissor, Mary E. | 12, Nov. 1836 | F |
| Mender, Patrick | McDonald, Mary | 29, Apr. 1849 | GG |
| Mendler, Philipp | Eickert, Catharine | 4, Nov. 1841 | RCH |
| Menebrocker, Friedr. | Dremeier, Elisabeth | 31, Aug. 1849 | RCH |
| Menge, Georg | Neun, Gertrud | 27, Mar. 1848 | G |
| Mengelkamp, Carl | Fering, Adelheid | 4, May 1845 | AA |
| Meniery, Bernard | ----, Anna Maria | 15, Dec. 1849 | RCH |
| Menig, Ferdinand | Kottmann, Catharine | 21, Nov. 1847 | EE |
| Meninger, John | Schurbrock, Maria | 6, July 1846 | RCH |
| Menke, Bernard | Lehring, Maria | 6, Feb. 1848 | FF |
| Menke, Bernard H. | Grewe, Elisabeth | 25, July 1847 | AA |
| Menke, Ernst | Koetting, Anna Cath. | 19, Nov. 1845 | F |
| Menke, Gerhard | Unkraut, Maria Cath. | 9, Jan. 1844 | FF |
| Menke, Johan Bernard | Meyer, Elisabeth | 27, Sept 1842 | AA |
| Menke, Johan Wilhelm | Cullott, Anna M.Cath | 10, Feb. 1835 | FF |
| Menke, Johan Wilhelm | Beckemeier, Henriett | 25, July 1844 | F |
| Menke, Johan Wilhelm | Fagge, M. Elis.(Mrs) | 13, Dec. 1849 | F |
| Menke, Joseph | Wilmsen, Elisabeth | 9, Jan. 1848 | EE |
| Menke, Rudolph | Schumacher, Elis. | 25, Aug. 1835 | FF |
| Menke, Theodor | Werrick, Elisabeth | 27, Jan. 1846 | FF |
| Menkhaus, David | Kreienbrink, Anna M. | 28, June 1836 | FF |
| Menkhaus, Heinrich | Dickmann, Maria Anna | 3, Sept 1848 | AA |
| Menninger, Carl | Steigert, Francisca | 12, Apr. 1847 | EE |
| Menninger, Eberhard | Kraft, Carolina | 17, July 1845 | AA |
| Menninger, Johan | Schierbeck, Maria | 6, July 1845 | AA |
| Mense, Matthias | Dubreien, Caroline | 3, Feb. 1842 | FF |
| Ment, George | Sacket, Elisabeth A. | 17, Mar. 1834 | RCH |
| Mentel, Bartholomew | Netter, Anna Maria | 12, June 1849 | EE |
| Mentonye, Zachariah | Shuff, Sarah | 22, Aug. 1816 | RCH |
| Mentz, | Rapp, Anna Maria | 11, June 1849 | RCH |
| Mentzel, Jacob | Rothert, Susanna | 16, Nov. 1849 | G |
| Menzer, Martin | Stecker, Charlotte | 26, July 1847 | AA |
| Mercer, Benjamin | Graham, Mary | 21, Nov. 1833 | RCH |
| Mercer, William | Kite, Frances | 1, Oct. 1846 | RCH |
| Merchant, John | Kinney, Elisabeth E. | 20, Mar. 1848 | RCH |
| Merckel, Georg | Kaerndorfer, Anna | 10, Sept 1845 | AA |
| Mercklin, George | Hautz, Margaret | 8, Aug. 1846 | RCH |
| Meredith, Charles | Simmons, Sarah E. | 4, Dec. 1849 | RCH |
| Meredith, David | Brees, Anna | 4, Dec. 1841 | RCH |
| Meredith, Ephraim | Jones, Elisabeth | 2, Mar. 1846 | RCH |
| Mergenthal, Casper | Fridler, M Josephina | 4, July 1842 | FF |
| Mergler, Andreas | Herberger, Margaret | 23, May 1837 | FF |
| Merkel, Johan | Hohneker, Francisca | 2, Mar. 1848 | EE |
| Merlin, Casper | Uphus, Dina | 8, May 1849 | II |
| Mernan, John | Seplaim, Julia | 15, Feb. 1847 | GG |
| Merrell, Ephraim | Robinson, Ellen | 14, Oct. 1844 | RCH |
| Merrell, H.C. | Stockbridge, Louise | 15, Apr. 1838 | RCH |
| Merret, | Bickel, Nancy | 26, May 1823 | RCH |
| Merrett, Debolt | Lemmon, Elisabeth | 7, Apr. 1844 | RCH |
| Merrett, John | Haythorn, Mary Ann | 1, July 1847 | RCH |

| Grooms<br>***** | Brides<br>***** | Date of Marriage<br>**** ** ******** | Code<br>**** |
|---|---|---|---|
| Merrick, Casper L. | Maddin, S.E. | 28, Apr. 1822 | RCH |
| Merrick, William | Enos, Isabel | 7, Oct. 1841 | RCH |
| Merrie, Hugh | Crooks, Margaret | 18, Sept 1843 | RCH |
| Merril, Jacob | Graham, Mary Ann | 24, Apr. 1820 | RCH |
| Merrill, James | Lawson, Hannah | 31, Jan. 1822 | RCH |
| Merriman, John | Cummins, Jane | 21, Feb. 1843 | RCH |
| Merring, John George | Hutwick, Mary | 17, Mar. 1841 | RCH |
| Merriott, Andrew | Conley, Elisabeth | 28, Dec. 1831 | RCH |
| Merritt, James | Crossley, Rachel | 28, Aug. 1822 | RCH |
| Merritt, James P. | Dunseth, Margaret | 3, Feb. 1833 | RCH |
| Merriweather, James | Juppenlatz, Louise | 22, Sept 1835 | RCH |
| Merriweather, Nick. | Yeatman, Sarah Jane | 17, Dec. 1839 | I |
| Merry, Nathaniel | Hunt, Sarah | 10, June 1847 | RCH |
| Merryweather, Fred. | Arnold, Sarah | 20, June 1837 | RCH |
| Merser, Robert | Dobson, Ann | 1, June 1847 | RCH |
| Mersmann, Ferdinand | Mueller, Anna Cath. | 23, Jan. 1844 | AA |
| Mersmann, Heinrich | Imsieke, Maria | 26, Apr. 1842 | FF |
| Mersmann, Heinrich | Tebbelmann, Adelheid | 19, Aug. 1845 | FF |
| Merten, Andreas | Scheper, Agnes | 11, June 1848 | FF |
| Mertens, George | Busse, Catharine | 31, May 1842 | RCH |
| Mertz, Carl | Wurst, Christina | 30, June 1847 | EE |
| Merwarth, Johan Geo. | Martin, Maria | 30, July 1846 | G |
| Merz, Gotthard | Gasser, Fridolina | 8, July 1844 | FF |
| Mescher, Bernard | Norre, M. Elisabeth | 25, Nov. 1849 | II |
| Mescher, Wilhelm | Moormann, Maria | 2, Nov. 1848 | A |
| Mescke, Peter Wm. | Struck, Johanna R. | 27, Sept 1846 | B |
| Mesger, Wilhelm | Meyers, Maria | 9, Dec. 1847 | A |
| Mesher, Johan | Sandermann, Elisabet | 12, Apr. 1836 | FF |
| Mesling, Johan | Wedding, Christina | 15, Oct. 1844 | AA |
| Mesmann, Johan Hein. | Weming, Maria Anna | 25, Apr. 1847 | AA |
| Messech, E. | Dean, Rebecca | 18, July 1841 | RCH |
| Messer, Benjamin | Parker, Mary Ann | 16, July 1835 | RCH |
| Messer, Peter | Skippermew, Elis. | 1, Dec. 1834 | RCH |
| Messick, George | Steel, Maria | 17, June 1847 | RCH |
| Messmann, Johan Bd. | Henning, M. Catharin | 21, Nov. 1847 | AA |
| Messmer, Heinrich | Strattmann, Elis. | 4, Feb. 1840 | FF |
| Metcalf, Joseph | Rogers, Harriet | 11, Jan. 1834 | RCH |
| Metcalf, Samuel | Pexton, Mary | 5, Oct. 1834 | RCH |
| Metcalf, Thomas | Dearsley, Margaret | 26, Mar. 1838 | RCH |
| Metcalfe, James | Edwards, Ann | 16, Mar. 1843 | I |
| Meteger, George H. | Deamond, Cecilia | 30, Jan. 1848 | BB |
| Metscher, Jacob | Donnersperger, Jos. | 12, Sept 1847 | CC |
| Mette, Heinrich | Goldkamp, Elisabeth | 11, Oct. 1842 | AA |
| Mette, Heinrich | Ossenbeck, Catharina | 26, Apr. 1842 | FF |
| Mettland, Charles | Adams, Emilia | 25, June 1822 | RCH |
| Mettles, Albert | Scogen, Amanda | 28, Aug. 1841 | RCH |
| Metz, Adam | Brunner, Francisca | 22, Feb. 1838 | FF |
| Metz, Johan | Morio, Catharina | 14, Apr. 1842 | FF |
| Metz, Johan | Weingaertner, Cath. | 22, Aug. 1843 | FF |
| Metz, Johan | Feiker, Mathilda | 22, Aug. 1844 | FF |
| Metz, Joseph | Reberger, Josephina | 13, Aug. 1839 | FF |
| Metz, Pancratz | Strez, Cunigunda | 15, Nov. 1847 | FF |
| Metz, Peter | Goerman, Catharine | 18, Feb. 1848 | RCH |
| Metz, Simon | Berger, Sophia | 25, Dec. 1848 | EE |
| Metzel, George | Huber, Catharine | 27, Oct. 1845 | RCH |
| Metzger, | Metzger, Appolonia | 20, Apr. 1835 | RCH |
| Metzger, Adam | Bechler, Catharina | 27, Aug. 1839 | G |
| Metzger, Wilhelm | Huhn, Friedricka | 2, Aug. 1847 | FF |
| Metzler, Heinrich | Jung, Catharine | 30, Nov. 1848 | EE |
| Metzler, Jacob | Gonner, Magdalena | 22, Sept 1848 | A |
| Meweny, David | Robison, Mary | 1822 | RCH |
| Meyer, Adam | Biehler, Barbara | 27, July 1841 | G |
| Meyer, Adam | Prugler, Catharine | 19, Apr. 1847 | CC |
| Meyer, Adam F. | Mosekamp, Louise M. | 20, June 1849 | B |
| Meyer, Anton | Goetz, Barbara | 20, June 1834 | RCH |
| Meyer, Anton | Sielinger, Barbara | 3, Aug. 1835 | FF |
| Meyer, Arnold Heinr. | Eickelmann, Maria | 30, Mar. 1843 | RCH |
| Meyer, Bernard | Kollage, Caroline | 21, June 1842 | FF |
| Meyer, Bernard | Jansen, Anna Maria | 18, Nov. 1849 | AA |
| Meyer, Bernard Hein. | Wiene, Anna M.L. | 3, Aug. 1843 | F |
| Meyer, Carl | Moennig, Elisabeth | 16, July 1844 | AA |

| Grooms<br>****** | Brides<br>****** | Date of Marriage<br>**** ** ******** | Code<br>**** |
|---|---|---|---|
| Meyer, Carl | Bahn, Aleid | 20, Mar. 1845 | C |
| Meyer, Carl | Henn, Dorothea | 16, Nov. 1848 | G |
| Meyer, Carl | Hentinges, Anna M. | 21, June 1849 | EE |
| Meyer, Casper Heinr. | Koenig, Cath. Marg. | 21, Oct. 1847 | F |
| Meyer, Clemens | ----, Anna Maria | 5, Mar. 1839 | RCH |
| Meyer, Dietrich H. | Menke, Catharina | 6, Dec. 1849 | C |
| Meyer, Francis | Beckmann, Josephina | 23, Oct. 1838 | FF |
| Meyer, Francis | Baumer, Agnes | 27, Sept 1842 | FF |
| Meyer, Francis | Brockamp, Anna Maria | 3, July 1849 | AA |
| Meyer, Francis | Schinzing, Maria A. | 29, Aug. 1848 | EE |
| Meyer, Francis Jos. | Klatte, Helena | 15, Apr. 1845 | FF |
| Meyer, Franz | Predick, Elisabeth | 5, Feb. 1846 | AA |
| Meyer, Franz Joseph | Weiskittel, Francis | 30, July 1848 | AA |
| Meyer, Franz Joseph | Brunning, Agnes(Mrs) | 19, Aug. 1849 | FF |
| Meyer, Friedrich | Henderson, Christina | 30, Nov. 1843 | A |
| Meyer, Friedrich | Gerholtz, Sophia | 21, Feb. 1842 | F |
| Meyer, Friedrich | Wehmann, Anna F. | 13, Oct. 1842 | F |
| Meyer, Friedrich | Marcke, Elisabeth | 1, Aug. 1847 | RCH |
| Meyer, Friedrich | Teben, Maria | 26, Oct. 1848 | F |
| Meyer, Friedrich | Kugel, Catharine | 21, July 1848 | G |
| Meyer, Friedrich | Macke, Elisabeth | 10, Aug. 1847 | AA |
| Meyer, Friedrich | Rodekamp, Maria Anna | 6, May 1849 | AA |
| Meyer, Friedrich C. | Balthaus, A. Gertrud | 29, Oct. 1846 | C |
| Meyer, Friedrich W. | Fricken, Charlotte | 23, Feb. 1848 | F |
| Meyer, Georg | Hiller, Catharina | 13, July 1838 | FF |
| Meyer, Georg | Trout, Eva Elisabeth | 29, Nov. 1848 | RCH |
| Meyer, Georg | Dewein, Susannah | 24, Oct. 1847 | A |
| Meyer, Georg | Heinrich, Philippina | 26, Apr. 1849 | C |
| Meyer, Georg | Willing, Clara | 27, Apr. 1849 | G |
| Meyer, George | Bohlke, Maria C. | 11, Nov. 1846 | RCH |
| Meyer, Gerhard | Hoefer, Elisabeth | 7, Sept 1841 | FF |
| Meyer, Gerhard | Drephagen, Johanna | 8, June 1849 | RCH |
| Meyer, Gerhard | Holster, Adelheid | 23, Sept 1845 | AA |
| Meyer, Gottlieb | Steib, Dorothea | 4, Mar. 1841 | G |
| Meyer, Gottlieb | Rosenfield, M.Sophia | 18, June 1846 | C |
| Meyer, Heinrich | Erdbrink, Sophia W. | 30, Dec. 1840 | F |
| Meyer, Heinrich | Elbert, Margaretha | 3, Mar. 1841 | F |
| Meyer, Heinrich | Lubbers, Sophia | 21, Oct. 1841 | F |
| Meyer, Heinrich | Tiemann, Maria | 12, Dec. 1844 | F |
| Meyer, Heinrich | Richter, Gertrud | 13, Sept 1842 | AA |
| Meyer, Heinrich | Mueller, Elisabeth | 12, Jan. 1843 | AA |
| Meyer, Heinrich | Raelling, Antonia | 25, Feb. 1840 | FF |
| Meyer, Heinrich | Berger, Theresa | 11, Jan. 1842 | FF |
| Meyer, Heinrich | Hanselmann, Sophia | 24, Sept 1846 | C |
| Meyer, Heinrich | Meyers, Elisabeth | 27, Jan. 1846 | C |
| Meyer, Heinrich | Huntemann, Christina | 15, June 1848 | C |
| Meyer, Heinrich | Stuebe, Hannah | 18, Nov. 1845 | F |
| Meyer, Heinrich | Brockschmidt, Maria | 30, Apr. 1846 | G |
| Meyer, Heinrich | Christmann, Maria A. | 2, Sept 1849 | AA |
| Meyer, Heinrich A. | Rennert, Margaretha | 22, Apr. 1849 | AA |
| Meyer, Heinrich Wm. | Heine, Maria | 27, Feb. 1841 | F |
| Meyer, Henry D. | Kregel, Margaretha | 30, Aug. 1841 | RCH |
| Meyer, Herman | Habighorst, Carolina | 22, Oct. 1840 | FF |
| Meyer, Herman H. | Meyer, Elisabeth | 27, Nov. 1838 | FF |
| Meyer, Herman H. | Telkamp, A Catharine | 5, July 1848 | F |
| Meyer, Herman Heinr. | Biber, Elisabeth | 5, July 1842 | FF |
| Meyer, Herman J. | Schaefer, Anna M. | 25, Oct. 1838 | FF |
| Meyer, Herman L. | Asbre, Anna M. Cath. | 10, Jan. 1847 | AA |
| Meyer, J. Dietrich | Aschen, Cath. Elis. | 31, Oct. 1844 | F |
| Meyer, J. Friedrich | Rottinghaus, M. Elis | 12, May 1840 | FF |
| Meyer, J. Friedrich | Fleddermann, Marg. | 25, Jan. 1842 | FF |
| Meyer, J. Friedrich | Bergisch, Agnes | 3, Sept 1847 | B |
| Meyer, Jacob | Thorp, Hannah | 14, Oct. 1824 | RCH |
| Meyer, Jacob | Huscher, Anna Maria | 3, May 1837 | FF |
| Meyer, Jacob | Kaufmann, Rebecca | 29, Dec. 1846 | RCH |
| Meyer, Jacob | Altinger, Catharine | 7, Nov. 1845 | G |
| Meyer, Jacob | Leitsch, Marg. (Mrs) | 28, Jan. 1847 | AA |
| Meyer, Johan | Spellmann, Elisabeth | 17, Mar. 1842 | F |
| Meyer, Johan | Lehmann, Christina | 25, Oct. 1842 | AA |
| Meyer, Johan | Schroeder, Theresa | 31, Aug. 1843 | FF |
| Meyer, Johan | Rondler, Catharine | 8, Nov. 1847 | C |

| Grooms<br>****** | Brides<br>****** | Date of Marriage<br>**** ** ******** | Code<br>**** |
|---|---|---|---|
| Meyer, Johan | Doerr, Maria | 26, Oct. 1847 | EE |
| Meyer, Johan A. | Casner, Catharine | 28, Oct. 1844 | G |
| Meyer, Johan Adam | Dudenhofer, Apolonia | 4, Feb. 1838 | FF |
| Meyer, Johan Bernard | Herzog, Elisabeth | 13, Jan. 1846 | AA |
| Meyer, Johan Bernard | Bunker, Maria Elis. | 19, July 1846 | EE |
| Meyer, Johan Bernard | Lange, Anna Maria | 6, May 1845 | FF |
| Meyer, Johan Bernard | Buenker, M Elisabeth | 27, Jan. 1846 | FF |
| Meyer, Johan Dietric | Horsmann, Catharine | 21, Nov. 1843 | FF |
| Meyer, Johan Ernst | Brasen, Dorothea | 15, Nov. 1845 | RCH |
| Meyer, Johan Gerhard | Ratermann, Bernardin | 3, June 1841 | FF |
| Meyer, Johan Gerhard | Hevelmeyer, Theresa | 4, Nov. 1849 | AA |
| Meyer, Johan Gerhard | Gausepohl, Maria | 20, Nov. 1849 | AA |
| Meyer, Johan H. | Helling, Maria Adel. | 20, June 1847 | EE |
| Meyer, Johan H. | Koebbink, Bernardina | 5, Mar. 1848 | EE |
| Meyer, Johan Heinric | Hoevermeyer, Maria | 16, Dec. 1840 | F |
| Meyer, Johan Heinric | Wenning, Catharine | 24, Oct. 1844 | F |
| Meyer, Johan Heinric | Lankering, Anna M.F. | 13, Mar. 1847 | RCH |
| Meyer, Johan Heinric | Prenton, Margaretha | 10, Sept 1846 | B |
| Meyer, Johan Heinric | Meyer, Catharine | 14, Nov. 1846 | E |
| Meyer, Johan Heinric | Schuermann, M Louise | 1, Oct. 1849 | F |
| Meyer, Johan Heinric | Austing, Maria Agnes | 6, May 1845 | AA |
| Meyer, Johan Heinric | Hoegemann, A. Maria | 7, May 1848 | FF |
| Meyer, Johan Joseph | Meyer, Elisabeth | 9, Oct. 1849 | AA |
| Meyer, Joseph | Hagerty, Catharine | 1, Apr. 1845 | AA |
| Meyer, Louis | Riemeier, Anna | 15, Nov. 1846 | B |
| Meyer, Louis | Duensing, Sophia | 9, Dec. 1847 | F |
| Meyer, Martin | Peter, Rosalia | 9, Aug. 1846 | AA |
| Meyer, Martin | Feuerstein, Margaret | 14, Nov. 1848 | FF |
| Meyer, Michael | Liegel, Catharine | 25, Nov. 1844 | AA |
| Meyer, Moses | Glasser, Henrietta | 10, Sept 1849 | RCH |
| Meyer, Peter | Lohmann, Catharine | 16, July 1844 | FF |
| Meyer, Valentin | Gottmann, Maria Eva | 13, Apr. 1845 | FF |
| Meyer, Valentine | Leist, | 5, Feb. 1841 | RCH |
| Meyer, W. Christian | Kries, A. Maria | 7, Sept 1843 | G |
| Meyer, Werner | Kramer, Elisabeth | 16, Apr. 1844 | AA |
| Meyer, Wilhelm | Pruss, Maria | 19, May 1842 | F |
| Meyer, Wilhelm | Metting, Margaretha | 18, July 1844 | F |
| Meyer, Wilhelm | Rosengarden, Cath. | 23, Apr. 1846 | C |
| Meyer, Wilhelm | Luetkemeyer, Cath. | 2, Nov. 1847 | F |
| Meyer, Wilhelm | Steins, Anna | 24, Oct. 1849 | F |
| Meyer, Wilhelm | Klatte, Elisabeth | 14, Jan. 1845 | AA |
| Meyer, William | Klitta, Elisabeth | 13, Nov. 1844 | RCH |
| Meyer, William Chr. | Fries, Anna Maria | 2, Sept 1843 | RCH |
| Meyer, Xavier | Hanna, Matilda | 23, Aug. 1847 | EE |
| Meyerhoefer, Wilhelm | Schierberg, Wilhel. | 31, Oct. 1847 | EE |
| Meyerhoff, Georg H. | Scheidemann, Elis. | 8, Sept 1847 | F |
| Meyerholz, Wilhelm | Engelkotte, Anna M. | 2, July 1840 | F |
| Meyering, Anton | Gess, Elisabeth | 11, Jan. 1845 | AA |
| Meyering, Joseph | Wiszmann, M. Gertrud | 20, July 1845 | AA |
| Meyerrose, Herman F. | Bertelsman, Marg. W. | 9, Apr. 1846 | F |
| Meyers, Adam | Hill, Henrietta | 16, July 1837 | RCH |
| Meyers, Andrew | Kitts, Julia | 7, Nov. 1843 | RCH |
| Meyers, Anthony | Reinert, Margaret | 21, Apr. 1849 | RCH |
| Meyers, Bernard | Lebbermann, Louise | 8, Jan. 1845 | RCH |
| Meyers, Carl | Decker, A. Catharine | 1, Oct. 1846 | RCH |
| Meyers, Frederick | ----, Ann L. | 26, Dec. 1836 | RCH |
| Meyers, George | Clark, Mary E. | 10, Jan. 1838 | RCH |
| Meyers, Grean B. | Thompson, Mary Jane | 11, Oct. 1836 | RCH |
| Meyers, Heinrich | Welling, Catharine | 22, Mar. 1849 | B |
| Meyers, Jacob | Stimis, Mary Louise | 18, May 1849 | RCH |
| Meyers, Johan | Shaller, Mary Ann | 2, Jan. 1846 | RCH |
| Meyers, Johan | Rush, Rachel | 25, Feb. 1847 | RCH |
| Meyers, John | McFall, Catharine | 3, Oct. 1839 | BB |
| Meyers, John | Bevins, Hannah | 3, Aug. 1845 | RCH |
| Meyers, John | Young, Elisabeth | 25, Nov. 1846 | RCH |
| Meyers, John R. | Gulick, Mary A. | 28, Mar. 1843 | RCH |
| Meyers, Jonathan | Sentney, Asa | 10, Jan. 1836 | RCH |
| Meyers, Jonothan | Park, Matilda B. | 27, Sept 1833 | RCH |
| Meyers, Peter | Martin, Amanda | 6, Feb. 1842 | RCH |
| Meyers, Samuel | McGinnity, Maria | 26, Dec. 1844 | RCH |
| Meyers, Samuel | Alward, Jemmina | 27, Dec. 1846 | RCH |

| Grooms | Brides | Date of Marriage | Code |
|--------|--------|------------------|------|
| Meyhoff, Johan D. | Bode, Anna Elisabeth | 21, Nov. 1844 | F |
| Meyleben, Georg | Wolten, Christina | 22, May 1849 | EE |
| Meymann, Heinrich | Laumann, Lisette | 7, May 1848 | AA |
| Meynek, John H. | Smith, Catharine | 23, July 1818 | RCH |
| Mi---, Jacob | Foreman, Margaret | 28, Sept 1820 | RCH |
| Micener, | Debensh, Margaret | 7, Mar. 1822 | RCH |
| Michael, Carl | Rohle, Barbara | 4, June 1843 | RCH |
| Michael, Christoph | Decker, Maria | 14, Sept 1841 | FF |
| Michael, Georg | Hauser, Barbara | 26, Sept 1847 | C |
| Michael, Heinrich | Wellmann, Maria | 29, Apr. 1843 | AA |
| Michael, Joseph | Wegis, Elisabeth | 19, Mar. 1839 | RCH |
| Michael, Joseph | Wiges, Elisabeth | 19, Nov. 1839 | FF |
| Michael, Philip Jac. | Ennes, Catharine | 10, Sept 1835 | RCH |
| Michall, Daniel | Bell, | 1, Aug. 1839 | RCH |
| Michel, Francis | Roding, Regina | 29, Sept 1839 | FF |
| Michel, Jacob | Mundorf, Margaretha | 26, Dec. 1848 | A |
| Mickel, Philipp | Tuchfarber, Rosina | 11, Feb. 1847 | EE |
| Micklin, Henry | McCardle, Bridget | 30, Sept 1845 | BB |
| Middeldorfer, Johan | Ewigmann, Maria A. | 12, Jan. 1849 | EE |
| Midden, Gerhard | Rutter, Anna M. | 6, May 1849 | AA |
| Midden, Herman D. | Wilmes, Anna Maria | 7, Aug. 1845 | RCH |
| Midden, Herman Theo. | Weberg, Cath. E(Mrs) | 31, Aug. 1845 | FF |
| Middendorf, Gehrard | Heger, Regina | 6, Oct. 1847 | EE |
| Middendorf, Herman | Ostendorf, Maria C. | 16, July 1848 | EE |
| Middendorf, Johan | Soenkers, Maria Anna | 4, Jan. 1848 | AA |
| Middlebeck, Clemens | Hineo, Maria | 15, Apr. 1834 | RCH |
| Middleton, Elijah | Lovejoy, Mary Jane | 19, Apr. 1848 | RCH |
| Middleton, Robert | Lynch, Catharine | 15, July 1849 | RCH |
| Middleton, Thomas | Kirby, Elisabeth | 23, Feb. 1833 | RCH |
| Middleton, William | Mason, Ann | 13, Feb. 1822 | RCH |
| Middlewood, | Whitehead, Sarah | 18, Oct. 1842 | RCH |
| Midlen, William | McBride, Elisabeth | 13, Sept 1842 | RCH |
| Mieder, Joseph | Keller, Ottilia | 17, Nov. 1849 | EE |
| Miedke, August | Hellmann, Babette | 30, June 1846 | RCH |
| Miggenburg, Joseph | Lueker, Elisabeth | 25, Jan. 1848 | EE |
| Mighel, John | Bell, Mary | 25, May 1847 | RCH |
| Migul, Bernard | Knese, Maria Anna | 15, Apr. 1849 | FF |
| Milbis, Nathan | Graham, Mary Jane | 28, Feb. 1844 | RCH |
| Milburn, John | Smith, Matilda | 18, Aug. 1835 | RCH |
| Miles, Benjamin | Stilwell, Catharine | 4, Apr. 1833 | RCH |
| Miles, Henry | Ayres, Rachel | 10, July 1848 | RCH |
| Miles, James | Thomas, Mary | 14, July 1836 | RCH |
| Miles, Marsh | Ferril, Chalena | 17, Feb. 1820 | RCH |
| Miles, Reese | Tatem, Catharine | 23, Feb. 1847 | RCH |
| Miley, William | Dennan, Margaret | 13, Apr. 1841 | BB |
| Milig, John | Schmidt, Julia | 14, Jan. 1846 | RCH |
| Milins, William | Wolf, Daphine | 10, Feb. 1846 | RCH |
| Miller, Abner | Miller, Jane | 18, Apr. 1844 | RCH |
| Miller, Abraham | Cornell, Mary A. | 13, May 1824 | RCH |
| Miller, Alfred | Guild, Emily M. | 12, June 1834 | RCH |
| Miller, Allen | Boget, Sophia | 27, Nov. 1843 | RCH |
| Miller, Amos | Kitchell, Margaret | 14, Feb. 1826 | RCH |
| Miller, Andreas | Menninger, Maria | 20, Feb. 1844 | AA |
| Miller, Anthony | Kincaid, Mary | 6, Apr. 1849 | RCH |
| Miller, Charles | Conover, Levina A. | 3, Sept 1846 | RCH |
| Miller, Charles | Dodsworth, Hannah | 30, Aug. 1849 | RCH |
| Miller, Constantin | Crippen, Sarah | 23, Sept 1846 | RCH |
| Miller, Daniel | Arthurs, Anna E. | 22, Aug. 1844 | RCH |
| Miller, David | Colven, Elisabeth | 17, Oct. 1824 | RCH |
| Miller, David H. | Kibourne, Damand M. | 28, June 1833 | RCH |
| Miller, Edward | Harris, Mary Jane | 5, May 1839 | RCH |
| Miller, Emanuel | Taylor, Sarah H. | 12, June 1839 | I |
| Miller, Francis | Moore, Rebecca | 26, Sept 1849 | RCH |
| Miller, George | Carson, Acksa | 14, Feb. 1822 | RCH |
| Miller, George | Mappin, Isabella | 3, Oct. 1833 | RCH |
| Miller, George S. | Haan, Barbe | 20, June 1834 | RCH |
| Miller, George W. | Semings, Catharine | 1, Sept 1834 | RCH |
| Miller, Heinrich E. | Kiens, Maria Anna | 24, Jan. 1847 | RCH |
| Miller, Henry | Austin, Elisabeth | 28, July 1839 | RCH |
| Miller, Henry | Bell, Jane | 13, Aug. 1844 | RCH |
| Miller, Henry | Heuer, Christina | 22, Dec. 1847 | A |

| Grooms | Brides | Date of Marriage | Code |
|--------|--------|------------------|------|
| ****** | ****** | **** ** ******** | **** |
| Miller, Henry B. | Reeves, Mary | 2, June 1841 | RCH |
| Miller, Henry B. | Jones, Elisabeth | 6, Apr. 1849 | RCH |
| Miller, Henry T. | Jungman, Fanny | 7, Aug. 1848 | RCH |
| Miller, Isaac | McMillan, Mary H. | 28, June 1838 | RCH |
| Miller, Isaac | Fowler, Penelope | 1, Jan. 1843 | RCH |
| Miller, Jacob | Dobbling, Dorothea | 2, May 1837 | RCH |
| Miller, Jacob | Reeb, Dorothea | 14, Jan. 1847 | A |
| Miller, James | Eddington, Jane | 29, July 1833 | RCH |
| Miller, James | Edwards, Sarah | 9, July 1839 | RCH |
| Miller, James | Kelsey, Maria | 18, Dec. 1839 | RCH |
| Miller, James | Bonte, Sarah | 9, May 1847 | RCH |
| Miller, Job W. | Brooks, Caroline | 1, June 1839 | RCH |
| Miller, Johan | Wilhelm, Columbia | 18, Apr. 1843 | AA |
| Miller, Johan | Deter, Catharine | 11, Jan. 1844 | AA |
| Miller, John | Norris, Temperence | 18, Oct. 1818 | RCH |
| Miller, John | Tucker, Anna | 4, June 1821 | RCH |
| Miller, John | Bowman, Mary Ann | 19, Feb. 1824 | RCH |
| Miller, John | Lindley, L. | 11, May 1826 | RCH |
| Miller, John | Felter, Lucy | 4, Aug. 1833 | RCH |
| Miller, John | Patton, Hannah | 18, Feb. 1838 | RCH |
| Miller, John | Holmes, Selina | 16, Sept 1841 | RCH |
| Miller, John | Griffith, Nancy Jane | 16, Mar. 1842 | RCH |
| Miller, John | Kincade, Julia | 23, June 1842 | RCH |
| Miller, John | Armstrong, Isabella | 30, July 1846 | RCH |
| Miller, John | Fountain, Sarah | 10, Oct. 1847 | RCH |
| Miller, John | Grannis, Sarah | 2, Jan. 1849 | RCH |
| Miller, John | Mueller, Margaretha | 25, Aug. 1846 | AA |
| Miller, John B. | Nichols, Hulda | 1, Apr. 1844 | RCH |
| Miller, John H. | Parker, Sarah Jane | 29, Jan. 1842 | RCH |
| Miller, John Henry | Meyer, Margaret | 3, Jan. 1847 | RCH |
| Miller, John W. | Whipple, Lucinda | 9, Jan. 1848 | RCH |
| Miller, Joseph | Ewing, Anna | 24, Mar. 1821 | RCH |
| Miller, Joseph | Harris, Sarah | 17, May 1838 | RCH |
| Miller, Joseph | Brittainharm, Mary | 16, Aug. 1845 | RCH |
| Miller, Joshua | Lamphear, Lida | 17, June 1834 | RCH |
| Miller, Louis | Bamber, Elisabeth | 3, Feb. 1836 | RCH |
| Miller, Martin | Williams, Mary Jane | 1, Jan. 1845 | RCH |
| Miller, Michael | Brater, Catharine | 29, July 1844 | RCH |
| Miller, Milton | Fox, Charlotte | 12, Dec. 1841 | RCH |
| Miller, Morton F. | Decoursey, Mary A. | 23, June 1834 | RCH |
| Miller, Nicolaus | Corp, Catharina | 26, May 1838 | FF |
| Miller, Perry | Fahling, Mary | 21, Apr. 1842 | RCH |
| Miller, Peter | Miller, Lylia | 3, Jan. 1833 | RCH |
| Miller, Peter | Klein, Margaretha | 23, June 1839 | G |
| Miller, Peter W. | Sheon, Charlotte | 10, May 1836 | RCH |
| Miller, Reuben | Jones, Ruth | 7, June 1837 | RCH |
| Miller, Richard | Gro---, Margaret | 7, Jan. 1820 | RCH |
| Miller, Richard | Sherwin, Ellen | 14, Feb. 1848 | RCH |
| Miller, Robert | Moss, Sarah | 27, Aug. 1846 | RCH |
| Miller, Samuel | Pickering, Emeline | 15, May 1839 | RCH |
| Miller, Sebastian | Martin, Catharine | 23, Jan. 1849 | RCH |
| Miller, Selden | Mah---, Margaret | 19, Jan. 1837 | RCH |
| Miller, Sidney | Harper, Jemima | 4, Sept 1847 | RCH |
| Miller, Sylvester | Foster, Emeline | 16, Dec. 1849 | RCH |
| Miller, Theodor | Krieger, Helena | 13, Apr. 1845 | AA |
| Miller, Theodore | Conner, Sarah | 7, July 1834 | RCH |
| Miller, Thomas | Miller, Matilda | 11, Oct. 1832 | RCH |
| Miller, Thomas | Henning, Julia A. | 7, May 1835 | RCH |
| Miller, Thomas | Woonee, Sarah | 10, May 1837 | RCH |
| Miller, Tobias | Wolverton, Jane | 4, Feb. 1820 | RCH |
| Miller, Washington | Miller, Nancy | 22, June 1846 | RCH |
| Miller, William | Spring---, Sarah | 23, Mar. 1837 | RCH |
| Miller, William | Bell, Elisabeth | 23, July 1844 | RCH |
| Miller, William | Wilson, Sarah | 22, Oct. 1846 | RCH |
| Miller, William | Hill, Nancy Jane | 16, Apr. 1847 | RCH |
| Miller, William | Givens, Sarah E. | 6, Dec. 1848 | RCH |
| Miller, William | Young, Mary Ann | 3, July 1849 | RCH |
| Millikin, Daniel | Osborne, Sarah Jane | 21, Feb. 1843 | RCH |
| Millman, Samuel | Frame, Ann | 4, Oct. 1835 | RCH |
| Mills, Aaron | Wilson, Mary Jane | 12, Sept 1843 | RCH |
| Mills, Abner | Dunham, Mary | 13, July 1835 | RCH |

| Grooms | Brides | Date of Marriage | Code |
|--------|--------|------------------|------|
| ****** | ****** | **** ** ******** | **** |
| Mills, Charles | Price, Elisabeth | 19, Mar. 1843 | RCH |
| Mills, David | Chamberlin, Jerusha | 17, Dec. 1845 | RCH |
| Mills, Henry | Stoup, Catharine | 31, Jan. 1822 | RCH |
| Mills, Hope | Armstrong, Rebecca | 31, Mar. 1844 | RCH |
| Mills, Horace | Palmerton, Diana | 8, Apr. 1833 | RCH |
| Mills, James | Mahoney, Elisabeth | 2, Feb. 1844 | RCH |
| Mills, Joseph | Sterges, Mary B. | 7, June 1843 | RCH |
| Mills, Martin S. | Matting, Julia | 22, Dec. 1831 | RCH |
| Mills, Noah | Beach, Hannah | 13, June 1849 | I |
| Mills, Peter | Doherty, Lucinda | 14, Feb. 1836 | RCH |
| Mills, Thaddeus | Logan, Harriet | 27, Nov. 1832 | RCH |
| Mills, Thomas J. | McCollum, Mary | 9, Jan. 1843 | RCH |
| Mills, Thornton | Gaulay, Hulda | 12, Sept 1837 | RCH |
| Mills, William | Yetter, Nancy P. | 25, Dec. 1833 | RCH |
| Millspaugh, Benjamin | Jones, Maria | 29, July 1819 | RCH |
| Millspaugh, Nathan. | Bodine, Susan | 4, Oct. 1823 | RCH |
| Millspaugh, William | Riggle, Sarah Jane | 29, Aug. 1844 | RCH |
| Milner, Jonathan | Wilsey, Lovina | 3, Feb. 1819 | RCH |
| Milton, Asa | ----, Mary | 17, Dec. 1824 | RCH |
| Mindermann, Albert | Junkle, Johanna A. | 26, Dec. 1849 | F |
| Miner, Henry | Gerard, Honora J. | 26, Oct. 1847 | RCH |
| Miner, John L. | Wright, Mary | 26, Oct. 1837 | I |
| Minester, Robert | McGregor, Elisabeth | 17, Sept 1839 | RCH |
| Minett, Julius | Thompson, Sarah | 15, July 1837 | I |
| Minister, George | Campbell, Hester A. | 24, Sept 1846 | RCH |
| Mink, Theodor H. | Albers, Clara | 4, Apr. 1837 | FF |
| Mink, Xistus | Afatter, Elisabeth | 16, Jan. 1849 | RCH |
| Minnekin, Manan | Arnold, Catharine | 29, July 1847 | RCH |
| Minniear, John | Bowman, Margaret | 20, Mar. 1847 | RCH |
| Minor, John D. | McLean, Mary B. | 26, Dec. 1843 | RCH |
| Minor, Robert | Thomson, Sophia | 16, Dec. 1844 | RCH |
| Minor, Thomas | Baldridge, Rebecca | 28, Nov. 1844 | RCH |
| Minsall, John | Don, Mary | 17, Dec. 1822 | RCH |
| Minshall, Robert | Payne, Mary Ann | 16, Dec. 1839 | RCH |
| Minshall, Thomas | Huffman, Amelia | 24, Feb. 1820 | RCH |
| Minster, Washington | Ravencraft, Ellen R. | 30, June 1833 | RCH |
| Mischet, J. Dietrich | Meyer, Catharina | 4, Oct. 1836 | FF |
| Mitchell, Austin | Smith, Sarah | 27, June 1847 | RCH |
| Mitchell, Cyrus | Gest, Mary A. | 3, Apr. 1838 | RCH |
| Mitchell, Francis | Seamon, Harriet | 31, Mar. 1847 | RCH |
| Mitchell, George W. | Hull, Eunice | 2, June 1833 | RCH |
| Mitchell, Jacob | Columbia, Susannah | 14, Aug. 1842 | RCH |
| Mitchell, James | Dawson, Sarah | 28, Sept 1836 | RCH |
| Mitchell, James | Hall, Mary Ann | 19, Dec. 1849 | RCH |
| Mitchell, John S. | Black, Nancy | 25, Oct. 1837 | RCH |
| Mitchell, Joseph | Mason, Sarah | 10, Sept 1845 | RCH |
| Mitchell, Micajah | Ward, Frances | 3, May 1846 | RCH |
| Mitchell, Thomas | Mullen, Mary | 31, Dec. 1848 | RCH |
| Mitchell, Thomas | Coffin, Martha E. | 15, Oct. 1846 | I |
| Mitchell, Thomas | Kearney, Catharine | 21, June 1847 | GG |
| Mitchell, William | Cook, Rebecca | 25, Apr. 1819 | RCH |
| Mitchell, William | Scott, Jane A. | 28, Mar. 1848 | RCH |
| Mitte, Henry | Elinghausen, Augusta | 24, Mar. 1844 | RCH |
| Mittendorf, Adam | Otting, Anna Engel | 11, Jan. 1844 | F |
| Mittendorf, Herman | Mess, Anna Margaret | 17, Nov. 1849 | EE |
| Mittendorp, Herman H | Niemann, Margaretha | 15, Oct. 1849 | F |
| Mittigan, Samuel | Mallott, Julia | 24, Oct. 1841 | RCH |
| Mix, Jairus | Snyder, Mourning | 20, Apr. 1847 | RCH |
| Mix, Joseph S. | Miller, Mary | 24, Jan. 1833 | RCH |
| Mix, William F. | Freeman, Ann | 6, Oct. 1833 | RCH |
| Moak, Philipp | Bowers, Susannah | 17, Mar. 1841 | RCH |
| Moake, Philipp | Nobles, Elisabeth | 21, Jan. 1836 | RCH |
| Moakey, John | Farrer, Isabella | 12, July 1834 | RCH |
| Mocheh, Jacob | Eckart, Catharine | 9, Aug. 1836 | RCH |
| Modlinger, Joseph | Heller, Adelia | 25, Apr. 1837 | FF |
| Moebus, William F. | Peene, Louise | 19, Aug. 1849 | G |
| Moedicker, Heinrich | Dumeier, Catharine | 20, Nov. 1848 | F |
| Moehle, Johan | Hole, Theresa | 10, Apr. 1849 | EE |
| Moehler, Johan | Trepp, Johanna | 27, Sept 1842 | FF |
| Moehlhop, Friedrich | Xavers, Adelheid | 17, May 1849 | RCH |
| Moehring, Friedrich | ----, ---- | 11, Feb. 1849 | A |

| Grooms<br>****** | Brides<br>****** | Date of Marriage<br>**** ** ******** | Code<br>**** |
|---|---|---|---|
| Moehringer, Heinrich | Hoffmann, Margaretha | 9, Apr. 1849 | EE |
| Moeller, Christian | Kruger, Wilhelmina | 10, Feb. 1846 | RCH |
| Moeller, Edward | Markt, Maria | 30, Apr. 1848 | FF |
| Moeller, Gerhard F. | Wichmann, Anna Clara | 14, Jan. 1847 | F |
| Moeller, Herman | Dunker, Gertrud | 21, June 1846 | AA |
| Moeller, J Friedrich | Rodering, Dorothea M | 14, Oct. 1847 | F |
| Moeller, Johan | Knauf, Dorothea | 24, July 1843 | G |
| Moeller, Mathias | Rolfer, Catharine | 15, Aug. 1848 | II |
| Moeller, Peter | Grefer, Elisabeth | 24, Mar. 1845 | AA |
| Moeller, Philipp | Tegeler, M Catharine | 3, Feb. 1846 | FF |
| Moeller, Theodor | VonderHaar, Gertrud | 25, Oct. 1846 | AA |
| Moellering, Heinrich | Arings, Maria E. | 18, Jan. 1844 | G |
| Moellmann, Bernard | Dirker, Margaretha | 6, June 1843 | AA |
| Moellmann, Herman H. | Juetten, Anna Maria | 17, Nov. 1840 | FF |
| Moellmann, Joseph | Holthaus, Elisabeth | 4, Sept 1849 | II |
| Moenig, Johan Heinr. | Finge, M. Catharina | 23, Apr. 1839 | FF |
| Moennig, Francis | Hessen, Louise | 10, Nov. 1844 | FF |
| Moenning, Gerhard H. | Mehring, Anna Maria | 20, Feb. 1844 | FF |
| Moenter, Gerhard H. | Hehmeyer, Elisabeth | 27, Dec. 1842 | F |
| Moenter, J Friedrich | Freyen, Elisabeth | 17, Apr. 1845 | F |
| Moerlein, Christian | Adam, Sophia | 10, Sept 1843 | C |
| Moerlein, Christian | Oeh, Barbara | 3, Aug. 1849 | C |
| Moerschel, Philipp | Schatt, Elisabeth | 10, Apr. 1848 | G |
| Moesch, Mathias | Steiert, Sophia | 26, Nov. 1846 | EE |
| Moesenmeier, Bernard | Ortmann, Angela | 22, Feb. 1848 | FF |
| Moesle, Jacob | Seeger, Christina | 13, May 1847 | C |
| Moessner, Anton | Romeissen, Friedrika | 6, Feb. 1846 | C |
| Mohan, George | Beatty, Amelia | 7, Mar. 1841 | BB |
| Mohlenbach, Philipp | Fischvogt, Sophia | 13, Feb. 1849 | B |
| Mohlenkamp, G. Fried | Stuckwisch, Anna M. | 9, Dec. 1847 | F |
| Mohlenkamp, J Christ | Hensch, Friedricka | 31, June 1845 | A |
| Mohlenkamp, Johan | Knapkenhowe, Cath. | 5, Nov. 1846 | F |
| Mohlenkamp, Johan C. | Noehler, Wilhelmina | 28, Sept 1848 | F |
| Mohling, Martin | McCann, Catharine | 16, Sept 1841 | G |
| Mohlmeyer, Friedrich | Kern, Johanna | 17, Oct. 1844 | A |
| Mohn, Christopher | Urban, Regina | 10, Sept 1844 | FF |
| Mohnlein, Caspar | Meyer, Eva Margaret | 2, July 1848 | EE |
| Mohr, Johan August | Macksum, Elisabeth | 9, Feb. 1839 | FF |
| Mohrhaus, J. Gerhard | Strubbe, A. Juliana | 24, Sept 1846 | F |
| Mohrhoff, Heinrich | Bueckers, Catharine | 12, Oct. 1843 | F |
| Molitor, Francis | Krapp, Anna Maria | 17, May 1849 | AA |
| Molleran, Joseph | Wessel, M. Gertrud | 8, Sept 1846 | FF |
| Mollmann, Anton | Speckbauch, Anna M. | 22, May 1845 | FF |
| Molloy, Daniel | Fitzsimmons, Mary | 16, Aug. 1847 | BB |
| Molloy, Daniel | Diamond, Hannah | 12, May 1849 | BB |
| Molloy, Hugh | Molloy, Honora | 21, Sept 1847 | BB |
| Molloy, John | Mitchell, Martha | 16, May 1847 | BB |
| Molloy, John | Molloy, Jane | 5, Sept 1847 | BB |
| Molloy, John | Corcoran, Mary | 7, Jan. 1849 | BB |
| Molloy, Peter | Tobin, Margaret | 27, Jan. 1844 | BB |
| Molloy, William | Cahill, Esther | 22, May 1839 | BB |
| Moloney, John | ----, Eleanor | 1, June 1835 | RCH |
| Molster, Cornelius | Finch, Sarah | Nov. 1844 | RCH |
| Molter, Jacob | Darr, Margaretha | 14, Aug. 1849 | C |
| Moltiz, Michael | Thompson, Elisabeth | 18, Sept 1838 | RCH |
| Monaghan, James | Borroughton, Mary | 12, Sept 1837 | RCH |
| Monahan, Lawrence | Mulvey, Elisabeth | 16, Aug. 1843 | BB |
| Monday, John | McDonald, Sarah Jane | 19, Mar. 1842 | RCH |
| Monday, Samuel | McBride, Polly | 26, Aug. 1819 | RCH |
| Mondmann, Bernard H. | Wilke, Maria Engel | 30, May 1843 | AA |
| Monfort, Henry | Featherling, Marcinn | 3, Apr. 1825 | RCH |
| Monfort, John | Parker, Elmira | 10, Sept 1834 | RCH |
| Monjan, Peter | McElroy, Margaret | 7, Feb. 1843 | RCH |
| Monk, Samuel | Case, Harriet R. | 1, Jan. 1847 | D |
| Monkhof, Christian F | Luebbers, Marg. Elis | 22, Oct. 1840 | F |
| Monkhoff, Christian | Willmer, Regina M.E. | 21, Mar. 1847 | F |
| Monliet, Peter | Nieder, Theresa | 5, June 1848 | EE |
| Monoghan, Lawrence | Gannon, Bridget | 8, Oct. 1849 | BB |
| Monroe, George | Randall, Elisabeth | 8, June 1846 | RCH |
| Monroe, John | Colvin, Martha | 19, July 1847 | RCH |
| Monroe, Joseph B. | Kennard, Sarah | 21, Sept 1848 | RCH |

| Grooms | Brides | Date of Marriage | Code |
|--------|--------|------------------|------|
| ****** | ****** | **** ** ******** | **** |
| Monroe, Nathan | Buxton, Jane | 20, May 1819 | RCH |
| Monroe, William | Reed, Ann Elisabeth | 1, Feb. 1838 | RCH |
| Monsch, Anton | Bermann, Maria | 2, Nov. 1835 | FF |
| Monson, | Loe, Fancy | 2, Jan. 1823 | RCH |
| Monson, Jacob | Meddock, Anna | 19, Dec. 1842 | RCH |
| Mont---, | Parving, Margaret | 30, Jan. 1838 | RCH |
| Montag, Johan Carl | Stadtmueller, Anna | 1, Feb. 1848 | EE |
| Montague, Thomas | Bacon, Sarah | 11, Dec. 1847 | RCH |
| Montfort, Lawrence | Harris, Martha | 11, May 1822 | RCH |
| Montfort, William | Conahan, Mary Ann | 7, Feb. 1847 | BB |
| Montforte, Peter | ----, ---- | 5, June 1835 | RCH |
| Montgomery, | Stewart, Elisabeth | 15, Nov. 1839 | RCH |
| Montgomery, James | Pickering, Ann | 18, June 1826 | RCH |
| Montgomery, John | Hardin, Martha | 10, Oct. 1845 | RCH |
| Montgomery, John C. | Bates, Mary Ann | 25, Apr. 1843 | RCH |
| Montgomery, Leland | ----, Mary | 9, Oct. 1837 | RCH |
| Montgomery, William | Pease, Abigail | 29, Oct. 1846 | RCH |
| Montsarral, David | Ruffin, Harriet | 29, May 1834 | I |
| Montz, Gottfried | Albers, Anna Maria | 4, Nov. 1849 | EE |
| Monyer, Jacob | Wood, Ann | 8, July 1839 | RCH |
| Moody, George | Bringhurst, Mary | 28, June 1842 | RCH |
| Moody, Samuel | Wigglesworth, Mary A | 8, Feb. 1844 | RCH |
| Moody, William | Morehead, Susan | 9, Apr. 1826 | RCH |
| Moody, William | Truss, Hannah | 17, Aug. 1845 | RCH |
| Mooers, Levi | Carver, Margaret | 26, Feb. 1835 | RCH |
| Mooh, John | White, Sarah | 13, Oct. 1825 | RCH |
| Mook, Jacob | Weaver, Mary Ann | 23, Mar. 1837 | RCH |
| Moon, Daniel | Kerr, Jane | 7, Mar. 1847 | RCH |
| Moonert, August | Seymour, Sarah | 6, Sept 1848 | I |
| Moonert, Charles | Plunket, Margaret | 29, July 1844 | BB |
| Mooney, Andrew | Roberts, Anna Maria | 2, Sept 1841 | RCH |
| Mooney, Michael | Fitzpatrick, Sarah | 18, Oct. 1848 | BB |
| Mooney, Thomas | Harding, Ann | 18, Feb. 1844 | BB |
| Moore, Abraham | Laroy, Elisabeth | 8, Sept 1833 | RCH |
| Moore, Adrion | Hood, Jane | 23, Mar. 1837 | RCH |
| Moore, Albert | Tredway, Amelia P. | 9, Sept 1839 | RCH |
| Moore, Asher | Balange, Elisabeth | 21, May 1846 | RCH |
| Moore, Benjamin | Charlton, Nancy | 24, Sept 1818 | RCH |
| Moore, Bernard | Shea, Honora | 8, Feb. 1846 | BB |
| Moore, Charles | Go---, Margaret | 31, Oct. 1822 | RCH |
| Moore, Charles L. | Rigor, Prudence | 29, Nov. 1840 | RCH |
| Moore, Christopher | Deppe, Catharine C. | 1, Dec. 1835 | RCH |
| Moore, Daniel | Leonard, Catharine | 29, Dec. 1845 | RCH |
| Moore, David | Scofield, Sarah Ann | 26, Aug. 1846 | RCH |
| Moore, Edward | Palmer, Sarah | 13, June 1849 | RCH |
| Moore, Ellis | Cattle, Martha | 22, Feb. 1833 | RCH |
| Moore, Ezekiel | Gaston, Anna C. | 6, Jan. 1820 | RCH |
| Moore, George | Shaw, Sarah J. | 29, June 1846 | RCH |
| Moore, George W. | Ferry, Sarah | 8, Feb. 1826 | RCH |
| Moore, George W. | Moore, Emily | 26, Jan. 1847 | RCH |
| Moore, Henry C. | McHugh, Mary | 20, Dec. 1849 | RCH |
| Moore, Henry F. | Cox, Mary | 22, Oct. 1833 | RCH |
| Moore, Henry H. | Swain, Emeline | 19, Sept 1848 | RCH |
| Moore, Hugh | Martin, Rosina | 7, Apr. 1825 | RCH |
| Moore, Hugh | Thompson, Isabella | 14, Mar. 1836 | RCH |
| Moore, Isaac | Gosney, Frances | 1, Dec. 1842 | RCH |
| Moore, James C. | Sutton, Sarah | 16, Aug. 1849 | RCH |
| Moore, John | Ferris, Rebecca | 24, Dec. 1820 | RCH |
| Moore, John | Langley, Mary | 22, Feb. 1838 | RCH |
| Moore, John | Taylor, Emeline | 5, Apr. 1842 | RCH |
| Moore, John | Moore, Elisabeth Ann | 15, May 1844 | RCH |
| Moore, John | Bussell, Catharine | 13, June 1849 | RCH |
| Moore, John E. | Young, Mary | 26, June 1836 | RCH |
| Moore, John F. | Wilson, Rebecca | 4, May 1848 | RCH |
| Moore, John R. | Boyd, Martha A. | 20, Feb. 1843 | RCH |
| Moore, John W. | McGilliard, Mary | 17, Nov. 1824 | RCH |
| Moore, Joseph | Jackson, Mary | 7, Mar. 1844 | RCH |
| Moore, Joseph | Cox, Elizabeth | 27, Nov. 1849 | RCH |
| Moore, Joseph M. | Palmer, Deborah | 23, Apr. 1835 | RCH |
| Moore, Lines | Jenkins, Phoebe Jane | 28, July 1839 | RCH |
| Moore, Michael | Slotham, Mary Jane | 6, May 1849 | RCH |

| Grooms | Brides | Date of Marriage | Code |
|--------|--------|------------------|------|
| ****** | ****** | **** ** ******** | **** |
| Moore, Morris | B---d, Mary | 21, Sept 1832 | RCH |
| Moore, Nathan | Kelley, Clarissa | 1, Sept 1818 | RCH |
| Moore, Patrick | Hughes, Ellen | 9, Oct. 1848 | RCH |
| Moore, Robert | Osborne, Harriet | 17, Nov. 1833 | RCH |
| Moore, Robert | Price, Ann Elisabeth | 1, May 1843 | RCH |
| Moore, Thomas | Hicks, Elisabeth | 9, Aug. 1849 | RCH |
| Moore, Thornton | Bird, Leona | 9, Nov. 1839 | RCH |
| Moore, Turner | Evans, Charlotte | 7, July 1836 | RCH |
| Moore, William | Band, Elisabeth | 9, Feb. 1824 | RCH |
| Moore, William | Winter, Ann | 22, Apr. 1824 | RCH |
| Moore, William | Gates, Mary A. | 28, Oct. 1838 | RCH |
| Moore, William | Irwin, Ann | 7, Aug. 1844 | RCH |
| Moore, William | Keys, Elizabeth Ann | 4, Aug. 1847 | RCH |
| Moore, William | Forbis, Elizabeth | 14, Oct. 1847 | RCH |
| Moore, William | McCluskey, Catharine | 4, Mar. 1848 | BB |
| Moore, William B. | Cobb, Elisabeth | 3, Apr. 1833 | RCH |
| Moore, William R. | Vanarsdale, Jane | 9, Apr. 1848 | RCH |
| Moores, Henry | Willis, Charlotte | 1, Nov. 1846 | RCH |
| Moores, Henry F. | Jenkins, Permelia | 9, July 1836 | RCH |
| Moores, John D. | Alston, Abigal | 5, Apr. 1818 | RCH |
| Moorhaus, Bernard | Zumbahlen, Elis. | 10, Jan. 1847 | AA |
| Moorhead, Peter | Tee, Susan | 9, June 1836 | RCH |
| Moorhead, Thomas | Bevis, Ann | 11, Oct. 1838 | RCH |
| Moorherm, Heinrich | Beck, Maria Adelheid | 15, Nov. 1846 | AA |
| Moormann, Bernard | Brune, Catharine | 6, Oct. 1846 | AA |
| Moormann, Bernard J. | Reneker, Catharina M | 9, Feb. 1846 | FF |
| Moormann, Christian | Scheinhorst, Doroth. | 25, Nov. 1847 | F |
| Moormann, Ernst | Weber, Phoebe | 29, Nov. 1849 | G |
| Moormann, Francis H. | Siemer, Lisette | 14, May 1848 | AA |
| Moormann, Gerhard | Winkeljohan, A. Elis | 4, Nov. 1849 | II |
| Moormann, Heinrich | Osterfeld, Elisabeth | 14, Aug. 1845 | AA |
| Moormann, Heinrich | Siefke, Catharine | 23, May 1847 | FF |
| Moormann, Herman H. | VonderHeide, A Cath. | 26, May 1835 | FF |
| Moormann, J. Bernard | Zimmer, M. Dorothea | 22, Aug. 1844 | FF |
| Moormann, J. Jacob | Dickmann, Gesina A. | 16, May 1848 | AA |
| Moormann, Joseph | Kitzeroh, Elisabeth | 21, July 1846 | AA |
| Moormann, Joseph | Egbers, Sophia | 6, Jan. 1848 | EE |
| Moormann, Theodor | Huelsmann, Catharina | 3, Sept 1848 | EE |
| Mooton, Jacob | Malnee, Elisabeth | 2, Aug. 1831 | RCH |
| Moran, Hugh | Sefton, Ann | 17, Aug. 1836 | RCH |
| Moran, John | Moore, Ellen | 11, June 1848 | BB |
| Moran, Michael | Brohan, Ellen | 7, June 1849 | BB |
| Moran, Patrick | Callahan, Bridget | 9, Dec. 1849 | BB |
| Moran, Thomas | Kays, Bridget | 24, Nov. 1849 | RCH |
| Morbach, Peter | Kiehl, Maria | 14, May 1848 | FF |
| Morbrink, Gerhard | Wellmann, Elisabeth | 30, Sept 1849 | II |
| More, John | Morrison, Levinda | 19, Sept 1832 | RCH |
| Morehead, Jonathan | Pratt, Julia | 28, Apr. 1841 | RCH |
| Morehead, Samuel | Lotton, Elisabeth | 25, Oct. 1835 | RCH |
| Morehouse, William | Rees, Mary Ann | 22, Mar. 1836 | RCH |
| Moreley, William | VanderBerg, Mary | 10, Mar. 1848 | RCH |
| Morey, John | Hall, Phile | 13, Oct. 1846 | RCH |
| Morffett, James | Hoffner, Elisabeth | 2, Mar. 1843 | RCH |
| Morford, Samuel | Marshall, Mary | 14, Aug. 1834 | RCH |
| Morgan, | Neville, Catharine | 23, June 1849 | RCH |
| Morgan, Andrew | Wright, Elisabeth | 18, Dec. 1847 | RCH |
| Morgan, Archibald | McCallister, Elinder | 19, May 1846 | RCH |
| Morgan, Daniel | Ewing, Elisabeth | 7, Nov. 1835 | RCH |
| Morgan, David | Snedley, Mary | 7, Nov. 1836 | RCH |
| Morgan, David | Mitchell, Emily | 7, Aug. 1848 | RCH |
| Morgan, David H. | Merrick, Elisabeth | 2, Oct. 1832 | RCH |
| Morgan, Edward | Smith, Elizabeth G. | 31, May 1847 | I |
| Morgan, George | Gosset, Sarah | 27, Jan. 1844 | RCH |
| Morgan, George | Jewitt, Sarah | 10, June 1849 | RCH |
| Morgan, Henry | Yeatman, Elizabeth | 27, Apr. 1843 | I |
| Morgan, Hugh | Smith, Ann | 14, May 1842 | RCH |
| Morgan, Isaac | Wood, Elisabeth F. | 13, Nov. 1817 | RCH |
| Morgan, Isaac | Brown, Lucinda | 8, Nov. 1841 | RCH |
| Morgan, Jacob | Nelson, Lucy | 14, Feb. 1844 | RCH |
| Morgan, John | Hazer---, Parthena | 3, Apr. 1821 | RCH |
| Morgan, John | ----, June A. | 22, Mar. 1823 | RCH |

| Grooms<br>****** | Brides<br>****** | Date of Marriage<br>**** ** ******** | Code<br>**** |
|---|---|---|---|
| Morgan, John | Hunn, Catharine | 9, Oct. 1842 | RCH |
| Morgan, John | Glenn, Elisabeth | 20, July 1843 | RCH |
| Morgan, John | Jones, Mary | 30, Oct. 1844 | RCH |
| Morgan, John | Harris, Lucinda | 26, Oct. 1848 | RCH |
| Morgan, John | Samuel, Elisabeth | 13, Apr. 1846 | I |
| Morgan, Joseph | Freeman, Sarah | 18, Sept 1841 | RCH |
| Morgan, Lewis | Wright, Sarah Ann | 9, July 1823 | RCH |
| Morgan, Nathaniel | Harrison, Amelia | 24, Sept 1835 | RCH |
| Morgan, Nelson | Williams, Mary Ann | 1, Jan. 1846 | RCH |
| Morgan, Patrick | Brennan, Ann | 4, Sept 1840 | BB |
| Morgan, Patrick | Brethet, Elisabeth | 29, May 1849 | BB |
| Morgan, Stephan | Griffith, Margaret | Apr. 1846 | I |
| Morgan, Thomas | Champion, Patsey | 9, Nov. 1824 | RCH |
| Morgan, Timothy | Johnson, Sarah | 23, Oct. 1839 | RCH |
| Morgan, Timothy | Griffith, Rachel | 11, Apr. 1846 | I |
| Morgan, William | Burns, Fanny | 24, Aug. 1848 | RCH |
| Morgan, William | Whallon, Caroline | 2, May 1849 | RCH |
| Morgans, Morgan | Daniel, Ann | 27, Apr. 1848 | RCH |
| Morgenroth, Heinrich | Wieghaus, Catharine | 13, Jan. 1846 | AA |
| Morgenroth, Simon | Steifel, Babette | 22, May 1849 | RCH |
| Morgenthal, Henry | Gugenheimer, Adel. | 4, Apr. 1849 | RCH |
| Morgenthaler, Heinr. | Huston, Carolina | 3, Nov. 1847 | A |
| Morgenthaler, Jacob | Traeger, Anna Maria | 10, June 1847 | A |
| Moriarty, Daniel | Sullivan, Mary | 1, Nov. 1845 | RCH |
| Moritz, Carl | Wiesmann, Sophia | 18, Feb. 1849 | CC |
| Moritz, Christoph | Heidkamp, Catharina | 26, Sept 1837 | FF |
| Moritz, Christoph | Wischmann, Christina | 31, Oct. 1847 | CC |
| Moritz, Christoph | Walters, M. Theresa | 24, Oct. 1846 | EE |
| Moritz, Godfried | Bextermann, Anna M. | 10, Jan. 1847 | EE |
| Moritz, Joseph M. | Debbi, Josephina | 26, Apr. 1836 | FF |
| Morman, Jacob | Beckmann, Maria | 27, Nov. 1847 | RCH |
| Moroney, Patrick | Kelly, Ellen | 6, June 1839 | BB |
| Morrell, Abraham | Ware, Anna Maria | 3, Dec. 1840 | RCH |
| Morrell, James C. | Johnston, A.R. | 10, Dec. 1823 | RCH |
| Morrell, Thomas | Beaty, Elisabeth | 18, Aug. 1849 | RCH |
| Morrill, | Knight, Nancy | 14, Nov. 1824 | RCH |
| Morris, Alexander | Apgar, Charity | 26, May 1847 | RCH |
| Morris, Benjamin | Dea, Belinda | 20, Sept 1837 | RCH |
| Morris, Calvin | Nickols, Achsah | 23, June 1842 | RCH |
| Morris, Edward | Jones, Jane | 7, Oct. 1830 | RCH |
| Morris, Edward | Bird, Margaret | 2, Dec. 1839 | RCH |
| Morris, Edward | Watson, Jane | 1, Feb. 1847 | BB |
| Morris, George | Batters, Nancy Ann | 18, Mar. 1844 | RCH |
| Morris, Henry C. | Hanter, Charlotte | 21, Oct. 1845 | RCH |
| Morris, Henry H. | Williams, Mickell | 20, Jan. 1836 | RCH |
| Morris, Jacob | Thomas, Caroline | 30, Sept 1835 | RCH |
| Morris, John | Thompson, Catharine | 24, Oct. 1839 | RCH |
| Morris, John | Beaman, Mary | 20, May 1847 | RCH |
| Morris, John J. | Hageman, Lucinda | 20, May 1835 | RCH |
| Morris, John M. | Wilson, Helen Ann | 6, Aug. 1848 | RCH |
| Morris, Joseph | Whipple, Harriet | 11, July 1844 | RCH |
| Morris, Morgan | Sloan, Mary | 5, Dec. 1841 | RCH |
| Morris, Phineas | Packer, Eunice | 8, Dec. 1845 | RCH |
| Morris, Samuel W. | Martin, Charlotte | 6, Mar. 1820 | RCH |
| Morris, Shelton | Barker, Catharine | 1, Mar. 1847 | RCH |
| Morris, Smith | Bowman, Hannah | 8, Feb. 1844 | RCH |
| Morris, Thomas | Harper, Ann E. | 2, May 1842 | RCH |
| Morris, Thomas | McQuinley, Mary | 19, Dec. 1848 | RCH |
| Morris, W.H. | Barke, Malissa | 18, Sept 1832 | RCH |
| Morris, Walthan | Moreland, Penance | 9, June 1839 | RCH |
| Morris, William | Baxter, Ann | 1, Sept 1846 | RCH |
| Morris, William H. | Ross, Charlotte | 8, Oct. 1833 | RCH |
| Morris, William R. | Powers, Lydia S. | 12, May 1823 | RCH |
| Morrison, Abram | McCord, Ellen M. | 2, June 1847 | RCH |
| Morrison, Andrew | Miller, Mary | 2, Mar. 1843 | RCH |
| Morrison, J. Warren | Tobin, Ann | 20, Oct. 1842 | BB |
| Morrison, James | Wheeler, Jane | 18, June 1844 | RCH |
| Morrison, James | Tully, Ellen | 20, Apr. 1846 | BB |
| Morrison, James B. | Jones, Nancy | 23, Dec. 1847 | RCH |
| Morrison, Lemuel | Cash, Mary M. | 21, Mar. 1849 | RCH |
| Morrison, Moses | Stump, Miriam | 22, Dec. 1842 | RCH |

| Grooms | Brides | Date of Marriage | Code |
|--------|--------|------------------|------|
| ****** | ****** | **** ** ******** | **** |
| Morrison, Thomas | Rutter, Elisabeth | 28, Mar. 1839 | RCH |
| Morrison, William | Burt, Anna Rebecca | 30, July 1846 | RCH |
| Morrow, Alexander | Lewis, Susannah | 21, Oct. 1842 | RCH |
| Morrow, Francis | Scott, Jane | 16, May 1836 | RCH |
| Morrow, Francis | Ballard, Mary | 16, July 1844 | RCH |
| Morrow, James | Belt, Sarah | 20, Sept 1832 | RCH |
| Morrow, John | Clark, Margaret | 14, Feb. 1833 | RCH |
| Morrow, Joseph | Brown, Sarah | 14, Feb. 1822 | RCH |
| Morrow, Thomas | Lee, Elisabeth | 21, June 1846 | RCH |
| Morse, Benjamin | Manley, Elisabeth | 5, Nov. 1843 | RCH |
| Morse, Charles | Hardie, Sarah | 27, Aug. 1846 | RCH |
| Morse, Charles C. | Thomas, Sarah R. | 11, Oct. 1838 | RCH |
| Morse, George W. | Hemphill, Mary | 15, Sept 1845 | RCH |
| Morse, Henry | Ryan, Phoebe | 28, Oct. 1820 | RCH |
| Morse, John | Swallow, Anna | 28, Oct. 1843 | RCH |
| Morse, Joseph | Teeany, Louise | 6, Jan. 1846 | RCH |
| Morse, Lewis | Brown, Elisabeth | 7, Oct. 1832 | RCH |
| Morse, Lewis | Sorter, Mary J. | 28, Dec. 1837 | RCH |
| Morse, Samuel | Silbermann, Babette | 2, Apr. 1849 | RCH |
| Morse, William | Opplender, Mary | Nov. 1844 | RCH |
| Morsell, James | Hankens, Martha L. | 31, Oct. 1848 | RCH |
| Morten, George | Booth, Mary | 23, Jan. 1846 | RCH |
| Morten, James L. | Drake, Isabella | 27, Oct. 1848 | RCH |
| Morten, John S. | Ramsdale, Charlotte | 23, Feb. 1837 | RCH |
| Mortimer, Joseph | McCormick, Elisabeth | 9, Mar. 1838 | RCH |
| Mortimer, Thomas | Pine, Elisabeth | 15, Sept 1847 | RCH |
| Morton, Aaron | Spencer, Mary | 6, Dec. 1843 | RCH |
| Morton, James | Grinton, Judy Ann | 17, Oct. 1848 | RCH |
| Morton, John | Jones, Caroline | 13, Dec. 1837 | RCH |
| Morton, Joseph | Boyd, Margaretha J. | 17, Aug. 1837 | RCH |
| Morton, Joseph A. | Ross, Jane | 24, Oct. 1833 | RCH |
| Morton, Thomas | Booth, Elisabeth | 10, Nov. 1847 | RCH |
| Morton, Wellington | Collins, Jane Ann | 25, Feb. 1841 | RCH |
| Morton, William | Garrett, Rhoda Jane | 3, Feb. 1843 | RCH |
| Morton, William | Henderson, M. Agnes | 31, Dec. 1846 | RCH |
| Morton, Zalmunna | Marshall, Mary | 24, Mar. 1824 | RCH |
| Mosby, Napoleon | Mosby, Ann | 11, Apr. 1844 | RCH |
| Mosch, Johan Herman | Bolmer, Anna Gertrud | 31, Oct. 1847 | EE |
| Moser, John | Kareth, Anna M. | 25, Nov. 1845 | RCH |
| Moses, Benjamin | ----, ---- | 13, Jan. 1836 | RCH |
| Moses, Morris | Johnson, Elisabeth | 29, Oct. 1845 | RCH |
| Moses, Morris | Oppenheim, Maria | 13, Oct. 1847 | RCH |
| Mosier, Cato | Robertson, Hetty | 5, 1822 | RCH |
| Mosley, James A. | Davis, Melinda | 3, Sept 1848 | RCH |
| Mosly, Nelson | Murphy, Elisabeth | 19, Nov. 1843 | RCH |
| Mosmuenster, Johan | Schleicher, Laura A. | 8, Nov. 1849 | G |
| Moss, Daniel | Coleman, Harriet | 10, Feb. 1833 | RCH |
| Moss, Gordon | Pettit, Lydia Ann | 7, June 1846 | RCH |
| Moss, Lewis | Smith, Martha | 1, Feb. 1849 | RCH |
| Moss, William | Vernon, Emily | 27, Sept 1842 | RCH |
| Moss, William | Strong, Mary | 22, Apr. 1844 | RCH |
| Mossett, August | Clemment, Rosetta | 5, July 1834 | RCH |
| Mossman, James | Lang, Elisabeth | 2, Jan. 1844 | RCH |
| Mostello, Michael | McAuley, Amanda | Apr. 1844 | RCH |
| Motherry, William | Morris, Ann | 12, Aug. 1834 | RCH |
| Motsch, Johan | Wuest, Elisabeth | 9, Nov. 1837 | FF |
| Mott, John | Dedrick, Catharine | 11, July 1833 | I |
| Mott, John E. | Yeaman, Anna E. | 3, Aug. 1848 | RCH |
| Mott, Sayres | Bassit, Sarah | 28, Nov. 1820 | RCH |
| Mott, William S. | Dill, Sarah | 12, Mar. 1834 | RCH |
| Motter, Michael | Houchard, Maria | 5, Jan. 1836 | FF |
| Motz, George | Dennison, Mary A. | 22, Apr. 1844 | RCH |
| Motz, Johan | Gerber, Agatha | 24, July 1843 | FF |
| Mougey, Desere | Clement, Felicitas | 1, Jan. 1838 | FF |
| Mould, Hiram | Lee, Rachel | 6, Sept 1836 | RCH |
| Mount, Henry | Fort, Julia Ann | 13, Nov. 1845 | RCH |
| Mount, James | Tenley, Catharine | 28, May 1846 | RCH |
| Mount, James G. | Gorman, Margaret | 29, May 1834 | RCH |
| Mount, Obadiah | Skillman, Gilly Ann | 7, Sept 1826 | RCH |
| Mount, Robert | Shepherd, Nancy | 4, Jan. 1844 | RCH |
| Movici, Thomas | Quigley, Mary | 6, Aug. 1849 | GG |

| Grooms<br>****** | Brides<br>****** | Date of Marriage<br>**** ** ******** | Code<br>**** |
|---|---|---|---|
| Mow---, Levi W. | Buckman, Sarah Ann | 19, Oct. 1826 | RCH |
| Mowrey, Elias H. | Wallace, J. | 20, May 1832 | RCH |
| Moyer, Philipp | Wood, Columbia | 27, June 1847 | RCH |
| Muchmore, Abner | Bennett, Mary | 5, Mar. 1835 | RCH |
| Muchmore, David | Jening--, Harriet | 30, Oct. 1819 | RCH |
| Muchmore, Eli | Ward, Agnes | 22, Oct. 1845 | RCH |
| Muchmore, Elias | Hetzler, Matilda | 21, Sept 1842 | RCH |
| Muchmore, Israel | Gerard, Elisabeth | 10, Oct. 1846 | RCH |
| Muchmore, John | Ferguson, Catharine | 1822 | RCH |
| Muchmore, Samuel | Connet, Jane | 11, Apr. 1822 | RCH |
| Muchmore, Stephen | Williams, Harriet | 17, Dec. 1843 | RCH |
| Muchmore, William | Stiles, Sarah | 29, Sept 1841 | RCH |
| Muckerheide, Heinric | Kalvelage, Elisabeth | 17, Jan. 1846 | AA |
| Muckerheide, Heinric | Korte, Elisabeth | 25, Sept 1849 | II |
| Muehel, Heinrich | Hahnhauser, Catharin | 24, Aug. 1843 | AA |
| Muehl, Andreas | Duttenhofer, Apolon. | 1, May 1843 | AA |
| Muehl, Edward | Strehley, Paulina | 9, Oct. 1841 | RCH |
| Muehle, Johan Fried. | Emphoff, Maria | 9, July 1846 | F |
| Muehlherr, Ottmar | Naegele, Carolina | 10, Dec. 1848 | EE |
| Mueller, Adam | Emmet, Catharine | 25, Apr. 1839 | FF |
| Mueller, Adam | Bender, Barbara | 24, Jan. 1846 | G |
| Mueller, Andreas | Flickinger, Anna M. | 3, Aug. 1847 | C |
| Mueller, Bernard | Witte, Maria Theresa | 20, Jan. 1849 | CC |
| Mueller, Bernard | Wallmann, Maria Elis | 15, Apr. 1847 | EE |
| Mueller, Carl | Korte, Christina | 26, Feb. 1848 | F |
| Mueller, Carl | Welkers, Johanna | 8, June 1848 | F |
| Mueller, Carl | Mueller, Franzisca | 31, Dec. 1846 | G |
| Mueller, Christian | Jaekle, Anna | 1, Apr. 1848 | A |
| Mueller, Christoph | Scheidemann, Emilia | 4, Mar. 1841 | F |
| Mueller, Christoph | Slick, Catharine | 4, July 1849 | RCH |
| Mueller, Conrad | Hock, Maria Anna | 11, Sept 1838 | FF |
| Mueller, Conrad | Meinhard, Catharine | 7, Mar. 1848 | CC |
| Mueller, Daniel | Germann, Donisa | 24, Apr. 1845 | G |
| Mueller, David | Thomin, Louise | 4, June 1845 | G |
| Mueller, Ferdinand | Zurwellen, Anna M. | 6, Apr. 1847 | G |
| Mueller, Francis | Ackermann, Catharina | 8, May 1838 | FF |
| Mueller, Frank | Neidemeier, Maria | 24, Sept 1845 | RCH |
| Mueller, Franz | Borgeding, Gertrud | 26, Oct. 1845 | AA |
| Mueller, Friedrich | Schlesinger, Barb. | 23, Sept 1845 | AA |
| Mueller, Georg | Kronister, Margaret | 28, Oct. 1844 | A |
| Mueller, Georg | Schulz, Anna Maria | 17, Oct. 1847 | CC |
| Mueller, Georg | Knopf, Anna | 28, Oct. 1849 | EE |
| Mueller, Heinrich | Knapke, Catharine | 23, Jan. 1849 | C |
| Mueller, Heinrich | Kunzle, Cath. Elis. | 23, Jan. 1849 | C |
| Mueller, Heinrich | Helmig, Elisabeth | 18, May 1847 | CC |
| Mueller, Heinrich | Ploess, Anna Gertrud | 7, Oct. 1849 | EE |
| Mueller, Jacob | Wirt, Elisabeth | 9, Apr. 1839 | G |
| Mueller, Jacob | Hulsmann, | Nov. 1844 | RCH |
| Mueller, Jacob Henry | Hines, Friedricka | 22, Sept 1846 | RCH |
| Mueller, Johan | Goettker, Anna Maria | 31, May 1838 | FF |
| Mueller, Johan | Hoffmann, Magdalena | 23, Aug. 1840 | F |
| Mueller, Johan | Goss, Maria | 9, May 1843 | AA |
| Mueller, Johan | Schaffer, Margaretha | 14, Feb. 1847 | EE |
| Mueller, Johan Geo. | Michel, Walburga | 29, Oct. 1848 | II |
| Mueller, Johan Adam | Steinmann, Johanna | 22, Apr. 1845 | AA |
| Mueller, Johan Bd. | Burlage, Maria Elis. | 10, Oct. 1848 | CC |
| Mueller, Johan Hein. | Mueller, Marilius | 17, June 1848 | A |
| Mueller, Johan Wm. | Steinkamp, M. Elis. | 21, July 1846 | AA |
| Mueller, John | Gindling, Maria | 11, Nov. 1844 | G |
| Mueller, Joseph | Wurst, Maria Magdal. | 22, Apr. 1844 | AA |
| Mueller, Joseph | Schmidt, Crescentia | 10, Apr. 1849 | AA |
| Mueller, Joseph | Auer, Maria Anna | 8, June 1847 | CC |
| Mueller, Joseph | Eisinger, Theresa | 17, Oct. 1847 | EE |
| Mueller, Lawrence | Hochwolt, Elisabeth | 18, Sept 1848 | EE |
| Mueller, Leonard | Bohr, Magdalena | 20, Nov. 1838 | FF |
| Mueller, Leonard | Fischer, Anna Maria | 25, June 1838 | FF |
| Mueller, Leonard | Schoenig, Catharine | 6, Nov. 1843 | AA |
| Mueller, Melchior | Wenzel, Anna Maria | 19, Sept 1847 | EE |
| Mueller, Nicholas | Bausen, Margaretha | 26, Dec. 1846 | G |
| Mueller, Peter | Schubert, Anna | 22, May 1843 | AA |
| Mueller, Peter | Frieker, Elisabeth | 21, Sept 1841 | FF |

| Grooms<br>****** | Brides<br>****** | Date of Marriage<br>**** ** ******** | Code<br>**** |
|---|---|---|---|
| Mueller, Philipp | Klein, Julia Ann | 6, Oct. 1845 | G |
| Mueller, Philipp | Reis, Elisabeth | 19, Sept 1848 | FF |
| Mueller, Sebastian | Remisch, Josephina | 29, Dec. 1849 | FF |
| Mueller, Seraphim | Schoenenberger, Fran | 14, Aug. 1837 | FF |
| Mueller, Theodor | Ordemann, Maria | 4, Sept 1846 | F |
| Mueller, Theodor | Feldcamp, Maria | 26, July 1846 | EE |
| Mueller, Wilhelm | Bender, Elisabeth | 24, July 1848 | C |
| Mueller, Wilhelm | Luetke, Theresa | 15, Apr. 1845 | AA |
| Mueller, Wilhelm H. | Sicks, Catharine | 17, June 1843 | C |
| Mueller, Wilhelm M. | Cawson, Maria Anna | 16, Apr. 1837 | FF |
| Mueller, William | Havekotte, Maria | 5, Oct. 1836 | F |
| Muench, Georg | Beyer, Crescens | 24, Oct. 1848 | G |
| Muench, Michael | Wagner, Maria Regina | 26, Apr. 1842 | FF |
| Mueters, Heinrich | Moeller, Maria | 25, Mar. 1847 | G |
| Mugel, Peter | Wayer, Maria | 22, Oct. 1845 | C |
| Muhle, Bernard | Korte, Catharine | 16, Jan. 1844 | FF |
| Muhlhauser, Ulrich | Muhlhauser, Christin | 1, May 1849 | C |
| Muhrmann, Johan | Boeshe, Anna | 25, Nov. 1842 | F |
| Muirhead, John | Williamson, Mary | 22, July 1821 | RCH |
| Mulalley, John | Connor, Sarah | 20, Oct. 1817 | RCH |
| Mulally, Cornelius | Cooke, Margaret | 15, Aug. 1849 | GG |
| Mulcahy, Dennis | Byron, Bridget | 3, June 1849 | GG |
| Muldore, John | Mason, Sarah | 30, Nov. 1837 | RCH |
| Mulfeather, William | Delahunt, Mary | 22, May 1845 | BB |
| Mulford, Daniel | Stootnee, Amelia | 25, May 1834 | RCH |
| Mulford, Howell | Riddle, Lucinda | 27, May 1844 | RCH |
| Mulford, John P. | Parvin, Ruth H. | 1, Jan. 1838 | RCH |
| Mulford, Richard | Davenport, Harriet | 17, July 1839 | RCH |
| Mulholland, William | Wever, Elisabeth | 14, Oct. 1837 | RCH |
| Mulholland, William | Hagerman, Maria L. | 11, Mar. 1844 | RCH |
| Mulholley, George | Jones, Jane | 7, Aug. 1842 | RCH |
| Mullally, John H. | Vincent, Nancy Jane | 2, Feb. 1843 | RCH |
| Mullally, Richard | Ludlum, Hannah | 10, Oct. 1848 | RCH |
| Mullaly, Joseph | Marshall, Elisabeth | 20, May 1838 | RCH |
| Mullane, James | Sullivan, Julia | 9, Jan. 1849 | BB |
| Mullen, Dominick | Ryan, Ellen | 11, Jan. 1849 | GG |
| Mullen, Ephraim | Meyers, Rhoda | 14, Oct. 1837 | RCH |
| Mullen, Hugh | Casey, Fanny | 31, July 1849 | BB |
| Mullen, Isaac | Parker, Mary | 23, July 1844 | RCH |
| Mullen, Isaac N. | Burdsall, Hannah E. | 19, Nov. 1835 | RCH |
| Mullen, James | Polser, | 3, Oct. 1826 | RCH |
| Mullen, James | Lucas, Mary Ann | 5, July 1838 | RCH |
| Mullen, James | Burton, Ann C. | 8, Jan. 1844 | BB |
| Mullen, James | Shinn, Margaret | 23, Aug. 1849 | RCH |
| Mullen, Johan B. | Aydelott, Mathilda | 22, Mar. 1849 | RCH |
| Mullen, John | Cummings, Rebecca | 1, Nov. 1848 | RCH |
| Mullen, Joseph | Bavis, Sarah Ann | 20, Sept 1835 | RCH |
| Mullen, Robert | Stout, Catharine | 14, June 1825 | RCH |
| Mullen, Simon | Hudley, Mary | 8, June 1849 | GG |
| Muller, Joseph L. | Kinyon, Hannah | 24, Mar. 1833 | RCH |
| Mulling, John | Strubble, | 28, Oct. 1823 | RCH |
| Mullrey, John | Heaton, Jane | 15, Mar. 1838 | RCH |
| Mulrain, Francis | Anderson, Charlotte | 10, Feb. 1849 | RCH |
| Mulsbery, Jacob | Conrey, Lucinda | 3, Mar. 1836 | RCH |
| Mulsbury, Joel | Snider, Sanderson | 25, Oct. 1838 | RCH |
| Mulvey, Michael | Reagan, Mary Ann | 3, Feb. 1845 | BB |
| Mulvihill, William | Lynch, Bridget | 14, Oct. 1849 | GG |
| Mund, Conrad | Housefield, Catharin | 20, Jan. 1847 | RCH |
| Munday, Gilbert | Knox, Clarissa | 28, Nov. 1846 | RCH |
| Munday, William | Holcomb, Lorena | 29, Apr. 1847 | RCH |
| Mundell, John | Mundell, Catharine | 8, Oct. 1842 | RCH |
| Mundell, William | Butler, Martha | 30, Mar. 1845 | RCH |
| Mundi, Conrad | Grieble, Ottilia | 25, July 1842 | FF |
| Mundie, Patrick | House, Margaret | 9, Feb. 1823 | RCH |
| Mundory, Jeremiah | Liverpool, Dorcus | 2, Jan. 1834 | RCH |
| Mundy, Freeman | Lockman, Martha | 10, Oct. 1833 | RCH |
| Mundy, John | McGinley, Elisabeth | 7, Jan. 1847 | BB |
| Munford, Manly | Miller, Elis. Jane | 12, May 1834 | RCH |
| Mungall, John | Goddin, Anna | 2, Feb. 1846 | RCH |
| Munn, Thomas | Quick, Jane | 4, Apr. 1833 | RCH |
| Munrath, Philipp | Young, Magdalena | 16, Dec. 1843 | RCH |

| Grooms<br>****** | Brides<br>****** | Date of Marriage<br>**** ** ******** | Code<br>**** |
|---|---|---|---|
| Munroe, John R. | Sheldon, Rhoda | 11, Sept 1833 | RCH |
| Munsell, Henry | Mussett, Rosannah | 20, Dec. 1835 | RCH |
| Munson, Henry | Glackin, Adelphina | 14, June 1838 | RCH |
| Munson, Rodick | Shaw, Ann | 10, Nov. 1825 | RCH |
| Munson, Samuel B. | Sellew, Hannah | 27, Apr. 1838 | RCH |
| Muntel, Johan Hein. | Brinkhaus, Maria A. | 14, May 1848 | AA |
| Muntzenberger, Conr. | Rahke, Elisabeth | 18, May 1845 | G |
| Muny, Luke | Hewson, Elisabeth | 22, Nov. 1843 | RCH |
| Murdock, Charles | Wallace, Amanda | 27, Dec. 1843 | RCH |
| Murdock, Joseph | Fanning, Margaret | 10, Jan. 1849 | BB |
| Murgar, William | Flesh, Mary | 18, May 1820 | RCH |
| Murley, John | Morrigan, Mary | 15, May 1844 | BB |
| Murnahan, James | Clark, Diana | 14, Apr. 1846 | RCH |
| Murphy, Anthony | McCormack, Ann | 16, Oct. 1849 | BB |
| Murphy, Archibald | McCane, | 30, Jan. 1825 | RCH |
| Murphy, Cornelius | Donovan, Mary | 5, Oct. 1843 | BB |
| Murphy, Daniel | Finnerty, Ellen | 28, Nov. 1848 | BB |
| Murphy, Edward | Mahoney, Nora | 28, Feb. 1843 | BB |
| Murphy, Edward | Cummings, Catharine | 31, Oct. 1848 | BB |
| Murphy, Isaiah | Bradgley, Elisabeth | 1, Nov. 1847 | RCH |
| Murphy, Jacob | Martin, Emily | 26, Apr. 1823 | RCH |
| Murphy, James | Parent, Mary | 3, Dec. 1818 | RCH |
| Murphy, James | Boyle, Catharine | 14, Sept 1839 | RCH |
| Murphy, James | Roache, Ann | 9, May 1841 | BB |
| Murphy, James | Taylor, Jane | 11, Feb. 1849 | BB |
| Murphy, James | Taylor, Jane | 11, Feb. 1849 | BB |
| Murphy, James | Conlin, Margaret | 10, Sept 1848 | GG |
| Murphy, James M. | Davis, Elmira | 29, June 1843 | RCH |
| Murphy, John | Vincent, Louisa | 19, Mar. 1824 | RCH |
| Murphy, John | Stuart, Margaret | 30, June 1842 | RCH |
| Murphy, John D. | Clark, Emily Ann | 12, Jan. 1843 | RCH |
| Murphy, Michael | Conlon, Bridget | 9, Feb. 1841 | BB |
| Murphy, Michael | Desmond, Margaret | 30, Jan. 1842 | BB |
| Murphy, Michael | Ryan, Mary | 4, June 1848 | BB |
| Murphy, Michael | McCarter, Alice | 9, Aug. 1849 | BB |
| Murphy, Michael | Pugh, Mary (Mrs) | 14, Jan. 1849 | BB |
| Murphy, Michael | Foy, Mary | 28, Oct. 1849 | GG |
| Murphy, Myles | Carey, Catharine | 8, Jan. 1838 | RCH |
| Murphy, Patrick | Cole, Elisabeth | 12, June 1849 | RCH |
| Murphy, Patrick | McAntee, Sarah | 6, Feb. 1848 | GG |
| Murphy, Richard G. | Hedding, Elisabeth | 30, May 1832 | RCH |
| Murphy, Thomas | Edwards, Susan J. | 15, Dec. 1837 | RCH |
| Murphy, Thomas | Shaley, Elisabeth | 16, Aug. 1848 | BB |
| Murphy, William | Miller, Ann | 8, Dec. 1825 | RCH |
| Murphy, William | Mollenny, Elisabeth | 20, Dec. 1841 | RCH |
| Murray, Henry | McGilligan, Bridget | 12, Aug. 1847 | RCH |
| Murray, James | Murdock, Mary Ann | 7, May 1836 | RCH |
| Murray, James | Maddox, Mary Ann | 2, Aug. 1847 | RCH |
| Murray, James H. | Castner, Margaret | 5, Dec. 1847 | BB |
| Murray, James W. | Demmitt, Amanda | 24, Dec. 1848 | RCH |
| Murray, John | Fitzsimmons, Mary | 11, Aug. 1841 | BB |
| Murray, John | Wiley, Rose | 9, Aug. 1849 | RCH |
| Murray, John | Keeler, Mary | 17, Dec. 1849 | RCH |
| Murray, Patrick | Griffiin, Elisabeth | 14, July 1844 | RCH |
| Murray, Patrick | Kelly, Elizabeth | 28, June 1848 | GG |
| Murray, Thomas | Levet, Harriet | 13, June 1838 | RCH |
| Murray, Thomas | Brannan, Catharine | 12, Mar. 1849 | GG |
| Murtaugh, Patrick | Kavey, Margaret | 21, June 1839 | BB |
| Muscroft, George | Thomas, Christina | 15, Feb. 1836 | RCH |
| Musgrave, Hiram | Dougherty, Maria P. | 11, Jan. 1848 | RCH |
| Mushaben, Anton | Kloegfel, Maria Anna | 15, July 1844 | RCH |
| Mushaben, Anton | Zifle, Maria | 28, July 1844 | AA |
| Musser, Jacob | Shippen, Martha Ann | 5, Oct. 1835 | RCH |
| Mussing, Joseph | Affing, Adelheid | 4, July 1847 | AA |
| Mussler, Adrian | Gerth, Rosina | 18, Apr. 1844 | AA |
| Mussmann, Joseph P. | Stilling, Maria Adel | 10, Sept 1848 | EE |
| Mustard, Alexander | Gaither, Sophia | 14, Dec. 1843 | RCH |
| Muster, Samson C. | Garbet, Rebecca | 27, Dec. 1832 | RCH |
| Mustofsky, Simon | Hicks, Hannah | 8, Jan. 1833 | RCH |
| Musurole, Alexander | Stewart, Sarah A. | 30, July 1835 | RCH |
| Muth, August | Eitelgeorge, Carolin | 26, Nov. 1836 | F |

| Grooms<br>****** | Brides<br>****** | Date of Marriage<br>**** ** ******** | Code<br>**** |
|---|---|---|---|
| Muthert, Christian | Rehme, Maria | 8, June 1843 | G |
| Muthert, Gerhard Wm. | Kruse, Jane | 10, July 1845 | F |
| Mutzler, Adam | Weber, Catharine | 13, Jan. 1844 | AA |
| Myers, | Smith, Mary | 1, Nov. 1821 | RCH |
| Myers, Andrew | King, Emeline | 25, Dec. 1823 | RCH |
| Myers, Daniel | Simmonds, Elisabeth | 30, Aug. 1818 | RCH |
| Myers, Elkanah | Owens, Mary Jane | 4, July 1849 | RCH |
| Myers, Erastus | Redinbo, Charlotte | 28, Feb. 1846 | RCH |
| Myers, Freedom | Grant, Elisabeth | 3, Mar. 1842 | RCH |
| Myers, Gideon | Phillips, Matilda | 25, Apr. 1849 | RCH |
| Myers, Henry Lewis | Tressel, Sarah Mary | 10, Aug. 1823 | I |
| Myers, Isaac | Cole, Rachel | 25, Dec. 1841 | RCH |
| Myers, Isaac | Graham, Jane | 8, Jan. 1846 | RCH |
| Myers, Jacob | Buler, Ann | 23, Feb. 1822 | RCH |
| Myers, Joel | Roll, Lydia | 15, Dec. 1825 | RCH |
| Myers, John | Davis, Elisabeth | 13, Feb. 1846 | RCH |
| Myers, John | Hetzel, Hannah | 20, Dec. 1849 | RCH |
| Myers, Jonathan | Clarke, Dean-- | 7, Nov. 1824 | RCH |
| Myers, Joseph V. | Hatt, Margaret | 13, July 1848 | D |
| Myers, Levi | Morton, Rebecca | 11, Mar. 1835 | RCH |
| Myers, Robert | Runyan, Elisabeth | 29, Mar. 1846 | RCH |
| Myers, Samuel | ----, ---- | 11, Mar. 1819 | RCH |
| Myers, Theophilus | Garrett, Elisabeth | 14, Feb. 1843 | RCH |
| Myers, Thomas | Wolf, Nancy | 10, Oct. 1832 | RCH |
| Myres, Andrew | Crossan, Jane | 12, Nov. 1834 | RCH |
| Myres, Cornelius | Graham, Sarah | 23, Jan. 1834 | RCH |
| Myres, John | Brooks, | 15, Oct. 1820 | RCH |
| Myrick, Thomas | Fight, Catharine | 3, July 1843 | RCH |
| | | | |
| Nabe, Herman Heinric | Egleas, Anna Maria | 27, Feb. 1847 | RCH |
| Naber, Clement | Hundepohl, Anna M. | 15, Feb. 1843 | AA |
| Naber, Gerhard H. | Wellmann, Catharine | 20, June 1844 | AA |
| Naber, Herman | Haverkamp, Maria | 20, Nov. 1838 | FF |
| Naber, Johan Gerhard | Ruhls, Josephine | 16, Apr. 1844 | AA |
| Nabers, Bernard E. | Otte, Maria Catharin | 28, Jan. 1845 | AA |
| Nachen, Johan | Bennert, Margaretha | 12, Oct. 1848 | C |
| Naegel, Johan | Feck, Catharina | 21, May 1848 | AA |
| Naegele, Fidel | Schege--, Karolina | 30, Oct. 1847 | RCH |
| Naegele, Fidel | Schmidt, Maria | 27, Feb. 1848 | FF |
| Nagel, Georg | Gegner, Charlotte | 6, May 1849 | C |
| Nageleisen, Fidel | Schueler, Rosa | 4, Apr. 1848 | AA |
| Naighinger, Friedric | Long, Christina | 20, Apr. 1837 | RCH |
| Nailon, Thomas | Costello, Catharine | 23, Oct. 1843 | BB |
| Nalton, Thomas | Ath, Charlotte | May 1839 | RCH |
| Nann, Bernard | Lipps, Caroline | 9, Nov. 1846 | FF |
| Nann, Johan N. | Ort, Maria Anna | 14, Nov. 1842 | FF |
| Napoleon, Louis | Jackson, Sarah | 9, Oct. 1843 | RCH |
| Nash, Benjamin | Roosa, Julia Ann | 28, Mar. 1839 | RCH |
| Nash, David S. | Sweeney, Dorcus | 21, Mar. 1848 | RCH |
| Nash, John | ----, ---- | 22, Sept 1825 | RCH |
| Nash, Sheldon H. | Gaines, Mary Ann | 20, Sept 1832 | RCH |
| Nast, Gottlob | Kettner, Jeanette | 12, Nov. 1845 | RCH |
| Nast, William | McDowell, Elisabeth | 1, Aug. 1836 | RCH |
| Nathorst, John | Ross, Charlotte | 9, Apr. 1844 | RCH |
| Nau, Joseph | Enne, Elphie | 19, Oct. 1848 | RCH |
| Naumann, Georg | Gasser, Albina | 10, Apr. 1849 | DD |
| Nayler, Elmore | Ellis, Lucina | 8, Nov. 1847 | RCH |
| Naylor, Elmer | Ellis, Ruth | 26, Feb. 1848 | RCH |
| Naylor, John E. | Wilson, Rachel | 23, Jan. 1833 | RCH |
| Naylor, William | Ryan, Rebecca | 22, May 1825 | RCH |
| Naylor, William | Anderson, Isabella | 16, July 1837 | RCH |
| Naylor, William B. | Kinney, Ann | 2, Jan. 1833 | RCH |
| Neal, William | Vincent, Elisabeth | 8, Apr. 1844 | RCH |
| Nealeaus, Andrew | Cook, Catharine | 13, May 1846 | RCH |
| Neamon, John | Dodd, Elisabeth C. | 26, Sept 1839 | RCH |
| Nearre, Amos | Wiath, Lydia | 6, Oct. 1835 | RCH |
| Neas, James | Jeffers, Martha | 23, Sept 1844 | RCH |
| Neaves, Hezekiah | Keys, Rebecca | 30, Nov. 1845 | RCH |
| Neavs, William | Ward, Sarah Jane | 10, Sept 1846 | RCH |
| Nebel, William | Getzendanner, Esther | Feb. 1839 | RCH |
| Neblett, George | Murphy, Margaret | 23, Dec. 1848 | RCH |

| Grooms<br>****** | Brides<br>****** | Date of Marriage<br>**** ** ******** | Code<br>**** |
|---|---|---|---|
| Neblett, James | Feckley, Catharine | 21, July 1844 | RCH |
| Neckermann, Michael | Brand, Juliana | 14, Nov. 1846 | RCH |
| Neddermann, G Albert | Scholling, Adelheid | 17, Dec. 1843 | F |
| Neeley, John | Broadwell, Melvina | 30, Apr. 1844 | RCH |
| Neely, James | Frilliner, Catharine | 21, Jan. 1843 | RCH |
| Neff, Jacob | Dietrich, Maria(Mrs) | 9, Aug. 1842 | FF |
| Neff, William | ----, Elisabeth | 20, Mar. 1822 | RCH |
| Neff, William | Williams, Narcissa | 14, Dec. 1846 | RCH |
| Nehus, Heinrich | Meyer, Josephina | 26, Apr. 1849 | AA |
| Neibert, Georg | Reise, Margaretha | 18, July 1848 | C |
| Neidel, Johan Georg | Hartmann, Margaretha | 22, Aug. 1843 | C |
| Neidhart, Valentin | Vollmann, Maria | 22, Nov. 1846 | EE |
| Neidig, Michael | Kohl, Elisabeth | 5, Sept 1843 | C |
| Neighbors, Samuel | Gordon, Elisabeth | 2, Nov. 1848 | RCH |
| Neighbours, James | Hopkins, Caroline | 28, Aug. 1825 | RCH |
| Neighbours, William | Malney, Mary Ann | 15, Oct. 1846 | RCH |
| Neihring, Heinrich | Schulte, Anna M. | 3, Oct. 1847 | AA |
| Neili, John | Bugner, Barbara | 22, Aug. 1841 | RCH |
| Neinaeger, Friedrich | Rose, Catharina | 1, Feb. 1849 | G |
| Neisbaum, Juta | Wolfe, Josephine | 24, Mar. 1842 | RCH |
| Neizer, John | Allen, Elisabeth | 23, Feb. 1824 | RCH |
| Nell, John | Bradford, Jane | 7, Dec. 1823 | RCH |
| Neller, Conrad | Kuhn, Maria | 25, June 1848 | FF |
| Nelsen, Anton | Desch, Maria | 28, Nov. 1844 | AA |
| Nelson, Clark | Carrigan, Anna Jane | 16, Aug. 1836 | RCH |
| Nelson, Edwin | Smith, Polly | 18, Feb. 1838 | RCH |
| Nelson, Francis | Tice, Dorothea | 15, June 1839 | RCH |
| Nelson, George | Petterson, Martha | 3, Dec. 1848 | RCH |
| Nelson, James | Walker, Rosannah | 27, Apr. 1849 | RCH |
| Nelson, James A. | Kemper, Judith | 7, Oct. 1836 | RCH |
| Nelson, John Joseph | Pinger, Mary | 26, Oct. 1843 | RCH |
| Nelson, Joseph S. | Bowman, Nancy | 29, Sept 1823 | RCH |
| Nelson, Levi F. | Grad---, Sarah | 3, Oct. 1824 | RCH |
| Nelson, Robert | Connely, Bridget | 18, Sept 1819 | RCH |
| Nelson, William | Strenhover, Martha | 29, Aug. 1838 | RCH |
| Nelson, William | Horton, Mary | 31, Dec. 1843 | RCH |
| Nelson, William G. | Sand, Elisabeth | 9, Dec. 1837 | RCH |
| Nemeier, Herman H. | Palberg, Wilhelmina | 3, Oct. 1848 | II |
| Nemire, | Copeland, Lovena | 14, Feb. 1839 | RCH |
| Nendel, Kasper | Fleckenstein, Susana | 15, Nov. 1843 | AA |
| Nentrup, Heinrich | Besuden, Margaretha | 10, Apr. 1845 | F |
| Nerger, Edward | Serg, Lydia | 2, Oct. 1832 | RCH |
| Nerney, John | Jones, Elisabeth | 24, May 1834 | RCH |
| Nesmith, James | Wright, Harriet | 29, Jan. 1826 | RCH |
| Nesney, John | Horman, Lucinda | 8, July 1832 | RCH |
| Ness, John | Whalon, Lydia | 8, Apr. 1841 | RCH |
| Netter, Johan | Siefert, Maria Anna | 7, June 1848 | EE |
| Netterfield, William | Williams, Harriet | 21, June 1849 | RCH |
| Neubauer, Georg | Bengler, Barbara | 31, May 1847 | EE |
| Neubauer, Jacob | Krebs, Elisabeth | 25, Nov. 1841 | FF |
| Neuber, Simon | Kapl, Maria Theresa | 10, Feb. 1846 | EE |
| Neuckam, Conrad | Ceprer, Johanna | 16, May 1842 | RCH |
| Neuer, Daniel | Klein, Lucy | 20, July 1844 | RCH |
| Neuhaus, Anton | Felken, A. Catharine | 7, Feb. 1846 | RCH |
| Neuhaus, Bernard H. | Bruns, Elisabeth | 13, May 1845 | G |
| Neuhaus, Heinrich | Schroeder, M Angela | 19, Nov. 1835 | FF |
| Neuhaus, J. Bernard | Sanders, Elisabeth | 24, Apr. 1838 | FF |
| Neuhaus, Philipp | Oliger, Barbara | 18, Sept 1838 | FF |
| Neuheufer, Jacob | Treymann, Ernestina | 6, July 1847 | EE |
| Neukam, Johan | Schmidt, Margaretha | 10, Nov. 1844 | C |
| Neukam, John | Pope, Margaret | 11, Feb. 1844 | RCH |
| Neumann, August | Wilhelmi, Francisca | 26, Sept 1848 | B |
| Neumann, Johan Bapt. | Haarmeyer, Maria Ann | 3, Nov. 1841 | FF |
| Neumann, Johan Bd. | Traesenberg, Elis. | 12, Feb. 1839 | FF |
| Nevers, Elijah | Cox, Elisabeth | 2, Nov. 1847 | RCH |
| Neves, John | ----, Elisabeth | 25, Oct. 1838 | RCH |
| Neville, Ira | Williams, Mary J. | 16, June 1846 | RCH |
| Neville, Morgan | Dennison, Caroline | 17, Nov. 1840 | RCH |
| Neville, William | Taylor, Anna Elis. | 5, Jan. 1847 | RCH |
| Nevitt, W.F. | Mathews, Johanna | 15, Mar. 1848 | RCH |
| Newal, Jefferson | Newal, Mary Elis. | 24, Jan. 1837 | RCH |

| Grooms | Brides | Date of Marriage | Code |
|--------|--------|------------------|------|
| ****** | ****** | **** ** ******** | **** |
| Newal, William T. | Hoel, Euphemia | 6, Mar. 1834 | RCH |
| Newall, William | Charters, Jane | 2, Sept 1837 | RCH |
| Newberger, Jacob | Wise, Gottam | 17, Jan. 1843 | RCH |
| Newberry, William O. | Putnam, Clarinda | 14, Feb. 1833 | RCH |
| Newcomb, Henry | Applegate, Matilda | 13, June 1837 | RCH |
| Newcomb, John | Shield, Julia M. | 9, Jan. 1846 | RCH |
| Newcomer, Jacob | Clark, Nancy | 12, Feb. 1820 | RCH |
| Newel, Daniel | Carters, Mary | 9, Oct. 1834 | RCH |
| Newell, Alfred | McClure, Susan | 30, Aug. 1845 | RCH |
| Newell, James | Attenborough, Elis. | 5, Apr. 1842 | RCH |
| Newell, Stephen W. | Vance, Mary | 26, Apr. 1844 | RCH |
| Newell, William | Nappin, Elisabeth | 17, Aug. 1820 | RCH |
| Newgass, Henry | Bailey, Mary | 31, May 1836 | RCH |
| Newhouse, Henry | Ezekiel, Matilda | 2, July 1844 | RCH |
| Newhouse, Joseph | Werberink, Elisabeth | 18, Oct. 1842 | RCH |
| Newkirk, Cornelius S | Lackey, Mary | 11, Dec. 1823 | RCH |
| Newkirk, George W. | Halstead, Abigail | 3, Jan. 1847 | RCH |
| Newkirk, Matthew | St.Clair, Nancy | 2, Mar. 1837 | RCH |
| Newman, Abner | Abergust, Elisabeth | 14, Mar. 1822 | RCH |
| Newman, Daniel | Stilt, Maria | 1, July 1838 | RCH |
| Newman, Eli | Bently, Lusand | 9, Sept 1832 | RCH |
| Newman, Gideon | Wardall, Elisabeth | 19, Nov. 1848 | RCH |
| Newman, Henry | Hayman, Mary | 26, Jan. 1844 | RCH |
| Newman, Jerome | Stillwell, Catharine | 23, Mar. 1848 | RCH |
| Newman, John | Duvell, Elisabeth A. | 27, Dec. 1847 | RCH |
| Newman, Reloyd | Lilly, Rebecca | 6, Apr. 1843 | RCH |
| Newman, Reuben | Harris, Frances | 19, July 1842 | RCH |
| Newman, Reuben | Cooper, Caroline | 19, Dec. 1845 | RCH |
| Newman, Solomon | Hyner, Susan | 13, Mar. 1834 | RCH |
| Newman, William | Benton, Elisabeth | 4, Dec. 1843 | RCH |
| Newman, William | Brown, Nancy | 7, Aug. 1844 | RCH |
| Newmann, Joseph | Simon, Mary Ann | 22, Sept 1847 | RCH |
| Newmeist, John | Gattsurr, Taraty | 25, Dec. 1841 | RCH |
| Newson, Edward | Cruit, Sarah | 9, July 1844 | RCH |
| Newson, Edward | Fisher, Keziah | 8, Dec. 1849 | RCH |
| Newson, John | Myers, Mary | 12, Nov. 1842 | RCH |
| Newson, Thomas | Hays, Frances | 3, Apr. 1843 | RCH |
| Newton, Bazel | Man, Nancy | 25, Dec. 1825 | RCH |
| Newton, Calvin | Wilson, Sarah | 24, Dec. 1823 | RCH |
| Newton, David | Merrell, Roby | 1, June 1843 | RCH |
| Newton, Henry | Brown, Maria | 11, Nov. 1841 | RCH |
| Newton, Isaac | Strops, Sereda | 3, Jan. 1834 | RCH |
| Newton, John | Stogdon, Elisabeth | 26, Feb. 1844 | RCH |
| Newton, John C. | Connor, Hannah | 7, July 1833 | RCH |
| Newton, Nelson | Armistead, Maria | 9, Feb. 1844 | RCH |
| Newton, Thomas | Miranda, Angela | 18, Apr. 1833 | RCH |
| Neyer, Johan Gerhard | Fasse, Elisabeth | 2, Feb. 1845 | AA |
| Niblick, Alexander | Lane, Ann | 6, July 1844 | RCH |
| Nicel, Francis | Bittner, Anna Maria | 7, Jan. 1849 | EE |
| Niceway, Henry | Brown, Rebecca | 10, Mar. 1844 | RCH |
| Nichles, Friedrich | Fries, Barbara | 12, Apr. 1847 | EE |
| Nichol, Johan | Buttern, Anna M. | 6, Nov. 1838 | FF |
| Nicholls, Samuel | Atlee, Elisabeth J. | 22, Feb. 1841 | D |
| Nichols, David C. | Crooke, Mary W. | 26, Nov. 1824 | RCH |
| Nichols, James | Jones, Susan | 12, Apr. 1820 | RCH |
| Nichols, Joseph | Thompson, Martha | 17, Sept 1843 | RCH |
| Nichols, Larkin | Hays, Mary | 2, Jan. 1844 | RCH |
| Nichols, Luther | Whittaker, Anna | 30, June 1846 | RCH |
| Nichols, Samuel | Wayman, Charlotte | 4, July 1818 | RCH |
| Nichols, Vesper | Brown, Eunice | 18, Aug. 1832 | RCH |
| Nichols, Vesper | Robinson, Sally | 24, July 1836 | RCH |
| Nichols, Vesper | Harris, Phebe | 12, Oct. 1843 | RCH |
| Nicholson, Daniel | Costigan, Catharine | 26, May 1842 | BB |
| Nicholson, John | Thompson, Mary | 11, Mar. 1819 | RCH |
| Nicholson, William | Maher, Bridget | 12, Jan. 1848 | I |
| Nickal, James | Rutherford, Frances | 21, Apr. 1822 | RCH |
| Nickens, T.B. | Stewart, Elisabeth | 4, Jan. 1837 | RCH |
| Nickerson, Charles | DeGray, Ellen | 4, July 1848 | RCH |
| Nickerson, Uriah | Kelly, Elisabeth | 28, Dec. 1821 | RCH |
| Nickles, Friedrich | Frees, Barbara | 12, Apr. 1847 | RCH |
| Nickol, Xavier | Peter, Anna Maria | 15, May 1847 | RCH |

| Grooms<br>***** | Brides<br>***** | Date of Marriage<br>**** ** ******** | Code<br>**** |
|---|---|---|---|
| Nicolai, Adam | Trap, Ann | 15, Nov. 1842 | AA |
| Nicolai, Heinrich | Brethauer, Elisabeth | 9, Nov. 1845 | C |
| Nicolai, Heinrich | Brethauer, Philippin | 19, Nov. 1848 | C |
| Nicolaus, Valentin | Schmidt, Margaretha | 16, Sept 1839 | FF |
| Niebrugge, Johan H. | Hussemann, Maria L. | 9, Feb. 1849 | F |
| Niebrugge, Wilhelm | Kramer, Elisabeth | 8, Feb. 1846 | A |
| Niedfeld, J. Arnold | Seger, Maria Agnes | 6, Apr. 1842 | FF |
| Niedheimer, Carl | Erd, Caroline | 14, May 1848 | EE |
| Niegengerd, Herman | Rothers, Elisabeth | 28, Dec. 1843 | RCH |
| Niehart, Jacob | Vosgre, Maria | 14, Jan. 1847 | RCH |
| Niehaus, Bernard | Schulte, Margaretha | 16, Apr. 1844 | AA |
| Niehaus, Bernard | Heikemper, Clara | 13, Oct. 1846 | EE |
| Niehaus, Bernard | Kerhoff, Agnes | 10, Sept 1848 | FF |
| Niehaus, Christoph | Goerres, Agnes | 1, Oct. 1848 | AA |
| Niehaus, Gerhard | Rumping, Catharine | 5, Sept 1843 | FF |
| Niehaus, Gerhard L. | Lambers, Euphemia | 8, Nov. 1842 | AA |
| Niehaus, Johan Hein. | Emke, Elisabeth | 17, Jan. 1847 | AA |
| Niehaus, John Conrad | Bloch, Cath. Wilhel. | 13, Dec. 1845 | B |
| Niehaus, Joseph G. | Meyer, Catharine | 17, Oct. 1848 | EE |
| Niehof, Herman J. | Roettering, Theresa | 21, Sept 1845 | AA |
| Niehof, Johan Hein. | Bram, Gesina | 13, Apr. 1845 | AA |
| Nieland, Andreas | Bencken, Margaretha | 2, Sept 1849 | AA |
| Niemann, Francis H. | Huelsmann, Catharine | 24, Nov. 1844 | FF |
| Niemann, Heinrich | Jung, Maria Angela | 23, June 1840 | FF |
| Niemann, Heinrich | Brueggemann, Gertrud | 26, Sept 1847 | AA |
| Niemann, Heinrich W. | Lakamp, M. Elisabeth | 12, Apr. 1849 | B |
| Niemann, Heinrich W. | Bruns, Wilhelmina | 15, Feb. 1849 | F |
| Niemann, Johan | Vorbrinck, Catharine | 10, July 1849 | F |
| Niemann, Johan Hein. | Meling, Maria Clara | 4, June 1840 | FF |
| Niemeier, Friedrich | Sleboms, Engel | 25, Apr. 1848 | RCH |
| Niemeier, Johan Hein | Kerk, M. Catharina | 22, Sept 1846 | FF |
| Niemer, Wilhelm | Beltert, Elisabeth | 11, Apr. 1837 | FF |
| Niemerg J. Bernard | Brueggemann, Anna M. | 4, Nov. 1849 | FF |
| Niemerg, Johan Bd. | Luecken, Maria Anna | 26, Apr. 1842 | FF |
| Niemeyer, Andreas | Kockmeyer, Anna M. | 3, Feb. 1847 | AA |
| Niemeyer, Carl Hein. | Rippe, Maria | 24, Sept 1849 | F |
| Niemeyer, Friedrich | Niemann, Catharine | 7, May 1846 | AA |
| Niemeyer, Heinrich | Wellmann, Elisabeth | 17, Nov. 1846 | AA |
| Niemeyer, Johan | Beck, Maria | 28, Jan. 1845 | AA |
| Niemeyer, Johan H. | Lammers, Margaretha | 28, Jan. 1845 | AA |
| Niemoller, Heinrich | Meyer, Maria Elis. | 3, Feb. 1842 | F |
| Nienaber, Carl F. Wm | Meyer, M. Friedricka | 26, Aug. 1847 | A |
| Nienaber, Gerhard | Feldkamp, Elisabeth | 6, Sept 1846 | AA |
| Nienaber, J Heinrich | Specker, A. Gertrud | 4, June 1848 | FF |
| Nienaber, J. Bernard | Heying, Maria | 18, Jan. 1846 | FF |
| Nienberg, Johan H. | Niemerg, Christina | 17, Sept 1848 | FF |
| Niencher, Jacob | Harsch, Dorothea B. | 18, Nov. 1849 | A |
| Nienhuser, John Adam | Hesper, Maria Elis. | 8, July 1846 | RCH |
| Nies, John K. | Poiner, Mary Ann | 29, May 1820 | RCH |
| Nieske, Heinrich Ed. | Bartling, Wilhelmina | 20, Dec. 1847 | AA |
| Nieters, Gerhard | Broecker, Maria Anna | 9, July 1848 | FF |
| Nieters, J. Herman | Bram, M. Adelheid | 22, Oct. 1848 | FF |
| Nieters, Johan | Lange, Maria Anna | 7, Feb. 1843 | FF |
| Nietert, Heinrich | Loreyn, Louise | 3, Feb. 1848 | B |
| Niewedde, Gerhard H. | Stukenberg, Margaret | 14, Jan. 1845 | F |
| Niewedde, Heinrich | Vollmer, Maria A. | 2, Feb. 1843 | F |
| Niewedde, Johan | Stuckenberg, Cath. | 15, Oct. 1846 | F |
| Niewett, Friedrich | Derricks, Eliza | 30, Nov. 1849 | RCH |
| Night, Samuel | ----, ---- | 11, May 1834 | RCH |
| Nikel, Francis | Mathes, Maria Anna | 14, Nov. 1849 | FF |
| Nilbert, Charles C. | Shields, Mary Jane | 1, Apr. 1848 | RCH |
| Niles, Barnabus | Land, Parmelia | 20, Nov. 1835 | RCH |
| Niles, Jesse | Moore, Lydia | 26, May 1842 | RCH |
| Niles, Nathaniel | Burget, Sarah Jane | 1, July 1846 | RCH |
| Niles, Solomon | Foans, Amanda | 24, Mar. 1842 | RCH |
| Nilling, Joseph | Vaske, Maria | 5, Sept 1847 | EE |
| Nimmo, Edward | Henderson, Ellen | 18, May 1842 | RCH |
| Ninel, John | Chana, Catharine | 30, Nov. 1826 | RCH |
| Nip, John | Cartle, Elisabeth | 30, Jan. 1833 | RCH |
| Nipper, Joseph | Ruhler, Elisabeth | 9, May 1847 | AA |
| Nisbet, William | Farris, Elisabeth | 27, Oct. 1845 | RCH |

| Grooms<br>****** | Brides<br>****** | Date of Marriage<br>**** ** ******** | Code<br>**** |
|---|---|---|---|
| Nischwitz, J. Philip | Maertz, Dorothea | 1, Oct. 1846 | G |
| Nistler, Casper | Cloppenberg, Elis. | 26, Mar. 1840 | FF |
| Niten, Levi | Dodge, Susanna | 4, Nov. 1819 | RCH |
| Nix, Edward | Edward, Nancy | 22, Apr. 1824 | RCH |
| Nixon, Josiah | Harrison, Susan | 16, Oct. 1848 | RCH |
| Nixon, Martin | Brown, Catharine M. | 18, Feb. 1847 | I |
| Nixon, William | Gordon, Sarah | 2, July 1821 | RCH |
| Noa, Adam | Freinking, Wilhelmin | 19, July 1848 | RCH |
| Nobbe, Francis | Beckmann, Catharine | 30, Apr. 1845 | AA |
| Nobbe, Friedrich | Aumann, Catharina | 6, July 1841 | FF |
| Nobbeler, Johan | Beckmann, Angela | 26, Jan. 1836 | FF |
| Nobbemeier, Gerhard | Kerdels, A. Adelheid | 16, Nov. 1848 | C |
| Nobenberger, Andreas | Wellmann, Margaretha | 18, June 1848 | EE |
| Noble, Alexander | Steed, Mahala | 8, Sept 1842 | RCH |
| Noble, Edward | Ross, Sarah | 11, Jan. 1821 | RCH |
| Noble, Edward | Mills, Charlene | 26, Aug. 1826 | RCH |
| Noble, Harrison | Cook, Abby | 21, Mar. 1833 | RCH |
| Noble, Henry | Townsend, Rosanna | 18, Feb. 1841 | RCH |
| Noble, Jackson | Francisco, Louise | 17, Feb. 1842 | RCH |
| Noble, John | Case, Mary Ann | 31, Mar. 1846 | RCH |
| Noble, Nathan | Picket, Ada Ellen | 8, Aug. 1849 | RCH |
| Nobles, Henry | Archer, L.A. | 7, Aug. 1835 | RCH |
| Nodell, George | Wiebering, Regina | 23, Nov. 1845 | RCH |
| Noe, Ellis | Smith, Mary | 12, Feb. 1833 | RCH |
| Noe, Job | Tibbets, Ebelind | 26, Dec. 1818 | RCH |
| Noe, Jonathan | Maselander, Rachel | 23, Nov. 1837 | RCH |
| Noecker, August | Gott, Sophia | 7, May 1848 | AA |
| Noel, Heinrich | Rimmel, Francisca | 9, Aug. 1839 | FF |
| Noel, Henry | Waterman, Susan | 27, June 1844 | RCH |
| Noelker, Georg | Schaefer, Anna Maria | 29, Sept 1842 | F |
| Noelp, Friedrich | Kirscher, Magdalena | 29, Dec. 1849 | A |
| Noelp, J. Andreas | Kreiselmann, Babette | 17, July 1849 | A |
| Noes, Friedrich | Laton, Sarah | 16, Sept 1841 | RCH |
| Noeth, Francis | Strohhefer, Dorothea | 23, Apr. 1849 | AA |
| Noetker, Gerhard | Pohlmann, Theresa | 14, May 1848 | FF |
| Noetmer, Egidius | Wagenheimer, Theresa | 2, Sept 1849 | CC |
| Noftsgar, Nelson | Clark, Mary | 5, Aug. 1841 | RCH |
| Nohe, Johan | Harte, Barbara | 11, Nov. 1845 | AA |
| Nol---, Job | Tibbatt, Sarah | 5, Mar. 1826 | RCH |
| Nol---, William | Butler, Mary Ann | 20, Nov. 1823 | RCH |
| Noland, George B. | McDowell, Mary Jane | 8, Sept 1836 | RCH |
| Nold, Jacob | McCash, Cynthia A. | 8, Apr. 1844 | RCH |
| Nolden, James | Gunkle, Betsey Ann | 18, Nov. 1841 | RCH |
| Nolen, Lewis | Philipps, Martha A. | 27, Mar. 1848 | RCH |
| Nolke, J. Friedrich | Schnedeker, Catharin | 20, Feb. 1845 | F |
| Noll, Jacob | Knoelle, Christina | 25, Dec. 1849 | RCH |
| Nolte, Friedrich | Grave, Maria | 21, Dec. 1847 | F |
| Nolte, Henry | Puhmann, Dorothea S. | 24, Mar. 1848 | G |
| Nolte, Johan | Biemann, Meta Sophia | 2, June 1847 | F |
| Noltman, John G. | Sampson, Mary | 17, June 1841 | RCH |
| Noon, Daniel | McGuire, Elisabeth | 22, Oct. 1843 | BB |
| Noonan, Patrick | O'Connor, Jane | 4, July 1838 | RCH |
| Nopper, Ludwig | Kraemer, Magdalena | 18, Apr. 1847 | FF |
| Norcap, Edmund | Wilson, Ann | 4, Jan. 1849 | RCH |
| Nordhoff, Stephan | Sticker, Anna | 11, June 1848 | AA |
| Nordick, Henry | Welch, Elisabeth | 10, Apr. 1843 | RCH |
| Nordick, Henry P. | Luhrmann, Anna C. | 22, Dec. 1847 | RCH |
| Nordloh, Heinrich | Hollmann, Margaretha | 11, Nov. 1845 | A |
| Nordloh, Johan Hein. | Droppelmann, Gertrud | 11, May 1847 | AA |
| Nordlohne, Heinrich | Dolle, M. Anna | 24, Oct. 1848 | II |
| Nordmann, Gerhard F. | Wiewingers, A Louise | 21, Mar. 1844 | F |
| Nordmann, Gerhard H. | Campbell, Mary C. | 5, Sept 1838 | RCH |
| Nordmann, J Heinrich | Freye, Maria | 30, Dec. 1841 | F |
| Nordmeyer, Andreas | Mueller, Anna Maria | 28, Oct. 1845 | AA |
| Nordmeyer, Andreas | Kettels, Christina | 18, Jan. 1848 | AA |
| Nordmeyer, Heinrich | Schalk, Theresa | 13, Feb. 1844 | AA |
| Nordmeyer, Henry | Schulte, Theresa | 13, Feb. 1844 | RCH |
| Noring, Cord | Sou, Anna Elisabeth | 31, July 1845 | C |
| Norkmann, Richard | Bowers, Mary Ann | 5, Dec. 1841 | RCH |
| Normann, William B. | Warr, Sarah A. | 21, June 1849 | RCH |
| Norre, Bernard | Schillmoeller, Elis. | 22, May 1849 | II |

| Grooms ****** | Brides ****** | Date of Marriage **** ** ******** | Code **** |
|---|---|---|---|
| Norris, Benjamin | Heely, Abigail | 6, Oct. 1824 | RCH |
| Norris, Benjamin | Cobb, Rosetta H. | 20, Aug. 1844 | BB |
| Norris, Charles C. | Yeatman, Sarah Lucy | 10, Apr. 1839 | RCH |
| Norris, Culver | LaBoyteaux, Hannah | 7, Apr. 1838 | RCH |
| Norris, E.S. | Sampson, Mary J. | 27, Nov. 1842 | RCH |
| Norris, Harvey | Young, Julia | 25, May 1847 | RCH |
| Norris, William R. | Thompson, Nancy | 29, Jan. 1835 | RCH |
| North, Alfred | Miner, America | 9, Feb. 1847 | RCH |
| North, Lewis | Brownlow, Lucinda | 20, Aug. 1846 | RCH |
| North, Peter | McCann, Ellen | 25, Jan. 1844 | BB |
| North, Peter | Stall, Emma | 14, Mar. 1847 | RCH |
| North, Robert | Hey, Ann | 22, Dec. 1845 | RCH |
| Northrop, William | Aydelott, Margaret | 23, June 1842 | RCH |
| Nortker, Theodor | Kamphaus, Anna Maria | 26, Oct. 1848 | AA |
| Norton, D.M. | Swain, Adelia | 21, Dec. 1849 | RCH |
| Not, Joseph H. | C---, Elisabeth | 3, May 1837 | RCH |
| Notcher, Henry O. | Sawyer, Mary F. | 25, May 1841 | I |
| Notlow, Johan H. | Buebe, Maria | 4, Oct. 1846 | EE |
| Notmeyer, Friedrich | Lorey, Wilhelmina L. | 11, Feb. 1841 | F |
| Novaski, Alexander | Cleavon, Eleanor | 18, Apr. 1839 | RCH |
| Nubling, Georg | Kirschmer, Catharine | 18, Feb. 1849 | G |
| Nuekel, Francis | ----, Mary | 13, Dec. 1849 | RCH |
| Nuesert, August | Brock, Mary Ann | 18, July 1848 | RCH |
| Nufer, Martin | Schnitzer, Maria A. | 20, Feb. 1849 | EE |
| Nugent, Edward | Byrne, Sarah | 18, June 1848 | BB |
| Nulte, Johan Heinric | Niekamp, Anna Maria | 19, Oct. 1845 | AA |
| Nunneker, Wilhelm | Heinemann, Wilhelmin | 29, Dec. 1847 | E |
| Nunnick, Bernard | Kockmann, Anna | 6, May 1849 | EE |
| Nunninger, Ignatz | Oehler, Margaretha | 13, May 1845 | FF |
| Nurre, Heinrich | Fehring, Anna Maria | 9, Apr. 1844 | AA |
| Nurre, Henry | Feldmann, Agnes | 8, July 1843 | RCH |
| Nurth, Friedrich | Kenner, Friedricka | 29, Dec. 1846 | RCH |
| Nusbaum, Jude | Meyer, Hannah | 2, Apr. 1847 | RCH |
| Nuss, Johan | Stephan, Johanna | 18, Sept 1848 | EE |
| Nusse, Johan H. | Siemer, Gertrud | 14, May 1848 | AA |
| Nussel, Michael | Heiss, Anna Maria | 12, Feb. 1844 | RCH |
| Nussmeyer, Wilhelm | Steinkamp, Johanna | 20, Dec. 1849 | C |
| Nutter, George | Roach, Deborah | 26, Oct. 1844 | RCH |
| Nutting, Henry W.G. | Dean, Sarah Ann | 11, Nov. 1835 | RCH |
| Nutts, Jacob | Blair, Sarah E. | 18, Nov. 1845 | RCH |
| Nutz, Leonard | Likens, Mary Ellen | 17, Aug. 1844 | RCH |
| Nutz, Leonard | Cochran, Susan | 27, Nov. 1846 | RCH |
| Nutz, Leonard N. | Clutch, Rebecca | 17, Apr. 1836 | RCH |
| Nye, Joseph | Wilson, Rosanna | 16, Feb. 1843 | RCH |
| Nye, Stephen | Harding, Susan | 2, May 1836 | RCH |
| O'Berne, John | Kemp, Sarah Ann | 18, May 1846 | BB |
| O'Brian, Thomas T. | McHenry, Mary | 30, Jan. 1848 | I |
| O'Brien, Daniel | Eagen, Catharine | 7, May 1848 | GG |
| O'Brien, Edmund | Mitchell, Rebecca J. | 14, Dec. 1848 | RCH |
| O'Brien, Edward | Sullivan, Mary Jane | 1, June 1846 | RCH |
| O'Brien, Edward | Keiser, Jane | 26, Aug. 1849 | BB |
| O'Brien, George | McCormick, Mary | 9, June 1845 | BB |
| O'Brien, James | Neary, Mary | 4, May 1835 | RCH |
| O'Brien, James | Spencer, Johanna | 21, Feb. 1836 | RCH |
| O'Brien, John | Doran, Ellen | 7, Oct. 1839 | BB |
| O'Brien, John | Brasee, Rosanna | 19, Aug. 1844 | RCH |
| O'Brien, John | O'Brien, Catharine | 25, May 1847 | RCH |
| O'Brien, John | Shanning, Catharine | 21, Apr. 1849 | RCH |
| O'Brien, John | Morgan, Mary | 21, Aug. 1849 | GG |
| O'Brien, Maurice | Ryan, Mary ann | 1, Feb. 1844 | BB |
| O'Brien, Thomas | Ryan, Catharine | 20, Aug. 1844 | BB |
| O'Brien, Thomas | Fogarty, Catharine | 31, May 1846 | BB |
| O'Conner, Michael | Murphy, Ann | 21, June 1841 | BB |
| O'Conner, Michael | Eagan, Honora | 5, Feb. 1843 | BB |
| O'Conner, Rudolph | Dooley, Mary | 21, Apr. 1845 | BB |
| O'Conner, William | Watson, Hannah | 2, May 1821 | RCH |
| O'Connor, Edward | McGrath, Bridget | 25, Aug. 1838 | RCH |
| O'Connor, James | McGanahan, Julia | 21, Oct. 1841 | BB |
| O'Connor, John | Russell, Margaret | 1, July 1847 | GG |
| O'Connor, Stephan | McDermott, Catharine | 1, Nov. 1848 | BB |

| Grooms<br>****** | Brides<br>****** | Date of Marriage<br>**** ** ******** | Code<br>**** |
|---|---|---|---|
| O'Connor, Thomas | Fleming, Ann | 16, Nov. 1837 | RCH |
| O'Connor, Thomas | McDonough, Catharine | 7, Feb. 1838 | RCH |
| O'Connor, Thomas | Keenan, Anna | 13, Sept 1841 | BB |
| O'Connor, Timothy | Newell, Margaret | 12, May 1845 | BB |
| O'Dell, William | Putthoff, M. Engel | 2, Sept 1839 | FF |
| O'Donald, John | Fitzpatrick, Mary | 19, Sept 1849 | RCH |
| O'Donnell, Hugh | Pitcher, Laura | 2, Oct. 1837 | RCH |
| O'Donnell, John | Carroll, Mary | 23, Apr. 1844 | BB |
| O'Donnell, Patrick | Adkins, Sarah | 9, Sept 1847 | RCH |
| O'Donnell, Thomas | Coffee, Bridget | 17, June 1841 | BB |
| O'Donnell, Thomas | Hane, Catharine | 18, Sept 1849 | GG |
| O'Donnen, Peter | Cronan, Bridget | 18, Sept 1849 | GG |
| O'Garra, Patrick | Rooney, Mary | 30, May 1842 | BB |
| O'Hara, Henry | Donnegan, Sarah | 2, Nov. 1848 | RCH |
| O'Hara, John | Rogers, Mary | 6, July 1840 | BB |
| O'Hara, Patrick | Mullen, Mary | 7, Jan. 1849 | GG |
| O'Hara, William A. | Hughes, Jane | 10, May 1840 | BB |
| O'Hare, Edward | Waters, Mary | 15, Apr. 1849 | GG |
| O'Hare, John | Lynch, Mary Ann | 24, July 1848 | BB |
| O'Kane, Henry | Hillegefort, Maria | 27, Feb. 1838 | FF |
| O'Keefe, James | Watson, Ella | 22, Feb. 1846 | BB |
| O'Keefe, Thomas | McAvoy, Elisabeth | 2, Nov. 1841 | BB |
| O'Keefe, Thomas J. | Payne, Trilinda | 23, Jan. 1849 | RCH |
| O'Leary, Timothy | Cunningham, Mary | 23, Aug. 1846 | BB |
| O'Maley, Thomas | Reily, Mary | 16, July 1849 | RCH |
| O'Meara, John | Baxter, Margaret | 23, June 1849 | RCH |
| O'Meara, Thomas | Sweeney, Jane | 16, June 1842 | RCH |
| O'Meara, Thomas | Cottam, Ann | 5, Feb. 1841 | BB |
| O'Meara, William | Murray, Julia | 15, Aug. 1849 | GG |
| O'Meara, William P. | Bradley, Mary | 23, May 1841 | BB |
| O'Neal, Dennis | Fitzgerald, Mary | 2, July 1842 | BB |
| O'Neal, Henry | Hart, Catharine | 26, Dec. 1844 | RCH |
| O'Neil, Joseph | Ferguson, Mary | 26, 1836 | RCH |
| O'Neil, Patrick | O'Reilly, Mary | 10, May 1842 | BB |
| O'Neil, Timothy | Brady, Ann | 25, Jan. 1849 | GG |
| O'Neil, William | Moore, Henrietta | 23, Dec. 1845 | RCH |
| O'Neill, Cornelius | Hildebrand, Mary | 19, Aug. 1849 | GG |
| O'Neill, Jesse | Greenleaf, Caroline | 19, Feb. 1826 | RCH |
| O'Neill, John | Kelly, Mary | 14, Jan. 1844 | BB |
| O'Neill, Thomas | Shield, Rosannah | 25, Mar. 1848 | RCH |
| O'Rourke, Timothy | Parsons, Louise | 3, Aug. 1845 | BB |
| O'Rourke, Timothy | Murtha, Alice | 18, Feb. 1849 | BB |
| O'Shaughnessy, Nick. | O'Neil, Ellen | 8, Jan. 1848 | GG |
| Oakes, Lewis | Broun, Alice M. | 15, Dec. 1836 | RCH |
| Oakley, Elias | Turner, Mary Ann | 12, Apr. 1835 | RCH |
| Oakley, Lester | Reese, Parmelia | 8, Feb. 1844 | RCH |
| Oates, William | Cartwright, Ann | 18, Feb. 1844 | BB |
| Oatley, William | Ragenna, Nancy | 5, June 1834 | RCH |
| Obear, Elezer | Morton, Jane | 20, Mar. 1823 | RCH |
| Obear, Horatio | Ayers, Anna Maria | 24, Dec. 1846 | RCH |
| Ober, Heinrich | Wessels, Angela | 26, Nov. 1848 | II |
| Oberdorf, Francis | Whitehouse, Jane | 23, June 1844 | RCH |
| Oberdorfer, Elias | Lewis, Fanny | 13, July 1843 | RCH |
| Oberhelmann, Fried. | Wiepker, Catharine | 19, Jan. 1846 | RCH |
| Oberhelmann, Wilhelm | Schulte, Friedricka | 15, Jan. 1845 | F |
| Oberklaus, Johan G. | Treier, Elisabeth | 26, Nov. 1848 | EE |
| Oberklein, Georg | Ludwig, Anna S. | 27, Mar. 1844 | RCH |
| Oberklein, Gerhard H | Mollen, Wilhelmina | 10, Nov. 1843 | RCH |
| Oberle, Balthasar | Gardner, Magdalena | 19, Nov. 1846 | RCH |
| Obermann, Henry | Lampson, Louise | 17, Aug. 1849 | RCH |
| Obermeyer, August | VonHagen, Anna Maria | 5, Aug. 1847 | FF |
| Obermeyer, Franz | Kralmeyer, Mary Elis | 3, Feb. 1848 | G |
| Obermeyer, Johan H. | Feder, Maria | 3, Feb. 1842 | FF |
| Obermeyer, Wilhelm | Bockstedde, Margaret | 15, Feb. 1849 | II |
| Ocheltree, John | Churchill, Hannah H. | 14, June 1834 | RCH |
| Oclierman, David | S---, Elisabeth | 3, Mar. 1835 | RCH |
| Octeman, Daniel | Adams, Selinda | 3, Apr. 1825 | RCH |
| Odenbach, Johan | Bohlander, Maria | 30, Mar. 1846 | C |
| Oder, David | Miller, Ann | 22, July 1843 | RCH |
| Odiet, Joseph | Matteer, Margaret | 13, June 1846 | RCH |
| Odor, Barnett | Havernierly, Martha | 24, July 1835 | RCH |

| Grooms | Brides | Date of Marriage | Code |
|--------|--------|------------------|------|
| Oechsle, Johan | Schmidt, Magdalena | 26, Dec. 1849 | C |
| Oedermann, Bernard | Meyer, Catharine | 24, June 1845 | AA |
| Oehler, Alois | Fluk, Magdalena | 24, Aug. 1848 | A |
| Oehler, Andreas | Garrison, Louise | 23, June 1842 | FF |
| Oehler, Joseph | Pistner, Margaretha | 11, Feb. 1839 | FF |
| Oehler, Philipp | Adam, Magdalena | 27, Jan. 1846 | HH |
| Oehling, Johan G. | Kamproch, Anna Adel | 19, Sept 1847 | EE |
| Oehs, Georg | Hoffmann, Anna | 4, Sept 1845 | C |
| Oelgatz, | Gross, Barbara | 27, Aug. 1849 | RCH |
| Oelmann, Friedrich H | Bohringer, Elis. C. | 5, Nov. 1840 | F |
| Oesper, George | Engelhart, Catharine | 27, Aug. 1847 | RCH |
| Oesper, Johan | Meckel, Maria | 29, Apr. 1848 | RCH |
| Oesterle, Bernard | Riester, Maria | 3, Sept 1844 | RCH |
| Oesterle, Johan | Hoeske, Louise | 26, Aug. 1847 | RCH |
| Oesting, J. Dietrich | Schmersal, Juliana A | 8, Feb. 1844 | F |
| Oesting, J. Wilhelm | Wiechmann, Maria | 23, May 1848 | F |
| Oesting, Johan | Bettenbrock, Elis. | 10, June 1841 | F |
| Oesting, Johan Hein. | Strubbe, Anna Helena | 15, Feb. 1840 | F |
| Oestmann, Heinrich | Evers, Anna Margaret | 17, Jan. 1849 | F |
| Oevermann, Casper H. | Lange, M. Elisabeth | 30, Jan. 1838 | FF |
| Oevermann, Casper H. | Lang, Maria Elis. | 15, Sept 1840 | FF |
| Oevermann, Heinrich | Boeckmann, Agnes | 12, June 1838 | FF |
| Oevermann, Wilhelm | Tintrupp, Paulina | 13, Jan. 1842 | FF |
| Offenbach, Herman B. | Lamping, Maria Engel | 18, June 1847 | RCH |
| Offenberger, Franz H | Brockmeyer, Catharin | 29, Oct. 1842 | F |
| Ogan, James | Gardner, Anna Maria | 30, Dec. 1834 | RCH |
| Ogden, Benjamin | Tibbits, Adelia | 13, Dec. 1849 | RCH |
| Ogden, Ezekiel | Wood, Harriet | 11, July 1848 | RCH |
| Ogden, James S. | Wright, Eliza | 24, Oct. 1822 | RCH |
| Ogden, Jonathan | Gorham, Elizabeth | 21, Nov. 1834 | I |
| Ogden, Lewis | Hardy, Isabella | 10, June 1847 | RCH |
| Ogden, Samuel E. | Kline, Malinda | 26, Aug. 1848 | RCH |
| Ogden, Thomas | Hilton, Mahala | 27, Aug. 1845 | RCH |
| Ogg, Joel | Kugler, Sarah | 25, Sept 1836 | RCH |
| Ogg, Reuben | McCleary, Jane | 17, June 1824 | RCH |
| Ogle, John | Rust, Mary | 15, May 1836 | RCH |
| Ogle, William H. | Smith, Christine | 5, Mar. 1833 | RCH |
| Oglesby, Willis | Glore, Zerilda | 31, Aug. 1847 | RCH |
| Ohl, Wendel | Matel, Catharine | 12, Jan. 1847 | EE |
| Ohler, Edward | Koehl, Friedricka | 23, Oct. 1838 | FF |
| Ohler, Johan | Reichli, Julia | 5, Nov. 1848 | CC |
| Ohlhoff, Louis | Brengelmann, Cath. | 19, Jan. 1846 | F |
| Ohlmann, Herman H. | Poos, Hannah Maria | 10, Oct. 1845 | F |
| Ohm, Heinrich | Tonn, Sophia Carolin | 1, Dec. 1846 | RCH |
| Ohmann, Eberhard H. | Portner, Maria Anna | 11, July 1849 | RCH |
| Ohrbrand, J Philipp | Horekort, Maria | 5, Oct. 1841 | RCH |
| Olberding, Herman H. | Kruse, Josephine | 16, Oct. 1845 | AA |
| Olberding, Johan H. | Meyer, Elisabeth | 12, Sept 1847 | FF |
| Oldemeier, Franz H. | Oppings, Anna Maria | 14, Sept 1848 | A |
| Olden, John | Shumard, Mary | 31, Oct. 1841 | RCH |
| Olden, John | Bratton, Mary | 18, June 1846 | RCH |
| Oldendick, Heinrich | Dey, Dina | 23, Sept 1849 | AA |
| Oldenick, J. Herman | Rabke, Cath. Agnes | 16, May 1848 | FF |
| Oldenschmidt, Dietr. | Ewers, Caroline W. | 23, Nov. 1845 | B |
| Olges, Anton | Dramann, M. Anna | 6, May 1847 | AA |
| Oliger, Andreas | Brunner, Christina | 18, Aug. 1840 | FF |
| Oliger, Johan | Stammer, Helena | 12, Oct. 1841 | FF |
| Oliger, Nicolaus | Paul, Barbara | 18, May 1841 | FF |
| Oliger, Peter | Rutz, Magdalena | 26, May 1835 | FF |
| Oliger, Wendel | Neuhausel, Anna M. | 18, Oct. 1841 | FF |
| Oliver, Alexander | Pierce, Jane | 26, July 1841 | RCH |
| Oliver, Richard | Zerhuny, Mary | 25, Dec. 1843 | RCH |
| Oliver, Robert | Manan---, Sarah | 23, Mar. 1823 | RCH |
| Oliver, Thomas | Brashier, Catharine | 2, July 1843 | RCH |
| Oliver, William | Davis, Mary Jane | 6, May 1847 | RCH |
| Ollendick, Heinrich | Hackas, Maria | 18, July 1837 | FF |
| Ollis, Matthias | Stokes, Elisabeth | 12, Apr. 1819 | RCH |
| Olmstead, Thadeus | Bell, Lucinda | 9, Apr. 1846 | RCH |
| Olmstead, William | Holland, Malinda | 11, Oct. 1848 | RCH |
| Olmsted, John | Paxton, Margaret | 17, Jan. 1849 | RCH |
| Olphen, Bernard H. | Nodrup, Maria A. | 1, Oct. 1848 | AA |

| Grooms<br>****** | Brides<br>****** | Date of Marriage<br>**** ** ******* | Code<br>**** |
|---|---|---|---|
| Ong, | Ross, Sarah | 19, Sept 1849 | RCH |
| Onken, Otto | Karrmann, Dorothea | 3, Feb. 1848 | C |
| Onnewehr, Freidrich | Meyer, Catharine | 27, Feb. 1848 | A |
| Onnewehr, Friedrich | Kolkmeier, Catharine | 10, Jan. 1843 | AA |
| Opermann, Wendel | Leitner, Barbara | 3, Apr. 1837 | FF |
| Opitz, John | Zeilman, Catharine | 30, Nov. 1845 | RCH |
| Opmann, Gerhard | Wortmann, Maria | 18, Nov. 1849 | CC |
| Opp, William R. | Ewing, Laura | 28, Dec. 1832 | RCH |
| Oppenheimer, Samuel | Levi, Dianna | 17, Feb. 1849 | RCH |
| Oppenheimer, Solomon | Schuhl, Hannah | 4, Mar. 1844 | RCH |
| Oppenlander, Christ. | Holmann, Mary | 29, May 1847 | RCH |
| Orange, Benjamin | Beresford, Elizabeth | 1827 | I |
| Orange, Samuel | Clayton, Deborah | 18, May 1848 | RCH |
| Orange, Thomas | Conover, Mary | 13, Apr. 1820 | RCH |
| Orange, William | Allern, Betsy | 19, June 1823 | RCH |
| Orcott, Alvin | Bruen, Emeline | 30, Apr. 1842 | RCH |
| Ordemann, Herman | Dolle, Maria | 6, June 1848 | F |
| Oresell, Henry | Strong, Martha | 10, May 1841 | RCH |
| Orme, John | Barnett, Anna | 27, Dec. 1847 | RCH |
| Ormond, John | Lahey, Mary | 14, Jan. 1840 | BB |
| Ormsby, Thomas | Flanagan, Ann | 6, Sept 1841 | BB |
| Ormsby, Thomas | Eagin, Catharine | 25, Oct. 1845 | RCH |
| Orr, Arthur | Clingman, Elisabeth | Sept 1844 | RCH |
| Orr, David C. | Seaman, Johanna | 28, July 1846 | RCH |
| Orr, Henry | Carr, Anna | 14, Mar. 1846 | RCH |
| Orr, Robert | Weir, Esther | 11, July 1844 | RCH |
| Orr, Samuel | Scott, Fanny | 7, Aug. 1834 | RCH |
| Orr, Thomas | Leech, Elisabeth | 7, Dec. 1820 | RCH |
| Orr, Thomas | Munford, Elis. Jane | 29, July 1844 | RCH |
| Orr, William | Pierson, Amelia | 14, Nov. 1837 | RCH |
| Orsborn, Caleb | Walker, Martha | 6, Apr. 1845 | RCH |
| Ort, Michael | Hesselbach, Wilhel. | 18, Nov. 1845 | AA |
| Orth, Georg | Wiederich, Christina | 17, Oct. 1848 | FF |
| Orth, John Adam | Mong, Catharine | 8, June 1848 | RCH |
| Ortmann, Christoph | Borges, Catharina | 24, Oct. 1847 | FF |
| Ortmann, Heinrich | Groten, Catharina | 1, Oct. 1839 | FF |
| Ortmann, Herman H. | Langhorst, Catharine | 24, Sept 1848 | II |
| Ortwerth, Franz H. | Kallmeier, Wilhelmin | 5, Sept 1848 | F |
| Os---, Hiram M. | Turner, Charlotte | 7, Nov. 1826 | RCH |
| Osborn, Archibald | Marshall, Missouri | 3, Nov. 1846 | RCH |
| Osborn, Benjamin | Claypool, Mary | 8, Nov. 1843 | RCH |
| Osborn, David | McKee, Cynthia | 1, Jan. 1834 | RCH |
| Osborn, Fielding | Stuck, B. | 5, Oct. 1835 | RCH |
| Osborn, Jesse | Robinson, Jemima | 24, Oct. 1843 | RCH |
| Osborn, Stephan | Hearn, Martha Jane | 31, Mar. 1847 | RCH |
| Osborn, Stephan | Schribner, Sarah | 17, Oct. 1847 | RCH |
| Osborn, Thomas | Allibone, Mary | 22, Oct. 1822 | I |
| Osborne, William | Townley, Joanna | 10, Feb. 1846 | RCH |
| Osburn, William | McCash, Harriet | 17, July 1834 | RCH |
| Oser, Johan | Krieg, Carolina | 9, June 1840 | FF |
| Osgood, David | Israel, Sarah Jane | 5, Mar. 1846 | RCH |
| Osgood, Henry D. | Robinson, Sarah | 21, Nov. 1837 | RCH |
| Osgood, James | Vance, Margaret | 3, Sept 1844 | RCH |
| Osgood, T.M. | Taylor, Sarah | 31, Mar. 1834 | RCH |
| Osius, John William | Stegner, Anna | 22, Oct. 1846 | G |
| Oskamp, Clement | Fischer, Mary | 23, May 1847 | GG |
| Oskamp, Theodor | Frey, Margaret | 29, Oct. 1848 | BB |
| Oslage, Ernst F. | Sieckmeyer, Maria D. | 10, May 1849 | C |
| Osner, Georg | Rickert, Susanna | 23, Oct. 1849 | DD |
| Ossege, Heinrich | Placke, Elisabeth | 11, Nov. 1849 | AA |
| Ossege, Wilhelm | Buter, Angela | 9, June 1849 | II |
| Ossenbeck, Friedrich | Hardinghaus, Maria | 13, Sept 1836 | FF |
| Ossenbeck, H. Johan | Burghardt, Elisabeth | 6, Feb. 1849 | FF |
| Ossing, Heinrich | Lucas, Elisabeth | 23, Feb. 1841 | FF |
| Ostendarp, Francis H | Siefke, Katharine | 15, Nov. 1842 | AA |
| Ostendorf, Heinrich | Siemer, Maria Anna | 8, Feb. 1842 | FF |
| Ostendorf, Heinrich | Kramer, Bernardina | 15, Apr. 1849 | FF |
| Ostendorf, Johan F. | Tegge, Magdalena | 14, Feb. 1847 | AA |
| Ostenfeld, Francis | Timmers, M Catharina | 27, May 1849 | FF |
| Oster, Andrew | Davis, Amanda | 1, May 1848 | RCH |
| Oster, Friedrich | Schatz, Anna Maria | 12, June 1849 | A |

| Grooms<br>***** | Brides<br>***** | Date of Marriage<br>**** ** ******** | Code<br>**** |
|---|---|---|---|
| Osterbrink, Johan H. | Toerner, Anna Maria | 1, Oct. 1848 | AA |
| Osterhoff, Bernard | Raeling, Agnes | 15, Sept 1840 | FF |
| Osterloh, Johan | Wehrmann, Josephina | 8, Nov. 1836 | FF |
| Ostermann, Francis | Klene, Margaretha | 3, Aug. 1841 | FF |
| Ostermann, Francis | Keutz, Margaretha | 21, Apr. 1846 | FF |
| Ostermann, Johan | Kasler, Catharina | 21, Nov. 1848 | AA |
| Ostertag, Christian | Luethy, Lisette | 20, Nov. 1849 | A |
| Ostheimer, Adam | Seitz, Christina | 29, Feb. 1848 | AA |
| Ostheimer, Georg A. | Steigerwald, Marg. | 25, Feb. 1838 | FF |
| Ostrander, John C. | Kelly, Catharine M. | 7, May 1840 | BB |
| Oswald, Matthew | Bennett, Lucy | 15, Dec. 1844 | RCH |
| Others, Abraham | Miller, Julia Ann | 27, June 1837 | RCH |
| Ott, Francis | Bredel, Rosina | 19, Jan. 1847 | AA |
| Ott, Fridolin | Forner, Kunigunda | 20, June 1848 | EE |
| Ott, Heinrich | Oeh, Cunigunda | 24, Jan. 1847 | C |
| Ott, Johan | Bender, Johanna | 22, Oct. 1846 | EE |
| Ott, Johan | Rexath, Juliana | 18, Nov. 1847 | EE |
| Ott, Johan Friedrich | Grane, Anna Maria | 28, Oct. 1846 | RCH |
| Ott, Johan M. | Birckopf, Kunigunda | 15, Mar. 1847 | RCH |
| Ott, John | Reyrott, Juliana | 18, Nov. 1847 | RCH |
| Ott, Martin | Ossegen, Katharina | 20, Jan. 1848 | G |
| Otte, Georg Heinrich | Reinhardt, Sophia | 8, Apr. 1840 | F |
| Otte, Gerhard Heinr. | Schmersals, Henriett | 27, Mar. 1845 | F |
| Otte, Gerhard Heinr. | Rittmann, Anna H. | 11, Apr. 1849 | F |
| Otte, Johan | Schneider, A. Maria | 27, Apr. 1843 | F |
| Otte, Johan Heinrich | Mohlenkamp, Anna M. | 5, Mar. 1846 | F |
| Otten, Johan Dietric | Buening, Anna Maria | 7, Oct. 1841 | F |
| Ottenjohan, Wilhelm | Meyers, Margaretha | 23, Jan. 1848 | B |
| Ottermann, Heinrich | Rehms, Maria E. | 27, Jan. 1842 | F |
| Otterson, James | Bingham, Elisabeth | 21, Sept 1849 | RCH |
| Otting, Christoph | Minnecker, Fanny | 24, Apr. 1849 | F |
| Otting, Conrad M. | Stuenkel, Wilhelmina | 7, Dec. 1843 | F |
| Otting, Friedrich W. | Kruse, Bernardina | 11, Feb. 1849 | CC |
| Otting, Johan Hein. | Fuller, Catharine M. | 18, Nov. 1847 | F |
| Ottmann, Cyril | Geker, Rosina | 15, May 1848 | EE |
| Otto, Heinrich | Peters, Sophia | 9, Oct. 1849 | C |
| Otto, Herman Friedr. | Hollenbeck, Dorothea | 12, June 1845 | G |
| Ottoway, William | Bickerdyke, Ketura | 12, Sept 1846 | RCH |
| Outley, Alonzo | Fox, Margaret | 11, Sept 1843 | RCH |
| Outly, Thomas | Benham, Isabel | 20, Jan. 1834 | RCH |
| Overbeck, Francis H. | Lang, Anna M. Agnes | 31, Aug. 1841 | FF |
| Overbeck, Francis T. | VonderHaar, M. Cath. | 15, July 1849 | AA |
| Overbeck, Heinrich | Quarbmann, Catharin | 27, Apr. 1837 | FF |
| Overbeck, Herman | Frank, Louise | 24, Oct. 1844 | F |
| Overbeck, Johan H. | Buschmann, Anna M. | 20, Feb. 1838 | FF |
| Overberg, Anton | Feldmann, Catharine | 14, May 1848 | EE |
| Overdick, Heinrich | Caspers, Louise | 3, Mar. 1848 | C |
| Overmann, Anton | Holthaus, Elisabeth | 27, July 1845 | AA |
| Overmann, Friedrich | Eskake, Elisabeth | 8, May 1844 | AA |
| Overmeier, Louis | Fromann, Fanny | 11, Mar. 1846 | RCH |
| Owcutt, Curtis | Norris, Euphemia | 6, Mar. 1835 | RCH |
| Owen, Allison | Miller, Caroline | 13, Dec. 1832 | RCH |
| Owen, Aquila | Sophila, Mathilda | 9, Mar. 1841 | RCH |
| Owen, John | Murray, Isabella | 6, Feb. 1838 | RCH |
| Owen, William | Nreng, Kiziah A. | 29, Apr. 1837 | RCH |
| Owen, William | Neves, Virginia | 3, Jan. 1847 | RCH |
| Owens, Asahel P. | Phelin, Harriet | 27, June 1848 | I |
| Owens, C. | Calvit, Mary M. | 4, July 1837 | RCH |
| Owens, John | Nead, Mary | 26, Dec. 1842 | RCH |
| Owens, John | Black, Jane | 25, Jan. 1843 | RCH |
| Owens, Martin | Powers, Ellen | 17, May 1849 | BB |
| Owens, Owen P. | Reese, Susanah | 18, Jan. 1834 | RCH |
| Owens, Patrick | Gridley, Mary | 31, Mar. 1833 | RCH |
| Owens, Patrick | Golden, Sarah | 7, July 1846 | RCH |
| Owens, Patrick | Ball, Mary | 14, Oct. 1847 | BB |
| Owens, Richard | Crane, Lydia | 4, Aug. 1842 | RCH |
| Owens, Richard | Cummings, Mary Ann | 14, Oct. 1846 | RCH |
| Owens, Robert | Leper, Margaret | 10, June 1840 | RCH |
| Owens, Thomas | Quilder, Catharine | 17, Apr. 1849 | RCH |
| Owin, John | Meeker, Eunice | 27, Apr. 1819 | RCH |
| Oyelzauer, Wilhelm | Meyer, Maria | 18, Oct. 1849 | C |

| Grooms | Brides | Date of Marriage | Code |
|--------|--------|------------------|------|
| ****** | ****** | **** ** ******** | **** |
| Oyler, David D. | Harper, Jane | 2, Nov. 1846 | RCH |
| Oyler, Edward | Bowles, Emily | 20, Nov. 1847 | RCH |
| Oyler, William | Dobell, Mary Ann | 14, Nov. 1845 | RCH |
| P---, Isaac | Holland, Anna Maria | July 1835 | RCH |
| P---, Job | Howard, Rebecca Wood | 12, May 1833 | RCH |
| Pa---, Thomas | Woolley, Elisabeth | 27, Dec. 1825 | RCH |
| Pabst, Casper H. | Oldendick, Catharine | 8, Sept 1846 | AA |
| Pace, Robert | Kennedy, Nancy C. | 9, Nov. 1834 | RCH |
| Pack, Armleder | Todd, Caroline | 27, Sept 1842 | RCH |
| Packard, Benjamin | Debolt, Nancy | 23, Feb. 1842 | RCH |
| Packard, Henry | Cohen, Sarah | 30, June 1846 | RCH |
| Packer, James | VanZant, Rachel | 19, Nov. 1842 | RCH |
| Packingham, | Hatharsley, Mary | 30, Aug. 1849 | RCH |
| Paddick, Johan Bern. | Lang, Elisabeth(Mrs) | 3, Mar. 1835 | FF |
| Paddock, Charles | Mahew, Olive | 8, Oct. 1817 | RCH |
| Paener, Adam | Lambert, Sophia | 25, Nov. 1845 | AA |
| Page, Andrew | Yocum, | Dec. 1844 | RCH |
| Page, Edwin V. Lee | L---, Mary | 28, Sept 1819 | RCH |
| Page, John | Stule, Charlotte | 1, Apr. 1838 | RCH |
| Page, Joseph | Ashcraft, Elisabeth | 28, Sept 1846 | RCH |
| Page, Michael | Schooley, Sarah C. | 14, Sept 1843 | RCH |
| Page, Thomas | McBride, Margaret | 17, Sept 1837 | RCH |
| Page, Thomas | Gordon, Elisabeth | 1, Jan. 1844 | RCH |
| Page, Walter | Kain, Minerva | 17, Aug. 1846 | RCH |
| Page, William L. | Phillips, Elisabeth | 5, July 1840 | RCH |
| Paget, Edward | Holmes, Mary Ann | 16, Feb. 1847 | RCH |
| Pahlmann, J Dietrich | Schroer, A Elisabeth | 3, June 1841 | G |
| Pahls, Johan | Freund, Maria | 26, Nov. 1840 | FF |
| Paige, John | Cook, Nancy | 24, Dec. 1845 | RCH |
| Pain---, John | Hubbs, Polly | 1, Sept 1820 | RCH |
| Paine, Luther | Manzy, Marietta | 24, Dec. 1844 | RCH |
| Painter, David | Wheeler, Permilia | 16, June 1836 | RCH |
| Painter, John | Corey, Anna Ophelia | 31, Oct. 1847 | RCH |
| Painter, Samuel | Higgins, Elisabeth | 14, Jan. 1847 | RCH |
| Palm, Cord Heinrich | Schmidt, Maria | 29, Jan. 1846 | G |
| Palmer, Abraham | Trutebuss, Manor | 18, June 1837 | RCH |
| Palmer, Abraham | Nehemiah, Sarah | 24, Apr. 1844 | RCH |
| Palmer, Edward | Maynard, Mary Jane | 3, June 1848 | RCH |
| Palmer, Henry | Brown, Margaret | 2, Feb. 1818 | RCH |
| Palmer, John E. | Brown, Lucy Ann | 8, Dec. 1824 | RCH |
| Palmer, Joseph | Stillwell, Susan | 23, June 1848 | RCH |
| Palmer, Richard | Smith, Rosanna | 10, Sept 1849 | RCH |
| Palmer, Seneca | Palmer, Mary | 18, May 1839 | RCH |
| Palmer, Thomas | Smith, Sally Ann | 11, Aug. 1833 | RCH |
| Palmer, William | Rice, Sarah | 14, Mar. 1846 | RCH |
| Palmerton, John | Wilcox, Evemond | 11, Mar. 1824 | RCH |
| Palser, Alexander | Anderson, Mary | 24, May 1822 | RCH |
| Pam---, John | Demand, Sarah | 27, Apr. 1818 | RCH |
| Pamader, Georg | Stutzler, Kundigunda | 22, Aug. 1837 | FF |
| Pancera, Anton | Weimann, Margaretha | 10, Aug. 1849 | RCH |
| Pancoast, George | Hovey, Caroline | 12, Nov. 1843 | RCH |
| Pancoast, Jonathan | Powell, Delilah | 9, Feb. 1843 | RCH |
| Pandelo, Lambert | Meyer, Maria Engel | 5, Oct. 1845 | AA |
| Panning, Johan Georg | Sponsel, Catharine | 14, Dec. 1845 | C |
| Pape, Heinrich | Stuever, Catharine | 20, Feb. 1838 | FF |
| Pape, Heinrich | Ginde, Louise | 2, Nov. 1848 | A |
| Pape, Herman | Tiersbers, Sophia | 25, Feb. 1847 | F |
| Papenbrock, Everhard | Iserhinke, Gertrud | 23, Sept 1848 | FF |
| Papenbrock, Wilhelm | Harmann, Elisabeth | 18, Feb. 1849 | AA |
| Pardum, Walter | Greenham, Dinah | 22, Mar. 1833 | RCH |
| Parent, Hiram | Ready, Ann | 28, June 1821 | RCH |
| Paris, Peter | Reese, Mary J. | 20, May 1847 | RCH |
| Parish, William | VanWinkle, Dorcas | 1, Apr. 1847 | RCH |
| Park, Isaac | Hutchinson, Hannah | 23, Jan. 1842 | RCH |
| Park, John D. | Price, Susan | 17, Dec. 1845 | RCH |
| Park, Thomas L. | Young, Elisabeth | 26, Apr. 1849 | RCH |
| Parker, | Struble, Mary | 16, Apr. 1837 | RCH |
| Parker, Alexander | Noble, Melissa | 26, Sept 1848 | RCH |
| Parker, Alfred | Tigar, Christina | 22, Mar. 1848 | RCH |
| Parker, Alvah | Heaslitt, Eliza Jane | 2, Feb. 1846 | RCH |

| Grooms | Brides | Date of Marriage | Code |
|--------|--------|------------------|------|
| ****** | ****** | **** ** ******** | **** |
| Parker, David | Patton, Amanda M. | 2, Oct. 1834 | RCH |
| Parker, David | Evinger, Sarah | 27, Apr. 1843 | RCH |
| Parker, David | Dungan, Harriet | 19, Feb. 1844 | RCH |
| Parker, David | Garnder, Mary | 25, Apr. 1844 | RCH |
| Parker, Francis | Jones, Elisabeth | 18, Jan. 1818 | RCH |
| Parker, Franklin | Carr, Catharine | 27, Oct. 1834 | RCH |
| Parker, Frederick | Langland, Margaret | 24, Feb. 1846 | RCH |
| Parker, George H. | Witt, Lydia | 5, Oct. 1836 | RCH |
| Parker, George W. | Patten, Rachel | 1, June 1843 | RCH |
| Parker, Isaac P. | Burnet, Hannah | 27, June 1822 | RCH |
| Parker, J. | Kincaid, Hannah | 27, Apr. 1837 | RCH |
| Parker, J.H. | Laidley, Jonna | 5, Oct. 1823 | RCH |
| Parker, Jacob | Hoffner, Mary | 29, Sept 1833 | RCH |
| Parker, Jacob | Larew, Catharine | 3, Mar. 1842 | RCH |
| Parker, James | Burns, Ann | 24, Jan. 1825 | RCH |
| Parker, James | Severn, Charlotte | 17, Jan. 1847 | RCH |
| Parker, John | Harris, Emeline | 9, Apr. 1834 | RCH |
| Parker, John | Banks, Lydia | 13, Oct. 1834 | RCH |
| Parker, John J. | Riggs, Elisabeth | 16, Sept 1833 | RCH |
| Parker, Joshua | Kincaid, Francis | 28, Mar. 1844 | RCH |
| Parker, Lewis | Sawyer, Elisabeth | 19, Nov. 1843 | RCH |
| Parker, Lucius H. | Holyoke, Elisabeth | 31, Aug. 1836 | RCH |
| Parker, Samuel | Perry, Jane | 15, Aug. 1849 | RCH |
| Parker, Thomas | Ewans, Elisabeth | 26, Dec. 1841 | RCH |
| Parker, Trebulon | Simpson, Matilda | 29, May 1841 | RCH |
| Parker, W.B. | Scott, Actia Jane | 6, Aug. 1837 | RCH |
| Parker, William | Leeds, Rhoda Ann | Apr. 1844 | RCH |
| Parkhurst, S.L. | Wing, Elisabeth | 12, May 1833 | RCH |
| Parkinson, John H. | Weaver, Catharine | 16, Jan. 1848 | I |
| Parkinson, Martin | Arlington, Frances | 23, June 1833 | RCH |
| Parkinson, Richard | Surguy, Mary Ann | 30, Dec. 1843 | RCH |
| Parks, Austin B. | Shaw, Louise | 24, July 1840 | RCH |
| Parks, Daniel | Layton, Mary Ann | 22, Sept 1842 | RCH |
| Parks, David | Hanna, Margaret | 24, Sept 1841 | RCH |
| Parks, M. | Smith, Margaret | 29, Mar. 1836 | RCH |
| Parks, Nathaniel | Nesbit, Charlotte | 20, Dec. 1841 | RCH |
| Parks, Thomas | Mason, Mary | 9, Mar. 1834 | RCH |
| Parma, Francis | Baer, Catharina | 1, June 1841 | FF |
| Parmela, E. | Crowley, Nancy | 7, Aug. 1821 | RCH |
| Parmer, | Underwood, Mary | 6, June 1822 | RCH |
| Parnell, John | Fish, Louise | 1, Feb. 1835 | RCH |
| Parr, Johan | Gilz, Antonia | 28, Jan. 1849 | EE |
| Parram, William | Ely, Martha | 9, Dec. 1846 | RCH |
| Parrich, Samuel | Park, Lucinda | 3, June 1838 | RCH |
| Parry, Owen | Goodhue, Miranda | 27, Nov. 1845 | RCH |
| Parry, William | Moore, Minerva | 2, Oct. 1842 | RCH |
| Parsell, George | Crowell, Lucy | 1, Mar. 1836 | RCH |
| Parvin, David H. | Winston, Francisca | 22, Oct. 1837 | RCH |
| Parvin, Samuel | Brown, Lucinda | 6, Sept 1848 | RCH |
| Pasckert, Bernard | Kloster, M Catharine | 12, May 1845 | FF |
| Pasely, Benjamin | Herron, Mary Elis. | 17, Sept 1846 | RCH |
| Pasker, Bernard | Hollermann, Matilda | 22, July 1849 | CC |
| Pasley, Henry | Brown, Elisabeth | 22, June 1826 | RCH |
| Paslich, J. Albert | Sohlmann, Catharina | 18, Feb. 1849 | AA |
| Pasmore, Elias | Lambert, Lucinda | 9, Apr. 1848 | RCH |
| Pasqueen, Lawrence | Coddington, Cynthia | 23, Aug. 1845 | RCH |
| Pasquier, Charles | Packard, Martha | 29, Sept 1843 | RCH |
| Passmore, | Remier, Lillie Ann | 25, Sept 1849 | RCH |
| Past, Nicolaus | Goetz, Maria Anna | 4, Nov. 1841 | FF |
| Patberg, Casper H. | Suhrkamp, Catharina | 22, Dec. 1849 | RCH |
| Patmor, Jacob | Coldo, Sarah Ann | 23, May 1844 | RCH |
| Patmor, James | Sotcher, Marion | 5, Sept 1847 | RCH |
| Patmore, Jacob | Pierson, Margaret | 3, Dec. 1848 | RCH |
| Patmore, Mathias | Felton, Elisabeth | 19, Aug. 1824 | RCH |
| Patten, Johan | Schutz, Anna | 7, Sept 1847 | EE |
| Patter, Jonathan | McKer---, Elisabeth | 16, Apr. 1822 | RCH |
| Patterson, Alexander | Long, Elisabeth | 29, Mar. 1821 | RCH |
| Patterson, Andrew | Nelson, Bridget | 25, Feb. 1819 | RCH |
| Patterson, David | Butterfield, Sarah | 17, Jan. 1822 | RCH |
| Patterson, Eli | Cox, Harriet | 28, Dec. 1837 | RCH |
| Patterson, Elijah | Bowman, Nancy | 2, Aug. 1838 | RCH |

| Grooms | Brides | Date of Marriage | Code |
|--------|--------|------------------|------|
| Patterson, George | Lawrie, Jane | 20, Nov. 1845 | RCH |
| Patterson, Henry | Cole, Mary | 14, Dec. 1847 | RCH |
| Patterson, James | Whitcomb, Sarah | 23, Sept 1819 | RCH |
| Patterson, James | Patterson, Hannah | 16, Oct. 1833 | RCH |
| Patterson, John | Williams, Mary A. | 2, Feb. 1839 | RCH |
| Patterson, John | Charter, Elisabeth | 11, Dec. 1844 | RCH |
| Patterson, John D. | Blair, Minerva | 14, Nov. 1844 | RCH |
| Patterson, John S. | Ball, Emily A. | 8, Dec. 1835 | I |
| Patterson, Joseph | Gales, Nancy | 20, Sept 1849 | RCH |
| Patterson, Joshua | Williams, Mary Ann | 2, Feb. 1837 | RCH |
| Patterson, Ludlum | Davis, Hannah M. | 8, Mar. 1832 | RCH |
| Patterson, Richard | Smith, Mary A. | 22, June 1844 | RCH |
| Patterson, Richard | Clark, Lucy | 25, July 1848 | RCH |
| Patterson, Samuel | Felter, Isabella | 31, Mar. 1846 | RCH |
| Patterson, Thomas | Linton, Sarah | 30, May 1835 | RCH |
| Patterson, William | Robins, Adaline | 16, June 1844 | RCH |
| Patterson, William | Kirkpatrick, Elis. | 28, Oct. 1847 | RCH |
| Pattie, William | Phillips, Sarah | 14, Aug. 1836 | RCH |
| Pattison, R.E. | Wilson, Frances | 13, Nov. 1834 | RCH |
| Patton, Alpheus | Davis, Amanda | 23, Sept 1846 | RCH |
| Patton, David | Mefuly, Mary | 18, Jan. 1834 | RCH |
| Patton, David | Danby, Catharine | 1, Mar. 1838 | RCH |
| Patton, Isaac L. | Hall, Jane | 22, June 1825 | RCH |
| Patton, John | Lockwood, Lydia | 8, Mar. 1821 | RCH |
| Patton, John | Rybolt, Abby | 9, Apr. 1835 | RCH |
| Patton, Joseph | Armstrong, Jane | 10, May 1842 | RCH |
| Patton, Joseph | Buskirk, Jane | 11, May 1842 | RCH |
| Patton, Marsh | Isgrig, Rhoda Ann | 9, Aug. 1832 | RCH |
| Patton, William | Dolph, Philinda | 19, Mar. 1831 | RCH |
| Patton, William | Henry, Harriet | 2, Nov. 1846 | RCH |
| Patz, Wilhelm Robert | Fischer, Henrietta C | 3, Nov. 1849 | F |
| Paul, Alexander | Thomas, Margaret | 6, Oct. 1845 | RCH |
| Paul, Casper | Knitel, Margaret | 20, Feb. 1844 | RCH |
| Paul, James M. | Hill, Jane Charlotte | 16, Nov. 1848 | RCH |
| Paul, Joseph | Becht, Apollonia | 7, Jan. 1849 | FF |
| Paul, Robert | Featherland, Elis. | 16, July 1843 | RCH |
| Paul, William | Menke, Mary | 30, May 1843 | RCH |
| Pauland, Heinrich | Schumacher, M. Dina | 19, Oct. 1841 | FF |
| Pauli, Anton | Schoen, Crescentia | 18, Sept 1848 | II |
| Paulite, Joseph | Swift, Mary | 8, Feb. 1836 | RCH |
| Paulsen, Peter Corn. | Dyrssen, Ovedine S. | 20, Oct. 1848 | C |
| Pauly, Anton | Schein, Anna Theresa | 8, May 1848 | RCH |
| Paver, George W. | Hoffman, Nancy Ann | 16, Aug. 1836 | I |
| Pawen, George | Hoffmann, Nancy Ann | 16, Aug. 1837 | RCH |
| Paxton, Samuel | Willer, Elisabeth | 14, June 1821 | RCH |
| Pay, Oscar | Ingersoll, Hester | 17, May 1846 | RCH |
| Payne, Arthur | Huntley, Rebecca E. | 5, Jan. 1842 | RCH |
| Payne, Benjamin | Bolles, Harriet | 10, Aug. 1848 | RCH |
| Payne, Bracket | Miller, Hannah | 29, Oct. 1836 | RCH |
| Payne, Edward | Smith, Frances | 27, Dec. 1840 | RCH |
| Payne, Enoch | Hall, Martha | 27, June 1847 | RCH |
| Payne, John M. | Hageman, Catharine | 10, Dec. 1834 | RCH |
| Payne, William | Morgan, Martha | 10, Feb. 1848 | D |
| Payne, William James | Jardine, Elisabeth | 6, Apr. 1846 | RCH |
| Payton, John | Holliday, Hannah | 22, Dec. 1837 | RCH |
| Peables, William | Stevenson, Lucy | 28, Oct. 1841 | RCH |
| Peace, Horace | Price, Lucretia | 23, Feb. 1826 | RCH |
| Peacock, John George | Murphy, Mary Elis. | 3, Apr. 1845 | BB |
| Peacock, William | Browner, Sophia J. | 8, June 1847 | RCH |
| Pealer, George | Stewart, Elisabeth | 11, June 1835 | RCH |
| Pearce, Benjamin | Cross, Thesiah | 18, May 1822 | RCH |
| Pearce, Henry | Pearson, Elisabeth | 26, Mar. 1835 | RCH |
| Pearce, Henry | Lee, Elisabeth | 12, Feb. 1842 | RCH |
| Pearce, Henry | Owens, Elisabeth | 9, Aug. 1847 | RCH |
| Pearce, James | Goss, Mary | 18, May 1847 | D |
| Pearce, John | Campbell, Sally | 15, Sept 1835 | RCH |
| Pearce, Samuel | Parks, Elisabeth | 2, Nov. 1841 | RCH |
| Pearse, Albert | Williams, Hannah | 25, Jan. 1849 | RCH |
| Pearson, Benjamin | Mofford, Lucinda | 7, Mar. 1847 | RCH |
| Pearson, Charles | Ramsten, Sophia | 6, Aug. 1849 | RCH |
| Pearson, Charles D. | Laterhell, Sarah | 9, Aug. 1824 | RCH |

| Grooms | Brides | Date of Marriage | Code |
|--------|--------|------------------|------|
| Pearson, Frederick | Dill, Ann | 17, Sept 1832 | RCH |
| Pearson, Jesse | Sampson, Martha | 17, Oct. 1822 | RCH |
| Pearson, John | Nightengale, Betsey | 11, Sept 1843 | RCH |
| Pearson, John | Brokenshire, Mary A. | 24, Sept 1846 | RCH |
| Pearson, John | Lemmon, Millison | 21, Nov. 1847 | RCH |
| Pearson, Levi | Emmon, Hannah | 6, July 1820 | RCH |
| Pearson, Richard | Hanes, Martha | 7, May 1837 | RCH |
| Pearson, William | Nash, Abba | 20, Mar. 1836 | RCH |
| Peas, Henry | Padgett, Elisabeth | 27, June 1833 | RCH |
| Peas, Horace | Stitts, Ann | 26, July 1821 | RCH |
| Pease, Henry B. | Morrison, Theresa | 24, Mar. 1836 | RCH |
| Peasse, John | Baget, Alice | 5, Aug. 1841 | RCH |
| Peavey, Joseph | Vetile, Mary | 19, Sept 1846 | RCH |
| Peavy, Eliphalet | Miller, Roxanna | 25, Dec. 1841 | RCH |
| Peck, Bernard | Heidkamper, Gertrud | 17, Feb. 1846 | RCH |
| Peck, Charles | Potter, Adeline | 8, Mar. 1842 | RCH |
| Peck, Eli | Schuyler, Abby | 14, Apr. 1846 | RCH |
| Peck, Georg | Hayden, Almira J. | 13, June 1847 | RCH |
| Peck, Homer | Jones, Elisabeth J. | 9, Dec. 1843 | RCH |
| Peck, John | Reick, Dorothea | 3, Dec. 1843 | RCH |
| Peck, O.W. | Cropper, Angelina | 22, Nov. 1843 | RCH |
| Peck, William | Brown, Elisabeth J. | 12, Nov. 1843 | RCH |
| Peckenpaugh, Michael | Hathorn, Susan | 26, May 1847 | RCH |
| Peckinpaugh, Fred. | Livingston, Delilah | 9, Dec. 1834 | RCH |
| Peebles, James | Farmer, Mary Elis. | 12, June 1847 | RCH |
| Peebles, Joseph R. | Straub, M. Carolina | 20, Feb. 1844 | RCH |
| Peek, Bernard | Heitkemper, Gertrud | 24, Feb. 1846 | AA |
| Peek, William | ----, Catharine | 4, Oct. 1838 | RCH |
| Peel, Samuel | Cupsey, Margaret Ann | 22, June 1837 | RCH |
| Peepen, Friedrich W. | Bahn, M. Dorothea | 28, Dec. 1843 | RCH |
| Peeper, A. | Miller, Catharine | 2, Oct. 1834 | RCH |
| Peerce, John | Hazgard, Charlotte | 13, May 1841 | RCH |
| Peers, Henry | Coppin, Elmira | 28, Oct. 1837 | RCH |
| Peers, William | Reed, Grace | 19, Apr. 1847 | RCH |
| Peht, Alexander H. | Sells, Lydia | 28, May 1833 | RCH |
| Pelch, Alfred | Taylor, Jane | 25, Dec. 1841 | RCH |
| Pelham, William | Phelps, Almira | 4, Sept 1823 | RCH |
| Pelking, Bernard H. | Weise, Maria | 12, May 1840 | FF |
| Pell, John | Cresland, Martha | 20, July 1839 | RCH |
| Pell, Nicolaus | Day, Catharine | 2, Aug. 1838 | RCH |
| Pell, Nicolaus | Pelton, Amelia | 1, Jan. 1849 | RCH |
| Pellewessel, Herman | Wellbrink, Elisabeth | 9, Apr. 1839 | FF |
| Pelser, Friedrich H. | Schroeder, Theresa | 21, Nov. 1847 | FF |
| Pelser, Gerhard | Plaspohl, Maria Anna | 28, Oct. 1849 | EE |
| Pelton, George | Corder, Sarah | 8, May 1846 | RCH |
| Pelton, John | Grant, Mary Ann | 15, Feb. 1846 | RCH |
| Pelton, Lorenzo | Campbell, Martha | 14, Apr. 1843 | RCH |
| Pelton, Mahlon | Turner, Sarah Ann | 11, Apr. 1844 | RCH |
| Pelzer, Francis | Tegenkamp, Lucia | 13, Oct. 1835 | FF |
| Pelzer, Gerhard H. | Ossenbeck, Dorothea | 28, Nov. 1843 | AA |
| Pelzer, Theodor | Duevel, Maria | 13, May 1849 | FF |
| Pemberton, Thomas | Centhinger, Louise | 26, Nov. 1848 | RCH |
| Pemrell, George W. | Miles, Cath. Elis. | 27, Dec. 1842 | I |
| Pendergast, John G. | Mc---, Hannah | 30, Nov. 1818 | RCH |
| Pendery, Alexander | Williamson, Sarah | 27, Aug. 1838 | RCH |
| Pendery, James | Dunn, Naomi | 11, May 1848 | RCH |
| Pendery, John | Rockey, Catharine | 10, June 1847 | I |
| Pendery, Ralph | Weatherby, Susan S. | 15, Dec. 1846 | RCH |
| Pendery, William D. | Skillman, Mary Ann | 6, Nov. 1833 | RCH |
| Pendleton, Edmund | Morgan, Cornelia | 13, Jan. 1845 | I |
| Pendleton, Nathaniel | Hunt, Jane F. | 10, May 1820 | RCH |
| Pengemann, Gerhard B | Wilkemacke, Anna M. | 26, June 1849 | AA |
| Penn, James | Moors, Ann | 2, Aug. 1838 | RCH |
| Penn, James | Ruse, Margaret | 24, July 1839 | RCH |
| Penn, James | Langston, Ann | 21, Aug. 1849 | RCH |
| Penn, John W. | McDougal, Catharine | 19, Sept 1835 | RCH |
| Pennefather, William | Nugent, Margaret | 17, Mar. 1849 | GG |
| Pensky, Michael | Brandt, Henrietta | 11, Feb. 1849 | G |
| Penter, George Adam | Stauss, E.M. | 9, Oct. 1841 | RCH |
| Pentermann, Herman H | Hone, Margaretha | 4, Nov. 1847 | F |
| Peoples, Samuel | Stafford, Mahala | 21, May 1836 | RCH |

| Grooms<br>****** | Brides<br>****** | Date of Marriage<br>**** ** ******** | Code<br>**** |
|---|---|---|---|
| Peper, Carl | Niermann, Louisa | 26, Oct. 1841 | F |
| Pepperkorn, Heinrich | Niehaus, Catharina | 31, July 1849 | II |
| Pepperkorn, J Heinr. | Lienesch, M. Gertrud | 8, Jan. 1845 | FF |
| Perckes, Johan | Kehl, Magdalena | 29, July 1849 | AA |
| Perdee, Alfred | Conover, Ann | 19, Mar. 1837 | RCH |
| Perien, August | Kline, Maria Cath. | 2, May 1839 | RCH |
| Perin, Franklin | McMicken, Mary | 28, June 1844 | RCH |
| Pering, Rannd | Thomas, Elisabeth | 27, Aug. 1832 | RCH |
| Perkey, David | Symons, Mary Ann | 10, June 1844 | RCH |
| Perkey, David | Rusk, Ellen | 19, Apr. 1847 | RCH |
| Perkins, Askner | Eort, Josephine | 17, Sept 1841 | RCH |
| Perkins, August | Wadsworth, Fanny | 25, Jan. 1844 | RCH |
| Perkins, James H. | Elliot, Sarah H. | 17, Dec. 1834 | D |
| Perkins, Manuel | Wade, Elisabeth | 21, Aug. 1845 | RCH |
| Perkins, Thomas H. | McCullough, Elisabet | 14, Jan. 1847 | RCH |
| Perkins, William | Robinson, Elisabeth | 7, Apr. 1833 | RCH |
| Perle, John | Pierson, Mariah | 31, Dec. 1835 | RCH |
| Perret, Philipp H. | Pernet, Cecilia | 11, June 1824 | RCH |
| Perrine, Amos | Decor, Jerusha | 23, Jan. 1833 | RCH |
| Perrine, William H. | Long, Mary | 27, Dec. 1825 | RCH |
| Perrish, Edmund | Smith, Margaret | 29, June 1821 | RCH |
| Perry, Aaron | Williams, Elisabeth | 15, Mar. 1843 | RCH |
| Perry, Fountain | Keenes, Julia Ann | 20, Jan. 1832 | I |
| Perry, Gardner M. | Stewart, Margaret | 14, Dec. 1834 | RCH |
| Perry, Georg Fried. | Davis, Susan | 1, May 1849 | RCH |
| Perry, James | Demming, Emilia | 22, Mar. 1821 | RCH |
| Perry, John | Strout, Mary | 4, Mar. 1821 | RCH |
| Perry, John | Hinnan, Sophia | 8, Oct. 1835 | RCH |
| Perry, John | Ashton, Elisabeth | 1, Oct. 1837 | RCH |
| Perry, John | Harris, Mary | 17, Dec. 1843 | RCH |
| Perry, Joseph | Marriott, Sarah | 10, Oct. 1822 | RCH |
| Perry, Louis | Donley, Ellen | 18, May 1847 | RCH |
| Perry, Mason | Stroughten, Anna | 25, Dec. 1847 | RCH |
| Perry, Richard | Guthrie, Nancy | 25, Dec. 1817 | RCH |
| Perry, Richard | Edwards, Mary | 28, May 1840 | RCH |
| Perry, Richard | Gambriel, Maria | 6, Oct. 1845 | RCH |
| Perry, Samuel R. | Pancoast, Louise | 29, Aug. 1826 | RCH |
| Perry, Stacy | Hathorn, Amanda | 18, Sept 1846 | RCH |
| Perry, William | Hulse, Maria | 27, Nov. 1844 | RCH |
| Perry, William A. | Lee, Caroline B. | 25, Oct. 1835 | RCH |
| Perry, William J. | Burroughs, Rosanna | 21, Jan. 1838 | RCH |
| Perryman, John W. | Constable, Margaret | 22, Mar. 1848 | RCH |
| Persell, Joseph | Rollson, Hetty Ann | 29, Dec. 1822 | RCH |
| Persons, | Carbar, Rachel | 25, Nov. 1844 | RCH |
| Perterfield, James | Newborough, Lavina | 24, Dec. 1835 | RCH |
| Peter, Georg Adam | Noll, Regina | 27, June 1839 | FF |
| Peter, Heinrich | Schneider, Catharine | 22, Aug. 1849 | B |
| Peter, Jacob W. | Gettier, Josephine | 8, June 1848 | G |
| Peter, Johan Heinric | VonderHeide, Anna M. | 23, Mar. 1843 | F |
| Peter, Meinrad | Albert, Catharina | 29, Nov. 1849 | G |
| Petermann, Heinrich | Schmidt, A. Adelheid | 9, Mar. 1848 | F |
| Peters, Christopher | Uphof, Elisabeth | 18, Aug. 1848 | II |
| Peters, Gerhard | Rusche, Catharine | 10, Jan. 1847 | AA |
| Peters, Gerhard | Hoping, Catharine | 21, Aug. 1849 | FF |
| Peters, Heinrich | Dunker, Anna Cath. | 7, Oct. 1849 | CC |
| Peters, Isaac | Lusk, Sarah | 2, Aug. 1832 | RCH |
| Peters, Jacob | Peace, Mary | 5, Jan. 1827 | RCH |
| Peters, James S. | Dunn, Sarah | 31, July 1849 | RCH |
| Peters, Johan Hein. | Huerstmann, Anna M. | 28, Jan. 1845 | AA |
| Peters, Joseph | Rogers, Lucretia | 24, Aug. 1834 | RCH |
| Peters, Joseph | Kaspers, Catharine | 5, Mar. 1848 | II |
| Peters, Joseph F. | Kennedy, Eleanor | 25, Sept 1835 | RCH |
| Peters, Simon | Turner, Elisabeth | 2, May 1842 | RCH |
| Peters, Wilhelm | Espel, Sophia F. | 23, Nov. 1843 | RCH |
| Peters, William | Shy, Ann C. | 13, Oct. 1844 | RCH |
| Petersohn, Jacob | Klostermann, Maria | 10, July 1845 | G |
| Peterson, Christian | Becker, Catharine | 2, Oct. 1846 | G |
| Peterson, Elisha | Brown, Elisabeth | 2, Jan. 1834 | RCH |
| Peterson, Isaac | Conover, Mary Ann | 3, Oct. 1837 | RCH |
| Peterson, Johan Wm. | Meyer, M. Elisabeth | 26, Dec. 1846 | G |
| Peterson, John S. | Sentney, Mary A. | 28, Jan. 1849 | RCH |

| Grooms<br>****** | Brides<br>****** | Date of Marriage<br>**** ** ******** | Code<br>**** |
|---|---|---|---|
| Peterson, Peter | Williams, Abigail | 9, Oct. 1832 | RCH |
| Peterson, Peter | Williams, Mary | 13, Oct. 1837 | RCH |
| Peterson, Philipp | Bechtell, Charlotte | 28, Mar. 1848 | RCH |
| Peterson, Ralph | Hardingbrook, Sarah | 30, May 1822 | RCH |
| Peterson, Wilhelm | Woellmann, M. Cath. | 10, Mar. 1846 | G |
| Peterson, William | Albers, Elisabeth | 5, Nov. 1841 | RCH |
| Petri, Jacob | Morhaus, M Elisabeth | 30, Oct. 1846 | A |
| Petrie, Joseph | Kelly, Mary | 24, Nov. 1825 | RCH |
| Petteida--, Theodore | Woodruff, Caroline | 24, Dec. 1823 | RCH |
| Pettet, Cornelius | Morrison, Effie | 23, Nov. 1848 | RCH |
| Pettibone, Andrew | Blohm, Maria | 6, June 1848 | F |
| Pettiford, Lewis | Basil, Artemesia | 11, Sept 1849 | RCH |
| Pettis, Andrew | McCarthy, Sarah | 1, July 1847 | RCH |
| Pettis, Simon | Boyer, Elisabeth | 28, June 1847 | RCH |
| Pettit, David | Fair, Elisabeth | 31, Aug. 1832 | RCH |
| Pettit, Elnathan | Benhana, Harriet | 11, July 1840 | RCH |
| Pettit, John | Alexander, Mary | 2, Feb. 1834 | RCH |
| Petton, William | Edes, Permelia | 4, Feb. 1847 | RCH |
| Peyer, Samuel | Scheis, Lena | 6, Sept 1849 | A |
| Peyton, Blewfort | Cookenar, Elisabeth | 15, Feb. 1843 | RCH |
| Peyton, Daniel | Hazelton, Debora | 14, May 1843 | RCH |
| Peyton, Levi | Franks, Barbara A. | 27, Dec. 1847 | RCH |
| Pfaff, John | Holt, Louise | 15, Mar. 1842 | RCH |
| Pfaff, Nicolaus | Spies, Genofeva | 12, Sept 1839 | FF |
| Pfaffenberger, Georg | Hahn, Barbara | 24, Oct. 1847 | EE |
| Pfalzgraf, Philipp | Waldmann, Eva | 7, Mar. 1848 | A |
| Pfalzgraf, Philipp | Martin, Magdalena | 6, Nov. 1849 | A |
| Pfarr, Johan | Franzheim, Magdalena | 17, Mar. 1846 | C |
| Pfau, Philipp | Crepeter, Elisabeth | 27, May 1847 | B |
| Pfau, Sylvester | Nadler, Charlotte | 25, Sept 1838 | FF |
| Pfautsch, Johan | Pfaff, Catharine | 9, Sept 1845 | AA |
| Pfeifer, Christian | Dunker, Melina | 26, Jan. 1847 | FF |
| Pfeifer, Friedrich | Panthoefer, Christ. | 5, Mar. 1848 | EE |
| Pfeifer, Georg | Neuhart, Victoria | 2, June 1846 | EE |
| Pfeifer, Heinrich | Thomas, Anna Elis. | 2, Dec. 1847 | C |
| Pfeifer, Marc | Hippen, Lucia | 15, June 1848 | EE |
| Pfeiffer, Georg | Sutter, Maria | 7, Oct. 1849 | EE |
| Pfeister, Franz | Reis, Magdalena | 11, Apr. 1839 | G |
| Pfetzer, Joseph | Amberg, Maria | 28, May 1849 | AA |
| Pfiermann, Conrad | Schmidt, Margaretha | 24, Oct. 1844 | C |
| Pflug, William | Erkmann, Eva | 3, July 1842 | RCH |
| Pflum, Johan | Laut, Sophia | 22, Nov. 1848 | EE |
| Pflum, Wolfgang | Bogenschultz, Kunig. | 18, Sept 1843 | AA |
| Phares, Amos | Herron, Elisabeth | 7, May 1835 | RCH |
| Phares, John | Butler, Hannah | 7, Oct. 1842 | RCH |
| Phares, John | Pritchard, Martha | 9, Dec. 1845 | RCH |
| Phares, Matthew | Martin, Rebecca | 24, Sept 1849 | RCH |
| Phares, R.T. | ----, Elisabeth | 22, Mar. 1835 | RCH |
| Phares, Robert | Brown, Jane | 9, Apr. 1818 | RCH |
| Phares, Samuel | Hutchinson, Polley | 14, Nov. 1824 | RCH |
| Phares, Samuel | Gould, Jane | 26, Dec. 1846 | RCH |
| Pharran, William | Casey, Nancy | 25, Oct. 1842 | RCH |
| Phelan, Philip | Powers, Bridget | 15, Apr. 1849 | GG |
| Phelps, John | Shaw, Mary | 3, Dec. 1818 | RCH |
| Phelps, Samuel W. | Ball, Ann | 22, Feb. 1835 | I |
| Phester, Chester | Shearer, Catharine | 24, May 1839 | RCH |
| Philbin, John | Manly, Mary | 31, Oct. 1849 | GG |
| Philhour, Philip | Sears, Catharine | 26, Apr. 1821 | RCH |
| Philipp, Abraham | Steinaugh, Caroline | June 1849 | RCH |
| Philipp, Georg | Stengen, Margaretha | 28, Apr. 1846 | EE |
| Philipps, William | Lister, Hannah | 15, Jan. 1842 | RCH |
| Philips, | Durkey, Betsey | 11, June 1818 | RCH |
| Philips, B. | Purlier, Elisabeth | 24, Aug. 1845 | RCH |
| Philips, Spencer | Robinson, Hannah | 27, Dec. 1821 | RCH |
| Philips, Thomas H. | McCoy, Ann | 6, Feb. 1822 | RCH |
| Philips, William G. | Gifford, Josephine | 17, Sept 1848 | RCH |
| Philley, Erastus | Griffin, Mary | 20, Sept 1836 | RCH |
| Phillip, John | McEwen, Catharine | 5, Dec. 1849 | RCH |
| Phillip, Robert C. | Smith, Maria | 28, Aug. 1834 | RCH |
| Phillips, | Hagemann, Catharine | 28, Nov. 1849 | RCH |
| Phillips, Andrew | Wyatt, Elisabeth J. | 7, Sept 1848 | RCH |

| Grooms | Brides | Date of Marriage | Code |
|--------|--------|------------------|------|
| ****** | ****** | **** ** ******** | **** |
| Phillips, Asa | Norholtz, Elisabeth | 3, Oct. 1819 | RCH |
| Phillips, Elias | Sharp, Sarah | 20, Mar. 1826 | RCH |
| Phillips, George W. | Lynes, Susan | 24, Apr. 1825 | RCH |
| Phillips, Henry | Thomas, Margaret | 13, June 1825 | RCH |
| Phillips, James | Douglass, Elisabeth | 11, Jan. 1821 | RCH |
| Phillips, James | Rosenburgh, Nancy | 9, May 1840 | RCH |
| Phillips, Joel | Goldsmith, Charlotte | 3, July 1837 | RCH |
| Phillips, John | Dusheef, Betsy | 18, June 1818 | RCH |
| Phillips, John | Dandy, Maria | 21, Mar. 1842 | RCH |
| Phillips, John R. | Beeler, Nancy | 22, Nov. 1849 | RCH |
| Phillips, Mark | Morrison, Sarah | 1, Apr. 1824 | RCH |
| Phillips, Moses | Noble, Elisabeth | 16, Aug. 1835 | RCH |
| Phillips, Moses | Silvers, Sarah | 21, Feb. 1838 | RCH |
| Phillips, Richard | Gest, Sally | 12, Nov. 1820 | RCH |
| Phillips, Robert | Humber, Mary S. | 2, Aug. 1843 | RCH |
| Phillips, Thomas | Harris, Mary | 27, Aug. 1845 | RCH |
| Phillips, William | Long, Mary Ann | 15, Feb. 1841 | RCH |
| Phillips, William C. | Finnigan, Mary | 9, Nov. 1840 | BB |
| Phillips, William H. | Hill, Martha | 8, Nov. 1847 | RCH |
| Phillis, Jacob | Brundenge, Murilda | 7, Nov. 1833 | RCH |
| Phillis, Thomas | Ross, Emeline | 5, June 1836 | RCH |
| Phiper, John | Shearer, Elisabeth | 14, Feb. 1837 | RCH |
| Phipps, Christopher | Gilmore, Angeline | 26, Dec. 1847 | RCH |
| Phipps, Elias | Pierson, Hulda | 26, Sept 1842 | RCH |
| Phipps, Tobias | Miller, Sophia | 27, Oct. 1847 | RCH |
| Phipps, William | Dernerice, Emily | 3, Feb. 1836 | RCH |
| Phipps, William | Dixon, Margaret | 27, Nov. 1842 | RCH |
| Piatt, Donn | Kirby, Louise | 18, Aug. 1847 | BB |
| Piatt, Jacob W. | Devalcourt, Martha | 29, Aug. 1837 | RCH |
| Piatt, John | Hybeman, Hannah | 22, May 1834 | RCH |
| Pickelheimer, David | Sharp, Susan | 20, Jan. 1846 | RCH |
| Pickens, John | Porter, Elisabeth | 8, Dec. 1841 | RCH |
| Picker, Johan Chris. | Horsemann, Catharina | 21, Apr. 1836 | FF |
| Pickering, George M. | Seamore, Maria | 5, June 1833 | RCH |
| Pickering, Thomas | Kendall, Elisabeth | 1, Apr. 1838 | RCH |
| Picket, John M. | Williams, Elinor P. | 7, Oct. 1833 | RCH |
| Pickett, Thomas | Fennemore, Harriet | 2, Apr. 1848 | RCH |
| Pickham, Andrew | Holland, Mary Jane | 24, Nov. 1842 | RCH |
| Pickins, Alexander | Baumeister, Lucinda | 22, Oct. 1842 | RCH |
| Pickle, Anton | Dueringer, Antonia | 3, July 1849 | EE |
| Pieper, Bernard | Faehr, Barbara | 20, June 1844 | AA |
| Pieper, J. Gerhard | Holtmeyer, Catharina | 13, May 1849 | AA |
| Piepmeyer, Johan F. | Huermann, Maria | 11, Nov. 1846 | AA |
| Pierce, Charles H. | Chase, Harriet | 9, Nov. 1847 | RCH |
| Pierce, Isaac | Millne, Jane | 23, July 1834 | RCH |
| Pierce, John | Stoyden, Ruth | 20, Aug. 1837 | RCH |
| Pierce, Samuel R. | Comstock, Sylvia | 24, Apr. 1834 | RCH |
| Pierce, Thomas | Wheeler, Mary Jane | 29, Sept 1845 | RCH |
| Pierce, William | Sloop, Maria | 11, Mar. 1849 | RCH |
| Pierce, William H. | Jackson, Eveline | 8, Sept 1836 | RCH |
| Pierson, Charles | Marrow, Jane | 29, July 1845 | RCH |
| Pierson, David | C---, Elisabeth | 6, Jan. 1825 | RCH |
| Pierson, James | Roseboom, Sarah Jane | 29, Oct. 1846 | RCH |
| Pierson, Jesse | Wood, Almira | 16, Mar. 1833 | RCH |
| Pierson, Jesse | Schenck, Margaret | 15, Nov. 1843 | RCH |
| Pierson, Jonathan | Hill, Phoebe | 16, Mar. 1843 | RCH |
| Pierson, Moses B. | Barr, Lucy | 26, Mar. 1833 | RCH |
| Pierson, Simon | Layman, Harriet | 6, June 1841 | RCH |
| Pierson, William | Couse, Isabella | 13, Oct. 1836 | RCH |
| Pierson, William | Schanck, Rebecca | 10, Feb. 1842 | RCH |
| Pieser, Jacob | Pfister, Elisabeth | 1, Sept 1845 | C |
| Pigman, Harrison T. | ----, Phoebe | 21, June 1835 | RCH |
| Pike, George | Ross, Prudence | 29, Sept 1842 | RCH |
| Pike, Samuel | Miller, Ellen | 29, Oct. 1846 | RCH |
| Pike, Wesley | Drake, Lu. | 19, Apr. 1835 | RCH |
| Pilage, Heinrich | Hemmer, Anna Maria | 10, Feb. 1846 | AA |
| Piles, Andrew J. | Wilson, Nancy | 12, Nov. 1836 | RCH |
| Pilkington, George | Crary, Martha | 10, Mar. 1842 | RCH |
| Pille, Friedrich | Witteriede, Catharin | 16, July 1848 | FF |
| Piller, John Bernard | Becker, Maria | 27, Jan. 1835 | FF |
| Pilmore, Eben H. | Smith, Mary H. | 25, Dec. 1832 | RCH |

| Grooms | Brides | Date of Marriage | Code |
|--------|--------|------------------|------|
| ****** | ****** | **** ** ******** | **** |
| Pilsing, Friedrich | Kreke, Maria | 10, Aug. 1841 | FF |
| Pincheon, W. | Mathers, Nancy | 25, Nov. 1825 | RCH |
| Pindell, Daniel | Storlig, Elisabeth | 12, Oct. 1841 | RCH |
| Pindell, Richard | Beard, Amanda M. | 17, Feb. 1833 | RCH |
| Pine, Benjamin | Hoogland, Mary | 30, Apr. 1819 | RCH |
| Pine, Lazarus | Holden, Elisabeth | 11, Apr. 1822 | RCH |
| Pinger, Jacob | Bohl, Mary | 17, Nov. 1845 | EE |
| Pingstrauss, Herman | Woltmann, Maria Cath | 28, Aug. 1849 | EE |
| Pining, Joseph | Strieker, Agnes | 29, Apr. 1849 | AA |
| Pinney, Sidney | Johnson, Elisabeth | 25, Apr. 1839 | RCH |
| Piper, Charles | Engelking, Christina | 7, June 1836 | RCH |
| Piper, Conrad | Braun, Anna Maria | 15, Nov. 1849 | G |
| Piper, George | Cattrill, Tamar | 17, Sept 1847 | RCH |
| Pisenti, Peter | Bust, Mary | 9, Dec. 1839 | I |
| Pisters, Joseph | Geisler, Catharine | 15, May 1844 | AA |
| Pistner, Adam | Brand, Carolina | 6, May 1845 | AA |
| Pistner, Johan | Reis, Margaretha | 3, Mar. 1840 | FF |
| Pistner, Martin | Walte, Elisabeth | 17, Jan. 1837 | FF |
| Pitabone, Albert | Wyatt, Frances | 30, Jan. 1836 | RCH |
| Pitman, Jonathan | Argardine, Jane | 2, Dec. 1825 | RCH |
| Pitroff, Georg | Gratz, Margaretha | 13, May 1849 | EE |
| Pittman, Ephraim | McClellan, Hannah | 19, Feb. 1818 | RCH |
| Pittman, Nathan | Chandler, Mary | 11, Nov. 1818 | RCH |
| Plack, Henry | Lampe, Sophia | 1, Sept 1841 | RCH |
| Placke, Friedrich | Soelmann, Catharina | 21, May 1846 | G |
| Plagemann, Joseph | Sonderhaus, M. Agnes | 16, Apr. 1844 | FF |
| Plagemann, Joseph | Schroeder, Anna M. | 7, Oct. 1849 | AA |
| Planck, Johan | Heit, Margaretha | 11, Dec. 1847 | EE |
| Plaspohl, Andreas | Helmes, Maria Helena | 7, Aug. 1844 | AA |
| Plate, Hannabel | Brown, Hannah | 3, Nov. 1841 | RCH |
| Platfant, Gerhard | Sanders, A. Adelheid | 1, Nov. 1849 | II |
| Platt, Alfred J. | Harrison, Mary Ann | 23, Apr. 1839 | RCH |
| Platt, James | Ginsley, | 8, June 1834 | RCH |
| Platt, William | Herbert, Sarah Ann | 18, Aug. 1840 | RCH |
| Pleasants, Samuel E. | Biggs, Mary | 17, May 1821 | I |
| Pleickert, Carl H. | Dotgen, Catharine | 5, Sept 1846 | G |
| Plevins, James | ----, ---- | 10, June 1826 | RCH |
| Plimridge, Thomas | McIntosh, Margaret | 17, Feb. 1842 | RCH |
| Ploehs, Johan Hein. | Wellmann, Carolina | 1, Feb. 1846 | AA |
| Plogmann, Heinrich | Frommeyer, M.G. | 17, June 1849 | AA |
| Plogmann, Johan | Elixmann, Maria | 11, July 1847 | AA |
| Plosner, Daniel | Albright, Rosina | 22, Apr. 1841 | RCH |
| Plow, Joseph | ----, Mary | 19, Sept 1839 | RCH |
| Plowman, Edward | Jones, Elisabeth | 25, Aug. 1846 | RCH |
| Plucker, Heinrich | Bille, Anna Maria | 23, Feb. 1839 | FF |
| Plum, Gotfried | Metz, Carolina | 26, Nov. 1839 | FF |
| Plummer, Daniel | Hunt, Ann | 3, Dec. 1837 | RCH |
| Plummer, Henry | Connel, Mary | 29, May 1839 | RCH |
| Plump, Daniel | Hildebrand, Cath. | 8, May 1838 | FF |
| Plump, Herman Hein. | Fricke, Elisabeth | 30, Apr. 1840 | F |
| Plump, Johan Heinric | Henkentin, M. Engel | 2, May 1840 | F |
| Plunket, Matthew | Dolan, Catharine | 20, Aug. 1848 | BB |
| Plunket, Peter | O'Brien, Ann | 3, June 1845 | BB |
| Podesta, Bartholomew | Williams, Anna | 6, Dec. 1842 | BB |
| Poe, George | Topf, Lucina | 2, June 1846 | RCH |
| Poehner, Andrew | Roeter, Margaretha | 24, Dec. 1843 | RCH |
| Poehner, Heinrich | Stimmermann, Cath. | 4, Dec. 1843 | C |
| Poerjer, Johan | Selm, Maria | 20, June 1848 | EE |
| Poeslash, Benedict | Straub, Elisabeth | 22, Sept 1834 | RCH |
| Pogendick, Heinrich | Gerdsen, Caroline | 30, May 1844 | F |
| Pohl, Herman H. | Alvdrosen, Margaret | 2, July 1848 | EE |
| Pohlmann, Bernard | Rusche, Agnes | 29, Oct. 1843 | FF |
| Pohlmann, Carl Fried | Baum, Eva Catharina | 18, Nov. 1847 | A |
| Pohlmann, Heinrich | Nienaber, Maria | 8, Sept 1844 | FF |
| Pohlmann, Heinrich | Hackmann, Catharine | 4, Nov. 1845 | AA |
| Pohlmann, Herman H. | Gerke, A.M. Louise | 2, Sept 1847 | F |
| Pohlmann, Johan Herm | Faring, Maria Anna | 24, Feb. 1838 | FF |
| Pohlmann, Joseph H. | Sundermann, Cath. M. | 3, Apr. 1845 | C |
| Pohlmann, Nicolaus | Kitter, Hannah Cath. | 9, Aug. 1842 | RCH |
| Pohlmann, Paul | Zeitler, Sophia | 16, Jan. 1848 | A |
| Pohlmeyer, Heinrich | Kuhlmann, Bernardina | 1, Aug. 1848 | FF |

| Grooms | Brides | Date of Marriage | Code |
|--------|--------|------------------|------|
| ****** | ****** | **** ** ******** | **** |
| Pohlschneider, Bern. | Asbrede, Margaretha | 20, Feb. 1848 | AA |
| Poindexter, Joel | Davis, Elisabeth Ann | 22, Apr. 1841 | RCH |
| Poinier, Isaac | Hanniss, Amanda | 9, May 1844 | RCH |
| Poireier, Henry | Wallace, Mary | 19, Nov. 1848 | GG |
| Poklet, Philipp | Voll, Anna | 29, Aug. 1848 | EE |
| Poland, Nathan | McChesney, Eleanor | 26, Dec. 1817 | RCH |
| Poland, Patrick | Ryan, Mary | 8, Feb. 1846 | BB |
| Pole, James | McDonald, Anna | 11, Sept 1847 | RCH |
| Polinger, Stephan | Klein, Eva Maria | 2, July 1848 | EE |
| Pollack, Thomas | Ay---, Rachel | 8, Apr. 1820 | RCH |
| Pollee, William | Preston, Elisabeth | 27, Feb. 1832 | RCH |
| Pollock, | Sherrer, Margaret | 15, Apr. 1838 | RCH |
| Pollock, Collin | Amos, Margaret | 27, Aug. 1846 | RCH |
| Pollock, Cyrus | Sutton, | 15, Jan. 1825 | RCH |
| Pollock, Hamilton | Apgar, Margaret | 16, Nov. 1846 | RCH |
| Pollock, John | Rude, Rachel | 16, Oct. 1817 | RCH |
| Pollock, John | Butler, Martha | 12, Aug. 1845 | RCH |
| Polly, Charles | Orr, Mary Jane | 1, Oct. 1846 | RCH |
| Polser, John | Rofelter, Peggy | 25, Dec. 1820 | RCH |
| Polster, George | Hartlein, Barbara | 23, May 1849 | C |
| Pomroy, Caleb M. | Simpson, Nancy | 8, Oct. 1834 | RCH |
| Pontius, Peter | Loeffel, Maria | 22, Nov. 1842 | A |
| Pool, George | Smith, Mahala | 23, June 1846 | RCH |
| Pool, Robert | Tibbs, Sarah | 30, Apr. 1833 | RCH |
| Pool, Stephen | Messick, Elisabeth | 5, Jan. 1836 | RCH |
| Pool, William | Hardin, Rebecca | 30, June 1823 | RCH |
| Poole, Thomas | Care, Mary | 30, Jan. 1838 | RCH |
| Poor, Henry | Cramsey, Elisabeth | 26, Oct. 1848 | BB |
| Pope, Conrad | Schmidt, Wilhelmina | 14, Oct. 1847 | A |
| Pope, Isaac | Lindsey, Roberta | 15, Aug. 1846 | RCH |
| Popp, | Mory, Mary | 4, Aug. 1849 | RCH |
| Popp, Andrew | Zehbegen, Elisabeth | 29, July 1844 | RCH |
| Popp, Georg | Popp, Margaretha | 23, June 1840 | FF |
| Poppe, Adolph | Christoph, Maria | 20, Nov. 1849 | F |
| Poppe, Conrad | Speckmann, Sophia | 15, Feb. 1848 | F |
| Poppe, Dietrich | Brengelmann, Maria | 28, July 1846 | G |
| Poppe, Heinrich | Bahrs, Maria | 11, Oct. 1844 | F |
| Poppe, Michael | Schrenger, Barbara | 24, Jan. 1848 | EE |
| Poppe, Wilhelm | Moritz, Elisabeth | 9, Dec. 1847 | F |
| Poppen, Arnold | Stalhaus, M.A. | 14, Oct. 1841 | RCH |
| Poppers, August | Hannebaum, Elisabeth | 24, Jan. 1847 | A |
| Pork, Johan Eduard | Bielfeld, Maria Anna | 21, Oct. 1849 | AA |
| Pornerkmann, Heinric | Huger, Margaretha | 5, Dec. 1849 | B |
| Porning, Johan Georg | Oeh, Margaretha | 11, Oct. 1849 | C |
| Porrow, William | Kuhn, Elisabeth | 16, Jan. 1834 | RCH |
| Porschet, Leonard | Leherzer, Margaretha | 29, July 1844 | RCH |
| Porter, Edward | Sullivan, Lydia Ann | 20, Apr. 1849 | RCH |
| Porter, Henry Austin | Jackson, Sarah Ann | 24, Dec. 1843 | RCH |
| Porter, James | McKinsey, Margaret | 21, Aug. 1845 | RCH |
| Porter, John H. | Bonsall, Lydia | 22, Mar. 1849 | RCH |
| Porter, Jonathan | Smith, | 3, May 1825 | RCH |
| Porter, Morgan | Elder, Christina | 3, Dec. 1848 | RCH |
| Porter, Peter N. | Hoghland, Martha | 12, Apr. 1837 | RCH |
| Porter, Richard | Barnes, Catharine | 13, Aug. 1846 | RCH |
| Porter, William | Smith, Mary Ann | 16, Mar. 1837 | RCH |
| Portner, K. Adolph | Hesping, Cath. Elis. | 9, Feb. 1847 | RCH |
| Poschert, Wendel | Prausch, Catharine | 22, Feb. 1848 | EE |
| Post, Aaron | Gondy, Mary Ann | 15, June 1846 | RCH |
| Post, Herman | Gellenbeck, Adelheid | 10, Nov. 1844 | AA |
| Post, James | ----, Amelia | 7, Aug. 1821 | RCH |
| Post, Joseph | Brown, Eleanor | Nov. 1832 | RCH |
| Post, William | Wescott, Caroline | 2, July 1846 | RCH |
| Postel, Georg Jacob | Leininger, Emilia | 1, Jan. 1839 | G |
| Postell, James | Fitzgerald, Mary | 16, Nov. 1832 | RCH |
| Postlethwaite, John | Anthony, M. Adelheid | 4, Feb. 1843 | RCH |
| Postner, Adam | Lakamp, Margaretha | 28, Nov. 1843 | RCH |
| Pott, Johan Heinrich | Buhrmann, Catharine | 14, Sept 1843 | F |
| Pott, Johan Heinrich | Norkamp, Catharine W | 1, June 1848 | B |
| Pottenger, James W. | ----, Mary | 19, Jan. 1835 | RCH |
| Potter, James | Gulick, Mary | 18, Sept 1843 | RCH |
| Potter, John | Kelpan, Tabitha | 11, July 1847 | RCH |

| Grooms<br>****** | Brides<br>****** | Date of Marriage<br>**** ** ******** | Code<br>**** |
|---|---|---|---|
| Potter, Joseph | Miller, Mary | 21, Jan. 1819 | RCH |
| Potter, Joseph | Robinson, Mary Jane | 29, Oct. 1845 | RCH |
| Potter, Joseph F. | Alston, Caroline W. | 26, Sept 1848 | I |
| Pottinger, | Williamson, Cathriin | 5, Jan. 1826 | RCH |
| Pottinger, D.H. | Atherton, Elisabeth | 20, Oct. 1847 | RCH |
| Pottinger, John | Huston, Lucy Ann | 12, Jan. 1843 | RCH |
| Pottle, William B. | Boran, Mary Jane | 5, July 1849 | RCH |
| Potts, William | Dotten, Phoebe | 5, Aug. 1825 | RCH |
| Pouder, Lemuel | Aston, Mary | 14, Jan. 1849 | RCH |
| Powell, | Merritt, Elisabeth | 13, Sept 1821 | RCH |
| Powell, George | Collins, Catharine | 14, May 1844 | RCH |
| Powell, Gibson | Stockham, Catharine | 3, Oct. 1836 | RCH |
| Powell, James | McDonald, Joanne | 12, Sept 1847 | GG |
| Powell, John | Lamburn, Mary | 30, Apr. 1818 | RCH |
| Powell, John | Rashal, Elizabeth | 5, Feb. 1846 | RCH |
| Powell, Joseph | Winston, Rebecca | 25, Aug. 1837 | RCH |
| Powell, Joseph | Hallowell, Louise | 20, June 1843 | RCH |
| Powell, Thomas | Clawson, Maria | 9, Apr. 1835 | RCH |
| Powell, Thomas | Bates, Margaret | 26, July 1838 | I |
| Powell, William | Pugh, Elisabeth | 16, May 1841 | RCH |
| Powell, William B. | Wallace, Nancy | 3, July 1837 | RCH |
| Powell, William F. | Dulhagen, Elisabeth | 14, Dec. 1848 | RCH |
| Powell, William T. | Walker, Elisa | 14, May 1848 | RCH |
| Powers, Archilles | Stewart, Sarah | 24, Apr. 1847 | RCH |
| Powers, Benjamin F. | Bosson, Catharine M. | 6, Nov. 1818 | RCH |
| Powers, Biven | Hubbard, Mary | 28, Sept 1845 | RCH |
| Powers, Earl | McGaughey, Rebecca | 25, June 1835 | RCH |
| Powers, Esh. | Miller, Phebe | 1, Apr. 1841 | RCH |
| Powers, Henry P. | Brehtel, Lydia Ann | 6, Sept 1832 | RCH |
| Powers, John | Boon, Jane | 20, Dec. 1832 | RCH |
| Powers, John | Lebman, Sybilla | 23, Nov. 1834 | RCH |
| Powers, John | Trindle, Isaac | 1, Dec. 1844 | RCH |
| Powers, Manuel | Powers, Bridget | 17, July 1841 | BB |
| Powers, Michael | Rochford, Catharine | 8, Oct. 1849 | GG |
| Powers, Philipp | Hart, Elizabeth | 16, May 1848 | GG |
| Powers, Samuel | Haines, Arietta | 29, Mar. 1833 | RCH |
| Powers, Samuel | Legune, Rebecca | 4, Feb. 1845 | RCH |
| Powers, Thomas | VanSant, Jane L. | 30, Dec. 1837 | RCH |
| Powers, William | Cross, Parmelia | 19, June 1842 | RCH |
| Powner, Andrew | Kelsay, Lydia | 4, May 1839 | RCH |
| Powner, John | Stoughton, Mary Ann | 17, Mar. 1836 | RCH |
| Powner, William M. | Watson, Anna Delia | 13, May 1841 | RCH |
| Praino, James H. | Turner, Mary | 25, Nov. 1834 | RCH |
| Pranton, Friedrich | Wesselmann, Louise | 3, May 1849 | B |
| Praters, Johan Bd. | Bove, Helena | 12, Aug. 1849 | EE |
| Prather, James | Pratt, Clarissa | 14, Oct. 1841 | RCH |
| Pratt, Micah | ----, Nancy | 17, May 1823 | RCH |
| Prell, Sebastian | Wittenbauer, Johanna | 29, Aug. 1848 | EE |
| Prem, Georg | Busbacher, Dorothea | 12, Jan. 1849 | EE |
| Prematha, Mathias | Auerbacker, M. Elis. | 12, Jan. 1841 | FF |
| Prescott, Levi | King, Mary C. | 14, Aug. 1848 | RCH |
| Prescott, Thomas | Crofts, Charlotte | 4, Oct. 1847 | RCH |
| Preston, Abijah | Roll--, Patsy | 23, Sept 1818 | RCH |
| Preston, E.J. | Bryant, Lydia | 8, Dec. 1847 | RCH |
| Preston, Joseph | Thornton, Hannah | 21, June 1836 | RCH |
| Preston, William | Whalon, Sarah | 3, Oct. 1822 | RCH |
| Preston, William | Stewart, Louise | 23, June 1842 | RCH |
| Price, David | Langdon, Elisabeth | 1, Feb. 1843 | RCH |
| Price, Edward | Maderia, Martha | 27, Apr. 1843 | RCH |
| Price, George | Thomas, Elisabeth | 7, Jan. 1844 | RCH |
| Price, J. | Davis, Elisabeth | 23, July 1821 | RCH |
| Price, Jacob | Paton, Dorcus A. | 10, July 1847 | RCH |
| Price, John | Kale, Mary Ann | 10, Nov. 1841 | RCH |
| Price, John | Cohen, Maria Anna | 12, May 1846 | RCH |
| Price, John R. | Judd, Mary Ann | 15, July 1833 | RCH |
| Price, Nimrod | Peckinpaugh, Rachel | 19, Jan. 1823 | RCH |
| Price, Rees E. | Matson, | 9, Dec. 1825 | RCH |
| Price, Stephen | Vroom, Cornelia | 28, July 1846 | RCH |
| Price, Thomas | Austin, Sidney N. | 12, Mar. 1835 | RCH |
| Price, Thomas | Hindman, Susan | 22, Feb. 1844 | RCH |
| Price, William | Johnston, Sarah | 9, Dec. 1821 | RCH |

| Grooms | Brides | Date of Marriage | Code |
|--------|--------|------------------|------|
| ****** | ****** | **** ** ******** | **** |
| Price, William | McGalw--, Mary | 30, Oct. 1834 | RCH |
| Price, William A. | Leever, Martha | 8, Feb. 1849 | RCH |
| Price, William T. | McHenry, Elisabeth A | 12, Oct. 1826 | RCH |
| Pricket, Nicholas | Nash, Elisabeth | 18, Feb. 1849 | RCH |
| Pricket, Paul | Hinkle, | 5, July 1823 | RCH |
| Prickett, John | Frank, Maria | 15, July 1847 | RCH |
| Prickett, William | McManaman, Minerva | 1, June 1848 | RCH |
| Prier, James A. | Horton, Maly Ann | 19, Sept 1822 | RCH |
| Priesmeyer, Friedric | Quebe, Charlotte W. | 7, June 1849 | C |
| Priesmeyer, John C. | Spreel, Dorothea | 9, Nov. 1848 | RCH |
| Priete, Johan H. | Aspre, Elisabeth | 3, June 1849 | EE |
| Prince, Lucas | Maxmeller, Susanna | Dec. 1844 | RCH |
| Prindeville, Garrett | Lynch, Honora | 16, June 1846 | BB |
| Prindle, George B. | Williams, Sarah Ann | 7, June 1835 | RCH |
| Prior, Friedrich | Ahring, Charlotte | 17, July 1841 | F |
| Prior, James | Shanks, Cassandra | 21, Nov. 1845 | RCH |
| Prish, Daniel | Beckenbragh, Elis. | 31, Dec. 1820 | RCH |
| Pritchard, Ezekiel | Eglester, Caroline | 4, Dec. 1843 | RCH |
| Pritchard, Moses | Stewart, Casey Jane | 4, Apr. 1847 | RCH |
| Pritchard, R. | Hunitton, Margaret | Sept 1845 | RCH |
| Pro---, R.M. | Kelly, Ellen Jane | 21, Jan. 1846 | RCH |
| Probst, John George | Ritter, Catharine | 1, Nov. 1842 | RCH |
| Proctor, Thomas H. | Norris, Anna | 22, Oct. 1840 | RCH |
| Proctor, William | Norris, Olivia | 5, Nov. 1833 | I |
| Proessler, Andreas | Koerner, Anna Maria | 22, Feb. 1841 | FF |
| Progaska, Johan | Freund, Elisabeth | 27, Mar. 1849 | AA |
| Proshun, Friedrich | Frieern, M Elisabeth | 9, May 1840 | G |
| Pross, George W. | Rafferty, Adelheid | 20, Mar. 1849 | RCH |
| Pross, Peter | Stegner, Catharine | 25, Nov. 1845 | AA |
| Prossart, J. Martin | Helfers, Margaretha | 27, Aug. 1848 | EE |
| Prosser, Henry | Hicox, Mary | 7, Sept 1837 | RCH |
| Prout, Thomas | Little, Ann | 3, Dec. 1849 | GG |
| Prows, Sylvester | Ryley, Ellen | 4, Dec. 1849 | RCH |
| Pruden, Andrew | Powell, Mary Ann | 19, Aug. 1841 | RCH |
| Pruden, Henry | Green, Mary | 9, Apr. 1846 | RCH |
| Prues, Bernard H. | Gisting, Elisabeth | 10, Nov. 1846 | AA |
| Prues, Heinrich | Huelskamp, Wilhelmin | 29, July 1848 | AA |
| Prues, Wilhelm | Schreiber, Anna | 11, Jan. 1837 | FF |
| Pryer, Andrew | Cole, Mary | 5, Jan. 1823 | RCH |
| Puck, Henry | Manning, Hannah | 17, Sept 1845 | RCH |
| Pucker, Jacob | Springer, Susannah | 9, July 1838 | RCH |
| Pucker, Peter | Christian, Prudence | 16, Aug. 1837 | RCH |
| Puckett, John | Leeds, Susan | 22, Jan. 1846 | RCH |
| Puckner, John | Oliver, Elisabeth | 29, May 1838 | RCH |
| Puesch, Joseph | Fin, Rosina | 3, Oct. 1848 | EE |
| Puetz, Johan Joseph | Hoefel, Maria Jos. | 6, Nov. 1849 | EE |
| Puffmann, Philip | Maas, Magdalena | 17, May 1843 | RCH |
| Pugh, Elias | French, Elisabeth | 31, Aug. 1843 | RCH |
| Pugh, Jordan A. | Miller, Sarah Belle | 31, May 1842 | I |
| Pugh, Richard | Evans, Ann | 11, Apr. 1844 | RCH |
| Pulk, Peter | Whitmore, Sarah | 6, June 1818 | RCH |
| Pullan, James | Stephen, Anna | 4, June 1846 | RCH |
| Pullan, Joseph | Purinton, Elisabeth | 2, Aug. 1847 | RCH |
| Pullen, William | Dickinson, Abby | 15, Feb. 1842 | RCH |
| Pullman, John | Maloney, Fidelia | 2, May 1844 | RCH |
| Puls, Johan Herman | Luhn, Maria Anna | 25, Apr. 1843 | FF |
| Puls, Wilhelm | Splinters, Margaret | 30, Apr. 1844 | FF |
| Puls, Wilhelm | Schulte, Anna Maria | 4, Nov. 1849 | CC |
| Pulse, David | VanCleve, Rebecca | 3, Sept 1843 | RCH |
| Punch, David | Hulbert, Harriet | 30, July 1848 | RCH |
| Pund, Anton | Wobbler, Catharine | 6, May 1845 | AA |
| Pund, Carl | Metha, Elisabeth | 21, June 1836 | FF |
| Pund, John Henry | Stuckenborg, A. Cath | 20, Nov. 1848 | RCH |
| Pundsack, Joseph | Enneking, Maria Elis | 2, Aug. 1846 | FF |
| Punshon, | Langdon, Ruth | 21, Nov. 1844 | RCH |
| Punt, Johan Heinrich | Noble, Elisabeth | 3, Feb. 1841 | FF |
| Purcel, Samuel | Whipple, Emily | 27, Aug. 1835 | RCH |
| Purcell, Brison | Johnson, Priscilla | 10, July 1835 | RCH |
| Purcell, James | Holahan, Ellen | 27, Apr. 1840 | BB |
| Purcell, James | McGrath, Ann | 13, July 1847 | GG |
| Purcell, Robert | Burns, Mary | 22, Apr. 1849 | GG |

| Grooms | Brides | Date of Marriage | Code |
|--------|--------|------------------|------|
| ****** | ****** | **** ** ******** | **** |
| Purdy, Benjamin | Johnson, Achsah | 18, Oct. 1842 | RCH |
| Purdy, Jeremiah | Disbrowne, Rebecca | 14, Oct. 1821 | RCH |
| Purel, Joseph S. | Ross, Mary | 9, Sept 1818 | RCH |
| Purlee, Peter | ----, Elisabeth | 18, Apr. 1823 | RCH |
| Purlier, | Watson, Sarah | 17, June 1849 | RCH |
| Purnell, John M. | Wilson, Eliza Jane | 9, Sept 1848 | RCH |
| Pursel, Brisen | Snowden, Hannah | 21, Apr. 1846 | RCH |
| Pursel, Stephen L. | Washington, Ann | 18, May 1834 | RCH |
| Purser, John | Dunlap, Elisabeth | 23, Aug. 1845 | RCH |
| Purvis, John | Douglass, Elisabeth | 21, Nov. 1843 | RCH |
| Puthof, David | Vogelsang, Maria | 3, Aug. 1841 | FF |
| Puthof, Francis H. | Boetemann, Margaret | 4, June 1847 | AA |
| Puthoff, Bernard F. | Feldmann, Maria A. | 9, Jan. 1844 | FF |
| Puthoff, Heinrich | Cruse, M. Elisabeth | 17, July 1838 | FF |
| Puthoff, Johan Hein. | Gers, Maria Agnes | 30, Oct. 1845 | AA |
| Putthof, Heinrich | Fairmann, Anna Maria | 18, Aug. 1835 | FF |
| Puttmann, Wilhelm | Puttmann, Elisabeth | 11, Nov. 1849 | FF |
| Pyfrin, John | McCoy, Hester | 25, Dec. 1849 | RCH |
| Pygrle, George | Clements, Belinda | 13, Dec. 1845 | RCH |
| Pyle, George | Wilson, Mary Jane | 2, Nov. 1843 | RCH |
| Pyle, Isaac | Lake, Ann | 7, Mar. 1843 | RCH |
| Pyle, Jeremiah | Burdge, Elisabeth | 5, May 1846 | RCH |
| Pyle, Milton E. | Howard, Margaret | 4, Oct. 1838 | RCH |
| Pyle, Smith | Capidor, Catharine | 19, Oct. 1845 | RCH |
| | | | |
| Quaing, Gerhard H. | Foppen, Anna Margar. | 31, Oct. 1847 | EE |
| Quall, William | Shrouds, Susan | 14, Mar. 1833 | RCH |
| Qualls, William | Lonsdale, Susanna | Jan. 1823 | RCH |
| Quante, Heinrich | Lorey, Sophia | 31, Oct. 1844 | F |
| Quarmby, John | Savill, Jane | 29, Jan. 1849 | RCH |
| Quartmann, Joseph | Drees, Angela | 4, Feb. 1841 | FF |
| Quatmann, Joseph | Otten, Maria | 16, Apr. 1844 | AA |
| Quebbemann, Heinrich | Holthaus, Elisabeth | 28, Sept 1845 | FF |
| Quebbemann, Heinrich | Wiebold, Gertrud C. | 21, May 1848 | FF |
| Quebemann, Joseph | Heckmann, Bernardina | 18, Oct. 1846 | FF |
| Queen, William P. | Russell, Mariah | 16, Nov. 1820 | RCH |
| Quensel, Johan F. | Schwenning, Christ. | 31, Aug. 1847 | EE |
| Querner, Heinrich | Friedeborn, Catharin | 7, Apr. 1840 | G |
| Quick, Jacob | Chivington, Mary | 5, May 1834 | RCH |
| Quick, Joseph | Applegate, Anna | 28, Dec. 1847 | RCH |
| Quick, Richard | ----, Catharine | 18, Jan. 1820 | RCH |
| Quigley, Peter | McOngey, Ann | 18, Aug. 1849 | GG |
| Quigley, Samuel | Hall, Margaret | 29, Nov. 1832 | RCH |
| Quincy, John | Dorst, Mary Ann | 14, Feb. 1847 | BB |
| Quinlan, James | Fogarty, Margaret | 18, Apr. 1842 | BB |
| Quinlan, Thomas | Sweeney, Mary | 5, Aug. 1845 | BB |
| Quinlin, Thomas | Smitherne, Virginia | 21, Aug. 1847 | RCH |
| Quinn, Hugh | Nugent, Bridget | 22, May 1848 | BB |
| Quinn, James | Borden, Mary Ann | 16, July 1849 | RCH |
| Quinn, John | Barnbridge, | 4, July 1825 | RCH |
| Quinn, Michael | Nicholas, Mary | 7, Jan. 1847 | BB |
| Quinn, Patrick | Grogan, Mary | 6, Jan. 1843 | BB |
| Quinn, Thomas | Nordike, Mary | 27, July 1848 | RCH |
| Quinn, Thomas | Haney, Bridget | 2, May 1847 | BB |
| Quinn, William | Williams, Harriet | 22, May 1839 | RCH |
| Quinn, William | O'Neil, Sarah | 1, May 1847 | GG |
| Quint, Heinrich F. | Brockmann, Charlotte | 10, May 1849 | G |
| Quire, Charles | Thompson, Julia Ann | 6, Nov. 1842 | RCH |
| Quire, Charles | Phipps, Cordelia | 31, Dec. 1849 | RCH |
| Quire, William | Harris, Caroline | 20, Dec. 1841 | RCH |
| | | | |
| R---, Deloss | Cummins, Mary | 8, May 1834 | RCH |
| R---, Joseph | Loge, Mary | 27, Feb. 1837 | RCH |
| R---, Moses | Orr, Eliza | 1, Mar. 1848 | RCH |
| R---, Samuel | McKim, Lydia | 11, Nov. 1826 | RCH |
| R---, Vere. | Zuemers, Maria | 12, Apr. 1826 | RCH |
| R---, William | King, Sarah | 29, Mar. 1821 | RCH |
| R---, William | Fanmire, Hannah | 16, Nov. 1826 | RCH |
| R---, William | Wilson, Catharine S. | 11, Sept 1833 | RCH |
| Raabe, Conrad | Walter, Martha | 28, Sept 1845 | G |
| Rabe, Clemens | Shillis, Catharine | 12, Feb. 1835 | FF |

| Grooms<br>***** | Brides<br>***** | Date of Marriage<br>**** ** ******** | Code<br>**** |
|---|---|---|---|
| Rabe, Clemens | VanHusen, Gertrud | 5, Aug. 1845 | RCH |
| Raber, Georg | Bopp, Margaretha | 2, Feb. 1842 | G |
| Raber, Georg | Riegler, Apollonia | 24, Feb. 1848 | G |
| Raber, J. Sebastian | Kramer, Elisabeth | 19, July 1848 | G |
| Raborg, Samuel | Leggett, Mary Jane | 10, Oct. 1835 | RCH |
| Race, Abraham | Bennett, Mary Jane | 31, Oct. 1833 | RCH |
| Rack, Anton | Rennert, Barbara | 27, Feb. 1848 | AA |
| Racoe, William | Miller, Mary Ann | 12, Oct. 1834 | RCH |
| Radabaugh, Clarkson | Sampson, Mary Ann | 16, Dec. 1844 | RCH |
| Rademacher, Johan H. | Schulten, Helena | 30, Sept 1849 | EE |
| Rademacher, Wilhelm | Heitgies, Christina | 6, Aug. 1848 | EE |
| Rader, Lewis | Massan, Mary | 13, May 1837 | RCH |
| Radester, Wilhelm | Stamber, Philippina | 29, Jan. 1849 | C |
| Radley, William | String, Louisa | 15, Feb. 1849 | RCH |
| Radloff, Wilhelm | Besuden, Anna | 11, Nov. 1847 | F |
| Rady, Joseph | Morton, Isabella | 14, Sept 1845 | RCH |
| Raechtin, Bernard | Dieker, Adelheid | 15, July 1845 | FF |
| Raechtin, Gerhard | Raechtin, Catharine | 10, July 1845 | FF |
| Rafferty, James | Moore, Rebecca | 15, Feb. 1849 | GG |
| Rafflaub, Nicolaus | Bernard, Margaretha | 3, Nov. 1842 | FF |
| Ragin, Robert | Jewell, Sarah | 9, Oct. 1842 | RCH |
| Rago, Domenigo | Ringe, Sarah A. | 29, Mar. 1839 | RCH |
| Ragot, Dominique | Antonie, Catharine | 28, Aug. 1843 | RCH |
| Rah, Johan | Oderbeck, Katharine | 17, Sept 1844 | AA |
| Rahe, Johan Heinrich | Brinkmann, Catharine | 6, Feb. 1844 | AA |
| Rahe, Johan Heinrich | Teepen, Maria Louise | 18, June 1849 | F |
| Raible, Carl | Schweitzer, Phil. | 6, May 1841 | FF |
| Raipe, | Summons, Ellen J. | 17, July 1849 | RCH |
| Raisler, Charles | Hill, Mary | 8, Sept 1849 | RCH |
| Rakers, Gerhard | Koen, Anna Catharine | 14, Feb. 1847 | EE |
| Rall, Louis | Cahow, Mary Jane | 20, Dec. 1835 | RCH |
| Rall, Wick | VanDyke, Elisabeth | 4, Feb. 1836 | RCH |
| Ralle, Charles | Stewart, Elisabeth | 12, Mar. 1849 | RCH |
| Ralston, Peter | Picken, Margaret | Oct. 1844 | RCH |
| Ralston, William | Brown, Janet | 3, Aug. 1843 | RCH |
| Rambart, August | Burman, Sarah | 21, Dec. 1842 | RCH |
| Rambo, Francis | Richardson, Joan | 11, Feb. 1827 | RCH |
| Ramley, Daniel | Cochran, Mary | 19, Oct. 1818 | RCH |
| Ramme, Heinrich | Bickmann, Maria | 14, May 1839 | FF |
| Rammeler, Heinrich | Harvinghorst, Carol. | 6, July 1847 | FF |
| Rammelsberg, Friedr. | Lape, Sarah M. | 12, Apr. 1842 | RCH |
| Rammet, G. Leonhard | Roedter, Catharine | 8, Apr. 1845 | A |
| Rampe, Joseph | Notebrock, Elisabeth | 21, Sept 1845 | FF |
| Ramsay, Charles | Roberts, Betsy Ann | 13, June 1848 | RCH |
| Ramsay, John M. | Bevis, Mary | 8, May 1834 | RCH |
| Ramsay, Thomas | Passons, Lydia | 21, Nov. 1832 | RCH |
| Ramsbeck, Valentin | Suhr, Theresa | 24, Sept 1848 | FF |
| Ramsdell, Joshua | Baker, Clarissa | 8, Jan. 1836 | RCH |
| Ramsden, Daniel | Barrow, Ann H. | 27, Sept 1843 | RCH |
| Ramsey, Allen | Heaps, Hester | 12, Jan. 1842 | RCH |
| Ramsey, Aquilla | Milay, Priscilla | 6, Oct. 1833 | RCH |
| Ramsey, James | Arbuckle, Minerva | 4, Nov. 1847 | RCH |
| Ramsey, John | Buckingham, Ann | 17, Dec. 1846 | RCH |
| Ramsey, Sample | Peters, Anna Maria | 9, Sept 1841 | RCH |
| Ramsey, Samuel | Guthrie, Mary | 20, Nov. 1845 | RCH |
| Ramsey, Simon | ----, Margaret | 18, Nov. 1818 | RCH |
| Ramsey, Thomas | Punshan, Mary | 29, Sept 1825 | RCH |
| Ramsey, Thomas | Heap, Ann | 15, Jan. 1842 | RCH |
| Ramsey, William | Gambrel, Phebe | 9, May 1846 | RCH |
| Ramsey, William | Punshon, Mary | 31, Aug. 1847 | RCH |
| Rand, Elbrigid | Rand, Sarah Ann | 6, Apr. 1837 | RCH |
| Randal, Richard | Filter, Rosalia | 9, Mar. 1842 | RCH |
| Randal, William S. | Hildreth, Hannah | 30, Apr. 1833 | RCH |
| Randall, Cyrus C. | Penckston, Margaret | 6, Aug. 1839 | RCH |
| Randall, David | Carmichael, Grace | 19, May 1842 | RCH |
| Randall, George W. | Duval, Ellen | 5, Jan. 1846 | RCH |
| Randall, John | Newell, Mary Ann | 23, June 1842 | RCH |
| Randall, Joshua | Southerland, Mary | 10, Mar. 1842 | RCH |
| Randall, Joshua | Freshower, Sophia | 14, Aug. 1845 | RCH |
| Randall, William | Watts, Sarah | 22, Jan. 1844 | RCH |
| Randle, William | Hindman, Ellen | 1, May 1843 | RCH |

| Grooms<br>****** | Brides<br>****** | Date of Marriage<br>**** ** ******** | Code<br>**** |
|---|---|---|---|
| Randolph, Benjamin | Davis, Sarah | 13, Sept 1848 | RCH |
| Randolph, David F. | H---, Jemima | 24, Dec. 1818 | RCH |
| Randolph, Lewis | Steele, Sarah | 19, July 1846 | RCH |
| Randolph, Peter | Jefferson, Mary A. | 27, Dec. 1848 | RCH |
| Rands, Charles | Coleman, Rachel | 3, Jan. 1837 | RCH |
| Raney, Moses | Luckey, Catharine M. | 9, Mar. 1837 | RCH |
| Raney, Peter | Lidle, Elisabeth | 4, Jan. 1844 | RCH |
| Rankin, Charles | Dodsworth, Nancy | 7, Apr. 1844 | RCH |
| Rankin, Thomas | Scott, Matilda | 17, Apr. 1834 | RCH |
| Rankin, William | Stevens, Ellen H. | 1, June 1841 | RCH |
| Rankstirt, Lewis | Menkin, Rosina | 2, Feb. 1846 | RCH |
| Rannels, Richard | West, Betsey | 23, Sept 1839 | RCH |
| Ransch, Philipp | Droste, Anna Maria | 1, May 1849 | C |
| Ransly, Charles E. | Looker, Emeline | 1, Apr. 1826 | RCH |
| Ransom, | Steel, Elisabeth | 24, Apr. 1849 | RCH |
| Ransom, William | Robinson, Sarah | 19, Apr. 1848 | RCH |
| Raper, Joseph | Tudor, Johanna | 25, Oct. 1842 | RCH |
| Rapp, Friedrich J. | Ganz, Sophia Christ. | 3, July 1845 | G |
| Rapp, George | Leininger, Margaret | 23, June 1835 | RCH |
| Rapp, George Michael | Steiner, Maria | 15, Nov. 1836 | RCH |
| Rapp, Jacob | Sohn, Elisabeth | 16, Aug. 1849 | G |
| Rapp, John | Haslop, Elisabeth | 27, May 1841 | BB |
| Rapp, John | Meier, Dorothea | 16, Feb. 1846 | A |
| Rapp, John | Dick, Catharine | 20, Jan. 1849 | G |
| Rapp, Leopold | Katz, Amelia | 1, Aug. 1837 | FF |
| Rapp, Peter | Imhoff, Anna | 13, Apr. 1837 | FF |
| Rapp, Peter | Loux, Catharine | 7, Oct. 1847 | RCH |
| Rapp, Valentine | Ovedunch, Catharine | 16, Oct. 1849 | GG |
| Rappalee, Thomas | Schammaborne, Mary A | 25, Feb. 1823 | RCH |
| Rappott, Anton | Krimm, Catharine | 9, Jan. 1845 | RCH |
| Rasche, Johan Theo. | Lines, Catharine | 6, May 1849 | EE |
| Raschig, F. Maurice | Meyer, Catharine | 29, Aug. 1835 | RCH |
| Raske, Heinrich | Kennepohl, Catharine | 7, Jan. 1846 | AA |
| Ratcliff, James | Booth, Catharine | 28, Dec. 1849 | RCH |
| Rates, George | Hollingshead, Elis. | 20, Oct. 1843 | RCH |
| Rath, Georg | Ries, Johanna | 12, Nov. 1848 | A |
| Rathauser, Friedrich | Zink, Helena | 29, June 1843 | FF |
| Rathbone, Jonathan | Cliff, Sarah | 17, May 1821 | RCH |
| Rathjins, Johan C. | Brost, Katharina | 8, Oct. 1848 | A |
| Ratigan, James | Burke, Bridget | 2, Feb. 1849 | BB |
| Ratliff, Joseph H. | Thomas, Saran Ann | 31, Dec. 1844 | RCH |
| Rattan, Friedrich L. | Wesemann, Lisette | 30, May 1843 | F |
| Rattmann, Francis | Strotkamp, Maria | 21, Aug. 1838 | FF |
| Rau, Heinrich | Herrmann, Maria | 14, Feb. 1839 | G |
| Rauber, Jacob | Souders, Rachel | 24, Oct. 1848 | A |
| Raukopf, Carl | Bostede, Catharine | 24, Sept 1846 | F |
| Rausch, J. Friedrich | Lintsch, Mathilda | 20, Aug. 1848 | C |
| Rauscher, John M. | Eisenbert, Maria | 18, Aug. 1849 | RCH |
| Raut, Friedrich | Dietrich, Maria Anna | 7, Feb. 1837 | FF |
| Rawdon, Horace | Bartlett, Catharine | 10, Sept 1844 | RCH |
| Rawlings, James | Hulick, Augusta A. | 7, May 1848 | RCH |
| Rawlings, Richard | McCarty, Jane | 22, Dec. 1849 | RCH |
| Rawlings, William | Wiggins, Elisabeth | 23, May 1844 | RCH |
| Rawlins, John H. | Higbee, Jane | 26, Mar. 1844 | RCH |
| Rawlins, Robert | Ross, Alice | 18, June 1842 | RCH |
| Ray, James B. | Riddle, Mary | 10, Dec. 1818 | RCH |
| Ray, William | Hoon, Barbara | 17, Dec. 1824 | RCH |
| Raymond, Burr | Morrison, Mary A. | 8, Sept 1837 | RCH |
| Raymond, Calvin | Oliver, Sarah | 8, Feb. 1849 | RCH |
| Raymond, Daniel | Bonte, Jane M. | 31, Oct. 1833 | RCH |
| Raymond, David S. | Facemer, Mat. | 7, May 1822 | RCH |
| Raymond, George M. | Bonte, Elisabeth Ann | 5, Oct. 1836 | RCH |
| Rays, John | Campbell, Keziah | 13, Apr. 1834 | RCH |
| Read, Ezra | Young, Louisa Budd | 8, Sept 1836 | RCH |
| Read, John A. | Staggmann, Lucy | 29, Apr. 1844 | RCH |
| Read, Robert | Cubberly, Mary Ann | 15, Nov. 1836 | RCH |
| Reade, David J. | Preston, Maria | 25, Oct. 1832 | RCH |
| Reader, William | Rude, Sarah | 30, June 1842 | RCH |
| Ready, Benjamin | Hazen, Harriet | 31, May 1838 | RCH |
| Ready, Lain | Beckley, Mary Ann | 19, Jan. 1842 | RCH |
| Ready, William | Prunt, Ruthinda | 18, Mar. 1837 | RCH |

| Grooms | Brides | Date of Marriage | Code |
|--------|--------|------------------|------|
| ****** | ****** | **** ** ******** | **** |
| Ready, William | Hueston, Margaret | 4, Jan. 1845 | RCH |
| Reagan, Hamilton | Wright, Rosanna | 6, Mar. 1843 | RCH |
| Reagan, Patrick | Reilly, Bridget | 25, June 1848 | BB |
| Reagan, Reason | Goodwin, Margaret | 2, Feb. 1843 | RCH |
| Reagen, John | Richardson, Betsey | 22, Dec. 1820 | RCH |
| Reamy, George | Zumwald, Sarah | 12, Apr. 1849 | RCH |
| Reaney, Johan | Robinson, Esther A. | 6, May 1849 | RCH |
| Reany, William | Vaughn, Susan | 15, Dec. 1843 | RCH |
| Rearden, Michael | Lynch, Catharine | 3, Sept 1848 | BB |
| Reber, Johan Caspar | Linne, Maria | 15, Feb. 1849 | EE |
| Reberger, John | Mueller, Elisabeth | 20, Apr. 1844 | RCH |
| Rebstock, Carl | Schneider, Caroline | 11, Nov. 1845 | G |
| Recam, Herman Heinr. | Guelker, Maria Adel. | 17, Nov. 1840 | FF |
| Rech, Christian | Ackermann, Margaret | 18, Mar. 1849 | RCH |
| Rechas, Herman | Schmude, Elisabeth | 28, Apr. 1840 | FF |
| Rechtin, Gerhard H. | Hubbers, A. Barbara | 16, Jan. 1848 | FF |
| Rechtin, Johan Bd. | Midden, Theresa | 22, Feb. 1846 | AA |
| Rechtin, Johan Bd. | Schulte, Maria Adel. | 27, Feb. 1848 | AA |
| Rechtin, Johan Phil. | Zurline, Katharina | 19, Nov. 1848 | AA |
| Rechtin, Phillip | Heidemann, Anna | 28, Oct. 1845 | AA |
| Recker, Heinrich | Schomaker, Margaret | 31, Mar. 1843 | AA |
| Recker, Johan | Zumgrunde, Maria | 12, June 1843 | FF |
| Reckmann, Friedrich | Reckmann, Maria | 21, Dec. 1848 | RCH |
| Red, Georg | Schmid, Elisabeth | 8, Sept 1840 | FF |
| Red, William | Arrens, Emeline | 18, Mar. 1846 | RCH |
| Reddick, Elisha | Bence, Mary | 20, Oct. 1842 | RCH |
| Reddick, Martin | Walker, Jane | 10, Dec. 1835 | RCH |
| Reddick, Martin | Creagan, Matilda | 23, Mar. 1837 | RCH |
| Reddick, Richard | Dilks, Catharine | 13, Feb. 1846 | RCH |
| Reddish, John W. | Hay, Susan | 20, June 1849 | RCH |
| Redelmann, Georg H. | Oldendick, Mathilda | 22, Feb. 1848 | AA |
| Redelmann, Matthias | Bergstermann, Elis. | 12, Jan. 1847 | AA |
| Reder, Heinrich | Videmann, Maria | 6, June 1844 | F |
| Redermann, Francis | Holt, Maria  Anna | 9, May 1848 | EE |
| Redette, John | Lenon, Isabella | Nov. 1844 | RCH |
| Redford, Alfred | Bush, Elisabeth | 11, Oct. 1839 | RCH |
| Redinbo, Henry | Cassidy, Abigail | 21, Mar. 1837 | RCH |
| Redman, Dr. | Mills, Elisabeth | 16, Mar. 1836 | RCH |
| Redman, James | Colgate, Mary | 25, Oct. 1832 | RCH |
| Redman, Robert S. | Hier, Mary Elisabeth | 8, Oct. 1843 | RCH |
| Redman, Thomas | Bracy, Francis | 27, Sept 1849 | RCH |
| Redmore, Richard | Wilson, Mary Ann | 30, Sept 1841 | RCH |
| Redroo, James | Ross, Mary | 14, Jan. 1835 | RCH |
| Redrow, Enoch | Snowhill, Mary Jane | 16, Apr. 1837 | RCH |
| Redwisch, Cord Hein. | Koch, Margaretha F. | 25, Nov. 1842 | F |
| Ree, Heinrich | Sieker, M. Gertrud | 5, May 1836 | FF |
| Ree, John | Huffman, Hannah | 2, July 1837 | RCH |
| Reed, | Runion, Mary | 10, Nov. 1832 | RCH |
| Reed, Abijah | George, Mahala | 27, May 1819 | RCH |
| Reed, Benjamin | Phares, Adelphia | 25, June 1835 | RCH |
| Reed, Charles | Ward, Minerva | 13, June 1839 | RCH |
| Reed, Daniel | Boilean, Melvina C. | 22, July 1842 | RCH |
| Reed, David | Keegan, Catharine | 4, Oct. 1849 | BB |
| Reed, Enos | Rose, Martilla | 27, May 1843 | RCH |
| Reed, Henry | Pettit, Catharine | 3, Nov. 1837 | RCH |
| Reed, Hiram | Longshore, Mary Ann | 12, Sept 1839 | RCH |
| Reed, James | ----, ---- | 25, Feb. 1819 | RCH |
| Reed, James | Long, Mary Ann | 27, Sept 1832 | RCH |
| Reed, James | Johnson, Caroline | 2, Apr. 1846 | RCH |
| Reed, Jesse C. | Cazey, Wilea M. | 5, Dec. 1832 | RCH |
| Reed, John | Hugle, Sophia B. | 14, July 1835 | RCH |
| Reed, Joseph | Sedam, Elisabeth | 24, Jan. 1847 | RCH |
| Reed, Joseph | McQuillan, Mary Ann | 26, Apr. 1846 | BB |
| Reed, Peter | Bedel, Jane | 27, Sept 1833 | RCH |
| Reed, Reuben | Hackeleander, Christ | 23, Nov. 1826 | RCH |
| Reed, Reuben | Shaw, Hannah | 21, Jan. 1827 | RCH |
| Reed, Robert | Abbott, Elisabeth | 29, July 1819 | RCH |
| Reed, Robert | M---, Mary | 11, Mar. 1835 | RCH |
| Reed, Robert C. | Hale, Julia | 17, May 1818 | RCH |
| Reed, Rosswell | Stonebraker, Matilda | 9, Oct. 1834 | RCH |
| Reed, Thomas J. | Shaw, Emily | 14, Apr. 1834 | RCH |

| Grooms | Brides | Date of Marriage | Code |
|--------|--------|------------------|------|
| ****** | ****** | **** ** ******** | **** |
| Reed, William | Whiteside, Sarah | 23, Dec. 1832 | RCH |
| Reed, William | Bodine, Catharine | Sept 1834 | RCH |
| Reed, William | Elkins, Laura | 19, Mar. 1846 | RCH |
| Reeder, Alaric | Strickler, Sarah J. | 24, June 1847 | RCH |
| Reeder, Alfred A. | Brown, Amelia S. | 22, July 1835 | RCH |
| Reeder, Allen | Elliott, Lydia | 8, Dec. 1841 | RCH |
| Reeder, David | Pierce, Elisabeth | 6, July 1843 | RCH |
| Reeder, Joseph | Roth, Margaret | 15, Aug. 1847 | BB |
| Reeder, Joseph A. | Langdon, Olive | 2, Apr. 1818 | RCH |
| Reeder, William | Morris, Nancy | 18, Sept 1834 | RCH |
| Reel, John | Fitzpatrick, Elis. | 2, Sept 1844 | BB |
| Reese, Robert | Richards, Martha | 21, Apr. 1842 | RCH |
| Reese, William | Reese, Catharine | 15, Nov. 1845 | RCH |
| Reese, William | Gambrel, Elisabeth | 29, Nov. 1846 | RCH |
| Reeve, William | Greming, Joann | 27, Apr. 1836 | RCH |
| Reeves, Aaron | Warmistin, Sarah | 5, Nov. 1837 | RCH |
| Reeves, B. | McLain, Elisabeth | 20, Sept 1836 | RCH |
| Reeves, John M. | Holmes, Deborah | 31, Mar. 1839 | RCH |
| Reeves, Spender | Morris, Mary | 8, Nov. 1846 | RCH |
| Reeves, Thomas | Smith, Anna Maria | Dec. 1842 | RCH |
| Reeys, Andrew | Tinhoff, Bertha | 13, Dec. 1835 | RCH |
| Regan, David | Roberts, Cynthia | 18, Jan. 1818 | RCH |
| Regan, George Henry | McLaughlin, | 20, Aug. 1833 | RCH |
| Regan, John | Jones, Elisabeth | Feb. 1843 | RCH |
| Regan, John | McGrath, Margaret | 12, Sept 1846 | BB |
| Regland, Benjamin | Ellis, Jane | 17, Nov. 1845 | RCH |
| Reglein, Peter | Feist, Theresa | 25, Feb. 1847 | A |
| Rehbrock, Heinrich F | Schlottmann, Maria | 20, May 1847 | C |
| Rehe, Johan Joseph | Meyer, Anna Maria | 16, May 1848 | AA |
| Rehfuss, Ludwig | Frank, Catharine | 19, Dec. 1843 | G |
| Rehling, Bernard H. | Fettlage, Catharine | 26, Sept 1844 | AA |
| Rehling, Friedrich | Ahlers, Anna Elis. | 5, Sept 1847 | AA |
| Rehling, Gerhard H. | Luehn, Anna Margaret | 29, July 1849 | AA |
| Rehling, Heinrich | Schone, Gertrud | 12, Sept 1843 | AA |
| Rehm, Simon | Muhlin, Anna | 16, May 1838 | FF |
| Rehner, J. Friedrich | Brockmann, Catharine | 24, Dec. 1849 | F |
| Rehres, Joseph | Backs, M. Gertrud | 28, Oct. 1849 | II |
| Reibel, Friedrich | Hopstetter, Margaret | 10, Jan. 1842 | G |
| Reichart, Johan | Koehler, Martha | 25, Oct. 1849 | G |
| Reid, Alexander | Laing, Jane | 4, Dec. 1835 | RCH |
| Reid, Benjamin | Ackley, Mary | 7, May 1824 | RCH |
| Reid, Robert | Blakeley, Mary | 20, Apr. 1843 | RCH |
| Reidel, Georg | Meyer, Babette | 24, May 1849 | C |
| Reidel, Michael | Hedel, Maria Anna | 10, Oct. 1848 | RCH |
| Reidenbach, Friedric | Krausch, Barbara | 30, Oct. 1845 | G |
| Reif, Adam | Kleinmann, Margaret | 13, Nov. 1838 | FF |
| Reif, Carl | Graf, Barbara | 25, Oct. 1846 | FF |
| Reif, Joseph | Daringer, Catharina | 23, Nov. 1835 | FF |
| Reif, Joseph | Wolfzahn, Eva | 20, Nov. 1843 | FF |
| Reife, Ignatz | Mueller, Maria Anna | 3, Nov. 1834 | FF |
| Reifschneider, Johan | Keppler, Catharine | 22, Oct. 1844 | G |
| Reike, Friedrich | Rahn, Elisabeth | 30, Mar. 1848 | RCH |
| Reikert, G. Heinrich | Speick, M. Elisabeth | 17, Sept 1839 | FF |
| Reikert, Jacob | Heiselman, Magdalena | 11, Oct. 1841 | RCH |
| Reile, Georg | Goff, Catharina | 31, Dec. 1835 | FF |
| Reiley, John W. | Ready, Mary | 30, Sept 1835 | RCH |
| Reiling, Johan | Doeppe, Agnes | 8, June 1848 | G |
| Reilly, Christopher | McAdams, Ann | 15, Sept 1847 | RCH |
| Reilly, Eugene | Mitchell, Ellen | 13, May 1849 | BB |
| Reilly, James | Green, Julia | 8, Sept 1841 | BB |
| Reilly, James | French, Lucia Ann | 3, May 1848 | I |
| Reilly, John C. | Lynch, Ellen | 1, May 1845 | BB |
| Reilly, Michael | Donahue, Mary | 29, Sept 1844 | BB |
| Reilly, Michael | Connelly, Ann | 8, June 1846 | BB |
| Reilly, Patrick | Cassidy, Mary | 4, Sept 1840 | BB |
| Reilly, Patrick | Smith, Mary | 10, Jan. 1847 | BB |
| Reilly, Thomas | Pendergast, Mary | 3, May 1843 | BB |
| Reilly, Thomas | Meyers, Susannah | 27, Dec. 1849 | BB |
| Reilly, Washington | Bird, Mary | 28, Sept 1841 | RCH |
| Reilly, William | Rails, Louise | 29, Nov. 1834 | RCH |
| Reily, Benjamin | Pauner, Hannah | 16, Nov. 1820 | RCH |

| Grooms<br>****** | Brides<br>****** | Date of Marriage<br>**** ** ******** | Code<br>**** |
|---|---|---|---|
| Reily, Dennis | McManus, Ann | 25, Aug. 1842 | BB |
| Reinberg, John | Darwerger, Catharine | 9, Nov. 1841 | RCH |
| Reinbold, Johan | Braun, Magdalena | 2, May 1844 | AA |
| Reindt, J. Friedrich | Erstrol, Christina H | 6, Feb. 1845 | C |
| Reineke, Michael | Klanken, Henrietta | 16, June 1842 | FF |
| Reiner, James | Simonson, Julia A. | 21, Apr. 1839 | RCH |
| Reiner, John | Stollen, Anna C. | 9, Nov. 1841 | RCH |
| Reiner, Ludwig | Kraft, Katharina | 23, July 1848 | A |
| Reiners, Johan | Deinger, Maria | 10, Sept 1848 | CC |
| Reinhard, Balthasar | Kuntz, Catharina | 1, Oct. 1839 | FF |
| Reinhard, Carl | McDonough, Emily | 25, Aug. 1849 | RCH |
| Reinhard, Carl | Robert, Maria | 25, Aug. 1849 | C |
| Reinhard, Gottfried | Deller, Barbara | 31, Oct. 1843 | AA |
| Reinhardt, Friedrich | Hoffmeyer, Sophia | 23, Jan. 1845 | F |
| Reinhardt, Georg | Reitz, Magdalena | 10, Apr. 1845 | G |
| Reinhardt, Heinrich | Bergmann, Maria | 12, Jan. 1846 | RCH |
| Reinhardt, Michael | Meyer, Barbara | 4, Aug. 1849 | RCH |
| Reinhart, Carl | Eicker, Barbara | 6, Jan. 1835 | FF |
| Reinhart, John | Cotton, Margaret | 5, Mar. 1843 | RCH |
| Reinhart, Nicolaus | Geisendorfer, Anna M | 7, Jan. 1849 | EE |
| Reinhart, Nicolaus | Efers, Sophia | 20, Feb. 1849 | EE |
| Reinhart, Wilhelm | Hagedorn, Margaretha | 23, Nov. 1844 | F |
| Reinheimer, Adam | Reich, Christina | 4, Apr. 1848 | C |
| Reinheir, Simon | Woodruff, Sarah | Mar. 1839 | RCH |
| Reining, Johan | Wupker, Maria Cath. | 20, Apr. 1847 | AA |
| Reinke, Friedrich | Lukens, Maria Sophia | 13, Oct. 1845 | RCH |
| Reinke, Friedrich W. | Lukens, Dorothea | 22, Feb. 1849 | F |
| Reinke, Johan Heinr. | Burmann, Catharine D | 26, Sept 1849 | B |
| Reinking, Wilhelm | Scheidemann, Sophia | 2, Feb. 1843 | F |
| Reinlein, Anton | Kitzenschwab, M Anna | 29, Sept 1840 | FF |
| Reira, James J.S. | Moeller, Matilda | 2, Apr. 1845 | BB |
| Reiring, Herman | Ravekamp, Anna Maria | 16, Feb. 1841 | FF |
| Reis, Ignatz | Gress, Catharine | 10, Oct. 1844 | AA |
| Reis, Johan Georg | Heine, Anna Maria | 29, May 1838 | FF |
| Reis, Louis | Lambert, Margaretha | 25, July 1847 | EE |
| Reis, Nicolaus | Pletner, Elisabeth | 13, Feb. 1849 | AA |
| Reis, Nicolaus | Kammer, Barbara | 11, Nov. 1845 | EE |
| Reis, Peter | Nichten, Sibylla | 12, Nov. 1839 | FF |
| Reischel, Andreas | Enderle, Theresa | 3, Apr. 1845 | AA |
| Reisel, John | Schilfling, Barbara | 9, Aug. 1847 | RCH |
| Reiser, Seraphin | Birsch, Othilia | 18, June 1848 | CC |
| Reising, Adam | Springer, Aloysia | 23, May 1848 | EE |
| Reising, Adam | Oestern, Christina | 5, Sept 1848 | EE |
| Reising, Johan | Beyer, Margaretha | 7, Jan. 1840 | FF |
| Reising, Johan | Hafner, Magdalena | 22, Feb. 1848 | EE |
| Reising, Johan Adam | Hemmer, Catharine | 7, Oct. 1845 | AA |
| Reising, Johann | Lamai, Magdalena | 14, Jan. 1840 | FF |
| Reising, Leonard | Fink, Catharine | 4, Feb. 1849 | II |
| Reisinger, John | Feiss, Affara | 27, July 1848 | G |
| Reisinger, Joseph | Wessendorf, Anna M. | 7, Mar. 1848 | CC |
| Reisler, Wilhelm | Kolkmeyer, Maria | 1, Nov. 1845 | C |
| Reiss, Conrad | Muehl, M. Elisabeth | 16, Feb. 1841 | FF |
| Reiss, Joseph | Bauermann, Catharine | 10, Aug. 1842 | G |
| Reiss, Ludwig | Schmidt, Eva | 25, Feb. 1847 | A |
| Reiss, Philipp | Starkel, Catharine | 27, Feb. 1840 | G |
| Reiter, Friedrich H. | Dammeier, Christina | 24, Mar. 1848 | C |
| Reiter, Mathias | McElroy, Clara | 1, July 1848 | RCH |
| Reiters, Francis | Hukert, Helena | 2, Mar. 1848 | EE |
| Reith, Francis | Hug, Francisca | 25, July 1847 | EE |
| Reith, Johan Georg | Menz, Eva Elisabeth | 7, Jan. 1840 | FF |
| Reitz, Conrad | Bertsche, Caroline | 23, May 1847 | EE |
| Reitz, Georg | Bartholomai, A. Elis | 26, Sept 1848 | A |
| Reitz, John William | VanWarburg, Magdalen | 10, Sept 1848 | RCH |
| Reitzammeier, Peter | Zimmer, Margaret | 18, Nov. 1846 | RCH |
| Reken, Gerhard | Hellhaus, Anna Maria | 5, Feb. 1839 | FF |
| Rekers, Herman | Pohlmann, Catharine | 6, Oct. 1846 | AA |
| Relkers, Heinrich | Bueckle, Maria Elis. | 24, Nov. 1835 | FF |
| Remey, Richard | Herron, Susan | 7, May 1835 | RCH |
| Remis, Marvin | Knight, Jane | 28, Apr. 1836 | RCH |
| Remme, Heinrich W. | Leimann, Catharine W | 2, Sept 1841 | F |
| Remmert, Heinrich | Reper, Maria L. | 10, Oct. 1845 | RCH |

| Grooms<br>****** | Brides<br>****** | Date of Marriage<br>**** ** ******** | Code<br>**** |
|---|---|---|---|
| Remmert, Heinrich | Kalthaus, M. Louise | 11, Feb. 1847 | F |
| Rempe, Franz | Mueller, Elisabeth | 12, Nov. 1848 | II |
| Renart, Johan | Paul, Magdalena | 6, Aug. 1848 | EE |
| Rendings, Johan H. | Braun, Elisabeth | 7, Aug. 1849 | RCH |
| Renecker, Jacob Th. | Wittkamp, Margaret | 23, Sept 1849 | FF |
| Reneke, Johan | Niemeyer, Maria | 10, Jan. 1841 | FF |
| Rennecker, Heinrich | Obenstadt, Catharina | 4, Nov. 1840 | FF |
| Rennekamp, Bernard | Francis, Christina | 28, Oct. 1845 | FF |
| Rennekamp, Georg | Krieger, A.M. Elis. | 5, Aug. 1849 | EE |
| Rennekamp, Georg | Mescher, Elisabeth | 2, Nov. 1847 | FF |
| Rennekamp, Heinrich | Busse, Elisabeth | 21, Mar. 1846 | AA |
| Rennekamp, Heinrich | Mascher, Catharine | 9, Sept 1849 | FF |
| Rennekamp, Heinrich | Tolsche, Wilhelmina | 16, Oct. 1849 | II |
| Renneker, Johan H. | Aumann, Josephina | 22, Oct. 1848 | AA |
| Rennemeier, Friedric | Tienig, Maria Elis. | 11, Oct. 1849 | F |
| Renner, Jacob | Scheurer, Susanna | 4, Feb. 1841 | G |
| Renner, Wendel | Knaebel, Carolina | 31, May 1841 | FF |
| Renner, William | Devasack, Catharine | 24, Feb. 1842 | RCH |
| Rennicks, John | Gray, Susanna | 24, Feb. 1819 | RCH |
| Reno, Lewis | McGlahan, Mary | 26, July 1844 | RCH |
| Renont, Charles E. | Harrison, Elisabeth | 14, Dec. 1846 | RCH |
| Rensford, Thomas C. | Williams, Margaret | 24, Dec. 1844 | RCH |
| Renshen, Johan Hein. | Decken, M. Elisabeth | 28, Feb. 1843 | FF |
| Rentz, Ferdinand | Hermann, Maria | 5, Nov. 1839 | FF |
| Rentz, Joseph | Mueller, Margaretha | 19, Nov. 1844 | FF |
| Rentz, Michael | Erhart, Veronica | 11, Oct. 1836 | FF |
| Rentz, Peter | Eckstein, Sarah | 14, Aug. 1839 | FF |
| Renz, August | Schneider, Rosa B. | 8, June 1848 | G |
| Renzenbiber, Johan H | Wildenhaus, Catharin | 8, Feb. 1848 | EE |
| Renzenbrink, Christ. | Brockmann, Charlotte | 4, Nov. 1847 | F |
| Renzenkuper, Johan G | Lammers, Maria Anna | 4, June 1848 | EE |
| Renzing, Heinrich | Wiggers, Theresa | 12, Sept 1849 | AA |
| Rerenger, Casper | Fagly, Jemima | 4, May 1819 | RCH |
| Rerirvan, John | McDonald, Mary | 8, Nov. 1849 | GG |
| Rerk, William | Meek, Catharine | 14, Dec. 1833 | RCH |
| Resener, Christian | Seifreid, Julianna | 31, Oct. 1848 | A |
| Resing, Heinrich | Bley, Elisabeth | 28, Jan. 1849 | FF |
| Resing, Louis Heinr. | Koch, Sophia Maria | 25, Mar. 1847 | B |
| Resink, Friedrich | Tenbrink, Genidina | 31, Aug. 1843 | RCH |
| Resor, Jacob | Silsbee, Anna | 15, Oct. 1845 | RCH |
| Resor, Reuben P. | Lovel, Sarah | 11, Sept 1834 | RCH |
| Reuschel, Andreas | Freis, Magdalena | 29, Feb. 1848 | EE |
| Reutelmann, Herman | Winger, Anna Maria | 11, Nov. 1846 | AA |
| Reutemann, Heinrich | Messmann, Elisabeth | 17, Nov. 1846 | AA |
| Reutepohler, Christ. | Darpe, Mary A. | 16, Oct. 1845 | RCH |
| Reutepohler, Herman | Sollmann, Catharine | 8, Sept 1842 | F |
| Reutepohler, Johan | Steinkers, M. Louise | 18, Apr. 1849 | RCH |
| Rewe, William | Sutton, Sarah | 18, Feb. 1844 | RCH |
| Rewel, Heinrich | Finzer, Maria | 30, Apr. 1848 | C |
| Rewz, Francis | Cummings, Rebecca | 27, Feb. 1832 | RCH |
| Rex, Daniel | Helmig, Catharine | 13, Jan. 1847 | RCH |
| Reynolds, Allen B. | Bradbury, Louise | 8, June 1831 | RCH |
| Reynolds, Daniel | Taylor, Milly | 21, Mar. 1819 | RCH |
| Reynolds, Isaac | Sessions, Margaret | 5, Aug. 1833 | RCH |
| Reynolds, James | Horne, Bridget | 22, Mar. 1842 | RCH |
| Reynolds, James | McLean, Nancy | 25, Jan. 1844 | RCH |
| Reynolds, James | Beagen, Margaret | 2, Jan. 1849 | RCH |
| Reynolds, Joseph | Este, Lucy Ann | 9, Feb. 1843 | I |
| Reynolds, Owen | Nolen, Ann | 1, Aug. 1847 | BB |
| Reynolds, R.G. | Londsdale, Martha | 9, Sept 1823 | RCH |
| Reynolds, Robert | Montgomery, Mary | 26, Aug. 1837 | RCH |
| Reynolds, Robert | Weeks, Matilda | 20, May 1844 | RCH |
| Reynolds, Robert | Lilley, Elisabeth | Nov. 1844 | RCH |
| Reynolds, Royland | Slude, Delsina | 22, Mar. 1838 | RCH |
| Reynolds, Walter | Pearson, Mary Jane | 7, May 1834 | RCH |
| Reynolds, Whitney | Mills, Julia Anna | 9, Aug. 1837 | RCH |
| Reynolds, Wiley | Johns, Catharine | 20, June 1833 | RCH |
| Reynolds, William | Campbell, Elisabeth | 8, Oct. 1840 | RCH |
| Reynolds, William | Cross, Charity C. | 23, Apr. 1846 | RCH |
| Reynolds, William | Simmons, Elizabeth | 17, July 1848 | GG |
| Rhea, John | Groves, Rosetta | 25, Oct. 1842 | RCH |

| Grooms<br>****** | Brides<br>****** | Date of Marriage<br>**** ** ******** | Code<br>**** |
|---|---|---|---|
| Rhegennes, Jacob | Mulford, Irene | 11, June 1832 | RCH |
| Rhegness, John | Sullivan, Sarah | 30, June 1844 | RCH |
| Rheinberger, J. Adam | Mehl, Maria | 11, Dec. 1849 | C |
| Rhineo, Henry | Geise, Elisabeth | 15, Apr. 1834 | RCH |
| Rhoton, Leonard | Shyrock, Sarah | 7, Oct. 1844 | RCH |
| Rice, Elipalet | Harrison, Sallie | 30, Dec. 1847 | RCH |
| Rice, George | Way, Ellen | 12, Aug. 1837 | RCH |
| Rice, Henry | Fields, Sylvia | 21, Sept 1847 | RCH |
| Rice, Jacob | Sterin, Anna | 29, Aug. 1842 | RCH |
| Rice, James | Price, Clarissa D. | 14, Dec. 1841 | RCH |
| Rice, John | Brown, Hannah | 19, Mar. 1839 | RCH |
| Rice, John | Camp, Julia | Oct. 1844 | RCH |
| Rice, John Henry | Lightfoot, Martha | 11, June 1846 | RCH |
| Rice, Joseph | Getz, Magdalena | 2, May 1844 | RCH |
| Rice, Michael | Ginn, Ann | 3, June 1849 | BB |
| Rice, Reuben | Wiggins, Sarah | 12, Mar. 1835 | RCH |
| Rice, Rufus | Picket, Aley | 20, Dec. 1841 | RCH |
| Rice, Solomon | Edwards, Margaret | 30, Dec. 1846 | RCH |
| Rice, William | Lee, Anna | 9, Dec. 1841 | RCH |
| Rich, John B. | Humphrey, Elliott | 27, Nov. 1841 | RCH |
| Rich, Joseph | Black, Lucretia | 19, Dec. 1843 | RCH |
| Rich, Nathan F. | Manning, Hannah | 20, Oct. 1845 | BB |
| Rich, Robert | Morley, Rosetta | 15, July 1849 | RCH |
| Richard, George | Allen, Jane Margaret | 3, Feb. 1838 | RCH |
| Richard, J. Theodor | Reckelhoff, Anna M. | 11, Oct. 1836 | FF |
| Richard, Richard | Humphrey, Mary | 10, June 1837 | RCH |
| Richard, William | Corrington, Nancy | 10, June 1844 | RCH |
| Richards, Channing | Williamson, Lydia H. | 9, Mar. 1837 | I |
| Richards, Charles | Reck, Martha | 7, May 1839 | RCH |
| Richards, Dennis | Roy, Margaret | 6, June 1848 | RCH |
| Richards, Dickson | Wirk, Nancy | 18, May 1847 | RCH |
| Richards, Erastus | Alexander, Susan | 18, Dec. 1848 | RCH |
| Richards, George | Quinn, Elisabeth | 26, Apr. 1838 | RCH |
| Richards, Giles | Hankinson, Eleanor | 1, Nov. 1820 | RCH |
| Richards, James | Hill, Margaret | 31, Jan. 1846 | RCH |
| Richards, John | Richards, Harriet | 16, Nov. 1845 | RCH |
| Richards, John | Northrop, Adaline | 2, Aug. 1846 | RCH |
| Richards, John | Beaufort, Jane | 21, Apr. 1849 | RCH |
| Richards, Jonathan | Latta, Elizabeth | 7, July 1825 | RCH |
| Richards, Samuel | Williamson, Jane | 2, July 1832 | RCH |
| Richards, Thomas | Jenkins, Elisabeth | 18, Dec. 1843 | RCH |
| Richards, Thomas | Heiring, Amanda | 15, Dec. 1849 | RCH |
| Richards, Timothy | Sanders, Martha | 3, June 1848 | RCH |
| Richards, William | Woodburn, Lucinda | 14, Oct. 1846 | RCH |
| Richardson, Francis | Conclin, Louise | 19, Apr. 1847 | RCH |
| Richardson, Frederic | Harris, Sarah | 6, Mar. 1846 | RCH |
| Richardson, Georg | Campbell, Mary | 29, Mar. 1849 | RCH |
| Richardson, Henry | Hobbs, Mary | 21, Sept 1847 | RCH |
| Richardson, Isaac | Biddle, Rebecca | 3, June 1824 | RCH |
| Richardson, James | Waggoner, Mary | 30, May 1844 | RCH |
| Richardson, James | Bates, Jane | 21, May 1846 | RCH |
| Richardson, John | Doel, Sarah | 11, Aug. 1845 | RCH |
| Richardson, Jonathan | Richards, Sarah | 6, Feb. 1835 | RCH |
| Richardson, Joseph | Fuller, Mary C. | 13, Aug. 1847 | RCH |
| Richardson, Noah | Brown, Mary | 15, Feb. 1825 | RCH |
| Richardson, Pearson | Schillinger, Elis. | 15, June 1836 | RCH |
| Richardson, Philipp | Doney, Nancy | 26, Oct. 1844 | RCH |
| Richardson, Robert | Richardson, Cath. | 30, Aug. 1820 | RCH |
| Richardson, Robert | Gilman, Ann | 21, Mar. 1832 | RCH |
| Richardson, Robert | Russell, Catharine | 16, May 1842 | RCH |
| Richardson, Roswell | Spears, Matilda | 1, Jan. 1845 | RCH |
| Richardson, Samuel | Lawrence, Elisabeth | 18, Sept 1847 | RCH |
| Richardson, William | Richardson, Jane | 2, Feb. 1842 | RCH |
| Richart, Johan | Schoen, Wilhelmina | 17, Oct. 1848 | EE |
| Riche, John F. | Walker, Parmela | 29, May 1819 | RCH |
| Richer, Karl | Niehof, Henrietta | 25, May 1848 | RCH |
| Richert, Philipp | Bigham, Elisabeth | 24, June 1849 | BB |
| Richey, | Borradail, Rebecca | 31, Aug. 1831 | RCH |
| Richimer, Michael | Boellinger, Francis | 31, Aug. 1843 | FF |
| Richter, Bernard | Wibbel, Catharine | 29, Mar. 1845 | AA |
| Richter, Dietrich | Riehm, Elisabeth | 13, Apr. 1847 | AA |

| Grooms | Brides | Date of Marriage | Code |
|--------|--------|------------------|------|
| ****** | ****** | **** ** ******** | **** |
| Richter, Dietrich | Schroeder, Elisabeth | 14, Aug. 1849 | EE |
| Richter, Ernst | Buldmann, Bernardina | 11, June 1848 | A |
| Richter, Friedrich | Langemeier, Elisabet | 23, Jan. 1848 | FF |
| Richter, Heinrich | Bellmann, Adelheid | 17, Sept 1839 | FF |
| Richter, Heinrich | Freisen, Cath. Adel. | 6, June 1847 | FF |
| Richter, Joseph | Fischer, Maria Elis. | 7, May 1846 | AA |
| Richter, Joseph | Wuebbel, Friedricka | 25, Jan. 1848 | EE |
| Rick, William | Gray, Elisabeth | 25, Mar. 1819 | RCH |
| Ricke, Herman Heinr. | Kunnemann, Charlotte | 7, Jan. 1847 | B |
| Ricke, J. Heinrich | Timpermann, M. Cath. | 16, June 1840 | FF |
| Rickeling, Johan H. | Schippers, Susanna | 16, Apr. 1844 | AA |
| Rickenbach, Joseph | Hirzelberger, Marg. | 11, Nov. 1849 | AA |
| Ricker, Joel | Williamson, Sarah | 24, Dec. 1835 | RCH |
| Rickert, Peter | Selm, Anna Maria | 19, Dec. 1846 | RCH |
| Rickert, Peter | Imbot, Magdalena | 9, Feb. 1847 | G |
| Ricket, John | Williams, Nancy | 24, Dec. 1818 | RCH |
| Rickets, Greenbury | Ray, Mary | 6, June 1833 | RCH |
| Rickey, | Clark, Elisabeth | 9, Jan. 1823 | RCH |
| Rickhof, Albert | Poelking, Margaretha | 4, June 1848 | II |
| Ricking, Heinrich | Sieve, Dina | 13, Aug. 1848 | FF |
| Rickoff, Andrew | Black, Elisabeth | 18, Aug. 1842 | RCH |
| Ricoff, Aron | Roll, Margaret | 18, Apr. 1836 | RCH |
| Riddell, Neal | Tandy, Mildred | 11, Sept 1832 | RCH |
| Ridder, Friedrich H. | Lohmeyer, Marg. D. | 4, May 1843 | F |
| Riddle, Adam N. | Cook, Elisabeth | 28, Apr. 1835 | RCH |
| Riddle, Alfred | Oliver, Anna M. | 25, July 1844 | RCH |
| Riddle, Andrew | Miller, Martha | 23, Nov. 1847 | RCH |
| Riddle, Andrew J. | Skillman, Levine | 17, Feb. 1848 | RCH |
| Riddle, August | Loose, Catharine | 4, Oct. 1835 | RCH |
| Riddle, Benjamin | Patterson, Nancy | 14, June 1820 | RCH |
| Riddle, David | Fox, Caroline | 22, Dec. 1837 | RCH |
| Riddle, Hiram | VanAusdol, Lucretia | 21, Oct. 1846 | RCH |
| Riddle, Hiram B. | Tuttle, Mary Ann | 29, Feb. 1835 | RCH |
| Riddle, Jacob | Tucker, Ol. | 7, Aug. 1823 | RCH |
| Riddle, John | Ross, Jane | 30, Sept 1834 | RCH |
| Riddle, John | Hilts, Elisabeth | 6, Apr. 1843 | RCH |
| Riddle, Samuel | French, Sickey | 8, Nov. 1825 | RCH |
| Riddle, Thomas | Tice, Catharine | 1, Dec. 1818 | RCH |
| Riddle, Thomas J. | Cooper, Martha Ann | 12, May 1841 | RCH |
| Ridgely, Abraham | Hayes, Frances A. | 5, Sept 1843 | I |
| Ridgely, William | Flinthan, Charlotte | 4, June 1844 | RCH |
| Ridgeway, John | Hicks, Mary Jane | 21, Sept 1845 | RCH |
| Ridgeway, John N. | McGinnis, Anna L. | 9, May 1835 | RCH |
| Ridgway, Samuel | Robins, Carolina A. | 29, Nov. 1842 | RCH |
| Riebe, George Mich. | Brodbeck, Maria | 28, May 1837 | RCH |
| Riebel, Georg | Erdmann, Maria | 3, Feb. 1843 | G |
| Riebel, George | Alexander, Catharine | 13, May 1846 | G |
| Rieck, John | Hagemann, Sarah J. | 19, Sept 1849 | RCH |
| Rieddinghack, H. | Ternwald, Margaretha | 17, Apr. 1834 | RCH |
| Riedel, Christian | Schneidering, Marg. | 19, Aug. 1848 | RCH |
| Riedel, Martin | Arnold, Barbara | 9, July 1842 | G |
| Rieger, Christian | Juppenlatz, Elisabet | 20, Nov. 1842 | A |
| Riegler, Leonard | Rubner, Rosina | 14, Oct. 1845 | AA |
| Riehl, Charles H. | Ruerden, Clarissa | 2, May 1841 | RCH |
| Riehl, Ludwig | Nau, Elisabeth | 10, Aug. 1842 | RCH |
| Rieker, Michael Adam | Weismann, Barbara | 16, Aug. 1845 | RCH |
| Rieker, Samuel C. | Cochran, Amanda | 19, May 1841 | RCH |
| Rielage, Franz | Zumbahlen, Maria A. | 16, Nov. 1845 | AA |
| Rielage, Johan | Zumbahlen, Carolina | 24, Oct. 1847 | AA |
| Rielage, Wilhelm | Wischmeyer, Catharin | 20, Sept 1842 | AA |
| Riemann, Friedrich | Henke, Dorothea | 20, May 1849 | AA |
| Riemann, Gerhard | Kleier, Maria Elis. | 7, Nov. 1847 | FF |
| Riemenschneider, H. | Nicklaus, Maria | 9, Mar. 1849 | RCH |
| Riemeyer, Friedrich | Sollmann, Caroline | 19, Oct. 1843 | F |
| Riemeyer, J. David | Woellmer, Maria | 3, Oct. 1844 | F |
| Ries, Adam | Geisler, Magdalena | 29, Dec. 1840 | FF |
| Ries, Francis | Hoffmann, Maria | 10, Oct. 1848 | AA |
| Ries, Georg Adam | Weber, Elisabeth | 7, Oct. 1847 | G |
| Ries, Jacob | Morio, Elisabeth | 13, June 1848 | FF |
| Riewe, Clement | Vonhus, | 24, Aug. 1845 | AA |
| Riffy, George | Dunseth, Elisabeth | 17, Mar. 1848 | RCH |

| Grooms ****** | Brides ****** | Date of Marriage **** ** ******** | Code **** |
|---|---|---|---|
| Rigdon, Charles | Dalton, Ann L. | 20, Jan. 1820 | RCH |
| Riggen, Algier | Durham, Rebecca | 29, Jan. 1847 | RCH |
| Riggle, George | ----, ---- | 24, Feb. 1833 | RCH |
| Riggs, Isaac | Franklin, Mary Ann | 20, Feb. 1842 | RCH |
| Riggs, Milan | Douthwaite, Sarah | 30, Nov. 1845 | RCH |
| Right, John | Burns, Mary | 15, Jan. 1835 | RCH |
| Rigle, Benjamin | Edwards, Eveline | 31, Oct. 1833 | RCH |
| Rihm, Johan | Gnaebel, Josephina | 13, Feb. 1840 | FF |
| Riker, James | Voorhes, Jennett | 4, Aug. 1845 | RCH |
| Riker, Johan Dietric | Schade, Maria Anna | 18, Aug. 1846 | AA |
| Riker, John | Johnson, Phoebe | 20, Nov. 1828 | RCH |
| Riker, John | Riker, Sarah Jane | 12, Nov. 1843 | RCH |
| Riker, Thomas | Bramble, Eleanor | 1, Nov. 1834 | RCH |
| Riker, William | Ferris, Rachel | 16, Apr. 1818 | RCH |
| Rilen, Isaac | King, Caroline | 16, Sept 1849 | RCH |
| Riley, Andrew | McGlinn, Margaret | 21, July 1841 | BB |
| Riley, Harrison | Spergon, Martha | 30, Mar. 1845 | RCH |
| Riley, Irvin | Shaw, Nancy | 21, Sept 1833 | RCH |
| Riley, James | Purvis, Elisabeth | 27, Feb. 1844 | RCH |
| Riley, James | Kramer, Henrietta | 22, Dec. 1845 | RCH |
| Riley, Jesse | Adams, Lucinda | 29, Nov. 1841 | RCH |
| Riley, John | Barnes, Susan | 13, Apr. 1837 | RCH |
| Riley, John | Wallace, Helen | 20, Sept 1849 | RCH |
| Riley, John C. | Lewis, Martha | 15, Feb. 1847 | RCH |
| Riley, Jonathan | Lamber, Elisabeth | 10, June 1833 | RCH |
| Riley, Shepherd | Ward, Harriet | 6, Aug. 1847 | RCH |
| Riley, Thomas | Bloomer, Virginia | 31, Dec. 1841 | RCH |
| Riley, William H. | Carter, Rosetta | 21, June 1839 | RCH |
| Rilmemann, Ludwig | Jones, Marsa | 19, Dec. 1848 | RCH |
| Rin, William P. | Voses, Mary A. | 4, Dec. 1839 | RCH |
| Rincke, Friedrich W. | Helten, Anna Maria | 13, Nov. 1849 | C |
| Rinear, Samuel | Enos, Martha | 25, Dec. 1846 | RCH |
| Rinear, Thomas J. | Tumpaugh, Margaret | 28, Dec. 1848 | RCH |
| Rinehart, William | Hoffmann, Ruth | 30, July 1842 | RCH |
| Rinehart, William | Rue, Roxinda | 9, Jan. 1849 | RCH |
| Ring, John | Night, Margaret | 28, Sept 1847 | RCH |
| Ringel, Johan | Lutz, Kunigunda | 28, June 1848 | EE |
| Ringen, Gilbert | Domhof, Maria E. | 16, Mar. 1843 | F |
| Ringer, Joseph | Kasings, Maria | 20, Dec. 1846 | F |
| Ringer, Joseph | Kasting, Engel | 27, Oct. 1849 | F |
| Ringer, Leonard | Held, Margaretha | 26, Oct. 1847 | AA |
| Rinkenberger Philipp | Gross, Magdalena | 25, Nov. 1846 | G |
| Rinkenmeyer, Heinric | Benninghaus, Anna M. | 5, Nov. 1846 | EE |
| Rinkhorst, Ludwig | Wienke, Anna Maria | 22, Dec. 1842 | F |
| Rinnfus, Joseph | Schmidt, Barbara | 30, Jan. 1844 | AA |
| Rinschler, Anton | Schuh, Wilhelmina | 16, July 1844 | AA |
| Riorden, Cornelius | Durken, Ann | 26, Dec. 1849 | RCH |
| Ripley, George | Hallgath, Sarah | 13, Apr. 1843 | RCH |
| Ripley, Joseph D. | Gardner, Sarah Ann | 6, May 1835 | RCH |
| Riplo, Wilhelm | Stevert, Gertrud | 28, July 1849 | CC |
| Ripolt, John | Rice, Amelia | 28, Nov. 1844 | BB |
| Rippenberg, Charles | Ziegler, Catharine | 29, Apr. 1847 | RCH |
| Ripperger, Adam | Hock, Eva | 18, Jan. 1843 | AA |
| Ripperger, Adam | Winter, Regina | 17, Oct. 1843 | AA |
| Rippey, Wesley | Weeks, Catharine | 9, Nov. 1845 | RCH |
| Riscau, John Theodor | Kluenenberg, M. Elis | 27, Nov. 1838 | FF |
| Risch, Heinrich | Landemann, Elisabeth | 6, Aug. 1846 | A |
| Risch, Heinrich | Diez, Magdalena | 4, June 1848 | A |
| Rise, Heinrich | Meilhoff, Maria | 21, Dec. 1848 | B |
| Rishley, Elvy | Tibbs, Sarah D. | 21, July 1836 | RCH |
| Risingsun, Henry | Given, Rebecca | 26, Nov. 1818 | RCH |
| Risk, E.F. | Murdock, Jane | 3, May 1846 | RCH |
| Risk, Samuel | Mineis, Christina | 30, Dec. 1841 | RCH |
| Risp, Conrad | Henninger, Elisabeth | 30, Apr. 1842 | RCH |
| Risschan, J. Theodor | Klunenberg, Elis. | 27, Nov. 1839 | RCH |
| Rissey, James H. | Kelly, Mary | 5, Nov. 1833 | RCH |
| Ritchie, Charles | Terry, Rebecca | 29, June 1843 | RCH |
| Ritemann, Johan | Bonnet, Maria Anna | 7, June 1842 | FF |
| Rithaly, Blasius | Enger, Theresa | 10, Oct. 1848 | CC |
| Ritt, Nicolaus | Staub, Apollonia | 3, Jan. 1843 | FF |
| Rittenhouse, Adam | Steames, Janette | Sept 1844 | RCH |

| Grooms<br>****** | Brides<br>****** | Date of Marriage<br>**** ** ******** | Code<br>**** |
|---|---|---|---|
| Rittenhouse, David | McCammins, Sarah | 25, Mar. 1821 | RCH |
| Rittenhouse, Eli F. | Herakle, Lydia | 17, Nov. 1818 | RCH |
| Rittenhouse, Freeman | Robinson, Margaret P | 11, June 1843 | BB |
| Rittenhouse, George | Cormick, Elisabeth | 8, July 1849 | RCH |
| Rittenhouse, Samuel | Layton, Margaret | Nov. 1841 | RCH |
| Ritter, Anton | Ohnemiller, Catharin | 31, Aug. 1841 | FF |
| Ritter, Friedrich W. | Ensfelder, Maria A. | 9, Oct. 1849 | FF |
| Ritter, Hosea | Collins, Rachel | 16, Feb. 1841 | RCH |
| Ritter, Hubert | Spengler, Margaretha | 1, June 1843 | AA |
| Ritter, J. William | Casser, Anna M. | 1, Nov. 1845 | RCH |
| Ritter, John G. | Mann, Elisabeth | 1, Aug. 1843 | RCH |
| Ritter, Philipp | Martin, Charlotte | 6, Mar. 1849 | DD |
| Ritter, Rupert | Schnacher, Anna M. | 5, Aug. 1847 | EE |
| Ritterath, Peter | Druhmann, Agnes | 22, Apr. 1849 | CC |
| Ritting, Francis | Brumler, Elisabeth | 29, Apr. 1849 | EE |
| Rittinger, Johan | Schmidt, Philippina | 4, Jan. 1844 | G |
| Rittinger, Philipp | Kuckenheim, Rosina | 28, Nov. 1847 | G |
| Rittmann, J. Fried. | Trentmann, Maria | 19, Apr. 1847 | F |
| Rittweger, Georg C. | Scheinhof, Eva Wal. | 25, Jan. 1842 | G |
| Rittweger, Philipp | Langenstrass, Maria | 7, May 1839 | G |
| Ritzenberger, Joseph | Wies, Fanny | 13, Nov. 1843 | RCH |
| Rivers, Francis | Huston, Elisabeth | 25, Feb. 1847 | RCH |
| Rivers, Joshua | Stromp, Permilia | 18, June 1836 | RCH |
| Rix, Heinrich | Guenther, Christina | 26, Apr. 1845 | A |
| Roach, Thomas | Woodruff, Elisabeth | 27, Nov. 1845 | RCH |
| Roach, William | Heffernan, Bridget | 25, Jan. 1846 | BB |
| Roaren, John | Harrington, Ellen | 8, Nov. 1848 | GG |
| Roas, Jacob R. | Addison, Mary | 1, July 1841 | RCH |
| Roasey, Charles | Forainer, Mary | 8, Feb. 1836 | RCH |
| Roat, Samuel | Crawford, Laura | 6, Aug. 1846 | RCH |
| Robb, James | Smith, Jane | 19, Sept 1822 | RCH |
| Robbe, Heinrich | Alf, Euphemia Maria | 17, Apr. 1849 | II |
| Robben, Martin | Planware, Anna Maria | 19, Sept 1839 | RCH |
| Robbins, Dan | Leverett, Charlotte | 14, June 1819 | I |
| Robbins, Francis | Tuttle, Sarah | 18, Apr. 1843 | RCH |
| Robbins, James | Bierer, Mary | 3, July 1848 | BB |
| Robbins, Josiah | Hamilton, Elisabeth | 25, Dec. 1846 | RCH |
| Robe, Herman H. Jos. | Essenbeck, M. Elis. | 5, Jan. 1836 | FF |
| Robers, Johan | Schold, Theresa | 9, Jan. 1849 | EE |
| Robert, Louis | Clark, Ann (Mrs) | 1, Sept 1836 | RCH |
| Robert, Robert H. | Burk, Tempy | 20, Aug. 1822 | RCH |
| Roberts, Britton | Martin, Hester Ann | 4, May 1843 | RCH |
| Roberts, Charles J. | LeBoutillier, Anne | 6, July 1848 | D |
| Roberts, David | Edwards, Elisabeth | 18, Dec. 1847 | RCH |
| Roberts, Ebenezer | Covey, Ann | 10, Feb. 1846 | RCH |
| Roberts, Elijah | Birdges, Julia | 15, Aug. 1849 | RCH |
| Roberts, Jacob | Curtis, Sarah | 31, Mar. 1847 | RCH |
| Roberts, James | Clear, Mary | 25, Sept 1836 | RCH |
| Roberts, James | Rensten, Matilda | 8, Oct. 1842 | RCH |
| Roberts, John | Bohn, Nancy | 23, Apr. 1833 | RCH |
| Roberts, John | Sisco, Rebecca | 20, May 1838 | RCH |
| Roberts, John | Anderson, Martha | 25, May 1840 | RCH |
| Roberts, John | Wright, Dorcas | 29, Nov. 1842 | RCH |
| Roberts, John | Smith, Anna Elis. | 19, Nov. 1846 | RCH |
| Roberts, John | Tappan, Mary Elis. | 28, Mar. 1847 | RCH |
| Roberts, John W. | Phillips, Anna Maria | 12, Mar. 1844 | RCH |
| Roberts, Joseph | Hughes, Elisabeth | 19, Apr. 1837 | RCH |
| Roberts, Leonard | Smith, Elisabeth | 29, Jan. 1836 | RCH |
| Roberts, Lewis | Runyon, Mary | 4, July 1835 | RCH |
| Roberts, Michael | Wagstaff, Margaret | 13, July 1849 | RCH |
| Roberts, Robert | Jones, Charlotte | 12, Mar. 1833 | RCH |
| Roberts, Samuel | Wilkinson, Hannah | 20, Nov. 1845 | RCH |
| Roberts, Thomas | Watson, Maria | 31, Dec. 1837 | D |
| Roberts, Thomas | Jones, Eleanor | 12, Dec. 1843 | RCH |
| Roberts, Thomas | Doyle, Bridget | 19, Jan. 1843 | BB |
| Roberts, Thomas | Bryant, Elisabeth | 2, Dec. 1845 | RCH |
| Roberts, Timothy | Rodgers, Lavina | 23, July 1821 | RCH |
| Roberts, Turner | Wilson, Elisabeth | 28, July 1834 | RCH |
| Roberts, William | Johnson, Sarah | 1, May 1842 | RCH |
| Roberts, William | Fryer, Dorothea Ann | 26, Apr. 1842 | I |
| Robertson, Alexander | Johnson, Mary | 23, May 1848 | D |

| Grooms<br>****** | Brides<br>****** | Date of Marriage<br>**** ** ******** | Code<br>**** |
|---|---|---|---|
| Robertson, Green W. | Trotter, Matilda | 13, Feb. 1844 | RCH |
| Robertson, Isaac | Newman, Rhody | 7, Apr. 1825 | RCH |
| Robertson, Israel | Redenbaugh, Elisabet | 21, Dec. 1843 | RCH |
| Robertson, James | Bennett, Abigail | 12, Jan. 1843 | RCH |
| Robertson, John | Jinks, Ann | 14, June 1836 | RCH |
| Robertson, John | Edwards, Elisabeth | 2, Nov. 1843 | RCH |
| Robertson, John W. | Hull, Mary | 30, Nov. 1837 | RCH |
| Robertson, Jonathan | Davison, Ann | 22, Dec. 1833 | RCH |
| Robertson, Junius | Perralliat, Angela S | 12, Sept 1848 | BB |
| Robess, Henry | Ellermann, Mary | 10, Mar. 1836 | RCH |
| Robinson, Alfred C. | Criswell, Isabella | 29, Oct. 1835 | RCH |
| Robinson, Benjamin | Ferguson, Rachel | 2, July 1849 | RCH |
| Robinson, Charles | Barret, Maria | 19, Apr. 1843 | RCH |
| Robinson, Charles | Tuttle, Elisabeth | 31, Aug. 1846 | RCH |
| Robinson, Cuthbert | Bouser, Jane Ann | 14, Jan. 1836 | RCH |
| Robinson, Daniel | Stachhouse, Emeline | 5, May 1840 | RCH |
| Robinson, David | Gale, Jane | 2, July 1835 | RCH |
| Robinson, Francis L. | Donovan, Lydia | 20, June 1833 | RCH |
| Robinson, Frank | Milam, Julia | 21, Jan. 1844 | RCH |
| Robinson, Gabriel | Jacks, Malinda | 24, July 1836 | RCH |
| Robinson, Gabriel | Turner, Elisabeth | 12, Oct. 1842 | RCH |
| Robinson, George C. | Streelon, Jane | 3, Sept 1837 | RCH |
| Robinson, Henry | Johnson, Elisabeth | 6, Aug. 1846 | RCH |
| Robinson, Henry | Turner, Elisabeth | 28, Jan. 1847 | RCH |
| Robinson, Henry | Lowry, Sarah L. | 13, Nov. 1848 | RCH |
| Robinson, Henry | McAndrew, Joann | 24, Sept 1848 | BB |
| Robinson, J.M. | Bakes, Margaret | 4, July 1847 | RCH |
| Robinson, James | Barnum, Mary | 2, Dec. 1843 | RCH |
| Robinson, James C. | Crarey, Mary Ann | 3, July 1834 | RCH |
| Robinson, John | ----, Catharine | 27, Dec. 1821 | RCH |
| Robinson, John | Davis, Elisabeth | 7, Feb. 1832 | RCH |
| Robinson, John | Secret, Julia A. | 30, Jan. 1838 | RCH |
| Robinson, John | Wilmington, Mary J. | 26, Dec. 1846 | RCH |
| Robinson, John | Hays, Lizzie | 14, Jan. 1849 | RCH |
| Robinson, John | Klise, Elisabeth | 14, Mar. 1849 | RCH |
| Robinson, John B. | Challey, Maria | 10, Apr. 1834 | RCH |
| Robinson, John C. | Porter, Margaret | 4, Dec. 1835 | RCH |
| Robinson, John H. | Ogden, Amelia | 14, Aug. 1845 | RCH |
| Robinson, Joseph | Crowder, Maria | 3, Dec. 1846 | RCH |
| Robinson, Joseph | Markley, Ruth Ann | 4, July 1847 | RCH |
| Robinson, Joshua | Gates, M. Caroline | 13, Sept 1849 | RCH |
| Robinson, M.F. | Reede, Rachel | 27, Dec. 1832 | RCH |
| Robinson, Marens | Rokistem, Emily | 13, Nov. 1836 | RCH |
| Robinson, Nathaniel | Schafers, Charlotte | 20, July 1848 | RCH |
| Robinson, Nicolaus | Schnell, Maria | 25, Nov. 1847 | G |
| Robinson, Richard | Moore, Louise | 29, Jan. 1837 | RCH |
| Robinson, Richard | Dukes, Elisabeth Ann | 26, Dec. 1842 | RCH |
| Robinson, Robert | Wetzel, Margaret | 19, Mar. 1847 | RCH |
| Robinson, Samuel | Sears, Mary | 5, Mar. 1818 | RCH |
| Robinson, Samuel | Capp, Lucy | 1, Apr. 1841 | RCH |
| Robinson, William | Ayers, Julia Ann | 20, Mar. 1843 | RCH |
| Robinson, William | Jitler, Mary | 22, Jan. 1846 | RCH |
| Robinson, William | Epply, Julia Ann | 12, May 1847 | RCH |
| Robison, James | Courtney, Matilda | 4, June 1839 | RCH |
| Robison, John | ----, ---- | 22, Dec. 1824 | RCH |
| Robison, John | Doherty, Elisabeth | 25, Nov. 1841 | RCH |
| Robison, Joshua V. | Kinsey, Hannah J. | 19, Jan. 1819 | RCH |
| Robison, Michael | Ginty, Mary | 16, Apr. 1849 | RCH |
| Robson, George | Steelman, Mary | 23, Feb. 1834 | RCH |
| Rocap, Eli | Stake, Catharine | 29, May 1849 | BB |
| Roche, Thomas | Munday, Margaret A. | 19, Apr. 1849 | BB |
| Rockenfield, Abraham | Johns, Mary | 18, Aug. 1842 | RCH |
| Rockenfield, Jacob | Samm, Hannah | 26, Dec. 1833 | RCH |
| Rockenfuss, Huldrich | Fullroth, Maria | 30, Sept 1849 | C |
| Rocker, Felix | Hilder, Christine | 8, Aug. 1836 | RCH |
| Rockey, Henry | Ruffin, Mary | 9, Nov. 1820 | I |
| Rockingfield, John | Hildreth, Asenath | 14, Feb. 1834 | RCH |
| Rockwell, Henry | Hopper, Louise | 21, Aug. 1847 | RCH |
| Rockwood, Nathan | Chaloner, Anna Elis. | 26, Jan. 1843 | RCH |
| Rodabaugh, Peter | Fields, Mary Jane | 15, Aug. 1847 | RCH |
| Roddin, William | Martin, Susan | 13, Sept 1839 | BB |

| Grooms | Brides | Date of Marriage | Code |
|--------|--------|------------------|------|
| ****** | ****** | **** ** ******** | **** |
| Rode, Johan | Seelinger, Margaret | 21, Apr. 1835 | FF |
| Rodecker, Matthias | Martin, Elisabeth | 6, Jan. 1842 | RCH |
| Rodefeld, J Heinrich | Meyers, Maria | 19, Oct. 1848 | F |
| Rodefeld, Johan H. | Mollenkamp, Anna M. | 3, Sept 1846 | F |
| Rodefer, Christopher | Smith, Elisabeth | 30, Dec. 1841 | RCH |
| Rodekamp, Gerhard | Gramann, Anna M. | 6, May 1849 | AA |
| Rodemann, Georg | Bratenmacher, Chris. | 2, July 1848 | AA |
| Rodenbeck, Johan H. | Grobmeier, Bernardin | 2, Mar. 1848 | FF |
| Rodgers, Walter | Bowen, Margaret | 22, Feb. 1820 | RCH |
| Rodifer, Joseph | Loomis, Susan | 6, Aug. 1835 | RCH |
| Rodine, William | Hinton, Matilda | 14, Sept 1820 | RCH |
| Rodocker, Jacob | Craig, Crecy Ann | 17, May 1827 | RCH |
| Rodocker, William | Bell, Mary | 27, Nov. 1824 | RCH |
| Rodriquez, Francis | Maggini, M Josephina | 3, Nov. 1844 | BB |
| Roe, Daniel | Ma---, Mary | 2, Aug. 1824 | RCH |
| Roe, John J. | Wright, Martha | 10, Aug. 1837 | RCH |
| Roedel, Michael | Sengel, Caroline | 22, July 1847 | C |
| Roeder, John | Ilstrots, Christina | 4, Feb. 1845 | RCH |
| Roeder, Joseph | Schoenstein, Agatha | 4, Dec. 1846 | EE |
| Roedter, Heinrich | Lempert, Theresa | 1, Nov. 1842 | G |
| Roedter, Simon | Leiner, Maria Anna | 21, Feb. 1846 | EE |
| Roeger, John | Dressenberger, Marg. | 8, Jan. 1843 | G |
| Roegge, Gerhard H. | Ninker, Anna Maria | 9, Sept 1847 | F |
| Roehle, Martin | Eckstein, Anastasia | 8, Oct. 1846 | EE |
| Roehm, Johan Georg | Keller, Fridolina | 17, June 1846 | A |
| Roehr, Dietrich Herm | Drees, Catharina M. | 29, June 1841 | FF |
| Roelke, Georg W.H. | Bode, Caroline | 18, May 1849 | G |
| Roelker, Friedrich | Hastings, Emily | 24, Feb. 1846 | RCH |
| Roelker, Heinrich | Meyers, Wilhelmina | 13, Nov. 1849 | F |
| Roelker, Johan Heinr | Steinkamp, Regina M. | 20, Oct. 1842 | F |
| Roell, Martin | Fleckstein, Maria | 18, Feb. 1842 | RCH |
| Roemer, Francis | Bleckmann, Gertrud | 9, Apr. 1839 | FF |
| Roemer, Heinrich | Brinning, Maria Anna | 24, Jan. 1843 | FF |
| Roemer, Herman Heinr | Trimpe, Maria Agnes | 18, Jan. 1842 | FF |
| Roemer, J. Bernard | Griefenkamp, M Agnes | 7, Aug. 1838 | FF |
| Roemer, Johan Heinr. | Sannerhaus, M. Agnes | 22, Jan. 1839 | FF |
| Roemer, Joseph | Thorner, Friedricka | 5, Dec. 1842 | RCH |
| Roemer, William | Hunt, Mary Ann | 2, Nov. 1834 | RCH |
| Roeschmann, Bernard | Stratmann, Catharine | 8, Feb. 1842 | FF |
| Roese, Balthasar | Heister, Margaret | 7, July 1846 | RCH |
| Roese, Georg | Altemann, Maria | 14, Feb. 1847 | G |
| Roettger, Frank | Toppie, Maria Regina | 1, Sept 1849 | F |
| Roettger, Wilhelm | Takelberg, Charlotte | 8, Nov. 1849 | B |
| Rofelty, William | Markland, Catharine | 15, Nov. 1848 | RCH |
| Roff, Ferdinand | Fuller, Louise | 30, Dec. 1846 | RCH |
| Roff, William W. | Spranger, Hoppy Ann | 26, Aug. 1834 | RCH |
| Rogers, Alfred | Dixon, Louise | 20, Aug. 1846 | BB |
| Rogers, Andrew | Whipple, Harriet | 20, Feb. 1833 | RCH |
| Rogers, Charles E. | Phillips, Susan | 13, Sept 1832 | RCH |
| Rogers, Clark | Markland, Anna Maria | 5, Apr. 1847 | RCH |
| Rogers, Daniel D. | Harris, Rachel | 11, Apr. 1837 | RCH |
| Rogers, David | Sefton, Harriet | 24, Apr. 1825 | RCH |
| Rogers, Edmund | Gild, Celia | 18, Mar. 1837 | RCH |
| Rogers, Francis | Briggs, Jane | 5, July 1849 | RCH |
| Rogers, George W. | Brecount, Ruth | 16, Mar. 1843 | RCH |
| Rogers, Hiram | Harding, Cordelia D. | 19, Aug. 1833 | RCH |
| Rogers, James | Kerr, Adaline | 24, May 1846 | RCH |
| Rogers, James | McMillan, Mary | 7, July 1849 | RCH |
| Rogers, John | Larone, Rebecca | 1, Apr. 1839 | RCH |
| Rogers, John | Bradley, Jerusha | 18, July 1839 | RCH |
| Rogers, John | Shane, Mary Jane | 7, Apr. 1847 | RCH |
| Rogers, Michael | Markey, Bridget | 25, Nov. 1849 | GG |
| Rogers, Nathaniel | Evans, Sarah | 10, July 1826 | RCH |
| Rogers, W.A. | Smith, Elisabeth | 6, Sept 1837 | RCH |
| Rogers, William | Gildea, Ellen | 20, Mar. 1848 | RCH |
| Rohe, Fr. H. | Tabel, Josephina | 21, Jan. 1849 | II |
| Rohe, Heinrich | Hergenruther, Marg. | 30, May 1843 | AA |
| Rohe, Joseph | Bremer, Maria Angela | 23, Jan. 1848 | FF |
| Rohlfing, Carl Fried | Jungblut, Friedricka | 25, Apr. 1844 | G |
| Rohlfing, Christian | Andreas, Elisabeth | 2, Nov. 1848 | C |
| Rohlfing, Christian | Schmidt, Dorothea L. | 9, Sept 1847 | F |

| Grooms | Brides | Date of Marriage | Code |
|--------|--------|------------------|------|
| ****** | ****** | **** ** ******** | **** |
| Rohlfing, Christian | Rohlfing, Sophia | 12, Dec. 1848 | F |
| Rohlfing, Wilhelm | Rohlfing, Sophia L. | 5, Dec. 1849 | F |
| Rohlhepp, Georg | Schimmelpfennig, M. | 1, May 1849 | RCH |
| Rohmann, Francis J. | Hudepohl, Wilhelmina | 28, May 1849 | AA |
| Rohmann, Herman Bd. | Kedeler, Catharina | 15, Oct. 1839 | FF |
| Rohn, Philipp | Findling, Maria | 1, Sept 1846 | G |
| Rohrbacher, Philipp | Hessler, Carolina | 2, June 1840 | FF |
| Rohrer, Georg | Cutler, Eliza | 29, Nov. 1849 | RCH |
| Rohrkasse, Friedrich | Fenkhaus, Louise | 10, Jan. 1848 | B |
| Rohrkasse, Friedrich | Kostermann, Margaret | 13, Jan. 1849 | F |
| Rohrkasse, Johan H. | Peper, Caroline | 12, Nov. 1846 | B |
| Rohs, John | Waggoner, Margaretha | 10, Apr. 1849 | RCH |
| Roland, Jacob | West, Cynthia Ann | 26, Apr. 1841 | RCH |
| Rolands, William | Evans, Mary | 31, Oct. 1846 | RCH |
| Rolf, Bernard | Barlage, Elizabeth | 20, Nov. 1849 | RCH |
| Rolf, Robert | Jackson, Ann | 14, Apr. 1845 | BB |
| Rolfes, Johan Fried. | Schulte, Anna Maria | 4, Feb. 1845 | AA |
| Rolfmeier, Herman H. | Dammermann, Cath. M. | 10, Nov. 1836 | F |
| Rolfs, Bernard | Borlage, Elisabeth | 20, Nov. 1849 | II |
| Rolfs, Rudolph | Melcher, Catharina M | 27, July 1841 | FF |
| Rolfsen, Bernard | Moorkamp, Margaretha | 19, Aug. 1849 | CC |
| Rolfsen, Johan Hein. | Brockamp, Agnes | 16, Sept 1847 | AA |
| Roling, Heinrich | Brinkers, Maria A. | 6, Oct. 1846 | AA |
| Roll, | Jones, Polly | 6, Mar. 1823 | RCH |
| Roll, David | Leinhard, Maria | 1, Dec. 1840 | G |
| Roll, Edward | Riddle, Elis. Jane | 6, Jan. 1846 | RCH |
| Roll, Edward C. | Kelley, Julia Ann | 16, Nov. 1836 | RCH |
| Roll, Georg | Mohr, Elisabeth | 12, Nov. 1849 | AA |
| Roll, John | Cranson, Diantha | 28, Feb. 1844 | RCH |
| Roll, John | Miller, Hannah | 1, July 1844 | RCH |
| Roll, Mathias | Miller, Ann | 31, Oct. 1844 | RCH |
| Roll, Paul | Bettinger, M Theresa | 11, Dec. 1837 | FF |
| Roll, Peter G. | Newell, Sarah Jane | 11, Aug. 1836 | RCH |
| Roll, Philipp | Lochkinfin, Barbara | 28, Nov. 1848 | RCH |
| Roll, S.V. | Knof, Nancy | 2, Oct. 1834 | RCH |
| Roll, William | George, Margaret M. | 21, Mar. 1847 | RCH |
| Rollart, Friedrich | Brose, Mary | Aug. 1836 | RCH |
| Rolling, Gerhard H. | Pengemann, M. Adel. | 19, May 1840 | FF |
| Rolling, Heinrich | Settlage, Gertrud | 23, June 1840 | FF |
| Rollins, James | Thompson, Emma | 18, Nov. 1842 | RCH |
| Rollmann, Johan | Hackmann, Elisabeth | 5, Mar. 1839 | RCH |
| Rolls, James | Campbell, Mary | 29, Nov. 1835 | RCH |
| Rolls, Lewis | Goins, Theresa | 12, Dec. 1846 | RCH |
| Rollwage, Fritz | Kibers, Ernestina | 3, June 1849 | C |
| Rolof, John | Frazer, Jane | 6, May 1841 | RCH |
| Roloff, Friedrich | Getz, Wilhelmina | 5, Sept 1844 | RCH |
| Rolper, Heinrich | Leas, Elisabeth | 25, Aug. 1834 | RCH |
| Rolster, Heinrich R. | Voin, M. Christina | 18, Dec. 1849 | F |
| Rolves, Wilhelm | Uphoff, Elisabeth | 16, Oct. 1838 | FF |
| Rolves, Wilhelm | Meyer, Catharina | 24, Jan. 1843 | FF |
| Rom, Georg | Ponatz, Theresa | 4, July 1844 | AA |
| Romben, Anthony | Hleck, Carol | 15, Aug. 1847 | GG |
| Rombone, Garrett | Conrelly, Mary S. | 10, Jan. 1837 | RCH |
| Romeis, Heinrich | Hoppmann, Catharina | 7, Jan. 1841 | FF |
| Romer, Johan Fried. | Kraemer, Catharine | 2, Sept 1845 | AA |
| Romig, Johan Andreas | Fink, Magdalena | 26, Feb. 1847 | G |
| Romweber, Anton | Brockmann, Catharine | 26, Oct. 1842 | AA |
| Ron---, James | Harrison, Nancy | 14, Apr. 1818 | RCH |
| Ronan, James | Ronan, Anastasia | 25, Feb. 1843 | BB |
| Ronan, Matthew | Delaney, Ann | 28, Jan. 1849 | BB |
| Ronan, Maurice | Flevehan, Rose Ann | 19, July 1846 | BB |
| Ronnald, Jacob | Trout, Phoebe | 25, Dec. 1832 | RCH |
| Ronnebaum, Francis | Schaffstall, Clara | 12, June 1849 | II |
| Ronnebaum, Francis | Trennekamp, Maria A. | 21, Oct. 1849 | II |
| Ronnebaum, Heinrich | Reutemann, Elisabeth | 24, Sept 1840 | FF |
| Ronnebaum, J Bernard | Michael, Anna Maria | 7, Jan. 1841 | FF |
| Ronnebaum, Johan H. | Maehler, Anna Maria | 18, Aug. 1835 | FF |
| Ronnebaum, Johan H. | Feldmann, Agnes | 23, Apr. 1844 | AA |
| Ronnebaum, Johan H. | Thedick, Mina | 15, May 1849 | DD |
| Ronninger, Georg | Koehler, Elisabeth | 19, Nov. 1848 | EE |
| Rook, John | Garrison, Leah | 1, Dec. 1819 | RCH |

| Grooms | Brides | Date of Marriage | Code |
|--------|--------|------------------|------|
| Rooney, Henry | Canfield, Dorothy E. | 15, Mar. 1843 | BB |
| Rooney, James | Dempsey, Elisabeth | 27, Aug. 1834 | RCH |
| Rooney, Peter | Sheridan, Frances | 26, Nov. 1849 | GG |
| Roos, Johan | Schaefer, Maria | 15, Mar. 1849 | CC |
| Roos, Joseph | Lux, Agatha | 8, Jan. 1838 | FF |
| Roos, Joseph | Seifried, Catharine | 16, Aug. 1842 | RCH |
| Roosa, John T. | Patton, Elisabeth | 1, Dec. 1842 | RCH |
| Root, Daniel | Marty, Sarah Ann | 27, Mar. 1837 | RCH |
| Root, James | Baxter, Almira | 20, Mar. 1843 | RCH |
| Roots, Philander | Brown, Susan | 17, Oct. 1837 | RCH |
| Roots, Thomas | Turvin, Mary L. | 8, Feb. 1849 | RCH |
| Ropes, Samuel | Breeland, Maria | 20, Oct. 1822 | RCH |
| Roppelberger, Tobias | Stilwell, Elisabeth | 16, May 1841 | RCH |
| Roppert, Johan | Herrmann, Agnes | 31, Oct. 1842 | FF |
| Rork, Daniel | Morgan, Charlotte | 3, Mar. 1847 | RCH |
| Rosborough, William | Mahard, Mary | 23, May 1833 | RCH |
| Rosbrough, William | Ayres, Hannah | 6, Nov. 1823 | RCH |
| Rose, | Kuhn, Sarah | 6, Apr. 1849 | RCH |
| Rose, Abraham | Mole, Blandina | 4, Feb. 1819 | RCH |
| Rose, Christian F. | Shomaker, Maria | 30, May 1844 | F |
| Rose, Francis | Wang, Magdalena | 20, May 1838 | FF |
| Rose, Francis A. | Orr, Sarah Jane | 22, Aug. 1848 | RCH |
| Rose, George | Edington, Alice | 29, July 1844 | RCH |
| Rose, Heinrich | VonBrocke, Elisabeth | 10, Oct. 1847 | FF |
| Rose, Hugh R. | Wolcott, Catharine | 28, Sept 1832 | RCH |
| Rose, Isaac | Harvey, | 5, May 1825 | RCH |
| Rose, James | Henderson, Sarah | 16, Dec. 1846 | RCH |
| Rose, Jesse | Williams, Susanna | 26, Feb. 1843 | RCH |
| Rose, Johan Peter | Bruns, Maria Elis. | 14, Feb. 1847 | AA |
| Rose, John | Douglass, Jane | 20, July 1823 | RCH |
| Rose, John | Crosley, Belinda | 6, Sept 1847 | RCH |
| Rose, Joseph M. | Irwin, Rachel | 2, Aug. 1821 | RCH |
| Rose, Ludwig | Wernitscheck, Barb. | 26, Sept 1847 | G |
| Rose, Nathaniel | Byington, Elisabeth | 7, Nov. 1842 | RCH |
| Rose, Oliver | Williams, Maria | 28, June 1849 | RCH |
| Rose, Samuel S. | Geraldine, Caroline | 22, Oct. 1840 | BB |
| Rose, Stites | Hughes, Lydia | 15, Mar. 1827 | RCH |
| Rose, Thomas | Fawcett, E. | 5, May 1836 | RCH |
| Rose, Thomas | Drake, Rebecca | 10, May 1848 | RCH |
| Roseberry, Isaac | Bellew, Nancy Ann | 7, Feb. 1833 | RCH |
| Rosebone, John | Hole, Phoebe | 11, Nov. 1819 | RCH |
| Roseboom, William | Bacon, Mary L. | 21, Oct. 1846 | RCH |
| Rosemeyer, Johan H. | Bierhorst, Anna M. | 9, Oct. 1846 | F |
| Rosen, John | Foil, Catharine | 7, Apr. 1842 | RCH |
| Rosenbaum, Johan H. | Callmaner, Maria E. | 12, Oct. 1836 | F |
| Rosenberg, Julius | Finck, Sybilla | 21, Sept 1849 | RCH |
| Rosenberger, Alex. | Kaufmann, Babette | 22, July 1842 | RCH |
| Rosenberger, Leonard | Dieck, Maria | 10, Apr. 1849 | CC |
| Rosenberger, Nichol. | Stadtmueller, Barb. | 10, Nov. 1846 | EE |
| Roseners, John Henry | Hermmelings, Carolin | 26, Aug. 1847 | RCH |
| Rosenkranz, D Christ | Boulkan, M. Sophia | 27, Jan. 1843 | C |
| Rosenthal, August | Aber, Friedricka | 27, Dec. 1846 | G |
| Rosenthaler, Lewis | Rindskopp, Anna | 21, Mar. 1849 | RCH |
| Roseyboom, Daniel | Harrison, Mary | 19, Sept 1846 | RCH |
| Rosfeld, Heinrich | Vockenholz, Maria | 27, Nov. 1838 | FF |
| Roskin, Henry | Maline, Josephine | 8, Oct. 1835 | RCH |
| Roslein, George | Kelhmeier, Anna M. | 6, Mar. 1848 | RCH |
| Rosnagel, Samuel | Lacony, Catharine | 11, Oct. 1842 | RCH |
| Ross, Alvah | Whitehead, Abaline | 4, Feb. 1843 | RCH |
| Ross, Apollos | Campbell, Anna Elis. | 6, May 1844 | RCH |
| Ross, Brooks | Ridlin, Elisabeth | 1, Oct. 1836 | RCH |
| Ross, Charles | Conklin, Harriet | 12, July 1835 | RCH |
| Ross, Daniel | Gittier, Mary Louise | 3, Apr. 1843 | RCH |
| Ross, David | Heckler, Barbara | 13, Apr. 1849 | G |
| Ross, F. | Dicks, Catharine | 27     1834 | RCH |
| Ross, Georg | Dalheim, Margaretha | 23, June 1845 | G |
| Ross, Georg | Withacke, M. Anna | 6, June 1847 | AA |
| Ross, George E. | Orr, Nancy | 10, Sept 1835 | RCH |
| Ross, Isaiah | Singleton, Maria | 28, Sept 1839 | RCH |
| Ross, Jacob | Greg, Rebecca M. | 2, Nov. 1837 | RCH |
| Ross, James J. | Harper, Jane | 9, Apr. 1833 | RCH |

| Grooms<br>***** | Brides<br>***** | Date of Marriage<br>**** ** ******** | Code<br>**** |
|---|---|---|---|
| Ross, James J. | Boswell, Mary Jane | 2, Oct. 1834 | RCH |
| Ross, John L. | Brenner, Catharine | 23, Oct. 1843 | RCH |
| Ross, Joseph | Humphrey, Hepsey | 30, June 1825 | RCH |
| Ross, Joseph | Speckbauch, Anna M. | 10, Jan. 1847 | AA |
| Ross, Joseph S. | Bradstreet, M. | 12, Dec. 1825 | RCH |
| Ross, Mulford | Guyune, Martha | 25, July 1835 | RCH |
| Ross, Oliver | Whipple, Matilda | 11, Apr. 1842 | RCH |
| Ross, Richard M. | Eastburn, Elisabeth | 15, Apr. 1846 | I |
| Ross, Stephan | Eshpan, Polly T. | 24, June 1822 | RCH |
| Ross, Valentine | Siltz, Maria Anna | 19, Aug. 1836 | FF |
| Ross, William | Jenkins, Martha | 23, Aug. 1839 | RCH |
| Ross, William | Hawthorn, Georgiana | 25, Nov. 1843 | D |
| Ross, William | Ladley, Mary Ann | 16, Jan. 1847 | RCH |
| Ross, William | West, Electa | 9, Sept 1847 | RCH |
| Ross, William B. | Roe, Frances | 12, June 1836 | RCH |
| Ross, William R. | Flagg, Ann | 14, May 1834 | RCH |
| Ross, Williamson | Stewart, Margaret | 11, Apr. 1823 | RCH |
| Rosselot, Francis | South, Nancy | 6, Oct. 1843 | RCH |
| Rossfeld, John Anton | Steinmetz, Catharina | 30, Dec. 1847 | AA |
| Rossler, Thomas | McGinnis, Mary | 5, Dec. 1836 | RCH |
| Rost, Carl | Grau, Barbara | 10, June 1848 | A |
| Rost, Henry S. | Emmons, Mary | 3, Dec. 1848 | RCH |
| Rote, Peter | Beer, Catharina | 6, Oct. 1835 | FF |
| Rotert, Heinrich | Boehl, Maria Elis. | 3, June 1847 | EE |
| Rotert, Johan Fried. | Lake, Maria Cath. | 19, Apr. 1846 | FF |
| Rotert, Johan Heinr. | Aubke, Anna Maria | 9, June 1842 | RCH |
| Roth, Balthasar | Schaefer, Thekla | 29, Apr. 1844 | AA |
| Roth, Conrad | Hellmann, Elisabeth | 22, Sept 1838 | FF |
| Roth, Francis | Lambert, Rosina | 2, Feb. 1841 | FF |
| Roth, Franz | Strohvers, Maria | 21, Apr. 1849 | RCH |
| Roth, Gregor | Schuler, Elisabeth | 22, July 1845 | FF |
| Roth, Heinrich | Birger, Juliana | 17, Feb. 1848 | G |
| Roth, Johan | Pister, Eva | 13, June 1836 | FF |
| Roth, Johan | Winkler, Elisabeth | 14, Sept 1848 | A |
| Roth, Joseph | Carbin, Emma | 23, Apr. 1843 | RCH |
| Roth, Joseph | Hahnwaker, | 9, Jan. 1848 | EE |
| Roth, Leonard | Hammel, Eva | 17, Apr. 1849 | G |
| Roth, Peter | Kline, Margaret | 28, Apr. 1842 | RCH |
| Rothan, | Rose, Francisca | Apr. 1849 | RCH |
| Rothan, Johan | Reising, M. Gertrud | 28, Apr. 1842 | FF |
| Rothemel, Valentin | Bens, Cunigunda | 16, Mar. 1848 | RCH |
| Rothenbusch, Philipp | Doerr, Maria Amalia | 27, Dec. 1847 | C |
| Rothert, Christian F | Kruse, Christina | 7, Mar. 1844 | F |
| Rothert, Franz H. | Bramlage, Josephine | 27, June 1843 | AA |
| Rothert, Heinrich L. | Ellerbruck, Cath. M. | 6, Sept 1849 | B |
| Rothert, J Friedrich | Osterhaus, Lisette | 28, Apr. 1847 | E |
| Rothert, Johan H.Wm. | Dickmann, Maria | 11, Oct. 1849 | B |
| Rothert, Johan Heinr | Hartmann, A.M. Elis. | 17, Oct. 1844 | F |
| Rothmann, Carl Jos. | Hilsmann, Maria A. | 18, July 1843 | FF |
| Rothschild, Joseph | Rothschild, Cecilia | 18, Sept 1843 | RCH |
| Rothwell, Elkanah | Waddingham, Elis. | 27, July 1848 | RCH |
| Rothwell, John | Steel, Mahala | 25, Jan. 1847 | RCH |
| Rott, Herman Martin | Haidkamp, Elisabeth | 18, Apr. 1847 | AA |
| Rottam, Michael | Graf, Francisca | 17, Apr. 1849 | FF |
| Rous, Mathelbert | Crosby, Nancy Jane | 24, June 1846 | RCH |
| Rouse, Philipp | Hudson, Sarah Ann | 3, Oct. 1842 | RCH |
| Rouse, Simeon | Sargent, Dolly | 6, Dec. 1846 | RCH |
| Rover, Charles | Kilgore, Maria | 24, Dec. 1845 | RCH |
| Rovers, John Gerhard | Becker, Maria Adel. | 19, July 1842 | FF |
| Row, Conrad | Lambdin, Elisabeth | 21, Mar. 1822 | RCH |
| Row, Samuel H. | Heath, Mary | 28, Aug. 1836 | RCH |
| Rowan, John D. | ----, Jane | 16, Apr. 1835 | RCH |
| Rowan, Michael | Morten, Martha | Oct. 1824 | RCH |
| Rowan, Robert | Snider, Margaret | 22, Mar. 1849 | RCH |
| Rowan, Thomas | ----, Margaret | 30, May 1822 | RCH |
| Rowan, William | Bogart, Ann | 14, Sept 1820 | RCH |
| Rowe, Stanhope | Thomas, Frances Mary | 28, July 1841 | D |
| Rowe, Thomas M. | Oliver, Margaret | 19, Aug. 1846 | RCH |
| Rowen, James D. | Arnold, Mary Elis. | 22, Mar. 1848 | RCH |
| Rowland, | Winshell, Waty Ann | 22, Feb. 1821 | RCH |
| Rowland, George | Sheeler, Kate | 29, May 1849 | RCH |

| Grooms | Brides | Date of Marriage | Code |
|--------|--------|------------------|------|
| ****** | ****** | **** ** ******** | **** |
| Rowland, Richard | Berger, Mary Ann | 12, Nov. 1846 | RCH |
| Rowland, William | Bailey, Catharine W. | 17, June 1843 | RCH |
| Rowse, John B. | Silver, Margaret | 16, Dec. 1845 | RCH |
| Roxborough, Charles | Briscka, Eveline | 8, Aug. 1843 | RCH |
| Roy, James | Hill, Hannah J. | 22, Mar. 1847 | RCH |
| Roy, Phillip | Nicholet, Elizabeth | 23, July 1849 | GG |
| Royer, Theodor | Rodgers, Elisabeth | 5, Dec. 1843 | RCH |
| Roys, John | Boyland, Nancy | 24, May 1833 | RCH |
| Rubenbaur, Nicolaus | Poetter, Anna Maria | 15, Aug. 1848 | EE |
| Ruberg, Francis | Getiker, M. Adelheid | 16, June 1842 | FF |
| Ruble, Benjamin | Wilcox, Mary | 28, Mar. 1833 | RCH |
| Rubly, Jacob | Hein, Catharine | 10, Oct. 1837 | FF |
| Ruch, John | Tomer, Elisabeth | 29, Apr. 1847 | RCH |
| Ruck, Joseph | Schulz, Catharine J. | 18, July 1847 | EE |
| Rucker, Henry L. | Heckwelder, Mary J. | 11, Apr. 1833 | RCH |
| Ruckle, Charles | Roberts, Celia | 10, Dec. 1818 | RCH |
| Ruckman, Shephard | Patterson, Rachel | 3, June 1839 | RCH |
| Rude, William | ----, C. | 2, Sept 1834 | RCH |
| Rudiger, August Ferd | Niebuhr, M. Sophia | 12, Dec. 1849 | B |
| Rudisel, John | Shots, Mary | 13, Jan. 1825 | RCH |
| Rudisell, George | Ackley, Ellen | 19, Aug. 1824 | RCH |
| Rudisell, Jacob | Little, Patty | 11, Mar. 1819 | RCH |
| Rudisil, Reuben | Rudisil, Betsey | 3, Sept 1843 | RCH |
| Rudolph, Lawrence | Sheeouf, Catharine | 29, Sept 1823 | RCH |
| Ruecke, Friedrich W. | Rahen, Elisabeth | 30, Mar. 1848 | B |
| Rueff, Johan | Erwin, Maria | 14, Mar. 1843 | A |
| Ruesselmann, Ludwig | Steinke, M. Adelheid | 3, Feb. 1841 | FF |
| Ruf, Peter | Biger, Victoria | 1, Aug. 1847 | EE |
| Rufe, James | Crammond, Alice | 30, Aug. 1849 | RCH |
| Ruffin, James | Griffith, Sarah | 24, Aug. 1836 | RCH |
| Ruffin, John | Williamson, Rachel | 24, May 1842 | RCH |
| Ruffin, Louis | Knapp, Viola | 2, Dec. 1843 | I |
| Ruffner, Daniel | Singleton, Elisabeth | 11, Nov. 1844 | RCH |
| Ruffner, Henry | Kirby, Laura Jane | Nov. 1849 | RCH |
| Ruffner, Marine | Odell, Susan | 1, Dec. 1833 | RCH |
| Ruffner, Morgan | Letter, Mary Elis. | 25, Oct. 1843 | RCH |
| Ruffner, Sylvester | Wilson, Alsee J. | 27, June 1838 | RCH |
| Rufuss, Christian | Stoevan, Anna | 19, Oct. 1848 | F |
| Rugg, Elisha | Heritage, Sarah P. | 22, Jan. 1843 | RCH |
| Ruhe, Theodor | Schwegmann, Maria A. | 26, Apr. 1842 | FF |
| Ruhl, Conrad | Grimmer, Maria | 11, May 1837 | FF |
| Ruhl, Heinrich | Behrens, Dorothea | 17, Jan. 1844 | C |
| Ruhl, Peter | Davis, P. | 24, Aug. 1819 | RCH |
| Ruhrwein, Friedrich | Hanselmann, Elis. | 26, Mar. 1846 | C |
| Ruhrwein, Jacob | Hausmann, Elisabeth | 19, July 1842 | RCH |
| Ruhrwein, Jacob | Mans, Louise | 21, Sept 1843 | RCH |
| Rule, Thomas | Cully, Prudence | 15, May 1834 | RCH |
| Rulison, Hiram | Barcley, Sarah E. | 25, Oct. 1848 | RCH |
| Rull, Herman Martin | Lammers, Elisabeth | 23, Nov. 1845 | AA |
| Rulmann, Christoph | Merhoff, M. Engel | 17, Jan. 1846 | F |
| Rumbach, Francis X. | Bessenhurst, Gertrud | 20, Aug. 1843 | AA |
| Runck, Henry | Houser, Sophia | 3, Nov. 1845 | RCH |
| Rune, Johan H. | Stukenberg, Katharin | 22, Nov. 1848 | AA |
| Rungan, Christian | Rademan, Elisabeth | 18, July 1839 | RCH |
| Runge, Wilhelm | Linnemann, Wilhelmin | 16, Oct. 1849 | F |
| Runk, Friedrich | Kiefer, Barbara | 29, Oct. 1849 | G |
| Runk, Heinrich | Runk, Margaretha | 16, Dec. 1841 | G |
| Runk, Heinrich | Buehler, Maria | 11, Apr. 1848 | G |
| Runnel, Joseph | Howard, Sarah | 24, Oct. 1833 | RCH |
| Runtz, Georg | Schitt, Salome | 6, May 1845 | FF |
| Runyan, Alfred | Nichols, Sarah B. | 20, Feb. 1844 | RCH |
| Runyan, Courtland | Towner, Abigail | 9, Aug. 1849 | RCH |
| Runyan, Elias P. | Curle, Catharine | 16, Dec. 1836 | RCH |
| Runyan, Freeman | Woodruff, M. Louise | 15, Sept 1847 | RCH |
| Runyan, George | Rhinehart, Mary | 27, June 1840 | RCH |
| Runyan, Goerge | Pierson, Huldah | 17, July 1834 | RCH |
| Runyan, Jonathan | Smith, Sarah | 1, May 1842 | RCH |
| Runyan, Lewis | VanSickle, Milla | 5, Jan. 1834 | RCH |
| Runyan, Robert | McAuley, Mary | 13, May 1826 | RCH |
| Runyan, Solomon | Hanley, Sarah Jane | 12, Sept 1847 | RCH |
| Runyon, James M. | Ogden, Nancy | 2, Dec. 1835 | RCH |

| Grooms<br>****** | Brides<br>****** | Date of Marriage<br>**** ** ******* | Code<br>**** |
|---|---|---|---|
| Runyon, John | Loery, Prudence | 4, June 1835 | RCH |
| Rupert, Johan | Duroth, Maria | 29, May 1849 | II |
| Ruply, Jacob | Denzler, A. Barbara | 5, Sept 1848 | FF |
| Rupner, Joseph | Stein, Barbara | 9, Jan. 1848 | EE |
| Rupp, Frederick | Ohler, Catharine | 29, Feb. 1848 | RCH |
| Rupp, Jacob | Dorst, Maria | 20, Apr. 1840 | G |
| Rupp, Joseph | Smith, Martha | 12, Aug. 1839 | RCH |
| Ruppel, Johan | Hornung, Barbara | 18, Nov. 1849 | AA |
| Ruppell, John | Ryland, Mary | 4, Dec. 1848 | RCH |
| Rupprecht, J. Peter | Linken, Elisabeth | 28, Feb. 1846 | RCH |
| Rupprecht, Lawrence | Schuster, Barbetta | 22, July 1847 | RCH |
| Rupprich, Christoph | Theis, Sophia | 28, Jan. 1847 | F |
| Rurod, Peter F. | Wedenonione, Maria | 23, July 1832 | RCH |
| Rusche, Bernard H. | Dickhaus, M. Anna | 5, Mar. 1848 | AA |
| Rusche, Francis | Schildmeyer, Cath. | 30, May 1846 | EE |
| Rusche, Johan H. | Glins, Christina | 30, Oct. 1849 | EE |
| Rusche, Joseph | Buerger, Anna Maria | 23, Jan. 1848 | EE |
| Ruscher, Ludwig | Moellers, Sophia | 11, Aug. 1845 | RCH |
| Ruse, Henry | McCane, Jane | 12, Dec. 1825 | RCH |
| Rush, Alfred | Tury, Rachel | 19, May 1835 | RCH |
| Rush, William | Buckingham, Elisabet | 13, Sept 1849 | RCH |
| Rusk, David | Snider, Rebecca | 18, July 1830 | RCH |
| Rusk, James | Castill, Eliza Jane | 26, Aug. 1849 | RCH |
| Ruske, Johan H. | Sonnenberg, Maria A. | 21, Sept 1847 | EE |
| Rusland, Christopher | Wolf, Mary | 15, Feb. 1848 | RCH |
| Russ, Jacob | Frey, Christina | 30, Sept 1849 | G |
| Russ, Johan | Litz, Barbara | 20, June 1847 | EE |
| Russe, Heinrich | Kassens, Anna | 24, Dec. 1849 | F |
| Russekup, Bernard H. | Bendermann, Catharin | 11, Aug. 1849 | F |
| Russell, Henry | Tate, Jane | 3, Sept 1841 | RCH |
| Russell, Henry | French, Elisabeth | 22, July 1847 | RCH |
| Russell, James H. | Jorden, Charlotte | 8, Aug. 1824 | RCH |
| Russell, Job | Schwischer, Mary Ann | 15, Jan. 1848 | RCH |
| Russell, John | Winter, Maria | 5, Nov. 1845 | RCH |
| Russell, John | Dale, Eleanor | 7, Sept 1848 | RCH |
| Russell, Joseph | Walker, Rhoda | 29, July 1823 | RCH |
| Russell, Moses | Roberson, Sarah | 28, July 1818 | RCH |
| Russell, Samuel | Nicklaus, Jane | 26, Jan. 1832 | RCH |
| Russell, Samuel V. | Crane, Mary | 9, Oct. 1825 | RCH |
| Russell, Thomas M. | Curry, Clarissa | 20, Dec. 1849 | RCH |
| Russell, William | Dunlap, Sarah | 29, May 1844 | RCH |
| Russell, William | Long, Elizabeth | 22, Feb. 1847 | RCH |
| Russell, William | L'Hommidieu, Elis. | 16, June 1847 | RCH |
| Russell, William | Lawson, Susan | 27, Apr. 1848 | RCH |
| Russell, Zane W. | Hardy, Mary Ann | 26, Dec. 1841 | RCH |
| Rust, Abraham | Emmet, Mary | 3, July 1821 | RCH |
| Rust, Abraham | Ennerett, Jane | 14, Oct. 1835 | RCH |
| Rust, August | Gross, Catharine | 28, May 1849 | G |
| Rust, Benjamin | McDaniel, Mary Ann | 7, May 1835 | RCH |
| Rust, Friedrich A. | Schulte, Jenny | 20, Oct. 1835 | RCH |
| Rust, James | Willmore, Delila | 1, Aug. 1842 | RCH |
| Rust, Joseph G. | Morris, Jane | 5, June 1836 | RCH |
| Rust, Thomas | Sanders, Drucilla | 19, July 1846 | RCH |
| Rust, Thomas | Bonham, Clara | 20, Mar. 1849 | RCH |
| Rust, Wilhelm | Schuermann, Catharin | 20, Feb. 1845 | F |
| Ruwe, Francis Hein. | Schoettmer, Gesina | 25, Jan. 1848 | AA |
| Ruwe, Friedrich | Scheper, Catharina | 24, Sept 1848 | FF |
| Ruwe, Johan Gerhard | Wellinghoff, Gertrud | 3, June 1849 | EE |
| Ruwers, Johan | Teipen, Helena | 11, Nov. 1849 | AA |
| Ryan, Charles | Bell, Susan | 15, Aug. 1847 | RCH |
| Ryan, Dennis | Dougherty, Mary Ann | 20, Apr. 1845 | BB |
| Ryan, Dennis | McDermott, Christina | 22, June 1845 | BB |
| Ryan, Dennis | Carrigan, Mary | 6, July 1845 | BB |
| Ryan, George W. | Bowan, Mary | 3, July 1834 | RCH |
| Ryan, James | Barry, Margaret | 16, Aug. 1842 | BB |
| Ryan, James | Roberts, Mary | 17, Feb. 1849 | BB |
| Ryan, James | Roberts, Mary | 17, Feb. 1849 | BB |
| Ryan, Jefferson | Schenck, Rhoda Ann | 23, Apr. 1843 | RCH |
| Ryan, John | Kenney, Winnifred | 4, Nov. 1849 | BB |
| Ryan, Joseph | Cunningham, Harriet | 4, July 1847 | RCH |
| Ryan, Matthew | Beresford, Mary | 29, May 1844 | RCH |

| Grooms<br>****** | Brides<br>****** | Date of Marriage<br>**** ** ******** | Code<br>**** |
|---|---|---|---|
| Ryan, Michael | Hammond, Lydia H. | 11, June 1840 | BB |
| Ryan, Patrick | McAvoy, Mary | 16, Sept 1843 | BB |
| Ryan, Thomas | Davis, Joanne | 6, Feb. 1843 | BB |
| Ryan, Thomas | ----, Catharine | 3, May 1846 | BB |
| Ryan, Thomas | Dooley, Bridget | 19, Feb. 1849 | BB |
| Ryan, Thomas | Murray, Elisabeth | 21, Aug. 1848 | GG |
| Ryan, William | Gray, Sarah | 18, Mar. 1819 | RCH |
| Ryan, William | Wood, Elisabeth | 3, Feb. 1839 | RCH |
| Ryan, William | Porter, Harriet | 17, Oct. 1842 | RCH |
| Ryan, William | Downy, Bridget | 30, Oct. 1848 | GG |
| Ryan, William M. | Murray, Ellen | 23, Feb. 1843 | BB |
| Rybolt, H.S. | Devoy, Elizabeth | 27, Nov. 1849 | RCH |
| Rybolt, Jacob | Johnson, Mary Jane | 27, Feb. 1836 | RCH |
| Rybolt, John | Moore, Amelia | 8, Aug. 1845 | RCH |
| Rybolt, Stephen | Scudder, Phoebe | 5, Feb. 1821 | RCH |
| Rybolt, Willis | Crowl, Adelheid | 11, May 1843 | RCH |
| Ryder, Charles | Elem, Harriet | 4, May 1844 | RCH |
| Ryland, James S. | Hallam, Mary | 3, Dec. 1837 | RCH |
| Ryle, Joseph | Vinton, Sarah | 30, Nov. 1834 | RCH |
| Rynar, Henry | Jocelyn, Maria | 27, Feb. 1837 | RCH |
| Rynearson, George | Sweethard, Nancy | 16, Aug. 1837 | RCH |
| Rynearson, George | Locy, Martha Jane | 11, Mar. 1849 | RCH |
| Rynearson, Isaac | Crosson, Susan | 15, July 1834 | RCH |
| Rynearson, Jacob | Sharp, Phoebe | 21, Dec. 1820 | RCH |
| Rynearson, James | Brwon, Sarah | 13, July 1844 | RCH |
| | | | |
| S---, Amos | Carroll, Jane | 18, June 1818 | RCH |
| S---, Daniel | Leary, Margaret Ann | 6, Aug. 1845 | RCH |
| S---, David | Hickman, Catharine | 16, July 1826 | RCH |
| S---, George | Rogers, Mary Ann | 19, Oct. 1823 | RCH |
| S---, James | Tauph, Frances | 18, Aug. 1826 | RCH |
| S---, James | Clapp, Amelia Ann | 24, Sept 1835 | RCH |
| Saalmann, Joseph | Spaltmann, Johanna | 24, Sept 1845 | AA |
| Saatkamp, Adolph | Dodhagen, Charlotte | 14, Sept 1849 | C |
| Saatkamp, Friedrich | Schobengers, Friedr. | 10, Oct. 1846 | C |
| Sabb, John | ----, ---- | 7, Aug. 1817 | RCH |
| Sabbert, Peter Hein. | Boesmann, Catharine | 12, Aug. 1849 | C |
| Sachs, Caspar | Wiest, Theresa | 13, Nov. 1849 | EE |
| Sachs, Christian D. | Hauck, Margaretha | 15, Aug. 1841 | G |
| Sachs, Henry | Thurmour, | 22, Mar. 1847 | RCH |
| Sachs, Johan Georg | Bogen, Johanna | 11, Jan. 1849 | C |
| Sachstetter, Peter | Schak, Elisabeth | 20, July 1847 | EE |
| Sack, Henry | Brandmeier, Maria | 27, Dec. 1845 | RCH |
| Sack, Henry | Moellers, Mary | 27, Apr. 1847 | RCH |
| Sackey, William | O'Brien, Julia | 6, Jan. 1849 | RCH |
| Sackhoff, Heinrich | Kisner, Augusta | 24, Feb. 1846 | F |
| Sackman, Henry | Sallman, Anna Maria | 26, Sept 1836 | RCH |
| Sacks, Christian D. | Houck, Margaretha | 15, Aug. 1841 | RCH |
| Sackstetter, Francis | Stoll, Barbara | 7, Jan. 1840 | FF |
| Sackstetter, Johan | Strapel, Johanna | 17, Jan. 1841 | FF |
| Sadler, David | Sweet, Abigail | 23, July 1843 | RCH |
| Sadler, Joseph W. | Mitchell, Margaretha | 21, May 1835 | RCH |
| Saeling, Johan | Kelch, Catharina | 7, Jan. 1840 | FF |
| Saerger, Georg | Schmidt, Catharine | 16, Mar. 1847 | G |
| Saffin, James | Horton, Elisabeth B. | 6, Apr. 1826 | RCH |
| Sagassur, Gillingham | Sheets, Mary | 14, Nov. 1826 | RCH |
| Sage, Charles | Black, Eliza | 19, Dec. 1849 | RCH |
| Sage, Joseph | Stuemann, Catharine | Oct. 1844 | RCH |
| Sage, Samuel | Flemming, Mary | 27, Dec. 1832 | RCH |
| Sage, Samuel | Dugan, Temperance | 18, Sept 1845 | RCH |
| Sailer, Michael | Dennis, Maria | 11, Jan. 1842 | FF |
| Saker, Henry | Andrews, Mary | 14, Mar. 1848 | RCH |
| Saller, Joseph | Young, Mary J. | 14, July 1838 | RCH |
| Salley, August G. | Hunter, Matilda | 11, 1837 | RCH |
| Salman, Daniel | Carson, Hannah | 18, June 1825 | RCH |
| Salmon, James | Turner, Elcey | 13, Dec. 1821 | RCH |
| Salmon, Robert | Pine, Priscilla | 29, Apr. 1845 | RCH |
| Salt, Francis M. | Frazer, Emily | 23, Apr. 1848 | RCH |
| Salter, Thomas | Foster, Elisabeth | 20, June 1833 | RCH |
| Saltes, Christian | Kubel, Maria | 22, Feb. 1844 | A |
| Samanahorn, Luke | ----, Rachel | 28, May 1837 | RCH |

| Grooms ****** | Brides ****** | Date of Marriage **** ** ******** | Code **** |
|---|---|---|---|
| Saming, John Bernard | Hanefeld, A Margaret | 3, June 1849 | RCH |
| Sammons, J. | Spence, Susannah | 15, Nov. 1835 | RCH |
| Sammons, James | ----, Abigail | 29, June 1822 | RCH |
| Sampson, Franklin | Long, Lydia G. | 26, Feb. 1843 | RCH |
| Sampson, George | Ellis, Hannah | 7, Nov. 1846 | RCH |
| Sampson, Henry | Young, Josephine | 9, Oct. 1848 | RCH |
| Sampson, James | Day, Ellen | 18, Nov. 1834 | RCH |
| Sampson, James | Patmore, Mary Ann | 16, Feb. 1847 | RCH |
| Sampson, James | Irvin, Mary Frances | 3, May 1847 | RCH |
| Sampson, John E. | Philley, Mary | 12, May 1836 | RCH |
| Sampson, Joseph | McDaniel, Mary | 13, Nov. 1835 | RCH |
| Sampson, Joseph | Baxter, Lucinda | 27, Jan. 1847 | RCH |
| Sampson, Senneca | Thocker, Jane | 25, Aug. 1836 | RCH |
| Sampson, William | Clafton, Submit | 22, Nov. 1832 | RCH |
| Sampson, William | Perryman, Sarah B. | 18, Nov. 1848 | RCH |
| Samuels, Solomon | Gratz, Rachel | 30, Aug. 1843 | RCH |
| Sanaey, Frederick | Whipple, Mary | 15, Mar. 1818 | RCH |
| Sanborn, John | Dawson, Phebe | 4, July 1834 | RCH |
| Sanborn, John | Cooke, Elisabeth | 23, Dec. 1846 | RCH |
| Sand, Herman | Brunsmann, Juliana | 28, Apr. 1847 | AA |
| Sandbrink, Georg | Havikurst, Margaret | 2, Aug. 1842 | FF |
| Sandburn, Abraham | White, Sarah | 27, July 1841 | RCH |
| Sandel, Valentin | Geissen, Anna Maria | 12, May 1846 | C |
| Sander, Anton | Storck, Theresa | 10, Jan. 1843 | FF |
| Sander, Bernard H. | Luebkers, Angela | 24, Nov. 1840 | FF |
| Sander, C.G. | Lauber, M. Elisabeth | 9, Jan. 1838 | FF |
| Sander, Clement | Penke, Maria Helena | 9, Jan. 1848 | EE |
| Sander, Henry | Dutrit, Mary | 12, July 1834 | RCH |
| Sander, Herman | Horstmann, Catharine | 23, Jan. 1848 | EE |
| Sander, Johan Ch. | Dammermann, Margaret | 3, Oct. 1844 | F |
| Sander, Johan H. | Gladen, Maria Anna | 24, Apr. 1849 | EE |
| Sander, Johan P. | Friedeborg, Marg. | 6, Dec. 1849 | C |
| Sander, Wilhelm | Meikenhaus, Margaret | 30, July 1846 | F |
| Sanderlin, Holland | Bradley, Susan | 18, Aug. 1846 | RCH |
| Sandermann, | Rectine, Elisabeth | 4, Feb. 1845 | AA |
| Sandermann, Heinrich | Kleve, Angela | 30, Jan. 1849 | II |
| Sanders, | Guion, Sarah | 11, Apr. 1849 | RCH |
| Sanders, Eli | Lingo, Orpha | 10, Feb. 1820 | RCH |
| Sanders, Francis | Jones, Elisabeth | 11, Oct. 1837 | RCH |
| Sanders, George | Davis, Margaret | 3, May 1847 | RCH |
| Sanders, Gerhard H. | Lammers, Clara | 22, June 1848 | AA |
| Sanders, James | Harris, Mary | 8, Aug. 1837 | RCH |
| Sanders, James | Conger, Rachel | 13, Jan. 1843 | RCH |
| Sanders, James | Cusick, Catharine | 21, Dec. 1848 | RCH |
| Sanders, Johan Hein. | Deters, Elisabeth | 9, May 1848 | AA |
| Sanders, Washington | Butler, Elisabeth | 14, Oct. 1841 | RCH |
| Sanders, William | Marand, Susan | 5, Mar. 1837 | RCH |
| Sanders, William H. | Dunn, Margaret | 26, Dec. 1848 | RCH |
| Sanderson, John | Lofthouse, Jane | 13, Aug. 1837 | RCH |
| Sanderson, John | Butler, Draden | 5, Apr. 1838 | RCH |
| Sanderson, Joseph | Buckton, Ann | 28, Nov. 1836 | RCH |
| Sanderson, Joseph | Trainer, Emeline | 19, Aug. 1848 | RCH |
| Sanderson, William | Wheeler, Abeline | 21, Sept 1834 | RCH |
| Sandford, Edwin | Miller, Jennett | 18, Feb. 1848 | RCH |
| Sandford, Seth | Sumner, Margaret E. | 25, Nov. 1844 | RCH |
| Sandler, Meyer | Mack, Regina | 25, July 1843 | RCH |
| Sandman, Gerhard H. | Snier, Wilhelmina | 4, Mar. 1847 | RCH |
| Sandmann, Friedrich | Schwepmann, Maria | 16, Mar. 1848 | B |
| Sandmann, J Heinrich | Helmich, Anna Regina | 1, July 1847 | F |
| Sandmann, Wilhelm | Dobbeling, Friedrika | 28, May 1846 | G |
| Sandoe, John | Palser, Elisabeth | 4, Dec. 1823 | RCH |
| Sands, Ephraim | McCoy, Elisabeth W. | 27, Sept 1833 | RCH |
| Sands, Joshua | Cook, Eleanor Ann | 28, Aug. 1847 | RCH |
| Sands, Robert M. | Dicks, Cecilia | 8, Feb. 1835 | RCH |
| Sane, Isaac | Cill, Margaret | 18, Aug. 1839 | RCH |
| Sanning, Johan Bd. | Keitz, Susanna Marg. | 30, Oct. 1843 | FF |
| Sanning, Johan Bd. | Hanfeld, Anna Marg. | 3, June 1849 | CC |
| Sanschie, George | Becker, Elisabeth | 9, May 1847 | G |
| Sapp, Thomas | Williams, Nancy | 24, June 1826 | RCH |
| Sappington, Thomas | Eaverson, Matilda | 21, May 1844 | RCH |
| Sargent, Charles | Lawson, Hannah | 15, June 1842 | RCH |

| Grooms<br>****** | Brides<br>****** | Date of Marriage<br>**** ** ******** | Code<br>**** |
|---|---|---|---|
| Sargent, David | Batchelor, Patty | 7, Jan. 1819 | RCH |
| Sargent, Edward | Smith, Mary J. | 1, Oct. 1845 | RCH |
| Sargent, John M. | Sharp, Elisabeth | 10, Sept 1834 | RCH |
| Sargent, William | Wilson, Sarah Ellen | 7, Mar. 1842 | RCH |
| Sarick, Peter | Hof, Elisabeth | 6, Jan. 1839 | FF |
| Sarison, Jacob | Waters, Elisabeth | 8, Nov. 1821 | RCH |
| Sarke, C. | Pistner, Margaretha | 17, Jan. 1837 | FF |
| Sarreo, Philip W. | VanLier, Mary Ann | 9, Jan. 1835 | RCH |
| Sarsfield, Michael | Dixon, Mary | 14, Jan. 1849 | GG |
| Sarver, John | Scales, Elisabeth | 12, Apr. 1846 | RCH |
| Sarver, Philipp | McLean, Elisabeth | 16, Aug. 1846 | RCH |
| Sasse, August | Vornholtz, M. Engel | 19, Nov. 1846 | C |
| Sasse, Heinrich | Andreas, Maria | 13, Apr. 1848 | C |
| Sasse, Heinrich F. | Fisse, Anna Maria | 4, Aug. 1846 | AA |
| Sassen, Tobias | Linnemann, Gesina | 14, May 1848 | FF |
| Sater, John J. | Larison, Nancy | 19, Feb. 1834 | RCH |
| Sater, Joseph | Pottinger, Elisabeth | 30, Jan. 1820 | RCH |
| Sater, Joseph | Hedges, Elisabeth A. | 29, Mar. 1849 | RCH |
| Sater, Joseph L. | Allen, Sarah P. | 10, Dec. 1833 | RCH |
| Sater, William | Skillman, Sarah Jane | 29, Feb. 1844 | RCH |
| Satter, Joseph | Gilb, Genofeva | 3, Sept 1846 | EE |
| Sattershall, Thomas | Isgrigg, Nancy Ann | 4, June 1835 | RCH |
| Satterthwaite, Georg | Chenoweth, Rebecca | 22, June 1849 | RCH |
| Sattler, John | Dopmeier, Catharine | 7, July 1848 | RCH |
| Sauer, Adam | Sommer, Margaretha | 18, May 1835 | FF |
| Sauer, Adam | Bargel, Magdalena | 7, July 1840 | G |
| Sauer, Anton | Heiberg, Catharina | 9, May 1848 | FF |
| Sauer, Aquilin | Staub, Elisabeth | 26, Oct. 1843 | FF |
| Sauer, Conrad | Amann, Louise | 30, Jan. 1845 | AA |
| Sauer, Francis | Schmidt, M. Barbara | 11, Feb. 1849 | CC |
| Sauer, Georg | Herz, Helena | 31, Jan. 1849 | CC |
| Sauer, Heinrich Wm. | Grell, Eva | 13, Sept 1849 | EE |
| Sauer, Johan | Mueller, Margaretha | 16, Nov. 1846 | EE |
| Sauer, Johan | Weber, Maria | 16, Sept 1849 | EE |
| Sauer, John | Ruebler, Gottlieba | 13, Oct. 1847 | RCH |
| Sauley, Alexander | Chatman, Harriet | 18, Sept 1843 | RCH |
| Saulman, Peter S. | Schweinhart, Carolin | 6, Oct. 1836 | RCH |
| Saundermann, Heinric | Schaperklaus, Sophia | 3, May 1842 | RCH |
| Saunders, John | Turner, Sarah Ann | 6, June 1841 | D |
| Saunders, John | Dickson, Elisabeth | 15, Nov. 1846 | RCH |
| Saunders, Samuel | Parker, Sarah | 31, May 1843 | RCH |
| Saunders, Wesley | Witacker, Henrietta | 25, Feb. 1842 | RCH |
| Savage, James | Jolly, Mary A. | 9, Apr. 1843 | RCH |
| Savage, John | Houser, Harriet | 30, May 1847 | RCH |
| Sawyer, Freeman | Slack, Cornelia | 23, June 1847 | RCH |
| Saxton, | Harding, Sarah B. | 8, Jan. 1825 | RCH |
| Saxton, Benjamin | Hunt, Elisabeth | 17, Aug. 1845 | RCH |
| Sayer, Joseph | Aman, Sophia | 24, Feb. 1846 | RCH |
| Sayers, John | Brooks, Jane | 30, Apr. 1843 | RCH |
| Saylor, Jacob | In---, Barbara | 11, Mar. 1819 | RCH |
| Sayre, Lewis G. | Alexander, Elisabeth | 27, June 1848 | RCH |
| Sayre, William | Hamilton, Juliana | 12, Feb. 1821 | RCH |
| Scallin, John | Scully, Mary | 17, Aug. 1825 | RCH |
| Scanlan, John | Kavanaugh, Margaret | 11, June 1848 | BB |
| Schababerle, Leopold | Rapp, Louisa | 26, Nov. 1848 | AA |
| Schaber, Andreas | Nollen, Susanna | 28, Oct. 1849 | AA |
| Schaber, Johan | Bichler, Catharine | 25, Feb. 1849 | C |
| Schacherer, Johan | Stammer, Catharina | 28, Nov. 1848 | FF |
| Schacht, William | Tappin, Maria | 17, Mar. 1842 | RCH |
| Schachtmann, Andreas | Daubert, A. Margaret | 18, Jan. 1849 | A |
| Schade, John | Doerfler, Elisabeth | 22, Jan. 1842 | RCH |
| Schaecker, Michael | Meyer, Elisabeth | 26, Sept 1839 | G |
| Schaefer, Adam | Weber, Caroline | 21, Mar. 1843 | G |
| Schaefer, Christoph | Gehrlich, Margaretha | 3, May 1842 | FF |
| Schaefer, Christoph | Hoppmann, Dorothea | 12, Apr. 1847 | EE |
| Schaefer, Conrad | Orlet, Barbara | 13, May 1849 | AA |
| Schaefer, Everhard | Pena, Walburga | 27, Oct. 1834 | FF |
| Schaefer, Georg | Seifert, Margaretha | 11, Dec. 1838 | FF |
| Schaefer, J. Philipp | Mathias, Catharine | 20, Dec. 1848 | A |
| Schaefer, Johan | Brossard, Theresa | 21, Nov. 1837 | FF |
| Schaefer, Johan | Kramer, Elisabeth | 21, Jan. 1847 | RCH |

| Grooms | Brides | Date of Marriage | Code |
|--------|--------|------------------|------|
| ****** | ****** | **** ** ******** | **** |
| Schaefer, Johan | Kuhlmann, Babette | 13, Nov. 1845 | G |
| Schaefer, Johan | Barranier, Gertrud | 14, Nov. 1847 | G |
| Schaefer, Johan | Bruns, Catharine | 15, May 1849 | CC |
| Schaefer, Johan Adam | Besler, Mary | 16, July 1844 | AA |
| Schaefer, John Henry | Young, Maria | 24, Feb. 1848 | G |
| Schaefer, Leonhardt | Diehl, Philippina | 30, May 1843 | G |
| Schaefer, Nicolaus | Landwehr, Margaretha | 18, Apr. 1842 | RCH |
| Schaefer, Peter | Bondeter, Elisabeth | 22, Sept 1838 | FF |
| Schaefer, Udalrich | Beckermann, Maria A. | 18, Sept 1849 | DD |
| Schaeffer, Carl | Schwarderer, Rosina | 12, Oct. 1843 | C |
| Schaeffer, Friedrich | Westerhaus, Cath. | 10, Nov. 1840 | F |
| Schaeffer, Joseph | Rach, Mary | 18, Nov. 1839 | BB |
| Schaetzlein, Friedr. | Voney, Margaretha | 1, June 1846 | G |
| Schaf, Johan | Hoeltinger, Maria | 22, Feb. 1848 | EE |
| Schafer, Anton | Frisch, Catharine | 12, Nov. 1848 | EE |
| Schafer, Christian | Rieder, Elisabeth | 2, May 1848 | EE |
| Schafer, Johan H. | Jung, Anna Maria | 24, Apr. 1849 | EE |
| Schaffel, Georg C. | Wollenhaupt, Emilia | 1, June 1846 | C |
| Schaffer, Michael | Eschmann, Francis | 21, Dec. 1848 | RCH |
| Schaffner, Valentin | Kopf, Catharine | 10, Mar. 1849 | RCH |
| Schafstahl, Gerhard | Westerhaus, Gertrud | 18, May 1846 | EE |
| Schafstall, Heinrich | Engelhard, Margaret | 25, June 1846 | B |
| Schafstall, Heinrich | Schmidt, Katharina | 16, May 1848 | AA |
| Schafstall, Philipp | Hoene, A.M. Adelheid | 1, Oct. 1846 | B |
| Schaid, Philip Jacob | Hauck, Barbara | 14, Aug. 1835 | RCH |
| Schall, Joseph | Baumann, Catharine | 28, July 1849 | G |
| Schallcross, Hiram | Quick, Elisabeth | 27, Feb. 1847 | RCH |
| Schalze, William | Haas, Christine | 1, June 1848 | RCH |
| Schamerloh, Heinrich | Weiss, Elisabeth | 2, Nov. 1845 | F |
| Schandonney, George | Cheek, Mary | 10, Mar. 1842 | RCH |
| Schank, Woodhull | Miller, Jeanette | 14, Oct. 1841 | I |
| Schantz, Michael | Fahner, Elisabeth | 14, June 1849 | C |
| Schaperklaus, Herman | Packers, Maria | 24, Apr. 1842 | RCH |
| Schar, Samuel | Bertel, Anna | 7, June 1849 | RCH |
| Schardein, Adam | Marshall, Friedricka | 28, May 1835 | RCH |
| Scharf, Carl | Nolte, A. Christina | 15, Nov. 1849 | F |
| Scharf, Conrad | Pist, Margaretha | 12, June 1849 | EE |
| Scharfscher, Heinric | Stegemueller, Louise | 17, Feb. 1846 | F |
| Scharherer, Jacob | Oswald, Margaretha | 1, Nov. 1842 | AA |
| Scharinghausen, Wm. | Stadtlander, Anna M. | 30, Mar. 1845 | G |
| Scharmann, Heinrich | Nuelke, Maria | 7, Sept 1848 | G |
| Scharnhorst, Heinric | Eist, Anna Maria | 19, Jan. 1847 | C |
| Scharold, Philipp | Schriml, Anna Marg. | 19, Jan. 1847 | EE |
| Schattinger, Peter | Kaige, Catharine | 2, Nov. 1848 | C |
| Schatzman, John | Governeur, M. | 17, Nov. 1846 | GG |
| Schaub, Conrad | Chreist, Catharine | 15, July 1844 | RCH |
| Schaub, Dionysius | Beiser, Magdalena | 2, July 1838 | FF |
| Schaue, John Henry | Wingermuhler, Elis. | 18, Mar. 1846 | RCH |
| Schauler, Michael | Wagner, Maria | 8, July 1837 | FF |
| Schaurer, Michael | Baurer, Maria Anna | 30, Jan. 1844 | AA |
| Schaurer, Peter | Zipp, Catharine | 27, Sept 1846 | A |
| Schbahe, Everhard | Lies, Catharine A. | 3, Jan. 1844 | RCH |
| Scheble, Heinrich | Eliger, Anna Maria | 27, Nov. 1835 | FF |
| Scheck, Lorenz | Cramer, Josephine | 2, May 1843 | AA |
| Scheele, Gerhard | Drasing, Maria | 2, June 1842 | RCH |
| Scheele, Otto | Bruding, Catharine | 13, Sept 1842 | F |
| Scheibel, Friedrich | Baltz, Dorothea | 8, June 1843 | G |
| Scheible, Nicolaus | Hylser, Dorothea | 28, July 1849 | II |
| Scheid, Nicolaus | Riesbeck, Barbara | 16, May 1843 | FF |
| Scheidemantel, Johan | Koch, Magdalena | 18, July 1837 | FF |
| Scheiler, Joseph | Fassel, Brigitta | 11, Sept 1837 | FF |
| Scheiml, Heinrich | Koch, Catharine M. | 10, Nov. 1846 | EE |
| Scheiner, Andrew | Deuchter, Isabella | 15, Mar. 1847 | RCH |
| Scheiss, Johan B. | Mittnacht, Anna M. | 16, Sept 1849 | A |
| Schekelhoff, Johan W | Kennebeck, Maria E. | 5, Nov. 1848 | EE |
| Schel, Johan Anton | Schick, Regina | 12, May 1846 | EE |
| Scheldering, Heinric | Hux, Gesina | 14, Nov. 1849 | AA |
| Schell, Jacob | Laudick, Anna Maria | 1, Oct. 1848 | EE |
| Schellenberg, Jacob | Fuchs, Magdalena | 11, Feb. 1849 | AA |
| Schellmueller, Ger. | Dirsen, Wilhelmina | 16, Nov. 1845 | AA |
| Schenck, John | Schenck, Phebe | 9, Oct. 1843 | RCH |

| Grooms<br>***** | Brides<br>***** | Date of Marriage<br>**** ** ******** | Code<br>**** |
|---|---|---|---|
| Scheneberger, Lorenz | Everns, Francisca | 16, Feb. 1836 | FF |
| Scheninger, Johan | Rudel, Anna | 22, May 1843 | C |
| Schenk, Aaron L. | Wood, Maria P. | 25, July 1822 | RCH |
| Schepas, Johan | Knagg, Dina | 9, Sept 1849 | EE |
| Scheper, Anton | Broegelmann, Henriet | 7, Jan. 1847 | AA |
| Scheper, Bernard | Mehmert, Elisabeth | 23, Jan. 1844 | AA |
| Scheper, Francis H. | Schroeder, Catharina | 24, Nov. 1834 | FF |
| Scheper, Herman H. | Meyer, Bernardina | 23, Jan. 1848 | AA |
| Scheper, Johan | Deken, Elisabeth(Mrs | 4, Nov. 1849 | CC |
| Schepker, Herman G. | Meyer, Katharina M. | 11, July 1848 | AA |
| Schepmann, J. | Freudenbargh, Elis. | 13, Feb. 1845 | A |
| Schepmann, Johan H. | Voregge, Catharine | 12, Nov. 1846 | F |
| Schepper, Heinrich | Brinkmann, Caroline | 27, Nov. 1848 | F |
| Schepper, J. Francis | Brueggemann, Elis. | 23, Apr. 1844 | FF |
| Scherbrock, Heinrich | Breckweth, Catharina | 10, Nov. 1836 | FF |
| Scherck, Francis | Aulals, Maria | 21, Apr. 1844 | A |
| Scherer, Georg | Schmidt, Susanna | 30, June 1845 | A |
| Scherer, Joseph | Reising, Barbara | 17, Jan. 1843 | AA |
| Schermer, Johan | Schreiner, Julia | 9, June 1846 | EE |
| Schetter, Heinrich | Ringmann, Anna | 9, May 1837 | FF |
| Scheuing, Christian | Henn, Anna Maria | 16, Aug. 1849 | II |
| Scheurer, J. Jacob | Meinhardt, Catharine | 13, Feb. 1848 | G |
| Scheurer, Michael | Knabb, Elisabeth | 11, Nov. 1817 | RCH |
| Scheve, Bernard | Huelsmann, Catharine | 30, Sept 1849 | FF |
| Scheve, Johan | Luebbe, Catharina | 19, Sept 1847 | AA |
| Schewe, J. Dietrich | Ruse, Anna Maria | 6, Feb. 1849 | F |
| Schey, J. Christoph | Leider, Catharina | 31, Mar. 1839 | G |
| Scheyt, Johan | Vollherbst, Luitgard | 6, Sept 1846 | FF |
| Schick, Joseph | Werner, Elisabeth | 19, Oct. 1845 | AA |
| Schickedanz, Christ. | Mallen, Mary Ann | 3, Nov. 1846 | RCH |
| Schidmiah, Philipp | Schwab, Catharine | 28, May 1837 | RCH |
| Schie, Johan Adam | Tenzer, Maria | 4, July 1846 | EE |
| Schierberg, Bernard | Lange, Agnes | 16, May 1843 | AA |
| Schierberg, Friedric | Harmeier, Catharine | 4, Aug. 1840 | FF |
| Schiering, Gerhard | Rassing, Christina | 23, Jan. 1848 | EE |
| Schiering, Johan H. | Dopphor, Margaretha | 20, Feb. 1848 | EE |
| Schiermann, Johan H. | Egbert, Maria Angela | 27, Apr. 1841 | FF |
| Schiff, Heinrich | Zerfass, Elisabeth | 17, Oct. 1847 | AA |
| Schiff, Johan | Hauck, Maria | 16, Dec. 1839 | G |
| Schill, Bernard | Lang, Barbara | 29, Oct. 1846 | RCH |
| Schill, Bernard | Viux, Pauline | 7, Oct. 1847 | EE |
| Schill, Sebastian | Reibing, Theresa | 24, Aug. 1847 | FF |
| Schiller, Ludwig | Knau, Anna | 20, Sept 1838 | FF |
| Schilling, Michael | Stenger, Maria | 22, June 1847 | EE |
| Schillinger, William | Lovejoy, Mary | 19, Oct. 1836 | RCH |
| Schillinger, William | Cones, Frances Mary | 26, May 1841 | RCH |
| Schindeldecker, Geo. | Sieg, Elisabeth | 16, Jan. 1848 | A |
| Schindeldecker, H. | Lautemann, Bena | 13, Nov. 1842 | G |
| Schipner, Joseph | Droll, Maria Anna | 28, Jan. 1840 | FF |
| Schipper, J. Bernard | Schulte, M Catharina | 9, Nov. 1841 | FF |
| Schipper, J. Theodor | Frecking, M. Agnes | 7, Jan. 1840 | FF |
| Schirberg, Bernard | Niemer, Elisabeth | 6, Feb. 1848 | II |
| Schirer, Georg | Schilling, Christina | 11, Oct. 1838 | FF |
| Schiring, Gerhard | Quain, Anna Adelehid | 13, May 1847 | EE |
| Schirmann, Francis | Neddermann, Anna M. | 11, Oct. 1842 | FF |
| Schirmer, Philipp | Doermann, Wilhelmina | 27, Aug. 1846 | G |
| Schits, John | Featherlin, Joanna | 22, Feb. 1846 | RCH |
| Schlacke, Bernard | Verwick, Margaretha | 24, June 1849 | CC |
| Schlaegel, Anton | Lambur, Catharina | 29, Sept 1840 | FF |
| Schlageter, Martin | VanDuzer, Catharine | 3, Nov. 1845 | G |
| Schlaghenn, Georg | Hille, Elisabeth | 14, May 1848 | AA |
| Schlaich, Gregory | Speers, Gottlieba | 21, Sept 1849 | RCH |
| Schlake, Heinrich | Voss, Maria | 27, Jan. 1842 | FF |
| Schlat, Johan | Ziegler, Anna Maria | 30, Jan. 1840 | FF |
| Schlauch, Friedrich | Kehrt, Susannah | 18, Oct. 1846 | A |
| Schlebaum, Heinrich | Peters, Louise | 13, Nov. 1845 | F |
| Schlebbe, Theodor | Rehe, M. Catharina | 1, Nov. 1849 | FF |
| Schlecht, Johan | Doll, Magdalena | 31, July 1837 | FF |
| Schleebaum, Gerhard | Hoberg, Marg. Regina | 14, Nov. 1847 | F |
| Schleheim, Georg L. | Walter, A. Barbara | 28, Oct. 1843 | G |
| Schleich, Anton | Bobb, Magdalena | 30, Aug. 1846 | EE |

| Grooms | Brides | Date of Marriage | Code |
|------|------|------|------|
| Schleich, Joseph | Feldkamp, Gertrud | 26, Sept 1847 | AA |
| Schleight, Henry | Divley, Rachel | 2, Feb. 1845 | BB |
| Schlemme, Christoph | Borrmann, Catharina | 28, May 1846 | G |
| Schlemmer, Johan H. | Rabe, Maria Elis. | 10, Nov. 1846 | AA |
| Schlenz, J Friedrich | Westhoff, Maria(Mrs) | 7, Oct. 1849 | F |
| Schleppe, Herman H. | Korte, Anna M. Elis. | 21, Oct. 1849 | FF |
| Schleppey, John | Hart, Ruth E. | 6, June 1849 | RCH |
| Schlesinger, Michael | Niemeyer, Friedricka | 2, June 1847 | RCH |
| Schlessinger, Debolt | Autmann, Lena | 5, Feb. 1844 | RCH |
| Schlessinger, Johan | Friedlin, Christina | 8, May 1838 | FF |
| Schlessinger, Lebolt | Hausenbusch, Hansch. | 14, Apr. 1843 | RCH |
| Schleter, Theodor | Buscher, Catharina M | 12, Nov. 1839 | FF |
| Schleucher, Valentin | Rheinlander, Maria | 28, Feb. 1847 | G |
| Schleutker, Friedric | Burbaner, Elisabeth | 24, Jan. 1844 | RCH |
| Schlicht, Johan | Hoffmann, Anna Maria | 1, Nov. 1847 | FF |
| Schlicht, Joseph | Deifus, Margaretha | 7, Aug. 1848 | EE |
| Schlichter, Ernst | Vasker, Catharine | 24, Aug. 1845 | FF |
| Schlicker, Jacob | Lang, Elisabeth | Sept 1845 | RCH |
| Schlickmann, Heinr. | Showen, Catharine | 10, Oct. 1844 | C |
| Schling, Henry | Lubbens, Catharine | 18, June 1841 | RCH |
| Schlocke, Dietrich | Nolker, Adelheid | 26, Nov. 1848 | AA |
| Schloeffel, Johan | Lampen, Louise | 28, Sept 1848 | F |
| Schloemer, Friedrich | Bahlmann, Catharina | 15, May 1849 | AA |
| Schloemer, Johan Bd. | Bolke, Maria Elis. | 21, Nov. 1848 | AA |
| Schloer, Friedrich | Ridinsheverin, Apol. | 24, Nov. 1847 | A |
| Schloer, Michael | Moor, Barbara | 26, July 1846 | C |
| Schlopper, Johan | Schilling, Katharina | 1, June 1848 | AA |
| Schloss, Philipp J. | Schmidt, Catharina | 15, Aug. 1837 | FF |
| Schlosser, Francis | Ziegler, Dorothea | 31, Dec. 1844 | AA |
| Schlosser, Henry | Sponsel, Margaretha | 24, Apr. 1848 | G |
| Schlotmann, Dietrich | Harmann, Gertrud | 12, July 1842 | FF |
| Schlotmann, Gerhard | Landwehr, Gertrud | 23, Jan. 1848 | EE |
| Schlotmann, Gerhard | Duerstock, Catharine | 22, Oct. 1848 | EE |
| Schlotter, Johan | Hipp, Maria | 18, Nov. 1849 | AA |
| Schlottmann, Johan H | Leppold, Maria | 30, Apr. 1846 | RCH |
| Schluete, Herman | Huppmann, Maria Anna | 23, July 1846 | AA |
| Schlueter, Wilhelm | Lages, Elisabeth | 13, July 1841 | FF |
| Schluetker, Heinrich | Grove, Margaretha | 7, Nov. 1837 | FF |
| Schlutmann, Johan J. | Kleinebahnhofl, Kath | 12, Nov. 1848 | AA |
| Schlutte, Johan H. | Richter, Bernardina | 28, Jan. 1845 | AA |
| Schmale, Heinrich F. | Gorkens, M Elisabeth | 28, Sept 1848 | B |
| Schmehling, Joseph | Hirchkorn, Margaret | 14, Mar. 1842 | FF |
| Schmerling, Joseph | Goss, Catharina | 1, May 1849 | HH |
| Schmid, Lewis | Scher, Caroline | 5, Nov. 1846 | RCH |
| Schmid, Michael | Fladung, Catharine | 29, May 1849 | EE |
| Schmidlapp, Fredrick | Raye---, Mary Ann | 25, Nov. 1826 | RCH |
| Schmidlapp, Peter | Goll, Catharina | 21, Oct. 1839 | G |
| Schmidt, Adolph | Meyer, Maria | 8, May 1847 | F |
| Schmidt, Albert | Eiglisheimer, Barb. | 17, Feb. 1842 | G |
| Schmidt, Andreas | Nicole, Catharina | 15, May 1838 | FF |
| Schmidt, Andreas | Hunt, Adilia | 2, July 1839 | FF |
| Schmidt, Anton | Pflum, Christina | 18, Oct. 1836 | FF |
| Schmidt, Anton | Huber, Catharina | 6, Mar. 1848 | AA |
| Schmidt, Bernard | Lambers, Anna | 7, Jan. 1835 | FF |
| Schmidt, Bernard | Stockhof, Catharine | 19, Apr. 1846 | AA |
| Schmidt, Carl | Kirchner, Rosa | 22, Sept 1849 | B |
| Schmidt, Charles | Griffin, Susan | 18, Sept 1839 | RCH |
| Schmidt, Christian | Hoffmeister, Pauline | 21, Feb. 1849 | A |
| Schmidt, Christian | Wagner, Eva | 3, July 1845 | G |
| Schmidt, Christian | Mueller, Elisabeth | 12, July 1846 | G |
| Schmidt, Christoph | Schneider, Friedrika | 29, July 1849 | A |
| Schmidt, Conrad | Witt, Barbara | 14, Feb. 1843 | AA |
| Schmidt, Daniel | Wing, Dorothea Maria | 23, Jan. 1848 | G |
| Schmidt, David | Eckstein, Thecla | 17, Nov. 1840 | FF |
| Schmidt, Dietrich | Meiers, A. Maria | 21, Sept 1843 | G |
| Schmidt, Francis | Mans, Magdalena | 2, Jan. 1849 | EE |
| Schmidt, Francis | Voll, Gertrud | 25, Oct. 1849 | EE |
| Schmidt, Friedrich | Wesemann, Sophia | 12, Oct. 1843 | F |
| Schmidt, Friedrich | Lang, Maria | 9, July 1848 | C |
| Schmidt, Georg | Scheu, Maria Anna | 9, Mar. 1842 | FF |
| Schmidt, Georg | Schmidt, Elisabeth | 7, Jan. 1849 | A |

| Grooms | Brides | Date of Marriage | Code |
|--------|--------|------------------|------|
| Schmidt, Georg | Theis, Margaretha | 2, Sept 1849 | A |
| Schmidt, Georg | Loeffler, Lydia | 4, Oct. 1849 | C |
| Schmidt, Georg | Ken, Maria | 16, Sept 1849 | EE |
| Schmidt, George | Ruver, Anna | 23, Aug. 1836 | RCH |
| Schmidt, George | Hoffmann, Maria | 10, Jan. 1847 | RCH |
| Schmidt, George | Lamarche, Elisabeth | 15, Apr. 1848 | RCH |
| Schmidt, Heinrich | Friege, Elisabeth | 20, June 1837 | F |
| Schmidt, Heinrich | Gernand, Maria | 30, June 1840 | G |
| Schmidt, Heinrich | Weindel, Barbara | 20, Oct. 1842 | FF |
| Schmidt, Heinrich | Franzen, M. Theresa | 14, May 1848 | AA |
| Schmidt, Heinrich | Mueller, Elisabeth | 11, June 1848 | AA |
| Schmidt, Henry | Friedechen, Cath. | 3, Oct. 1845 | RCH |
| Schmidt, Herman H. | Stadtlander, Sophia | 6, Feb. 1849 | F |
| Schmidt, Herman H. | Depenbrock, M. Elis. | 21, Nov. 1847 | AA |
| Schmidt, J. Heinrich | Koch, Louisa | 3, Oct. 1849 | A |
| Schmidt, J. Rudolph | Fangmeyer, Anna M. | 4, Nov. 1841 | F |
| Schmidt, Jacob | Huegel, Christina | 25, July 1844 | G |
| Schmidt, Jacob | Reiss, Magdalena | 6, Nov. 1843 | FF |
| Schmidt, Jacob | Baron, M. Elisabeth | 1, July 1845 | G |
| Schmidt, Johan | Sindermann, Catharin | 29, May 1849 | RCH |
| Schmidt, Johan | Muckenhaupt, Magd. | 19, Jan. 1847 | AA |
| Schmidt, Johan Adam | Quint, Johanna | 23, July 1848 | C |
| Schmidt, Johan Bd. | Vornhage, M. Gertrud | 23, Sept 1849 | AA |
| Schmidt, Johan Bd. | Wibling, Adelheid | 23, Oct. 1849 | AA |
| Schmidt, Johan Hein. | ----, ---- | 10, Feb. 1847 | RCH |
| Schmidt, Johan Hein. | Hilman, Louisa W.C. | 23, Sept 1847 | A |
| Schmidt, Johan Hein. | Esselmann, Maria A. | 16, Aug. 1846 | FF |
| Schmidt, John | Steckel, Margaret | 22, Oct. 1844 | RCH |
| Schmidt, John Georg | Meier, Rosina | 19, Feb. 1846 | RCH |
| Schmidt, Joseph | Roth, Kunigunda | 19, May 1849 | II |
| Schmidt, Kilian | Betz, Maria | 17, Apr. 1838 | FF |
| Schmidt, Leonard | Wellmeyer, Theresa | 18, May 1847 | EE |
| Schmidt, Martin | Kirn, Maria Anna | 16, May 1847 | FF |
| Schmidt, Nicolaus | Speck, Veronica | 9, May 1849 | EE |
| Schmidt, Peter | Goll, Cath. Barbara | 2, Apr. 1842 | FF |
| Schmidt, Peter | Roeble, Kunigunda | 3, Aug. 1845 | RCH |
| Schmidt, Peter | Rust, Barbara | 20, Aug. 1848 | C |
| Schmidt, Peter | Koch, Catharine | 30, July 1848 | G |
| Schmidt, Peter | Schmidt, Maria | 15, Nov. 1847 | EE |
| Schmidt, Peter H. | Schindler, Sophia W. | 22, June 1849 | A |
| Schmidt, Valentin | Wagner, Catharine | 15, Dec. 1844 | C |
| Schmidt, Valentin | Kopp, Victoria | 7, Mar. 1842 | FF |
| Schmidt, Valentin | Thrasher, Martha | 5, Feb. 1848 | RCH |
| Schmidt, Wilhelm | Hemmelgarn, Catharin | 13, Oct. 1846 | AA |
| Schmidt, Wilhelm | Mentler, Barbara | 13, Oct. 1849 | CC |
| Schmidtlein, Johan | Diethorn, Margaretha | 9, May 1847 | AA |
| Schmidtlein, Nic. | Wagner, Kunigunda | 22, Feb. 1846 | EE |
| Schmied, J Friedrich | Boesch, Anna | 20, July 1847 | A |
| Schmieding, Carl H. | Wiegrewe, Wilhelmina | 3, Mar. 1837 | RCH |
| Schmieding, Carl H. | Brand, Johanna | 13, Dec. 1840 | G |
| Schmiesing, Johan H. | Flothmann, Elisabeth | 24, Apr. 1849 | CC |
| Schmit, Peter | Roemelin, Anna | 17, Aug. 1847 | AA |
| Schmith, Philipp | Wemyer, Margaret | 7, Sept 1841 | RCH |
| Schmitt, Bernard | Hilgelmann, Cath. | 1, Sept 1835 | FF |
| Schmitt, Dietrich | Stricker, Anna Maria | 3, Nov. 1835 | FF |
| Schmitt, George | LaMarche, Anna Elis. | 8, May 1848 | GG |
| Schmitt, Jacob | Schranck, Francisca | 3, Nov. 1835 | FF |
| Schmitt, Jacob | Stembler, Charlotte | 30, Dec. 1842 | RCH |
| Schmitt, Karl | Wollan, Maria | 17, May 1849 | RCH |
| Schmitz, Nicolaus | Tarmann, Elisabeth | 31, Oct. 1837 | FF |
| Schmitzer, John | Brobeck, Veronica | 17, Dec. 1847 | RCH |
| Schmolsmeier, Casper | Hovelmeier, Margaret | 21, May 1842 | F |
| Schmucker, Ludwig | Frey, Barbara | 13, Oct. 1846 | C |
| Schnarre, Casper | Rodert, Maria | 21, Oct. 1847 | C |
| Schneers, Friedrich | Jorings, Maria | 20, Feb. 1849 | II |
| Schneider, Adam | Weber, Susannah | 15, June 1843 | C |
| Schneider, Balthasar | Popp, Magdalena | 27, July 1848 | EE |
| Schneider, Carl A. | Ballauf, Louise | 28, July 1842 | G |
| Schneider, Carl Fr. | Surenkamp, Marg. E. | 16, Feb. 1841 | F |
| Schneider, Casper | Lotz, Anna M. | 18, Oct. 1841 | RCH |
| Schneider, Charles | Willmer, M. Angela | 21, Mar. 1847 | F |

| Grooms | Brides | Date of Marriage | Code |
|--------|--------|------------------|------|
| Schneider, Christian | Leile, Augusta | 22, Oct. 1848 | A |
| Schneider, Christoph | Molitor, Anna Maria | 6, Aug. 1844 | AA |
| Schneider, Christoph | Berg, Catharine | 8, Aug. 1848 | CC |
| Schneider, Conrad | Schultz, Angela | 28, May 1844 | FF |
| Schneider, Daniel | Weber, Louise | 26, Nov. 1848 | A |
| Schneider, Georg | Stinger, Maria | 19, Dec. 1843 | G |
| Schneider, Heinrich | Baumann, Wilhelmina | 4, July 1848 | A |
| Schneider, Heinrich | Mesloh, Dorothea L. | 14, Mar. 1847 | F |
| Schneider, Jacob | Schmidt, Elisabeth | 3, Mar. 1840 | FF |
| Schneider, Jacob | Raus, Mary | 26, Nov. 1849 | RCH |
| Schneider, Jacob | Traub, Catharine | 24, Feb. 1848 | G |
| Schneider, Jacob | Orlet, Anna Maria | 29, Nov. 1849 | AA |
| Schneider, Johan | Bechtold, Maria | 27, Oct. 1840 | FF |
| Schneider, Johan | Erhard, M. Antonia | 22, Apr. 1841 | FF |
| Schneider, Johan | Schmidt, Margaretha | 24, June 1841 | FF |
| Schneider, Johan | Stevens, Margaretha | 26, Apr. 1842 | FF |
| Schneider, Johan | Heid, Margaretha | 15, Feb. 1849 | G |
| Schneider, Johan | Utz, Clara | 30, Sept 1845 | AA |
| Schneider, Johan A. | Weindel, Anna | 28, Jan. 1845 | AA |
| Schneider, Johan F. | Schmidt, Eva | 20, Aug. 1848 | CC |
| Schneider, Johan H. | Goldmeyer, Gertrud | 11, July 1848 | EE |
| Schneider, John | Schilling, Mary | 7, Apr. 1846 | RCH |
| Schneider, Joseph | Widmann, Christina | 17, Feb. 1835 | FF |
| Schneider, Joseph | Goetz, Elisabeth | 30, June 1846 | AA |
| Schneider, Joseph | Gutzwiller, Maria U. | 7, Jan. 1849 | EE |
| Schneider, Julius | Scheuct, Catharine | 23, July 1848 | C |
| Schneider, Leopold | Wellenbrink, G.(Mrs) | 30, Apr. 1845 | AA |
| Schneider, Louis | Hack, M. Catharine | 28, Jan. 1840 | FF |
| Schneider, Mathias | West, Maria Anna | 4, Feb. 1839 | FF |
| Schneider, Max. | Pister, Catharina | 21, May 1835 | FF |
| Schneider, Nicolaus | Bohlander, Margaret | 18, June 1844 | C |
| Schneider, Philipp | Amann, Elisabeth | 9, May 1844 | G |
| Schneider, Philipp | Kortzdorfer, Marg. | 14, June 1846 | G |
| Schneider, Sanderlin | Foll, Anna (Mrs) | 2, Oct. 1837 | FF |
| Schneider, Wilhelm | Dingfelder, Margaret | 14, Oct. 1844 | C |
| Schneider, Wilhelm | Otberg, Anna | 30, Sept 1847 | F |
| Schneider, Wilhelm | Bluemer, Carolina | 31, Dec. 1846 | G |
| Schneidermann, Carl | Schmidt, Catharina | 23, Dec. 1847 | E |
| Schneidermann, Henry | Otten, Anna Maria | 16, Nov. 1843 | RCH |
| Schneidermann, Wm. | Butchers, Clara Elis | 3, Jan. 1844 | RCH |
| Schnell, Friedrich J | Hornberger, Maria | 7, July 1847 | F |
| Schnell, Jacob | Langer, Francisca | 6, Dec. 1846 | C |
| Schnench, John | Wood, Lucy | 2, Mar. 1837 | RCH |
| Schnepferling, John | Hofecker, Barbara | 1, Feb. 1847 | RCH |
| Schneppel, Bernard | Egbers, Catharine | 4, June 1844 | AA |
| Schners, Francis | Leiverling, Margaret | 27, Feb. 1848 | EE |
| Schnett, Gregor | Koch, Sophia | 16, Sept 1849 | EE |
| Schnetz, Martin | Pistner, Maria Eva | 29, Aug. 1839 | FF |
| Schnetzer, Georg | Fuchs, Elisabeth | 23, May 1839 | G |
| Schnetzer, Johan | Witz, Maria | 27, Sept 1842 | FF |
| Schnicke, Carl Hein. | Neufarth, Catharine | 14, Nov. 1846 | C |
| Schnierwitz, Johan | Dorsch, Margaretha | 13, Dec. 1846 | C |
| Schnitger, Heinrich | Sonnenmann, Maria A. | 20, Sept 1836 | FF |
| Schnitger, Heinrich | VonWalde, Catharine | 26, Feb. 1838 | FF |
| Schnitger, Johan H. | Becker, Maria Agnes | 20, Nov. 1839 | FF |
| Schnitker, Victor | Kleinborn, Elisabeth | 23, Jan. 1845 | F |
| Schnitzer, Godfried | Baner, Catharine | 19, July 1847 | EE |
| Schnuck, Bernard | Kendorf, Sophia | 15, Aug. 1849 | FF |
| Schnurr, Heinrich | Habermann, Caroline | 2, Dec. 1847 | C |
| Schoat, Stephan | Roberts, Ann | 8, June 1837 | RCH |
| Schober, Jacob | Evans, Caroline | 25, Feb. 1847 | RCH |
| Schobert, J Wolfgang | Paulus, Margaret | 8, Oct. 1845 | RCH |
| Schockel, Francis | Klueber, Maria Anna | 11, Jan. 1848 | CC |
| Schodde, Johan Fried | Rolwes, Charlotte | 8, Aug. 1849 | F |
| Schodel, Theodor | Wessel, Gertrud | 21, Oct. 1849 | EE |
| Schodert, Johan | Hehn, Maria | 26, Oct. 1845 | AA |
| Schoeber, Francis J. | Niemann, Elisabeth | 20, Feb. 1849 | EE |
| Schoenbaum, Heinrich | Neddersen, Dorothea | 21, Jan. 1846 | F |
| Schoenberg, Elias | Rothschild, Fanny | 23, Mar. 1849 | RCH |
| Schoenberg, Markus | Hecht, Theresa | 15, Apr. 1847 | RCH |
| Schoenberger, Anton | Schmidt, Catharine | 26, Aug. 1849 | EE |

| Grooms<br>****** | Brides<br>****** | Date of Marriage<br>**** ** ******** | Code<br>**** |
|---|---|---|---|
| Schoenberger, Conrad | Keller, Christina | 29, Aug. 1845 | RCH |
| Schoenberger, Georg | Hamilton, Sarah | 9, June 1835 | RCH |
| Schoene, Christian F | Busche, Maria Gesche | 23, Apr. 1849 | F |
| Schoenebaum, Heinric | Cruse, Sophia | 26, Nov. 1846 | B |
| Schoenenberger, Hein | Jaeger, Margaretha | 22, May 1838 | FF |
| Schoener, Christian | Cammann, Maria | 16, Oct. 1838 | FF |
| Schoener, Paul | Bruch, Catharina | 21, Oct. 1844 | G |
| Schoenfeld, Bernard | Goodman, Fanny | 19, June 1848 | RCH |
| Schoenhaus, Louis | Hallstein, Barbette | 14, Nov. 1846 | RCH |
| Schoenhoft, Bernard | Bemer, Elisabeth | 19, July 1836 | FF |
| Schoenhoft, Joseph | Engelke, Anna M. | 11, May 1841 | FF |
| Schoenhorst, Christ. | Deeg, Maria | 22, Aug. 1848 | G |
| Schoening, Carl | Gessert, Catharine | 10, Jan. 1846 | G |
| Schoenlaub, Franz | Gruber, Maria Elis. | 10, June 1844 | C |
| Schoenlaub, Johan | Schoepner, Eva | 5, Apr. 1847 | RCH |
| Schoenluecke, Wilhel | Weddendorf, Elisabet | 14, Dec. 1848 | C |
| Schoenstadt, Heinric | Stinger, Louise | 9, Mar. 1847 | G |
| Schoenthaler, Johan | Doll, Magdalena | 7, Nov. 1842 | G |
| Schoepf, Nicholas | Hofmann, Anna | 10, June 1849 | CC |
| Schoepner, Joseph | Betts, Theresa | 26, Oct. 1849 | CC |
| Schoering, Gerhard H | Schrotz, Maria | 6, Nov. 1849 | EE |
| Schoester, Johan H. | Widhorn, Catharine | 16, Jan. 1844 | AA |
| Schoetmer, Johan H. | Beckmann, Anna M. | 26, Jan. 1847 | AA |
| Schoette, Heinrich | Behn, Margaret | 26, Apr. 1838 | FF |
| Schoettelkot, Johan | Korte, M. Catharina | 19, Nov. 1849 | HH |
| Schoettinger, Conrad | Baesel, Elisabeth | 6, Jan. 1848 | G |
| Schoevoght, Friedric | Schmidt, Catharine | 7, July 1849 | A |
| Schofield, Andrew | Powers, Sarah | 9, June 1839 | RCH |
| Schofield, Robert | McLaughlin, Sarah | 6, Aug. 1846 | RCH |
| Schofield, William | Brown, Lucy | 27, Mar. 1846 | RCH |
| Schole, William | Ford, Anna Elisabeth | 4, July 1841 | BB |
| Scholl, Christian | Weiss, Barbara | 12, May 1845 | C |
| Scholl, Mathias | Mueller, Walburga | 21, Nov. 1848 | EE |
| Schomacher, Eulard | Jansen, Wilhelmina | 10, Apr. 1847 | FF |
| Schomacher, Johan H. | Imbusch, Catharine | 28, Jan. 1845 | AA |
| Schon, Peter | Knerr, Magdalena | 22, Feb. 1846 | EE |
| Schone, Johan Heinr. | Winkelmueller, Elis. | 21, Mar. 1846 | AA |
| Schone, John Henry | Sonken, Maria | 9, Aug. 1849 | RCH |
| Schontrup, Johan | Wilmers, Adelheid | 24, Sept 1848 | AA |
| Schook, Isaac | Ashton, Mary Ann | 9, Mar. 1844 | RCH |
| Schooley, Israel | Sturgess, Marietta | 18, July 1824 | RCH |
| Schooley, James | Jackson, Mary | 22, Feb. 1847 | RCH |
| Schooley, John | Isham, Elisabeth | 22, May 1844 | RCH |
| Schoolfield, John | Sims, Honora | 24, Dec. 1845 | RCH |
| Schoolman, William | Ziegler, Elisabeth | 18, Sept 1832 | RCH |
| Schooner, Simon | Cooper, Caroline | 5, Apr. 1849 | RCH |
| Schoonover, Joseph | Mains, Mary | 9, Nov. 1834 | RCH |
| Schopf, Nicholas | Hoffmann, Lena | 10, June 1849 | RCH |
| Schopmann, Johan Bd. | Kuhne, Anna Maria | 8, June 1847 | AA |
| Schoppenhorst, Wm. | Rathenbrink, Maria | 13, May 1847 | C |
| Schopper, Paul | Bitter, Philippina | 3, Nov. 1849 | C |
| Schoppner, Johan | Weber, Cath. Elis. | 17, July 1849 | FF |
| Schorling, Christian | Lohrmann, Gesche A. | 31, July 1844 | F |
| Schorr, Johan | Reiss, Barbara | 1, Nov. 1846 | G |
| Schoseph, | Gimbel, Babette | 6, Apr. 1849 | RCH |
| Schoster, Ulrich | Bakerhaus, Maria | 30, Aug. 1849 | RCH |
| Schotsmann, John | Jelliff, Amelia | 9, Sept 1849 | BB |
| Schott, John | Gottfried, Margaret | 17, Feb. 1846 | RCH |
| Schott, Ludwig | Brosmer, Ottilia | 29, May 1845 | FF |
| Schottelkot, Gerhard | Schwenker, M. Elis. | 15, Aug. 1843 | FF |
| Schottmueller, Fried | Kinzel, Johanna | 27, Sept 1849 | G |
| Schotts, Henry | Rudisell, Jane | 6, Aug. 1846 | RCH |
| Schrader, Friedrich | Schrader, Leonora | 11, Sept 1849 | C |
| Schrader, Herman Wm. | Schrader, Adolphina | 26, Aug. 1847 | G |
| Schrader, Michael | Ross, Elisabeth | 9, Apr. 1823 | RCH |
| Schrag, Ludwig | Stein, Sarah | 16, July 1843 | G |
| Schrage, Gerhard | Schuermann, Margaret | 7, Nov. 1837 | FF |
| Schram, Johan | Schneider, Catharine | 11, Aug. 1840 | FF |
| Schramm, J. Leonard | Benker, Catharine M. | 2, Apr. 1842 | RCH |
| Schrand, Bernard | Pelzer, M. Elisabeth | 14, Oct. 1849 | FF |
| Schrand, Conrad | Resing, Gertrud | 27, May 1849 | FF |

| Grooms | Brides | Date of Marriage | Code |
|--------|--------|------------------|------|
| ****** | ****** | **** ** ******** | **** |
| Schrandenbach, Hein. | Renz, Theresa | 20, June 1847 | EE |
| Schrant, Wilhelm | Sanders, Gertrud | 11, Aug. 1844 | AA |
| Schrauder, Charles | Cothe, Catharine | 12, Feb. 1849 | G |
| Schreiber, Bernard | Arn, Margaretha | 29, Feb. 1848 | G |
| Schreiber, Ludwig | Brueggemann, Anna | 25, Apr. 1849 | F |
| Schreiber, Martin | Trimpe, M. Angela | 11, Nov. 1840 | FF |
| Schreiber, Martin | Heuer, Sophia | 17, Jan. 1847 | F |
| Schreifer, Heinrich | Immgarten, Sophia | 2, Sept 1841 | F |
| Schreiner, Jacob | Sauer, Margaretha | 6, June 1847 | CC |
| Schreiner, Jacob | Kuhn, Maria Anna | 14, May 1848 | CC |
| Schreiner, Wilhelm | Klingler, Veronica | 9, Oct. 1849 | EE |
| Schrelmann, Friedric | Bader, Barbara | 28, Oct. 1845 | AA |
| Schremker, Johan | Sohnlein, Kunigunda | 14, June 1847 | EE |
| Schrender, Mathias | Duskey, Sarah | 29, Sept 1844 | RCH |
| Schrener, Stephan H. | Essel, Catharia M. | 25, Oct. 1849 | C |
| Schrett, Anton | Lipger, Maria Anna | 7, Jan. 1840 | FF |
| Schreyer, Carl Fr. | Stoehl, Maria Anna | 10, Jan. 1846 | FF |
| Schriefer, Heinrich | Brandt, Sophia | 13, Jan. 1841 | F |
| Schrimpp, Casper | Allen, Ann | 10, Sept 1840 | BB |
| Schriver, Francis | Roberg, Louisa Jos. | 16, Jan. 1840 | FF |
| Schroeder, Bernard | Hostmann, Catharina | 22, Jan. 1835 | FF |
| Schroeder, Bernard | Herbeck, Margaretha | 6, Nov. 1838 | FF |
| Schroeder, Bernard | Darstiege, Maria | 8, May 1838 | FF |
| Schroeder, Bernard | Willing, Gertrud | 25, Apr. 1843 | FF |
| Schroeder, Bernard | Moses, Poylenna | 10, Feb. 1846 | RCH |
| Schroeder, Bernard | Humman, Maria | 11, Jan. 1849 | RCH |
| Schroeder, Bernard | Dramann, Angela | 14, Jan. 1849 | AA |
| Schroeder, Carl | Baumer, Elisabeth | 10, Aug. 1841 | FF |
| Schroeder, Carl | Wittmer, Christina | 22, Nov. 1849 | F |
| Schroeder, Caspar | Ulrich, Aloysia | 14, Sept 1846 | EE |
| Schroeder, Christian | Kruse, Louise | 11, Feb. 1848 | F |
| Schroeder, Christoph | Desser, Maria | 9, Nov. 1837 | FF |
| Schroeder, Dietrich | Thielbar, Gesche M. | 19, Feb. 1849 | F |
| Schroeder, Dietrich | Troste, Henrietta | 24, Oct. 1849 | F |
| Schroeder, Ernst R. | Kucks, Sophia | 14, Mar. 1840 | G |
| Schroeder, Friedrich | Finke, Margaretha | 28, July 1847 | B |
| Schroeder, Friedrich | Gruber, Catharine | 23, May 1847 | F |
| Schroeder, Friedrich | Holste, Christina W. | 24, Sept 1846 | G |
| Schroeder, Friedrich | Burger, Elisabeth | 1, May 1849 | AA |
| Schroeder, Georg | Hanselmann, Catharin | 5, Mar. 1848 | G |
| Schroeder, Georg | Altenschulten, Anna | 29, Oct. 1848 | CC |
| Schroeder, Gerhard | VonLaar, Adelheid | 26, Aug. 1849 | AA |
| Schroeder, Heinrich | Korte, Anna | 12, Dec. 1844 | F |
| Schroeder, Heinrich | Caseman, Maria | 11, Sept 1845 | F |
| Schroeder, Heinrich | Lambers, Elisabeth | 28, Jan. 1845 | AA |
| Schroeder, Henry | Bruns, Sophia | 25, Nov. 1847 | RCH |
| Schroeder, J Gerhard | Schmolsmeier, Elis. | 21, July 1842 | F |
| Schroeder, Johan F. | Stueve, Margaretha | 7, May 1846 | F |
| Schroeder, Johan G. | Kuhl, Louisa | 12, Aug. 1849 | AA |
| Schroeder, Johan H. | Paters, A.M. Elis. | 1, June 1843 | F |
| Schroeder, Johan H. | Varel, Maria Adel. | 23, Jan. 1848 | AA |
| Schroeder, Joseph | Korte, Anna M. | 17, May 1849 | AA |
| Schroeder, Karl | Limbold, Lena | 3, Jan. 1847 | RCH |
| Schroeder, Louis | Meyers, Judith | 9, May 1841 | RCH |
| Schroeder, Martin | Willer, Sophia | 14, May 1848 | AA |
| Schroeder, Peter | Reineke, Dorothea | 13, Nov. 1848 | F |
| Schroeder, Rudolph | Kruse, Christina | 3, July 1844 | RCH |
| Schroeder, Wilhelm | Ladekotter, Elis. | 20, Feb. 1838 | FF |
| Schroer, Heinrich | Pelster, Elisabeth | 30, Sept 1849 | II |
| Schroer, Herman H. | Schoppenhorst, Elis. | 9, Sept 1841 | G |
| Schroer, Herman Wm. | Lutterbeck, Catharin | 28, July 1848 | C |
| Schroerlucke Herman | Gentrup, Catharine | 29, Oct. 1846 | C |
| Schroerlucke, Hein. | Borhells, Regina | 13, Apr. 1849 | C |
| Schroerlucke, Henry | Ohmann, Louise | 22, Apr. 1847 | F |
| Schroll, Matthias | Fleckenstein, Doroth | 8, Feb. 1842 | FF |
| Schrorten, Friedrich | Biedinger, Louise | 23, Oct. 1847 | C |
| Schroth, Jacob | Beckley, Walburga | 27, Feb. 1843 | AA |
| Schroth, John | Schontz, Catharine | 1, Mar. 1842 | RCH |
| Schruck, Philipp | Taylor, Lucy D. | 25, Dec. 1833 | I |
| Schrunk, Michael | Doll, Christina | 10, Jan. 1837 | FF |
| Schuck, Johan Jacob | Pfalzgraf, Eva | 20, Aug. 1840 | G |

| Grooms | Brides | Date of Marriage | Code |
|--------|--------|------------------|------|
| ***** | ***** | **** ** ******** | **** |
| Schuder, Heinrich | Verwolth, Christina | 25, Jan. 1848 | CC |
| Schuderer, George | Biegler, Maria C. | 27, Nov. 1845 | RCH |
| Schueler, Zacharias | Schulze, M. Gertrud | 27, Apr. 1847 | CC |
| Schuepferling, John | Voelkel, Eleanor | 15, July 1843 | RCH |
| Schuer, Johan | Schwarz, Dorothea | 25, Feb. 1848 | F |
| Schuerberg, Bernard | Thile, Agnes | 5, Feb. 1839 | FF |
| Schuermann, Bernard | Ernstes, Maria Cath. | 3, June 1845 | AA |
| Schuermann, Johan H. | Moentkehaus, Anna | 24, Apr. 1845 | F |
| Schuette, Albert | Haverkamp, Dina | 7, Feb. 1849 | II |
| Schuette, Arnold | Noelkers, Elisabeth | 27, Dec. 1838 | FF |
| Schuette, J. Gerhard | Hilgefort, Cath. E. | 31, Oct. 1848 | FF |
| Schuh, Christian | Hofegert, Barbara | 16, Aug. 1846 | RCH |
| Schuh, Conrad | Metzger, Barbara | 20, June 1844 | G |
| Schuh, Joseph | Schinner, Francisca | 28, Aug. 1845 | AA |
| Schuh, Nicolaus | Ader, Catharine | 26, Sept 1847 | EE |
| Schuhmacher, Johan | Thamans, Anna M. | 18, Feb. 1849 | RCH |
| Schuhmacher, Theodor | Thamann, A. Gertrud | 18, Feb. 1849 | CC |
| Schuhmaker, Jacob | Seass, Margaret | 18, Dec. 1844 | RCH |
| Schulenberg, Heinric | Schwalemeier, Anna | 21, May 1848 | EE |
| Schulenberg, Wilhelm | Raskin, Caroline | 23, Sept 1849 | A |
| Schuler, Conrad | Wolf, Barbara | 9, Mar. 1846 | G |
| Schuler, Georg | Hutte, Maria Anna | 9, Oct. 1849 | CC |
| Schuler, Johan | Ahrens, Margaretha | 26, Oct. 1847 | EE |
| Schuler, Johan Georg | Haas, Catharine | 18, July 1847 | FF |
| Schuler, Theodor | Haerdel, Josephine | 10, Aug. 1840 | FF |
| Schulhof, Mathias | Dickmann, Catharine | 22, Jan. 1839 | FF |
| Schulte, Bernard | Nordmeyer, Agnes | 18, July 1843 | AA |
| Schulte, Bernard H. | Gessen, Maria Adel. | 23, Sept 1849 | EE |
| Schulte, Casper | Schander, Victoria | 12, Oct. 1837 | FF |
| Schulte, Ernst H.W. | Guenther, A.M. Elis. | 15, Jan. 1845 | F |
| Schulte, Francis F. | Rabbe, Maria Agnes | 17, May 1846 | AA |
| Schulte, Gerhard | Buhmann, Sophia | 26, Oct. 1842 | RCH |
| Schulte, Gerhard H. | Hetlage, Maria | 11, Feb. 1847 | F |
| Schulte, Gerhard H. | Zurline, Theresa | 5, Feb. 1849 | AA |
| Schulte, Gerhard H. | Haverland, Maria M. | 2, Feb. 1846 | EE |
| Schulte, Gerhard R. | Olemueller, Johanna | 1, Feb. 1848 | F |
| Schulte, Heinrich | Naenkers, Maria | 26, Oct. 1841 | F |
| Schulte, Heinrich | Apke, Elisabeth | 8, Feb. 1846 | EE |
| Schulte, Heinrich W. | Heinz, Wilhelmina C. | 10, Feb. 1849 | G |
| Schulte, J. Gerhard | Otten, Elis. (Mrs) | 10, Jan. 1847 | AA |
| Schulte, Johan Bd. | Werri, Catharine | 27, Sept 1842 | AA |
| Schulte, Johan Herm. | Baumann, Anna M. | 1, Feb. 1848 | AA |
| Schulte, John Henry | Koch, Louise | 8, July 1847 | RCH |
| Schulte, Joseph | Stieve, Catharina | 1, Nov. 1836 | FF |
| Schulte, Joseph | Roves, A. Margaretha | 10, Oct. 1848 | FF |
| Schulte, Wilhelm | Meyer, Sophia | 8, Dec. 1842 | F |
| Schulte, Wilhelm | Renne, Catharine M. | 18, Aug. 1846 | AA |
| Schulten, Johan Bd. | Hoppenjans, Christin | 12, Sept 1843 | FF |
| Schultgers, Johan | Linnemann, Thecla | 19, Jan. 1847 | FF |
| Schults, George | Bray, Ellen | 4, Feb. 1834 | RCH |
| Schultz, George | Fasey, Barbara | 12, Oct. 1846 | RCH |
| Schultz, Henry | Litherbury, Mathilda | 10, Sept 1846 | RCH |
| Schultz, John | Berbrecht, Theresa | 28, June 1849 | RCH |
| Schultz, Peter | Weingaertner, Cath. | 24, Nov. 1840 | FF |
| Schultz, Philipp | Dickmeyer, Caroline | 15, Feb. 1848 | G |
| Schulz, Adam | Seibert, Gertrud | 3, Oct. 1848 | EE |
| Schulz, Adrian | Muehl, Apollonia | 8, Mar. 1847 | AA |
| Schulz, Andreas | Reis, Carolina | 9, Oct. 1845 | AA |
| Schulz, Casper | Fuerst, Catharine | 10, May 1846 | AA |
| Schulz, Georg | Weis, Theresa | 7, Nov. 1849 | B |
| Schulz, Johan Martin | Hackel, Margaretha | 2, Sept 1849 | B |
| Schulz, Martin | Zumbahlen, Bernar. | 23, Aug. 1846 | EE |
| Schulz, Michael | Henke, Agnes | 14, Nov. 1847 | AA |
| Schumacher, Caspar | Kuesters, Anna | 3, Sept 1848 | AA |
| Schumacher, Eilert | Johnson, Amelia | 2, Apr. 1847 | RCH |
| Schumacher, Franz H. | Reinecker, Catharina | 28, Jan. 1840 | F |
| Schumacher, Johan | Biermann, Anna Maria | 8, Aug. 1836 | FF |
| Schumacher, Johan | Gerse, Catharine M. | 13, Nov. 1838 | FF |
| Schumacher, Johan | Rapp, Amalia | 10, Apr. 1845 | C |
| Schumacher, Johan A. | Kippes, Maria Anna | 7, Jan. 1849 | EE |
| Schumacher, Johan B. | Metz, Caroline | 19, Sept 1843 | RCH |

| Grooms | Brides | Date of Marriage | Code |
|--------|--------|------------------|------|
| ****** | ****** | **** ** ******** | **** |
| Schumard, Joseph | Crandle, Amanda | 10, July 1849 | RCH |
| Schumard, Thomas | Knott, Mary Ann | 31, Dec. 1842 | RCH |
| Schumpe, Henry Wm. | Niehaus, Anna Elis. | 5, Aug. 1847 | RCH |
| Schun, Georg | Bohl, Elisabeth | 30, May 1848 | AA |
| Schurmann, Gerhard | Husing, Anna Maria | 9, Jan. 1848 | FF |
| Schurmeyer, Friedric | Theilen, Louise | 24, Dec. 1846 | F |
| Schussler, Johan D. | Kobelmann, Friedrika | 24, Feb. 1848 | C |
| Schuster, Friedrich | Henschel, Catharine | 18, Jan. 1844 | C |
| Schuster, Georg | Dick, Maria | 17, Feb. 1849 | G |
| Schute, Heinrich | Uphaus, Maria Anna | 30, Oct. 1843 | FF |
| Schute, Johan Bern. | Hermes, M. Adelheid | 21, Oct. 1849 | FF |
| Schute, Samuel | Nealy, Catharine | 7, Apr. 1847 | RCH |
| Schutt, Johan Bern. | Denger, Anna Maria | 17, Jan. 1847 | EE |
| Schutte, Anton | Warburg, A. Maria | 6, June 1848 | II |
| Schutte, August | Meyer, Anna Maria | 11, July 1848 | EE |
| Schutter, Johan | Berkley, Crescentia | 8, Feb. 1841 | FF |
| Schuvert, Michael | Steinmueller, Barb. | 17, Aug. 1835 | FF |
| Schuyler, Alfred | Brown, Ann E. | 26, Dec. 1843 | RCH |
| Schwab, Georg | Vorgott, Maria | 17, Apr. 1843 | G |
| Schwab, Heinrich | Kuetting, Theresa | 20, Aug. 1846 | EE |
| Schwab, Lebold | Baumann, Sarah | 2, Oct. 1848 | RCH |
| Schwab, Severin | Herzog, Paulina | 1, Oct. 1848 | AA |
| Schwager, Jacob | Guenzel, Anna Maria | 30, Sept 1849 | G |
| Schwake, Heinrich | Degner, Maria | 11, Apr. 1844 | F |
| Schwaller, Francis | Trautmann, Agatha | 4, Oct. 1847 | CC |
| Schwallie, Jacob | Krenner, Magdalena | 19, Jan. 1849 | EE |
| Schwalmeyer, Heinric | Strueve, Maria | 2, Mar. 1843 | F |
| Schwaneke, J. Georg | Kranhold, Adelheid | 28, Sept 1848 | F |
| Schwanholt, Friedric | Rahe, Mary Engel | 28, Oct. 1845 | F |
| Schwarts, August | Moore, Julianna | 13, Oct. 1822 | RCH |
| Schwartz, Bernard | Mansheim, Catharine | 31, Jan. 1843 | FF |
| Schwartz, Dominick | Dumont, Margaret | 16, July 1844 | FF |
| Schwartz, Friedrich | Wollens, Margaretha | 10, Feb. 1837 | F |
| Schwartz, Friedrich | Weatherby, Mary | 8, Apr. 1847 | RCH |
| Schwartz, Johan | Halmi, Anna Elis. | 11, July 1847 | RCH |
| Schwartz, Johan | Heilmann, Barbara | 25, Nov. 1849 | EE |
| Schwartze, August J. | Moore, Maria | 4, Feb. 1818 | RCH |
| Schwartzmann, Albert | Meyers, Lisette | 17, Sept 1848 | G |
| Schwarz, Alexander | Ganda, Catharina | 2, May 1848 | FF |
| Schwarz, Coelestin | Dieters, Agnes | 16, July 1844 | FF |
| Schwarz, Frank | Schmidt, Anna Maria | 1, July 1845 | AA |
| Schwarz, Georg | Shives, Maria | 31, Dec. 1847 | G |
| Schwarz, Georg Hein. | Stroebel, Margaretha | 1, Sept 1844 | G |
| Schwarz, Johan | Beuenermann, Mina | 25, June 1843 | C |
| Schwarz, Johan | Wald, Matilda | 18, Jan. 1848 | EE |
| Schwarz, Max | Kukumas, Cecilia | 7, Jan. 1849 | RCH |
| Schwarz, Wenselaus | Linnemann, Christina | 29, July 1847 | FF |
| Schwecke, Ludwig | Wesselmann, Amalia | 4, Sept 1845 | F |
| Schwegmann, Bernard | Huels, Anna Maria | 23, Sept 1846 | AA |
| Schwegmann, Christ. | Fossgroene, Maria | 26, May 1840 | FF |
| Schwegmann, Heinrich | Retmer, Maria | 18, July 1836 | FF |
| Schwegmann, Heinrich | Tegeler, M Elisabeth | 7, Nov. 1837 | FF |
| Schwegmann, Heinrich | Kroeger, Helena | 24, Nov. 1844 | FF |
| Schwegmann, Johan G. | Brogmann, Anna Maria | 28, Nov. 1837 | FF |
| Schwegmann, Johan H. | Hobestadt, Elisabeth | 1, Feb. 1842 | FF |
| Schwegmann, Joseph | Klaus, Clara | 5, Jan. 1836 | FF |
| Schwegmann, Joseph | Lahmers, Lisette | 13, Apr. 1846 | RCH |
| Schweibel, Joseph | Dilick, Margaretha | 9, May 1847 | G |
| Schweigert, Joseph P | Veit, Gertrud | 17, Oct. 1847 | EE |
| Schwein, Ernst M. | Schroer, Wilhelmina | 8, Mar. 1849 | C |
| Schwein, Friedrich | Heyl, Maria | 18, June 1848 | C |
| Schwein, Jacob | Keddel, Elisabeth | 14, Mar. 1842 | RCH |
| Schweine, Jacob | Seigwolf, Anna M. | 27, Nov. 1848 | RCH |
| Schweinfuss, Anton | Rottinghaus, Agnes | 14, Jan. 1836 | FF |
| Schweir, Michael | Schamerloh, Sophia | 26, Apr. 1849 | G |
| Schweitzer, Heinrich | Deirmann, Christina | 19, Nov. 1848 | RCH |
| Schweitzer, J. Jacob | Hess, Johanna | 23, Sept 1849 | G |
| Schweizer, Adam | Keller, Rosina | 10, Aug. 1835 | FF |
| Schweizer, Blasius | Nunn, Francisca | 22, July 1839 | FF |
| Schweizer, Gottlieb | Metzger, Friedricka | 15, Nov. 1849 | A |
| Schwenck, J. Martin | Weishaupt, Agnes | 13, Sept 1847 | RCH |

| Grooms<br>****** | Brides<br>****** | Date of Marriage<br>****, ** ******** | Code<br>**** |
|---|---|---|---|
| Schwengel, Heinrich | Enghaus, Caroline | 27, Nov. 1845 | F |
| Schwenker, Adam | Weismueller, Marg. | 20, Jan. 1849 | CC |
| Schwenker, Fried. Wm | Schumacher, Maria E. | 18, May 1843 | F |
| Schwenker, Wilhelm | Bruning, Johanna | 24, Nov. 1846 | F |
| Schwenter, Christ. F | Rosengarten, M. Elis | 30, Nov. 1847 | C |
| Schwepmann, Bernard | Winstring, Sophia F. | 5, Oct. 1848 | B |
| Schwermann, Franz J. | Fresenberg, Catharin | 7, Feb. 1849 | II |
| Schwermann, Joseph | Epke, Elisabeth | 21, Nov. 1847 | FF |
| Schwertmann, Heinric | Bleckmann, A.M. | 16, Sept 1849 | II |
| Schwettmann, Heinr. | Winterberg, Theresa | 17, June 1848 | FF |
| Schwiers, Georg Hein | Schwiers, M Adelheid | 25, July 1844 | F |
| Schwind, Christian | Fricker, Catharine | 8, Aug. 1847 | RCH |
| Schwindt, Philipp | Meier, Elisabeth | 23, Feb. 1849 | RCH |
| Schwineker, Heinrich | Huessing, M. Theresa | 14, Nov. 1843 | FF |
| Schwinheer, Johan H. | Schottelkotte, Maria | 5, Nov. 1844 | FF |
| Schwitzer, Johan | Fischer, Anna | 31, Dec. 1843 | RCH |
| Schwitzle, George | Hester, Catharine | 21, Sept 1836 | RCH |
| Schwoeppe, Edward | Lenges, Catharine | 9, Jan. 1844 | AA |
| Schwor, Louis | Schrokamp, Louisa | 16, June 1849 | FF |
| Sclicker, Jacob | Kop, Margaretha | 9, Feb. 1847 | RCH |
| Scofield, David | Phyfrin, Elisabeth | 3, Oct. 1844 | RCH |
| Scofield, John | Lindley, Maranda | 14, Apr. 1839 | RCH |
| Scofield, John | Ketchum, Phebe | 21, Mar. 1848 | RCH |
| Scofield, Richard | Paton, Nancy | 1, Aug. 1834 | RCH |
| Scoggin, Hiram | Stone, Emily | 18, Aug. 1846 | RCH |
| Scogin, Levi | Nugen, Mary | 21, Jan. 1838 | RCH |
| Scogin, William | Kerr, Margaret | 29, Dec. 1836 | RCH |
| Scoites, Theodor | Kovermann, Sophia | 24, June 1849 | EE |
| Scolins, James | Cassner, Margaret | 13, May 1838 | RCH |
| Scolp, Joseph | Porter, Mary | 3, Apr. 1832 | RCH |
| Sconce, George S. | Cheesman, Susan | 27, Mar. 1836 | RCH |
| Scothorn, Esrom | Mills, Lydia | 26, Nov. 1845 | RCH |
| Scott, Alex. | Rowe, Mary J. | 23, Mar. 1847 | RCH |
| Scott, Alexander | Whitehouse, Dinah | 14, Feb. 1843 | RCH |
| Scott, Andrew | Williams, Catharine | 20, June 1833 | RCH |
| Scott, Charles | Hawkins, Mary | 4, June 1835 | RCH |
| Scott, Charles | O'Hara, Mary | 16, Feb. 1846 | RCH |
| Scott, Edgar | Armstrong, Martha A. | 13, May 1842 | RCH |
| Scott, George W. | Ballard, Mary E. | 11, May 1848 | RCH |
| Scott, Gustav | Dunolds, Elisabeth | 21, Jan. 1847 | RCH |
| Scott, Hardy | Horton, Hannah | 1, Jan. 1844 | RCH |
| Scott, Herod | Wolf, Catharine | 12, Dec. 1833 | RCH |
| Scott, Jacob | Amos, Cynthia | 29, Oct. 1836 | RCH |
| Scott, John | Stevens, Jane | 12, Oct. 1841 | RCH |
| Scott, John | Brown, Milley | 24, June 1846 | RCH |
| Scott, John | Harris, Margaret | 28, June 1846 | RCH |
| Scott, John | Dudley, Mary | 23, Dec. 1849 | RCH |
| Scott, John Gray | Doggin, Jane | 23, Dec. 1822 | I |
| Scott, John W. | Sargent, Elisabeth | 7, Dec. 1835 | RCH |
| Scott, Josiah | Austin, Susan | 4, May 1846 | RCH |
| Scott, Parker | Munroe, Julia Ann | 12, Mar. 1837 | RCH |
| Scott, Richard | Cook, Jane | 16, Sept 1841 | RCH |
| Scott, Samuel | Scott, Jane | 21, July 1847 | RCH |
| Scott, Thomas A. | Pelsor, Margaret | 6, May 1838 | RCH |
| Scott, Thomas J. | Wayts, Sarah | 12, Aug. 1846 | RCH |
| Scott, William | Ogden, Martha | 2, Mar. 1842 | RCH |
| Scott, William | Reilly, Anna | 17, Apr. 1848 | RCH |
| Scott, William | Dickson, Jane | 3, Mar. 1849 | RCH |
| Scovill, Amon | Whipple, Harriet A. | 19, Dec. 1842 | RCH |
| Scowden, Theodore | Stewart, Rosetta | 16, June 1836 | RCH |
| Scraggs, Thomas B. | Calaway, Elisabeth | 30, May 1835 | RCH |
| Scribner, Orison | Carson, Sarah Jane | 3, Apr. 1847 | RCH |
| Scudder, Alfred | Lence, Ann | 7, May 1836 | RCH |
| Scudder, B. Sidney | Potter, Anne J. | 10, Feb. 1847 | D |
| Scudder, Clark | Dunn, Mary | 28, Sept 1818 | RCH |
| Scudder, Moses | Patterson, Anna | 5, June 1821 | RCH |
| Scudder, William | Carter, Polly | 12, Nov. 1818 | RCH |
| Scudder, William | Bruster, Ruth | 22, Apr. 1821 | RCH |
| Scudmore, Godwin | Colly, Caroline | 15, Sept 1849 | RCH |
| Scull, | Hamel, Eliza | 23, May 1822 | RCH |
| Scull, David M. | Lee, Margaret | 6, Dec. 1833 | RCH |

| Grooms<br>***** | Brides<br>***** | Date of Marriage<br>**** ** ******* | Code<br>**** |
|---|---|---|---|
| Scull, James | Mullin, Almira | 31, Dec. 1848 | RCH |
| Scull, John | James, Phoebe | 8, Feb. 1835 | RCH |
| Scull, John H. | Ware, Elisabeth | 27, Mar. 1849 | RCH |
| Scully, John | Kain, Joann M. | 16, Nov. 1843 | BB |
| Seal, Enoch H. | Riss, Mary Ann | 6, May 1839 | RCH |
| Seales, Alexander | Haley, Catharine | 16, May 1847 | RCH |
| Seaman, Francis | Cunningham, Sarah | 15, Apr. 1824 | RCH |
| Seaman, Henry | Smith, Georgetta | 30, June 1840 | RCH |
| Seams, Philipp | Clang, Julia | 25, Sept 1834 | RCH |
| Searle, John | Ostler, Ann | 13, Aug. 1849 | RCH |
| Sears, Abraham | Philherber, Elis. | 29, July 1819 | RCH |
| Sears, Abraham | Buchanan, Matilda | 6, Mar. 1821 | RCH |
| Sears, Cephas | Perry, Georgianna | 28, May 1848 | RCH |
| Sears, Clinton | Brooks, Angeline | 1, June 1842 | RCH |
| Sears, Gideon | Thompson, Catharine | 20, Nov. 1842 | RCH |
| Sears, Joseph | Pollack, Matilda | 14, Sept 1844 | RCH |
| Searuger, Christian | Kollmeyer, Maria | 13, Apr. 1846 | G |
| Seashotts, George | Love, Mary Jane | 14, Nov. 1847 | RCH |
| Sebastian, Benjamin | Lebille, Harriet | 15, Feb. 1846 | RCH |
| Sebold, John G. | Noble, Catharine | 12, June 1840 | BB |
| Secretan, Mark L. | Dutort, Charlotte | 2, July 1849 | RCH |
| Secrist, Hamilton | Eidemeier, Sarah | 9, June 1846 | RCH |
| Secrist, James | Spencer, Emily | 26, Oct. 1843 | RCH |
| Secrist, John | Corbin, Elisabeth | 2, Dec. 1832 | RCH |
| Secrist, Joseph | VanSant, Theresa A. | 23, Dec. 1840 | RCH |
| Secrist, Peter | Munkey, Lydia Ann | 13, July 1843 | RCH |
| Sedam, Cornelius | ----, ---- | 5, Feb. 1824 | RCH |
| Sedam, Henry W. | Seeds, | 1, July 1824 | RCH |
| Seddens, James | Williams, Remitha | 3, Aug. 1842 | RCH |
| Sedela, Joseph | Adam, Elisabeth | 10, May 1847 | RCH |
| Sedgwick, Barney | Duncan, Lucinda | 2, Sept 1834 | RCH |
| See, Erasmus | Buchanan, Isabella | 17, Apr. 1848 | RCH |
| Seebee, John | Daley, Selina | 21, June 1837 | RCH |
| Seeberger, Isaac | Schnell, Louise | 27, May 1844 | G |
| Seebers, Herman | Kohl, Mary | 16, Nov. 1849 | F |
| Seed, Samuel | Garner, Jane | 24, Jan. 1846 | RCH |
| Seeger, Daniel | Stevens, Elisabeth | 26, Feb. 1846 | C |
| Seeger, J. Theodor | Rolfers, Wilhelmina | 9, Oct. 1845 | FF |
| Seeger, Ludwig | Langots, Christina | 12, July 1847 | C |
| Seegers, Francis | Mueller, Eva | 11, Jan. 1848 | AA |
| Seele, August | Wrassmann, Maria | 18, Oct. 1846 | F |
| Seelhorst, Johan H. | Olding, Anna Gertrud | 5, June 1849 | FF |
| Seelig, Conrad | Wiest, Theresa | 5, Oct. 1847 | EE |
| Seelig, Samuel | Winter, Amelia | 29, Mar. 1849 | RCH |
| Seeling, Heinrich | Dubmann, Maria E. | 28, Dec. 1843 | G |
| Seely, Alfred | Spahr, Rachel | 13, Feb. 1844 | RCH |
| Seely, Silas M. | Harris Ann | 11, Oct. 1832 | RCH |
| Seely, William | Spaulding, Sophronia | 30, Oct. 1848 | BB |
| Seemueller, Georg | Meyer, Kunigunda | 17, Aug. 1845 | AA |
| Seevers, Heinrich | Zurmuhlen, Maria | 3, Apr. 1845 | F |
| Sefert, Charles H. | Lohmann, Catharine | 2, Sept 1847 | RCH |
| Seffert, Henry Wm. | Krenning, M. Louise | 15, July 1847 | F |
| Seger, Bernard | Mueller, M. Adelheid | 27, Oct. 1840 | FF |
| Seger, Heinrich | Firkamp, Elisabeth | 13, Oct. 1840 | FF |
| Segers, Johan Herman | Niebuhr, Maria Anna | 8, Feb. 1842 | FF |
| Sehi, Gottfried | Jung, Maria Anna | 1, Feb. 1844 | FF |
| Sehlhorst, Joseph | Reineke, Gertrud | 1, Nov. 1848 | II |
| Sehon, Edwin W. | McLean, Caroline | 4, Sept 1833 | RCH |
| Seiberling, Adam | Ott, Barbara | 10, Jan. 1843 | FF |
| Seibert, Adam | Gass, Regina | 16, Nov. 1846 | EE |
| Seibert, Joseph | Geble, Elisabeth | 17, Nov. 1849 | EE |
| Seibert, Martin | Fischer, Anna Maria | 31, May 1842 | FF |
| Seibert, Nicolaus | Leistmaein, Catharin | 23, Feb. 1848 | C |
| Seidenbach, Lehman | Siegel, Caroline | 30, May 1849 | RCH |
| Seidenfaden, George | Schlenck, Margaretha | 17, Aug. 1845 | RCH |
| Seifert, Adam | Hefte, Margaretha | 25, Nov. 1841 | FF |
| Seifert, Andreas | Reinhart, Catharina | 27, Oct. 1840 | FF |
| Seifert, Philipp | Seifert, Margaretha | 27, Nov. 1845 | C |
| Seifner, Peter | Likich, Anna Maria | 20, Feb. 1848 | EE |
| Seifried, Adam | Gebhardt, Margaretha | 11, July 1841 | G |
| Seifried, Johan | Littig, Margaretha | 13, Dec. 1849 | A |

| Grooms | Brides | Date of Marriage | Code |
|--------|--------|------------------|------|
| Seiger, Franz | Winters, Margaret | 2, Dec. 1844 | RCH |
| Seigerl, Wendel | Fischer, Elisabeth | 14, May 1848 | EE |
| Seiler, Gregor | Joerker, Wilhelmina | 3, Nov. 1846 | AA |
| Seiler, Joseph | Grundmann, Susanna | 1, Nov. 1848 | AA |
| Seim, Johan Casper | Wackenrod, Anna M. | 9, July 1846 | C |
| Seiner, Ferdinand | Horst, Barbara | 6, Dec. 1836 | FF |
| Seip, John | Moog, Catharine | 1841 | RCH |
| Seissle, Thomas | Seward, Mary | 21, Oct. 1846 | RCH |
| Seiter, Joseph | Woeffel, Maria | 18, Aug. 1845 | FF |
| Seiter, Nicolaus | Stadelmann, Margaret | 13, Nov. 1845 | FF |
| Seitz, Conrad | Puhl, Barbara | 8, Nov. 1843 | C |
| Seitz, Conrad | Haberline, Margaret | 27, Nov. 1845 | RCH |
| Seitz, J. Friedrich | Weibel, Anna Maria | 20, Aug. 1848 | C |
| Seitzer, Georg | Pistner, Margaretha | 22, Feb. 1846 | AA |
| Seivers, Heinrich | Kuers, Elisabeth | 28, Nov. 1849 | F |
| Selden, Alanson | Johnson, Louisa D. | 19, Sept 1822 | RCH |
| Selden, Charles | Gellingham, Henriett | 4, Nov. 1845 | RCH |
| Selig, Johan | Schneider, Dorothea | 10, Apr. 1845 | C |
| Selinger, Johan | VonderHeide, A.(Mrs) | 16, June 1840 | FF |
| Selinger, Valetin | Hovestadt, Sophia | 2, Apr. 1839 | FF |
| Selker, Wenceslaus | Kramer, Elisabeth | 16, June 1846 | AA |
| Sellers, Jacob | Campbell, Frances | 4, Dec. 1844 | RCH |
| Sellmeyer, J. Heinr. | Bruckenschmidt, El. | 21, May 1840 | FF |
| Sellwood, James | Dawe, Elisabeth H. | 2, Oct. 1837 | RCH |
| Selman, Franklin | Noble, Priscilla | 22, June 1837 | RCH |
| Selmon, Garrett | Howell, Alice | 5, Dec. 1841 | RCH |
| Selmon, Garrett | Lee, Anna Elisabeth | 26, June 1844 | RCH |
| Selmon, John | Nuts, Mary Ellen | 14, July 1846 | RCH |
| Selser, Lewis | Greenhaw, Rachel | 2, Feb. 1838 | RCH |
| Selves, George | Luck, Sarah | 1, May 1834 | RCH |
| Semon, Friedrich | Salzner, Sophia | 9, June 1846 | RCH |
| Semon, Palemon | McClain, Martha J. | 7, Jan. 1846 | RCH |
| Sen, Philipp | Hand, Thekla | 27, Jan. 1846 | RCH |
| Senard, James | Cobon, Lucinda | 14, Aug. 1834 | RCH |
| Sendelbach, Johan F. | Illig, Catharine | 2, May 1848 | EE |
| Sendfeld, Herman | Tenkamp, Mina | 30, Sept 1849 | EE |
| Senger, Tobias | Keller, Josephina | 25, Sept 1849 | EE |
| Senico, James | Finkbine, Mary | 14, Jan. 1835 | RCH |
| Sening, Martin D. | Holt, Hannah | May 1839 | RCH |
| Senior, Abraham | Mayfield, Regina | 24, May 1848 | RCH |
| Senior, William | Fisher, Martha | 26, Mar. 1845 | RCH |
| Senk---, J. | Creach, Charlotte | 16, Aug. 1845 | RCH |
| Senn, Philipp | Hund, Thekla | 27, Jan. 1845 | AA |
| Senz, Valentin | Stoehr, Anna Maria | 6, Aug. 1848 | EE |
| Seopold, James | Hasper, Elisabeth | 20, Mar. 1820 | RCH |
| Sepp, Wilhelm | Baer, Catharine | 27, Mar. 1845 | A |
| Septimus, Nimrod | Goshorn, Rachel | 7, Sept 1841 | RCH |
| Serenbitz, Florenz | Voelker, M Catharina | 29, Aug. 1848 | C |
| Serriskotter, Theo. | Riegelmeyer, Clara | 30, Dec. 1849 | AA |
| Serter, Arthur | Malone, Mary | 26, Jan. 1837 | RCH |
| Serves, Heinrich | Lammer, Maria Magdal | 15, Oct. 1846 | EE |
| Service, Henry | Kinney, Keziah | 18, Mar. 1847 | RCH |
| Settle, William | Henn, Mary Jane | 21, May 1847 | RCH |
| Sevain, | Burchill, Mary Ann | 20, Sept 1849 | RCH |
| Severs, Johan | Molendick, Henrietta | 1, Jan. 1847 | EE |
| Seward, Daniel | Wolverton, Theodocia | 20, Jan. 1833 | RCH |
| Seward, Daniel | Greenleaf, Matilda | 22, Apr. 1843 | RCH |
| Seward, F. Heinrich | Sliming, Anna Maria | 9, Jan. 1848 | RCH |
| Seward, James | Richey, Elisabeth | 12, Aug. 1837 | RCH |
| Seward, Martin | Cox, Ann | 3, Oct. 1841 | RCH |
| Seward, Martin | Littell, Mary Jane | 22, Jan. 1846 | RCH |
| Seward, Matthew | King, Margaret | 26, Feb. 1835 | RCH |
| Seward, Matthew | Covill, Sophia | 9, Jan. 1848 | RCH |
| Seward, William | Hachwelder, Jerasha | 5, Sept 1849 | RCH |
| Sewards, John B. | Swallow, Mary W. | 7, Feb. 1818 | RCH |
| Sewe--, John | Morgan, Sarah | 16, Apr. 1825 | RCH |
| Sexton, Richard | Clypoole, Ann | 7, Feb. 1835 | RCH |
| Seybold, Emanuel | Zimmermann, Catharin | 31, May 1847 | RCH |
| Seymour, Manville | Taylor, Catharine | 3, Sept 1842 | RCH |
| Sh---, James | Coons, Elisabeth | 7, Dec. 1826 | RCH |
| Shaddinger, George | Ford, Ellen | Oct. 1844 | RCH |

| Grooms | Brides | Date of Marriage | Code |
|--------|--------|------------------|------|
| ****** | ****** | **** ** ******** | **** |
| Shaddinger, George | Rose, Isabella | 13, Aug. 1846 | RCH |
| Shaddinger, Joseph | Dupont, Charlotte | 2, Nov. 1842 | RCH |
| Shaff, David | Runion, Lucinda | 23, Sept 1836 | RCH |
| Shaffer, Adam | Weaver, Caroline | 20, Mar. 1843 | RCH |
| Shaffer, Daniel | Prisco, Rosanna | 3, Feb. 1818 | RCH |
| Shaffer, David H. | Robinson, Jane C. | 7, Oct. 1835 | RCH |
| Shaffer, Johan | Henke, A. Adelhei | 1, Oct. 1846 | RCH |
| Shais, Knowles | Andrew, Hannah | 14, Mar. 1822 | RCH |
| Shallow, Patrick | Thorp, Elizabeth | 23, Sept 1849 | GG |
| Shaman, John | Filson, Elisabeth | 26, Feb. 1818 | RCH |
| Shanahan, Daniel | Brown, Honora | 3, Oct. 1847 | BB |
| Shanahan, John | Carroll, Catharine | 22, Nov. 1849 | GG |
| Shanar, Henry | Kelsay, Susannah | 7, Aug. 1847 | RCH |
| Shane, Henry | Pearson, Sarah | 18, Aug. 1846 | RCH |
| Shane, Patrick | Crowley, Nancy | 29, Mar. 1842 | BB |
| Shane, Samuel W. | Leake, Mary | 26, Sept 1848 | RCH |
| Shaner, Stephan | Dunbar, Tamson | 13, Jan. 1842 | RCH |
| Shanklin, William | Hamonell, Rebecca | 26, Mar. 1838 | RCH |
| Shannon, Martin A. | Lewis, Catharine E. | 7, May 1840 | I |
| Shannon, Samuel | Stewart, Elisabeth | 20, Apr. 1823 | RCH |
| Sharkey, Patrick | Flanagan, Catharine | 1, Aug. 1839 | BB |
| Sharp, Abraham | Souter, Charity | 3, Jan. 1833 | RCH |
| Sharp, James | Jordan, Rebecca Ann | 29, Feb. 1832 | RCH |
| Sharp, Jefferson | Duncan, Mugary | 23, Mar. 1834 | RCH |
| Sharp, John | Marsh, Nancy | 14, June 1821 | RCH |
| Sharp, John | Jordon, Harriet J. | 2, Jan. 1833 | RCH |
| Sharp, John M. | Mahardy, Mary | 9, Aug. 1845 | BB |
| Sharp, Morris | Williams, Parthena | 25, Apr. 1833 | RCH |
| Sharp, Nathan | Morrell, Charlotte | 1, Oct. 1835 | RCH |
| Sharp, Orrice | Cennen, Eleanor | 26, Feb. 1833 | RCH |
| Sharp, Peter | Bevins, Polley | 2, June 1824 | RCH |
| Sharp, Thomas | Wood, Elisabeth | 22, Mar. 1836 | RCH |
| Sharp, William | Osburn, Phoebe | 22, July 1834 | RCH |
| Sharpless, | Laye---, Margaret | 21, Nov. 1822 | RCH |
| Sharpless, Alfred J. | Holmes, Ellen | 26, Dec. 1848 | D |
| Sharpless, Nicolaus | Simmons, Frances | 2, June 1836 | RCH |
| Sharrer, Jacob | McNeeley, Rebecca | 11, May 1824 | RCH |
| Sharret, August | Garretson, Sarah(Mrs | 15, Sept 1840 | BB |
| Shaver, Stephen | Williams, Josephine | 13, Oct. 1844 | RCH |
| Shaw, | Tice, Sally | 2, Apr. 1818 | RCH |
| Shaw, Abner | Lemare, Mary Ann | 6, June 1842 | RCH |
| Shaw, Albin | Griffith, Huldah | 7, Mar. 1833 | RCH |
| Shaw, Alvin | Breitenstein, Rachel | 18, Feb. 1849 | RCH |
| Shaw, Artemus | Coat, Elisabeth H. | 21, Jan. 1836 | RCH |
| Shaw, B.J. | Smith, Sarah | 30, Apr. 1832 | RCH |
| Shaw, Charles G. | Milford, Susannah | 6, Dec. 1832 | RCH |
| Shaw, Denison | Bloxom, Margaret | 2, July 1835 | RCH |
| Shaw, Denison | Higdon, Sarah | 28, May 1844 | RCH |
| Shaw, Henry | Coddan, Elisabeth | 17, Jan. 1841 | RCH |
| Shaw, Henry S. | Baymiller, Mary T. | 29, Sept 1836 | D |
| Shaw, Jesse | Moore, Catharine | 23, June 1844 | RCH |
| Shaw, John | Webb, Ida | 14, Apr. 1837 | RCH |
| Shaw, Joseph E. | Tapp, Emily Jane | 19, Apr. 1849 | RCH |
| Shaw, Plinn | Cassage, Julia A. | 28, Dec. 1837 | RCH |
| Shaw, Sacher | Grimes, Massa | 2, May 1838 | RCH |
| Shaw, Silas | Folick, Mary Ann | 16, Nov. 1845 | RCH |
| Shaw, Thomas | Ogg, Eveline | 12, May 1834 | RCH |
| Shaw, William | McKane, Mary | 3, Sept 1843 | RCH |
| Shawk, Abel | Marsh, Phoebe Ann | 2, May 1849 | RCH |
| Shay, James D. | Murphy, Mary | 9, Dec. 1849 | GG |
| Shay, John | Hill, Sarah | 10, Jan. 1841 | RCH |
| Shay, John R. | Pook, Ellen M. | 25, Mar. 1838 | RCH |
| Shay, William | Hill, Martha | 6, Apr. 1842 | RCH |
| Shaylock, Hezekiah | Sayres, Hannah | 14, Oct. 1832 | RCH |
| Shays, John W. | Crane, Susan T. | 4, Mar. 1844 | RCH |
| Shea, James | Lynch, Elisabeth | 9, Sept 1849 | GG |
| Shea, Robert | Wright, Mary | 18, Sept 1836 | RCH |
| Shearer, Ebenezer | Conklin, Elisabeth | 25, May 1826 | RCH |
| Shearer, Henry | Kleabern, Catharine | 7, Feb. 1847 | RCH |
| Shearer, Jacob | Imhoff, Mary Ann | 15, Dec. 1833 | RCH |
| Shearer, Job | Isgrigg, Fanny | 22, Aug. 1849 | RCH |

| Grooms<br>***** | Brides<br>***** | Date of Marriage<br>**** ** ******** | Code<br>**** |
|---|---|---|---|
| Shearer, John | Watkins, Sarah Jane | 5, Sept 1848 | RCH |
| Shearon, Roland | Jennings, Lucinda | 17, June 1832 | RCH |
| Sheehan, David | Burke, Ann | 29, Apr. 1849 | BB |
| Sheehan, John | Buckley, Mary | 27, Apr. 1849 | RCH |
| Sheeler, Leonard | Gustaden, Sophia | 30, Oct. 1845 | RCH |
| Sheets, Adam | Karnes, Mary | 30, Nov. 1833 | RCH |
| Sheets, Jacob | Ashbury, Anna Maria | 1, Jan. 1849 | RCH |
| Sheets, William | Heritage, Cornelia | 24, Apr. 1842 | RCH |
| Shehan, Michael | Shandley, Margaret | 1, Nov. 1845 | BB |
| Shekin, John | Bonnel, Jane | 1, Oct. 1835 | RCH |
| Shelby, James E. | Duennen, Margaret | 22, Aug. 1833 | RCH |
| Sheldon, David | Cameron, Mary | 2, July 1844 | RCH |
| Sheldon, George | Jones, Harriet | 20, May 1847 | RCH |
| Sheldon, James | Merry, Emeline | 14, June 1842 | RCH |
| Sheldon, Moses | Hundford, Mary | 27, Apr. 1842 | RCH |
| Sheldon, William B. | Ewing, Rody | 27, Aug. 1818 | RCH |
| Shell, Jonas | Warren, Catharine | 15, May 1833 | RCH |
| Shelleck, M. | Storms, Mary | 3, May 1838 | RCH |
| Shelman, John | Cochran, Sarah | 28, Apr. 1837 | RCH |
| Shelterly, John | Gamon, Sarah | 24, Feb. 1820 | RCH |
| Shepeklaus, Friedric | Pott, Mina | 11, May 1848 | RCH |
| Sheperd, Chauncey | Armstrong, Elisabeth | 5, Apr. 1841 | RCH |
| Shephard, John | Barry, Joanne | 27, June 1842 | BB |
| Shephard, William | Mahoney, Mary | 1, Nov. 1841 | BB |
| Shepherd, Daniel | Story, Rachel | 12, Dec. 1844 | RCH |
| Shepherd, David | Engloth, Elisabeth | 18, Jan. 1821 | RCH |
| Shepherd, George | Stibbins, Sarah | 26, Jan. 1819 | RCH |
| Shepherd, Stebbens | Moore, Elisabeth | 11, Dec. 1841 | RCH |
| Shepherd, Stibbins | Skillmann, Mary Jane | 2, Nov. 1848 | RCH |
| Sheppard, Belle R. | Hinkle, Elisabeth | 28, Mar. 1836 | RCH |
| Sheppard, Casper | Ward, Anna Jordan | 22, Dec. 1842 | BB |
| Sheppard, Charles | Stoughton, Mary Jane | 19, Dec. 1844 | RCH |
| Sheppard, Edwin | Ewing, Mary | 19, Dec. 1848 | RCH |
| Sheppard, Isaac | White, Mary | 1, Apr. 1842 | RCH |
| Sheppard, James | Brown, Ann | 25, May 1844 | RCH |
| Sheppard, John | Corbly, Elisabeth | 15, Apr. 1846 | RCH |
| Sheppard, Morris | Reilly, Catharine | 9, Jan. 1838 | RCH |
| Sheppard, Samuel | Jones, Nancy | 29, Aug. 1835 | RCH |
| Sherder, Jacob | Jerger, Elisabeth | 3, Nov. 1842 | AA |
| Sherer, John | Cardingley, Mercian | 22, July 1842 | RCH |
| Sherer, William | Williams, Polly | 3, Sept 1822 | RCH |
| Sheridan, Charles | McCoy, Mary | 28, May 1838 | D |
| Sheridan, Martin | Mullan, Ann | 30, Jan. 1849 | RCH |
| Sheriff, Anthony | Lovejoy, Sarah | 31, Dec. 1846 | RCH |
| Sherlock, Thomas | Redhead, Martha A. | 27, Mar. 1847 | RCH |
| Sherlock, Thomas J. | Bruen, Jane | 24, Dec. 1847 | RCH |
| Sherman, Abel | McGuyne, Ann | 5, May 1831 | RCH |
| Sherman, Henry | Blodgett, Elisabeth | 4, Nov. 1843 | RCH |
| Sherman, Ira | Sq---, Amelia | 24, Mar. 1819 | RCH |
| Sherman, Robert | Norton, Margaret(Mrs | 1, Sept 1836 | RCH |
| Sherod, James | Allison, Mary Ann | 2, Apr. 1844 | RCH |
| Sherrod, Calvin | Hoffmann, Caroline | 30, Aug. 1840 | BB |
| Sherwood, Orison | Keyler, Deborah | 3, Feb. 1820 | RCH |
| Sherwood, Robert R. | Hughes, Charlotte | 8, Apr. 1844 | BB |
| Shettinger, Johan | Schaefer, Appolonia | 22, Aug. 1844 | C |
| Sheven, Thomas | Anderson, Sarah Jane | 23, June 1836 | RCH |
| Shewa--, Albert | Addis, Isabella | 1, May 1839 | RCH |
| Shewan, George | Mason, | 27, June 1839 | RCH |
| Shey, E. | Katon, Martha | 7, Sept 1834 | RCH |
| Shield, George | Tiley, Elisabeth | 20, Oct. 1833 | RCH |
| Shields, Charles | Soliffe, Lavina | 7, Dec. 1826 | RCH |
| Shields, Edwin | Mooney, Jane | 12, Sept 1837 | RCH |
| Shields, John | Huffmann, Margaret | 6, July 1842 | RCH |
| Shields, John | Phelan, Mary | 3, Sept 1849 | BB |
| Shields, John F. | Denison, Elis. Jane | 9, Oct. 1834 | RCH |
| Shields, Patrick | Kennedy, Elisabeth | 20, Feb. 1844 | RCH |
| Shields, Patrick | Holliby, Elisabeth | 17, Mar. 1844 | BB |
| Shields, William | Jones, Ann | 21, May 1833 | RCH |
| Shillito, George | Bernard, Sarah Elis. | 17, Mar. 1836 | I |
| Shinder, Valentin | Giltel, Mary | 26, Jan. 1843 | RCH |
| Shiner, Thomas | Shoben, Elisabeth | 11, Sept 1832 | RCH |

| Grooms ****** | Brides ****** | Date of Marriage **** ** ******** | Code **** |
|---|---|---|---|
| Shinn, Vincent | Nile, Mary | 21, May 1838 | RCH |
| Ship, Gerhard | Rose, Clara | 11, Sept 1838 | FF |
| Ship, Thomas | Thornton, Ellen | 13, Oct. 1844 | RCH |
| Shiplee, John | Snyder, Mary | 16, Nov. 1837 | RCH |
| Shipley, | Kiles, Sarah Ann | 23, Aug. 1825 | RCH |
| Shipley, David | Lacey, Mary E. | 4, Dec. 1849 | RCH |
| Shipley, Henry H. | Bonsall, Anna H. | 21, June 1848 | RCH |
| Shipley, John P. | Russell, Emeline | 8, Oct. 1848 | RCH |
| Shipman, Horace | Bennett, Maria J. | 28, Nov. 1849 | RCH |
| Shipman, Nicolaus | Bennet, | 21, July 1825 | RCH |
| Shipper, Bernard | Schum, Catharine | 23, Jan. 1844 | FF |
| Shires, John | Allen, Mary | 3, Dec. 1844 | RCH |
| Shirly, Michael | LaBoiteaux, Keziah | 10, May 1832 | RCH |
| Shively, John | Flood, Clarissa | 17, Jan. 1825 | RCH |
| Shively, John | Oliver, Mary Jane | 1, Dec. 1849 | RCH |
| Shober, Godfrey | Felter, Amanda | 8, Dec. 1819 | RCH |
| Shockley, William | Armstrong, Elisabeth | 10, June 1844 | RCH |
| Shoeknepy, Patrick | Hayden, Winnifred | 29, July 1849 | GG |
| Shoemaker, Nicolaus | Snider, Sarah | 30, Sept 1819 | RCH |
| Shofs, George | Haney, Jane | 26, Oct. 1835 | RCH |
| Sholl, David | Edwards, Rachel | 27, Mar. 1843 | RCH |
| Sholl, George W. | Hunter, Emily | 9, Jan. 1844 | RCH |
| Sholl, John D. | James, Sarah J. | 16, May 1843 | RCH |
| Shomaker, J. | Brown, | 19, Feb. 1821 | RCH |
| Shomp, Clemmerther | Borden, Hannah | 7, July 1833 | RCH |
| Shope, | Wheeler, Amanda M. | 8, Aug. 1849 | RCH |
| Shoppell, Carry | Doty, Ella Ann | 23, Mar. 1837 | RCH |
| Shorm, Frederick | King, Mary | 4, Feb. 1837 | RCH |
| Short, | Mitchell, Mary Ann | 26, July 1849 | RCH |
| Short, Charles | Smith, Mary | 1, May 1847 | RCH |
| Short, James | Holley, Rebecca | 23, Oct. 1834 | RCH |
| Short, John | Botkin, Margaret | 17, Jan. 1845 | RCH |
| Short, Jonathan | Graham, Adelia | 30, Dec. 1847 | RCH |
| Short, Joseph | Courney, Sarah | 28, Feb. 1849 | RCH |
| Short, Samuel | Rowan, Elisabeth | 16, Nov. 1837 | RCH |
| Shorten, William | Hill, Elisabeth | 20, June 1839 | RCH |
| Shortle, Thomas | Harris, Rebecca | 18, May 1842 | RCH |
| Shotsman, Edward | Risinger, Phebe | 1, Jan. 1842 | RCH |
| Shott, Moses | Meyer, Harriet | 28, Aug. 1849 | RCH |
| Shotwell, George H. | Tudor, Mary E. | 8, Nov. 1836 | RCH |
| Shotwell, John | Cains, Elisabeth G. | 16, Feb. 1843 | RCH |
| Shotwell, John T. | Foote, Mary W. | 23, Oct. 1832 | I |
| Shotwell, L. | Sedam, Nancy | 17, Mar. 1825 | RCH |
| Showell, Elisha | Waldsmith, Catharine | 25, Jan. 1836 | RCH |
| Shower, Charles | Roberts, Emma | 3, Apr. 1841 | RCH |
| Showers, Elisha | Leogis, Caroline | 16, Aug. 1837 | RCH |
| Shren, Michael R. | Grinsto, Ann | 24, Apr. 1839 | RCH |
| Shueler, Amand | Fell, Maria | 1, Aug. 1843 | FF |
| Shuff, Jacob | Miller, Nancy | 10, Oct. 1833 | RCH |
| Shuff, John | Cunningham, Deborah | 25, Sept 1844 | RCH |
| Shull, John | Devin, Mary | 7, Mar. 1824 | RCH |
| Shull, John | Edmonds, Lucy Ann | 12, Nov. 1846 | RCH |
| Shulto, George W. | Kugler, Elisabeth | 9, May 1839 | RCH |
| Shultz, Charles | Bowers, Ann Eliza | 12, Feb. 1827 | I |
| Shum, Jacob | Whallon, Eleanor | 30, Nov. 1843 | RCH |
| Shuman, Friedrich | Sexton, Ann | 15, Dec. 1845 | RCH |
| Shuman, Jacob | Weit, Elisabeth | 18, July 1844 | RCH |
| Shumate, John | Stage, Anastasia | 22, Jan. 1846 | RCH |
| Shunk, Isaac | Wolf, Maria Anna | 5, July 1836 | RCH |
| Shurt, Bonaparte | Wirtz, Catharine | 11, Aug. 1834 | RCH |
| Shuster, William | Bates, Elisabeth | 26, Nov. 1842 | RCH |
| Shute, Samuel | Rogers, Rebecca | 2, June 1848 | RCH |
| Shutter, Christian | Matter, Anna | 7, Jan. 1847 | EE |
| Shuwan, Horatio G. | Shuwan, Ruth | 9, Oct. 1819 | RCH |
| Sibsey, John | Renby, Susannah | 20, Mar. 1836 | RCH |
| Sice, Hiram | Letter, Esther | 1, June 1820 | RCH |
| Sick, Crispin | Urban, Agatha | 24, Apr. 1843 | FF |
| Sick, Friedrich | Homann, Dorothea | 10, Nov. 1847 | C |
| Sick, Jacob | Meier, Anna | 23, May 1849 | RCH |
| Sickemeyer, Friedric | Ossendarp, Elisabeth | 1, Apr. 1845 | AA |
| Sicker, Anton | Messing, Johanna | 16, May 1848 | FF |

| Grooms | Brides | Date of Marriage | Code |
|--------|--------|------------------|------|
| ***** | ***** | **** ** ******** | **** |
| Sickle, Albert | Hopkins, Julia | 28, Mar. 1822 | RCH |
| Sickler, Levi | Keith, Elisabeth J. | 2, July 1842 | RCH |
| Sickles, Isaac | Borum, Jane | 15, May 1847 | RCH |
| Sides, William | Newton, Elisabeth | 2, Nov. 1845 | RCH |
| Siebel, Julius | Friedeborn, Augusta | 7, May 1842 | G |
| Siebenthal, Halvet. | Halstead, Elisabeth | 2, May 1849 | RCH |
| Sieber, Joseph | Kronbitter, Josephin | 20, Aug. 1848 | EE |
| Siebern, Johan N. | Steinkamp, Anna M.E. | 23, Jan. 1845 | F |
| Siebern, Peter Hein. | Wellmann, Cath.(Mrs) | 30, Sept 1845 | F |
| Siebert, Christian | McKim, Sarah | 24, Dec. 1844 | RCH |
| Siebert, Francis | Loacks, Margaretha | 27, Apr. 1839 | FF |
| Siebrock, Johan | Reiting, Margaretha | 28, Nov. 1837 | FF |
| Siedenberg, Johan C. | Bandemann, Charlotte | 1, Dec. 1842 | F |
| Siederer, Anton | Vogt, Francisca | 1, Nov. 1847 | EE |
| Siedle, Engelbert | Walzer, Aloisa | 24, July 1849 | EE |
| Sieferle, Gervasius | Ernst, Victoria | 25, Aug. 1840 | FF |
| Siefers, Georg | Haionair, Anna Maria | 11, June 1845 | A |
| Siefert, Aloys | Reis, Catharine | 15, Feb. 1849 | EE |
| Siefert, Francis Jos | Link, Maria Anna | 25, Nov. 1840 | FF |
| Siefert, Joseph | Brosemer, Elisabeth | 7, Jan. 1836 | FF |
| Siefert, Lorenz | Schwendemann, Theres | 8, July 1845 | AA |
| Siefert, Martin | Steinmelering, Barb. | 15, Feb. 1836 | FF |
| Siefert, Michael | Baer, Cornelia | 11, Apr. 1837 | FF |
| Siefert, Valentin | Deidille, Maria | 21, July 1844 | AA |
| Siefert, Wilhelm | Hundepohl, Gertrud | 3, Oct. 1843 | FF |
| Siefke, Heinrich | Tepe, Catharine | 7, May 1844 | FF |
| Siefter, Friedrich | Frieschen, Maria | 20, July 1841 | G |
| Sieg, Gottfried | Wagner, Margaretha | 30, Oct. 1842 | A |
| Siegel, Lazarus | Reis, Babette | 24, Mar. 1849 | RCH |
| Siegele, Joseph | Sauer, Barbara | 11, Dec. 1849 | II |
| Sieger, Johan Joseph | Rieder, Anna Maria | 14, Aug. 1849 | EE |
| Siegle, Michael | Schmietzer, Barbara | 19, July 1840 | G |
| Siegler, Anton | Richard, Maria | 9, Jan. 1840 | G |
| Siegmann, Wilhelm | Stahl, Maria | 26, Aug. 1847 | EE |
| Sielschatt, Johan | Rodert, Catharine | 6, Sept 1846 | C |
| Siemann, J Friedrich | Hillmann, Sophia C. | 29, Nov. 1849 | B |
| Siemann, Johan Hein. | Bruns, Anna Margaret | 15, Apr. 1849 | CC |
| Sieme, Caspar Hein. | Duettmann, Catharina | 25, Apr. 1847 | AA |
| Siemer, Joseph | Meier, Maria Engel | 26, Dec. 1847 | CC |
| Siermann, Edward | Minnzinger, Friedr. | 20, July 1848 | G |
| Sieronski, John | Digan, Bridget | 18, July 1849 | BB |
| Sierp, Bernard H.F. | Leitenburg, Cath. E. | 28, Sept 1848 | B |
| Sierp, Georg | Siefert, Maria M. | 27, Dec. 1842 | F |
| Sierp, Henry | Holthaus, Catharine | 6, May 1847 | RCH |
| Sierp, Wilhelm | Kramers, Caroline | 30, Nov. 1843 | RCH |
| Sieve, Heinrich | Kohorst, Sophia | 15, Feb. 1849 | EE |
| Sievre, Francis | Niehaus, Maria Agnes | 8, Sept 1849 | CC |
| Sigerson, John | Schillinger, Philom. | 25, Oct. 1836 | RCH |
| Silbeck, Johan | Karmann, Charlotte | 9, Feb. 1843 | F |
| Silberman, Susman | Reinman, Esther | 22, Aug. 1845 | RCH |
| Silberuggel, Michael | Meyer, Eva Catharina | 25, Nov. 1849 | G |
| Silen, Uriah | Glissin, Mary Ann | 29, Nov. 1835 | RCH |
| Siler, Peter | Wells, Clarissa | 23, May 1844 | RCH |
| Silies, Gerhard H. | Libbers, Francisca C | 16, Nov. 1847 | AA |
| Sill, William H. | Barker, Matilda | 10, Dec. 1848 | RCH |
| Silsbee, H. | Burt, Ann | 22, Apr. 1819 | RCH |
| Silsbee, John | Houston, Isaleen | 9, May 1844 | RCH |
| Silsbee, William | Leyman, Charlotte | 21, Mar. 1837 | RCH |
| Silsby, John | Whiteside, Amanda | 20, Mar. 1844 | RCH |
| Silschotte, Bernard | Kessen, Carolina | 4, Feb. 1845 | FF |
| Silver, Samuel | Johnson, | 4, Apr. 1824 | RCH |
| Sim---, Aaron | Pasmore, Margaret | 30, Aug. 1826 | RCH |
| Simister, Abel | Clayton, Mary | 9, June 1849 | D |
| Simmandel, John Geo. | Mosmeyer, M. Barbara | 10, Sept 1843 | G |
| Simmes, Raphael | Spencer, Anne E. | 2, May 1837 | I |
| Simmonds, James | Frost, Anna | 16, Mar. 1819 | RCH |
| Simmonds, Samuel | Clark, Amilia | 30, July 1837 | RCH |
| Simmons, Benjamin | Young, Harriet | 22, May 1833 | RCH |
| Simmons, Benjamin | McMurray, Eleanor | 2, July 1844 | RCH |
| Simmons, John B. | Green, Prudence Ann | 26, Mar. 1818 | RCH |
| Simmons, John H. | Collins, Polly | 24, July 1834 | RCH |

| Grooms<br>****** | Brides<br>****** | Date of Marriage<br>**** ** ******** | Code<br>**** |
|---|---|---|---|
| Simmons, John J. | Gunner, Elisabeth | 8, Oct. 1835 | RCH |
| Simmons, Joseph | Russell, Mary | 23, July 1823 | RCH |
| Simmons, Joseph | Urmston, Mary | 14, July 1839 | RCH |
| Simmons, Moses | Riggs, Ann | 17, Apr. 1844 | RCH |
| Simmons, Moses | Bradley, Sarah | 18, Apr. 1844 | RCH |
| Simmons, Sylvanus | VanLiew, Catharine | 16, Sept 1845 | RCH |
| Simms, William | Jones, Ann | 13, Nov. 1840 | BB |
| Simon, Adam | Par, Elisabeth | 16, Feb. 1841 | FF |
| Simon, Friedrich | Brokamp, Maria Anna | 26, Nov. 1844 | AA |
| Simon, Hiram | Clark, Mary | 22, Nov. 1834 | RCH |
| Simon, Isaac | Haas, Sarah | 15, Sept 1846 | RCH |
| Simon, John Michael | Rozner, Maria A. | 24, Aug. 1845 | RCH |
| Simon, Joseph | Levy, Regina | 17, Jan. 1842 | RCH |
| Simon, Marcus | Thurnouer, Lotta | 9, Dec. 1844 | RCH |
| Simons, Thomas | Nowlan, Mary | 14, Mar. 1844 | RCH |
| Simonton, Hiram | Jewitt, Elisabeth | 6, Feb. 1849 | RCH |
| Simonton, Richard | Smith, | Nov. 1844 | RCH |
| Simonton, William | Cameron, Caroline | 5, Nov. 1840 | RCH |
| Simpson, Alexander | Clark, Lorgin | 18, May 1843 | RCH |
| Simpson, Alexander | McCune, Maranda J. | 11, Nov. 1846 | RCH |
| Simpson, Asbury | Hukill, Nancy | 21, Oct. 1846 | RCH |
| Simpson, Charles | Gest, Sarah | 20, June 1844 | RCH |
| Simpson, G.M. | Jones, Emily J. | 26, Oct. 1841 | RCH |
| Simpson, Isaac | Grace, Lavina Ann | 16, Aug. 1846 | RCH |
| Simpson, James H. | Warnis, | 2, June 1825 | RCH |
| Simpson, Jeremiah | Hoppins, Sarah | 12, June 1849 | RCH |
| Simpson, John | Hall, Phoebe | 8, Dec. 1840 | RCH |
| Simpson, John | Campbell, Mary | 31, May 1842 | RCH |
| Simpson, John H. | Martin, Sidney M. | 1, June 1826 | RCH |
| Simpson, Jonathan | Davis, Matilda | 6, Dec. 1835 | RCH |
| Simpson, Joseph H. | Sullivan, Emily | 12, Apr. 1835 | RCH |
| Simpson, Langhorn | Hoffmann, Harriet W. | 5, Oct. 1835 | RCH |
| Simpson, Miles | Joel, Nancy | 18, June 1846 | RCH |
| Simpson, Nathaniel | Woods, Henrietta | 1, Nov. 1843 | RCH |
| Simpson, William | Holland, Charlotte | 19, Mar. 1834 | RCH |
| Simpson, William | Yates, Mary | 20, Sept 1849 | RCH |
| Sims, Samuel | Johnson, Achsa | 26, Oct. 1846 | RCH |
| Simson, Samuel | Riddle, | 27, Mar. 1823 | RCH |
| Sinclair, | Tindall, Margaret | 27, Feb. 1823 | RCH |
| Sinclair, John | Winter, Emma | 16, Mar. 1846 | RCH |
| Sine, Xenophen | Wilson, Susan Maria | 15, Nov. 1843 | RCH |
| Singer, Michael | Mueller, Catharine | 11, Aug. 1846 | EE |
| Singer, Nicolaus | Zeits, Augusta | 26, Jan. 1846 | A |
| Singer, William | Guthrie, Sarah | 27, May 1846 | RCH |
| Singler, Johan | Allbeck, Margaretha | 16, Nov. 1835 | FF |
| Singleton, Henry | Fitzgerald, Elisabet | 3, Dec. 1849 | RCH |
| Singsang, J. Mathias | Kohl, Anna Maria | 21, Nov. 1847 | AA |
| Sins, Martin | Spartz, Caroline | 27, Apr. 1846 | RCH |
| Sinsabaugh, Henry | Fitter, Maria | 25, Mar. 1822 | RCH |
| Sipple, Johan Wm. | Schupferling, Cath. | 6, Nov. 1843 | RCH |
| Sirazey, Hazen | Alten, Sophia | 5, Sept 1822 | RCH |
| Sirwell, Richard | Moore, Mary | 7, May 1846 | BB |
| Sitel, Christian | Becker, Caroline | 13, Aug. 1848 | G |
| Siya, Samuel | Anderson, Mary | 13, Jan. 1825 | RCH |
| Sizelove, David | Jack, Susannah | 4, Feb. 1820 | RCH |
| Sizelove, George | Weaver, Sarah | 15, Apr. 1821 | RCH |
| Skaats, Garrett | Mahon, Catharine A. | 27, May 1841 | BB |
| Skerrett, David | Voaglan, Mary Ann | 21, Dec. 1844 | RCH |
| Skidmore, Wesley | VanGorder, Elisabeth | 28, July 1848 | RCH |
| Skillman, | Palmer, Elisabeth A. | 7, Sept 1849 | RCH |
| Skillman, Abraham | Hardenbrook, Phebe | 1, Dec. 1842 | RCH |
| Skillman, Samuel | Strong, Sarah Ann | 5, Apr. 1832 | RCH |
| Skillman, Theodore | Albright, Catharine | 31, Dec. 1819 | RCH |
| Skillman, Thomas | Davis, Mary Ann | 2, Mar. 1843 | RCH |
| Skillman, William | Albright, Polley | 21, Oct. 1824 | RCH |
| Skillman, William | Collins, Catharine | 18, Oct. 1843 | RCH |
| Skinner, Phillip | Kelly, Harriet | 17, Nov. 1820 | RCH |
| Skinner, Thomas M. | Miller, Lucinda | 27, Sept 1836 | RCH |
| Slabeck, Samuel | Robinson, Sarepta M. | 9, Apr. 1834 | RCH |
| Slack, Benjamin | Cook, Christina | 13, June 1848 | RCH |
| Slack, Daniel | Berry, Margaret Ann | 6, Aug. 1845 | RCH |

| Grooms<br>\*\*\*\*\*\* | Brides<br>\*\*\*\*\*\* | Date of Marriage<br>\*\*\*\* \*\* \*\*\*\*\*\*\*\* | Code<br>\*\*\*\* |
|---|---|---|---|
| Slack, Friedrich | Baldwin, Harriet | 12, June 1846 | RCH |
| Slack, Ralph | Bagley, Catharine | 17, Oct. 1847 | GG |
| Slane, Alexander | Bradford, Mary Ann | 13, July 1847 | RCH |
| Slane, William | Sprague, Rapena | 16, June 1839 | RCH |
| Slate, Henry | Phares, Caroline | 5, Nov. 1846 | RCH |
| Slater, John F. | St.Julian, Elisabeth | 31, Mar. 1849 | RCH |
| Slayback, Solomon | Day, Phoebe | 16, Apr. 1818 | RCH |
| Sleath, Gabriel | Hyde, Elisabeth | 23, Sept 1835 | D |
| Slemmer, George | McManaway, Elisabeth | 28, Aug. 1845 | RCH |
| Sleter, Theodor | Busch, Catharine M. | 5, Mar. 1839 | RCH |
| Sloan, Isaac | ----, Elisabeth | 19, Feb. 1819 | RCH |
| Sloan, Samuel | Adamson, Jane | 10, Dec. 1839 | D |
| Sloan, Samuel | Dawson, Mary | 30, May 1847 | RCH |
| Sloan, William | Morse, Ann | 14, June 1847 | RCH |
| Sloane, George | Simmonds, Soenty | 25, July 1839 | RCH |
| Sloat, John | Lockwood, Hannah | 26, Dec. 1844 | RCH |
| Sloat, John | Foster, Eveline | 18, Jan. 1847 | RCH |
| Slocum, B.W. | Matthews, Pamelia | 15, June 1843 | RCH |
| Slocum, William | Collins, Sarah | 20, Feb. 1834 | RCH |
| Sloop, Hiram | Schultz, Anna Maria | 16, June 1826 | RCH |
| Sloop, Jacob B. | Harrison, Frances | 27, Jan. 1825 | RCH |
| Slott, Jacob | Dennis, Elisabeth | 3, June 1847 | RCH |
| Smal, Joseph | Volterings, Catharin | 27, Aug. 1849 | EE |
| Small, John | McCurdy, Nancy | 31, Aug. 1836 | RCH |
| Smallhouse, Christ. | Neville, Harriet | 18, Aug. 1845 | RCH |
| Smallwood, Richard | O'Keefe, Elisabeth | 20, Sept 1848 | BB |
| Smallwood, Samuel | Curtis, Elisabeth | 24, Dec. 1845 | RCH |
| Smart, Richard | Webb, Martha J. | 28, June 1843 | RCH |
| Smead, Wesley | McKennan, Amelia | 6, May 1832 | RCH |
| Smgey, John | Lumfey, Ann | 19, Feb. 1835 | RCH |
| Smidell, Jonathan | Johnson, Mary | 4, May 1836 | RCH |
| Smiley, John J. | Taylor, Elisabeth | 23, May 1843 | RCH |
| Smiley, John R. | Skillman, Mary Ann | 21, Dec. 1841 | RCH |
| Smiley, Robeson | Iliff, Clara | 1, Oct. 1845 | RCH |
| Smith, | Hutchinson, Rebecca | 11, Jan. 1835 | RCH |
| Smith, Abel M. | Reading, M. Margaret | 27, June 1847 | RCH |
| Smith, Abraham | Chambers, Charlotte | 17, Oct. 1826 | RCH |
| Smith, Adam | Miller, Margaret | 1, Mar. 1844 | RCH |
| Smith, Adolph | Bates, Sarah | 13, Sept 1842 | RCH |
| Smith, Albert | Brown, Sirena | 24, Mar. 1847 | RCH |
| Smith, Alpheus | Betts, Esther | Feb. 1821 | RCH |
| Smith, Ambrose | Tridway, Elisabeth | 4, July 1844 | RCH |
| Smith, Andrew | Balding, Lucinda | 17, Mar. 1847 | RCH |
| Smith, Arthur | Ball, Susan | 25, Oct. 1842 | RCH |
| Smith, Austin | English, Margaret | 19, Aug. 1844 | RCH |
| Smith, Bartholomew | Reagan, Jane | 30, Aug. 1845 | BB |
| Smith, Benjamin | Slater, Mary | 16, Oct. 1823 | RCH |
| Smith, Benjamin | Walton, Abigail | 12, Aug. 1841 | RCH |
| Smith, Benjamin | Kastner, Frances | 17, Dec. 1844 | RCH |
| Smith, Beriah | Goudy, Jane H. | 19, Oct. 1835 | RCH |
| Smith, Bernard | Smith, Margaret | 11, Dec. 1841 | RCH |
| Smith, Buckner | Cox, Rachel Amanda | 18, Nov. 1845 | RCH |
| Smith, Charles P. | Addis, Amelia | 10, Aug. 1822 | RCH |
| Smith, Charles W. | Pancoast, Frances | 24, Nov. 1847 | RCH |
| Smith, Chester | Preston, Mary Ann E. | 4, Apr. 1849 | D |
| Smith, Cyrus | McFeely, Nancy | 18, Mar. 1836 | RCH |
| Smith, Daniel | Brickley, Sarah | 5, Apr. 1849 | RCH |
| Smith, David | Lee, Sarah | 13, Jan. 1833 | RCH |
| Smith, David | Rawlins, Matilda A. | 13, Jan. 1835 | RCH |
| Smith, DeWitt C. | Getz, Elisabeth | 20, Oct. 1847 | D |
| Smith, Dennis | Jones, Johanna | 25, Jan. 1844 | RCH |
| Smith, Dwight | Glisson, Harriet | 29, Mar. 1839 | RCH |
| Smith, Edward | Hook, Esther | 6, July 1826 | RCH |
| Smith, Edward | Sullivan, Sarah | 9, July 1844 | RCH |
| Smith, Elias | Hickman, Mary Ann | 13, Mar. 1834 | RCH |
| Smith, Elisha | Muchmore, Mary | 1, Nov. 1842 | RCH |
| Smith, Ezekiel | Cain, Deborah | 21, Mar. 1846 | RCH |
| Smith, F. | Matthews, Martha | 20, Jan. 1822 | RCH |
| Smith, Francis | Rice, Louisa T. | 9, May 1822 | RCH |
| Smith, Frank | Shelton, Ruthy | 25, June 1818 | RCH |
| Smith, Franklin | Hanna, Martha | 3, Nov. 1843 | RCH |

| Grooms<br>****** | Brides<br>****** | Date of Marriage<br>**** ** ******** | Code<br>**** |
|---|---|---|---|
| Smith, Garret | Hustin, Amanda | 1, Sept 1825 | RCH |
| Smith, George | Runyan, Abiah | 9, Apr. 1819 | RCH |
| Smith, George | Colvin, Hester | 26, Feb. 1824 | RCH |
| Smith, George | Scofield, Nancy | 15, Nov. 1842 | RCH |
| Smith, George | Leon, Mary J. | 6, Jan. 1846 | RCH |
| Smith, George | Bray, Mary | 8, May 1847 | RCH |
| Smith, George A. | Rava, Anna | 12, Mar. 1849 | RCH |
| Smith, George W. | Smith, Margaret | 18, Apr. 1826 | RCH |
| Smith, George W. | Jones, Mary A. | 3, Feb. 1842 | RCH |
| Smith, H. | Hankle, Elisabeth | 9, Nov. 1820 | RCH |
| Smith, Hartman | Ames, Elisabeth | 18, Nov. 1847 | RCH |
| Smith, Henry | Main, Elizabeth | 31, July 1825 | RCH |
| Smith, Henry | Brauman, Jane | 27, Mar. 1837 | RCH |
| Smith, Henry | Scrivener, Orodine | 16, May 1843 | RCH |
| Smith, Henry H. | Peace, Jane | 8, Dec. 1844 | RCH |
| Smith, Henry M. | Powell, Nancy | 15, Dec. 1844 | RCH |
| Smith, Hiram | Babbett, Elisabeth | 20, May 1832 | RCH |
| Smith, Ida | Ramsey, Elisabeth | 8, Feb. 1835 | RCH |
| Smith, Isaac | Tucker, Candis | 11, May 1837 | RCH |
| Smith, Isaac | Fithian, Elisabeth | 17, Aug. 1846 | RCH |
| Smith, Isaac | Baker, Sarah Ann | 7, Sept 1849 | RCH |
| Smith, Jacob | Mays, Sarah | 20, Jan. 1833 | RCH |
| Smith, Jacob | Linkmyre, Mary Ann | 28, Sept 1845 | RCH |
| Smith, Jacob | Zimmermann, Mary A. | 4, Nov. 1848 | RCH |
| Smith, James | Conrad, Elisabeth | 5, Apr. 1819 | RCH |
| Smith, James | Mayor, Sophia | 15, Aug. 1836 | RCH |
| Smith, James | Hillborough, Sarah | 26, Nov. 1837 | RCH |
| Smith, James | Ferris, Margaret | 15, July 1840 | RCH |
| Smith, James | James, Angela | 16, May 1843 | RCH |
| Smith, James | Dawson, Anna | 17, Oct. 1843 | RCH |
| Smith, James | Nixon, Elisabeth A. | 6, Apr. 1847 | RCH |
| Smith, James | Jeremiah, Martha | 11, Apr. 1847 | RCH |
| Smith, James | Wagner, Julia Ann | 5, July 1847 | RCH |
| Smith, James | Montight, Elisabeth | 1, Nov. 1847 | GG |
| Smith, James B. | Dare, Helen M. | 21, Mar. 1839 | RCH |
| Smith, James W. | Moore, M. | 29, Dec. 1834 | RCH |
| Smith, Jeremiah | Lee, Pauline | 23, Dec. 1847 | RCH |
| Smith, Jesse | Butt, Ann | 13, Oct. 1842 | RCH |
| Smith, Jesse S. | Murray, Sarah | 14, May 1818 | RCH |
| Smith, John | Scammahorn, Elis. | Apr. 1823 | RCH |
| Smith, John | Smith, Mary | 17, Dec. 1825 | RCH |
| Smith, John | Tucker, Elisabeth | 2, Feb. 1832 | RCH |
| Smith, John | Brown, Elisabeth | 25, Sept 1834 | RCH |
| Smith, John | Bun---, Sarah | 17, May 1837 | RCH |
| Smith, John | Foulks, Keeter | 15, Jan. 1838 | RCH |
| Smith, John | Miller, Elisabeth | 27, July 1838 | RCH |
| Smith, John | Kinder, Margaret | 24, Apr. 1842 | RCH |
| Smith, John | Hoffman, Lucinda | 5, June 1842 | RCH |
| Smith, John | Nelson, Olena | 9, June 1842 | RCH |
| Smith, John | Riker, Phebe | 22, Nov. 1842 | RCH |
| Smith, John | Kennedy, Harriet | 28, May 1846 | RCH |
| Smith, John | Murphy, Isabella | 18, Nov. 1846 | RCH |
| Smith, John | Gueth, Eva Barbara | 20, May 1847 | RCH |
| Smith, John | Lyon, Susan | 20, Apr. 1849 | RCH |
| Smith, John | McGrath, Mary | 18, Nov. 1849 | GG |
| Smith, John C. | Dana, Mary | 28, Oct. 1823 | RCH |
| Smith, John Freeman | Woods, Phoebe M. | 24, Aug. 1845 | RCH |
| Smith, John H. | Jenkins, Clarinda J. | 27, May 1838 | RCH |
| Smith, John J. | Arkins, Ruth | 4, Feb. 1841 | RCH |
| Smith, John W. | Posey, Mary Jane | 14, June 1848 | RCH |
| Smith, Jonas | Rice, Harriet | 26, Mar. 1846 | RCH |
| Smith, Joseph | Yateman, Indiana | 6, May 1837 | RCH |
| Smith, Joseph | Weaver, Barbara | 12, Apr. 1840 | RCH |
| Smith, Joseph | Harris, Mary | 8, Feb. 1844 | RCH |
| Smith, Joseph | Smith, Eliza Jane | 14, Feb. 1847 | RCH |
| Smith, Josiah T. | Cummings, Nancy | 6, Dec. 1832 | RCH |
| Smith, Lemuel | Winskip, Matilda | 2, July 1826 | RCH |
| Smith, Levi | Job, Sarah | 29, July 1820 | RCH |
| Smith, Lindsay | Wilson, Ann | 1, July 1835 | RCH |
| Smith, Martin | Darough, Nancy | 3, Aug. 1826 | RCH |
| Smith, Mason | Gwynn, Mary Ann | Jan. 1843 | RCH |

| Grooms<br>****** | Brides<br>****** | Date of Marriage<br>**** ** ******** | Code<br>**** |
|---|---|---|---|
| Smith, Mason | Blain, Harriet | 13, Sept 1849 | RCH |
| Smith, Mathew | Martin, Abigail | Nov. 1844 | RCH |
| Smith, Moses | Gerard, Hulda | 11, July 1848 | RCH |
| Smith, Nathan | Wheeler, Naomi | 23, Mar. 1847 | RCH |
| Smith, Nathan S. | Balser, Mary | 28, July 1825 | RCH |
| Smith, Nathaniel | Dyer, Elisabeth | 28, Sept 1834 | RCH |
| Smith, Nathaniel | Lovett, Elisabeth | 15, Feb. 1847 | RCH |
| Smith, Nicolaus | Armer, Catharina | 28, Apr. 1837 | RCH |
| Smith, Olian | McFadden, Nancy | 31, July 1839 | RCH |
| Smith, Oren | Cruger, Frances | 1, May 1847 | RCH |
| Smith, Patrick | Connell, Ann | 7, Dec. 1841 | RCH |
| Smith, Peter | Smith, Alice | 9, Apr. 1842 | BB |
| Smith, Philipp | Ayer, Lucy Ann | 7, Oct. 1847 | RCH |
| Smith, Powuel | Lupe, Catharine | 2, Feb. 1818 | RCH |
| Smith, Richard | Wood, Mary Ann | 6, June 1844 | RCH |
| Smith, Richard | Quinn, Mary | 26, Oct. 1846 | RCH |
| Smith, Robert | Holmes, Sarah | 6, Oct. 1846 | RCH |
| Smith, Robert | Gordon, Elisabeth | 2, Nov. 1847 | RCH |
| Smith, Samuel | Brown, Margaret | 5, Sept 1818 | RCH |
| Smith, Samuel | Ellison, Jane | 28, July 1833 | RCH |
| Smith, Samuel | Ferguson, Mary | 20, Mar. 1834 | RCH |
| Smith, Samuel | Wolt, Martha | 31, Dec. 1837 | RCH |
| Smith, Samuel | Gilbert, Ellen | 16, Sept 1841 | RCH |
| Smith, Samuel | Rice, Susan | 1, Sept 1842 | RCH |
| Smith, Samuel | Smith, Sarah | 19, Mar. 1846 | RCH |
| Smith, Samuel R. | Adams, Elisabeth | 4, Mar. 1821 | RCH |
| Smith, Samuel S. | Andress, Elisabeth | 11, Nov. 1832 | RCH |
| Smith, Samuel T. | Hildreth, Sarah | 5, Aug. 1835 | RCH |
| Smith, Sidney | Cremer, Sarah Jane | 24, July 1832 | RCH |
| Smith, Silas | Hutchins, Elisabeth | 11, Dec. 1845 | RCH |
| Smith, Solomon | Marshall, Jane | 15, Feb. 1820 | RCH |
| Smith, Thomas | Thorp, Mary Ann | 9, Dec. 1824 | RCH |
| Smith, Thomas | Dollin, Jane | 8, Nov. 1820 | I |
| Smith, Thomas | Otsen, Margaret | 3, Mar. 1848 | RCH |
| Smith, Thomas K. | McCullough, Elis. | 2, May 1848 | BB |
| Smith, Thomas W. | Smith, Mary C. | 7, Mar. 1837 | RCH |
| Smith, Walter | Irwin, Elisabeth | 29, Dec. 1846 | BB |
| Smith, William | Folger, Elisabeth | 25, Dec. 1820 | RCH |
| Smith, William | Carr, Margaret | 20, July 1826 | RCH |
| Smith, William | Peters, Barbara | 1, Feb. 1832 | RCH |
| Smith, William | Morris, Jane | 24, Sept 1832 | RCH |
| Smith, William | Hoffman, Harriet M. | 21, Oct. 1832 | RCH |
| Smith, William | Veler, Rachel | 24, Mar. 1833 | RCH |
| Smith, William | Mathews, Margaret | 18, Aug. 1836 | RCH |
| Smith, William | Hoffmann, Ellen | 14, June 1837 | RCH |
| Smith, William | Webber, Elisabeth | 14, June 1837 | RCH |
| Smith, William | Barlow, Nancy | 23, Aug. 1841 | RCH |
| Smith, William | Scotherland, Rebecca | 11, Sept 1841 | RCH |
| Smith, William | Bowen, Mary | 22, Nov. 1842 | RCH |
| Smith, William | Crawford, Martha | 26, June 1844 | RCH |
| Smith, William | Broadwell, Elisabeth | 27, June 1844 | RCH |
| Smith, William | Sharit, Frances A. | 17, July 1844 | RCH |
| Smith, William | McMullen, Catharine | 9, Aug. 1844 | BB |
| Smith, William | Hennessy, Hannah | 8, Jan. 1843 | BB |
| Smith, William | Whittaker, Sarah | 14, July 1845 | RCH |
| Smith, William | Reed, Lucinda | 26, Dec. 1845 | RCH |
| Smith, William | Hervey, Frances | 8, Oct. 1846 | RCH |
| Smith, William | Young, Julia Sophia | 19, Aug. 1847 | RCH |
| Smith, William | Payler, Elisabeth | 15, Nov. 1847 | RCH |
| Smith, William | Hill, Sophia | 25, May 1848 | RCH |
| Smith, William | Beatty, Sarah | 18, Nov. 1848 | RCH |
| Smith, William | Lamb, Elisabeth | 20, Mar. 1849 | RCH |
| Smith, William | Freeman, Sarah | 16, Aug. 1849 | RCH |
| Smith, William A. | Robertson, Mary | 15, July 1839 | RCH |
| Smith, William A. | Lucas, Ann | 11, July 1848 | D |
| Smith, William C. | Nemish, Betsey | 17, Feb. 1825 | RCH |
| Smith, Winthrop | ----, ---- | 4, Nov. 1834 | RCH |
| Smith, Wright | Walker, Matilda C. | Nov. 1835 | I |
| Smithers, John | Cox, Susan Jane | 13, Sept 1845 | BB |
| Smithey, Curtis | Pierce, Louisa | 6, Dec. 1833 | RCH |
| Smithurst, William | Ayers, Sarah Ann | 11, Nov. 1846 | RCH |

| Grooms<br>****** | Brides<br>****** | Date of Marriage<br>**** ** ******** | Code<br>**** |
|---|---|---|---|
| Smucker, William | Ackermann, Catharine | 18, Oct. 1846 | RCH |
| Smyser, Josiah | Carver, Sarah Ann | 11, Oct. 1846 | RCH |
| Smyzer, Cornelius | Davis, Ann Elisabeth | 19, Aug. 1845 | RCH |
| Snedecker, Samuel | Turner, Ann | 11, Aug. 1845 | RCH |
| Sneidewind, Heinrich | Meyer, Friedricka | 8, Dec. 1846 | F |
| Sneiller, William | Shearman, Fanny | 23, May 1839 | RCH |
| Snell, Abraham | Vallandingham, Cyr. | 6, Mar. 1844 | RCH |
| Snell, Lorenzo | Glisson, Martha M. | 19, Sept 1846 | RCH |
| Snezbacher, Martin | Holzstein, Dorothea | 11, Jan. 1842 | RCH |
| Snezer, August | Witzel, Maria | 4, Mar. 1849 | C |
| Snider, Alexander | Apgar, Lydia | 31, Jan. 1844 | RCH |
| Snider, Charles | Chandler, Mary Jane | 1, Jan. 1844 | RCH |
| Snider, Conrad | Felter, Synthy | 10, Nov. 1821 | RCH |
| Snider, Cornelius | Cochran, Sally Ann | 11, June 1843 | RCH |
| Snider, Daniel | Bickman, Susannah | 7, Mar. 1822 | RCH |
| Snider, Frederick | Jester, Mary | 11, Nov. 1832 | RCH |
| Snider, George | Dowd, Rosanna | 29, Mar. 1842 | BB |
| Snider, Isaac | Hastings, Mercy | 22, Mar. 1821 | RCH |
| Snider, Jacob | Baiden, Jane | 7, Dec. 1820 | RCH |
| Snider, Jacob | Williams, Rebecca | 22, Aug. 1821 | RCH |
| Snider, James | Wilder, Elisabeth | 27, Aug. 1844 | RCH |
| Snider, John | Miller, Mary | 2, Feb. 1819 | RCH |
| Snider, John | Auten, Mary | 19, Sept 1833 | RCH |
| Snider, John | Jonte, Elisabeth | 26, Sept 1839 | D |
| Snider, John | Hayslip, Sarah | 1, June 1847 | RCH |
| Snider, John W. | Davis, Martha | 2, Apr. 1835 | RCH |
| Snider, Mathias | Dawson, Julia | 12, Feb. 1837 | RCH |
| Snider, William | Littell, Sarah | 13, June 1846 | RCH |
| Snodgrass, John S. | Hoffner, Catharine | 3, Apr. 1836 | RCH |
| Snodgrass, Joseph | Hathorn, Margaret | 4, Oct. 1841 | RCH |
| Snodgrass, Joseph S. | Spring, Emily Ann | 14, Nov. 1833 | RCH |
| Snook, William | Parker, Mary Ann | 14, Aug. 1843 | RCH |
| Snow, Jacob | Criger, Mary | Apr. 1849 | RCH |
| Snowden, Sidney | Mitchell, Elisabeth | 23, Aug. 1837 | RCH |
| Snowfield, Benjamin | Amos, Susan M. | 22, Feb. 1844 | RCH |
| Snyder, Charles | Norris, Mary E. | 15, Dec. 1842 | RCH |
| Snyder, Charles | Welmers, M. Angeline | 21, Mar. 1847 | RCH |
| Snyder, Peter | Goff, Anna | 8, Oct. 1846 | RCH |
| Snyder, Richard H. | Griffin, Ann L. | 17, Oct. 1836 | I |
| Snyder, William | Williams, Ann | 8, Jan. 1824 | RCH |
| Snyder, William | Server, Elisabeth | 20, Oct. 1842 | RCH |
| Snyder, William | Irwin, Mathilda | 1, Jan. 1845 | RCH |
| Societo, Friedrich | Stephani, Magdalena | 13, July 1846 | AA |
| Soechting, August | Logemann, A Margaret | 15, Feb. 1847 | G |
| Soenig, Herman | Kluesner, Catharine | 7, Jan. 1840 | FF |
| Soete, Heinrich | Weding, Anna Maria | 7, Nov. 1837 | FF |
| Sofley, William | Mathews, Sarah Jane | 11, Aug. 1848 | RCH |
| Sohn, Georg | Raaber, Barbara | 15, Mar. 1847 | B |
| Sohnlein, Georg C. | Grafen, Kunigunda | 17, Aug. 1845 | C |
| Soiph, William D. | Russell, Mary | 3, Nov. 1834 | RCH |
| Solar, Joseph | Goodwin, Roxanda | 13, Jan. 1820 | RCH |
| Solar, Stephen | McDonald, Margaret | 4, Sept 1846 | RCH |
| Sollmann, Joseph H. | Groene, M. Elisabeth | 6, May 1847 | AA |
| Solmann, Christian | Meyers, Maria | 20, June 1837 | F |
| Solomon, Christian | Hetzel, Magdalena | 24, Aug. 1841 | RCH |
| Solomon, E.T. | Weyman, Eva | 24, Nov. 1849 | RCH |
| Solomon, John | Hudson, Nancy | 24, Jan. 1833 | RCH |
| Sombrink, Heinrich | Steinermann, Elis. | 12, July 1836 | FF |
| Somerkam, Peter | Hemph, Anna Catharin | 12, Jan. 1849 | EE |
| Sommer, A. | Spaeth, Kunigunda | 15, Feb. 1845 | A |
| Sommer, Anton | Geissert, Mathilda | 28, Nov. 1840 | FF |
| Sommer, Herman Hein. | Ketting, A.M. Gesina | 19, Nov. 1848 | FF |
| Sommer, J. Friedrich | Schmitherms, Elis. | 10, June 1846 | AA |
| Sommer, Johan Fried. | Steinemann, Anna M. | 12, Oct. 1847 | AA |
| Sommer, Johan H. | Zurline, Elisabeth | 3, Jan. 1847 | AA |
| Sommer, Joseph | Mueller, Catharina | 8, May 1838 | FF |
| Sommer, Julius | Erst, Walburga | 26, Dec. 1849 | RCH |
| Sommer, Wilhelm | Rechting, Theresa | 11, Nov. 1847 | FF |
| Sommerkamp, Casper H | Oberklein, Amanda H. | 11, Nov. 1847 | RCH |
| Sommermeyer, Johan H | Schulte, Elisabeth | 13, July 1846 | EE |
| Sonderdick, Herman | Luebbermann, Agatha | 2, May 1847 | AA |

| Grooms | Brides | Date of Marriage | Code |
|--------|--------|------------------|------|
| ****** | ****** | **** ** ******** | **** |
| Sonderhaus, Francis | Dickhaus, Anna Cath. | 29, Apr. 1849 | AA |
| Sondermann, Heinrich | Schmale, M. Theresa | 5, Nov. 1848 | AA |
| Sonding, William | Sandweir, Caroline | 15, May 1841 | RCH |
| Sope, Thomas | Lester, Jane | 4, Jan. 1834 | RCH |
| Soper, Enoch | Heath, Elisabeth | 4, Feb. 1820 | RCH |
| Sorter, Arthur S. | Tucker, Fanny | 26, Nov. 1819 | RCH |
| Sorter, Peterson | Heath, Amanda | 2, July 1843 | RCH |
| Soshen, Jacob J. | Camoner, Hannah | 21, Feb. 1835 | RCH |
| Sothora, Michael | Thomas, Hester Ann | 4, Mar. 1847 | RCH |
| Sotton, Alfred | Stiles, Almira | 27, Dec. 1846 | RCH |
| Souggs, S. | Davis, Catharine | 27, May 1833 | RCH |
| Sound, August | Feyman, Christine | 3, May 1849 | GG |
| Sour, Andrew | Davis, Melissa | 27, May 1845 | BB |
| Southard, Hugh | James, Catharine | 1, Jan. 1846 | RCH |
| Southard, Isaac | Mitchell, Sarah Ann | 4, Sept 1846 | RCH |
| Southgate, H.H. | Smith, Maria C. | 23, Sept 1834 | D |
| Southgate, James | Smith, Jane | 24, Jan. 1835 | D |
| Southgate, James | Brigham, Cornelia M. | 11, May 1831 | I |
| Southgate, Richard | Watson, Julia | 28, Dec. 1843 | RCH |
| Southward, John | McCarty, Agnes J. | 28, May 1818 | RCH |
| Sowards, John | Mongar, Sarah | 16, Apr. 1825 | RCH |
| Sowder, John | Rose, Henrietta | 6, June 1827 | RCH |
| Sower, J. | Stout, Johanna | 1, Jan. 1837 | RCH |
| Sowers, Andrew | Garrison, Sarah A. | 11, June 1848 | RCH |
| Sowers, William | Leurs, Margaret | 7, July 1849 | RCH |
| Sowester, Johan H. | Helmig, Maria Engel | 27, Aug. 1848 | CC |
| Sozinski, Lewis | Dorr, Olive | 19, Mar. 1846 | RCH |
| Sp---, Max | Meyffous, Cecilia | 28, July 1845 | RCH |
| Spacke, Friedrich | Trier, Catharine | 18, Oct. 1842 | RCH |
| Spaeth, Christoph | Weber, Anna Maria | 1, May 1849 | A |
| Spaeth, John | Bittinger, Catharine | 25, May 1847 | RCH |
| Spaeth, Philipp | Minken, Margaretha | 29, Jan. 1839 | FF |
| Spaeth, Wolfgang | Mineri, Francisca | 27, Sept 1849 | EE |
| Spahn, Joseph | Ning, Maria Anna | 30, Jan. 1837 | FF |
| Spahr, Benjamin | Plummer, Mary B. | 2, Jan. 1845 | RCH |
| Spain, Josiah | Payton, Rebecca | 30, May 1819 | RCH |
| Spake, Conrad | Fullhart, Charlotte | 21, Apr. 1844 | A |
| Spalding, John W. | White, Adolphina | 2, Sept 1844 | BB |
| Spanaugle, John | Cole, Elisabeth | Sept 1849 | RCH |
| Spangenberg, Lewis | Mason, Elisabeth | 17, June 1847 | RCH |
| Spangenberg, Peter | Umlauf, Philippina | 9, Jan. 1844 | G |
| Spar, Henry | Weatherby, Edith | 10, June 1835 | RCH |
| Sparks, David | Holmes, Lucy Ann | 12, July 1849 | RCH |
| Sparks, Ephraim | Tuley, Rebecca | 31, July 1845 | RCH |
| Sparks, Isaac | Leggett, Sarah | 18, Apr. 1826 | RCH |
| Sparks, Jesse W. | Pierson, Harriet | 10, Nov. 1836 | RCH |
| Sparks, Rudolphus | Epley, Sarah | 13, Jan. 1848 | RCH |
| Sparks, Samuel | Richardson, | 8, Nov. 1825 | RCH |
| Sparks, William | Wiggins, Jane | 14, Oct. 1819 | RCH |
| Sparks, William | Podesta, Ann | 1, Oct. 1845 | RCH |
| Sparkson, William | Barns, Catharine | 26, Dec. 1820 | RCH |
| Spatz, Bernard | Marks, Miriam | 11, Jan. 1842 | RCH |
| Speagh, David | Dennis, Mary | 27, June 1837 | RCH |
| Spear, Samuel | Carey, Rachel | 14, July 1842 | RCH |
| Spears, Henry | Flowers, Mary | 12, June 1841 | RCH |
| Specht, Carl | Miller, Henrietta | 25, Dec. 1849 | RCH |
| Specht, Jacob | Enichen, Caroline | 1, June 1848 | RCH |
| Speck, Francis Jos. | Lugel, Louisa | 31, Oct. 1847 | AA |
| Speckbauch, Joseph | Ragge, Anna Maria | 16, Feb. 1847 | EE |
| Speckmann, Friedrich | Vodden, Henrietta | 5, May 1849 | F |
| Speckmann, Herman F. | Johannes, Gesina C. | 22, Oct. 1846 | F |
| Speers, Harrison | Webb, Elisabeth | 8, May 1846 | RCH |
| Speers, Henry | Mulford, Betsy | 15, Sept 1836 | RCH |
| Speers, William | Sargent, Mary | 18, Apr. 1841 | RCH |
| Speilmann, Friedrich | Friend, Rachel | 1, July 1846 | RCH |
| Speis, Andreas | Werner, Catharine | 20, Apr. 1846 | RCH |
| Spelger, Johan | Flick, Cath. Ursula | 2, May 1847 | EE |
| Spellman, Daniel | Rourk, Honora | 15, Oct. 1848 | GG |
| Spellman, Henry | King, Mary M. | 22, Oct. 1843 | RCH |
| Spellman, James | Warren, Angela | 8, Dec. 1842 | RCH |
| Spellman, John | Evans, Maria Louise | 4, Mar. 1847 | RCH |

| Grooms | Brides | Date of Marriage | Code |
|--------|--------|------------------|------|
| Spellman, Michael | Hinkle, Lydia | 23, Oct. 1847 | BB |
| Spellmann, Charles | Noftsger, Susannah | 19, July 1846 | RCH |
| Spellmeier, Francis | Schmidts, Maria | 12, Sept 1839 | FF |
| Spellmeyer, Francis | Waltemann, Gertrud | 19, Jan. 1847 | EE |
| Spellmeyer, Johan H. | Schmidt, Elis. (Mrs) | 21, Jan. 1845 | AA |
| Spellmeyer, Johan H. | Mehlmann, Catharine | 4, Sept 1849 | EE |
| Spen---, Eli F. | Draper, Edith | 30, Nov. 1837 | RCH |
| Spence, Thomas | Jones, Elisabeth | 22, Oct. 1845 | RCH |
| Spencer, Benjamin | Martin, Angela | 26, Aug. 1844 | RCH |
| Spencer, Caleb C. | Kibby, Lavina S. | 12, Apr. 1825 | RCH |
| Spencer, Charles | Riggle, Ruth T. | 29, July 1833 | RCH |
| Spencer, Henry | Hull, Sophia | 11, Sept 1846 | RCH |
| Spencer, Henry R. | Ingram, Mary Ann | 26, Aug. 1848 | RCH |
| Spencer, Jarvis | Easly, Rebecca | 1, Aug. 1846 | RCH |
| Spencer, John | Bland, Alice | 24, Dec. 1832 | RCH |
| Spencer, John C. | Barr, Susan | 19, Aug. 1835 | I |
| Spencer, Lawton | Reeder, Elisabeth | 2, Jan. 1833 | RCH |
| Spencer, Oded | Turner, Theodosia | 23, Dec. 1837 | RCH |
| Spencer, Oliver M. | Barton, Anna Elis. | 2, Nov. 1832 | RCH |
| Spencer, Oliver M. | Coombs, Emily | 28, Sept 1837 | I |
| Spencer, Peter | Butterworth, Mary A. | 7, Apr. 1844 | RCH |
| Spencer, Samuel | Peck, Emily | 26, May 1833 | RCH |
| Spencer, Samuel A. | Keating, Mary | 15, Feb. 1841 | BB |
| Spencer, Warner | Miller, Catharine | 4, Aug. 1845 | RCH |
| Spencer, William | Schultz, Eliza Jane | 2, Apr. 1848 | RCH |
| Spering, John S. | Gibson, Margaret | 2, Oct. 1839 | RCH |
| Spicer, James W. | Walker, Matilda | 4, Jan. 1846 | RCH |
| Spicker, Herman H. | Westenbeck, Carolina | 24, Oct. 1847 | CC |
| Spieker, J. Gerhard | Niehoff, M. Theresa | 4, July 1847 | AA |
| Spiekermann, Heinric | Kustermeyer, Gertrud | 27, Feb. 1848 | AA |
| Spies, Andreas | Dariens, Margaret | 23, Oct. 1841 | RCH |
| Spies, Robert | Molitor, Barbara | 11, May 1848 | AA |
| Spiess, Carl | Heim, Maria | 11, Apr. 1847 | C |
| Spilker, J. Mathias | Enneking, Maria Anna | 6, June 1848 | AA |
| Spiller, James | Pridham, Fanny F. | 25, May 1848 | RCH |
| Spillman, James | Martin, Rachel | 29, July 1832 | RCH |
| Spillman, Samuel | Risky, Harriet | 1, Dec. 1832 | RCH |
| Spills, Johan | Schneider, Angela | 22, Oct. 1840 | FF |
| Spils, Johan Herman | Sommer, M.G. | 23, Sept 1849 | AA |
| Spink, Ebenezer | Bailey, Fanny | 12, July 1843 | RCH |
| Spinner, Carl | Bonnert, Ricka | 9, July 1839 | FF |
| Spinner, Mathias | Riele, Mary | 20, June 1843 | AA |
| Spinning, Charles | Baker, Mary | 12, May 1846 | RCH |
| Spinning, Ebenezer | Letter, Maria D. | 6, Nov. 1833 | RCH |
| Spinning, Isaac | French, Elisabeth | 5, Mar. 1818 | RCH |
| Spinning, Jonathan | Johnston, | Mar. 1827 | RCH |
| Spinning, William | Worley, Margaret E. | 20, May 1849 | RCH |
| Spitzfaden, Peter | Schifer, Elisabeth | 10, Dec. 1847 | A |
| Splete, Johan F. | Hubbert, Catharine | 24, Sept 1846 | G |
| Splinter, Heinrich | Gewerige, Maria | 16, Sept 1849 | EE |
| Splinters, Heinrich | Windels, Margaretha | 23, Nov. 1845 | AA |
| Splinters, Johan H. | George, Maria | 16, Sept 1849 | RCH |
| Spoengelmeyer, J.S. | Degder, M.E. | 27, Sept 1834 | RCH |
| Spoffard, Jacob | Springer, Elisabeth | 20, Sept 1846 | RCH |
| Spooner, Jacob | Riser, Hannah | 10, Dec. 1833 | RCH |
| Spooner, Reed | Hinman, Sarah P. | 19, Sept 1833 | RCH |
| Spotswood, Isaac | Maynard, Julia | 15, Apr. 1846 | RCH |
| Spotswood, James | Jones, Lydia Ann | 8, July 1846 | RCH |
| Sprague, Ambrose D. | Bloomer, Sarah | 7, July 1837 | RCH |
| Sprague, Andrew | Watkins, Lydia | 10, Feb. 1842 | RCH |
| Sprague, Elisha | Wallace, Jemima | 26, Jan. 1842 | RCH |
| Sprague, Henry | Belt, Elisabeth | 31, Dec. 1843 | RCH |
| Sprague, John N. | Moore, Henrietta | 30, Dec. 1840 | RCH |
| Sprague, Jonathan | Keys, Elisabeth | 14, June 1842 | RCH |
| Sprauer, Joseph | Tshingtschang, (Mrs) | 9, Aug. 1845 | AA |
| Spriggs, Thomas | Ferguson, Jane | 1, May 1844 | RCH |
| Spring, David | Patton, Isabella | 9, Nov. 1826 | RCH |
| Spring, John | Harris, Rebecca | 17, May 1840 | RCH |
| Spring, Sydney | Tait, Margaret | 1, Nov. 1847 | RCH |
| Spring, William | Dyer, Louise | 16, May 1844 | RCH |
| Springer, Charles | Kilgour, Catharine | 6, May 1840 | BB |

| Grooms<br>****** | Brides<br>****** | Date of Marriage<br>**** ** ******** | Code<br>**** |
|---|---|---|---|
| Springer, Ernst | Wellmann, Magdalena | 24, May 1836 | RCH |
| Springer, Jacob | Sarver, Sarah | 9, Aug. 1821 | RCH |
| Springer, John | Jerys, Esther | 3, Sept 1818 | RCH |
| Springer, Lehman | Simon, Amelia | 5, June 1848 | RCH |
| Springmeier, Heinric | Kallmeier, Henrietta | 6, Jan. 1840 | F |
| Springmeier, Heinric | Weddermann, Catharin | 29, Nov. 1849 | C |
| Springmier, Heinrich | Ruese, Wilhelmina | 26, Nov. 1846 | C |
| Springsteel, William | Emmons, Mary | 16, Mar. 1836 | RCH |
| Sprong, Cornelius | Quire, M. Elisabeth | 17, July 1844 | RCH |
| Sprong, Cornelius | Perkins, Ruth | 14, Sept 1845 | RCH |
| Sprong, David | Cary, Anna | 13, Mar. 1847 | RCH |
| Sprong, James | Pierson, Isabella | 7, Feb. 1847 | RCH |
| Sprong, Ward F. | Ranesville, Sarah A. | 26, Nov. 1835 | RCH |
| Sprouse, George | Simpson, Jane | 26, Nov. 1845 | RCH |
| Sprung, Johan Wm. | Eggers, Louisa | 7, Nov. 1844 | C |
| Spun, Avery | Gordon, Rachel | 1, May 1833 | RCH |
| Spunion, Reason | Banks, Mary | 23, Feb. 1825 | RCH |
| Spurgeon, Samuel | Hulings, Elisabeth | 14, Aug. 1849 | RCH |
| Spurgin, John M. | Salsbury, Phebe | 15, Feb. 1833 | RCH |
| Spurlock, Thomas | Neves, Melissa Jane | 19, Aug. 1847 | RCH |
| Squires, David | Alley, Mary | 8, Apr. 1832 | RCH |
| Squires, Serice | Roberts, Elisabeth | 13, Mar. 1838 | RCH |
| St.Clair, John | St.Clair, Lydia | 22, Sept 1832 | RCH |
| St.John, Deyo | Hoffner, Delila | 25, Apr. 1847 | RCH |
| Staab, Adam | Metzger, Anna Maria | 20, July 1848 | EE |
| Staab, Johan | Engel, Maria | 8, Oct. 1839 | FF |
| Stabler, David | Temy, Catharine | 4, Mar. 1836 | RCH |
| Stabler, John | Decker, Susan | 13, Jan. 1833 | RCH |
| Stabler, Solomon | Holland, Sarah Ann | 13, Mar. 1836 | RCH |
| Stacker, John | Thompson, Patty | 24, Mar. 1825 | RCH |
| Stackhouse, George | DeGraff, Sarah | 10, Feb. 1848 | RCH |
| Stadler, Anton | Hipoltsteiner, Johan | 26, Oct. 1847 | EE |
| Stadler, Max | Lauer, Mathilda | 27, Mar. 1847 | RCH |
| Stadtlander, Fried. | Luhring, Maria | 14, Dec. 1847 | F |
| Stadtlander, Wilhelm | Masmann, Maria | 15, Sept 1848 | F |
| Stadtmueller, Adam | Langer, Francisca | 15, Feb. 1848 | FF |
| Stadtmueller, Mich. | Krug, Catharina | 15, Oct. 1839 | FF |
| Stadtmueller, Nicol. | Holzmeister, Anna M. | 5, Dec. 1837 | FF |
| Stadts, Richard | Neeves, Mary | 21, Dec. 1834 | RCH |
| Staebles, John | Justice, Susan | 7, Feb. 1846 | RCH |
| Staemle, Stephan | Schuh, Magdalena | 7, Jan. 1840 | FF |
| Stafford, William | Ladd, Harriet | 25, Oct. 1846 | RCH |
| Stagamann, Friedrich | Quinn, Elisabeth C. | 24, Sept 1848 | F |
| Stagen, Christoph | Jefger, Margaretha | 16, Feb. 1837 | F |
| Stagg, Henry | Davis, Hannah Isabel | 20, Nov. 1842 | RCH |
| Stagg, James | Poor, Rachel | 3, Mar. 1846 | RCH |
| Stagg, Richard | Shephardson, Elis. | 31, May 1840 | RCH |
| Stagge, Christoph | Hellmich, Margaretha | 1, Feb. 1842 | F |
| Stagge, Friedrich | Driehaus, Catharine | 13, Oct. 1842 | F |
| Stagge, Johan Hein. | Rothert, Catharina M | 3, Feb. 1848 | F |
| Stagman, Jacob | Stake, Mary | 15, Apr. 1819 | RCH |
| Stahl, August | Pfarr, Catharine | 10, Mar. 1840 | G |
| Stahl, Dietrich | ---seher, Sophia | 7, Jan. 1846 | B |
| Stahl, Ernst | Niemann, Louise | 30, May 1849 | F |
| Stahl, Friedrich | Wiehl, Louise | 28, Sept 1843 | C |
| Stahl, Friedrich | Kodern, Elisabeth | 7, Dec. 1843 | F |
| Stahl, Ludwig | Teckelburg, Friedr. | 12, Oct. 1848 | C |
| Stahmann, Heinrich | Kueker, Dorothea | 26, Nov. 1846 | F |
| Stal, John B. | Morford, Mary | 23, Mar. 1836 | RCH |
| Stalcamp, Heinrich | Pelzer, Maria | 10, Oct. 1848 | EE |
| Staley, Samuel | Wright, Margaret | 16, Jan. 1827 | RCH |
| Stalkamp, John | Wendel, Maria E. | 30, Apr. 1844 | RCH |
| Stall, Gerhard | Marien, Agnes | 9, Oct. 1849 | AA |
| Stall, Herman Jacob | Kolkmeyer, Maria | 24, Nov. 1842 | AA |
| Stall, Herman Jacob | Bergmann, Catharine | 2, Feb. 1843 | AA |
| Stall, Philipp | Kepler, Sarah | 27, Nov. 1841 | RCH |
| Stallard, William | Moore, Elisabeth | 22, Jan. 1849 | RCH |
| Stallo, Bernard | Busche, M. Gertrud | 30, Aug. 1846 | EE |
| Stallo, Francis | Koenig, Elisabeth | 15, Aug. 1847 | EE |
| Stallo, Franz Joseph | Deie, M. Agnes | 7, Jan. 1849 | II |
| Stallo, Heinrich | Kleine, Engel | 8, May 1849 | CC |

| Grooms<br>****** | Brides<br>****** | Date of Marriage<br>**** ** ******** | Code<br>**** |
|---|---|---|---|
| Stallo, Johan B. | Zimmermann, Helena | 1, Feb. 1849 | RCH |
| Stamburg, Friedrich | Reily, Catharine M. | 26, Nov. 1835 | FF |
| Stambusch, Bernard | Bagge, Maria Angela | 22, July 1839 | FF |
| Stambusch, Heinrich | Wessel, Elisabeth | 13, Aug. 1846 | AA |
| Stambuske, Clemens | Meier, Maria Anna | 14, Jan. 1841 | FF |
| Stamp, Daniel | Blakemore, Lucy | 10, Feb. 1846 | GG |
| Stamp, Eeza | Noelblet, Margaret | 1, July 1838 | RCH |
| Stams, Michael | Hertkorn, Maria | 23, Oct. 1849 | AA |
| Stan, Abner | Whitehead, Ann | 5, Aug. 1819 | RCH |
| Stanberry, Henry | Bond, Celia R. | 14, July 1841 | I |
| Standeford, Edmund | Andrews, Caroline | 22, Mar. 1838 | RCH |
| Stang, Johan Georg | Stang, Maria Gertrud | 6, July 1849 | RCH |
| Stange, Christian | Breich, Clara | 19, Sept 1847 | G |
| Stanhope, Benjamin | Stevens, Amelia | 9, Dec. 1849 | RCH |
| Stanley, Charles | Wickham, Margaret | 16, Sept 1847 | RCH |
| Stanley, David | Compton, Jane | 16, Nov. 1848 | RCH |
| Stanley, Frederick | Lanphear, Mary A. | 28, Sept 1843 | RCH |
| Stanley, Georg | Duvenel, Mary | 21, June 1849 | RCH |
| Stanley, Jonathan | Tunison, Ann | 14, Apr. 1844 | RCH |
| Stanley, Meredith | Seymore, Elisabeth | 31, July 1844 | RCH |
| Stanley, Stephen | Saunders, Elisabeth | 28, Dec. 1842 | RCH |
| Stannus, Thomas | Shield, Helen | 30, Oct. 1844 | RCH |
| Stansberry, Johan | Combs, Hannah | 12, July 1843 | RCH |
| Stansbery, Osnal | Norris, Nancy | 24, Sept 1846 | RCH |
| Stansbury, Adam | Belvial, Susan | 11, Sept 1834 | RCH |
| Stansbury, John | Burch, Caroline | 28, Nov. 1844 | RCH |
| Stansbury, John S. | Coffin, M. | 6, Sept 1836 | RCH |
| Stansbury, M. | Thornton, Fanny | 27, Aug. 1818 | RCH |
| Stapler, John | Marrner, Barbara | 24, Nov. 1835 | RCH |
| Stapleton, James | Murphy, Honora | 23, July 1848 | BB |
| Stapleton, Robert | Campbell, Ann | 20, Apr. 1846 | BB |
| Stapp, Edwin | Akers, Elvira | 16, Feb. 1845 | RCH |
| Stappe, Heinrich | Baker, Catharine | 3, Dec. 1836 | F |
| Star, Emmanuel | Levi, Mena | 12, Sept 1843 | RCH |
| Starbuck, Calvin | Webster, Nancy | Jan. 1845 | RCH |
| Stardeur, Heinrich | Gerson, M. Elisabeth | 13, June 1837 | FF |
| Stark, Simon | Maier, Maria | 8, Oct. 1849 | DD |
| Starke, Thomas | Murphy, Margaret | 6, June 1844 | RCH |
| Starkey, Benjamin | Croul, Martha | 30, Nov. 1843 | RCH |
| Starkey, William | Carr, Maria | 30, Oct. 1821 | RCH |
| Starks, Thomas | Grason, Rachel | 4, June 1848 | RCH |
| Starks, William | McManus, Mary Ann | 8, Jan. 1846 | RCH |
| Starling, John F. | Poe, Barbara | 26, Aug. 1838 | RCH |
| Starr, Charles | Palmer, Mary | 4, Mar. 1847 | RCH |
| Starr, D.L. | Hauser, Sarah J. | 22, May 1849 | RCH |
| Starr, George | Gordon, Mary | 6, Aug. 1842 | RCH |
| Starr, James | Hackett, Elisabeth | 28, Apr. 1846 | BB |
| State, Peter L. | Penra, Hannah | 11, June 1834 | RCH |
| Staten, Joseph | Torrence, Cindria | 21, May 1818 | RCH |
| Stathem, Joseph | Crowell, Louise | 2, July 1842 | RCH |
| Stathem, Thomas | Gridley, Mary E. | 1, Feb. 1846 | RCH |
| Statsman, Andrew | Kinshallow, Ellen | 15, July 1834 | RCH |
| Staub, Joseph | Graf, Magdalena | 23, Apr. 1848 | G |
| Staubach, Ambrose | Leinster, Apollonia | 1, July 1849 | FF |
| Staup, William | McDonald, Christina | 7, Jan. 1846 | RCH |
| Staut, Georg | Sievertiny, Marg. | 19, Apr. 1836 | FF |
| Stauvermann, Johan D | Naber, Euphemia | 9, Nov. 1847 | CC |
| Stay, David M. | Coldwell, Maria | 16, May 1839 | RCH |
| Stead, George | Bliss, Charlotte | 4, Nov. 1832 | RCH |
| Stearns, William | Gambrel, Nancy | 7, June 1846 | RCH |
| Stecher, Francis | Meier, Kunigunda | 7, Jan. 1841 | FF |
| Stecher, Gerhard | Klanke, Maria | 4, Mar. 1842 | F |
| Stecher, Johan Peter | Tschaerter, Barbara | 13, Dec. 1849 | G |
| Stecker, Herman | Feldmann, Catharine | 7, Nov. 1843 | AA |
| Stedinger, Martin | Geisler, Eva | 29, Feb. 1844 | FF |
| Stedman, Samuel | Wells, Catharine V. | 28, Sept 1832 | RCH |
| Steege, Louis | Kelles, Elis. Jane | Dec. 1844 | RCH |
| Steel, Eliphalet | Clark, Mary | 9, Oct. 1825 | RCH |
| Steel, John | Bohlander, Anna E. | 18, Sept 1842 | RCH |
| Steel, Richard | Foster, Sarah | Dec. 1844 | RCH |
| Steele, John | Baker, Elizabeth | 19, Feb. 1827 | I |

| Grooms<br>***** | Brides<br>***** | Date of Marriage<br>**** ** ******** | Code<br>**** |
|---|---|---|---|
| Steele, Samuel | Collins, Sarah | 10, Nov. 1822 | RCH |
| Steele, Stephen | ----, Susannah | 18, Oct. 1839 | RCH |
| Steelman, James | Anderson, Nancy | 25, Nov. 1837 | RCH |
| Steem, Samuel | Hall, Mary | 22, Sept 1839 | RCH |
| Steemann, Heinrich | Hold, Bernardina | 30, Oct. 1849 | EE |
| Steen, Johan Herman | Wilpers, Anna Maria | 8, Sept 1846 | EE |
| Steen, John Friedric | Barlow, Ann | 24, July 1848 | RCH |
| Stefan, Sylvester | Germann, Elisabeth | 14, Nov. 1848 | FF |
| Steffe, Heinrich | Biemann, Margaretha | 5, Apr. 1849 | B |
| Steffe, Johan | Geisler, Elisabeth | 9, June 1836 | FF |
| Steffen, Alois | Birkly, Julia Anna | 5, Jan. 1836 | FF |
| Steffen, Mathias | Jergens, Anna Maria | 3, Nov. 1844 | FF |
| Steffens, Friedrich | Schutz, Susanna | 5, May 1849 | FF |
| Stegemann, Bernard | Broering, Catharina | 1, Dec. 1849 | AA |
| Stegemann, Gerhard | Lueken, Louise | 15, Oct. 1844 | AA |
| Stegemeier, Cord | Windhorst, Caroline | 13, Nov. 1848 | F |
| Steger, Michael | Schmidt, Margaretha | 6, Feb. 1848 | AA |
| Stehle, Vincenz | Schmidt, Isabella | 5, May 1847 | FF |
| Stehlin, Alois | Denhard, Anna Maria | 7, Aug. 1845 | AA |
| Stehteresch, Gerhard | Reineke, Maria | 17, June 1847 | RCH |
| Steidel, David | Peters, Margaretha | 2, Sept 1841 | RCH |
| Steidle, Johan | Hipp, Magdalena | 18, Nov. 1849 | AA |
| Steifel, Adam | Holler, Christina | 27, Oct. 1841 | RCH |
| Steigelmann, Jacob | Korzenborn, Anna | 1, Dec. 1846 | G |
| Steigerwald, Adam | Hagen, Maria | 13, June 1836 | FF |
| Steigerwald, Adam | Ballenger, Barb(Mrs) | 27, Jan. 1846 | EE |
| Steigerwald, Michael | Schumacher, Maria A. | 5, Nov. 1846 | EE |
| Stein, Albert | Kerr, Mary | 22, Nov. 1848 | RCH |
| Stein, Andreas | Fuhrmann, Maria | 15, Feb. 1842 | G |
| Stein, Johan | Manger, Maria | 17, July 1845 | FF |
| Stein, Mathias | Heistin, Eva Maria | 7, Sept 1848 | A |
| Stein, Michael | Singlewood, Mary | 14, July 1843 | RCH |
| Stein, Peter | Blum, Catharine | 28, July 1840 | FF |
| Stein, Peter | Hezel, Christina | 27, Dec. 1848 | A |
| Stein, Sebastian | Stab, Catharina | 7, Sept 1847 | AA |
| Steinagel, John | Mohn, Anna Margaret | 11, Apr. 1842 | RCH |
| Steinbach, John Adam | Huebner, Maria | 17, Oct. 1847 | AA |
| Steinbecker, Heinric | Massmann, A. Cath. | 25, Apr. 1847 | AA |
| Steinberg, William L | Hagen, Wilhelmina | 2, May 1848 | G |
| Steinbrink, Gerhard | Strunk, Anna Maria | 5, Nov. 1840 | F |
| Steineck, Bardol | Fryer, Elisabeth | 13, Feb. 1844 | RCH |
| Steineker, Wilhelm | Tiemann, Caroline | 14, Mar. 1848 | F |
| Steiner, Heinrich | Wuest, Apollonia | 15, Dec. 1836 | RCH |
| Steiner, Heinrich | Schneider, Sophia | 31, Dec. 1846 | C |
| Steiner, John | Pechhold, Margaret | 1, Jan. 1846 | RCH |
| Steiner, Michael | Cohen, Fanny | 24, Apr. 1846 | RCH |
| Steinfels, Lewis | Lems, Caroline | 26, July 1847 | RCH |
| Steinkamp, Ferdinand | Wessendorf, Gertrud | 14, June 1846 | AA |
| Steinkamp, Georg F. | Klein, Maria | 20, Sept 1848 | F |
| Steinkamp, Johan H. | Mueller, Louise | 30, Sept 1847 | F |
| Steinkamp, Nicolaus | VonderHaar, Elis. | 14, June 1846 | AA |
| Steinke, Johan H. | Sonderhaus, M. Agnes | 29, Sept 1840 | FF |
| Steinlage, Albert | Kock, Christina | 7, Oct. 1849 | II |
| Steinmann, Bernard | Tepe, Elisabeth | 7, June 1838 | FF |
| Steinmann, Friedrich | Bolte, Catharine M. | 30, Dec. 1845 | F |
| Steinmann, J Andreas | Weismann, Barbara | 27, June 1847 | G |
| Steinmann, Johan H. | Meyer, Cath. Gertrud | 29, Oct. 1835 | FF |
| Steinmann, Louis | Osmann, Maria | 27, Mar. 1849 | A |
| Steinmetz, Jacob | Maseram, Maria | 14, Dec. 1842 | AA |
| Steinmetz, Jacob | Hammerle, Elisabeth | 12, July 1849 | AA |
| Steinmetz, Wilhelm | Schmidt, Dorothea | 12, May 1846 | G |
| Steinriede, Johan H. | Siewe, Carolina | 12, Aug. 1849 | CC |
| Steinriede, Johan H. | Rolfs, Maria Angela | 25, Apr. 1847 | EE |
| Steins, Bernard | Kicking, Maria Anna | 28, Apr. 1842 | FF |
| Steirs, Matthew | Belts, Rachell | 15, Feb. 1838 | RCH |
| Stelle, Asa | Gould, Matilda | 10, Sept 1844 | RCH |
| Stelle, Joseph | Deeds, Julia | 15, Apr. 1849 | RCH |
| Steltenpohl, Herman | Bergmann, M. Agnes | 4, Feb. 1840 | FF |
| Stempfle, Johan | Meyer, Rufina | 27, Oct. 1846 | FF |
| Stenbach, | Kuthmann, Anna M. | 18, July 1847 | AA |
| Stengel, Andreas | Bras, Magdalena | 2, Feb. 1843 | FF |

| Grooms | Brides | Date of Marriage | Code |
|--------|--------|------------------|------|
| ****** | ****** | **** ** ******** | **** |
| Stengel, Nicolaus | Fritz, Apollonia | 13, Oct. 1835 | FF |
| Stenger, Andreas | Rittinger, Anna Eva | 22, Jan. 1846 | AA |
| Stenger, Christopher | Amann, Barbara | 27, Jan. 1846 | AA |
| Stenger, Heinrich | Stumvel, Maria | 29, Nov. 1845 | AA |
| Stenger, Heinrich | Scheinen, Dorothea | 20, June 1847 | EE |
| Stenger, Johan | Witt, Carolina | 16, Apr. 1844 | AA |
| Stenger, Lawrence | Mueller, Theresa | 26, Sept 1849 | EE |
| Stenglein, Johan | Nusslein, Kunigunda | 9, Sept 1849 | EE |
| Stenglein, Joseph | Obermeyer, Anna | 1, Jan. 1849 | EE |
| Stenzel, Wilhelm | Renndler, Francisca | 24, Oct. 1846 | EE |
| Steory, William | Singleton, Mary Ann | 14, Feb. 1832 | RCH |
| Stephan, Clement | Stehr, Carolina | 26, Mar. 1845 | AA |
| Stephans, William L. | Gall---, Sarah B. | 1, Jan. 1823 | RCH |
| Stephen, Isaac | Pullom, Eliza | 8, May 1839 | I |
| Stephen, James H. | Guisi, Elisabeth | 30, Dec. 1840 | RCH |
| Stephens, Daniel | Johnson, Mary | 17, Oct. 1832 | RCH |
| Stephens, Enoch | Barnes, Louise | 1, Dec. 1842 | RCH |
| Stephens, Isaac | Hays, Sarah M. | 23, Dec. 1845 | RCH |
| Stephens, Jonathan | Day, Harriet | 14, Feb. 1833 | RCH |
| Stephens, Lott B. | Miles, Amy | 6, Oct. 1833 | RCH |
| Stephens, Marcus | Cutter, Charlotte | 16, Feb. 1823 | RCH |
| Stephens, Reuben | Rickhoff, Mary Ann | 1, Jan. 1836 | RCH |
| Stephens, Samuel | Menatier, Wilhelmina | 26, Nov. 1848 | G |
| Stephens, Squire | Pummil, Martha | 14, June 1849 | RCH |
| Stephens, Thomas | Lockwood, Sarah | 9, Feb. 1820 | RCH |
| Stephens, William | Lucas, Mary A. | 10, Feb. 1843 | RCH |
| Stephens, William | McCartney, Elisabeth | 7, June 1849 | RCH |
| Stephens, Winthrop | Williams, Elisabeth | 1, June 1826 | RCH |
| Stephenson, Lorenzo | Simpson, Elisabeth | 28, Oct. 1837 | RCH |
| Stephenson, Reilly | Carman, Elisabeth | 28, Dec. 1820 | RCH |
| Stephenson, Richard | Rugg, Sarah | 14, Dec. 1847 | RCH |
| Stephenson, Samuel | Ferris, Elsey Ann | 22, Feb. 1844 | RCH |
| Stephenson, Thomas | Roll, Beatty | 4, Feb. 1843 | RCH |
| Steppen, Henry | Kerchner, Catharine | 5, Sept 1847 | RCH |
| Stepton, John | Heer, Carolina | 17, June 1834 | RCH |
| Sterlin, Louis | Letourneur, Sophia M | 11, Feb. 1846 | BB |
| Sterling, Samuel | Smith, Elisabeth | 11, Dec. 1842 | RCH |
| Sterling, Stephen | Cooper, Jane | 2, June 1841 | RCH |
| Stern, Aaron | Rosenthaler, Harriet | 22, July 1847 | RCH |
| Stern, Christoph | Milleri, Maria | 21, Feb. 1849 | CC |
| Sternweis, Johan F. | Schwartz, Magdalena | 6, Sept 1849 | C |
| Sternwerf, Herman | Schulze, Christina | 31, Jan. 1847 | EE |
| Sterrett, David | Wood, Phoebe Ann | 19, June 1837 | RCH |
| Stertmeyer, Joseph | Hoppen, Anna Maria | 16, July 1848 | EE |
| Stertsman, Samuel | Hicks, Anna Maria | 28, Dec. 1834 | RCH |
| Steth, Johan | Brausch, Maria | 22, Apr. 1845 | AA |
| Stetter, Lorenz | Weibel, Catharine | 17, May 1849 | II |
| Stettmeier, Heinrich | Winkelmann, Josephin | 17, Nov. 1849 | EE |
| Stettmeyer, Joseph H | Christel, Euphemia | 7, Oct. 1849 | EE |
| Steubbus, F. Anthony | Oben, Frances | 3, June 1842 | RCH |
| Steven, Gerhard J. | Bernsing, Catharne | 14, Sept 1845 | AA |
| Stevens, Charles | Boland, Emily | 11, Apr. 1841 | RCH |
| Stevens, Charles | Parker, Rachel | 5, Sept 1843 | RCH |
| Stevens, Edward | Williams, Elisabeth | 25, Mar. 1849 | RCH |
| Stevens, Eliphalet | Day, Margaret | 2, Nov. 1834 | RCH |
| Stevens, Enoch | Dunlap, Mary Ann | 21, Aug. 1843 | RCH |
| Stevens, Francis | Everhart, Mary Ann | 17, Sept 1844 | RCH |
| Stevens, George | Stephenson, Amelia | 30, May 1844 | RCH |
| Stevens, Gerhard H. | Deiper, Adelheid | 12, Oct. 1847 | AA |
| Stevens, Henry | Cass, Anna C. | 17, Sept 1839 | RCH |
| Stevens, Hiram | White, Wealthy Ann | 1, July 1844 | RCH |
| Stevens, Isaac | Harness, Harriet | 6, Aug. 1848 | RCH |
| Stevens, James | Fowler, Sarah | 29, Sept 1842 | RCH |
| Stevens, James F. | Hart, Harriet | 3, Mar. 1841 | RCH |
| Stevens, Johan Theo. | Ubschulten, Susanna | 28, May 1848 | EE |
| Stevens, John | Dixon, Rachel | 15, Apr. 1842 | RCH |
| Stevens, John | Mel, Barbara | 28, Jan. 1847 | RCH |
| Stevens, John | Lee, Ann | 7, Mar. 1849 | RCH |
| Stevens, Levi | Pierson, Emily J. | 26, Nov. 1842 | RCH |
| Stevens, Marcus | Smith, Harriet | 13, Apr. 1836 | RCH |
| Stevens, Martin | Schulhausen, Eva D. | 24, Dec. 1847 | G |

| Grooms | Brides | Date of Marriage | Code |
|--------|--------|------------------|------|
| Stevens, Montgomery | Price, Elisabeth | 4, Jan. 1846 | RCH |
| Stevens, Oliver | Biddle, Mary Ann | 11, June 1846 | RCH |
| Stevens, Ranna | VanDoran, Elisabeth | 14, Aug. 1846 | RCH |
| Stevens, Thomas | Applegate, Sarah | 18, Jan. 1846 | RCH |
| Stevens, William | Bruner, Caroline | 31, Jan. 1836 | RCH |
| Stevens, William | Brown, Frances | 13, Dec. 1849 | RCH |
| Stevens, William H. | Sweet, Frances | 21, Aug. 1849 | RCH |
| Stevenson, Francis | Harvey, Elisabeth | 1, Nov. 1833 | RCH |
| Stevenson, Henry | Hand, Elisabeth | 10, May 1848 | RCH |
| Stevenson, Hugh | Williamson, Adrian | 26, Jan. 1832 | RCH |
| Stevenson, Isaac | Stokes, Matilda | 20, July 1844 | RCH |
| Stevenson, John | Martin, Sarah | 14, Oct. 1819 | RCH |
| Stevenson, Joseph | Boone, Hester | 20, Oct. 1841 | RCH |
| Stevenson, T. | Hart, Martha J. | 22, May 1849 | RCH |
| Stever, Johan Heinr. | Briggemeyer, Anna M. | 15, July 1841 | FF |
| Stevit, David | Hickman, Mary | 22, Apr. 1843 | RCH |
| Steward, Ephraim | Mills, Rachel | 1822 | RCH |
| Steward, James | Hawkins, Lucinda | 6, Apr. 1834 | RCH |
| Steward, James | Dunham, Margaret | 3, Mar. 1836 | RCH |
| Steward, Nathan | Bryant, Ellen | 16, Nov. 1842 | RCH |
| Stewart, Alexander | Stephens, Hannah | 10, May 1832 | RCH |
| Stewart, Alexander | Sutton, Susan | 12, June 1832 | RCH |
| Stewart, Arthur | Moore, Mary Jane | 28, Feb. 1844 | RCH |
| Stewart, Benjamin | ----, H. | 21, Sept 1819 | RCH |
| Stewart, Charles | ----, ---- | Dec. 1834 | RCH |
| Stewart, Charles | Ireland, Susan | 21, Feb. 1836 | RCH |
| Stewart, Charles | Dawson, Martha Ann | 1, Apr. 1849 | RCH |
| Stewart, Daniel | Williams, Mary C. | 14, Mar. 1833 | RCH |
| Stewart, Daniel | Miller, Alsey | 27, Mar. 1834 | RCH |
| Stewart, George | Swales, Rachel | 15, May 1831 | RCH |
| Stewart, Henry | Lawmons, Jane | 2, July 1839 | RCH |
| Stewart, Henry | Stillman, Barbara | 5, Jan. 1840 | RCH |
| Stewart, Israel | Slayback, Margaret | 30, Oct. 1817 | RCH |
| Stewart, Jacob | Sutton, Elisabeth | 17, Oct. 1820 | RCH |
| Stewart, Jacob | Crosby, Lois | 29, Mar. 1832 | RCH |
| Stewart, Jacob | Conklin, Sarah | 6, Jan. 1833 | RCH |
| Stewart, James | Williams, Susannah | 25, Aug. 1835 | RCH |
| Stewart, James | McCann, Martha | 4, Dec. 1841 | BB |
| Stewart, Jealous | Carel, Elisabeth | 12, July 1838 | RCH |
| Stewart, John | ----, Dorcus | 7, Nov. 1826 | RCH |
| Stewart, John | Kinney, Ann | 29, Oct. 1834 | RCH |
| Stewart, John | Wass, Sarah | 28, Feb. 1837 | RCH |
| Stewart, John | Beeler, Elisabeth | 23, Nov. 1837 | RCH |
| Stewart, John | Worth, Elsy | 9, June 1849 | RCH |
| Stewart, Joseph | Grady, Elisabeth | 5, July 1821 | RCH |
| Stewart, Joseph | Walton, Elvinia | 29, Jan. 1826 | RCH |
| Stewart, Joseph | Richardson, Elis. | 22, Aug. 1839 | RCH |
| Stewart, Myron Alson | Meara, Catharine | 29, May 1845 | BB |
| Stewart, Philipp G. | Bowen, Jane | 18, Nov. 1832 | RCH |
| Stewart, Samuel | Meeks, Isabella | 12, Feb. 1837 | RCH |
| Stewart, Samuel | Stratthan, Sarah M. | 20, Mar. 1839 | RCH |
| Stewart, Samuel | Statham, Sarah | 24, Dec. 1841 | RCH |
| Stewart, Samuel | Riley, Amanda | 1, May 1844 | RCH |
| Stewart, Samuel M. | Ferguson, Peninah | 8, Nov. 1832 | RCH |
| Stewart, Thomas | Gentle, Margaret | 20, Oct. 1846 | RCH |
| Stewart, Thomas Alex | Williams, Caroline | 15, June 1848 | RCH |
| Stewart, William | Martin, Elisabeth | 10, May 1835 | RCH |
| Stewart, William | Could, Jane | 8, Apr. 1838 | RCH |
| Stewart, William | Homer, Elisabeth | 14, Oct. 1841 | RCH |
| Stewart, William | Smith, Caroline | 26, Sept 1846 | RCH |
| Steyart, Pankranz | Menninger, Anna M. | 16, Nov. 1845 | FF |
| Steyert, Martin | Menninger, Catharine | 28, May 1848 | EE |
| Stibbs, Samuel | Gibbs, Mary Jane | 20, June 1842 | RCH |
| Stibe, Joseph | Arkenberg, Carolina | 11, Sept 1847 | EE |
| Stickel, Amand | Friz, Apollonia | 15, Feb. 1844 | AA |
| Stickel, Samuel | Ackley, Tamsion | 8, Aug. 1837 | RCH |
| Stickeling, Christ. | Dehren, Elizabeth | 31, Dec. 1849 | RCH |
| Sticker, Johan Bd. | Claasmann, Bernardin | 2, May 1847 | AA |
| Stickler, George | Dicks, Ellen | 17, Feb. 1842 | RCH |
| Stickney, Daniel | Lewis, Sarah Ann | 27, May 1847 | RCH |
| Stickney, David | Plummer, Mary J. | 15, May 1839 | RCH |

| Grooms | Brides | Date of Marriage | Code |
|--------|--------|------------------|------|
| Sticksel, Peter | Fink, Susanna | 4, Feb. 1841 | FF |
| Stiedel, Georg | Bohlander, Margaret | 4, Mar. 1845 | G |
| Stiefel, Adolph C. | Kroebe, Margaretha | 10, Oct. 1845 | C |
| Stiefel, Meyer | Goetz, Fanny | 29, May 1849 | RCH |
| Stiegeler, Anton | Bachtler, Barbara | 15, Apr. 1849 | II |
| Stiene, Johan D. | Krolage, Cath. (Mrs) | 7, Jan. 1845 | AA |
| Stieneker, Ernst | Schoppenhorst, Lou. | 6, May 1847 | C |
| Stienker, Heinrich P | Burlage, M Elisabeth | 24, Apr. 1845 | F |
| Stiens, Arnold Hein. | Hubbert, Christina | 19, July 1846 | FF |
| Stiens, Gerhard H. | Timmermann, Maria | 18, Jan. 1842 | FF |
| Stiens, Johan Hein. | Stueve, Maria Anna | 22, Jan. 1839 | FF |
| Stiens, Johan Hein. | Barhorst, M. Gertrud | 6, Oct. 1842 | AA |
| Stiere, Johan H. | Ortmann, Margaretha | 10, Feb. 1835 | FF |
| Stifel, Christian | Hudrick, Lydia | 23, Sept 1845 | RCH |
| Stikes, A.F. | Hart, Catharine | 29, Nov. 1836 | RCH |
| Stiles, Benjamin | ----, Sarah | 5, Aug. 1819 | RCH |
| Stiles, Benjamin T. | Davis, Sidney V. | 22, Aug. 1833 | RCH |
| Stiles, Washington | Southerner, Kitty | 19, Feb. 1839 | RCH |
| Stille, Ernst | Dickmann, Henrietta | 4, May 1848 | C |
| Stille, John | Hamilton, Caroline | 10, May 1842 | RCH |
| Stilley, James | Russell, Ann Elis. | 20, May 1841 | RCH |
| Stilley, James | Folger, Eleanor | 5, June 1844 | RCH |
| Stillman, George | Nottingham, Mary | 9, Feb. 1846 | RCH |
| Stillman, Oliver | Talbott, Hester | 17, July 1838 | RCH |
| Stillwell, Major | P---, Phebe | 16, Mar. 1835 | RCH |
| Stilwell, Amos | Cooper, Polly | 4, Mar. 1841 | RCH |
| Stilwell, James | Lewis, Catharine | 25, Jan. 1847 | RCH |
| Stilwell, Joseph | Thompson, Mary | 1, Aug. 1818 | RCH |
| Stilwell, Robert | Dimick, Catharine | 4, Nov. 1843 | RCH |
| Stimpson, Charles | Graham, Rachel | 7, Oct. 1837 | RCH |
| Stimweis, Johan | Schwarz, Magdalena | 6, July 1845 | C |
| Stineke, Ernst Wm. | Dieckmann, Louise A. | 27, Apr. 1847 | E |
| Stinger, Andreas | Stinger, Anna Maria | 23, Feb. 1841 | FF |
| Stingsley, Thomas | Wiley, Catharine | 20, June 1819 | RCH |
| Stins, Francis | Busch, Elisabeth | 15, May 1834 | RCH |
| Stinson, William G. | Morgan, Margaret | 11, Aug. 1818 | RCH |
| Stints, Henry J. | Higdon, Julia A. | 15, Dec. 1837 | RCH |
| Stirge, Daniel | McKee, Mary | 1, Apr. 1819 | RCH |
| Stites, Alexander | Varley, Ellen | 31, Oct. 1847 | RCH |
| Stites, Casper | Harper, Mary Ann | 8, July 1834 | RCH |
| Stites, George W. | Stites, Abigail | Dec. 1840 | RCH |
| Stites, Hezekiah | Ferris, Mary | 2, Sept 1846 | RCH |
| Stites, James | Ward, Charlotte | 25, Nov. 1845 | RCH |
| Stites, James | Muchmore, Harriet | 10, Feb. 1847 | RCH |
| Stites, James | Boyer, Elisabeth | 15, Oct. 1848 | RCH |
| Stites, John | Hart, Mary | 7, May 1836 | RCH |
| Stites, Michael | Rudeeph, Elenor | 19, Jan. 1834 | RCH |
| Stites, William | Carney, Elisabeth | 13, Jan. 1820 | RCH |
| Stites, William | Murburger, Elisabeth | 4, July 1846 | RCH |
| Stitwell, William | Helm---, Nancy | 17, 1823 | RCH |
| Stoat, George W. | Atkinson, Lucinda | 3, July 1834 | RCH |
| Stobbe, John M. | Goeke, Anna M. Elis. | 26, Nov. 1848 | BB |
| Stobbers, Clemens | Nordlohn, M. Helena | 27, May 1849 | II |
| Stock, Heinrich | Tube, M. Anna | 4, Sept 1849 | AA |
| Stock, Peter | Stephan, Anna Maria | 14, Mar. 1848 | CC |
| Stockbrink, Heinrich | Hoening, Elisabeth | 16, Nov. 1846 | EE |
| Stockham, William | Jones, Ann | 17, May 1834 | RCH |
| Stockhof, Carl Fried | Hugerkampf, Sophia L | 28, Oct. 1847 | A |
| Stockhove, Gerhard F | B---mann, Dorothea | 19, Mar. 1840 | F |
| Stocking, Daniel | B---, Prudence | 17, Jan. 1823 | RCH |
| Stockmann, Johan H. | Robinson, Lucretia | 13, Dec. 1845 | RCH |
| Stockton, Joseph | McWright, Catharine | 18, Apr. 1821 | RCH |
| Stoddard, Avery | Burse, Sarah Ann | 22, June 1847 | G |
| Stoddard, James | Waggoner, Hannah | 25, July 1822 | RCH |
| Stoeckel, Joseph | Kraisick, Barbara | 19, Sept 1842 | RCH |
| Stoecker, Conrad | Grammann, Anna | 1, July 1845 | AA |
| Stoeckle, Anton | Dunkes, Mary E. | 2, Oct. 1846 | RCH |
| Stoehr, Johan | Walz, Margaretha | 8, Sept 1846 | AA |
| Stoehr, Leonardt | Bender, Helena | 8, Oct. 1848 | C |
| Stoekel, Wendel | Fritz, Apollonia | 15, Feb. 1844 | RCH |
| Stoel, William | May, Julia Ann | 24, May 1822 | RCH |

| Grooms<br>****** | Brides<br>****** | Date of Marriage<br>**** ** ******** | Code<br>**** |
|---|---|---|---|
| Stoellner, Georg | Noelle, Margaretha | 3, Sept 1848 | A |
| Stoemer, William | Stewart, Milly | 1, Jan. 1823 | RCH |
| Stoer, John | Dyday, Mary | 29, Sept 1834 | RCH |
| Stoet, Daniel C. | Byrne, Lucinda | 30, Nov. 1837 | RCH |
| Stofel, William | Marks, Elisabeth | 22, Jan. 1845 | RCH |
| Stoff, Valentin | Koefers, Agnes | 10, Sept 1848 | EE |
| Stokes, Clayton | West, Sarah | 19, Nov. 1846 | RCH |
| Stokes, Edward | Hon, Mary | 14, June 1846 | RCH |
| Stokes, Richard | Meyers, Julia Ann | 5, Oct. 1845 | RCH |
| Stokes, Theodor | Marshall, Sarah | 17, Jan. 1849 | RCH |
| Stoll, John | McClure, Mary Jane | 14, June 1843 | RCH |
| Stoll, Michael | Rossfeld, Apollonia | 28, Dec. 1847 | AA |
| Stolz, Bernard | Bressler, Anna Maria | 20, June 1847 | EE |
| Stolz, Carl | Wingerder, Margaret | 4, Apr. 1837 | FF |
| Stolz, Johan | Kenna, Maria | 18, Feb. 1849 | C |
| Stolzer, Andreas | Spaeth, Frances(Mrs) | 15, Nov. 1849 | FF |
| Stombs, Daniel | Noland, Nancy | 3, Sept 1848 | RCH |
| Stombs, Thomas | Taylor, Esther | 3, May 1846 | RCH |
| Stone, | Dusky, Cynthia | 25, Apr. 1822 | RCH |
| Stone, Ashel | Preston, Lydia | 24, Sept 1837 | RCH |
| Stone, James F. | Kessler, Christina | 21, Dec. 1844 | RCH |
| Stone, James S. | Phenen, Mary E. | 13, June 1838 | RCH |
| Stone, Joseph | McFeely, Elisabeth | 19, Nov. 1833 | RCH |
| Stone, Landon | Gross, Susan | 4, Jan. 1835 | RCH |
| Stone, Richard | Landrum, Sarah | 26, Nov. 1846 | RCH |
| Stone, Theodore | Carson, Margaret | 15, Nov. 1847 | RCH |
| Stone, William | Edda, Ann | 30, Jan. 1819 | RCH |
| Stone, William | Matson, Joanna | 11, Dec. 1822 | RCH |
| Stone, William | Bartlette, Margaret | 28, May 1844 | RCH |
| Stonemelt, David | Allen, Willey | 14, Jan. 1847 | RCH |
| Stoner, Alfred | ----, Elisabeth | 21, May 1835 | RCH |
| Stoops, Hugh | Carr, Elisabeth | 15, Aug. 1833 | RCH |
| Stoops, John | Dawson, Mary Ann | 4, Aug. 1847 | RCH |
| Stoops, William | Linsley, Hannah | 26, Oct. 1835 | RCH |
| Stopher, Jacob | Ray, Elisabeth | 23, May 1833 | RCH |
| Stops, Sampson | Clark, Margaret | 18, Aug. 1847 | RCH |
| Storch, Johan | Keck, Francisca | 25, Nov. 1849 | CC |
| Storch, Joseph | Muth, Margaretha | 24, Aug. 1847 | AA |
| Storck, Paul | Denie, Theresa | 7, Sept 1841 | FF |
| Stordeur, Martin | Wuebbelsmann, Elis. | 11, Nov. 1849 | CC |
| Storer, Bellamy | Bartow, Euretta Lou. | 20, Sept 1820 | I |
| Storer, Bellamy | Comstock, Sarah | 27, Dec. 1842 | I |
| Storer, Bellamy | Drinker, Elisabeth | 12, May 1846 | I |
| Stork, Basil | Rhea, Sarah | 14, Feb. 1836 | RCH |
| Stork, Christian | Landon, Jane | 5, Mar. 1837 | RCH |
| Storkey, Abraham | Carr, Martha | 24, June 1820 | RCH |
| Storm, John | Whiteman, Margaret | 14, July 1842 | RCH |
| Storms, William | Means, Elisabeth | 12, Oct. 1837 | RCH |
| Stort, Heinrich | Flederjohann, Cath. | 26, Oct. 1848 | C |
| Story, Jacob | Hutmacher, Salome | 9, Mar. 1841 | G |
| Story, James | Johnson, Hannah | 1, Apr. 1848 | RCH |
| Story, Peter | Voelker, Appolonia | 18, Mar. 1848 | G |
| Storz, Francis X. | Boellinger, Theresa | 14, Feb. 1847 | EE |
| Stossmeister, Fried. | Mueller, Friedricka | 3, June 1849 | G |
| Stoud, Franklin | Conley, Lydia | 7, Sept 1835 | RCH |
| Stouder, Samuel | Knicely, Zipporah | 1, Oct. 1848 | RCH |
| Stout, Aaron G. | Adams, Lydia | 24, Jan. 1838 | RCH |
| Stout, Daniel | McLaughlin, Diana | 25, July 1822 | RCH |
| Stout, Ephraim | Pool, Ellen | 23, Dec. 1847 | RCH |
| Stout, Esra | Robinson, Fanny | 31, Mar. 1825 | RCH |
| Stout, George | Satnatt, Catharine | 8, Apr. 1838 | RCH |
| Stout, Horace | Agnew, | 23, 1834 | RCH |
| Stout, Ira | Evans, Ann | 30, Aug. 1835 | RCH |
| Stout, James | Coore, Rachel | 4, May 1839 | RCH |
| Stout, Jesse D. | Thomas, Mary A. | 23, Nov. 1848 | RCH |
| Stout, John | Money, Sarah Ann | 24, Dec. 1826 | RCH |
| Stout, John S. | Cogswell, Anna | 15, Feb. 1835 | RCH |
| Stout, John W. | Powell, Hester | 23, Apr. 1834 | RCH |
| Stout, Jonathan | Cunning, | 12, Sept 1835 | RCH |
| Stout, Nathaniel | Peck, Emily | 4, May 1847 | RCH |
| Stout, Oliver | Gulich, Jane | 2, Mar. 1846 | RCH |

| Grooms | Brides | Date of Marriage | Code |
|--------|--------|------------------|------|
| ****** | ****** | **** ** ******** | **** |
| Stout, William | Minor, Keziah | 18, Apr. 1846 | RCH |
| Stover, Johan Conrad | Doepke, Catharine | 27, Feb. 1848 | F |
| Stow, William | Ingersoll, Elisabeth | Dec. 1844 | RCH |
| Stowers, Henry | Henry, Levina | 20, Feb. 1832 | RCH |
| Strader, Jacob | Dunseth, Julia | 16, May 1827 | RCH |
| Stradtmann, Carl | Armeding, Maria | 5, Oct. 1849 | C |
| Stradtmann, Heinrich | Wuelles, Elisabeth | 30, Jan. 1838 | FF |
| Straeber, Georg | Rapsin, Elisabeth | 23, June 1844 | C |
| Strahmann, Theodor | Schulte, Anna | 26, Aug. 1849 | II |
| Stralkamp, Bernard | Dres, Anna | 3, June 1849 | AA |
| Stranger, William | Sutton, Caroline | 21, Aug. 1848 | RCH |
| Strantlin, Friedrich | Ottemans, Wilhelmina | 25, Oct. 1847 | C |
| Straper, Friedrich | Meyer, Catharina | 3, Aug. 1837 | FF |
| Strassel, Michael | Schorr, Katharine | 25, June 1848 | EE |
| Strasser, Johan | Dickmann, Kunigunda | 25, June 1848 | AA |
| Strassner, Heinrich | Somer, Caroline | 25, Mar. 1848 | C |
| Strateger, Johan H. | Broemann, Maria | 17, Nov. 1846 | AA |
| Stratmann, Bernard | Bohlmann, Elisabeth | 19, Nov. 1844 | AA |
| Stratmann, Casper | Weiger, Anna Maria | 12, Oct. 1845 | AA |
| Strattmann, Theodor | Meyer, Catharine | 4, May 1843 | AA |
| Stratton, Eli | Wait, Ann | 24, Dec. 1824 | RCH |
| Stratton, Jeriel R. | Babb, Emeline | 27, Aug. 1846 | RCH |
| Stratton, Job | Pipet, Ann | 10, June 1818 | RCH |
| Stratton, John | Mevall, Belinda | 15, Dec. 1837 | RCH |
| Stratton, Noah | White, Louise | 16, Nov. 1843 | RCH |
| Stratton, Orange | Long, S. | 30, Sept 1824 | RCH |
| Straub, Felix | Bodmer, Eva | 19, Oct. 1845 | AA |
| Straube, William H. | Nouss, Phebe | 1, Sept 1836 | RCH |
| Strauble, Heinrich | Wuest, Wilhelmina | 26, Jan. 1843 | RCH |
| Straubuck, John | Horton, Sophia | 24, July 1820 | RCH |
| Strauhruner, George | Smead, Jane C. | 29, Mar. 1834 | RCH |
| Straukamp, Francis J | Sommer, Catharina | 25, Nov. 1847 | FF |
| Straupart, Joseph | Hutzler, Rosina | 25, Apr. 1837 | FF |
| Straus, Abraham | Sputz, Fanny | 15, Feb. 1842 | RCH |
| Straus, Moses | Moeller, Julia | 9, Dec. 1844 | RCH |
| Straus, Samuel | Guttmann, Ricke | 15, Sept 1842 | RCH |
| Strauss, Johan | Schetter, Judith | 7, Aug. 1849 | EE |
| Strautker, Friedrich | Otmans, Wilhelmina | 28, Oct. 1847 | RCH |
| Strecker, Johan | Schmalz, Walburga | 16, June 1842 | FF |
| Street, George | Pond, Elisabeth | 7, Mar. 1833 | RCH |
| Street, Marvin B. | Mount, Elisabeth | 10, July 1834 | RCH |
| Strehle, Conrad | Kuhn, Barbara | 4, June 1844 | AA |
| Strehle, Joseph | Bodenkircher, | 1, Sept 1839 | FF |
| Streibich, Michael | Harbich, Margaret | 19, Dec. 1849 | RCH |
| Streife, Francis Jos | Gisler, Walburga | 19, Apr. 1836 | FF |
| Streiff, Thomas | Klein, Catharine | 23, Sept 1845 | C |
| Streile, Anton | Knopf, Ursula | 27, Apr. 1847 | AA |
| Streitmeyer, Heinric | Ross, Catharine | 22, Jan. 1846 | C |
| Stremenn, Clamor | Wering, Anna M.Elis. | 10, Feb. 1835 | FF |
| Stretz, Andreas | Deglemann, Magdalena | 22, Feb. 1841 | FF |
| Streutker, Heinrich | Fesbeck, Lisette | 16, Oct. 1845 | C |
| Streutker, J. Heinr. | Wiemand, Sophia | 26, Sept 1844 | F |
| Strewe, Francis Con. | Bulthof, Maria Agnes | 17, June 1841 | FF |
| Stribing, Mathias | Knebel, Magdalena | 4, Nov. 1844 | AA |
| Strick, Isaac | Brotherton, Sarah | 31, Oct. 1833 | RCH |
| Strickelmeyer, Johan | Weipert, Maria Anna | 16, Feb. 1840 | FF |
| Stricker, Anton | Prune, Maria | 28, July 1835 | FF |
| Stricker, Charles | Thompson, Belthia | 23, Feb. 1838 | RCH |
| Stricker, F. | Price, Angela | 3, Oct. 1844 | RCH |
| Stricker, Henry F. | Robinson, Ernestine | 7, June 1843 | BB |
| Stricker, Johan H. | Wensing, Gertrud | 30, Sept 1849 | AA |
| Strickler, John | Kuckle, Catharine C. | 14, Aug. 1842 | RCH |
| Striecker, Peter | Utz, Magaretha | 23, May 1847 | AA |
| Striefler, Georg M. | Fromholt, Margaretha | 9, July 1848 | EE |
| Strieker, Francis M. | Renk, Magdalena | 7, Feb. 1848 | AA |
| Strietelmeier, Adolf | Gerse, Maria | 28, Feb. 1848 | E |
| Strietelmeier, Johan | Busemeyer, Maria E. | 27, Oct. 1842 | RCH |
| Strietelmeier, Rud. | Bohrmann, Margaretha | 9, Mar. 1849 | E |
| Striff, Michael | Hennie, Margaret | 30, Dec. 1843 | RCH |
| Strigel, Paul | Gert, Genofeva | 18, July 1847 | EE |
| Strimple, Henry | Stewart, Mary | 21, Nov. 1820 | RCH |

| Grooms | Brides | Date of Marriage | Code |
|--------|--------|------------------|------|
| ****** | ****** | **** ** ******** | **** |
| Stringe, Thomas | Edwards, Mary G. | 27, Mar. 1843 | RCH |
| Strob, Christian | Schirlo, Elisabeth | 3, Nov. 1840 | FF |
| Strobel, Johan | Baillert, Christina | 7, Nov. 1844 | AA |
| Strobridge, Hines | Wright, Jane Isabell | 2, Oct. 1845 | RCH |
| Strobridge, Matthew | Riley, Ann J. | 15, Aug. 1839 | RCH |
| Stroh, Conrad | Klump, Barbara | 21, May 1845 | A |
| Stroher, Michael | Schmidt, Elisabeth | 22, Mar. 1849 | RCH |
| Strohmeyer, F Xavier | Casper, M. Catharina | 5, Dec. 1839 | FF |
| Strome, George W. | Williams, Elisabeth | 14, Jan. 1846 | RCH |
| Strome, John R. | Murray, Keziah | 13, Dec. 1849 | RCH |
| Strong, David | Harris, Elisabeth | 1, May 1837 | RCH |
| Strong, Ebenezer | Glover, Catharine | 2, Mar. 1846 | RCH |
| Strong, Eber | McCarty, Martha | 5, Apr. 1842 | RCH |
| Strong, Henry | Collins, Mary W. | 6, May 1847 | RCH |
| Strong, Simon | Watgen, Friedricka | 27, May 1837 | RCH |
| Strong, Truman B. | Booth, Rachel | 4, May 1827 | RCH |
| Strong, William | Salor, Sarah | 11, July 1843 | RCH |
| Stronk, Heinrich | Leibsuch, Elisabeth | 5, Feb. 1835 | FF |
| Stronninger, Casper | Rehberger, Barbara | 26, Dec. 1847 | EE |
| Stropel, Peter | Ingert, Elisabeth | 7, Mar. 1837 | FF |
| Stroten, Eli | Scofield, Emeline | 1, Nov. 1845 | RCH |
| Strothmann, Theodore | Trentmann, M. Elis. | 14, Apr. 1843 | RCH |
| Strotmann, Georg | Meyer, Margaretha | 7, Jan. 1838 | FF |
| Strouder, Zachariah | Harrison, Elisabeth | 23, Jan. 1843 | RCH |
| Stroup, Heinrich Wm. | Boyer, Elisabeth | 16, Aug. 1848 | RCH |
| Stroup, Washington | Baker, Hester | 11, Dec. 1848 | RCH |
| Strowbridge, William | Abbott, Eveline | 1, June 1843 | RCH |
| Strowhover, H.A. | Merryfield, Irene | 31, July 1834 | RCH |
| Strub, George | Witgresse, Margaret | 1, Dec. 1846 | RCH |
| Strubb, John | Boierl, Christina | 7, Nov. 1844 | RCH |
| Strubbe, Herman | Schepmann, Catharine | 6, Oct. 1842 | F |
| Strubbe, Johan | Kunnemann, Catharine | 30, July 1846 | F |
| Strubbe, Johan Hein. | Hausfeld, Elisabeth | 4, June 1846 | F |
| Strubbe, Joseph | Hunt, Clara | 4, May 1835 | RCH |
| Strubble, James | ----, Sarah Ann | 1822 | RCH |
| Strubele, George | Parker, Elinida | 17, Sept 1836 | RCH |
| Struble, Andrew | Stout, Sarah | 31, May 1834 | RCH |
| Strunk, Friedrich | Ellermann, Maria E. | 9, Dec. 1841 | F |
| Strunk, Heinrich | Ohhe, Maria Elis. | 30, Apr. 1839 | FF |
| Strunk, Simon | Wayter, Friedricka | 2, June 1837 | RCH |
| Stryker, Asher | Collington, Caroline | 1, May 1843 | RCH |
| Stryker, Joseph M. | Gardner, Elisabeth A | 1, May 1848 | RCH |
| Stryker, Joseph M. | Clark, Mary Jane | 25, Oct. 1849 | BB |
| Stryker, William | McCandliss, Isabella | 21, Aug. 1847 | RCH |
| Stu---, Robert | Knox, Margaret | 11, Dec. 1821 | RCH |
| Stuart, James A. | Bruley, Elisabeth | 3, Apr. 1834 | RCH |
| Stubbie, Friedrich | Seneber, Angela | 1, Sept 1835 | FF |
| Stubblemann, Francis | Gossling, Elisabeth | 22, Apr. 1849 | FF |
| Stubbs, Isaac | Metcalf, Alice | 30, July 1835 | RCH |
| Stubert, John | Ballard, Rebecca | 17, Sept 1826 | RCH |
| Stubert, John | Bidelle, Clarissa | 21, May 1835 | RCH |
| Stuck, John | Pryer, Mary | 9, Oct. 1832 | RCH |
| Stuckmann, Friedrich | Heidorn, Sophia | 25, Nov. 1848 | F |
| Stuckmeyer, Herman H | Schulte, Henrietta | 12, June 1845 | F |
| Stuckmeyer, Johan H. | Nothmann, A.M. Engel | 27, Nov. 1845 | F |
| Studer, Fidel | Gasser, Martina | 25, Jan. 1848 | EE |
| Studer, Fidel | Brunner, Anna Maria | 9, Jan. 1849 | EE |
| Studley, Nathaniel | Stephens, Susan | 6, Jan. 1825 | RCH |
| Studt, Friedrich | Sandermann, Regina | 19, June 1849 | C |
| Study, John | VanZant, Sarah | 22, Aug. 1844 | RCH |
| Stuempel, Bernard | Kuhlmann, Anna Maria | 30, July 1849 | AA |
| Stuenkel, Heinrich | Cook, Hannah | 9, Sept 1845 | F |
| Stuerenberg, Heinric | Meyer, Maria Agnes | 23, Nov. 1848 | FF |
| Stuermer, Francis | Raedinger, Anna M. | 28, Apr. 1846 | FF |
| Stuessel, Heinrich C | Stadeckers, Maria | 14, June 1845 | C |
| Stueve, G. Heinrich | Tormoehlen, Anna M. | 7, Sept 1843 | F |
| Stueve, Heinrich | Mesch, Maria Anna | 31, Aug. 1841 | FF |
| Stueve, Johan Herman | Moellers, Wilhelmina | 14, May 1846 | F |
| Stuevel, Georg | Butke, Anna | 21, Dec. 1849 | C |
| Stuewe, Bernard Wm. | Luebbermann, Phil. | 9, May 1847 | AA |
| Stuhrenberg, Joseph | Kemper, Maria | 12, Jan. 1847 | FF |

| Grooms | Brides | Date of Marriage | Code |
|--------|--------|------------------|------|
| Stulhamb, Johan H. | Windel, Elisabeth | 30, Apr. 1844 | AA |
| Stull, Abraham | Wilson, Mary | 16, Sept 1837 | RCH |
| Stump, John | Burd, Amanda | 8, July 1826 | RCH |
| Stump, Samuel | Reagan, Nancy | 29, Aug. 1822 | RCH |
| Stumpe, Herman Fried | Kollmeyer, Wilhelmin | 17, Oct. 1849 | F |
| Stumpel, Bernard | Kuhlmann, Maria A. | July 1849 | RCH |
| Stumpf, Adam | Kellermann, Catharin | 26, Sept 1844 | AA |
| Stumpf, Conrad | Bechtholdt, Maria | 13, Aug. 1848 | G |
| Stumpf, Francis | Meyer, Margaretha | 3, Nov. 1846 | FF |
| Stumpf, Johan | Lindner, Margaretha | 24, Sept 1844 | AA |
| Stumpf, Valentin | Seifert, Eva | 27, Oct. 1840 | FF |
| Stundebeck, Francis | Trenkamp, M. Agnes | 29, July 1848 | AA |
| Stunfield, Thomas | Peebles, Nancy | 27, Dec. 1841 | RCH |
| Stuns, William | Jones, Priscilla | 1, July 1849 | RCH |
| Sturges, Levi C. | Ayres, Louisa | 25, Apr. 1833 | RCH |
| Sturs, William | Pierson, Mary | 21, Sept 1846 | RCH |
| Sturwald, Johan M. | Kock, Anna Maria | 23, Apr. 1844 | AA |
| Stutch, Georg | Grossen, Margretha | 30, Oct. 1846 | C |
| Stutelberg, Albert | Lanfersick, Elis. | 10, Jan. 1837 | FF |
| Stuttelberg, Arnold | Weuhler, Carolina | 25, May 1839 | FF |
| Stutters, Edward | Thompson, Ann | 28, Apr. 1846 | RCH |
| Stuve, Clemens | Vogt, Elisabeth | 9, Jan. 1849 | II |
| Sudbeck, Francis A. | Dollmann, Catharina | 21, Aug. 1838 | FF |
| Sudbeck, Johan Hein. | Elking, Anna Maria | 10, Oct. 1847 | AA |
| Sudbeck, Johan Hein. | Alert, M. Catharina | 6, Jan. 1849 | AA |
| Sudfeld, Carl | Warning, Charlotte | 31, May 1847 | RCH |
| Suding, Herman Hein. | VonLehmen, Katharina | 17, Sept 1848 | AA |
| Sudmeyer, Johan | Hoppenjans, A. Cath. | 12, May 1846 | EE |
| Sudmeyer, Johan Wm. | Bogmann, Anna Maria | 21, Apr. 1846 | EE |
| Suelter, Bernard H. | Lehing, Sophia Fried | 27, June 1848 | F |
| Suesen, Johan | Bruner, Theresa | 8, Aug. 1836 | FF |
| Suhr, Ernst | Wehking, Caroline | 24, Sept 1846 | F |
| Suhr, Heinrich Wm. | Ordemann, Meta Adel. | 8, June 1845 | G |
| Suhr, Jacob | Brig, Mary | 8, Feb. 1846 | AA |
| Suhrheinrich, Wm. | Kreizer, Christina | 9, Mar. 1847 | C |
| Suidole, George | Shoily, Amelia | 21, Aug. 1835 | RCH |
| Sulan, John | Stover, Anna B. | 26, Nov. 1842 | RCH |
| Sulier, Samuel | Hermann, Magdalena | 15, Nov. 1836 | FF |
| Sullivan, Herbert | Carmichael, Isabella | 8, Jan. 1842 | RCH |
| Sullivan, Hiram | Haven, Georgitta | 21, May 1846 | RCH |
| Sullivan, James | Lynch, Mary | 9, Aug. 1839 | BB |
| Sullivan, James | Carnes, Catharine | 24, Sept 1846 | BB |
| Sullivan, Jeremiah | Kelly, Elisabeth | 15, June 1847 | BB |
| Sullivan, John | Bowman, Lydia | 26, Apr. 1838 | RCH |
| Sullivan, John | Adams, Margaret | 4, Nov. 1845 | RCH |
| Sullivan, Mordecai | Lee, Virginia | 29, Sept 1846 | RCH |
| Sullivan, Samuel | Corrill, Loretta | 4, July 1849 | RCH |
| Sullivan, Septimus | Cutter, Elisabeth | 16, Sept 1849 | RCH |
| Sullivan, Timothy | Don---, Ann | 24, Jan. 1838 | RCH |
| Sullivan, William | Monahan, Ann | 20, July 1846 | BB |
| Sulter, Christian | Hardegg, Louise M. | 7, June 1849 | G |
| Sulter, Johan H. | Lothmann, Clara M. | 15, Jan. 1843 | F |
| Sum---, David | Gazlay, Tharenda | 17, Aug. 1826 | RCH |
| Summens, James | Bogert, Elisabeth | 8, Feb. 1819 | RCH |
| Summer, John | Reinerg, Caroline | 23, Feb. 1849 | RCH |
| Summers, | Trow, Lydia | 5, July 1849 | RCH |
| Summers, David | Blumer, Tryphene | 20, Nov. 1842 | RCH |
| Summers, George | Rowen, Catharine | 13, Oct. 1846 | GG |
| Summers, John | Trump, Vanelia | 9, Sept 1824 | RCH |
| Summons, James | Lovell, Elisabeth M. | 7, Dec. 1842 | RCH |
| Sumpter, Robert | Griffith, Elisabeth | 2, Dec. 1825 | RCH |
| Sumwalt, William | Parsons, Jane | 20, Jan. 1825 | RCH |
| Sunderhaus, Johan F. | Moeller, M. Angela | 28, Nov. 1844 | AA |
| Sunderland, John J. | Stewart, Martha E. | 27, Jan. 1844 | RCH |
| Sundermann, Adam H. | Harlams, Friedricka | 23, Aug. 1842 | RCH |
| Sundermann, Friedric | Winkelmann, Mina | 8, May 1845 | F |
| Sundermann, Heinrich | Steinkamp, Julia Ann | 14, Sept 1843 | F |
| Suple, Charles | Thompson, Mary | 9, July 1826 | RCH |
| Surenbrock, Bernard | Wanstert, Gertrud | 27, Jan. 1846 | AA |
| Surin, Joseph | Babach, Sarah | 19, Aug. 1819 | RCH |
| Susan, Mark | Longfellow, C.H. | 21, Dec. 1848 | RCH |

| Grooms | Brides | Date of Marriage | Code |
|--------|--------|------------------|------|
| ****** | ****** | **** ** ******** | **** |
| Suthe, Andreas Clem. | Niemann, M. Johanna | 2, Nov. 1848 | AA |
| Suthe, Clemens | Stricker, Carolina | 27, Nov. 1849 | FF |
| Sutherland, Adolph | Wilkinson, Charlotte | 27, Apr. 1848 | RCH |
| Sutherland, Robert | Sutherland, Catharin | 28, June 1844 | RCH |
| Sutherland, William | Martin, Elisabeth | 18, Oct. 1848 | RCH |
| Sutten, Henry | Shipley, Sarah | 26, Apr. 1847 | RCH |
| Sutthof, Francis | Rippe, Maria Angela | 30, June 1840 | FF |
| Sutton, Andrew | Oldfield, Sarah Ann | 29, June 1837 | RCH |
| Sutton, Cornelius | Ellison, Rachel | 25, July 1842 | RCH |
| Sutton, Isaac | Townsend, Catharine | 25, Nov. 1821 | RCH |
| Sutton, John | McGraw, Catharine | 15, Apr. 1849 | BB |
| Sutton, John D. | McGraw, Catharine | 15, Apr. 1849 | BB |
| Sutton, John S. | Addis, Mary | 30, Oct. 1832 | RCH |
| Sutton, Joseph M. | Nichols, Lydia | 19, May 1849 | RCH |
| Sutton, Reeder | Thompson, Mary | 1, May 1836 | RCH |
| Sutton, Samuel | Babbage, Elisabeth | 7, Sept 1821 | RCH |
| Sutton, Timothy | Frost, Julia Ann | 26, Nov. 1824 | RCH |
| Swain, Friedrich C. | Bamard, Lucretia | 20, Apr. 1836 | RCH |
| Swain, Henry | Abercrombie, Mary | 17, June 1849 | RCH |
| Swain, Robert | Smith, Lydia | 12, Nov. 1818 | RCH |
| Swain, Solomon | Bowen, Lydia | 17, Sept 1834 | RCH |
| Swain, William | Cugar, Elisabeth | 6, Nov. 1834 | RCH |
| Swainey, Jonas | Smith, Nancy | 25, Dec. 1832 | RCH |
| Swales, George | Burke, Mary | 24, Mar. 1849 | RCH |
| Swales, Wilson | Pruden, Sarah Ann | 1, Feb. 1842 | RCH |
| Swallow, Benjamin | Hutchinson, Cath. | 27, Nov. 1834 | RCH |
| Swallow, Isaac | Rinehart, Elisabeth | 13, Mar. 1843 | RCH |
| Swallow, Jacob | Perryman, Returah | 17, Dec. 1836 | RCH |
| Swallow, John | Miller, Mary Ann | 7, Jan. 1844 | RCH |
| Swancot, John | Jones, Mary | 28, May 1821 | RCH |
| Swarzwolder, Sebast. | Findling, Barbara | 21, Aug. 1845 | RCH |
| Sweat, John | Moore, Matilda | 30, Nov. 1844 | RCH |
| Sweeney, John | Wheeland, Elvira | 15, Jan. 1845 | RCH |
| Sweeney, Patrick | New, Mary | 19, Feb. 1849 | BB |
| Sweeney, William | Weaver, Mary Ann | 25, May 1848 | RCH |
| Sweet, Benone | Smith, Margaret | 21, Feb. 1833 | RCH |
| Sweet, Edward | Coleman, Sarah Jane | 15, Aug. 1842 | RCH |
| Sweet, Henry | Walker, Adeline | 17, Aug. 1847 | RCH |
| Sweet, Paul | Stockham, Rachel | 20, Dec. 1835 | RCH |
| Sweet, Paul | Shipley, Elisabeth | 19, May 1844 | RCH |
| Swelts, John | Getzendanner, Elis. | 18, Oct. 1832 | RCH |
| Swem, William | Reed, Elinor | 5, May 1848 | RCH |
| Swendler, Matthew | Leesby, Martha | 3, Mar. 1833 | RCH |
| Swift, Briggs | Hubbel, Martha | 17, Sept 1846 | RCH |
| Swift, John | Kelly, Joann | 30, July 1846 | BB |
| Swift, Patrick | Kelly, Dermot | 27, Mar. 1849 | RCH |
| Swift, Thomas T. | Holabird, Jenette | 3, Sept 1849 | RCH |
| Swim, George | McQuillan, Louisa | 8, Oct. 1846 | RCH |
| Swinburn, James | Kendall, Lucy D. | 25, June 1849 | RCH |
| Swing, John | Rinkle, Catharine | 7, Nov. 1846 | RCH |
| Switzer, John | Gottlieb, Hannah | 15, Feb. 1842 | RCH |
| Swots, John | Tarrance, Charlotte | 15, Feb. 1844 | RCH |
| Swoup, Joseph | Tucker, Mary | 5, Jan. 1819 | RCH |
| Sykes, Charles | Jones, Martha Ann | 27, Mar. 1849 | RCH |
| Sylvester, Emery | Thacker, Mary | 29, July 1841 | RCH |
| Sylvester, Wiloughby | Macy, Rachel | 24, Apr. 1849 | RCH |
| Sym, Zachariah | Day, Elizabeth | 25, Apr. 1825 | RCH |
| Symmes, Henry | Sedam, Belinda | 10, Sept 1846 | RCH |
| Symmes, Stephen | Pleasant, Mary | 7, Oct. 1833 | RCH |
| Symmes, Timothy | Spurrier, Ruth | 1, Oct. 1818 | RCH |
| Sypher, David | Speer, Elisabeth Ann | 17, Aug. 1847 | RCH |
| Syselin, Samuel | Badger, Jane | 1, Jan. 1846 | RCH |
| | | | |
| T---, Enoch | Apple, Elisabeth | 23, Nov. 1831 | RCH |
| T---, Jacob | Buckman, Maria | 5, Aug. 1827 | RCH |
| T---, James | Brown, Louise | 8, Dec. 1821 | RCH |
| Taber, Asa | Gorman, Sarah | 7, Oct. 1834 | RCH |
| Taber, Jertho Wright | Come, Esther H. | 21, Dec. 1836 | RCH |
| Tabler, Johan Heinr. | Gesling, Catharine | 5, May 1840 | FF |
| Tabler, Theodor | Eisenbach, Barbara | 1, May 1838 | FF |
| Tackenberg, Ernst H. | Hasemeyer, M. Elis. | 11, Mar. 1847 | G |

| Grooms<br>***** | Brides<br>***** | Date of Marriage<br>**** ** ******** | Code<br>**** |
|---|---|---|---|
| Tackenberg, John Hy. | Meyer, Anna Regina | 30, Aug. 1849 | G |
| Taft, George W. | Steel, Rebecca M. | 8, Oct. 1843 | BB |
| Taft, Samuel H. | Dixon, Waitse | 11, Oct. 1838 | RCH |
| Tagart, Alexander | Lindsey, Mary | 6, May 1844 | RCH |
| Talbert, John | Winters, Nancy | 4, Aug. 1836 | RCH |
| Talbot, Samuel | Taylor, Eliza | 11, Nov. 1824 | RCH |
| Talbott, Isaac | Rutherford, Sarah A. | 29, Dec. 1846 | RCH |
| Talbott, Robert | Miller, Leonora | 22, Mar. 1832 | RCH |
| Talbott, William H. | Tinker, Elisabeth | 22, Mar. 1848 | I |
| Talent, Henry L. | Hall, Sarah Ann | 29, Oct. 1833 | RCH |
| Talor, John | Berry, Ann | 29, Oct. 1833 | RCH |
| Taney, Jonas | Thompson, Elisabeth | 30, Apr. 1846 | RCH |
| Tangeman, John H. | Patterson, Elisabeth | 21, Mar. 1844 | RCH |
| Tangemann, Friedrich | Kenkel, Catharine | 6, Jan. 1846 | FF |
| Tangemann, Heinrich | Kenne, Elisabeth | 3, Feb. 1835 | FF |
| Tangemann, Herman H. | Leive, Mary | 22, Dec. 1846 | RCH |
| Tanner, Bernard | Bogenschuetz, Cres. | 28, Nov. 1843 | FF |
| Tanner, Charles | Gordon, Sarah Jane | 23, May 1848 | RCH |
| Tanner, James | Smith, Rebecca | 17, Oct. 1844 | RCH |
| Tanner, Michael | Kauer, Margaretha | 21, Oct. 1844 | C |
| Tanner, Pernel | Garrett, Margaret | 14, Apr. 1836 | RCH |
| Tanner, William | Mahon, Sarah | 15, Oct. 1843 | BB |
| Tanquary, Benjamin | Bierbaum, Elisabeth | 10, July 1846 | RCH |
| Tape, Friedrich | Holtvoight, Elisabet | 1, Oct. 1846 | FF |
| Taph, William | Starlin, Christina | 10, Sept 1837 | RCH |
| Taphorn, Gerhard | Deters, Catharine | 26, Nov. 1846 | AA |
| Tapke, Otto Heinrich | Doelker, Elisabeth | 2, Oct. 1849 | AA |
| Tappemeier, Heinrich | Zeidenberg, Louise C | 1, Apr. 1849 | F |
| Tapscott, Joseph | See, Mary Jane | 23, Nov. 1836 | RCH |
| Tarbell, William | Newton, Amelia H. | 5, June 1848 | I |
| Tarlton, Robert | Cowine, Hannah Jane | 24, Sept 1835 | RCH |
| Tarpot, George | Lucas, Susan | 4, Sept 1834 | RCH |
| Tarquin, John | Finney, Sarah | 10, Nov. 1840 | RCH |
| Tarr, Thomas | Hill, Elmira | 20, July 1842 | RCH |
| Tarrant, M. | Tunis, Emeline | 19, Jan. 1826 | RCH |
| Tarrill, Herman | Dayton, Thala | 21, Mar. 1842 | RCH |
| Tarvin, Samuel | Johnston, Elisabeth | 10, Nov. 1836 | RCH |
| Tarvin, Samuel | Barney, Hannah | 16, May 1849 | RCH |
| Tasker, Benjamin | Davis, Lydia | 25, Nov. 1845 | RCH |
| Tate, James | Lane, Elisabeth | 16, Oct. 1817 | RCH |
| Tate, Richard | Scott, Catharine | 28, Nov. 1832 | RCH |
| Tatem, John | Lilley, Mary | 19, Aug. 1823 | RCH |
| Tatham, W.H. | Williams, Ann | 27, Mar. 1834 | RCH |
| Tattershall, Benj. | Isgrigg, Barbara | 18, Sept 1836 | RCH |
| Tattershall, James | Hubbard, Susannah | 7, Mar. 1844 | RCH |
| Taulk--, Thomas | Smith, A. | 26, July 1827 | RCH |
| Taulman, Calvin | McKee, Elisabeth | 10, Mar. 1844 | RCH |
| Tavlin, Peter | Foley, Mary | 17, June 1849 | GG |
| Tayler, Richard | Bell, Martha | 18, Mar. 1849 | RCH |
| Taylor, Abraham | Smith, Sarah | 8, Dec. 1832 | RCH |
| Taylor, B.P. | Doan, Eveline A. | 5, Nov. 1835 | RCH |
| Taylor, Calvin | Crary, Almira | 5, Nov. 1840 | RCH |
| Taylor, Edward | Brown, Annis | 9, Dec. 1819 | RCH |
| Taylor, Edward | Barler, Elisabeth | 2, May 1847 | RCH |
| Taylor, Eli | Marsh, Hannah M. | 22, Dec. 1835 | RCH |
| Taylor, Gabriel | Miller, Sarah Jane | 20, Sept 1847 | RCH |
| Taylor, Garrett | Jack, Sinthia A. | 20, Mar. 1838 | RCH |
| Taylor, George | Porter, Elisabeth | 16, Sept 1819 | RCH |
| Taylor, George | Taylor, Elisabeth | 30, Oct. 1821 | RCH |
| Taylor, George | Nesmith, Margaret | 30, May 1844 | RCH |
| Taylor, George | Creach, Mary Ann | 26, Aug. 1847 | RCH |
| Taylor, George W. | Wilson, Harriet | 24, Aug. 1834 | RCH |
| Taylor, George W. | Rose, Hester Ann | 18, Apr. 1843 | RCH |
| Taylor, Hiram | Stonebraker, Martha | 7, Feb. 1846 | GG |
| Taylor, Isaac | Bastable, Emma | 30, Dec. 1841 | RCH |
| Taylor, Isaac | Babcock, Sarah | 18, Oct. 1845 | RCH |
| Taylor, Jacob | Mesach, Sarah | 6, Oct. 1824 | RCH |
| Taylor, James | Monjar, Mary Jane | 9, Oct. 1847 | RCH |
| Taylor, Jeremiah | Willis, Caroline | 26, June 1841 | RCH |
| Taylor, John | Habis, Mary Ann | 10, Oct. 1818 | RCH |
| Taylor, John | Bebinger, Charlotte | 31, July 1823 | RCH |

| Grooms<br>\*\*\*\*\*\* | Brides<br>\*\*\*\*\*\* | Date of Marriage<br>\*\*\*\* \*\* \*\*\*\*\*\*\*\* | Code<br>\*\*\*\* |
|---|---|---|---|
| Taylor, John | Jackson, Mary | 12, Oct. 1841 | RCH |
| Taylor, John | Linter, Mary Ann | 17, Dec. 1846 | RCH |
| Taylor, Jonah | Ward, Elisabeth Ann | 28, June 1842 | BB |
| Taylor, Mahlon R. | Lyon, Elisabeth | 1, Dec. 1836 | RCH |
| Taylor, Michael | Richardson, Mary | 8, Oct. 1846 | RCH |
| Taylor, Robert | Preston, Margaret | 21, Mar. 1844 | RCH |
| Taylor, Samuel | Hubbard, Eliza | 27, Oct. 1825 | RCH |
| Taylor, Samuel | Hayelton, Dorothy | 10, Jan. 1833 | RCH |
| Taylor, Thomas | Carroll, Ellen | 8, Aug. 1843 | RCH |
| Taylor, Thomas H. | Westlake, Susan | 15, May 1833 | RCH |
| Taylor, Thomas J. | Lynchard, Sarah A. | 20, June 1841 | RCH |
| Taylor, Wesley | Caun---, Louise Jane | 23, Nov. 1837 | RCH |
| Taylor, William | ----, Sally | 4, May 1821 | RCH |
| Taylor, William | Hughes, Sarah | 14, Aug. 1845 | RCH |
| Taylor, William H. | Harrison, Anna T. | 22, June 1836 | I |
| Teal, Jesse | Gallagher, Mary | 25, Oct. 1843 | RCH |
| Tealin, | Parker, Ann | 23, Dec. 1838 | RCH |
| Teanthorpe, James | Morgan, Sarah | 6, Dec. 1846 | RCH |
| Teasdale, William | Butterworth, Ann | 21, Feb. 1838 | RCH |
| Tebbe, Johan Bernard | Kroeger, M Catharina | 3, Feb. 1842 | FF |
| Tebbell, Sand. | Summerville, Mary | 25, Aug. 1839 | RCH |
| Tebblemann, Heinrich | Kuhlmann, Elisabeth | 26, Aug. 1845 | FF |
| Tebbs, Joseph | Burk, Rebecca | 22, Apr. 1846 | RCH |
| Tebelmann, Heinrich | Long, Maria | 27, Apr. 1849 | B |
| Teckemeier, Christ. | Myers, Mary | 3, Apr. 1846 | RCH |
| Teckenbrock, Fried. | Heuers, Sophia F. | 4, Oct. 1846 | RCH |
| Teder, Johan | Schippers, Catharina | 27, Oct. 1840 | FF |
| Tedrich, | Marshall, Fanny | 28, Oct. 1816 | RCH |
| Tedrow, Asa W. | Davis, Sarah Elis. | 5, Jan. 1837 | RCH |
| Tedtmann, Martin F. | Schmidt, Elisabeth | 6, June 1849 | F |
| Teeken, Gerhard Geo. | Burlagen, Catharina | 31, Oct. 1849 | AA |
| Tegge, Johan H. | Detmer, Bernardina | 1, May 1849 | AA |
| Telerac, Nathan | Banks, Mary Ann | Apr. 1839 | RCH |
| Telgemeier, Johan H. | Elstrots, Wilhelmina | 3, Aug. 1843 | F |
| Telke, Franz H. | Wehage, Catharina | 20, June 1848 | II |
| Telker, Heinrich | Ohns, Maria | 1, Apr. 1847 | RCH |
| Telking, John Albert | Eckof, Anna M. (Mrs) | 9, June 1835 | FF |
| Telskamp, Friedrich | Meyer, Maria | 13, Sept 1836 | FF |
| Teman, George | Ponder, Malinda A. | 11, Mar. 1847 | RCH |
| Temme, Johan | Grewe, Mina | 26, July 1843 | F |
| Temmelmann, Herman H | Lutmer, M. Maria | 14, Oct. 1849 | II |
| Temple, Alexander | Knowles, Elmira | 25, Sept 1832 | RCH |
| Temple, Jesse H. | Patton, Jane | 28, June 1835 | RCH |
| Temple, Tillison | Carson, Ann Elis. | 9, Apr. 1835 | RCH |
| Templeton, William C | Hawkins, Eliza | 12, Dec. 1833 | I |
| Tenant, Louis | Epperson, Susan | 10, June 1825 | RCH |
| Tenbusch, Johan | Hoeper, Wilhelmina | 20, May 1845 | AA |
| Tencke, Nelson | Haines, Martha | 31, Jan. 1841 | RCH |
| Teneick, Abraham | ----, ---- | 10, July 1834 | RCH |
| Teneleger, John E. | Jones, Elisabeth | 7, Apr. 1836 | RCH |
| Tennen, Johan Herman | Kamprolves, Elisabet | 24, Oct. 1846 | EE |
| Tensing, Albert | Kemper, M. Magdalena | 29, June 1841 | FF |
| Tepe, Gerhard | Imhoff, Veronica | 11, Oct. 1846 | AA |
| Tepe, Heinrich | Niemann, Elisabeth | 24, Sept 1839 | FF |
| Tepe, Heinrich | VanLuehrte, Anna G. | 13, May 1846 | C |
| Tepe, Herman Heinric | Nurnberns, Adelheid | 23, June 1840 | FF |
| Tepe, Johan Bernard | Kipp, Theresa | 26, Nov. 1846 | AA |
| Tepker, Johan Heinr. | Morrarend, Maria | 31, Mar. 1846 | F |
| Terdink, Johan | Muntel, Anna Maria | 9, May 1848 | AA |
| Terlert, Joseph | Embertson, Catharine | 19, Sept 1838 | RCH |
| Teron, Joseph | ----, Cordelia Ann | 20, Mar. 1839 | RCH |
| Terrel, | Meisener, Gabriella | 25, Dec. 1810 | RCH |
| Terrell, Edmund | Lytle, Elisabeth | 13, June 1844 | RCH |
| Terrell, John | Harris, Elvira | 23, Dec. 1832 | RCH |
| Terry, James | Terry, Henrietta | 24, Feb. 1842 | RCH |
| Terry, James | Every, Maria | 23, Mar. 1842 | RCH |
| Terry, John | Harvey, Martha | 2, Sept 1819 | RCH |
| Terry, Washington | Zericks, Catharine | 10, Feb. 1833 | RCH |
| Terry, William | Leockmann, Louise | Oct. 1844 | RCH |
| Terttle, Hazel | Greenwell, Elisabeth | 18, Apr. 1839 | RCH |
| Terwilliger, John C. | Graham, Eliza | 2, Nov. 1825 | RCH |

| Grooms<br>***** | Brides<br>***** | Date of Marriage<br>**** ** ******** | Code<br>**** |
|---|---|---|---|
| Terwilliger, Nathan | Hogeman, Charlotte | 30, June 1825 | RCH |
| Terwilliger, Stewart | Perkins, Nancy | 31, Oct. 1822 | RCH |
| Terwilliger, William | Shatton, Mary Ann | 25, May 1837 | RCH |
| Terwisch, Theodor | Meyer, Francisca | 31, Oct. 1836 | FF |
| Tesh, Henry | Newly, Mary | 11, Nov. 1832 | RCH |
| Tetrich, Joseph | Hooper, Elisabeth | 11, Nov. 1834 | RCH |
| Tettenhorst, Christ. | Soll, Hannah | 23, Oct. 1846 | F |
| Tey, Heinrich | Lammers, Elisabeth | 4, May 1845 | AA |
| Thaber, Theodor | Heilmann, Gesina | 27, June 1849 | II |
| Thale, Bernard | Stordeur, Dina | 16, Nov. 1845 | AA |
| Thale, Herman H. | Backhorst, Catharine | 24, Feb. 1846 | AA |
| Thaler, Jacob | Haid, Barbara | 7, May 1849 | II |
| Thalheimer, Nathan | Oberndorfer, Rosa | 9, Oct. 1845 | RCH |
| Thanartha, Charles | Mayhew, Rebecca | 22, Feb. 1838 | RCH |
| Thaney, Michael | Murphy, Bridget | 26, June 1849 | GG |
| Tharp, Jacob | VanMatre, Mary A. | 24, June 1844 | RCH |
| Tharp, Oliver | Barnes, Rachel | 29, Nov. 1843 | RCH |
| Tharpe, Franklin | Lucker, Frances | 19, Jan. 1842 | RCH |
| Thatcher, Henry | Wakefield, Sarah | 20, Nov. 1817 | RCH |
| Thatcher, Richard | Kobson, Catharine | 21, Nov. 1833 | RCH |
| Thay, David A. | Dunn, Mary Ann | 25, Nov. 1832 | RCH |
| Thayer, Henry | Wood, Susan | 14, Apr. 1840 | RCH |
| Thayre, George | Williams, Nancy | 11, Nov. 1841 | RCH |
| Thayres, George W. | Doty, Theodosia | 20, June 1839 | RCH |
| Thedy, August | Zwickgi, Wilhelmina | 18, July 1848 | RCH |
| Theile, Heinrich | Fischer, Catharine | 10, Nov. 1846 | EE |
| Theiring, Francis | Widenbach, Anna M. | 19, Aug. 1849 | EE |
| Theis, Carl | Ulm, Maria | 22, Apr. 1839 | G |
| Theis, Henry | Dunhelt, Louise | 21, Feb. 1842 | RCH |
| Theis, Jacob | Vester, Catharine | 2, July 1846 | A |
| Theobald, August | Hendricks, Catharine | 15, July 1847 | RCH |
| These, Herman | Ortmann, Elisabeth C | 28, May 1848 | II |
| These, Johan Heinric | Bergmann, A.M. Elis. | 14, Jan. 1840 | FF |
| Thibero, Joseph | Uphaus, Maria | 23, Jan. 1838 | FF |
| Thieke, Friedrich | Loers, Catharine | 25, Nov. 1847 | RCH |
| Thieke, Johan | Beyer, Catharine | 4, Apr. 1844 | F |
| Thieke, Ludwig H. | Huntemann, A. Elis. | 12, Apr. 1842 | F |
| Thiel, Johan | Wulferkuhl, Elis. | 25, Sept 1849 | AA |
| Thielbahr, Dietrich | Barm, M. Dorothea | 12, July 1845 | A |
| Thielmann, Julius | Spieker, Justina | 11, May 1846 | RCH |
| Thiemann, Heinrich | Rixmann, Elisabeth | 17, Jan. 1849 | AA |
| Thiemann, Herman H. | Hagemann, Elisabeth | 7, Jan. 1845 | AA |
| Thiemann, Johan H. | Stevens, Elisabeth | 23, Apr. 1844 | AA |
| Thiemann, Johan H. | Woltering, A. Maria | 5, Apr. 1842 | FF |
| Thiene, Bernard H. | Hackmoeller, Elis. | 30, Apr. 1848 | AA |
| Thiese, Gottlieb | Becker, Dorothea C. | 18, Nov. 1847 | F |
| Thiesing, Ernst | Stagmann, Christina | 14, Feb. 1849 | F |
| Thiesing, Friedrich | Oelmann, Sophia | 10, Dec. 1840 | F |
| Thiesing, Herman | Ludeke, Catharine E. | 20, Mar. 1849 | F |
| Thiez, Michael | Heinrich, Margaretha | 8, Feb. 1849 | C |
| Thike, Jacob | Connor, Elisabeth | 19, Mar. 1835 | RCH |
| Thile, Werner | Toerningens, Elis. | 14, May 1839 | FF |
| Thimber, Samuel | Lawrence, Mary Ann | 18, Dec. 1842 | RCH |
| Thin, B. Heinrich | Bertke, M. Elisabeth | 30, Sept 1849 | II |
| Thinnes, Peter | Bauer, Josephina | 12, May 1835 | FF |
| Thirkield, Thornton | Mooney, Mary | 17, Dec. 1844 | RCH |
| Thiser, Johan | Heck, Katharine | 18, Oct. 1849 | EE |
| Thistle, Robert | Bell, Jane | 1, Oct. 1841 | RCH |
| Thistlewaite, James | Punshon, Rachel | 12, Feb. 1836 | RCH |
| Thiston, Tennat | Howard, Elisabeth | 5, Nov. 1818 | RCH |
| Tho---, Price | Morrison, Martha | 6, Apr. 1824 | RCH |
| Thoele, Heinrich | Macke, Agnes | 17, Oct. 1848 | II |
| Thoele, Johan Herman | Kraft, Catharine | 29, Apr. 1849 | A |
| Thoele, Johan Peter | Starr, Anna Maria | 8, Nov. 1842 | AA |
| Thoele, Theodor | Imwalde, Elisabeth | 14, Jan. 1840 | FF |
| Thoerner, Heinrich | Hamlage, Margaretha | 30, July 1848 | AA |
| Thole, Francis | Abelinck, Maria Anna | 22, Nov. 1846 | EE |
| Thole, Francis | Westendorf, Theresa | 23, May 1848 | EE |
| Thole, Francis Jos. | Spells, Maria | 11, Sept 1849 | II |
| Thole, Joseph | Kenkel, Maria Elis. | 7, May 1848 | EE |
| Thole, Theodor | Krister, Adelheid | 27, May 1849 | II |

| Grooms | Brides | Date of Marriage | Code |
|--------|--------|------------------|------|
| ***** | ***** | **** ** ******** | **** |
| Thom, Frederick | Hoops, Lucy | 22, Jan. 1826 | RCH |
| Thom---, John | Graham, Jane | 7, Aug. 1836 | RCH |
| Thom---, Joseph M. | Messuck, Mary Ann | 8, Mar. 1826 | RCH |
| Thom---, William | Collins, Sarah E. | Sept 1845 | RCH |
| Thoma, Heinrich | Knoth, Barbara | 18, Sept 1845 | G |
| Thoma, Henry | Hartmann, Margaretha | 12, Feb. 1847 | G |
| Thoman, Charles L. | Tyman, Hannah | 1, Jan. 1849 | I |
| Thoman, Joseph | Huller, Barbara | 10, Apr. 1849 | EE |
| Thomas, | Mere---, Emily | May 1837 | RCH |
| Thomas, | Bun---, Margaret | 19, Nov. 1844 | RCH |
| Thomas, Alexander | Shepherdson, Mary | 27, May 1847 | RCH |
| Thomas, Alfred | Reynolds, Julia | 29, Apr. 1846 | RCH |
| Thomas, Alpheus | Neville, Elisabeth | 11, Apr. 1839 | RCH |
| Thomas, Aron | Empson, Elisabeth A. | 4, July 1834 | RCH |
| Thomas, Benjamin | Bunker, Marian | 1, May 1839 | RCH |
| Thomas, Benjamin | Lovejoy, Susan | 25, Oct. 1842 | RCH |
| Thomas, Bryant | Malry, Mary | 13, Apr. 1842 | RCH |
| Thomas, Carl Edward | Schoen, Wilhelmina | 18, Apr. 1844 | G |
| Thomas, Charles | Simpson, Mary | 3, Apr. 1834 | RCH |
| Thomas, Christopher | Margan, Elisabeth | 22, Sept 1844 | RCH |
| Thomas, David | Matlack, Mary W. | 17, Nov. 1836 | RCH |
| Thomas, E. Sydney | Morris, Rebecca E. | 25, Jan. 1848 | D |
| Thomas, Edward | Wiscott, Amanda | 8, May 1823 | RCH |
| Thomas, Enoch | Isaac, Margaret | 7, Sept 1843 | RCH |
| Thomas, Henry | Hancock, Susan Ann | 3, Jan. 1844 | RCH |
| Thomas, Henry | Madison, Sophia | 4, Aug. 1847 | RCH |
| Thomas, Jacob | Armstrong, Neona | 27, Mar. 1834 | RCH |
| Thomas, James | Smith, Anna Maria | 17, Apr. 1839 | RCH |
| Thomas, Jesse | Thompson, Sarah | 8, Dec. 1821 | RCH |
| Thomas, John | Bridge, Mary Ann | 4, Mar. 1823 | RCH |
| Thomas, John | Nichabron, Mary | 15, Sept 1833 | RCH |
| Thomas, John | McGeorge, Jane | 8, May 1837 | RCH |
| Thomas, John | Peterson, Malinda | 15, Sept 1846 | RCH |
| Thomas, John | Jones, Mary | 27, Sept 1849 | RCH |
| Thomas, John B. | Gowers, Elisabeth | 3, Aug. 1836 | RCH |
| Thomas, John R. | Hager, Abigail | 27, Dec. 1821 | RCH |
| Thomas, Jonathan | Thompson, Lydia J. | 28, Feb. 1844 | RCH |
| Thomas, Joseph | Lounks, Abigail | 28, Feb. 1822 | RCH |
| Thomas, Joseph | Hopple, Mary | 14, Oct. 1841 | RCH |
| Thomas, Joseph H. | Campbell, Wilhelmina | 26, Mar. 1835 | RCH |
| Thomas, Lorenzo | Horn, Rebecca Ann | 21, Aug. 1845 | RCH |
| Thomas, Osborn | McNeal, Rebecca | 19, Mar. 1833 | RCH |
| Thomas, Philipp | Holzmann, Elisabeth | 12, Sept 1847 | G |
| Thomas, Reuben | Sprague, Bowman | 5, Sept 1824 | RCH |
| Thomas, Richard | Clark, Martha | 10, Feb. 1847 | RCH |
| Thomas, Robert | Whitney, Elisabeth | 13, May 1847 | RCH |
| Thomas, Russell | Wells, Sarah | 12, Feb. 1846 | RCH |
| Thomas, Samuel | Gould, Elisabeth | 20, Dec. 1821 | RCH |
| Thomas, Samuel | Brewer, Adaline | 30, May 1846 | RCH |
| Thomas, Sandy | Smith, Pleasant | 25, Sept 1842 | RCH |
| Thomas, Washington | Rockerfellow Charlot | 19, Nov. 1835 | RCH |
| Thomas, William | Alcott, Elisabeth | 31, Mar. 1839 | RCH |
| Thomas, William | Cabel, Elisabeth | 24, Feb. 1842 | RCH |
| Thomas, William | Godden, Jane | 29, June 1848 | RCH |
| Thomer, Johan | Rausch, Margaretha | 22, Aug. 1847 | G |
| Thomin, Conrad F. | Follenius, Catharine | 19, May 1844 | G |
| Thompson, --nard | Neighbors, Amanda | 17, July 1837 | RCH |
| Thompson, Alexander | Edwards, Mary Ann | 6, Jan. 1848 | I |
| Thompson, Andrew | Horton, Elizabeth | 10, Sept 1848 | RCH |
| Thompson, Benjamin | VanTrees, Magdalena | 18, Dec. 1817 | RCH |
| Thompson, Caleb | Murphy, Elisabeth | 2, Nov. 1817 | RCH |
| Thompson, Cornelius | Jones, Sarah | 23, Jan. 1834 | RCH |
| Thompson, David | Holberg, Ann | 1, Jan. 1824 | RCH |
| Thompson, David | Mayhew, Agnes | 18, May 1842 | RCH |
| Thompson, Edward | Edwards, Clarissa | 2, Nov. 1843 | RCH |
| Thompson, Elijah | McGuire, Cynthia | 2, July 1826 | RCH |
| Thompson, Ezra | Nichols, | 15, Apr. 1838 | RCH |
| Thompson, Ezra F. | Dunseth, Mathilda | 11, July 1833 | RCH |
| Thompson, Francis | Norris, Martha | 7, Sept 1847 | RCH |
| Thompson, Henry | Mills, Elisabeth | 11, Jan. 1847 | RCH |
| Thompson, Hiram | Wilson, Anna | 6, June 1835 | RCH |

| Grooms | Brides | Date of Marriage | Code |
|--------|--------|------------------|------|
| ****** | ****** | **** ** ******** | **** |
| Thompson, Hiram | Wynn, Nancy | 23, Apr. 1844 | RCH |
| Thompson, Ira | Wells, Margaret | 9, Apr. 1820 | RCH |
| Thompson, Jackson | Apple, Naomi | 27, May 1842 | RCH |
| Thompson, Jackson | Scheckles, Hannah | 26, Nov. 1848 | RCH |
| Thompson, Jacob | Edwards, Atlantic | 16, Apr. 1833 | RCH |
| Thompson, Jacob | Meyer, Magdalena | 21, Dec. 1839 | G |
| Thompson, James | Oliver, Elisabeth A. | 20, Mar. 1834 | RCH |
| Thompson, James | Hartley, Rachel | 7, Oct. 1841 | RCH |
| Thompson, James | Cummisky, Catharine | 26, Oct. 1841 | BB |
| Thompson, James B. | McGuire, Mary | 1, May 1834 | RCH |
| Thompson, John | Scogin, Ruth | 16, Mar. 1819 | RCH |
| Thompson, John | Davis, Mary | 11, Jan. 1821 | RCH |
| Thompson, John | Ross, Maria | 31, May 1827 | RCH |
| Thompson, John | Fathergail, Mary Ann | 7, June 1835 | RCH |
| Thompson, John | Langlands, Janet | 21, Mar. 1837 | RCH |
| Thompson, John | Richardson, Lestina | 15, Dec. 1844 | RCH |
| Thompson, John | Hancock, Sarah Jane | 31, Dec. 1846 | RCH |
| Thompson, John | Wait, Agnes | 15, Sept 1847 | RCH |
| Thompson, John | Crail, Mary Ann | 16, July 1848 | RCH |
| Thompson, John S. | Aik--, Rachel | 5, Dec. 1818 | RCH |
| Thompson, Joseph | Doane, Sarah | 31, Aug. 1823 | RCH |
| Thompson, Joseph | Morris, Mary Ann | 22, Mar. 1848 | RCH |
| Thompson, Joshua | Fowler, Rachel | 3, Dec. 1846 | RCH |
| Thompson, Marcus | Gorum, Matilda | 9, Feb. 1842 | RCH |
| Thompson, Oliver | Johnston, Sarah | 10, Jan. 1846 | RCH |
| Thompson, Price | Ritter, Elisabeth | 5, June 1838 | RCH |
| Thompson, Quinton | Cathcart, Charlotte | 31, May 1844 | RCH |
| Thompson, R.E. | Ryland, Caroline | 28, Aug. 1849 | RCH |
| Thompson, Ralph | Lyle, Mary Ann | 25, Feb. 1819 | RCH |
| Thompson, Richard | Leonard, Ann | 5, Oct. 1844 | BB |
| Thompson, Robert | Carr, Mary S. | 10, May 1837 | RCH |
| Thompson, Robert | Cooper, Cynthia | 9, Sept 1842 | RCH |
| Thompson, Samuel | Durham, Margaret | 12, June 1842 | RCH |
| Thompson, Samuel | Smith, Mary Ann | 22, Mar. 1847 | RCH |
| Thompson, Samuel P. | Donnall, Sarah | 24, Mar. 1825 | RCH |
| Thompson, Thomas | Hilford, Mary | 13, Oct. 1834 | RCH |
| Thompson, Thomas | McClure, Margaret | 25, Sept 1836 | RCH |
| Thompson, Thomas | Young, Julia Ann | 7, July 1844 | RCH |
| Thompson, Thomas | Sanders, Sarah | 1, May 1847 | RCH |
| Thompson, Thomas H. | ----, Tamer | 9, July 1822 | RCH |
| Thompson, William | Kinett, Mary | 14, Mar. 1834 | RCH |
| Thompson, William | Oldfield, Elisabeth | 25, Sept 1849 | RCH |
| Thompson, William H. | Nehemiah, Ann | 25, May 1836 | RCH |
| Thompson, William H. | Graham, Laura | 15, 1845 | I |
| Thomson, | Benben, Matilda | 16, May 1839 | RCH |
| Thomson, James | Richardson, Sarah | 25, Dec. 1843 | RCH |
| Thomson, James | Fetute, Sarah | 30, Dec. 1843 | RCH |
| Thomson, William | Gray, Elisabeth | 23, Dec. 1845 | RCH |
| Thomson, William | Skeno, Margaret | Mar. 1849 | RCH |
| Thood, Misham | Reed, Eva | 23, Nov. 1838 | RCH |
| Thorburn, Robert | Stanley, Charlotte | 15, July 1847 | RCH |
| Thorn, George W. | McCoy, Martha Jane | 18, Sept 1840 | RCH |
| Thornell, Angus | Little, Margaret | 16, Oct. 1847 | RCH |
| Thornell, Angus W. | Cochran, Ann M. | Dec. 1832 | RCH |
| Thornhill, George D. | Thiener, Gertrud | 25, Jan. 1848 | BB |
| Thorninton, Henry | McNair, Abigail | 14, June 1841 | RCH |
| Thornley, Philipp | Anderson, Mary P. | 13, Sept 1848 | BB |
| Thornton, Benjamin | Hollowell, Eliza | 14, May 1833 | I |
| Thornton, Hiram | Fryer, Sarah | 10, Oct. 1846 | RCH |
| Thornton, James | Milfon, | 1, Mar. 1825 | RCH |
| Thornton, Joseph | West, | 20, Dec. 1825 | RCH |
| Thornton, Richard | Kirby, Hannah | 9, May 1840 | RCH |
| Thornton, Tyrral | Murray, Rosetta Jane | 14, Dec. 1835 | I |
| Thorp, Albert | Sigsworth, Ann | 15, May 1849 | RCH |
| Thorp, Charles W. | Earnst, Catharine | 12, June 1836 | RCH |
| Thorp, David | Jacobs, Catharine | 10, May 1818 | RCH |
| Thorp, Ezekiel | Clark, Elvira | 19, May 1825 | RCH |
| Thorp, Franklin | Tyler, Emeline | 19, May 1833 | RCH |
| Thorp, George | Philpot, Mary | 28, Dec. 1837 | I |
| Thorp, George | Kemper, Isabella | 6, Dec. 1843 | RCH |
| Thorp, J. | Chamberlain, Emaline | 17, Sept 1825 | RCH |

| Grooms | Brides | Date of Marriage | Code |
|--------|--------|------------------|------|
| ****** | ****** | **** ** ******** | **** |
| Thorp, John | Tiley, Emma | 17, July 1836 | RCH |
| Thorp, Oliver | Adkins, Julia Anna | 16, Sept 1848 | RCH |
| Thorp, Silas | Bailey, Susan W. | 16, Oct. 1836 | RCH |
| Thorp, Stokes | Gumsalles, Emily | 1, Apr. 1839 | RCH |
| Thorp, Thomas J. | Morrow, Abigail | 17, Sept 1836 | RCH |
| Thorp, William | Carter, Elisabeth | 13, Sept 1845 | RCH |
| Thorp, William | Muntz, Mary | 11, June 1849 | RCH |
| Thorpe, Alexander | Smith, Emily | 14, Aug. 1849 | RCH |
| Thorpe, Henry | Manifold, Mary A. | 20, Aug. 1844 | RCH |
| Thorpe, John | Flintham, Margaret | 21, July 1847 | RCH |
| Thorpe, Taber C. | Henteworth, Maria | 5, Mar. 1835 | RCH |
| Thorpe, William | Thorpe, Sarah | 18, June 1837 | RCH |
| Though, Daniel | ----, ---- | 19, Sept 1839 | RCH |
| Thraenle, Damian | Donnersperger, Elis. | 10, Jan. 1848 | CC |
| Thrasher, Charles | Vincent, Hannah | 26, Mar. 1848 | RCH |
| Thrau, Carl | Wolfneyer, Louise | 3, Feb. 1846 | RCH |
| Threlkeld, William | Drescher, Ellen | 27, Sept 1837 | I |
| Threm, Francis | Denies, Elisabeth | 16, May 1848 | AA |
| Thropp, James | Markland, Anna M. | 24, Dec. 1849 | RCH |
| Thuerauf, John | Schlech, Elisabeth | 1, Dec. 1845 | RCH |
| Thuet, Georg | Pfleger, M Magdalena | 11, Nov. 1849 | AA |
| Thullen, Philipp | Rodenkirch, Regina | 27, Nov. 1847 | AA |
| Thurston, Joshua | Applegate, Caroline | 7, May 1846 | RCH |
| Thyer, Richard | Brothers, Mary | 30, Dec. 1817 | RCH |
| Tibbets, Robert | Pangburn, Martha Ann | 13, Mar. 1823 | RCH |
| Tibbetts, Ephraim | Timmermann, Elisabet | 28, Nov. 1843 | RCH |
| Tibbetts, John | Wharton, Sarah | 23, Oct. 1817 | RCH |
| Tibbs, Andrew | Mays, Hester | 20, Apr. 1848 | RCH |
| Tice, Jacob | Smith, Charlotte | 29, Nov. 1849 | RCH |
| Tickmann, Wilhelm | Luken, Maria | 10, Nov. 1846 | EE |
| Tiemann, Casper Hein | Hagemeyer, M. Elis. | 2, June 1847 | E |
| Tiemann, Francis | Bruns, Anna Gertrud | 9, July 1848 | FF |
| Tiemann, Gerhard | Brandewiede, Anna M. | 14, Apr. 1844 | FF |
| Tiemann, Heinrich | Barger, Bernardina | 15, Nov. 1847 | FF |
| Tiemann, J. Gerhard | Thoele, Elisabeth | 9, July 1848 | II |
| Tiemann, J. Heinrich | Dirker, Elisabeth | 22, Oct. 1848 | II |
| Tiemann, Johan | Schmerge, Elisabeth | 1, May 1849 | II |
| Tiemann, Johan Hein. | Konersmann, Angela E | 25, Nov. 1845 | FF |
| Tiemann, Joseph | Nordmann, Anna Maria | 18, May 1841 | FF |
| Tiemeyer, Georg H. | Kattemeyer, Elisabet | 16, Apr. 1844 | AA |
| Tien, Bernard | Emger, A. Maria | 25, Aug. 1846 | AA |
| Tiernan, Thomas | Collins, Ann | 21, Oct. 1843 | BB |
| Tierney, Michael | Scully, Elisabeth | 3, Feb. 1845 | BB |
| Tierney, Patrick | Ryan, Margaret (Mrs) | 3, Sept 1849 | BB |
| Tiger, Nicolaus | Allpaugh, Charlotte | 16, Mar. 1836 | RCH |
| Tigges, Theodor | Schlemann, A. Maria | 23, June 1842 | FF |
| Tighe, Francis | Leonard, Catharine | 19, Dec. 1847 | GG |
| Tillard, Samuel | Esnot, Sabrina | 19, July 1818 | RCH |
| Tillotson, Edward | Schooley, Augusta | 28, Nov. 1844 | RCH |
| Timbermann, John | Strout, Indiana | 16, Sept 1838 | RCH |
| Timbermann, John | Meeker, Amanda | 24, Apr. 1849 | RCH |
| Timmer, Heinrich | Rabe, Maria Anna | 31, Oct. 1847 | AA |
| Timmer, Herman | Gruen, M. Elisabeth | 26, Nov. 1839 | FF |
| Timmer, Johan | Richter, Antoinette | 28, Jan. 1845 | AA |
| Timmermann, Dietrich | Meyer, Catharine | 16, Sept 1841 | RCH |
| Timmermann, Johan | Christopher, Sophia | 18, Mar. 1840 | F |
| Timmermann, Johan | Schlichte, Anna M. | 11, July 1843 | AA |
| Timmermann, Johan F. | Schmidt, Margaretha | 14, Nov. 1847 | F |
| Timmermann, Johan H. | Bengelmann, Maria A. | 4, May 1841 | FF |
| Timmermann, Theodor | Bokopf, Elisabeth | 23, Nov. 1845 | FF |
| Timmermeister, Wm. | Strube, Mary Jane | 14, Feb. 1846 | RCH |
| Timmers, Bernard | Hackemoeller, Angel. | 8, Nov. 1846 | AA |
| Timmers, Bernard Wm. | Helmann, Anna Maria | 9, Sept 1849 | AA |
| Timmers, Gerhard H. | Sondermann, Gertrud | 11, Nov. 1845 | AA |
| Timmers, Gerhard H. | Hackemoeller, Cath. | 28, Oct. 1849 | AA |
| Timmers, Johan G. | Herzog, Anna Maria | 7, July 1846 | AA |
| Timmons, William | Bodine, Ann W. | 13, Nov. 1833 | RCH |
| Timpermann, Johan H. | Krues, Anna Maria | 24, Jan. 1847 | AA |
| Tindall, Isaac | Conley, Catharine | 15, Nov. 1821 | RCH |
| Tindall, Jackson | Walker, Zelphia | 24, Oct. 1841 | RCH |
| Tinden, Thomas | Ar, Elizabeth | 21, Aug. 1849 | GG |

| Grooms | Brides | Date of Marriage | Code |
|--------|--------|------------------|------|
| ****** | ****** | **** ** ******** | **** |
| Tinnemeyer, Heinrich | Kruse, Maria | 6, Dec. 1848 | F |
| Tinsley, John | Webb, Susan | 18, June 1834 | RCH |
| Tipmore, John | Babb, Sarah | 2, July 1842 | RCH |
| Tippenbauer, John | Dalmatch, Elisabeth | 10, May 1846 | RCH |
| Tisk, Robert M. | Ransom, Orphey | 17, Aug. 1834 | RCH |
| Titel, Martin | Beckel, Lucinda | 28, Aug. 1849 | FF |
| Titsworth, | Davis, Maria | 11, Feb. 1835 | RCH |
| Tittle, | Weirmeis, Mary C. | 7, June 1849 | RCH |
| Titus, Ethan | Wisong, Barbara | 14, Oct. 1838 | RCH |
| Titus, Samuel | Seward, Elisabeth | 12, June 1842 | RCH |
| Titus, Smith | Cox, Sarah | 7, Jan. 1844 | RCH |
| Tobet, Herman | Holmann, Agnes | 5, Oct. 1845 | FF |
| Tobey, Cornelius | Armstrong, Sarah J. | 20, Sept 1849 | RCH |
| Tobin, Adam | McCarthy, Rosanna | 13, Aug. 1840 | BB |
| Tobin, John | Coleman, Ellen | 26, Nov. 1842 | BB |
| Tobin, William | Corbett, Julia | 26, Aug. 1849 | BB |
| Tobling, Clement | Stallo, Maria | 5, Feb. 1848 | EE |
| Tocum, Enoch | Jenner, Mary Ann | 9, Dec. 1847 | RCH |
| Todd, George W. | Murphy, Elizabeth | 15, Mar. 1846 | RCH |
| Todd, John | Down, Elisabeth | 19, Sept 1839 | RCH |
| Todd, John G. | Williams, Mary | 3, Feb. 1846 | RCH |
| Todd, Nicolaus | Harper, Elisabeth | 14, June 1831 | RCH |
| Todd, Samuel | Wallace, Henrietta H | 8, Sept 1818 | RCH |
| Todd, Solomon | Gleason, Henrietta | 30, Oct. 1847 | RCH |
| Todd, Tracey | Marshall, Nancy | 27, May 1844 | RCH |
| Todd, William | Ward, Lydia | 4, Nov. 1834 | RCH |
| Toddhunter, William | Herzog, Elisabeth | 1, Nov. 1846 | RCH |
| Todhunter, Louis | Stokes, Catharine M. | 31, Jan. 1843 | RCH |
| Todhunter, Rees | ----, Margaret | 16, Nov. 1824 | RCH |
| Toelke, Gerhard | Gude, Theresa | 21, Feb. 1843 | AA |
| Toennis, Johan G. | Kellermann, Elisabet | 24, Sept 1848 | AA |
| Toerner, J Christoph | Laudicks, Catharina | 30, Jan. 1838 | FF |
| Toettel, Johan | Kestler, Maria | 4, Feb. 1849 | FF |
| Tohbuhrin, Claus | Boetemann, Meta Adel | 21, Jan. 1841 | F |
| Toland, George | Francisco, Mary E. | 7, June 1836 | RCH |
| Tolbert, Allen | Smith, Mary | 15, Oct. 1837 | RCH |
| Tollman, Henry | Burns, Sarah | 30, Sept 1841 | RCH |
| Tomlinson, John G. | Garrison, Mary Ann | 1, Jan. 1833 | RCH |
| Tomlinson, L.C. | Powers, Elis. Jane | 23, May 1839 | RCH |
| Tomlinson, Samuel | Sparks, Elisabeth | 1, Aug. 1835 | RCH |
| Tomlinson, Samuel | Norris, Abigail | 13, Dec. 1842 | RCH |
| Tompkins, Amos | Ball, Flora | 16, Dec. 1846 | RCH |
| Tonbrink, Heinrich | Hodes, Maria | 18, July 1847 | AA |
| Tons, Hieronymus | Hunt, Margaretha | 4, Sept 1836 | FF |
| Topie, Friedrih | Grautmann, Maria | 11, June 1846 | F |
| Topkins, Daniel | Jeffers, Ellen | 25, May 1844 | RCH |
| Topmueller, Herman | Morwessels, Maria A. | 16, Jan. 1848 | CC |
| Torline, Georg | Schweinfuss, Maria | 25, Apr. 1838 | FF |
| Torline, Johan Georg | Kidden, Elisabeth | 15, Apr. 1847 | FF |
| Torline, Theodor | Heseker, Dorothea | 5, July 1846 | FF |
| Tormann, Herman H. | Feldhaus, Anna Maria | 16, Apr. 1844 | AA |
| Tormohler, Gerhard H | Niehaus, Maria Engel | 26, Apr. 1848 | F |
| Torsony, Barney | O'Byrne, Bridget | 1, July 1849 | GG |
| Tosso, Julius | Lafferty, Francis | 25, Dec. 1849 | RCH |
| Tosspot, Jonathan | Gist, Elisabeth | 14, Mar. 1849 | RCH |
| Totten, Alfred | Stites, Almira | 27, Dec. 1846 | RCH |
| Totten, William | Nash, Martha | 20, Jan. 1847 | RCH |
| Totton, Jasper | ----, Sarah | 13, Oct. 1818 | RCH |
| Totton, Samuel | Matthews, Matilda | 9, Aug. 1819 | RCH |
| Tout, James | Munroe, Sarah | 6, Apr. 1848 | RCH |
| Towers, Thomas N. | Burnham, Margaret | 15, Nov. 1835 | RCH |
| Towne, Henry | Markland, Sarah | 5, July 1835 | RCH |
| Townes, Robert J. | Eggleston, Pattie C. | 8, Jan. 1846 | D |
| Townley, Asa | Reed, Catharine | 18, Apr. 1847 | RCH |
| Townley, George M. | Vonice, Phebe | 18, Nov. 1834 | RCH |
| Towns, Watson | Selvis, Mary | 11, Nov. 1837 | RCH |
| Townsen, Kurnel | Miller, Abby | 12, May 1834 | RCH |
| Townsend, | Stuart, Sarah | 16, Aug. 1835 | RCH |
| Townsend, Albert | Black, Honora | 14, May 1846 | RCH |
| Townsend, Edmond | Booth, Maria | 5, Apr. 1843 | RCH |
| Townsend, Edward | Eackred, Elisabeth | 13, Jan. 1849 | RCH |

| Grooms<br>****** | Brides<br>****** | Date of Marriage<br>**** ** ******** | Code<br>**** |
|---|---|---|---|
| Townsend, Marshall | Martin, Ann | 6, Nov. 1835 | RCH |
| Townsend, Thomas | McMullen, Mary | 4, Nov. 1845 | RCH |
| Townsend, William | Parks, Jane | 7, Aug. 1834 | RCH |
| Townsky, Nathaniel | Cowen, Elizabeth | 30, Mar. 1825 | RCH |
| Toy, Benjamin | Housel, Catharine | 27, Apr. 1847 | RCH |
| Toy, Isaiah | Noble, Sarah Ann | 9, Nov. 1843 | RCH |
| Toy, Napoleon | Walker, Catharine | 22, June 1840 | RCH |
| Tracy, Michael | Henry, Rose Ann | 7, Jan. 1845 | BB |
| Tracy, Patrick | Henry, Elisabeth | 26, Nov. 1848 | BB |
| Traeger, Christian | Cawein, Sophronia | 9, July 1844 | C |
| Traeger, Johan | Walter, Josephine | 14, June 1849 | G |
| Tragesser, Thomas | Nichtern, Sibylla | 12, Oct. 1841 | FF |
| Trainor, Thomas | Boyd, Mary Jane | 10, Oct. 1841 | BB |
| Tranel, Johan Bern. | Mueller, Adelheid | 28, Jan. 1845 | AA |
| Tranel, Johan Herm. | Huelsebeck, Euphemia | 18, Feb. 1849 | AA |
| Trap, Jonathan | Herkin, Sarah | 3, Nov. 1836 | RCH |
| Trapl, Gerhard | Mueller, Maria | 23, May 1846 | EE |
| Trarbach, J. Michael | Hartmann, Maria E. | 27, Mar. 1849 | C |
| Trast, Casper | Ellis, Greatful | 2, Dec. 1821 | RCH |
| Traubaldt, Georg | Kress, Elisabeth | 18, Dec. 1845 | G |
| Trautman, J. Peter | Schmidt, Barbara | 7, Jan. 1840 | FF |
| Trautmann, Gottfried | Schierholz, Anna | 2, Nov. 1846 | C |
| Trautmann, Leonard | Brickmann, Elisabeth | 1, Apr. 1849 | C |
| Trautmann, Peter | Schmidt, Barbara | 26, Nov. 1839 | FF |
| Trautwein, Mathias | Hoffmann, Eva | 13, Oct. 1845 | RCH |
| Trauzottheipe, Carl | Worsner, Anna Maria | 7, Oct. 1849 | C |
| Traver, John | Wilson, Mary | 2, Oct. 1834 | RCH |
| Travers, John | McCabe, Mary | 12, Jan. 1848 | BB |
| Travis, Abram | Milson, Catharine | 11, Sept 1833 | RCH |
| Traxel, Johan | Dillmann, Elisabeth | 12, Sept 1843 | G |
| Trayme, George | Breen, Sally | 21, Dec. 1841 | BB |
| Treadway, John | Dodge, Mercy | 6, Mar. 1821 | RCH |
| Treadway, John | McCane, Rebecca | 30, Dec. 1822 | RCH |
| Treadway, William | Weed, Juliana | 4, July 1841 | RCH |
| Treat, Isaac | Crawford, Elisabeth | 26, Sept 1847 | RCH |
| Treat, John | Jones, Elisabeth | 15, Nov. 1847 | RCH |
| Treat, Theodor | Colvin, Dacy Ann | 11, June 1849 | RCH |
| Trebein, Christian | Scheidemann, Louise | 23, Aug. 1849 | C |
| Tredway, William | Jobe, Mary Jane | 13, Oct. 1842 | RCH |
| Trefzer, Jacob | Kramer, Barbara | 14, Aug. 1842 | RCH |
| Tremble, John | Perry, Sarah | 14, July 1844 | RCH |
| Trembur, Nicolaus | Laut, M. Magdalena | 21, Nov. 1836 | FF |
| Trentmann, Bernard | Rennis, Maria | 30, Oct. 1838 | FF |
| Trentmann, Franz | Kudinghaus, Agnes | 12, May 1844 | AA |
| Trentmann, Johan F. | Zumbrink, Louisa | 2, May 1848 | AA |
| Trentmann, Johan H. | Nordmann, A.M. Cath. | 17, Feb. 1842 | F |
| Trerking, Wilhelm G. | Hinke, Augusta | 16, Oct. 1839 | FF |
| Trester, Simon | Huff, Sarah | 19, Dec. 1849 | RCH |
| Trever, Samuel | Bidwell, Margaret | 24, May 1848 | RCH |
| Tri---, Nathan | Roberts, M.A. | 9, Dec. 1833 | RCH |
| Tricke, Charles | Daughaday, Rebecca | 14, June 1848 | BB |
| Triffs, Joseph | Michael, Frances | 26, Dec. 1844 | RCH |
| Trim, Nathaniel | Clark, Sarah L. | 27, June 1844 | RCH |
| Trimble, Harvey | Dustin, Diana | 30, Apr. 1842 | RCH |
| Trimble, Henry | Boleyn, Susan Ayres | 7, Nov. 1823 | I |
| Trimble, Johan Hein. | Busch, Anna Maria | 8, Sept 1835 | FF |
| Trimpe, Anton | Thiele, Anna Maria | 16, Dec. 1838 | FF |
| Trimpe, Friedrich | Thiele, Elisabeth | 23, May 1838 | FF |
| Trimpe, Heinrich | Tenemann, Elisabeth | 10, Nov. 1836 | F |
| Trimpe, Herman H. | Borgstede, Maria A. | 5, Aug. 1843 | F |
| Trimpe, Johan | Hill, Maria | 16, Oct. 1838 | FF |
| Trimpe, John Gerhard | Moormann, Catharine | 14, Apr. 1846 | F |
| Trimper, William | Trimper, Mary | 29, Aug. 1835 | RCH |
| Triplet, Alfred | Steard, Elisabeth | 28, June 1839 | RCH |
| Trivin, James | Knighton, Margaret | Aug. 1835 | RCH |
| Trollmann, Johan | Zeller, Maria | 23, Oct. 1849 | EE |
| Trom, Peter | Vance, M. Josephine | 29, Dec. 1847 | BB |
| Trond, Joseph | Peterson, Louise | 8, Aug. 1839 | RCH |
| Trotber, Daniel | Hamilton, Maria L. | 2, Oct. 1832 | RCH |
| Trotter, Joseph | Johnson, Hannah | Sept 1836 | RCH |
| Trotter, Samuel | Whitehead, Scion | 21, Apr. 1844 | RCH |

| Grooms<br>****** | Brides<br>****** | Date of Marriage<br>**** ** ******** | Code<br>**** |
|---|---|---|---|
| Trowbridge, David | Dolph, Catharine | 29, Oct. 1823 | RCH |
| Trowbridge, Watson | Krummel, Susanna | 13, Nov. 1846 | G |
| Trowbridge, William | Pease, Mary Ann | 8, Oct. 1848 | RCH |
| Troxell, William | Little, Jane | 5, June 1844 | RCH |
| Troy, Daniel | Repske--, Mary Ann | 1, Oct. 1818 | RCH |
| Troy, Vincent S. | Justice, Rebecca | 20, Dec. 1832 | RCH |
| Trueman, Aaron | Stewart, Margaret | 15, May 1832 | RCH |
| Trueman, John | Ludlow, Harriet | 1, Feb. 1837 | RCH |
| Truesdale, Charles | Sennett, Helen M. | 19, July 1849 | RCH |
| Truet, Fedock | Helmeth, Margaret | 28, Oct. 1819 | RCH |
| Trum, Bernard | Luster, Louise | 25, Aug. 1840 | FF |
| Trumber, Johan | Oliger, Maria | 10, Nov. 1834 | FF |
| Trumeter, John | Wagerlin, Margaret | 27, Nov. 1845 | RCH |
| Trump, John | Williamson, Margaret | 30, June 1836 | RCH |
| Trunck, Bardol | Walton, Margaret | 2, Oct. 1843 | RCH |
| Trunck, Bartol | Trap, Catharine | 8, Apr. 1844 | RCH |
| Trunk, J. Michael | Lutze, Maria | 15, July 1845 | AA |
| Trunnell, Thomas | Paylor, Mary Ann | 12, Mar. 1845 | RCH |
| Tryant, John | Gallagher, Margaret | 30, Sept 1843 | RCH |
| Tubbesing, Herman H. | Meiers, Anna Louise | 5, July 1849 | E |
| Tuchfarber, Anton | Ripberger, Maria A. | 11, Feb. 1840 | FF |
| Tuchfarber, Stephan | Rubem, Apollonia | 13, Apr. 1847 | EE |
| Tucker, Albert | Evans, Elisabeth J. | 15, June 1842 | RCH |
| Tucker, Amos | Glascoe, Sarah | 7, Oct. 1847 | RCH |
| Tucker, Elisha | Loughlin, Emeline | 10, Oct. 1832 | RCH |
| Tucker, George | Coltharon, Sarah | 1, May 1833 | RCH |
| Tucker, George W. | Huntman, Sarah Ann | 4, July 1841 | RCH |
| Tucker, Henry | Crisser, Lucy | 19, Aug. 1825 | RCH |
| Tucker, Jonas | Tucker, Sarah | 2, May 1822 | RCH |
| Tucker, Lewis | Miles, Lavina | 28, Mar. 1822 | RCH |
| Tucker, Richard | Nott, Mary | 19, Dec. 1835 | RCH |
| Tucker, Squire | Carson, Eleanor | 9, Aug. 1832 | RCH |
| Tucker, William | Mack, Mary | 25, Sept 1834 | RCH |
| Tudor, Edward | Smallwood, Virginia | 14, Sept 1847 | BB |
| Tudor, John M. | Hill, Ann R. | 18, June 1839 | RCH |
| Tudor, William | Morgans, Sarah | 19, Apr. 1838 | RCH |
| Tuebben, Johan Bd. | Zurline, Gesina | 7, Sept 1845 | AA |
| Tuenemann, Heinrich | Otto, Theresa | 27, Aug. 1846 | AA |
| Tuerk, Johan | Dilg, Elisabeth | 12, June 1849 | G |
| Tuffley, Peter | Blese, Catharine | 11, Feb. 1846 | GG |
| Tuggar, William H. | Gordon, Mary | 16, Feb. 1848 | RCH |
| Tull, Henry | Robertson, Parmetia | 11, Dec. 1845 | RCH |
| Tull, Joseph | Graham, Sarah A. | 22, Feb. 1838 | RCH |
| Tullis, David | Moore, Jane | 7, Sept 1843 | RCH |
| Tullis, David | Miller, Mary Ann | 13, June 1846 | RCH |
| Tullis, Moses | Carpenter, Sarah Ann | 22, Aug. 1837 | RCH |
| Tullis, Samuel | Hood, Dianna | 7, June 1826 | RCH |
| Tumy, John | Johnson, Lucy | 27, Feb. 1834 | RCH |
| Tunnicliff, John | English, Affalina | 6, June 1846 | RCH |
| Turner, Daniel | Wagner, Elisabeth | 10, Aug. 1844 | RCH |
| Turner, Duncan | Carnes, Hannah | 31, Oct. 1847 | RCH |
| Turner, E.A. | Vickers, Sarah Ann | 21, June 1834 | RCH |
| Turner, Fobs | Bunk, Polly | 22, Jan. 1821 | RCH |
| Turner, Francis | Gray, Letitia | 8, Dec. 1849 | RCH |
| Turner, Georg | McMillen, Mary J. | 2, Nov. 1845 | RCH |
| Turner, George | English, Susan | 24, Mar. 1844 | RCH |
| Turner, Henry | Lindley, Jane | 1, Nov. 1846 | RCH |
| Turner, Herman | Grimm, Maria E. | 26, Mar. 1839 | RCH |
| Turner, James | Thrasher, Elisabeth | 25, Sept 1836 | RCH |
| Turner, Jesse | Smith, Sarah Jane | 26, July 1848 | RCH |
| Turner, Michael | Flinn, Nancy | 9, Dec. 1835 | RCH |
| Turner, Samuel | Wiltse, Rachel | 7, Mar. 1844 | RCH |
| Turner, William | Graham, Mariah | 6, Mar. 1820 | RCH |
| Turner, Zedekiah | Cooper, Susannah | 15, Aug. 1820 | RCH |
| Turnpan, James | Jeffries, Lobelia | 22, Sept 1845 | RCH |
| Turpin, Edward J. | Kugler, Christina | 20, May 1839 | RCH |
| Turpin, Robert | Stewart, Frances M. | 23, Sept 1846 | RCH |
| Turtle, Goerge | Bartlett, Lydia | 20, Nov. 1823 | RCH |
| Turvin, Thomas S. | Kercher, Winifred G. | 23, Feb. 1836 | RCH |
| Tussey, John | Wilson, Sarah | 4, Apr. 1833 | RCH |
| Tussey, William | Welding, Louise | 14, Sept 1846 | RCH |

| Grooms<br>****** | Brides<br>****** | Date of Marriage<br>**** ** ******** | Code<br>**** |
|---|---|---|---|
| Tutlin, Simon Chas. | Sheiner, Sarah F. | 31, Aug. 1845 | BB |
| Tuttle, Alexander | Smith, Elisabeth | 27, Dec. 1842 | RCH |
| Tuttle, George | Hays, Mary | 25, Sept 1820 | RCH |
| Tuttle, John | Ellis, Elisabeth | 3, Apr. 1834 | RCH |
| Tuttle, John | Gilman, Mary | 19, Apr. 1849 | RCH |
| Tuttle, Thomas C. | Anderson, Elisabeth | 31, Mar. 1836 | RCH |
| Twachtmann, Christ. | Droege, Sophia | 8, Mar. 1842 | F |
| Tweed, James | Bradbury, Sarah | 27, Feb. 1848 | RCH |
| Tweed, John P. | VanDyke, Jane Carol. | 13, Oct. 1836 | RCH |
| Twente, Wilhelm | Walhaker, Maria | 16, Feb. 1843 | RCH |
| Twente, Wilhelm | Kollmeier, Sophia | 10, July 1845 | C |
| Twentyman, John | Wood, Angeline | May 1847 | RCH |
| Twohey, Jeremiah | Nead, Mary | 23, July 1849 | RCH |
| Twohey, Thomas | Fitzpatrick, Marg. | 8, Mar. 1848 | BB |
| Tye, Johan Gerhard | Groneke, Catharine | 27, May 1845 | AA |
| Tyley, Francis | Hughes, Sarah | 13, Oct. 1841 | RCH |
| Tyner, Silas | Bent, Hannah Ann | 9, Oct. 1845 | RCH |
| Tyrack, James | Conkling, Sarah | 6, May 1847 | RCH |
| Tyre, Whitefield | Hinton, Jane | 26, Oct. 1837 | RCH |
| Tyre, William | Phinney, Jemima | 30, Nov. 1849 | RCH |
| Tyson, Joseph L. | Drinham, Caroline | 26, Mar. 1840 | I |
| | | | |
| Uckotter, Herman | Kenkel, Catharina | 4, July 1847 | AA |
| Ucmans, Joseph | McElva, Mary Ann | 8, June 1834 | RCH |
| Udry, Lorenz | Schindler, Magdalena | 11, May 1840 | FF |
| Uhland, Johan Heinr. | Landwehr, Fina Adel. | 17, Nov. 1846 | F |
| Uhlaren, Johan | Withar, Bernardina | 13, June 1847 | AA |
| Uhlenbrock, Bernard | Ballmann, Catharina | 18, Apr. 1847 | AA |
| Uhlhorn, Herman H. | Feldmann, Rebecca M. | 17, Nov. 1835 | FF |
| Ulicke, Herman H. | Kampmann, Elisabeth | 22, Oct. 1848 | FF |
| Ullmann, Henry | Loeb, Babette | 22, Aug. 1846 | RCH |
| Ullmer, Andreas | Schmidlapp, Maria A. | 17, Mar. 1839 | G |
| Ulmer, Friedrich | Flinschbach, Marie | 16, Sept 1849 | G |
| Ulmer, Joseph | Lippert, Barbara | 29, Dec. 1839 | G |
| Ulrey, John | Turner, Mary | 16, Sept 1832 | RCH |
| Ulrey, Stephen | McDonald, Casandra | 27, Apr. 1842 | RCH |
| Umbach, Joseph Hein. | Vogel, Elisabeth | 13, Nov. 1849 | G |
| Umberger, John | O'Brien, Caroline | 31, Mar. 1847 | RCH |
| Umlauf, Philipp | Banlitz, Caroline | 25, Oct. 1845 | RCH |
| Underhill, Richard | Lavercombe, Mary A. | 1, Aug. 1849 | D |
| Underwood, Hiram | Kemp, Louise | 20, Dec. 1835 | RCH |
| Underwood, John | Smith, Eva | 19, May 1842 | RCH |
| Underwood, John | Dean, Harriet | 16, June 1842 | RCH |
| Unger, Johan Heinric | Boehning, Sophia | 15, Nov. 1842 | AA |
| Unkraut, Heinrich | Joering, Elisabeth | 2, May 1843 | FF |
| Unluecke, Georg H. | Strickers, Maria Ann | 10, May 1846 | FF |
| Unterbottom, John | Roberts, Mary A. | 8, Dec. 1847 | RCH |
| Untereiner, Paul | Hardcope, Carolina | 27, Feb. 1836 | FF |
| Unverzagt, Johan G. | Lerch, Friedricka | 1, July 1846 | C |
| Unzicker, Joseph | Wellmann, Anna M.D. | 9, Dec. 1841 | F |
| Uphaus, Friedrich | Tegler, Louise | 13, Apr. 1848 | C |
| Upheil, Joseph Anton | Rudmann, Maria Anna | 1, Nov. 1840 | FF |
| Uphof, Heinrich Geo. | Meier, Anna Gertrud | 12, Jan. 1845 | FF |
| Uphof, Johan Heinric | Doth, Margaretha | 29, Aug. 1847 | FF |
| Upjohn, Sylvester | Argedine, Elisabeth | 22, Mar. 1838 | RCH |
| Upmar, Herman Hein. | Barhorst, Catharine | 20, June 1839 | FF |
| Upson, Ashel A. | Weeks, Dorinda A. | 9, Apr. 1849 | RCH |
| Uptmann, Clemens | Niehaus, Elisabeth | 24, Sept 1839 | FF |
| Urban, George | Fox, Helen | 3, Mar. 1842 | RCH |
| Urban, Johan | Wilhelm, Maria Magd. | 5, May 1846 | EE |
| Urlage, Johan Bern. | VonWalde, Maria | 27, Nov. 1849 | AA |
| Urmston, John | Teter, Maria | 3, Dec. 1837 | RCH |
| Urmston, Joseph | Hickmann, Martha A. | 5, Jan. 1843 | RCH |
| Uster, J. Ludwig Fr. | Schlueter, Charlotte | 15, Nov. 1849 | F |
| Utz, Casimer | Vollherbst, Sybilla | 11, Nov. 1845 | FF |
| | | | |
| Vactor, John | Weeks, Sarah | 1, July 1842 | RCH |
| Vagedes, Anton | Soeger, Catharine | 28, July 1849 | CC |
| Vaghinger, Gustav | Schwerkler, Margaret | 9, Feb. 1837 | RCH |
| Vaiel, Daniel H. | Todd, Harriet | 30, Oct. 1822 | RCH |
| Vail, Stephen | Shepherd, Elanor | 1, Feb. 1821 | RCH |

| Grooms<br>****** | Brides<br>****** | Date of Marriage<br>**** ** ******** | Code<br>**** |
|---|---|---|---|
| Vail, Stephen | Netta, Susan | 30, Aug. 1849 | RCH |
| Vale, James | Laxton, Lydia C. | 31, Mar. 1839 | RCH |
| Valendahmen, Anthony | Paul, Regina | 20, Dec. 1845 | BB |
| Valentine, Charles | Baird, Ann | 30, Mar. 1842 | RCH |
| Valentine, John | Funk, Mary Ann | 25, Dec. 1837 | RCH |
| Valentine, John | Walton, Phebe | 17, Jan. 1844 | RCH |
| Valentine, Lafayette | Chandler, Nancy | 25, Mar. 1849 | RCH |
| Valentine, Lewis | Dunn, Elisabeth | 12, Apr. 1842 | RCH |
| Valentine, Samuel | Jessup, Mary | 1, June 1843 | RCH |
| Vallandingham, Nel. | Pangburn, Matilda | 30, Apr. 1843 | RCH |
| Vallandingham, Oliv. | Stiltz, Elisabeth | 10, Aug. 1848 | RCH |
| Vallis, Stephen | Taylor, Elisabeth | 4, June 1842 | RCH |
| Vallo, Christopher | Hudepohl, M. Anna | 7, Sept 1847 | AA |
| Valmer, Frederick | Duffy, Margaret | 22, May 1842 | BB |
| Valtair, Christian | Deck, Diss | 31, July 1841 | RCH |
| Van, Valentine | Lindenmeyer, Friedr. | 7, Apr. 1849 | RCH |
| VanAdam, Peter | McLean, Sarah | 29, Dec. 1836 | RCH |
| VanAmberg, Nelson | Roberts, Nancy | 25, June 1846 | RCH |
| VanAusdal, | Bernard, Ellen | 30, Aug. 1849 | RCH |
| VanAusdol, Angus | King, Mary | 13, Aug. 1848 | RCH |
| VanAusdol, Garrett | Gasley, Julia Ann | 5, Aug. 1847 | RCH |
| VanBlaricum, David | Douglass, Margaret | 9, Sept 1849 | RCH |
| VanBlaricum, Henry | Coon, Elisabeth Jane | 12, Nov. 1848 | RCH |
| VanBronkhorst, Johan | Salomen, Maria Cath. | 27, Aug. 1846 | EE |
| VanCamp, Cornelius | Hahn, Mary | 31, Dec. 1844 | RCH |
| VanCamp, Garrett | Baker, Harriet | 23, May 1847 | RCH |
| VanCeyac, Godfrey | Brown, Carry | 28, Oct. 1832 | RCH |
| VanCuran, Charles | McCreary, Mary | 1, Apr. 1824 | RCH |
| VanDike, William | Sintney, Martha Ann | 29, Oct. 1834 | RCH |
| VanDiver, Emmett | Price, Martha Jane | 25, Aug. 1846 | RCH |
| VanDoren, Dominick | Sentney, Jane | 27, Sept 1842 | RCH |
| VanDusen, Edward | Duncan, Susan | 10, June 1849 | RCH |
| VanDusen, James | Smith, Sophia | 4, May 1845 | BB |
| VanDusen, Sylvanus | Bryant, Mary | 10, Dec. 1843 | RCH |
| VanDuzen, Benjamin | Cook, Ann | 25, Mar. 1849 | RCH |
| VanDuzen, Ezra | Dowd, Ann E. | 16, Oct. 1844 | RCH |
| VanDuzen, F. | Robinson, Polly | 24, July 1822 | RCH |
| VanDuzen, John | Harper, Mary Ann | 14, Apr. 1836 | RCH |
| VanDyke, Abijah | Lawrence, Sylvia | 8, May 1843 | RCH |
| VanDyke, William | Auter, Elisabeth | 21, Mar. 1821 | RCH |
| VanEaton, David | McMahon, Susannah | 13, June 1823 | RCH |
| VanEaton, James | Cox, Hannah | 11, June 1833 | RCH |
| VanFrees, Isaac | Orr, Jane Elisabeth | 15, June 1844 | RCH |
| VanGooden, Abraham | Hoslet, Anny | 16, Feb. 1834 | RCH |
| VanGorder, | Pierson, Sarah | 26, Aug. 1849 | RCH |
| VanGorder, Abram | Guinra, Matel H. | 13, Aug. 1839 | RCH |
| VanGorder, Herman | Stewart, Mary Ann | 6, July 1842 | RCH |
| VanGorder, John | Fox, Pamila | 5, Aug. 1824 | RCH |
| VanGordon, Alexander | Kincaid, Margaret | 21, July 1825 | RCH |
| VanHart, Jacob | Buck, Jane | 1, June 1841 | RCH |
| VanHart, Samuel | Quick, Catharine | 12, May 1844 | RCH |
| VanHart, Thomas | Bowers, Susannah | Jan. 1845 | RCH |
| VanHolle, Johan Bd. | Kessling, Anna Maria | 3, June 1849 | CC |
| VanHorne, John | Williams, Elisabeth | 11, Apr. 1839 | RCH |
| VanKindorfe, Hiram | Harris, Ann | 19, Oct. 1835 | RCH |
| VanKirk, John D. | Spader, Mary | 7, Jan. 1819 | RCH |
| VanLiew, Dennis | Hanson, Mary | 9, Mar. 1842 | RCH |
| VanLiew, John | Guynn, Ellen | 24, Feb. 1844 | RCH |
| VanLoon, Samuel | McDowell, Lucinda | 11, Oct. 1843 | RCH |
| VanMatre, Daniel | Henderson, Maria A. | 25, Apr. 1833 | RCH |
| VanMiddlesworth, P. | Miles, Elisa | 21, Sept 1820 | RCH |
| VanNastin, Abram | Cook, Margaret | 10, Nov. 1821 | RCH |
| VanPelt, John | Gresmore, Sarah | 11, May 1820 | RCH |
| VanRe, Andreas | Kunters, Anna | 25, July 1847 | EE |
| VanRoon, Benjamin | Danbury, Sarah | 21, May 1839 | RCH |
| VanS---, Stephen | Jessup, Lydia | 16, Aug. 1836 | RCH |
| VanScoyve, William | Davis, Nancy L. | 3, July 1843 | RCH |
| VanSeele, Alexander | Baughman, Mary | 12, Jan. 1837 | RCH |
| VanSickle, William | Jones, Rachel | 29, Jan. 1818 | RCH |
| VanSlyck, Peter | Mitchell, Nancy | 7, Sept 1843 | RCH |
| VanSycke, John | Rensford, Susannah | 4, June 1844 | RCH |

| Grooms<br>****** | Brides<br>****** | Date of Marriage<br>**** ** ******** | Code<br>**** |
|---|---|---|---|
| VanSyell, William | Berry, Catharine | 1, Sept 1839 | RCH |
| VanTruse, Solomon | Mintor, Lucinda | 26, Nov. 1837 | RCH |
| VanTuyle, Isaac | Carnahan, Ellen | 5, Aug. 1847 | RCH |
| VanVaulkenburg, Wm. | Ogg, Sarah | 1822 | RCH |
| VanVliet, John | Beard, Jane | 25, Apr. 1846 | RCH |
| VanWerden, Carl | Henke, M. Elisabeth | 12, Oct. 1843 | F |
| VanZant, Benjamin | Kane, Rebecca | 20, Nov. 1834 | RCH |
| VanZant, George C. | Cunningham, Jane | 4, Feb. 1838 | RCH |
| VanZant, James | Coleman, Elisabeth | 10, Sept 1842 | RCH |
| VanZant, John | Runyan, Nancy | 1, July 1824 | RCH |
| VanZant, Lorenzo | Aikens, Caroline | 10, Mar. 1842 | RCH |
| VanZant, Richard | Iliff, Elisabeth | 20, Dec. 1818 | RCH |
| VanZant, William | Morges, Ann | 26, July 1833 | RCH |
| VanZile, Abraham | Butter, Julia | 27, Nov. 1849 | RCH |
| Vanan, Miles | Bartlett, Charlotte | 15, Dec. 1845 | RCH |
| Vance, Alexander | Dean, Harriet | 6, May 1819 | RCH |
| Vance, Andrew | Norris, Harriet | 9, Feb. 1836 | RCH |
| Vance, Charles | Peck, Catharine | 10, Nov. 1842 | RCH |
| Vance, E. | Doaks, Catharine A. | 4, May 1837 | RCH |
| Vance, James | Williamson, Asha | 6, May 1849 | RCH |
| Vance, John | Whallon, Jane | 11, Apr. 1833 | RCH |
| VandeGriff, William | Stevens, Letitia | 13, June 1844 | RCH |
| VandeGrift, Abraham | Tracy, Margaret | 19, May 1836 | RCH |
| Vanlein, Ira | Windlin, Mariah | 10, Jan. 1847 | RCH |
| Vannaken, Joseph | Dresback, Leah | 31, Dec. 1833 | RCH |
| Vannekle, Ralph | Snyder, Sarah | 1, Apr. 1834 | RCH |
| Vantile, Oliver | Auter, Mary | 1822 | RCH |
| Vantrees, Israel | Sellors, Betsey | 29, Apr. 1824 | RCH |
| Vantreese, Daniel | Pierson, Rebecca | 6, Jan. 1846 | RCH |
| Vantreese, Solomon | Williamson, Mary | 5, Aug. 1847 | RCH |
| Varcie, Herman Hein. | Trenkamp, J. | 22, Feb. 1838 | FF |
| Varhiss, Isaac | Grigg, Harriet | 5, Apr. 1841 | RCH |
| Varnall, August | Honeck, Barbara | 1, Oct. 1844 | FF |
| Varner, Alfred | Collins, Ruth | 10, Jan. 1839 | RCH |
| Varner, Thomas | Sassebre, Martha | 3, Mar. 1841 | RCH |
| Varney, Anson | Graham, Mary | 9, Aug. 1845 | RCH |
| Varwig, Georg | Tipken, Margaret S. | 15, Oct. 1846 | B |
| Vater, Thomas J. | Hey, Anna | 3, Sept 1848 | RCH |
| Vatier, John L. | Fowsatte, Margaret | 22, Sept 1828 | I |
| Vattier, John L. | Disney, Mary Frances | 20, June 1833 | RCH |
| Vattier, John L. | Moore, Anna Maria | 9, Dec. 1845 | RCH |
| Vaughan, Charles | Tucker, Catharine | 2, Oct. 1843 | RCH |
| Vaughan, Daniel | Mitchell, Ann | 7, Oct. 1832 | RCH |
| Vaughan, George W. | Shoemaker, Mary Ann | 15, Aug. 1847 | RCH |
| Vaughan, Jesse | Moor, Nancy | 1, July 1837 | RCH |
| Vaughan, John | Sisbruthal, Felicia | 23, Sept 1832 | RCH |
| Vaughn, James | Merriott, Rhoda | 6, Sept 1844 | RCH |
| Vaughn, John | Badger, Amanda | 4, July 1848 | RCH |
| Vaughn, Liberty | Briceland, Nancy | 15, Jan. 1827 | RCH |
| Vaul, Alois | Jaeger, Magdalena | 19, Apr. 1836 | FF |
| Vaulhorn, John K. | Stewart, Agnes | 9, Jan. 1848 | RCH |
| Vawter, William | Neave, Sarah | 8, Jan. 1834 | RCH |
| Vechterup, J Wilhelm | Mescher, Gertrud | 10, Feb. 1848 | FF |
| Vedder, Joseph | Kuhlmann, Elisabeth | 7, Jan. 1845 | FF |
| Veegmann, Jacob | Klein, Dorothea | 8, Feb. 1846 | FF |
| Veerkamp, Gerhard G. | Mussing, Sophia | 10, May 1844 | RCH |
| Vehebring, Herman | Dickmann, Bernardina | 24, Nov. 1839 | FF |
| Vehr, Gerhard | Diesenhorst, Elis. | 23, May 1848 | EE |
| Veil, John | Crist, Elisabeth | 21, Nov. 1819 | RCH |
| Venderson, Henry | Tinven, Christina | 29, Jan. 1821 | RCH |
| Vennedunker, Anton | Weber, Catharine M. | 21, Oct. 1846 | AA |
| Vennedunker, Anton | Fransmann, Theresa | 23, Jan. 1848 | AA |
| Vennedunker, Bernard | Beckerman, Elisabeth | 19, Sept 1847 | FF |
| Vennedunker, Johan | Woeste, Theresa | 3, Feb. 1847 | AA |
| Vennemann, Anton | Beidenharn, Cath. E. | 31, Jan. 1837 | FF |
| Vennemann, Gerhard | Woskefart, Catharina | 20, May 1838 | FF |
| Vennemann, Heinrich | Brodbeck, Helena | 6, Feb. 1844 | AA |
| Vennemann, Herman | Schroers, Christina | 10, May 1849 | RCH |
| Vennemann, J Theodor | Hoelscher, Isabella | 22, Oct. 1840 | FF |
| Vennemann, J. Anton | Schweer, Maria Cath. | 5, Nov. 1844 | FF |
| Vennemann, Theodor | Raters, Elisabeth | 10, Feb. 1835 | FF |

| Grooms<br>***** | Brides<br>***** | Date of Marriage<br>**** ** ******** | Code<br>**** |
|---|---|---|---|
| Verbold, Anton | Schildmeier, Cath. | 30, Sept 1849 | EE |
| Verdam, Friedrich | Mascher, Catharine | 30, Oct. 1843 | FF |
| Verdin, Aloysius N. | Werk, N. | 12, Nov. 1839 | FF |
| Verdin, Francis | Heimberger, Ricardin | 8, Jan. 1848 | EE |
| Verdin, Francis S. | Geargen, Josephina | 12, Nov. 1839 | FF |
| Verige, J. Friedrich | Greathaus, Anna J. | 29, Oct. 1846 | RCH |
| Verkamp, Franz | Schneiders, Theresa | 10, Aug. 1843 | AA |
| Verkamp, Heinrich | Stricker, Elisabeth | 4, June 1844 | FF |
| Verkamp, Lucas | Honermann, Maria | 18, Jan. 1842 | FF |
| Vervolan, Joseph | Moss, Elisabeth J. | 5, Mar. 1846 | RCH |
| Veske, Gerhard | Hemrock, Catharina | 20, Apr. 1841 | FF |
| Vetter, Carl | Gentner, Rosina | 6, June 1847 | EE |
| Vetter, Georg | Fritz, Maria Theresa | 12, Apr. 1842 | FF |
| Vetter, Peter | Licher, Margaretha | 6, Feb. 1842 | G |
| Vice, Franklin | Kilwell, Emily | 8, Apr. 1842 | RCH |
| Vickers, Garland | Vail, Mary Ann | 3, Feb. 1841 | RCH |
| Vidal, Francis | Shipley, Mary Jane | 28, July 1847 | RCH |
| Vierke, Johan Conrad | Lindemann, Dorothea | 12, Apr. 1842 | F |
| Vierling, Francis | Volmer, Caroline | 19, July 1849 | RCH |
| Vierschilling, Anton | Dikel, Helen (Mrs) | 26, Oct. 1847 | EE |
| Vieths, J. Dietrich | Schneider, Christina | 4, Feb. 1847 | RCH |
| Vinable, Samuel | McMuny, Anna | 6, Sept 1838 | RCH |
| Vincent, Atchilus | Davison, Nancy | 20, Apr. 1820 | RCH |
| Vincent, Bartlett C. | Sharkes, Mary | 14, Mar. 1824 | RCH |
| Vincent, Jeremiah | Pearce, Sophia | 30, Nov. 1845 | RCH |
| Vinhage, Joseph | Timmans, Maria | 24, Apr. 1838 | FF |
| Vinson, John | Phillips, Sarah | 17, June 1847 | RCH |
| Vinson, Lewis | McMahon, Louise | 6, Aug. 1837 | RCH |
| Vinson, William | McAdams, Nancy Ann | 31, July 1844 | RCH |
| Violett, William | Oldham, Penelope | 16, June 1846 | RCH |
| Virgin, Stephen | Carr, Ann | 1, July 1837 | RCH |
| Virgin, Thomas | Morrow, Sarah | 5, Apr. 1835 | RCH |
| Vischer, Carl A. | Mueller, Rosina B. | 6, Oct. 1848 | G |
| Visse, Bernard | Stilling, Catharine | 3, Nov. 1846 | FF |
| Vobler, Bernard | Neuhaus, Elisabeth | 20, Jan. 1835 | FF |
| Vocke, Bernard | Muhle, Maria | 12, Sept 1847 | CC |
| Vocke, Francis Hein. | Sandmann, Sophia M. | 11, June 1848 | AA |
| Vocke, Herman Hein. | Stegmann, Maria Elis | 15, Jan. 1846 | AA |
| Voelker, Heinrich | Schmidt, Lisette | 13, Aug. 1844 | AA |
| Voelker, Heinrich | Beyerle, Margaretha | 4, Apr. 1848 | G |
| Voet, Francis H. | Willenborg, Cathar. | 6, Nov. 1849 | AA |
| Vogeding, Gerhard | Helmig, Adelheid | 20, Nov. 1849 | II |
| Vogel, Abraham | Schroeder, | 1844 | RCH |
| Vogel, Albert | Sendlinger, Caroline | 15, July 1845 | G |
| Vogel, Edward | Emmert, Wendeline | 18, Nov. 1845 | F |
| Vogel, Heinrich | Ellermann, Dorothea | 29, Nov. 1841 | F |
| Vogel, Johan | Feldmann, Rosina | 12, Apr. 1846 | EE |
| Vogel, John | Guggenheim, Matilda | Nov. 1848 | RCH |
| Vogel, John | Zepf, Kunigunda | 20, Aug. 1849 | RCH |
| Vogel, Joseph | Bustart, Cath. (Mrs) | 23, Apr. 1838 | FF |
| Vogel, Peter | Kessel, Magdalena | 4, Jan. 1846 | A |
| Vogel, Valentin | Dresendorfer, Doroth | 18, Aug. 1845 | G |
| Vogel, William | Jais, Caroline | 4, June 1836 | RCH |
| Vogelbach, Johan | Schaefer, Margaretha | 7, Jan. 1841 | FF |
| Vogler, Michael | Pfisterer, Dorothea | 18, Dec. 1845 | G |
| Vogt, Bernard | Brun, Anna Maria | 21, Nov. 1837 | FF |
| Vogt, Christian L. | Koehne, Maria Elis. | 15, Dec. 1846 | G |
| Vogt, Friedrich | Morsch, Louise | 9, Oct. 1846 | F |
| Vogt, Heinrich | Flaspohler, M. Cath. | 12, May 1840 | FF |
| Vogt, Heinrich | Henke, Anna Elis. | 9, Oct. 1849 | AA |
| Vogt, Jacob | Gutzwiller, M. Magd. | 19, Apr. 1836 | FF |
| Vogt, Johan | Durst, M. Anna | 17, Oct. 1848 | FF |
| Voigt, Michael | Geblin, Maria Anna | 30, Jan. 1845 | AA |
| Voix, Conrad | Horst, Margaretha | 20, Nov. 1848 | RCH |
| Volant, Alexander | Bleem, Mary A. | 15, July 1844 | RCH |
| Volant, Alexander | Blaums, Maria | 31, May 1846 | C |
| Volk, Ferdinand | Poppolt, Margaretha | 18, Feb. 1847 | EE |
| Volk, Johan | Adam, Anna Maria(Mrs | 20, Nov. 1848 | EE |
| Volk, Nicolaus | Strowhuver, Susan | 7, Mar. 1833 | RCH |
| Volke, Jacob | Ross, Sybilla | 25, Mar. 1849 | C |
| Volker, Georg Heinr. | Schwerzwig, A. Maria | 21, Nov. 1842 | FF |

| Grooms ****** | Brides ****** | Date of Marriage **** ** ******** | Code **** |
|---|---|---|---|
| Voll, Caspar | Pistner, Maria | 16, July 1846 | EE |
| Voll, George | Rattermann, Anna | 11, Jan. 1849 | GG |
| Voller, Johan H. | Holtheimer, Elis. | 28, Aug. 1849 | CC |
| Vollmeier, Heinrich | Mueller, Henrietta E | 12, Dec. 1844 | F |
| Vollmer, Daniel | Burger, Barbara | 9, Jan. 1845 | FF |
| Vollmer, Heinrich | Kamphaus, Theresa | 17, Nov. 1846 | AA |
| Volpert, Francis | Baumer, Francisca | 20, Feb. 1848 | EE |
| Voltering, Johan H. | Robben, Maria Rosina | 7, Nov. 1847 | EE |
| Volz, Anton | Mueller, Francisca | 6, Jan. 1848 | HH |
| Volz, Benedict | Bechtel, Helena | 26, July 1841 | FF |
| Volz, Carl | Allbecker, Carolina | 14, Aug. 1838 | FF |
| Volz, Peter | Braun, Barbara | 24, June 1847 | G |
| Volz, Philipp | Kern, Eva Rosina | 30, Sept 1841 | FF |
| Volz, Trubert | Pfeifer, Carolina | 1, Feb. 1848 | AA |
| VonBehren, Heinrich | Hoffner, Margaretha | 8, Aug. 1848 | A |
| VonEye, Gerhardt | Magreten, Johanna | 18, Jan. 1844 | G |
| VonGeldern, Gerhard | Meyer, Maria | 27, Feb. 1845 | F |
| VonGerechten, Mich. | Velker, Maria | 3, Feb. 1847 | RCH |
| VonHafen, Bernard | Brogmann, Elisabeth | 16, Aug. 1846 | EE |
| VonHandorf, Bernard | Trimpe, Carolina | 18, Jan. 1842 | FF |
| VonHandorf, Bernard | Fortmann, Elis (Mrs) | 8, Feb. 1842 | FF |
| VonHandorf, Johan B. | Wilhauper, Anna M. | 15, Oct. 1844 | AA |
| VonHollen, Claus | Dupmann, Doretta | 30, Mar. 1847 | F |
| VonHolz, Leotes | Ameling, Charlotte | 26, Dec. 1849 | H |
| VonKeitz, Valentin | Frevel, Sophia | 1, Nov. 1847 | CC |
| VonKirk, John L. | ----, ---- | 1, Mar. 1832 | RCH |
| VonKnapp, Carl Theo. | Wendel, Margaret | 19, Feb. 1847 | RCH |
| VonLehmen, Carl | Poppelmann, Catharin | 12, Sept 1847 | AA |
| VonPuhl, Henry | Stout, Esther | 29, Mar. 1843 | RCH |
| VonSeggern, Christof | Wagner, Louise | 10, Aug. 1848 | F |
| VonSeggern, Friedr. | Wismann, Mary | 10, Aug. 1836 | RCH |
| VonSeggern, Herman | Kruse, Catharina M. | 27, Oct. 1840 | F |
| VonSeggern, Johan H. | Schlenker, Agnes | 24, Oct. 1847 | A |
| VonStein, Georg | Runk, Margaretha | 3, Oct. 1848 | G |
| VonStraton, Robert | Knight, Esther | 13, Apr. 1846 | RCH |
| VonWalde, Bernard | Evermann, Gertrud | 16, Nov. 1841 | FF |
| VondemBerge, Joseph | Lucker, Catharine | 22, June 1847 | EE |
| VondemFange, Gerhard | Ohmann, Maria | 18, Aug. 1841 | F |
| VondemFange, Herman | Holscher, Caroline | 9, Oct. 1849 | F |
| VondemWoom, Clement | Jessing, Gertrud | 18, July 1847 | EE |
| VondenFange, Heinric | Eckelmann, Maria | 3, Nov. 1842 | F |
| VonderHayde, Bernard | Meirose, Anna Maria | 16, Feb. 1841 | FF |
| VonderHeide, Bernard | Elsemann, M. Elis. | 28, July 1835 | FF |
| VonderHeide, Heinr. | Moormann, Elisabeth | 7, Feb. 1837 | FF |
| VonderHeide, Heinric | Enneking, Maria | 3, Feb. 1846 | AA |
| VonderHeide, Heinric | Stubemann, Wilhelmin | 27, Jan. 1847 | FF |
| VonderWoesten, Johan | Oehlschlaeger, Maria | 24, Aug. 1843 | C |
| Vonida, Philipp | Ferster, Christina | 23, Nov. 1841 | RCH |
| Voolts, Johan Joseph | Holencamp, Ger.(Mrs) | 24, Apr. 1849 | EE |
| Voorhees, Abraham L. | Jackson, Mary G. | 12, Apr. 1842 | I |
| Voorhees, Abraham V. | Holcomb, S. | 26, Jan. 1836 | RCH |
| Voorhees, Lorenzo | Mal---, Catharine | Nov. 1841 | RCH |
| Voorhes, Sylvester | Vorhes, Cornelia | 6, Feb. 1838 | RCH |
| Voorhis, Henry M. | Bernard, Louise A. | 21, Jan. 1838 | RCH |
| Vorbrinck, Johan | Lage, Maria Anna | 5, Oct. 1841 | FF |
| VordenBeumen, Anton | Mennomann, Louise | 26, Sept 1849 | RCH |
| VorderHack, Gerhard | Bohnen, Maria | 20, Oct. 1840 | F |
| Vordermann, Herman | Kahle, Friedricka | 25, Dec. 1846 | RCH |
| Vores, Holmes | Cooper, Elisabeth | 1, Jan. 1845 | RCH |
| Vorhees, | Pendry, Ruth | 23, Apr. 1818 | RCH |
| Vorhees, Albert | Homerfelt, Ann | 19, Sept 1821 | RCH |
| Vorhes, John | Harper, Martha | 11, Feb. 1846 | RCH |
| Vorhis, Theodor | Forden, Harriet | 4, July 1847 | RCH |
| Vorner, Martin | Ward, Abigail | 24, Oct. 1833 | RCH |
| Vornholt, Johan H. | Wissmann, Elisabeth | 20, Oct. 1842 | F |
| Vorwald, Francis | Reulmann, Catharine | 5, Jan. 1842 | FF |
| Vorwald, Joseph | Landwehr, Maria Anna | 18, Sept 1837 | FF |
| Vorwald, Joseph | Schlechten, Anna M. | 18, Jan. 1842 | RCH |
| Vorwald, Wilhelm | Laener, Catharina | 2, Dec. 1848 | G |
| Vorwalk, Johan | Sandmann, Francisca | 15, Nov. 1846 | EE |
| Vosch, Johan H.C. | Peters, Maria | 30, Apr. 1840 | F |

| Grooms | Brides | Date of Marriage | Code |
|--------|--------|------------------|------|
| ****** | ****** | **** ** ******** | **** |
| Voskuhle, Heinrich | Ludobeck, Friedricka | 30, Apr. 1846 | C |
| Voss, Carl Heinrich | Trentmann, Anna M. | 3, Aug. 1845 | AA |
| Voss, Francis | Kruse, Maria Anna | 9, June 1840 | FF |
| Voss, Georg Friedric | Lindemann, Catharina | 6, Sept 1848 | E |
| Voss, Heinrich | Rembeck, Maria | 22, Nov. 1842 | FF |
| Voss, Johan Bernard | Vennemann, Agnes | 8, Jan. 1839 | FF |
| Voss, Joseph | Heckvert, Maria | 9, Nov. 1841 | FF |
| Voss, William | Leiner, Anna | 3, Apr. 1849 | RCH |
| Vosse, Andrew | Tiser, Jane | 19, Dec. 1820 | RCH |
| Vossenkemper, Heinr. | AufdemBerge, Wilhel. | 21, Aug. 1844 | C |
| Vossgroene, Wilhelm | Timpermann, M. Elis. | 5, May 1840 | FF |
| Vosskort, Johan Jos. | Koene, Maria Elis. | 8, Nov. 1846 | AA |
| Voswinkel, Johan | Soechen, Elisabeth | 9, Jan. 1849 | EE |
| Vragge, Eberhard | Lammers, Maria Elis. | 25, Nov. 1847 | C |
| | | | |
| W---, George B. | Wakefield, Elisabeth | 13, Dec. 1817 | RCH |
| W---, James | Weldridge, Sarah | 25, Sept 1825 | RCH |
| W---, Joseph | Beaman, Martha H. | 3, July 1836 | RCH |
| W---, William | Susan, Jane | 13, Sept 1838 | RCH |
| Wabler, Bernard | Schulte, Bernardina | 28, Dec. 1844 | AA |
| Wabnitz, Daniel | Heit, Maria | 11, Sept 1845 | C |
| Wachendorf, Alfred H | Stuevers, Margaretha | 30, Oct. 1845 | F |
| Wachendorf, Heinrich | Cordes, Maria | 27, Nov. 1848 | F |
| Wacher, Carl | Schneider, Josephina | 12, Oct. 1837 | FF |
| Wacher, Max | Scherer, Amalia | 12, Mar. 1839 | FF |
| Wachtler, John | ----, Margaretha | 14, Feb. 1847 | RCH |
| Wackelmann, Johan H. | Bemmen, Anna Maria | 5, June 1838 | FF |
| Wackens, | Warren, Beulah | May 1839 | RCH |
| Wacker, John Philipp | Seibert, Appolonia | 13, July 1847 | A |
| Waddie, William | Mack, Lerina | 11, July 1842 | RCH |
| Wade, David | Conklin, Ann | 13, Oct. 1818 | RCH |
| Wade, David | Bartow, Ann (Mrs) | 28, Mar. 1826 | I |
| Wade, David E. | Snodgrass, Mary | 24, Dec. 1846 | RCH |
| Wade, John | Byetinowe, Sally | 17, Mar. 1818 | RCH |
| Wade, John | Martin, Catharine | 6, May 1832 | RCH |
| Wade, Joseph | McCormick, Jane | 8, Oct. 1840 | I |
| Wade, Melancthon | Armstrong, Elisabeth | 27, Aug. 1823 | RCH |
| Wade, Moses | Ferris, Rachel | 29, Mar. 1838 | RCH |
| Wade, Samuel | Watts, Ellen | 6, Apr. 1846 | RCH |
| Wade, Stephen J. | Ramsay, Harriet S. | 29, Jan. 1835 | RCH |
| Wade, William W. | Betts, Frances | 23, Aug. 1818 | RCH |
| Wadkins, Cyrus | Anderson, Elis. Jane | 12, Dec. 1845 | RCH |
| Wadsworth, Martin | Johnson, Lucinda | 11, Jan. 1845 | RCH |
| Waechler, Eberhard | Lueck, Maria Elis. | 15, Apr. 1847 | AA |
| Waechter, Eberhard | Krumpelbeck, M Elis. | 29, Sept 1840 | FF |
| Waechter, J. Adolph | Berte, Lisette | 7, Mar. 1848 | AA |
| Waer, Wellington | Dearmond, Sarah | 23, Feb. 1843 | RCH |
| Wagener, James | Mulligan, Mary A. | 16, May 1834 | RCH |
| Wagenhauser, Georg | Brockmann, Elisabeth | 28, Oct. 1845 | AA |
| Wagenhauser, Georg | Schwendemann, Carol. | 9, Feb. 1847 | EE |
| Wagenhauser, Michael | Reinhardt, Ursula | 3, Feb. 1842 | FF |
| Wager, William | Wade, Elisabeth | 6, May 1843 | RCH |
| Waggoner, Joseph | West, Sophia | 25, Oct. 1836 | RCH |
| Wagner, Adam | Schneider, Catharine | 8, Nov. 1847 | A |
| Wagner, Adrian | Steffen, Angela | 4, Aug. 1844 | AA |
| Wagner, August | Nulsen, Philippina | 2, July 1842 | F |
| Wagner, Christopher | Wald, Caroline | 21, July 1846 | BB |
| Wagner, Conrad | Reumlein, Elisabeth | 6, Feb. 1838 | FF |
| Wagner, Franz | Huber, Helena | 28, Sept 1844 | C |
| Wagner, Heinrich | Schmidt, Louise | 6, Oct. 1843 | C |
| Wagner, Heinrich | Kothi, Anna Elisabet | 22, Dec. 1844 | G |
| Wagner, Heinrich | Engenfeld, Maria | 3, Jan. 1846 | C |
| Wagner, Jacob | Diekmueller, Louisa | 15, Mar. 1838 | FF |
| Wagner, Jacob | Schmidt, Elisabeth | 25, Jan. 1848 | G |
| Wagner, John | Goldsmith, Catharine | 28, Jan. 1844 | RCH |
| Wagner, John | Kennedy, Susannah | 27, Nov. 1846 | RCH |
| Wagner, John N. | Seybold, Carol. | 28, June 1836 | RCH |
| Wagner, Michael | Kuhlmann, Margaretha | 3, June 1846 | G |
| Wagner, Nicolaus | Bachmann, Margaretha | 28, June 1848 | EE |
| Wagner, Peter | Quintin, Anna Maria | 14, July 1840 | FF |
| Wagner, Valentin | Herberger, Magdalena | 8, Nov. 1842 | FF |

| Grooms<br>***** | Brides<br>***** | Date of Marriage<br>**** ** ******** | Code<br>**** |
|---|---|---|---|
| Wagner, Valentin | Meier, Justina M. | 12, Aug. 1849 | II |
| Wagner, Valentine | Hett, Mary | 30, Mar. 1842 | RCH |
| Wagoner, August | Bailey, Mary Jane | 12, Apr. 1849 | RCH |
| Wagoner, Benjamin | Brown, Elisabeth | 29, Nov. 1842 | RCH |
| Wahl, Gerhard Heinr. | Tabelmann, M. Elis. | 16, May 1844 | G |
| Wahl, Jacob | Walker, Sarah | 7, Feb. 1847 | A |
| Wahler, Georg | Biber, Margaretha | 6, May 1849 | EE |
| Wahlmann, Georg | Brosmer, Helena | 22, Dec. 1842 | AA |
| Wahmes, Johan Herman | Kronkmann, Maria | 7, Oct. 1846 | RCH |
| Wahof, Simon Linus | Hambrock, Christina | 9, May 1848 | II |
| Wail, David | Benedick, Mina | 10, May 1849 | RCH |
| Wainright, Daniel | Grapevine, Prudence | 6, Nov. 1842 | RCH |
| Wainwright, Britton | Darby, Mary Elis. | 1, May 1847 | RCH |
| Wainwright, John | Raney, Elisabeth | 22, Dec. 1836 | RCH |
| Wainwright, Tyler | Phillips, Nancy Ann | 21, Sept 1845 | RCH |
| Wainwright, Vincent | Morrow, Mahitable | 2, May 1843 | RCH |
| Wainwright, William | Bickerdyke, Ann | 21, July 1844 | RCH |
| Waite, Richard | Morton, Martha | 13, June 1842 | RCH |
| Wakefield, John | Moody, Hannah E. | 17, Nov. 1840 | BB |
| Wakenroder, Christ. | Roehr, Maria | 31, Aug. 1841 | RCH |
| Waker, John C. | Miller, Amanda | 6, Sept 1840 | RCH |
| Walbillach, Leonard | Trautmann, Francisca | 29, May 1849 | II |
| Walbrige, | Chase, Helen | 17, Oct. 1839 | D |
| Wald, Andrew | Wareham, Elisabeth | 28, Apr. 1841 | BB |
| Waldberg, Francis | Butscha, Dina | 4, Apr. 1837 | FF |
| Walden, Gustav | Struve, Henrietta | 20, May 1841 | G |
| Walden, Jesse | Nelson, Jane | 27, May 1844 | RCH |
| Waldenand, William | Watkins, Joanna | 14, Oct. 1832 | RCH |
| Waldhaus, Martin | Knosp, Catharine | 27, June 1849 | RCH |
| Waldin, Elisha | Kitchell, Julia | 16, Feb. 1843 | RCH |
| Waldmann, Peter | Vester, Magdalena | 7, May 1846 | A |
| Waldon, Baltazer | Streeter, Julia A. | 27, Oct. 1838 | RCH |
| Waldon, Benjamin | Swaney, Matilda | 23, Dec. 1837 | RCH |
| Waldorf, John | Gallagher, Ellen | 15, Sept 1844 | RCH |
| Waldren, Benjamin | Cox, Lucinda | 21, Feb. 1821 | RCH |
| Waldron, David | Markward, Sarah | 7, Sept 1846 | RCH |
| Waldron, Ebenezer | Smith, Catharine | 8, Oct. 1818 | RCH |
| Waldschmidt, Heinric | Reising, Anna Maria | 11, Aug. 1846 | AA |
| Walelouf, Joseph | Wilson, Adelheid | 3, May 1835 | RCH |
| Wales, John W. | Noble, Matilda | 18, Apr. 1837 | RCH |
| Walkenhorst, Francis | Regeness, Mary | 29, July 1839 | RCH |
| Walker, Alexander | Walker, Elenora | 13, Mar. 1848 | RCH |
| Walker, Charles | Boffendeck, Rebecca | 3, Aug. 1848 | RCH |
| Walker, Chatfield | Snyder, Margaret | Apr. 1833 | RCH |
| Walker, Daniel | McClaren, Jane | 27, Oct. 1842 | RCH |
| Walker, David | Hammet, Lydia | 10, Oct. 1847 | RCH |
| Walker, Elias | Choate, Sarah Ann | 25, Feb. 1844 | RCH |
| Walker, Francis | Rouch, Rachel | 12, Nov. 1843 | RCH |
| Walker, Friedrich H. | Meier, A.M. Magdal. | 28, Oct. 1847 | F |
| Walker, George B. | Clark, Elisabeth | 23, June 1835 | D |
| Walker, George W. | Ward, Mary L. | 10, Mar. 1841 | RCH |
| Walker, Gerhard | Rodges, Maria Anna | 26, May 1841 | FF |
| Walker, H. | Spinnings, Frances | 23, May 1836 | RCH |
| Walker, Jacob | McLaughlin, Nancy | 11, Dec. 1834 | RCH |
| Walker, John | Shane, Mary | 19, May 1820 | RCH |
| Walker, John | Garrison, Aggy | 12, Sept 1820 | RCH |
| Walker, John | Osborn, Abigail | 9, June 1843 | RCH |
| Walker, John | Wilson, Amanda | 8, May 1849 | RCH |
| Walker, John H. | Black, Mary | 11, June 1842 | RCH |
| Walker, John J. | Brokaw, Sarah | 31, Oct. 1818 | RCH |
| Walker, Joseph | Campbell, Hannah | 9, Dec. 1824 | RCH |
| Walker, Joseph | Orr, Martha E. | 22, Sept 1836 | RCH |
| Walker, Lewis | Taylor, Mary | 10, Nov. 1841 | RCH |
| Walker, Morrison | Joyce, Elis. | 10, Sept 1835 | RCH |
| Walker, Richard | Caldwell, Isabell | 17, Dec. 1837 | RCH |
| Walker, Robert | Sellers, Susan | 3, Nov. 1843 | RCH |
| Walker, Robert | Beesley, Hannah | 13, Mar. 1846 | RCH |
| Walker, Shelby | Horan, Margaret | 2, Nov. 1848 | RCH |
| Walker, Warren | Hammond, Hannah | 16, Mar. 1843 | RCH |
| Walker, William | Constable, Elisabeth | 12, Sept 1843 | RCH |
| Walket, William | Roberts, Mary | 8, June 1834 | RCH |

| Grooms<br>****** | Brides<br>****** | Date of Marriage<br>**** ** ******** | Code<br>**** |
|---|---|---|---|
| Wall, James | Schultz, Mary | 3, June 1849 | GG |
| Wall, John H. | Cole, Magdalena | 17, June 1824 | RCH |
| Wallace, Alexander | Mitchell, Helen | 3, Mar. 1836 | RCH |
| Wallace, David | Oakson, Demis | 31, Mar. 1818 | RCH |
| Wallace, Michael | Montfort, Elisabeth | 13, Sept 1843 | RCH |
| Wallace, Moses | Hardick, Nancy | 17, Mar. 1826 | RCH |
| Wallace, Thomas | Lancaster, Sarah | 19, Aug. 1834 | RCH |
| Wallace, Thomas | Crane, Ann | 5, Apr. 1847 | GG |
| Wallace, William | Alcorn, Jane | 5, Sept 1821 | RCH |
| Wallace, William | Bush, Barbary | 14, Aug. 1834 | RCH |
| Wallace, William | Weatherby, Elisabeth | 4, May 1842 | RCH |
| Wallas, W. | Beachim, Elisabeth | 28, May 1839 | RCH |
| Wallen, Daniel | Kan---, Mary | 13, Nov. 1821 | RCH |
| Waller, Bernard | Schalch, Philippina | 13, Sept 1849 | A |
| Waller, Emery | Parker, Rebecca | 31, Jan. 1833 | RCH |
| Waller, Wilhelm | Grimm, Margaretha | 18, Jan. 1848 | EE |
| Walley, Oliver | Burke, Mary | 14, Nov. 1849 | GG |
| Wallin, Monroe | Bard, Elisabeth | 30, Dec. 1846 | RCH |
| Wallin, William | Lauter, Caroline | 25, Dec. 1845 | RCH |
| Wallis, Heinrich | Schuler, Elisabeth | 26, Mar. 1839 | RCH |
| Wallmann, Bernard J. | Feldhaus, Elisabeth | 13, Sept 1846 | FF |
| Walsch, Johan Wm. | Best, Catharine | 17, Nov. 1849 | EE |
| Walsh, Daniel | Maguire, Julia | 31, Mar. 1845 | BB |
| Walsh, Henry | Ludguider, | June 1835 | RCH |
| Walsh, James | Howard, Deborah | 21, Nov. 1842 | RCH |
| Walsh, James | Kennedy, Rebecca | 22, Oct. 1849 | D |
| Walsh, Michael | McDonald, Susan | 21, June 1849 | RCH |
| Walsh, Patrick | Rourke, Julia | 9, Sept 1838 | RCH |
| Walsh, Patrick | McCormack, Lucy | 4, Oct. 1845 | RCH |
| Walsh, Sebastian | Kirchred, Elisabeth | 11, July 1846 | EE |
| Walsh, Thomas | Whelpley, Ann | 14, Dec. 1849 | RCH |
| Walsh, Thomas | Farley, Ann | 9, Sept 1849 | BB |
| Waltenrath, Jacob | Stoll, Catharine(Mrs | 25, Nov. 1841 | G |
| Walter, Jacob | Gebhardt, Sarah | 20, Nov. 1848 | G |
| Walter, Jacob | Kluber, Margaretha | 6, May 1845 | FF |
| Walter, Johan | Leppert, Catharina | 15, June 1841 | FF |
| Walter, John | Brahm, Christina | 30, Dec. 1841 | RCH |
| Walter, John | McIntire, Margaret | 11, Oct. 1846 | RCH |
| Walter, Peter | Schlotterbeck, Barb. | 13, June 1848 | C |
| Walter, Samuel | Myers, Amelia | 22, Oct. 1846 | RCH |
| Walter, Thomas | Sleight, Jane E. | 18, June 1844 | RCH |
| Walter, Wilhelm | Meyner, Caroline A. | 2, Mar. 1846 | C |
| Walter, William | McCall, Mary Ann | 21, June 1842 | RCH |
| Walters, Gerhard | Timmermann, Maria A. | 14, May 1839 | FF |
| Walters, Heinrich | Schulte, Elisabeth | 26, Nov. 1839 | FF |
| Walters, Heinrich | Thielbers, G. Maria | 7, Sept 1843 | F |
| Walters, Johan Wm. | Reddelmann, Anna E. | 26, Oct. 1847 | AA |
| Walters, John | Hays, Catharine | 29, Sept 1840 | BB |
| Walters, John | Cole, Catharine | 21, July 1846 | RCH |
| Walters, Marcus | Brittingham, Elenora | 2, May 1847 | RCH |
| Walters, Owen | Maher, Elisabeth | 23, July 1839 | BB |
| Walters, William | Lewis, Mary Jane | 5, Aug. 1846 | RCH |
| Waltgerman, Friedric | Schaeffer, Elisabeth | 22, Mar. 1847 | RCH |
| Walthall Albert | Wilson, Sarah Jane | 9, July 1839 | RCH |
| Walton, Abraham | Robson, Mary | 16, May 1821 | RCH |
| Walton, George | Woodruff, Mary Ann | 24, Feb. 1847 | RCH |
| Walton, Joshua | Swain, Elisabeth | 31, Dec. 1846 | RCH |
| Walton, Nathan | Cunningham, | 24, Apr. 1834 | RCH |
| Walz, Francis | Riss, Catharina | 9, Feb. 1841 | FF |
| Walz, Valentin | Meyer, Catharine | 1, Feb. 1847 | EE |
| Wambsgans, Friedrich | Schneider, Ursula | 2, Sept 1849 | G |
| Wampser, Jacob | Nieder, Theresa | 25, Apr. 1844 | AA |
| Wamser, Jacob | Elbe, Eva | 20, Oct. 1841 | FF |
| Wamsley, Samuel | Groendyke, Catharine | 31, Jan. 1844 | RCH |
| Wamsley, Stephen | VanGorder, Mary | 17, Dec. 1846 | RCH |
| Wamsley, William | Madby, Fanny | 22, Nov. 1824 | RCH |
| Wandell, William | Hadman, Leah | 28, Aug. 1825 | RCH |
| Wandhorst, Friedrich | Stanecker, Sophia | 17, Feb. 1847 | F |
| Wanee, West C. | Lacy, Rachel | 26, Oct. 1845 | RCH |
| Wang, Matthias | Schindler, Maria Ann | 24, May 1841 | FF |
| Wannell, William | Styles, Sarah | 13, Aug. 1834 | RCH |

| Grooms<br>****** | Brides<br>****** | Date of Marriage<br>**** ** ******** | Code<br>**** |
|---|---|---|---|
| Wanstrath, Gerhard N | Oevermelle, Elis. | 19, May 1840 | FF |
| Wanstrath, Heinrich | Holthaus, Maria | 23, Feb. 1841 | FF |
| Wanstrath, Johan H. | Frommann, Henrietta | 22, Oct. 1846 | F |
| Wappenstein, Joseph | Markbreit, Johanna | 31, July 1849 | RCH |
| Warburg, Johan Bd. | Hoppenjans, Susanna | 8, Feb. 1848 | EE |
| Warburg, Johan Bd. | Gerwe, Elisabeth | 7, May 1848 | EE |
| Ward, Aaron | Cochran, Mary | 3, Oct. 1847 | RCH |
| Ward, Albert | VanHook, Emily | 12, Sept 1839 | RCH |
| Ward, Athanasius | Applegate, Jane | Nov. 1844 | RCH |
| Ward, Charles | Tunis, Henrietta | 8, Mar. 1842 | RCH |
| Ward, Charles E. | Irvin, Caroline A. | 4, Dec. 1849 | RCH |
| Ward, Christopher | Carnahan, Frances | 28, June 1844 | RCH |
| Ward, Christopher | Connelly, Bridget | 16, Sept 1849 | GG |
| Ward, Edward | Applegate, Catharine | 16, Nov. 1846 | RCH |
| Ward, Elon | VanMiddlesworth, A. | 26, Jan. 1845 | RCH |
| Ward, George | Luslie, Mary | 12, Oct. 1841 | RCH |
| Ward, Homer | Todhunter, Hannah | 14, Dec. 1845 | RCH |
| Ward, James | Davis, Lavina | 23, Aug. 1821 | RCH |
| Ward, James W. | Lea, Catharine | 29, June 1848 | RCH |
| Ward, John | Warner, Margaret | 20, Feb. 1834 | RCH |
| Ward, Joshua | Fisher, Nancy | 9, Aug. 1832 | RCH |
| Ward, Josiah | Mead, Rebecca | 15, Oct. 1846 | RCH |
| Ward, M. | Kogan, Mary | 9, Dec. 1849 | GG |
| Ward, Patrick | Bryan, Sarah | 29, May 1849 | RCH |
| Ward, Patrick | Dophy, Catharine | 11, Sept 1848 | GG |
| Ward, Richard | Baumeister, Harriet | 27, Aug. 1843 | RCH |
| Ward, Samuel | Kilbuck, Mary | 23, Dec. 1837 | RCH |
| Ward, Thomas | Fuller, Marietta | 6, Aug. 1839 | RCH |
| Ward, Thomas | Kearney, Catharine | 1, July 1845 | BB |
| Ward, William | Fagien, Cordelia Ann | 2, Jan. 1834 | RCH |
| Ward, William | Ray, Louise | 8, Nov. 1842 | RCH |
| Ward, William | Carter, Elisabeth | 23, Nov. 1846 | BB |
| Ward, William Milton | Yeatman, Caroline | 29, May 1849 | I |
| Wardall, Charles | Wise, Sarah | 28, Dec. 1837 | RCH |
| Warden, Lanson | Pearson, Sarah | 16, May 1833 | RCH |
| Warden, Leo Lewis | Cameron, Louise | 4, Apr. 1841 | BB |
| Warder, Robert A. | Kerdolff, Catharine | 8, Sept 1844 | BB |
| Ware, George W. | Saunders, Ann | 2, June 1842 | RCH |
| Ware, Henry | Johnson, Isabell | 6, Oct. 1847 | RCH |
| Ware, James | Amley, Maria | 2, Sept 1841 | RCH |
| Ware, Samuel | Wells, Marnetta | 10, June 1847 | RCH |
| Ware, William | Conner, Rebecca | 10, Nov. 1844 | RCH |
| Ware, William G. | Ryland, Emily V. | 6, Apr. 1841 | RCH |
| Warfield, Alonzo | Smith, Malinda | 29, Mar. 1849 | RCH |
| Warfield, Thomas B. | Carneal, Alice | 17, July 1838 | I |
| Waring, Isaac F. | Nelson, Jane | 30, Sept 1824 | RCH |
| Warject, Elisha | Ware, Catharine Ann | 24, Jan. 1833 | I |
| Warner, Adam | Nahwald, Louise | 9, July 1846 | F |
| Warner, Edward | Decker, Nancy Ann | 9, May 1841 | RCH |
| Warner, Henderson | Carter, Rosannah | 19, Oct. 1837 | RCH |
| Warner, Horatio | Smith, Mary Jane | 22, Dec. 1849 | GG |
| Warner, Samuel | Woodland, Emily(Mrs) | 25, Nov. 1846 | D |
| Warner, William | Thompson, Susan | 31, Aug. 1846 | RCH |
| Warnington, William | Little, Nancy | 4, Feb. 1836 | RCH |
| Warnke, Johan | Fay, Anna | 14, Nov. 1849 | F |
| Warr, George | Rickerson, Elisabeth | 9, Nov. 1844 | RCH |
| Warren, George | Ware, Abigail | 19, Aug. 1819 | RCH |
| Warren, George | McCracken, Elisabeth | 7, Jan. 1836 | RCH |
| Warren, Ichabod | Clavin, Sarah | 12, Aug. 1832 | RCH |
| Warren, Israel T. | Goldson, Ann | 5, Sept 1833 | RCH |
| Warren, John Berlace | Bussey, Julia | 5, Oct. 1835 | RCH |
| Warren, Luther | M---, Elizabeth | 25, Apr. 1825 | RCH |
| Warren, Stephen | Cassat, Elisabeth | 22, Dec. 1836 | RCH |
| Warren, Sylvannus | Morrill, Susannah | 7, Oct. 1846 | RCH |
| Warrington, Warburt. | Garrison, Susan | 29, June 1843 | RCH |
| Warsel, John | Goodwin, Jane | 12, July 1821 | RCH |
| Wartcki, Moses | Brul, Flora | 1, Jan. 1842 | RCH |
| Warth, Heinrich | Straub, Charlotte | 14, Nov. 1843 | G |
| Wartman, William | Coffmann, Lucinda | 19, Feb. 1846 | RCH |
| Wartwine, Christoph | Fisher, Josephine | 1, Sept 1844 | RCH |
| Warwick, Isaac | Buckingham, Harriet | 24, Oct. 1843 | RCH |

| Grooms<br>****** | Brides<br>****** | Date of Marriage<br>**** ** ******** | Code<br>**** |
|---|---|---|---|
| Warwick, Lewis H. | Badgely, Sarah R. | 12, Feb. 1835 | RCH |
| Warwick, Louis | Eady, Margaret E. | 13, Mar. 1843 | RCH |
| Waschefort, J. Ferd. | Drees, Maria Gertrud | 22, Jan. 1839 | FF |
| Washborn, Martin | Minor, Adelia | 1, Sept 1842 | RCH |
| Washburn, Alvan | Noble, Margaret | 11, May 1808 | RCH |
| Washburn, Ira | McKnight, Mary Ann | 28, May 1843 | RCH |
| Washburn, Jabez | Wood, Mary Ann | 22, Oct. 1824 | RCH |
| Washburn, Jerome B. | Grandall, Christina | 17, June 1838 | D |
| Washburn, Timothy | Freeman, Mary | 5, July 1833 | RCH |
| Washington, Andrew | Bell, Adelheid | 12, May 1847 | RCH |
| Washington, George | Curtis, Lucinda | 31, May 1836 | RCH |
| Washington, George | Howard, Nancy | 13, May 1846 | RCH |
| Wasmer, Sebastian | Render, Maria Eva | 4, Oct. 1842 | FF |
| Wasson, William | Kendall, Caroline | 7, Oct. 1845 | RCH |
| Waten, George | Colton, Nancy | 12, Aug. 1819 | RCH |
| Water, Herman H. | Rueters, Elisabeth | 8, Apr. 1845 | AA |
| Waterb--, John | Jackson, Mary | 31, July 1838 | RCH |
| Waterbury, William | Humphrey, Mary E. | Sept 1844 | RCH |
| Waterfall, James | Thompson, Helen | 22, Nov. 1834 | RCH |
| Waterhouse, Charles | Waterhouse, Hannah | 15, Mar. 1847 | RCH |
| Waterhouse, Jonas | Sloop, Elisabeth | 7, Feb. 1822 | RCH |
| Waterman, Gerhard | Borenkamp, Anna M. | 8, Apr. 1837 | F |
| Waterman, Robert | Pusoll, Elisabeth | 26, Sept 1833 | RCH |
| Waters, Jacob | Dennison, Dolly | 9, Jan. 1826 | RCH |
| Waters, John | Clark, Florilla | 2, May 1842 | RCH |
| Waters, Otis | Biddle, Julia | 19, Aug. 1849 | RCH |
| Watersly, J. | Turner, Emma | 11, May 1849 | RCH |
| Waterson, Thomas W. | Moore, Jane | 7, Mar. 1833 | RCH |
| Wates, Peter | Moore, Sarah | 5, June 1841 | RCH |
| Watkins, Charles | Lewis, Rebecca | 31, May 1849 | RCH |
| Watkins, Daniel | Sperlock, Hester | 20, Sept 1849 | RCH |
| Watkins, Henry | Jones, Rachel | 9, Oct. 1847 | RCH |
| Watkins, J. | Hiddun, Esther | 11, July 1822 | RCH |
| Watkins, James | Harris, Mary | 26, July 1844 | RCH |
| Watkins, Matthew | Brown, Hannah | 7, Dec. 1837 | RCH |
| Watkins, Morris | Meals, Mary Ann | 29, Oct. 1845 | RCH |
| Watkins, Thomas | Spiller, Elisabeth | 10, May 1846 | RCH |
| Watkins, William | Hawkins, Elisabeth | 31, May 1832 | RCH |
| Watson, Elias James | Carter, Susan | 2, Nov. 1837 | RCH |
| Watson, George | Hubley, Sarah Ann | 3, Sept 1832 | RCH |
| Watson, Henry | Clemmons, Mary | 22, Feb. 1846 | RCH |
| Watson, Henry | Simonton, Louise | 13, June 1848 | RCH |
| Watson, James | Vorhees, Mary Ann | 23, Feb. 1836 | RCH |
| Watson, James | Thomas, Frances Ann | 11, June 1836 | RCH |
| Watson, John | Simpson, Mary Ann | 12, July 1835 | RCH |
| Watson, John | Geeding, Ruanna | 16, June 1842 | RCH |
| Watson, John | Hummel, Mary Ann | 16, June 1842 | BB |
| Watson, John | Murphy, Arena | 1, Dec. 1845 | RCH |
| Watson, Joseph | Stone, Elisabeth | 28, Jan. 1849 | RCH |
| Watson, Peter | Stewart, Sarah | 6, Oct. 1847 | RCH |
| Watson, Richard | Robins, Mary | 27, May 1838 | RCH |
| Watson, Thomas | Lendon, Rachel | 27, Feb. 1834 | RCH |
| Watson, William | Baxter, Nancy | 9, Feb. 1841 | RCH |
| Watson, William | Skillman, Catharine | 6, Dec. 1843 | RCH |
| Watson, William | Thompson, Elizabeth | 9, Oct. 1848 | GG |
| Watt, William | Oliphant, Ann | 29, May 1847 | RCH |
| Watters, Mitchell | Hilton, Caroline | 27, Nov. 1842 | RCH |
| Watts, Henry | Cunningham, Julia | 31, May 1849 | RCH |
| Watts, Hiram | Miller, Matilda | 26, May 1839 | RCH |
| Watts, Joseph | Taylor, Melissa | 5, July 1847 | RCH |
| Watts, Robert | Shaw, Hannah Ann | 6, June 1849 | RCH |
| Watts, William | Thomson, Amelia L. | 16, Dec. 1844 | RCH |
| Waugh, John M. | Ellis, Mary Ann | 20, Aug. 1843 | BB |
| Way, Charles | Fogelmann, Louise | 15, Nov. 1842 | RCH |
| Way, Joshua | Lampher, Elisabeth | 25, Mar. 1819 | RCH |
| Waybrigs, Solomon | Ward, Elisabeth | 26, Jan. 1843 | RCH |
| Wayland, William | Stagg, Nancy | 12, Jan. 1837 | RCH |
| Wayne, Anthony | Werrie, Sallie | 29, Aug. 1841 | RCH |
| Wayne, Clifford G. | Avery, Eliza A. | 4, Apr. 1839 | I |
| Wearts, Jacob | Shaffer, Julia Ann | 5, Sept 1846 | RCH |
| Weasner, Thomas | Dickinson, Olive | 19, Nov. 1846 | RCH |

| Grooms | Brides | Date of Marriage | Code |
|--------|--------|------------------|------|
| Weatherby, Luther | Timbermann, M. | 31, July 1839 | RCH |
| Weatherby, Philipp | Jackson, Mary Jane | 1, Sept 1847 | RCH |
| Weatherby, Thomas B. | VanZant, Macy | 20, Oct. 1825 | RCH |
| Weatherling, John | Pickens, Clarissa | 28, Dec. 1826 | RCH |
| Weaver, John | Fuller, Julia Ann | 20, Aug. 1837 | RCH |
| Weaver, John | Linkmeier, Elisabeth | 16, Jan. 1838 | RCH |
| Weaver, Joseph A. | Weaver, Louise | 17, Sept 1837 | RCH |
| Weaver, Levi D. | Mefford, Fanny | 2, Oct. 1834 | RCH |
| Weaver, Louis | Mitchell, Mary Ann | 5, Nov. 1835 | RCH |
| Weaver, Philipp | Dokes, Elisabeth | 12, July 1849 | RCH |
| Weaver, Samuel | Winters, Margaret | 18, Jan. 1843 | BB |
| Weaver, Samuel W. | VanGundy, Magdalena | 30, July 1846 | RCH |
| Weaver, Thomas | Clark, Sarah M. | 12, Feb. 1842 | RCH |
| Webb, Arthur | Hogan, Elisabeth | 10, Apr. 1849 | BB |
| Webb, Arthur | Hogan, Elisabeth | 10, Apr. 1849 | BB |
| Webb, Asborn | Reynolds, Catharine | 1, July 1822 | RCH |
| Webb, G.M. | Dodson, Elisabeth | 2, Aug. 1838 | RCH |
| Webb, Harmon | Putman, Abby | 22, Feb. 1821 | RCH |
| Webb, Henry | Holley, Mary | 30, Jan. 1826 | RCH |
| Webb, John | Armstrong, Hannah | 19, Dec. 1833 | RCH |
| Webb, John H. | Chappell, Harriet | 24, Aug. 1843 | RCH |
| Webb, Leonard | Frost, Penthesilea | 16, May 1847 | RCH |
| Webb, Peter | Black, Elisabeth | 8, July 1834 | RCH |
| Webb, Theodore | Farmer, Sarah | 22, Mar. 1838 | RCH |
| Webb, Zebulon B. | Goinfinsey, Hepsylah | 20, Nov. 1823 | RCH |
| Webber, Bloomfield | Griffith, Harriet | 16, Dec. 1849 | RCH |
| Webber, Gideon C. | Rybolt, Barbara | 8, Oct. 1832 | RCH |
| Weber, Adam | Doll, Margaretha | 25, May 1841 | FF |
| Weber, Adam | Bilbelheim, Carolina | 5, Nov. 1848 | A |
| Weber, Andreas | Langenkamp, Katharin | 1, May 1849 | AA |
| Weber, Benedict | Bopp, Elisabeth | 20, Sept 1847 | EE |
| Weber, Bernard | Sailer, Veronica | 5, June 1838 | FF |
| Weber, Bernard Hein. | Robenkamp, Catharina | 18, July 1847 | FF |
| Weber, Carl | Brandt, Eva | 30, Sept 1845 | G |
| Weber, Christoph | Dunken, Margaretha | 5, Feb. 1839 | FF |
| Weber, Dominick | Spergelmann, Cath. | 16, June 1847 | RCH |
| Weber, Francis H. | Ruters, Clara Cath. | 23, May 1847 | AA |
| Weber, Francis H. | Duddei, J.H. | 28, Oct. 1849 | AA |
| Weber, Franz | Leffel, Catharine | 1, May 1849 | RCH |
| Weber, Friedrich | Mueller, Louise | 27, Feb. 1848 | RCH |
| Weber, Friedrich | Brandt, Catharine | 27, Oct. 1846 | G |
| Weber, Friedrich | Grieser, Elisabeth | 4, Feb. 1849 | II |
| Weber, Friedrich H. | Lindemann, Louisa | 25, Jan. 1849 | C |
| Weber, Friedrich Wm. | Hilgermann, M Sophia | 20, Apr. 1847 | F |
| Weber, George M. | Stewart, Jane M. | 21, Mar. 1849 | RCH |
| Weber, Gottfried | Wenzel, Margaretha | 26, Nov. 1844 | AA |
| Weber, Heinrich | ----, ---- | 15, Dec. 1847 | RCH |
| Weber, Heinrich | Hombach, Elisabeth | 1, Apr. 1848 | G |
| Weber, Heinrich | Timpe, Anna Maria | 25, Aug. 1846 | EE |
| Weber, Henry | Weber, Margaretha | 14, Mar. 1847 | A |
| Weber, Henry | Zumbusch, Louise | 27, Feb. 1849 | G |
| Weber, Herman Hein. | Stricker, M. Cath. | 12, Oct. 1847 | AA |
| Weber, Herman Heinr. | Kemper, Maria Anna | 21, Nov. 1847 | FF |
| Weber, Jacob | Thien, Barbara | 26, Jan. 1842 | FF |
| Weber, Johan | Emmert, Catharine | 18, June 1844 | FF |
| Weber, Johan | Ginter, Maria Magd. | 7, Jan. 1847 | CC |
| Weber, Johan | Fuchs, Margaretha | 27, Nov. 1849 | CC |
| Weber, Johan | Hoffmann, Maria | 19, Aug. 1847 | EE |
| Weber, Johan | Lueticke, Theresa | 4, Aug. 1846 | FF |
| Weber, Johan Herman | Ossing, Maria | 26, Nov. 1839 | FF |
| Weber, John | Ganter, M. Magdalena | 7, Jan. 1847 | RCH |
| Weber, Joseph | Linnert, Catharine | 16, Jan. 1845 | AA |
| Weber, Joseph | Hemmelgarn, Elis. | 24, Apr. 1849 | AA |
| Weber, Joseph | Weiler, Rosina | 6, June 1847 | EE |
| Weber, Joseph A. | Walz, Genofeva | 3, Nov. 1847 | EE |
| Weber, Joseph Anton | Konen, Maria Anna | 25, Nov. 1849 | FF |
| Weber, Mathias | Hune, Elisabeth | 31, May 1846 | AA |
| Weber, Michael | Ehrhart, Monica | 2, Oct. 1843 | AA |
| Weber, Michael | Reis, Maria Josephin | 1, Dec. 1846 | EE |
| Weber, Peter | Reifschneider, Cath. | 1, Oct. 1848 | G |
| Weble, Jacob | Earheart, Sarah | 5, May 1820 | RCH |

| Grooms<br>***** | Brides<br>***** | Date of Marriage<br>**** ** ******** | Code<br>**** |
|---|---|---|---|
| Webster, Edmund | Corey, Jane H. | 6, Mar. 1848 | RCH |
| Webster, George | Grimes, Elisabeth | 27, Aug. 1846 | RCH |
| Webster, Joel | Miller, Jane | 8, Sept 1842 | RCH |
| Webster, John | Lord, Norah | 29, Nov. 1848 | RCH |
| Webster, Joseph | Mullen, Jane | 17, Jan. 1842 | BB |
| Webster, Robert | Wilson, Ellen | 16, Aug. 1849 | RCH |
| Weckers, Johan G. | Wilgens, Anna Marg. | 16, July 1848 | CC |
| Weddendorf, Friedric | Hilgemann, Wilhelmin | 11, Nov. 1841 | RCH |
| Wedell, George | Miller, Margaret | 17, Dec. 1849 | RCH |
| Wedig, Friedrich Wm. | Meyer, Louise | 17, Jan. 1846 | F |
| Wedkamp, Wilhelm | Hetlage, Dorothea | 19, Dec. 1848 | C |
| Wedrich, Johan | Saladin, Rosa | 1, Oct. 1849 | DD |
| Weeks, Eben | Conkling, Ann | 15, Oct. 1845 | RCH |
| Weeks, Henry | Cocks, Rebecca M. | 20, Feb. 1823 | RCH |
| Weeks, Henry J. | Shepherd, Sarah C. | 4, Apr. 1833 | RCH |
| Weeks, Matthew | Robinson, Elisabeth | 4, Aug. 1842 | RCH |
| Weeks, Steven | Sinton, Rachel | 14, Jan. 1837 | RCH |
| Weeks, Walter | King, Martha Lavina | 20, Mar. 1843 | RCH |
| Weele, Lorenz | Leetz, Maria | 17, Apr. 1834 | RCH |
| Wegelin, Emil Adolf | Siebenthal, Jane P. | 7, Oct. 1849 | G |
| Weghorst, Christian | Wildehaus, Angela | 22, Nov. 1836 | FF |
| Weghorst, Heinrich G | Bueckers, Catharina | 10, Aug. 1841 | FF |
| Wegmann, Johan | Lobmeyer, Catharine | 14, Feb. 1843 | AA |
| Wegmann, Johan Wm. | Klostermann, Anna M. | 28, Sept 1847 | EE |
| Wehage, Johan Herm. | Ruhol, Catharina M. | 5, Mar. 1848 | AA |
| Wehbrink, Heinrich H | Greve, Elisabeth | 25, Nov. 1848 | II |
| Wehe, John | Berg, Christina | 12, Oct. 1848 | RCH |
| Wehler, Francis A. | Tieke, Maria Gertrud | 9, Jan. 1848 | AA |
| Wehmeier, Gottlieb | Eggert, Henrietta | 10, Aug. 1849 | RCH |
| Wehmer, Carl Friedr. | Mollenkamp, Charlott | 12, Aug. 1847 | F |
| Wehmes, Herman | Kruetzmann, Maria | 8, Oct. 1846 | AA |
| Wehmig, Johan H. | Steinriede, Anna M. | 5, Nov. 1848 | CC |
| Wehming, Joseph | Keven, Maria Anna | 27, Nov. 1849 | FF |
| Wehn, Heinrich | Gerbes, Anna Gesina | 26, Sept 1847 | AA |
| Wehner, Joseph | Raabe, Elisabeth | 11, June 1846 | RCH |
| Wehning, John Henry | Steuerniele, Anna M. | 5, Nov. 1848 | RCH |
| Wehring, Bernard | Hollkamp, Anna | 20, Aug. 1849 | II |
| Wehrkamp, Georg H. | Dickroeger, Sophia D | 7, Nov. 1844 | F |
| Wehrkamp, Johan Bd. | Frohning, Maria Anna | 27, Oct. 1849 | CC |
| Wehrle, Pancratus | Holz, Margaretha | 12, Dec. 1837 | FF |
| Wehrle, Xavier | Schroeck, Maria | 2, Aug. 1841 | FF |
| Wehrmann, Bernard | Knapke, Elisabeth | 21, Sept 1841 | FF |
| Wehrmeyer, August | Bahlmann, A. | 14, Jan. 1849 | AA |
| Weibel, Francis | Hopp, Maria | 1, Jan. 1838 | FF |
| Weibel, Georg | Schoster, Catharina | 7, Mar. 1839 | G |
| Weibking, Henry | Brosse, Leonora | 13, Aug. 1845 | RCH |
| Weidemann, Christian | Kreidler, Magdalena | 28, June 1842 | FF |
| Weidenbach, Wendel | Rosenberg, Margaret | 11, Jan. 1842 | FF |
| Weidenweber, Johan A | Mass, Cecilia | 14, Sept 1847 | EE |
| Weidinger, Johan G. | Deuerlein, Anna | 28, Nov. 1847 | C |
| Weidman, Joseph | Enos, Martha Ann | 2, Sept 1832 | RCH |
| Weidner, Johan | Dickmann, Catharina | 26, May 1838 | FF |
| Weigel, Joseph | Leonard, Mary | 24, Apr. 1849 | RCH |
| Weigel, Joseph | Wicher, Maria | 24, Apr. 1849 | HH |
| Weigler, Arnold | Tappe, Sophia | 22, Oct. 1843 | AA |
| Weigler, Christian | ----, Rebecca | 15, May 1834 | RCH |
| Weiher, G. Heinrich | Weber, Bernardina | 9, July 1848 | II |
| Weikinger, Georg | Kuder, Barbara | 26, June 1837 | FF |
| Weil, | Nufauth, Maria | 8, June 1848 | A |
| Weil, Charles | Cole, Elisabeth | 26, Jan. 1845 | RCH |
| Weil, John | Eichert, Friedricka | 6, Feb. 1849 | RCH |
| Weilemann, Johan | Wirmel, Margaretha | 15, Apr. 1849 | EE |
| Weiler, Dominick | Herzog, Mary Magd. | 17, Sept 1843 | BB |
| Weiler, Dominick | Bedel, Mary Eva | 25, June 1848 | BB |
| Weiler, Michael | Maas, Babette | 16, Apr. 1844 | RCH |
| Weiler, Solomon | Mack, Hetty | 10, Apr. 1847 | RCH |
| Weiling, B. Heinrich | Felbing, A. Margaret | 17, May 1848 | II |
| Weiller, Georg F. | Frittner, Anna Maria | 6, Jan. 1848 | EE |
| Weimer, Bernard | Fai---, Hannah | 30, Sept 1837 | RCH |
| Weinantz, Konrad | Stewan, Katharina | 7, Mar. 1848 | A |
| Weinberg, Simon | Irgens, Louise | 30, Dec. 1845 | F |

| Grooms<br>****** | Brides<br>****** | Date of Marriage<br>**** ** ******** | Code<br>**** |
|---|---|---|---|
| Weincamp, Peter | Bergmann, Anna Maria | 25, July 1847 | EE |
| Weindel, Johan | Schreim, Margaretha | 7, Feb. 1842 | FF |
| Weinel, Heinrich | Lerch, Elisabeth | 24, Jan. 1849 | G |
| Weiner, John | Koch, Apollonia | 16, Apr. 1844 | RCH |
| Weingaertner, Casper | Schwarz, Catharina | 1, May 1848 | FF |
| Weingaertner, Lorenz | Bechtold, Magdalena | 7, Apr. 1839 | FF |
| Weingardner, Joseph | Smeyer, Catharine | 18, Mar. 1834 | RCH |
| Weingarth, Jacob | Weber, Barbara | 28, Sept 1848 | A |
| Weingartner, Franz J | Schweizer, Catharina | 18, Nov. 1834 | FF |
| Weingartner, Lorenz | Becker, Magdalena | 6, Feb. 1838 | FF |
| Weinheimer, Anton | Loewen, Theresa | 10, Aug. 1847 | EE |
| Weinreiter, Ignatz | Roth, Elisabeth | 4, Aug. 1835 | FF |
| Weirich, Philipp | Junker, Anna Maria | 16, Apr. 1840 | G |
| Weis, Georg | Siefert, M. Ursula | 8, Sept 1842 | AA |
| Weis, Jacob | Keister, Fanny | 13, July 1848 | RCH |
| Weis, Jacob | Weis, Maria | 19, June 1848 | A |
| Weis, Jacob | Ekert, Margaretha | 3, May 1846 | EE |
| Weis, Valentin | Klein, Catharine | 29, Nov. 1838 | FF |
| Weisel, Joseph | Sched, Anna Maria | 22, Nov. 1846 | EE |
| Weisel, Valentin | Barbick, Elisabeth | 19, Apr. 1847 | EE |
| Weisen, Jacob | Ward, Charlotte | 16, Apr. 1849 | RCH |
| Weisenbaum, Johan | Marks, Sarah | 29, Sept 1846 | F |
| Weisensell, Johan | Schmar, Gertrud | 15, Apr. 1844 | AA |
| Weisgerber, Johan | Guetemann, Anna M. | 24, Aug. 1847 | EE |
| Weisler, Jacob | Metz, Maria Elis. | 31, May 1836 | FF |
| Weismann, Peter | Eichelberger, Ther. | 7, Feb. 1838 | FF |
| Weismohr, John | Mahne, Barbara | 7, Apr. 1842 | G |
| Weiss, Adam | Betzold, Eva | 12, Nov. 1846 | AA |
| Weiss, Daniel | Scheeler, Maria | 23, Aug. 1835 | RCH |
| Weiss, Johan Louis | Russ, Christina | 21, Nov. 1846 | G |
| Weiss, Joseph | Schacherer, Theresa | 1, Feb. 1842 | FF |
| Weiss, Martin | Seidner, Barbara | 1, Nov. 1847 | AA |
| Weissel, Mathias | Brummer, Maria | 19, Jan. 1843 | AA |
| Weisslogen, Jacob | Mauer, Minna | 19, May 1848 | C |
| Weissmueller, Ignatz | Kamer, Maria | 17, May 1842 | FF |
| Weitkamp, Bernard | Drulmann, Maria | 19, June 1838 | FF |
| Weitzel, Francis | Williams, Susan | 19, Aug. 1846 | BB |
| Weitzel, Jacob | Shaler, Mary | 4, Nov. 1841 | RCH |
| Weitzel, Peter | Foerst, Theresa | 24, June 1848 | EE |
| Weizenecker, Friedr. | Jung, Catharina | 9, Sept 1849 | II |
| Welage, Bernard H. | Engelbert, Maria | 13, Oct. 1846 | AA |
| Welage, Friedrich J. | Meyer, Catharina M. | 2, Nov. 1836 | FF |
| Welber, Bernard | Vorre, Elizabeth | 25, Nov. 1849 | RCH |
| Welbring, J. Arnold | Hessmann, Maria Elis | 5, May 1836 | FF |
| Welbrun, William | Adams, Ellen | 19, Feb. 1847 | RCH |
| Welch, Charles | Simmonds, Narcissa | 3, Dec. 1845 | RCH |
| Welch, Cyrus | McGinnis, Maretta | 1, Nov. 1835 | RCH |
| Welch, John | Branly, Jean | 29, Oct. 1848 | GG |
| Weldam, Friedrich | Schumacher, Margaret | 16, Oct. 1838 | FF |
| Weldam, Heinrich J. | Schroeder, Catharine | 21, Feb. 1843 | AA |
| Welding, Oliver | Wilie, Virginia | 15, Jan. 1846 | RCH |
| Weldy, John | Meyers, Elisabeth | 26, Nov. 1844 | RCH |
| Wellenkamp, Heinrich | Inderstroth, Anna M. | 19, Sept 1844 | F |
| Weller, Daniel | Snyder, Elisabeth | 13, June 1849 | RCH |
| Weller, James | Johnson, Elisabeth | 20, June 1845 | RCH |
| Welling, Heinrich | Haubrock, Maria Elis | 27, Apr. 1848 | A |
| Welling, Herman H. | Moormann, Anna M. | 28, Aug. 1838 | FF |
| Wellinghoff, Joseph | Westerhaus, Catharin | 6, Sept 1846 | FF |
| Wellis, William H. | Brown, Hester | 20, Nov. 1836 | RCH |
| Wellmann, Anton Jos. | Oevermann, Maria | 22, May 1838 | FF |
| Wellmann, Anton Jos. | Fick, Anna Catharina | 1, Sept 1840 | FF |
| Wellmann, Anton Jos. | Schawen, Engel | 1, Dec. 1849 | AA |
| Wellmann, Bernard | Westemeyer, Louisa | 27, June 1847 | AA |
| Wellmann, Conrad | Settage, Elisabeth | 29, Sept 1846 | AA |
| Wellmann, Gerhard | Fischer, Maria Anna | 28, Jan. 1849 | EE |
| Wellmann, Heinrich | Bunnemeyer, Elisabet | 20, Apr. 1847 | AA |
| Wellmann, Heinrich F | Knapke, Cath. Elis. | 19, Apr. 1849 | B |
| Wellmann, Herman | Koenig, Sophia | 29, Nov. 1848 | F |
| Wellmann, Herman H. | Rippstein, Maria C. | 24, Sept 1849 | F |
| Wellmann, J Heinrich | Amann, Catharina | 3, Nov. 1834 | FF |
| Wellmann, Mathias | Brossart, Catharine | 7, Dec. 1843 | FF |

| Grooms<br>****** | Brides<br>****** | Date of Marriage<br>**** ** ******** | Code<br>**** |
|---|---|---|---|
| Wellmann, Nicolaus | Hollinger, Genofeva | 29, May 1843 | AA |
| Wellmann, S Heinrich | Boekmann, Maria Anna | 6, Aug. 1837 | FF |
| Wellmeyer, F Wilhelm | Temmen, Wilhelmina | 13, Jan. 1847 | E |
| Wellner, Heinrich | Kerner, Anna | 9, Sept 1849 | II |
| Wells, Armsted | Wilson, Sarah | 18, Apr. 1833 | RCH |
| Wells, Darius | Weaver, Julia | 1, Mar. 1821 | RCH |
| Wells, Erastus | Hyatt, Maria Anna | 22, Oct. 1843 | RCH |
| Wells, Horace | Whipple, Sarah H. | 10, Mar. 1822 | RCH |
| Wells, Joe C. | Wilson, Clarissa | 30, Jan. 1834 | RCH |
| Wells, Lemuel | Foster, Mary Frances | 29, Oct. 1845 | RCH |
| Wells, Thomas | ----, ---- | 8, Oct. 1823 | RCH |
| Wells, William | Stewart, Anna M. | 23, Nov. 1837 | RCH |
| Wells, William | Sannon, Susan | 11, Aug. 1840 | RCH |
| Wells, William | Henderson, Charlotte | 14, Dec. 1843 | RCH |
| Welpley, John | Lane, Sarah | 13, Aug. 1848 | RCH |
| Welsch, Johan | Ludwig, Catharine | 12, May 1844 | G |
| Welsh, Henry | Allen, Levena | 8, Jan. 1821 | RCH |
| Welsh, Henry | Graves, Catharine | 8, July 1844 | RCH |
| Welsh, Jacob | Spencer, Patty | 26, Aug. 1819 | RCH |
| Welsh, James | Butler, Joann | 2, Oct. 1842 | BB |
| Welsh, James | Baily, Ellen | 11, Nov. 1849 | GG |
| Welsh, John | Kelly, Elisabeth A. | 1, June 1838 | I |
| Welsh, John | Kelly, Catharine | 10, Oct. 1840 | BB |
| Welsh, John | Clancy, Margaret | 23, June 1842 | BB |
| Welsh, John | Kelly, Jane | 26, Sept 1847 | GG |
| Welsh, Patrick | Cosgrove, Mary | 7, Jan. 1849 | BB |
| Welsh, Patrick | Horde, Mary | 11, June 1848 | GG |
| Welsh, Thomas | Donnolly, Mary | 23, Apr. 1843 | BB |
| Welsh, Thomas | Lamb, Mary | 12, June 1849 | RCH |
| Welsh, Thomas | Cooper, Bridget | 3, June 1849 | GG |
| Welten, Andrew | Felten, Harriet | 1, Dec. 1826 | RCH |
| Wemeyer, Johan And. | Koke, Anna Maria | 20, Aug. 1848 | EE |
| Wemhoff, Bernard | Kruse, Margaretha | 17, Jan. 1847 | AA |
| Wempe, Herman Heinr. | Johnson, Maria Sarah | 26, Jan. 1837 | FF |
| Wempe, J. Gerhard H. | Cordes, Anna Maria | 12, May 1835 | FF |
| Wempe, Wilhelm | Stuckenborg, Anna | 18, Apr. 1847 | AA |
| Wempe, Wilhelm | Evers, M. Elisabeth | 4, Nov. 1849 | II |
| Wendel, Wilhelm | Diekmann, Elisabeth | 9, Oct. 1839 | FF |
| Wendeler, J. Friedr. | Frommeyer, M. Elis. | 11, Nov. 1840 | FF |
| Wendeler, Jacob | Eveslage, Catharina | 13, Oct. 1840 | FF |
| Wendell, Pius | Rathemueller, Barb. | 20, Feb. 1838 | FF |
| Wendell, William | Haller, Ann | 24, Dec. 1841 | RCH |
| Wendelmann, Fritz | Brandt, Adelheid | 9, Aug. 1849 | F |
| Wendeln, Johan Hein. | Duetmann, M. Elis. | 8, Oct. 1839 | FF |
| Wendlandt, Philipp | Duffke, Friedricka | 1, Dec. 1848 | F |
| Wendle, Johan | Hinkle, Catharine | 23, Apr. 1839 | FF |
| Wendling, Jacob | Gossting, Matilda | 17, Nov. 1844 | RCH |
| Wendt, John Henry | Wiechert, Louise | 1, May 1847 | RCH |
| Wenger, Michael | Thines, Catharine | 21, Aug. 1843 | FF |
| Wenig, Joseph | Willers, Theresa | 6, Sept 1842 | AA |
| Wenner, Philipp | Seger, Catharine | 4, Dec. 1844 | C |
| Wenning, Herman | Kleinenberg, Elis. | 18, Apr. 1847 | AA |
| Wenning, Wilhelm | Goos, Lisette | 23, Sept 1849 | CC |
| Wenstrup, Johan H. | Brockmann, Catharine | 19, May 1846 | AA |
| Wente, Clemens | Albers, Catharine | 17, Jan. 1847 | AA |
| Wentehold, Bernard | Grave, Elisabeth | 16, Feb. 1847 | EE |
| Wentling, John | McCurdy, Phoebe | 10, June 1846 | RCH |
| Wentlon, John | Reuth, Margaret M. | 17, Nov. 1833 | RCH |
| Wentworth, James | Burrows, Phebe | 26, July 1846 | RCH |
| Wentzell, Washington | Sharp, Bulia | 20, Nov. 1832 | RCH |
| Wenzel, Johan | Gessert, Sophia | 18, Feb. 1849 | G |
| Werbel, Johan | Schindler, Julia | 20, Jan. 1846 | FF |
| Werick, Balthasar | Graff, Margaretha | 11, Apr. 1847 | EE |
| Werk, Asher | Carson, Margaret | 29, Dec. 1841 | RCH |
| Werle, Joseph | Phillips, Anna Maria | 12, Jan. 1843 | FF |
| Werlen, Herman Anton | Kolb, Margaret Elis. | 8, July 1849 | II |
| Wermann, Christian | Spellman, Maria | 1, Sept 1841 | RCH |
| Wermann, J Friedrich | Menke, M. Catharina | 20, Apr. 1841 | FF |
| Wermann, Louis | Lichte, Catharine | 4, Oct. 1846 | EE |
| Werndt, Johan Joseph | Fleddermann, Cath. | 24, May 1846 | AA |
| Werner, Adam | Hulmann, Catharine | 9, Jan. 1848 | EE |

| Grooms | Brides | Date of Marriage | Code |
|--------|--------|------------------|------|
| ****** | ****** | **** ** ******** | **** |
| Werner, Jacob | Weghorn, Christina | 1, Mar. 1847 | RCH |
| Werner, Jacob | Reil, Catharine | 13, Nov. 1849 | A |
| Werner, Johan | Hauck, Maria | 4, Aug. 1840 | G |
| Werner, Laurenz | Demand, Catharine | 11, Jan. 1841 | FF |
| Werner, Michael | Hahn, M. Magdalena | 22, Sept 1846 | G |
| Werner, Michael | Schindler, Magdalena | 29, Oct. 1848 | FF |
| Werning, Bernard | ----, ---- | Dec. 1849 | RCH |
| Werning, Herman Bd. | Kolden, Anna Maria | 14, Sept 1845 | AA |
| Werning, Phil. Jacob | Diehl, Christina | 21, June 1849 | G |
| Wernke, Bernard | Ostendorf, Anna | 25, Nov. 1849 | EE |
| Wernke, Frederick | Uphaus, Elisabeth | 14, Jan. 1843 | RCH |
| Wernsing, Heinrich | Brogmann, Anna Maria | 29, Nov. 1837 | FF |
| Werr, Lawrence | Gosser, Margaret | 25, Mar. 1848 | RCH |
| Werry, Johan Heinric | Rennekamp, Elisabeth | 17, May 1846 | FF |
| Werry, Johan Heinric | Kunstler, Caroline | 23, Oct. 1847 | FF |
| Werselmann, Heinrich | Tecker, Maria | 3, July 1849 | II |
| Wertermann, Lambert | Robben, Margaretha | 31, Oct. 1847 | FF |
| Werth, Georg | Bauer, Elisabeth | 4, Sept 1848 | G |
| Werth, Johan | Pist, Gertrud | 4, Feb. 1849 | EE |
| Wertheim, David | Elsasser, Sarah | 22, Mar. 1847 | RCH |
| Wertheim, David | Goldstein, Cecilia | 12, Sept 1849 | RCH |
| Wertheimer, Joseph | Lemlein, Hannah | 20, Sept 1842 | RCH |
| Wertheimer, Joseph | Schiff, Jennette | 17, Feb. 1847 | RCH |
| Werthman, Isaac | Benjamin, Theresa | 13, Dec. 1842 | RCH |
| Wertmueller, Andreas | Hoppe, Theresa | 5, June 1849 | EE |
| Werts, Theodore | Cable, Anna Elis. | 22, Nov. 1841 | RCH |
| Wertz, Adam | Lakas, Katharine | 17, Nov. 1849 | EE |
| Wesbey, William | Muir, Elisabeth | 14, July 1836 | RCH |
| Wescot, Charles | Borgett, Susan | 8, May 1836 | RCH |
| Wescot, Nehemiah | Ludlum, Tilphid | 11, Feb. 1819 | RCH |
| Wescott, John | Espe, May | 3, Aug. 1824 | RCH |
| Wesemann, Johan | Droeger, Maria | 11, June 1841 | F |
| Weshear, William | Compton, Polly | 25, Oct. 1832 | RCH |
| Wess, Heinrich | Harcas, Anna Engel | 24, Feb. 1838 | FF |
| Wessel, Bernard | Thiemann, Maria | 17, Nov. 1841 | FF |
| Wessel, Bernard | Bocklage, Maria Anna | 8, Aug. 1846 | FF |
| Wessel, Bernard H. | Hermasch, M. Agnes | 19, Nov. 1835 | FF |
| Wessel, Friedrich | Limberg, Lena Wilhel | 8, Aug. 1844 | A |
| Wessel, H. Herman | Ostendorf, A Gertrud | 29, Nov. 1849 | II |
| Wessel, Heinrich | Martin, Maria Anna | 4, Feb. 1840 | FF |
| Wessel, Heinrich | Hermeske, M. Elis. | 12, Jan. 1841 | FF |
| Wessel, J. Gerhard | Tibben, Marg. Elis. | 26, Feb. 1849 | F |
| Wessel, Johan Adam | Thomas, Elisabeth | 3, Nov. 1847 | RCH |
| Wessel, Johan Herman | Brittinger, Eva T. | 14, Sept 1848 | RCH |
| Wessel, John | Retter, Rachel | 14, Feb. 1842 | RCH |
| Wessel, Joseph | Wehrmann, Elisabeth | 27, Jan. 1846 | FF |
| Wessel, William | Hasger, Sophia | 26, Oct. 1842 | RCH |
| Wesseling, J. Heinr. | Lutkenhof, Margaret | 6, Nov. 1849 | FF |
| Wesselkock, Herman | Niemeyer, Veronica | 25, Nov. 1849 | AA |
| Wesselmann, | Budemeier, Johanna | 27, Aug. 1849 | RCH |
| Wesselmann, Herman | Schmidt, Gertrud | 10, July 1838 | FF |
| Wesselmann, Johan | Tegelers, Catharine | 5, Oct. 1843 | F |
| Wesselmann, Johan H. | Thoele, Adelheid | 10, Mar. 1842 | F |
| Wesselmann, Joseph | Moehlmann, Maria | 10, Nov. 1842 | AA |
| Wessels, Heinrich | Meyer, Maria | 1, May 1838 | FF |
| Wessels, Heinrich | Schilmela, Anna M. | 9, Jan. 1848 | EE |
| Wessels, J. Martin | Rump, Catharine | 1, Oct. 1846 | FF |
| Wessels, Johan H. | Eifilers, Louise E. | 6, May 1849 | EE |
| Wessels, Johan Hein. | Goetke, Elisabeth | 21, June 1846 | AA |
| Wessels, Johan Hein. | Doetmer, Anna Marg. | 25, June 1848 | EE |
| Wessels, Johan Jos. | Seepe, Elisabeth | 23, Apr. 1839 | FF |
| Wessling, Heinrich | Meyer, Maria | 4, May 1843 | FF |
| Wessling, Heinrich | Schmidt, Maria Jos. | 28, May 1848 | EE |
| Wessling, Johan | Grueshof, | 17, Sept 1848 | EE |
| West, Alfred | Duning, Milley | 20, July 1844 | RCH |
| West, Buchard | Compton, Armand | 22, Oct. 1835 | RCH |
| West, Caleb R. | Dousa, Elisabeth T. | 12, July 1834 | RCH |
| West, Christopher | Alford, Betsey | 7, Jan. 1821 | RCH |
| West, Daniel | Gillespie, Clara | 19, Apr. 1842 | RCH |
| West, David | Balser, Rebecca | 6, Oct. 1836 | RCH |
| West, Elijah | Waters, Catharine | 23, Dec. 1841 | RCH |

| Grooms<br>****** | Brides<br>****** | Date of Marriage<br>**** ** ******** | Code<br>**** |
|---|---|---|---|
| West, George | Miner, Sarah Jane | 6, Sept 1847 | RCH |
| West, Isaac | Norris, Nancy | 29, Oct. 1835 | RCH |
| West, James M. | Parks, Sarah Ann | 9, May 1833 | RCH |
| West, Jefferson | Patterson, Betsy | 10, Nov. 1836 | RCH |
| West, Joseph | Miller, Elisabeth | 29, Dec. 1834 | RCH |
| West, Manning | Stout, Amanda | 11, Apr. 1838 | RCH |
| West, Stockton | Bevis, Catharine | 12, May 1842 | RCH |
| West, William | Compton, Mary | 27, Dec. 1832 | RCH |
| Westcott, John D. | Willis, Margaret S. | 26, Feb. 1823 | RCH |
| Westcott, William | Slelin, Alexandra | 17, Nov. 1833 | RCH |
| Weste, Theodor | Albers, Elisabeth | 26, Sept 1837 | FF |
| Westendarp, Joseph | Frommeier, A. Maria | 10, Sept 1848 | II |
| Westendorf, Francis | Bocklage, Bernardina | 4, Feb. 1849 | AA |
| Westendorf, Joseph | Simmer, Elisabeth | 5, Nov. 1839 | FF |
| Wester, Herman H. | Schleper, Catharine | 2, June 1846 | AA |
| Westerbusch, Wilhelm | Husmann, Maria | 16, Oct. 1838 | FF |
| Westerfield, David J | Hansel, Jane | 28, June 1835 | RCH |
| Westerheide, Johan H | Mackhof, Catharina | 21, Jan. 1849 | AA |
| Westerkamp, Heinrich | Otte, Catharine | 7, Nov. 1849 | F |
| Westermann, Carl H. | Froehlking, Sophia | 13, Jan. 1848 | F |
| Westermann, Friedric | Moormann, Maria | 20, Sept 1849 | C |
| Westermann, John H. | Berwick, Amalia | 7, Apr. 1842 | G |
| Western, George | Gray, Harriet | 24, May 1838 | RCH |
| Western, Silas | Adams, Sarah | 10, Aug. 1839 | RCH |
| Western, William | Brown, Mary A. | 16, May 1841 | RCH |
| Westheimer, Heinrich | Goetz, Carolina | 19, June 1849 | RCH |
| Westing, Friedrich | Meyer, Dorothea | 29, June 1845 | F |
| Westing, Georg Hein. | Heikmann, Maria H. | 25, May 1848 | F |
| Westing, Heinrich | Heckmanns, Maria | 25, July 1846 | F |
| Westing, Heinrich | Witcombs, Henrietta | 13, Oct. 1848 | F |
| Westjohan, Heinrich | Heirmann, Maria Anna | 2, Feb. 1837 | FF |
| Westjohann, Anton | Weichler, Theresa | 3, Feb. 1844 | FF |
| Westmeyer, Heinrich | Rasch, Anna | 11, Nov. 1849 | AA |
| Westmeyer, Herman H. | Plogmann, A. Elis. | 9, Sept 1849 | AA |
| Westmeyer, Johan H. | Oehrbrock, Catharine | 19, Jan. 1846 | F |
| Weston, Burd | Hill, Susan | 26, Sept 1818 | RCH |
| Weston, James | Barbin, Rachel | 27, Mar. 1841 | RCH |
| Weston, Lewis | Murphy, Seynthe | 5, Nov. 1833 | RCH |
| Weston, Simon | Rafferty, Margaret | 16, Jan. 1844 | BB |
| Weston, Willard | Barnhisel, Catharine | 8, Jan. 1837 | RCH |
| Westover, Allen | Tatem, Mary | 31, Mar. 1844 | RCH |
| Westover, Jonathan | Bean, Mary | 13, Nov. 1842 | RCH |
| Westphal, Heinrich | Meyer, Charlotte | 23, Aug. 1849 | A |
| Westphal, Nicholas | Brem, Catharine | 15, Nov. 1848 | C |
| Westphalen, Anton | Hegger, Helena | 23, Oct. 1849 | II |
| Westrich, Louis | Mueller, Catharine | 24, May 1847 | EE |
| Westrup, Henry | Krauss, Catharine | 25, Oct. 1846 | RCH |
| Wetteler, Joseph | Stertinkamp, Elis. | 7, Jan. 1845 | FF |
| Wettich, Heinrich | Freund, Anna Maria | 27, Nov. 1849 | C |
| Wetzel, August | Hook, Magdalena | 21, Aug. 1845 | AA |
| Wetzel, Ludwig | Rieder, Margaretha | 22, Nov. 1846 | AA |
| Wetzel, Wilhelm | Becker, Catharine | 15, Oct. 1848 | A |
| Wewer, Carl | Caspers, Anna Adel. | 19, Sept 1847 | CC |
| Weyer, Herman Hein. | Brink, Anna Adelheid | 11, Jan. 1848 | AA |
| Weygandt, Philipp | Littemann, Susannah | 25, Mar. 1846 | RCH |
| Weythman, John B. | Watterer, Frances | 2, June 1840 | RCH |
| Wh---, James M. | Gorman, Julia Ann | 14, Jan. 1836 | RCH |
| Wh---, William | Hastry, Ellen | 13, Sept 1838 | RCH |
| Whal, Anthony | Herman, Mary | 6, Sept 1834 | RCH |
| Whaley, Wilford | Gibson, Ann | 13, Mar. 1849 | RCH |
| Whallon, James | Prater, Julia Ann | 8, June 1848 | RCH |
| Whallon, James J. | Westlake, Ann | 8, Nov. 1834 | RCH |
| Whalon, Robert | Carver, Margaret | 15, Mar. 1837 | RCH |
| Whalon, Simon | Preston, Levina | 2, Mar. 1826 | RCH |
| Whann, George | Huntsman, Mary | 8, June 1841 | RCH |
| Whaton, William | Gray, | 13, June 1826 | RCH |
| Whe, Abraham | Newbaum, E.W. | 17, Dec. 1835 | RCH |
| Whe---, Chesley | Bellinger, Margaret | 1, Aug. 1844 | RCH |
| Wheatley, Isaac | Winans, Sarah | 1, Oct. 1840 | RCH |
| Wheatley, Martin | Hawkins, | 10, Aug. 1826 | RCH |
| Wheatley, Robert | Barrow, Maria | 9, Aug. 1846 | RCH |

| Grooms | Brides | Date of Marriage | Code |
|--------|--------|------------------|------|
| Wheatley, Thomas | Barrow, Aletha | 30, Oct. 1836 | RCH |
| Wheatley, William | Miller, Rachel Ann | 19, Dec. 1846 | RCH |
| Wheeler, | Piatt, Catharine G. | 24, Jan. 1822 | RCH |
| Wheeler, August | Gano, Elisabeth S. | 3, Sept 1843 | RCH |
| Wheeler, Benjamin | Allen, Elisabeth | 14, Mar. 1843 | RCH |
| Wheeler, Daniel W. | Pierce, Eunice | 30, Oct. 1817 | RCH |
| Wheeler, Jackson | DeGear, Harriet | 3, Oct. 1842 | RCH |
| Wheeler, Joseph | Jackson, Susannah | 2, Aug. 1846 | RCH |
| Wheeler, Michael | Carroll, Ellen | 2, Nov. 1845 | RCH |
| Wheeler, Milton G. | Rosaline, Ann | 24, Jan. 1838 | RCH |
| Wheeler, Samuel W. | Ashton, Sarah S. | 2, Apr. 1821 | RCH |
| Wheeler, William Hy. | Cooper, Ann | 9, May 1847 | RCH |
| Wheelwright, James R | Irwin, Sarah Frances | 12, Nov. 1839 | I |
| Whelan, August | Stevens, Arabell E. | 29, Aug. 1842 | RCH |
| Whelan, Barry S. | Anderson, Sarah A. | 12, Mar. 1832 | RCH |
| Whelan, Jonathan | Williams, Elisabeth | 26, Mar. 1843 | RCH |
| Whelan, Thomas | Coyle, Jane | 14, Oct. 1839 | BB |
| Whelan, Thomas | McCarthy, Mary A. | 4, Aug. 1849 | BB |
| Whelan, William | Johnson, Marg. (Mrs) | 17, Mar. 1848 | BB |
| Whetsel, Henry B. | Skillman, Sarah | 16, July 1841 | RCH |
| Whetstone, Richard | Smith, Marion | 3, May 1847 | RCH |
| Whetty, Joseph | Crosby, Hannah | 21, Dec. 1817 | RCH |
| Whilley, Charles | Hey, M. | 6, Oct. 1834 | RCH |
| Whipper, Abel | Matsonwell, Mary Ann | 4, Oct. 1836 | RCH |
| Whipple, Emor | Hanks, Julia | 22, Mar. 1836 | RCH |
| Whipple, John L. | Smith, Frances M. | 8, July 1842 | I |
| Whipple, Lucius | Trump, Emily | 31, Mar. 1844 | RCH |
| Whipple, Samuel D. | Conklin, Elisabeth | 14, Oct. 1819 | RCH |
| Whiste---, John | Sturr, Mary | 29, Mar. 1838 | RCH |
| Whitaker, Daniel | Bennett, Anna Maria | 16, Mar. 1836 | RCH |
| Whitaker, James | Hunt, Francis | 13, Jan. 1820 | RCH |
| Whitaker, John | Phillips, Jane | 16, Oct. 1823 | RCH |
| Whitaker, Jonathan | ----, ---- | 24, Feb. 1825 | RCH |
| Whitaker, Jonathan | Potter, Mary | 7, June 1836 | RCH |
| Whitaker, Joseph | Beresford, Sarah | 11, Aug. 1847 | RCH |
| Whitcher, William | Patterson, Sarah | Nov. 1844 | RCH |
| Whitcom, George | Barclay, A. Ellen | 16, Sept 1846 | RCH |
| Whitcomb, David | Welton, Magdalena | 11, Dec. 1833 | RCH |
| White, | Forde, Mary | 25, June 1818 | RCH |
| White, | McLain, Sophronia | 2, Sept 1849 | RCH |
| White, Amos | Luckmeyer, Esther | 9, May 1836 | RCH |
| White, Archibald | McColin, Nancy | 11, Dec. 1848 | RCH |
| White, Barton | Mullen, Mary Ann | 25, Nov. 1840 | RCH |
| White, Bernard | Powers, Margaret | 27, May 1848 | RCH |
| White, Burton | Law, Eleanor Adel | 18, June 1833 | RCH |
| White, Daniel | Williams, Mary M. | 28, Feb. 1843 | RCH |
| White, Edward | Case, Carolina | Nov. 1849 | RCH |
| White, Francis | Garrison, Rebecca | 14, July 1835 | RCH |
| White, George | Stedman, Elisabeth J | 20, Feb. 1844 | RCH |
| White, Henry | French, Nancy | 25, Aug. 1838 | RCH |
| White, Horace | ----, Xenia | 7, Nov. 1837 | RCH |
| White, Isaac | Ballard, Olive | 17, Apr. 1822 | RCH |
| White, Isaac | Ringle, Lucy | 3, Sept 1832 | RCH |
| White, Jacob | Kerley, Rhodah | 24, Nov. 1817 | RCH |
| White, James | Waters, Ann | 7, Oct. 1820 | RCH |
| White, James | Miller, Keziah | 27, Jan. 1836 | RCH |
| White, James | Howard, Sarah | 29, July 1843 | RCH |
| White, James | Maloney, Hester | 12, Dec. 1843 | RCH |
| White, James | Bushnell, Abby | 9, Oct. 1845 | RCH |
| White, James | Parker, Theresa A. | 16, Apr. 1849 | RCH |
| White, James | Clancy, Margaret | 12, Nov. 1847 | BB |
| White, James S. | Stewart, Sarah | 27, Nov. 1845 | RCH |
| White, Joel | Hutchinson, Eliza M. | 27, Mar. 1849 | RCH |
| White, John | Staunton, Catharine | 21, Nov. 1839 | BB |
| White, John F. | Wade, Harriet | 18, Mar. 1845 | I |
| White, John R. | Arnold, Sarah | 4, Dec. 1836 | RCH |
| White, Joseph | Gardener, Charlotte | 7, Mar. 1848 | RCH |
| White, Joseph | Egner, Elisabeth | 15, Jan. 1849 | RCH |
| White, Joseph R. | Smith, Rachel | 6, July 1849 | RCH |
| White, Levi | Ross, | 20, Dec. 1824 | RCH |
| White, Michael | Ryan, Joann | 19, Oct. 1843 | BB |

| Grooms<br>****** | Brides<br>****** | Date of Marriage<br>**** ** ******** | Code<br>**** |
|---|---|---|---|
| White, Michael | Fahey, Catharine | 1, Jan. 1849 | RCH |
| White, Michael | Crosson, Mary | 13, Oct. 1849 | BB |
| White, Michael | Sheedy, Catharine | 17, Sept 1848 | GG |
| White, Moses | Palmer, Margaret M. | 8, July 1833 | I |
| White, Moses D. | McQueeny, Susan | 3, Feb. 1825 | RCH |
| White, Samuel | Luckey, Harriet | 26, Aug. 1843 | RCH |
| White, Stephen | Manhallen, Patience | 21, June 1833 | RCH |
| White, Thomas | Seward, Elsey | 10, Oct. 1820 | RCH |
| White, Thomas | Sacwell, Elisabeth | 21, Feb. 1836 | RCH |
| White, Thomas | Cones, Jane | 14, Oct. 1843 | RCH |
| White, Thomas A. | Grinstead, Mary Ann | 5, Oct. 1833 | RCH |
| White, Uriah | Duffy, Susan | 9, Nov. 1843 | RCH |
| White, Washington | Simpson, Sarah | 22, July 1847 | RCH |
| White, William | ----, ---- | 18, Feb. 1847 | RCH |
| White, William E. | Seymour, Eureta(Mrs) | 28, Feb. 1821 | I |
| White, William H. | Sharpe, Sarah | 1, Mar. 1821 | RCH |
| White, William J. | Stoughton, Mary | 19, Feb. 1843 | RCH |
| White--, Benjamin | Casselly, Henrietta | 13, Sept 1838 | I |
| Whitehead, Charles | Ramsey, Sarah Jane | 12, Jan. 1843 | RCH |
| Whitehead, George | Hodgson, Mary | 13, Apr. 1847 | D |
| Whitehead, John | Gray, Catharine | 30, July 1818 | RCH |
| Whitehead, Ralph | Ogden, Esther | 31, July 1848 | RCH |
| Whitehead, Thomas | Walters, Maria | 26, Mar. 1838 | RCH |
| Whitehead, William | Arthurs, Charlotte | 28, Nov. 1848 | RCH |
| Whiteman, Lewis | Irwin, Louise | 12, May 1824 | RCH |
| Whiteman, Lewis | Harrison, Jane | 30, June 1842 | RCH |
| Whiteman, Nathan M. | Thornton, | 16, Nov. 1824 | RCH |
| Whiteside, John | ----, Catharine | 5, Feb. 1835 | RCH |
| Whiteside, Robert | Balona, Isabella | 22, Apr. 1849 | RCH |
| Whiteside, Samuel | Lemon, Mary | 8, Oct. 1843 | RCH |
| Whitesides, Jaems | Morrison, Elisabeth | 18, Apr. 1839 | RCH |
| Whitesides, Samuel | Johnson, Caroline | 12, Aug. 1847 | RCH |
| Whitewell, Isaac S. | Browntree, Ann Jane | 16, July 1835 | I |
| Whiting, Edward A. | Johnson, Margaret | 2, Oct. 1834 | RCH |
| Whitlock, Stephen | Pitman, Sarah | 11, Mar. 1834 | RCH |
| Whitmann, Adam | Adam, Elisabeth | 8, Dec. 1835 | FF |
| Whitmore, John | Mahne, Barbara | 7, Apr. 1842 | RCH |
| Whitmore, Moses N. | Heddington, Elis. J. | 15, Nov. 1836 | RCH |
| Whitney, Daniel E. | Thompson, Elisabeth | 8, Oct. 1824 | RCH |
| Whitney, Nathan | Moore, Mary Jane | 27, Apr. 1837 | RCH |
| Whitney, Samuel | Miller, Rachel | 20, Apr. 1835 | RCH |
| Whitsit, | Mathers, Ann | 2, Jan. 1827 | RCH |
| Whitten, Francis | Johnson, Nancy | 20, Mar. 1846 | RCH |
| Whitten, Richard | Davey, Sarah | 2, June 1848 | RCH |
| Whittier, | Barber, Charlotte | 9, Sept 1849 | RCH |
| Whittington, Nathan | Thomas, Biddy | 7, Feb. 1848 | RCH |
| Whitvige, William | Hook, Mary | 25, Sept 1834 | RCH |
| Wholy, Oliver | Stewart, Sarah | 29, May 1834 | RCH |
| Wiatt, Thomas | Flogg, Betsy | 1, Oct. 1825 | RCH |
| Wiatt, William B. | Smith, Elsey | 7, June 1820 | RCH |
| Wibben, B. Herman | Rottermann, Gertrud | 4, Feb. 1849 | II |
| Wichmann, Theodor A. | Wichmann, Emelia W. | 6, Sept 1849 | E * |
| Wicht, Aaron | Landis, Louise | 2, Mar. 1848 | G |
| Wick, Michael | Scheering, Margaret | 10, Sept 1846 | EE |
| Wickelmann, Clemens | Broecker, Anna Maria | 18, Feb. 1844 | FF |
| Wicker, James H. | Morton, Mary A. | 30, Apr. 1849 | RCH |
| Wickham, John | Dedrick, Elisabeth | 3, May 1847 | RCH |
| Wickmann, Friedrich | Roth, Margaretha | 26, Jan. 1848 | G |
| Wickmann, Johan | Utill, Gertrud | 7, Jan. 1840 | FF |
| Widemeyer, Friedrich | Kneppenberger, Cath. | 29, Nov. 1849 | RCH |
| Widich, Georg | Kraus, Christina | 24, Sept 1846 | C |
| Widman, John | Crowley, Sarah | 22, Aug. 1839 | BB |
| Widmer, Fidel | Lambers, Maria | 7, July 1840 | FF |
| Widney, Stephen | Williams, Elis. Jane | Jan. 1845 | RCH |
| Widt, C. Ernst F. | Schaetle, Augusta | 28, Jan. 1849 | G |
| Wiebert, Wilhelm | Burkhardt, Charlotte | 21, Oct. 1849 | C |
| Wiebring, Heinrich | Messmann, Angela | 17, Feb. 1835 | FF |
| Wiecher, Heinrich | Grelle, Rachel | 17, Nov. 1848 | G |
| Wiecher, Herman F. | Kinghorst, Christine | 17, Nov. 1847 | G |
| Wiechter, Herman | Lange, Theresa | 24, Oct. 1846 | EE |
| Wiedemer, Ignatz | Wurst, Maria | 1, Sept 1840 | FF |

| Grooms<br>****** | Brides<br>****** | Date of Marriage<br>**** ** ******** | Code<br>**** |
|---|---|---|---|
| Wiedholter, H Adolph | Duvall, Cath. Carol. | 9, Sept 1845 | G |
| Wiedmann, August | Wiesz, Louisa | 16, Feb. 1847 | EE |
| Wiegelmann, Johan | Moormann, A.M. Cath. | 19, Apr. 1836 | FF |
| Wieghaus, Bernard | Grave, Maria Elis. | 9, Jan. 1848 | EE |
| Wiehoff, Bernard | Schawing, Adelheid | 23, Nov. 1847 | EE |
| Wiemann, Christian H | Niehaus, M. Engel | 3, May 1845 | F |
| Wiemann, Friedrich | Rodefeld, Anna Maria | 31, Aug. 1843 | F |
| Wiemann, Heinrich | Decker, Maria Engel | 26, Jan. 1847 | C |
| Wiemann, Henry | Wietholters, Sophia | 23, Jan. 1843 | RCH |
| Wiemann, Herman Geo. | Kruse, Regina Cath. | 23, June 1847 | C |
| Wiemann, Herman H. | Geismann, A. Louise | 31, Dec. 1844 | F |
| Wiemann, J. Heinrich | Rohlfing, Wilhelmina | 6, Jan. 1846 | B |
| Wiemann, Johan Bd. | Strattmann, Gertrud | 16, Feb. 1847 | EE |
| Wiemann, Johan Hein. | Stadtlander, Louise | 9, Aug. 1844 | A |
| Wiemann, Wilhelm | Pottebaum, M. Anna | 9, Jan. 1849 | AA |
| Wiemeier, Gerhard H. | Lubke, Catharine | 11, Feb. 1847 | F |
| Wiemer, Andrew | Rose, Barbara | 27, Aug. 1845 | RCH |
| Wiemeyer, Francis | Dacken, Wilhelmina | 20, Oct. 1846 | AA |
| Wiemeyer, Heinrich | Temme, Louise | 14, Nov. 1841 | F |
| Wierty, John | Case, Mary | 25, Aug. 1834 | RCH |
| Wieser, Heinrich | Deveny, Catharine M. | 4, Aug. 1845 | C |
| Wiethauper, John | Driehaus, Friedricka | 20, July 1844 | RCH |
| Wieverich, Frank | Balde, Margaretha | 29, Nov. 1849 | G |
| Wieweiner, Heinrich | Droege, Maria | 3, Nov. 1846 | C |
| Wigand, Michael | Hack, Maria Elis. | 28, Jan. 1840 | FF |
| Wigant, Francis | Lapp, Rosina (Mrs) | 27, Nov. 1845 | FF |
| Wigbels, Johan Hein. | Thole, Anna Margaret | 18, June 1848 | AA |
| Wigbels, Johan Wm. | Bosing, Johanna | 8, Nov. 1846 | AA |
| Wigert, Johan | Werner, Anna Maria | 19, Jan. 1847 | EE |
| Wiggermann, Bernard | Reismann, Anna Maria | 15, June 1843 | AA |
| Wiggermann, H. Johan | Behrmann, M. Gertrud | 9, Jan. 1849 | FF |
| Wiggers, Heinrich | Naber, Adelheid | 14, Jan. 1849 | II |
| Wiggers, Louis | Meyer, Anna Margaret | 14, Dec. 1849 | G |
| Wiggins, David | Platt, Betsey | 7, Jan. 1824 | RCH |
| Wiggins, Harrison | Nicholson, Catharine | 11, June 1846 | RCH |
| Wiggins, James | Emmett, Elisabeth C. | 9, Mar. 1844 | RCH |
| Wiggins, Josiah | Goodhue, Jane | 24, Apr. 1839 | RCH |
| Wiggins, Philemon | Burr, Mary | 1, Mar. 1848 | RCH |
| Wightman, Alexander | VonGundy, | Oct. 1844 | RCH |
| Wiglesworth, Ferd. | Day, A. Elisabeth | 28, Sept 1848 | RCH |
| Wigley, Henry | Kemball, Susan | 17, Jan. 1846 | RCH |
| Wigmann, Gerhard H. | Brinkmeyer, M. Anna | 16, July 1848 | AA |
| Wigmann, Johan Mich. | Bohle, Crescentia | 27, Feb. 1848 | EE |
| Wilard, Roland | Borland, Elisabeth S | 27, June 1832 | RCH |
| Wilberding, Heinrich | Overmuehle, Adelheid | 13, July 1841 | FF |
| Wilbers, Bernard H. | Trentmann, Anna M. | 14, Jan. 1845 | AA |
| Wilbes, Gerhard H. | Fering, Catharine | 8, Aug. 1847 | CC |
| Wilby, Joseph | Hinman, Mary H. | 31, Aug. 1847 | RCH |
| Wilcox, Alexander | Young, Nancy | 8, Oct. 1844 | RCH |
| Wilcox, James | Sullivan, Polly | 1, Oct. 1820 | RCH |
| Wilcox, Moses | Taylor, Sarah | 2, Sept 1847 | RCH |
| Wilcox, Peter | Thomas, Prescilla | 4, Apr. 1822 | I |
| Wilcox, William | Brannon, Harriet | 28, Sept 1848 | RCH |
| Wild, Mathias | Enderle, Regina | 14, Nov. 1848 | EE |
| Wild, Peter | Schmidt, Margaretha | 5, Dec. 1844 | AA |
| Wilde, Jacob | Espert, Maria | 26, Nov. 1846 | G |
| Wildenhaus, Johan Bd | Lisner, Anna Marg. | 12, Jan. 1847 | EE |
| Wilder, Ira | Morris, Elisabeth | 2, Jan. 1839 | RCH |
| Wildermann, Bernard | Haring, Maria | 24, Feb. 1838 | FF |
| Wildman, Thomas | Hoel, Delilah | 24, Aug. 1848 | RCH |
| Wildy, August | Fenner, Margaretha | 12, Jan. 1843 | G |
| Wile, Andrew | Williams, Mary Ann | 25, July 1847 | RCH |
| Wile, Henry | Jones, Elisabeth | 8, Mar. 1827 | RCH |
| Wile, Jubale | Hill, Elisabeth | 25, Feb. 1819 | RCH |
| Wiles, Frisbe | S---, Eleanor (Mrs) | 28, Jan. 1827 | RCH |
| Wiley, Decator | Budd, Hannah | 10, Mar. 1842 | RCH |
| Wiley, Francis | Bradley, Ellen | 2, Mar. 1842 | RCH |
| Wiley, James | VanDyke, Elmira | 24, Mar. 1842 | RCH |
| Wiley, John | Anderson, Alaney | 9, Apr. 1820 | RCH |
| Wiley, John | Runnels, Mary | 19, Oct. 1848 | RCH |
| Wiley, Joseph | Bell, Jane | 23, July 1835 | RCH |

| Grooms | Brides | Date of Marriage | Code |
|--------|--------|------------------|------|
| Wiley, William | Waldsmith, Jane | 29, Aug. 1824 | RCH |
| Wilhelm, Carl Fried. | Gerbel, Margaretha | 14, Jan. 1841 | FF |
| Wilhelm, George | Ovlim, Catharine | 10, Nov. 1843 | RCH |
| Wilhelm, Michael | Ulrich, Catharine | 9, June 1845 | C |
| Wilhorn, Friedrich | Heidbrings, Catharin | 23, June 1837 | RCH |
| Wilhorn, Johan Herm. | Puthoff, Maria Engel | 30, July 1844 | AA |
| Wilke, Friedrich | Tapkins, Margareth D | 1, June 1848 | B |
| Wilke, Johan Gerhard | Atte, Anna M. Engel | 2, Aug. 1849 | C |
| Wilke, Theodor | Meyer, Maria Anna | 15, Oct. 1848 | FF |
| Wilkemeyer, Johan H. | Baumann, Catharine | 10, Nov. 1846 | AA |
| Wilken, Dietrich | Rutker, Angela | 29, May 1839 | FF |
| Wilken, Gerhard H. | Kessen, Maria Adel. | 19, Sept 1847 | EE |
| Wilken, Heinrich | Drollmann, Elisabeth | 3, July 1849 | II |
| Wilkening, Wilhelm | Nietert, Dorothea S. | 4, Mar. 1847 | F |
| Wilkens, Asa | Binnington, Sarah | 30, May 1837 | RCH |
| Wilker, Johan Joseph | Woermeyer, M. Elis. | 27, June 1847 | AA |
| Wilkerson, William | Ewing, Amelia | 7, Dec. 1837 | RCH |
| Wilkes, Gerhard | Tensching, Angela | 6, Sept 1846 | EE |
| Wilkie, Georg | Johnston, Elisabeth | 7, Dec. 1820 | RCH |
| Wilkin, John | Nicholson, Beatrice | 10, Aug. 1837 | RCH |
| Wilkins, Albert | Featherling, Mary A. | 2, Dec. 1849 | RCH |
| Wilkins, Harrison | Miller, Mathilda | 12, Mar. 1843 | RCH |
| Wilkins, J. Dietrich | Graevenkamp, Angela | 14, Sept 1841 | FF |
| Wilkinson, Benjamin | Johnson, Margaret | 20, Jan. 1845 | RCH |
| Wilkinson, Daniel | Shepherd, Louise | 4, Apr. 1847 | RCH |
| Wilkinson, Hugh | Marsh, Abbey | 9, Feb. 1843 | RCH |
| Wilkinson, Ira | Strong, Martha | Jan. 1839 | RCH |
| Wilkinson, Isaac | Strong, Susan | 7, Apr. 1836 | RCH |
| Wilkinson, James | Mason, Elisabeth | 10, Nov. 1836 | RCH |
| Wilkinson, James | Wirt, Elizabeth | 28, Mar. 1847 | RCH |
| Wilkinson, John | D---, Christina | 18, Dec. 1822 | RCH |
| Wilkinson, John | Oliver, Angela | 22, June 1846 | RCH |
| Wilkinson, John N. | ----, Anna | 1, July 1819 | RCH |
| Wilkinson, Murwine | Barnes, Rachel | 16, Dec. 1817 | RCH |
| Wilkinson, Nat. | Brown, Letitia | 8, Oct. 1846 | RCH |
| Wilkinson, Samuel | Beeler, Ruth Ann | 2, Nov. 1842 | RCH |
| Wilkinson, Stephan | Moak, Lois | 14, Feb. 1847 | RCH |
| Wilkison, Jacob | Strong, Rebecca | 31, Dec. 1848 | RCH |
| Will, Jacob | Zittel, Susannah | 16, July 1846 | A |
| Will, Magnus | Krug, Elisabeth | 11, Aug. 1840 | FF |
| Will, Valentin | Hartkopf, Caroline | 9, Oct. 1846 | A |
| Willard, Franklin | Regan, Sarah | 29, Nov. 1848 | BB |
| Willard, Morgan | Perry, Eliza Jane | 24, May 1847 | RCH |
| Willard, Simon | Cooper, Anna H. | 8, May 1848 | RCH |
| Willcox, Charles | Blauvelt, Jane | 20, May 1846 | RCH |
| Willem, Jacob | Roeler, Barbara | 14, Sept 1845 | A |
| Willen, Heinrich | Sunneberg, Catharina | 1, Feb. 1842 | FF |
| Willen, Heinrich | Wilkes, Angela M. | 11, Feb. 1849 | EE |
| Willen, J. Wilhelm | Gravenkamp, Maria A. | 25, May 1841 | FF |
| Willenbach, Bernard | VanHusen, Henriette | 4, Feb. 1849 | EE |
| Willenborg, Johan H. | Krumpelmann, Elis. | 9, Nov. 1845 | FF |
| Willenbring, Friedr. | Knapke, M.A. Gertrud | 12, Jan. 1841 | FF |
| Willer, Gerhard H. | Worthmann, Elisabeth | 25, Apr. 1848 | FF |
| Willert, David | Beebe, Charlotte | 4, July 1830 | RCH |
| Willey, David | VanMitdlen, Cath. | 25, Sept 1834 | RCH |
| Willey, Richard | Eck, Mary | 30, Mar. 1847 | RCH |
| Willholz, Carl | Wetzheimer, Margaret | 4, Dec. 1844 | A |
| Williams, | Roberts, Hannah | 1, Mar. 1827 | RCH |
| Williams, ---lius | Spicer, Esther | 3, Aug. 1820 | RCH |
| Williams, Alfred | Jackson, Sophia | 23, May 1833 | RCH |
| Williams, Asa | Harrison, | 15, Sept 1831 | RCH |
| Williams, Benjamin | Nye, Lucy | 16, Feb. 1847 | RCH |
| Williams, Calvin | Darst, Mary E. | 9, Apr. 1849 | RCH |
| Williams, Carlisle B | Foster, Martha | 9, Mar. 1820 | RCH |
| Williams, Charles | Lee, Virginia | 22, Apr. 1846 | RCH |
| Williams, Charles | Daugherty, Ann | 8, June 1849 | RCH |
| Williams, Claudius | Crawford, Mary | 21, Nov. 1836 | RCH |
| Williams, Columbus | Todd, Sarah | 16, Mar. 1833 | RCH |
| Williams, David | Jessup, Louise | 4, Oct. 1838 | RCH |
| Williams, David | Bosley, Delila | 20, Feb. 1842 | RCH |
| Williams, David | Jones, Mary | 13, June 1844 | RCH |

| Grooms<br>****** | Brides<br>****** | Date of Marriage<br>**** ** ******** | Code<br>**** |
|---|---|---|---|
| Williams, David | Bishop, Jane | 8, Oct. 1845 | RCH |
| Williams, Didemus | McMicken, Matilda | 1, Sept 1848 | RCH |
| Williams, Elijah | Coplen, Mary S. | 19, Oct. 1848 | RCH |
| Williams, Elmore | Grand---, Lucy Ann | 22, May 1823 | RCH |
| Williams, Enos | Nase, Lydia | 22, Nov. 1845 | RCH |
| Williams, Ephraim D. | Mills, Mana | 25, Dec. 1818 | RCH |
| Williams, Fisby | Luxon, Jane | 28, Aug. 1835 | RCH |
| Williams, Franklin | Addison, Sarah | 15, May 1836 | I |
| Williams, G. | McLean, Mary Ann | 15, Feb. 1837 | RCH |
| Williams, George W. | Foster, Martha Jane | 12, Dec. 1847 | RCH |
| Williams, George W. | Lockla, Mary Ann | 27, Dec. 1849 | RCH |
| Williams, Henry | Nicholas, Emeline | 4, Feb. 1834 | RCH |
| Williams, Henry | Harris, Sarah (Mrs) | 10, Oct. 1835 | RCH |
| Williams, Henry | Brown, Betsy | 21, Nov. 1839 | I |
| Williams, Ignatius | Bradbury, Rachel | 8, June 1836 | RCH |
| Williams, Isaac P. | Bernard, Louise | 7, Aug. 1834 | RCH |
| Williams, J.P. | Harvey, Margaret | 15, Mar. 1849 | RCH |
| Williams, James | Dunlap, Phillis | 15, Sept 1836 | RCH |
| Williams, James | Thompson, Sophia | 25, Apr. 1844 | RCH |
| Williams, James | Henry, Sarah Ann | 30, July 1846 | RCH |
| Williams, James | Hains, Hester Ann | 29, Aug. 1847 | RCH |
| Williams, James B. | Thomas, Sarah | 25, Dec. 1834 | RCH |
| Williams, James B. | Loder, Bathsheba | 24, Jan. 1849 | RCH |
| Williams, James S. | Bell, Mary | 4, Aug. 1833 | RCH |
| Williams, Jason | Stout, | Nov. 1844 | RCH |
| Williams, Jeremiah | Howarth, Susan | Dec. 1840 | RCH |
| Williams, John | Hunter, Phoebe | 7, Aug. 1818 | RCH |
| Williams, John | Brocaw, Catharine | 11, May 1819 | RCH |
| Williams, John | Johnson, Louise | 1, Oct. 1835 | RCH |
| Williams, John | Bailey, Susan | 8, Oct. 1836 | RCH |
| Williams, John | Reeder, Elisabeth | 25, Feb. 1844 | RCH |
| Williams, John | Griffin, Mary | 2, Oct. 1844 | RCH |
| Williams, John | Rees, Hannah | 10, Dec. 1846 | RCH |
| Williams, John | Evans, Sarah | 8, Jan. 1849 | RCH |
| Williams, John | Murphy, Nancy | 25, June 1849 | RCH |
| Williams, John A. | Arnold, Adaline | 3, June 1838 | RCH |
| Williams, John M. | Noble, Harriet | 4, Dec. 1849 | RCH |
| Williams, Joseph | Wilson, Prudence | 3, Jan. 1822 | RCH |
| Williams, Joseph | Willey, Lucy | 30, Jan. 1823 | RCH |
| Williams, Joseph | Kitchen, Mary | 28, Feb. 1834 | RCH |
| Williams, Joseph | Brisbun, Sally | 9, Nov. 1836 | RCH |
| Williams, Joseph | Manley, Dicey A. | 18, June 1844 | RCH |
| Williams, Joseph B. | Bailey, Mary | 12, Feb. 1844 | RCH |
| Williams, Joshua | Gwynne, Catharine | 7, Mar. 1836 | RCH |
| Williams, Korts | Smith, Ann Elisabeth | 28, Dec. 1844 | RCH |
| Williams, Lambert | Howe, Fanny Tyler | 8, Apr. 1840 | D |
| Williams, Lewis | Smith, Rachel | 27, May 1819 | RCH |
| Williams, Lewis | Olden, Mary | 5, Mar. 1846 | RCH |
| Williams, Lewis W. | Smith, Ann C. | 3, Dec. 1835 | RCH |
| Williams, Louis | Price, Catharine | 9, Nov. 1842 | RCH |
| Williams, Mathias C. | Crookshank, Julia M. | 31, Jan. 1827 | RCH |
| Williams, Matthew M. | Hammond, Elizabeth | 26, Oct. 1848 | I |
| Williams, Michael | Wright, Sophia | 28, Mar. 1849 | RCH |
| Williams, Milton | Moody, Mary Ann | 4, Apr. 1843 | RCH |
| Williams, Milton L. | Moxer, Nancy | 23, Oct. 1835 | RCH |
| Williams, Nathaniel | Ore, Margaret | 13, Sept 1818 | RCH |
| Williams, Noah | Cormes, Abigail | 27, Apr. 1834 | RCH |
| Williams, Noah P. | Brown, Maria | 8, May 1833 | RCH |
| Williams, Otho | Quail, Araminta | 13, Dec. 1846 | RCH |
| Williams, Owen | Rees, Mary | 18, Feb. 1840 | RCH |
| Williams, Pardon | ----, ---- | 3, Jan. 1819 | RCH |
| Williams, Peter | Vincent, Catharine E | 11, Dec. 1844 | RCH |
| Williams, R.R. | Langdon, Delilah | 13, Dec. 1834 | RCH |
| Williams, Reason | E---, Sophia | 5, Nov. 1818 | RCH |
| Williams, Samuel | Davis, Margaret | 4, Aug. 1845 | RCH |
| Williams, Shedrack | Swisher, Elvira | 17, Dec. 1832 | RCH |
| Williams, Simon | Edmondson, Cynthia | 29, May 1843 | RCH |
| Williams, Simon B. | Johnston, Cornelia | 29, June 1848 | D |
| Williams, Thomas | Williams, Margaret | 24, Aug. 1820 | RCH |
| Williams, Thomas | Short, Elisabeth | 13, Jan. 1825 | RCH |
| Williams, Thomas | Goodwin, Anna Maria | 27, July 1832 | RCH |

| Grooms<br>****** | Brides<br>****** | Date of Marriage<br>**** ** ******** | Code<br>**** |
|---|---|---|---|
| Williams, Thomas | Skinner, Emily Ann | 23, Dec. 1840 | RCH |
| Williams, Thomas | Thomas, Cecilia | 3, May 1843 | RCH |
| Williams, Thomas | Jacobs, Kesiah | 29, Mar. 1844 | RCH |
| Williams, Thomas | Edwards, Ann | 5, July 1844 | RCH |
| Williams, Thomas | Collier, Fanny | 9, July 1846 | RCH |
| Williams, William | Knapp, Sarah | 6, June 1826 | RCH |
| Williams, William | Harris, Anna | 9, June 1827 | RCH |
| Williams, William | Graney, Euphemia | 27, Sept 1836 | RCH |
| Williams, William | Foster, Catharine | 18, Jan. 1847 | RCH |
| Williams, William | Davis, Mary Ann | 16, Aug. 1847 | RCH |
| Williams, William T. | Garo---, Milliner | 18, Apr. 1820 | RCH |
| Williamson, | Shaw, Araminta | 13, Oct. 1847 | RCH |
| Williamson, Alfred | Kyle, Mary | 16, June 1842 | RCH |
| Williamson, Amos | Skillman, Catharine | 12, Feb. 1818 | RCH |
| Williamson, Amos | Hear, Clarissa | 12, Apr. 1834 | RCH |
| Williamson, Asbury H | Norris, Sarah | 14, May 1834 | RCH |
| Williamson, Cornel. | Teople, Sarah | 9, July 1818 | RCH |
| Williamson, David | Satcher, Martha | 6, Nov. 1824 | RCH |
| Williamson, David | Huston, Elisabeth | 2, May 1833 | RCH |
| Williamson, David | Duncan, Agnes | 24, Jan. 1844 | RCH |
| Williamson, Elias | Smith, Barbara | 13, Oct. 1836 | RCH |
| Williamson, Ellis | Babcock, Sophia | 6, Dec. 1821 | RCH |
| Williamson, Ephraim | Falkington, Elisabet | 17, Dec. 1848 | RCH |
| Williamson, Euclid | Kirby, Mary | 6, Apr. 1842 | RCH |
| Williamson, Henry | Gullich, Getty | 22, Feb. 1838 | RCH |
| Williamson, James | Heights, Maria | 15, Dec. 1842 | RCH |
| Williamson, James | Montfort, Phebe Ann | 1, Nov. 1843 | RCH |
| Williamson, James | Talkington, Rebecca | 19, Nov. 1848 | RCH |
| Williamson, John | Wheeler, Cordelia | 27, Oct. 1848 | RCH |
| Williamson, Joseph | Radley, Mary Jane | 11, Jan. 1835 | RCH |
| Williamson, Joseph M | Boyle, Mary | 18, Dec. 1833 | I |
| Williamson, Levi | Musser, Elisabeth | 18, Oct. 1843 | RCH |
| Williamson, Nelson | Tuttle, Jane | 6, Mar. 1836 | RCH |
| Williamson, Peter | ----, Mary | 22, June 1839 | RCH |
| Williamson, Richard | Swift, A. Elisabeth | 20, Sept 1846 | RCH |
| Williamson, Richard | O'Meara, Bridget | 30, Nov. 1848 | BB |
| Williamson, Samuel | Beresford, Anna | 23, June 1847 | RCH |
| Williamson, William | Shannon, Rebecca | 18, May 1841 | RCH |
| Williamson, William | Farmer, Harriet | 27, June 1843 | RCH |
| Williamson, William | Hobert, Caroline | 23, Nov. 1848 | RCH |
| Willies, William | Langhorst, Caroline | 22, Aug. 1849 | RCH |
| Willig, Daniel | Schoepfel, Francisca | 1, Mar. 1849 | AA |
| Willing, Gerhard H. | Niemeier, Maria A. | 4, Nov. 1848 | CC |
| Willis, | Arnold, Virginia | 19, Sept 1849 | RCH |
| Willis, Benjamin | Lenshor, Mary | 23, Mar. 1842 | RCH |
| Willis, Johnson | Thornton, Mary | 8, June 1844 | RCH |
| Willis, Lewis | Cox, Jane | 26, Feb. 1846 | RCH |
| Willis, Nathaniel | Williams, Anna M. | 14, Feb. 1844 | RCH |
| Willits, William | Trainor, Mary Jane | 4, Oct. 1845 | RCH |
| Willmann, Adam | Runck, Anna Maria | 21, Sept 1849 | G |
| Willmann, Carl F. | Miters, Henrietta | 23, Jan. 1849 | C |
| Willmeier, Henry Wm. | Kruse, Christina | 5, Aug. 1842 | RCH |
| Willming, J. Gerhard | Gels, Margaretha | 19, July 1842 | FF |
| Willmington, Bloom. | Terril, Nancy A. | 4, Sept 1845 | RCH |
| Willmuth, Warren | Wright, Nancy | 25, Dec. 1845 | RCH |
| Willoh, Bernard | Mossmann, Catharine | 19, May 1840 | FF |
| Wills, Andrew | Degraw, Elisabeth | 12, Nov. 1846 | RCH |
| Wills, John | Long, Lucinda | 24, Aug. 1818 | RCH |
| Wills, John S. | Hervy, Mary Jane | 4, Oct. 1839 | RCH |
| Wills, Lewis | Dinn, Jane | 27, June 1849 | RCH |
| Wills, Oliver | Maisk, Miranda | 31, Aug. 1826 | RCH |
| Willsey, | Warwick, Priscilla | 2, June 1822 | RCH |
| Willsey, William | Slingsby, Sarah | 6, Jan. 1842 | RCH |
| Willy, August | Fenner, Margaret | 10, Jan. 1843 | RCH |
| Wilmer, Francis | Wibbels, Maria Cath. | 21, Apr. 1846 | AA |
| Wilmer, Lucas | Schwegmann, Clara | 13, Sept 1842 | RCH |
| Wilmer, Theodor | Schroeder, Elisabeth | 12, Feb. 1839 | FF |
| Wilmes, Rudolph | Jansen, Gesina | 22, Nov. 1846 | AA |
| Wilmot, Thomas | Tomnson, Elisabeth | 7, Jan. 1821 | RCH |
| Wils, Conrad | Schram, Anna Maria | 26, Nov. 1848 | CC |
| Wilsey, Henry | Ogle, Hannah Jane | 18, Feb. 1844 | RCH |

| Grooms<br>****** | Brides<br>****** | Date of Marriage<br>**** ** ******** | Code<br>**** |
|---|---|---|---|
| Wilsey, Isaac | Leggett, Harriet | 8, Feb. 1835 | RCH |
| Wilsey, Rufus | Dunseth, Elisabeth | 8, Mar. 1847 | RCH |
| Wilshire, William | Wilkins, Frances | 24, Aug. 1843 | RCH |
| Wilson, | Milton, Elisabeth | 20, Dec. 1821 | RCH |
| Wilson, Abraham | Ballard, Mathilda | 5, July 1832 | RCH |
| Wilson, Alexander | Cipler, Martha L. | 14, Nov. 1843 | RCH |
| Wilson, Allen | Christie, Jane | 9, June 1836 | RCH |
| Wilson, Andrew | McNulty, Lucy Ann | 22, Jan. 1842 | RCH |
| Wilson, Andrew | Billingsly, Barbara | 23, June 1844 | RCH |
| Wilson, Bertrand | Case, Mary | 25, July 1849 | RCH |
| Wilson, Cradduck | Watson, Mary | 3, Oct. 1822 | RCH |
| Wilson, Curtis | Gray, Isabel | 28, Nov. 1833 | RCH |
| Wilson, Daniel | Bateman, Melissa | 2, Apr. 1843 | RCH |
| Wilson, David | Gibson, Ann | 1, June 1818 | RCH |
| Wilson, David | Coleman, Lucy Rice | 23, Feb. 1823 | RCH |
| Wilson, Edward | Peck, Amanda | 14, Sept 1847 | RCH |
| Wilson, Elias | Witt, Eleanor | 22, Mar. 1821 | RCH |
| Wilson, Enoch | Baily, Margaret | 12, Nov. 1835 | RCH |
| Wilson, George | Gosung, Harriet | 31, Dec. 1840 | RCH |
| Wilson, George | Sykes, Amanda | 25, Apr. 1849 | RCH |
| Wilson, George | Robinson, Ann | 31, July 1849 | RCH |
| Wilson, Hiram | Hobb, Elisabeth H. | 25, Oct. 1846 | RCH |
| Wilson, Hiram G. | Newton, Eliza Jane | 17, Oct. 1849 | D |
| Wilson, Isaac | Biggle, Charlotte | 12, Jan. 1837 | RCH |
| Wilson, Isaac | Wilson, Martha | 22, Dec. 1841 | RCH |
| Wilson, Isaac B. | Arnot, Harriet | 9, June 1836 | RCH |
| Wilson, Israel | Gano, Phoebe | 11, July 1836 | RCH |
| Wilson, Jacob | Murphy, America | 8, Mar. 1846 | RCH |
| Wilson, Jacob P. | James, Amanda M. | 3, Feb. 1848 | I |
| Wilson, James | Anderson, Margaret | 24, Dec. 1821 | RCH |
| Wilson, James | B---, Elisabeth K. | 22, Apr. 1823 | RCH |
| Wilson, James | Outley, Nancy | 7, Dec. 1843 | RCH |
| Wilson, James | Martin, Mary A. | 25, June 1846 | RCH |
| Wilson, James | Smith, Harriet | 20, May 1847 | RCH |
| Wilson, James | Bassett, Rachel | 11, June 1849 | RCH |
| Wilson, James A. | McDonough, Ann | 14, June 1841 | I |
| Wilson, James P. | Fox, Margaret | 25, May 1818 | RCH |
| Wilson, Jesse | Allhoezer, Charlotte | 16, Sept 1832 | RCH |
| Wilson, Jesse | Ruffner, Minerva | 23, Feb. 1848 | RCH |
| Wilson, John | Clark, Mary | 6, Jan. 1824 | RCH |
| Wilson, John | Park, Elisabeth | 2, Feb. 1833 | RCH |
| Wilson, John | Hess, Isabella | 8, July 1838 | RCH |
| Wilson, John | Carmon, Susan | 29, June 1841 | RCH |
| Wilson, John C. | Spears, Frances | 14, July 1843 | I |
| Wilson, John C. | Stewart, Mary | 2, June 1849 | RCH |
| Wilson, John James | Nicholson, Susannah | 28, June 1847 | RCH |
| Wilson, John S. | Whosley, Phebe | 4, Sept 1832 | RCH |
| Wilson, Joseph | Stanton, Maria | 16, Jan. 1840 | FF |
| Wilson, Joseph | Homer, Caroline | 8, Dec. 1845 | RCH |
| Wilson, Joseph R. | Hart, Margaret | 15, Jan. 1835 | RCH |
| Wilson, Lauchlin | Cowan, Mary | 31, May 1843 | RCH |
| Wilson, Lemuel | Churchill, Caroline | 20, Oct. 1831 | RCH |
| Wilson, Lewis J. | Merritt, Rhea Sylvia | 8, Nov. 1846 | RCH |
| Wilson, M. | Conner, Elizabeth | 29, July 1847 | RCH |
| Wilson, Nathan | Badgly, Euphemia | 24, Nov. 1833 | RCH |
| Wilson, Nathan | Bywater, Amanda | 7, Oct. 1841 | RCH |
| Wilson, Nelson | Tolliver, Frances | 11, Oct. 1842 | RCH |
| Wilson, Oliver | Barlow, Elisabeth | 6, July 1842 | RCH |
| Wilson, Philander | Hobbs, Nancy | 7, Sept 1847 | RCH |
| Wilson, Richard | Nehemiah, Catharine | 19, Nov. 1846 | RCH |
| Wilson, Robert | Sherman, Peggy | 21, Aug. 1845 | RCH |
| Wilson, Robert | Sullivan, Maria | 23, Mar. 1847 | RCH |
| Wilson, Rolan | Johns, Mary | 24, Mar. 1843 | RCH |
| Wilson, Samuel | Brohard, Maria | 22, Aug. 1822 | RCH |
| Wilson, Samuel | White, Elisabeth | 1, Jan. 1835 | RCH |
| Wilson, Samuel | Laird, Rebecca | 8, Aug. 1845 | RCH |
| Wilson, Samuel | West, Miranda | 5, Apr. 1846 | RCH |
| Wilson, Samuel B. | Johnston, Nancy | 26, Mar. 1841 | RCH |
| Wilson, Somerville | Groves, Mary Ann | 9, Nov. 1843 | RCH |
| Wilson, Stewart | Calhoun, Sarah | 9, Oct. 1845 | RCH |
| Wilson, Stewart | Fulton, Lavina | 10, Sept 1849 | RCH |

| Grooms | Brides | Date of Marriage | Code |
|--------|--------|------------------|------|
| Wilson, Theophilus | Paddock, Lydia | 2, Nov. 1843 | RCH |
| Wilson, William | Updike, Mary | 24, Apr. 1836 | RCH |
| Wilson, William | Miller, Elisabeth | 28, Feb. 1842 | RCH |
| Wilson, William | Paty, Hetty | 29, Apr. 1846 | RCH |
| Wilson, William B. | Keys, Mary B. | 12, Apr. 1827 | RCH |
| Wilson, William J. | Nelson, Elisabeth | 29, May 1848 | RCH |
| Wilson, William M. | Lindly, Julia B. | 11, Sept 1835 | RCH |
| Wiltberger, Jacob | Horton, Susan | 6, June 1818 | RCH |
| Wiltsee, John | Lyon, Susan | 12, Oct. 1845 | RCH |
| Wiltsee, John W. | Kown, Martha | 2, Dec. 1847 | RCH |
| Wiltsee, Simon | Littell, Mary | 25, Dec. 1845 | RCH |
| Wilwern, Johan Heinr | Grothaus, A Margaret | 9, Aug. 1848 | F |
| Wimmer, Isaac | Ross, | 13, June 1824 | RCH |
| Win, Edward | Sullivan, Susan | 10, Feb. 1833 | RCH |
| Winall, Samuel | Harper, Sarah | 24, Dec. 1848 | RCH |
| Winall, Stuart | Robinson, Mary A. | 2, Dec. 1845 | RCH |
| Winans, James M. | Knowles, Angeline | 11, Aug. 1849 | RCH |
| Winatt, George W. | Maders, Susannah | 9, July 1840 | RCH |
| Winchel, Benjamin | Reed, Esther | 28, June 1827 | RCH |
| Winchell, George | Weeks, Susan Ann | 28, Apr. 1847 | RCH |
| Windel, Jonas | McKenna, Alice | 16, July 1846 | RCH |
| Windemuth, J August | Schneider, Maria | 13, Sept 1845 | A |
| Winderricht, Georg | Brossam, Maria | 15, Sept 1846 | C |
| Windhoffer, Heinrich | Kidder, Anna M. Elis | 11, Aug. 1847 | FF |
| Windler, John | Belmess, Margaret | 22, Aug. 1836 | RCH |
| Windmeyer, Gerhard | Beinkmann, Anna M. | 9, July 1848 | AA |
| Windsor, Thomas | Monjar, Martha | 4, Aug. 1842 | RCH |
| Windswall, Samuel | Woolley, Lydia | 17, Oct. 1844 | RCH |
| Winens, John | Walker, Levina | 6, June 1833 | RCH |
| Wingbermuehle, Diet. | Arns, Gesina | 16, Oct. 1838 | FF |
| Winings, Joseph | Mullen, Jane | 3, Mar. 1836 | RCH |
| Winkelmann, Benjamin | Boehmer, Margaretha | 14, July 1842 | RCH |
| Winkelmann, Gerhard | Deters, Maria Elis. | 27, Oct. 1845 | RCH |
| Winkelmann, Johan H. | Baumer, Anna M. | 12, June 1838 | FF |
| Winkelmueller, Herm. | Holters, Elisabeth | 8, Aug. 1843 | FF |
| Winkler, Andreas | Trennel, Dorothea | 19, Oct. 1846 | EE |
| Winkler, J. Heinrich | Schaefer, Maria Elis | 5, Nov. 1839 | FF |
| Winland, Thomas B. | Bailey, Ann | 9, Sept 1832 | RCH |
| Winnans, William | Maginty, Margaret | 20, Jan. 1849 | RCH |
| Winneys, James | Wilson, Ann | 25, Jan. 1838 | RCH |
| Winnings, | Jones, Harriet | 24, Dec. 1837 | RCH |
| Winslow, Martin | Clark, Emily | 12, Feb. 1849 | RCH |
| Winsor, Alfred | Vail, Amy | 26, Jan. 1833 | RCH |
| Winston, John P. | Smith, Julia S. | 30, Aug. 1837 | RCH |
| Winter, August | Joachim, Maria | 26, Aug. 1849 | C |
| Winter, Benjamin | Cooley, Sarah | 31, May 1821 | RCH |
| Winter, Conrad | Schwaneberger, Maria | 17, Nov. 1846 | RCH |
| Winter, Edwin Theo. | Farmer, Luzena Coal | 13, Dec. 1849 | D |
| Winter, Friedrich | Garen---, Wilhelmina | 27, Aug. 1840 | F |
| Winter, Georg | Bittmann, Margaretha | 16, June 1847 | A |
| Winter, Georg | Meiler, Theresa | 23, Jan. 1848 | HH |
| Winter, H. August | Degener, M. Sophia | 5, Nov. 1840 | F |
| Winter, Heinrich | Neinzenwilzen, Elis. | 9, Mar. 1847 | C |
| Winter, Henry | Pennington, H. | 10, Nov. 1832 | RCH |
| Winter, Henry | Minchweiler, Fanny | 1, Sept 1847 | RCH |
| Winter, Johan | Kenkel, Elisabeth | 28, Oct. 1849 | II |
| Winter, John | Bartolet, Catharine | 17, Dec. 1818 | RCH |
| Winter, Nicolaus | Braun, Magdalena | 4, Feb. 1849 | EE |
| Winter, Robert | Super, Cynthia | 4, Aug. 1836 | RCH |
| Winter, Samuel | Remme, Elisabeth | 6, Sept 1847 | RCH |
| Winter, Thomas | Wingert, | 24, Sept 1823 | RCH |
| Winterholter, Georg | Ball, Theresa | 23, Apr. 1839 | FF |
| Wintermann, Lucas | Heinen, Maria | 30, Jan. 1844 | FF |
| Winters, Asa | Hamel, Julia A. | 31, Dec. 1846 | RCH |
| Winters, Edward | Smith, Mary | 14, Jan. 1849 | BB |
| Winters, Elisha | Dickson, Jane | 5, Apr. 1844 | RCH |
| Winters, Johan | Creley, Martha | 8, May 1848 | II |
| Winters, John | Flanagan, Ann | 14, Aug. 1839 | BB |
| Winters, Moses W. | Rogers, Sarah | 27, Jan. 1825 | RCH |
| Winters, William | Willis, Jane F. | 30, Jan. 1835 | RCH |
| Winters, William | Philipps, Nancy B. | 26, Dec. 1835 | RCH |

| Grooms<br>***** | Brides<br>****** | Date of Marriage<br>**** ** ******** | Code<br>**** |
|---|---|---|---|
| Winters, William | Mitchell, Elisabeth | 31, Aug. 1842 | RCH |
| Winton, John | Bond, Frances E. | 22, Feb. 1827 | I |
| Winton, Matthew | ----, Mary Jane | 15, July 1837 | RCH |
| Winton, Thomas | McAthin, Nancy | 13, Dec. 1823 | RCH |
| Wintrich, Ludwig | Henke, Carolina | 15, Feb. 1848 | AA |
| Wintrode, John | Kinney, Lucy | 20, Aug. 1846 | RCH |
| Wintz, Johan Nicol. | Mary, Margaret | 13, Apr. 1836 | FF |
| Wippen, Gerhard H. | Kramer, Anna Maria | 6, May 1849 | EE |
| Wirbel, Anton | Spatrohr, Anna Maria | 13, Feb. 1848 | EE |
| Wirbling, Herman | Nemers, Margaretha | 27, Jan. 1837 | F |
| Wirsching, Gottlieb | Stising, Margaretha | 24, Apr. 1848 | G |
| Wirsel, Francis | Baumgartner, Elis. | 11, Sept 1849 | II |
| Wirtel, Leonard | Schraft, Catharine | 11, Feb. 1849 | II |
| Wirthlein, Thadeus | Wombell, Clara J. | 12, July 1842 | RCH |
| Wirthlin, Nicolaus | Schlosser, Juliana | 3, Feb. 1846 | FF |
| Wirthlin, Stephen | Kugler, Barbara | 7, Jan. 1840 | FF |
| Wirtz, Johan | Steinmetz, Elisabeth | 25, Nov. 1847 | AA |
| Wirtz, Johan G. | Pea, Elisabeth | 31, Jan. 1844 | RCH |
| Wirtzel, Francis | Williams, Susan | 18, Aug. 1846 | RCH |
| Wisbey, Louis | Cartwright, Margaret | 2, June 1844 | BB |
| Wischmeier, Heinrich | Ohe, Marg. Wilhelmin | 8, July 1847 | F |
| Wise, Albert R. | Townsend, Josana | Apr. 1839 | RCH |
| Wise, Johan | Latz, Elisabeth | 27, Feb. 1838 | FF |
| Wise, Peter | Enos, Mary | 10, Oct. 1841 | RCH |
| Wise, Silvester Ross | Grogan, Mary Jane | 28, Dec. 1842 | BB |
| Wise, Thomas | Gaines, Susan | 20, Nov. 1834 | RCH |
| Wise, William | Miller, Elisa | 21, Oct. 1848 | RCH |
| Wise, William | Martin, Amelia | 24, June 1849 | RCH |
| Wiseman, John | Dirkes, Maria E. | 3, Sept 1841 | RCH |
| Wiseman, John A. | Harrison, Mary | 1, Jan. 1826 | RCH |
| Wisert, Johan | Spehrer, Barbara | 18, Jan. 1847 | EE |
| Wisker, Theodor | Quatermann, A. Cath. | 20, Sept 1839 | FF |
| Wisner, John | Stevens, Ann | 19, July 1848 | GG |
| Wisscot, William | Dastien, Amanda | 7, Oct. 1821 | RCH |
| Wissel, Johan Adam | Thoma, Elisabeth | 21, Nov. 1847 | HH |
| Wissman, Peter | Eschelberger, Theres | 7, Feb. 1838 | RCH |
| Wist, Andreas | Gaesner, Magdalena | 26, Oct. 1847 | EE |
| Witham, Manner | Worthington, Mary | 8, Feb. 1833 | RCH |
| Witham, Zenas | Bachelder, Mary Jane | 5, July 1838 | RCH |
| Withan, Gideon | Burnside, Jane | 30, Sept 1845 | RCH |
| Withar, Herman | Wielenberg, Agnes | 7, Nov. 1847 | AA |
| Withay, Heinrich | Fild, Anna Adelheid | 28, Jan. 1845 | AA |
| Withorn, John | Puthoff, Mary | 30, July 1844 | RCH |
| Withron, William | Lefevre, Mary Jane | 15, Dec. 1848 | RCH |
| Witt, Anton | Tetampel, Angela | 13, Feb. 1848 | EE |
| Witte, Caspar | Kohorst, Bernardina | 23, Sept 1849 | CC |
| Witte, Heinrich | Bischelmann, Maria A | 13, July 1845 | AA |
| Witte, Herman | Mansheim, M Elisabet | 2, Feb. 1843 | FF |
| Witte, Herman H. | Weiste, Charlotte | 4, July 1848 | RCH |
| Witte, Johan Friedr. | Simons, Catharine S. | 13, Nov. 1845 | A |
| Witte, Johan Friedr. | Boeseler, Wilhelmina | 6, Sept 1849 | A |
| Witte, Johan Heinric | Romat, Bernardina | 18, Nov. 1845 | AA |
| Witte, John Henry | Groener, Catharine G | 31, Aug. 1847 | RCH |
| Wittkemper, Friedric | Wittkemper, A. Cath. | 7, Jan. 1849 | RCH |
| Wittmann, Francis | Graf, Christina | 20, Apr. 1841 | FF |
| Wittmers, Hein. Ferd | Born, Dorothea | 25, Sept 1847 | B |
| Wittrick, John | Dailey, Eliza | 29, Jan. 1824 | RCH |
| Wittruck, Abraham | Borgerding, Elisabet | 22, Apr. 1849 | AA |
| Witz, Henry | Weis, Mary | 6, Dec. 1849 | RCH |
| Wo---, John S. | Bowen, Mary | 21, Dec. 1832 | RCH |
| Wobeler, Heinrich | Buenning, Christina | 24, Oct. 1848 | II |
| Wobkenberg, Heinrich | Meyer, Angela | 29, Jan. 1835 | FF |
| Wochefort, Johan H. | Buschle, Anna Maria | 18, May 1835 | FF |
| Wocher, Adolph | Fieber, Catharine | 15, Feb. 1849 | C |
| Wode, Ludwig | Ahlers, Friedricka | 13, Jan. 1848 | A |
| Woegemann, Matthias | Timpe, Elisabeth | 30, Sept 1845 | FF |
| Woehler, Bernard | Dierken, Mary | 9, Apr. 1844 | AA |
| Woehlers, August L. | Brinkmann, Wilhelmin | 26, Oct. 1848 | B |
| Woelfel, John | Frelinger, Magdalena | 28, Sept 1847 | BB |
| Woelfel, Joseph | Schipper, Elisabeth | 4, May 1847 | AA |
| Woelpers, Bernard | Massing, Anna Cath. | 30, July 1848 | EE |

| Grooms<br>***** | Brides<br>***** | Date of Marriage<br>**** ** ******** | Code<br>**** |
|---|---|---|---|
| Woenert, Herman Bd. | Heike, Catharine | 5, Oct. 1845 | FF |
| Woermann, Johan Bd. | Hackmann, Elisabeth | 15, Nov. 1846 | AA |
| Woesten, J. Wilhelm | Mohlenkamp, A Gesina | 27, June 1848 | FF |
| Wohlers, Henry | Heise, Rebecca | 19, Mar. 1849 | F |
| Wohlferth, Michael | Rohracker, Margaret | 25, Nov. 1847 | EE |
| Wohnker, Johan F. | Buldmann, Anna | 23, Sept 1849 | AA |
| Wolber, Herman | Koch, Catharina L. | 17, Jan. 1843 | F |
| Wolberth, Adam | Oberle, Rosina | 25, Nov. 1845 | AA |
| Wolever, Perry | Russell, Eunice | 1, June 1848 | RCH |
| Wolf, Abraham | Benjamin, Hannah | 5, Nov. 1842 | RCH |
| Wolf, Christian | Weber, Elisabeth | 14, Mar. 1847 | A |
| Wolf, Conrad | Sachs, Sophia | 29, May 1849 | G |
| Wolf, Daniel | Brand, Elisabeth | 14, Apr. 1837 | RCH |
| Wolf, Daniel | Bruel, Rebecca | 14, Jan. 1847 | RCH |
| Wolf, Georg Michael | Enginger, Magdalena | 17, Feb. 1848 | G |
| Wolf, Isaac | Kahn, Theodora | 15, June 1848 | RCH |
| Wolf, J. Georg | Dewein, Catharine | 7, Nov. 1844 | C |
| Wolf, Johan | Kirhoff, Elisabeth | 10, May 1849 | A |
| Wolf, Joseph | Beck, Paulina | 8, Feb. 1847 | FF |
| Wolf, Philipp | Rupp, Catharine | 20, Apr. 1840 | G |
| Wolf, Philipp | Fuchs, Magdalena | 7, Dec. 1847 | A |
| Wolf, Samuel | Brown, Margaret | 29, Mar. 1844 | RCH |
| Wolfe, Carl H Ludwig | Kolbe, Louise | 4, Nov. 1847 | F |
| Wolfe, Marvin | Briggs, Mary | 8, Apr. 1843 | RCH |
| Wolfer, Michael | Oehler, Barbara | 24, Feb. 1846 | FF |
| Wolff, Carl | Pelser, Friedricka | 8, June 1835 | RCH |
| Wolff, Charles | Swormsted, Sarah | 16, Oct. 1845 | RCH |
| Wolff, John C. | Skillman, Elisabeth | 17, Dec. 1837 | RCH |
| Wolff, Louis | Fristmann, Esther | 24, Dec. 1844 | RCH |
| Wolford, Joseph | Mavie, Maria | 14, Apr. 1834 | RCH |
| Wolfram, Joseph | Husser, Johanna | 17, May 1842 | FF |
| Wolfrom, Anton | Klausmann, Maria | 19, Feb. 1849 | II |
| Wolfser, Leonard | Hoffner, Christina | 27, Mar. 1838 | RCH |
| Wolfson, Israel | Heidelbach, Sarah | 27, Apr. 1844 | RCH |
| Wolfson, Richard D. | ----, Sarah | 25, June 1835 | RCH |
| Wolke, J. Herman G. | Fox, Charlotte | 20, May 1845 | A |
| Wolke, Wilhelm | Niewedde, Maria Anna | 25, Nov. 1847 | F |
| Wolking, Friedrich | Wehrmann, Maria | 13, Oct. 1842 | F |
| Wolkotter, Bernard H | Feldschneider, Eva M | 25, Jan. 1842 | FF |
| Woll, Jacob | Schoch, Maria | 30, May 1848 | EE |
| Wollenweber, Wilhelm | Jackee, Minna | 2, Dec. 1847 | G |
| Wollinghoff, Heinr. | Kohls, Marg. Elis. | 3, Apr. 1845 | FF |
| Wolpert, Friedrich | Mueller, Crescentia | 1, Sept 1846 | AA |
| Wolss, Martin C.D. | Stanss--ss, Sophia J | 13, Nov. 1849 | C |
| Wolter, Andreas | Rohlfing, Maria S. | 20, Aug. 1846 | F |
| Woltermann, Bernard | Moeller, Elisabeth | 25, Nov. 1849 | FF |
| Wolters, Gerhard H. | Haseker, Maria | 14, June 1843 | RCH |
| Wolters, Heinrich | Segemann, Lena | 11, May 1848 | B |
| Wolters, Johan G. | Fischer, A. Theresa | 21, Oct. 1849 | AA |
| Wolverton, Amos | Carl, Rebecca | 19, Jan. 1833 | RCH |
| Wolverton, C. | Frazee, Jane | 15, Feb. 1827 | RCH |
| Wonderlin, Amos | Montgomery, Nancy | 15, Feb. 1844 | RCH |
| Wonnell, John | Evans, Louise | 21, Nov. 1842 | RCH |
| Wood, Aaron | Miller, Emeline | 10, June 1838 | RCH |
| Wood, Alexander | McChesney, Ann | 16, Oct. 1821 | RCH |
| Wood, Alfred | Clark, Nancy Ann | 20, Oct. 1836 | I |
| Wood, Alfred | Lamb, Virginia | 14, Dec. 1845 | RCH |
| Wood, Ansel | Conlin, Mary Alice | 1, Oct. 1848 | BB |
| Wood, Anthony | ----, Peggy Ann | 4, Apr. 1835 | RCH |
| Wood, Archibald | Blackwell, May | 11, Nov. 1819 | RCH |
| Wood, Daniel | Willis, Mary | 3, Sept 1817 | RCH |
| Wood, Eleazar | Cary, Roxey | 21, Mar. 1822 | RCH |
| Wood, Elijah | Davis, Elisabeth | 16, Nov. 1837 | RCH |
| Wood, Elisha | Barker, Nancy | 22, Jan. 1818 | RCH |
| Wood, Emson | Parks, Emily | 16, Feb. 1842 | RCH |
| Wood, Henry | Service, Amanda K. | 16, Nov. 1848 | RCH |
| Wood, James | Conner, Charlotte | 24, Aug. 1837 | RCH |
| Wood, James | Cooper, Mary | 29, Oct. 1837 | RCH |
| Wood, James | Bardsley, Elisabeth | 11, Dec. 1845 | RCH |
| Wood, James | Foutz, Sophia | 5, Feb. 1848 | RCH |
| Wood, James M. | Greathouse, Nancy | 3, Sept 1846 | RCH |

| Grooms | Brides | Date of Marriage | Code |
|--------|--------|------------------|------|
| ****** | ****** | **** ** ******** | **** |
| Wood, Joel | Nesbit, Amanda | 20, Mar. 1834 | RCH |
| Wood, John | Spicer, Nancy | 10, July 1821 | RCH |
| Wood, John | Gutney, Lucinda | 4, July 1831 | RCH |
| Wood, John | Hughes, Judah | 5, Mar. 1836 | RCH |
| Wood, John C. | Cortleyou, Sarah | 15, Mar. 1843 | RCH |
| Wood, John M. | Copelan, Isabella | 17, Jan. 1844 | RCH |
| Wood, Jonathan | Storer, Mary Jane | 28, July 1847 | RCH |
| Wood, Jonathan M. | Goslin, Clarissa | 31, Oct. 1832 | RCH |
| Wood, Joseph | Cain, Jane | 27, Mar. 1849 | RCH |
| Wood, Lelly | Burnet, Nancy | 20, Apr. 1842 | RCH |
| Wood, Levi | Sharp, | 24, Mar. 1824 | RCH |
| Wood, Philander | Kirkpatrick, Martha | 16, Sept 1846 | RCH |
| Wood, Redmon | Wood, Mercy | 6, July 1842 | RCH |
| Wood, Samuel | Rusk, Jane | 3, May 1825 | RCH |
| Wood, Thompson | Pool, Rebecca M. | 31, Oct. 1847 | RCH |
| Wood, Timothy | B---, Mary | 11, May 1822 | RCH |
| Wood, William | Craven, Abigail | 29, May 1843 | RCH |
| Wood, William | Gould, Jane | 19, Apr. 1844 | RCH |
| Wood, William | Seston, Judith | 10, Sept 1846 | RCH |
| Wood, William | Roush, Nancy | 10, Aug. 1847 | RCH |
| Wood, William B. | Worthington, Abby A. | 30, Oct. 1835 | I |
| Woodard, Benjamin | Higgins, Mary Ann | 9, Dec. 1834 | RCH |
| Woodard, Francis H. | Cox, Elisabeth | 25, Sept 1832 | RCH |
| Woodford, Daniel | Morrison, Nancy | 8, June 1836 | RCH |
| Woodin, William | Newton, Elisabeth | 6, June 1840 | RCH |
| Woodington, Jacob | Kelley, Mary Jane | 3, Nov. 1846 | RCH |
| Woodman, John | Long, Elisabeth | 17, Aug. 1821 | RCH |
| Woodrow, David T. | Cromwell, Louise | 28, Sept 1840 | I |
| Woodruff, Albert | Hooper, Catharine | 30, July 1834 | RCH |
| Woodruff, Ezra | Parson, Maria | 8, Aug. 1822 | RCH |
| Woodruff, Henry P. | Cooper, Ann | 8, Feb. 1838 | RCH |
| Woodruff, Isaac | Smith, Mary | 5, Nov. 1833 | RCH |
| Woodruff, Jacob | Robbins, Sarah Ann | 16, Dec. 1841 | RCH |
| Woodruff, Joel | Wilkinson, Elisabeth | 4, Dec. 1836 | RCH |
| Woodruff, John | Henderson, Margaret | 2, Dec. 1840 | RCH |
| Woodruff, Joseph H. | Sullivan, Sarah | 29, June 1834 | RCH |
| Woodruff, Lafayette | Reed, Elizabeth | 15, Oct. 1846 | RCH |
| Woodruff, Samuel | Townley, Elizabeth | 28, June 1846 | RCH |
| Woodruff, Seth | Lewis, Charlotte | 21, Apr. 1822 | RCH |
| Woodruff, Stephen | Markley, Elisabeth | 11, Jan. 1818 | RCH |
| Woodruff, William | Mason, Sarah | 18, Sept 1841 | RCH |
| Woodruff, William | Rogers, Cath. Jane | 17, May 1848 | RCH |
| Woodruff, William H. | Foster, Margaret | 3, Dec. 1837 | RCH |
| Woodruff, William H. | Jackson, Julia H. | 18, Jan. 1848 | RCH |
| Woods, Alfred | Irick, Margaret | 25, Nov. 1849 | RCH |
| Woods, Andrew | Evans, Margaret | 17, Feb. 1848 | RCH |
| Woods, Isaac | Evans, Margaret | 25, Jan. 1849 | RCH |
| Woods, Jacob | Billingsley, Nancy | 30, Apr. 1833 | RCH |
| Woods, John R. | Morrison, Sarah | Apr. 1835 | RCH |
| Woods, Luther | Annabel, Ludinca | 4, Jan. 1849 | RCH |
| Woods, Robert | Parker, Mary Elis. | 8, Mar. 1841 | RCH |
| Woodside, John | McElroy, Ellen | 7, July 1847 | RCH |
| Woodson, John | Clark, Eveline | 18, July 1833 | RCH |
| Woodward, Francis | Donovan, Elvira | 20, Mar. 1834 | RCH |
| Woodward, George R. | Wury, Edith | 17, June 1832 | RCH |
| Woodward, James | Thrasher, Sarah J. | 4, Feb. 1841 | RCH |
| Woodward, Washington | Tibbits, Caroline S. | 1, Apr. 1835 | RCH |
| Woodworth, Benjamin | McCray, Mary S. | 22, June 1825 | RCH |
| Woodworth, Benjamin | Jenks, Malinda | 15, Aug. 1847 | RCH |
| Woodworth, Caleb | Holman, Abigail | 20, Jan. 1834 | RCH |
| Woof, John | Johnson, Elisabeth | 18, Jan. 1844 | RCH |
| Woolcot, William G. | Ewing, Juliet | 8, Jan. 1833 | RCH |
| Woold, Absalom | Sersior, Ellen | 12, Oct. 1824 | RCH |
| Wooleaver, Jacob | Cross, Elizabeth | 27, Sept 1847 | RCH |
| Woolen, Jacob | Wilsey, Elisabeth | 27, Mar. 1833 | RCH |
| Wooley, James | ----, Rachel | 19, Apr. 1820 | RCH |
| Wooley, James | Shaw, Nancy | 13, Sept 1832 | RCH |
| Wooley, James | Symonds, Esther E. | 17, Sept 1842 | RCH |
| Wooley, Oliver | McHatton, Vetura | 2, Oct. 1843 | RCH |
| Wooley, Stiles | Creatch, Martha | 20, Oct. 1835 | RCH |
| Wooley, Thomas | Craven, Mary | 1, May 1818 | RCH |

| Grooms<br>****** | Brides<br>****** | Date of Marriage<br>**** ** ******** | Code<br>**** |
|---|---|---|---|
| Wooley, Thomas | Wiltsee, Catharine | 31, May 1849 | RCH |
| Wooley, William | ----, ---- | 21, Sept 1820 | RCH |
| Wooley, William | Stevenson, Mary Ann | 9, May 1839 | RCH |
| Wooley, William M. | Neare, Hannah | 22, Aug. 1826 | RCH |
| Woolley, Joseph | Church, Elisabeth | 11, May 1848 | RCH |
| Woolly, Charles | Forman, Eliza | 26, Sept 1823 | RCH |
| Wormann, Heinrich | Singer, Catharine | 26, June 1845 | C |
| Wormley, Samuel | Seden, Amatha | 21, Oct. 1846 | RCH |
| Worn, Henry | Evans, Margaret | 8, Sept 1842 | RCH |
| Worpenberg, Gerhard | Westmeyer, A. Maria | 11, Jan. 1848 | AA |
| Worpenberg, Johan F. | Frommeyer, Anna M. | 7, May 1848 | AA |
| Worstel, Samuel | Steel, Elisabeth | 4, July 1849 | RCH |
| Worth, Joseph | Hayden, Anna | 18, July 1824 | RCH |
| Worth, William | Herrington, Sarah | 19, Sept 1832 | RCH |
| Worthington, Amos | Wilson, Jane | 6, July 1842 | RCH |
| Worthington, Ismael | Smith, Martha Jane | 23, June 1842 | RCH |
| Worthington, Jacob | French, Mary R. | 23, Mar. 1837 | RCH |
| Worthington, Levicus | Pisna, Sally Ann | 3, Oct. 1837 | RCH |
| Worthington, Vachel | Burnet, Mary Ann | 31, May 1825 | RCH |
| Worthington, Vachel | Wiggins, Julia | 10, Jan. 1839 | D |
| Worthington, William | P---, Sarah | 18, Aug. 1822 | RCH |
| Worthington, William | Brown, Mary | 1, Dec. 1833 | RCH |
| Wortman, Isaac | Childers, | 16, Aug. 1817 | RCH |
| Wortmann, Georg C. | Ortmann, Wilhelmina | 25, Oct. 1846 | F |
| Woskefort, Casper | Bockhold, Theresa | 30, Nov. 1837 | FF |
| Wosser, Richard | Murtough, Margaret | 6, Apr. 1845 | BB |
| Woters, Jacob | Prudence, Hester Ann | 20, Oct. 1833 | RCH |
| Wozencraft, William | Carter, Margaret | 1, Nov. 1846 | RCH |
| Wragg, Benjamin | Owens, Susannah E. | 1, Oct. 1840 | RCH |
| Wrampelmeier, John H | Boegel, Theresa | 17, Dec. 1845 | B |
| Wray, James | Shull, Catharine | 26, Jan. 1846 | RCH |
| Wrench, James | Ra---, Phebe | 16, July 1839 | RCH |
| Wrench, John | Lafferty, Hannah | 5, May 1842 | RCH |
| Wrench, John | Brown, Martha Ann | 2, July 1846 | RCH |
| Wrench, William | Hall, Eliza | 11, Oct. 1843 | RCH |
| Wrenn, George L. | Duffild, Mary J. | 4, Sept 1833 | RCH |
| Wright, Alexander | Earnest, Ellen | 16, Dec. 1837 | RCH |
| Wright, Arthur W. | Dunn, Harriet L. | 1, Jan. 1846 | D |
| Wright, Benjamin | Workman, Maria | 28, June 1834 | RCH |
| Wright, Benjamin | Belt, Mary | 24, Apr. 1847 | GG |
| Wright, Charles | Franklin, Alvina | 17, Jan. 1820 | RCH |
| Wright, Charles | Vorus, Ellen | 20, Jan. 1846 | RCH |
| Wright, Charles | Doerer, Pauline | 13, May 1847 | RCH |
| Wright, Coleman | ----, Mary | 25, Jan. 1827 | RCH |
| Wright, Curtis | Garvin, Hester | 27, Mar. 1849 | RCH |
| Wright, Elijah | Britton, Jane | 29, Feb. 1844 | RCH |
| Wright, Elijah | Jolley, Emeline | 12, Aug. 1846 | RCH |
| Wright, Frederick | Jones, Nancy | 4, July 1823 | RCH |
| Wright, Henry | Cox, Sarah | 16, June 1842 | RCH |
| Wright, Hugh | Taphs, Elisabeth | 3, Dec. 1819 | RCH |
| Wright, Isaac | Colle, Harriet | 1, Aug. 1837 | RCH |
| Wright, Isaac | Taylor, Maria L. | 26, July 1846 | RCH |
| Wright, Jacob | Tompkins, Mary | 19, July 1846 | RCH |
| Wright, James | Phares, Mary | 17, Apr. 1821 | RCH |
| Wright, James | Lacey, Sarah Ann | 26, Feb. 1843 | RCH |
| Wright, James | Low, Sareptha | 21, Mar. 1844 | RCH |
| Wright, John | Chamberlain, Martha | 8, Nov. 1837 | RCH |
| Wright, John | Graff, Mary Ann | 25, June 1842 | RCH |
| Wright, John | Gould, Amelia | 16, Nov. 1841 | I |
| Wright, John | Carter, Elisabeth | 31, Mar. 1847 | RCH |
| Wright, John | McGill, Jane | 13, Sept 1849 | RCH |
| Wright, John F. | Smith, Elisabeth B. | 4, Feb. 1846 | RCH |
| Wright, John F. | Baird, Ellen | 8, Feb. 1849 | RCH |
| Wright, John H. | Brown, Ann | 21, Sept 1837 | RCH |
| Wright, Jonathan | Hollingsworth, Marg. | 27, Mar. 1849 | RCH |
| Wright, Joseph | Roark, Theodosia E. | 16, June 1840 | RCH |
| Wright, Moses | Looker, L.V. | 21, Oct. 1833 | RCH |
| Wright, Nathaniel | Thew, Caroline A. | 19, Apr. 1820 | RCH |
| Wright, Noah | Ferris, Maria L. | 3, Sept 1845 | RCH |
| Wright, Robert | Sedam, Mary | 11, Feb. 1838 | RCH |
| Wright, Samuel | Cook, Mary Ann | 13, Aug. 1846 | RCH |

| Grooms | Brides | Date of Marriage | Code |
|--------|--------|------------------|------|
| ****** | ****** | **** ** ******** | **** |
| Wright, Thomas | Hines, Mary | 1, June 1848 | BB |
| Wright, Thomas D. | Goodwin, Emily | 26, May 1841 | RCH |
| Wright, Wendel | Hopkins, Sarah | 6, June 1833 | RCH |
| Wright, Wendel | Pitman, Jane B. | 31, Dec. 1844 | RCH |
| Wright, William | Startin, Elisabeth | 20, Aug. 1843 | RCH |
| Wright, William | Taylor, Lydia | 12, Sept 1844 | RCH |
| Wright, William | Vale, Catharine | 29, Apr. 1848 | RCH |
| Wright, William | Gregg, Mary Ann | 28, Sept 1845 | BB |
| Wuebbels, Johan Bd. | Stephens, Gesina | 20, Jan. 1849 | CC |
| Wuelfing, J. Daniel | Lockdrops, Doris | 18, Feb. 1845 | G |
| Wueller, Andreas | Timmerwilke, Adel. | 16, May 1847 | FF |
| Wuellner, Carl H. | Woehle, Friedricka | 29, Oct. 1848 | RCH |
| Wuepke, Friedrich | Ronnebaum, Anna | 12, Nov. 1848 | AA |
| Wuermel, Ignatz | Schultheis, Maria E. | 28, Jan. 1849 | EE |
| Wuersheimer, Wilhelm | Deubel, Sibilla | 8, July 1848 | A |
| Wuerth, Johan | Wilsch, Catharina | 29, Oct. 1849 | G |
| Wuertz, Matthias | Lightner, Catharine | 5, Jan. 1841 | RCH |
| Wuertz, Nicolaus | Goetz, Maria Anna | 19, Aug. 1836 | FF |
| Wuerz, Johan | Spies, Rosina | 3, May 1846 | AA |
| Wuest, Conrad | Ziegler, Margaretha | 24, June 1845 | FF |
| Wuest, Emil | Phillips, Clarissa | 3, Sept 1842 | RCH |
| Wuest, Heinrich | Saumenicht, Augusta | 3, Dec. 1846 | G |
| Wuest, J. Dietrich | Hayserin, Eva | 25, Aug. 1847 | RCH |
| Wuest, Jacob | Scheidt, Magdalena | 24, Mar. 1845 | G |
| Wuest, Jacob | Becker, Margaretha | 31, Mar. 1845 | G |
| Wuest, Johan Adam | Geis, Anna Maria | 9, May 1848 | EE |
| Wuest, Johan Georg | Voigt, Appolonia | 7, Mar. 1847 | C |
| Wuest, Michael | Walter, Catharine | 26, Dec. 1844 | G |
| Wuestefeld, Carl | Nordmann, Margaretha | 25, May 1848 | EE |
| Wukly, Charles | Foley, Louise | 12, Nov. 1835 | RCH |
| Wulfhorst, Johan H. | Nolte, Catharine | 19, Dec. 1848 | F |
| Wullenweber, Nicol. | Biermann, Louise | 10, Apr. 1846 | RCH |
| Wullmeier, Frederich | Huers, Rebecca | 19, Nov. 1849 | F |
| Wumer, Friedrich A. | Schaling, Margaretha | 25, May 1848 | G |
| Wunder, Vanaken | Barger, Elisabeth | 28, Oct. 1835 | RCH |
| Wunderle, Rufus | Lambert, Salome | 7, Aug. 1838 | FF |
| Wunderle, Sebastian | Gasser, Agatha | 2, July 1844 | AA |
| Wurman, Jeremiah | Sedam, Margaret | 20, Jan. 1844 | RCH |
| Wurmser, Daniel | Dreifuss, Lena | 8, Apr. 1844 | RCH |
| Wurster, Christian | Schaffer, Friedricka | 23, Apr. 1849 | A |
| Wurtzer, Christoph | Schueler, Anna | 26, Sept 1848 | EE |
| Wurz, Matthias | Leichner, Catharina | 2, Feb. 1841 | FF |
| Wurzbeck, Johan | Derr, Margaretha | 9, Oct. 1844 | A |
| Wurzberger, Anton | Stenger, Catharine | 5, Mar. 1848 | EE |
| Wusler, Georg | Lethermann, Dorothea | 10, Aug. 1835 | FF |
| Wyatt, Francis | Gray, Mary Ann | 28, May 1849 | RCH |
| Wyatt, Kary C. | Bachus, Laura | 10, Feb. 1848 | RCH |
| Wyatt, Thomas | Ellis, Martha | 4, Dec. 1836 | RCH |
| Wyatt, Washington | Nelson, Cordelia | 15, Dec. 1844 | RCH |
| Wyatt, York | Flemnon, Ann | 2, June 1849 | RCH |
| Wyckoff, Isaac | Irvin, Elisabeth | 23, Feb. 1843 | RCH |
| Wyckoff, Nicholas | Martin, Harriet | 21, Dec. 1848 | RCH |
| Wyeth, Francis B. | Potuare, Elisabeth | 4, July 1835 | RCH |
| Wyeth, Nelson | Fowler, Elisabeth | 26, May 1836 | RCH |
| Wykoff, Jacob | Cunningham, Louise | 23, Mar. 1848 | RCH |
| Wynne, John | Barnard, Sarah | 21, May 1849 | I |
| Wynne, Patrick | Moran, Julia | 15, Oct. 1838 | RCH |
| Xaver, Christian | Koch, Elisabeth | 5, Oct. 1841 | FF |
| Y---, Nason | ----, ---- | July 1835 | RCH |
| Yaeger, Heinrich | Morebaugh, Barbara | 31, Dec. 1846 | RCH |
| Yager, Andrew | Carter, Levinia | 26, Mar. 1825 | RCH |
| Yager, Joseph | ----, ---- | 11, Sept 1832 | RCH |
| Yancy, Joseph | Bowers, Mary E. | 12, Feb. 1846 | RCH |
| Yancy, Lewis | Starkey, Maria | 18, Aug. 1846 | RCH |
| Yaney, Genl. | VanGernaben, Anna | July 1834 | RCH |
| Yang, Jacob | VanGorder, Eleanor | 19, Jan. 1833 | RCH |
| Yanney, Samuel | Timeus, Catharine | 18, Dec. 1845 | RCH |
| Yarbrough, John | Rice, Isabella | 30, Mar. 1849 | RCH |
| Yark, Jacob | Tapp, Elisabeth Ann | 19, Jan. 1843 | RCH |

| Grooms | Brides | Date of Marriage | Code |
|--------|--------|------------------|------|
| Yarnall, Eli | Sortwell, Miranda | 17, Dec. 1845 | RCH |
| Yates, Charles | Sayer, Mary Ann | 6, Mar. 1844 | RCH |
| Yates, Strother | Murphy, Ellen | 22, Jan. 1842 | RCH |
| Yeager, George | Gibson, Ann | 1, Oct. 1846 | RCH |
| Yeatman, John | Schooley, Elisabeth | 28, Aug. 1822 | RCH |
| Yenny, Friedrich | Dressel, Louise | 8, Mar. 1849 | G |
| Yerkes, Joshua | Brown, Elisabeth | 11, Mar. 1847 | RCH |
| Yoden, Henry | Snudee, Elisabeth | 28, Nov. 1833 | RCH |
| Yonarn, John | Roderick, Jane | 29, Dec. 1843 | RCH |
| Yopst, Michael | Dee, Mary | 19, Mar. 1833 | RCH |
| Yost, Conrad | Bachmann, Margaretha | 12, Apr. 1842 | RCH |
| Yost, James | Clark, Amelia | 26, Mar. 1834 | RCH |
| Yost, Peter | Rabe, Catharine | 28, Nov. 1844 | C |
| Yost, Peter | Becker, Elisabeth | 20, Nov. 1843 | FF |
| Youel, James | Shuen, Ann | 15, June 1842 | RCH |
| Youmans, Isaac | Barton, Mary | 3, Jan. 1833 | RCH |
| Young, Abner | Smith, | 13, Nov. 1823 | RCH |
| Young, Andrew J. | Britt, Catharine | 25, Jan. 1844 | BB |
| Young, Anton | Windler, Elisabeth | 26, Apr. 1842 | RCH |
| Young, Benjamin | Westcott, Hannah | 15, May 1827 | RCH |
| Young, Charles | Chamberlin, Mary L. | 15, Dec. 1842 | RCH |
| Young, Elias | Punch, Elisabeth | 10, Mar. 1846 | RCH |
| Young, George | Patterson, Margaret | 24, July 1834 | RCH |
| Young, George W. | Secount, Emma | 14, May 1843 | RCH |
| Young, Harvey | Hashburger, Delilia | 9, Sept 1849 | RCH |
| Young, J.B. | Hemenway, Margaret | 20, Jan. 1846 | RCH |
| Young, James R. | McHenry, Frances | 25, Sept 1832 | RCH |
| Young, John | Chamberlain, Carol. | 4, May 1836 | RCH |
| Young, John | Long, M. | 13, Aug. 1838 | RCH |
| Young, John | Flack, Ellen | 17, June 1846 | RCH |
| Young, John N. | Walters, Elisabeth | 12, Aug. 1834 | RCH |
| Young, Joseph | Nelson, Delia | 6, Dec. 1843 | RCH |
| Young, Nicolaus | Shepard, Esther | 30, Mar. 1846 | RCH |
| Young, Peter | Selden, Emeline | 7, Oct. 1845 | RCH |
| Young, Robert | Logan, Sarah | 9, Dec. 1824 | RCH |
| Young, Robert | Heoney, Catharine | 19, Sept 1834 | RCH |
| Young, Sylvester | Woodside, Lucinda | 23, Feb. 1844 | RCH |
| Young, William | Davis, Charlotte | 20, July 1844 | RCH |
| Young, William | Orr, Ann W. | 31, May 1849 | RCH |
| Yuncy, Charles | Howard, Mary Jane | 21, Aug. 1848 | RCH |
| | | | |
| Zabrisky, Abraham | Brumer, Susanna | 19, Feb. 1818 | RCH |
| Zachmeier, Johan H. | Goldschmidt, Theresa | 1, July 1849 | DD |
| Zahn, Edward | Settelmeyer, Elis. | 4, Feb. 1847 | AA |
| Zahn, Elias | Kuhlmann, Louise | 10, July 1849 | G |
| Zahn, Herman Heinric | Ahrmann, Elisabeth | 25, Mar. 1841 | F |
| Zahn, Herman Heinric | Ahrmann, Regina | 4, Aug. 1842 | F |
| Zaiser, J. Wilhelm | Tron, Maria | 9, Apr. 1849 | G |
| Zambelle, Bazilo | Hof, Mary | 16, June 1842 | RCH |
| Zambelli, Christoph | Landwehr, Elisabeth | 3, Apr. 1845 | FF |
| Zambelli, John | Moosmeyer, Anna | 11, June 1844 | RCH |
| Zankel, Johan Georg | Rumler, Margaret | 9, Sept 1847 | RCH |
| Zapf, Johan | Metzger, Margaretha | 2, May 1848 | G |
| Zapf, Johan | Schellenbaum, Eva | 2, Dec. 1849 | G |
| Zech, Johan Friedric | Hupp, Charlotte | 31, Oct. 1847 | A |
| Zeigenbein, Christ. | Diedrichs, Maria | 5, Sept 1849 | RCH |
| Zeigler, Adam | Bohrer, Maria | 9, July 1849 | RCH |
| Zelger, Ferdinand | Zelger, Francisca | 22, Apr. 1849 | A |
| Zeller, Franz | Salome, Maria | 12, June 1845 | C |
| Zeller, Johan | Tracheser, Rosina | 31, Oct. 1847 | EE |
| Zeller, Joseph | Haug, Barbara | 12, Feb. 1839 | FF |
| Zeltner, Johan | Braun, Anna Maria | 2, July 1845 | A |
| Zenone, Anthony | Heutheres, Martha | 21, Nov. 1837 | RCH |
| Zentner, Philipp | Renner, Catharina | 5, Sept 1847 | AA |
| Zenwon, Reuben | Strister, Sarah | 11, July 1839 | RCH |
| Zerhusen, Herman H. | Gervers, Gertrud | 6, Aug. 1839 | FF |
| Zerhusen, Herman H. | Vennemann, Helena | 24, Nov. 1840 | FF |
| Zeuner, Carl | Charles, Elisabeth | 17, May 1849 | G |
| Ziegenmueller, Jos. | Deutschle, Carolina | 12, Nov. 1848 | AA |
| Ziegler, Adam | Caprau, Sophia | 9, Jan. 1838 | FF |
| Ziegler, Anton | Pfefferle, Catharine | 8, Feb. 1848 | EE |

| Grooms<br>****** | Brides<br>****** | Date of Marriage<br>**** ** ******** | Code<br>**** |
|---|---|---|---|
| Ziegler, Johan | Schuh, Johanna Marg. | 16, June 1847 | C |
| Ziegler, Martin | Hofgesang, Margaret | 17, Sept 1846 | EE |
| Ziegler, Valentin | Eichelberger, Eva C. | 31, July 1838 | FF |
| Zilch, Paul | Dirk, Antonia | 16, Nov. 1841 | FF |
| Zimmer, John | Heinlein, Anna Maria | 27, June 1847 | RCH |
| Zimmer, Martin | Juntt, Maria | 23, Oct. 1848 | RCH |
| Zimmermann, Gottlieb | Bichler, Barbara | 9, Sept 1846 | RCH |
| Zimmermann, Jacob | Ha---, Barbara | 1, May 1849 | RCH |
| Zimmermann, Johan | Brink, Mary | 18, Apr. 1844 | AA |
| Zimmermann, Johan | Diemert, Catharina | 6, Dec. 1849 | A |
| Zimmermann, John P. | Schneider, Anna | 2, Mar. 1840 | RCH |
| Zimmermann, Lewis | McAlment, Jane | 7, Apr. 1846 | RCH |
| Zink, John | Neidig, Eva | 2, Feb. 1846 | RCH |
| Zinn, Peter | Goodin, Margaret | 17, July 1849 | BB |
| Zinninger, Francis | Hahn, Anna Maria | 12, Aug. 1847 | EE |
| Zivi, Isaac | Bloch, Rachel | 6, Oct. 1843 | RCH |
| Zoeh, Michael | Fischer, Anna | 4, June 1848 | RCH |
| Zoll, Burghard | Rothenhofer, Cath. | 16, Feb. 1841 | FF |
| Zoller, Andreas | Witz, Margaretha | 3, Sept 1846 | FF |
| Zoller, Benjamin J. | Lambert, Barbara | 22, Apr. 1839 | FF |
| Zoller, Blasius | Wernert, Elisabeth | 24, July 1843 | FF |
| Zoller, Carl | Muehl, Barbara | 13, Aug. 1846 | G |
| Zoller, Georg | Cornelius, Harriet | 22, Apr. 1841 | G |
| Zorn, Zacharias | Halts, F. | 10, Nov. 1839 | BB |
| Zoss, Johan Heinrich | Moellers, Anna Maria | 8, Feb. 1848 | F |
| Zottmann, Jacob | Wolf, Cath. Louise | 25, Oct. 1849 | G |
| Zowren, John | Jones, Mary | 27, June 1849 | RCH |
| Zuber, David | Friedmann, Regina | 28, Dec. 1849 | RCH |
| Zuest, Jacob | Ott, Maria Anna | 21, Sept 1848 | EE |
| ZumBraegel, Francis | Bruns, Anna Maria | 13, June 1847 | AA |
| Zumbahlen, Ferdinand | Bergkotter, Helena | 8, Oct. 1848 | AA |
| Zumbrink, Anton | Dunnhoft, Louisa | 9, Feb. 1847 | AA |
| Zumbroegel, Franz | Krugmann, Mary | 3, Sept 1844 | AA |
| Zumbusch, Anton | Bieler, Elisabeth | 24, Jan. 1843 | AA |
| Zunger, Anton | Wollfert, Sibella | 4, Nov. 1843 | AA |
| Zurline, Bernard H. | Werry, Maria Gertrud | 21, Nov. 1847 | FF |
| Zurline, J. Gerhard | Overmann, Elisabeth | 27, May 1849 | AA |
| Zurline, Johan | Thiemann, Theresa | 27, Aug. 1840 | FF |
| Zurline, Phillip | Hudepohl, Elisabeth | 23, Nov. 1845 | AA |
| Zurmuhlen, Cord H. | Weinberg, Anna | 30, May 1849 | F |
| Zurmuhlen, Johan D. | Wulkamper, Hannah | 30, May 1849 | F |
| Zwicker, August | Fenner, Margaretha | 8, Dec. 1840 | G |